PRINCETON READINGS IN AMERICAN POLITICS

PRINCETON READINGS IN AMERICAN POLITICS

• • •

Edited by Richard M. Valelly

PRINCETON UNIVERSITY PRESS

PRINCETON AND OXFORD

Published by Princeton University Press,
41 William Street,
Princeton, New Jersey 08540

In the United Kingdom:
Princeton University Press,
6 Oxford Street,
Woodstock, Oxfordshire OX20 1TW

ISBN: 978-0-691-12471-1
ISBN (pbk.): 978-0-691-12472-8

Library of Congress Control Number: 2009927649

British Library Cataloging-in-Publication Data is available

This book has been composed in Sabon
Printed on acid-free paper ∞

press.princeton.edu

Printed in the United States of America
1 3 5 7 9 10 8 6 4 2

To Madison, our first political scientist

CONTENTS

A New Kind of Introduction to American Politics   1

SECTION 1. WHO GOVERNS?

1. Robert A. Dahl, "A Critique of the Ruling Elite Model"   17

2. Murray Edelman, "Symbolism in Politics"   24

3. Deborah A. Stone, "Causal Stories and the Formation of Policy Agendas"   34

4. Paul Pierson, "When Effect Becomes Cause: Policy Feedback and Political Change"   51

SECTION 2. CONSTITUTIONALISM AND THE SEPARATION OF POWERS

5. Michael J. Klarman, "What's So Great About Constitutionalism?"   81

6. Rick Valelly, "An Overlooked Theory on Presidential Politics"   124

7. Michael Nelson, "The Curse of the Vice-Presidency"   129

8. David R. Mayhew, "Legislation"   136

9. Paul Burstein, "Is Congress Really for Sale?"   164

10. Howard Gillman, "Judicial Independence Through the Lens of Bush v. Gore: Four Lessons from Political Science"   172

11. Gerald N. Rosenberg, "Judicial Independence and the Reality of Political Power"   186

12. Martha Derthick, "The Enduring Features of American Federalism"   206

13. Jack L. Walker, "The Diffusion of Innovations among the American States"   212

SECTION 3. GOVERNANCE AND PUBLIC POLICY

14. Joseph Stiglitz, "Central Banking in a Democratic Society"   243

15. R. Kent Weaver, "The Politics of Blame Avoidance"   268

16. Jacob S. Hacker, "Privatizing Risk without Privatizing the Welfare State: The Hidden Politics of Social Policy Retrenchment in the United States"   291

SECTION 4. PUBLIC OPINION AND ITS ROLES

17. Paul Burstein, "The Impact of Public Opinion on Public Policy:
    A Review and an Agenda"   325

18. Sidney Verba, "The Citizen as Respondent: Sample Surveys
    and American Democracy"   346

19. Donald R. Kinder and Don Herzog, "Democratic Discussion"   358

20. John R. Zaller, "Monica Lewinsky's Contribution to
    Political Science"   380

SECTION 5. FORMING GROUPS

21. John Mark Hansen, "The Political Economy of Group
    Membership"   395

SECTION 6. ELECTIONS

22. Larry M. Bartels, "Electoral Continuity and Change, 1868–1996" 421

23. Michael P. McDonald, "The Turnout Rate Among Eligible
    Voters in the States, 1980–2000"   447

24. Barbara Norrander, "The Evolution of the Gender Gap"   460

25. Matthew Soberg Shugart, "The American Process of Selecting
    a President: A Comparative Perspective"   468

26. Kay Lehman Schlozman and Sidney Verba, "Sending Them a
    Message—Getting a Reply: Presidential Elections and
    Democratic Accountability"   492

SECTION 7. POLITICAL PARTIES AND THE PARTY SYSTEM

27. Rick Valelly, "Who Needs Political Parties?"   513

28. Danny Hayes and Seth C. McKee, "Toward a One-Party South?"   519

29. Nathaniel Persily and Bruce E. Cain, "The Legal Status of
    Political Parties: A Reassessment of Competing Paradigms"   542

SECTION 8. CHALLENGES TO AMERICAN DEMOCRACY

30. Larry M. Bartels, "The Partisan Political Economy"   577

31. Marta Tienda, "Demography and the Social Contract"   607

ACKNOWLEDGMENTS

THIS VOLUME began with an invitation from Peter Dougherty and Chuck Myers—who then brainstormed very helpfully with me about this volume. The book acquired its basic outlines during a fellowship at the Center for the Study of Democratic Politics at Princeton University. Subsequently, Sarah Pachner and Taira Blankenship at Princeton University Press very competently handled the logistics for the book. Brigitte Pelner, the production editor at the Press, exercised a firm touch in keeping the book's physical production on schedule. Marsha Kunin proved to be an excellent copy editor. My thanks, too, to the many contributors whose cooperation aided the volume's composition.

PRINCETON READINGS IN AMERICAN POLITICS

A NEW KIND OF INTRODUCTION TO AMERICAN POLITICS

IN AN ERA when American government has taken on extraordinary policy responsibilities, you may be particularly focused on how American government and politics work. To help you with that inquiry this volume mixes challenge and enjoyment. The "challenge" part is in the academic selections—about 90 percent of the book comes from political science and the rest from law and sociology. The "enjoyment" part comes from a political scientist/author grabbing you by the lapels and saying, "Hey, *you*: Look at this part of American politics and the puzzles it presents, and look at how I clarified them for you." The authors, speaking as specialists, effectively treat you as perfectly competent to understand their specialty—and to learn comprehensively about American politics through reading them.

In other words you will survey American politics differently than most people do. The standard way to conduct an overview of American politics is through a textbook, which typically features attractive visual extras—pictures of the American Founding's philosophical forebears, such as John Locke (whose portrait Thomas Jefferson hung at Monticello), the great presidents and Supreme Court justices, views of the Capitol, and the like. The Constitution and the Declaration are reproduced in the book (though you can easily find them on-line). A textbook will have a "big theme" and gesture here and there to a controversy or two.

But a standard textbook of course hides the vital fact that most of what we know about American politics comes from the hard work of political science. With this book you are going to get the basics, rest assured. Every contribution covers several fundamentals, artfully and rigorously. But you'll also get much more than the basics. In fact, you'll become something of a political scientist yourself (if you are not one already).

"But *wait just a minute*," some of you might be thinking, "that's really not what I signed up for." "Okay—that's a valid rejoinder," I respond (imagine me speaking in soothing, laid-back tones). Seriously, here's what I'm going to do next: give you a crash "minicourse" in political science. I think you'll look forward to what this book has to offer after you hear me out. And if you happen to be a political scientist already, you will find this refresher quite useful. What comes next is an essential introduction to the articles in this volume.

WHAT DO POLITICAL SCIENTISTS DO?

What do political scientists do? They study power and its uses, good and bad.

Consider such processes and outcomes as the allocation of government benefits and burdens, the mobilization of votes, the focusing of public attention on some issues and not on others, the celebration by public officials and citizens of things that their countries hold dear, and the identification of national enemies real and imagined. They are all accomplished by ordinary (and extraordinary) people trying to make these processes and outcomes happen. In each of these cases there is some causal relationship between, on the one hand, the people who have preferences about some real-world outcome and the outcome itself. It is there, in that causal relationship, that one finds power.

When one looks closely, one sees that the source of the power to realize preferences lies in some *resource(s)* available to the people who have the preferences. In the case of a presidential election that results in a Democrat going to the White House, for example, Democratic voters had the power to translate their preferences for a Democratic victory into that outcome largely because they, as voters, formed part of a distribution of partisan allegiances among the states in the Electoral College that was large enough, on election day, to generate a Democratic winner.

Very often, then, political scientists try to figure out which resources are decisive, and under what conditions. They try, too, to figure out where the resources came from and how likely they will continue to be available to people who have preferences for a political outcome.

With me so far? By now it should be clear that I am using "power" differently from how it is more commonly used. Power often stands in for subterfuge, coercion, and intimidation. These are real elements of politics, and they are not attractive. Living in places like Belarus, North Korea, or Zimbabwe—where power is concentrated in the hands of thuggish or totalitarian despots—is hard. But political science is about studying power in its several forms, the disturbing *and* the creative manifestations.

To take another instance, power can involve someone or some people focusing the attention of citizens on an issue that they are glad to consider, once they do so. A person who writes an op-ed for the *New York Times* or the *Wall Street Journal* about a fresh plan for trading carbon emissions is exercising influence. Same goes for someone who blogs well about a political campaign or American policy toward the Middle East. She or he is deploying such political resources as imagination, access to fresh facts, and skill in writing.

Power can also be about setting things up right, or trying to. The Founders exercised power—their patriotism, the cogency of their ideas, their social influence, their reputations, their linkages to each other in informal networks across the thirteen states, their resources for publicity—when they met in Philadelphia in 1787 to challenge the viability of the Articles of Confederation and to propose the alternative charter that we still have, the Constitution.

This reader thus directs you to consider *both* aspects of power, aspects that cause some unease and aspects that inspire admiration. It asks you to think subtly about the various influence mechanisms in American democracy.

The selections also will suggest, over and over, that there are no simple generalizations about power in American politics. There is no ruling elite, for instance—some set of people who *really* run the country. The American political system is just too complex for that idea to be convincing, except as a matter of paranoia or theology.

GETTING HELP

The second thing to know about political science, besides its focus on the complex uses of influence and power, is that it cannot analyze politics all by itself. *It needs help*—specifically from disciplines that, like political science, require getting accurate information about people and their interactions with each other. Political science is shameless about putting these other disciplines to use.

Economics is today the most important of the allied disciplines that help political scientists study power and its uses. Economists focus on individual responses to material incentives. Adopting the concept of incentives, and adapting it to the terrain of politics, political scientists often try to figure out what parts of governmental processes create behavioral if not precisely material incentives for public officials and for citizens.

What does this mean? Political scientists think, for instance, that constitutional rules that allow legislators to gain reelection indefinitely—until they are defeated, die in office, or retire in order to lead a less stressful or more lucrative life—will create incentives for them to blanket their districts with literature about themselves and to do that at public expense. They don't do that anymore, partly because political scientists publicized the practice. But the general point holds: If you are going to have a career, you want to make sure that you don't get pushed out of your career track.

So today, members of Congress (through what are often called "earmarks") make sure that some public money somehow goes to schools, colleges, hospitals, and companies in their districts or states—and that they can claim credit for this. This sort of thing isn't new, really. In the nineteenth century, many members of Congress provided free seed to farmers in their states or districts.[1]

This all sounds terribly self-serving. But political scientists also think that the reelection incentive that leads to shameless self-promotion and earmarks in federal appropriations encourages careerist politicians to do something else with their careers besides just managing their election prospects and handing out goodies. After a while, they get pretty good at getting reelected. What do career politicians do then? They specialize. In fact they started specializing when they got to Congress and asked for their committee assignments. They therefore acquire very detailed knowledge about policy and governance.

On balance, then, the operation of the reelection incentive fosters the voter selection of representatives who aren't making it up as they go along and who have the kind of self-discipline and commitment to hard work that any professional career requires. What *this* means, in turn, is that *our* power as citizens to elect a competent government is somewhat enhanced. This doesn't come free—and earmarks are the most visible price we pay. Consider, though, that earmarks add up to, oh, about 1–2 percent of total federal outlays—and while many are wasteful (you may have heard of bridges or roads that have been built to go nowhere at all, or to benefit expensive residential developments or resorts), the vast majority of earmarks are *not* wasteful. The actual social cost of congressional careerism is really very, very small.[2]

---

[1] For an introduction to earmarking, see Robert Porter and Sam Walsh, "Earmarks in the Federal Budget Process," Briefing Paper No. 16, May 1, 2006, briefing papers on federal budget policy, prepared by Harvard Law School students under the supervision of Professor Howell E. Jackson, available at http://www.law.harvard.edu/faculty/hjackson/budget.php, accessed 20 June 2008. For a succinct blog entry on the subject, link to: http://www.brendan-nyhan.com/blog/2008/09/gail-collins -vs.html. As for seed distribution—describing the Congressional Free Seed Distribution Program, Daniel Carpenter writes "Congressional free seed distribution was the dominant agricultural program of the late nineteenth century." Daniel P. Carpenter, *The Forging of Bureaucratic Autonomy: Reputations, Networks, and Policy Innovation in Executive Agencies, 1862-1928* (Princeton: Princeton University Press, 2001), p. 183.

[2] Porter and Walsh, "Earmarks in the Federal Budget Process," p. 19.

As you can see, borrowing from economics can help political science. But it is not the only allied discipline that helps political scientists. Sociologists study class and status; anthropologists study myths, symbols, and rituals. These concepts, too, are available to political scientists as they puzzle over power—who has it and how it is used.

Take the local police bureaucracies. African American and many Latino citizens have mixed feelings about the police because for a very long time the police were used by white politicians to intimidate minority citizens. Sociology sorts that out, since it emphasizes enduring social divisions and their effects on government. Whites long desired racial hierarchy, and they used government to scare people of color into staying down in the hierarchy. This isn't ancient history either. Countless African Americans have been pulled over in their cars for "d-w-b"—driving while black.

On the whole, however, most American citizens trust most government agencies and agents. That's a bit of a puzzle. You and I simply don't have a lot of *direct* influence on a bureaucracy—say the Environmental Protection Agency or the FBI. We would in fact seem utterly powerless against them. Oddly, the people in such agencies seem to behave every day as if we actually do have a lot of influence over them. They perform their jobs creditably day in and day out; they rarely think about ripping off the taxpayers, and even more rarely actually do so; they very seldom gang up on a vulnerable small-business owner, say, to shake him or her down for money or free goods. Why?

Part of the answer, of course, is to be found by borrowing from economics. With a free press, enterprising reporters have incentives to write shocking stories. The prospect of publicity deters or corrects bureaucratic misbehavior to some degree.

Still, in many countries with a fairly free press, citizens nonetheless find that bureaucrats and public servants take bribes and steal stuff that belongs to ordinary people or the government and then sell it on the side. They abuse their formal power and accumulate material resources and informal power. Yet most (though hardly all) Americans go their entire lives as citizens and never encounter such behavior.

Why? Borrowing from anthropology helps to illuminate the relative overall absence of bureaucratic abuse. Political scientists who study bureaucracies have noticed that effectively motivating people in nonprofit organizations is quite possible—particularly through inculcating *loyalty* to the organization's purposes. This is done, in turn, partly through carefully selecting new hires and charismatic leadership (although that of course is rare), and partly through ritual: ceremonies and activities that bestow honor and esteem within the organization or that accompany career ladders within the organization. Such experiences in turn inspire an organization's people and deepen their affection for the institutions they give their energies to every day.

There are yet other allied disciplines that we borrow from. Psychologists study emotions, rationality, cognitive patterns, and mental illness and health. These preoccupations have in turn helped political science make sense out of an interesting, power-creating phenomenon known as "rally around the flag." If the United States is attacked, as it was on 9/11, the public rushes to support the president—even though one could argue that it instead should rake the president over the coals for not having prevented such a catastrophic attack. In fact, from an economics perspective, "agents" (that is, the people in government) have failed to perform their contract with us, "the principals," to keep us safe. If we were rational, we would punish them. Yet no one was punished for 9/11—even when it became known that many high public officials, and even the president, were warned of some sort of attack before it happened. In fact, President George W. Bush was reelected by a comfortable margin in the popular vote. This is an instance in which economics doesn't explain what happens; instead, psychology does—and it predicts "rallies," sometimes rallies that last long enough to help with a president's reelection.

Such rallies furthermore change who has power. They increase the influence of a president over Congress and ensure deference from reporters and editors—quite a lot, and for a measurable period of time. Again, psychology can help political scientists study power. Social psychology can explain something that matters in the study of power—the mass (if temporary) delegation of additional power to the president and those who work for him or her.

To sum up, political scientists study power—where it comes from, how it is used. Most of the time the role of power, particularly in democracies, is so innocuous that we refer to it as influence, not power. This is a slight tweak in language that in turn generates a useful shading of the concept of power. Whichever shade we study, however, we need help—and we get a lot of help from allied social sciences.

THEORY AND METHOD

Political science has at least two more parts to it—and you should know about them too before plowing into the selections in this volume. These other two parts of political science are self-conscious inquiry and discussion about both *theory* and *method*.

Theory and method are the two things that tend to make political science somewhat technical. But by thinking about them as you read the selections in this book you will also appreciate the challenging intricacy of American politics. Theory and method are in fact essential to making sense of American democracy.

What is theory? Theory is based on simplifying premises. If you wanted to anthropomorphize it, think of theory as a person yelling, "Pay attention to *this* and *not that*!" Or think of theory as a pair of eyeglasses that allows you to see certain things *very* clearly but simultaneously leaves everything else hazy or blurry because they are, according to theory, not worth worrying about. Political scientists sometimes joke, as well, that theory is like a hammer: Once you believe in a theory, you see nails everywhere to use your theory on.

How would this notion of theory work in connection with studying politics? Recall the point about simplifying premises. You could assume that it is alarmingly easy in politics for people to pointlessly fight with one another over just about anything—unless their institutional environment somehow demanded that they find ways to address big issues that really matter without constantly "defaulting" to bitter division. This would be a theory that states something like the following: People will strike up fruitless conflict in the absence of a well-designed institutional environment, but good institutional design can force productive political interaction among the elected political representatives of an otherwise potentially fractious public. As it turns out, this is the theory enunciated by James Madison, Alexander Hamilton, and John Jay in *Federalist*, the collection of essays that they wrote to persuade voters in the state of New York to ratify the Constitution (and that is today easily available in several paperback editions). In these famous essays, one reads over and over how the institutions that we still have were carefully designed to elicit enough checking and balancing to simultaneously force national officeholders to start talking with each other in the language of public values and interests, even as they conduct much of their business according to majority rule.

Most (though hardly all) political scientists currently subscribe to a rather different theory—certainly for understanding professional politicians. They use a simple motivational theory borrowed from microeconomics, namely, that people choose to realize their goals "rationally." That is, given constraints on their knowledge (after all, they may be unaware of certain options or not have enough time, energy, or skill to learn about all of them) and given known constraints to realizing their goals (for example, time, money, the rules of the game accepted by all other players), most politicians act strategically to realize their goals. They can make mistakes, of course, but since they are professionals they tend to make relatively few, otherwise they get weeded out of politics and better politicians take their place.

In this view, politicians' ultimate goals are *not* regularly in danger of defaulting to small-minded parochialism. The Founders worried far more than modern political scientists about pettiness and small-mindedness among politicians—not surprisingly, given the need to build a new national government. Now that we have got a successful national government of long standing it is more sensible to assume that professional politicians have quite strong policy goals and little trouble "thinking big," as long as they can stay in office or move up to even more important office. Part of this is due as well to party affiliation, since both national political parties have clear and detailed policy platforms.

In the more modern view, then, the institutional setting that the Founders created for the pursuit of policy goals might invite or induce interbranch deliberation but it *also* creates "costs" for transacting political business with other politicians. The original plan was to force consensus around broad national values—but we now think that that is not the hard part. The hard part is getting anything done. Coalitions have to be assembled in congressional committees, for instance, and controlling the floor in the House or Senate long enough to put together a bill takes an enormous amount of time and energy. Policies have to repeatedly attract majorities in both the Senate and House *and* appeal to the president *and* appear likely to withstand judicial scrutiny, if that occurs, in order for policy ideas to become law.

Institutional structure thus certainly requires that policy proposals and well-crafted bills encode desirable and attractive values and symbols. But it also generates what economists might call transaction costs. The modern perspective emphasizes trade-offs, frictions, false starts, delays, and the omnipresence of inaction in the face of public needs. The modern resort to economic analysis suggests that there is a certain cost to our fondness for the institutions bequeathed to us by the Founders. Politicians need to take those costs into account when they try to make public policy. We as citizens need to be patient about these costs, since we hardly know what switching to an alternative system would do to the relative predictability of our politics.

What about ordinary citizens? What theory of their behavior and decision-making could one adopt? For instance, could one extend the way we think about professional politicians to include them as well? Are *they* rational choosers too? Yes and no, it turns out.

In large groups, ordinary citizens *act* as if they are rational. Thus voters punish presidents for appearing to ruin the economy. (Incidentally, such accountability places enormous pressure on presidents, particularly first-term presidents, to find some way of credibly taking credit for good economic performance.) But if we move from voters as a whole to individuals, then the basic fact about citizens that immediately comes through is that levels of political knowledge *vary*, both *across groups* that are defined by, for example, levels of education or partisanship, and for individuals *across time*, say over the course of a presidential campaign.

Most of the time most citizens are *inattentive*. Citizen attention is in fact one of the great variables of American politics. Consequently, most citizens fall back on pretty basic predispositions and desires when they think about government. It turns out that the most adopted framework is wanting politics and government to operate *fairly*.

Individual citizens are not, in other words, particularly strategic, in contrast to full-time, careerist politicians or unelected officials running a government agency. In a way, of course, this is perfectly rational: How could any sane citizen think that she or he could, through strategic behavior, nudge the ship of state even a millimeter in one direction or another?

To tally up for the moment, we have two basic theoretical premises on offer for the study of American politics: (1) Politicians are rational and strategic and (2) Busy citizens will fit most issues into a few basic templates or questions, such as, "What's fair?" Notice, by the way, that from these premises we can observe the persistent discontent with politicians among ordinary citizens. Citizens want "fairness" and politicians want careers and policies. Not exactly a marriage made in heaven. But the mismatch is, for better or worse, central to American politics and unlikely to change.

Let's take a couple of more steps as long as we are talking about theory. The next step is pointing out that working premises—such as the two I just sketched— are not cast in stone.

There is in fact a lot of "metatheoretical" activity in political science. By this I mean that there is a constant prowl, as it were, to find something useful from some new quarter of intellectual life. You already have a sense of that from the discussion above concerning the adaptation of economics, psychology, sociology, and anthropology for political analysis.

Many political scientists also read deeply in history, for instance. They do this in order to test hunches about motivations and behavior, and how various sorts of common historical events or sequences (for example, formal transfers of power, war, international competition for markets) can affect the motivations and behavior of important or ordinary people. Others read what lawyers say about the same issues (which is why you will find articles from law reviews in the book). Yet others find that they can get a lot from reading the famous (and not so famous) philosophers of politics. These are people like Aristotle, Saint Thomas Aquinas, and Alexis de Tocqueville or W.E.B. DuBois, Jurgen Habermas, Jane Addams, and Simone de Beauvoir—people who have written about and debated how men and women *ought* to behave politically. Reading them helps, in a deep way, with figuring out the enduring questions of what makes people tick in politics.

In a different vein, there is a serious interest emerging among many political scientists in the role of emotions in politics. Here neuroscience is seen as a source of inspiration. There is also, relatedly, interest in genetics. Recently political scientists have seriously asked whether political affiliations have genetic bases, predisposing some people toward becoming Democrats and others toward becoming

Republicans, given the differences between parties that people will observe as they mature emotionally and intellectually during childhood and adolescence.

Now what does all I have said to this point about "theory"—what it is and how it has a tendency to evolve—mean for you? As you read the selections in this book, you might ask yourself: What theoretical premise is implicit or explicit in the selection that I am reading? Each author is working from some perspective that says—for this is what a theory does—"Pay attention to these sorts of things about people and what makes them tick, not those sorts of things that you *could* focus on but that won't really clarify what you are studying." Why does the author seem to have this premise? What part of American politics does it frame and why does it do so usefully or interestingly? To repeat, think about these matters from time to time. You will notice that you will start thinking more synthetically and clearly about current events as you start using theory to make sense of what you learn about public affairs.

There is still "method" to discuss. To test premises about behavior, and to fit them to experiments, observations, and data, political scientists spend a lot of time discussing good *measurement of behavior* and debating *what counts as reliable and replicable information* about politics. Happily for them, and you, democratic governments provide copious information about themselves, executive officials answer questions from reporters or legislators, legislatures record their debates and roll calls, and election administrators provide reliable counts of winners and losers of elections. Also, communications systems that are not controlled by public officials allow researchers to contact citizens directly and ask them what they think and why—and citizens answer back without fear. Census data and other statistics, furthermore, are relatively accurate—and corrected when they are shown to be defective. There are no strongly vested interests in these data taking any particular form. Finally, there are no politically incorrect research findings. In principle, both reassuring and disturbing evidence about how the polity is working is welcome, and it is subject to scrutiny by other researchers without fear for the safety of those who do the research, or the scrutiny. Given such conditions for social science research, lots of highly educated people do political science in democracies. Democracy *breeds* political scientists.

To get useful information out of the political system in which they do their work, American political scientists ask several sorts of questions. Should we interview powerful or ordinary people? How many? Which ones? When? Can we get them to speak candidly if we also feel obliged to make the results available to other scholars on our websites?

Or, should we observe congressional committee hearings? Should we collect lots of newspaper stories and figure out how often something seems to be on the agenda of the newspapers? What will we learn by collecting and analyzing measurable data, such as election results? Once we start to draw inferences, how do we do that *honestly*, so that other people, using the same rules of inference, would get the same results we do?

Given the many opportunities for freely studying, writing about, and discussing American politics, the results of what political scientists discover are inevitably contradictory and ambiguous—and open to correction by better evidence, more elegantly conceived frameworks for analysis, or better math. Political science, like American democratic life, is pragmatic, pluralistic and open-ended. You will notice these qualities immediately as you read the selections in this reader and as you appreciate the varieties of information and techniques for handling information.

DOES POLITICAL SCIENCE ACCUMULATE RELIABLE KNOWLEDGE?

However, at this point you might be worried that there is way too much pluralism in political science. If it is so pluralistic—lots of borrowing from allied social sciences and even law, lots of techniques and data sources, and lots of searching for yet new ways to cross-fertilize the study of politics with some other nonpolitical field of study—then can it really be a *science*? Why is it even called a "science"?

If by science you mean something like molecular biology, then no, it is not a science. If by science you mean rigorous inquiry that accumulates reliable knowledge, then yes, it is a science. The pluralistic nature of political science actually guarantees progress. Since ideas are constantly tested, the ones that hold up are certain to become recognized as enduring insights.

The case of an American president—Woodrow Wilson—illustrates the point. He wrote one of the first Ph.D. dissertations about American politics, at Johns Hopkins University, which he later published as *Congressional Government*.[3] That work strongly emphasized the centrality of congressional committees in American national government, and, by the same token, a need for centralized, integrating mechanisms in national government. Because there were few such mechanisms, or so Wilson believed (because he did not think congressional political parties did the trick), there were few public activities that the ordinary citizen could focus on. Unfortunately, she or he was stuck with party slogans and partisan newspapers—and Wilson did not think this was good enough. So, when he became president, Wilson consciously changed how presidents spoke in public. He revived the practice of giving the State of the Union address in person to Congress, and in his first inaugural address, he announced that such speeches should project a "vision" from which to "approach new affairs." Wilson wanted to enrich the experience of citizenship by making the presidency an easy "focal point" for the average person. Later presidents expanded Wilson's innovation—FDR, for instance, with his "fireside chats" on the radio.[4]

With a little reflection, one can see that Woodrow Wilson's political science ideas about American politics are still quite relevant. Politics and policy *are* hard to follow if you are not involved with them full-time. It *does* help us as citizens when presidents get on television and explain things to us. Yet Wilson's insights are well over one hundred years old, which exemplifies how a smart political scientist can generate lasting ideas—and institute reforms or new practices—that stand the test of time.

To sum up once again, political science is about how people influence one another and why they try to do so in the ways that they do. There are a huge variety of influence mechanisms in American politics, and people use them with a wide array of goals in mind. Making sense of such a buzzing reality—and making sense of the different conceptual traditions and techniques for acquiring evidence about that reality—is what political scientists do, with considerable success in generating enduring insights.

---

[3] Woodrow Wilson, *Congressional Government: A Study in American Politics* (Boston and New York: Houghton, Mifflin and Company, 1885).

[4] For a more extended discussion, see Jeffrey K. Tulis, *The Rhetorical Presidency* (Princeton: Princeton University Press, 1987).

READING WHAT'S INSIDE THIS READER

So let's turn now to what's inside the reader itself. How does it start?

It opens by considering whether there is a "power elite" in American politics—some exclusive club made up of, say, billionaires, generals, and media tycoons who *run everything*. Is there such a network of people who protect one another's interests and make sure that democracy never fundamentally threatens their wealth and power?

According to the American public, the answer is a resounding *yes*. The American National Election Studies (ANES) surveys have documented in detail that most Americans believe that power is very concentrated. Since 1964 the ANES has asked a random sample of Americans the following question: "Would you say that the government is pretty much run by a few big interests looking out for themselves or that it is run for the benefit of all the people?" The answer that "government is pretty much run by a few big interests" has varied from a low of 29 percent (in 1964) to a high of 76 percent (1994), but since 1970 it has never dropped below about 50 percent. Between 1970 and 2004 the "paranoid percentage"—or perhaps it should be more charitably called the "populist percentage"—has averaged 63 percent.[5]

But the possibility of a power elite is just that, as the opening article by Robert Dahl concisely argues. The idea relies so much on positing the existence and significance of mysterious and unobservable processes that it borders on nonsense. Nevertheless, the succeeding article (by Murray Edelman) does cleverly sketch how the people at the top might manipulate symbols in ways that shape what the public thinks.

But wait—it gets more complicated still. If you think about it, there's an awful lot of *discussion* in American public life. As Deborah Stone shows, just about anyone with a lot of time, energy, and skill can get into the business of telling one of Stone's "causal stories," for the simple reason that there are lots of public problems that require—and end up getting—discussion and scrutiny. Hmm...doesn't look so good for the power elite, you would have to concede.

The last piece in the opening section, by Paul Pierson, complicates the power discussion even further. It shows that public policy choices are constantly disrupting and restructuring politics in the United States. If policy does this, then the distribution of power is constantly changing.

The bottom line of the reader's opening section is clear enough. The relative concentration of power is quite indeterminate. American politics is in fact full of activities and processes that make it *complex*. The articles and arguments in the *rest* of the reader therefore *have to* come into the conversation about how American politics works.

That American politics is indeed complex is not entirely accidental, of course. American politics is intricately designed to disperse power. The reader turns, in Section 2, to treating basic features of American politics that *tame* power: constitutionalism and the separation of powers across the presidency, Congress, the Supreme Court, federalism, and the fifty states.

What one sees by the end of Section 2 is that the American polity is institutionally differentiated—in fact, *elaborately* differentiated. Power and conflict are

---

[5] See http://www.electionstudies.org/nesguide/toptable/tab5a_2.htm.

tamed and regularized by American institutional design and evolution. This protects freedom: Each of us can get on with our busy lives and have some sense that we control our lives to some degree. America is very much a busy free-enterprise republic—by design.

Do we go too far with this business of pushing politics and government—the search to acquire and use influence—to one side? We are often not aware of it but many of the issues that we *could* be talking about in our politics are simply absent from the public arena or are turned into a matter of regulatory management. The American polity indeed contains many institutions and programs that are not obviously directly politically controlled by anyone.

We often think that politicians constantly dream up ways to take credit for pleasant outcomes. This is what the constant hullabaloo about congressional "earmarks" presumes. In fact, governance and policy are not that simple. They involve trade-offs or doing things that a politician would prefer *not* to be associated with. Accountable politicians might thus rationally assign key governance tasks to experts—say the experts who run the Federal Reserve system—and they might rationally establish "automatic government," which features (for example) the regular, nondiscretionary inflation adjustment of Social Security old-age insurance payments to senior citizens.

Also, American politicians—particularly (but not always) those in the Republican party—like to put as much government as they can into partnerships with the private sector. Much of our social policy is based on such a partnership. Working Americans get health insurance or old-age income insurance through tax credits that invite the companies for which they work to join forces with government to provide health or old-age income insurance.

All of these strategies—the depoliticization of extremely important policy choices, automatic government, and routing social policy through the private sector—have a huge effect on us as citizens. They probably make it harder for us to be attentive citizens. And attention to politics is already fairly hard for American citizens.

This brings us to *public opinion*—what it is, whether it is well-informed, and whether and how it affects policy and government. H. L. Mencken, the great political satirist of Baltimore, once quipped that "democracy is the theory that holds that the common people know what they want, and deserve to get it good and hard."[6] But how can America's "common people" possibly "know what they want?" Most adults toil five, six, even seven days a week in commercial, service-sector, and professional jobs. To get to and from work they crawl along in bumper-to-bumper traffic. Perhaps they dutifully listen to political talk radio or National Public Radio—but more likely they are cursing the congestion and flipping channels to find a decent song. Some of the country rides buses and trains, yes—and it is a common sight to see commuters with their noses in a newspaper. But this is a tiny fraction of the citizenry (public transportation is after all a very small part of the country's daily commute). What about after work or on the weekend? Most exhausted adults surely find it difficult to use their free time for *civic* homework—reading the national news pages, watching Washington's talking heads on Sunday-morning television, logging onto political blogs—when they also have shopping, laundry, and other errands to do.

[6] H. L. Mencken, *A Mencken Chrestomathy,* edited and annotated by the author (New York: Alfred A. Knopf, 1949), p. 622.

In short, on most days of the week, for months at a time, a huge number of Americans are simply unlikely to "know what they want" from politics with any specificity. That translates into quite a bit of ignorance concerning the basic political facts that every citizen should probably know. About half of Americans do not know who exactly the chief justice of the United States Supreme Court is. Most constituents in a congressional district do not know who represents them in the United States House of Representatives. Fewer than half of all Americans appear to know that the first ten amendments to the Constitution compose the Bill of Rights.

In 2001 and 2003 President George W. Bush signed extremely large tax cuts that cost the Treasury about $1.3 trillion in foregone revenue. Yet about 40 percent of the American public told survey researchers that they had not thought much about these tax cuts.

As the ANES has shown, people freely admit that they have trouble following politics and policy. Between 1952 and 2000, the ANES asked a random sample of respondents if they agreed or disagreed with the following statement: "Sometimes politics and government seem so complicated that a person like me can't really understand what's going on." Over the course of about half a century, the percentage of respondents who agreed with the idea "that a person like me can't really understand what's going on" never dropped below 59 percent—and it averaged 68 percent.[7]

In short, while political involvement by ordinary people is essential to democracy, that requirement runs up against the reality that most of the time most of us are too busy with our lives. "We the people" might better be called "We the part-time citizens." As "part-time citizens" the vast majority of us have *at best* an episodic (though it is also, via elections, a regularly scheduled) role in affecting public decisions. And we seem to recognize that about ourselves, too.

So it makes great sense to carefully consider just how the *linkages* and interactions between politicians and public officials and voters and citizens actually work—and also to explore what ordinary people and citizens bring to the operations of these linkages.

Here the reader looks closely at:

- The scientific survey of public opinion as a democratic institution
- The impact of public opinion on policy and government
- Whether public opinion *can* be well-informed (despite the data concerning the ordinary citizen's sense of bafflement about politics and policy)—and the implications of scientific measurement of voter ignorance for democratic theory
- How sensible the public seems to be when it *does* pay attention to politics and, more generally, whether media politics fundamentally distracts democratic citizens

In addition, the reader treats the role of formally organized groups in political representation. This type of participation occurs *between* elections, and it requires resources. Thus, to use John Mark Hansen's phrase, group membership has a certain political economy. Here, too, you will wish to reread Paul Pierson's article (in Section 1), Kent Weaver's piece (Section 3) on how politicians try to avoid blame, and the piece by Sidney Verba (Section 4), which contrasts participation in groups

[7] See http://www.electionstudies.org/nesguide/toptable/tab5b_1.htm.

and participation in opinion surveys. These discussions round out Hansen's treatment of what formally organized groups do in American politics.

Then the reader considers:

- Whether the national electoral process ever gets unbalanced or tilted in favor of one party or another (it does not) and why not
- Voter turnout (it is higher than many think—but that may not be good news)
- Whether men and women relate to the electoral process differently (and by implication how voter characteristics mediate their attachment to political parties)
- How we pick the president of the United States
- What elections communicate, or do not communicate, to politicians and to the public at large

After considering these matters, the focus of the reader pivots again toward a related set of readings, this time toward selections that focus on *political parties*. Many people think that they do not like political parties, and think that huge numbers of Americans agree with them by calling themselves "independents." Political scientists disagree; they *love* political parties—they really do. They really do not think that political democracy could work without political parties. They very much like the fact that most people, when pressed by survey researchers, will think of themselves as either a Republican or a Democrat. Political scientists like parties so much because they connect the ordinary citizen to government and politics and consistently and regularly offer them broad policy choices, thereby giving voters a chance to direct and to control government through party competition.

After you have worked through public opinion, groups, voting and elections, and political parties, you will end with *problems*—issues that are not going to go away anytime soon. The first of these is income inequality; the second is immigration. Both problems reframe American politics and democracy.

The piece by Larry Bartels is a chapter from his pathbreaking analysis of how American political processes independently contribute to income inequality. It shows that the party system refracts genuine class conflict—and has the potential to make the people at the top of the income distribution better off over time, while not doing all that much for the people at the bottom.

The piece by Marta Tienda shows that the American political system does a poor job of representing and incorporating immigrants. We now have more legal and undocumented immigrants in the United States than we have had in a century. Immigrants are likely to continue arriving. As Tienda shows, from the perspective of democratic theory these facts pose hard questions about American politics that are here to stay.

"But why does the book end with problems?" you might ask. It's a great country, after all. Why end on a downbeat note?

The answer is: Our politics is a work in progress. It always has been, it always will be. Democracy is not an endowment, or a legacy so secure that our role now, over two hundred years after the Founding, is simply to keep on trucking, as it were. On the contrary, democracy is a constant and collective project for all of us. You know that already, in fact—otherwise you wouldn't have cared enough to pick up this book and read this far.

One last word about the contents of the reader. You will see that there is a short *headnote* for each piece. What I do in these headnotes is explain in some detail why I picked that particular reading. But the headnotes are not particularly long—I step aside as quickly as I can so that you can dig into the material yourself.

IN CONCLUSION . . .

Let me end this introduction with the following thought: If you read this book carefully, you will develop an enduring desire to follow the recurring operations of American politics. By training you in thinking and reading about American politics in the manner of a political scientist, this reader will leave you better equipped for attentive (and, if you choose, participatory) citizenship. Political scientists of all stripes constantly pay attention to the public sphere—reading blogs, watching the news, reading newspapers, doing simple back-of-the-envelope econometrics to test out hunches. You will, too.

Although most politicians have backgrounds in law, business, or military service, even political scientists get caught up in the public sphere and end up in local, state, and national government. One of the greatest political scientists, Woodrow Wilson, served two terms as president. Ph.D. political scientists have served in the U.S. House and the U.S. Senate. Vice-President Dick Cheney meant to be a Ph.D. political scientist, and did course work toward that end. He even coauthored a still-cited article on Congress, before he discovered his deep interest in governmental service. (Of course, some of you may think that it's too bad he left graduate school!) The point is, you will care more about American politics after working with this book, and you will follow its dynamics far more easily and with greater appreciation.

The same ANES study documenting that most people consider politics and policy confusing also shows that those with college degrees *disagree* that politics is too complicated. The rate of disagreement has ranged from a high of 66 percent in 1956 to a low of 36 percent in 1998, and since 1980 has averaged 47 percent. You're going to be in that 47 percent. You might even come up with some idea (besides the obvious one of making everyone read this book!) for how to kick the figure back up to its earlier level of 66 percent.

Now let's get started.

Who Governs?

1

A CRITIQUE OF THE RULING ELITE MODEL
Robert A. Dahl

Dahl argues that figuring out who has power in American politics requires testable propositions and convincing evidence. Is Dahl denying, however, that some people in American society have more capacity to influence politics than most? Not really. Dahl is simply insisting that questions about who causes what, where, how, why, and when in American politics lack obvious answers. If American politics could be easily explained in a convincing way it would be.

How might Dahl's perspective frame contemporary issues? Here is an example: During the period of the War in Iraq, the policy domain of defense procurement was apparently dominated by the Pentagon, a very large corporation (Halliburton—a kind of twenty-first century version of the East India Company), and by relevant committees in Congress. The governance of this policy domain produced huge overpayments by the U.S. government to Halliburton for its services. This seems like a clear example of private actors hijacking a public process for their own benefit. Dahl's analysis in this article clearly implies, though, that someone studying such a "subsystem of power" (1) has to show where the power of the private actors who seem so potent comes from and (2) whether it is stable or temporary. Dahl's analysis also suggests that finding a subsystem of power in one part of American politics does not mean that all parts of American politics resemble it.

Thus, to get back to the example, one might wonder why Congress and the Pentagon allowed Halliburton to dominate defense procurement. Because members of Congress received campaign funds from Halliburton? Maybe—but when you read the piece by Paul Burstein ("Is Congress Really For Sale?") later in the volume you will find that the campaign contribution explanation for why Congress does something is rather weak. An equally good explanation might simply be that the Defense Department needed private corporate help as fast as possible for provisioning American troops who were initially (if foolishly) expected to stay in Iraq for only a brief period. By now you get the idea here: The most accurate answers about power only come from the hard work of studying where it comes from. And, by the same token, the right answers about American politics come from studying its various parts—as you will do with this volume.

• • •

A GREAT MANY PEOPLE seem to believe that "they" run things: the old families, the bankers, the City Hall machine, or the party boss behind the scene. This kind of view evidently has a powerful and many-sided appeal. It is simple, compelling,

American Political Science Review 52 (June 1958): 463–469. Copyright © 1958 by the American Political Science Association. Reprinted with the permission of Cambridge University Press.

dramatic, "realistic." It gives one standing as an inside-dopester. For individuals with a strong strain of frustrated idealism, it has just the right touch of hard-boiled cynicism. Finally, the hypothesis has one very great advantage over many alternative explanations: It can be cast in a form that makes it virtually impossible to disprove.

Consider the last point for a moment. There is a type of quasi-metaphysical theory made up of what might be called an infinite regress of explanations. The ruling elite model can be interpreted in this way. If the overt leaders of a community do not appear to constitute a ruling elite, then the theory can be saved by arguing that behind the overt leaders there is a set of covert leaders who do. If subsequent evidence shows that this covert group does not make a ruling elite, then the theory can be saved by arguing that behind the first covert group there is another, and so on.

Now whatever else it may be, a theory that cannot even in principle be controverted by empirical evidence is not a scientific theory. The least that we can demand of any ruling elite theory that purports to be more than a metaphysical or polemical doctrine is, first, that the burden of proof be on the proponents of the theory and not on its critics; and, second, that there be clear criteria according to which the theory could be disproved.

With these points in mind, I shall proceed in two stages. First, I shall try to clarify the meaning of the concept "ruling elite" by describing a very simple form of what I conceive to be a ruling elite system. Second, I shall indicate what would be required in principle as a simple but satisfactory test of any hypothesis asserting that a particular political system is, in fact, a ruling elite system. Finally, I shall deal with some objections.

I. A SIMPLE RULING ELITE SYSTEM

If a ruling elite hypothesis says anything, surely it asserts that within some specific political system there exists a group of people who to some degree exercise power or influence over other actors in the system. I shall make the following assumptions about power:[1]

1. In order to compare the relative influence of two actors (these may be individuals, groups, classes, parties, or what not), it is necessary to state the scope of the responses upon which the actors have an effect. The statement, "A has more power than B," is so ambiguous as to verge on the meaningless, since it does not specify the scope.

2. One cannot compare the relative influence of two actors who always perform identical actions with respect to the group influenced. What this means as a practical matter is that ordinarily one can test for differences in influence only where there are cases of differences in initial preferences. At one extreme, the difference may mean that one group prefers alternative A and another group prefers B, A and B being mutually exclusive. At the other extreme, it may mean that one group prefers alternative A to other alternatives, and another group is indifferent. If a political system displayed complete consensus at all times, we should find it impossible to construct a satisfactory direct test of the hypothesis that it was a ruling elite system, although indirect and rather unsatisfactory tests might be devised.

[1] See Robert A. Dahl, "The Concept of Power," *Behavioral Science*, Vol. 2 (July 1957), pp. 201–215.

Consequently, to know whether or not we have a ruling elite, we must have a political system in which there is a difference in preferences, from time to time, among the individual human beings in the system. Suppose, now, that among these individuals there is a set whose preferences regularly prevail in all cases of disagreement, or at least in all cases of disagreement over key political issues (a term I propose to leave undefined here). Let me call such a set of individuals a "controlling group." In a full-fledged democracy operating strictly according to majority rule, the majority would constitute a controlling group, even though the individual members of the majority might change from one issue to the next. But since our model is to represent a ruling elite system, we require that the set be *less than a majority in size.*

However, in any representative system with single member voting districts where more than two candidates receive votes, a candidate *could* win with less than a majority of votes; and it is possible, therefore, to imagine a truly sovereign legislature elected under the strictest "democratic" rules that was nonetheless governed by a legislative majority representing the first preferences of a minority of voters. Yet I do not think we would want to call such a political system a ruling elite system. Because of this kind of difficulty, I propose that we exclude from our definition of a ruling elite any controlling group that is a product of rules that are actually followed (that is, "real" rules) under which a majority of individuals could dominate if they took certain actions permissible under the "real" rules. In short, to constitute a ruling elite a controlling group must not be *a pure artifact of democratic rules.*

A ruling elite, then, is a controlling group less than a majority in size that is not a pure artifact of democratic rules. It is a minority of individuals whose preferences regularly prevail in cases of differences in preference on key political issues. If we are to avoid an infinite regress of explanations, the composition of the ruling elite must be more or less definitely specified.

II. SOME BAD TESTS

The hypothesis we are dealing with would run along these lines: "Such and such a political system (the U.S., the U.S.S.R., New Haven, or the like) is a ruling elite system in which the ruling elite has the following membership." Membership would then be specified by name, position, socio-economic class, socio-economic roles, or what not.

Let me now turn to the problem of testing a hypothesis of this sort, and begin by indicating a few tests that are sometimes mistakenly taken as adequate.

The first improper test confuses a ruling elite with a group that has a high *potential for control*. Let me explain. Suppose a set of individuals in a political system has the following property: there is a very high probability that if they agree on a key political alternative, and if they all act in some specified way, then that alternative will be chosen. We may say of such a group that it has a *high potential for control*. In a large and complex society like ours, there may be many such groups. For example, the bureaucratic triumvirate of Professor Mills would appear to have a high potential for control.[2] In the City of New Haven, with which I have some acquaintance, I do not doubt that the leading business figures together with the leaders of both political parties have a high potential

---

[2] C. Wright Mills, *The Power Elite* (New York, 1956), *passim*.

for control. But a potential for control is not, except in a peculiarly Hobbesian world, equivalent to actual control. If the military leaders of this country and their subordinates agreed that it was desirable, they could most assuredly establish a military dictatorship of the most overt sort; nor would they need the aid of leaders of business corporations or the executive branch of our government. But they have not set up such a dictatorship. For what is lacking are the premises I mentioned earlier, namely agreement on a key political alternative and some set of specific implementing actions. That is to say, a group may have a high potential for control and a *low potential for unity*. The actual *political effectiveness* of a group is a function of its potential for control *and* its potential for unity. Thus a group with a relatively low potential for control but a high potential for unity may be more politically effective than a group with a high potential for control but a low potential for unity.

The second improper test confuses a ruling elite with a group of individuals who have more influence than any others in the system. I take it for granted that in every human organization some individuals have more influence over key decisions than do others. Political equality may well be among the most Utopian of all human goals. But it is fallacious to assume that the absence of political equality proves the existence of a ruling elite.

The third improper test, which is closely related to the preceding one, is to generalize from a single scope of influence. Neither logically nor empirically does it follow that a group with a high degree of influence over one scope will necessarily have a high degree of influence over another scope within the same system. This is a matter to be determined empirically. Any investigation that does not take into account the possibility that different elite groups have different scopes is suspect. By means of sloppy questions one could easily seem to discover that there exists a unified ruling elite in New Haven; for there is no doubt that small groups of people make many key decisions. It appears to be the case, however, that the small group that runs urban redevelopment is not the same as the small group that runs public education, and neither is quite the same as the two small groups that run the two parties. Moreover the small group that runs urban redevelopment with a high degree of unity would almost certainly disintegrate if its activities were extended to either education or the two political parties.

III. A PROPOSED TEST

If tests like these are not valid, what can we properly require?

Let us take the simplest possible situation. Assume that there have been some number—I will not say how many—of cases where there has been disagreement within the political system on key political choices. Assume further that the hypothetical ruling elite prefers one alternative and other actors in the system prefer other alternatives. Then unless it is true that in all or very nearly all of these cases the alternative preferred by the ruling elite is actually adopted, the hypothesis (that the system is dominated by the specified ruling elite) is clearly false.

I do not want to pretend either that the research necessary to such a test is at all easy to carry out or that community life lends itself conveniently to strict interpretation according to the requirements of the test. *But I do not see how anyone can suppose that he has established the dominance of a specific group in a community or a nation without basing his analysis on the careful examination of a series of concrete decisions.* And these decisions must either constitute the universe or a fair sample from the universe of key political decisions taken in the political system.

Now it is a remarkable and indeed astounding fact that neither Professor Mills nor Professor Hunter has seriously attempted to examine an array of specific cases to test his major hypothesis.[3] Yet I suppose these two works more than any others in the social sciences of the last few years have sought to interpret complex political systems essentially as instances of a ruling elite.

To sum up: The hypothesis of the existence of a ruling elite can be strictly tested only if:

1. The hypothetical ruling elite is a well-defined group.
2. There is a fair sample of cases involving key political decisions in which the preferences of the hypothetical ruling elite run counter to those of any other likely group that might be suggested.
3. In such cases, the preferences of the elite regularly prevail.

IV. DIFFICULTIES AND OBJECTIONS

Several objections might be raised against the test I propose.

First, one might argue that the test is *too weak*. The argument would run as follows: If a ruling elite doesn't exist in a community, then the test is satisfactory; that is, if every hypothetical ruling elite is compared with alternative control groups, and in fact no ruling elite exists, then the test will indeed show that there is no minority whose preferences regularly prevail on key political alternatives. But—it might be said—suppose a ruling elite *does* exist. The test will not *necessarily* demonstrate its existence, since we may not have selected the right group as our hypothetical ruling elite. Now this objection is valid; but it suggests the point I made at the outset about the possibility of an infinite regress of explanations. Unless we use the test on every possible combination of individuals in the community, we cannot be certain that there is not some combination that constitutes a ruling elite. But since there is no more *a priori* reason to assume that a ruling elite does exist than to assume that one does not exist, the burden of proof does not rest upon the critic of the hypothesis, but upon its proponent. And a proponent must specify what group he has in mind as his ruling elite. Once the group is specified, then the test I have suggested is, at least in principle, valid.

Second, one could object that the test is *too strong*. For suppose that the members of the "ruled" group are indifferent as to the outcome of various political alternatives. Surely (one could argue) if there is another group that regularly gets its way in the face of this indifference, it is in fact the ruling group in the society. Now my reasons for wishing to discriminate this case from the other involve more than a mere question of the propriety of using the term "ruling elite," which is only a term of convenience. There is, I think, a difference of some theoretical significance between a system in which a small group dominates over another that is opposed to it, and one in which a group dominates over an indifferent mass. In the second case, the alternatives at stake can hardly be regarded as "key political issues" if we assume the point of view of the indifferent mass; whereas in the first case it is reasonable to say that the alternatives involve a key political issue from the standpoint of both groups. Earlier I refrained from defining the concept "key

[3] Mills, *op. cit.*; Floyd Hunter, *Community Power Structure* (Chapel Hill, 1953).

political issues." If we were to do so at this point, it would seem reasonable to require as a necessary although possibly not a sufficient condition that the issue should involve actual disagreement in preferences among two or more groups. In short, the case of "indifference vs. preference" would be ruled out.

However, I do not mean to dispose of the problem simply by definition. The point is to make sure that the two systems are distinguished. The test for the second, weaker system of elite rule would then be merely a modification of the test proposed for the first and more stringent case. It would again require an examination of a series of cases showing uniformly that when "the word" was authoritatively passed down from the designated elite, the hitherto indifferent majority fell into ready compliance with an alternative that had nothing else to recommend it intrinsically.

Third, one might argue that the test will not discriminate between a true ruling elite and a ruling elite together with its satellites. This objection is in one sense true and in one sense false. It is true that on a series of key political questions, an apparently unified group might prevail who would, according to our test, thereby constitute a ruling elite. Yet an inner core might actually make the decisions for the whole group.

However, one of two possibilities must be true. Either the inner core and the front men always agree at all times in the decision process, or they do not. But if they always agree, then it follows from one of our two assumptions about influence that the distinction between an "inner core" and "front men" has no operational meaning; that is, there is no conceivable way to distinguish between them. And if they do not always agree, then the test simply requires a comparison at those points in time when they disagree. Here again, the advantages of concrete cases are palpable, for these enable one to discover who initiates or vetoes and who merely complies.

Fourth, it might be said that the test is either too demanding or else it is too arbitrary. If it requires that the hypothetical elite prevails in *every single case*, then it demands too much. But if it does not require this much, then at what point can a ruling elite be said to exist? When it prevails in 7 cases out of 10? 8 out of 10? 9 out of 10? Or what? There are two answers to this objection. On the one hand, it would be quite reasonable to argue, I think, that since we are considering only key political choices and not trivial decisions, if the elite does not prevail in every case in which it disagrees with a contrary group, it cannot properly be called a ruling elite. But since I have not supplied an independent definition of the term "key political choices," I must admit that this answer is not wholly satisfactory. On the other hand, I would be inclined to suggest that in this instance as in many others we ought not to assume that political reality will be as discrete and discontinuous as the concepts we find convenient to employ. We can say that a system approximates a true ruling elite system, to a greater or lesser degree, without insisting that it exemplify the extreme and limiting case.

Fifth, it might be objected that the test I have proposed would not work in the most obvious of all cases of ruling elites, namely in the totalitarian dictatorships. For the control of the elite over the expression of opinion is so great that overtly there is no disagreement; hence no cases on which to base a judgment arise. This objection is a fair one. But we are not concerned here with totalitarian systems. We are concerned with the application of the techniques of modern investigation to American communities, where, except in very rare cases, terror is not so pervasive that the investigator is barred from discovering the preferences of citizens. Even in Little Rock, for example, newspaper men seemed to have had little difficulty in finding diverse opinions; and a northern political scientist of my acquaintance has managed to complete a large number of productive interviews with White and Negro Southerners on the touchy subject of integration.

Finally one could argue that even in a society like ours a ruling elite might be so influential over ideas, attitudes, and opinions that a kind of false consensus will exist—not the phony consensus of a terroristic totalitarian dictatorship but the manipulated and superficially self-imposed adherence to the norms and goals of the elite by broad sections of a community. A good deal of Professor Mills' argument can be interpreted in this way, although it is not clear to me whether this is what he means to rest his case on.

Even more than the others this objection points to the need to be circumspect in interpreting the evidence. Yet here, too, it seems to me that the hypothesis cannot be satisfactorily confirmed without something equivalent to the test I have proposed. For once again either the consensus is perpetual and unbreakable, in which case there is no conceivable way of determining who is ruler and who is ruled. Or it is not. But if it is not, then there is some point in the process of forming opinions at which the one group will be seen to initiate and veto, while the rest merely respond. And we can only discover these points *by an examination of a series of concrete cases where key decisions are made*: decisions on taxation and expenditures, subsidies, welfare programs, military policy, and so on.

It would be interesting to know, for example, whether the initiation and veto of alternatives having to do with our missile program would confirm Professor Mills' hypothesis, or indeed any reasonable hypothesis about the existence of a ruling elite. To the superficial observer it would scarcely appear that the military itself is a homogeneous group, to say nothing of their supposed coalition with corporate and political executives. If the military alone or the coalition together is a ruling elite, it is either incredibly incompetent in administering its own fundamental affairs or else it is unconcerned with the success of its policies to a degree that I find astounding.

However I do not mean to examine the evidence here. For the whole point of this paper is that the evidence for a ruling elite, either in the United States or in any specific community, has not yet been properly examined so far as I know. And the evidence has not been properly examined, I have tried to argue, because the examination has not employed satisfactory criteria to determine what constitutes a fair test of the basic hypothesis.

2

SYMBOLISM IN POLITICS
Murray Edelman

Edelman is the perfect thing to read after Dahl because Edelman succinctly suggests that citizens' generally nonideological predispositions and their understandable concerns for nonpolitical pursuits (work, recreation, family, religion) create some opportunity for politicians and officials to shape citizens' beliefs about government. Shaping citizens' beliefs is obviously a very powerful exercise in influence! The colloquial term is "mind control."

But ask yourself: Isn't Edelman assuming that people pay enough attention to politics and government to have their views decisively and permanently shaped by government officials? If people hardly ever pay much attention to politics and government, then how much room is there for psychological influence of any sort by governmental officials?

Still, Edelman provocatively emphasizes that many of us assume much of the time that government is competent enough for us to get on with our lives—and we do so in part because government constantly advertises its competence. Think here of the Marine Corps recruiting ad you may have recently seen at the movie theater—America is protected by elite warriors, it suggests. Perhaps you remember seeing the logo of the Federal Deposit Insurance Corporation (FDIC) at your bank when depositing money: it helped you think that your deposits are insured and therefore safe (at least if you did not immediately remark to yourself that your money is only safe as long as the entire banking system is safe and free from crisis or if you have less than $250,000 on deposit.)

There is a subtle implication here, one that is well worth noting at the outset of this volume. A lot of contemporary democratic citizenship is a combination of, on the one hand, our trust in government and, on the other, discounting the risk that our trust might be misplaced. Those people who are simply unwilling to experience democratic citizenship in this way have to do weird things like put their money under their beds—or move to a country where they feel safer. That does happen—a few thousand Americans emigrated to Canada, for instance, during the years that George W. Bush was president. But that was a ten-thousandth of one percent of the population, or about half the population of the tiny little college town in which I live.

• • •

THE SHAPING OF BELIEFS THROUGH POLITICS

AMERICANS ARE TAUGHT early in life that the policies of their government reflect what the people want, but few adults can be unaware today that governments

In Leon N. Lindbergh, ed., *Stress and Contradiction in Modern Capitalism* (Lexington, MA: Lexington Books, 1975), pp. 309–320. Reprinted with the permission of Lauren Edelman on behalf of Murray Edelman.

create public opinion as well as respond to it, or that they sometimes respond to it only after they shape it.

Governments influence both the quality of people's lives and their states of mind, although until recently political science paid relatively little attention to the latter process. Public policies help the poor, kill people in wars, and make some rich through depletion allowances; they also evoke common beliefs and perceptions among large segments of the population: a belief, for example, that a foreign country is planning aggression, that antitrust laws protect consumers against unfair prices, that crime is increasing or declining, that welfare recipients need to be controlled or forced to work. Such common beliefs in turn justify far-reaching public policies.

The beliefs are frequently accurate, but often they are inaccurate or problematic even though everyone likes to think of himself or herself as a political realist. Usually the beliefs are a mixture of fact and myth, and there is no way most citizens can learn which components are which. The social and psychological processes through which public beliefs come into being regardless of verifiable evidence are systematic in character, however, and we are learning what these processes are through the study of political symbolism.[1]

These symbolic processes more easily maintain confidence in the status quo than they promote disaffection and change, for the most powerful and most subtle cues come from established authorities. Though public officials and policies often become targets of criticism, the existing social structure and existing patterns of authority and status relationships typically benefit from political symbolism in advanced industrial societies. Increasing social complexity, more sophisticated electronic communications media, and greater knowledge of psychology are likely to provide authorities with ever more potent resources for reassuring the public and for socializing people into roles useful to elites.

When change serves elite interests, myths and rituals readily justify that too, typically employing traditional symbols to do so. Old nationalisms serve the interests of the new multinational corporations. Summit visits in Moscow and Peking create a widespread belief that detente has been achieved, although there is no lessening in the arms race or in the occurrence of confrontations.

The political creation of strong mass beliefs about controversial public issues takes many forms, but there are common elements whenever it occurs. There is always widespread anxiety about a potential threat (foreign attack, domestic subversion, economic insecurity, moral blight), and there is always substantial ambiguity about the facts and the causes of the problem. In consequence a large public very much wants to believe that the authorities know how to cope with the issues that they themselves find both threatening and bewildering.

For most people most of the time politics is, paradoxically, both a distraction from their chief interests and a source of deep-seated anxiety. Political leaders who appear to be competent, strong, and resolute therefore find a large audience eager to be reassured by their dramaturgical performances even if the social, economic, and foreign problems they attack remain unsolved or grow worse. Because

---

[1] I have discussed the issues raised in this article in more extended fashion in these publications: *The Symbolic Uses of Politics* (Urbana: University of Illinois Press, 1964); *Politics as Symbolic Action* (New York: Academic Press, 1971); "The Political Language of the Helping Professions," *Politics and Society*, vol. 4, no. 3; "Language and Social Problems," Institute for Research on Poverty Discussion Paper 207–74, May 1974.

of the pervasive ambiguity about the nature of the problems and the ready possibility of creating misleading benchmarks either of progress or of growing threat, dramaturgy rather than demonstrable results can easily shape public opinion and win a political following.

Through this psychological incentive to treat top government officials and official actions as symbols of effective and benevolent leadership, governments continuously evoke widespread beliefs about the entire range of our social and political concerns. They evoke perceptions of escalating threats and reassure us that threats are being dealt with; they create beliefs about what problems face us and what their causes are; and they instill beliefs about which people are meritorious and should be rewarded and which are incompetent or untrustworthy and need to be controlled. In short, they shape our political worlds far more completely than we recognize. Symbolically evoked beliefs are not necessarily false, but it is social cues rather than their factual accuracy or demonstrability that brings them into being; and they often *are* invalid. The mode of creation of each of these forms of politically cued beliefs is worth examination.

In the wake of Watergate and the Pentagon Papers it is obvious that governments sometimes evoke false beliefs deliberately. While outright public lying can profoundly affect people's lives, it is neither as long lasting in shaping states of mind nor as scientifically challenging as those political symbols that engage the political actors themselves at least as deeply as their audiences. The discussion that follows focuses upon the evocation of public beliefs that are not consciously deceptive: those that are typically seen both by officials and by the public as having different consequences from their demonstrable ones.

THE SYMBOLIC EVOCATION OF THREATS

Some political enemies hurt their adversaries; some help their adversaries by winning wider political support for them; and some do both. For the German Jews under Hitler, the Nazis were enemies who tortured and killed; for the Nazis, the Jews were enemies who helped solidify domestic opinion behind Hitler and so were politically useful, even though the typical Nazi doubtless perceived Jews as the enemy in just as real a sense as the Jews saw Nazis as their enemies. Because political opponents *can* marshal support for a leader or a cause, it is tempting for those who share a political ideology to perceive some group as the enemy and to evoke the same perception in the population generally. In view of the ready possibility of real conflicts and the constant temptation to create symbolic enemies, it is easy to understand why so much political history is a chronicling of mass violence in the form of wars, genocidal operations, riots, rebellions, and police actions.

The forms of action and of rhetoric that create enemies in this way are readily identified. A physical attack on the alleged enemy by a government recognized by its people as legitimately holding power is the most potent way to create a symbolic enemy. When the Johnson Administration fired upon North Vietnamese ships in the Tonkin Gulf and began bombing North Vietnam, most Americans accepted that action as evidence for the claim that North Vietnamese ships had fired upon American ships on routine maneuvers and that North Vietnam was aggressive, dangerous, and had to be contained. When the Chicago police beat up demonstrators at the 1968 Democratic National Convention, survey research showed that most Americans at once perceived the demonstrators as subversive types needing forceful containment. To try representatives of a group for alleged subversion in publicized court proceedings similarly convinces at least a part of the public that the group is indeed subversive.

In general, any social movement most effectively enlarges its political support by identifying as the enemy a group widely regarded as different and alien and therefore not sharing the human qualities of the people we know well. Differences in color, in religion, in nationality, in ideology, and in life-style have all served as a reason for picturing some target as subhuman or, occasionally, as uncannily superhuman. Because these grounds are so readily available for the creation of support to battle symbolic enemies, it is a constant temptation for political regimes and for others who need political support to convince themselves that whatever goals they have in the way of power, status, or money for themselves are in fact means to cope with powerful threats to the population generally: that their own interest is identical with the public interest.

Once particular people are identified in the public mind as actual or potential enemies, the intensification of conflict with them can stem from other symbolic cues rather than from demonstrable aggression. "Hawks" convinced a showdown is inevitable gain wider public support for escalation and larger military budgets by observing, publicizing, and exaggerating the militant behavior of the actual or potential adversary. In this sense the hawks in the Pentagon and in the Kremlin, for example, unwittingly serve each other's domestic political interests. Doves in rival countries do too, though in their case it is typically a conscious strategy.

Escalation and detente therefore bring with them new patterns of political support and new winners of material rewards. Heightened racial tension in the cities attracts wider support for the more militant groups and tactics, both among police and among blacks. It also means larger budgets for police weapons and more support for police discretion, power, and wage increases. On the other side escalation means larger public contributions and higher status for groups like the Black Panthers and less for moderate groups like the Urban League, while detente means the opposite. Because it is easy for governments to create beliefs in threats and enemies, and because the resulting escalation brings material and political benefits, the confusion between real and symbolic enemies can be useful to authorities. Ritualistic engagement with enemies based upon plots that are often mythical brings real rewards for some, though the rewards are conventionally perceived as public costs or deprivations.

If some enemies muster political support, there is reason to change enemies from time to time, to evoke new ones who will muster even wider support in the light of new popular anxieties. And that is exactly what happens with symbolic enemies. At various periods in the nineteenth century the Pope and Roman Catholicism were widely feared enemies for Americans worried about internal subversion from alien sources. In the early decades of the twentieth century anarchists assumed this role. After the Russian Revolution it became the communists. Sometimes an ally becomes an enemy overnight. Soviet Russia, which fought on our side during World War II, became the chief foreign threat to America almost instantly after V.E. Day; and our erstwhile enemies, the Germans, became allies almost as quickly. The inevitable ambiguity about how much of the threat from such enemies is real is a prerequisite to their symbolic potency, as noticed earlier.

By a curious paradox it is the opponents who are most widely and universally feared who most easily undergo such fast conversions. When there is political debate over a public issue or the definition of an enemy, beliefs and perceptions change slowly. Public controversy forces people on both sides to defend their opinions and find reasons to espouse and maintain them. But when there is a consensus the government is the chief, sometimes the only, source of cues, and social pressures are so strong that people adopt the common view with great facility, without having to defend it or even think about it with care. This is often the case in the foreign policy area. When the government begins to redefine the situation a new consensus is as easily formed as the old one was. There is little or no ground for resistance; social pressures to conform are still overwhelming; and so the change is just as noncontroversial as was the previous consensus.

THE CREATION OF REASSURANCE

Just as people are induced to see enemies who help politically but may not hurt physically, so are they induced to accept real deprivations without political resistance. Here again the possibility of symbolic response arises because the actual impacts of governmental actions are ambiguous and because people are eager to believe that the problems they fear are being effectively countered by governments they can trust.

Economists typically have little confidence, for example, that public utility laws, antitrust laws, and other statutes regulating business prices and practices in the interest of consumers make much difference for long. The regulatory agencies begin before long to reflect the interests and the point of view of the business corporations they are supposed to regulate, their information and their contacts are chiefly with these businesses, and the commissioners typically come from the same social and economic circles as the business management. Consumers, by contrast, are not organized to pursue their interests, to exert political sanctions if they are ignored, or even to see themselves as a distinct pressure group.

Laws regulating business in the interest of consumers do serve an important function, but it is chiefly political and psychological in character rather than economic. To people worried about the power of business monopolies or conglomerates to exploit them, the establishment and the publicized operations of a regulatory agency are reassurance that the government is protecting them. Politicians have often built constituencies upon these fears and their symbolic appeasement through "regulation," even if economists conclude that the regulation is largely ceremony, freeing the regulated industries to set prices and quality of service without political resistance. Because there is no other benchmark of fairness, consumers readily accept the pronouncements of the authoritative regulatory agency as constituting objective, scientific analysis, not responsiveness to the perspective and the interests of sellers.

In the same way a great deal of "law enforcement" masks bargaining, or arbitrariness, or concessions to elites behind a facade of legal certainty and objective fact-finding that render the outcomes psychologically acceptable. Law enforcement is often best understood as a game in which the basic rule is that most "violations" will not be detected or punished, but the authorities are free to decide which will be, in accordance with social norms, formal and informal bargains, and political strength. At the same time legal language and procedures legitimize the process and the outcome because they serve so potently as symbols of objectivity, blindness to privilege, and certainty. In filling out income tax forms, in observing or ignoring speed limits, in coping with antitrust laws, and in hundreds of other encounters with each other, citizens and public administrators regularly engage in a form of risk taking and bargaining while justifying the process and the result with the symbol of the rule of law. For this reason publicized emphasis upon the justice or the democratic character of a governmental proceeding is often a signal that the procedures are significant chiefly for their psychological effect: that they are justifying concessions in line with bargaining power.

A dramaturgy of zealous coping by leaders in behalf of the mass of the citizens is another powerful source of reassurance. Like formal procedures and formal declarations that the consumer is being protected, it is typically effective psychologically whether the leader's coping is real or make-believe and even when the outcome is an obvious failure. President Kennedy's popularity actually rose after the Bay of Pigs fiasco, as did President Nixon's after the 1971 wage-price freeze. When a leader's action looks resolute and decisive, it wins approval, for it reassures people that the chief executive knows how to deal with a problem or threat that worries them but also baffles most of them. A shake-up in the form of a governmental reorganization or the dismissal of subordinates; the publicized assumption by the chief of state of personal "responsibility" for a problem even though only subordinates are actually penalized for mistakes; the vigorous pursuit of a course of action that brings no results or counterproductive results—all of these have often increased a leader's popularity. President Nixon's rapid decline in popularity after the Watergate scandal is evidence that tough rhetoric and action cannot help a leader when the public perceives them as *refusal* to assume responsibility or as self-serving or self-contradictory. This stance leaves the impression of inability to cope and so creates anxiety. But a leader has wide leeway to shape a dramaturgy of competence. The test lies in how he acts, for by creating confidence in himself he also creates confidence in his own interpretation of the results of his acts, which are always ambiguous.

Symbolic gestures not only reassure the general public, but can continue to do so indefinitely, even in the face of authoritative evidence that the reassurance is not warranted. The federal antitrust laws are more than eighty years old. Public utilities regulation and other controls over business in the interest of consumers date from the early years of the twentieth century. Almost from their inception economists have questioned the effectiveness of such controls; but they continue to win votes for politicians, and any effort to repeal them would certainly bring widespread and intense protests. Tokenism has similarly been the order of the day over many decades in other areas of public policy, including many civil rights protections and guarantees of the health and safety of workers. Publicized administration and token enforcement continuously reemphasize the message people want to believe. The hard-nosed skepticism of serious students of these policies becomes known to some and even ambivalently accepted; but in a setting of uncertainty and concern, public actions in behalf of the consumer are easier to grasp, and they exercise a psychological magic that retains its potency.

GOVERNMENTAL LANGUAGE AS REASSURANCE

George Orwell once observed that political rhetoric usually lulls people into an uncritical and accepting state of mind, as church liturgy does.

By what psychological devices can the language of government play its part in stilling qualms and focusing the mind upon those facets of public policy that justify it? All language is metaphorical in the sense that it highlights some aspects of a situation while ignoring or masking others. In speaking of a farm policy as "parity" we concentrate upon its alleged function of raising farm income to an equitable level but divert attention from the demonstrable fact that it chiefly helps corporate farmers rather than family farmers and that consumers pay for it. In discussing a "war on poverty" we focus upon the intention of helping the poor, but in consequence fail to notice that the war is a border skirmish at best: that its benefits to the poor are meager and highly selective, while it provides much larger benefits to such affluent groups as slum landlords, highway builders in Appalachia, and physicians whose patients are covered by Medicaid or Medicare.

The *form* of political language has an even more subtle, and probably more powerful, impact upon our beliefs about government than its content does. As politicians and public officials appeal to us to support candidates and policies, their exhortations implicitly convey the message that our opinions count; and that reassuring message builds support for government and public policies whether or not we like particular regimes and particular actions. The legal language of constitutions, statutes, and treaties is rigorous in its form, commanding officials to carry out the precisely expressed will of the people and their elected representatives. This linguistic style is also strongly reassuring, for it tells us that it is the people, not officials, who make policy. But legal language is highly ambiguous in application. There are always conflicting precedents conferring wide and sometimes total discretion upon governmental regimes. Nonetheless the *form* of constitutions and laws continuously reassures us that we have a government of laws and not of men.

Banality and jargon in official language are also reassuring, even when they are exasperating and objects of irony. The bureaucrat who speaks in "officialese" is certainly avoiding fresh ideas and is telling us through his language style that just as his words are banal, so will his ideas be the conventional ones in the organization he serves. He can be counted on not to question the accepted values of his organization or rock the boat; and those who absorb such jargon smoothly, without qualms or protest, convey the same message about their own values. Hannah Arendt's observation that Adolf Eichmann expressed himself chiefly in cliches therefore helps us understand Eichmann's willingness to accept the shocking goals of the organization he served; in this sense Eichmann was the archetypical bureaucrat. By the same token people who refuse to use the conventional language forms of an organization or a social group are declaring their independence of the values of their associates.

THE SYMBOLIC EVOCATION OF MERIT AND DEVIANCE

One of the most powerful, yet least obvious, symbolic functions of government is the creation of widespread impressions about the level of merit or competence of particular groups of people. Who are incompetent, undeserving, criminal, mentally sick, or otherwise deviant; and who are normal, intelligent, admirable, or authoritative? In some degree, of course, we base such judgments upon objective evidence, but to a considerable extent we also base them upon governmental cues that are subtle, yet arbitrary. When government defines the consumption of alcohol as legal and the consumption of marijuana as criminal, it shapes public opinion regarding the respectability of consumers of the first and the deviance of consumers of the second. Similarly, the Eighteenth (prohibition) Amendment to the United States Constitution legitimized the way of life of rural, fundamentalist Protestants while debasing the culture of urban Catholics, just as repeal of that amendment twelve years later conveyed the reverse message about the relative status and respectability of these different groups of Americans. Government constantly influences status by exalting or condoning some norms while condemning others; and these influential judgments often differ over time and place, as the current state of obscenity and abortion laws illustrate.

In many other ways as well, agencies of the state determine people's status through procedures that purport to be scientific but are in some measure arbitrary or problematic. Elementary school teachers and counselors define children as intelligent or dull, high or low achievers, normal or psychologically disturbed, using tests and observations whose validity and reliability have repeatedly been shown to be low or doubtful. For one thing they often measure how well the children conform to middle-class norms of behavior, demeanor, and speech. Yet, there is impressive psychological evidence that the classifications tend to become self-fulfilling prophecies, for they shape the attitudes of others toward the child and the child's self-esteem and self-conception.

Studies of the classification of people as mentally ill and of the decision to charge them with crime similarly show very low reliability and the strong tendency to believe the worst of the poor and those whose social norms differ from those of psychiatrists, social workers, policemen, and judges. An overwhelming proportion of psychiatric patients involuntarily committed to hospitals and of persons charged with crime are poor or black, while a far higher proportion of middle-class crime and unconventional behavior is either overlooked or labeled as something else, such as individuality, resourcefulness, or eccentricity. In the first case we are cued to see a major defect of character or of mind; in the second, either something laudatory or a yielding to transient temptation, much less serious in its causes and in the rehabilitation measures that are appropriate. The state not only punishes people who are categorized as deviant, but in doing so reinforces beliefs about what is normal and what is deviant in the population generally. Governmental and professional actions create popular fears of the ex–mental patient or the ex-con whose original labeling was often problematic. In doing so they strengthen biases against the subcultures of the poor and the unconventional and so force the victims to continue to play the stigmatized role authorities have defined for them. It is understandable that recidivism rates for prisoners and mental patients are high, no matter what the mode of their "treatment" or the actual threat they pose. A five-year study in New York of the arrest rate of 5,000 former mental patients found it was one-twelfth that of the general population; and most of the arrests were for loitering, vagrancy, and public intoxication, the charges that confer the widest discretion upon police.

This role of the government in classifying people's level of merit and then making the labels a self-fulfilling prophecy works for the exalted as well as for the demeaned. As already noted, behavior is often officially or professionally judged according to who engages in it. The management and stockholders of most forms of business receive large governmental subsidies in the form of tax benefits, free public services, or direct grants. The subsidies are justified on the ground that their recipients are serving the public interest, and they symbolize a high level of merit, while the resulting wealth of the recipients further guarantees their high status.

THE EVOCATION OF BELIEFS ABOUT THE CHARACTER OF PUBLIC PROBLEMS AND THEIR CAUSES

Governmental acts and rhetoric also shape beliefs about the nature of public problems and about their causes. Such beliefs underlie many of the differences just noticed in the symbolic and material consequences of governmental programs. What we see as a public problem is not an empirical observation, but rather a function of subtle cues. While a comparatively small group of liberal intellectuals saw the segregation of schoolchildren by color as a serious problem before 1954, it was the widely publicized Supreme Court decision in the *Brown* case in that year that defined it as a major public issue for a much wider segment of the population. The proclamation of a "War on Poverty" in 1964 made poverty in America a conspicuous and serious problem for a large number of people for whom the poor had been invisible earlier, even though there had long been as many or more poor people suffering just as intensely.

Government strongly influences perceptions of the causes of problems as well as perceptions of their existence. The 1962 amendments to the Social Security Act requiring some classes of welfare recipients to accept counseling from social caseworkers created or strongly reinforced a widespread belief that there is far more wrong with the poor than low wages, unemployment, or inability to work: a belief that they suffer from cognitive deficiencies and need control and guidance in how to raise their children, run their homes, and spend their money. The work requirement in the 1972 amendments created or reinforced a belief that a major cause of poverty is laziness, even though it had long been known that a very small fraction of the recipients were physically able to work, did not have to care for small children, and could find jobs when the unemployment rate was close to five percent. In this instance the symbolic function of the statute came close to being its only function.

During World War II gasoline rationing was quite deliberately used not only to conserve fuel but also to create and maintain a strong sense of urgency in the population: to remind people in a compelling way that we were at war and that a spirit of austerity and self-denial was appropriate. The shortage was in fact never serious and the rationing program flexible enough that virtually everyone who was sufficiently persistent and demanding could secure extra rations. As a wisecrack among employees of the Office of Price Administration put it, "The meek shall inherit the dearth."

It has long been clear to sociologists that reality is socially created: that people differ radically in their perceptions of the same situations because of different cues from others. But we rarely recognize or remember that fact as we go about our everyday affairs. We naturally think our perceptions are objective, identical with those of other rational people. We see the world as fact, not as a creation of "significant others" who provide cues that resolve thousands of confusing sense perceptions into simplified patterns that tell us what kinds of situations confront us and even who we are. The belief that our perceptions are objective gives us confidence in them, whether or not the confidence is warranted.

Cues from others are especially powerful in shaping beliefs and perceptions when they deal with matters that create anxiety, when they are not countered by conflicting cues from other sources, and, above all, when the cues are covert. On all kinds of issues that concern us deeply government is our chief or only source of information. When governmental leaders debate publicly among themselves or with nongovernmental opinion leaders, their views are influential because the idea that government is legitimate is inculcated in us early in life. But the very fact of open debate signals the possibility that government can be wrong and in some degree makes us skeptical and alert for confirming or falsifying evidence.

The case is otherwise when the cues from government reach us without our becoming aware that we are being influenced, as is true of most of the symbolic cues discussed in this chapter: rituals of imminent threat to national or personal security and of protection against threats; metaphors and syntactic forms embodied in the language that "describes" issues and governmental institutions; authoritative labels that demean or exalt groups of people and define the causes of their behavior and their problems; myths we learn as children that give us our political identities and roles.

ISSUES IN NEED OF FURTHER EXPLORATION

Though it is apparent that many tenaciously held political beliefs are not empirically based, we need to know a great deal more about the social-psychological processes and the conditions that generate such beliefs. In what respects are the language and the acts of public officials distinctive in their consequences for public opinion and in what respects do they exemplify a link between language and cognition that also appears in other social interactions?

Comparison of political symbolism and its consequences in different countries and cultures should prove especially fruitful in this regard. Manifestly, the content of symbols differs among nations in the light of their respective histories, social and economic conditions, internal social conflicts, and national myths. But such differences may be fairly superficial, changing readily as new interpretations of history, new economic circumstances, and new ideologies appear. They may also be superficial, in the sense that symbols with different content are functionally equivalent, generating similar cognitive structures, as the work of Noam Chomsky and of Claude Lévi-Strauss suggests.

These issues also arise with respect to comparisons of symbols over time. Words and acts that once had powerful effects upon belief lose their potency, and new ones appear. We need to learn considerably more about the conditions of such change and the extent to which new symbols are functional equivalents of their predecessors.

One of the questions that needs investigation in this connection deals with the symbolic correlates of social and economic complexity, urbanization, and functional differentiation in contemporary life. Social scientists have long suggested that these secular trends have entailed a loss in individual autonomy and increasing alienation and anomie. As people's lives are increasingly affected by remote decisions (or nondecisions), does susceptibility to political mystification grow as well? And is there a corresponding increase in the range of behaviors defined as deviant by authorities and therefore by a mass public?

In the study of individual psychology systematic exploration of the non-rational and the irrational has become an essential complement to the study of human intelligence and reason. A similar emphasis in the study of political behavior is past due.

People typically pride themselves on their realism where politics is at issue, but our political worlds are symbolically created to a greater extent than are most aspects of our lives: a joint consequence of psychological needs and of the communications implicit in governmental actions and language. Political mystification is most powerful and most dangerous when, as is usually true, it is not deliberate; and so it is vital that we apply our knowledge of politics and of social psychology to throw light on the mechanisms that create and maintain widely held political cognitions whether or not they are valid.

3

CAUSAL STORIES AND THE FORMATION
OF POLICY AGENDAS

Deborah A. Stone[*]

Despite the fact that government constantly advertises its competence, disturbing events happen all the time for which there is no government role at all. To take three leading examples: Asthma, autism, and obesity all appear to be on the rise among children in the United States. Why is any one of them apparently more widespread than before? Who can do something about any one of them? Can government do something about any one of them? Ought it to? Why and how?

These questions imply the existence of a certain kind of politics—the politics of causal stories, to use Deborah Stone's apt formulation. Trying to get the public or some set of politicians or government officials to accept the proposition that upsetting phenomena have causes that they can effectively address is what the politics of causal stories is all about. The result is a lot of talking, arguing, and reasoning in American public life.

In identifying and succinctly characterizing such aspects of American politics, Stone underscores that the power to shape the public agenda can be highly dispersed. The capacity to tell a causal story, and get people to pay attention to it, is hardly universal. There are skill and resource requirements for telling compelling "causal stories." On the other hand, if acquiring influence can often come down to getting others—one way or another and through sheer persistence—to pay attention to a "causal story," then how concentrated is power and how undemocratic is American society?

• • •

THERE IS AN OLD SAW in political science that difficult conditions become problems only when people come to see them as amenable to human action. Until then, difficulties remain embedded in the realm of nature, accident, and fate—a realm where there is no choice about what happens to us. The conversion of difficulties into problems is said to be the *sine qua non* of political rebellion, legal disputes, interest-group mobilization, and of moving policy problems onto the public agenda.[1] This article is about how situations come to be seen as caused by human actions and amenable to human intervention. Despite the acknowledged

Reprinted by permission from *Political Science Quarterly* 104 (Summer 1989): 281–300.

[*] The author would like to thank the A. Alfred Taubman Center for Public Policy of Brown University for support of an earlier version of this article.

[1] On litigation, see William Felstiner, Richard Abel, and Austin Sarat, "The Emergence and Transformation of Disputes: Naming, Blaming, Claiming," *Law and Society Review* 15 (1980–81): 631–654; on interest groups, the locus classicus is David Truman, *The Governmental Process* (New York: Knopf, 1951); on agenda formation, see John Kingdon, *Agendas, Alternatives and Public Policies* (Boston: Little, Brown, 1984), 115–121.

importance of this phenomenon as a precursor to political participation and to agenda setting, there is little systematic inquiry about it in the political science literature. For the most part, the question is dealt with under the rubric of agenda setting, even though the transformation of difficulties into problems takes place in something of a black box prior to agenda formation. Three strands of thinking in the agenda literature contribute indirectly to an understanding of this topic. One strand focuses on the identity and characteristics of political actors—leaders, interest groups, professionals, bureaucrats. It looks at the actors' attitudes, resources, and opportunities to account for the appearance of policy problems and their particular formulations at any given time.[2] A second strand focuses on the nature of the difficulties or harms themselves—for example, whether they are serious or mild, new or recurring, short-term or long-term, health effects or economic effects.[3] Finally, a third strand focuses on the deliberate use of language and of symbols in particular as a way of getting an issue onto the public agenda or, alternatively, keeping it off.[4]

While each of these approaches gives us some insight into the processes of problem definition and agenda setting, they miss what I think is the core substance of the transformation of difficulties into political problems: causal ideas. Problem definition is a process of image making, where the images have to do fundamentally with attributing cause, blame, and responsibility. Conditions, difficulties, or issues thus do not have inherent properties that make them more or less likely to be seen as problems or to be expanded. Rather, political actors *deliberately portray* them in ways calculated to gain support for their side. And political actors, in turn, do not simply accept causal models that are given from science or popular culture or any other source. They compose stories that describe harms and difficulties, attribute them to actions of other individuals or organizations, and thereby claim the right to invoke government power to stop the harm. Government action might include prohibition of an activity, regulation, taxation, economic redistribution, criminal sanctions, education campaigns, direct compensation of victims (through social insurance or special funds), and mandated compensation of victims (through litigation).

In thinking about how causal argument works in politics, I have borrowed from all three strands of the agenda-setting literature. I take a social constructionist view of policy problems. That is to say, I believe our understanding of real situations is always mediated by ideas; those ideas in turn are created, changed, and fought over in politics. I will show how political actors use narrative story lines and symbolic devices to manipulate so-called issue characteristics, all the while making it seem as though they are simply describing facts.[5] I have created a typology of causal stories, and I hope to demonstrate with a variety of examples that

[2] I see this approach as the main thrust of Kingdon's *Agendas, Alternatives and Public Policies*, ibid., though he certainly incorporates the second and third approaches mentioned below.

[3] This strand is best exemplified by Roger Cobb and Charles Elder, *Participation in American Politics: The Dynamics of Agenda-Building* (Boston: Allyn and Bacon, 1972), chaps. 6 and 7. Cobb and Elder also pay attention to the nature of the participants and to symbolic language (see esp. chaps. 8 and 9), but I think their distinctive contribution is the argument that certain characteristics of a difficult situation determine whether it is likely to expand.

[4] The work of Murray Edelman dominates this tradition. See his *The Symbolic Uses of Politics* (Urbana: University of Illinois Press, 1964); *Politics as Symbolic Action* (Chicago: Markham Publishing Company, 1971); and *Constructing the Political Spectacle* (Chicago: University of Chicago Press, 1988).

[5] The best analysis I know of using this perspective is Joseph Gusfield, *The Culture of Public Problems* (Chicago: University of Chicago Press, 1981).

there is in fact a systematic process with fairly clear rules of the game by which political actors struggle to control interpretations and images of difficulties.

Causal stories have both an empirical and a moral dimension. On the empirical level, they purport to demonstrate the mechanism by which one set of people brings about harms to another set. On the normative level, they blame one set of people for causing the suffering of others. On both levels, causal stories move situations intellectually from the realm of fate to the realm of human agency. This intellectual step is the key trigger for moving a condition onto what Roger Cobb and Charles Elder call the "systemic agenda," the set of issues up for general discussion in a polity.[6] The great books that launched public issues, such as Ralph Nader's *Unsafe at Any Speed*, all performed this intellectual transformation, as I will show later. But the competition to control causal stories does not stop once an issue reaches either the systemic or the formal agenda. Causal stories continue to be important in the formulation and selection of alternative policy responses, because they locate the burdens of reform very differently.

In politics, causal theories are neither right nor wrong, nor are they mutually exclusive. They are ideas about causation, and policy politics involves strategically portraying issues so that they fit one causal idea or another. The different sides in an issue act as if they are trying to find the "true" cause, but they are always struggling to influence which idea is selected to guide policy. Political conflicts over causal stories are, therefore, more than empirical claims about sequences of events. They are fights about the possibility of control and the assignment of responsibility.

A TYPOLOGY OF CAUSAL STORIES

We have two primary frameworks for interpreting the world—the natural and the social. In the natural world, we understand occurrences to be "undirected, un-oriented, unanimated, unguided, 'purely physical.'"[7] There may be natural determinants—the clash of a cold front and a warm front causes a storm. But there is no willful intention behind the occurrences, at least not without invoking a purposeful God. The natural world is the realm of fate and accident, and we believe we have an adequate understanding of causation when we can describe the sequence of events by which one thing leads to another. In the social world, we understand events to be the result of *will*, usually human but perhaps animal. The social world is the realm of control and intent. We usually think we have an adequate understanding of causation when we can identify the purposes or motives of a person or group and link those purposes to their actions. Because we understand causation in the social sphere as related to purpose, we believe that influence works. Coaxing, flattering, bribing, and threatening make sense as efforts to change the course of events; and it is possible to conceive of preventing things from happening in the first place. In the natural world, influence has no place. We laugh at those who would bring rain with their dances or sweet talk their computer into compliance. In the natural world the best we can do is to mitigate effects.

In everyday discourse, as Erving Goffman points out, we use the term "causality" to refer to both "the blind effect of nature and intended effect of man, the first seen as an infinitely extended chain of caused and causing effects and the

---

[6] Cobb and Elder, *Participation*, 14.
[7] Erving Goffman, *Frame Analysis* (New York: Harper and Row, 1974), 22.

TABLE 1
Types Of Causal Theories

Consequences		
Actions	Intended	Unintended
	Mechanical Cause	*Accidental Cause*
Unguided	intervening agent machines trained animals brainwashed people	nature weather earthquakes machines that run amok
	Intentional Cause	*Inadvertent Cause*
Purposeful	assault oppression conspiracies that work programs that work	intervening conditions unforeseen side effects neglect carelessness omission

second something that somehow begins with a mental decision."[8] Yet in politics, the distinction between actions that have purpose, will, or motivation and those that do not is crucial. So, too, is the distinction between effects that are intended and those that are not, since we know all too well that our purposeful actions may have unintended consequences.

These two distinctions—between action and consequences and between purpose and lack of purpose—can be used to create a framework for describing the causal stories used in politics. (See Table 1.) Each box contains a different kind of story about causality. The four types are rough categories with fuzzy boundaries, not clear dichotomies. The table is meant to serve as a map to show how political actors push an issue from one territory to another.

The most important feature of the table is that there are two relatively strong, pure positions—accident and intent—and two relatively weak, mixed positions— mechanical and inadvertent cause. In the struggle over problem definition, the sides will seek to stake out the strong positions but will often move into one of the weaker positions as a next-best option.

In the upper right box are accidental causes. These include natural disasters such as floods, earthquakes, droughts, and hurricanes. Here we might also put machines run amok—the car that careens out of control or the CAT scanner that crushes its captive patient. These phenomena are devoid of purpose, either in their actions or consequences. In fact, one cannot properly speak of actions here, but only of occurrences. This is the realm of accident and fate.

Since our cultural understanding of accidents defines them as events beyond human control, causal politics is centrally concerned with moving interpretations of a situation from the realm of accident to one of the three realms of control. This is not to say that government action is limited to the realm of human control; we often call upon government to mitigate the effects of natural disasters, for example, by providing famine relief or aid for flood and storm victims. Yet even for natural disasters, where there is probably the strongest cultural agreement that they are

[8] Ibid., 23.

indeed accidents, there is sometimes a political struggle over even that consensus as victims call for government aid. For example, government-subsidized flood insurance has been opposed because it artificially lowers the true cost of residing or doing business in a flood plain; it thus gives people an incentive to do something that an informed rational calculus would prevent. Government, too, is often called upon to prevent accidents; but almost always the debate then turns on whether and how human action contributes to accident or exacerbates its effects.[9]

In the lower left box are intentional causes, where an action was willfully taken by human beings in order to bring about the consequences that actually happened. When the consequences are perceived as good, this is the domain we know as rational action, apotheosized by the professional schools of public policy. When the consequences are perceived as bad, we have stories of oppressors and victims. In this box also belong conspiracy stories; here the argument is that problems are the result of deliberate but concealed human action. For example, the Johns Manville company knew about the dangers of asbestos exposure but concealed them from its employees.

In the lower right box are inadvertent causes, or the unintended consequences of willed human action. (Actions often have good side effects, but I will ignore these, since we are talking about problems here.) One type of story in this box is the tale of harmful side effects of well-intentioned policy. Here, the consequences are predictable but still unforeseen. Lester Thurow tells such a story about inflation during the Nixon era. Richard Nixon imposed wage and price controls to stem inflation, but didn't realize that in the context of expansionary fiscal and monetary policies, the controls would only create even bigger price increases when they were lifted. Economic theory would predict exactly these results.[10]

Stories of inadvertent cause are common in social policy; problems such as poverty, malnutrition, and disease are "caused" when people do not understand the harmful consequences of their willful actions. The poor do not realize how important it is to get education or save money; the elderly do not understand how important it is to eat a balanced diet even if they are not hungry; the sick do not understand that overeating leads to diabetes and heart disease. Inadvertence here is ignorance; the consequences are predictable by experts but unappreciated by those taking the actions. These stories are soft (liberal) versions of blaming the victim: if the person with the problem only changed his or her behavior, the problem would not exist. The conservative version of blaming the victim is intentional causation: the victim actually chooses to have the problem. Thus, as President Ronald Reagan said about the homeless, there are those who sleep on grates by choice.[11]

Another type of inadvertence is carelessness or recklessness. Problems in occupational safety and health are often explained in this rubric, although carelessness is alternately attributed to labor or management. In management's version, workers understand the dangers of machines or chemicals; but they decline to use protective gear and safety devices because their tasks are easier, more comfort-

---

[9] See, for example, Anders Wijkman and Lloyd Timerlake, *Natural Disasters: Acts of God or Acts of Man?* (Washington, D.C.: International Institute for Environment and Development, 1984), arguing that the event, if not the consequences, in most floods, droughts, famines, etc. can be prevented or mitigated by human action.

[10] Lester Thurow, *Dangerous Currents*, 2nd ed. (New York: Vintage Books, 1984), 54–56.

[11] Reagan speech, 31 January 1984, cited in Herbert Block, *Through the Looking Glass* (New York: W. W. Norton, 1984), 123.

able, or faster without the precautions. In labor's version, management understands the hazards; but it does not monitor equipment conscientiously or provide safety gear, hoping it can keep productivity up without any undue mishaps. And in a more radical labor version, management knowingly stints on safety in the interests of profits, a conscious trade-off that pushes the problem into the sphere of intent.

In the upper left box are mechanical causes. It contains things that have no will of their own but are designed, programmed, or trained by humans to produce certain consequences. The idea of mechanical cause is that the effects of actions are intended, but the actions are guided only indirectly; someone's will is carried out through other people or through machines. There is an intervening agent. The notion of planned obsolescence is such a causal story: manufacturers design light bulbs, appliances, and tools to wear out so that consumers will have to buy new ones. The story asserts that a problem once thought to be unintended machine failure (accident) is really a case of intended machine failure (mechanism). In this category might also fit situations—common in tort law—where one person frightens another; the frightened person acts reflexively, almost mechanically, in a way that creates a harm. For example, a person frightened by one danger dashes into an oncoming car or drives his own car into someone else's.

In mechanical cause, the exact nature of human guidance or control is at issue. Often a fight about the cause of a problem is a debate about whether certain people are acting out of their own will or carrying out the will of others. To return to the example of malnutrition, one liberal causal story rests on unintended consequences of purposeful action: malnourished people do not know how to eat a proper diet or, alternatively, unwittingly sacrifice good nutrition in trying to stretch their meager resources. A conservative story rests on intended consequences of purposeful action: malnourished people knowingly choose to spend their food money on beer and junk food. And a radical causal story rests on indirect control: food processors and advertisers, in their quest for profits, manipulate people into eating junk food and unbalanced diets.

If the nature of human control over other humans is problematic, so is human control over machines. Debates about nuclear power, chemical plants, airplane accidents, and toxic chemical spills usually center on this issue. After a chemical leak at the Union Carbide plant in Institute, West Virginia, in 1985, company officials blamed a computer for their delay in notifying local authorities. The computer had erroneously predicted that the aldicarb oxime gas cloud would not leave the plant site. Officials told a story of accidental breakdown. Then the president of the company that had made the computer safety system said the computer had never been programmed to detect aldicarb oxime. "The computer worked exactly the way it was supposed to," he affirmed, changing the story to pure mechanism. He revealed that his company could have provided a more expensive safety system that would have detected the leak, predicted the flow of the cloud, and automatically notified local authorities; but Union Carbide had ordered only the "basic model."[12]

By the end of the week, the Union Carbide story had grown hopelessly complex. The injuries from the leak could be traced to a tank that wasn't designed to hold aldicarb oxime, faulty meters on another tank, defective safety valves, weak

[12] David Sanger, "Carbide Computer Could Not Track Gas That Escaped," *New York Times*, 14 August 1985.

gaskets, pipes too small for the job, mistaken transmission of steam to the tank, failure of control room operators to notice pressure and temperature gauges, failure of the computer to detect the spreading gas cloud, failure of executives to purchase a program that could detect the chemical, and failure of government to regulate the chemical industry.[13]

The Union Carbide "accident" suggests a type of causal story far more complex than can be contained in the table. The ideas of accidental, mechanical, intentional, and inadvertent cause all conjure up images of a single actor, a single action, and a direct result. This underlying image remains even when the ideas are applied to corporations, agencies, and large groups—or to sequences of identifiable actions and results. Many policy problems—the toxic hazard problem notable among them—require a more complex model of cause to offer any satisfying explanation. There is a wide variety of such models, but let me paint three broad types.

One might be called "complex systems."[14] It holds that the social systems necessary to solve modern problems are inherently complex. Today's technological systems, such as chemical production, involve parts that serve multiple functions, juxtaposition of different environments (high and low temperatures), complicated feedback loops, and interactions between different parts of a system. In such complex interactive systems, it is impossible to anticipate all possible events and effects; so failure or accident is inevitable. Failures also involve so many components and people that it is impossible to attribute blame in any fashion consistent with our cultural norm that responsibility presupposes control.

A second type of complex cause might be called "institutional." It envisions a social problem as caused by a web of large, long-standing organizations with ingrained patterns of behavior. The problem of cost overruns and "gold-plating" in weapons acquisition—symbolized by $630 toilet seats—has been explained in these terms. The armed services operate with a basic drive to have the edge in operational performance over the other side. They believe that it pays to develop the best quality weapons during peacetime, because Congress will certainly authorize high quantity production during wars. The different service branches gain by colluding for overall increases in the defense budget rather than competing with each other for a fixed pie. The services also gain by colluding with industry contractors to push programs through Congress on the basis of low initial cost estimates and by coming back later for increases once costs have been sunk. As one analyst says, "the causes of gold plating in its broadest sense are rooted in the institutional interests and professional outlooks of the military."[15]

A third type of complex cause might be called "historical" or "structural." Quite similar to institutional explanations, this model holds that social patterns tend to reproduce themselves. People with power and resources to stop a problem (for example, mining accidents) benefit from the social organization that keeps them in power and maintain it through control over selection of elites and socialization of both elites and non-elites. People who are victimized by a problem do not seek

---

[13] See, in addition to Sanger article, ibid., Stuart Diamond, "Carbide Blames a Faulty Design for Toxic Leak," *New York Times*, 13 August 1985; Stuart Diamond, "Chemical Pipe Size Called Key Safety Factor," *New York Times*, 14 August 1985; and Robert E. Taylor, "Carbide Tank Wasn't Designed to Hold Chemicals That Leaked," *Wall Street Journal*, 16 August 1985.

[14] For an excellent statement and exploration of this theory, see Charles Perrow, *Normal Accidents* (New York: Basic Books, 1984).

[15] Robert J. Art, "Restructuring the Military-Industrial Complex: Arms Control in Institutional Perspective," *Public Policy* 22 (Fall 1974): 423–459.

political change because they do not see the problem as changeable, do not believe they could bring about change, and need the material resources for survival provided by the status quo. Causal explanations of poverty that blame economic inequality or capitalism would be examples of such a structural explanation.[16]

Images of complex cause are in some sense analogous to accidental or natural cause. They postulate a kind of innocence, in that no identifiable actor can exert control over the whole system or web of interactions. Without overarching control, there can be no purpose and no responsibility. Complex causal explanations are not very useful in politics, precisely because they do not offer a single locus of control, a plausible candidate to take responsibility for a problem, or a point of leverage to fix a problem. Hence, one of the biggest tensions beween political science and real-world politics. The former tends to see complex causes of social problems, while the latter searches for immediate and simple causes.

STRATEGIES OF CAUSAL ARGUMENT

There are many strategies for pushing responsibility onto someone else. For the side that believes it is the victim of harm, the strongest claim it can make is to accuse someone else of intentionally causing the problem. Short of being able to make that claim stick, the victim group will allege either mechanical causation or inadvertent causation. Mechanical causation is a somewhat stronger claim, because it implies intended consequences, even if only through indirect guidance such as management instructions to floor supervisors or explicit decisions to design a safety system for some contingencies but not others.

Books and studies that catalyze public issues have a common structure to their argument. They claim that a condition formerly interpreted as accident is actually the result of human will, either indirectly (mechanical or inadvertent cause) or directly (intentional cause); or they show that a condition formerly interpreted as indirectly caused is actually pure intent. Crystal Eastman's *Work Accidents and the Law*, usually deemed the trigger event for Workmen's Compensation, showed that workplace injuries were not primarily caused by worker carelessness (inadvertence) but by employer refusal to provide safe machines and working conditions (intent). Eastman's framing of the problem is illustrative of the political logic in all these arguments:

> If adequate investigation reveals that most work-accidents happen because workmen are fools, like Frank Koroshic, who reached into danger in spite of every precaution taken to protect him, then there is no warrant for direct interference by society in the hope of preventing them. If on the other hand, investigation reveals that a considerable proportion of accidents are due to insufficient concern for the safety of workmen on the part of their employers, . . . then social interference in some form is justified.[17]

Rachel Carson's *Silent Spring* argued that the deterioration of animal and plant life was not a natural phenomenon (accident) but the result of human pollution

---

[16] A well thought-out example of this type of argument is Joshua Cohen and Joel Rogers's explanation of how capitalist democracy reproduces itself, in their *On Democracy* (Harmondsworth, England: Penguin Books, 1983), chap. 3. On historicist causal theories, see also Arthur Stinchcomb, *Constructing Social Theories* (New York: Harcourt Brace, and World, 1986), 101–130.

[17] Crystal Eastman, *Work Accidents and the Law* (New York: Russell Sage, 1910), 5.

(inadvertence).[18] Ralph Nader's *Unsafe at Any Speed* claimed that automobile crashes were not primarily due to unpredictable mechanical failures (accidents) or even to reckless drivers (inadvertence), but to car manufacturers' decisions to stint on safety in design (intention).[19] Jonathan Schell's book on nuclear holocaust, *The Fate of the Earth*, is a twist on this genre of policy writing, because it has to begin by imagining, predicting, estimating, and portraying consequences of an event that has not yet occurred. Having done that, Schell argues that this new "knowledge" moves our actions into the sphere of intent, and we can no longer regard the effects of nuclear holocaust as accident.[20]

A common strategy in causal politics is to argue that the effects of an action were secretly the intended purpose of the actor. If people sleep on grates or work in dangerous jobs, they must have chosen to do so because they get more satisfaction out of those activities than anything else (to pick a conservative version of the argument). Or (to pick a liberal version), since the deficit incurred by the Reagan administration has united liberals and conservatives around reduced government spending, Reagan must have run up the deficit deliberately in order to force Democratic support for his program of government retrenchment.[21]

To assume that the effects of an action are its purposes is to commit the teleological fallacy. Purpose must always be demonstrated with evidence of the actor's wishes or motives, apart from the effects of his actions. Still, teleological reasoning is a good political ploy, because the person who turns out to have willed harm while concealing his malevolent intent is a doubly despicable character; the symbolism of the disguised malefactor is a potent rallying cry.

The concept of risk has become a key strategic weapon for pushing a problem out of the realm of accident into the realm of purpose. Risk serves this function in two ways. First, when the harms at issue are medical, as in food and drug regulation, occupational safety, consumer product safety, environmental pollution, or nuclear power, the probabilistic association of harmful outcomes with human actions is widely accepted as a demonstration of a cause-and-effect relationship.[22] If the harms associated with an action or policy are predictable, then business and regulatory decisions to pursue a course of action in the face of that knowledge appear or can be made to appear as a calculated risk. Similarly, business and regulatory decisions justified by risk/benefit analysis can be portrayed as the intentional causation of harms in the pursuit of benefits to oneself.[23]

Increasingly, courts are willing to hold companies liable for calculated risks. The Ford Pinto automobile case is especially notable because the court construed Ford's business decision to trade off safety for cost as "conscious disregard of the *probability* that [its] conduct will result in injury to others," and, therefore,

[18] Rachael Carson, *The Silent Spring* (New York: Fawcett, 1978).

[19] Ralph Nader, *Unsafe at Any Speed* (New York: Bantam Books, 1973).

[20] Jonathan Schell, *The Fate of the Earth* (New York: Avon Books, 1982).

[21] Daniel Moynihan, letter to the editor, *Wall Street Journal*, 15 August 1985.

[22] On the predominance of the probabilistic interpretation of causation in twentieth-century scientific culture, see Jacob Brownowski, *The Common Sense of Science* (London: William Heinemann, 1951). On the increasing acceptance of statistical and epidemiological evidence in American courts, see Richard E. Hoffman, "The Use of Epidemiological Data in the Courts," *American Journal of Epidemiology* 120 (1982): 190–202; and Berk Black and David Lilienfeld, "Epidemiological Proof in Toxic Tort Litigation," *Fordham Law Review* 52 (1984): 732–785.

[23] See Richard Bogen, "Quantitative Risk-Benefit Analysis in Regulatory Decision-Making," *Journal of Health Politics Policy and Law* 8 (1983): 120–143.

as "malicious intent."[24] Calculated risk is also the crux of the plaintiffs' argument in the asbestos and Agent Orange litigation. In short, predictable stochastic outcomes have been transformed by reformers into conscious intent. The idea of calculated risk is a way of pushing a problem from inadvertence to intent.

A second way that risk serves to push harms into the realm of purpose is in the area of civil rights. Statistical evidence is now the primary tool to prove discrimination in employment, jury selection, schools, voting districts, housing, and other government service programs.[25] Until the 1970s the only way minorities could win discrimination suits was to show evidence of intent to discriminate on the part of an employer, a prosecutor, a school superintendent, and so forth. In cases where a policy or rule did not explicitly mention race or gender as a criterion, this requirement usually meant adducing evidence of a person's motives and intentions (evil-motive analysis), showing that a seemingly neutral rule was really a pretext for discrimination or showing that a rule was administered in an obviously discriminatory fashion.

In 1971, the U.S. Supreme Court for the first time allowed statistical evidence of a rule's "disproportionate impact" on a minority group to stand as proof of discrimination without a showing of purpose.[26] Since then, plaintiffs can sometimes succeed in discrimination suits if they can show that the result of a selection process (for jobs, juries, school assignment, public housing) could not have occurred by chance. If the risk of not being selected is higher for a minority group than for another group or higher than it would be with random selection from a pool of both groups, then a court may find discrimination, assuming some other tests are also met.[27]

The significance of this change in legal doctrine is that it broadens the concept of discrimination to encompass systematic effects without a direct link to human intent and motivation. Civil rights advocates have long argued that contemporary economic and occupational differences between blacks and whites or women and men, though not attributable to contemporary bias or intended discrimination, *are* attributable to differences created by past intentionally discriminatory treatment. In effect, they have successfully pushed the problem of institutional discrimination from the realm of accident to the realm of inadvertence. The acceptance of statistical evidence by courts as proof of discrimination converts discriminatory impact into the moral and political equivalent of calculated risk.

As one side in a political battle seeks to push a problem into the realm of human purpose, the other side seeks to push it away from intent toward the realm of nature or to show that the problem was intentionally caused by someone else.

[24] *Grimshaw v. Ford Motor Co.*, 119 Cal. App. 3d 757, 174 Cal. Rptr. 348 (1981), citing language from *Dawes v. Superior Court*, 111 Cal. App. 3d. 82 (1980). (Emphasis added.)

[25] Caroline Peters Egli, "Judicial Refinement of Statistical Evidence in Title VII Cases," *Connecticut Law Review* 13 (1981): 515–548; and Julia Lamber, Barbara Reskin, and Terry Dworkin, "The Relevance of Statistics to Prove Discrimination: A Typology," *Hastings Law Journal* 34 (January 1983): 553–598.

[26] *Griggs v. Duke Power Co.*, 401 U.S. 424 (1971). Duke Power Company required either a high school diploma or a minimum score on an intelligence test as a condition for internal transfer. The Court found that neither requirement was related to ability to learn or perform jobs. Far fewer blacks than whites (proportionately) could satisfy either of these requirements, and so blacks fared poorly in job advancement.

[27] An employer can maintain a rule that has a discriminatory impact if he can show that its criteria are job-related or necessary for the business. Even after Griggs, statistical arguments do not always win the day, but it is fair to say that they are increasingly victorious in discrimination cases.

The side accused of causing the problem is best off if it can show the problem was accidentally caused. Hence, after the leak at its West Virginia plant, Union Carbide began with a story about failed safety valves and a malfunctioning computer. Second best is to show that the problem was caused by someone else. This strategy is only second best, because anyone else accused of causing the problem will fight back and resist the interpretation, whereas the accidental causal story does not generate a live opponent.

The weakest defense is to show inadvertence, especially of the unforeseen consequences variety. Carelessness and neglect do not look very good, but they are probably better defenses than planned or designed failures. For example, Union Carbide chose to program its computer to detect only ten of the hundreds of chemicals it produces and had purchased programs for only three of the ten at the time of the leak. Aldicarb oxime wasn't even on the list of ten. In the aftermath, management talked of faulty pipes and valves but not of its decision not to purchase a warning system for the chemical that leaked.

The struggle between interpretations of accidental cause and controllable cause frequently takes the form of a debate about heredity versus environment. This debate has long been prominent with respect to intelligence and its supposed correlates of academic, economic, and political success.[28] More recently, the propensity to commit crime has also been debated in this framework.[29] Accepting heredity as a determinant of a social problem usually means adopting a policy of laissez-faire, while finding environmental determinants, such as education or income, means investment of social resources to equalize the benefits or burdens of a problem.

Complex cause is sometimes used as a strategy to avoid blame and the burdens of reform. When a company comes under fire and appears to be losing in the struggle to prove itself innocent—Manville and asbestos litigation, for example—it may argue that the problem is really due to a complex structural cause and can only be "solved" by larger institutions. By insisting that the federal government deal with compensating asbestos victims, Manville attempted to spread out the costs onto society at large. The widespread adoption of Workers' Compensation in the early twentieth century can be seen as a successful move by employers, who were increasingly losing liability suits, to define the problem of industrial accidents as the "natural" result of modern technology and to socialize the costs through insurance.[30]

THE LIMITS OF CAUSAL ARGUMENT

Causal stories need to be fought for, defended, and sustained. There is always someone to tell a competing story, and getting a causal story believed is not an easy task. American automobile and steel producers, for example, blame their declining market share on unfair Japanese competition. They try to sustain their claims by lobbying Congress for import tariffs and domestic content legislation, petitioning the International Trade Commission for restrictions on Japanese imports, and advertising about their market difficulties. Meanwhile, others (including the Japanese) are trying to define the problem as caused by failure of steel

[28] See Stephen J. Gould, *Mismeasure of Man* (New York: W. W. Norton, 1981).

[29] See James Q. Wilson and Richard J. Herrnstein, *Crime and Human Nature* (New York: Simon and Schuster, 1985).

[30] Lawrence Friedman and Jack Ladinsky, "Social Change and the Law of Industrial Accidents," *Columbia Law Review* 67 (1967): 50–82; and James Weinstein, *The Corporate Ideal and the Liberal State: 1900–1918* (Boston: Beacon Press, 1968), chap. 2.

companies to innovate; failure of car manufacturers to offer small, fuel-efficient cars; overly generous union contracts; and poor management. Auto and steel producers, for all their apparent political strength, have not succeeded in making their story stick, however. In a recent poll, 53 percent of American respondents thought the United States makes Japan a scapegoat for its trade problems, and only 30 percent thought Japan engaged in unfair trading practice.[31]

Most citizens have and can articulate explanations of national problems such as poverty, unemployment, or terrorism. But recent research suggests that causal beliefs are quite sensitive to the way television news coverage portrays problems. For example, when people watch news stories about poverty that show a homeless family, they are much more likely to think of individual explanations of poverty, such as lack of motivation or lack of skills. When they see news stories that portray a high rate of unemployment or reductions in federal social spending, they are more apt to give societal or governmental explanations of poverty.[32]

If problem definition is a great tug of war between political actors asserting competing causal theories, one wants to know what makes one side stronger than another. What accounts for the success of some causal assertions but not others? What are the political conditions that make one causal theory seem to resonate more than others?

Many of the constraints that have been identified for agenda setting hold for causal argument in problem definition as well.[33] Assertions of a causal theory are more likely to be successful—that is, become the dominant belief and guiding assumption for policy makers—if the proponents have visibility, access to media, and prominent positions; if the theory accords with widespread and deeply held cultural values; if it somehow captures or responds to a "national mood";[34] and if its implicit prescription entails no radical redistribution of power or wealth. One major causal story—that the capitalist economic and political system is the cause of innumerable social ills—is consistently shut out.[35]

The political success of causal theories is also constrained by two powerful social institutions for determining cause and legitimating claims about harms: law and science. Law is a whole branch of government devoted to hearing claims, examining evidence, pronouncing verdicts, and enforcing them. Science is an intellectual enterprise with its own vast social and economic organization devoted to determining cause-and-effect relationships. And if law carries greater formal authority by virtue of its status as part of government, science commands enormous cultural authority as the arbiter of empirical questions. Not all battles over causal stories will be resolved in the court of law or science, but most significant ones will find their way into one or both of these forums.

Tort law (sometimes called accident or personal injury law) is the branch of law concerned with injurious behavior that is not regulated via criminal law or formal contracts. It has to do with the informal standard of care for one another

[31] Susan Chira, "Poll Blames U.S. on Japan Trade," *New York Times*, 13 August 1985.

[32] Shanto Iyengar, "Television News and Citizens' Explanations of National Affairs," *American Political Science Review* 81 (September 1987): 815–831.

[33] See Kingdon, *Agendas*, 138–46; and Roger Cobb and Charles Elder, "Communications and Public Policy" in Dan Nimmo and Keith Sanders, eds., *Handbook of Political Communications* (Beverly Hills, Calif.: Sage, 1981).

[34] Kingdon, *Agendas*, 153–57.

[35] For both the story and an analysis of the reasons why it is shut out, see Cohen and Rogers, *On Democracy*.

that a community expects of its members. Since there is no formal set of rules, only case-by-case decision making, tort law is fuzzy and constantly evolving. Tort law arbitrates issues of causation, because it is concerned with deciding what harmful consequences of people's actions the people should be expected to control. It therefore defines the political boundaries between the realm of fate (what harmful effects are considered natural or plain bad luck) and the realm of human control (what harmful effects will trigger the attribution of responsibility).

The tort suit is a primary vehicle in the United States for asserting a causal theory about harm and demanding a remedy. It has been used for all manner of harms—dangerous consumer products, drug side effects, radiation exposure, incompetent professional services, occupational hazards, and emotional distress. Discrimination and affirmative action suits under constitutional and statutory laws are another legal vehicle for asserting and defining socially caused harms. Large class action suits make the law a forum for group warfare, not merely individual disputes. The Agent Orange cases, for example, in addition to being individual claims, are an organized protest by Vietnam veterans against their treatment during and after the war.[36]

All of this is to say that the rules of the game in law are crucial determinants of the political success of causal theories, even theories with the stamp of approval of science. Although epidemiological studies had shown a link between asbestos and cancer by the late 1940s, it was not until 1973 that the courts first allowed a verdict against an asbestos manufacturer. The scientific evidence for the cigarette-cancer link is even stronger, and yet it was first in 1988 that a cigarette manufacturer was held liable for smokers' lung cancer.[37]

Science serves as an arbiter of causal theories for an even broader array of issues than law. Proponents of causal theories—whether about disease or poverty, crime or inflation, car accidents or homelessness—appeal to scientific studies and the canons of scientific inquiry in their quest for political support. Often academics and scientists are the chief proponents of a theory. But to say the enterprise of science exercises some kind of constraint on the successful assertion of causal theories is not to say that its judgments are any more consistent, any less confusing, and any less political than those of law. We can only say that having some science on your side may help; it will not guarantee that a causal theory will become the guiding assumption of public policy.

An extended analysis of the role of law and science in problem definition is beyond the scope of this article. Here I only want to make the point that a theory of how problems come to be defined in politics must include a more extended analysis of how these two social institutions support and constrain causal argument.

THE POLITICAL FUNCTIONS OF CAUSAL THEORIES

Causal theories, if they are successful, do more than convincingly demonstrate the possibility of human control over bad conditions. First, they can either challenge or protect an existing social order. Second, by identifying causal agents, they can assign responsibility to particular political actors so that someone will have to stop an activity, do it differently, compensate its victims, or possibly face punishment. Third, they can legitimate and empower particular actors as "fixers" of the

[36] See Peter Schuck, *Agent Orange on Trial* (Cambridge, Mass.: Harvard University Press, 1986).
[37] *Cipollone v. Liggett Group, Inc.,* 683 F. Supp. 1487 (DNS 1988).

problem. And fourth, they can create new political alliances among people who are shown to stand in the same victim relationship to the causal agent.

Bringing a condition under human control often poses a challenge to old hierarchies of wealth, privilege, or status. In the nineteenth and early twentieth century, many poor rural whites in the South were afflicted with a chronic sickness later discovered to be caused by the hookworm parasite. People with the disease were listless and eventually became slow-witted. Popular belief held that the condition reflected the laziness and lax moral character of the victims. When Charles Stiles demonstrated in 1902 that hookworm was the cause and that the disease could easily be cured with a cheap medicine, he was widely ridiculed in the press for claiming to have discovered the "germ of laziness." The discovery was resisted because it meant that southern elites had to stop blaming "poor white trash" for their laziness and stupidity and stop congratulating themselves for their superior ability to work hard and think fast—a supposed superiority that served to justify political hierarchy.[38]

The abortion issue is a more recent example of political resistance to the extension of human control into an area formerly deemed natural. Much of the rhetoric against abortion is couched in terms of "interference with nature" and the "sanctity of life." Religious beliefs aside, the control over childbearing made possible by abortion threatens the social order in which a woman's status and social protection is determined by her role in the family, at the same time as it enables a social order in which her status is determined by her role in the workforce. And in fact, women who actively oppose permissive abortion policies tend to be those who do not work and whose social identity is tied to motherhood, while those who actively support abortion tend to be career women whose identity depends on work outside the home.[39]

Causal theories are also used as an instrument of social control to maintain existing patterns of dominance. For example, the theory that poor, pregnant women "cause" premature and unhealthy babies through their dietary deficiencies justifies official monitoring of their shopping and dietary habits as a condition of social aid. The theory of maternal deprivation (that children whose mothers work suffer developmental deficits and delays) arose just as middle-class women entered the workforce in large numbers. The maternal deprivation theory, consciously or unconsciously, served as a brake on disintegration of the standard middle-class pattern in which the man is breadwinner and the woman is childbearer. Struggles over causal definitions of problems, then, can be seen as contests over basic structures of social organization.[40]

Any bad situation offers multiple candidates for the role of "cause." In the old nursery rhyme, the fall of a kingdom can be traced back through a lost battle, a fallen soldier, an injured horse, a loose horseshoe all the way to a missing nail and a careless blacksmith. In the real world, problems rarely come with such neat lineage, but, like the leak at Union Carbide, always are replete with possible causes.

---

[38] Deborah A. Stone, *The Disabled State* (Philadelphia: Temple University Press, 1984), 93–94. The history of medicine is full of stories of resistance to discoveries that would make disease controllable. See, for example, Charles Rosenberg, *The Cholera Years* (Chicago: University of Chicago Press, 1962).

[39] Kristin Luker, *The Politics of Motherhood* (Berkeley: University of California Press, 1984).

[40] I borrow these illustrations from Mary Douglas, *Risk Acceptability According to the Social Sciences* (New York: Russell Sage, 1985), 53–60.

In the world of policy there is always choice about which causal factors in the lineage to address, and different choices locate the responsibility and burden of reform differently. In the issue of deaths and injuries resulting from drunk driving, both our laws and cultural beliefs place responsibility with the drunk driver. There are certainly alternative ways of viewing the problem: we could blame vehicle design (for materials and structure more likely to injure or kill in a crash); highway design (for curves likely to cause accidents); lack of fast ambulance service or nearby hospitals; lax enforcement of drunk driving penalties by police; or even availability of alcoholic beverages.[41] Grassroots organizations of victims (such as Mothers Against Drunk Driving) have successfully moved the issue beyond moral exhortation by looking for targets of responsibility other than the driver. They have sued the people who served drinks to the driver—restaurants, taverns, private hosts, and even governments; pressured legislatures to pass laws making hosts and servers liable for damages caused by drunk drivers; and lobbied to ban "happy hours" in bars.[42]

Even when there is a strong statistical and logical link between a substance and a problem—such as between alcohol and car accidents, handguns and homicides, tobacco and cancer deaths, or cocaine and overdose deaths—there is still a range of places to locate control and impose sanctions. Each of these problems has a virtually identical chain of causation: substance-user-seller-manufacturer-raw-materials supplier. In the case of alcohol, we have traditionally seen drinkers as the cause and limited sanctions to them, though sellers have more recently been made to bear the costs. In lung cancer deaths, we have blamed the smoker primarily; but to the extent people have sought to place the blame elsewhere, they have gone after cigarette manufacturers, not sellers or tobacco growers. With handgun homicides, we have limited blame to the users of guns rather than imposing sanctions on either the sellers or manufacturers. And with cocaine, we cast the widest net with attacks against users, sellers, (importers, street peddlers, pharmacies, physicians), and growers. Finding the true or ultimate cause of harms in these policy areas is not what is at issue. Rather, the fight is about locating moral responsibility and real economic costs on a chain of possible causes. The location is dictated more by the political strength of different groups (tobacco growers, the gun lobby) than by any statistical proof or causal logic.

Just as different causal stories place the burden of reform on some people rather than others, they also empower people who have the tools or skills or resources to solve the problem in the particular causal framework. People choose causal stories not only to shift the blame but to enable themselves to appear able to remedy the problem.

Lloyd Ethridge tells a wonderful story about the problem of unreturned cafeteria trays when he was president of his high school student council. The student council, not wanting to get involved in policing other students but still needing to oblige the principal's request for help, chose to adopt the theory that offending students were ignorant of the consequences of their actions (inadvertent cause). That way the student council could offer to run an awareness campaign without accepting any form of coercion. The principal, believing in the school as a training ground for life and having at his disposal a host of teacher-employees and disciplin-

[41] The drunk driving issue is the topic of Gusfield's *The Culture of Public Problems*.
[42] Jilian Mincer, "Victims of Drunken Driving Press Suits on Drivers' Hosts," *New York Times*, 9 August 1985.

ary powers, adopted instead an intentional cause theory. He asserted that students left trays on tables because "it wasn't worth it" to them to walk the trays back to the kitchen. Not surprisingly, he instituted a system of teacher monitors, moralistic lectures, and "the familiar repertoire of high school discipline."[43]

Like the famous six characters in search of an author, people with pet solutions often march around looking for problems that need their solutions. Causal stories then become mechanisms for linking a desired program to a problem that happens to be high on the policy agenda. Health Maintenance Organizations (HMOs) were sold as reforms to increase health care for the poor during the liberal 1960s on the theory that limited access of poor people to health care was caused by the inefficient solo-practice system of delivery. The same advocates of HMOs then pushed them to the Nixon administration as answers to the cost-containment problem on the theory that high health care costs were caused by fee-for-service payment.[44] Urban mass transit was billed as the answer to traffic congestion during the urban-growth-conscious 1950s and early 1960s; to pollution during the environmental-conscious late 1960s and early 1970s; and to conservation during the energy-conscious late 1970s.[45] Causal theories serve as devices for building alliances between groups who have problems and groups who have solutions.

Shifting the location of responsibility on a causal chain can restructure alliances. Under the old view of drunk driving, where the driver bore sole responsibility for accidents, the drunk driver was pitted against everybody else. In the new view the driver becomes a victim (of the server's negligence) along with the people he injured, and the server is cast outside this alliance. The relationship between taverns and their customers is altered, because all customers—indeed especially the best customers—are now a potential liability. Tavern owners may seek new alliances with other anti-regulation groups. One can also imagine alcoholic beverage manufacturers facing a difficult political choice whether to ally themselves with the taverns (their most important customers) or with the injured victim and the driver (in the hopes that victims won't go after manufacturers next).

Causal theories predicated on statistical association can create alliances by mobilizing people who share a risk factor but otherwise have no natural communication or association. In the DES cases, organizations of mothers and their daughters exposed to DES some twenty or more years ago sprang up out of nowhere as soon as the initial publicity about the DES-cancer link occurred. The trigger for Vietnam veterans' mobilization around the Agent Orange issue was a benefits counselor in the Chicago Veterans Administration (VA) office who thought she saw a pattern of illnesses and exposure to Agent Orange. She collected her own statistics, publicized them on television in 1978, and soon Agent Orange–based disability claims began rolling in to the VA.[46] Irving Selikoff's early studies of cancer in asbestos workers stimulated unions to sponsor more studies, organize their members for research and litigation, and ally with other unions on issues of

[43] Lloyd S. Etheredge, *The Case of the Unreturned Cafeteria Trays* (Washington, D.C.: American Political Science Association, 1976).

[44] Paul Starr "The Undelivered Health System," *The Public Interest* 42 (Winter 1976): 66–85.

[45] This example comes from Kingdon, *Agendas*, 181. Kingdon calls the phenomenon of hooking problems to causes "coupling." It has also been called "A Garbage Can Model of Organizational Choice" by Michael Cohen, James March, and Johan Olsen in *Administration Science Quarterly* 17 (March 1972): 1–25.

[46] Schuck, *Agent Orange on Trial*, 23.

occupational safety.[47] Causal theories, thus, can be both a stimulus to political organization and a resource for political leaders seeking to create alliances.

CONCLUSION

It is only recently that political scientists have produced a literature on the question of how problems move onto policy agendas. The question of how difficult conditions become defined as problems in the first place has received very little attention in the public policy literature. In this article I have tried to develop a theory of problem definition, starting from the conventional social science wisdom that a bad condition does not become a problem until people see it as amenable to human control.

First, causal argument is at the heart of political problem definition. Problem definition is centrally concerned with attributing bad conditions to human behavior instead of to accident, fate, or nature.

Second, the process of problem definition cannot be explained by looking solely at political actors, the nature of bad conditions, or the characteristics of issues. Problem definition is the active manipulation of *images* of conditions by competing political actors. Conditions come to be defined as problems through the strategic portrayal of causal stories.

Third, these portrayals can be categorized as four causal theories: intent (direct control); mechanistic cause (indirect control exercised through an intervening agent); inadvertent cause (control mediated by intervening conditions); and accident (total absence of human control).

Fourth, actors seeking to define a problem attempt to push the interpretation of a bad condition out of the realm of accident and into the realm of human control. The three causal stories of human control all assign responsibility for the condition to someone else and so create a burden of reform. People blamed for a problem and saddled with the burden of reform will resist the new causal theory (assuming they benefit from the status quo) by portraying the condition as accidental, as caused by someone else, or as one of the indirect forms of causation.

Fifth, political actors have increasingly used probabilistic notions of causation in addition to mechanistic concepts, and arguments based on probabilistic cause are increasingly successful. (The world of policy seems to parallel the world of science with about a fifty-year lag.)

Sixth, the competition over causal theories in problem definition is bounded not only by the usual political conditions that constrain agenda setting, but also by law and science, two social institutions that are each in their own fashion charged with arbitrating disputes about causal theories.

Finally, causal theories have important consequences for politics beyond the mere demonstration of human control. They have a strong normative component that links suffering with an identifiable agent, and so they can be critical of existing social conditions and relationships. They implicitly call for a redistribution of power by demanding that causal agents cease producing harm and by suggesting the types of people who should be entrusted with reform. And they can restructure political alliances by creating common categories of victims.

[47] Paul Brodeur, *Expendable Americans* (New York: Viking, 1974).

4

WHEN EFFECT BECOMES CAUSE
Policy Feedback and Political Change
Paul Pierson*

The article by Stone emphasizes that politics often means pushing for a policy. But once there is a policy, the resulting allocation of governmental resources or approval "feeds back" into the political system. New symbols of governmental competence exist, perhaps, for some new policy—affecting (Edelman would say) how people think about the issue connected to the symbol. Also, many policies require new governmental agencies that are not certain to be popular or well liked beyond the "target" population served by that agency. The "feedback" from a policy choice may in fact be quite politically disruptive and generate new divisions in society or harden those that already exist.

Environmental regulation during the 1970s, for example, helped to mobilize private businesses into lobbying for changes in environmental regulations. The Supreme Court's decision in Roe v. Wade *made it a policy of the United States that women could control the fate of the fetuses they carry. In making this decision, the Supreme Court helped to create "abortion politics"—which has often been very bitter.*

What might Pierson's unusual perspective mean for thinking about the distribution of power? It suggests that policy-making—which is constant—is constantly rearranging what politically active people pay attention to, and thereby changing how and why they mobilize political resources. Policy feedback, due to active government, reinforces Dahl's essential point: If American politics could be simply explained in a convincing way it would be. If the polity "sat still" or were in some sort of equilibrium, such explanation might eventually become possible. But as Pierson demonstrates quite succinctly, American politics is dynamic because government is active.

• • •

Gøsta Esping-Andersen. *The Three Worlds of Welfare Capitalism.* Princeton: Princeton University Press, 1990, 248 pp.

Peter Hall, ed. *The Political Power of Economic Ideas: Keynesianism across Countries.* Princeton: Princeton University Press, 1989, 406 pp.

Douglass C. North. *Institutions, Institutional Change and Economic Performance.* Cambridge: Cambridge University Press, 1990, 152 pp.

Paul Pierson, "When Effect Becomes Cause: Policy Feedback and Political Change," *World Politics* 45 (July 1993): 595–628. © The Johns Hopkins University Press. Reprinted with permission of The Johns Hopkins University Press.

  * For helpful comments on earlier versions of this paper I would like to thank Richard Valelly and the participants in the State and Capitalism and the American Political Development Seminars at Harvard University.

Theda Skocpol. *Protecting Soldiers and Mothers: The Political Origins of Social Policy in the United States.* Cambridge: Belknap Press of Harvard University Press, 1992, 714 pp.

ACTIVE GOVERNMENT is a central feature of modern life. In advanced industrial democracies, anywhere from 30 to 60 percent of GNP is filtered through government programs. In addition to these massive public systems of resource extraction and deployment, governments exert a major influence on social relations through an unquantifiable but pervasive set of prohibitions and requirements. This extensive activity makes it very likely that, as E. E. Schattschneider argued over a half century ago, "new policies create a new politics."[1] Yet political scientists were slow to incorporate Schattschneider's insight into their models of politics, treating policy as the result of political forces (the dependent variable), but rarely as the cause of those forces (the independent variable). In the past decade or so, this has ceased to be true. Scholars working on a range of empirical issues have begun to emphasize that "policies produce politics."

The massive twentieth-century expansion of the role of government has clearly contributed to this new orientation. Increasing government activity made it harder to deny that public policies were not only outputs of but important inputs into the political process, often dramatically reshaping social, economic, and political conditions. Intellectual developments have also fostered this shift in research. The "postbehavioralist" turn toward investigating the structural constraints facing individual actors has led scholars working from a variety of perspectives to begin identifying the ways in which the formal and informal rules of the game in political and social life influence political behavior. To date, most analysis has centered on formal governmental institutions and political organizations.[2] However, major public policies also constitute important rules of the game, influencing the allocation of economic and political resources, modifying the costs and benefits associated with alternative political strategies, and consequently altering ensuing political development.

The increased scope of public policy and the close fit between the concept of policy feedback and a new social science agenda has fueled a growth of research on the topic. The emergence of a substantial and broadly persuasive literature on policy feedback represents a considerable achievement for what might be called a "historical institutionalist" approach to comparative politics.[3] Historical institutionalist analysis is based on a few key claims: that political processes can best be understood if they are studied over time; that structural constraints on individual

[1] E. E. Schattschneider, *Politics, Pressures and the Tariff* (New York: Prentice-Hall, 1935), 288.

[2] For a range of "new institutionalist" analyses, see Peter B. Evans, Dietrich Reuschemeyer, and Theda Skocpol, eds., *Bringing the State Back In* (Cambridge: Cambridge University Press, 1985); James G. March and Johan P. Olsen, *Rediscovering Institutions: The Organizational Basis of Politics* (New York: Free Press, 1989); Kenneth A. Shepsle, "Studying Institutions: Some Lessons from the Rational Choice Approach," *Journal of Theoretical Politics* 1 (April 1989); and Stephen Skowronek, *Building a New American State: The Expansion of National Administrative Capacities, 1877–1920* (Cambridge: Cambridge University Press, 1982).

[3] In addition to the scholarship of Theda Skocpol reviewed in this essay, see, for example, Skowronek (fn. 2); Peter A. Hall, *Governing the Economy: The Politics of State Intervention in Britain and France* (Oxford: Oxford University Press, 1986); and Sven Steinmo, Kathleen Thelen, and Frank Longstreth, eds., *Structuring Politics: Historical Institutionalism in Comparative Analysis* (Cambridge: Cambridge University Press, 1992).

actions, especially those emanating from government, are important sources of political behavior; and that the detailed investigation of carefully chosen, comparatively informed case studies is a powerful tool for uncovering the sources of political change. Yet if the scholarship discussed below suggests the strengths of this approach, it also reveals important limitations.

This new research raises the prospect of significantly improving our understanding of politics. However, while recent scholarship has emphasized that past policies themselves influence political struggles, moving from this general statement to more specific propositions about *how* policy structures matter has proven to be difficult. It is too easy to let a label substitute for an argument—a dangerous practice when the label is in fact an umbrella term covering a wide range of sometimes incompatible propositions about the political world. Asking how previous policy decisions are being used to explain later developments quickly reveals not one argument but many. Either these specific arguments are often not clearly spelled out, or the scope of their application remains unexplored.

This essay investigates the range of arguments that lie behind the general label of policy feedback. Part of my purpose is to indicate the sheer range of existing work, which provides compelling evidence that the analysis of policy feedback constitutes a major research frontier in comparative politics. The discussion also seeks to help scholars expand their investigations of policy feedback. Because researchers have not clearly specified the range of ways in which policies can affect politics, they have often failed to identify important paths of influence. I will argue that there are significant feedback processes—particularly those directly affecting mass publics rather than bureaucrats, politicians, or organized groups—that have yet to receive sufficient attention. Indeed, there is reason to expect that the effects on mass publics may turn out to be the most important political consequences of government growth.

The main goal of this article, however, is to encourage improved use of an increasingly popular type of explanation. The broad claim that "policies produce politics" has been important. Now that we know policy choices have political consequences, however, what needs to be determined is precisely how, when, and where particular effects are likely to occur. We need to ask more complex questions about the extent and operation of feedback. Providing empirical support for specific claims is beyond the scope of this essay. However, it is possible to raise some central questions that deserve attention and to outline some plausible and testable hypotheses about the range and impact of various feedback effects that would reward further study. A close investigation of existing research reveals that particular routes of inquiry are more promising than others. It also suggests that some of the most promising lines of research must draw heavily on work in other traditions, especially rational-choice theory, and that many of the most pressing questions will be difficult to answer through the case study approach that has been the favored tool of historical institutionalists.

The following discussion makes no attempt to offer a comprehensive evaluation of the works considered. In several instances, a focus on policy feedback was not the author's central interest. Yet each has made important contributions to an understanding of the political consequences of public policies. I begin by considering arguments about the ways in which policies provide resources and incentives for political actors, before turning to arguments that concentrate on the cognitive consequences of public policies.

POLICIES AS PRODUCERS OF RESOURCES AND INCENTIVES

Analyses that stress the ways in which political systems confer resources on individuals and create incentives for them are the bread and butter of contemporary political science. By virtue of their location within a political system, particular actors may have direct access to significant political assets. These may be material, but an even more important asset may be access to authority—the capacity to issue commands and take other steps with a reasonable expectation that others will accept these actions as legitimate. Political systems also create incentives, which do not directly confer resources but help to define the alternatives available to individual actors. Incentive structures influence the probability of particular outcomes and the payoffs attached to those outcomes. Individuals choose, but the conditions that frame their decisions provide strong inducements to make particular choices.

While often associated with rational-choice theory, it is worth stressing that these arguments are compatible with the central claims of many investigations operating outside that tradition. Often, the difference between rational-choice and ostensibly competing approaches concerns the explicitness of certain assumptions and the preferred methodologies rather than more fundamental disagreements about the major determinants of political action. For most political scientists operating both within and outside rational-choice frameworks, resources and incentives are key.

Given the scope of modern government, it would be hard to deny that public policies provide resources and incentives that may influence political action. Yet how, and how often, are these feedback effects important? Resource/incentive arguments have been used to support claims of significant policy feedback on social groups, government elites, and mass publics. Perhaps the most successful line of research on policy feedback emphasizes the resource/incentive effects of policies on *social groups*. If interest groups shape policies, policies also shape interest groups. The organizational structure and political goals of groups may change in response to the nature of the programs they confront and hope to sustain or modify.

INTEREST GROUP EFFECTS

The activity of interest groups often seems to follow rather than precede the adoption of public policies. This is a central theme in Theda Skocpol's *Protecting Soldiers and Mothers*, which represents both a major contribution to our understanding of American social policy before the New Deal and a considerable theoretical achievement. More than any other scholar, Skocpol has been at the center of efforts to use historical institutionalist analysis to understand the dynamics of policy feedback. *Protecting Soldiers and Mothers* provides her most sustained effort to show how these processes work in a particular historical case. The prominence Skocpol gives to this variable suggests that, even before the arrival of "big government," policy choices could have major political consequences.

Skocpol identifies "changes in social groups and their political goals and capabilities" (p. 58) as one of two major types of policy feedback. In emphasizing the linkage between policies and interest groups, she echoes a common theme. Jack Walker's detailed investigation of interest groups in the United States, for example, noted that "the steady expansion of the federal government figures as one of the major causes of the recent growth of new organizational devices for linking citizens with their government."[4]

As in much of the research on policy feedback, however, arguments about the relationship between previous policies and patterns of interest articulation are quite diverse, and analysts have not always been careful to specify precisely what the relationship between the two variables might be. Policies provide both incentives and resources that may facilitate or inhibit the formation or expansion of particular groups. The incentives stem primarily from the major social consequences of specific government actions. Public policies often create "spoils" that provide a strong motivation for beneficiaries to mobilize in favor of programmatic maintenance or expansion. Skocpol cites the case of Civil War pensions: "After initial legislative liberalizations, veterans became self-consciously organized and mobilized to demand ever improved benefits" (p. 59).

Exactly who is induced to mobilize will often depend on the precise nature of policy interventions. In an influential article, Weir and Skocpol suggested that a crucial difference between Swedish and U.S. social policies during the 1930s was that the former helped to cement a farmer/worker political alliance while the latter did not. The Swedish Social Democrats devised a system of price supports without production controls that was attractive to small farmers. The structure of New Deal agricultural policies, by contrast, activated affluent farmers who had little inclination to establish common cause with urban workers:

> Rather than enduringly uniting labor with those farmers who would benefit most from increased domestic consumption and state interventions in agriculture, the New Deal ended up joining together larger, commercially well-established, export-oriented southern cotton producers with better-off midwestern corn and wheat farmers oriented to domestic as well as international markets. This cross-regional alliance, which took shape from the middle 1930s, was embodied in the American Farm Bureau Federation (AFBF), an organization that became very influential in Congress . . . [and] frequently cooperated with the conservative alliance of southern Democrats and Republicans in Congress to oppose many urban liberal Democratic initiatives.[5]

It is important to stress that new policies do not only provide incentives for supporters. Initiatives may also fuel countermobilizations involving novel forms of political organization. David Vogel's analysis of the response of American

---

[4] Jack L. Walker, Jr., *Mobilizing Interest Groups in America: Patrons, Professions and Social Movements* (Ann Arbor: University of Michigan Press, 1991), 54.

[5] Margaret Weir and Theda Skocpol, "State Structures and the Possibilities for 'Keynesian' Responses to the Great Depression in Sweden, Britain and the United States," in Evans, Reuschemeyer, and Skocpol (fn. 2), 143–44. The Farm Bureau's development has been widely linked to policy feedback, even by scholars not inclined to emphasize the independent role of government activity. In his classic study of interest groups, Mancur Olson argues that "the Farm Bureau was created by the government." Olson, *The Logic of Collective Action: Public Goods and the Theory of Groups* (Cambridge: Harvard University Press, 1965), 149. David B. Truman also identified "the aid of federal officials" as important in launching the Farm Bureau. Truman, *The Governmental Process* (New York: Alfred A. Knopf, 1971), 87–93. On policy feedback in agriculture, see also Terry M. Moe, *The Organization of Interests: Incentives and the Internal Dynamics of Political Interest Groups* (Chicago: University of Chicago Press, 1980), 181–91; Richard Valelly, *Radicalism in the States: The Minnesota Farmer-Labor Party and the American Political Economy* (Chicago: University of Chicago Press, 1989); and John Mark Hansen, *Gaining Access: Congress and the Farm Lobby, 1919–1981* (Chicago: University of Chicago Press, 1991), chaps. 2–3.

business to the regulatory initiatives of the late 1960s and early 1970s provides an excellent example of how policy feedback generated new structures of interest representation:

> Among the most distinctive features of the regulatory statutes enacted during the first half of the 1970s was precisely that they were not directed toward specific industries. Rather, they sought to change the behavior of companies in a wide variety of different industries. This made many business executives much more conscious of their common or class interests, which in turn led to both the formation and revival of political organizations that represented firms in many different industries, such as the Business Roundtable, the United States Chamber of Commerce, and the National Federation of Independent Business.[6]

Policy designs can also create niches for political entrepreneurs, who may take advantage of these incentives to help "latent groups" overcome collective action problems.[7] The history of the now-formidable American Association of Retired People (AARP) illustrates this feedback process. The inadequacy of health care benefits for the elderly provided the AARP with a niche for activity. The sale of health insurance prior to the enactment of Medicare, and of "Medigap" policies since then, has provided a strong "selective incentive" for individuals to join AARP. These conditions promoted the development of an elderly lobby that is unmatched in other countries.[8]

Not only do public policies create incentives for interest group activities, they may also provide resources that make that activity easier. The political influence of groups varies dramatically; some are central actors in the development of policy, while others are ineffectual, forced to accept gains and losses determined elsewhere. Public policies can clearly "feed back" into politics in this respect, too. Policies can have an effect on the resources of groups and the ability of groups to bring those resources to bear on decision makers.

Sometimes government policies create interest group resources in a straightforward sense, as when legislation provides funding to favored organizations or provides incentives for individuals to join particular groups (e.g., by banning or harassing alternative organizations). In a compelling essay on the development of the Swedish labor movement, Bo Rothstein has demonstrated that policy designs that gave unions authority over unemployment funds provided a crucial impetus to the development of powerful labor confederations.[9] Union administration of these funds gave workers a strong "selective incentive" to become union members. Rothstein's comparative analysis indicates that union density rose rapidly and stabilized at higher levels in countries that adopted this particular design for unemployment insurance.

---

[6] David Vogel, *Fluctuating Fortunes: The Political Power of Business in America* (New York: Basic Books, 1989), 13–14.

[7] On the importance of political entrepreneurs, see Mancur Olson (fn. 5); Russell Hardin, *Collective Action* (Baltimore: Johns Hopkins University Press, 1982), 35–37; and Moe (fn. 5), 37–39.

[8] See, for example, Christine L. Day, *What Older Americans Think: Interest Groups and Aging Policy* (Princeton: Princeton University Press, 1990). Thanks to Kent Weaver for bringing this example to my attention.

[9] Bo Rothstein, "Labor Market Institutions and Working-Class Strength," in Steinmo, Thelen, and Longstreth (fn. 3).

Policies may also strengthen particular groups by increasing their access to decision makers. The literature on corporatism contains many examples of this kind of process.[10] Governments pursuing a complicated social and economic agenda adopted policies that brought important social actors (usually business associations and labor confederations) directly into the decision-making process. Essentially, these governments tried to increase their effectiveness by trading expanded group access to policymakers for group acquiescence to current initiatives. Many critics of these initiatives argued that this expansion of group access eventually undermined the ability of state actors to govern effectively.[11] Students of regulatory "capture" have picked up on a similar phenomenon. Interventionist government policies often have the paradoxical effect of making the success of particular policies dependent upon group-controlled resources (e.g., information, skilled personnel). This dependence in turn enhances the ability of groups to turn their preferences into government policy.[12]

There is, then, significant research suggesting feedback effects on group formation and activity. All of this, however, remains illustrative. How common are these feedback effects? Under what circumstances are they likely to occur? The answer is that we do not know, and cannot know until research is designed specifically to address these questions. Progress can be made from two directions. In many cases, one can start with policies themselves and demonstrate the presence or absence of links to specific group activities. Where policies provide tangible resources (e.g., formalized access, financing), these connections should be easy to trace. At the same time, research can begin with the interest groups themselves and seek to draw linkages back toward policies. It is probably easier, for example, to first identify the selective incentives that groups are using to overcome collective action problems and then work backward to determine if government policies produced those selective incentives.

In addition, two more specific approaches may shed further light on how policy-created resources and incentives affect interest groups. First, policy feedback is likely to be most consequential in issue-areas (or in countries, e.g., those of post-communist Eastern Europe) where interest group activity is not yet well established. Recent research on "path dependency"—including the work of Douglass North to be discussed below—suggests the importance of focusing on the formative moments for institutions and organizations.[13] Even where the influences of policy on social groups seem relatively modest, small effects at crucial junctures may make a profound difference. Factors that give one set of organizations an initial advantage—even a small one—are likely to become self-reinforcing. Costs of starting up competing organizations are generally high, and as a result the incentives for

---

[10] Philippe Schmitter and Gerhard Lehmbruch, eds., *Trends toward Corporatist Intermediation* (Beverly Hills, Calif.: Sage, 1979); Suzanne Berger, ed., *Organizing Interests in Western Europe* (Cambridge: Cambridge University Press, 1981); and John H. Goldthorpe, ed., *Order and Conflict in Contemporary Capitalism* (Oxford: Oxford University Press, 1984).

[11] See, for example, Samuel Brittan, *The Role and Limits of Government: Essays in Political Economy* (London: Temple Smith, 1983).

[12] Grant McConnell, *Private Power and American Democracy* (New York: Random House, 1966); George J. Stigler, "The Theory of Economic Regulation," *Bell Journal of Economics and Management Science* 2 (Spring 1971).

[13] For interesting discussions of path dependency, see Stephen Krasner, "Approaches to the State: Alternative Conceptions and Historical Dynamics," *Comparative Politics* 16 (January 1984); and Ruth Berins Collier and David Collier, *Shaping the Political Agenda: Critical Junctures, the Labor Movement, and Regime Dynamics in Latin America* (Princeton: Princeton University Press, 1991), chap. 1.

individuals to invest in "proven" institutions are substantial. High "barriers to entry" mean that established interest organizations will tend to maintain themselves unless their performance is very poor. Recent research on the women's movement in the United States during the early 1960s is suggestive. In a context where interest organizations were largely absent, even the relatively weak policy initiatives of the federal government (such as the establishment of a network of state commissions that subsidized communications within the movement) proved consequential for patterns of interest group development.[14]

Circumstances where governments can use a variety of instruments to achieve the same policy goals provide another good opportunity to study resource/incentive feedback on social groups. For example, farm incomes can be maintained through government purchases of surplus produce, price supports, or transfer payments to farmers. Although each option would provide income for farmers, the different policies might have quite different consequences for interest group development. Comparative analyses that examine the use of different policy instruments to achieve similar goals can determine if the variation in instruments has political consequences. These investigations could clarify how specific characteristics of policies promote particular patterns of interest group formation and activity. Doing so would provide a stronger basis for moving beyond persuasive case studies to some broader propositions about the impact of policy feedback on interest groups.

POLICIES AND THE RESOURCES AND INCENTIVES
FOR GOVERNMENT ELITES

According to Skocpol, the second major type of policy feedback is the transformation of state capacities. "Because of the official efforts made to implement new policies using new or existing administrative arrangements," she writes, "policies transform or expand the capacities of the state. They therefore change the administrative possibilities for official initiatives in the future, and affect later prospects for policy implementation" (p. 58).

It does indeed seem plausible that policy initiatives—which are, after all, the central undertakings of public officials—may provide resources and incentives affecting the capacities of government elites. Yet of all the dimensions of policy influence reviewed in this essay, those linking the resources and incentives generated by existing policies to the actions of government elites seem the least well established. In part, this shortcoming reflects continuing uncertainty about the nature and limits of the political power wielded by government authorities.

Administrative resources are obviously important. The viability of policy initiatives often requires the presence of coherent bureaucratic organizations staffed by well-trained, experienced, and respected officials. A number of analysts have recently stressed the impact of policy feedback on state administrative capacities. For example, Weir and Skocpol's research on government responses to the Great Depression suggests that previous policy choices in Sweden helped to produce the administrative apparatus that allowed state actors to pursue a Keynesian agenda.[15] Unemployment insurance was not well established in Sweden, but public works

---

[14] Georgia Duerst-Lahti, "The Government's Role in Building the Women's Movement," *Political Science Quarterly* 104 (Summer 1989).

[15] Weir and Skocpol (fn. 5), 123–25, 129–32.

programs were, and the latter provided a good "bridge" to the development of Keynesian policies. Britain, by contrast, found that its preexisting administrative organizations, derived from the previous development of unemployment insurance policies, were far better suited to an expansion of unemployment benefits than to developing a new system of public works and other job creation efforts.

G. John Ikenberry's analysis of United States energy policy in the 1970s points to a similar dynamic.[16] Previous energy policies had hindered the development of administrative capacities that would have given political elites the knowledge and managerial experience necessary to intervene extensively in energy exploration and development. As Ikenberry concludes, when American policymakers sought responses to the energy crisis of the 1970s, "the institutional legacy of the past weighed heavily on proposals for change. In particular, the scarcity and fragmentation of bureaucratic expertise and operational capacities provided few bases from which to build new government powers and responsibilities."[17]

However, analyses that emphasize feedback effects on the administrative capacities of government actors are sometimes hazy about just what the critical features of these capacities might be. Most studies of the development of generalized bureaucratic competence (i.e., the establishment of a stable, prestigious civil service) have emphasized a range of contributing factors, such as the timing of democratization and the significance of external military pressures.[18] Specific policy initiatives, on the other hand, seem far more likely to have an impact on the development of specialized administrative skills. Thus, the significance of feedback turns on which type of administrative capacity is deemed to be important. Where general bureaucratic capacities are easily transferred from one domain to another, policy feedback is likely to be of little relevance. Future research could usefully concentrate on the circumstances under which policies generate an expansion of relatively specialized but important administrative skills. Such effects are likely to be limited to situations where new government actions require highly intrusive and complex actions for implementation and oversight.

Discussions of policy feedback on governmental elites share a problem common to this whole field of research. Illustrations of particular effects are easy to find and often persuasive, but general propositions about the frequency with which such effects will occur and the circumstances that make them more or less likely are rare. In this particular instance, limitations in our understanding of the position of state actors compound the problem. It has become a commonplace that states vary in their capacities to carry out particular activities.[19] However, our understanding of what the critical features are that make state actors "strong" or "weak" remains relatively limited. In this context, work on this dimension of policy feedback clearly has a long way to go.

---

[16] G. John Ikenberry, *Reasons of State: Oil Politics and the Capacities of American Government* (Ithaca, N.Y.: Cornell University Press, 1988).

[17] Ibid., 44.

[18] Perry Anderson, *Lineages of the Absolutist State* (London: Verso, 1974); Charles Tilly, *Coercion, Capital and European States*, A.D. 990–1992 (Oxford and Cambridge: Blackwells, 1992).

[19] Peter J. Katzenstein, "Conclusion: Domestic Structures and Strategies of Foreign Economic Policy," in Katzenstein, ed., *Between Power and Plenty: Foreign Economic Policies of Advanced Industrial States* (Madison: University of Wisconsin Press, 1978); John Zysman, *Governments, Markets and Growth: Financial Systems and the Politics of Industrial Change* (Ithaca, N.Y.: Cornell University Press, 1983).

Resource/incentive arguments have generally explored the impact of policy feedback on organized interests and government elites. However, public policies also provide resources and create incentives for mass publics. Unless these resources and incentives directly induce political action, they are unlikely to attract the attention of political scientists. Perhaps it is not surprising then that the most detailed examination of how the resources generated by public policies affect mass publics is the recent work of a sociologist, Gøsta Esping-Andersen. In *The Three Worlds of Welfare Capitalism*, Esping-Andersen makes a strong plea for greater attention to policy feedback:

> The present challenge for comparative research is to study welfare states in their role as independent, causal variables. . . . The welfare state is becoming deeply embedded in the everyday experience of virtually every citizen. Our personal life is structured by the welfare state, and so is the entire political economy. Given the magnitude and centrality of the welfare state, it is indeed unlikely that we shall understand much of contemporary society unless it becomes part of our models. (p. 141)

Welfare states provide resources and incentives to individuals that profoundly influence crucial life choices: what kind of job to take, when to retire or take time off from the paid labor force, how to organize and divide household tasks such as child rearing. The welfare state, Esping-Andersen argues, "is a midwife of post-industrial employment evolution." His central argument is that "different welfare-state/labor-market interactions produce different post-industrial trajectories" (p. 192).

Esping-Andersen's detailed investigation of social policy and occupational structures in the United States, Sweden, and Germany persuasively links public policy structures to the socioeconomic circumstances of mass publics. Emerging variations in the rate of growth of service industries, the relative weight of social services as opposed to personal services, the skill and occupational composition of the labor force, and the distribution of jobs by gender and racial or ethnic background can all be traced in part to previous policy choices. What *The Three Worlds of Welfare Capitalism* does not do in more than a cursory way is investigate how these shifts in the circumstances of mass publics influence political processes. But the importance of the transformations Esping-Andersen identifies suggests that such an investigation would probably yield rich returns.[20]

The most promising avenue for research is the possibility that policies provide incentives that encourage individuals to act in ways that *lock in a particular path of policy development*. This claim can be derived from the central arguments of Douglass North's *Institutions, Institutional Change and Economic Performance*. North's goal is to explain the failure of economic performance in different countries to converge over time. In a careful but wide-ranging analysis grounded in

---

[20] For an analysis that suggests how such links might be drawn, see Peter Swenson, "Labor and the Limits of the Welfare State: The Politics of Intraclass Conflict and Cross-Class Alliances in Sweden and West Germany," *Comparative Politics* 23, no. 4 (1991). Esping-Andersen himself did explore the political consequences of policy choices in an earlier work, *Politics against Markets: The Social Democratic Road to Power* (Princeton: Princeton University Press, 1985). This analysis is rather murky on the question of exactly how policy feedback influences political change. In Esping-Andersen's account policies seem to provide some combination of resources, material incentives, and cognitive signals that encourage certain patterns of political behavior.

rational-choice theory, he stresses the ways in which institutional arrangements, once adopted, may lead quite rational actors to behave in ways that are collectively suboptimal. In developing his argument, North draws heavily on economic historians' discussions of the development of technology. I will begin by summarizing this research, will review North's application of the analysis to institutions, and then will suggest how it can be extended to the study of policy feedback.[21]

Economic historians using the assumptions of neoclassical economics have recently demonstrated that under certain conditions the development of technology will not proceed toward the most economically efficient alternatives. The "QWERTY" typewriter keyboard is a classic example. Although more efficient alternatives to QWERTY quickly emerged, there were strong pressures to develop an industry standard. In this instance, being relatively well established was more important than being best. Alternative keyboard types could not gain a foothold in the industry, and the QWERTY standard was effectively locked in.[22] Under what conditions are such outcomes likely? Brian Arthur has identified the following factors:

- *Large set-up or fixed costs.* If initial costs are a high proportion of total expenses, there are likely to be increasing returns to further investment in a given technology, providing individuals with a strong incentive to identify and stick with a single option.
- *Learning effects.* Large learning effects, which may lower product costs or improve their use as prevalence increases, provide an additional source of increasing returns.
- *Coordination effects.* In many cases, the advantages an individual derives from a particular activity depend on the action of others. These effects may encourage coordination with others in adopting a single option.
- *Adaptive expectations.* If it is important for individuals to "pick the right horse"—because options that fail to win broad acceptance will have drawbacks later on—individual expectations about usage patterns may become self-fulfilling.[23]

The existence of lock-in effects in the development of technology is now generally accepted, but one can legitimately ask whether this excursion into economic history has any relevance to the current discussion. North argues persuasively that it does. The factors Arthur identifies as contributing to technological lock-in—increasing returns and high fixed costs, learning effects, coordination effects, and adaptive expectations—are often characteristic of institutions. Consequently, one could anticipate the same kinds of historical processes, in which initial choice of institutional design had long-term implications for economic and political performance.

This argument can easily be applied to public policies as well. North defines institutions broadly as "the rules of the game in a society or, more formally, . . . the humanly devised constraints that shape human interaction" (p. 3). This definition would seem to encompass public policies as well as what we conventionally recognize as institutions, since policies clearly do establish rules and create

[21] For a more complete summary, see North, 93–95.
[22] Paul David, "Clio and the Economics of QWERTY," *American Economic Review* 75 (May 1985).
[23] W. Brian Arthur, "Self-Reinforcing Mechanisms in Economics," in Philip W. Anderson, Kenneth J. Arrow, and David Pines, eds., *The Economy as an Evolving Complex System* (Reading, Mass.: Addison-Wesley, 1988); W. Brian Arthur, "Competing Technologies, Increasing Returns, and Lock-In by Historical Events," *Economic Journal* 99 (March 1989).

constraints that shape behavior. The specific example North uses to illustrate his argument about path dependence is instructive. The Northwest Ordinance was a quasi-constitutional initiative, outlining the basic rules of the game for "the governance and settlement of the vast area of land in the West and . . . a framework by which the territories would be integrated into the new nation" (p. 97). In this respect, it resembles a formal institution. However, the Northwest Ordinance was also "a specific legislative enactment"—that is, a public policy.

By choosing such a legalistic, foundational initiative that created such straightforward rules of the game, North obscures the broad application of his argument to policy feedback. Policies may create incentives that encourage the emergence of elaborate social and economic networks, greatly increasing the cost of adopting once-possible alternatives and inhibiting exit from a current policy path. Major policy initiatives have major social consequences. Individuals make important commitments in response to certain types of government action. These commitments, in turn, may vastly increase the disruption caused by new policies, effectively "locking in" previous decisions.

Like more formal institutions, public policies operating in a context of complex social interdependence will often generate increasing returns as well as high fixed costs, learning effects, coordination effects, and adaptive expectations. For example, housing and transportation policies in the United States after World War II encouraged massive investments in particular spatial patterns of work, consumption, and residence. Once in place, these patterns sharply constrained the alternatives available to policymakers on issues ranging from energy policy to school desegregation.[24]

Many of the individual commitments that locked in suburbanization were literally cast in concrete, but this need not be the case. Policies may encourage individuals to develop particular skills, make certain kinds of investments, purchase certain kinds of goods, or devote time and money to certain kinds of organizations. All these decisions generate sunk costs. That is to say, they create commitments. In many contexts, policies may push individual behavior onto paths that are hard to reverse.

Research on Reagan and Thatcher's social policies provides a good illustration of the wide scope of these policy feedbacks.[25] Reagan's inability to restructure public pensions can be partly attributed to lock-in processes. Since 1939, Social Security in the United States has operated on a pay-as-you-go basis: current benefits are paid out of current contributions; each working generation pays for the previous generation's retirement. Once such a system matures, it becomes essentially locked in. Because the currently retired generation has made irreversible commitments based on the existence of a public system of old-age pensions, moving to a private system (which would necessarily be financed by earnings on invested contributions) creates a "double-payment problem"; current workers would have to finance both their parents' retirement and their own. This made any major privatization initiative in the United States unthinkable. By contrast, because of the constant alternation of Conservative and Labour governments

---

[24] Kenneth T. Jackson, *Crabgrass Frontier: The Suburbanization of the United States* (Oxford: Oxford University Press, 1985), esp. chap. 11; Michael N. Danielson, *The Politics of Exclusion* (New York: Columbia University Press, 1976).

[25] Paul Pierson, "'Policy Feedbacks' and Political Change: Contrasting Reagan and Thatcher's Pension-Reform Initiatives," *Studies in American Political Development* 6 (Fall 1992).

during the 1960s and 1970s, Britain failed to develop a mature earnings-related scheme. With the "double-payment" problem far less prominent, the Thatcher government did not face the policy lock-in confronted by Reagan, and was able to engineer a major shift in policy toward private provision of retirement income.

In contrast to the other "feedback" examined here, this discussion of lock-in has generally not drawn on the political science literature concerned with public policy determination. Analysts have been slow to build an examination of lock-in processes into their models of political development.[26] Instead, groundbreaking work has been done by economic historians and students of industrial organization. One reason for this lack of attention is that feedback effects of this kind have a tendency to depoliticize issues. By accelerating the momentum behind one policy path, they render previously viable alternatives implausible. The result is often not conflict over the foregone alternative (which political scientists would generally be quick to identify), but the absence of conflict. In Bachrach and Baratz's terms, "lock-in" leads to "non-decisions."[27] Another problem is that comparative analysis is probably required to study policy lock-ins. An analyst needs a comparative case where lock-in has not occurred to identify the political effects of policy feedbacks.

Instances of "policy lock-in" are probably widespread. Many public policies create or extend patterns of complex social interdependence in which microeconomic models of isolated, independent individuals smoothly and efficiently adapting to new conditions do not apply.[28] Future research should strive to identify the circumstances under which policy initiatives are likely to produce lock-in, altering the prospects for new initiatives at a later date. The characteristics identified by David, modified to incorporate aspects of social as well as technological complexity, provide an excellent starting point for this research. Lock-in effects are likely to be important when public policies encourage individuals to make significant investments that are not easily reversed, and when actors have strong incentives to coordinate their activities and to adopt prevailing or anticipated standards. Policies that involve high levels of interdependence and where intervention stretches over long periods are particularly likely sites for lock-in effects. Infrastructure policies (communications, transportation, and housing) are good examples, but the pensions case considered above raises the prospect of considerably broader applications.

Policies do create powerful packages of resources and incentives that influence the positions of interest groups, government elites, and individual social actors in politically consequential ways. However, analysts have so far failed to tap the full range of these arguments, and efforts to develop and test clear claims about the generalizability of many of these feedback effects have hardly begun. I now want

[26] Interestingly, within political science the idea of "lock-ins" (though focusing on institutions rather than policies) has mainly been utilized in the field of international relations. See for example Robert O. Keohane, *After Hegemony: Cooperation and Discord in the World Political Economy* (Princeton: Princeton University Press, 1984), 100–106. Keohane draws on Arthur Stinchcombe's analysis of sunk costs. See Stinchcombe, *Constructing Social Theories* (New York: Harcourt, Brace, 1968), 120–25.

[27] Peter Bachrach and Morton Baratz, "Two Faces of Power," *American Political Science Review* 56 (1962).

[28] For a pathbreaking study of networks of social interdependence, see Thomas C. Schelling, *Micromotives and Macrobehavior* (New York: W. W. Norton, 1978). The contribution of public policies to the development of these social networks is discussed in more detail in Fred Hirsch, *Social Limits to Growth* (Cambridge: Harvard University Press, 1976); and Alfred E. Kahn, "The Tyranny of Small Decisions: Market Failures, Imperfections, and the Limits of Economics," *Kyklos* 19 (1966).

to suggest that the existence of a range of arguments emphasizing the "interpretive effects of public policies"—the impact of policies on the cognitive processes of social actors—further complicates the task. In some cases, these arguments constitute explanatory alternatives to the arguments already considered; in other cases, they offer promising opportunities to supplement or enrich those accounts.

POLICIES AS SOURCES OF INFORMATION AND MEANING

Interpretive arguments stress that an exclusive focus on material resources and incentives is psychologically anemic.[29] The process through which individuals choose a course of action does not involve a simple calculation of easily discernible costs and benefits. A viable theory of action must take into account the fact that all actors have to cope with overwhelming complexity and uncertainty, and that they use a wide range of cognitive shortcuts in order to make sense of the social world. Furthermore, analysts must recognize that knowledge itself is a critically scarce resource, distributed in a highly unequal fashion. Starting from an emphasis on problems of interpretation leads to quite different questions about the impact of "the rules of the game." How do these rules (in this case, public policies) influence the manner in which social actors make sense of their environment? How do policies influence the distribution of information, and the impact of that distribution on political outcomes?

PUBLIC POLICIES AND LEARNING EFFECTS

To date, applying an interpretive approach to policy feedback has generally meant depicting policy development as a process of political learning. A number of scholars have stressed the importance of "learning effects" in policy-making. Political learning arguments focus on individuals at or near the center of the policy-making process and emphasize problems of bounded rationality and uncertainty. Hugh Heclo summarized this perspective in an early but still influential formulation:

> Politics finds its sources not only in power but also in uncertainty—men collectively wondering what to do. Finding feasible courses of action includes, but is more than, locating which way the vectors of political pressure are pushing. Governments not only "power" (or whatever the verb form of that approach might be); they also puzzle. Policy-making is a form of collective puzzlement on society's behalf; it entails both deciding and knowing.[30]

Implicitly or explicitly, policy learning arguments build on work in decision-making and organizational theory that emphasizes the variety of techniques (e.g., satisficing, incrementalism) used to cope with limited cognitive capacities.[31]

---

[29] For an introduction to the ways in which these kinds of arguments are reshaping institutional analysis, see March and Olsen (fn. 2); and Walter W. Powell and Paul J. DiMaggio, eds., *The New Institutionalism in Organizational Analysis* (Chicago: University of Chicago Press, 1991).

[30] Hugh Heclo, *Modern Social Politics in Britain and Sweden* (New Haven: Yale University Press, 1974), 305.

[31] See, for example, Herbert A. Simon, *Models of Man* (New York: Wiley, 1957); Charles E. Lindblom, "The 'Science' of Muddling Through," *Public Administration Review* 19 (Spring 1959); and James G. March, "Bounded Rationality, Ambiguity, and the Engineering of Choice," *Bell Journal of Economics* 9 (Autumn 1978).

The depiction of political development as a learning process is sometimes presented in sweeping terms. Heclo, for example, talks of "social learning" and "political learning" and identifies a number of sources of such effects. Prominent among them, however, is the impact of previously adopted public policies, and it is these "policy-learning" effects that are relevant here. Important political actors may become aware of problems as a result of their experiences with past initiatives. The setting of a new agenda and the design of alternative responses may build on (perceived) past successes or may reflect lessons learned from past mistakes.

Heclo's study of the Swedish and British welfare states was the first sustained effort to investigate this dimension of policy feedback. Although he acknowledged that there were other important sources of learning, he identified the impact of previous policy as "probably [the] most pervasive manifestation of political learning in the development of social policy."[32] According to Heclo, policymakers have tended to frame new problems in terms that make it possible to draw on already established policy designs:

> Policymakers may not exactly salivate at the sound of the usual bell, but there is something of a conditioned reflex in a great deal of their behavior. Once implemented, a technique such as social insurance has tended to be readopted, to be considered the "natural" policy response for other types of income risk. . . . The incrementalism pervasive in policy making is one manifestation of the more general tendency to respond by analogizing. Typically, steps taken with regard to a new situation are small (compared to the almost infinite variety of possible responses) because the new situation is responded to like something already known, or some element of it. It is this facet of learning that more than anything lies at the heart of the essentially liberal continuity evident in social policy since the first insurance efforts to deal with the cumulative insecurity of industrial society. The inheritance of income maintenance policies has served as a path through the immense complexity facing social policy makers and has facilitated the creation of subsequent responses.[33]

In this passage, the link to the work of Simon, Lindblom, and others on incrementalism is particularly clear. Overwhelmed by the complexity of the problems they confront, decision makers lean heavily on preexisting policy frameworks, adjusting only at the margins to accommodate distinctive features of new situations.

These learning processes emerge as a significant theme in *The Political Power of Economic Ideas*, edited by Peter Hall. Noting that, despite perceptions of a sweeping "Keynesian revolution," the reception of Keynes' ideas was highly uneven across nations, Hall and his collaborators seek to uncover the reasons for this variation. Among the factors considered in this rich volume is the impact of "prior experience with related policies . . ."—the hypothesis that "states will be predisposed towards policies with which they already have some favorable experience, and even the demands of political parties and interest groups may be based on their conceptions of . . . existing policy legacies" (p. 11). Bradford Lee, for example, argues that the resistance of French, British, and American policymakers to proto-Keynesian ideas in the early 1930s was rooted in "lessons" learned from

[32] Heclo (fn. 30), 315.
[33] Ibid., 315–16.

previous experiences, such as the inflationary policies followed after World War I and the escalating demands for redistribution that many political actors linked to the growth of the modern state.[34]

Lee's argument suggests that an incremental, cumulative process is not the only possible form of policy learning. Policymakers may also react negatively to previous policies, fashioning new initiatives to address perceived failures. Heclo makes room in his account for negative learning, noting that "probably the single most important force molding the policies discussed in this volume was the reaction against the poor law. Without exception, the point of departure for reformers of all parties in both Britain and Sweden was the desire to find something better than the opprobrious poor law for the deserving poor."[35]

Although she does not employ the language of policy learning, this is in essence the process described in Skocpol's analysis of Civil War pensions in the United States (pp. 155–58, 531–33).[36] Perceived by key middle-class reformers as a scandalous example of patronage politics, Civil War pensions were not used as a blueprint for new, incremental extensions of government activity. On the contrary, important political actors drew negative conclusions, which served as a check on the emergence of significant federal social expenditure programs in the pre–New Deal era. Negative learning had a major impact on the policy agendas and political strategies of middle-class reform groups.

Despite the appeal of this line of argument, there are several difficulties in the work on policy learning. First, there are uncertainties about who is doing the learning. Heclo's account stresses the role of civil servants: "Forced to choose one group among all the separate political factors as most consistently important . . . the bureaucracies of Britain and Sweden loom predominant in the policies studied." Most influential, he adds, are "middlemen at the interfaces of various groups. These have been men with transcendable group commitments, in but not always of their host body."[37] The process Heclo describes is one populated by experts working in small groups to develop new policy blueprints. However, social groups, like bureaucrats and politicians, may derive lessons from previous initiatives. It is the former who are judged to be of particular importance in Skocpol's account.

There are questions, then, about the circumstances under which "learning effects" on state actors or social groups will be most important. Hall makes progress on this issue in a recent essay, distinguishing three levels of policy change, and arguing that the learning process will not be identical in the three cases.[38] First-order change alters the settings of policy instruments while the instruments used and the goals of policy remain constant. Second-order change modifies instruments as well as settings; while third-order change, which marks a clear

[34] Bradford A. Lee, "The Miscarriage of Necessity and Invention: Proto-Keynesianism and Democratic States in the 1930s," in Hall, 129–70.

[35] Heclo (fn. 30), 317.

[36] See also Ann Shola Orloff and Theda Skocpol, " 'Why Not Equal Protection?': Explaining the Politics of Public Social Spending in Britain, 1900–1911, and the United States, 1880s–1920," *American Sociological Review* 49 (December 1984); and Ann Shola Orloff, "The Political Origins of America's Belated Welfare State," in Margaret Weir, Ann Shola Orloff, and Theda Skocpol, eds, *The Politics of Social Policy in the United States* (Princeton: Princeton University Press, 1988).

[37] Heclo (fn. 30), 301, 308.

[38] Peter A. Hall, "Policy Paradigms, Social Learning and the State: The Case of Economic Policy-Making in Britain," *Comparative Politics* (forthcoming). See also idem, "Conclusion: The Politics of Keynesian Ideas," in Hall, 361–91.

break with past practice, involves simultaneous shifts in settings, instruments, and goals. Hall argues that in the relatively incremental processes of first- and second-order change, the learning process is likely to be highly technical and relatively insulated, with bureaucrats playing a central role. Third-order change, by contrast, involves a wider range of actors and is more "sociological" and "political" in character.

Hall's effort to disaggregate broad concepts like policy-learning and develop more specific propositions about when a particular feedback will operate is precisely what is needed to push the discussion forward. Although one would need to look beyond Hall's single case of macroeconomic policymaking for further support, this claim that major departures from past policies are likely to involve a broader range of political actors and increased contestation seems plausible. But Hall's account does raise the serious question of whether the most interesting process (third-order change), which involves the mobilization of substantial political resources in favor of a new policy agenda, can best be described as a process of learning.

A second difficult issue for policy-learning arguments regards the dynamics of the learning process. Why does "learning" sometimes produce positive conclusions and incremental policy change and at other times generate negative conclusions and reactive policy shifts? As Hall acknowledges, "It is all very well to say that policy makers are influenced by the lessons drawn from past policy experiences, but the lessons that history provides us with are always ambiguous" (p. 362). Although hindsight may lead one to say "success" encourages repetition, defining success and failure is necessarily a sociological and political process. Two prominent examples from recent American history illustrate the problem. The key policy decisions of the Johnson administration—the pursuit of a war in Vietnam and the pursuit of a "War on Poverty" at home—have been widely held to contain "lessons" of relevance to future policy. However, the nature of the appropriate lessons is unclear and bitterly contested.[39]

Hall's account does offer some suggestions about when policies are likely to be perceived as failures. Drawing on Kuhn's concept of scientific paradigms, he argues that learning connected to third-order change (paradigm shifts, or what I have here termed negative learning) is likely "to involve the appearance of anomalies, . . . developments that are not fully comprehensible, even as puzzles, within the terms of the [existing] paradigm." But it remains unclear whether this provides a clear guide, except perhaps *ex post*, to the circumstances when policies will be regarded as failures. The complexity and multiplicity of policy interventions, combined with the uncertainty of the links between interventions and outcomes, will generally leave considerable room for dispute.[40]

The fact that policy "success" is often contested suggests a substantial indeterminacy to the learning process. Perhaps the best way to describe the impact of public policies is to say that they provide part of what Ann Swidler has called a

[39] On Vietnam, see David Fromkin and James Chace, "What *Are* the Lessons of Vietnam?" *Foreign Affairs* 63 (Spring 1985). On the War on Poverty, consider the contrasting lessons drawn in Charles Murray, *Losing Ground: American Social Policy, 1950–1980* (New York: Basic Books, 1984); and John E. Schwartz, *America's Hidden Success: A Reassessment of Public Policy from Kennedy to Reagan*, rev. ed. (New York: W. W. Norton, 1987). I am grateful to Peter Hall for suggesting these examples to me.

[40] Henry J. Aaron, *Politics and the Professors: The Great Society in Perspective* (Washington, D.C.: Brookings Institution, 1978).

"tool kit" of symbols and arguments that actors use in their efforts to assemble meaningful interpretations of the world around them.[41] Robert Jervis has stressed that because individuals seek to maintain cognitive consistency, they are strongly inclined "to fit incoming information into pre-existing beliefs and to perceive what they expect to be there," to "ignore information that does not fit," or to "twist it so that it confirms" beliefs already held.[42] Swidler's and Jervis's arguments suggest that proponents of policy-learning arguments face a daunting task. Past policies do help frame discussions of new initiatives, but not in any straightforward fashion. To be convincing, policy learning arguments must offer clearer propositions about the conditions that lead particular actors to view previous initiatives in positive or negative terms. Further, they need to show that the policies have some significant *independent* impact on actors' political behavior, rather than simply contributing to actors' accounts of their actions.

Finally, there is a pressing need to establish the range of circumstances under which policy-learning arguments are likely to be persuasive. If governments both "power" and "puzzle," when should we expect to see one process or the other predominate? In this respect, policy-learning arguments have also suffered from an emphasis on *illustrating* processes rather than establishing the frequency of those processes. Because arguments about policy learning have been developed largely through single case studies (or, for Heclo, a multicase study in which learning was claimed to be central in each instance), the question of this phenomenon's scope has hardly been asked, much less answered. Yet surely this is a critical concern.

Amenta et al.'s study of the early development of unemployment insurance in individual states in the United States is a promising first attempt to confront this problem.[43] By adopting a multicase study design, involving five relatively developed states, the authors were able to assess the usefulness of policy-learning arguments for explaining the timing and design of state initiatives. Wisconsin's early adoption of unemployment insurance is plausibly attributed, in part, to the prior development there of an extensive policy network with experience in the promotion of such policies. At the same time, Amenta et al.'s analysis suggests that a full explanation of policy outcomes must move beyond policy-learning arguments to examine prospects for successful coalition formation. Support among experts for unemployment insurance was of limited use in the absence of strong backing within state legislatures.

The Hall volume represents a second effort to place policy-learning arguments in a broad comparative framework, since it investigates the dissemination of Keynesian ideas in a number of countries. On my reading, the results are disappointing for those who would stress this dimension of policy feedback. Of the empirical essays, only Lee's puts heavy emphasis on policymakers' experience with prior policies, and his efforts to link specific policies with later political processes are sketchy at best. In Hall's concluding essay, which advances a complex explanation for the reception of Keynesian ideas, policy-learning arguments re-

[41] Ann Swidler, "Culture in Action: Symbols and Strategies," *American Sociological Review* 51 (April 1986).

[42] Robert Jervis, *Perception and Misperception in International Politics* (Princeton: Princeton University Press, 1976), 143.

[43] Edwin Amenta, Elisabeth S. Clemens, Jefren Olsen, Sunita Parikh, and Theda Skocpol, "The Political Origins of Unemployment Insurance in Five American States," *Studies in American Political Development* 2 (1987).

cede into the background. Hall lists "collective associations with similar policies" as one of several factors affecting the political viability of Keynesian proposals, but his account places more weight on party structures, the interests of potential coalition partners, and the reputations of Keynesianism's exponents. Further, he stresses that political viability is only one part of a complete explanation: Keynesian proposals needed to pass tests of economic and administrative viability as well. In contrast to Hall's single-case study of British policy-making, this cross-national investigation suggests a limited role for policy-learning effects.

While making some progress on the question of how learning effects may interact with other variables, even these multicase studies could make limited progress on the scope question because they looked at only one type of policy. Determining when learning effects are likely to be prominent will require carefully designed research projects comparing different types of policies and different policy-making environments. While a detailed examination of such a research agenda is not possible here, a few plausible and illustrative hypotheses can be suggested.

First, the degree of *insulation of decision makers* is likely to be important. Learning processes are more likely to be prominent when a small number of actors are involved.[44] Widening the scope of conflict increases the chances for disagreement and hence the decisiveness of political resources.[45] Analysts need to think about the characteristics of policies that are conducive to relatively insulated policy-making.

A second factor of significance may be *policy complexity*. The greater the technical proficiency required to understand an issue and possible policy responses, the greater the likelihood that learning effects stemming from social investigation and analysis will be prominent. As I will discuss in more detail below, some government activities involve rather direct connections between policy and outcomes (e.g., the relationship between the legality of abortion and the options available to pregnant women; the relationship between pension benefits and the financial status of the elderly), while in other cases the causal chains are more complex and uncertain (e.g., the relationship between educational policy and economic competitiveness). Where policies are not complex, "puzzling" is likely to give way to "powering." An argument about the role of policy learning may be far more persuasive in accounting for changes in educational policy than it will be in explaining policy covering abortion.

Finally, it is very likely that policy learning plays a different role at different *stages of the policy-making process*. Learning effects will be most apparent in the specification of alternatives, since this is when detailed knowledge is most crucial.[46] The heavy weight Heclo gives to learning effects and bureaucratic influence stems partly from his desire to account for the identification and development of specific policy alternatives rather than more general policy orientations.[47]

[44] This perhaps explains why students of foreign policy–making, which often features decision making by small groups or even single individuals, have had a particular interest in learning processes. See the literature reviewed in Yuen Foong Khong, *Analogies at War: Korea, Munich, Dien Bien Phu, and the Vietnam Decisions of 1965* (Princeton: Princeton University Press, 1992), chap. 1. Khong's work offers an ambitious and thoughtful attempt to address many of the objections to learning arguments.

[45] On the importance of the scope of conflict, see E. E. Schattschneider, *The Semisovereign People* (New York: Holt, Rinehart, and Winston, 1960).

[46] Kingdon makes this point in his careful study of the policy-making process. John Kingdon, *Agendas, Alternatives, and Public Policies* (Boston: Little, Brown, 1984).

[47] See Heclo's discussion of party and interest group influence (fn. 30), 293–301.

Agenda-setting and the final choice of policies are likely to be the result of other kinds of influences. If so, this suggests an important limit to the scope of policy-learning arguments.

The work of Hall, Amenta, and their colleagues indicates a growing interest in fleshing out the insights of a policy-learning approach; but they only begin the process of producing answers to the questions of when, where and how policy-learning effects might be important. To determine the scope of learning arguments, scholars need to disaggregate policy-making along two dimensions. Disaggregating policy-making *temporally* (along the standard lines of agenda setting, alternative specification, policy choice, and implementation) will permit an evaluation of policy learning's role at different stages of the political process. The design of alternatives is clearly important, but to date we know little about the role of policy learning beyond that realm. To what extent are learning effects important in explaining the agendas, or final policy choices, made by governments? Disaggregating *across policies* will also contribute to an understanding of the true scope of learning arguments. Past investigations have often examined areas of very complex policy-making where expertise is at a premium (Hall's work on macroeconomic policy being a good example). To what extent, if any, can learning arguments be applied to policy areas where expertise may play a less important role (e.g., abortion, immigration, industrial relations)? Should efforts to address these questions be pursued, it is far from clear how powerful policy learning arguments will turn out to be. To date, what we have are plausible accounts of isolated cases.

POLICIES AS SOURCES OF INFORMATION FOR MASS PUBLICS

Given the serious problems with policy-learning arguments, it may be that interpretive accounts, like investigations of resource/incentive feedback, could benefit from a shift in focus towards mass publics rather than policymakers. Policy-learning arguments concentrate on those with a continuing active role in policy-making: high-level bureaucrats and politicians, policy experts, and the leaders of interest groups. But interpretive arguments may help to account for the behavior of a broader set of actors, who are also engaged in efforts to understand the social world and the consequences of their own actions. For the electorate, policies may produce cues that help them develop political identities, goals, and strategies. While policy-learning arguments see policies as the source of models or analogies for policymakers, what is likely to be important for mass publics is the informational content of policies. As James Kuklinski has recently written, "The idea of information has overtaken political scientists."[48] Political actions must be based on understanding, but our understandings are necessarily constrained by the sheer complexity of the social world and our own limitations of time and cognitive capacity. Yet if there is a growing recognition that knowledge is a scarce and critical political commodity, the integration of this insight into understandings of politics remains more an aspiration than an accomplishment. Nonetheless, the role of public policies in the production and dissemination of information recently has received increased attention.

[48] James H. Kuklinski, "Information and the Study of Politics," in John Ferejohn and James H. Kuklinski, *Information and Democratic Processes*, 391.

The specific design of programs may heighten the visibility of some social and political connections while obscuring others. In a context of great social complexity, policies may generate "focusing events" or cues that help social actors to interpret the world around them.[49] Policy-induced cues may influence an individual's awareness of government activity. For example, when the National Aeronautics and Space Administration chose to pursue a manned space shuttle program rather than unmanned alternatives, one important consequence was to greatly increase the attention paid to individual flights. NASA supporters hoped that the heightened visibility would strengthen political support for the space program. The creation of "focusing events" backfired with the *Challenger* disaster, which gravely damaged NASA's reputation. The opposite process can operate as well. Some programs are "quiet"—they do not produce events that generate attention. For instance, many countries provide massive subsidies for various private activities through their tax codes. Unlike on-budget outlays, "tax expenditures" are not subjected to annual legislative scrutiny. Despite their importance, policies designed this way do not produce the focusing events that might place their reform on the political agenda.[50] It is probably no accident that the benefits of such programs tend to be far more heavily concentrated on small groups of wealthy individuals than are on-budget expenditures.

Harold Wilensky has extended this argument about tax visibility to the whole range of a nation's tax policies. He suggests that whether these policies serve to heighten or obscure tax burdens may be more important politically than the actual level of taxation.[51] Prospects for the development of "tax backlash" movements depend on public perceptions of burdensome taxation. Because indirect taxes are less visible to voters, governments relying on them can maintain higher tax levels than countries that depend more heavily on highly visible taxes such as the income tax.

This argument may be widely applicable. In *The Rise and Fall of the Great Powers*, Paul Kennedy devotes a chapter to the European conflicts from 1660 to 1815, with particular attention to the struggles between Britain and France. Kennedy's explanation for Britain's ultimate triumph in the lengthy and costly competition places significant weight on Britain's superior financial position. That superiority, in turn, is attributed in large part to the difference in visibility between the tax systems of the two rivals, which allowed a less populous Britain to produce more revenue with less public discontent.

> While it is true that its general taxation system was more regressive than that of France—that is, it relied far more upon indirect than direct taxes— particular features seem to have made it much less resented by the public. For example, there was in Britain nothing like the vast array of French tax farmers, collectors, and other middlemen; many of the British duties were "invisible" (the excise duty on a few basic products), or appeared to hurt the foreigner (customs); there were no *internal* tolls, which so irritated French merchants . . . the British land tax—the chief direct tax for so much of the

[49] On focusing events, see Kingdon (fn. 46), 99–105.

[50] See, for example, Herman B. Leonard, *Checks Unbalanced: The Quiet Side of Public Spending* (New York: Basic Books, 1986), chap. 4.

[51] Harold Wilensky, *The New Corporatism, Centralization, and the Welfare State* (Beverly Hills, Calif.: Sage, 1976). See also Douglas A. Hibbs, Jr., and Henrik Jess Madsen, "Public Reactions to the Growth of Taxation and Government Expenditure," *World Politics* 33 (April 1981).

eighteenth century—allowed for no privileged exceptions and was also "invisible" to the greater part of society.[52]

In common with policy-learning arguments, these analyses focus on the signals that policies send to political actors. These signals may influence individuals' perceptions about what their interests are, whether their representatives are protecting those interests, who their allies might be, and what political strategies are promising. Besides broadening the range of actors considered, this approach has a significant additional advantage over a focus on policy learning. Not only does it acknowledge that all policy-making takes place in a context of information constraints, but it recognizes that the distribution of this information is often highly unequal. The emphasis of these arguments is on how *information asymmetries* create space for the strategic manipulation of policy design. Knowledge is indeed power, and the fact that policy structures can influence the role and availability of information makes this an important and contested aspect of policy development. To rephrase Heclo, "powering" and "puzzling" are often part of the same process; power can be utilized to facilitate or impede actors' efforts to understand the consequences of public policies.

Yet beyond rather vague formulations, such as the suggestions that some policies are "visible" and others are not or that some policies generate "focusing events" and others do not, there was until recently little systematic discussion of the characteristics of initiatives that produce particular "cues" for social actors. However, political scientists are now making significant progress on several fronts. R. Kent Weaver's work on blame avoidance indicated that policymakers will take steps, including the redesign of policies, to modify public awareness of their actions, depending on whether or not they expect those actions to be popular.[53] Douglas Arnold has stressed the importance of the electorate's capacity to link particular effects, whether positive or negative, with the actions of individual politicians.[54]

According to Arnold, two conditions must hold for public policies to generate a response from mass publics. The first condition is *visibility*: voters must experience some discernible outcome that leads them to inquire about the cause of this outcome. The second condition is *traceability*: to respond by rewarding or punishing politicians, the electorate must be able to link that outcome to some governmental action. The critical point is that both visibility and traceability can vary independently of a policy's actual impact and that this variation may be a product of policy design. Specific features determine a policy's *informational content*, influencing both these determinants of the electorate's reaction. Policies that distribute benefits widely and intermittently are less likely to be visible than policies that distribute benefits to a concentrated group and in a single package. Whether those affected are part of a network (e.g., geographical or occupational) allowing communication with others affected (what Arnold has called *proximity*) is another important factor. Homeowners living near a toxic dump and dairy farmers sharing a common profession are each likely to be part of networks that facilitate communication and therefore improve the chances that they will become aware of outcomes that affect them; recipients of disability payments who have their benefits cut are not.

[52] Paul Kennedy, *The Rise and Fall of the Great Powers* (New York: Random House, 1987), 80–81.

[53] R. Kent Weaver, "The Politics of Blame Avoidance," *Journal of Public Policy* 6 (October–December 1986).

[54] Douglas Arnold, *The Logic of Congressional Action* (New Haven: Yale University Press, 1990).

The traceability of policies varies as well. Traceability really involves two distinct tests: can visible outcomes be linked to government policy and can those policies be linked to someone who can be given credit or blame? A crucial factor in linking outcomes to policy, as Arnold notes, is the "length of the causal chain." The more stages and uncertainties that lie between a policy's enactment and a perceived outcome, the less likely it is that those affected will respond politically. Producers, who see a direct link between tariff levels and their own profitability, are much more likely to be activated than consumers, for whom the causal chain is longer. Consumers may not like the prices they pay for goods, but they are unlikely to attribute those prices to government trade policies. In general, the more difficult it is to sort out causal arguments—the more complex the policy—the less likely it is that voters will trace even major problems to specific government decisions.

Policymakers have a significant degree of control over this aspect of traceability. They may choose interventions that create causal chains of varying lengths. Ideally, they would like to design programs for which the benefits involve short causal chains and the costs involve long ones. Time lags, for example, add greatly to the length and complexity of causal chains, so policymakers favor policy designs that front-load benefits and back-load costs.

The second aspect of traceability, linking government action to specific decision makers, may also depend on policy design.[55] Policies can either illuminate or obscure the role of decision makers. As Weaver has argued, indexation mechanisms, which put particular policies on "automatic," have proven attractive precisely because they reduce the traceability of outcomes to particular decision makers.[56] To take another recent example, the intricate legislative history surrounding the evolution of U.S. policy regulating savings and loan institutions made it practically impossible for even the most incensed taxpayer to know which politicians to hold accountable for the massive costs imposed on the Treasury.

There is significant evidence that the information content of policies is important for mass publics and that these feedback effects deserve careful attention. Certainly the ability to raise or lower the profile of their actions for different constituencies would seem to give politicians an important political resource. Unfortunately, the methodological problems associated with this kind of analysis are substantial. It is often difficult enough to measure the most concrete consequences of policies, let alone things as intangible as traceability and visibility. While Arnold's concept of "causal chains" offers a promising beginning, he acknowledges that the efforts of actors to create these chains are a "subjective process" likely to be highly complex and culturally contingent.[57] However, one could certainly begin, as scholars have with tax policy, with some fairly simple measures of visible and traceable policy designs and could seek to identify the political consequences of each.

The potential payoff seems well worth the effort. Recall the discussion of resource/incentive feedback on government elites, where I argued that it has been

---

[55] This is much more likely to be true in an institutional setting like that of the United States, where the location of accountability is often uncertain. See Paul Pierson and R. Kent Weaver, "Political Institutions and Loss Imposition: Pensions Policy in Britain, Canada and the United States," in R. Kent Weaver and Bert Rockman, eds., *Do Institutions Matter? Government Capabilities in the U.S. and Abroad* (Washington, D.C.: Brookings Institution, 1993).

[56] R. Kent Weaver, *Automatic Government: The Politics of Indexation* (Washington, D.C.: Brookings Institution, 1988).

[57] Arnold (fn. 54), 48n. For an interesting effort to explore this issue, see Deborah Stone, "Causal Stories and the Formation of Policy Agendas," *Political Science Quarterly* 104 (Summer 1989).

very difficult to establish strong claims about the impact of policy feedback. By contrast, the arguments of Wilensky and others about tax visibility, if correct, would significantly contribute to our understanding of the fiscal resources of states, which Skocpol has claimed tells us "more than could any other single factor about [the state's] existing (and immediately potential) capacities to create or strengthen state organizations, to employ personnel, to coopt political support, to subsidize economic enterprises, and to fund social programs."[58]

That potential underscores the basic point of this discussion of interpretive arguments about policy feedback. Policies indeed allocate large quantities of resources and create powerful incentives, but some of their most important effects may be cognitive. The massive scope of public policies assures that they play a significant role in our efforts to understand and act in an enormously complex political world.

AN AGENDA FOR RESEARCH ON POLICY FEEDBACK

The scholarship reviewed in this essay shares a common feature: the claim that policies themselves must be seen as politically consequential structures. The rise of active government leaves little room for doubt about this general proposition. Nonetheless, the fact that policy feedback arguments are now widely applied in divergent national contexts and across a variety of issue-areas drives home the growing importance of this concept to the study of comparative politics.[59] To take only a few of the examples discussed in this essay, policy feedback arguments have been used to help account for Britain's triumph over France in the eighteenth century, the development of Sweden's powerful labor movement, and the failure of New Deal reformers to cement a farmer/worker alliance. In a wide range of circumstances and in numerous ways, policies restructure politics.

This lengthy discussion also reveals the diversity of arguments that lies behind a general claim. Based on the preceding discussion, Figure 1 offers a summary of the dimensions of policy feedback. The summary utilizes a distinction between two main feedback *mechanisms* (resource/incentive effects and interpretive effects) and among three *sets of actors* affected by these mechanisms (government elites, social groups, and mass publics). The framework suggests six separate pathways of influence running from policies to politics, although several pathways (e.g., the impact of resource/incentive mechanisms on social groups) may involve multiple sources of influence.

This framework indicates where scholars might expect to find significant causal connections between public policies and political developments. It is not, however,

---

[58] Theda Skocpol, "Bringing the State Back In: Strategies and Analysis in Current Research," in Evans, Reuschemeyer, and Skocpol (fn. 5), 17.

[59] For those uninterested in the roots of current politics, policy feedback arguments may nonetheless be useful. The fact that such political consequences of policy design are likely to be discernible to policymakers raises an additional issue that deserves attention: the extent to which decision makers self-consciously design policies to produce particular feedback effects. Especially as government activity becomes widespread, politicians are likely to become aware that policy choices have political consequences. This suggests that feedback effects should not only be incorporated into political analysis because previous policies influence current politics. Current political struggles may well reflect concern over the *future* political consequences of contemporary policy choices. Cognizance of the possible range of such consequences may give analysts important insights into the strategic choices facing contemporary political actors.

Type of Mechanism	Actors Affected by Feedback Mechanism: government elites	Actors Affected by Feedback Mechanism: interest groups	Actors Affected by Feedback Mechanism: mass publics
resource and incentive effects	administrative capacities	"spoils" organizing niches financing access	"lock-in" effects
interpretive effects	policy learning	policy learning visibility/ traceability	visibility/ traceability

FIGURE 1. The Dimensions of Policy Feedback

an effort to follow the well-known attempts of analysts like Lowi and Wilson to develop an extremely parsimonious theory linking specific policy "types" to particular political outcomes.[60] The current discussion suggests two reasons why such efforts are unlikely to provide a sound basis for theory building. First, as Figure 1 indicates, individual policies may have a number of politically relevant characteristics, and these characteristics may have a multiplicity of consequences. Second, as a number of studies discussed in this essay suggest, policy feedback rarely operates in isolation from features of the broader political environment (e.g., institutional structures, the dynamics of party systems).[61] The impact of policies is likely to occur in interaction with other variables. For both these reasons, it seems doubtful that we can expect to develop sweeping theories that link a few policy "types" to clearly defined political outcomes. Instead, a more promising strategy is to develop middle-range theories that acknowledge both the complexity of feedback and its context-specific qualities.

This discussion carries some specific implications for research agendas. A greater recognition of the wide scope of possible feedback—and, in particular, of how policy feedback affects mass publics—can strengthen work on the political consequences of public policies. Too often, analysts interested in feedback effects

[60] Theodore J. Lowi, "American Business, Public Policy, Case Studies, and Political Theory," *World Politics* 16 (July 1964); idem, "Four Systems of Policy, Politics, and Choice," *Public Administration Review* 32 (July–August 1972); James Q. Wilson, *Political Organizations* (New York: Basic Books, 1973), 330–37; and idem, *American Government*, 4th ed. (Lexington, Mass.: D. C. Heath, 1989), 422–47, 590–604.

[61] It is probably no coincidence that the two significant efforts to develop "policies produce politics" typologies have been developed in American politics rather than comparative politics, which allows Lowi and Wilson at least to attempt to "hold constant" elements of the broader political environment. Instructively, Elizabeth Sanders's study of natural gas regulation argues that Lowi's typology starts to break down when one studies the dynamics of policy struggles over time. "Regulatory" policy seems to produce different politics in different historical contexts. Sanders, *The Regulation of Natural Gas: Policy and Politics 1938–1978* (Philadelphia: Temple University Press, 1981).

have looked at only one or two possible pathways of influence. Although many of the processes sketched out here will not be important in particular cases, each should be explored. Attention to the impact of policies on individual actors outside the circuit of bureaucrats, politicians, and interest groups is especially urgent. Policies have a major influence on mass publics, generating patterns of behavior (lock-in effects) and interpretive efforts (attempts to identify policy effects and trace those effects to government decisions) that have significant political repercussions.

THE DIMENSIONS OF POLICY FEEDBACK

The informational content of public policies deserves particular attention. Increasingly, political scientists have recognized that the staggering complexities of modern life make information a critical factor in politics. There has been growing attention to the ways in which institutional structures facilitate or impede information flows and to the role of politicians, parties, and interest groups as transmitters of information to various actors.[62] Yet we still know relatively little about the contribution of policies themselves to such processes. Because both the visibility and traceability of policies can vary so widely, the informational content of policies is likely to have significant effects on the mobilizing potential of political actors.

Analysts need not give up a concern with the material resources and incentives created by public policies. Indeed, arguments about informational feedback pose far less of a challenge to standard political science frameworks than do arguments that focus on policy learning.[63] The latter require a significant reevaluation of the psychological foundations of individual choice, leading to a thicket of intriguing but perhaps intractable questions. By contrast, the former approach calls only for the incorporation of information into the universe of relevant political resources.

It is no accident that both the arguments I have advanced about policy feedback on mass publics (the production of lock-in effects and the provision of information) draw heavily on work in rational-choice theory. While historical institutionalists have studied state structures and social groups, the use of microeconomic theory leads naturally to a focus on *individual* behavior. Economists have developed powerful models for exploring how different institutional frameworks and resource distributions influence both individual choices and the ways in which individual choices lead to particular aggregate outcomes. Wedded to historical institutionalist arguments about the prominence of public policies and the importance of tracing historical processes, these insights from rational-choice theory offer promising openings for the study of policy feedback on mass publics.

Finally, the diversity of the arguments identified here and the uncertainty regarding the scope of many of them also suggests the need for a more fundamental reexamination of research agendas. While the utility of policy feedback arguments seems clear, there are a great many unanswered questions about the circumstances under which preexisting policies are likely to influence political processes, and about the particular types of influence that are most important.

[62] Ferejohn and Kuklinski (fn. 48); Keith Krehbiel, *Information and Legislative Organization* (Ann Arbor: University of Michigan Press, 1991); Mathew M. McCubbins and Terry Sullivan, eds., *Congress: Structure and Policy* (Cambridge: Cambridge University Press, 1987).

[63] For a summary of that challenge, see March and Olsen (fn. 2), chap. 1.

Resolving these issues will require a reformulation of questions. Rather than asking "Do policies produce politics?" we need to ask more precise questions about how policies matter and under what conditions. Getting at the answers will often require careful attention to research design.

This conclusion highlights both the merits and limitations of recent work in historical institutionalism. By now, the merits should be clear. The emergence of arguments about policy feedback has stemmed largely from research that takes structural constraints imposed by government seriously, that utilizes detailed case studies, and that emphasizes that history matters—that political processes should be analyzed over time. As Skocpol puts it:

> Too often social scientists . . . forget that policies, once enacted, restructure subsequent political processes. Analysts typically look only for synchronic determinants of policies—for example, in current social interests or in existing political alliances. In addition, however, we must examine patterns unfolding over time. . . . We must make social policies the starting points as well as the end points of analysis. (p. 58)

Because historical institutional analysis encourages intensive scrutiny of specific historical paths, it has been ideally suited to identify the existence of policy feedback mechanisms. The same approach, however, has had greater difficulty in moving to the next phase: establishing the scope of particular mechanisms, and the specific characteristics of policies and the broader context that are likely to make particular mechanisms relevant.

Much can probably be done within a historical institutionalist framework to cope with these problems. More specific questions need to be asked and hypotheses need to be carefully stated. Insights from rational choice theory need to be incorporated. But it is difficult to see how many of these more specific questions can be answered through the use of single-case studies. Investigating many of the most pressing questions may require a reorientation toward the investigation of large samples that would allow the application of statistical techniques.

Political scientists study what they do because they believe that politics matters—that government decisions have major social consequences. It is surely ironic that among the least understood of these consequences are the feedback effects on political life. Much like the formal institutions that have recently received extensive scholarly attention, major policies frame the choices of political actors both by creating resources and incentives and by influencing the efforts of individuals to interpret the social world. Incorporating this insight more systematically into research will greatly enrich our understanding of politics.

Constitutionalism and the Separation of Powers

5

WHAT'S SO GREAT ABOUT CONSTITUTIONALISM?
Michael J. Klarman[*]

American politics seems to be distinguished by the quite considerable extent to which politicians and citizens take the Constitution seriously—and have done since the document's ratification. Taking the Constitution seriously in turn means that politicians and citizens try to make their own sense of what it means. Everybody is on the same page—even if they disagree about what they read on the page. With constitutionalism, therefore, certain kinds of political actions, decisions, and interpretive statements about the Constitution are both possible and legitimate, others are not, and yet others are in a gray zone for shorter or longer periods of time until people constitutionalize those actions and interpretations. What better way, in the end, to tame power than for everyone to consult the Constitution in case they have reservations about what a public official is doing? They won't get clear answers. But the more important fact is that everyone turns to the same authority . . . the Constitution. Right?

Wrong, says Michael Klarman, a renowned legal historian. What constitutionalism actually is and how it actually works in American politics are really hard to pin down.

What's terrific about this article is how it forces one to appreciate the weaknesses in all of the leading arguments meant to canonize constitutionalism. And, just to be really frustrating, Klarman proposes a provocatively "realistic" account of constitutionalism —that it is ultimately a matter of broad social consensus. What constitutionalism does is to legally transmute what the best-educated and best-placed people in American society think about the relationships between the Constitution and the issues of the day: what the CEO's of the Fortune 500 companies want from fundamental law, what people at the top law schools take seriously, what federal judges and Supreme Court justices agree about the Constitution, what national politicians care about when they consider constitutional values, what the leaders

Northwestern University Law Review 93 (1998–1999): 145–194. Reprinted by special permission of Northwestern University School of Law, *Northwestern University Law Review*.

* James Monroe Professor of Law and F. Palmer Weber Research Professor of Civil Liberties and Human Rights, University of Virginia School of Law. I owe a special debt of gratitude to Mike Seidman, who not only provided his usual incisive comments on an earlier draft but also has exerted a profound influence on my thinking about constitutional theory generally. I am also grateful to Daryl Levinson, David Strauss, and George Cohen for their helpful comments. Versions of this paper were presented at a panel of the same title at the 1997 annual meeting of the American Political Science Association in Washington, D.C., and at faculty workshops at the DePaul College of Law, the University of Virginia School of Law, and the Marshall-Wythe School of Law at the College of William and Mary. I benefited from the comments and criticism that I received on each of those occasions. Last but not least, Jason Carey provided outstanding research assistance.

*of large voluntary organizations want to see protected by fundamental law,
and so forth. Take that, Robert Dahl!*

*The obvious retort to Klarman's suggestion, however, is that what "elites"
think is fundamentally shaped by their experience of the separation of powers across the president (and presidency), Congress, the Supreme Court,
federalism, and the fifty states. Accordingly, the articles that come after Klarman, in this section of the volume, cover those institutions.*

• • •

MISSING FROM THE VAST CONSTITUTIONAL LAW LITERATURE is a comprehensive
account of the different purposes served by constitutionalism. This Article aims
to fill that gap by identifying and evaluating ten leading accounts of constitutionalism that can be garnered from the cases and commentary: enforcement of a
principal-agent relationship; enforcement of societal pre-commitments; providing
a mechanism for checks and balances; protection of minority rights; maintenance
of continuity or tradition; symbolizing national unity; serving an educational
function; securing finality for disputed issues; providing a rule of recognition for
law; satisfying a majoritarian preference for constitutionalism.

In addition to describing these ten leading accounts of constitutionalism, Part
I offers positive and normative criticism of each. I shall argue, first, that none of
these accounts provides a very satisfactory description of how our constitutional
system operates. Second, I shall argue that none of these proffered justifications
for constitutionalism is unambiguously attractive. Specifically, each justification
possesses virtues and vices, the balancing of which entails controversial value
judgments. Thus, if one core function of constitutionalism is to provide some
common area of agreement for those who disagree about the merits of particular
controversies, such as abortion or affirmative action, I shall argue that it fails in
its objective. The normative evaluation of any particular account of constitutionalism requires value judgments no different in kind from those that infuse our
disagreements regarding the merits of particular constitutional controversies.

Part II of the article offers a concise alternative description of our constitutional
practices, which I believe to be more accurate than the accounts considered in Part I:
The Supreme Court, in *politically unpredictable* ways, imposes *culturally elite* values in *marginally countermajoritarian* fashion. In Part III, I offer a brief normative
assessment of this alternative description of American constitutionalism.

One preliminary point warrants brief attention. Throughout this essay, when
I discuss constitutionalism I am principally concerned with its judicially enforceable variety. I do not, of course, mean to deny the possibility of constitutionalism
without judicial review. Most American states experienced precisely that version
of constitutionalism in the decade before the Philadelphia Convention,[1] and numerous constitutional commentators recently have investigated the question of
constitutional interpretation outside the courts.[2] Still, constitutionalism without

---

[1] The first unambiguous instances of judicial review in the states did not come until just before
the meeting of the Philadelphia Convention—*Bayard v. Singleton*, 1 N.C. 5 (Mart. 1787), and *Trevett
v. Weeden* (RI 1786). For in-depth discussion of these and other more ambiguous early exercises of
the judicial review power in the states, see CHARLES GROVES HAINES, THE AMERICAN DOCTRINE OF
JUDICIAL SUPREMACY ch. 5 (1932).

[2] *See, e.g.*, Paul Brest, *The Conscientious Legislator's Guide to Constitutional Interpretation*, 27 STAN.
L. REV. 585 (1975); Lawrence Sager, *Fair Measure: The Legal Status of Underenforced Constitutional
Norms*, 91 HARV. L. REV. 1212 (1978); Robin West, *Progressive and Conservative Constitutionalism*,

judicial enforceability poses a less interesting question because so much less is at stake. A constitution as textually open ended as our own allows even constitutionally conscientious legislators to do pretty much as they please. As we shall see, constitutionalism without judicial review shares many of the virtues and vices of its judicially enforceable variety, but usually in less robust form.

I. TEN LEADING ACCOUNTS OF CONSTITUTIONALISM

A. Agency

On one prominent account, constitutionalism consists primarily of an agency relationship: the sovereign People constrain their government agents through the instrument of a written constitution. Judicial review, from this perspective, is the enforcement mechanism for that agency relationship. This is pretty much the view of constitutionalism espoused by Alexander Hamilton in *Federalist No. 78*[3] and by Chief Justice John Marshall in *Marbury v. Madison*.[4] It also suffuses Bruce Ackerman's notion of "constitutional dualism," in which the sovereign will of the People voiced through "constitutional politics" constrains the actions of legislative agents engaged in "ordinary politics" through the mechanism of "preservationist" courts.[5]

Descriptively, this agency conception of constitutionalism suffers both from the Supreme Court's failure to enforce agency restrictions that are specified in the Constitution and its willingness to manufacture restrictions that are not. As to the former, consider the Court's substantial evisceration of the Contracts Clause in the twentieth century,[6] its general unwillingness (until very recently) to supply any concrete content to the Tenth Amendment,[7] its refusal to enforce the constitutional

---

88 MICH. L. REV. 641, 717–21 (1990); Hal Krent, The (Un)intended Consequences of Underenforcing Constitutional Norms (1997) (unpublished manuscript, on file with author); Mark V. Tushnet, The Constitution Outside the Courts ch.1 (1996) (unpublished manuscript, on file with author).

[3] THE FEDERALIST No. 78, at 526 (Alexander Hamilton) (Jacob E. Cooke ed., 1961) (because "the prior act of a superior ought to be preferred to the subsequent act of an inferior and subordinate authority . . . , whenever a particular statute contravenes the constitution, it will be the duty of the judicial tribunals to adhere to the latter, and disregard the former").

[4] 5 U.S. (1 Cranch) 137, 176 (1803) (observing that judicial review empowers courts to invalidate legislation inconsistent with "fundamental" principles embraced by the "supreme" will of the sovereign People).

[5] BRUCE ACKERMAN, WE THE PEOPLE: FOUNDATIONS chs. 1, 9–11 (1991). *See also* Akhil Reed Amar, *Philadelphia Revisited: Amending the Constitution Outside Article V*, 55 U. CHI. L. REV. 1043, 1085 (1988).

[6] The critical decision here was *Home Building & Loan Ass'n v. Blaisdell*, 290 U.S. 398 (1934). The Court has not, of course, completely extinguished the Contracts Clause. *See, e.g.*, Allied Structural Steel v. Spannaus, 438 U.S. 234 (1978); United States Trust Co. v. New Jersey, 431 U.S. 1 (1977); David A. Strauss, *Common Law Constitutional Interpretation*, 63 U. CHI. L. REV. 877, 904 (1996) (noting that the Contracts Clause has been "interpreted to reach the narrowest range of cases that it could reach without being effectively read out of the Constitution").

[7] *Compare* Garcia v. San Antonio Metro. Transit Auth., 469 U.S. 528 (1985) (Tenth Amendment is a truism) *with* New York v. United States, 505 U.S. 144 (1992) (construing the Tenth Amendment to forbid congressional commandeering of state legislatures) *and* Printz v. United States, 117 S. Ct. 2365 (1997) (construing the Tenth Amendment to forbid congressional commandeering of state executive officers). *See, e.g.*, Gary Lawson, *The Rise and Rise of the Administrative State*, 107 HARV. L. REV. 1231, 1236 (1994) (noting that "the Court has effectively acquiesced in Congress's assumption of general legislative powers").

requirement that wars be declared by Congress,[8] and its unwillingness to require that Congress rather than the president legislate.[9] As to the Court's willingness to manufacture new agency restrictions, consider the entire doctrine of substantive due process in both its *Lochner*-era and modern privacy incarnations,[10] the expansion of the Equal Protection Clause to cover unanticipated beneficiaries,[11] or the application of the First Amendment to a plenitude of subjects never contemplated by the Framers, such as commercial speech, pornography, campaign finance, and hate speech.[12]

To a certain extent, judicial expansion and contraction of the original agency relationship seems inevitable given the relative indeterminacy of the Constitution, which, for this very reason, comprises a lousy set of agency instructions. Given such an open-textured document, it seems inevitable that courts entrusted with its enforcement will be imposing their own notion of the appropriate agency relationship rather than enforcing the one designed by the Constitution's Framers. Terms such as "necessary and proper," "commerce," "freedom of speech," and "equal protection" seem to invite, indeed require, judicial creativity.[13] Yet it is uncertain whether the cause of popular sovereignty is better served by having unelected judges impose their own view of an appropriate agency relationship than by having the imperfectly constituted sovereign People redefine the agency relationship through popular elections. So the first normative objection to the agency conception of constitutionalism inheres in the relative indeterminacy of our Constitution; a document drafted with greater precision might ameliorate the problem of the enforcement mechanism inventing rather than enforcing agency restrictions.

Yet more specific agency instructions would exacerbate a second normative problem: the deadhand objection to enforcing an agency relationship that was, in substantial part, designed over two hundred years ago. Why should the People of 1998 be bound by a set of agency restrictions designed by a People possessed of

---

[8] *See* U.S. CONST. art. I, § 8, cl. 11. The numerous cases in which the Supreme Court declined to hear challenges to the constitutionality of the Vietnam War are itemized in Rodric B. Schoen, *A Strange Silence: Vietnam and the Supreme Court*, 33 WASHBURN L.J. 275, 278–98 (1994). *See also* The Prize Cases, 67 U.S. (2 Black) 635, 668–71 (1863) (noting that the Court is obliged to defer to the president's determination that the nation is at war, even in the absence of a congressional declaration to that effect); Bas v. Tingy, 4 U.S. (4 Dall.) 37 (1800) (endorsing the national government's authority to wage an undeclared war with France). For a useful discussion of *Bas v. Tingy*, see WILLIAM R. CASTO, THE SUPREME COURT IN THE EARLY REPUBLIC: THE CHIEF JUSTICESHIPS OF JOHN JAY AND OLIVER ELLSWORTH 120–24 (1995). *See generally* JOHN HART ELY, WAR AND RESPONSIBILITY: CONSTITUTIONAL LESSONS OF VIETNAM AND ITS AFTERMATH 54–67 (1993).

[9] *See* JOHN HART ELY, DEMOCRACY AND DISTRUST 131–34 (1980); DAVID SCHOENBROD, POWER WITHOUT RESPONSIBILITY: HOW CONGRESS ABUSES THE PEOPLE THROUGH DELEGATION (1993); Lawson, *supra* note 7, at 1237–41. The Court has not used the nondelegation doctrine to invalidate a congressional statute since the New Deal period. *See* A.L.A. Schechter Poultry Corp. v. United States, 295 U.S. 495 (1935); Panama Refining Co. v. Ryan, 293 U.S. 388 (1935).

[10] *See, e.g.*, Roe v. Wade, 410 U.S. 113 (1973) (abortion); Griswold v. Connecticut, 381 U.S. 479 (1965) (contraception); Lochner v. New York, 198 U.S. 45 (1905) (liberty of contract).

[11] *See, e.g.*, Romer v. Evans, 116 S. Ct. 1620 (1996) (gays and lesbians); Plyler v. Doe, 457 U.S. 202 (1982) (children of illegal aliens); Reed v. Reed, 404 U.S. 71 (1971) (women); Graham v. Richardson, 403 U.S. 365 (1971) (aliens); Levy v. Louisiana, 391 U.S. 68 (1968) (nonmarital children).

[12] *See, e.g.*, R.A.V. v. City of St. Paul, 505 U.S. 377 (1992) (hate speech); Virginia State Bd. of Pharmacy v. Virginia Citizens Consumer Council, 425 U.S. 748 (1976) (commercial speech); Buckley v. Valeo, 424 U.S. 1 (1976) (campaign finance); Roth v. United States, 354 U.S. 476 (1957) (pornography).

[13] *See, e.g.*, ELY, *supra* note 9, at 12–14; Michael J. Klarman, *The Puzzling Resistance to Political Process Theory*, 77 VA. L. REV. 747, 769–70 (1991).

radically different ideas and confronted with radically different circumstances?[14] For example, the principals of 1787 plainly possessed a limited conception of national government power that was appropriate to a world with primitive transportation and communication, little mobility among the citizenry, a barely developed market economy, and a paranoid fear of distant government power. It is unclear why the principals of 1998, inhabiting a radically changed world, should presumptively be bound by the original set of agency restrictions imposed upon the national government. Nor does the possibility of constitutional amendment solve this deadhand problem, though it does ameliorate it. The supermajority requirements of Article V unduly privilege the status quo and thus confound any argument that today's principals have manifested their consent to deadhand agency restrictions by acquiescing in them.[15]

The agency conception of constitutionalism is subject to another objection with both positive and normative dimensions. Usually, to be effective, agency restrictions require an impartial enforcement mechanism. But there is no such mechanism available for enforcing the federal Constitution. Federal courts are part of the federal government and state courts are part of their state governments, with corresponding incentives to expand and contract the powers conferred by the agency relationship upon their respective governments. Both Antifederalist opponents of the original Constitution and Jeffersonian critics of the Marshall Court's great nationalizing decisions raised precisely this objection to the claim that the federal courts would be the arbiter of federal/state conflicts.[16]

[14] I have elaborated at length upon the deadhand problem of constitutionalism in Michael J. Klarman, *Antifidelity*, 70 S. Cal. L. Rev. 381, 383–87 (1997).

[15] *See, e.g.,* Robert A. Dahl, Democracy and Its Critics 136–37, 153 (1989); Elaine Spitz, Majority Rule 151, 173 (1984); Amar, *supra* note 5, at 1073–74; Ian Shapiro, *Three Fallacies Concerning Majorities, Minorities and Democratic Politics, in* Majorities and Minorities, NOMOS XXXII, 79, 83 (1990).

[16] For Madison's claim that the federal courts would be the final arbiter of such disputes, see The Federalist No. 39, at 256 (James Madison) (Jacob E. Cooke ed., 1961) ("[I]n controversies relating to the boundary between the two jurisdictions [state and federal], the tribunal which is ultimately to decide, is to be established under the general [federal] government."); *see also* Jack N. Rakove, Original Meanings: Politics and Ideas in the Making of the Constitution 76 (1996) (noting a similar statement by Edmund Randolph at the Philadelphia Convention). For Antifederalist criticism, see G. Edward White, *Recovering Coterminous Power Theory,* 14 Nova L. Rev. 155, 168–72 (1989) (discussing the views of the Antifederalist Brutus). For Jeffersonian criticism, see, for example, Dwight Wiley Jessup, Reaction and Accommodation: The United States Supreme Court and Political Conflict 1809–1835, at 145–46, 218–19, 226, 359 (1987); *A Virginian's "Amphictyon" Essays, reprinted in* John Marshall's Defense of McCulloch v. Maryland (Gerald Gunther ed., 1969) [hereinafter *A Virginian's "Amphictyon" Essays*]:

> [T]he states never could have committed an act of such egregious folly as to agree that their umpire should be altogether appointed and paid by the other party. The supreme court may be a perfectly impartial tribunal to decide between two states, but cannot be considered in that point of view when the contest lies between the United States, and one of its members.

Id. at 58. Madison remained committed to his initial view—that the federal courts were the arbiters of federal/state conflicts—notwithstanding Jefferson's imprecations to the contrary and Madison's qualms about the overly nationalist bent of the Marshall Court in the decade after the end of the War of 1812. *See* Letter from James Madison to Thomas Jefferson (June 27, 1823), *in* 3 The Republic of Letters: The Correspondence Between Thomas Jefferson and James Madison 1776–1826, at 1867–70 (James Morton Smith ed., 1995) [hereinafter The Republic of Letters]. Madison's later views on this subject are usefully discussed in Drew R. McCoy, The Last of the Fathers: James Madison and the Republican Legacy 70 (1989); 1 Charles Warren, The Supreme Court in

Not only might federal courts have an abstract bias in favor of expanding the power of the government with which they are affiliated, but they also might possess a concrete incentive to expand national government power and thereby augment their own jurisdiction vis-à-vis state courts. Specifically, Article III's "arising under" head of jurisdiction[17] creates the possibility that expanded national *legislative* power will result in expanded national *judicial* power. Antifederalist and Jeffersonian critics repeatedly made this point as well.[18] Indeed, the theoretical underpinning of southern nullification and secession arguments was the absence of any neutral arbiter of the agency relationship.[19] Because neither federal nor state courts were neutral with regard to construing Congress's powers under the federal constitution, only the sovereign People, meeting in their state conventions, could arbitrate federal/state conflicts.[20]

The lack of neutrality of federal courts is especially significant when one recalls that they are not only the enforcement mechanism for the agency relationship, but also are among the agents supposedly constrained by that relationship. If, as Chief Justice Marshall warned, Congress cannot be trusted with construing its

---

UNITED STATES HISTORY, 1789–1835, at 554–55 (1922); Ralph Ketcham, *James Madison and Judicial Review*, 8 SYRACUSE L. REV. 158, 160–61 (1956).

[17] U.S. CONST. art. III, § 2, cl. 1.

[18] *See* RAKOVE, *supra* note 16, at 187; White, *supra* note 16, at 168–69.

[19] *See* JESSE CARPENTER, THE SOUTH AS A CONSCIOUS MINORITY 1789–1861, at 136–38, 209–10 (1930); JESSUP, *supra* note 16, at 339–40 (noting the Virginia legislature's resolution in 1828 denying the existence of any neutral arbiter on federal/state disputes and proclaiming that each state had a right to construe the compact for itself); *id.* at 377 (noting Calhoun in 1828 denying that the Supreme Court had authority to determine federal/state conflicts); Lacy Ford, Jr., *Inventing the Concurrent Majority: Madison, Calhoun and the Problem of Majoritarianism in American Political Thought*, 60 J. S. HIST. 19, 49 (1994). This notion that the federal courts lacked neutrality in resolving conflicts between federal and state power also inspired numerous proposals early in the nineteenth century to create a more impartial tribunal to resolve such disputes, including awarding appellate jurisdiction to the United States Senate. *See. e.g.*, JESSUP, *supra* note 16, at 145–46, 218–19, 384–85; WARREN, *supra* note 16, at 388–89, 518–19, 657–58. There was possibly some hypocrisy here, because many southerners in the 1850s—when the Court was firmly in the control of southerners—were happy to accept the Supreme Court as final arbiter of constitutional disputes involving congressional power to regulate slavery in the federal territories. *See* DON E. FEHRENBACHER, THE *DRED SCOTT* CASE: ITS SIGNIFICANCE IN AMERICAN LAW AND POLITICS 418 (1978); Barry Friedman, *The History of the Countermajoritarian Difficulty, Part One: The Road to Judicial Supremacy*, 73 N.Y.U. L. REV. 333, 422–23 (1998) (collecting statements to this effect); *see also* CARPENTER, *supra*, at 162–63.

[20] *See* John C. Calhoun, South Carolina Exposition, *in* X THE PAPERS OF JOHN C. CALHOUN 422–23 (Clyde N. Wilson & W. Edwin Hemphill eds., 1977):

> [T]o divide power, and to give to one of the parties the exclusive right of judging of the portion allotted to each, is in reality not to divide at all; and to reserve such exclusive right to the General Government (it matters not by what department it be exercised), is in fact, to constitute it one great consolidated government, with unlimited powers, and to reduce the States to mere corporations.

Id.; *see also* John C. Calhoun, Fort Hill Address, *in* XI THE PAPERS OF JOHN C. CALHOUN 506 (Clyde N. Wilson & W. Edwin Hemphill eds., 1977) [hereinafter Calhoun, Fort Hill Address] (noting that federal judges represent the same national majority as Congress and the president, and thus cannot be trusted to defend the prerogatives of the states from national usurpation); *Kentucky Resolution of 1798, in* 2 THE REPUBLIC OF LETTERS, *supra* note 16, at 1080 ("[a]s in all other cases of compact among powers having no common judge, each party has an equal right to judge for itself, as well of infractions as of the mode and measure of redress"). *Cf.* McCoy, *supra* note 16, at 69–70 (noting Jefferson's argument that a convention of the people called either by Congress or two-thirds of the states must be the arbiter of state/federal conflicts).

own powers,[21] it is not clear why federal courts are better entrusted with defining their own powers. Much of our constitutional history confirms the notion that federal judges possess strong incentives to augment their powers by distorting the agency relationship in their favor.[22] Consider the following examples, which are meant to be illustrative rather than exhaustive. First, the relaxation and eventual near-abandonment of federalism restrictions on Congress[23] might confirm the Antifederalist suspicion that federal courts benefit, both abstractly and concretely, from expanded national legislative power. Second, consider the Court's century-long experiment in the making of federal common law under *Swift v. Tyson*[24]—an especially striking illustration of judicial self-aggrandizement because it occurred in an era when the Court almost certainly would have invalidated congressional efforts to impose similar rules through legislation.[25] Third, note the revolutionary expansion of federal equity jurisprudence in the context of railroad receiverships[26] and labor union injunctions[27] near the end of the nineteenth century, extending judicial oversight to bankruptcy and labor policy in the absence of congressional authorization. Finally, the Supreme Court's stunning expansion of individual rights protections over the past four decades, from the political left and right simultaneously, seems to corroborate the imperialist impulses of the nation's judiciary.[28] Every time the Supreme Court declares the existence of a new constitutional right—a right to use contraceptives or to obtain abortions, a right against affirmative action or regulatory takings[29]—it seizes judicial control over a new area of public policy. One must not forget that courts too are agents theoretically bound by the agency relationship;[30] to invest them with authority definitively to construe that relationship is normatively problematic, given their

---

[21] *See* Marbury v. Madison, 5 U.S. (1 Cranch) 137, 178 (1803) (noting that in the absence of judicial review, legislatures would enjoy "a practical and real omnipotence"); *see also* City of Boerne v. Flores, 117 S. Ct. 2157, 2162 (1997) (same).

[22] *See* Robert G. McCloskey, The American Supreme Court 129 (2d ed. 1994) (noting "the old urge to monarchize" of the Supreme Court).

[23] The crucial decisions were *United States v. Darby*, 312 U.S. 100 (1941), and *Wickard v. Filburn*, 317 U.S. 111 (1942), and only recently has the Court evinced any inclination to reenter the field. *See* United States v. Lopez, 115 U.S. 1624 (1995).

[24] 41 U.S. (16 Pet.) 1 (1842).

[25] *See* Erie R.R. Co. v. Tompkins, 304 U.S. 64, 78–80 (1938) (holding that federal courts have no constitutional power to apply rules of general federal common law in diversity cases); *cf.* Warren, *supra* note 16, at 164 (noting Thomas Jefferson making a similar objection to the notion of a federal common law of crimes).

[26] *See* Quincy, Mo. and Pac. R.R. Co. v. Humphreys, 145 U.S. 82 (1892). For a brief discussion, see James W. Ely, Jr., The Chief Justiceship of Melville W. Fuller 1888–1910, at 203–04 (1995).

[27] *See In re* Debs, 158 U.S. 564 (1895); *see also* Owen M. Fiss, Troubled Beginnings of the Modern State, 1888–1910, at 65–73 (1993); David Currie, *The Constitution in the Supreme Court: Protection of Economic Interests, 1889–1910*, 52 U. Chi. L. Rev. 325, 343–46 (1985); Daniel Novak, *The Pullman Strike Cases: Debs, Darrow, and the Labor Injunction, in* American Political Trials (Michael R. Belknap ed., 1981).

[28] I have developed this theme, with numerous examples, in Michael J. Klarman, *Majoritarian Judicial Review: The Entrenchment Problem*, 85 Geo. L.J. 491, 544–51 (1997) [hereinafter Klarman, Majoritarian Judicial Review].

[29] *See, e.g.*, Adarand Constructors, Inc. v. Pena, 115 S. Ct. 2097, 2114–17 (1995) (affirmative action); Lucas v. South Carolina Coastal Council, 505 U.S. 1003 (1992) (regulatory takings); Roe v. Wade, 410 U.S. 113 (1973) (abortion); Griswold v. Connecticut, 381 U.S. 479 (1965) (contraceptives).

[30] *See, e.g.*, Richard S. Kay, *Preconstitutional Rules*, 42 Ohio St. L.J. 187, 187 (1981); *see also* James Madison, *Report on the Resolutions, reprinted in* VI The Writings of James Madison 341 (Gaillard Hunt ed., 1906) (noting that "dangerous powers, not delegated, may not only be usurped and executed by the other departments, but that the Judicial Department may also exercise or sanction

obvious incentive to distort their interpretations in favor of expanding their own power. The relative political insulation of courts only exacerbates this problem by diluting the most powerful constraint upon this self-aggrandizing tendency—direct electoral accountability.

B. Precommitment

A second, related account holds that the Constitution consists of a set of precommitments undertaken by the sovereign People. Courts, because of their relative insulation from short-term passions, are entrusted with enforcement of those precommitments against repudiations manifested in the form of legislation inconsistent with the Constitution. This precommitment notion of constitutionalism differs from the agency conception in this sense: The latter conceives of legislators as agents and the People, speaking through their Constitution, as sovereign, while the former understands both the Constitution and legislation to represent the will of the People, though one takes the form of long-term precommitments and the other the form of short-term preferences that may be inconsistent with those precommitments. This precommitment notion of constitutionalism is widely embraced. Consider, for example, Alexander Bickel's notion of courts enforcing "enduring values" as against "the current clash of interests,"[31] Alexander Hamilton's vision of courts checking the "ill humours" frequently manifested in legislation,[32] or Justice Brennan's notion of courts passing "sober constitutional judgment" because legislators sometimes are influenced "by the passions and exigencies of the moment."[33]

---

dangerous powers, beyond the grant of the Constitution"); *A Virginian's "Amphictyon" Essays, supra* note 16 (same).

[31] ALEXANDER BICKEL, THE LEAST DANGEROUS BRANCH 24–26 (1962).

[32] THE FEDERALIST No. 78, at 527 (Alexander Hamilton) (Jacob E. Cooke ed., 1961). Hamilton noted that courts will

> guard the Constitution and the rights of individuals from the effects of those ill-humours which . . . though they speedily give place to better information and more deliberate reflection, have a tendency, in the meantime, to occasion dangerous innovations in the government, and serious oppressions of the minor party in the community.

[33] Marsh v. Chambers, 463 U.S. 783, 814 (1983) (Brennan, J., dissenting). For additional examples of this view, see New York v. United States, 505 U.S. 144, 187 (1992) (noting that the Constitution "divides power among sovereigns and among branches of government precisely so that we may resist the temptation to concentrate power in one location as an expedient solution to the crisis of the day"); Rutan v. Republican Party, 497 U.S. 62, 95 (1990) (Scalia, J., dissenting) ("The provisions of the Bill of Rights were designed to restrain transient majorities from impairing long-recognized personal liberties."); American Communications Ass'n v. Douds, 339 U.S. 382, 453 (1950) (Black, J., dissenting) (observing that the Court's role is to intervene when "the fog of public excitement obscures the ancient landmarks set up in our Bill of Rights"); West Virginia State Bd. of Educ. v. Barnette, 319 U.S. 624, 665 (1943) (Frankfurter, J., dissenting) (noting that judicial review enables men "freed from the influences of immediacy . . . to take a view of longer range than the period of responsibility entrusted to Congress and legislatures"); *Ex parte Milligan*, 71 U.S. (4 Wall.) 2, 109 (1866) ("During the late wicked Rebellion, the temper of the times did not allow that calmness in deliberation and discussion so necessary to a correct conclusion of a purely judicial question."); McCLOSKEY, *supra* note 22, at 212 (noting that "[a]n impulsive nation like ours, much given to short-run fads, enthusiasms and rages, can little afford to dispense with the one governmental element that is disposed by its nature to take the long-run into account"); Albert M. Sacks, *The Supreme Court 1953 Term—Foreword*, 68 HARV. L. REV. 96, 96 (1954) (noting that the Court's function "is to seek to reflect the sober second thought of the community").

This precommitment model also fails to account adequately for our constitutional practices. Very few of the Court's recent landmark individual rights decisions fit the precommitment paradigm. When the Court invalidated race discrimination,[34] sex discrimination,[35] school prayer,[36] abortion restrictions,[37] malapportionment in legislatures,[38] or obscenity regulations,[39] it plainly was not restraining short-term departures from long-term precommitted values. Quite to the contrary, each of these practices was deeply entrenched in American tradition when the Supreme Court ruled against it.

Conversely, the Court frequently has *declined* to intervene when this paradigm calls for judicial involvement—when legislatures perpetrate short-term departures from long-term principles. The most notable illustrations here are the Justices' refusal to invalidate Japanese-American internment during World War II[40] or virtually unprecedented speech restrictions during World War I[41] and the early Cold War.[42]

Normatively, proponents of this conception of constitutionalism generally fail to justify the privileging of long-term precommitments over short-term efforts to repudiate them. Yet both decisionmaking contexts have something to be said for them. Abstract long-term precommitments have the advantages of relative impartiality (because the concrete consequences of such decisions may be unknowable)[43] and of affording time for deliberation and insulation from passion. On the other hand, a concrete short-term decisionmaking context affords the advantages of experience, awareness of changed circumstances, and knowledge of the concrete consequences of abstract principles, which can be an advantage as well as a disadvantage.[44] Thus, for example, one plausibly might argue that unforeseeable changed circumstances may warrant either a temporary exemption or a permanent departure from a precommitted value. As to the former, consider, for example, President Lincoln's argument that an otherwise unconstitutional

---

[34] *See, e.g.*, Brown v. Board of Educ., 347 U.S. 483 (1954).

[35] *See, e.g.*, Reed v. Reed, 404 U.S. 71 (1971).

[36] *See, e.g.*, Engel v. Vitale, 370 U.S. 421 (1962).

[37] *See, e.g.*, Roe v. Wade, 410 U.S. 113 (1973).

[38] *See, e.g.*, Reynolds v. Sims, 377 U.S. 533 (1964).

[39] *See, e.g.*, Roth v. United States, 354 U.S. 476 (1957).

[40] *See* Korematsu v. United States, 323 U.S. 214 (1944).

[41] *See, e.g.*, Schenck v. United States, 249 U.S. 47 (1919).

[42] *See, e.g.*, Dennis v. United States, 341 U.S. 494 (1951). I regard the Court's invalidation after the Civil War of military trials of civilians, after declining to reach the question during the war, as further support for my claim. *Compare Ex parte* Milligan, 71 U.S. (4 Wall.) 2 (1866) *with Ex parte* Vallandigham, 68 U.S. (1 Wall.) 243 (1863).

[43] This is the basic idea behind Rawls's famous veil of ignorance. *See* John Rawls, A Theory of Justice 136–42 (1971); *see also* Frederick Schauer, *Judicial Review of the Devices of Democracy*, 94 Colum. L. Rev. 1326, 1336–37 (1994) (noting the objections to decisions about procedure being taken with knowledge of their substantive effects). Interestingly, as early as the 1790s, proponents of originalism were making precisely this argument in support of their interpretive methodology. *See* Rakove, *supra* note 16, at 359, 365.

[44] *Cf.* Letter from Thomas Jefferson to Samuel Kercheval (July 12, 1816), *in* 15 The Writings of Thomas Jefferson 32, 40 (Andrew Lipscomb ed., 1903) (criticizing the tendency to "ascribe to the men of the preceding age a wisdom more than human" and noting that their age "was very like the present, but without the experience of the present"). The importance of weighing the concrete consequences of abstract principles is the notion behind Rawls's "reflective equilibrium." Rawls, *supra* note 43, at 20–21, 48–51; *see also* Bickel, *supra* note 31, at 26 (noting that concern "with the flesh and blood of an actual case . . . provides an extremely salutary proving ground for all abstractions").

presidential suspension of the writ of habeas corpus might be justified in light of the South's massive insurrection against the Union and the Constitution,[45] or the Supreme Court's acknowledgement in *Blaisdell* that the Constitution temporarily might assume new meaning during an economic calamity as severe as the Great Depression.[46] Contemporaneously, it will be difficult, if not impossible, to judge whether a particular governmental action is a product of passions run amok that a court should resist or of short-term exigencies justifying drastic solutions that a court should accommodate. Think of how difficult it would have been to distinguish between these scenarios for one charged with making contemporaneous evaluations of the Japanese-American internment or McCarthyism.[47]

As to permanent repudiations of precommitted principles in light of changed circumstances, consider President Franklin Roosevelt's criticism of the "Nine Old Men" for foisting a "horse and buggy" conception of commerce on a radically transformed nation[48] or the Supreme Court's eventual acquiescence in the virtual elimination of the "public purpose" requirement from its substantive due process and takings jurisprudence.[49] It is far from obvious in either of these contexts— temporary departures or permanent repudiations—that abstract precommitted principles normatively should trump inconsistent subsequent concrete preferences. Problematically, any choice between the advantages and disadvantages of these two decisionmaking contexts is likely to be influenced by the context in which it is made; there is no neutral vantage point from which to make the assessment.[50]

---

[45] Abraham Lincoln, *Special Message to Congress, reprinted in* 2 ABRAHAM LINCOLN: SPEECHES AND WRITINGS 1859–1865, at 253 (Don E. Fehrenbacher ed., 1989) ("[A]re all the laws, *but one*, to go unexecuted, and the government itself go to pieces, lest that one be violated?"). Lincoln did not concede that his action was unconstitutional, but rather argued that it was justifiable *even if* it was unconstitutional. *See id.* (arguing that the Framers must have intended to allow the President to suspend the writ of habeas corpus, because "the provision was plainly made for a dangerous emergency" and Congress might not be in session).

[46] Home Bldg. & Loan Ass'n v. Blaisdell, 290 U.S. 398, 439 (1934) (Contracts Clause should not be interpreted "to prevent limited and temporary interpositions with respect to the enforcement of contracts if made necessary by a great public calamity"); *see also* Korematsu v. United States, 323 U.S. 214, 216 (1944) ("[P]ressing public necessity may sometimes justify the existence of . . . legal restrictions which curtail the civil rights of a single racial group.").

[47] I have argued elsewhere that the background social and political contexts of *Korematsu* and *Dennis* made contrary outcomes in the Supreme Court virtually unthinkable. *See* Michael J. Klarman, *Rethinking the Civil Rights and Civil Liberties Revolutions*, 82 VA. L. REV. 1, 28–31 (1996) [hereinafter Klarman, *Rethinking*]; *cf. Dennis*, 341 U.S. at 551 (Frankfurter, J., concurring) ("To make validity of legislation depend on judicial reading of events still in the womb of time—a forecast, that is, of the outcome of forces at best appreciated only with knowledge of the topmost secrets of nations—is to charge the judiciary with duties beyond its equipment.").

[48] FRANK FREIDEL, FRANKLIN D. ROOSEVELT: A RENDEZVOUS WITH DESTINY 163 (1990) (quoting FDR's statement at a 1935 press conference in which he criticized the Court's decision in *Schechter Poultry Corp. v. United States*, 295 U.S. 495 (1935), invalidating the National Industrial Recovery Act).

[49] On substantive due process, see Nebbia v. New York, 291 U.S. 502, 536 (1934) ("The phrase 'affected with a public purpose' can, in the nature of things, mean no more than that an industry, for adequate reason, is subject to control for the public good."); *see also* Williamson v. Lee Optical, 348 U.S. 483 (1955); Railway Express Agency v. New York, 336 U.S. 106 (1949). On takings, see Hawaii Housing Auth. v. Midkiff, 467 U.S. 229, 239–41 (1984) (emphasizing the extent of the Court's deference to legislative determinations of "public purpose" in the context of the eminent domain power).

[50] *See* Louis Michael Seidman, *Ambivalence and Accountability*, 61 S. CAL. L. REV. 1571, 1590– 1591 (1988); Louis Michael Seidman, *Reflections on Context and the Constitution*, 73 MINN. L. REV. 73, 81–82 (1988).

Moreover, the precommitment conception of constitutionalism suffers from the same indeterminacy and deadhand problems already considered in connection with the agency account. Specifically, if constitutional precommitments are indeterminate, and in our tradition they generally are, then the precommitment's enforcer (the judiciary) is as likely to be imposing its own preferences as interpreting those of the precommitment's maker (the People). And even if constitutional precommitments are determinate, they tend to be very old; to invalidate the will of a contemporary generation on the basis of a past generation's precommitments is normatively problematic.

C. Checks and Balances

A third defense of constitutionalism relies on the notion of checks and balances. This conception is distinct from the agency account, under which courts impose restrictions designed by the People on their legislative agents; it is also distinct from the precommitment notion, under which courts use the People's long-term precommitments to constrain the same People's short-term passions. Rather, this checks-and-balances account of constitutionalism conceives of judicial review as one set of agents (courts) controlling another (legislatures and executives). On this view, to be effective, the paper separation of powers contained in the Constitution requires a checking mechanism in the form of judicial review. In the absence of such a mechanism, one is left with ineffectual "parchment barriers."[51] Such a scenario would be especially unsettling for a Founding generation preoccupied with fears of the legislative "vortex"[52]—the plausible notion that the most powerful branch of the government would simply accumulate additional power once the system was up and running. Thus judicial review confers a salutary checking power upon the "least dangerous" branch,[53] regardless of whether one understands that branch to be enforcing agency restrictions as originally designed or simply making them up in its efforts to check legislative self-aggrandizement. On this view, judicially enforceable constitutionalism is analogous to the presidential veto; it is a mechanism that confers discretionary power on less threatening institutional actors in order to check more powerful ones.[54]

Descriptively, the checks-and-balances version of constitutionalism fails to account for the most fundamental shifts in governmental powers over the course of our constitutional history. The Court occasionally intervenes at the margin, but

---

[51] THE FEDERALIST No. 48, at 333 (James Madison) (Jacob E. Cooke ed., 1961) (disparaging "parchment barriers" as insufficient checks upon "the more powerful members of the government"). This skepticism of parchment barriers also informed the Federalists' generally lukewarm response to a proposed bill of rights. *See* RAKOVE, *supra* note 16, at ch. 10; Paul Finkelman, *James Madison and the Bill of Rights: A Reluctant Paternity*, 1990 SUP. CT. REV. 301, 310, 319, 326, 332.

[52] THE FEDERALIST No. 48, at 333 (James Madison) (Jacob E. Cooke ed., 1961) (expressing concern about the legislature "drawing all power into its impetuous vortex"); *see also* THE FEDERALIST No. 51, at 350 (James Madison) (Jacob E. Cooke ed., 1961) ("In republican government, the legislative authority, necessarily, predominates."); THE FEDERALIST No. 71, at 483 (Alexander Hamilton) (Jacob E. Cooke ed., 1961) (noting the "tendency of the legislative authority to absorb every other [authority]"); RAKOVE, *supra* note 16, at 281–83.

[53] THE FEDERALIST No. 78, at 522 (Alexander Hamilton) (Jacob E. Cooke ed., 1961).

[54] At the Philadelphia Convention, an extended debate occurred on whether the executive and judiciary should jointly exercise the proposed veto power over congressional legislation. *See, e.g.,* 2 RECORDS OF THE FEDERAL CONVENTION OF 1787, at 73–80 (Max Farrand ed., 1911) [hereinafter CONVENTION OF 1787]; *see also* RAKOVE, *supra* note 16, at 261–62 (describing this debate).

rarely resists fundamental changes that reflect an altered material reality. The Court has not resisted the growth of an imperial presidency by, for example, consistently enforcing the nondelegation doctrine.[55] The Court generally has acquiesced in the exponential increase in national government power vis-à-vis the states.[56] And the Court has shown little inclination to check the growth of the modern administrative state by insisting on the compartmentalization of executive, legislative, and judicial power apparently contemplated by Articles I, II, and III.[57]

In all three of these areas, the Court's interventions can accurately be described, I think, as fairly trivial. The Court occasionally and unpredictably intervenes in separation-of-powers cases, but allows to go unchecked the more significant departures from the original design.[58] Recently, the Court has begun reinvigorating its federalism jurisprudence, but thus far the result has been trivial compared to the massive centralization of power that the Court has legitimized since the New Deal.[59] And the Court has made no effort to check the concentration of legislative, executive, and judicial power in the hands of administrative agencies.[60] Generally speaking, the Court has interpreted the Constitution to permit fundamental adjustments to the original structural scheme in order to accommodate changing reality.

The principal normative objection to the checks-and-balances conception of constitutionalism is this: When the Court does intervene to check the power of other institutional actors, inevitably it augments its own power (at least in one sense), which is not so easily checkable because of the federal courts' relative insulation from politics. Chief Justice Marshall sought to evade this objection in *Marbury* by conceiving of judicial review as an objective enforcement mechanism for determinate constitutional text.[61] But, as I already have suggested, the constitutional text is sufficiently indeterminate to permit any number of plausible

[55] *See supra* note 9.

[56] *See supra* note 7.

[57] *See, e.g.,* Touby v. United States, 500 U.S. 160, 167–68 (1991) (separation of powers doctrine "does not speak to the manner in which authority is parceled out within a single Branch"); Lawson, *supra* note 7, at 1248–49 ("The destruction of this principle of separation of powers is perhaps the crowning jewel of the modern administrative revolution.").

[58] Thus the Court essentially permits the president to make law and to fight undeclared wars but gets bent out of shape when Congress permits legislative appointees to serve on commissions vested with "executive" functions. *See* Metropolitan Washington Airports Auth. v. Citizens for the Abatement of Aircraft Noise, 501 U.S. 252 (1991); Buckley v. Valeo, 424 U.S. 1 (1976); *see also* Bowsher v. Synar, 478 U.S. 714 (1986); *cf.* Strauss, *supra* note 6, at 917 n.93 (noting that the Court has been most "notoriously formalistic" in its recent separation of powers cases where the stakes were the lowest).

[59] The Court has struck a blow for federalism on several recent occasions. *See, e.g.,* Printz v. United States, 117 S. Ct. 2365 (1997); City of Boerne v. Flores, 117 S. Ct. 2157 (1997); Seminole Tribe v. Florida, 116 S. Ct. 1114, 1127 (1996); United States v. Lopez, 115 S. Ct. 1624 (1995); New York v. United States, 505 U.S. 144 (1992). It remains uncertain, though, whether any of these decisions genuinely affect the substance rather than the form of congressional power. Justices Kennedy and O'Connor went out of their way in *Lopez* to reject the notion that the Court was undertaking any fundamental reconsideration of post–New Deal national power. *See Lopez,* 115 U.S. at 1637 (Kennedy, J., with O'Connor, J., concurring) (noting that the history of the Court's Commerce Clause jurisprudence reveals "that the Court as an institution and the legal system as a whole have an immense stake in the stability of our Commerce Clause jurisprudence as it has evolved to this point"); *see also Printz,* 117 S. Ct. at 2385 (O'Connor, J., concurring) (emphasizing the limited reach of the Court's ruling and noting that Congress is free to reach the same result by other means). Nor has the Court yet been willing to place significant restrictions on what is Congress's arguably most important grant of power—spending. *See* South Dakota v. Dole, 483 U.S. 203 (1987).

[60] *See supra* note 57.

[61] Marbury v. Madison, 5 U.S. (1 Cranch) 137, 178–80 (1803).

interpretations, and judges may possess the same incentive as legislators to expand their power.

Nor is it obvious that the federal judiciary is any longer the least dangerous branch that the Founders and Chief Justice Marshall assumed it to be.[62] Federal courts had a far more limited stature and jurisdiction in the early years of the Republic than they do today.[63] Moreover, the Founding generation seems to have possessed a dramatically more limited conception of judicial review than that generally entertained today.[64] Specifically, the Framers apparently believed that the practice would be limited to cases of the "clear constitutional violation," such as the examples Chief Justice Marshall invokes in *Marbury v. Madison* to demonstrate that the existence of a written constitution *logically* implies the practice of judicial review.[65] Further, they probably conceived of judicial review in classically Madisonian separation-of-powers terms. That is, courts would invalidate only legislation involving matters of "peculiar judicial concern," such as the jurisdictional issue in *Marbury*, the non-judicial duties thrust upon federal judges by the statute invalidated in *Hayburn's Case*[66] or the divestiture of jury trial rights implicated in most of the early state cases that raised the issue of judicial review.[67]

When one considers the breadth and importance of the social policy questions constitutionalized by the Supreme Court in the last few decades, it is far from clear that the Court plays the sort of "least dangerous branch" role that might render palatable an uncabined checking function. Abortion, the death penalty, school desegregation, affirmative action, gay rights, women's rights, the role of religion in public life, the right to die, campaign finance reform—these are only the issues that head the list. If judicial review manifests the same self-aggrandizing tendency as does legislative power—and the course of American constitutional history suggests that it may[68]—then the checks-and-balances conception of judicially reviewable constitutionalism is normatively problematic.

Another normative objection to the checks-and-balances account relates to the deadhand problem. The Constitution's Framers saw legislative abuse, as manifested in the debtor relief and paper money schemes enacted by state legislatures in the 1780s, as the principal vice of the existing scheme of government.[69] One

---

[62] *See* ELY, *supra* note 9, at 45–48.

[63] *See* CASTO, *supra* note 8, at 27–53; McCLOSKEY, *supra* note 22, at 19–20; R. KENT NEWMYER, THE SUPREME COURT UNDER MARSHALL AND TANEY 18–19, 25–27 (1968).

[64] On these points I follow CASTO, *supra* note 8, at 222–27; ROBERT CLINTON, *MARBURY V. MADISON AND JUDICIAL REVIEW* 18–30 (1989); SYLVIA SNOWISS, JUDICIAL REVIEW AND THE LAW OF THE CONSTITUTION 23–44 (1990).

[65] *Marbury*, 5 U.S. (1 Cranch) at 179. On the notion of judicial review being limited to cases of the "clear constitutional violation," see James B. Thayer, *The Origin and Scope of the American Doctrine of Constitutional Law*, 7 HARV. L. REV. 129 (1893) (arguing for this limitation and collecting numerous cases from the early republic that embraced it).

[66] 2 U.S. (2 Dall.) 409 (1793). On *Hayburn's Case*, see the valuable discussion in WARREN, *supra* note 16, at 69–84.

[67] The best discussion of these cases is HAINES, *supra* note 1, at ch. 5.

[68] *See supra* notes 22–30 and accompanying text.

[69] *See* James Madison, *The Vices of the Political System of the United States, in* 9 THE PAPERS OF JAMES MADISON 345–58 (Robert A. Rutland ed., 1975). The best discussion of this state legislative activity is ALLAN NEVINS, THE AMERICAN STATES DURING AND AFTER THE REVOLUTION 1775–1789, at 470–543 (1924); *see also* Edward S. Corwin, *The Progress of Constitutional Theory Between the Declaration of Independence and the Meeting of the Philadelphia Convention*, 30 AM. HIST. REV. 511 (1926), *reprinted in* 1 CORWIN ON THE CONSTITUTION 56 (Richard Loss ed., 1981). For the impact

of Madison's principal objectives in Philadelphia was to curb state legislatures, preferably through adopting a national government veto on state legislation, but alternatively through a combination of Article I, section 10's bar on state redistributive tendencies, the Supremacy Clause of Article VI, and the mechanism of judicial review.[70] Thus, for Founders appalled by what they regarded as the confiscatory tactics of overly populist state legislatures, judicial review might play a useful checking function.

Today, however, we live in a very different world. The redistributive tendencies that the Framers sought to curb have been largely sanctified in the modern welfare state. In such a world, judicial checks on the legislative "vortex" may be undesirable. It all depends on one's normative perspective as to whether the unregulated market or legislative intervention will produce better results. The Framers feared legislative redistribution, so naturally they approved of judicial checks, which, at a minimum, were unlikely to make things worse. For those possessed of a more beneficent vision of legislative redistribution, though, it is not obvious that this checking function is normatively attractive.[71] It depends on whether one believes that courts or legislatures are more likely to accomplish one's redistributive objectives. There is substantial reason to doubt that courts are likely to redistribute wealth more aggressively than legislatures. Indeed, for most of our constitutional history, they have checked redistribution rather than compelling it.[72]

D. Minority Rights

One popular justification for judicially enforceable constitutionalism is the need to protect minority rights from majoritarian overreaching. To the extent that the minority rights being protected derive from the text of the Constitution, this account is just one application of the precommitment conception of constitutional-

---

of this activity on the Framers' conception of how the existing political regime needed to be changed, see RAKOVE, *supra* note 16, at 35–56; GORDON WOOD, THE CREATION OF THE AMERICAN REPUBLIC 403–09 (1969); GORDON WOOD, THE RADICALISM OF THE AMERICAN REVOLUTION 251–55 (1992) [hereinafter Wood, RADICALISM].

[70] *See* RAKOVE, *supra* note 16, at 171–77; Charles F. Hobson, *The Negative on State Laws: James Madison, the Constitution, and the Crisis of Republican Government*, 36 WM. & MARY Q. 215 (1979).

[71] *Cf.* Kay, *supra* note 30, at 201–02 (recognizing that one's preference for rigid as opposed to flexible constraints on governmental power is likely to be a function of one's calculation of the likelihood that that power will be effectively deployed for beneficent purposes).

[72] *See, e.g.*, Coppage v. Kansas, 236 U.S. 1 (1915); Lochner v. New York, 198 U.S. 45 (1905); Pollock v. Farmers Loan & Trust Co., 158 U.S. 601 (1895); Bronson v. Kinzie, 42 U.S. (1 How.) 311 (1843); Sturges v. Crowninshield, 17 U.S. (4 Wheat.) 122 (1819). *See generally* MCCLOSKEY, *supra* note 22, chs. 3–6. Only for a very brief period in its history did the Court construe the Constitution to require governmental subsidization of fundamental rights, and even then only in contexts in which the government coerced participation in the criminal process or monopolized an area such as voting or divorce. *See* Boddie v. Connecticut, 401 U.S. 371 (1971); Harper v. Virginia, 383 U.S. 663 (1966); Douglas v. California, 372 U.S. 353 (1963); Gideon v. Wainwright, 372 U.S. 335 (1963); Griffin v. Illinois, 351 U.S. 12 (1956). The Burger Court quickly and decisively put a halt to these redistributive tendencies, rejecting claimed constitutional rights to welfare and decent housing and denying that wealth was a suspect classification. *See* San Antonio Sch. Dist. v. Rodriguez, 411 U.S. 1 (1973); Lindsey v. Normet, 405 U.S. 56 (1972); James v. Valtierra, 402 U.S. 137 (1971); Dandridge v. Williams, 397 U.S. 471 (1970). I have argued elsewhere that repudiation of the incipient notion that the Constitution mandates wealth redistribution was among the most significant accomplishments of the Burger Court. *See* Michael J. Klarman, *An Interpretive History of Modern Equal Protection*, 90 MICH. L. REV. 213, 285–91 (1991).

ism. But most advocates of this minority rights notion do not limit themselves to judicial enforcement of the constitutional text. Rather, they argue more generally for a judicial role in protecting minority rights from majoritarian interference—whether those rights derive from natural law, societal consensus, or some other source. Consider, for example, Justice Black's famous statement that courts stand "as havens of refuge for those who might otherwise suffer because they are helpless, weak, outnumbered, or because they are nonconforming victims of prejudice and public excitement"[73] or Justice Jackson's proclamation in his celebrated opinion in the second flag salute case that "[t]he very purpose of a Bill of Rights was to withdraw certain subjects from the vicissitudes of political controversy, to place them beyond the reach of majorities."[74] This minority rights conception of constitutionalism also differs from the simple checks-and-balances notion, which focuses on legislative self-aggrandizement rather than on whether legislatures are protecting or persecuting minority groups.

Descriptively, this minority rights account of constitutionalism is surprisingly deficient, given its prevalence in conventional wisdom. Much as the Court has been unwilling to enforce precommitted values after they have lost their attraction, so has it generally declined to protect minority rights against dominant majoritarian norms.[75] The limited countermajoritarianism of the Court is partly attributable to political checks that constrain the Justices' *capacity* to frustrate strong public opinion but perhaps more significantly to internal cultural checks that limit their *inclination* to do so.[76]

The romantic image of the Court as countermajoritarian savior is shattered by historical reality. The Supreme Court sanctioned rather than attacked slavery, legitimized segregation for much of the Jim Crow era, validated the Japanese-American internment during World War II, sanctioned McCarthyism, and approved sex discrimination until after the emergence of the modern women's movement.[77] The most celebrated examples of the Court's supposed countermajoritarian heroics are less than compelling. The *Brown* decision was the product of a broad array of political, social, economic and ideological forces inaugurated or accelerated by World War II; by the time of the Court's intervention, half the nation no longer supported racial segregation.[78] Similarly, *Roe v. Wade* was decided at the crest of the modern women's movement and was supported by half

---

[73] Chambers v. Florida, 309 U.S. 227, 241 (1940).

[74] West Virginia State Bd. of Educ. v. Barnette, 319 U.S. 624, 638 (1943). For other strong statements of this view, see, for example, Employment Div. v. Smith, 494 U.S. 872, 902–03 (1990) (O'Connor, J., concurring); Minersville Sch. Dist. v. Gobitis, 310 U.S. 586, 606 (1940) (Stone, J., dissenting); United States v. Carolene Prods. Co., 304 U.S. 144, 153 n.4 (1938); *see also* Klarman, *Rethinking, supra* note 47, at 1–3 & nn.1–14 (collecting additional statements of this view).

[75] *See* McCLOSKEY, *supra* note 22, at 14 ("[T]he Supreme Court has seldom, if ever, flatly and for very long resisted a really unmistakable wave of public sentiment."); Klarman, *Rethinking, supra* note 47, at 17–18 ("[T]he Court identifies and protects minority rights only when a majority or near majority of the community has come to deem those rights worthy of protection.").

[76] *See* McCLOSKEY, *supra* note 22, at 209 ("We might come closer to the truth if we said that the judges have often agreed with the main current of public sentiment because they were themselves part of that current, and not because they feared to disagree with it."); Klarman, *Rethinking, supra* note 47, at 16 & n.72; Steven L. Winter, *An Upside/Down View of the Countermajoritarian Difficulty,* 69 TEX. L. REV. 1881, 1925 (1991) ("[J]udges cannot even think without implicating the dominant normative assumptions that shape their society and reproduce their political and cultural context.").

[77] *See* Klarman, *Rethinking, supra* note 47, at 23–24.

[78] *See* Michael J. Klarman, Brown, *Racial Change, and the Civil Rights Movement,* 80 VA. L. REV. 7, 13–71 (1994) [hereinafter Klarman, *Racial Change*].

the nation's population from the day it was handed down.[79] Finally, the Court protected gay rights for the first time in *Romer v. Evans*[80] only after a social and political gay rights movement had made substantial inroads against traditional attitudes toward homosexuality.

None of this is to deny that the Supreme Court possesses some marginal countermajoritarian capacity.[81] Clearly the Court's decisions invalidating school prayer or flag-burning prohibitions and protecting the procedural rights of alleged criminals have not commanded majority support.[82] Even with regard to these decisions, though, it is important to appreciate the limits of the Court's countermajoritarian thrust. For example, the Justices invalidated school prayer only after the relative demise of the nation's unofficial Protestant establishment.[83] And the countermajoritarian force of the Court's criminal procedure revolution has been largely blunted by the unwillingness of legislatures to adequately fund defense counsel.[84]

Normatively, perhaps we should applaud, rather than lament, the Court's failure to fulfill its heroic countermajoritarian role, given the absence of any uncontroversial theory of which minority rights deserve protection.[85] A countermajoritarian Court can appear either as hero or villain, depending on one's political preferences and the flow of history. It is not clear why one would expect the Justices to do a better job than majoritarian politics of selecting the *right* minority groups for protection. *Brown* probably has deluded us into thinking the Court has some comparative advantage in this enterprise, but taking a broader historical perspective corrects that misimpression.

For much of its history, the Court protected the minority group for which the Framers entertained the greatest sympathy—property owners. Madison candidly revealed his minority rights sympathies in *Federalist No. 10*, when he identified as a principal virtue of the large republic its capacity to inhibit "a rage for paper money, for an abolition of debts, for an equal division of property, or for any

---

[79] For the opinion polls, see DAVID J. GARROW, LIBERTY AND SEXUALITY: THE RIGHT TO PRIVACY AND THE MAKING OF *ROE V. WADE* 513, 539, 562, 605 (1994); GERALD N. ROSENBERG, THE HOLLOW HOPE: CAN COURTS BRING ABOUT SOCIAL CHANGE? 261 (1991); Barry Friedman, *Dialogue and Judicial Review*, 91 MICH. L. REV. 577, 607 n.148 (1993). David Garrow challenges the notion that *Roe* rode the crest of a wave of public opinion. *See* GARROW, *supra*, at ch. 8 (arguing that the abortion rights movement had stalled in the political arena by the early 1970s and that *Roe* rescued it). A recent article by Robert Karrer lends some support to Garrow's interpretation. *See* Robert N. Karrer, *The Formation of Michigan's Anti-Abortion Movement 1967–1974*, 22 MICH. HIST. REV. 67, 82 (1996).

[80] 517 U.S. 620 (1996).

[81] *See* McCLOSKEY, *supra* note 22, at 140–41 ("The nation's respect for the judiciary has been great enough . . . so that the Court can affect policy in marginal ways."); Robert A. Dahl, *Decision-Making in a Democracy: The Supreme Court as a National Policy-Maker*, 6 J. PUB. L. 279, 293–94 (1957) (observing that within the "somewhat narrow limits set by the basic policy goals of the dominant alliance, the Court can make national policy"); Klarman, *Rethinking, supra* note 47, at 18 & n.84.

[82] For the polls on flag burning and school prayer, see Friedman, *supra* note 79, at 606 n.142, 607 n.148.

[83] *See* Klarman, *Rethinking, supra* note 47, at 46–62.

[84] *See* William J. Stuntz, *The Uneasy Relationship Between Criminal Procedure and Criminal Justice*, 107 YALE L.J. 1 (1997); *see also* Klarman, *Rethinking, supra* note 47, at 62–66 (arguing that the criminal procedure revolution of the 1960s was rendered possible by changing conceptions of race and poverty as well as popular revulsion against methods of criminal law enforcement identified with totalitarian regimes).

[85] *See* HENRY BERTRAM MAYO, AN INTRODUCTION TO DEMOCRATIC THEORY 187–88 (1960).

other improper or wicked project."[86] Until the New Deal constitutional revolution, the Court established a track record of protecting certain property-owning minorities from majoritarian redistribution, whether in the form of debtor relief laws, a mildly progressive national income tax, or protective union legislation.[87] In perhaps its most infamous decision, the Court in *Dred Scott* protected the rights of one of American history's classic minority groups, southern slave owners.[88] More recently, the Court in *City of Richmond v. J. A. Croson Co.*[89] secured the equal protection rights of Richmond's minority white population by invalidating a city council affirmative action plan that awarded racial preferences in construction contracts. The point, to reiterate, is that protecting minority rights is normatively attractive only if the Court protects the "right" minorities. It is unclear why the Court should possess some inherent institutional advantage over legislatures in that enterprise, and the historical record confirms that the Justices have blundered as often as they have succeeded.

E. Continuity

Another justification for constitutionalism is that it promotes continuity within a political community.[90] This is related to, but distinct from, the enforcement-of-precommitments function already discussed. There, the emphasis was on preserving specific precommitted values from impulsive repudiation. The continuity account of constitutionalism, though, emphasizes the importance of protecting

[86] THE FEDERALIST No. 10, at 66 (James Madison) (Jacob E. Cooke ed., 1961); *see also* RAKOVE, *supra* note 16, at 314 (noting how Madison's "analysis of the dangers to property was paradigmatic for the program of reform he carried to Philadelphia in May 1787").

[87] *See* sources cited *supra* note 72; *see also* SPITZ, *supra* note 15, at 182 (noting that historically majority rule meant that the majority of poor people would seek to redistribute wealth in their favor).

[88] For the classic version of the southerners' states rights argument, see Calhoun, Fort Hill Address, *supra* note 20. For elaboration of Calhoun's conceptualization of the South as a potentially permanent national minority in need of constitutional protection, see WILLIAM W. FREEHLING, PRELUDE TO CIVIL WAR: THE NULLIFICATION CONTROVERSY IN SOUTH CAROLINA 1816–1836, at 154–55 (1965); Ford, *supra* note 19; *see also* DAVID M. POTTER, THE IMPENDING CRISIS, 1848–1861, at 475–76 (1976) (describing increasing reality and perception of the South's minority status over time). *See generally* CARPENTER, *supra* note 19 (describing different strategies deployed by the antebellum South over time to secure protection for its interests at the national level despite its minority status).

[89] 488 U.S. 469 (1989).

[90] *See* THE FEDERALIST No. 49, at 340 (James Madison) (Jacob E. Cooke ed., 1961) (noting that "frequent appeals" to the People "would in great measure deprive the government of that veneration, which time bestows on every thing, and without which perhaps the wisest and freest governments would not possess the requisite stability"); Letter from James Madison to Thomas Jefferson (Feb. 4, 1790), *in* 13 THE PAPERS OF JAMES MADISON 22 (Charles F. Hobson & Robert A. Rutland eds., 1981) (raising the objection to Jefferson's notion of an intragenerational constitution that "a Government so often revised [would] become too mutable and novel to retain that share of prejudice in its favor which is a salutary aid to the most rational Government" and that "such a periodical revision [would] engender pernicious factions that might not otherwise come into existence, and agitate the public mind more frequently and more violently than might be expedient"); Charles Fried, *Constitutional Doctrine*, 107 HARV. L. REV. 1140 (1994); Strauss, *supra* note 6, at 891–94; *see also* Rutan v. Republican Party, 497 U.S. 62, 96 (1990) (Scalia, J., dissenting) (arguing that constitutional interpretation must reflect "the principles adhered to, over time, by the American people"); Pollock v. Farmers Loan & Trust Ass'n, 157 U.S. 429, 650 (1895) (White, J., dissenting) ("The conservation and orderly development of our institutions rests on our acceptance of the results of the past, and their use as lights to guide our steps in the future.").

custom, mores, and tradition (as opposed to conscious precommitments) from evisceration (whether impulsive or deliberate).

It is worth noting a preliminary oddity in this conception of constitutionalism: The American constitution of 1787 represented a dramatic departure from tradition. Madison's theory of the large republic, the creation of a powerful executive branch, the very notion of federalism, the conceptual shift from state to popular sovereignty—all of these aspects of American constitutionalism represented momentous shifts from the political status quo. It was the Antifederalists, far more than the Federalists, who embodied continuity and tradition in their political and constitutional theory.[91] So if American constitutionalism does serve this preservation-of-continuity function, it is only in a forward-looking sense.

Empirically, it is hard to say whether having a written constitution makes America more tradition-bound than it otherwise would be; there is no control group against which to run this experiment. Americans frequently observe that the British seem more constrained by tradition, yet they have no written constitution.[92] This hardly constitutes compelling proof, though it may be suggestive.

Descriptively, it seems plain that *judicial review* makes little contribution to preserving continuity with the past. Most of modern constitutional law doctrine challenges tradition, much to Justice Scalia's chagrin.[93] *Brown* (school segregation), *Roe* (abortion restrictions), *Engel v. Vitale* (school prayer), *VMI* (exclusion of women from a military academy), *Reynolds v. Sims* (legislative malapportionment), *Davis v. Bandemer* (political gerrymandering), *Rutan* (political patronage)—just to note several prominent examples—illustrate the tradition-frustrating tendency of American constitutional law. Not only does modern judicial review frequently intervene against tradition, but it also generally *declines* to intervene against departures from tradition. Thus, as we already have noted, the Court generally has refused to enforce traditional notions of federalism and separation-of-powers to inhibit the growth of the modern welfare state and the imperial presidency.[94] Similarly, the Court has declined to enforce traditional constitutional notions that

[91] *See, e.g.*, Rakove, *supra* note 16, at 150–55; Cecelia M. Kenyon, *Men of Little Faith: The Anti-Federalists on the Nature of Representative Government*, 12 Wm. & Mary Q. 3, 38–43 (1955). Gordon Wood takes a different view of the Antifederalists, though he is referring both to different individuals and to the different issue of whether any class of persons was sufficiently disinterested to rule dispassionately. *See* Wood, Radicalism, *supra* note 69, at 255–56, 258–59, 296 (arguing that the Antifederalists paved the way for modern liberalism by espousing the view that no class of persons lacked interests and thus could serve as an impartial arbiter of society's conflicts).

[92] *Cf.* Strauss, *supra* note 6, at 923–24 (noting that the United States has more in common with a country such as Great Britain, which has no written constitution but shows great deference toward tradition, than with other countries that do have a written constitution).

[93] *See, e.g.*, United States v. Virginia, 518 U.S. 515, 568 (1996) (Scalia, J., dissenting) (arguing that "whatever abstract tests we may choose to devise, they cannot supersede—and indeed ought to be crafted *so as to reflect*—those constant and unbroken traditions that embody the people's understanding of ambiguous constitutional texts"); Romer v. Evans, 517 U.S. 620, 652 (1996) (Scalia, J., dissenting) (criticizing the majority not only for "inventing a novel and extravagant constitutional doctrine to take the victory away from traditional forces," but also for "verbally disparaging as bigotry adherence to traditional attitudes"); Lee v. Weisman, 505 U.S. 577, 632 (1992) (Scalia, J., dissenting) (arguing that "our Nation's protection, that fortress which is our Constitution, cannot possibly rest upon the changeable philosophical predilections of the Justices of this Court, but must have deep foundations in the historic practices of our people"); Rutan v. Republican Party, 497 U.S. 62, 96 (1990) (Scalia, J., dissenting) (noting that "traditions are themselves the stuff out of which the Court's principles are to be formed").

[94] *See supra* notes 7, 9.

would have inhibited undeclared wars,[95] military conscription,[96] imperial acquisitions,[97] Japanese-American internment,[98] debtor relief laws,[99] mandatory drug testing,[100] and so forth.

Normatively, we might have cause for concern had the Court done a better job of maintaining continuity with the past. Continuity does have its advantages—predictability, stability, the fulfillment that derives from having integrated projects over time (what Charles Fried calls "constitutive rationality" and Ronald Dworkin labels "integrity").[101] Yet the continuity conception of constitutionalism suffers from the same deadhand problem we already have encountered. When decisions made in the past presumptively determine the course of the present, one sacrifices the benefits of experience and runs the risk that the accumulated wisdom of the past will have been rendered obsolete by changed circumstances. Thus, it seems plausible that the normative force of tradition should be greater in a society not experiencing dramatic change—that is, someplace other than nineteenth- and twentieth-century America.[102] The problem is compounded when the normative force of tradition is compromised by past generations' now-antiquated conception of who should count in constituting its traditions—in our experience, predominantly white Anglo-Saxon male property-holders. Finally, it is worth noting that tradition exercises an inexorable pull on the present even in the absence of any constitutional bulwark; barring weighty reasons to the contrary, the political regime generally will continue to conduct business as usual.[103] It is not obvious that the virtues of continuity warrant supplementing this inexorable weight of tradition with the further entrenching effect of constitutionalism.

[95] *See supra* note 8.

[96] Selective Draft Law Cases, 245 U.S. 366 (1918). For a convincing argument that the Constitution's Framers would have thought that military conscription by the national government was unconstitutional, see Leon Friedman, *Conscription and the Constitution: The Original Understanding*, 67 MICH. L. REV. 1493 (1969).

[97] *See, e.g.,* Downes v. Bidwell, 182 U.S. 244 (1901) (limiting the Constitution's applicability to newly acquired territory). On the extent to which the *Insular Cases* represented a repudiation of traditional notions of the Constitution following the flag, see GERALD L. NEUMAN, STRANGERS TO THE CONSTITUTION: IMMIGRANTS, BORDERS AND FUNDAMENTAL LAW 72–89 (1996).

[98] *See* Korematsu v. United States, 323 U.S. 214 (1944). For valuable discussion of the background to *Korematsu*, see PETER IRONS, JUSTICE AT WAR (1983).

[99] *See* Home Bldg. & Loan Ass'n v. Blaisdell, 290 U.S. 398 (1934). For the extent to which *Blaisdell* contravened traditional Contracts Clause jurisprudence, see BENJAMIN WRIGHT, JR., THE CONTRACT CLAUSE OF THE CONSTITUTION 101–12, 211–13, 248 (1938); *see also Blaisdell*, 290 U.S. at 472 (Sutherland, J., dissenting) ("The defense of the Minnesota law is made upon grounds which were discountenanced by the makers of the Constitution and have many times been rejected by this court.").

[100] *See* Vernonia Sch. Dist. v. Acton, 515 U.S. 646 (1995); National Treasury Employees Union v. Von Raab, 489 U.S. 656 (1989); Skinner v. Railway Labor Executives Ass'n, 489 U.S. 602 (1989).

[101] *See* RONALD DWORKIN, LAW'S EMPIRE ch. 7 (1986); Fried, *supra* note 90.

[102] *See* MORTON J. HORWITZ, THE TRANSFORMATION OF AMERICAN LAW, 1780–1860, at 1–4, 43–47 (1977) (noting how, in a time of rapid economic and technological change, early nineteenth-century American judges transformed traditional common-law rules to accommodate a changing reality); G. EDWARD WHITE, THE MARSHALL COURT AND CULTURAL CHANGE, 1815–1835, at 975 (1988) ("The years of the Marshall Court may have been the first time in the history of American culture in which the possibility that the future might never replicate the past was truly grasped.").

[103] *See* DAHL, *supra* note 15, at 140 ("The status quo always has so many built-in advantages that surely it doesn't need the additional advantage of a biased decision rule!"); Christopher L. Eisgruber, *The Living Hand of the Past: History and Constitutional Justice*, 65 FORDHAM L. REV. 1611, 1615 (1997) ("Whether we have a written, obdurate constitution or not, we inherit our politics from the past; no people writes upon a blank slate.").

Many scholars and judges have sought to preserve the virtues of continuity while ameliorating its vices by embracing some version of "moderate" or "soft" originalism.[104] That is, they argue that principles embraced by past generations ought to be "translated" into modern contexts to reflect changed circumstances.[105] This position has acquired renewed currency in recent years.[106] Unfortunately, as I have endeavored to show elsewhere, this translation enterprise is fatally flawed.[107] It solves neither the deadhand problem of originalist interpretive methodologies nor the judicial subjectivity problem of nonoriginalist methods.

Consider an example.[108] Scholars committed to the translation enterprise might ask how the Framers' commitment to federalism principles should be adjusted to reflect the reality of a modern, industrial, highly integrated economy.[109] Perhaps the right question to ask, however, is whether the Framers would retain their commitment to federalism at all in light of these radically changed circumstances. After all, at least some of the Founders embraced federalism less out of political principle than political necessity—the fact that state legislatures, which could not be entirely cut out of the Constitution's ratifying process, would be loath to relinquish too much of their power.[110] This is not to deny that federalism retains many of its virtues even today. For example, it fosters experimentation, encourages competition between states, arguably maximizes preference satisfaction in a geographically diverse nation, enhances citizen participation in government, and ensures the existence of competing governmental power sources.[111] Yet federalism also has many disadvantages, some of which are simply the flip sides of its advantages. Federalism permits races to the bottom, prevents realization of efficiencies of scale, frustrates efforts to create an economic common market, arguably creates greater opportunities for minority oppression (the converse of Madison's point in *Federalist No. 10*) and obstructs implementation of federally guaranteed rights (think of massive resistance to *Brown*). Plainly, balancing the competing virtues

---

[104] Paul Brest, *The Misconceived Quest for the Original Understanding*, 60 B.U. L. Rev. 204, 205 (1980) (explaining but not defending "moderate" originalism); Cass R. Sunstein, *Five Theses on Originalism*, 19 Harv. J.L. & Pub. Pol'y 311, 313 (1996) (defending "soft" originalism); *see also* Trop v. Dulles, 356 U.S. 86, 101 (1958) (plurality opinion) ("evolving standards of decency" define scope of Eighth Amendment); McCulloch v. Maryland, 17 U.S. (4 Wheat.) 316, 415 (1819) ("a constitution intended to endure for ages to come, and, consequently, to be adapted to the various *crises* of human affairs").

[105] Lawrence Lessig, *Understanding Changed Readings: Fidelity and Theory*, 47 Stan. L. Rev. 395 (1995) [hereinafter Lessig, *Understanding Changed Readings*]; Lawrence Lessig, *Fidelity in Translation*, 71 Tex. L. Rev. 1165 (1993).

[106] *See, e.g.*, Randy E. Barnett, *Reconceiving the Ninth Amendment*, 74 Cornell L. Rev. 1, 25–26 (1988); Martin S. Flaherty, *The Most Dangerous Branch*, 105 Yale L.J. 1725, 1821, 1824–25, 1828–32 (1996); Abner S. Greene, *Checks and Balances in an Era of Presidential Lawmaking*, 61 U. Chi. L. Rev. 123, 131–35, 153–58, 182–85 (1994); Michael W. McConnell, *Originalism and the Desegregation Decisions*, 81 Va. L. Rev. 947, 1103–05 (1995); Peter B. McCutchen, *Mistakes, Precedent and the Rise of the Administrative State: Toward a Constitutional Theory of the Second Best*, 80 Cornell L. Rev. 1 (1994).

[107] *See* Klarman, *Antifidelity, supra* note 14.

[108] Here I draw on my lengthier critique of the translation enterprise. *See* Klarman, *Antifidelity, supra* note 14, at 396–97, 402–03, 406–07.

[109] *See* Lawrence Lessig, *Translating Federalism*: United States v. Lopez, 1995 Sup. Ct. Rev. 125; Lessig, *Understanding Changed Readings, supra* note 105.

[110] *See, e.g.*, Rakove, *supra* note 16, at 162, 169–70.

[111] *See, e.g.*, Steven G. Calabresi, *"A Government of Limited and Enumerated Powers": In Defense of* United States v. Lopez, 94 Mich. L. Rev. 752, 774–84 (1995); Larry Kramer, *Understanding Federalism*, 47 Vand. L. Rev. 1485, 1498–99 (1994); Andrzej Rapaczynski, *From Sovereignty to Process: The Jurisprudence of Federalism After* Garcia, 1985 Sup. Ct. Rev. 341, 380–414.

and vices of federalism is a complicated enterprise. My only point here is that freed from the political reality that made federalism commitments unavoidable and apprised of the massive political, social, and economic changes that arguably render federalism obsolete, it is entirely plausible that the transplanted Founders would choose to reject federalism altogether rather than to translate it.

Nor does translation solve the problem of uncabined judicial rule. There are two distinct problems. First, when asking what the Framers would have done under modern circumstances, which aspects of their world do we vary and which do we leave in place? Second, assuming we can answer the question of which changed circumstances are relevant to the translation, how do we calculate what the Founders would have done in light of those changes?

Consider first the question of which changed circumstances to incorporate into the translation. A rather large problem immediately presents itself: If we treat *all* changed circumstances as relevant variables, then we simply will have converted the Framers into us, and asking how they would resolve a problem is no different from asking how we would resolve it. Yet a decision to treat some changed circumstances as variables and others as constants seems entirely arbitrary. For example, it is wholly uncontroversial to vary the existing state of technology when translating the congressional power to regulate interstate commerce. I am aware of nobody who argues that Congress cannot regulate airplanes because they did not exist when the Constitution was adopted; airplanes are a modern analogue of ships, so certainly Congress can regulate their interstate movement. Yet in translating Congress's Commerce Clause power, why is it any less justifiable to treat as relevant variables all of the other changed circumstances that might influence one's attitude toward federalism—for example, the modern proliferation of national and international markets, the transportation and communications revolutions, the nation's growing international role, the increased mobility of the American population, and so forth?

Even if we could agree on which changed circumstances are relevant, we still would need to figure out whether the extent of the change has been sufficient to justify a translation. For example, Lawrence Lessig has argued that by the 1930s changed circumstances—both conceptions of the nature of law and political and social variables, the most notable of which was the Great Depression—justified the Supreme Court's repudiation of the *Lochner* era's commitment to laissez-faire economics and limited national government power.[112] Lessig's empirical claim about changed circumstances seems convincing. The pathologies of a complex urban, industrial society plainly did reduce the allure of laissez-faire and increase support for national government regulation by the 1930s. Yet a court charged with the complex task of translating the Framers' intentions needs to know more than the general direction of changing circumstances; it needs to identify with precision the point at which those changes have become sufficient to justify a translation. The problem is that at any particular point in time, reasonable people will disagree about whether the change in circumstances has been sufficient to justify a translation of the Framers' intentions. As late as 1937, the Four Horsemen still had not spotted sufficient changes in circumstance to justify translation of laissez-faire and federalism concepts.[113] On the other hand, as early as 1905 or 1910, some

[112] Lessig, *Understanding Changed Readings, supra* note 105, at 443–70.
[113] *See* NLRB v. Jones & Laughlin Steel Corp., 301 U.S. 1, 76 (1937) (McReynolds, J., dissenting); West Coast Hotel v. Parrish, 300 U.S. 379, 400 (1937) (Sutherland, J., dissenting).

Justices and scholars already had identified sufficient change to warrant a translation.[114] Furthermore, it is difficult to believe that one's view of the sufficiency of changed circumstances does not reflect, to a substantial degree, one's normative commitments. The Four Horsemen, for example, would have been unconvinced of the sufficiency of changed circumstances in 1937 largely because they liked things better the old way. Measuring the extent of changed circumstances and assessing whether they are sufficient to justify a translation are tasks certain to yield controverted conclusions. One can phrase this in terms of translation—would the Framers have considered the changed circumstances sufficient to justify altering their constitutional commitments? Because the answer to that question, however, is so obviously indeterminate, it appears that the real ground of controversy is over what *we* think should be done, rather than over what the Framers would have done in our changed circumstances. Translation solves the judicial subjectivity problem no better than it does the deadhand problem.

F. Symbolizing National Unity

The American Constitution is sometimes praised as a unifying symbol.[115] Just as the continuity conception of constitutionalism stressed the importance of securing unity across time, so the "symbolic" account emphasizes the value of promoting unity across geography and culture. Especially in a country as racially, religiously, and ethnically diverse as the United States, one might deem indispensable a set of shared symbols such as our Constitution.

Descriptively, it is uncertain whether the Constitution and judicial review have played this role in American history. Again, in the absence of a control group, it is hard to tell. Conversely, some countries, such as Great Britain, have cohered for much longer than the United States without a written constitution or judicial review. Other countries possessed of a written constitution, such as the Soviet Union, have been burst asunder. But, of course, those other countries faced different circumstances, making it difficult to draw reliable inferences from their experiences about the importance of constitutionalism to maintaining national unity. My own suspicion is that James Madison was right in his basic insight in *Federalist No. 10*: Racial, religious, and ethnic diversity actually help rather than hinder national unity by fostering a culture of relative tolerance.[116] On this view, it is pluralism rather than constitutionalism—"parchment barriers," in Madison's

---

[114] *See, e.g.,* Lochner v. New York, 198 U.S. 45, 75 (1905) (Holmes, J., dissenting); Learned Hand, *Due Process and the Eight-Hour Day*, 21 HARV. L. REV. 495, 506–07 (1908); Roscoe Pound, *Liberty of Contract*, 18 YALE L.J. 454, 464, 467 (1909).

[115] *See, e.g.,* McCLOSKEY, *supra* note 22, at 5 (noting that the Constitution rapidly was "transfigured . . . into a venerated symbol of Americanism"); Max Lerner, *Constitution and Court as Symbols*, 46 YALE L.J. 1290, 1298 (1937); Strauss, *supra* note 6, at 915 ("[T]he Constitution has been a central unifying symbol for Americans."); *cf.* RAKOVE, *supra* note 16, at 367 (suggesting that one appeal of originalism may be its reference to a Founding era "set of consensual political symbols that come closest to universal acceptance").

[116] *See* THE FEDERALIST No. 10, at 63 (James Madison) (Jacob E. Cooke ed., 1961) (noting that a "greater number of citizens and extent of territory . . . renders factious combinations less to be dreaded"); *id.* at 64 (noting that "a greater variety of parties and interests . . . make it less probable that a majority of the whole will have a common motive to invade the rights of other citizens"); *see also* THE FEDERALIST No. 51, at 352–53 (James Madison) (Jacob E. Cooke ed., 1961) (noting that security for religious rights "consists . . . in the multiplicity of sects").

pejorative term—which promotes national unity.[117] Further, even if the Constitution played an important symbolic role when the nation was in its infancy, filling a vacuum created by the absence of a common tradition and ancestry, the significance of this function is open to doubt in a nation with two centuries of history, tradition, and mythmaking under its belt.[118]

Finally, it would be odd if the Constitution has performed this unifying function because it is very much a false symbol of unity. To the extent that the Constitution succeeds in producing national consensus, it does so only by embodying principles at such a high level of abstraction as to generate little controversy.[119] The Constitution guarantees "equal protection" but does not tell us whether this bars racial segregation in public schools, the exclusion of women from the Virginia Military Institute or gays from the military, or the malapportionment and gerrymandering of state legislatures. The Constitution guarantees "freedom of speech" but does not tell us how this affects regulation of subversive speech, commercial speech, campaign finance, smut on the Internet, or flag burning. Thus, southerners and northerners in the 1850s could both believe that the Constitution legitimized their diametrically opposed positions on congressional power to prohibit slavery in the territories,[120] while a hundred years later they could continue to believe that the Constitution supported their respective positions on school segregation.[121] Can it be true that consensus secured on principles articulated at this level of abstraction has any genuine unifying effect on the nation?

Occasionally the Constitution does take a stand on a particular issue at a much greater level of specificity. Most post-1791 constitutional amendments,

---

[117] Madison and Jefferson believed that it was the relatively greater religious diversity of Virginia that rendered possible enactment of Jefferson's beloved Statute for Religious Freedom in the mid-1780s. See RAKOVE, supra note 16, at 333; Finkelman, supra note 51, at 326 (quoting Madison at the Virginia ratifying convention); see also THOMAS CURRY, THE FIRST FREEDOMS: CHURCH AND STATE IN AMERICA TO THE PASSAGE OF THE FIRST AMENDMENT 197 (1986) (noting that Edmund Randolph made a similar claim at the Virginia ratifying convention). For the argument that the growing religious pluralism of America in the late nineteenth and early twentieth centuries led to greater religious toleration and an accompanying revolution in Establishment Clause doctrine, see Klarman, Rethinking, supra note 47, at 46–62.

[118] Cf. Strauss, supra note 6, at 924 ("When a nation does not have well established traditions, the words of its constitution are correspondingly more important in providing something on which people can agree.").

[119] See, e.g., Steven G. Calabresi, The Crisis in Constitutional Theory, 83 VA. L. REV. 247, 264 (1997) ("[I]t is our collective, social ability to see ourselves and our views in the Constitution when they are not there that unites us.").

[120] Most southerners believed that the Fifth Amendment's Due Process Clause protected slavery in the territories from congressional interference (John C. Calhoun's "common property" doctrine). Northern Republicans argued that the very same Due Process Clause required Congress to bar slavery from the territories, because slavery was a denial of "liberty" (the "free soil" position). Northern Democrats argued that Congress was barred from resolving the slavery-in-the-territories issue one way or the other because of the limited scope of its Article IV power to govern the territories (Stephen A. Douglas's "popular sovereignty" position). For these doctrines, see FEHRENBACHER, supra note 19, at 139–47; Robert R. Russel, Constitutional Doctrines with Regard to Slavery in Territories, 32 J. S. HIST. 466 (1966).

[121] Southerners after Brown reaffirmed their "reliance on the Constitution as the fundamental law of the land," while denouncing the Court's decision as a "clear abuse of judicial power" because the Constitution consistently had been interpreted to permit racial segregation. 102 CONG. REC. 4515–16 (1956) (Southern Manifesto). For additional examples of the Constitution's fundamental indeterminacy, see Michael J. Klarman, Fidelity. Indeterminacy, and the Problem of Constitutional Evil, 65 FORDHAM L. REV. 1739, 1740–42 (1997) [hereinafter Klarman, Fidelity].

though not the Fourteenth, are examples of this phenomenon. Interestingly, though, these highly specific constitutional provisions tend to be so consonant with public opinion that it is hard to say that their embodiment in the Constitution produced rather than reflected national unity. The Eleventh Amendment overruling *Chisholm v. Georgia*,[122] the Twelfth Amendment responding to the electoral debacle of 1800,[123] the Sixteenth Amendment overruling *Pollock v. Farmers Loan & Trust Co.*,[124] the Seventeenth Amendment altering the method of selecting senators,[125] the Nineteenth Amendment enfranchising women,[126] the Twenty-fourth Amendment forbidding poll taxes,[127] and the Twenty-sixth Amendment enfranchising eighteen-year-olds[128] all illustrate this phenomenon.

On the relatively rare occasions when the Constitution takes a clear stand on a still contested issue, it plainly fails to secure national unity.[129] Prohibition is one such instance; the Eighteenth Amendment quickly was repealed by the Twenty-first. The Fifteenth Amendment, forced upon southerners against their will,[130] is

[122] (2 U.S. (2 Dall.) 419 (1793); *see* Casto, *supra* note 8, at 200 (noting lopsided congressional majorities of approximately ten-to-one in favor of the Eleventh Amendment); David E. Kyvig, Explicit and Authentic Acts: Amending the United States Constitution, 1776–1995, at 113 (1996).

[123] The Twelfth Amendment was contested almost entirely in party terms. Thus it barely achieved the necessary two-thirds majority in the House and Senate, but easily secured ratification in the states, where the Jeffersonian Republican party had become ascendant by 1804. *See* Tadahisa Kuroda, The Origins of the Twelfth Amendment: The Electoral College in the Early Republic, 1787–1804, at 142–61 (1994); Kyvig, *supra* note 122, at 116.

[124] 158 U.S. 601 (1895). On the ease with which the Sixteenth Amendment was ratified in the state legislatures, see Kyvig, *supra* note 122, at 204–08; Robert Stanley, Dimensions of Law in the Service of Order: Origins of the Federal Income Tax 1861–1913, at 211–12 (1993).

[125] By the time Congress approved the Seventeenth Amendment, well over half the states already had enacted mechanisms for circumventing the Constitution and ensuring that senators were effectively popularly elected. *See* Kris W. Kobach, *Rethinking Article V: Term Limits and the Seventeenth and Nineteenth Amendments*, 103 Yale L.J. 1971, 1978–79 (1994); *see also* George H. Haynes, The Senate of the United States: Its History and Practice 103–04 (1938) (noting the broad popularity by 1910 of the "Oregon Plan" for effectively achieving popular election of senators); Kyvig, *supra* note 122, at 210–11.

[126] *See* Kobach, *supra* note 125, at 1982–83 (noting the large number of states that had adopted women's suffrage before Congress endorsed the Nineteenth Amendment and the consequent ease with which the amendment was ratified in the state legislatures); Aileen S. Kraditor, *Tactical Problems of the Woman-Suffrage Movement in the South*, 5 La. Stud. 289, 301 (1966) (noting that by the time the Nineteenth Amendment went into effect, over half the states already had embraced women's suffrage on their own); *see also* Eleanor Flexner, Century of Struggle: The Woman's Rights Movement in the United States ch. 21 (rev. ed., 1975) (noting the burst of popular support for the Nineteenth Amendment in the years immediately preceding congressional approval). The Nineteenth Amendment may be best understood as the imposition of a national consensus on southern outliers. *See* Kyvig, *supra* note 122, at 234–39.

[127] The Twenty-fourth Amendment plainly is an instance of a national consensus being deployed to suppress southern outliers. *See* Kyvig, *supra* note 122, at 353–57.

[128] *See* Kyvig, *supra* note 122, at 363–68.

[129] *Cf.* Ely, *supra* note 9, at 99–100 (noting that the few conspicuous efforts to enshrine substantive values in the Constitution—most notably, slavery and prohibition—have not been resounding successes).

[130] Southern state ratification of both the Fourteenth and Fifteenth Amendments was rendered possible only by forcible congressional reconstruction of southern state governments. *See, e.g.,* Eric Foner, Reconstruction 271–80 (1988). For the four former Confederate states remaining outside the Union in 1870, Congress conditioned readmission on ratification of the Fifteenth Amendment. *See, e.g.,* William Gillette, The Right to Vote: Politics and Passage of the Fifteenth Amendment 93, 98–103 (1965); Emma Lou Thornbrough, The Negro in Indiana Before 1900, at 247 (1957). Given the peculiar political history of the Fifteenth Amendment, it is entirely possible that a majority

another; by the turn of the century, white southerners effectively had disfranchised blacks through a combination of force, fraud, and evasion.[131]

Ordinarily, though, the Constitution is fairly abstract, and only judicial interpretations make it concrete. More frequently than is commonly acknowledged, those interpretations are consonant with dominant national norms and thus are best described as reflecting rather than producing national unity. This is the phenomenon I have elsewhere described as deploying a national consensus to suppress outliers,[132] and it accurately accounts for landmark Supreme Court cases such as *Griswold v. Connecticut*,[133] *Harper v. Virginia Board of Elections*,[134] *Moore v. City of East Cleveland*,[135] *Coker v. Georgia*,[136] *Plyler v. Doe*,[137] and *United States v. Virginia*.[138]

On numerous other occasions, the Court's efforts to supply concrete meaning to abstract constitutional phraseology are genuinely controversial. In these cases, the Court confronts social disputes that genuinely rend the nation in half and awards victory to one side or seeks to split the difference. I believe this is a fairly accurate description of *Prigg v. Pennsylvania*,[139] *Dred Scott v. Sandford*,[140] *Brown v. Board of Education*,[141] *Furman v. Georgia*,[142] *Roe v. Wade*,[143] *Regents of the University of California v. Bakke*,[144] and *Romer v. Evans*.[145] On these occasions, the Court plainly is not reflecting national unity. But neither do its decisions produce that unity.[146] Once *Prigg v. Pennsylvania* rendered concrete the meaning of the Fugitive Slave Clause, northern states found ways to evade or even to defy the decision.[147] *Dred Scott* hardly settled the slavery-in-the-territories question

---

of the nation opposed the Amendment when it was passed. *See* Michael J. Klarman, Brown, *Originalism, and Constitutional Theory: A Response to Professor McConnell*, 81 Va. L. Rev. 1881, 1922–24 (1995). On ratification of the Fifteenth Amendment, see generally Gillette, *supra*, at chs. 3–8.

[131] The classic account of black disfranchisement in the South remains J. Morgan Kousser, The Shaping of Southern Politics: Suffrage Restriction and the Establishment of the One-Party South, 1880–1910 (1974). Other useful sources are Edward L. Ayers, The Promise of the New South: Life After Reconstruction 283–309 (1992); John Dittmer, Black Georgia in the Progressive Era, 1900–1920, at 90–109 (1977); Darlene Clark Hine, Black Victory: The Rise and Fall of the White Primary in Texas (1979); Neil R. McMillen, Dark Journey: Black Mississippians in the Age of Jim Crow 35–71 (1989); Frederic D. Ogden, The Poll Tax in the South 1–31 (1958).

[132] *See* Klarman, *Rethinking, supra* note 47, at 16–17.

[133] 381 U.S. 479 (1965) (right to use contraceptives).

[134] 383 U.S. 663 (1966) (poll tax).

[135] 431 U.S. 494 (1977) (familial relationships).

[136] 433 U.S. 584 (1977) (proportionality requirement in the death penalty).

[137] 457 U.S. 202 (1982) (right of children of illegal aliens to free public education).

[138] 518 U.S. 515 (1996) (right of women to attend Virginia Military Institute).

[139] 41 U.S. (16 Pet.) 539 (1842) (fugitive slave renditions).

[140] 60 U.S. (19 How.) 393 (1857) (slavery in the territories).

[141] 347 U.S. 483 (1954) (school desegregation).

[142] 408 U.S. 238 (1972) (death penalty).

[143] 410 U.S. 113 (1973) (abortion).

[144] 438 U.S. 265 (1978) (affirmative action).

[145] 116 S. Ct. 1620 (1996) (gay rights).

[146] *See, e.g.*, Calabresi, *supra* note 119, at 264 ("The constitutional opinions of Supreme Court Justices do not unite us as a people; rather, they give us something to argue and disagree about.").

[147] *See* Thomas D. Morris, Free Men All: The Personal Liberty Laws of the North, 1780–1861 (1974); Arthur Bestor, *State Sovereignty and Slavery: A Reinterpretation of Proslavery Constitutional Doctrine, 1846–1860*, 54 J. Ill. Hist. Soc'y J. 122, 137–38 (1961); Paul Finkelman, Prigg v. Pennsylvania *and Northern State Courts: Anti-Slavery Use of a Pro-Slavery Decision*, 25 Civ. War Hist. 5, 21–35 (1979). Southerners generally were outraged by what they perceived to be northern repudiation of a sacred constitutional obligation, and these personal liberty laws frequently were identified as

by rendering concrete constitutional language from which both northerners and southerners previously had drawn sustenance; if anything, the decision mobilized Republicans to defend the legitimacy of their party, which the Court essentially had ruled unconstitutional.[148] *Brown* crystallized southern white resistance to changes in the racial status quo,[149] and *Roe v. Wade* arguably mobilized a right-to-life movement that previously had not played a prominent role in politics.[150] Examples might easily be multiplied, but the point seems evident: The Justices may believe that their pronouncements "call[] the contending sides of a national controversy to end their national division,"[151] but there is little evidence that such disputes are so easily solved.

Normatively, is it clear that achieving a false, or even a genuine, national consensus is an unambiguous good? The "consensus" historians of the 1950s arguably reflected the apparent lack of conflict in the broader society of which they were a part.[152] From the perspective of the conflict-ridden 1960s,[153] though, the consensus of the preceding decade was very much one of appearance rather than reality. That appearance of consensus was rendered possible only through the suppression of minority viewpoints, such as those of African-Americans, feminists, gays and lesbians.[154] To consider one constitutional manifestation of this phenomenon, Jews and other religious minorities were inhibited during the McCarthy era from raising Establishment Clause challenges to public displays of (Protestant) religiosity.[155] Similarly, black leaders, consciously or subconsciously, reined in the aggressive civil rights campaign of the late 1940s to avoid the tincture of Communist complicity.[156] Furthermore, securing a false consensus has the

---

among the leading justifications for southern secession. *See* SECESSION DEBATED: GEORGIA'S SHOW-DOWN IN 1860, at viii (William W. Freehling & Craig M. Simpson eds., 1992) [hereinafter SECESSION DEBATED]; *id.* at 27 (statement of Thomas R.R. Cobb); *id.* at 41–42 (statement of Robert Toombs); *id.* at 70–71 (statement of Alexander H. Stephens); *id.* at 83–84 (statement of Benjamin H. Hill); *see also* CARPENTER, *supra* note 19, at 163 (noting complaint of South Carolina Secession convention).

[148] *See* FEHRENBACHER, *supra* note 19, at 561–67 (concluding that the combination of *Dred Scott* and the furor raised over the Lecompton Constitution probably explains the momentous Republican gains in the lower North between 1856 and 1858, which ultimately enabled Lincoln to win the presidency in 1860).

[149] *See* Klarman, *Racial Change, supra* note 78, at 75–150.

[150] *See* JOHN C. JEFFRIES, JR., JUSTICE LEWIS F. POWELL, JR. 354–59 (1994); ROSENBERG, *supra* note 79, at 188, 341–42; Ruth Bader Ginsburg, *Speaking in a Judicial Voice*, 67 N.Y.U. L. REV. 1185, 1205 (1992).

[151] Planned Parenthood v. Casey, 505 U.S. 833, 867 (1992) (plurality opinion).

[152] For a brief discussion, see LAURA KALMAN, THE STRANGE CAREER OF LEGAL LIBERALISM 23–26 (1996).

[153] *See, e.g.,* JOHN MORTON BLUM, YEARS OF DISCORD: AMERICAN POLITICS AND SOCIETY, 1961–1974 (1991).

[154] *See* RICHARD M. FRIED, NIGHTMARE IN RED: THE MCCARTHY ERA IN PERSPECTIVE 29–36 (1990) (noting how during the 1950s any social, political, or cultural movement challenging the status quo was susceptible to being labeled communist-inspired).

[155] *See* FRANK J. SORAUF, THE WALL OF SEPARATION: THE CONSTITUTIONAL POLITICS OF CHURCH AND STATE 46–47 (1976); *cf.* SAMUEL WALKER, IN DEFENSE OF AMERICAN LIBERTIES: A HISTORY OF THE ACLU 222 (1990) (noting that even the American Civil Liberties Union, stung by charges of being antireligious, "quietly downplayed church-state issues in the mid-1950s"); Klarman, *Rethinking, supra* note 47, at 61 (explaining the Court's "dramatic tilt toward separationism" in the school prayer cases of the early 1960s partly in terms of "the relative demise of domestic anti-communism").

[156] *See* FRIED, *supra* note 154, at 164–65; HARVARD SITKOFF, THE STRUGGLE FOR BLACK EQUALITY, 1954–1980, at 17 (1981); NEIL A. WYNN, THE AFRO-AMERICAN AND THE SECOND WORLD WAR 120 (1976).

consequence of deluding us into believing that real problems do not exist. The race riots of the 1960s reflected conditions that had existed in the 1950s but had gone unredressed partially because they had gone unacknowledged in an era of false consensus.

Even *genuine* national consensus may not always be so normatively attractive. It really depends on the substance of the consensus. To a certain extent, the original Constitution did help foster consensus on the question of national government power over slavery in existing states. At the time of the Philadelphia Convention, there was virtually no sentiment in favor of national abolition;[157] thus, initially, the Constitution reflected rather than produced a consensus against national government power to interfere with slavery in the states. Yet over the course of the antebellum period, as the abolitionist movement deepened and broadened its support, the existence of the Constitution may well have inhibited many anti-slavery souls from advocating national interference with slavery in the states. The anti-slavery Republican Party, founded in opposition to the spread of slavery into the Kansas and Nebraska territories, consistently conceded the absence of congressional power to suppress slavery in existing states.[158] Possibly it was the Constitution that fostered this national consensus; alternatively, it may have been northerners' awareness that southerners instantly would have seceded from a Union that treated this question as open to debate.[159] In either event, is it obvious that national consensus on this question was desirable? Perhaps William Lloyd Garrison and his followers were right—that the Constitution's protection of slavery rendered it "a covenant with death, and an agreement with hell"[160]—and that the North would have been better off without slavery and without the South than as part of a unified nation with slavery.

In sum, even if judicially reviewable constitutionalism does promote national unity, a supposition that I have argued is doubtful, the normative attraction of this conception of constitutionalism depends entirely on the substantive values being advanced by the nation.

G. Educational

Another related justification for constitutionalism and judicial review focuses on their educational function. Many Federalists and Antifederalists understood

---

[157] *See* Donald L. Robinson, Slavery in the Structure of American Politics, 1765–1820, at 233–34, 245 (1971); James Oakes, *"The Compromising Expedient": Justifying a Proslavery Constitution*, 17 Cardozo L. Rev. 2023, 2025, 2035, 2045 (1996).

[158] *See, e.g.*, Abraham Lincoln, First Inaugural Address, *in* 2 Abraham Lincoln: Speeches and Writings 215, 215–16 (Don E. Fehrenbacher ed., 1989); *Republican Party Platform of 1860*, § 4, *reprinted in* National Party Platforms, 1840–1872, at 31, 32 (Donald B. Johnson & Kirk H. Porter eds., 5th ed., 1973); *see also* Fehrenbacher, *supra* note 19, at 548; Potter, *supra* note 88, at 423, 532, 550.

[159] *See* Potter, *supra* note 88, at 44–45 (noting that even anti-slavery northerners were impelled to make concessions to both the Constitution and the Union); *cf.* R. Kent Newmyer, Supreme Court Justice Joseph Story: Statesman of the Old Republic 377–78 (1985) (noting that Justice Story's concessions to slavery in *Prigg v. Pennsylvania* may have been based on his desire to preserve the Union).

[160] The phrase comes from a resolution Garrison introduced before the Massachusetts Anti-Slavery Society in 1843. *See* J. M. Balkin, *Agreements with Hell and Other Objects of Our Faith*, 65 Fordham L. Rev. 1703, 1708 n.15 (1997) (quoting Walter M. Merrill, Against Wind and Tide: A Biography of William Lloyd Garrison 205 ([1963]).

the Constitution primarily in this way. Reflecting their skepticism of the utility of "parchment barriers," many Founders argued that the principal value of constitutional text lay in its capacity to educate the citizenry regarding important values and to serve as a banner around which to organize opposition in times of government oppression.[161] Many scholars similarly have emphasized the educational function of the Supreme Court in its capacity as constitutional interpreter.[162]

The descriptive objections to this educational conception of constitutionalism are similar to those raised against the unifying-symbol conception. The Constitution generally is written at such a high level of abstraction that one doubts whether it could have much educational effect. In the abstract, just about everyone agrees that "freedom of speech" and "equality" are good things; the citizenry does not require much educating on the worth of these concepts. Yet when the constitutional text becomes more specific, it risks alienating rather than educating those who disagree with its commitments. The original Constitution plainly sanctioned the institution of slavery, yet this failed to impede the rise of abolitionism by "educating" citizens to believe that slavery was morally acceptable. Presumably, the Prohibition amendment should have educated the nation into believing that alcohol was an evil, yet it plainly failed in that objective. The Thirteenth Amendment failed to educate white southerners out of the view that they had a proprietary interest in black labor, as evidenced by the panoply of legal and extralegal mechanisms used to perpetuate black peonage well into the twentieth century.[163] Likewise, the Fifteenth Amendment failed to educate white southerners into respecting black suffrage, as evidenced by the resolute, and ultimately successful, southern disfranchisement campaigns of the late nineteenth and early twentieth centuries.[164]

If the Constitution itself fails to fulfill this educational function to any significant degree, what about the Supreme Court in its role as constitutional interpreter? Many commentators have argued that the Court does indeed play an

---

[161] See Letter from James Madison to Thomas Jefferson (Oct. 17, 1788), in 1 REPUBLIC OF LETTERS, supra note 16, at 562, 565 (noting that a bill of rights in a republic serves two functions—stating "political truths" in a "solemn manner" so that they will "acquire by degrees the character of fundamental maxims of free Government" and serving, in cases of government oppression, as "a good ground for an appeal to the sense of the community"); 1 ANNALS OF CONG. 456 (1789) (statement of James Madison) (observing that while a Bill of Rights does consist of "paper barriers," such provisions would at least "have a tendency to impress some degree of respect for them, to establish the public opinion in their favor, and rouse the attention of the whole community"); RAKOVE, supra note 16, at 309, 323–24 (noting numerous statements by the Founding generation to this effect); see also Eakin v. Raub, 12 Serg & Rawle 330, 354 (Pa. 1825) (Gibson, J.) (noting that a written constitution "is of inestimable value . . . in rendering its principles familiar to the mass of the people").

[162] See BICKEL, supra note 31, at 26; Christopher L. Eisgruber, Is the Supreme Court an Educative Institution?, 67 N.Y.U. L. REV. 962 (1992); Ralph Lerner, The Supreme Court as Republican Schoolmaster, 1967 SUP. CT. REV. 127; Eugene V. Rostow, The Democratic Character of Judicial Review, 66 HARV. L. REV. 193, 208 (1952) (noting that Supreme Court Justices "are inevitably teachers in a vital national seminar").

[163] See United States v. Reynolds, 235 U.S. 133 (1914); Bailey v. Alabama, 219 U.S. 219 (1911); WILLIAM COHEN, AT FREEDOM'S EDGE: BLACK MOBILITY AND THE SOUTHERN WHITE QUEST FOR RACIAL CONTROL, 1861–1915 (1991); PETE DANIEL, THE SHADOW OF SLAVERY: PEONAGE IN THE SOUTH, 1901–1969 (1972); DANIEL A. NOVAK, THE WHEEL OF SERVITUDE: BLACK FORCED LABOR AFTER SLAVERY (1978).

[164] See Giles v. Harris, 189 U.S. 475 (1903); Williams v. Mississippi, 170 U.S. 213 (1898); sources cited supra note 131.

educational role, and *Brown v. Board of Education* frequently is cited as proof of that proposition. On this view, *Brown* played a vital role in educating Americans, especially whites, on the evils of racial segregation.[165]

Yet the historical accuracy of this account of the Court's educational function is dubious. On fundamental questions of social policy, it seems that Americans tend to make up their minds for themselves, heedless of the Court's instruction. As we have seen, while *Prigg v. Pennsylvania* invalidated northern states' personal liberty laws as inconsistent with the Fugitive Slave Clause, in the 1850s these same states evaded or even defied the Court's ruling with increasingly aggressive personal liberty laws.[166] *Dred Scott* failed to persuade northerners to acquiesce in the Court's judgment that Congress lacked constitutional power to bar slavery from the federal territories; quite to the contrary, the Republican Party after 1857 grew stronger, achieved majority status in the North, and during the Civil War simply ignored the Court's decision and excluded slavery from the federal territories.[167] Similarly, it seems doubtful that *Roe v. Wade* educated many Americans out of their right-to-life position or that *Bowers v. Hardwick*[168] convinced many who were not already convinced of the immorality of homosexuality. Indeed, one might argue that all of these Supreme Court decisions were more successful at mobilizing opposition than at rallying support by educating the citizenry.[169]

Even *Brown* is less persuasive evidence of the Court's educational function than is commonly supposed. With regard to white opinion in the South, *Brown*, if anything, crystallized resistance to altering the racial status quo.[170] In the nation as a whole, opinion polls conducted in the years after *Brown* registered only minor movement in attitudes toward racial segregation—a gradual shift in opinion that plausibly is attributable more to political, social, economic, and ideological trends inaugurated or accelerated by World War II than to the educational impact of *Brown*.[171] The only incontrovertible educational effect of *Brown* was in teaching African-Americans, who surely appreciated the injustice of Jim Crow without Supreme Court instruction, that their racial grievances might now be redressable in court.[172]

A defender of the educational conception of constitutionalism might respond that even if the Court is not always successful in shaping public opinion, at least the Justices manage to get public policy debates started, which is a good thing.

---

[165] *E.g.*, David J. Garrow, *Hopelessly Hollow History: Revisionist Devaluing of* Brown v. Board of Education, 80 VA. L. REV. 151, 152–53 (1994); C. Herman Pritchett, *Equal Protection and the Urban Majority*, 58 AM. POL. SCI. REV. 869, 869 (1964); Mark Tushnet, *The Significance of* Brown v. Board of Education, 80 VA. L. REV. 173, 175–77 (1994).

[166] *See supra* note 147.

[167] *See supra* note 148. On the Republicans' disregard of *Dred Scott* during the Civil War, see JAMES M. MCPHERSON, BATTLE CRY OF FREEDOM: THE CIVIL WAR ERA 496–97, 506 (1988).

[168] 478 U.S. 186 (1986).

[169] *See* Klarman, *Fidelity, supra* note 121, at 1751–52.

[170] *See* Klarman, *Racial Change, supra* note 78, at 75–150; Michael J. Klarman, *How* Brown *Changed Race Relations: The Backlash Thesis*, 81 J. AM. HIST. 81 (1994).

[171] On the opinion polls, see ROBERT F. BURK, THE EISENHOWER ADMINISTRATION AND BLACK CIVIL RIGHTS 202 (1984). I have described in detail these background extralegal forces in Klarman, *Racial Change, supra* note 78, at 13–71. For other very useful discussions, see DOUG MCADAM, POLITICAL PROCESS AND THE DEVELOPMENT OF BLACK INSURGENCY, 1930–1970, ch. 5 (1982); ROSENBERG, *supra* note 79, at 107–56.

[172] *See* Michael J. Klarman, Brown v. Board of Education: *Facts and Political Correctness*, 80 VA. L. REV. 185, 187–89 (1994).

Yet how plausible is it to believe that courts are responsible for commencing these debates? Conventional wisdom to the contrary notwithstanding,[173] the Court in *Brown* did not inaugurate the debate over American race relations. Indeed, the Justices who participated in the school segregation cases appreciated far better than have many subsequent commentators how significant were the advances in race relations that preceded the Court's intervention.[174] Similarly, the Court's sex discrimination cases of the 1970s plainly reflected, rather than inspired, the dramatic reconsideration of gender roles spawned by the women's movement.[175] Even *Roe v. Wade* culminated a half-dozen years' worth of frenetic legislative reform activity on the abortion issue.[176] The Court almost never inaugurates these sorts of fundamental public policy debates; the Justices are too much a part of popular culture to play that vanguard role. Rather, their interventions tend to come later—either when public opinion has become roughly evenly divided, or after a new consensus has emerged and the Justices use it to suppress lingering outliers.[177]

As a normative matter, we should be glad that the Supreme Court's pronouncements do not have much educational effect. Over the long haul, the educational lessons conveyed by the Court are as likely to be bad as good. The same Court that gave us *Brown* also gave us *Dred Scott, Plessy, Buck v. Bell,*[178] *Korematsu,* and *Bowers.* We should applaud the Court's educational function only to the extent that we believe the Court's decisions are likely to be normatively better than those of the political branches. And why, in general, should one believe this? Moreover, while there is little reason to believe that the Court's educational lessons are likely to be better on some consensus normative standard than those of the political branches, they certainly are likely to reflect more culturally elite values. It is this basic fact, I shall suggest in Part III, that constitutes the most fundamental objection to judicially reviewable constitutionalism in a democracy.

H. Finality

Another supposed virtue of constitutionalism is that it promotes finality.[179] Finality is a virtue, on this view, because endless reconsideration of the same issues

---

[173] *See, e.g.,* Aryeh Neier, Only Judgment, The Limits of Litigation in Social Change 241–42 (1982) ("*Brown* launched the public debate over racial equality. . . ."); Howard A. Glickstein, *The Impact of* Brown v. Board of Education *and Its Progeny,* 23 How. L.J. 51, 55 (1980) (asserting that *Brown* served "as the foundation of our quest for equal justice in the United States").

[174] *See, e.g.,* Richard Kluger, Simple Justice: The History of Brown v. Board of Education and Black America's Struggle for Equality 684 (1976) (reporting Justice Frankfurter's observation in a private memorandum regarding "the great changes in the relations between white and colored people since the first World War" and his remark that "the pace of progress has surprised even those most eager in its promotion"); Mark V. Tushnet, Making Civil Rights Law: Thurgood Marshall and the Supreme Court, 1936–1961, at 143 (1994) (quoting Justice Jackson's statement in a letter to constitutional historian Charles Fairman that the 1950 university segregation cases "show[ed] pretty conclusively that the segregation system is breaking down of its own weight and that a little time will end it in nearly all States"). For additional statements by the Justices to this effect, see Michael J. Klarman, *Civil Rights Law: Who Made It and How Much Did It Matter?* 83 Geo. L.J. 433, 458 (1994) (book review).

[175] *See* Jeffries, *supra* note 150, at 511; Klarman, *Rethinking, supra* note 47, at 9.

[176] *See* Garrow, *supra* note 79, at 335–472; Rosenberg, *supra* note 79, at 262–64.

[177] *See supra* notes 132–45 and accompanying text.

[178] 274 U.S. 200 (1927).

[179] *See, e.g.,* Planned Parenthood v. Casey, 505 U.S. 833, 867 (1992) (plurality opinion); Larry Alexander & Frederick Schauer, *On Extrajudicial Constitutional Interpretation,* 110 Harv. L. Rev.

is wasteful, unsettling, and possibly destructive of social peace. James Madison defended such a view in opposing Jefferson's proposal for a new constitutional convention every generation.[180]

Descriptively, the Constitution itself—unadorned by judicial interpretation—plainly does not secure final resolution of controverted issues. People constantly struggle to amend the Constitution to accord with their own preferences—whether through formal Article V mechanisms for amendment or through judicial construction. The mere possibility of formal amendment means that nothing ever can be settled definitively by the Constitution, except for issues resolved through unamendable amendments[181] (and why should anyone pay attention to those?).[182] Southerners appreciated this fact when seceding from the Union in 1860–61: Even if disagreements with the North temporarily could be compromised, southerners ultimately must be at risk within the Union, because demographic trends eventually would enable antislavery states to secure the three-quarters supermajority necessary to amend the Constitution to forbid slavery even in the South.[183]

More important than formal amendment, as a practical matter, has been the possibility of changed construction, whether judicial or popular. Contemporaries plausibly might have believed that the original Constitution of 1787 conclusively resolved in the negative the question of the national government's power to regulate slavery in the existing states.[184] Yet this seemingly settled understanding did not prevent one strand of northern abolitionists from evolving a contrary interpretation.[185] On their view, the Due Process Clause of the Fifth Amendment—which, *Barron v. Mayor of Baltimore*[186] notwithstanding, was deemed applicable to the states[187]—barred slavery as inconsistent with "liberty." Similarly, the fact that the actions and intentions of the Founders seemed clearly to authorize Congress to bar

---

1359, 1371–77 (1997); Strauss, *supra* note 6, at 906–24 (explaining various aspects of our constitutional practice in terms of "conventionalism"—the notion that it is more important that some things be settled than that they be settled right").

[180] *See* Letter from James Madison to Thomas Jefferson (Feb. 4, 1790), *in* 13 THE PAPERS OF JAMES MADISON, *supra* note 69, at 22 (arguing that "such a periodical revision" as Jefferson proposed would "engender pernicious factions that might not otherwise come into existence; and agitate the public mind more frequently and more violently than might be expedient"); *see also* Letter from James Madison to Thomas Jefferson (June 27, 1823), *in* 3 THE REPUBLIC OF LETTERS, *supra* note 16, at 1868 (disagreeing with Jefferson's view that disputes between national and state power should be referred to conventions of the People on the ground that the process would be "too tardy, too troublesome, and too expensive; besides its tendency to lessen a salutary veneration for an Instrument so often calling for such explanatory interpositions").

[181] *See* U.S. CONST. art. V (providing that no amendment shall be made prior to 1808 to the ban on congressional interference with the foreign slave trade and that "no State, without its Consent, shall be deprived of its equal Suffrage in the Senate").

[182] *See* Klarman, *Majoritarian Judicial Review*, *supra* note 28, at 506 & nn.67–68.

[183] *See* CARPENTER, *supra* note 19, at 167–70 (noting several statements by southerners to this effect); SECESSION DEBATED, *supra* note 147, at 118–19 (statement of Henry Benning); *see also id.* at xx.

[184] *See supra* note 157.

[185] *See* MICHAEL KENT CURTIS, NO STATE SHALL ABRIDGE: THE FOURTEENTH AMENDMENT AND THE BILL OF RIGHTS 42–44 (1986); JACOBUS TENBROEK, EQUAL UNDER LAW 66–93 (1965); Howard J. Graham, *The Fourteenth Amendment and School Segregation*, 3 BUFF. L. REV. 1, 8–16 (1954). Supreme Court Justice Story regarded this abolitionist interpretation as a perversion of the Constitution. *See* NEWMYER, *supra* note 159, at 365.

[186] 32 U.S. (7 Pet.) 243 (1833).

[187] *See* CURTIS, *supra* note 185, at 29, 42, 48–51; FEHRENBACHER, *supra* note 19, at 631 n.58.

slavery from federal territories[188] did not inhibit most southerners by the 1840s and 1850s from embracing John C. Calhoun's "common property" view to the contrary.[189] One likewise might have thought that Article I, Section 10 would definitively establish the unconstitutionality of debtor relief legislation, yet state legislatures constantly were reopening the question,[190] until, in 1934, they finally convinced the Court to capitulate.[191] Nor did the Reconstruction amendments to the Constitution conclusively resolve matters of racial equality. Not only did some white southerners continue to call for repeal of those amendments into the early twentieth century,[192] but more importantly, they hoped to secure judicial acquiescence in the amendments' evisceration through interpretation—a strategy that proved generally successful for many years.[193]

Nor do *judicial interpretations* of the Constitution achieve final resolution of contested policy questions. Occasionally, those decisions are overruled by formal Article V methods.[194] More frequently, they are overruled by the course of events or by subsequent judicial decisions. *Dred Scott* was defied by Republicans during the Civil War and then was formally overruled by Section 1 of the Fourteenth Amendment. The interment of the Fourteenth Amendment's Privileges and Immunities Clause in the *Slaughter-House Cases*[195] was functionally overruled by the development of substantive due process, culminating in the famous *Lochner* decision,[196] which in turn was functionally overruled by *West Coast Hotel*.[197] *Plessy* ultimately yielded to *Brown*. Restrictive commerce clause interpretations[198]

---

[188] *See* Northwest Ordinance Act of 1789, ch. 8, 1 Stat. 50 (1789); FEHRENBACHER, *supra* note 19, at 83–84; POTTER, *supra* note 88, at 54; Bestor, *supra* note 147, at 152–54. Fehrenbacher convincingly argues that southerners were impelled to raise the constitutional argument against congressional regulation of slavery in federal territories only when it became plausible that they might lose the political struggle over the issue—around the time of the Missouri Compromise debates. *See* FEHRENBACHER, *supra* note 19, at 103–04, 138–39.

[189] On this view, the federal territories were deemed the common property of the states, and Congress, as trustee, was barred from imposing territorial regulations that discriminated against forms of property recognized only in some states. *See* FEHRENBACHER, *supra* note 19, at 133, 134.

[190] *See, e.g.*, Bronson v. Kinzie, 42 U.S. (1 How.) 311 (1843); Sturges v. Crowninshield, 17 U.S. (4 Wheat.) 122 (1819); WRIGHT, *supra* note 99, at 68–71; Steven R. Boyd, *The Contract Clause and the Evolution of American Federalism, 1789–1815*, 44 WM & MARY Q. 529 (1987).

[191] *See* Home Bldg. & Loan Ass'n v. Blaisdell, 290 U.S. 398 (1934).

[192] *See, e.g.*, Charles Wallace Collins, Jr., *The Failure of the Fourteenth Amendment as a Constitutional Ideal*, 11 S. ATLANTIC Q. 101 (1912); *see also* JOHN DITTMER, BLACK GEORGIA IN THE PROGRESSIVE ERA, 1900–1920, at 182 (1977) (noting southern congressman Thomas M. Hardwick offering resolutions in 1911 to repeal parts of the Fourteenth Amendment and all of the Fifteenth Amendment).

[193] *See* Giles v. Harris, 189 U.S. 475 (1903); Williams v. Mississippi, 170 U.S. 213 (1898); Plessy v. Ferguson, 163 U.S. 537 (1896).

[194] *See* U.S. CONST. amend. XXVI (barring abridgement of the right to vote based on age for those eighteen or older, and effectively overruling *Oregon v. Mitchell*, 400 U.S. 112 (1970)); U.S. CONST. amend. XVI (empowering Congress to collect income taxes without apportionment and effectively overruling *Pollock v. Farmers Loan & Trust Co.*, 158 U.S. 601 (1895)); U.S. CONST. amend. XIV (providing for birthright citizenship and effectively overruling this aspect of *Dred Scott v. Sandford*, 60 U.S. (19 How.) 393 (1857)); U.S. CONST. amend. XI (protecting states against suits in federal court and effectively overruling *Chisholm v. Georgia*, 2 U.S. (2 Dall.) 419 (1793)).

[195] Slaughter-House Cases, 83 U.S. (16 Wall.) 36 (1873).

[196] Lochner v. New York, 198 U.S. 45 (1905).

[197] West Coast Hotel Co. v. Parrish, 300 U.S. 379 (1937).

[198] *E.g.*, Hammer v. Dagenhart, 247 U.S. 251 (1918); United States v. E.C. Knight Co., 156 U.S. 1 (1895).

yielded to *Darby*[199] and *Wickard*.[200] Additional examples easily might be cited, but the point seems evident.[201] The Justices possess a far more limited capacity to "call the contending sides of a national controversy to end their national division"[202] than they apparently would like.

Normatively, this is good news, because it seems doubtful that finality frequently is more important than reaching the right result. The Constitution generally is not like the mailbox rule in contract law;[203] getting the rule right is more important than simply establishing a predictable rule. There may be occasional exceptions, such as the rule established in *Dartmouth College*[204] for treating corporate charters as contracts protected against impairment by Article I, Section 10; since the Court permitted corporate charters to reserve the state's right to change them at any time,[205] the ruling essentially functioned as a default rule for the parties to bargain around.

But this is not an accurate description of most constitutional rules. It matters greatly whether the Constitution sanctions slavery, permits establishment of a national church, or creates a national government of enumerated as opposed to inherent powers. The same is true for Court interpretations of the Constitution. It matters greatly whether racial segregation is consonant with the Equal Protection Clause, whether abortion regulation is consistent with the Due Process Clause, and whether school prayer is tolerable under the Establishment Clause. It strains credulity to suggest that it matters more that such issues be resolved finally than that they be resolved rightly. For this reason, the Court has been correct to treat the doctrine of stare decisis as less constraining in the constitutional context.[206]

Finality is normatively dubious for another reason. While there are undeniable virtues to finality—efficiency, predictability, preserving social peace—there are also undeniable vices. If constitutional issues are finally resolved, either by the Constitution or by judicial construction, what are subsequent generations left to decide for themselves? The finality account of constitutionalism, if accurate, diminishes the political autonomy of subsequent generations. Since constitutional law has co-opted many of our most fundamental public policy issues, it would drain much of the meaning from our politics to treat constitutional resolutions of those issues as final.[207] This is, of course, the classic Progressive critique of judicial

---

[199] United States v. Darby, 312 U.S. 100 (1941).

[200] Wickard v. Filburn, 317 U.S. 111 (1942). Barry Cushman persuasively argues that the Commerce Clause revolution occurred in 1941–42, not in 1937, as is conventionally thought. *See generally* BARRY CUSHMAN, RETHINKING THE NEW DEAL COURT: THE STRUCTURE OF A CONSTITUTIONAL REVOLUTION (1998).

[201] For additional examples, see Klarman, *Fidelity, supra* note 121, at 1741–42.

[202] Planned Parenthood v. Casey, 505 U.S. 833, 867 (1992) (plurality opinion).

[203] The "mailbox rule" establishes that acceptance of a contract is accomplished upon mailing, rather than upon receipt. It is generally understood to represent a paradigm example of where the content of a rule matters less than that the rule be clearly established so that parties can plan around it. *See* ROBERT E. SCOTT & DOUGLAS L. LESLIE, CONTRACT LAW AND THEORY 231–33 (2d ed., 1993).

[204] Dartmouth College v. Woodward, 17 U.S. (4 Wheat.) 518 (1819).

[205] *See id.* at 675, 680, 708, 712 (Story, J., concurring).

[206] *See, e.g.*, Seminole Tribe v. Florida, 517 U.S. 44, 63 (1996); Adarand Constructors, Inc. v. Pena, 515 U.S. 200, 229–35 (1995); Payne v. Tennessee, 501 U.S. 808, 834 (1991) (Scalia, J., concurring).

[207] *Cf.* ACKERMAN, *supra* note 5, at 41–44 (criticizing the traditional "professional narrative" of American constitutional history which downplays the constitutional creativity of the American people by treating the New Deal constitutional revolution as simply a *rediscovery* of Marshall era understandings).

review—that the People must learn to rule themselves rather than having courts or the constitutional Framers do it for them.[208] The finality conception of constitutionalism is also subject to the deadhand objections previously described.[209]

I. Rule of Recognition

On another account—call it the "rule-of-recognition"[210] conception—constitutionalism is not so much good as inevitable. That is, even in a system not authorizing judicial invalidation of statutes inconsistent with a written constitution, judges still require a set of background rules that establish the criteria for valid legislation—for example, to be valid, a law must be passed by which institution using what voting rule?[211] This is constitutionalism in the British sense.

Objections to this rule-of-recognition conception of constitutionalism are all descriptive; it seems pointless to offer normative criticisms of the inevitable. First, even if our Constitution does play this function, it also does a great deal more, and thus cannot simply be defended on inevitable, rule-of-recognition grounds. The Constitution ventures beyond a simple rule of recognition both in establishing substantive standards against which otherwise constitutional practices must be tested and by entrenching the rule of recognition against subsequent change.

The rule-of-recognition notion justifies, for example, constitutional provisions defining the conditions for the enactment of valid national legislation—passage by both houses of Congress and presidential acquiescence or congressional override of a presidential veto. But this limited conception of constitutionalism hardly justifies the numerous substantive limitations on the national lawmaking power contained in Article I, Sections 8 and 9, or in the Bill of Rights. While it is inevitable that even a system without a written constitution possess some background pre-constitutional rules, our own Constitution goes substantially farther in the multitude of fetters it places on national legislative power. Similarly, while the rule-of-recognition notion justifies Article VI's Supremacy Clause—because a court needs to know how to resolve conflicts between state and federal law—it cannot account for the numerous limitations on state legislative authority contained in Article I, Section 10, or in Section 1 of the Fourteenth Amendment.

Nor does the rule-of-recognition account of constitutionalism plainly justify the antimajoritarian amendment rule contained in Article V. While a rule of recognition itself may be inevitable, there is no reason that rule need be entrenched against change, which is precisely the effect of Article V with its supermajority

---

[208] *See, e.g.*, West Virginia State Bd. of Educ. v. Barnette, 319 U.S. 624, 668 (1943) (Frankfurter, J., dissenting) (noting that judicial review "is always attended with a serious evil, namely, that the correction of legislative mistakes comes from the outside, and the people thus lose the political experience, and the moral education and stimulus that come from fighting the question out in the ordinary way, and correcting their own errors"); Learned Hand, The Bill of Rights 73 (1958) ("For myself it would be most irksome to be ruled by a bevy of Platonic Guardians, even if I knew how to choose them, which I assuredly do not."); Thayer, *supra* note 65, at 155–56 (arguing that the People must be taught that the responsibility for wise constitutional interpretation ultimately lies with themselves).

[209] *See supra* notes 14–15 and accompanying text.

[210] For the classic account of rules of recognition, see H.L.A. Hart, The Concept of Law 100–10 (1961).

[211] *See id.* at 102; Kay, *supra* note 30, at 188–93; Frank I. Michelman, *Thirteen Easy Pieces*, 93 Mich. L. Rev. 1297, 1301 (1995) (noting that constitutionalism at a minimum prescribes "organizational and procedural prerequisites for valid ordinary lawmaking") (book review).

requirements.[212] In other words, why can't the rule of recognition be amended so long as the amendment process itself complies with the rule of recognition? Specifically, if our rule of recognition for national legislation requires consent by both houses of Congress plus presidential acquiescence, that rule should be amendable by legislation that secures consent of both houses of Congress and presidential acquiescence. The Article V requirement that changes in the rule of recognition must secure supermajority assent in Congress and in the state legislatures is not justified by the minimalist rule of recognition conception of constitutionalism.

Second, while some background rule of recognition is inevitable, a written constitution establishing it certainly is not. In other regimes, tradition and custom establish the rule of recognition. Again, this is constitutionalism in the British sense. British courts figure out what counts as valid parliamentary legislation without a written constitution specifying the criteria.

More importantly, though, a written constitution is not only unnecessary to fulfilling the rule-of-recognition function, but it is also insufficient. A written constitution that purports to establish the rule of recognition for valid legislation cannot, as a simple matter of logic, establish the rule of recognition for itself. That is, while the written constitution specifies the criteria for the validity of legislation, it cannot specify the criteria for its own validity.[213] This is an infinite regress problem; everything must stand on something. Ultimately, the rule of recognition can be validated only by the bare fact of political acceptance, not by compliance with some meta rule of recognition.[214]

Consider, more concretely, the legitimacy of the United States Constitution. That Constitution pretty clearly was illegal under the rule of recognition established by the preceding regime.[215] The Articles of Confederation required that amendments be approved *unanimously* by state *legislatures*, and made no provision for a *constitutional convention* of any sort. Yet the Philadelphia Convention, contrary to instructions under which many of its delegates labored, repudiated rather than amended the Articles, and provided that its handiwork go into effect upon ratification by nine out of thirteen special state ratifying conventions. Thus, our Constitution plainly was, at its inception, an illegal document. Yet arguments to this effect today would get one nowhere in public debate, much less in a court of law.[216] The reason is that the ultimate rule of recognition is public acceptance.

---

[212] Michelman raises but does not resolve the question of whether constitutionalism requires the absolute entrenchment of an amendment rule that relatively entrenches everything else in the constitution. *See* Michelman, *supra* note 211, at 1303 n.27.

[213] *See* Ronald Dworkin, *The Forum of Principle*, 56 N.Y.U. L. REV. 469, 472–74 (1981); Frederick Schauer, *Amending the Presuppositions of a Constitution, in* RESPONDING TO IMPERFECTION: THE THEORY AND PRACTICE OF CONSTITUTIONAL AMENDMENT 145, 145 (Sanford Levinson ed., 1995) ("Constitutions establish the grounds for constitutionality and unconstitutionality, and in so doing they simply cannot themselves be either constitutional or unconstitutional.").

[214] *See* HART, *supra* note 210, at 107–10; Kay, *supra* note 30, at 193; Michelman, *supra* note 211, at 1302; Schauer, *supra* note 213, at 150 ("The ultimate rule of recognition is a matter of social fact....").

[215] On this point, I find Ackerman & Katyal more convincing than Amar. *Compare* Bruce Ackerman & Neal Katyal, *Our Unconventional Founding*, 62 U. CHI. L. REV. 475 (1995) *with* Amar, *supra* note 5, at 1047–48 *and* Akhil Reed Amar, *The Consent of the Governed: Constitutional Amendment Outside Article V*, 94 COLUM. L. REV. 457, 462–87 (1994) [hereinafter Amar, *Consent of the Governed*]. *See also* RAKOVE, *supra* note 16, at 128–29 (agreeing with Ackerman); Richard S. Kay, *The Illegality of the Constitution*, 4 CONST. COMMENTARY 57, 64–70 (1987) (same).

[216] *See* Schauer, *supra* note 213, at 154 n.20.

The Antifederalists understood this fact quite well; thus, they generally ceased raising legitimacy arguments against the Constitution once the requisite number of states had ratified under Article VII.[217]

Thus, while constitutionalism in the rule-of-recognition sense is inevitable, it also is impossible. The ultimate rule of recognition inheres not in any constitutional provision, written or unwritten, but in the bare fact of political acceptance.

Finally, in addition to the descriptive objections already raised against the rule-of-recognition conception of constitutionalism, one should note that our Constitution does an especially bad job of establishing rules of recognition: It fails even to provide clear criteria as to what counts as part of the Constitution. For example, the constitutional text says nothing about what a constitutional convention, one of the two recognized routes for amendment, would look like—how its delegates would be apportioned among the states or whether and how its agenda might be limited.[218] This uncertainty surrounding Article V conventions plainly has inhibited use of this alternative route to constitutional change.[219] Similarly, the constitutional text provides no guidance as to how long pending amendments remain ripe for ratification (thus the controversy over the Twenty-seventh Amendment),[220] whether states are permitted to change their minds about ratification while an amendment remains pending,[221] whether Congress can exact state ratification as a condition for granting some benefit otherwise within its discretion,[222]

[217] See, e.g., ELY, supra note 9, at 6; Amar, Consent of the Governed, supra note 215, at 464, 486–87; Kay, supra note 215, at 77–78; see also RAKOVE, supra note 16, at 130 (noting that the ratification process "produced a completely unambiguous result that ensured that the Constitution would attain immediate legitimacy").

[218] Madison himself raised some of these objections at the Philadelphia convention. See 2 CONVENTION OF 1787, supra note 54, at 558. For scholarship identifying these problems, see Gerald Gunther, The Convention Method of Amending the United States Constitution, 14 GA. L. REV. 1 (1979); Laurence H. Tribe, Issues Raised by Requesting Congress to Call a Constitutional Convention to Propose a Balanced Budget Amendment, 10 PAC. L.J. 627, 632–40 (1979). Interestingly, the Confederate Constitution explicitly addressed the problem of "runaway" conventions by limiting constitutional conventions to a consideration of amendments proposed by the states calling the convention. CONFEDERATE CONST. art. V, § 1, reprinted in MARSHALL L. DEROSA, THE CONFEDERATE CONSTITUTION OF 1861, at 149 (1991) (constitutional conventions called by Congress upon petition of the requisite number of states shall "take into consideration such amendments to the Constitution as the said States shall concur in suggesting at the time when the said demand is made"). For useful discussion, see Aaron Kanter, Lessons from Montgomery—Revisiting the Debate over Runaway Constitutional Conventions (May 1997) (unpublished student paper) (on file with author).

[219] See KYVIG, supra note 122, at 210, 213 (noting the large number of states calling for a constitutional convention before Congress finally passed the Seventeenth Amendment (direct election of senators)); id. at 376–79 (noting widespread concerns of a convention "run amok" in light of the large number of state petitions for a constitutional convention to consider amendments to overrule the reapportionment cases); id. at 433–34, 440–43 (noting similar concerns with respect to calls for a convention to consider a balanced budget amendment).

[220] See Michael Stokes Paulsen, A General Theory of Article V: The Constitutional Lessons of the Twenty-Seventh Amendment, 103 YALE L.J. 677 (1993).

[221] This issue arose both with regard to the Fourteenth and Fifteenth Amendments, as well as more recently with regard to the Child Labor amendment and the ERA. With regard to the Reconstruction amendments, see CURTIS, supra note 185, at 155; GILLETTE, supra note 130, at 84 tbl. 2, 115; Paulsen, supra note 220, at 709–11. On the Child Labor Amendment, see Coleman v. Miller, 307 U.S. 433, 447–50 (1939). On the ERA, see KYVIG, supra note 122, at 408–09, 414–16.

[222] It was generally understood that southern states could not gain readmission to the Union without ratifying the Reconstruction amendments. See FONER, supra note 130, at 261, 276; GILLETTE, supra note 130, at 92, 98–103; EARL M. MALTZ, CIVIL RIGHTS, THE CONSTITUTION, AND CONGRESS, 1863–1869, at 122–23 (1990); KENNETH M. STAMPP, THE ERA OF RECONSTRUCTION, 1865–1877, at 14, 145 (1965).

or whether state ratification is valid when Congress has forcibly reconstructed the state government in order to obtain it.[223] The Constitution answers none of these questions, yet each is vital to determining the validity of actual constitutional amendments. If the need for a rule of recognition is what justifies our Constitution, it does a lousy job of justifying itself.

J. Majoritarianism

A final, possibly unconventional, justification for constitutionalism is majoritarianism. According to this view, a judicially enforceable constitution is a good thing because most people want it.[224] This account simply takes peoples' preferences at face value, rather than piercing the veil to investigate the reasons behind those preferences and whether they withstand investigation. In other words, this majoritarian account of constitutionalism builds upon the liberal premise that personal conceptions of the good require no objective justification; we simply aggregate individual preferences and make policy accordingly.[225] Again, on this view, constitutionalism is good simply because people want it; it requires no greater justification than, say, a preference for chocolate over vanilla ice cream.[226]

The descriptive plausibility of this majoritarian account of constitutionalism boils down to an empirical question, the answer to which we simply do not know: Do most Americans endorse our current system of judicially enforceable constitutionalism? We know that they do not revolt against it, and we know that they do not constitutionally amend it through Article V procedures. Yet one hardly can infer consent from failure to resort to revolutionary or supermajoritarian remedies.[227] It may well be that a majority of people do not endorse our current constitutional regime, but feel powerless to change it given the antimajoritarian amendment process enshrined in Article V. On the other hand, Americans today do seem to admire their Supreme Court, according to some opinion polls far more than they respect the other branches of the national government.[228] Further, some have argued that the Senate's defeat in 1987 of Judge Bork's Supreme Court nomination, given the candidate's strong endorsement of judicial restraint and an originalist interpretive methodology, indicates popular support for more activist, free-floating judicial review.[229]

[223] On congressional reconstruction of the southern states, see, for example, FONER, *supra* note 130, chs. 6–7.

[224] *See* DAHL, *supra* note 15, at 113, 154, 185 (noting that it is not undemocratic for the majority to adopt decisionmaking processes, including judicial review, that are not strictly majoritarian); SPITZ, *supra* note 15, at 111 (same); *cf.* Washington v. Seattle School Dist. Number 1, 458 U.S. 457, 470 (1982) ("[T]he political majority may generally restructure the political process to place obstacles in the path of everyone seeking to secure the benefits of governmental action."). *But see* Lucas v. Forty-Fourth Gen. Assembly, 377 U.S. 713 (1964) (rejecting a malapportionment scheme that had secured majority endorsement in a referendum).

[225] *See, e.g.*, ROBERT H. BORK, THE TEMPTING OF AMERICA: THE POLITICAL SEDUCTION OF THE LAW 258–59 (1990) (noting that in the absence of any "objectively 'correct' hierarchy" for ranking "forms of gratification," we must simply "put such issues to a vote and . . . the majority morality prevails.").

[226] *See, e.g.*, Paul Brest, *The Fundamental Rights Controversy: The Essential Contradictions of Normative Constitutional Scholarship*, 90 YALE L.J. 1063, 1101–02 (1981); Silas J. Wasserstrom & Louis Michael Seidman, *The Fourth Amendment as Constitutional Theory*, 77 GEO. L.J. 19, 70 (1988).

[227] *See supra* note 15.

[228] *See, e.g.*, Gallup Poll, May 30–June 1, 1997, *reported in* USA TODAY, June 17, 1997, at 7A.

[229] *See, e.g.*, Richard Posner, *Bork and Beethoven*, 42 STAN. L. REV. 1365, 1381–82 (1990); Wasserstrom & Seidman, *supra* note 226, at 76; *see also* McCLOSKEY, *supra* note 22, at 118 (noting, in the

The principal normative objection to this majoritarian justification of judicially enforceable constitutionalism is that it has no logical limitation: it might be deployed to justify a dictatorship as easily as our own vaguely countermajoritarian constitutionalism. For example, had the Philadelphia Convention endorsed, and the nation ratified, Alexander Hamilton's proposals for a life-tenured presidency and Senate, that regime would possess a majoritarian pedigree and, on this account of constitutionalism, be unobjectionable.[230] The same would be true for majoritarian endorsement of slavery, religious persecution, and so on. Because most defenders of constitutionalism draw heavily upon the institution's countermajoritarian capacity,[231] I doubt that this overarching majoritarian justification has a very broad normative appeal. Only a thorough going majoritarian[232] would have trouble normatively rejecting this majoritarian account of constitutionalism, and even he or she could fall back upon the descriptive objection noted above.

II. A BETTER DESCRIPTION?

If none of the ten leading accounts adequately describes our system of judicially enforceable constitutionalism, what would be a better description, and is it normatively attractive? I believe that the American system of judicial review essentially boils down to this: The Supreme Court, in *politically unpredictable* ways, imposes *culturally elite* values in a *marginally countermajoritarian* fashion. Let me briefly elaborate on all three components of this description.

By politically unpredictable, I mean that judicial review possesses no inherent political bias. The Warren Court legacy has deluded many into thinking otherwise,[233] and contemporary political rhetoric generally perpetuates this myth.[234] But one must recognize that it is just a myth: Judicial review has no intrinsic liberal political bias.[235] A broader historical perspective plainly establishes this point. In the late nineteenth and early twentieth centuries, it was political Progressives who criticized the activist *Lochner* Court for invalidating social welfare legislation.[236]

---

context of the defeat of FDR's Court-packing plan, that Americans indicated their support for judicial review by "refusing to abet an assault on the Court even though it was carried on in their name to chastise the Court for thwarting their will").

[230] *See* 1 CONVENTION OF 1787, *supra* note 54, at 289–90 (Alexander Hamilton defending his proposal for a life-tenured Senate and president as consistent with republicanism so long as appointment is made by the People).

[231] *See supra* notes 73–74 and accompanying text.

[232] I have previously committed myself to such a position. *See* Klarman, *Antifidelity, supra* note 14, at 411–15; Klarman, *Majoritarian Judicial Review, supra* note 28.

[233] *See* KALMAN, *supra* note 152, at 1–10 (noting that the experience of the Warren Court has induced law professors and others to link activist judicial review with political liberalism—the "Faith of Our Fathers"); Ronald K. L. Collins & David M. Skover, *The Future of Liberal Legal Scholarship*, 87 MICH. L. REV. 189, 189 (1988) ("Earl Warren is dead. A generation of liberal legal scholars continues, nevertheless, to act as if the man and his Court preside over the present.").

[234] *See, e.g.*, David Bryden, *A Conservative Case for Judicial Activism*, 53 PUB. INTEREST 72 (1993).

[235] *See* KALMAN, *supra* note 152, at 130–31 (noting an exchange between Owen Fiss and Robert Cover in which the latter insisted that the "convergence" between judicial activism and political liberalism "was temporary and accidental").

[236] *See, e.g.*, Whitney v. California, 274 U.S. 357, 372 (1927) (Brandeis, J., concurring); Felix Frankfurter, *The Red Terror of Judicial Reform*, NEW REPUBLIC, Oct. 1, 1924, at 112, *reprinted in* FELIX FRANKFURTER ON THE SUPREME COURT: EXTRAJUDICIAL ESSAYS ON THE COURT AND THE CONSTITUTION 164 (Philip B. Kurland ed., 1970); Hand, *supra* note 114; Pound, *Liberty of Contract, supra* note 114; Theodore Roosevelt, *Criticism of the Courts*, THE OUTLOOK, Sept. 24, 1910, at 149. For a

Only since the *Carolene Products*[237] revolution in the conception of the Court's role has judicial review seemed even plausibly liberal in its implications. And since President Nixon reconstituted the Court around 1970, the performances of the Burger and Rehnquist Courts have corroborated the politically double-edged nature of activist judicial review. Conservative activism threatens affirmative action, minority voting districts, hate speech regulation, environmental land use restrictions, and campaign finance reform.[238] Liberal activism, on the other hand, invalidates school prayer, abortion regulation, restrictions on indecent speech, and discrimination against African Americans, women, and gays.[239] It is no accident that scathing critiques of the Court with the same title, *Government by Judiciary*, were written in 1932 by a left-wing critic and in 1977 by a right-wing one.[240] Judicial review has no intrinsic political bias.

To observe that judicially enforceable constitutionalism is a politically double-edged sword is not to deny that the practice has any systematic bias; it is only to suggest that the bias operates along an axis other than partisan politics. It is not my claim that judicial review is a simple crapshoot, yielding no systematic winners and losers. Indeed, very much to the contrary, I believe that judicial review is systematically biased in favor of culturally elite values.[241] Justice Scalia put the point with characteristic flair in his *Romer* dissent: "When the Court takes sides in the culture wars, it tends to be with the knights rather than the villeins—and more specifically with the Templars, reflecting the views and values of the lawyer class from which the Court's Members are drawn."[242]

Why this should be so is no mystery. Justices of the United States Supreme Court, indeed of any state or federal appellate court, are overwhelmingly upper-middle or upper-class and extremely well educated, usually at the nation's more elite universities. Moreover, unlike legislators who generally share a similar cultural background, federal judges enjoy a relative political insulation which significantly reduces any offsetting obligation to respond to the non-elite political preferences of their constituents. Throughout much of American history, this elite

---

comprehensive review of this Progressive criticism, see generally William G. Ross, A Muted Fury: Populists, Progressives, and Labor Unions Confront the Courts, 1890–1937 (1994).

[237] United States v. Carolene Prods. Co., 304 U.S. 144, 152 n.4 (1938). On the footnote's paradigmatic importance for modern constitutional theory, see Robert M. Cover, *The Origins of Judicial Activism in the Protection of Minorities*, 91 Yale L.J. 1287 (1982).

[238] *See, e.g.*, Shaw v. Reno, 509 U.S. 630 (1993) (minority voting districts); R.A.V. v. City of St. Paul, 505 U.S. 377 (1992) (hate speech restriction); Lucas v. South Carolina Coastal Council, 505 U.S. 1003 (1992) (environmental land use regulation); City of Richmond v. J.A. Croson Co., 488 U.S. 469 (1989) (affirmative action); Buckley v. Valeo, 424 U.S. 1 (1976) (campaign finance regulation).

[239] *See, e.g.*, Reno v. ACLU, 117 S. Ct. 2329 (1997) (indecent speech); Romer v. Evans, 517 U.S. 620 (1996) (sexual orientation discrimination); United States v. Virginia, 518 U.S. 515 (1996) (sex discrimination); Lee v. Weisman, 505 U.S. 577 (1992) (school prayer); Batson v. Kentucky, 476 U.S. 79 (1986) (race discrimination); Roe v. Wade, 410 U.S. 113 (1973) (abortion).

[240] *See* Raoul Berger, Government by Judiciary: The Transformation of the Fourteenth Amendment (1977); Louis B. Boudin, Government by Judiciary (2 vols. 1932).

[241] *See, e.g.*, Bork, *supra* note 225, ch. 11; Ely, *supra* note 9, at 59 & n.** (noting the danger that "upper-middle-class judges" will impose "flagrantly elitist" values); Paul Brest, *Who Decides?*, 58 S. Cal. L. Rev. 661, 664, 670 (1985); Lino A. Graglia, *The Constitution, Community and Liberty*, 8 Harv. J.L. & Pub. Pol'y 291, 295 (1995).

[242] Romer v. Evans, 517 U.S. 620, 652 (1996) (Scalia, J., dissenting); *see also* United States v. Virginia, 518 U.S. 515, 567 (1996) (Scalia, J., dissenting) (accusing the Court, in striking down VMI's exclusion of women, of inscribing "the counter-majoritarian preferences of the society's law-trained elite into our Basic Law").

cultural bias of the federal judiciary yielded a constitutional jurisprudence that was somewhat more protective of property rights than was majoritarian politics, and possibly more nationalistic as well.[243] Since the constitutional revolution of the 1930s, though, social or cultural issues largely have displaced economic ones from the forefront of the constitutional agenda.[244] And on these issues, a culturally elite bias has roughly correlated with a politically liberal one. That is, on today's culture war issues—the place of religion in public life, abortion, pornography, gay rights, flag burning—liberal opinion tends to be strongly correlated with years of education and economic class.[245] It is this phenomenon of cultural elitism that, I think, most plausibly explains the remarkably liberal aspects of the "conservative" Burger and Rehnquist Courts' activism—landmark sex discrimination cases, protection for abortion rights, constitutional suspicion manifested toward the death penalty, dramatic expansion of free speech rights, continued

[243] On the Court's pre-1937 predisposition toward protecting property rights, see *supra* note 72 (citing cases); *see also* McCloskey, *supra* note 22, at 69 (noting that a Court "composed of judges who were inevitably drawn largely from the ranks of the 'haves' . . . was almost certain to throw its weight against the regulatory movement and on the side of the business community"). With regard to the nationalist bias, it is revealing that President Jefferson's and President Madison's Republican appointments to the Court went along with the great nationalizing decisions in *McCulloch* and *Gibbons*—a fact that drove Jefferson to distraction. *See* Carpenter, *supra* note 19, at 62, 74–76; Jessup, *supra* note 16, at 413, 423; Warren, *supra* note 16, at 545–47, 557–58. Interestingly, as early as the 1820s, congressmen hostile to the Court were noting the culturally elite biases of Supreme Court Justices, specifically in the context of proposals to terminate the practice of circuit riding. *See* Jessup, *supra* note 16, at 308 (Senator White of Tennessee defending circuit riding on the ground that if the Justices were "locked up" in the capital they would become mere "bookworms, without any practical knowledge"); *id.* at 415 (noting additional similar statements); Warren, *supra* note 16, at 678 (noting that both Daniel Webster and James Buchanan argued against terminating circuit duty in the 1820s in order to keep the Justices in touch with popular opinion).

[244] On the dramatic transition from the pre-1937 Court's preoccupation with economic issues, see, for example, Walton H. Hamilton & George D. Braden, *The Special Competence of the Supreme Court*, 50 Yale L.J. 1319 (1941); Louis Lusky, *Minority Rights and the Public Interest*, 52 Yale L.J. 1, 11 (1942); Eugene V. Rostow, *The Democratic Character of Judicial Review*, 66 Harv. L. Rev. 193, 201–03 (1952).

[245] For example, a Roper public opinion poll from 1998 found that only 26% of those without a high school education favored the Court's decision in *Roe v. Wade*, compared with 44% of those with a high school degree, 53% of those with some college education, and 70% of those with a college degree. A similarly strong correlation holds with regard to economic class. The same Roper poll found that 33% of those with an annual income less than $15,000 supported *Roe*, compared with 55% of those earning between $30,000 and $50,000, and 70% of those earning $75,000 and over. For fascinating findings about voting patterns in university towns on Michigan's 1972 abortion reform referendum, see Karrer, *supra* note 79, at 95.

Similar correlations hold for school prayer. A Roper poll in 1995 asked respondents whether a constitutional amendment permitting organized school prayer should be a top priority of Congress. Forty percent of those lacking a high school degree said yes, compared with 26% of those with a high school degree, and only 8% of those with a college degree. Similarly with regard to economic class, 44% of those with annual incomes less than $15,000 thought such an amendment should be a top priority for Congress, compared with 21% of those earning between $30,000 and $50,000, and just 9% of those with incomes between $50,000 and $75,000.

The same sort of correlation holds with regard to attitudes about homosexuality. A Roper public opinion poll from 1998 asked respondents whether high school sex education courses should or should not tell students that homosexuality is immoral. Among those lacking a high school degree, 51% thought that they should, compared with 38% of those with a high school degree, 30% of those with some college, and 23% of those with a college degree. With regard to class, 48% of those with annual incomes under $15,000 thought sex education courses should teach that homosexuality is immoral, compared with 31% of those with incomes between $50,000 and $75,000, and 22% of those with incomes over $75,000.

commitment to a strong separation of church and state, and so on.[246] Yet when economic issues reappear on the constitutional agenda in a guise other than now-maligned substantive due process, the Justices' culturally elite biases produce no politically liberal spin, for on issues of economic redistribution the correlation between politically liberal attitudes and years of education/economic class no longer holds. Thus the Burger and Rehnquist Courts have produced markedly conservative results on issues such as campaign finance reform,[247] regulatory takings and exactions,[248] and commercial speech regulation.[249] And on structural constitutional issues like federalism, where there is no discernable culturally elite bias, the conservative Justices' political biases have, unsurprisingly, yielded politically conservative results.[250]

Finally, our judicially enforceable constitutionalism is only marginally countermajoritarian. That the Justices represent the elite segment of society should not blind us to the fact that they are products of the same cultural milieu that enacts the legislation they are called upon to review. It seems likely, to put the point somewhat differently, that the cultural differences that separate the elite Justices from popular opinion are generally less significant than the similarities they share as a result of inhabiting the same historical moment. To take one specific example, the racial views of culturally elite Justices in 1954 (the year of *Brown*) probably were more similar to those of the general population in 1954 than to those of the cultural elite in 1896 (the year of *Plessy*).

For this reason, judicial review has only marginally countermajoritarian potential.[251] Not only are judges subject to indirect political checks, but, more importantly, they are bound by internal cultural constraints. They are part of society, and thus are unlikely to interpret the Constitution in ways that radically depart

[246] *See, e.g.*, Richmond Newspapers, Inc. v. Virginia, 448 U.S. 555 (1980) (freedom of speech); Roe v. Wade, 410 U.S. 113 (1973) (abortion); Furman v. Georgia, 408 U.S. 238 (1972) (death penalty); Reed v. Reed, 404 U.S. 71 (1971) (sex discrimination); Lemon v. Kurtzman, 403 U.S. 602 (1971) (church-state separation); *see also* Klarman, *Majoritarian Judicial Review, supra* note 28, at 548. *See generally* THE BURGER COURT: THE COUNTER-REVOLUTION THAT WASN'T (Vincent Blasi ed., 1983). For a similar explanation of Justice Powell's vote in *Roe*, see JEFFRIES, *supra* note 150, at 350–51 (noting "the surprising lack of antiabortion sentiment inside the Court").

[247] *See* Colorado Republican Fed. Campaign Comm. v. Federal Election Comm'n, 116 S. Ct. 2309 (1996); Buckley v. Valeo, 424 U.S. 1 (1976).

[248] *See* Dolan v. City of Tigard, 512 U.S. 374 (1994); Lucas v. South Carolina Coastal Council, 505 U.S. 1003 (1992); Nollan v. California Coastal Comm'n, 483 U.S. 825 (1987).

[249] *See, e.g.*, 44 Liquormart, Inc. v. Rhode Island, 517 U.S. 484 (1996); Virginia State Bd. of Pharmacy v. Virginia Citizens Consumer Council, Inc., 425 U.S. 748 (1976).

[250] *See* Printz v. United States, 117 S. Ct. 2365 (1997); City of Boerne v. Flores, 117 S. Ct. 2157 (1997); Seminole Tribe v. Florida, 517 U.S. 44 (1996); United States v. Lopez, 514 U.S. 549 (1995); New York v. United States, 505 U.S. 144 (1992). I do not mean to suggest that attitudes toward federalism are intrinsically linked with liberal and conservative political philosophies either. Just as political liberals during the *Lochner* era criticized judicial activism, so did they praise federalism, which could insulate state social welfare legislation from the Court's constitutional axe. *See, e.g.*, New State Ice Co. v. Liebmann, 285 U.S. 262, 310–11 (1932) (Brandeis, J., dissenting). In the political context of the 1990s, though, political liberals tend to support national power (probably because of the national government's greater redistributive capacities), while conservatives praise federalism. For the argument that positions on constitutional issues like federalism or separation-of-powers generally act as a camouflage for policy preferences, see LOUIS MICHAEL SEIDMAN & MARK V. TUSHNET, REMNANTS OF BELIEF: CONTEMPORARY CONSTITUTIONAL ISSUES 181–89 (1996).

[251] *See generally* MCCLOSKEY, *supra* note 22; DAHL, *supra* note 15; Friedman, *supra* note 79; Klarman, *Rethinking, supra* note 47; Girardeau A. Spann, *Pure Politics*, 88 MICH. L. REV. 1971 (1990). *See also* ROSENBERG, *supra* note 79 (denying the capacity of courts to produce significant social change).

from contemporary popular opinion. Only one who thinks about judicial review ahistorically and acontextually could subscribe to the romantic vision of the Court as countermajoritarian hero.[252] As I have put the point on another occasion, it is unrealistic to believe that the Court could have

> invalidated racial segregation in public schools before the dramatic transformation in American racial attitudes spawned by World War II, . . . forbidden sex discrimination before the rise of the women's movement, articulated a constitutional right to sexual autonomy before the burgeoning of the gay rights movement, or banned prayer from the public schools before the gradual undermining of the unofficial Protestant establishment.[253]

Most of the Court's famous individual rights decisions of the past half century involve either the Justices seizing upon a dominant national consensus and imposing it on resisting outliers or intervening on an issue where the nation is narrowly divided and awarding victory to one side or seeking to split the difference.[254] Neither of these paradigms fits the romantic vision of a heroically countermajoritarian Court.

III. A NORMATIVE APPRAISAL

If this description of our judicially enforceable constitutionalism is accurate, what is its normative appeal? At first blush, this question would seem virtually to answer itself. How in a democratic society ostensibly committed to the notion that "all men are created equal" and that each person's vote should count the same,[255] can one justify entrusting resolution of fundamental questions of social policy to an institution possessed of a culturally elite bias? I do not mean to suggest that the Constitution's Framers would have balked at endorsing such a regime; a principal objective of their Founding project was to create a governmental structure that would facilitate rule by the "better sort."[256] Of course, they also endorsed race, sex, and wealth restrictions on the franchise—positions that our society long ago discarded as inconsistent with the democratic premise that the interests of all

---

[252] I have tried elsewhere to explain why the myth nonetheless has persisted. *See* Klarman, *Rethinking, supra* note 47, at 18–31.

[253] *Id.* at 31.

[254] *See supra* notes 132–45 and accompanying text.

[255] *See* Reynolds v. Sims, 377 U.S. 533 (1964).

[256] *See, e.g.,* Edmund S. Morgan, Inventing the People: The Rise of Popular Sovereignty in England and America 260–79, 305 (1988); Rakove, *supra* note 16, at 139 (suggesting that what Madison sought in the Constitution was "the neutralization of public opinion"); Hobson, *supra* note 70, at 221–25; Gordon S. Wood, *Interests and Disinterestedness in the Making of the Constitution, in* Beyond Confederation: Origins of the Constitution and American National Identity 69, 72–76 (Richard Beeman et al. eds., 1987). Only the Founders' limited conception of the scope of judicial review, *see supra* notes 64–67 and accompanying text, would have inhibited their fond embrace of an institution with such antidemocratic possibilities.

Years later, Chief Justice Marshall and Justice Joseph Story did endorse broad judicial power as a method of checking the spread of popular democracy, a development they detested. On Story, see Newmyer, *supra* note 159, at 158–59, 178, 197. On Marshall, see the fascinating commentaries by Democratic newspapers upon his death reproduced in Warren, *supra* note 16, at 807–12; *cf.* Jessup, *supra* note 16, at 443–44 (noting that Chancellor Kent of New York, who shared a similar perspective with Marshall and Story, saw the Court as the nation's only salvation from Jacksonian democracy and opposed universal suffrage as too violent for "our excitable people").

persons should count equally.[257] Nor do I mean to suggest that the culturally elite bias inherent in judicial review has dramatic consequences; the limited counter-majoritarian capacity of the Court rules out that possibility. Yet even if the consequences of the Court's culturally elite bias are small, how can they be defended consistently with democratic premises?

It seems to me that there are three possible responses to this line of argument. First, one might contend that we enjoy no more consensus in our society about what democracy consists of than about how to resolve controversial constitutional questions such as abortion, affirmative action, or school prayer. Thus, for a court to refrain from imposing its culturally elite values by deferring to the political process involves a value choice that is every bit as controversial.[258] This argument is flawed. While it is true that we lack a consensus definition of what democracy is, there is widespread agreement as to what it is *not*. The notion that one segment of society should enjoy disproportionate influence on public decisionmaking simply because of its members' greater education or wealth seems inconsistent with our basic commitment to the political equality of all. Such a practice is roughly equivalent to affording certain individuals multiple votes, a practice that few persons today would defend as consistent with democratic principles.

Second, one might defend judicially enforceable constitutionalism, notwithstanding its systematic biases, on the ground that the values of the cultural elite are good ones. There is nothing incoherent about such an approach, defending constitutionalism in terms of the results it achieves. The problem with this mode of defense, however, is that it is a conversation stopper; it leaves no ground for an appeal to common values. If a principal function of constitutionalism is to provide a broadly acceptable method of resolving our disputes over controversial issues such as abortion and affirmative action, then it has failed in its purpose when the ultimate defense proffered is in terms of those very disputed values. Concretely, those who reject culturally elite values have no reason to endorse constitutionalism if its ultimate justification is the advancement of the values they repudiate. It is for this very reason that most justifications of constitutionalism, such as those canvassed in Part I, defend the practice in terms of more abstract values upon which it is hoped a broader consensus can be achieved, such as "precommitment," "checks and balances," or "minority rights."

Finally, it is always possible, as we have seen,[259] to circumvent the anti-democratic objection by positing popular consent. That is, if the People endorse judicially enforceable constitutionalism notwithstanding its culturally elite bias, then the practice becomes democratic by definition. So the ultimate question for me is the empirical one—do the American people consent to this system of judicially enforceable constitutionalism? If they do, then it is hard to raise objections of the anti-democratic variety against it. Why they should want to do so is, of course, an entirely different matter.

[257] *See, e.g.*, DAHL, *supra* note 15, at 84–87 (arguing that the notion of intrinsic equality of human beings is central to the defense of democracy); MAYO, *supra* note 85, at 113 ("The history of the franchise in recent times has been one of widening the classes of persons entitled to vote, a process which everywhere was regarded as a nearer approach to democracy.").

[258] *See, e.g.*, Ronald Dworkin, *The Forum of Principle*, 56 N.Y.U. L. REV. 469, 502–04 (1981); Thomas Nagel, *The Supreme Court and Political Philosophy*, 56 N.Y.U. L. REV. 519, 520 (1981); Lawrence Sager, *Rights Skepticism and Process-Based Responses*, 56 N.Y.U. L. REV. 417, 423–34 (1981); Wasserstrom & Seidman, *supra* note 226, at 102, 104–05.

[259] *See supra* notes 224–26 and accompanying text.

6

AN OVERLOOKED THEORY ON PRESIDENTIAL POLITICS
Rick Valelly

We often think and say that the most powerful person in the world is the president of the United States. That's where a counterintuitive and elegant theory by Stephen Skowronek comes in. Described and summarized in this article, Skowronek's theory shows that all presidencies fit into one of four categories. There are simple regularities in presidential governance since the Founding. By the time presidents complete their tenure in office they have conformed to them more often than not. Skowronek's finding thus identifies one of the great paradoxes of American politics: Presidential leadership is very limited. It is tightly circumscribed by the relationships among the president, the national party system, and the resilience of the historical "regime" (here you have to see the article for a definition of the concept) that each incoming president encounters upon entering office. Since its publication, the theory's predictions have been eerily confirmed by events: President Clinton was impeached and tried, for instance, and President George W. Bush launched a war—both actions predicted by Skowronek's theory.

The presidents who occupy a particular type of presidency generally end up thinking about what they do (and presidents are intensely self-conscious) in very similar terms. When they compare themselves with previous presidents they often identify with presidents that happen to be their "type," or they talk about the truly agenda-setting presidents—Jefferson, Jackson, Lincoln, Franklin D. Roosevelt, and Ronald Reagan—in ways that reveal a clear recognition of how and why they are not and cannot be that kind of president. Presidents of each type also do things with the office in remarkably parallel fashion.

• • •

A LITTLE-DISCUSSED THEORY of the American presidency has had startling, if unnoticed, success as a crystal ball. Stephen Skowronek, a chaired professor at Yale, is the author of *The Politics Presidents Make: Leadership from John Adams to Bill Clinton* (Harvard University Press, 1997), which is a revision of his 1993 book with the same main title but a slightly different subtitle, *Leadership from John Adams to George Bush*. The books have foretold such major events as Bill Clinton's impeachment and George W. Bush's tax cuts, as well as his drive for a second Gulf war.

At recent conferences on the presidency in Princeton, N.J., and London, there was little mention of the theory or Skowronek, nor were there round tables or panels about his work at the annual meeting of the American Political Science Association in Philadelphia over Labor Day weekend. A survey of 930 or so hits

From *Chronicle of Higher Education*, 31 October 2003. Reprinted by permission of Rick Valelly.

on the Internet for Skowronek's name indicates that no one seems to be commenting on his predictive achievements. Instead, a previous book on the origins and evolution of federal bureaucracies is widely cited.

The quiet over Skowronek's presidency books is ironic—and also rather troubling. It is ironic because political scientists say that we want our discipline to become a predictive science of political behavior, yet we seem to have overlooked one of those rare instances of apparent success. It is troubling because it suggests that stereotypes about what constitutes predictive science may be clouding our vision. Skowronek's theory is historical and qualitative—it doesn't have the right "look" for such science.

In aspiring to predictive power, political science has become sharply formal and analytic, innovatively adapting aspects of microeconomics, psychology, and the mathematics of social choice and game theory. Despite the strong social and professional cues to be on the lookout for working predictive theories, the continuing accomplishment of Skowronek's approach to understanding the presidency has gone unremarked.

To be sure, Skowronek never said in print that Bill Clinton would be impeached. But reading his book before the event, a clever reader (though, alas, I was not that reader) would have seen that the book's typology of presidents clearly implied such a crisis—the second instance of impeachment in American history. Also, even as George W. Bush took the oath of office from the chief justice, Skowronek's theory foretold several salient features of the current administration. The theory suggested we should look for Bush to be treated more deferentially than his predecessor by both the news media and the political opposition. Expect Bush to replicate the massive, signature tax cuts of Ronald Reagan, his philosophical mentor. Expect, too, that Bush will press for a war somewhere. Finally, be prepared for the possibility that in agitating for war Bush will run the risk of misleading the public and Congress about the rationale.

The predictive strengths of Skowronek's work are rooted in a brilliantly simple scheme for classifying presidents and their impact on American politics. The framework assumes two things.

First, presidents are elected into the most powerful office in America against the backdrop of what Skowronek calls a "regime." In other words, they don't start history anew the day they walk into the Oval Office. A lot of their job has been defined beforehand.

Regimes comprise a particular public philosophy, like the New Deal's emphasis on government intervention on behalf of citizens. Another element of a regime is the mix of policies that further its public philosophy. And a regime contains a "carrier party," a party energized and renewed by introducing the new program. After the initial excitement of the regime's first presidential leader (for instance, Franklin Roosevelt or Ronald Reagan), the party becomes the vehicle for ideas with which everyone has had some experience—say, the Medicare amendment of the Social Security Act, or the tax cuts under the current administration. Late in the life of a regime, the once-dominant but actually quite brittle governing party stands for worn-out ideas.

Skowronek suggests that there have been five such regimes: The first was inaugurated by Thomas Jefferson, the next by Andrew Jackson, the third by Abraham Lincoln, the fourth by Franklin Roosevelt, and the most recent by Ronald Reagan.

Skowronek's second simple assumption has to do with a president's "regime affiliation." Affiliation with or repudiation of the regime comes from the incoming president's party identity. New presidents from a party that has been out of power can and will repudiate the rival party's regime if it appears bankrupt. Presidents inaugurated under those circumstances call the country to a new covenant or a new deal. Recall Ronald Reagan's famous subversion of a '60s catchphrase when he declared, in his first inaugural address: "In this present crisis, government is not the solution but the problem. . . . It is no coincidence that our present troubles parallel and are proportionate to the intervention and intrusion in our lives that result from unnecessary and excessive growth of government. . . . So, with all the creative energy at our command, let us begin an era of national renewal." Even if he is not particularly successful in realizing the new public philosophy to which he has pinned his colors, this kind of a repudiate-and-renew president is widely hailed as a great innovator.

Alternatively, an incoming president might affiliate with an existing, strong regime but seek to improve it. Think here of Lyndon Johnson, whose career began during the later phases of the New Deal. As president he pushed for Medicare, the Great Society, and the War on Poverty. He expressed his filial piety by signing Medicare, an amendment to the Social Security Act of 1935, in the presence of Harry Truman. Think, too, of George W. Bush, who has won Reaganesque tax cuts that—together with increases in military spending—are likely to force a great reduction in government social-policy obligations, thus furthering Reagan's dream of ending individual dependence on government. In essence, then, a president strongly affiliated with a regime is a defender of the faith.

Paradoxically, though, such presidents can break their party in two, or at least preside over serious factional disagreements. Skowronek sketches various ways that can happen. One scenario involves war. Deeply conscious of how important it is to hold his party in line, a president can find war useful—and in a dangerous world, it isn't hard to find real enemies. But a president pushing for war risks the appearance of possessing ulterior motives, or seeming impatient. In early August 1964, for example, Lyndon Johnson stampeded the Senate into the Gulf of Tonkin Resolution and then took the resolution, after his landslide over Goldwater, as Congressional authorization for a military buildup in Vietnam. Any subsequent military or diplomatic defeat following such an apparent manipulation of Congress will spark party factionalism, as the president's party colleagues scramble to keep control. It isn't hard, of course, to see how all this might apply to the current Bush administration. Criticism of Bush's plans for, and commitment to, reconstruction in Iraq influenced his call for a doubling in spending there.

To take a third general type, a new president may have no choice but to affiliate with a weak regime and try to muddle through. He characteristically does that by stepping away from the regime's stale public philosophy, emphasizing instead his administrative competence. Such was the approach of Herbert Hoover and Jimmy Carter. That sort of president is a caretaker of a threadbare public philosophy, doing his best with a bad historical hand, often with great ingenuity, as revisionist scholarship on Hoover has shown—for instance, the extent to which he had coherent programs for addressing unemployment and collapsing farm prices that foreshadowed key elements of the New Deal.

Yet another kind of president is someone who, like the innovator, repudiates the regime—but does so when it is still going strong in people's hearts and minds.

That kind of oppositional president seeks some "third way," even though other members of his party are convinced that there is little wrong with the reigning political philosophy. He quickly comes to seem disingenuous, even dangerous, to many of his contemporaries.

Andrew Johnson was unilaterally reconstructing the ex-Confederacy in ways that subverted Republican plans made by Congress during the Civil War. He was eventually impeached when he dismissed Secretary of War Edwin Stanton, the cabinet ally of Johnson's Congressional Republican opponents. Stanton's dismissal flouted the Tenure of Office Act giving the Senate say over dismissal of officials whose appointment it had approved. That provided the legal fodder for the impeachment. Richard Nixon advocated many liberal policies—proposing, for instance, a guaranteed national income, an idea that now seems hopelessly quaint. But he also disturbed and startled many of his opponents by openly regarding them as dangerous enemies warranting surveillance and dirty tricks, and that set the stage for his resignation. Clinton hired the dark prince of triangulation, Dick Morris. Clinton too was impeached and then tried after a desperately zealous independent prosecutor forced him into a public lie, under oath, about his affair with Monica Lewinsky.

Third-way presidents get the worst of both worlds—seeming untrustworthy both to the partisan opposition and to parts of their own base because they pursue policies that threaten to remove existing party polarities. It is striking that eventually they blunder into some act heinous enough to be plausibly treated as a crime.

In short, there is a simple two-by-two classification undergirding Skowronek's historical account. One dimension of classification is "strength of regime," which ranges from strong and commanding to collapsing and discredited. The other dimension is strength of the president's affiliation with the existing regime. That affiliation can range from none (repudiation, as with Reagan, or opposition, as with Clinton) through weak (Hoover or Carter) to strong (Lyndon Johnson or George W. Bush).

To be sure, a tale of recurring patterns that can be surmised from a two-by-two classification seems very distant from the presidency as it is experienced by the president, and by citizens, day by day. Conscious that a president's personal strengths matter greatly, specialists on the presidency, aided by recent theories of emotional intelligence, sort presidents according to their interpersonal skills. They also analyze the application of formal and informal powers: how presidents fare with Congress under different conditions of party control and by type of policy request, whether they move public opinion when they would like to, and how well they resist the inevitable undertow of public disillusionment. Scholars ask, as well, how the institutional evolution of the executive branch magnifies or frustrates such applications of temperament and skill. Finally, formal legal analysts assess any changes in the balance of executive and legislative power. In other words, in the subfield of presidency studies, most analysts look over the president's shoulder. They hew to the actual experience of being an overworked politician who makes literally thousands of anticipated and unanticipated decisions in the face of enormous ambiguity and uncertainty.

In the end, though, there is no gainsaying the performance of Skowronek's theory. Yes, there are lots of alternative explanations for the major events it has predicted. But that is precisely where the counterintuitive parsimony of Skowronek's theory comes in. By parsimony, political scientists mean successfully explaining the widest possible range of outcomes with the fewest possible variables. In 1993, there was no other coherent theory of presidential politics that anticipated the full range of events that Skowronek's theory did: impeachment of a Clinton-like president; and, if the Republicans recaptured the White House, tax cuts, war, and related outcomes like the news media's doting (at least for a while) on a chief executive who would use the rhetoric of common cause in a time of crisis.

Presidents, Skowronek's theory insists, are highly constrained actors, seemingly fated to replay variations on one of the four roles he outlines. That this seems fatalistic or cyclical—unlike the complicated lived experience of the presidency—doesn't lessen the theory's power. If the model works, then the right question to ask is not whether it is realistic, but why it works.

Of course, the prerequisite for such a discussion is adequate recognition that the theory *is* working—which is what seems to have eluded Skowronek. Here a subtle scientistic prejudice against his chosen scholarly identity may be in play. If so, the silence about his work raises an important question about the contemporary organization of American political science.

A bit of intellectual history is in order. The sort of work for which Skowronek is known is often called "American political development," or APD. (A disclosure: My own professional identity is closest to APD.) APD scholars roam interpretively across huge swaths of American political history. Their work so far has been qualitative, and thus tends to eschew any number-crunching beyond descriptive statistics.

For many years, APD's critics regularly knocked it as "traditional," and thus not "modern," political science. They often called it "bigthink"—speculative, broad rumination without any scientific value.

Those days are now happily over. APD is much less controversial than it was when Skowronek and Karen Orren, of the University of California at Los Angeles, founded the subfield's flagship journal, *Studies in American Political Development,* in 1985. Since then, other journals with the same focus have appeared—for example, the *Journal of Policy History*—and APD work has been published in mainstream refereed journals, too. The outgoing president of the American Political Science Association, Theda Skocpol of Harvard, a widely known social-policy scholar, has played an important role in mainstreaming APD work.

But does that acceptance disguise a lingering refusal to acknowledge that APD scholarship can say as much about the present and future of American politics as other kinds of research? I fear that many political scientists draw a line in their minds between "real," possibly predictive political science—work that requires lots of data, big computer runs, formal modeling, and regular National Science Foundation funds—and work that they consider pleasantly stimulating but not scientific enough to serve as a reliable guide to, or predictor of, events. It would be a sad paradox if, while honoring the appearance of science, we let that prejudice block powerful and elegant predictive theories like Skowronek's from coming to the fore.

7

THE CURSE OF THE VICE-PRESIDENCY
Michael Nelson

How did Dick Cheney come to be such a major player in American politics? This piece provides the answer by tracing the evolution of the vice-presidency. In doing this, its author, Michael Nelson, also communicates something subtle and vital about the office of the president, namely, that the president is at the center of a presidency, a complex web of organizations located in the executive branch.

The "presidency" is sufficiently complex and large that the president has considerable difficulty asserting control over its many parts—which is where the vice-president comes in. Unlike the cabinet officers and all of the other officers whom the president appoints, the vice-president is elected along with the president and his or her fortunes are tightly lashed to those of the president. Of the people in any president's presidency, the vice-president is among those likely to be particularly responsive and faithful to what the president wants to do, and is for that reason useful to the person who occupies the Oval Office. Paradoxically this has caused the office of vice-president to become increasingly influential—indeed to become a stepping stone to the presidency.

• • •

UNTIL THE ELECTION of George Bush the elder in 1988, no incumbent vice president had been elected president since Martin Van Buren in 1836. (Bush opened his first post-election news conference by saying, "It's been a long time, Marty.") Yet it also is true that, starting with Harry S. Truman in 1945, five of the last 10 presidents have been former vice presidents: Truman, Lyndon B. Johnson, Richard Nixon, Gerald Ford, and Bush. Death or resignation accounts for the ascensions of Truman, Johnson, and Ford, but each of them except Ford subsequently won at least one presidential election on his own.

Does being vice president make Al Gore a stronger contender for president or a weaker one? Until Gore agreed to be Bill Clinton's running mate in 1992, he was pursuing a different route to an eventual run at the White House. After youthful dalliances with journalism and the ministry, Gore had ascended rapidly, winning his father's old House seat in central Tennessee in 1976, then moving up to the Senate in 1984 and winning re-election by a landslide in 1990, when he carried every county in the state. In 1988 he'd made a presentable if premature run at the Democratic nomination. Gore was the youngest serious contender for a major-party nomination in this century, finishing third in a field of eight.

Reprinted with permission from Michael Nelson. "The Curse of the Vice-Presidency," *The American Prospect*, Volume 11, Number 17: July 31, 2000. The American Prospect, 2000 L Street NW, Suite 717, Washington DC 20036. All rights reserved.

The nature of Gore's springboard changed dramatically in May 1992. Clinton placed Gore on his list of 40 potential running mates, had him checked out by Democratic Party eminence Warren Christopher, then kept Gore on the list when he pared it down to five. On June 30, Clinton and Gore had the sort of two-souls-become-one meeting (incredibly, they had scarcely known each before then) that is scheduled for one hour and lasts for three. The call to Gore's Carthage, Tennessee, home came shortly before midnight on July 8.

The roots of the vice presidency's uncertain political status are embedded deeply in the Constitution and in two centuries of history. The Constitutional Convention of 1787 created the vice presidency as a weak office, but also a prestigious one. The Constitution empowered the vice president only to be "president of the Senate, but shall have no Vote, unless they be equally divided." It was the election system that brought the prestige. Every four years, presidential electors were charged to cast two votes for president: The first-place finisher in the electoral college won the office, and the person who finished second became vice president. In awarding the vice presidency to the runner-up in the presidential election, the Constitution thus made the vice president the presumptive heir to the presidency. Not surprisingly, the nation's first two vice presidents, John Adams and Thomas Jefferson, were elected to be its second and third presidents.

The arrival of political parties nominating not just a candidate for president, but a vice presidential candidate as well, rendered this system unworkable. The breakdown came in 1800 when, as a result of all of the Democratic-Republican electors faithfully discharging their duty to vote for both Jefferson and his vice presidential running mate, Aaron Burr, a tie vote for president occurred between the two nominees, and it took the House of Representatives weeks to resolve in Jefferson's favor.

The 12th Amendment, which was passed in time for the 1804 election, solved this problem neatly by instructing electors to cast one vote for president and a separate vote for vice president. But the amendment had a disastrous unintended side effect on the vice presidency: It left the office weak and, by stripping the vice president of his claim to be the second-most qualified person in the country to be president, took away its prestige as well. From 1804 on, talented and ambitious politicians shied away from vice presidential nominations. "I do not propose to be buried until I am dead," sniffed Daniel Webster when he was offered the Whig Party nomination in 1848. Ancient has-beens (six vice presidents died in office, all of natural causes, between 1812 and 1899) and middle-aged never-wases (George M. Dallas? Daniel D. Tompkins?) took their place.

RESURRECTING A DEAD OFFICE

Although the vice presidency is still constitutionally weak, the contrast between the political prestige of the nineteenth-century version of the office and the twentieth-century version is stark. Except for Van Buren, no nineteenth-century vice president was even renominated by his party's convention for a second term as vice president, much less nominated to run for president. Starting with William Howard Taft's vice president, James S. Sherman, however, every twentieth-century vice president who sought a second term has been renominated, and nine of them (nearly half) have gone on to receive a presidential nomination. Four nineteenth-century vice presidents succeeded to the presidency when the elected president died, but none of them was nominated to run for a full presidential term. The best of the four—Chester A. Arthur—was mediocre. The other three—John Tyler, Millard Fillmore, and Andrew Johnson—ran the gamut from bad to awful. In the twentieth century, not only were all five successor presidents—Theodore Roosevelt, Calvin Coolidge, Truman, Johnson, and Ford—renominated for president by their party, but all except Ford (who came very close) were elected. As a group, historians actually rank them higher than the century's elected presidents.

The record of vice presidential prestige has been even more compelling since the end of World War II. Starting in 1948, the vice presidential candidate as often as not has been the more experienced member of the ticket in high government office, including recent nominees such as Walter F. Mondale in 1976, Bush in 1980, Lloyd Bentsen in 1988, and Gore in 1992. Vice presidents have become the presumptive front-runners for their party's presidential nomination. Starting with Nixon in 1960, every elected vice president except Dan Quayle has led in a majority of the Gallup polls that measure the party rank and file's pre-convention preferences for president. Again excepting Quayle, all eight of the postwar vice presidents who have sought their party's presidential nomination have won it.

The roles and resources of the vice presidency also have grown in recent years. The office is larger and more prominent than in the past—in the terminology of political science, it has been "institutionalized." As recently as the mid-1970s, vice presidents hung their hats in the Capitol and the Old Executive Office Building, arranged their own housing, and were forced to crib speechwriters from the White House. Today they enjoy a large and professional staff, a West Wing office, a separate line item in the executive budget, and a grand official residence—the Admiral's House at the Naval Observatory. The office also has been institutionalized in the broader sense that more—and more substantial—vice presidential activities are now taken for granted. These include regular private meetings with the president, a wide-ranging role as senior presidential adviser, membership on the National Security Council, full intelligence briefings, access to the Oval Office paper flow, public advocacy of the administration's programs and leadership, a leadership role in the party second only to the president, sensitive diplomatic missions, attendance at cabinet meetings, and serving as a presidential liaison to congressional leaders and interest groups.

The reasons for the enhanced status of the vice presidency in government and politics are several. At the turn of the twentieth century, the rise of national news media (mass circulation magazines and newspaper wire services) and a new style of active political campaigning elevated the visibility and prestige of the vice president, which made the office more appealing to a better class of political leaders. In the 1900 election, the Republican nominee, Theodore Roosevelt, won widespread publicity and accumulated political IOUs from local politicians in nearly every state by becoming the first vice presidential candidate in history to campaign vigorously across the country. During the 1920s and 1930s, the roster of vice presidents included a speaker of the House, a Senate majority leader, and a Nobel Prize–winning cabinet member.

In 1940 Franklin D. Roosevelt, who had run (and lost) for vice president himself in 1920, successfully claimed for presidential candidates the right to name their running mates. In the past, party leaders had made that decision. They typically used it to pair the nominee for president with a vice presidential candidate from the opposite wing of the party, thereby discouraging the president from ever trusting the vice president personally or entrusting him with useful responsibilities in office. Voters want vice presidents to be loyal to the president as much as presidents do. This allows the president to choose his running mate virtually assured that such loyalty would be forthcoming.

Finally, after 1945, the combination of Truman's woefully unprepared succession to the presidency when Roosevelt died (Truman was at best dimly aware of the existence of the atom bomb and the Allies' plans for the postwar world) and the proliferation of nuclear weapons heightened public concern that the vice president be a leader who is ready and able to step into the presidency at a moment's notice.

A VICE PRESIDENTIAL CONSTITUTION

As voters increasingly have come to judge vice presidential nominees by their fitness to succeed to the presidency, most candidates for president have learned that, in filling the second slot on the ticket, they can do well politically by doing good for the country. As Hamilton Jordan put it in a 1976 memo to his candidate, Jimmy Carter, "The best politics is to select a person who is accurately perceived by the American people as being qualified and able to serve as president if that should become necessary."

The Constitution has been altered during the last half century in ways that have redounded to the benefit of vice presidents. The 25th Amendment, which was enacted in 1967, focused almost entirely on the vice presidency. The amendment declared, at last, that when the president dies, resigns, or is removed from office, "the Vice President shall become President" for the remainder of the four-year term. Vice presidents—nine in all (how's that for a stepping-stone to the presidency?)—had been doing exactly that since John Tyler, upon William Henry Harrison's untimely death (after one month in office) in 1841, declared himself president rather than acting president, ignoring the considerable congressional grumbling that ensued. At the time, this move had almost the character of a coup, since many thought the vice president had the right to serve only as interim chief executive until a special election could be called.

Indeed, until the 25th Amendment was enacted, the language of the Constitution remained vague enough to admit just that interpretation. James Madison's extensive notes of the debates at the Constitutional Convention indicate that a special presidential election was the framers' true intention. The key phrase that ended up in Article II of the original Constitution said that if the president dies, resigns, is removed by impeachment, or is unable "to discharge the Powers and Duties of the said Office, the Same shall devolve on the Vice President." The Same what? The president's "Powers and Duties" or "the said Office"—that is, the presidency itself? The framers meant only the powers and duties and only in a custodial capacity, but through careless drafting they did not say so clearly in the final text. Because Madison had embargoed his papers, his notes of the convention were not yet in circulation when Harrison died, and all the delegates were dead. Tyler's stubbornness constituted a successful fait accompli that set the precedent for all of his successors to follow. But it took the 25th Amendment to settle the succession question once and for all.

The amendment did more than tidy up a constitutional infelicity. It also made the vice president the crucial actor in determining whether a president is disabled: Unless the vice president agrees that the president is physically or mentally unable to serve, nothing can be done. Finally, the amendment provided that whenever the vice presidency becomes vacant (by 1967, this had happened 16 times during the nation's first 36 presidencies), the president will nominate a new vice president with congressional confirmation. So prestigious had the vice presidency become that in 1976, Americans barely noticed that their national bicentennial celebration was presided over by two men, President Ford and Vice President Nelson A. Rockefeller, who had attained their offices not through election but by being appointed vice president.

Equally significant in constitutional terms was the 22nd Amendment, which imposed a two-term limit on the president in 1951. Just as nobody had meant to damage the vice presidency politically with the enactment of the 12th Amendment in 1804, nobody was trying to enhance the vice president's political status when the 22nd Amendment limited presidential tenure. But the two-term limit made it possible for the vice president to step forward as a presidential candidate early in the president's second term, rather than wait in the wings until the president decided what he wanted to do. All three vice presidents who have served second-term presidents since the 22nd Amendment was enacted have made good use of this opportunity: Nixon in 1960, Bush in 1988, and now Gore.

In all, Gore inherited an impressive office when he became vice president in 1993. He has contributed to the power and prestige of the office as well: heading the administration's reinventing government initiative, serving as an important diplomatic channel to Russia and other former Soviet republics, filling the bureaucracy with political allies, deflating strong opposition to the North American Free Trade Agreement when he shredded Ross Perot in a televised debate, developing the Telecommunications Act of 1996 and persuading Congress to pass it, and stiffening the president's spine at crucial moments. "You can get with the goddamn program!" Gore famously told Clinton when the president was vacillating on his 1993 economic plan—and Clinton did. The conventional wisdom about the Gore vice presidency is absolutely true. No vice president in history has been more influential.

Still, the question remains: Is being vice president a blessing or a curse for a talented political leader like Gore who is trying to win the presidency? The answer comes in two parts, with the easy part first. Service as vice president is clearly the most direct route to winning a party's presidential nomination. There is a downside to the vice presidency, of course, especially the certain prospect of being a steady source of merriment for late-night television comedians. But consider what vice presidents seeking to be nominated for president have going for them.

In addition to the opportunity for early fundraising and organization-building that the 22nd Amendment affords and the likelihood that the vice president is already a leader of some stature, vice presidents derive two other benefits from the office in their pursuit of a presidential nomination. The first is that their ongoing activities as party leader—campaigning across the country during elections, raising funds at other times—and as public advocate of the administration and its policies uniquely situate them to win friends among the political activists who typically dominate the nominating process. (Such campaigning also is good experience for a presidential candidacy.) Second, the recent growth in the governmental responsibilities and resources of the vice presidency has made it a more prestigious position and thus a more plausible stepping-stone to the presidency. Substantive matters like international diplomacy and symbolic ones like the trappings of the office—not just the mansion and Air Force Two, but even the new vice presidential seal that displays an eagle, wings spread, with a claw full of arrows and a starburst at its head (the eagle in the old seal seemed rather sedentary)—attest to the prestige of the office.

Altogether, the modern vice president typically is an experienced and talented political leader who is loyal to the president and admired by the party—an ideal formula for securing a presidential nomination and one that Gore executed skillfully this spring. Exit surveys during the Democratic primaries and caucuses showed Gore winning overwhelming support from voters who approved of Clinton's performance as president. Needless to say, such voters made up the vast majority of those who turned out at the polls. Gore's worst moment in the nomination campaign was, in a sense, the exception that demonstrated the rule. The vice president's zeal as a fundraiser for Clinton and the Democratic National Committee in 1995 and 1996 ("Is it possible to do a reallocation for me to take more of the events and the calls?" he asked in a memo) gave former Senator Bill Bradley an opening among independent voters last fall. But it also strengthened Gore's bond with Democratic activists, which turned out to be much more important.

LOYAL TO A FAULT

Winning the party's nomination for president is no small thing, but it is not the main thing. For all their advantages in getting nominated, vice presidents have had an unusually hard time closing the deal in November. To be sure, the so-called Van Buren syndrome can be overstated: Of the 34 vice presidents who served between Van Buren and Bush, only seven even tried to run for president, and two of them—Nixon in 1960 and Humphrey in 1968—came very close to winning. But vice presidents carry burdens into the fall campaign that are as firmly grounded in their office as the advantages they bring to a nominating contest.

Indeed, some of the activities of the modern vice presidency that are most appealing to party activists may repel other voters. Days and nights spent fertilizing the party's grass roots with fervent, sometimes slashing rhetoric can alienate those who look to the presidency for leadership that unifies rather than divides. Gore's blurt to a postimpeachment rally of Democratic congressmen that Clinton "will be regarded in the history books as one of our greatest presidents" doubtless warmed the cockles of yellow dog Democratic hearts, but it seemed wildly excessive to almost everyone else. The woodenness that many people attribute to Gore is partly an artifact of the hundreds of vice presidential moments he has spent standing motionless and silent in the background while Clinton has spoken animatedly to the cameras.

Certain institutional qualities of the modern vice presidency also handicap the vice president turned presidential candidate. Vice presidents seldom get to take credit for the successes of the administration: That is a presidential prerogative. But they can count on being attacked for all of the administration's shortcomings. Such attacks allow no effective response. A vice president who tries to stand apart from the White House will alienate the president and cause voters to wonder why the criticisms were not voiced earlier. Gore did himself no good, for example, when he spent the evening of his official announcement for president telling the 20/20 audience that Clinton's behavior in the Monica Lewinsky affair was "inexcusable" or when he later dissented from administration policy on Elián Gonzalez. A vice president's difficulties are only compounded when it comes to matters of substantive public policy. Let Gore offer a new proposal, and Bush demands to know why he has hidden it under his hat until now.

Vice presidents can always say that loyalty to the president forecloses public disagreement, but that course is no less perilous politically. The public that values loyalty in a vice president disdains that quality as soon as he bids to become president. Strength, vision, and independence are what people look for then—the very qualities that vice presidents almost never get to display. Polls that show Gore trailing Bush by around 20 percentage points in the category of leadership are less about Bush and Gore than about the vice presidency. Bush's father trailed Michael S. Dukakis by a similar margin in the summer of 1988.

The political handicaps that vice presidents carry into the general election are considerable. They need not be insurmountable. As with all things vice presidential, much depends on the presidents they serve.

One of the main reasons that Nixon and Humphrey lost, for example, is that their presidents were so unhelpful. Every Poli Sci 100 student knows what Dwight D. Eisenhower said when a reporter asked him to name a single "major idea of [Nixon's] you had adopted" as president: "If you give me a week, I might think of one." (Less well-known is that a week later, Eisenhower still had nothing to say.) Johnson treated Humphrey with all the spitefulness of which he was capable as soon as it became clear that the Democratic convention was not going to draft him for another term despite his earlier withdrawal from the race. In true vice presidential style, Humphrey carried Johnson's water on Vietnam for four years, only to have the president threaten repeatedly that if he broke even slightly with the administration line, there would be political hell to pay. When Humphrey, ignoring yet another Johnson warning, finally did speak out in favor of a bombing pause just five weeks before the election, his poll numbers began a steep ascent. As Humphrey later said, he didn't lose the election to Nixon; he just ran out of time.

In contrast, Van Buren benefited enormously from his association with President Andrew Jackson, who regarded his vice president's election to the presidency as validation of the transformation he had wrought in American politics. Ronald Reagan was equally committed to Bush's success, putting ego aside to praise (even inflate) the vice president's contributions to what the president began calling the "Reagan-Bush administration." Reagan's popularity was of even greater benefit to his vice president. Bush won the votes of 80 percent of those who approved of Reagan's performance as president; he lost nine-to-one among those who disapproved. Eighty percent of many is more than 90 percent of few: Bush was elected.

Clinton combines Jackson's belief that his legacy is closely tied to his vice president's political success with Reaganesque approval ratings. If there is such a thing as "Clinton fatigue," it must be the exhaustion felt by those who have always hated him but have never been able to persuade the rest of the country that they are right. Clinton's job approval rating has been in the 60 percent-plus range for nearly four years—the highest and most enduring numbers for a second-term president in the history of polling. He has made it clear that all of his vast political talents are at Gore's disposal from now until November—including his ability, not often seen, to shine the spotlight on someone other than himself. Much to Clinton's credit, he remained steadfast last fall when Gore, in full panic mode, sometimes went out of his way to distance himself from the president.

As much as they will help, though, Clinton's efforts and popularity will not be enough to elect Gore. At the end of the day, candidates for president win or lose their own elections. "You're number two," says Gore, "and whether it's in politics or business or the professions, you have to make a transition from being number two to number one." But the president's assistance, joined with full use of the advantages the vice president derives from his own office, suggests that Gore's decision to seek the vice presidency instead of staying in the Senate eight years ago was his best available avenue to the White House.

8

LEGISLATION
David R. Mayhew

This article was long tucked away in an obscure publication—but it deserves a much broader readership than it has had. Mayhew covers a huge range of debates and questions about Congress very succinctly while sustaining a clear focus on who and what make Congress tick. But the article is much better than simply a learned tour of the issues that always come up when Congress is discussed within and without the profession of political science. It builds powerfully toward a dissection of the correspondence between the habits of mind and debate that pervade Congress, on the one hand, and those that can be found on editorial pages, in civics classes, and in ordinary conversation, on the other. As Mayhew says, this has to do with "language and style of thinking." He pictures Congress as a place "where ordinary-language, commonsense ways of thinking percolate upward from the public to permeate lawmaking processes and laws." Mayhew then briskly catalogues ten "cognitive grooves" (as he calls them), that is, ten recurring ways in which legislators talk as they legislate—and the far-reaching effects that these "cognitive grooves" have had on what American government has done and does.

Mayhew insists on treating Congress realistically and on drawing out the full implications of its basic institutional facts. It is a popularly elected assembly whose members paddle their own canoes and who are elected separately from the president and answer to a wide range of different kinds of people and places. Congress is one of the great legislatures of the world— but it is not a great legislature because it is a debating society or a model of deliberative rationality, as anyone who has spent anytime with C-SPAN knows. It is a great legislature because its members are pragmatic, energetic "doers" instinctively attuned to their constituencies and to how they think and talk about public issues.

• • •

STUDENTS OF GOVERNMENTS and of what they do apply both functional and structural typologies. "Rule-making," "rule application," and "rule adjudication" are contemporary terms designating some basic and familiar functions (see Almond and Powell 1966, chap. 6), and of course legislatures, executive or administrative organs, and courts make up a familiar set of structures. An early lesson in most courses in comparative politics teaches that functions do not reside according to any neat one-to-one pattern in structures.

Legislatures, for example, are commonly regarded as the bodies most responsible for rule-making, at least in constitutional states; but in fact they also act in other capacities not readily captured by the basic triad of functions; they commonly deal with citizen grievances, express public opinion, and oversee the administration of laws. General rule-making, the province of legislatures, is also exercised by executive officials, courts, and administrative agencies. In the case of civil rights regulations in the United States, the Supreme Court ordered in the mid-1950s that school systems be desegregated "with all deliberate speed"; the presidency initiated in the enactment of the Public Accommodations Act of 1964 and the Voting Rights Act of 1965; the Equal Employment Opportunity Commission and other administrative units led the development of national rules on affirmative action.

Since institutions evolve, and some new ones are even intentionally created, the question of the functions to be located in each structure is a live and practical one. American regulatory agencies, commonly mandated both to make general rules and to apply them and adjudicate disputes about them, are a multifunctional innovation of the industrial era, variously reshaped decade by decade. The presidency of the French Fifth Republic is an institution rich in functional capacity, designed to perform tasks not very well accomplished by any of the institutions of the Fourth Republic. The elected transnational parliament of the European Economic Community is a new structure in search of consequential functions, in some respects an interesting analogue to the fledgling United States Congress of the 1790s.

Common sense, ancient wisdom, and contemporary scholarship supply at least a number of considerations for any general statement on the appropriate structural location of functions. Within the context of the United States, such considerations turn, for example, on the capacities of legislatures, courts, and administrative agencies as makers of general rules. (For sources for this passage, see Horowitz 1977, chaps. 2, 7; Lorch 1969, chaps. 1, 2; Shapiro 1968, chap. 1; Huntington 1965.) Nine distinctions stand out.

1. In many policy areas, agency personnel are trained as professionals, whereas judges and legislators are not.
2. Agency personnel deal in their policy areas as specialists; so, to an important extent, do many legislatures; except in specialized courts, judges deal as generalists.
3. Bargaining and compromise are routine and legitimate in decision-making among formally equal legislators, but not—or not to a great extent—in agency hierarchies or among judges—though agencies bargain and compromise in dealing with each other, judges participate with other court personnel in plea bargaining, and juries commonly proceed by compromise.
4. Agencies and pertinent sets of legislators often build close relations with outside client groups; courts do not.
5. Agencies give sustained attention to what goes on in their policy areas; legislators, by comparison, give episodic attention; court attention is on an ad hoc basis.
6. Agencies and legislatures are capable of taking the initiative in policy areas; courts wait for cases to be brought.
7. Agencies can generate studies that turn up elaborate social information; legislators can do so as well, although their constructions of reality rely

heavily on what they learn from constituents and interest groups; courts ordinarily have before them only the facts of cases, which may supply poor guides to general social realities.

8. Agencies and legislatures commonly set out plans for the future, whereas courts ordinarily render judgments on situations of the past.

9. Most legislatures, like elected executives but unlike agency personnel and judges—in practice, even elected judges—serve in a relation of formal accountability to outside electorates.

In the eye of publics, this last circumstance confers legitimacy on legislators; it also makes them especially interesting to students of democracy and representation. The term "to legislate," it should be noted, is not, in ordinary Western parlance, an exact synonym of the functional term "to make rules." "Legislate" and its noun form "legislation" carry a connotation of structure as well as functions; to legislate is to make rules in a formal process, where one or more of the approving bodies constitute a "legislature" and where at least one of the bodies of the legislature is an elected assembly.

The actual role a legislature plays in legislating may be small or large. The role of the British Parliament is relatively small; in British lawmaking, cabinet and civil service carry most of the burden. The roles of postwar German and Italian parliaments are somewhat larger, those of the Swedish and Dutch parliaments substantially larger, and those of the United States Congress a great deal larger. These and other legislatures may be arranged along a continuum running from "arenas"—the British case—through "transformative assemblies"—legislatures that do a great deal of instigating on their own, the extreme example being the uniquely influential United States Congress (Polsby 1975; on the British case, see also Walkland 1968).

Congress warrants close inspection. For anyone interested in what happens when a legislature is established to write laws, freed from the obligation of sustaining a government, supplied an electoral base, and accorded considerable influence, the United States Congress furnishes the most rewarding testing ground. Having marshaled nine generalities, I shall proceed by delving into particularities, past and present, of the United States Congress, following what might be called a logic of the best-developed case.

Such logic would lead anyone with an interest in cabinet government to take a close look, covering past and present, at the Westminster model in Britain; those interested in decentralized federalism to inspect Canada; students of "consociational" politics to examine the Netherlands; those concerned with the functions of ombudsmen to track them down in Scandinavia; researchers on the evolution from authoritarian to democratic institutions to examine contemporary Spain; and so on. Studying a best-developed case risks identifying particularities that are no more than idiosyncrasies. Nevertheless, anyone concerned with what happens when a representative national assembly—or, more precisely, a two-part assembly—is allowed to function as a specialized legislative institution should ponder what the United States Congress has done and become over two centuries. (Unless specified otherwise, I shall use the term "Congress" to refer to both national houses—the constitutional and coequal partnership of the Senate and the House of Representatives.)

I shall write about legislation by writing about legislating—the process that generates the product. This course, natural to a political scientist, is, I trust, a useful one. In principle, the product is anything written formally into resolutions or laws—budgetary resolutions, laws authorizing expenditures or appropriating money, regulatory statutes covering corporate or individual behavior, laws prescribing the structure or functions of the branches of government, resolutions declaring judgments on events of the day, laws on pork barrel projects up through important matters of state. All these are formally enactments of Congress, although, of course, in recent decades, the presidency and the agencies have become increasingly important as suppliers of bills and ideas to Capitol Hill.

I shall frame my discussion of congressional process in a fashion that implies answers, or at least shapes speculation about possible answers, to two general questions of interest to students of law and society: What is the nature of whatever ends up on the statute books? How much legitimacy should be assigned to whatever emanates from legislative processes and ends up on the statute books? I shall set out briefly some major kinds of scholarly thinking on what congressional legislating amounts to or ought to amount to and indicate where fuller statements may be found.

The essay is in three parts. First, I shall consider some theories, assertions, accounts, prescriptions, and the like, in which Congress appears as a *passive* institution—a place where the influence of outside individuals, groups, and institutions is felt and recorded. The second section will offer a consideration of a number of scholarly organizing concepts in which Congress figures as an *active* institution—a set of members who make their own specifiable imprint on the law. Most of the treatments covered in these parts offer at least a grain of truth; it should be noted that the distinction between *active* and *passive* is sometimes blurred. The third part of the article consists of a piece of speculation on a subject insufficiently covered in scholarship—the impact of public opinion on congressional lawmaking.

CONGRESS AS A PASSIVE INSTITUTION

A vast amount of scholarship dealing with the United States Congress during the last century focuses on the outside forces that are said to influence congressional lawmaking, for better or worse, or that might usefully be induced to do so. This concern is not surprising, given that Congress was set up as a representative institution and that the term "representation" ordinarily implies external considerations. Most of the pertinent writing is laced in one way or another with normative notions; views on what the relations of influence are usually underlie views on whether or to what degree congressional lawmaking should be considered legitimate.

The question of what *influence* is—or what *power* is—is a source of unending confusion and controversy in the scholarship. A good state-of-the-art definition of a power relation, which I shall rely on in framing this section, states that a "power relation, actual or potential, is an actual or potential causal relation between the preferences of an actor regarding an outcome and the outcome itself" (Nagel 1975, p. 29).[1]

This definition casts a big enough net to include relations of anticipated reaction—that is, relations in which A has a preference about an outcome and B acts

---

[1] Nagel draws no distinction between "power" and "influence," and I shall make no effort to do so either.

to achieve the outcome because A wants it, but in which A makes no effort to induce B to act and, indeed, may never know that B has acted. Relations of this sort, though in principle detectable, present obvious empirical difficulties of a high order. Still, it is not possible to deal adequately with the subject of influence on legislatures without taking relations of anticipated reaction into account. An example is provided by the hypothetical instance in which a Mississippi congressman voted against a civil rights bill in 1950; hardly anyone back home noticed; nevertheless, people back home almost certainly would have noticed and erupted if he had voted the other way; he knew this and acted so as to minimize the probability of eruption; therefore, the (all white) electorate's preference caused the congressman's action.

Descriptive and prescriptive scholarship identifies four external actors or sets of actors as influencers of congressional activity.

Political Parties

The pertinent writing on parties is prescriptive and could defensibly be situated under either or both of the "active" and "passive" rubrics. I have in mind the "responsible parties" literature, the tradition of writing on Congress that has had the longest life and probably the greatest renown. Its central message is that Congress does not work very well and that it would work a great deal better if cohesive, programmatic, well-organized, electorally competitive, national parties existed and controlled its activities. The argument maintains that the American electorate's preferences are not properly expressed in Congress but that the existence of strong parties could provide such expression. Alternatively, the claim is made that the electorate's preferences are not very good anyway, but that better ones would be brought to bear if programmatic parties existed to generate them.

The founder of the tradition was Woodrow Wilson (1956), who discovered what he took to be British party government in the writing of Walter Bagehot and more or less advocated its American adoption in his 1885 work, *Congressional Government*—though without considering that the British electorate of the middle or late nineteenth century encompassed a much narrower stratum of society than did the American electorate. (For a general treatment of Wilson's views on parties, see Ranney 1954, chap. 3.) What Wilson urged—at least implicitly—was no less than an elitist counterrevolution, an abandonment of the Jacksonian mode of politics—with its localism and individualism, its corruption, its incoherence, its messiness, and its explosions of such public sentiment as the anti-Masonic movement, the antibank crusade, Know-Nothingism, abolitionism, the Greenback movement, and the Ku Klux Klan. Better the ritualized combat of a Gladstone and a Disraeli over broad "principles" and overall "programs" than such an unorganized free-for-all.

On the specifics, Wilson urged only a strengthening of parties within Congress itself, but subsequent writers have called for a forging of extraparliamentary party organizations—national and local—capable of keeping members of Congress in line. This recommendation was formalized in the American Political Science Association report, *Toward a More Responsible Party System* (1950), an audacious venture in Anglophilia. (For a retrospective reflection on the committee's statement, see Kirkpatrick 1971.) James MacGregor Burns, one of the leading contemporary exponents of the "responsible parties" cause, has urged a building of more influential extraparliamentary parties. (See, for example, Burns 1963, pp. 325–32.)

But none of this sort of exhortation has ever had much effect. The only American parties with a record of producing voting discipline in assemblies are local machines—such as Chicago's Democratic party organization under Mayor Richard Daley, with its servile board of aldermen. These are hardly the sorts of parties Wilson and his successors have had in mind. Members of Congress remain resolutely individualistic, very little influenced by party leaders inside Congress or by organizations properly called party organizations outside. Party loyalty on roll calls is loose by European standards, and during the twentieth century it has gradually grown looser. Such policy differences as there are between congressional Democrats and Republicans—and the two parties do have their distinctive centers of gravity on many issues—result, for the most part, from differences in personal views or ideologies and in the kinds of electoral constituencies members of either party must satisfy. The combination of Madisonian and Jacksonian traditions probably ruled out a long time ago a building of "party government" at the American national level and thereby ruled out the sort of lawmaking that might flow from it—arguably, a lawmaking more influenced than ours by experts and ideologies, more given to "planning," more abrupt and sweeping in its measures.

Interest Groups

While, in the United States, extraparliamentary parties do not exert much influence, interest groups do. Such groups range from tightly organized trade associations representing single industries through "public interest" groups, such as Common Cause, and mobilization of much of the general public by mail or media, such as the Moral Majority. Organized groups plainly wield a good deal of power in Congress and in lower-level assemblies. A generation ago, this circumstance was a cause of celebration among political scientists. "Group theorists" described and applauded a political world in which all people are free to coalesce in groups to further their interests and in which public policy is legitimately a resultant of group pressures. The classic statement of this brand of pluralism is contained in David B. Truman's *The Governmental Process* (1960). The heady claims of group theory are understandable, given the development of farmers in interest groups, finally, in the 1920s and industrial workers in the 1930s. For a time during the 1940s and 1950s, it seemed to some observers that interest groups, in place of parties, could offer a comprehensive set of linkages between the public and government. But major political problems since 1960 have not been comparably "solved" by the mobilization of interest groups of the farmer or labor kind, and political scientists, like most others, have retreated to a commonplace view of politics. (For a statement of disenchantment with "group theory" pluralism, see Lowi 1969.) This argument holds that some sets of people are better organized than others, that people in general are better organized in some of their roles than in others, and that better organization is likely to win better representation. The claim is certainly true for congressional representation. Minimum wage legislation, for example, a congressional staple, favors unionized adults over unorganized teenagers (whose source of jobs diminishes). Teachers have greater influence on education matters than do students or parents. Unorganized farm workers exercise little influence. In general people are better represented in their roles as producers than in their positions as consumers, as in the case of the tariff over most of American history—although the gap on producer and consumer matters has probably narrowed in the last two decades, with the mushrooming of public-interest groups on and around Capitol Hill.

The marked responsiveness of American legislative assemblies to organized groups raises chronic questions about the adequacy of ordinary lawmaking as a recourse for the relatively unorganized. Often, courts take up the slack, as in the case of general rule-making on racial matters during recent decades.

The scholarship on interest groups is only episodically an improvement on the American muckraking tradition—a genre in which some sets of people accuse other sets of constituting "special interests" (without defining very clearly what the label means), with the allegation that these "interests" get their way by rewarding or punishing politicians. (For an example of this genre, see Green et al. 1972, the flagship book of Ralph Nader's 1972 Congress project.) This scholarship does not cite much evidence or seem to realize that there are other ways of exercising influence—for example, by engaging in one-on-one persuasion and by expending resources to shape public opinion, which thereupon supplies a context in which politicians operate. In surprisingly few instances have scholars looked closely at the actual transactions between interest groups and politicians.[2] Such studies as exist suggest that persuasion—adducing information and making a case in Capitol Hill processes—is a more common means of exerting influence than is the offer of rewards or threats of punishment. Nor are students very sensitive to relations of anticipated reaction; the image of "pressure" is so strong that the influence of groups is ordinarily thought to be detectable only in actual transactions, though there is no good reason to suppose that a member of Congress from Oklahoma needs to receive any actual message from oil companies in order to be inspired to champion their interests. A final deficiency in the scholarship is its hangover image from the past that interest groups are private-sector organizations making claims on government; in fact, the world of interest groups is increasingly part of the public sector itself, with such organizations as mayors' and teachers' groups cutting a considerable swath on Capitol Hill (Beer 1976).

The President

Presidential influence on Congress is one of the hardiest concerns of American politics and the subject of a great many treatments, both positive and normative. Writing in the former vein—just how much and in what ways do presidents influence Congress—is rife with the problems and considerations inherent in discussing "power." Richard E. Neustadt's *Presidential Power* (1976), the standard analysis on the subject, makes the general case that presidents are most likely to be successful on Capitol Hill in two circumstances. The first is when their standing with the general public is high; members of Congress are then likely to see presidential claims as legitimate or to calculate that they themselves can profit, rather than lose, politically by going along with the White House. The second is when they build good "professional reputations" in the community of Washington politicians—that is, when they have records as forgers of good relations of reciprocal benefit with other political actors. In dealing with legislating, a sensible recourse is to note that president and Congress commonly weigh in at different stages of the

---

[2] The major study in which these transactions are inspected is Bauer et al. 1963, a study of the making of foreign trade policy in the mid-1950s.

process—initiation, information gathering, interest aggregation, and so on. (For a good discussion which picks up earlier scholarship, see Price 1972, chaps. 1, 8.)

Two hundred years of wrestling with the question of the matters on which presidents should exercise influence over Congress yields some clues to the inherent capabilities of representative assemblies. A simple distinction may be helpful. In a role envisioned in the Constitution and first fully exemplified by Lincoln as war leader, a president acts in the manner of a Roman consul—a manager, an executive, a doer of the sorts of tasks that seem to require quick action, centralized information gathering, day-to-day calculation, sometimes secrecy. The obvious examples are foreign policy in all eras of crisis management and economic policy since the mid-1930s—in the latter case, the kind of policy making that requires continuous watching of exchange rates, discount rates, price levels, and unemployment statistics. In playing consul, a president is not, strictly speaking, influencing Congress; rather, he is influencing events. The strengthening or weakening of the presidency as a managerial office—its weakening on foreign-policy matters since the early 1970s, for example—reflects judgments (popular and congressional) on the replacement of ordinary lawmaking processes by managerial processes in specified policy realms.

But many presidents take on a second role, not envisioned in the Constitution and first exemplified by Jackson. In this capacity they act like Roman tribunes. They speak, or claim to speak, for unorganized people not well enough represented in congressional lawmaking—either because too many members of Congress are hostile to what are claimed to be their interests or because congressional processes, for whatever reasons, fail to generate laws promoting what are claimed to be their interests. One thinks of Franklin Roosevelt and his "forgotten men" or Richard Nixon and his "silent majority." In this latter role, presidents do their work by trying to influence what Congress does in passing laws. All welfare-state builders are examples, but so is Ronald Reagan—a striking example, in the early part of his presidency, of a leader acting as tribune, rather than consul, in his all-consuming evocation of public opinion to foster a legislative program.

American views on whether the presidency or Congress should influence events, and on whether or how much presidents should influence congressional lawmaking, are based largely on perceptions of the country's managerial, as opposed to lawmaking, needs and, separately, perceptions of how well the unorganized are represented in Congress. One of the most conspicuous pieces of writing on Congress in recent decades, which argues that Congress should more or less give up trying to pass laws and spend its energies instead on oversight and casework, was written at a high-water mark of cold-war welfare-state liberalism (Huntington 1965).

Public Opinion

A century ago, James Bryce wrote of American legislators, "There is no country whose representatives are more dependent on public opinion, more ready to trim their sails to the last breath of it" (1959, vol. 1, p. 42). It does seem a reasonable assertion that public opinion exerts a greater influence on Congress than any other factor. This is an easier case to believe than to demonstrate, both because the tie between the public and members of Congress is largely (as in the case of the exemplary Mississippi district) a relation of anticipated reactions and because it is hard to decide what counts as a manifestation of public opinion. One study, based on interviews, conducted in the late 1960s in which a sizable number of House members were asked about the influences they felt in voting on a set of important issues, concluded (using some equations) that the perception or anticipation of constituency sentiment far outweighed interest groups, party leaders in Congress, and the presidential administration as an influence on roll call voting (Kingdon 1973, pp. 16–23 and, more generally, chaps. 1, 2).[3] The work's elaborate rendition of interview material makes the case more persuasively than any bare statement of it can. Again, however, the topic of public opinion has been insufficiently explored in the scholarship. It warrants more thinking and more scrutiny.

CONGRESS AS AN ACTIVE INSTITUTION

The next task is to consider Congress as a relatively autonomous institution, to ponder ways in which it makes its own predictable and distinctive imprint on the law. A fruitful approach takes a series of "organizing concepts" often said to capture processes, propensities, or attitudes of the institution or its members. The reason for treating these, once again, is to fuel speculation on the strengths and weaknesses of representative assemblies as generators of laws.

Particularism

There is a well-known legislators' propensity, probably detectable wherever members of assemblies have legislative powers and district roots, to pass out governmental benefits in small packets pleasing to districts or to groups or individuals within them. Such actions can cause—indeed, do cause, in the case of Congress—three kinds of "distortion" in the legislative product and one kind of distortion in members' activity.

Overspending

First, representative assemblies may "overspend" resources on some governmental programs—either rewarding some government programs (particularistic) over others (nonparticularistic) or spending more on some than the private sector would spend (on matters about which private-sector transactions supply a sensible standard). In fostering the Army Engineers' water projects, such as dams, for example, Congress works with a discount rate well under the market rate, thereby supplying more projects than the private market would. (See Ferejohn 1974, chap. 2.)

Inefficiency

Second, assemblies may inspire geographically inefficient allocation of resources within programs. The interesting argument on this matter has recently been set out along with some compelling evidence (Arnold 1979, especially chap. 9). The pertinent point is that for each program, its creators and sustainers—either legislative

---

[3] Kingdon sets out another equation (p. 20) in which he adds two other causal agents to the four specified here—that is, fellow congressmen (who supply "cues" on how to vote) and staff members (who supply information and advice). The four-variable equation is more interesting than the six-variable, for the reason that the two additional agents could supply a causal relation without its being a "power relation" (in Nagel's sense): we have no decisive reason to suppose that colleagues or staff members care how their cue-receivers vote.

leaders or the heads of agencies—must earn and keep the support of a majority coalition in Congress. (Agency leaders succeed largely by anticipating the reactions of members of Congress; that is to say, members influence agencies.) On a program offering collections of local goods or services, the way to nurture such a coalition is to spread funds thinly around many districts and states, often creating what can be regarded as inefficiencies. A program to deal with poverty in Appalachia develops over time an extraordinarily broad geographic definition of Appalachia.[4] A Model Cities program designed at the outset as a means of renovating a small set of urban disaster areas ends up as a source of modest and inconsequential funding for no fewer than 151 cities (*Public Interest* 1980). The National Endowments for the Arts and the Humanities start out, unsurprisingly, as patrons of New York City but end up, just as unsurprisingly, as funders of local ventures all over the country (Friedman 1979).

Design Bias

A third kind of "distortion" affects basic program design. Congress seems to prefer programs that offer geographically divisible benefits to other kinds, even if the former are not obviously more efficient. In times of economic downturn, for example, members of Congress reach instinctively for "accelerated public-works programs" rather than other sorts of macroeconomic levers—subsidies to the districts turn up as a way of dealing with water pollution. More generally, Congress prefers categorical grant programs to state and local aid that takes the form of generalized revenue sharing (the elected officials can claim credit for individual grants even if bureaucrats pass them out).

Casework

A fourth "distortion"—in congressional activity rather than directly, in legislative product—occurs in the extraordinary amounts of time and energy members spend on casework as a result of inducement from their home electorates (servicing constituents' requests) as compared with actually making laws. Emphasis on casework may reasonably be thought of as a nonstatutory brand of particularism. A survey conducted by the Obey Commission, a panel created by the House in the mid-1970s to study its internal organization, revealed that members of Congress and voters place approximately equal value on the legislative and service roles, that members themselves believe that the former role ought to be far more important than the latter, but that they admit to being induced by constituents' pressure to spend much more time and energy in the latter activity than they think they should (Cavanagh 1978).

These claims should not be taken as a judgment that members of Congress do nothing but build gratuitous dams and chase lost Social Security checks. In fact public-works programs—the old "pork barrel" standbys, with members of Congress retaining substantial discretion over item-by-item allocation—now take up only about 2 percent of the federal budget (Arnold 1978). The major growth in contemporary federal budgets has been in transfer programs—such as Medicare—rather than programs allocating benefits by discretionary or seemingly discretionary decision. And modern congressional offices, bulging with staff

---

[4] By 1980 nearly 85 percent of the country's population lived in "distressed areas" eligible for federal aid. See *Public Interest* 1980.

members, surely devote more resources to both legislating and casework than did the offices of a generation ago. Nevertheless, particularism is a propensity to watch for and wonder how to correct for.

Specialization

House and Senate members are organized into well over a hundred specialized committees and subcommittees in each house, where most of the essential work of legislating is done.[5] It is probable that no contemporary legislature can make a significant impact on the law without a division of labor to work out adequate methods, and in practice this requires committees. But delegation to committees creates its own sorts of problems, or is thought to do so. Three lines of criticism are worth setting out.

Special Interests

The first argues as follows. For electoral or other reasons, members of Congress ordinarily join committees dealing with programs in which they have a special interest (farm belt members, for example, join the agricultural committees);[6] committees ordinarily carry a great deal of weight on the floor; ergo, the congressional legislative product can come to resemble an unrepresentative collection of committee-centered programs. They may be unrepresentative in the senses both that, if asked, the general public might not approve the enacted individual programs and that, in a hypothetical world where all members of Congress are equally informed and equally influential on all matters, congressional floor majorities might also disapprove. This argument has a ring of truth. Following more or less the same line of reasoning, one scholar posits a budgetary effect—systematic "overspending" on committee programs (Niskanen 1971, chap. 14).

Committee Control

The second critique is a time-specific complaint often lodged by liberals against Congress from the late 1930s through the late 1960s. The argument went as follows: Democrats ordinarily controlled the Congress; committee chairmen (all Democrats) were chosen by seniority; committee chairmen had a great deal of influence; southern Democrats were chairmen in large numbers because they had safe seats and remained in Congress longer than northern Democrats; most southerners were conservatives; ergo, the current form of committee specialization resulted in Congress being controlled by a conservative oligarchy unrepresentative of the membership.

At one time this claim held a slight kernel of truth. Most of the time over these decades, however, the liberals' real problem lay in the fact that they lacked floor majorities, even though they made up a majority of the majority party; in fact, southern committee leaders tended to be fairly representative of cross-party floor majorities in their areas of specialty. But no matter, the argument has

[5] For sophisticated treatments of what goes on in sets of House and Senate committees see Fenno 1973 and Price 1972. Fenno covers both chambers but looks more closely at the House. Price concentrates on the Senate. On the building of the House committee system over time, see Polsby 1968.

[6] For a definitive analysis of how Democrats get to be members of committees in the House, see Shepsle 1978. On agriculture in particular, see Jones 1961.

become nothing more than historical curiosity now. Congress no longer has a southern tilt.[7]

Division

The third argument makes a persuasive case. Dividing up power among a multitude of committees makes legislating difficult, if not impossible, in the more complicated policy areas. Authorizing dams is easy enough, but arriving at a plan on the order of a congressional "energy policy" is extraordinarily difficult—indeed, more difficult now than it was a generation ago, because of "democratizing" reforms of the 1970s that weakened parent committees and strengthened more than a hundred subcommittees in the House (making the House more like the Senate). (For an account of the reforming of the House in the 1970s, see Dodd and Oppenheimer 1977.) Having legions of cooks stirring around makes for an unusual meal, a late meal, or no meal at all, even if most are working from more or less the same recipe. A few years ago, Jeffrey L. Pressman and Aaron B. Wildavsky wrote a book entitled *Implementation*, in which they pointed out the difficulty of carrying through a federal program that has to survive some seventy "decision points" between its statutory authorization and its final realization (Pressman and Wildavsky 1973). A still unwritten work, *Enactment*, could point out the difficulty of getting out of Congress anything worthy of the name of "energy policy" or anything of the sort, as long as literally scores of committees and subcommittees have a place in its making.

Careerism

Service in an assembly can fit into a lifetime career in many different ways. Members may serve a term or two before withdrawing to private life; this pattern is common in many American city councils and state legislatures. (See Prewitt 1970, pp. 5–17.) Membership in a legislature may be a preface to or a concomitant of holding a higher public position, as in the case of the eighteenth-century British House of Commons, a producer of cabinet members, generals, admirals, and bishops. Municipal and state legislative service may be a part-time occupation, an adjunct to a private career supplying a better and steadier source of income. The typical modern member of Congress, however, is what has been called a fully professionalized legislator, members ordinarily devote full time to their positions, and they aim to pursue lifelong careers on Capitol Hill—although, of course, many House members aim to abandon the House and move up to the Senate.[8]

Spending a full career in Congress requires multiple reelection, and this need shapes activities on Capitol Hill. Elsewhere I have argued that members seeking reelection—whatever the length of their term—are induced to engage relentlessly in three specifiable sorts of activity: *advertising*—"any effort to disseminate one's name among constituents in such a fashion as to create a favorable image but in messages having little or no issue content"; *credit claiming*—"acting so as to

---

[7] That the southern advantage would erode away was evident already in 1965. See Wolfinger and Heifetz 1965.

[8] Congressional service was not always so "professionalized." For a treatment of the evolution toward "professionalization," see Price 1975; and Polsby 1968.

generate a belief in a relevant political actor (or actors) that one is personally responsible for causing the government, or some unit thereof, to do something that the actor (or actors) considers desirable"; and *position taking*—"the public enunciation of a judgmental statement (which may take the form of a roll call vote) on anything likely to be of interest to political actors" (Mayhew 1974, pp. 49–77). Since members seeking reelection spend much time and energy engaging in these activities, the effects on the legislative product merit consideration.

One set of inferences is obvious. The need to "claim credit" can be expected to generate patterns of particularism. Its further effect of "clientelism"—working to achieve legislative ends in committees under the alert scrutiny of interest groups—has been discussed under "specialization."

Additionally, the politics of position taking has its legislative consequences. (The logic of this is set out in Mayhew 1974, pp. 61–73.) On broad matters, where no single member of Congress can believably claim credit for passing a law or for achieving its effect, the members' sense of craftsmanship or organizational incentives, rather than electoral considerations, must be relied on to yield workable laws. Where the electoral reward is for issue positions rather than programmatic effects, craftsmanship and internal incentives may have limited power. The contrast between the federal tax code and federal statutes regulating industry is illustrative. The tax code presents a history of the painstaking creation of precise, elaborate provisions—"loopholes" to some; this result is what one would expect in a process rife with particularism and clientelism. But regulatory statutes, until the mid-1960s, after which time they were put together by congressional staff members, have been notoriously brief, vague, and studded with internal contradictions. They are best considered as emanations of an amorphous public opinion rather than as exercises in instrumental rationality geared to produce programmatic effects.

The general distinction here is important. Making laws on matters on which members cannot easily claim individual credit can be a breathtakingly haphazard activity. One knowledgeable scholar writes, "Within the Congress words are equated with deeds. Votes represent final acts. There is a concern with administration, but it is focused primarily on those elements which directly affect constituency interests or committee jurisdictions. Legislative proposals seldom are debated from the viewpoint of their administrative feasibility" (Seidman 1970, pp. 65–66).

Coalition Formation

One line of theorizing in contemporary political science gives an arresting answer to the old question of the sort of winning coalitions likely to form where decisions are made by majority rule. William H. Riker has put forth what he calls a size principle, the gist of which is that "minimal winning coalitions" are likely to form in assemblies and other settings; people putting together victories will try to make them as narrow as possible (51 percent is the ideal under majority rule) so as to maximize per capita benefits on the winning side (Riker 1962). In a politics of dam building, for example, one might expect outcomes in which narrow majorities of legislators team up to supply dams for their own districts but impose tax burdens on all districts—or, indeed, merely on the districts of excluded minorities. Such a vision is less than edifying, and if members of assemblies routinely behaved as it predicts, it might reasonably be wondered whether assemblies are appropriate bodies for making decisions—or, if they are, whether they ought to make them by majority rule.

The primary objection to this "size principle" theory is that it generates a grotesque misconstruction of congressional reality on matters where it might be thought most directly to apply—that is, on what are often called "distributive" benefits: goods such as dams or block grants, which can be ladled out in piecemeal fashion, district by district. Benefits of this sort do indeed impose diffuse costs on taxpayers everywhere, but they need not of necessity be apportioned in a way that arouses hostility among excluded minorities anywhere. Processes can be arranged so as to allow every district its share of distributive goods at one time or another; impressive evidence suggests that Congress more or less does so arrange them. A statement of a member of the House Public Works Committee of the 1960s renders the spirit of the politics: "Any time any member of the Committee wants something, or wants to get a bill out, we get it out for him. . . . Makes no difference—Republican or Democrat. We are all Americans when it comes to that" (Murphy 1968, p. 23). (For a pertinent treatment of distributive politics on the House Interior Committee of the 1960s, see Fenno 1973, chaps. 3, 4; see also the discussion in Mayhew 1974, pp. 87–91.)

It seems likely that politicians who have to deal with each other over time find it more advantageous to devise long-term, "universalistic" standards of interaction than to exploit each other at the instant. (For a statement of this logic, see Barry 1965, pp. 255–56.) Bureaucrats, too, follow a logic of universalism; on some distributive federal programs, there is decisive evidence that, in doling out benefits so as to build congressional support, the aim of federal agencies is, not to service narrow majorities, but to spread goods around widely enough to silence all opposition (Arnold 1979).

Distributive politics poses its problems, of course, as the earlier discussion of particularism suggests. But injustice or idiosyncrasy brought on by the size principle is scarcely one of them.

It seems more probable that coalition builders try to squeeze out narrow majorities primarily on matters where conflict is unavoidable—on issues where two sides anchored in public opinion do battle on Capitol Hill and where "half a loaf" strategies can supply just enough votes to make one position or another prevail. Surely this happens sometimes (Stephen K. Bailey's classic account [1950] of the passage of the Employment Act of 1946 comes to mind), but how is this situation to be interpreted? Indeed, beyond the familiar ruminations about majority rule and minority rights, what considerations can be brought to bear on any situations in which congressional majorities vote down vocal minorities?

One good question, in line with concerns about coalition building and about the imprints assemblies distinctively make, is whether congressional decision processes tend to exacerbate or to diminish conflict naturally existing in the larger society. A reasonable answer suggests that ordinarily they diminish it. In the language of Capitol Hill, members trying to get a bill passed normally seek to "accommodate" the views of prospective opponents—that is, to shape legislation in ways that will head off objections and, if not to foreclose opposition, at least to reduce its intensity. Ordinarily, accommodation is a tactical necessity. There are in Congress so many dispersed decision points that legislation of any complexity can hardly be passed without it. The Senate, which operates procedurally by "unanimous consent" and where any inflamed Senator can hold up a bill, raises accommodation to a high art.[9] Thus, any image of Congress as a place where majorities routinely and wantonly trample on vocal minorities in passing bills is at variance with reality.

The need for "accommodation" nevertheless raises its own obvious difficulty: blocking bills is easier than passing them. On balance it is probably true that processes on Capitol Hill display a built-in bias for the status quo. Anyone can make up a list of issues on which the public—at least as its views are captured in opinion polls—pushes one way and Congress, by inaction, pushes the other. One such is gun control. Another is national health insurance, a public favorite but so far a congressional casualty to interest-group opposition and the sheer difficulty of maneuvering a bill through. School busing, affirmative action, and school prayer are all matters on which the Supreme Court or any agency handed down rulings that were unpopular with a majority of the public in the 1970s but which Congress did not overturn during that decade. The tendency toward stasis produces a demonstrable effect in the politics of the public sector; federal agencies and programs are hard to create, but once in place and bolstered by clients, they are very difficult to dismantle. (See Wilson 1975 and Kaufman 1976.)

A distinction is in order, however. No public majority or even vocal minority can now be said to be permanently barred from prevailing on Capitol Hill—permanently in the sense that obtained when advocates for blacks' equality were dealt out in the initial constitutional settlement, again in the Compromise of 1877 (giving the Republicans the presidency and the white South autonomy on racial matters, as a settlement of the disputed Hayes-Tilden election), and afterward, until the mid-1960s, by the race-saturated politics of the Senate filibuster. These persisting arrangements between northern and southern whites, embedded in congressional processes, probably belong in a class with the formulas of Dutch and Swiss consociationalism—long-standing quasi-constitutional agreements dividing governmental authority among ethnic, religious, or linguistic segments of the population. Since 1965, many senators of all ideological shades have used the filibuster, but no set of them has presumed to claim—probably none successfully could—that it can legitimately be used over and over again on the same issue. While a bias for the status quo clearly exists, Congress is no longer predictably static on any specifiable issue or set of issues.

And its members do, after all, pass a great number of bills, many of them controversial. A few members dedicated to a goal, fortified by staff work, and capable of shrewd maneuvering can often carry through a piece of legislation; the consumer statutes of the 1960s enacted over industry opposition supply some cases in point. (See, for example, the account in Price 1972, chap. 2.) Indeed, what Robert A. Dahl refers to in another context as a pattern of "minorities rule" is a fair characterization of much congressional bill passing (Dahl 1963, pp. 131–34). The accommodation required to conform House and Senate bills is also a matter of negotiated compromise.

Deliberation

Lawmakers may be said to be engaging in "deliberation" when the following set of circumstances characterize their activity: (a) they try to change or make up each

---

[9] Bernard Asbell makes the point with acuity and voluminous evidence in *The Senate Nobody Knows* (1978), a treatment of (among other things) Senate handling of clean air legislation in 1976.

other's minds about what, if anything, should be enacted into law; (b) they do so by adducing descriptive statements ("facts"), causal statements (for example, "Decontrolling gas prices will reduce demand"), normative statements (such as, "The government shouldn't interfere in people's lives"), or some combination of the three; and (c) the criterion they use, explicitly or implicitly, in arguing whether a bill should become law is whether it would be "good" for some reference group larger than themselves (for example, a district, the farmers, the nation, humanity). In principle, deliberation differs from bargaining—trying to get others to change their positions by making threats or offering inducements, although in practice the two forms of interaction are commonly entangled.

Operating on a premise that legislators register fixed positions or hone them to serve electoral ends, modern scholars have seldom paid much attention to deliberation or taken the process seriously. The oversight is curious, given the earlier emphasis accorded it by the authors of the Federalist papers and by Woodrow Wilson; the prominence of a twentieth-century "problem-solving" scholarship, from John Dewey through Harold Lasswell, that might have, but has not, made it a first-order concern; and the obvious fact that it does indeed take place. One thinks of the losing effort in the Senate in 1970 to confirm the nomination of G. Harrold Carswell to the Supreme Court, in which the arguments in his favor wore thin and in which the salient argument became Senator Roman L. Hruska's that "even if he were mediocre, there are a lot of mediocre judges and people and lawyers, and they are entitled to a little representation, aren't they?" Another illustration is furnished by President Carter's bill allowing election-day registration of voters, which lost its support when critics took a cold look at it and concluded that the potential for fraud was immense (*Congressional Quarterly Weekly* 1977). And there is President Nixon's Family Assistance Plan, impaled on its inconsistencies in the Senate Finance Committee; Senator John Williams adduced elaborate information and apparently persuaded the committee that "work incentives," predicted to be a product of the plan, were a mirage.[10] As a result of the scholarly oversight, political scientists have had little to say on such matters as the televising of congressional floor sessions; whether committee markup sessions (where decisions on particulars are hammered out) should be closed or open; whether treatment of legislative subjects should be scattered around many committees or concentrated in a few;[11] whether hiring of huge legislative staffs makes for better or worse consideration of bills (see Malbin 1977, 1980; Scully 1977); or, in general, what sorts of institutional arrangements make for a proper deliberative setting.

A heterogeneous collection of recent writings, however, offers promise that the topic of deliberation may become an object of scholarly interest. A paper by Joseph M. Bessette (1979) offers a careful probe of its nature.[12] Charles E. Lindblom

[10] See Bessette 1979, pp. 33–42. For an especially good account of deliberative activity at the committee and subcommittee levels, see Asbell 1978, pp. 10–17, 29–43, 121–27, 131–35, 176–79, 185–89, 198–207, 216–18, 224–28, 328–29, 333–36, 349–64, 371–74, 392–95; these scattered references, if strung together, supply a coherent narrative on the Senate Public Works Committee's handling of clean air legislation in 1976.

[11] See Davidson and Oleszek 1977, an account of the Bolling Committee's effort to make over the House committee system in 1973–74. Discussions among committee members and staff (the latter including some political scientists), reported in chapter 5, display traces of an interest in making committees better deliberative bodies.

[12] For a pertinent earlier offering see Barry 1965, pp. 87–88. Barry sets out seven methods of resolving disagreements, of which "discussion on merits" is one.

and David K. Cohen, exemplary of writers in a tradition outside congressional scholarship but relevant to it, have considered how social-scientific knowledge can usefully be inserted into decision-making processes in legislative and other settings (Lindblom and Cohen 1979). Nelson W. Polsby has given thought to the place of deliberation in presidential nominating conventions, settings from which it has virtually disappeared in recent decades as primaries and the mass media have become the realm and instruments of nominating (Polsby 1980). John W. Kingdon and Richard F. Fenno, Jr., both authors of books based on interviews with members of Congress, have told of a practice independent of deliberation but, on close inspection, arguably related to it—the members' standard, time-consuming practice of explaining their Capitol Hill activities, including their votes, to their constituencies (Fenno 1978, chap. 5; Kingdon 1973, pp. 46–53).

Taking positions is not enough: in order to show that they are performing well, members of Congress must travel around their districts and repeatedly make statements—descriptive, causal, and normative—about the legislative issues they deal with in Washington. Knowing that, back home, they will have to cite reasons for their stands on Capitol Hill, they worry and ruminate about how to explain later as they take their stands now. This circumstance, which may not be surprising, suggests the idea of a representative tie of some sophistication. Members can be judged, at least in part, in their home districts according to whether their statements are plausible; the statement making, so judged, is an attenuated form of the sort required in deliberation on Capitol Hill; the more alert constituents, in so judging, are therefore engaging in what amounts to a sampling activity, testing whether their representatives are likely to be much good at deliberating. Fenno argues that, in making explanations and performing the other actions they engage in back home, members of the House try, above all, to create a relation of "trust" with their constituents (Fenno 1978, passim). To carry the argument further, "trust" relations empower members to take part in arcane Washington discussions. It should further be remembered that argument on Capitol Hill, insofar as it is a rehearsal for explanations in the home district—and to some important degree it has this function—imparts popular styles of thinking into Congress's legislative activity.

BACK TO PUBLIC OPINION

The foregoing treatments of influence relations and processes will convey a sense of some of the achievements and difficulties when loosely structured elective assemblies generate laws. But there is a need for a general point of a different sort—one not covered in these treatments, not rooted in available scholarship or easily renderable by standard techniques or scholarship, but important nonetheless for what it suggests about American legislatures, Congress in particular, as distinctively popular institutions.

The point concerns language and style of thinking. As much as any, and probably more than most, American legislatures are places where ordinary-language, common-sense ways of thinking percolate upward from the public to permeate lawmaking processes and laws. This process can occur either because legislators embody public opinion or because they cater to it—probably as much the former as the latter. Capitol Hill terminology is normally no more complicated than the idiom of journalists or common-law lawyers. Styles of reasoning are ordinary; arguments in the *Congressional Record* are full of references to such images as mares' nests, entering wedges, camels' noses, last-mile walks, cans of worms, Pandora's boxes, stitches in time, golden eggs, roosting chickens, pigs in a poke, forests and trees, babies and bathwater. (See the discussion in Large 1973.)

This commonplace takes on importance with a view toward what the language of lawmaking could be but, at least in the American setting, normally is not—a "scientific" or otherwise inaccessible medium, a language of technical expertise (common, of course, in government agencies), of labyrinthine ideology, or of esoteric ethics.[13] Whatever else may be said about Congress and other American legislatures, they have little in common with task forces of economists or with seminars of Jesuits or Marxists or philosophy professors; their styles of thought and discourse are, by contrast, utterly prosaic.

A way to make this point is to set out some "cognitive grooves," some ordinary-language, common-sense ways of thinking about things, which unquestionably originate in public opinion and which, over and over again, infuse legislative discourse and give shape to American statutory law. I offer ten such "cognitive grooves."

Corrective Measures

"There Ought to Be a Law"

Conjuring up a "scientific" vision of legislating is easy enough; a body of lawmakers settles on some desirable ends and then builds statutes with a vigorous instrumental rationality to achieve them. A law is a "scientific" means to reach an end. But surely lawmaking rooted in public opinion is not likely to take this form, only with important qualifications. In the first place, to the average person, "law" is probably a kind of Mosaic mishmash—a mix of moral command and positive edict. Why pass a law proscribing marijuana or fornication? To set a standard or to abolish a practice? A "scientific" way to reduce air pollution might be to tax factory owners according to the amounts of poison they inject into the air; but this kind of remedy is hard to sell to American publics or their legislators because it appears immoral. If polluting the air is bad, why not simply pass a law stamping it out altogether?

In the second place, legislators rooted in public opinion are somewhat quicker on the draw in framing laws than, I suspect, "scientists" would have them be. They are casual, to say the least, in applying the tenets of instrumental rationality. If something is wrong, "there ought to be a law." The response is reflexive. An example of moralism intertwined with casual thinking is embodied in the Humphrey-Hawkins Act of 1978—an enacted national mandate, barren of instruction on means, to achieve a 4 percent unemployment rate as well as a 3 percent inflation rate by 1983. (See Singer 1978.) It is difficult to characterize such a venture; it can hardly be seen as an exercise in "scientific" lawmaking. The relentless currents of moralism and of quick, reflexive casualness in American lawmaking—at state and local levels in the nineteenth century, but extended to the national in the twentieth—almost certainly rule out a whole brand of economists' thinking as incompatible with popular democracy: the stark antistatist economics, that is, associated with Milton Friedman. Any collection of American legislators is likely to pass a great many laws in a short time that vigorously free-market economists

---

[13] The distinction here is akin to one Bruce A. Ackerman makes between "ordinary" and "scientific" legal language in *Private Property and the Constitution* (1977, chap. 1).

will find gratuitous or hateful; the public wants them. As long as a century and a half ago, Tocqueville reported on "American legislatures in a state of continual agitation," on the "continual feverish activity of the legislatures," and on the fact that "in America the legislator's activity never slows down" (Tocqueville 1969, pp. 243, 241, 249).

"Regulate It"

The reflexive American response to any malfunction in the private sector—most of the ills of the Industrial Revolution are cases in point—is to call for regulation. Such a recourse is simple, practical, and easily understood. It requires no theory. It flows from a judgment that some practices are good and others are bad.

At the legislative level, regulation is primarily expressed in lists of actions that people or organizations are mandated or forbidden to engage in. During the last two or three decades, when large staffs and "public interest advocates" have become fixtures on Capitol Hill, the lists have grown longer and more detailed. But they still cause despair among all sorts of economists on the ground that their means do not efficiently achieve their ends. (See, for example, the analysis in Ackerman et al. 1974.)

Furthermore, the American "regulatory" recourse has ruled out or taken the place of ways of dealing with the private sector that some would consider more basic or fundamental—for example, the Marxist recourse of "nationalizing the means of production." This is a message of intellectuals, rooted in a complicated body of theory, and it has never had much resonance in the American public or in American legislatures.

"Stamp It Out"

Reflecting public opinion, American lawmakers put a great deal of energy into trying to eliminate easily identifiable evils. Such targets may include slavery, drinking, Communism, drug addiction, vice, unemployment, inflation, pollution, hunger, and poverty.

But while "poverty" can become a fitting statutory target, it is more difficult, if not impossible, for any American legislature to ordain general societal rearrangements in the interest of realizing a complicated ethical theory. John Rawls and Robert Nozick may be captivating in university settings, but their lack of common-sense targets—they attack no manifest evil—makes them unsalable in an American political marketplace. George McGovern's "demogrant" plan of 1972 to give each person $1,000 a year as an incomes policy may have sounded persuasive in Cambridge, but it aroused bafflement and suspicion in the public and, as a result, would almost certainly have been unrealizable on Capitol Hill. Its intended underpinnings were not easy to convey.

"We're in a Crisis"; or, "This Is an Outrage"

There is a common inclination among American legislators, responding to public opinion, to frame measures as a quick reaction to events. One thinks of the "hundred days" legislation in response to the economic crisis of 1933; laws regulating drugs in 1938 and 1962 (the former brought on by a deadly sulfanilamide elixir, the latter by thalidomide) (see Harris 1964, pp. 181–245); the Tonkin Gulf resolution of 1964, giving President Lyndon Johnson what amounted to free rein in Vietnam; mining-safety laws passed in 1941, 1952, and 1969, all inspired by coal-mine disasters (see Lewis-Beck and Alford 1980); the National Defense Education

Act of 1958, brought on by Sputnik; the civil-rights laws of 1964 and 1965, triggered by violence in Birmingham and Selma. No one should be surprised by this reactiveness, of course, or even necessarily dismayed, but it does sometimes yield measures that are not very well thought out in their means or ends.

"Do It Once and for All"

Most of the natural sciences and some of the social sciences proceed by experimentation, either in laboratories or, with suitable application of rules, in real-life settings. Given the chance, therefore, scientists of various sorts might bring an experimental cast of mind to legislating. In many areas of lawmaking, there is no sure way of predicting the effects of a contemplated law. From a scientific standpoint, a reasonable—indeed, an obvious—course on such congressional subjects as campaign finance, minimum wage, water and air pollution, occupational safety, housing, and school busing would be experimentation with different laws in randomly selected parts of the country to observe the results. To be sure, such action would pose constitutional and other kinds of problems. But it is my impression that members of Congress almost never even consider such procedures. My guess is that their view of lawmaking as a substantially *moral* activity—a popularly rooted view—prevents them from contemplating experimentation: if there is a *right* solution to a problem, it must be universally imposed. By an accident of history, American lawmaking was more experimental half a century ago than it is now; fortuitous mixes of state laws on various subjects, at a time when states had greater autonomy, supplied what amounted to "natural experiments"—the individual states serving, in Louis D. Brandeis's phrase, as "laboratories." The current costly recourse at the federal level is, in effect, to try out solutions over time rather than across space.

"Wipe Out Corruption"

Nothing may be easier for people to understand than a charge of "corruption." Hence, a hypersensitivity on the subject has developed among American journalists and lawmakers. As a result, revelations of corruption produce laws; one thinks of the Watergate hearings and the subsequent overhaul of campaign-finance rulings.[14] Further, views on corruption give shape to laws; in important respects, the entire American public sector, with its elaborate civil-service requirements, its auditing arrangements, its reporting and disclosure constraints, its vast paperwork, is a monument to the memory and possibility of corruption. "There are watchdogs who watch watchdogs watching watchdogs." (See, for example, Kaufman 1977, p. 54; more generally pp. 50–56.) Initiative and flexibility can get lost in a quest for palpable honesty; agencies created by American legislatures may not always accomplish whatever else they are supposed to do, but they do manage to spend enormous amounts of money without much of it being illegally misused or stolen.

"Pin the Blame"

The gist of what might be called "blame theories" is that when something goes wrong, someone or a group of someones is intentionally and malevolently causing the situation; there may well be a conspiracy. This strain in American popular thinking has persisted from the beginning, the lineup of villains running from

[14] For a treatment of the Federal Election Campaign Act of 1974 and its follow-up litigation, see Polsby 1977, pp. 1–43. The act was among other things "a major legacy of [the Nixon] administration" (p. 1).

the Illuminati, the Masons, and the Pope up through such modern forces as the "Communist conspiracy," the "military industrial complex," and the Trilateral Commission. (For a general treatment, see Hofstadter 1967.) Some blame theories are more sophisticated than others, and some are surely true, but all probably win popular currency by their dealing in blame—one of the simplest of ideas.

A point worth making is that blame theories do not ordinarily achieve as much success in American legislatures as they do among the public; lawmakers seeking explanations, as a preface to writing statutes, are more likely to reach for impersonal causes. Their doing so may offer a good instance (and one that might, in social-science parlance, be "operationalizable"—survive rigorous definition of terms and scrutiny of evidence) of what James Madison expected of congressional representation: that it would "refine and enlarge the public views by passing them through the medium of a chosen body of citizens" (*Federalist Papers* 1961, p. 82).

Nevertheless, at times blame theories do make their mark on Capitol Hill. One thinks of a long line of noisy investigations: the Nye committee of the 1930s, with its theory that munitions makers brought on World War I; the McCarthy hearings and the three-decade run of the House Un-American Activities Committee; more recently, the House Select Committee on Assassinations and its unswerving conviction—evidence or the lack of it notwithstanding—that John F. Kennedy and Martin Luther King, Jr., were both victims of bizarre conspiracies. While such hearings occasionally result in laws, for the most part, the act of investigating in itself—authoritatively assigning the blame—seems to satisfy interested publics.

Anticipatory Measures

"We Need a Program"

The view that, if there is a problem, a government "program" can be created to "solve" it seems to be a twentieth-century idea, perhaps a remnant of the "problem-solving" strain in Progressivism. Sometimes the belief makes good sense; the space program, the Marshall Plan, and the effort of the 1970s to wipe out hunger come to mind. Sometimes it makes less sense; the crash program to wipe out cancer and most of the housing programs since the 1930s are cases in point. But the idea of "having a program" seems deeply ingrained in the popular mind and in politicians' minds. Anyone running for high office is obliged to set forth, for example, a "program for the cities." Consequently, the statute books fill up with plans for programs, whether or not there is good reason to suppose that labeling problems and creating programs to solve them will in fact achieve any intended ends.

"We've Got a Right"

The notion of rights has always been prominent in American culture, but since the mid-1960s, when southern obstruction of efforts to extend elementary rights to blacks finally gave way in Congress and in the southern state capitals, a new phenomenon has arisen—the persistent, frenetic invention of new rights. (For the treatment of the modern class of rights that amount to entitlements to government largesse, see Reich 1964.) Of course, the best way to establish a new right is to argue that it is an ancient one currently being traduced. Some of this invention has been carried on in Congress. The controversy on abortion, which, in principle, could be conducted on utilitarian lines—that is, on the presumed social effects of one policy or another—in fact, took the form of a competitive assertion of rights—as in the politically imaginative declaration of a "right to life" (with its conscious or unconscious appeal to the Declaration of Independence). An excellent current way to bring about large-scale social change is to label a desideratum a "right" by statute, specifying as little as possible about the costs or effects of implementation. In passing the Age Discrimination Act of 1975, for example, Congress "held no public hearings and left behind virtually no legislative history of its intentions to guide the government's policy makers" (Stanfield 1978, p. 2066; for a more extended treatment, see Schuck 1980). The Rehabilitation Act of 1973 included only one sentence barring discrimination against the handicapped in access to public transit; five years later, these few words had cost billions of dollars in public expenditure and filled the *Federal Register* with 51 pages of follow-up regulations (Clark 1973).

A vast potential exists for brief and cloudy laws producing expensive, enduring, and often surprising effects. Declaring "rights" may cause more notable results than creating "programs"; in the case of the handicapped, for example, a program in their behalf—a more traditional recourse—would probably have brought about less actual change. The congressional concern with rights has recently spilled over into foreign policy, where marking up foreign aid bills has sometimes taken the form of list bargaining—my Chile for your Mozambique. Each member has a distinctive list of countries argued to be too wicked on human-rights matters to deserve financial aid. (See Franck and Weisband 1979, chap. 4.)

"Balance the Budget and Stamp Out Waste"

An enduring substratum of public opinion seems to exist in American society that concentrates on money; its tenets are roughly as follows. Government budgets should be balanced. Agencies have an inherent tendency to waste money and should be stopped from doing so. Tax money is, in principle, citizens' property, and the burden is on government to prove it ought to be taken away. Running up a national debt is an improvident and, indeed, immoral act. The Proposition 13 movement in California, and similar initiatives in other states calling for reductions in public spending as a matter of law, have apparently built on a notion that a huge share of public expenditure is simply wasted. (For a good analysis based on national survey data, see Sussman 1978.) A publicly inspired constitutional amendment requiring that federal budgets be balanced may yet be enacted. (See Wildavsky 1980.)

To be sure, such a package of views hardly supplies an accurate prediction any more of what takes place on Capitol Hill: members of Congress, acting in the shadow of Keynesian theory, have not been hesitant to approve deficits and debts. Nevertheless, compared with other governmental organs—certainly the President's Council of Economic Advisers—Congress is a uniquely good reflector of public views on money matters. Decade after decade, the keynote of the House Appropriations Committee's activity has been the stamping out of governmental waste. (See Fenno 1966, especially pp. 98–108.) And deficits notwithstanding, it probably remains the case that no theory of budgeting other than a common-sense balancing theory has ever been decisively sold on Capitol Hill. Congress went along only half-heartedly with the Kennedy-Johnson tax cut of 1964—the first salient Keynesian instrument—and neither the statements nor the actions of its members since that time suggest any firm attachment to notions of counter-cyclicalism. The economic program of the Reagan administration in its early days was a powerful statement of mass opinion on government spending, budget balancing, and waste; but it is interesting that Reagan's macroeconomic proposal that encountered the strongest opposition in Congress was his tax scheme. The administration's Kemp-Roth plan, with its Laffer Curve justification of tax cuts unmatched by spending cuts, aroused suspicion of the sort inspired by the Democrats' Keynesianism of two decades earlier. And the opposition was rooted in public opinion; national surveys supplied evidence that unalloyed budget balancing is the macroeconomics of the mass public.[15] The main problem for economists on Capitol Hill is winning a lasting commitment to any theories at all, budget balancing aside.

These ten categories make my point about public opinion. Anyone examining the product of elective American assemblies, pondering what to make of it and how much to honor it, might consider not only the relations of influence and organizing concepts set out earlier, but also the infusion of raw public opinion into lawmaking. An inspection of congressional behavior on energy matters in the 1970s, for example, certainly warrants a consideration of pressure brought to bear by oil companies, the contemporary status of the presidency, the absence of disciplined national parties, patterns of coalition formation on Capitol Hill, the effects of hyperspecialization in the congressional committee system; but it must also consider the dogged, simultaneous expression on Capitol Hill of the conflicting demands of public opinion: big cars, low gas and oil prices, more investment in energy, more conservation, customary levels of energy consumption, nonintervention abroad, less dependence on imports, less government regulation, and lower taxes.

There is much to be said for the American model of rooting assemblies in public opinion. No doubt, it imparts a signal legitimacy to governmental actions, and it invests legislative enactments with a piecemeal cast of the kind advocated by Karl Popper—consider the "cognitive grooves" having to do with incremental regulation, obvious evils, and reaction to events.

The system also has its costs, however. A summary way of stating them is to cite a contrast drawn by Tocqueville (substituting, with some of the modern European regimes in mind, the phrase "party-centered technocracy" for his "aristocracy"):

> An aristocracy is infinitely more skillful in the science of legislation than the United States democracy ever can be. Being master of itself, it is not subject to transitory impulses; it has far-sighted plans and knows how to let them mature until the favorable opportunity offers. An aristocracy moves forward intelligently; it knows how to make the collective force of all its laws converge on one point at a time. A democracy is not like that; its laws are almost always defective or untimely. (Tocqueville 1969, p. 232)

He continued with a familiar assertion—"the great privilege of the Americans is to be able to make retrievable mistakes."

[15] See Samuelson 1978; Clymer 1978; Reinhold 1978. A nationwide election-day survey conducted in 1978 by the Times and CBS News turned up a 3–1 voter preference for spending cuts over tax cuts, and a 50 percent to 42 percent rejection of a "large Federal income tax cut, regardless of its effect on prices or government services"—a tendentious but recognizable rendition of Kemp-Roth (Clymer 1978, p. A19). In the same poll, 82 percent of Democratic voters and 86 percent of Republicans said they favored a constitutional amendment requiring federal budgets to be balanced (Reinhold 1978).

BIBLIOGRAPHY

Ackerman, Bruce A.
  1977 *Private Property and the Constitution.* New Haven: Yale University Press.
Ackerman, Bruce A., et al.
  1974 *The Uncertain Search for Environmental Quality.* New York: Free Press.
Almond, Gabriel A., and Powell, G. Bingham, Jr.
  1966 *Comparative Politics: A Developmental Approach.* Boston: Little, Brown.
American Political Science Association
  1950 *Toward a More Responsible Party System.* Report of the Committee on Political
    Parties. New York: Rinehart, especially pp. 21–22, 43, 56–65, and 72–73.
Arnold, R. Douglas
  1978 "Legislatures, Overspending and Government Growth." Paper delivered at the
    Conference on the Causes and Consequences of Public Sector Growth, Dorado
    Beach, Puerto Rico.
  1979 *Congress and the Bureaucracy.* New Haven: Yale University Press.
Asbell, Bernard
  1978 *The Senate Nobody Knows.* Garden City, N.Y.: Doubleday.
Bailey, Stephen K.
  1950 *Congress Makes a Law: The Story Behind the Employment Act of 1946.* New
    York: Columbia University Press.
Barry, Brian
  1965 *Political Argument.* London: Routledge & Kegan Paul, pp. 255–56.
Bauer, Raymond A., et al.
  1963 *American Business and Public Policy.* Chicago: Aldine-Atherton.
Beer, Samuel H.
  1976 "The Adoption of General Revenue Sharing: A Case Study of Public Sector
    Politics." *Public Policy* 14:127–95.
Bessette, Joseph M.
  1979 "Deliberation in Congress." Paper presented at the convention of the American
    Political Science Association, Washington, D.C.
Bryce, James
  1959 *The American Commonwealth.* New York: Putnam.
  [1888]
Burns, James MacGregor
  1963 *The Deadlock of Democracy.* Englewood Cliffs, N.J.: Prentice-Hall.
Cavanagh, Thomas E.
  1978 "The Two Arenas of Congress: Electoral and Institutional Incentives for Perfor-
    mance." Examination paper, Yale University.
Clark, Timothy B.
  1978 "Access for the Handicapped—A Test of Carter's War on Inflation." *National
    Journal,* October 21, p. 1673.
Clausen, Aage
  1973 *How Congressmen Decide: A Policy Focus.* New York: St. Martin's Press.
Clymer, Adam
  1978 "Most Voters Stay with Democrats but Republicans Make Gains in Governor-
    ships." *New York Times,* November 8, pp. A1, A19.
Congressional Quarterly Weekly
    March 26, 1977, pp. 561–63, 566–67; May 14, 1977, pp. 909–15; May 28,
    1977, pp. 1034–35; July 23, 1977, p. 1494; September 24, 1977, p. 2052.
Dahl, Robert A.
  1963 *A Preface to Democratic Theory.* Chicago: University of Chicago Press.
Davidson, Roger H., and Oleszek, Walter J.
  1977 *Congress Against Itself.* Bloomington: Indiana University Press.

Dodd, Lawrence C., and Oppenheimer, Bruce I.

    1977 "The House in Transition." In *Congress Reconsidered,* edited by Lawrence C. Dodd and Bruce I. Oppenheimer. New York: Praeger.

Fenno, Richard F., Jr.

    1966 *The Power of the Purse: Appropriations Politics in Congress.* Boston: Little, Brown.

    1973 *Congressmen in Committees.* Boston: Little, Brown.

    1978 *Home Style: House Members in Their Districts.* Boston: Little, Brown.

Ferejohn, John A.

    1974 *Pork Barrel Politics.* Stanford, Calif.: Stanford University Press.

Fiorina, Morris P.

    1977 *Congress: Keystone of the Washington Establishment.* New Haven: Yale University Press.

Fisher, Louis

    1972 *President and Congress: Power and Policy.* New York: Free Press.

Franck, Thomas M., and Weisband, Edward

    1979 *Foreign Policy by Congress.* New York: Oxford University Press.

Friedman, John

    1979 "A Populist Shift in Federal Cultural Support." *New York Times,* May 13, p. D1.

Green, Mark J., et al.

    1972 *Who Runs Congress?* New York: Grossman.

Harris, Richard

    1964 *The Real Voice.* New York: Macmillan.

Hayes, Michael T.

    1961 *Lobbyists and Legislators: A Theory of Political Markets.* New Brunswick, N.J.: Rutgers University Press.

Hofstadter, Richard

    1967 "The Paranoid Style in American Politics." In *The Paranoid Style in American Politics and Other Essays.* New York: Vintage Books.

Horowitz, Donald L.

    1977 *The Courts and Social Policy.* Washington, D.C.: Brookings Institution.

Huntington, Samuel P.

    1965 "Congressional Responses to the Twentieth Century." In *The Congress and America's Future,* edited by David B. Truman. Englewood Cliffs, N.J.: Prentice-Hall.

Jacobson, Gary C.

    1980 *Money in Congressional Elections.* New Haven: Yale University Press.

Jones, Charles O.

    1961 "Representation in Congress: The Case of the House Agriculture Committee." *American Political Science Review* 55:358–67.

Kaufman, Herbert

    1976 *Are Government Organizations Immortal?* Washington, D.C.: Brookings Institution.

    1977 *Red Tape: Its Origins, Uses, and Abuses.* Washington, D.C.: Brookings Institution.

Kingdon, John W.

    1973 *Congressmen's Voting Decisions.* New York: Harper & Row.

Kirkpatrick, Evron M.

    1971 "Toward a More Responsible Two-Party System: Political Science, Policy Science, or Pseudo-Science?" *American Political Science Review* 65:965–90.

Large, Arlen J.

    1973 "Pandora Opens a Can of Worms." *Wall Street Journal,* August 28, p. 10.

Lewis-Beck, Michael S., and Alford, John R.

    1980 "Can Government Regulate Safety? The Coal Mine Example." *American Political Science Review* 74:745–56.

Lindblom, Charles E., and Cohen, David K.
  1979 *Usable Knowledge: Social Science and Social Problem Solving.* New Haven:
      Yale University Press.
Lorch, Robert S.
  1969 *Democratic Processes and Administrative Law.* Detroit: Wayne State University
      Press.
Lowi, Theodore H.
  1969 *The End of Liberalism.* New York: Norton.
Madison, James, et al.
  1961 *The Federalist Papers.* No. 10. New York: New American Library.
  [1787–88]
Malbin, Michael
  1977 "Congressional Committee Staffs: Who's in Charge Here?" *Public Interest,*
      Spring, pp. 16–40.
  1980 *Unelected Representatives: Congressional Staff and the Future of Representative
      Government.* New York: Basic Books.
Manley, John F.
  1970 *The Politics of Finance: The House Committee on Ways and Means.* Boston:
      Little, Brown.
Mann, Thomas E.
  1978 *Unsafe at Any Margin: Interpreting Congressional Elections.* Washington, D.C.:
      American Enterprise Institute.
Mann, Thomas E., and Ornstein, Norman J., eds.
  1981 *The New Congress.* Washington, D.C.: American Enterprise Institute.
Mann, Thomas E., and Wolfinger, Raymond E.
  1980 "Candidates and Parties in Congressional Elections." *American Political Science
      Review* 74:617–32.
Matthews, Donald R.
  1960 *U.S. Senators and Their World.* Chapel Hill: University of North Carolina Press.
Mayhew, David R.
  1966 *Party Loyalty Among Congressmen: The Difference Between Democrats and
      Republicans, 1947–1962.* Cambridge, Mass.: Harvard University Press.
  1974 *The Electoral Connection.* New Haven: Yale University Press.
Murphy, James T.
  1968 "Partisanship and the House Public Works Committee." Paper presented at
      the annual convention of the American Political Science Association,
      Washington, D.C.
Nagel, Jack H.
  1975 *The Descriptive Analysis of Power.* New Haven: Yale University Press.
Neustadt, Richard E.
  1976 *Presidential Power.* Rev. ed. New York: Wiley.
Niskanen, William A.
  1971 *Bureaucracy and Representative Government.* New York: Aldine-Atherton.
Peabody, Robert L.
  1976 *Leadership in Congress: Stability, Succession and Change.* Boston: Little,
      Brown.
Peabody, Robert L., and Polsby, Nelson W., eds.
  1977 *New Perspectives on the House of Representatives.* Chicago: Rand McNally.
Polsby, Daniel D.
  1977 "Buckley v. Valeo: The Special Nature of Political Speech." In *The Supreme Court
      Review,* edited by Philip B. Kurland. Chicago: University of Chicago Press.
Polsby, Nelson W.
  1968 "The Institutionalization of the U.S. House of Representatives." *American Politi-
      cal Science Review* 62:144–68.

1975 "Legislatures." In *Governmental Institutions and Processes,* edited by Fred I. Greenstein and Nelson W. Polsby. Handbook of Political Science, vol. 5. Reading, Mass.: Addison-Wesley.

1980 "The News Media as an Alternative to Party in the Presidential Selection Process." In *Political Parties in the Eighties,* edited by Robert A. Goldwin. Washington, D.C.: American Enterprise Institute.

Pressman, Jeffrey L., and Wildavsky, Aaron B.

1973 *Implementation.* Berkeley: University of California Press.

Prewitt, Kenneth

1970 "Political Ambitions, Volunteerism, and Electoral Accountability." *American Political Science Review* 64:5–17.

Price, David

1972 *Who Makes the Laws?* Cambridge, Mass.: Schenkman.

Price, H. Douglas

1975 "Congress and the Evolution of Legislative 'Professionalism.' " In *Congress in Change,* edited by Norman J. Ornstein. New York: Praeger.

Public Interest

1980 "Poor America." *Public Interest,* Summer, pp. 148–49.

Ranney, Austin

1954 *The Doctrine of Responsible Party Government.* Urbana: University of Illinois Press.

Reich, Charles A.

1964 "The New Property." *Yale Law Journal* 73:733–87.

Reinhold, Robert

1978 "Poll Indicates Congress Candidates Were More Extreme Than Voters." *New York Times,* November 9, p. A21.

Riker, William H.

1962 *The Theory of Political Coalitions.* New Haven: Yale University Press.

Samuelson, Robert J.

1978 "Tax Cut May Come Back to Haunt House Members." *National Journal,* August 5, pp. 1245–47.

Schick, Allen

1980 *Congress and Money: Budgeting, Spending and Taxing.* Washington, D.C.: Urban Institute.

Schuck, Peter H.

1980 "The Graying of Civil Rights Law." *Public Interest,* Summer, pp. 69–93.

Scully, Michael A.

1977 "Reflections of a Senate Aide." *Public Interest,* Spring, pp. 41–48.

Seidman, Harold

1970 *Politics, Position, and Power: The Dynamics of Federal Organization.* New York: Oxford University Press.

Shapiro, Martin

1968 *The Supreme Court and Administrative Agencies.* New York: Free Press, chap. 1.

Shepsle, Kenneth A.

1978 *The Giant Jigsaw Puzzle.* Chicago: University of Chicago Press.

Singer, James W.

1978 "It's Not Over Till It's Over." *National Journal,* October 21, p. 1688.

Stanfield, Rochelle L.

1978 "Age Discrimination Regs—They're Turning the Rule Makers Gray." *National Journal,* December 30, p. 2066.

Sussman, Barry

1978 "Waste Angers Taxpayers, Poll Shows." *Los Angeles Times,* October 15, p. IV-2.

Tocqueville, Alexis de
   1969 *Democracy in America.* Garden City, N.Y.: Doubleday Anchor.
   [1835]
Truman, David B.
   1960 *The Governmental Process.* New York: Knopf.
Turner, Julius
   1970 *Party and Constituency: Pressures on Congress.* Edition revised by Edward V.
      Schneier, Jr. Baltimore: Johns Hopkins Press.
Walkland, S. A.
   1968 *The Legislative Process in Great Britain.* London: Allen and Unwin.
Wildavsky, Aaron B.
   1974 *The Politics of the Budgetary Process.* Boston: Little, Brown.
   1980 *How to Limit Government Spending.* Berkeley: University of California Press.
Wilson, James Q.
   1975 "The Rise of the Bureaucratic State." *Public Interest,* Fall, pp. 77–103.
Wilson, Woodrow
   1956 *Congressional Government.* New York: Meridian, especially pp. 77–82, 91–98,
      130–33, 147, 210–14.
Wolfinger, Raymond E., and Heifetz, Joan
   1965 "Safe Seats, Seniority, and Power in Congress." *American Political Science
      Review* 59:337–49.

9

IS CONGRESS REALLY FOR SALE?
Paul Burstein

Despite the picture Mayhew draws of Congress, it is not an institution that people say they like. Citizens might like particular people in the institution, usually a senator from their state or the representative from their district (if they happen to know who that is). But ordinary voters take it for granted that members of Congress do the bidding of lobbyists. Listen long enough to people who belittle Congress and you might fancifully imagine that sleek lawyers glide around the marble halls of the Capitol in tasseled loafers carrying suitcases full of cash and issuing detailed instructions to lazy legislators. As a matter of logic and evidence, Burstein shows, thinking this way—that Congress is a "market for legislation"—is plain wrong. This is hardly to deny that members of Congress pay attention to extremely wealthy people in their districts or states, particularly if they employ people and generate jobs in the district or the state, or that they or their staffers never meet with representatives of interest groups and advocacy organizations. Of course they do these things. In fact, doing them is part of their job. But if you want to know the answer to "who governs Congress?" then the answer is: the officeholders themselves. They structure its rules, learn its complexities, protect its prerogatives, and make it work to produce legislation and to serve as the institutional foundation on which they can do things like investigate and oversee other parts of the national government. The people who run Congress are the people in and of Congress, elected by majorities in their districts and states. They run it as an active legislature, just as Mayhew shows.

• • •

MANY AMERICANS lament the way special interests sway politicians with campaign contributions and lobbying, procuring privileged treatment even when the public is opposed. Research shows, however, that contributions and lobbying determine public policy much less than most people think. When major issues arise, party, ideology and public opinion matter much more.

"Lobbyists Are the Loudest in Health Care Debate," read the *New York Times* headline in August 1994. President Clinton's proposal for health care reform had provoked hundreds of interest groups into spending well over $100 million to influence the congressional response. Opposition was intense; political action committees (PACs) were reported to be spending over $2 million a month to modify the plan or kill it outright. And they got what they wanted; by the end of September Bill and Hillary Clinton's health plan was dead.

The fight over health care was unusually intense but otherwise typical, according to journalists' conventional wisdom about American politics: interest groups get what they want, regardless of the public's needs. Paul Krugman informed his readers in the *New York Times* last year, for example, that there would be no anti-pollution legislation under the Bush administration because "the big polluters get what they paid for in campaign contributions." Frank Rich, also in the *Times*, claimed that the Clinton administration did Enron's bidding on a power-plant project after getting $100,000 in Enron contributions. And Molly Ivins, writing from Texas, stated that CSX (formerly headed by Bush's new Treasury Secretary John Snow) got $164 million in federal tax rebates in return for the "investment" of a "mere $5.9 million in campaign contributions." The result, William Raspberry wrote in the *Washington Post*, is the "increased influence of moneyed interests while the ordinary voter seems to dwindle to insignificance."

Most Americans agree with this view. Three out of five people polled for the American National Election Studies said in 2000 that "the government is pretty much run by a few big interests looking out for themselves" rather than for the benefit of all the people, and almost as many agreed that public officials don't care much about what "people like me" think. Early in 2002, a Gallup poll showed that two-thirds of the public believe that no matter how campaign finance laws are reformed, "special interests will always find a way to maintain their power in Washington." Public cynicism about the federal government has become so pervasive that many observers fear the public is withdrawing from politics, leading to a self-fulfilling prophecy in which the public's retreat opens the way to even more special interest power.

Does anyone dissent from this view? Yes—many academic experts on American politics do, particularly those in political science and economics. For decades, a pattern of research has emerged that has surprised them as much as anyone else: A major study shows that campaign contributions or lobbying have little influence on policy. The findings are met with disbelief. Researchers refine their theories and methods, anticipating that more sophisticated studies—looking at more aspects of the policy process—will show that campaign contributions and lobbying have a powerful effect. Contrary to expectations, the new studies find that money and the efforts of special interest groups have little influence, and the cycle repeats.

One recent review (by political scientist Stephen Ansolabehere and his colleagues), found that on most issues studied PAC contributions have no effect on legislation. A review April Linton and I conducted considered the effect not only of PAC contributions, but of other ways of influencing policy as well—lobbying, demonstrating, union organizing—and found that they have no effect at all at least half the time. When groups do have an effect, it is typically slight. Even business lobbying and campaign contributions typically have little impact.

How can campaign contributions and lobbying have little or no effect on policy? Here it is important to be precise about what the issue is. Even though stories in the mass media highlight how much money is spent to influence policymakers, that is not what concerns the public most. The crucial questions are: Do campaign contributions and lobbying get legislators to act differently than they would have in the absence of contributions and lobbying? Do contributions and lobbying influence enough legislators to tip the balance on important votes? And, most critically, do contributions and lobbying enable interest groups to get what they want over the opposition of the public?

It turns out that the effect of campaign contributions and lobbying is limited for several reasons: Campaign contributions are not really that large; most lobbyists cannot even get to see members of Congress, much less influence them; members of Congress are more strongly affected by their parties, ideology, and constituents than by interest groups; and when some are influenced by campaign contributions or lobbying, the number is often too small to determine the outcome of key votes. The effect of campaign contributions and lobbying is overestimated because people tend to remember the egregious but atypical cases of apparent influence, ignore other influences on members of Congress, and not consider how the sheer complexity of modern politics affects policy change.

CAMPAIGN CONTRIBUTORS

In most accounts, interest groups have two ways to influence politicians: contributing to their campaigns and lobbying.

Campaign contributions are often seen as especially powerful, bordering on legalized bribery. We are told constantly that American political campaigns are awash in money. Every campaign costs more than the previous one, and the total amount spent on campaigns for Congress and the presidency—$3 billion in the 1999–2000 election cycle—seems astronomical. How can such huge sums not turn into tremendous interest group influence?

A closer look at the money—how much there is, where it comes from, and where it goes—provides some context. First, it may be argued that $3 billion isn't really all that much money, when Democrats' and Republicans' efforts to win "market share" are compared to other industries. All the money spent to influence candidates and campaigns amounted to less per year than the combined amount that corporations spent to influence our choice of soft drinks (Coca-Cola Corporation's advertising budget is $1.6 billion per year), phone companies (AT&T—$750 million) or computers (IBM—$650 million). In addition, only one-third of the total—about $1 billion—came from interest groups. 380 million dollars of this amount came directly, in the form of "soft money," from corporations, unions, and other groups. An additional $600 million came from PACs. The rest came from individuals' contributions directly to parties and candidates, and from government funds.

Most PACs contribute very little to campaigns. During the 2000 campaign, approximately 4,500 PACs were registered with the Federal Election Commission. Of these, one-third spent no money at all on the campaign. Of those that did, the average contribution to each candidate they aided was $1,700—approximately $1,400 from corporations, $1,700 from trade associations and membership groups, and $2,200 from labor unions. These amounts are not trivial, but considering that the average House candidate spent about $700,000 in 2000, and the average Senate candidate $5.7 million, it is difficult to see particular groups winning tremendous influence over most members of Congress through their campaign contributions. (Contributions from individuals aren't very large, either. Ansolabehere et al. estimate that the average political contribution from an individual was $115 in 2000, while a study of top executives showed them contributing—as individuals rather than through PACs—an average of $4,500.)

Of course, campaign contributions are only one way to influence office-holders. Lobbying—attempts to persuade politicians how to vote—is important to consider as well.

LOBBYING

What interest groups don't get through campaign contributions, they must get by lobbying, says the conventional wisdom. Indeed, there's an army of lobbyists around Capitol Hill—more than 20,000 registered in 2002.

The sheer number of lobbyists shows why it is believed that campaign contributions go simply to win access. No member of Congress and his or her entire staff could possibly see more than a tiny fraction of all the lobbyists over the course of a year, even if they stopped spending any time meeting ordinary constituents, visiting their districts, taking part in hearings and casting hundreds of votes.

It is also important to remember that many organizations that lobbyists represent are organizations of ordinary people, not the business organizations frequently cited in critiques of the system. Members of Congress hear not only from the National Association of Manufacturers, but also from organizations representing teachers, college students, minorities, crime victims, truck drivers and parochial schools—organizations that, taken together, represent a substantial proportion of the American people. Thus, when Congress is affected by interest groups, the groups may very well represent labor (unions sometimes affect congressional action on taxes), the elderly (who have influenced policy on pensions), or ordinary citizens concerned about guns (both the National Rifle Association and its opponent, Handgun Control, have at times influenced members of Congress).

It still may be said that it is not the typical lobbyist who distorts the political process, it is the well-connected lobbyist representing powerful groups with guaranteed access to members of Congress. Surely, there is something to this point of view. But when trying to determine whether access leads to influence, it is essential to return to the key questions: Do interest groups get members of Congress to act differently than they would otherwise? Do they get many members of Congress to do so? And do they win policies in opposition to what a majority of the public wants?

To answer these questions, it is necessary to ask how legislators would act in the absence of contributions and lobbying. What other factors influence their actions? Research consistently shows three factors to be especially important: ideology, party affiliation and public opinion.

IDEOLOGY AND PARTIES

Every year, the *Congressional Quarterly*, journalists' and academics' primary source of information about Congress, lists what it calls "key votes"—votes that, in the editors' opinion, determined the outcome on the most important and controversial issues Congress addressed. For 2002, it listed 11 votes in the House and 13 in the Senate. Some were on issues that most people wouldn't think are subject to interest group influence in a conventional sense, including the use of force against Iraq, establishment of an independent commission on 9/11 and some homeland security measures. Votes on these issues were probably determined by factors other than special interest actions. On most votes, though, interest groups had a strong interest in the outcome: pharmaceutical manufacturers and the American Association of Retired Persons (AARP) in votes on a Medicare prescription drug benefit; energy companies and environmental groups in votes on oil and gas drilling in the Arctic National Wildlife Refuge; agribusiness and small farmer groups in votes on farm subsidies, etc. What was most striking about many of the key votes was how often they were almost entirely along party lines. In the

House vote on prescription drug benefits, 16 representatives crossed party lines, out of 427 voting. In the Senate vote on farm subsidies, 11 of 97. On drilling in the Arctic National Wildlife Refuge, 13 of 99. Divisions were similar on defense spending, welfare reform, total government spending, campaign finance reform and the estate tax.

Why the differences between parties? One might argue that campaign contributions and lobbying led Republicans to vote one way and Democrats the other—that, for example, Republicans vote for Arctic drilling because of campaign contributions from the oil industry, and Democrats vote against it because of contributions from environmentalists. But if that were true, the energy companies could have outbid environmental groups and gotten what they wanted when the Democrats were in power. The party balance matters because the Republican party is ideologically committed to the needs of the oil industry, and the Democratic party to the environmental movement. Party and ideology matter far more than campaign contributions and lobbying.

But what about those who vote against their party, for example the eight Republicans who opposed drilling and the five Democrats who favored it? Campaign contributions and lobbying surely matter sometimes, but often those who vote against their parties are voting in line with their own long-standing, well-known views and with the views dominant in their regions. Among the five Democrats who favored drilling, three were rated by the League of Conservation voters as having voting records in 2002 (and for years before) very much like Republicans and very much in line with attitudes in their region, while three of the Republicans who defected consistently voted with Democrats on environmental issues, in line with the more liberal stance of the New Englanders they represent.

Also consider the Clinton health care plan. Among those who got the most in campaign contributions from health and insurance industries were Edward Kennedy and Newt Gingrich. Yet nothing could have turned Kennedy, a staunch Democrat, against health care reform, or dissuaded Gingrich from using opposition to the plan as the basis for the Republicans' ultimately successful fight for Congress in the 1994 election. These are not isolated examples. Though it is very difficult to separate the effect of party affiliation from ideology (because ideology influences choice of party and vice versa), there is little question that party and ideology together have far more effect on congressional action than interest groups do, even on issues usually seen as greatly influenced by interest groups, such as taxes on corporate profits and capital gains. Even when political scientists very carefully estimate how many legislators are affected by interest groups, they usually find the number too small to determine the result.

Political scientist John R. Wright's work provides a particularly interesting illustration. Wright gauged interest group influence on congressional voting on tobacco. He began his research soon after an article in the *Journal of the American Medical Association (JAMA)* claimed that congressional opposition to tobacco control was clearly due to tobacco-industry PAC contributions to members of Congress. Wright was dubious, however, because the *JAMA* article hadn't considered how voting might have been affected by members' political ideology. When he took ideology into account (using ratings by Americans for Democratic Action), it turned out that campaign contributions may have had some effect, but not as much as ideology and, most importantly, not enough to affect the outcome of the vote. Tobacco industry contributions went mostly to conservatives and Republicans who were already predisposed to vote against regulations of any kind.

The power of interest groups to get legislators to change their votes in the face of personal ideology and party commitments is real but very limited. But what is arguably the most important question remains: Do interest groups get what they want against the opposition of the public?

PUBLIC OPINION AND POLICY

According to the *New York Times*, the fate of the Clinton health care plan was a stark example of special interest lobbying "overwhelming the decision-making process." The process, in this case, is the democratic process. The claim is that interest groups won out over the public.

It is easy to see why people believe this. When Clinton's task force began developing plans for health care reform, 71 percent of the public said they approved of what they heard or read about it. When the plan was announced in September 1993, 59 percent of the public supported it. Yet it lost. What explanation could there be but interest group influence?

The explanation, many analysts have come to believe, is public opinion itself. In 1992, even before Clinton took office, health policy analyst Robert Blendon and his colleagues published an article in the *JAMA* describing public opinion on health care. They showed that the public was interested in health care reform, but was concerned about costs, coverage, the extent of government control and other issues. Presented with competing plans during the Clinton administration, the public turned out to be opposed to increasing income taxes to pay for universal coverage, and were much more interested in improving their own care than in providing care for the uninsured. Given a choice among possible plans, no single one was favored by a majority. By the time the plan was defeated, it had the support of only 43 percent of Americans. As Theda Skocpol has written, only "steadfast majority public support" could have gotten Congress to act, but such support "was gone by the time the Democratic congressional leaders finally got bills to the floor of the House and Senate."

Some observers have objected that although Congress acted in line with public opinion, public opinion itself had been influenced by interest groups pouring vast sums of money into media campaigns against the plan. This raises an interesting point. If interest groups devote great effort to changing public opinion, perhaps that is because they see public opinion as the prime mover behind policy change. In fact, as political scientist Ken Kollman has recently shown, that is how interest groups often see the political process. Interest groups of all types (labor, business, public interest, etc.) expend considerable resources on what he calls "outside lobbying"—attempts to mobilize citizens outside the policymaking community to pressure public officials. Naturally, interest groups would like to alter public opinion, but that is usually difficult. As a practical matter, what they try to do most often is take advantage of public opinion—to mobilize the public when it already favors their views.

It makes sense for interest groups to take public opinion seriously, because systematic studies comparing the effect of public opinion to that of lobbying and campaign contributions find consistently that public opinion matters more. For example, political scientist Mark A. Smith analyzed congressional action on over 2,300 issues on which the U.S. Chamber of Commerce took a stand between 1953 and 1996. He found that although business lobbying and PAC contributions had some effect on policy—it would be amazing if they had none—public opinion swayed Congress far more. Similarly, I found that interest group activity influenced employment discrimination legislation (which corporations were not enthusiastic about) far less than did public opinion. Similar results have been found for welfare policies and hate crime laws. Social scientists find it difficult practically to separate the effects of interest groups from that of public opinion, but the weight of the evidence to date clearly emphasizes the role of public opinion.

WHAT ABOUT COMMON SENSE?

In the face of findings that campaign contributions and lobbying have little effect on policy, and that party, ideology, and public opinion have far more, we still confront a key problem: the conclusions seem utterly contrary to everyone's experience and common sense. Is it possible to reconcile the conventional wisdom with what research shows?

The conventional wisdom may be mistaken for three reasons: people are especially likely to remember egregious examples of interest group power; it is difficult to sort out the multiple influences on policy change; and people often mistake their own policy preferences for those of the majority.

One reason most people think lobbying and campaign contributions are crucial is because reporters say they are; and reporters think they are important because of the striking cases they can't help but notice. But a focus on striking cases can be misleading. Discussions of interest group power return again and again to gun control, an issue on which a majority of the public, which favors gun control, is frustrated by the apparent power of the National Rifle Association. But the gun issue is an exception. Much less often do people systematically consider the role of interest groups on issues that matter more to most people but win less attention. Until very recently, the public was terribly afraid of crime and demanded government action; government at all levels responded by toughening laws, building prisons, and spending more money on police. The public always wants economic growth, and every administration works to bring it about. The quality of education rose in the public's list of concerns during the 1990s, and both state governments and Congress responded with reforms intended to improve K-12 education. Any fair assessment of the power of interest groups would have to take into account all these issues, not only blatant cases of interest group influence.

Common sense tells us that campaign contributions and lobbying matter because the influence seems so obvious—as with the Clinton health care example, we see that lobbyists were active and that they got what they wanted, so it seems only natural to conclude that Congress acted as it did because of special interest influence. But frequently, as with Wright's tobacco regulation example, it turns out that it is not really contributions or lobbying that matter most, but rather party, ideology or public opinion.

Finally, it sometimes seems obvious that interest groups control events because particular decisions seem so awful that there can be no other explanation—the decisions must have been opposed by a majority of the public. In fact, though, individuals are often mistaken about the majority's preference. What's more, on most of the hundreds of issues contemporary governments address, most people have no opinion at all. Most citizens neither know nor care about even some of the issues on which "key votes" occurred (such as competition in the telecommunications industry, fast-track trade procedures, farm subsidies or accounting standards). And the proportion that has meaningful opinions about the hundreds of other issues voted on by Congress every year (such as extension of copyright protection, tariffs on steel, federal funding of social science research, etc.) is small. The harsh truth is not that interest groups persistently win out over public opinion, but that on a wide range of issues, the public has no opinion. Many observers who view the results of decisions with dismay incorrectly assume that the general public shares their dismay—or would, if they only paid attention.

RECOMMENDED RESOURCES

Ansolabehere, Stephen, John de Figureiredo, and James M. Snyder, Jr. "Why Is There So Little Money in U.S. Politics?" *Journal of Economic Perspectives* (forthcoming). An analysis of how much money is given to political campaigns, the influence of campaign contributions on members of Congress and a discussion of why people contribute to campaigns.

Burstein, Paul, and April Linton. "The Impact of Political Parties, Interest Groups, and Social Movement Organizations on Public Policy." *Social Forces* 81 (December 2002):380–408. An overview of how strongly policy is affected by the party balance, interest groups and social movement organizations.

Smith, Mark A. *American Business and Political Power.* Chicago: University of Chicago Press, 2000. Smith analyzes how well bills supported by the U.S. Chamber of Commerce do in Congress, comparing the influence of business to that of public opinion.

Wright, John R. "Tobacco Industry PACs and the Nation's Health." In *The Interest Group Connection*, eds. Paul S. Herrnson, Ronald Shaiko and Clyde Wilcox. Chatham, NJ: Chatham House Publishers, 1997. Wright shows that the apparent impact of tobacco industry PACs on Congress has been greatly exaggerated.

10

JUDICIAL INDEPENDENCE THROUGH THE LENS OF *BUSH V. GORE*: FOUR LESSONS FROM POLITICAL SCIENCE

Howard Gillman[*]

How do political scientists get anywhere in studying the Court? It is an institution shrouded in secrecy. Interviewing the justices and clerks of the Supreme Court is out of the question for political scientists—only once, in fact, has a political scientist been able to do that. There are nonetheless ample materials from which analysts can draw inferences about the Court—and about whether and how it "has politics." They include (in no particular order) the written opinions, summary affirmances of lower court decisions, statements that are sometimes issued in connection with refusals to take a case, the justices' occasional public statements, judicial biographies written by historians, the personal papers that have become available, the vote tallies in cases, the briefs and other parts of a case record, commentary by members of Congress and the president that reveal the degree of conflict between a Court's majority and the occupants of other branches, the number and content of bills that members of Congress introduce to curb the Court, and the statutes (i.e., the many judiciary acts since the Founding) that have been enacted in order to develop the federal judiciary and to specify the jurisdiction of the Court.

Using these rich materials, political scientists have come to agree that the Supreme Court's members make public policy and that they do so strategically—at least in part—in the sense of carefully anticipating the reception of their decisions. This can come as a surprise for most people who are not political scientists and who tend to see the Court's justices as primarily legal—and not political—actors.

Indeed, people who are not political scientists readily distinguish the Court's members from the occupants of national elective office. They see members of the Court as reflective and even wise figures who, collectively, act as a saving grace for American politics. The Court, because it is independent, will do what is right for the country when the legislative-executive process is unable to—as in civil rights, to take a famous example.

It is precisely with this sort of example that political scientists become iconoclastic. Sure, the Court issued a unanimous decision in the landmark desegregation case, Brown v. Board—but did it not then refuse to implement the decision, holding in a follow-up decision that desegregation should occur with "all deliberate speed"? In fact, was it not until Congress and the

Originally published at 64 *Ohio St. L.J.* 249 (2003). Permission granted by the *Ohio State Law Journal.*

[*] Professor of Political Science and Law, University of Southern California. The author thanks Barry Friedman, Mark Graber, Michael Klarman, and Keith Whittington for their assistance, and happily relieves them of any responsibility for the ideas expressed in this essay.

president forced desegregation through withholding federal funding from segregated school districts that desegregation occurred? The justices of the Court are quite "political" in other words.

In this article Gillman carries such iconoclasm forward. He seriously considers whether a faction of justices of the Supreme Court would gain factional advantage by allying itself with party politicians. He does not offer direct evidence to support what actually amount to quite clever speculations. His article nonetheless forces one to think deeply about whether—at a critical moment in the nation's history, the election recount crisis of 2000—the justices of the Court engaged in "pressure-free, good-faith judging" (to use Gillman's words). How much of a saving grace is the Court in the end?

• • •

INTRODUCTION

THE EXPERIENCES with the 2000 election litigation, particularly the United States Supreme Court's decision in *Bush v. Gore*,[1] illustrate aspects of judicial independence that may be overlooked if too much focus is placed on linking the concept to the simple virtue of pressure-free, good-faith judging. This article explores the advantages of discussing judicial independence as if it was a subset of the more general practice of insulating policy-making institutions—like central banks or regulatory commissions—from conventional political pressures or mechanisms of political accountability.[2] Unfettered, neutral, professional decision-making may be one outcome that is desired whenever such independence is considered. However, these are not the only relevant political considerations or the only likely political consequences.

This article adopts a "regime politics" or "dominant coalition" view of institutional independence. This approach examines institutional structures, including the organization of judicial power, in terms of the political advantages for power-holders who are interested in promoting substantive political agendas.[3] This angle of analysis is not necessarily more accurate than one that emphasizes the relationship between judicial independence and values, such as the rule of law or impartiality. Nonetheless, an exclusive focus on these familiar tropes limits our field of vision. When too much focus is placed on judicial independence and the rule of law, it might mistakenly appear as if high courts are designed to be politically neutral. It is easy to forget that there is actually more room (by design) for ideological decision-making in the United States Supreme Court than there may

---

[1] 531 U.S. 98 (2000).

[2] For similar analyses of judicial politics and a review of the political science literature on the creation of politically insulated policy-making institutions, see Ran Hirschl, *The Political Origins of Judicial Empowerment Through Constitutionalization: Lessons from Four Constitutional Revolutions*, 25 LAW & SOC. INQUIRY 91, 102–05 (2000); Edward L. Rubin, *Independence as a Governance Mechanism, in* JUDICIAL INDEPENDENCE AT THE CROSSROADS: AN INTERDISCIPLINARY APPROACH 56, 69–77 (Stephen B. Burbank & Barry Friedman eds., 2002) [hereinafter JUDICIAL INDEPENDENCE].

[3] For additional examples of studies that place judicial politics in a larger political context, see Robert A. Dahl, *Decision-Making in a Democracy: The Supreme Court as a National Policy-Maker*, 6 J. PUB. L. 279 (1957); Howard Gillman, *How Political Parties Can Use Courts to Advance Their Agendas: Federal Courts in the United States, 1875–1891*, 96 AM. POL. SCI. REV. 511 (2002); Mark A. Graber, *The Nonmajoritarian Difficulty: Legislative Deference to the Judiciary*, 7 STUD. AM. POL. DEV. 35 (1993); Barry R. Weingast, *The Political Foundations of Democracy and the Rule of Law*, 91 AM. POL. SCI. REV. 245 (1997).

be for policy-making institutions such as central banks, whose missions are narrower or more well defined.[4]

Bush v. Gore is a useful starting point for thinking about judicial independence in terms of regime politics rather than the neutral application of law. Few scholars have been willing to defend the decision as an exemplar of impartial decision-making or as a stoic defense of the rule of law in the face of enormous political pressure, although some do make this argument.[5] It is already common to treat the case as an example of the sort of political agendas that might be pursued from within an institution that enjoys insulation from conventional mechanisms of political accountability.[6] Perhaps even those with a different view might find value in some of this article's more general points about judicial independence.

As this article will discuss, the analysis of *Bush v. Gore* reveals four major lessons about judicial independence and the Supreme Court that are sometimes overlooked in conventional discussions.

I. LESSON ONE:
THE DECISION TO GRANT INDEPENDENCE TO A POLICY-MAKING INSTITUTION HAS AS MUCH TO DO WITH INSULATING PREFERRED POLITICAL AGENDAS FROM ELECTORAL PRESSURE AS WITH ENSURING IMPARTIALITY

It is a basic assumption of political science that the United States Supreme Court is designed to be a national policy-making institution, not a forum for the routine and neutral resolution of everyday disputes.[7] Conventional ideological and political considerations dominate staffing decisions.[8] Justices may not always act in a way that is preferred by the appointing president, but political explanations usually exist for these relatively rare circumstances,[9] and they do not undermine

---

[4] For a canonical treatment of the United States Supreme Court as an ideological policy-making institution, see generally JEFFREY A. SEGAL & HAROLD J. SPAETH, THE SUPREME COURT AND THE ATTITUDINAL MODEL (1993).

[5] *See, e.g.*, Ronald D. Rotunda, *Yet Another Article on* Bush v. Gore, 64 OHIO ST. L.J. 283 (2003).

[6] Commentators disagree about what political agenda was being pursued. Some share Judge Richard Posner's belief that the decision was a salutary effort to forestall a potential constitutional crisis. *See* RICHARD A. POSNER, BREAKING THE DEADLOCK: THE 2000 ELECTION, THE CONSTITUTION, AND THE COURTS 3 (2001). Others believe that the conservative majority let partisan preferences trump their normal views of the law. *See* HOWARD GILLMAN, THE VOTES THAT COUNTED: HOW THE COURT DECIDED THE 2000 PRESIDENTIAL ELECTION 185–89 (2001). Still, there is a widespread consensus of opinion that some sort of political analysis is useful in understanding the Court's conduct during the 2000 election dispute.

[7] *See* TERRI JENNINGS PERETTI, IN DEFENSE OF A POLITICAL COURT 71–73 (1999) [hereinafter PERETTI, IN DEFENSE]. More recently, Peretti insists that if analysts persist in linking judicial independence to political neutrality, we all should be "dubious about the existence of judicial independence." Terri Jennings Peretti, *Does Judicial Independence Exist? The Lessons of Social Science Research, in* JUDICIAL INDEPENDENCE, *supra* note 2, at 103.

[8] For a discussion of the modern process, see DAVID ALISTAIR YALOF, PURSUIT OF JUSTICES: PRESIDENTIAL POLITICS AND THE SELECTION OF SUPREME COURT NOMINEES 12–19 (1999).

[9] Consider several political explanations for why justices do not always decide cases in a way that reflects the preferences of appointing presidents. One explanation is that the appointment may have been driven by non-ideological political considerations, such as geographical balance (more important in the nineteenth century than the twentieth) or other aspects of coalition politics. A second is that the President may face a Senate that does not share the President's ideology and insists on a compromise

the basic point. As Terri Peretti stated, ideological voting by justices "is not merely the arbitrary expression of a justice's idiosyncratic views [but] [r]ather . . . is the expression and vindication of those political views deliberately 'planted' on the Court" by policy-conscious presidents and senators.[10]

Because dominant coalitions are largely successful at planting trustworthy agents on the Supreme Court, the justices almost never engage in policy-making that challenges those power-holders who are in a position to assault their nominal independence. It is extremely rare, although not unheard of, for the Court to void an act of a current or "live" national majority.[11] It is more common for the justices to go after national legislation passed by a previous governing coalition or to impose a national policy consensus on local or regional "outliers."[12] In other words, judicial independence, defined as decision-making autonomy,[13] is largely a function of political alignment with potential adversaries rather than the maintenance of political neutrality.

However, inter-institutional alignment is not always perfect. During periods of prolonged inter-party competition, different political coalitions may control the White House and Congress, or the House and the Senate, and the justices may split among competing camps that reflect these broader, sustained divisions in the political system. A working majority on the Supreme Court may find itself in and out of sync with all or part of the federal government, especially if a wing of one of the parties has made efforts to entrench a politically tenuous agenda within the judiciary.[14] This condition does not necessarily put the Court's work at risk in the short term because it is likely that the Court's effective majority may be able to count on political allies who are in a position to veto any serious threats. However, under these circumstances, the Court's policy-making agenda can be placed at risk over the long term, especially if (a) that agenda is supported by only a narrow majority; (b) justices in that majority may be close to retirement (or worse); and (c) a chance exists that political opponents may take control of the presidency and the Senate and thus be in a position to use the appointment process to change the course of the Court's decision-making.

This is precisely the political context within which the 2000 election litigation evolved. While the justices were not aligned into opposing camps in all cases, a tenuous conservative majority emerged on several important constitutional issues,

---

candidate. Yet a third is that unanticipated issues may arise after an appointment that expose viewpoint differences between presidents and their appointees.

[10] PERETTI, IN DEFENSE, *supra* note 7, at 133.

[11] *See* Dahl, *supra* note 3 (providing a classical political science study of this issue); *see also* Michael J. Klarman, *Rethinking the Civil Rights and Civil Liberties Revolutions*, 82 VA. L. REV. 1, 7–18 (1996). For a similar analysis of the Marshall Court's decision-making, see Mark A. Graber, *Federalist or Friends of Adams: The Marshall Court and Party Politics*, 12 STUD. AM. POL. DEV. 229, 259–62 (1998).

[12] The Rehnquist Court's federalism decisions might be the best example of "cleaning up" legislation that was passed by earlier governing coalitions. The point about imposing a national consensus on local or regional outliers has been famously developed by Michael J. Klarman. *See* Klarman, *supra* note 11, at 7–18; *see also* Michael J. Klarman, *Majoritarian Judicial Review: The Entrenchment Problem*, 85 GEO. L.J. 491, 502–09 (1997). For a similar account of the Warren Court, see LUCAS A. POWE, JR., THE WARREN COURT AND AMERICAN POLITICS 485–87 (2000).

[13] For a defense of defining judicial independence as autonomy, see Charles M. Cameron, *Judicial Independence: How Can You Tell It When You See It? And Who Cares? in* JUDICIAL INDEPENDENCE, *supra* note 2, at 135–38.

[14] For an analysis of how economic nationalists in the post–Civil War Republican Party pursued this agenda in the late nineteenth century, see Gillman, *supra* note 3.

especially when Justice Sandra Day O'Connor found herself in agreement with Chief Justice William Rehnquist and Justices Antonin Scalia, Anthony Kennedy, and Clarence Thomas. Given the age and health of some of the justices, it seemed likely that the 2000 election would determine whether their decision-making agenda would be fortified (if Republicans controlled the next appointments) or possibly rolled back (if Democrats were in control). In the wake of the election, it was known that the incoming Senate would be evenly divided between Republicans and Democrats, and this meant that the outcome of the presidential election would determine which party controlled both the White House and the Senate and, thus, the appointment of Supreme Court justices.[15]

Thinking about judicial independence simply in terms of neutral, rule-of-law values, it may be a mystery why a narrow majority of Supreme Court justices took the remarkable step of involving themselves in the 2000 election controversy. It is possible to construct a story about how the justices were merely seeking to ensure that all those involved played by the rules. However, if it is accepted that the justices have personal and institutional interests in the configuration of power in the rest of the federal government, then the involvement of the *Bush v. Gore* majority can be seen as an effort to create a more favorable political climate for its (emergent but still vulnerable) constitutional agenda—that is, a political climate that would be less likely to trigger a negative response to conservative decisions and more likely to result in the appointment of justices who would maintain or solidify this agenda.

On this view, the Court's involvement in the 2000 election was not extraordinary simply because it revealed a rare instance of political bias. Political bias (or, more generously, political perspective) is revealed routinely in the ideological patterns of the justices' decision-making.[16] Rather, the Court's involvement was extraordinary because it demonstrated the Court's fortuitous ability to shape which candidates and parties would control the White House and the Senate, and thus make it less likely that political opponents would be able to interfere with its policy-making. Stated another way, this case is extraordinary because the policy alignment between the Court and the political system, which normally is established by the legislative and executive branches, was established by the Court.

II. LESSON TWO:
INDEPENDENT COURTS ARE OFTEN SUPPORTED BY OTHER POWER-HOLDERS BECAUSE THEY CAN ACT AS A FORUM WITHIN WHICH CONTENTIOUS POLITICAL QUESTIONS MAY BE CHANNELED

The desire of power-holders to insulate preferred political agendas is not the only reason that they may have an interest in establishing or deferring to the authority of relatively autonomous policy-making institutions such as agencies,

---

[15] This was before it was imagined that Republican Senator Jim Jeffords would bolt from the party and hand over control of the Senate to the Democrats.

[16] I have argued elsewhere, though, that what was different about the political dynamics of the Court's involvement was its overt partisanship. The justices routinely decide cases on the basis of their political ideologies, but it is not so common for the justices to set aside their normal policy positions on issues such as federalism or equal protection to promote the interests of a favored candidate. *See* GILLMAN, *supra* note 6, at 185–206.

commissions, central banks, or judicial bodies. Delegation is sometimes also a mechanism by which elected office-holders attempt to achieve political benefits by channeling contentious and potentially unpopular issues into the hands of "expert" decision-makers.[17]

The advantages of channeling are obvious when Congress sets up institutions, such as base-closing commissions, which are exclusively designed to facilitate decision-making on issues that raise political problems for elected officials.[18] More generally, institutions such as independent regulatory commissions (including the Federal Reserve Board) are also structured to enable more insulated policy-makers to pursue potentially controversial courses of action (such as an increase in interest rates). Legislators even benefit when they delegate more routine policy-making responsibilities to executive branch agencies. Traditional constitutional analysts are not wrong when they point out that delegation is often a natural and salutary part of the process by which the executive branch concretizes policy goals that are established by the legislature. However, this normative angle overlooks other political advantages for elected officials. Legislators also benefit when they put themselves in a position to claim credit for identifying important social problems without having to worry about the political costs of actually adopting specific policies that might alienate favored constituents. When bureaucracies adopt popular policies, legislators can take credit for results; when those same bureaucracies make unpopular decisions, legislators can join their constituents in complaining about bureaucrats and might even take steps to humiliate or punish the offending bureaucrats.[19]

As a general rule, the insulation or independence of courts is not best explained in terms of these political advantages. After all, most of what courts do (especially lower courts) is of little or no interest to policy-makers (beyond a general interest in relatively efficient case processing), which means that deference to courts is normally a byproduct of the overall political banality of the judiciary's work, rather than its sensitivity or salience. However, Mark Graber's path-breaking discussion of legislative deference to the Supreme Court has made it clear that under certain circumstances—such as the emergence of political disputes that threaten to disrupt established partisan coalitions—the Supreme Court's political insulation is self-consciously exploited by national party leaders.[20] To illustrate, Graber develops the following case studies: (1) the interest of beleaguered party leaders in the late 1850s to have the justices take the lead in addressing slavery politics; (2) the assumption among Congressional leaders in 1890 that the Supreme Court would make the final determination on key aspects of antitrust policy; and (3) the perceived advantages to national elites in the early 1970s for the justices to declare unconstitutional certain kinds of abortion statutes.[21] Some national political leaders in the 1950s may have believed that federal courts were in a better position to address certain civil rights controversies than other institutions of

---

[17] For an overview of the political calculations that go into the decision to delegate power, see Stefan Voigt & Eli M. Salzberger, *Choosing Not to Choose: When Politicians Choose to Delegate Powers*, 55 KYKLOS 289 (2002).

[18] *See* Defense Base Closure and Realignment Act of 1990, Pub. L. No. 101-510, §§ 2901–2911, 104 Stat. 1808, 1808–19 (1990).

[19] MORRIS P. FIORINA, CONGRESS: KEYSTONE OF THE WASHINGTON ESTABLISHMENT 67–71 (1977).

[20] Graber, *supra* note 3, at 41.

[21] *See id.* at 45–61.

the national government.[22] Additionally, conservatives who might have felt some political pressure to vote for laws such as the Gun-Free School Zone Act or the Violence Against Women Act may be silently grateful that the Rehnquist Court is attempting to reduce Congress's authority to pass laws for which they have little enthusiasm.[23] Whether this can be demonstrated in these cases, the overarching point is that it would not be unusual for elected officials to support courts when they insulate elected officials from having to make controversial decisions.

The justices in the *Bush v. Gore* majority may have revealed their own attachment to a political agenda when they decided to intervene in the presidential election dispute. However, the unwillingness of other power-holders to defend their own decision-making prerogatives suggests that they believed that there were perceived political advantages to having the Supreme Court take control of this dispute. Republican legislators in Florida were being pressured by legislative leaders to take the controversial step of challenging the Florida courts by appointing a new slate of Bush electors,[24] but there was some grumbling about the need to take this course of action, and there was a public expression of hope that the Washington justices would make it unnecessary for them to go on record with that vote.[25] Similarly, Republican congressional leaders had been preparing for some weeks to take control of the outcome in the event that Florida courts were able to complete a recount that resulted in a Gore victory, but there was not a lot of enthusiasm for this outcome, and a number of Republicans publicly expressed the view that

[22] The Truman Justice Department urged the Supreme Court to rule against segregated schools in *Brown v. Board of Education. See* MARY L. DUDZIAK, COLD WAR CIVIL RIGHTS: RACE AND THE IMAGE OF AMERICAN DEMOCRACY 90 (2000). Federal courts also addressed civil rights issues relating to workplace discrimination for decades after the New Deal, during a period when the Democratic Party felt constrained by its Dixiecrat contingent. *See* Paul Frymer, Courts, Electoral Politics, and Civil Rights Enforcement: Racial Integration in U.S. Labor Unions, 1935–1980, Lecture to the Washington University Department of Political Science (March 2002) (transcript on file with author) (arguing that, during this period, "while elected officials consistently avoided challenging union racism, courts succeeded in integrating resistant unions," in part because "elected officials during this time delegate[d] a great deal of institutional power to courts").

[23] *See* United States v. Morrison, 529 U.S. 598 (2000); United States v. Lopez, 514 U.S. 549 (1995).

[24] The *New York Times* reported on November 23, 2000 that "senior Republican legislators, led by men with strong political ties to the state's governor, Jeb Bush, searched with a partisan intensity today for a legislative stroke that would deliver Florida and the White House to George W. Bush." David Barstow & Somini Sengupta, *Florida Legislators Consider Options to Aid Bush*, N.Y. TIMES, Nov. 23, 2000, at A1; *see also* CORRESPONDENTS OF THE N.Y. TIMES, 36 DAYS: THE COMPLETE CHRONICLE OF THE 2000 PRESIDENTIAL ELECTION CRISIS 139 (John W. Wright et al. eds., 2001) [hereinafter 36 DAYS].

[25] On December 7, the *New York Times* reported that "Republicans here [in Florida] were worried about the potential fallout of convening a special session [of Bush electors]. They emphasized their reluctance in choosing this course and spoke of waiting until the very last moment." Dana Canedy & David Barstow, *Florida Lawmakers to Convene Special Session Tomorrow*, N.Y. TIMES, Dec. 7, 2000, at A35; *see also* 36 DAYS, *supra* note 24, at 252–53. Two days later, after the Florida Supreme Court ordered a state-wide recount of the undervote ballots, the paper reported that "if Mr. Bush's slim lead in the election dwindles during the recounting, the Republican leadership will have a much tougher time maintaining discipline among a rank and file composed largely of rookie legislators and those whose districts voted for Mr. Gore." Dana Canedy & David Barstow, *Ruling Fuels G.O.P. Resolve to Appoint Electors and Democrats' Will to Fight*, N.Y. TIMES, Dec. 9, 2000, at A14; *see also* 36 DAYS, *supra* note 24, at 271. Hours before the U.S. Supreme Court handed down its decision in *Bush v. Gore*, Republican state Senator Jim Horne said that he hoped "the Supreme Court would unilaterally slam dunk this thing so we could all go home." Jeffrey Gettleman, *Florida House OKs Slate of Electors Beholden to Bush*, L.A. TIMES, Dec. 13, 2000, at A28.

they would prefer it if the Supreme Court resolved the issue first.[26] It is reasonable to assume that the justices were quite aware that those other power-holders who might claim the prerogative to resolve the dispute nevertheless were in support of channeling the process into the federal courts, and it is no surprise that many of these legislators expressed relief rather than indignation after the justices decided the outcome.[27]

A related version of this interpretation is offered by those who characterize the Supreme Court's intervention as necessary and appropriate to avoid a constitutional crisis, or at least to end a prolonged political crisis that had tried the patience of the country and was not likely to result in a different outcome if it continued through the process of counting (and challenging) electoral votes in the Congress.[28] This version is different because it characterizes the political benefits for elected officials in a more bipartisan way. Rather than assume that Republican officials were supportive of the Court because it prevented them from having to face the possibility of handing the election to Bush after a Gore recount victory, the argument suggests that both Democrats and Republicans may have been relieved that the dispute was channeled into the Supreme Court rather than remaining in the legislative branches. This interpretation probably overstates the extent to which congressional Democrats actually supported the Court's intervention, although it might capture the sentiments of some Democrats—particularly more moderate or conservative Senate Democrats from states that supported Bush in the election—who had little enthusiasm for a Gore presidency and little interest in challenging House Republicans in a way that threatened a deadlock. Still, the argument offers another perspective on how the judiciary's independence can provide political benefits that would lead potentially competing power-holders to defer to judges when they address sensitive or controversial disputes.

III. LESSON THREE: BECAUSE INSTITUTIONAL INDEPENDENCE IS NEVER COMPLETE—AND IS EASILY OVERCOME BY DETERMINED POWER-HOLDERS—NOMINALLY INDEPENDENT DECISION-MAKERS STILL NEED TO ASSESS THEIR POLITICAL CONTEXT BEFORE CHOOSING POLITICALLY RISKY COURSES OF ACTION

Supreme Court justices are privileged to have an institutional setting that insulates them from direct political supervision or manipulation. "Good behavior" tenure, combined with having the last word on the interpretation of law in a given case cycle and the difficulties of mustering a consensus to retaliate against the Court, mean that the justices have enormous freedom to decide cases as they see fit. In fact, it is precisely these structural features that make it reasonable to assume that justices normally decide cases based mostly on their personal policy preferences

---

[26] House Republican Whip Tom Delay started organizing his colleagues just one week after election day. *See* 36 Days, *supra* note 24, at 83.

[27] *See* 36 Days, *supra* note 24, at 310 ("[M]ost politicians from both sides express relief that the drama is over. . . . [E]specially . . . members of the U.S. House and the Florida Senate, who would have been involved in making decisions that carried considerable political danger for all concerned.").

[28] *See* Posner, *supra* note 6, at 254–55.

(or views of the law) rather than other political motivations or influences, such as direct constituency pressures or the demands of party leaders.[29]

However, all structural protections for political independence can be overcome by sufficiently determined power-holders. Those who might threaten judicial autonomy are usually not tempted to interfere, both because judges typically decide cases that are of little interest to other power-holders (and thus benefit from the same considerations that protect low-level bureaucrats) and because judges typically decide more politically sensitive issues in a way that is broadly consistent with the preferences of other power-holders. Nonetheless, on occasion, judges find themselves in situations that threaten to disturb the hornet's nest of politics.[30] In such situations, the normal practice of deciding cases as a judge sees fit may give way to a more complicated set of strategic calculations.[31] This is why, despite their nominal structural independence, Supreme Court justices are demonstrably attentive to the political environment within which they operate.[32]

Sometimes this results in outright refusal to decide cases that might trigger political retaliation, as with the justices' initial decision to avoid the issue of miscegenation in the wake of the regional firestorm surrounding *Brown v. Board of Education*.[33] Sometimes these political calculations result in strategic retreats from incipient policies that are under assault, as with the Court's decision in the late 1950s to pull back from offering modest due process protections to those

---

[29] *See* Jeffrey A. Segal, *Separation-of-Powers Games in the Positive Theory of Congress and Courts*, 91 Am. Pol. Sci. Rev. 28, 42 (1997).

[30] One familiar example involved the reaction of leading Republicans and Democrats to a decision of District Court Judge Harold Baer, Jr., after an evidentiary ruling that resulted in the suppression of a large amount of cocaine. *See* United States v. Bayless, 913 F. Supp. 232, 242–43 (S.D.N.Y. 1996), *vacated on reconsideration*, 921 F. Supp. 211 (S.D.N.Y. 1996). President Clinton threatened to ask for the judge's resignation, and Senate Majority Leader Robert Dole indicated that the judge should be impeached if he did not reverse himself. The assault led this life-tenured judge to retreat on his ruling. For more on this and other examples, including House majority whip Tom DeLay's general threat to begin impeaching "activist" federal judges, see Stephan O. Kline, *Judicial Independence: Rebuffing Congressional Attacks on the Third Branch*, 87 Ky. L.J. 679, 714 (1998–99); Monroe H. Freedman, *The Threat to Judicial Independence by Criticism of Judges—A Proposed Solution to the Real Problem*, 25 Hofstra L. Rev. 729, 737–40 (1997); Don Van Natta, Jr., *Under Pressure, Federal Judge Reverses Decision in Drug Case*, N.Y. Times, Apr. 2, 1996, at A1.

[31] It is not always the case that judges will act cautiously or strategically when faced with potentially explosive issues. Consider the more recent case of *Newdow v. U.S. Congress*, in which the Ninth Circuit declared unconstitutional schoolchildren's exposure to the phrase "under God" in the Pledge of Allegiance. *See* 292 F.3d 597 (9th Cir. 2002). For an overview of the reaction to this decision, including Senator Frank Murkowski's plan to divide the Ninth Circuit in two, see Henry Weinstein, *Judge Defuses Tension over Court's Pledge Ruling*, L.A. Times, July 17, 2002, at B1; and Michelle Munn, *Don't Split 9th Circuit, House Panel is Told*, L.A. Times, July 24, 2002, at B8. Munn reports the following statement made by Democratic Rep. Howard L. Berman at a committee hearing on dividing the Ninth Circuit: "One could take these unique circumstances of the calling of the hearing and conclude it is an attempt to punish the Ninth Circuit for its decision on the Pledge of Allegiance." Munn, *supra* at B8. Of course, it is not possible to know whether the two judges who ruled against the phrase "under God" would have made the same decision if they had anticipated the political consequences.

[32] This aspect of Supreme Court politics is best captured in the literature on strategic decision-making by the justices. *See* Lee Epstein & Jack Knight, The Choices Justices Make 13 (1998). For an earlier treatment, see Walter F. Murphy, Elements of Judicial Strategy 245–68 (1964).

[33] *See* Naim v. Naim, 350 U.S. 891, 891 (1955); 350 U.S. 985, 985 (1956). Frankfurter expressed the view in conference that "[t]o thrust the miscegenation issue into 'the vortex of the present disquietude' would risk 'thwarting or seriously handicapping the enforcement of [*Brown*].'" Memorandum from Justice Felix Frankfurter (Nov. 4, 1955), *reprinted in* Dennis J. Hutchinson, *Unanimity and Desegregation: Decisionmaking in the Supreme Court, 1948–1958*, 68 Geo. L.J. 1, 64 (1979).

who refused to cooperate with the House Un-American Activities Committee.[34] And sometimes the justices' assessment leads them to conclude that the climate is conducive to risky courses of action, either because they believe there is not enough political will to challenge the Court on the issue or because they believe they can count on some protection from defenders who occupy strategically useful positions.

It is tempting to think that the political climate of the 2000 election was not conducive to a risky course of conduct by a bare majority of Court conservatives. No precedent existed for Supreme Court involvement in a dispute over a state's presidential electors.[35] Established processes were in place for resolving the dispute without the Court's participation—specifically, an initial resolution by state officeholders followed by a determination by the Congress. The legal issues raised were innovative and deeply disputed, and as it turned out, the justices were unable to arrive at a nominally non-partisan consensus on how best to address these issues. Moreover, despite arguments that there was a bipartisan interest in having the Court bring an end to a prolonged crisis, there was reason to believe that partisans on both sides would be upset with judges who took the wrong side.

In light of all this, it might be tempting to interpret the Court's involvement as an example of how structural mechanisms for political independence make it unnecessary for judges to take into account political considerations when deciding a course of conduct. In fact, though, the strategic political environment was actually quite hospitable to the course of conduct that the conservative majority set in motion around Thanksgiving when they voted to grant certiorari in the first Bush appeal of the Florida Supreme Court's decision to extend the deadline for hand recounts.[36] Assuming that the conservatives were interested in preventing any hand recounts that might overturn the initially reported results in favor of a Bush victory—an assumption that is consistent with the three anti-recount positions taken by these five justices across three separate legal issues[37]—then what they needed to assess was whether they had enough support in the political system to avoid retaliation for a set of decisions that either blocked recounts or rolled back the results of recounts. While the political environment might not have been

[34] See WALTER F. MURPHY, CONGRESS AND THE COURT 229–30 (1962); C. HERMAN PRITCHETT, CONGRESS VERSUS THE SUPREME COURT 48–53 (1961).

[35] Five justices (but not the Court as an institution) were involved in the Electoral Commission that addressed the disputed Hayes-Tilden election in 1876. Even this limited involvement by Court personnel was a byproduct of an explicit, formal invitation by congressional party leaders.

[36] The Florida Supreme Court's decision extending the recount deadline was *Palm Beach County Canvassing Board v. Harris*, 772 So. 2d 1220, 1240 (Fla. 2000). The U.S. Supreme Court granted certiorari on November 24 in an appeal of the newly titled case *Bush v. Palm Beach County Canvassing Board*, 531 U.S. 1004 (2000). In his *Bush v. Gore* dissent, in a part of his opinion that was joined by all four dissenters, Justice Souter declared that "[t]he Court should not have reviewed either Bush v. Palm Beach County Canvassing Board . . . or this case," which means that only the five most conservative justices supported the decision to intervene in the election 2000 controversy. *See* Gillman, *supra* note 6, at 145–46 (quoting Bush v. Gore, 531 U.S. 98. 130 [2000] [Souter, J., dissenting]).

[37] In *Bush v. Palm Beach County Canvassing Board*, the justices overturned the Florida Supreme Court's decision extending the deadline for manual recounts of votes using a legal argument based on Article II of the Constitution. *See* 531 U.S. 70, 78 (2000). In *Bush v. Gore*, the conservatives issued an injunction stopping the newly authorized statewide recount of undervote ballots using a legal argument based on whether new recounts represented an "irreparable harm" to Bush. *See* 531 U.S. 1046 (2000) (Scalia, J., concurring). And in the final *Bush v. Gore* decision, the conservatives declared a statewide recount to be unconstitutional using a legal argument based on the equal protection clause. *See Bush v. Gore*, 531 U.S. 98, 103, 110 (2000).

conducive to any imaginable course of conduct the Court might have adopted (such as one to require recounts), it was conducive to an anti-recount effort. The conservatives knew that they had a fully mobilized Republican constituency that would vehemently support such an intervention.[38] More importantly, Republicans were in control of virtually all of the potential competing political institutions, including the state legislature and executive branch of Florida and the U.S. House of Representatives. They also knew that the U.S. Senate and, of course, the presidency would be in Republican hands if they were successful in ensuring a Bush victory. Given this configuration of power, the conservatives could be confident that their decisions would not be met by any institutional resistance or short-term acts of retribution.

There were other strategic advantages as well. Immediately prior to the final decision, public opinion polls showed that 73% of respondents said they would consider any Supreme Court decision to be legitimate.[39] Conservatives also knew that a pro-Bush result would actually bring an immediate end to the dispute, since the Gore campaign had announced the weekend before *Bush v. Gore* that they would live with whatever decision the Court handed down.[40] While there might be lingering anger among disappointed partisans, there would not be the sort of ongoing struggle over judicial policy-making that one associates with the Court's most controversial decisions.

In considering the lessons for judicial independence presented by *Bush v. Gore*, it is too simple to assert that the formal, constitutional sources of the justices' independence were sufficient to give the conservative majority the political insulation it needed to intervene in the 2000 election controversy. Counterfactuals can only reach so far, but if the Court had been faced with a fully mobilized and determined Democratic Party in control of the U.S. Congress as well as Florida's legislative and executive branches, the *Bush v. Gore* majority would have had a lot more to consider before inserting themselves into this process. The main point is that Supreme Court independence is a function, not merely of formal structural protections, but also of historically contingent political alignments and the tendency of the justices to assess the strategic context within which they are operating. Without attention to these contextual and strategic variables, a lack of pressure, interference, or retribution might be explained as a function of well-functioning institutional barriers rather than the relation between these structural features and the constraints or opportunities generated by the background political climate.

IV. LESSON FOUR:
GREATER DEGREES OF STRUCTURAL INSULATION FROM ELECTORAL ACCOUNTABILITY DO NOT NECESSARILY MAKE GOOD FAITH DECISION-MAKING MORE LIKELY

It is tempting to assume that greater degrees of structural independence will reduce the likelihood that political considerations will shape decision-making. In other words, if independence is considered a good thing, then perhaps appointive

---

[38] For an account of the 2000 election that emphasizes the efforts of Republicans during the election crisis, see JEFFREY TOOBIN, TOO CLOSE TO CALL: THE THIRTY-SIX-DAY BATTLE TO DECIDE THE 2000 ELECTION (2001).

[39] GILLMAN, *supra* note 6, at 128.

[40] *Id.* at 129.

methods are better than elective methods; non-competitive retention elections are better than competitive elections; and longer terms of office are better than shorter terms. On this analysis, the federal structure of political appointment and life tenure might seem like a better way to reduce the corrupting effects of politics on judicial decision-making than state models that typically include some sort of electoral accountability.

It is a truism that when judges are insulated from elections, some of the dynamics of electoral politics are eliminated from their decision-making calculus. Judges who do not have to run for election or reelection will not have to raise money to run campaigns and may worry less about how their decisions might be used by electoral opponents in political advertising. However, it would be a mistake to assume that insulating judges from elections (or from easy removal by competing power-holders) will eliminate political motivations, pressures, or calculations from judicial decision-making. It would be more accurate to say that different structures of judicial selection and removal will produce slightly different political dynamics. Appointive systems marginally increase the influence of chief executives over the ideological make-up of the judiciary, although governors tend to dominate even elective and merit-based systems. Partisan election systems provide voters with one very salient cue that they would not be officially provided in non-partisan systems, although even in non-partisan systems parties may exert influence over the process by supporting particular candidates. Judges who enjoy life tenure have to worry less about whether voting their preferences will cause a political firestorm, although even life-tenured judges must pay attention to political opposition to their decisions.[41] It may be that there are good reasons to prefer the political dynamics associated with some of these structures and to oppose those created by others, especially in light of the increasing importance of money in some judicial elections.[42] However, in making these comparisons, we should debate the relative advantages and disadvantages associated with different political dynamics and try to avoid too much reliance on misleading, simplistic sloganeering about the elimination of political influence.

The role of state and federal judges during the 2000 election controversy provides a dramatic illustration of how greater degrees of political insulation do not necessarily lead to less political judicial decision-making. Examining the simple standard of whether judges were willing to decide cases inconsistently with their presumptive political preferences, it is clear that the judges who faced elections were much more willing to set aside their political preferences and offer good-faith interpretations of the law than judges who enjoyed the most structural "independence from politics."[43] For example, Florida Circuit Court Judge Terry Lewis, a Democrat, ruled that the Republican Secretary of State had the authority to disregard the results of manual recounts that were not completed until after a seven-day reporting deadline.[44] Lewis, along with another Democratic appointee,

[41] For an overview, see LAWRENCE BAUM, AMERICAN COURTS: PROCESS AND POLICY, 101–31 (5th ed. 1998).

[42] For "an investigation into how campaign cash is corrupting America's courts," see Frontline's "Justice For Sale" at http://www.pbs.org/wgbh/pages/frontline/shows/justice/ (last visited Nov. 9, 2002).

[43] For a more elaborate discussion of the issues raised in the next three paragraphs, see Gillman, *supra* note 3, at 172–96.

[44] *McDermott v. Harris*, No. 00-2700, 2000 WL 1714590, at *1 (Fla. Cir. Ct. Nov. 17, 2000) (order denying emergency motion to compel compliance with and for enforcement of injunction).

Circuit Court Judge Nikki Clark, also ruled against the Democrats in a lawsuit challenging the legality of certain Republican absentee ballots.[45] On the other side, when Republicans initially attempted to get a judge to throw out these absentee ballot challenges, they were disappointed by Judge Debra Nelson, who was a recent appointee of Republican Governor Jeb Bush.[46] At a time when the standards for evaluating chads were thought to be the difference between a Gore or a Bush victory, Republican state circuit Judge Jorge Labarga ruled that Palm Beach violated Florida law when it decided to only count those ballots with detached chads rather than any ballot where the intent of the voter could be discerned.[47]

Obviously, there was a storm of controversy surrounding some of the decisions of the Democratic Florida Supreme Court, especially when those justices frustrated Republicans by authorizing recounts that threatened Bush's nominal victory. It is reasonable to assume that the commitment of those justices to count ballots rather than disqualify ballots reflected their political attitudes. Still, in the five cases that this state high court decided that might have influenced the outcome of the controversy, the justices voted against Al Gore in three and gave Gore only partial victories in the other two. The justices voted against Gore on whether to order Miami-Dade to restart its recount after the local canvassing board suddenly decided to call it off; on whether to order a new election in Palm Beach County; and on whether to disqualify Republican absentee ballots.[48] Gore did get the state high court to approve an extension for when counties had to report the results of manually reviewed ballots. However, the extension was not as long as the Gore team hoped, and as it turned out, two of the three counties involved could not complete the recounts within the extended time frame.[49] A divided high court also authorized a statewide manual recount of the so-called undervote ballots, but this was less favorable to Gore (and set in motion a less predictable course of action) than the limited recount in Democratic counties that the Gore team had requested.[50] Whatever one's interpretation of the reasonableness of any of these decisions, it is beyond dispute that these judges were not single-minded about deciding cases in a manner that reflected a political preference for one candidate over another. In cases where they voted against the interests of Al Gore, it is reasonable to assume that the decision reflected their good faith understanding of the law.

Of all the judges who were involved in the 2000 election dispute, the ones whose behavior appeared the most partisan, and the least motivated by good faith understandings of the law, were the ones who enjoyed the most extreme insulation from conventional political pressure. The five conservatives in the *Bush v. Gore* majority were the only judges involved in this election dispute whose decisions

[45] *Taylor v. Martin County Canvassing Bd.*, No. 00-2850, 2000 WL 1793409, at *5 (Fla. Cir. Ct. Dec. 8, 2000) (final judgment for defendants); Scott Gold, *Judges Let Absentee Votes Stand*, L.A. TIMES, Dec. 9, 2000, at A26.

[46] Mitchell Landsberg, *Judge Upholds Democrat's Lawsuit over Absentee Applications*, L.A. TIMES, Nov. 21, 2000, at A16.

[47] *Florida Democratic Party v. Palm Beach County Canvassing Bd.*, No. 00-11078, 2000 WL 1728721 (Fla. Cir. Ct. Nov. 15, 2000) (declaratory order).

[48] The cases were as follows: *Gore v. Miami-Dade County Canvassing Bd.*, 780 So. 2d 913 (Fla. 2000); *Fladell v. Palm Beach County Canvassing Bd.*, 772 So. 2d 1240, 1242 (Fla. 2000); and *Taylor v. Martin County Canvassing Bd.*, 773 So. 2d 517, 519 (Fla. 2000).

[49] *Palm Beach County Canvassing Bd. v. Harris*, 772 So. 2d 1220 (Fla. 2000).

[50] *Gore v. Harris*, 772 So. 2d 1243, 1262 (Fla. 2000).

across a variety of legal issues were consistent with their political preferences and arguably inconsistent with their pre-election views on issues such as the meaning of the equal protection clause and the appropriateness of having federal courts second-guess state court interpretations of state law.[51] Whether these judges are viewed as loyal partisans, ideological policy-makers protecting their fragile constitutional agenda, or, most benignly, interested decision-makers exhibiting the influence of "motivated reasoning,"[52] it is hard to resist the conclusion that their actions were tainted by political considerations or motivations.[53] This is just another way of pointing out that, while judicial independence may sometimes free a judge from unwanted political pressure, those structures do nothing to prevent an insulated judge from indulging her or his own political preferences or private agendas. To guard against those unwanted influences, one has to focus more on the character of the decision-maker than the characteristics of the office.

None of this is to deny the importance of debating the practical consequences of adopting one set of institutional structures over another. All power-holders are affected in some way, whether positively or negatively, by the political architecture of the institutions within which they operate.[54] Moreover, as these issues are analyzed and debated, it is essential to consider the relationship between these structural questions and the promotion of rule-of-law norms. However, it also is useful to keep in mind the full range of motivations and consequences that are related to the question of whether judge-politicians should be given more or less decision-making autonomy. After all, "the choice of judicial selection and retention mechanisms is inherently a political choice with political implications,"[55] including unintended implications, such as the use of that independence to choose a president.

---

[51] The justices had no previously expressed views on the meaning of Article II as it relates to the authority of state courts to interpret state election law regulating the appointment of presidential electors. However, it is probably fair to say that no modern scholar of constitutional law had an opinion on that question before the 2000 election.

[52] For a general discussion of the insights of cognitive psychology on judicial decision-making, see Dan Simon, *A Psychological Model of Judicial Decision Making*, 30 Rutgers L.J. 1 (1998). Of course, one's susceptibility to the influences of motivated reasoning may itself be a byproduct of a preexisting willingness to indulge political preferences. Therefore, the phenomenon of motivated reasoning may not provide a persuasive defense against the charge of partisan decision-making. Obviously, not all judges involved in the 2000 election framed the legal issues in a politically convenient way.

[53] It should be emphasized that the charge of partisan bias is not easily applied to dissenting Justices David Souter and John Paul Stevens, each of whom was closely connected to the Republican Party before being appointed by Republican presidents.

[54] This is a central assumption of a political science school of thought known as "the new institutionalism." *See* Supreme Court Decision-Making: New Institutionalist Approaches (Cornell W. Clayton & Howard Gillman eds., 1999); *see also* The Supreme Court in American Politics: New Institutionalist Interpretations (Howard Gillman & Cornell W. Clayton eds., 1999).

[55] Lee Epstein, Jack Knight, & Olga Shvetsova, *Selecting Selection Systems*, in Judicial Independence, *supra* note 2, at 201.

11

JUDICIAL INDEPENDENCE AND THE
REALITY OF POLITICAL POWER
Gerald N. Rosenberg[*]

Compared to Howard Gillman, Gerald Rosenberg is, if anything, even more "realistic" in his assessment of judicial independence. Gillman, in his article, focuses on whether, how, and when justices will align themselves with a dominant policymaking coalition in the elected branches. As Gillman puts it, "It is a basic assumption of political science that the United States Supreme Court is designed to be a national policy-making institution." As such, the Court aligns itself with—and does not oppose (or long oppose)—other policymakers. But what if other policymakers will attack the civil liberties of unpopular groups or citizens? Does the Court's institutional independence mean that it will stand up for the rule of law? What if the Court itself is attacked when it does stand up for the rule of law? What do its members do then? Rosenberg explores these questions carefully—and the answers he provides are unsettling.

Please note that for more on the Supreme Court, you may wish to skip ahead at this point to read the piece by Nathaniel Persily and Bruce Cain on "the legal status of political parties," which shows that the Court has participated in the development of political thought about political parties. The Persily and Cain article thus helps to provide a fuller view of the Supreme Court.

• • •

DEFINING JUDICIAL INDEPENDENCE as the ability of courts to make decisions in the short term without regard for the preferences of officeholders, this article empirically examines the conditions under which judicial independence is and is not likely to be found. Nine periods of intense congressional hostility to the Supreme Court are identified and Court reactions are chartered along a continuum from pure independence to total subservience. Examination of the historical record highlights five key factors related to independence and shows that judicial independence existed in only three of the periods. In the remaining six periods, the Court either refrained from hearing certain cases, issued opinions more in line with congressional preferences, or reversed itself. The article rejects the hypothesis of judicial independence, concluding that in times of congressional opposition to the Court, only under special conditions identified in the analysis will it retain its independence.

From *Review of Politics* 54 (Summer 1992): 368–398. This material is published with permission of the editors of *The Review of Politics*, University of Notre Dame.

* I gratefully acknowledge helpful and extensive comments on an earlier draft from John Mark Hansen and Cass Sunstein of the University of Chicago and Rogers Smith and Stephen Carter of Yale University.

INTRODUCTION

The independence of the federal judiciary from political control is a hallmark of the American legal system. Institutionally separate and distinct from the other branches of the federal government, the judiciary is electorally unaccountable. Judges and justices are insulated from the political process through constitutional guarantees of life appointments and salaries that may not be diminished during their terms of office. In theory, this independence, plus the power to hold legislative and executive acts unconstitutional, allows courts to "stand as the ultimate guardians of our fundamental rights."[1] To laypeople, lawyers, and social scientists alike, judicial independence is central to American government.

While many social scientists are too "sophisticated" or cynical to put much stock in all but the weakest notions of judicial independence, the entire field of constitutional scholarship is based on it. Supporters and critics of judicial activism rely heavily on a strong notion of judicial independence. For proponents of judicial activism, independence allows courts to avoid the prejudice and short-sightedness to which elected officials sometimes succumb. Electorally unaccountable and institutionally insulated, federal judges can preserve rights under attack. An activist court is defensible in a democracy, then, precisely because it is independent. Its independence allows it to act to uphold rights where democratic majorities are paralyzed by prejudice. A nonindependent activist court would simply reinforce the discrimination and prejudice of the other branches. On the other hand, critics of judicial activism assume judicial independence as well. They argue that courts sometimes are carried away by the personal and political views of their members. Acting like "super-legislatures," these courts make policy decisions without the input of the democratic process. This occurs because courts are independent, free of the democratic process constraints that limit elected officials. A nonindependent activist court would not be dangerous because it would not act against the wishes of the other branches. Indeed, the debate over the countermajoritarian nature of judicial review is premised on meaningful judicial independence. Both supporters and critics of judicial activism assume judicial independence.

Constitutional structures, patterns of belief, and even the assumptions of much constitutional scholarship, do not always accurately reflect actual power relations. To assume judicial independence on these grounds is to overlook practice. And since the presence of power relations can only be judged in practice, the assertion of judicial independence must be tested empirically. This article attempts the task.

Although the reader may have a gut-level sense of the meaning of judicial independence, some elaboration is required. By judicial independence I mean the Supreme Court's relatively straightforward understanding of "judges who are free from potential domination by other branches of government."[2] If the judiciary is independent of the executive and the legislature, then independence must at least mean that court decisions are reached freely, without regard for the political preferences of members of the other branches. As Judge Kaufman put it, "the constitutional power to decide cases fairly in accordance with law can be exercised effectively *only* if the deliberative process of the courts is free from undue

---

[1] Charles A. Horsky, "Law Day: Some Reflections on Current Proposals to Curtail the Supreme Court," *Minnesota Law Review* 42 (1958): 1105, 1111.

[2] *U.S. v. Will*, 449 U.S. 200, 218 (1980). To the extent that public opinion is mediated through executive and legislative action, it is subsumed under the definition.

interference by the President or Congress."[3] The judiciary is independent, then, to the extent its decision-making is free from domination by the preferences of elected officials.

In a sense, though, this claims too much. Meaningful independence does not require the hermetic sealing off of one institution from another. There is overlap between and among the three branches of the federal government. The Congress and the president, for example, continually cajole and coerce each other in ways that are entirely appropriate to independent institutions. Similarly, courts function under laws enacted and executed by the other branches. The very questions courts often entertain are framed by the other branches. Also, judges, like elected officials and other human beings, have policy preferences on some issues. Judicial independence, then, does not require judges removed from the world around them. It does require that their decisions be unaffected, or at least minimally affected, by the strength of partisan positions among members of the other branches.

This article tests the hypothesis that courts are independent, that they reach decisions without regard to the preferences of politically accountable officials. The null hypothesis is that there is no judicial independence, that courts do take these preferences into account in reaching decisions. This formulation, however, is only a first step. Treating court decisions as either ignoring political preferences (judicial independence) or taking them into account (no judicial independence) creates an on/off, either/or variable that may miss much actual practice. It may be more helpful to treat court decisions as pictured in Figure 1, ranging along a continuum from total lack of regard for political preferences to absolute subservience to them.

Conceiving of judicial independence in this way allows for a more discriminating inquiry into the nature of judicial independence.

Numerous studies have attempted to conceptualize and measure judicial independence. In these studies, evidence is presented that suggests that courts act congruently with the wishes of a group or party which exerts pressure outside the confines of cases.[4] But how and why this occurs is left unspecified. The links between outside interests and court decisions are unclear.[5]

I test the hypothesis of judicial independence by isolating time periods during which congressional hostility to judicial decisions has been strong, and analyzing

---

[3] Irving R. Kaufman, "The Essence of Judicial Independence," *Columbia Law Review* 80 (1980): 671, 691, emphasis added.

[4] See, for example, Morton J. Horwitz, *The Transformation of American Law* (Cambridge, MA: Harvard University Press, 1977); Thomas R. Marshall, *Public Opinion and the Supreme Court* (Boston: Unwin Hyman, 1989); Note, "Government Litigation in the Supreme Court: The Roles of the Solicitor General," *Yale Law Journal* 78 (1969): 428; Steven Puro, "The United States as Amicus Curiae," in *Courts, Law, and Judicial Processes,* ed. S. Sidney Ulmer (New York: Free Press, 1981); Robert Scigliano, *The Supreme Court and the Presidency* (New York: Free Press, 1971); Martin Shapiro, "The Supreme Court: From Warren to Burger," in *The New American Political System,* ed. Anthony King (Washington, D.C.: American Enterprise Institute, 1978); S. Sidney Ulmer and David Willison, "The Solicitor General of the United States as *Amicus Curiae* in the U.S. Supreme Court, 1969–1983 Terms" (Paper presented at the annual meeting of the American Political Science Association, New Orleans, 1985).

[5] This is especially the case with electoral realignments. It has been argued that attempts to curb the Court are due to the periodic electoral realignments that sweep the United States. However, since their precise meaning and identity is unclear, and since this claim reduces to one of electoral pressure, it seems more sensible to focus on the broader indicator. Focusing directly on the positions of elected officials includes realigning periods but is not limited to them.

FIGURE 1
Variations in the Extent of Judicial Independence

Independence ↔ Subservience				
Lack of Regard		*Increasing Regard*		*Complete Regard*
for political preferences of Members of other branches—Continue development of case line	Slow down development of line	Stop development of line	Back-off line	for political preferences of Members of other branches— Reverse line

Supreme Court decisions reached then. Did the Court further or maintain the position(s) that engendered hostility? Did it back off from them? Overturn them? By examining a number of such periods of congressional hostility, patterns of Court responses may appear.

The attentive reader will have noticed that I have equated political hostility with congressional hostility and have focussed on the U.S. Supreme Court. Congressional hostility, although clearly not the only measure of judicial antipathy, is an appropriate measure of political hostility because Congress has the constitutional power to change certain institutional aspects of the federal judiciary (described, *infra*). While others can only complain, the Congress can affect the Court in direct ways. Also, congressional hostility receives nationwide media coverage. This focus on congressional hostility does not ignore the role of the president. Clearly, by commanding media coverage, and by refusing to implement Court decisions, the president can attack the Court.[6] Without substantial congressional support, however, the president risks alienating both of the other branches. Finally, focusing on the Supreme Court makes good sense because the Court, like the Congress and the presidency, while not the only institution of its kind in the American political system, is the most visible and important one. Sitting atop a hierarchical structure, it authors the most far-reaching of judicial opinions. If the Supreme Court cannot maintain its independence when threatened, then judicial independence has little meaning.

Identifying the preferences of elected officials about issues facing the courts is not simple. When are there threats to judicial independence? While legislation aimed at forcing the courts to decide cases in a certain way would be the ideal evidence, such bills have rarely been enacted. Thus, one must rely on "fuzzier" indicators such as the number of bills introduced clearly aimed at influencing court decisions and the strength of court opponents. However, members of Congress often act out of a variety of motives, from the furtherance of policy preferences to credit-claiming, publicity-seeking, turf-protecting, etc. The number of bills introduced and the number of opponents do not necessarily capture the whole picture. The intensity behind their action is important as well. Although intensity is difficult to measure, it's important to distinguish between *pro forma* actions to

---

[6] In addition, the president could order the army to arrest or detain judges, as was done by President Lincoln. Similarly, presidents, like governors in the 1950s and 1960s over the issue of desegregation, can order governmental institutions to ignore Court orders. But when this stage is reached, there is no constitutional government.

placate certain constituencies and serious attempts to influence judicial outcomes. Attention should also be paid to whether Court opponents or supporters can coalesce to increase their strength. Finally, elections may signal elected officials about the level of public support. Where the role of the Court is an election issue, the outcome can either embolden or deter Court opponents. These five factors, the number of bills introduced, the number and strength of their supporters, the intensity of the support, the likelihood of coalitions forming, and the results of elections, indicate political preferences. While several can be quantified easily, others cannot. Their presence and relative strength will be determined by the consensus of students of the period and by reference to historical records.

In examining threats to judicial independence, these five indicators will be the focus. The judicial independence hypothesis predicts that they are irrelevant to judicial decisions. In contrast, the null hypothesis suggests that the greater the strength of the indicators, the greater the threat to the Court, and the more subservient it will be.

It is important to note that this approach focuses on *attacks* on the Court over the *short term*. There are strong reasons for such an approach. First, given the difficulty social scientists have in assessing power relations, independence can best be judged when actual threats to it can be identified. When there is little or no hostility to the Court, it cannot be determined whether the Court is acting independently or simply going along with the preferences of the other branches. However, when Court action creates political opposition, independence is brought to the limelight. Second, a classic defense of judicial independence points to the ability of the Court to check the political system in the short term, allowing for a "sober second thought."[7] The Court, it is claimed, can protect us from the sway of short-sighted passions and mean-spirited but temporary legislative majorities by checking the legislative process long enough for calmer heads to prevail. This, in turn, argues for a focus on the short term. Liberties need protection when threatened and the Court can only play this protective, checking role, over the short term. There is no substantive meaning to judicial independence if courts only invalidate legislative acts years after their enactment, when the issues and passions that created them have passed and when the damage to liberties has already occurred. Finally, it is clear that through the appointment process, the Court lacks independence over the long term.

It might be contended, however, that any correlation between congressional hostility to the Court and Court action masks other effects. In particular, it might be suggested that the Court always backs away from major decisions and periods of activity regardless of congressional action. If so, any correlation between Court activism, congressional hostility, and Court reversal or change of direction would not be meaningful. Happily, this is not the case, as three kinds of examples demonstrate. First, not all periods of congressional hostility to the Court are marked by judicial activism. At times, it has been the fear of activism (1802–1804), or the continued support for a given line of reasoning (1922–1924), rather than activism per se that has ignited congressional opposition to the Court. Second, there are many instances where the Court developed a new line of reasoning in a generally controversial area and stuck to it for decades. Examples might include substantive due process, the defense of voting rights, and, perhaps, support for the procedural rights of criminal defendants. Third, as will be shown later, there are even periods

---

[7] Harlan F. Stone, "The Common Law in the United States," *Harvard Law Review* 50 (1936): 4, 25.

of congressional hostility to the Court during which the Court held fast to its activism and line of reasoning. It is unlikely that any relationship found between congressional hostility to the Court and Court behavior is spurious.

There are, however, some difficulties with this approach. Assuming periods of congressional hostility to the Court can be identified, it is only with great care that Court decisions can be characterized. Broad generalizations can do violence to subtle distinctions and artful legal reasoning. Yet, while cases may be distinguished by lawyers, the bottom line politically is how people react, and the political ramifications of decisions are often clear. It makes sense, then, if the data warrant it, to speak of judicial retreat or the Court's backing down. To the extent that changes in decisions can be identified, these characterizations can be made. But even with such characterizations, the analysis of how congressional hostility affects decisions is not straightforward. Correlation is not causation and such a showing will not demonstrate that the congressional action *caused* the shift in Court behavior. At best, then, the analysis will show that when there is congressional hostility, the Court conforms to congressional preferences. But it could be the case that both the Court and the Congress responded to a third force, perhaps public opinion, and that the Court would have modified its position regardless of congressional action. This means that the strongest conclusion this approach will allow (if the data support it) is that there is strong reason to believe that the Court responds to congressional hostility. But whether or not congressional hostility is the causal agent, the overriding point would be that judicial independence is weak or nonexistent at times of heightened political passion.

ATTACKS ON JUDICIAL INDEPENDENCE

Attacking the Court is an old congressional practice dating back to the early years of the nation. Murphy reports that by the close of Marshall's chief justiceship nearly all of the basic measures to dominate the Court had been tried.[8] Generally speaking, there are ten types of proposals that have been made to limit the power of the Court or demonstrate congressional displeasure.[9] They include: (1) using the Senate's *confirmation* power to select certain types of judges; (2) enacting *constitutional amendments* to reverse decisions or change Court structure or procedure; (3) *impeachment*; (4) *withdrawing Court jurisdiction* over certain subjects; (5) altering the *selection* and *removal* process; (6) requiring *extraordinary majorities* for *declarations* of *unconstitutionality*; (7) allowing *appeal* from the *Supreme Court* to a more "representative" tribunal; (8) *removing* the power of *judicial review*; (9) *slashing* the *budget*; (10) altering the *size* of the Court. The above list is not exclusive. Rather, it suggests the kinds of actions that Congress has utilized over the years to limit the independence of the Court. While several of the proposals raise serious questions of constitutionality, they have been introduced and seriously debated. Congress has acted as if it believes it can dominate the Court.

---

[8] Walter F. Murphy, *Congress and the Court* (Chicago: University of Chicago Press, 1962), p. 63.

[9] See, generally, Comment, "Congress Versus the Court: The Legislative Arsenal," *Villanova Law Review* 10 (1965): 347; Maurice S. Culp, "A Survey of the Proposals to Limit or Deny the Power of Judicial Review by the Supreme Court of the United States," 2 pts. *Indiana Law Journal* 4 (1929): 387; 474; Sheldon D. Elliot, "Court-Curbing Proposals in Congress," *Notre Dame Lawyer* 33 (1958): 597; Thomas Halper, "Supreme Court Responses to Congressional Threats: Strategy and Tactics," *Drake Law Review* 19 (1970): 292.

Court-attacking bills are not merely a historical occurrence. While there has been little serious talk recently of completely removing the power of judicial review or of requiring the votes of more than five justices for holdings of unconstitutionality, the other sorts of proposals have appeared. The late 1950s and early 1960s saw a flurry of Court-curbing bills and bills have been introduced in the 1970s and early 1980s withdrawing federal court jurisdiction over substantive areas such as school prayer, abortion, and busing. A resourceful Congress with a sense of history and a belief that the Court is wrong can act.

In order to test the strength of judicial independence, congressional attempts to limit the power and independence of the Court must be identified. Such attempts can be identified by employing the following definition of attacks on the Court:

> legislation introduced in the Congress having as its purpose or effect, either explicit or implicit, Court reversal of a decision or line of decisions, or Court abstention from future decisions of a given kind, or alteration in the structure or functioning of the Court to produce a particular substantive outcome.[10]

Court-attacking bills are distinct from bills intended to reverse a single decision on the grounds that the Court misinterpreted congressional intent.[11] While the latter are not aimed at limiting the power of the Court but only at correcting a mistaken judicial interpretation of congressional statutes, Court-attacking bills strike deeper political chords. They are intended to limit the independence of the Court and ensure that future decisions will be in accord with congressional preferences. Often they challenge decisions extending constitutional rights, decisions that are presumably immune from congressional action under the separation of powers doctrine. While in theory the distinction between the two may be hard to make, in practice the context makes the aim explicit.[12]

Employing this definition, approximately 560 bills were identified. Relying on the temporal distributions of the bills, the intensity of the debate they generated, and the consensus of historians, nine periods of major Court-attacking activity were found. Table I presents the periods.

PERIODS OF JUDICIAL SUBSERVIENCE

There is virtual consensus among students of the courts that in three of these periods the Court succumbed to congressional pressure. As the reader will soon see, in each of these periods several of the indicators of congressional hostility were present and strong. First, all followed the electoral victory of parties hostile to the

---

[10] This definition combines parts of several offered by Harry P. Stumpf, "Congressional Responses to Supreme Court Rulings: The Interaction of Law and Politics," *Journal of Public Law* 14 (1965): 377, 382. See, also, Torstein Eckhoff, "Impartiality, Separation of Powers, and Judicial Independence," *Scandinavian Studies in Law* 9 (1965): 9, 38.

[11] For an extensive compilation of data on recent statutory overrides, see William N. Eskridge, Jr., "Overriding Supreme Court Statutory Interpretation Decisions," *Yale Law Journal* 101 (1991): 331.

[12] See, generally, Stumpf, "Congressional Responses to Supreme Court Rulings" (1965). There is evidence that members of Congress are aware of the context in which bills are aimed at the Court. Schmidhauser et al. studied 147 House and Senate roll call votes from 1945 to 1968 dealing with Court-Congressional relations. Comparing Court-curbing to simple reversal bills, they found that members of Congress differentiated between the two in their voting patterns (John R. Schmidhauser, Larry L. Berg, and Albert Melone, "The Impact of Judicial Decisions: New Dimensions in Supreme Court-Congressional Relations, 1945–1968," *1971 Washington University Law Review*, p. 209).

TABLE 1

TABLE 1

High Frequency Periods of Court Attacks in American History

Years	Approximate # of bills
1802–1804	2
1823–1831	12
1858–1869	22
1893–1897	9
1922–1924	11
1935–1937	37
1955–1959	53
1963–1965	114
1977–1982	106
Total	366

Source: For the period from the beginning of the nation through 1959, I relied on Stuart Nagel, "Court-Curbing Periods in American History," *Vanderbilt Law Review* 18 (1965): 925. For the period 1960–1972, bills were identified through the *Congressional Record Index*. Bills introduced in the years 1973–1984 were found by the Library of Congress's "CG" computer file.

Note: The count reported here does *not* include constitutional amendments or joint or concurrent resolutions. This was done to follow Nagel and have a comparison across time. However, since such amendments tend to be introduced in times of heightened congressional hostility to the Court, their omission should not affect the analysis. Note, too, that the actual number of bills introduced is not important. What is important is the intensity and seriousness of attacks on the Court. Also, differences in the number of bills introduced across time bear little or no relationship to the intensity of the hostility towards the Court. The large number of bills introduced in the last two periods, for example, reflects the overall increase in legislation introduced in Congress and the breakdown of party control over the introduction of legislation.

prior actions or feared potential actions of the Court. Second, in each case opposition to those Court actions was intense. Third, there was a large enough block of Court opponents to make passage of Court-curbing bills possible. Finally, there was little opportunity for Court-supporters to play coalition politics or involve interest groups in changing minds. Brief review of these periods illustrates these conclusions.

In the first period, 1802–1804, the story is well known. The recently triumphant Jeffersonians battled the Federalists for control of the federal government. The conflict reached its height over the appointment of President Adams's so-called midnight judges, particularly one Justice of the Peace, Marbury, whose commission was signed and sealed but never delivered. The Jeffersonians, angered by this last-minute attempt to deny them the fruits of victory, responded in kind, enacting legislation preventing the Supreme Court from meeting for 14 months and abolishing the nationwide circuit court system set up by the Federalists during their last days in office (thus throwing Federalist-appointed judges out of office). The end result was that the Court, in an extraordinary opinion, did not order Jefferson to deliver the commission.[13] In a subsequent opinion, the Court upheld the abolition of the circuit courts and the subsequent loss of office of the

[13] *Marbury v. Madison*, 5 U.S. 49 (1 Cranch 137) (1803). While Chief Justice Marshall did seize the opportunity to assert the power of judicial review, little political attention was paid to it. The focus was on the more immediate Federalist-Republican battle, including the Court's holding that some actions of the executive branch were amenable to judicial oversight (Robert G. McCloskey, *The American Supreme Court* [Chicago: University of Chicago Press, 1960], pp. 44–45).

Federalist judges who sat on them despite the constitutional guarantee of life tenure for federal judges.[14] Clearly, the Court was subservient to the preferences of the Jeffersonians.

The 1858–1869 period is one of the more striking episodes of judicial acquiescence to congressional preferences. The crisis was ignited by the Supreme Court decision in *Dred Scott*,[15] invalidating the Missouri Compromise and holding that African-Americans were not citizens. Part of the 1860 presidential campaign involved attacks on the Court and, after Lincoln's election, leading papers such as the *Chicago Tribune* and the *New York Times* supported plans to limit the independence of the judiciary. Court-curbing action included the effective house arrest of one judge to prevent his issuing a writ, the abolition of the circuit court for the District of Columbia and its recreation with new judges, and reduction of the size of the Court from 10 to 8, preventing President Johnson from making three appointments.

In the most celebrated episode, the Congress, over the president's veto, enacted legislation aimed at preventing the Court from deciding the case of William McCardle, a Mississippi newspaper editor who had been arrested and tried before a military commission. Even though the Court had already heard full argument in the case, it ordered re-argument for the next term to consider the effect of the congressional action. Buckling to the Congress, the case was subsequently dismissed.[16] Again, it seems clear that in this period the Court succumbed to the political preferences of a large number of members of Congress.

The final episode where Court acquiescence to congressional preferences is clear is the 1935–1937 period. Here, the Court had continually invalidated New Deal legislation. After his 1936 landslide election, FDR attacked the Court, charging that its members were old men with old ideas. He proposed to remedy the situation by, in effect, packing the Court. Other Court-attacking bills were prepared as well. "As late as the final week of March," New Deal scholar Leuchtenburg reports, "publications hostile to the plan conceded that it would pass."[17] The tension was finally broken when Justice Roberts, who had consistently voted in the previous year and a half to invalidate New Deal legislation, switched sides in several key cases,[18] upholding the constitutionality of the legislation (the so-called switch in time that saved the nine). This seemed to take the steam out of the attack on the Court and none of the bills was enacted. However, their passage was no longer necessary as the Court had acquiesced to congressional hostility. So badly beaten was the Court that it did not hold another piece of federal legislation unconstitutional as violative of the commerce clause until 1976.

The New Deal Court–attack provides a good opportunity to remove several obstacles that have traditionally prevented some from accepting this conclusion. First, a skeptic might argue that since the Court-packing plan was not enacted, and, enlarging the argument with a dose of history, the overwhelming majority of

[14] *Stuart v. Laird*, 5 U.S. 95 (1 Cranch 299) (1803).

[15] 60 U.S. (19 How.) 393 (1857).

[16] *Ex Parte McCardle*, 74 U.S. (7 Wall.) 506 (1869).

[17] William E. Leuchtenburg, "The Court Packing Crisis of 1937," *News for Teachers of Political Science* 45 (1985): 12, 13.

[18] The cases include *West Coast Hotel Co. v. Parrish*, 300 U.S. 379 (1937), *NLRB v. Jones and Laughlin Steel Corp.*, 301 U.S. 1 (1937), and *Steward Machine Co. v. Davis*, 301 U.S. 548 (1937). In each case, Justice Roberts supplied the fifth vote, upholding the legislation. The decisions were handed down in March, April, and May of 1937.

Court-attack bills have not been enacted, why should anyone expect the Court to alter its decisions? The reply to the skeptic is severalfold. First, the fate of legislation is never entirely clear. The relationship between the Court and the Congress is dynamic, and members of the Court can only dimly perceive the future. It may be that justices, fearful of successful congressional action, act to mollify their congressional opponents by altering their decisions. Although as the spring of 1937 blossomed it appeared increasingly likely that FDR's bill would not pass, political hostility to the Court was running high. As one commentator put it, it was "likely" that "some sort of curb on the Court would have emerged under a compromise situation."[19] In the New Deal period, and in other periods of Court-attacking activity, a credible threat of passage is sufficient to limit the Court. Actual passage may not be required. This suggests that no legislation limiting the independence of the Court was passed in the New Deal period, and little has been passed in other periods, because the Court acquiesced to the Congress, removing the provocation. The lack of passage of Court-attacking bills, then, may be due in part to their effectiveness as a threat.

The second obstacle to accepting the success of Congress in limiting the Court involves studying it not as a political institution but rather as a collection of individual policymakers exercising power. Where I have asserted that the Court reversed itself, some might argue that the cases are simply different, or that the seeds of the new doctrine can be found in the old cases. Relying on such assertions in the 1946 Presidential Address to the American Political Science Association, for example, Walter Dodd said "there is *no basis* for the assertion that favorable opinions by the Court from January to June of 1937 were occasioned by the President's action, and there seems to be a *fair degree of certainty* that they were independent of such influence."[20] The problem is that we can never know the real reasons behind each individual justice's vote. But since no two cases are identical, cases can always be distinguished on some level. With hindsight, the seeds of current decisions can *always* be found in past decisions. The striking difference in the Court's opinions in 1937, coupled with congressional action, and the pattern of correlation that I am developing, strongly suggest that congressional attacks on the Court limit its independence.

Finally, it might be suggested that the Court's reactions can be explained by changing judicial personnel. However, this is not the case. In two of the three periods in which the Court was subservient to congressional wishes (1802–1804, 1935–1937), there were no changes in personnel. In the other period of subservience, 1858–1869, six justices left the bench and five new justices were appointed by Lincoln. However, the five did not invariably support Republican policies.[21] Similarly, in the three periods of independence, there were no changes (1963–1965), three changes (1922–1924), and three changes (1893–1897). And in the middle periods, there were four changes (1823–1831), three changes (1955–1959), and one change (1977–1982). The variation across all nine periods, and vote outcomes in cases during these periods, make it clear that changes in personnel are not crucial explanatory variables.

[19] Robert J. Steamer, *The Supreme Court in Crisis: A History of Conflict* (Amherst: University of Massachusetts Press, 1971), p. 21.

[20] Walter Dodd, "The United States Supreme Court, 1936–1946," *American Political Science Review* 41 (1947): 1, 4, emphasis added.

[21] *E.g., Ex Parte Milligan*, 71 U.S. (4 Wall.) 2 (1866), *Cummings v. Mo.*, 71 U.S. (4 Wall.) 277 (1867), *Ex Parte Garland*, 71 U.S. (4 Wall.) 333 (1867).

The first three periods discussed involved clear examples of the Court avoiding decisions opposed by elected officials, or backing-off or reversing decisions in response to congressional hostility (the right side of Figure 1). The next three periods show just the opposite. Here, instead, the Court ignored congressional opposition and continued to develop the principles and line of cases that engendered the opposition. Why was the Court able to maintain its independence?

At issue in the 1893–1897 period was the role of the Court as a protector of corporate interests. Through the transformation of the due process clause into a substantive check on legislative regulation of business, the creation of the labor injunction as an antistrike weapon, the near-emasculation of the Sherman Anti-Trust Act in the *E. C. Knight* case, and the invalidation of the federal income tax in the *Pollock* case, the Court angered many.[22] The presidential campaign of 1896 became the focus and battleground for competing views on the role of the Court, earning itself the characterization of one of the two "great 'anti-Supreme Court' campaigns of American party politics."[23] The Bryan campaign adopted three separate anti-Court planks as the anti-Court forces spread from the Populists to the Bryan coalition. These planks, and the campaign, represented a classic attack on the Court. In the end, however, they failed because Bryan was decisively defeated by McKinley, and the political energy attacking the Court dissipated.

In this period, the threat that legislation limiting the Court would be enacted was shown to be hollow. The defeat of Bryan demonstrated to Congress and Court alike that opposition to the Court's solicitous approach to business did not have strong support among voters. There was no need for the Court to retreat in the face of a hostile Congress and Executive because when the issue was pressed, in 1896, it turned out that the new Congress and the Executive weren't so hostile after all.

The second period where the Court retained its independence in the face of congressional hostility occurred in 1922–1924. Here, the attack on the Court was led by the Progressives, upset over continuing Court support of business and hostility to state regulation. In 1923, for example, Representative Frear of Wisconsin proposed a right of appeal from the Supreme Court to Congress for holdings of unconstitutionality, and Senator Borah introduced legislation requiring the agreement of at least seven justices to invalidate a congressional statute. Not surprisingly, La Follette, running as the Progressive candidate for president, injected the issue into the 1924 presidential campaign. His platform included a Court-curbing plank and the Progressives' anti-Court feelings were clear. But, when the votes were counted, La Follette finished a distant third, with slightly less than 17 percent of the popular vote and only 13 electoral votes. With his defeat came the end of the attacks on the Court. As with the 1893–1897 period, Court-attacking failed

---

[22] *U.S. v. E. C. Knight*, 156 U.S. 1 (1895), *Pollock v. Farmers Loan and Trust Co.*, 157 U.S. 429 (1895), *aff'd on rehearing*, 158 U.S. 601 (1895). See, generally, Arnold Paul, *Conservative Crisis and the Rule of Law* (Ithaca: Cornell University Press, 1960).

[23] Alan F. Westin, "The Supreme Court, the Populist Movement and the Campaign of 1896," *Journal of Politics* 15 (1953): 3, 38.

because, after the election, Congress lacked the political will to push it and the credibility of the threat was nil.

The final period where congressional anger at the Court had little influence occurred in the years 1963–1965. At issue were Court decisions involving the banning of prayer in public schools,[24] and requiring a "one person–one vote" standard for apportioning electoral districts.[25] Apportionment was the issue that was pressed the hardest and in August 1965, the *New York Times* editorialized that the role of the Supreme Court was "facing its gravest political threat in a generation."[26] A number of bills were seriously considered to reverse the decision and one, simply removing federal court jurisdiction over apportionment, passed the House on a vote of 218 to 175.[27] With the pressure mounting, Anthony Lewis concluded that passage of the most important Court-curbing bill, the Dirksen constitutional amendment, "might well depend on whether President Johnson is reelected."[28]

The crisis was indeed resolved by the election. Goldwater "chose to make the judiciary" a "significant campaign issue" and Johnson's landslide reelection helped to "decimate the array of those most likely to join an anti-Court movement."[29] It also demonstrated that hostility to the Court was not widely shared. The Court-attack period passed. The point, though, is that while the Congress came close to limiting the Court, the 1964 election effectively removed the issue. The threat of a successful congressional attack vanished.[30]

In examining why the Court was able to continue in each of these three cases, two of the indicators of political preferences come to the fore. First, in each period there was an election in which curbing the Court was a campaign issue. However, in contrast to the successful periods of Court-curbing, in these unsuccessful cases the forces seeking to limit the Court lost. Second, although opposition to the Court was intense, it was not spread among a large number of officeholders or the public at large.[31] The message to the Court, then, could have been that the opposition it had engendered was limited to a minority and it could continue with its cases without fear of politically significant opposition.

---

[24] *Engel v. Vitale*, 370 U.S. 421 (1962), *Abington School District v. Schempp*, 374 U.S. 203 (1963).

[25] *Baker v. Carr*, 369 U.S. 186 (1962), *Wesberry v. Sanders*, 376 U.S. 1 (1964), *Reynolds v. Sims*, 377 U.S. 203 (1964).

[26] Editorial, "Crisis for the Court," *New York Times*, 9 August 1965, sec. 4, p. 8.

[27] Emanuel Celler, the Chair of the House Judiciary Committee, called another bill a "vicious attack on the Supreme Court." E. W. Kenworthy, "House Votes Ban on Court Power to Reapportion," *New York Times*, 20 August 1964, p. 1.

[28] Anthony Lewis, "Congress vs. The Court—Issue Joined on Redistricting: Decision to Reapportion the State Legislatures Stirs Opposition," *New York Times*, 16 August 1964, sec. 4, p. 3.

[29] Robert G. McCloskey, *The Modern Supreme Court* (Cambridge, MA: Harvard University Press, 1972), p. 359.

[30] There is evidence to suggest that the Court acted during these years to mollify congressional opposition. Every November since 1949, the *Harvard Law Review* has compiled Supreme Court cases with full opinions involving the government (both state and federal). They show that by 1965, Supreme Court decisions supporting the government had risen 14 percent over the 1963 figure. While the annual number of cases is large, ranging from 70 to over 100, the inclusion of state government, and the variety of issues involved, make this weak evidence. However, it is in the direction supportive of the effectiveness of Court-attacking.

[31] While there was a good deal of opposition to the Court's apportionment decisions among office-holders, the public was rather oblivious to the issue.

PERIODS OF NEITHER INDEPENDENCE
NOR SUBSERVIENCE

The preceding six periods of Court-curbing activity have covered episodes in which the Court rather clearly took political preferences into account by avoiding, backing-off, or reversing its decisions on the one hand, or, on the other hand, ignoring the opposition and continuing. In pictorial terms, these six periods deal with the two ends of the continuum of Figure 1. The remaining three cases lie somewhere in the middle. In each of them, the Court did react to congressional opposition but not in clearly subservient or independent ways.

The earliest of these three periods, 1823–1831, saw a growing fight over states' rights. At issue was the power of the federal government vis-à-vis the states, particularly the Supreme Court under Section 25 of the Judiciary Act of 1789. Several types of bills were introduced to limit the Court, ranging from requiring the votes of more than a mere majority of the justices to hold state statutes unconstitutional to outright repeal of Section 25. Indeed, a repeal bill was favorably reported out of the House Judiciary Committee early in 1831, a bill that Chief Justice Marshall feared would become law.

The Court's reaction to these congressional attacks was to execute a withdrawal. It did not continue with Marshall's nationalizing decisions. Charles Warren found it "evident that the Supreme Court itself took warning" and changed some of its procedures.[32] For example, Marshall announced that only if an absolute majority of the Court (not just a majority of justices voting) agreed would any judgment on constitutional questions be announced. On the other hand, the Court did not renounce former decisions nor give up its power of judicial review over the acts of state institutions. Its response, then, was somewhere between the two extremes of independence and subservience.

What explains this mixed response? The forces that were most upset by Court decisions were states-righters. However, they showed a curious inability to coalesce. The Court was never forced to face a united opposition. While opposition from one state's congressional delegation might be intense, others were not often willing to join. So, there was neither a large number of congressional opponents nor a successful coalition facing the Court.[33] Similarly, although there was an election during the Court-curbing period, and Andrew Jackson was elected as a states-righter, his opposition to federal activity was selective. Members of the Court might well have believed that if they were careful not to galvanize opposition, if they retreated on some issues as detailed above, the Court could continue in the face of opposition.

In the 1977–1982 period, bills were proposed to limit the independence of the Court in a wide variety of fields. A major underlying issue, however, was access to legal abortion. Starting in 1973, and reaching a peak in the years between 1977 and 1982, a variety of bills sought to nullify the Supreme Court's abortion decisions. During this period, the Court issued four important opinions that provide the raw material for the analysis. In three 1977 companion cases, reversing lower court decisions, the Court freed states from paying for nontherapeutic (non-life-threatening) abortions or providing such abortion services in public

---

[32] Charles Warren, "Legislative and Judicial Attacks on the Supreme Court of the United States—A History of the Twenty-Fifth Section of the Judiciary Act," *American Law Review* 47 (1913): 1, 165.

[33] McCloskey, *American Supreme Court*, p. 59.

facilities.[34] Then, in 1980, with 238 members of Congress filing an *amicus* brief basically in support of the Hyde Amendment, the Court upheld its constitutionality, drastically limiting federal funding for abortions, including most medically necessary ones.[35]

It is not obvious how these decisions can best be characterized. On the one hand, they did not detract from the constitutional right to obtain an abortion. In this sense, then, they can be characterized as the Court's ignoring opposition and continuing. Yet, on the other hand, the decisions did make legal abortions harder to obtain, especially for poor women. That is, the Court can be seen as backing away from the logic of its holdings which guaranteed women access to legal abortion. That guarantee was less meaningful after these four decisions.

This middle position can best be understood in terms of the indicators of political preferences. For example, although both Presidents Carter and Reagan opposed abortion, neither took important steps, Reagan's rhetoric notwithstanding, to oppose it. Similarly, although the intensity of many abortion foes was high, their numbers were never large enough to effectively threaten the Court. While the Hyde Amendment was repeatedly reenacted, none of the more powerful antiabortion bills were. Abortion remained a single issue and no coalitions were formed around it. Thus, it is possible that by bowing to congressional preferences on access to legal abortion for poor women, members of the Court might have felt they were mollifying opposition and ensuring the continuation of the right to abortion.[36] As with the 1823–1831 period, then, moderate levels of opposition to the Court can produce Court decisions somewhat, but only somewhat, in line with congressional feelings.

The final period of Court-curbing activity to be considered occurred in the years 1955–1959. Because it presents the entire array of characteristics, and because the factual pattern is both complicated and fascinating, it will be treated in more depth. During the years 1955–1959, Court decisions in a number of fields, including desegregation, free speech and subversion, and criminal procedure, enraged many members of Congress and a concerted attack on the Court was launched. Over 50 Court-curbing bills were introduced into Congress as an alliance of segregationists, cold warriors, and right-to-workers coalesced to curb the Court.[37]

In response, the Court chose its ground carefully. In the area of free speech and subversion, the Court reversed decisions that engendered opposition. Yet with desegregation and criminal law reform, key decisions were not reversed. Rather, by simply not deciding cases, the Court maintained its ground, or backed off only slightly. The Court sacrificed independence in one area, and trimmed its sails in the others, to preserve its independence to forge ahead in those other fields later.

In the free speech and subversion area, the Court in the 1950s issued a number of decisions that gave protection to people espousing unpopular opinions.[38]

[34] *Beal v. Doe*, 423 U.S. 438 (1977), *Maher v. Roe*, 432 U.S. 464 (1977), *Poelker v. Doe*, 432 U.S. 519 (1977).

[35] *Harris v. McRae*, 448 U.S. 297 (1980).

[36] By 1982, Supreme Court decisions supporting the government rose slightly more than 10% over the period's low point. See *supra*, note 30, particularly the caveat on interpreting this data.

[37] See, generally, Murphy, *Congress and the Court*.

[38] Cases include *Pennsylvania v. Nelson*, 350 U.S. 497 (1956)—sedition; *Schware v. New Mexico*, 353 U.S. 232 (1957), *Konigsberg v. California*, 353 U.S. 252 (1957)—bar exclusions; *Jencks v. U.S.*, 353 U.S. 657 (1957)—access to government files.

Two cases of particular relevance were *Watkins v. U.S.*,[39] and *Sweezy v. New Hampshire*,[40] in which the Supreme Court overturned contempt convictions for refusal to testify before the House Un-American Activities Committee and a New Hampshire investigatory committee respectively. These, and a number of other decisions, stimulated much Court-curbing activity.[41]

The congressional response was quick and effective. In the summer of 1957, a bill drafted by the Justice Department codifying and limiting the *Jencks'* holding was enacted. Another important bill, introduced by Senator Jenner in July, 1957, removed Supreme Court jurisdiction over subversion in five areas including review of congressional inquiries, of the practices of state bar examining committees, and of the employment actions of school boards. In the summer of 1958, in a story that reads more like an adventure thriller than a legislative history, Court-curbing forces came within one vote, and a parliamentary maneuver, of passing legislation in the Senate.[42] With the 1958 elections coming up, the Court-attacking bills were temporarily shelved.

In the years 1958 and 1959, Court decisions backed away from those that had so angered the Congress. Perhaps the clearest examples occurred in *Uphaus v. Wyman*[43] and *Barenblatt v. U.S.*[44] where the Court upheld contempt convictions for refusal to cooperate with a New Hampshire investigatory committee and the House Un-American Activities Committee respectively. To many, these two cases seemed to reverse the earlier *Sweezy* and *Watkins* decisions. Those who "applauded" the earlier decisions were "dumfounded" by the latter ones.[45] As C. Herman Pritchett put it: "Barenblatt was before the same committee, which was operating under the same vague mandate and using the same tactics of exposure and publicity-seeking which the Court had castigated in *Watkins*."[46] Two cold warriors saw *Barenblatt* as having "completely reversed" *Watkins*.[47] While there are differences between *Sweezy* and *Uphaus* in terms of the alleged political affiliations and the type of activity involved, and attempts have been made to distinguish *Watkins* and *Barenblatt*, too much should not be made of them. The bottom line was that in response to congressional preferences the Court effectively reversed its earlier decisions.

In the areas of employment, legislative investigation, and bar exclusions, the Court retreated from its earlier positions too. As the *New York Times* editorialized, "what Senator Jenner was unable to achieve the Supreme Court has now virtually achieved on its own."[48] In the area of free speech and subversion, the

[39] 354 U.S. 178 (1957).

[40] 354 U.S. 234 (1957).

[41] See, Robert J. Steamer, "Statesmanship or Craftsmanship: Current Conflict over the Supreme Court," *Western Political Quarterly* 11 (1958): 265; Clifford M. Lytle, "Congressional Response to Supreme Court Decisions in the Aftermath of the School Segregation Cases," *Journal of Public Law* 12 (1963): 290.

[42] For a fascinating account of the bill's history, see Murphy, *Congress and the Court.*

[43] 360 U.S. 72 (1959).

[44] 360 U.S. 109 (1959).

[45] Adam Breckenridge, *Congress and the Court* (Lincoln: University of Nebraska Press, 1970), p. 15.

[46] C. Herman Pritchett, *Congress Versus the Supreme Court* (Minneapolis: University of Minnesota Press, 1961), p. 49.

[47] Roy M. Cohn and Thomas A. Bolan, "The Supreme Court and the A.B.A. Report and Resolutions," *Fordham Law Review* 28 (1959): 233, 273.

[48] Editorial, "A Regrettable Decision," *New York Times*, 2 March 1960, p. 36.

1955–1959 period shows the success of congressional attempts to limit the independence of the Court.[49]

In the area of desegregation, however, the story is somewhat different. What started with great fanfare in 1954 with *Brown v. Board of Education*[50] petered out under intense congressional pressure. The political response to the decision was not supportive. In Congress, the "Southern Manifesto" pledged its 101 signers to fight against desegregation, and governors and state legislatures throughout the South lashed out at the Court. Among the legal profession, the American Bar Association and both the National Association of State Attorneys General and the Conference of State Chief Justices criticized the Court.[51]

The Court heeded these attacks by avoiding major civil rights decisions until well into the 1960s. In education, it did not issue a full opinion from *Brown* until the Little Rock crisis of 1958.[52] After the crisis passed, there was silence again until 1963.[53] And, despite *Brown*, public schools in the South remained pristinely white, with barely one in a hundred African-American children in elementary and secondary school with whites by 1964, a decade after the ruling.[54] Only after there was a major change in the congressional climate with the passage of the 1964 Civil Rights Act did the Court reenter the field.[55] As Wasby et al. put it, after *Brown*, "either overreacting or feeling badly burned by the lesson, the justices beat an unseemly retreat from the public school education field which was to last, with a few exceptions, over a dozen years."[56] And the same pattern appeared in other civil rights areas from housing to public facilities to anti-miscegenation laws.[57]

The point this history makes is, I think, accessible. In the wake of congressional hostility the Court did not follow the logic and power of *Brown*. In the civil rights

<hr />

[49] Breckenridge, *Congress and the Court*; Harold W. Chase, "The Warren Court and Congress," *Minnesota Law Review* 44 (1960): 595; Roger Handberg and Harold F. Hill, "Court-Curbing, Court Reversals, and Judicial Review: The Supreme Court Versus Congress," *Law and Society Review* 14 (1980): 309; McCloskey, *Modern Supreme Court*; Murphy, *Congress and the Court*; Pritchett, *Congress Versus the Supreme Court*; Bernard Schwartz, "The Supreme Court—October 1958 Term," *University of Michigan Law Review* 58 (1959): 165; Steamer, *Supreme Court in Crisis*; Stephen L. Wasby, Anthony A. D'Amato, and Rosemary Metrailer, *Desegregation from Brown to Alexander* (Carbondale: Southern Illinois University Press, 1977).

[50] 347 U.S. 483 (1954).

[51] Louis H. Pollak, "The Supreme Court Under Fire," *Journal of Public Law* 6 (1957): 428.

[52] *Cooper v. Aaron*, 358 U.S. 1 (1958).

[53] *Goss v. Board of Education of Knoxville*, 371 U.S. 683 (1963).

[54] Southern Education Reporting Service, *A Statistical Summary of School Segregation—Desegregation in the Southern and Border States* (Nashville, TN: Southern Education Reporting Service, 1967), pp. 40–44.

[55] For full development of this argument, see Gerald N. Rosenberg, *The Hollow Hope: Can Courts Bring About Social Change?* (Chicago: University of Chicago Press, 1991), chap. 3.

[56] Wasby et al., *Desegration from Brown to Alexander*, p. 107.

[57] The Court declined to hear any housing cases from 1953 to 1967. Some of its refusals had the effect of upholding segregation (*e.g.*, *Cohen v. Public Housing Authority*, 358 U.S. 928 [1959]; *Barnes v. City of Gadsden*, 361 U.S. 915 [1959]). More generally, the refusal to hear *Rice v. Sioux City Memorial Park Cemetery*, 348 U.S. 880 (1954), *after Brown*, effectively upheld a cemetery's restrictive covenant limiting burial to Caucasians. In *Dawly v. City of Norfolk, Virginia*, 359 U.S. 935 (1959), refusal to hear the case left restrooms in a state courthouse segregated. Another denial of *certiorari*, *In re Girard College Trusteeship*, 357 U.S. 570 (1958), had the effect of allowing a segregated school administered by the state to remain segregated. And in *Naim v. Naim*, 350 U.S. 891 (1955), 350 U.S. 985 (1956), the Court declined to hear an attack on state laws prohibiting interracial marriage. While the Court did issue numerous *per curiam* opinions striking down segregation laws, they were mostly ignored.

area it avoided cases and side-stepped issues. Only after the passage of the 1964 Civil Rights Act did the Court reenter the field with vigor. Yet, in contrast to free speech and subversion, the Court did not reverse the key decisions that created the opposition.

The final area where some congressional anger was aroused involved criminal law. Decisions like *Jencks* and *Mallory v. U.S.*,[58] ordering a new trial for a 19-year-old African-American convicted of rape, brought congressional ire. While it is impossible to state definitively the effect of the congressional uproar in the criminal rights area, the major decisions reforming criminal procedure of *Mapp v. Ohio*,[59] *Gideon v. Wainwright*,[60] and *Miranda v. Arizona*[61] did not come until the early and mid 1960s. There was enormous congressional hostility to tentative steps at reform of criminal procedure and the Court did not continue the reforms started in *Jencks* and *Mallory* until the political climate changed in the 1960s.

The characteristics of the 1955–1959 period present an amalgam of factors associated with Court independence and subservience. As with periods of Court subservience, congressional opposition was both intense and numerous. Yet, like periods of Court independence, no single group of opponents was powerful enough to curb the Court. And, like the preceding periods where Court action lay somewhere between the two extremes, elections in this period, for the most part, did not squarely address the issue of the Court.

Given these circumstances, it appears that the Court did two things: it held off from further developing the case lines that created opposition until political support went one way or the other; and, it astutely picked apart the coalition opposing it by acquiescing to the views of one faction. By effectively reversing the free speech and subversion decisions, the Court may have been able to protect itself in civil rights and reform of criminal procedure. By satisfying one part of its opposition, it may have made it less likely that bills curbing its other activities would gain support. Like its opponents, the Court appeared to have played coalition politics. Yet, unlike them, it was able to keep a more united front. Thus, when the political climate changed in the 1960s, the Court was able to move ahead.[62]

CONCLUSION

This article set out to test the hypothesis of judicial independence, that courts are free to reach decisions without regard to the political preferences of elected officials. Nine periods of intense Court-curbing activity were identified and Court decisions during these periods were examined. In contrast to the hypothesis of judicial independence, in only three of the nine periods was the Supreme Court clearly independent of congressional preferences. In the remaining six periods, the Court either acquiesced to the Congress and reversed decisions, or backed off to some extent to mollify congressional opposition. In times of opposition to Court opinion, when the need for judicial independence is at its height, such

[58] 354 U.S. 449 (1957).
[59] 367 U.S. 643 (1961).
[60] 372 U.S. 335 (1963).
[61] 384 U.S. 436 (1966).

[62] By 1959, decisions supporting the government had risen 14 percent over the lowest figure in the 1955–1959 Court-attack period. See *supra*, note 30, particularly the caveat on interpreting this data.

independence is seldom found. The hypothesis of judicial independence must be rejected.[63]

On the other hand, the news is not all bad. Even in three of the periods of intense congressional hostility to the Court, it did preserve its independence. Further, since only nine periods of intense congressional anger with the Court were identified, most of the time the Court appears free of political pressure. While the findings suggest that judicial independence is least likely to be found when it is the most necessary, most of the time the Court is not under pressure to reach decisions preferred by members of the other branches. Both critics and supporters of judicial independence have grounds for celebration.

The analysis allows for further refinement of this conclusion. At first glance the refinement may appear obvious. Judicial independence is most likely to be found the more prevalent are four conditions. When congressional and presidential campaigns have a Court component and result in defeat for opponents of the Court, when opponents are few in number and unable to coalesce with others, and when opposition to the Court is not intensely felt, judicial independence is most likely. On the other hand, judicial independence is least likely to occur when elections to Congress and the presidency bring Court opponents to office, when opponents are many in number and/or able to coalesce with others, and when opposition is intensely felt. Table 2 highlights these findings.

Taking the indicators one at a time, it has been shown that if an election occurs within or just before a Court-attacking period, then the election results may determine the Court's reaction. Thus, in the periods 1802–1804, 1858–1869, and 1935–1937, where elections brought politicians hostile to the Court to power, the Court was successfully dominated. On the other hand, in the periods 1893–1897, 1922–1924, and 1963–1965, elections weakened foes of the Court, lessening the threat of successful action. In these periods the Court maintained its independent course. And, in the periods 1823–1831, 1955–1959, and 1977–1982, when election results did not squarely respond to the issue of the Court, the Court responded to congressional opposition by taking a middle course between independence and subservience.

Interestingly, it does not appear necessary for Court-curbing to be an issue in election campaigns for elections to play an important role. Changes in the ideological make-up of the Congress or the Executive appear sufficient. In part, this may be because Americans know little about the Court. Thus, for example, congressional ire over the reapportionment decisions was not based on public sentiment since it turned out that the general public was quite unaware of the decisions. However, where public opinion about the Court and/or recent decisions is strong, election results can take on added importance.

With number of opponents, as Table 2 summarizes, the obvious seems to be the case. When faced with many opponents in 1802–1804, 1858–1869, and 1935–1937, the Court was subservient. When opponents were few, as in 1893–1897 and 1922–1924, independence was maintained. And, when the number of opponents was somewhere in between, other variables came into play.

---

[63] Cf., William Lasser, *The Limits of Judicial Power: The Supreme Court in American Politics* (Chapel Hill: University of North Carolina Press, 1988), p. 262, who argues that the Supreme Court has "always been largely invulnerable to political assault." However, he never offers a definition of judicial independence, and at times his argument is contradictory.

TABLE 2

A. Court Response to Court-Curbing Periods

Independence		Subservience
1893–1897	1823–1831	1802–1804
1922–1924	1955–1959	1858–1869
1963–1965	1977–1982	1935–1937

B. Court-Curbing Periods by Presence of Indicators

Indicator	Range		
Election of Court Opponents	No	Unclear	Yes
	1893–1897	1823–1831	1802–1804
	1922–1924	1955–1959	1858–1869
	1963–1965	1977–1982	1935–1937
Number of Opponents	Few	↔	Many
	1893–1897	1823–1831	1802–1804
	1922–1924	1955–1959	1858–1869
		1963–1965	1935–1937
		1977–1982	
Intensity	Low	↔	High
		1823–1831	1802–1804
		1893–1897	1858–1869
		1922–1924	1935–1937
		1963–1965	1955–1959
		1977–1982	
Likelihood of Coalitions forming	Low	↔	High
	1802–1804	1823–1831	1955–1959
	1858–1869	1963–1965	
	1893–1897	1977–1982	
	1922–1924		
	1935–1937		

Variance in the intensity of opposition plays an interesting role. To start, there are no instances on the "low" end of the continuum because the periods were selected for congressional opposition to the Court. Given this parameter, periods of intense opposition to the Court resulted in the clearest cases of Court subservience to congressional opposition. When the intensity was somewhat less, the Court was more likely to be less subservient. Contrast, for example, the different congressional reactions to *Dred Scott*[64] and the invalidation of New Deal legislation on the one hand, and the abortion decisions on the other. Congressional actions in the 1858–1869 and 1935–1937 periods were much more threatening to the Court than was the enactment of the Hyde Amendment. Consequently, Court reactions were quite different, with the Court sacrificing independence in the two earlier periods while back-tracking only somewhat, if at all, in the latter period.

[64] 60 U.S. (19 How.) 393 (1857).

The likelihood of coalitions forming, though not always coming into play, brings an added dynamism to Court-Congress relations. Clearly, when Court opponents are either large in number or quite small, the question of coalition-building does not arise. However, where such a possibility does exist, it appears that the Court modifies its behavior to split an existing coalition or prevent one from forming. Thus, in the 1955–1959 period, the Court split the coalition while in the 1823–1831 and 1977–1982 periods the Court modified its position, removing potential coalition parties by mollifying them. While there was a potential for coalition in the 1963–1965 period, the 1964 election removed the need for Court concern.

Finally, the findings suggest that *enactment* of Court-curbing bills is not necessary to curb the Court. Arousing substantial opposition to the Court may be enough to dominate it. This may be due to the Court's reliance on political leaders for the implementation of its decisions. As Alexander Hamilton pointed out centuries ago, the Court has neither the power of the purse nor the sword and is uniquely dependent on the rest of the federal government. Without political support, Court decisions are unlikely to be implemented. If the Court is dependent on political elites for the implementation of its judgments, angering some portion of them may effectively stymie the implementation of Court decisions. To the extent that the justices perceive attacks on the Court, then, they may try to mollify their critics and conserve the goodwill the Court requires. Thus, "success" in dominating the Court may occur well before the passage of a Court-attack bill.

A final note of caution is necessary. While these findings present hypotheses that can be tested, they are based on imprecise indicators and on the slippery notion of the perceived credibility of congressional threats. When will a bill be successful? How hard is it being pushed? Which, among several issues, is of utmost concern? Does that point, or range, vary with the issue and the members of the Court?

Despite these difficulties, the analysis does suggest that the hypothesis of judicial independence is wrong. At times of congressional ire with the Court, the Court succumbs to congressional preferences. Depending on the Court, then, to defend unpopular minorities or opinion against political hostility is misplaced. The very American notion of the courts as the "ultimate guardians of our fundamental rights," may be dangerously wrong. Much recent constitutional scholarship that assumes judicial independence needs rethinking. The role of the Supreme Court as an independent institution needs to be reexamined.

12

THE ENDURING FEATURES OF AMERICAN FEDERALISM
Martha Derthick

Federalism is fundamental in American politics—and to the politics of many other countries as well, including Australia, Brazil, Canada, Colombia, Germany, Mexico, and India. It is an allocation of policy responsibilities between national and subnational governments. We do not, for instance, have a national police force that does all traffic control and criminal enforcement, nor do we have a national sanitation service. State governments operate universities, deploy environmental police, issue hunting permits, and register automobile drivers, among other things. Local governments also have distinctive and essential tasks—schooling, property tax assessment, police, garbage collection, public libraries, and the like. By the same token, the Commonwealth of Pennsylvania and the Borough of Swarthmore, Pennsylvania (where I live), do not print money, operate a central bank, or have a foreign policy.

All of these governments—national, state, and local—get along with and affect each other in complicated ways. But so what if they do? Why should you care? Answering those two questions is not easy: One has to say something simple, specific, and clear that will not be obsolete the minute it is said, and also, at the same time, one has to keep the audience awake and paying attention. Alas, federalism is a topic that, for many, offers a cure for insomnia, even if they recognize its importance. But Martha Derthick manages in this article to effectively underscore that the United States would fall apart in a minute if it did not have state and local governments.

• • •

IT IS A COMMONPLACE OF SCHOLARSHIP that American federalism constantly changes.

And it is a commonplace of contemporary comment that the states are enjoying a renaissance. Their historic role as laboratories of experiment is acknowledged with praise. Their executives and legislatures are increasingly active, seizing issues, such as economic development, that the federal government has failed to come to grips with. State courts are staking out positions on individual rights in advance of those defined by the U.S. Supreme Court, while state attorneys general pursue consumer protection and antitrust cases that federal agencies have ignored. The states' share of government revenue has gained slightly on that of the federal government in the 1980s, and considerably surpasses that of local governments, contrary to a pattern that prevailed until the 1960s. The states' standing with the public and with prospective employees has improved. The governors are getting their share of good press and, what may be almost as important, of presidential

Brookings Review (Summer 1989), pp. 34–38. Reprinted with permission of The Brookings Institution Press.

nominations. As a result, state governments are perceived to have improved their position in the federal system.

Yet it is worth recalling how different the impression was but a short time ago, and how little has changed in some respects. Early in 1984 the Advisory Commission on Intergovernmental Relations published a much-noticed report, *Regulatory Federalism*, detailing a wide range of new or expanded federal controls over state government. In 1985, in the case of *Garcia* v. *San Antonio Metropolitan Transit Authority*, the Supreme Court declined to protect the state governments from congressional regulation under the Constitution's commerce clause and then washed its hands of this crucial federalism question. In the spring of 1988 the court removed the constitutional prohibition on federal taxation of income from interest on state and local government bonds (*South Carolina* v. *Baker*).

Certain regulatory excesses of the federal government vis-à-vis the states have been modified in the past several years; rules regarding transportation of the disabled and bilingual education are two examples. Yet not even under Ronald Reagan did the federal government step back from the new constitutional frontiers mapped out in the last decade or two—frontiers such as the Clean Air Act of 1970, which addresses the states with the language of outright command ("Each state shall . . ."). The president's executive order of October 1987 on federalism may be interpreted as an attempt to draw back, with its rhetorical statement of federalism principles and its instructions to executive agencies to refrain from using their discretion to preempt state action. But to read it is to be reminded of how little unilateral power the president has. The drawing back can succeed only to the extent the national legislature and courts concur. Nor did the Reagan administration consistently adhere to its professed principles. Substantive policy goals often were in tension with devolution of power to the states; the Reagan administration could be counted on to opt for devolution only when that tactic was consistent with its pursuit of a freer market and lower federal spending.

American federalism is a very large elephant indeed, and it is hard for a lone observer to grasp the properties of the whole beast. One needs to be abreast of constitutional doctrines; of legislative, judicial, and administrative practices over the whole range of government activities, from taxation to protection of civil liberties to pollution control; of the development or disintegration of political parties (are they decaying at the grass roots? at the center? both? neither?); of the volume and locus of interest group activity; of trends in public opinion and public employment, and more. To understand the condition of federalism, one needs to comprehend the functioning of the whole polity.

Granting that the federal system is always in flux, it is harder than one might suppose even to detect the dominant tendencies. While most academic analysts probably would assert that centralization is the secular trend, such distinguished scholars as Princeton political scientist Richard P. Nathan and Brandeis historian Morton Keller have argued that centralization is not inexorable and that the evolution of American federalism follows a cyclical pattern, with the federal government and the states alternately dominating.

MAPPING THE TERRAIN

Fighting the customary temptation to concentrate on change, I want to try to identify some elemental and enduring truths of American federalism. I want to map the features of the terrain, a metaphor that may be in fact apt. Our federalism is much like a piece of earth that is subject to constant redevelopment. It can be bulldozed and built up, flattened and regraded, virtually beyond recognition. Yet certain elemental properties of it, the bedrock and the composition of the soil, endure. I will start with propositions that I take to be purely factual and then proceed to others that are more analytical and normative, hence debatable.

The states are governments in their own right. They have constitutions that derive from the people and guarantee specific rights. They have elected legislatures that make laws, elected executives that enforce laws, and courts that interpret them—and not incidentally interpret the laws of the United States as well. State governments levy taxes. Their territorial integrity is protected by the U.S. Constitution, which also guarantees them equal representation in the Senate and a republican form of government. These creatures that walk like ducks and squawk like ducks must be ducks.

Nevertheless, the states are inferior governments. In our pond, they are the weaker ducks. The stubbornly persistent mythology that governments in the American federal system are coordinate should not obscure that fact. The two levels of government are *not* coordinate and equal, nor did the winning side in 1787 intend them to be. One cannot deny the existence of the Constitution's supremacy clause and the prescription that state officers take an oath to uphold the Constitution of the United States, or the fact that the framers of the Constitution fully expected an instrumentality of the federal government, the Supreme Court, to settle jurisdictional issues in the "compound republic," as James Madison called it. See *Federalist* No. 39, in which Madison makes a feeble, unsuccessful attempt to deny that the Court's having this function gives the federal government a crucial advantage.

Whether the federal government has always been superior in fact can certainly be debated. At various times and places its writ did not run very strong. Ours was a different system in the 19th century, and it is significant that the full impact on federalism of the post–Civil War Amendments on civil rights was long delayed. Only recently has the South ceased to have a deviant social system. But on the whole, the federal government has won the crucial conflicts. Surely its ascendancy is not currently in dispute. Not only are the states treated as its administrative agents; they accept such treatment as a fact of life. Not since *Brown* v. *Board of Education* (1954) and *Baker* v. *Carr* (1962) have truly strenuous protests been heard from the states against their palpably inferior status.

The states' status as governments, even though inferior ones, gives Congress a range of choice in dealing with them. It may choose deference, displacement, or interdependence. In domestic affairs Congress always has the option of doing nothing, knowing that the states can act whether or not it does. Sometimes Congress consciously defers to the states, judging that the subject properly "belongs" to them. Perhaps just as often, Congress today is not deliberately deferential but fails to act for lack of time or the ability to reach agreement. It defaults. The area of congressional inaction, be it through deference or default, is reliably quite large. It normally includes new issues, such as AIDS or comparable worth. States remain on the front lines of domestic policy, the first to deal with newly perceived problems. Congress tends to defer or default on particularly difficult issues, such as the amount of support to be given to needy single mothers with children.

Congress rarely employs its second option, complete displacement, although explicit invocations of it, using the term "preemption," are more frequent now than they used to be. The third option, interdependence, is very common, I would think predominant. Through some combination of inducements, sanctions, or contractual agreements, Congress enters into collaborative arrangements with the states in the pursuit of national ends. The most common techniques are conditional grants-in-aid, which are characteristic of programs for income support and infrastructure development, and qualified preemptions, which are typical of the "new" regulation, including environmental protection and occupational health and safety. Congress sets standards but tells states that if they meet or exceed the national standards, they may retain the function, including administration.

The vigor and competence with which state governments perform functions left to them does not protect them against congressional incursions. Here I mean to challenge one of the leading canards of American federalism. Whenever Congress takes domestic action, that action is rationalized as a response to the failures of the states. Congress has had to step in, it is said, because states were not doing the job. The only thing one can safely say about the origins of nationalizing acts is that they are responses to the power of nationalizing coalitions. When Congress acts, in other words, it is not necessarily because states have failed; it is because advocates of national action have succeeded in mustering enough political force to get their way. State inaction may constitute part of their case, but state actions that are offensive to their interests may do so as well. Pathbreaking states have often demonstrated what can be done.

Congress's usual choice, moreover, is to cooperate with the states, not to displace them, and in the relationships of mutual dependence that result, it is a nice question just whose deficiencies are being compensated for. The federal government typically contributes uniform standards and maybe money. The states typically do the work of carrying out the function. The more they do and the better they do it, the more they are likely to be asked or ordered by Congress to do.

In cooperating with the states, Congress again has a choice. It can emphasize their status as governments, or it can emphasize their inferiority as such. Our ambiguous constitutional system enables Congress to view the states as equals or as agents. Congress gradually has abandoned the former view in favor of the latter. It has done so with the acquiescence of the Supreme Court, which once tried to defend "dual federalism"—that is, the notion that the states were sovereign, separate, and equal—but which has long since abandoned that doctrine. And Congress does not indulge its agents. Ask any federal bureau chief. Congress is very poor at balancing the ends and means of action. All major federal executive agencies—the Environmental Protection Agency, the Social Security Administration, the Immigration and Naturalization Service, to cite just a few—are laboring under a burden of excessive obligation.

Because states are governments, they may bargain with Congress. Bargaining is the usual mode of intergovernmental relations. State governments, even when treated by Congress as administrative agents, are agents with a difference. Unlike federal executive agencies, they are not Congress's creatures. Therefore they can talk back to it. They can influence the terms of cooperation.

This bargaining between levels of governments is good, depending on how the states use it. Here again I mean to challenge what I take to be a conventional view. Fragmentation of authority in the federal system is ordinarily portrayed, at least in academic literature, as a severe handicap to the federal government's pursuit of its goals. The federal government would be more effective, it is commonly said, if it did not have to rely so heavily on other governments. I believe, to the contrary, that the federal government needs a great deal of help, of a kind that can best be supplied—perhaps can only be supplied—by governments. It needs help with all aspects of governing, that is, with all the functions that legislatures, courts, and executives perform. Beyond that, it needs a great deal of help quite specifically in adjusting its goals to social and economic realities and to the capacities of administrative organizations.

Madison may be cited in support of this view—not the famous passage in *Federalist* No. 51 that one might anticipate, in which he argues that "the different governments will control each other, at the same time that each will be controlled by itself," but a passage less remarked, yet perhaps more prescient, in No. 62. In this essay on the Senate, Madison wrote: "A good government implies two things: first, fidelity to the object of government, which is the happiness of the people; secondly, a knowledge of the means by which that object can be best attained. Some governments are deficient in both these qualities; most governments are deficient in the first. I scruple not to assert, that in American governments too little attention has been paid to the last."

The deficiency in our attention to the means of government has never been more glaring. All institutions of the federal government—Congress, presidency, courts—have far more to do than they can do, but the executive agencies as the instruments of government action are arguably the most overburdened of all. Perhaps even more glaring today than the federal government's shortfall of institutional capacity is its shortfall of fiscal capacity. It has obligations far in excess of its willingness or ability to meet them. Whether that is a product of party politics or has other causes need not concern us here. The fact of the deficit is plain enough.

State governments help fill the federal government's performance gaps. They do much of the work of governing, as Madison anticipated. Even as an ardent nationalist, at the time of the Constitutional Convention, he held to the view that the national government would not be suited to the entire task of governing "so great an extent of country, and over so great a variety of objects." Just how right he was has never been clearer. But if the states help fill the federal government's implementation gaps, they also are very much at risk of being victimized by them. Congress will try to close the distance between what it wants and what the federal government is able to do independently by ordering the states to do it.

AN APPEAL TO TALK BACK

The states are entitled to talk back. As governments in their own right, they have an independent responsibility to set priorities and balance means against ends. Because they are closer to the practical realities of domestic problems and because they lack the power to respond to deficits by printing money, state governments are in a superior position to do that balancing.

This appeal to the states to talk back is not a call to defiance, but a call to engage federal officials in a policy dialogue—and, having done so, to address those officials with language suitable to governments. If states habitually present themselves as supplicants for assistance—supplicants like any other interest group—they will inevitably contribute to the erosion of their own status.

I believe that the states *are* increasingly using the language of governments, rather than supplicants, in their dialogue with the federal government. The enactment in 1988 of welfare reform legislation, which a working group of the National Governors Association helped to shape, is an example. The governors drew on the state governments' experience with welfare programs to fashion changes that would be both politically and administratively feasible, besides containing improved assurances of federal funding for welfare.

There are numerous explanations for the new, more authoritative voice of the states. One is that individually the states have heightened competence and self-confidence as governments, whatever the range among them (and the range between, say, Virginia and Louisiana is very great). Another is that the decline of federal aid under Presidents Carter and Reagan has compelled greater independence. A third is that self-consciousness and cohesion of the states as a class of governments have increased, as indicated by the development of organized, well-staffed mechanisms of cooperation. Their shared status as agents of Congress and objects of its influence has caused the states to cooperate with one another today to a degree unprecedented in history, even if they remain intensely competitive in some respects, such as the pursuit of economic development.

I have concentrated on relations between the states and Congress to keep the subject focused and relatively simple. But the federal judiciary rivals the legislature as a framer of federal-state relations. Federal courts, like Congress, can choose to emphasize the states' standing as governments or their inferiority as such. Like Congress, over time the courts have come to favor the latter choice, so that states today are routinely commanded to implement the detailed policy decisions of national courts as well as the national legislature.

For the states, it is one thing to talk back to Congress, quite another and much harder thing to talk back to the federal courts. Yet here as well, they have been trying to find ways to talk back more effectively. The National Association of Attorneys General and the State and Local Legal Center, both with offices in Washington, now offer advice and assistance to state and local governments involved in litigation before the Supreme Court. Such governments in the past have often suffered from a lack of expert counsel.

It is no use to portray these developments in federal-state relations as a transgression of the framers' intentions, at least if we take the *Federalist* as our authoritative guide to those intentions. Alexander Hamilton foresaw with evident satisfaction the federal-state relation that obtains today. In *Federalist* No. 27, he wrote that "the plan reported by the convention, by extending the authority of the federal head to the individual citizens of the several States, will enable the government to employ the ordinary magistracy of each, in the execution of its laws. . . . Thus the legislatures, courts, and magistrates, of the respective [states], will be incorporated into the operations of the national government . . . and will be rendered auxiliary to the enforcement of its laws." This is exactly what has happened.

What Hamilton would certainly not be satisfied with, however, is the federal government's management of its own administrative and fiscal affairs. One therefore feels entitled to invoke Madison on the states' behalf. It is not enough today that the states help the national government with governing, the function that both Hamilton and Madison foresaw. It is important as well that they perform a modern version of the balancing function that Madison in particular foresaw. This requires that in their policy dialogue with the federal government they assert, as governments in their own right, the importance of balancing ends and means.

13

THE DIFFUSION OF INNOVATIONS
AMONG THE AMERICAN STATES

Jack L. Walker*

Most of the time, federalism is thought about "vertically"—that is, in terms of intergovernmental conflict and cooperation from top to bottom, and back up, all involving national, state, and local governments. In this article, Walker takes a different, "horizontal" approach. Why are new policy ideas adopted by some states (i.e., by their state legislatures and governors) but not others? The "horizontal" answer is that officials in these legislatures and executive branches emulate and compete with each other in the adoption of policy ideas. Walker generates several suggestions about the factors that affect the diffusion of policy ideas among these public officials—and in doing so, he underscores a basic fact of American citizenship: Where you live affects how you experience being an American citizen. We ordinarily think that the Supreme Court defines our experience as citizenship. But if states and federalism are as important as the Derthick and Walker articles suggest, our citizenship is defined by federalism to a large extent as well.

If, for instance, you are gay, you already know that some states have adopted the policy idea of legally "defending" heterosexual marriage, while others have adopted the policy idea of permitting civil unions or same-sex marriage. Spatial variation in such marriage politics might, for example, prompt the two members of a gay partnership to pick up and move from Louisiana, which prohibits same-sex marriage, to Massachusetts, which permits it.

But Walker goes further than simply connecting place and the experience of citizenship: He also shows that the connection between place and citizenship has been, is, and will continue to be renegotiated and redefined by the "diffusion of innovations among the American states." The connections between place and citizenship change over time.

• • •

WE ARE NOW IN THE MIDST of a notable revival of interest in the politics of the American states. During the last decade many studies have been conducted of the

From *American Political Science Review* 63 (September 1969): 880–899. Copyright © 1969 by the American Political Science Association. Reprinted with the permission of Cambridge University Press.

*Thanks are due to the Committee on Governmental and Legal Processes of the Social Science Research Council, the Carnegie Corporation, the Michigan Legislative Intern Program, and the Rackham Faculty Research Fund of the University of Michigan for grants which made this study possible; to Mrs. Adarsh Trehan, Doyle Buekwalter, Michael Traugott, Mrs. Jennifer Drew Campbell, and Terry Bender who assisted in the collection and analysis of the data; and to H. Douglas Price, Rufus Browning, Warren Miller, Lawrence Mohr, Robert Friedman, Joel Aberbach, Robert Putnam, Ronald Brunner, Dennis Riley, Gail MacColl, and my wife, Linda Walker, whose criticisms and comments have helped me avoid several errors of inference and judgment.

social, political and economic determinants of state policy outcomes.[1] Several of these writers have argued that the relative wealth of a state, its degree of industrialization, and other measures of social and economic development are more important in explaining its level of expenditures than such political factors as the form of legislative apportionment, the amount of party competition, or the degree of voter participation.[2] It has been claimed that such factors as the level of personal income or the size of the urban population are responsible *both* for the degree of participation and party competition in a state, *and* the nature of the system's policy outputs. By making this argument these writers have called into question the concepts of representation and theories of party and group conflict which, in one form or another, are the foundations for much of American political science.[3]

There is a growing awareness, however, that levels of expenditure alone are not an adequate measure of public policy outcomes. Sharkansky has shown, for example, that levels of expenditure and levels of actual service are seldom correlated; presumably, some states are able to reach given service levels with much less expenditure than others.[4] Besides establishing the appropriate level of expenditure for a program, policy makers must also decide about the program's relative scope, provisions for appeal from administrative orders, eligibility requirements, the composition of regulatory boards and commissions, and many other matters which have little to do with money. Before we can evaluate the relative importance of structural and political factors as determinants of policy, therefore, we need to investigate decisions outside the budgetary process. In order to advance that object this study will focus on one of the most fundamental policy decisions of all: whether to initiate a program in the first place.

States have traditionally been judged according to the relative speed with which they have accepted new ideas. Wisconsin, because of its leadership during the Progressive period and its early adoption of the direct primary, the legislative reference bureau, and workmen's compensation, gained a reputation as a pioneering state which it has never lost. Reputations of this kind are usually based only on random impressions and they may be inaccurate or misleading, but if it is true

---

[1] Beginning with Richard E. Dawson and James A. Robinson, "Inter-Party Competition, Economic Variables, and Welfare Policies in the American States," *Journal of Politics* (May, 1963), 265–289, there have been numerous articles and books on the subject. The most recent summary is: John H. Fenton and Donald W. Chamberlayne, "The Literature Dealing with the Relationships Between Political Processes, Socio-economic Conditions and Public Policies in the American States: A Bibliographical Essay," *Polity* (Spring, 1969), 388–394.

[2] For examples see: Herbert Jacob, "The Consequences of Malapportionment: A Note of Caution," *Social Forces* (1964), 260–266; the chapters by Robert Salisbury, Robert Friedman, Thomas Dye, and Dawson and Robinson in: Herbert Jacob and Kenneth Vines (eds.), *Politics in the American States: A Comparative Analysis* (Boston, 1965); Richard I. Hofferbert, "The Relation Between Public Policy and Some Structural and Environmental Variables in the American States," this REVIEW (March, 1966), 73–82; and Thomas Dye, *Politics, Economics and the Public: Policy Outcomes in the American States* (Chicago, 1966).

[3] For an evaluation of the significance of this literature and its implications for political science see: Robert Salisbury, "The Analysis of Public Policy: A Search for Theories and Roles," in Austin Ranney (ed.), *Political Science and Public Policy* (Chicago, 1968), pp. 151–178.

[4] Ira Sharkansky, "Government Expenditures and Public Services in the American States," this REVIEW (1967), 1066–1077. Sharkansky also identifies important political variables in his: "Economic and Political Correlates of State Government Expenditures: General Tendencies and Deviant Cases," *Midwest Journal of Political Science* (1967), 173–192.

that some states change more readily than others a study of the way states adopt new ideas might lead to some important insights into the whole process of political change and development.

This essay is primarily an exercise in theory building. My aim is to develop propositions which might be used as guides to the study of the diffusion of innovations and which might also apply to budgeting and other forms of decision making.[5] Limitations in the data I have collected do not allow empirical testing of all the explanations I propose; the currently untestable propositions are presented in the hope that they may help in preparing the ground for future research. The study begins with an effort to devise a measure of the relative speed with which states adopt new programs. Once a measure of this phenomenon is created efforts are made to discover its principal demographic and political correlates. The article concludes with an effort to devise an explanation for the adoption of innovations based on insights gathered from studies of decision making, reference group theory, and the diffusion of innovations. The major questions being investigated are: (1) why do some states act as pioneers by adopting new programs more readily than others, and once innovations have been adopted by a few pioneers, (2) how do these new forms of service or regulation spread among the American states?

I. DEFINITIONS AND DISTINCTIONS

Several terms have already been used here which have ambiguous meanings and it is important to make clear just how they are to be defined. The most important, and potentially misleading, is the term "innovation." An innovation will be defined simply as a program or policy which is new to the states adopting it, no matter how old the program may be or how many other states may have adopted it. Even though bureaucratic innovations or new departures by regulatory commissions or courts may be mentioned in the course of the discussion, the data used to measure the relative speed of adoption of innovations consist exclusively of legislative actions, simply because the data were readily available only in that form.

We are studying the relative speed and the spatial patterns of *adoption* of new programs, not their invention or creation. Invention, or bringing into being workable, relevant solutions to pressing problems, is an important activity and has been the subject of fascinating research.[6] We will concentrate on the way in which organizations select from proposed solutions the one which seems most suited to their

---

[5] There is a well-established body of research on the diffusion of innovations from which I have drawn many insights. For general reviews of this literature see: Everett M. Rogers, *Diffusion of Innovations* (New York, 1962), Elihu Katz, Martin L. Levin, and Herbert Hamilton, "Traditions of Research in the Diffusion of Innovations," *American Sociological Review* (1963), 237–252. For early attempts to study the American states from this perspective see: Ada J. Davis, "The Evolution of the Institution of Mothers' Pensions in the United States," *American Journal of Sociology* (1930), 573–582; Edgar C. McVoy, "Patterns of Diffusion in the United States," *American Sociological Review* (1940), 219–227; and E. H. Sutherland, "The Diffusion of Sexual Psychopath Laws," *American Journal of Sociology* (1950–51), 144–156. Also see: Torsten Hagerstrand, *Innovation Diffusion as a Spatial Process* (Chicago, 1967); and Robert Mason and Albert N. Halter, "The Application of a System of Simultaneous Equations to an Innovation Diffusion Model," *Social Forces* (1968), 182–193.

[6] For examples see: Gary A. Steiner (ed.), *The Creative Organization* (Chicago, 1965); and Tom Burns and G. M. Stalker, *The Management of Innovation* (London, 1961).

needs, and how the organizations come to hear about these new ideas in the first place.[7] We are not trying to specify the circumstances under which new ideas or programs will be conceived or developed; we are studying instead the conditions under which state decision makers are most likely to adopt a new program.

The object of this analysis is the process of diffusion of ideas for new services or programs. Sometimes new legislation is virtually copied from other states. The California fair trade law, adopted in 1931, "was followed either verbatim or with minor variations by twenty states; in fact, ten states copied two serious typographical errors in the original California law."[8] No assumption is being made, however, that the programs enacted in each state are always exactly alike or that new legislation is written in exactly the same way by every legislature. It is unlikely that the highway department established in Wisconsin in 1907 had the same organizational format as the one adopted by Wyoming in 1917, or that the council on the performing arts created in New York in 1960 bears an exact resemblance to the one created by Kentucky in 1966. In each case, however, a commitment was made to offer a new service, establish a new principle of regulation, or create an agency which had never existed before. Our concern is the origin and spread of the idea to provide public subsidies for the arts, not the detailed characteristics of institutions created in each state to implement the policy.

No ideological bias was employed in selecting issues for study. The patterns of diffusion for each issue have been treated equally, and no effort was made to develop any method of determining the relative importance or desirability of the programs.[9] Programs are sometimes enacted only to provide symbolic rewards to groups within the population and once created are left with inadequate funds or otherwise disabled.[10] Oklahoma's legislature, for example, emulated other states by creating a state civil rights commission, but once the commission was established, only $2,500 was appropriated for its operation.[11] For the purposes of this study, however, all adoptions are equal. My goal is to provide an explanation of the relative speed of adoption and the patterns of diffusion of innovations; I am not interested in the effectiveness of Oklahoma's civil rights commission, but in where the legislature got the idea to create such a commission and why it acted when it did.

II. THE INNOVATION SCORE

My first aim is to explain why some states adopt innovations more readily than others. I assume that the pioneering states gain their reputations because of the

---

[7] There is much confusion over this distinction in the literature on diffusion. For an excellent discussion of the problem see: Lawrence B. Mohr, "Determinants of Innovation in Organizations," this REVIEW (1969), 111–126.

[8] Once the mistake was discovered, the Arkansas statute, which reproduced a model prepared by the National Association of Retail Druggists, was copied either verbatim or with minor changes by seventeen states. Ewald T. Grether, *Price Control Under Fair Trade Legislation* (New York, 1937), pp. 19–20.

[9] In later work I will report the results of comparisons of the diffusion patterns of issues from different subject matter areas. Preliminary efforts at such comparisons, however, have not revealed significant variations. There does not seem to be much difference in the diffusion patterns of issues of different types.

[10] For a discussion of this phenomenon see: Murray Edelman, *The Symbolic Uses of Politics* (Urbana, 1964), chapters 2 and 9.

[11] Duane Lockard, *Toward Equal Opportunity* (New York, 1968), p. 23.

speed with which they accept new programs. The study must begin, therefore, with an attempt to devise an innovation score that will represent the relative speed with which states adopt innovations.

The innovation score is based on the analysis of eighty-eight different programs (see the Appendix for a list) which were enacted by at least twenty state legislatures prior to 1965, and for which there was reliable information on the dates of adoption. In order to make the collection of programs as comprehensive and representative as possible, I adopted a list of basic issue areas similar to the one employed by the Council of State Governments in its bi-annual reports included in the *Book of the States*. I tried to study six to eight different pieces of legislation in each of these areas: welfare, health, education, conservation, planning, administrative organization, highways, civil rights, corrections and police, labor, taxes, and professional regulation. In the course of my analysis I studied issues ranging from the establishment of highway departments and the enactment of civil rights bills to the creation of state councils on the performing arts and the passage of sexual psychopath laws. Most of the programs were adopted during the twentith century, but sixteen of them diffused primarily during the latter half of the nineteenth century.

Once the eighty-eight lists of dates of adoption were collected they were used to create an innovation score for each state. The first step was to count the total number of years which elapsed between the first and last recorded legislative enactment of a program. Each state then received a number for each list which corresponded to the percentage of time which elapsed between the first adoption and its own acceptance of the program. For example, if the total time elapsing between the first and last adoption of a program was twenty years, and Massachusetts enacted the program ten years after the first adoption, then Massachusetts received a score of .500 on that particular issue. The first state to adopt the program received a score of .000 and the last state received a 1.000. In cases in which all the states have not yet adopted a program, the states without the program were placed last and given a score of 1.000.[12] The innovation score for each state is simply 1.000 minus the average of the sum of the state's scores on all issues. The larger the innovation score, therefore, the faster the state has been, on the average, in responding to new ideas or policies. The issues may be divided into groups according to subject matter areas or time periods, and separate scores can be created for these smaller groupings of issues by following the same procedure. The results of this scoring procedure, using all eighty-eight issues, are presented in Table 1.

A note of caution should be sounded before the results of this exercise are analyzed. We are endeavoring to measure a highly complex process in which an enormous number of idiosyncratic influences are at work; an official with an unusually keen interest in a particular program, a chance reading of an article or book by a governor's aide, or any number of other circumstances peculiar to any one issue might lead to the rapid adoption of a piece of legislation by a state which is usually reluctant to accept new programs. Mississippi, which has the lowest average score and ranks last among the states in relative speed of adoption, was nonetheless the first state to adopt a general sales tax.

---

[12] The beginning point for the existence of each state was the date upon which it was officially organized as a territory. Using this system, Oklahoma is the last state to come into being, having been organized in 1890. If a program began its diffusion before a state came into existence, that issue was not included in figuring the innovation score for the state.

TABLE 1
Composite Innovation Scores for the American States[13]

New York	.656	New Hampshire	.482	Idaho	.394
Massachusetts	.629	Indiana	.464	Tennessee	.389
California	.604	Louisiana	.459	West Virginia	.386
New Jersey	.585	Maine	.455	Arizona	.384
Michigan	.578	Virginia	.451	Georgia	.381
Connecticut	.568	Utah	.447	Montana	.378
Pennsylvania	.560	North Dakota	.444	Missouri	.377
Oregon	.544	North Carolina	.430	Delaware	.376
Colorado	.538	Kansas	.426	New Mexico	.375
Wisconsin	.532	Nebraska	.425	Oklahoma	.368
Ohio	.528	Kentucky	.419	South Dakota	.363
Minnesota	.525	Vermont	.414	Texas	.362
Illinois	.521	Iowa	.413	South Carolina	.347
Washington	.510	Alabama	.406	Wyoming	.346
Rhode Island	.503	Florida	.397	Nevada	.323
Maryland	.482	Arkansas	.394	Mississippi	.298

If this reservation is kept in mind, the data in Table I provide a crude outline of the standard or typical pattern of diffusion of new programs or policies among the American states. The states at the top of the list tend to adopt new programs much more rapidly than those at the bottom of the list. Having provided a preliminary measurement of this phenomenon, we must now try to explain it. Why should New York, California and Michigan adopt innovations more rapidly than Mississippi, Wyoming and South Dakota?

III. THE CORRELATES OF INNOVATION

Demographic Factors: After studying the acceptance of technological innovations by both individuals and organizations, several writers have concluded that the decision maker's relative wealth, or the degree to which "free floating" resources are available, are important determinants of the willingness to adopt new techniques or policies.[14] If "slack" resources are available, either in the form of money or a highly skilled, professional staff, the decision maker can afford the luxury of experiment and can more easily risk the possibility of failure.[15] Other studies, especially in the areas of agriculture and medicine, have also shown organizational size to be a strong correlate of innovation.[16] Given these results from prior studies in other fields we might expect to find that the larger, wealthier states, those

[13] Alaska and Hawaii were omitted from the analysis because data for their years of adoption were often missing.

[14] Everett M. Rogers, *Diffusion of Innovations* (New York, 1962), pp. 40, 285–292. Also see: S. N. Eisenstadt, *The Political Systems of Empires* (New York, 1963), p. 27, 33–112.

[15] For a discussion of "slack" resources and innovation see: Richard M. Cyert and James G. March, *A Behavioral Theory of the Firm* (Englewood Cliffs, N.J., 1963), pp. 278–279.

[16] Rogers, *op. cit.*, Mohr, *op. cit.*; and also: Edwin Mansfield, "The Speed of Response of Firms to New Techniques," *Quarterly Journal of Economics* (1963), 293–304; Jerald Hage and Michael Aiken, "Program Change and Organizational Properties: A Comparative Analysis," *American Journal of Sociology* (1967), 516–517; and Richard J. Hall, S. Eugene Haas, and Norman J. Johnson, "Organizational Size, Complexity and Formalization," *American Sociological Review* (1967), 903–912.

with the most developed industrial economies and the largest cities, would have the highest innovation scores. It would seem likely that the great cosmopolitan centers in the country, the places where most of the society's creative resources are concentrated, would be the most adaptive and sympathetic to change, and thus the first to adopt new programs.

In order to test these assumptions several measures of social and economic development were correlated with the innovation score. As we can see in Table 2, there is evidence that the larger, wealthier, more industrialized states adopt new programs somewhat more rapidly than their smaller, less well-developed neighbors. Fairly strong relationships exist between the innovation score and the value added by manufacturing, the average per acre value of farms, the size of the urban population, and the average per capita income. These relationships remain virtually unchanged in all time periods. In fact, the only relationship which changes substantially over time is that between innovation and the percentage of illiterates in the population which declines steadily across the three time periods. This declining relationship and the low correlation between innovation and the median school year completed is caused primarily by the states in the Rocky Mountain region which have the highest rankings on median school years completed and yet are among the slowest to adopt new programs.[17] The median of educational attainment in the states with the highest innovation scores is pulled down by the presence of a large, poorly educated, lower class, living primarily in the inner cities. The highly industrialized states with large urban concentrations are characterized by great inequality of social status and attainment. It would seem, however, that the elements necessary to foster innovation are present in these states even though they do not have highest average level of educational achievement.

Political Factors: Although students of policy making have begun to doubt the importance of the political system as an independent determinant of the behavior of decision makers, it seems likely that both the degree of party competition and a state's system of legislative apportionment would affect its readiness to accept change. It would seem that parties which often faced closely contested elections would try to out-do each other by embracing the newest, most progressive programs and this would naturally encourage the rapid adoption of innovations. Lowi argues that new departures in policy are more likely at the beginning of a new administration, especially when a former minority party gains control of the

---

[17] Regional affects of this kind appear frequently in analyses of data from the American states. In many studies, especially those which involve measures of political participation or party competition, strong relationships appear which are actually only a result of the distinctive nature of the southern states. In order to insure that the correlations in this analysis were not merely a result of the social and political peculiarities of the South, the eleven states of the confederacy were removed from all distributions. Since the Southern states do not cluster at one extreme of the innovation scale, no great changes occurred in correlation coefficients based upon data from the thirty-nine states outside the South. Within the eleven Southern states, however, almost all the relationships were substantially reduced in size. Because only eleven states are involved, this fact is difficult to interpret, but will be treated more fully in later work. For an example of this problem discussed in another context see: Raymond Wolfinger and John Osgood Field, "Political Ethos and the Structure of City Government," this REVIEW (1966), 306–326. For a more extensive discussion of the methodological implications see the discussion of "interaction effects" in Hugh Donald Forbes and Edward R. Tufte, "A Note of Caution in Causal Modelling," this REVIEW (1968), pp. 1261–1262; and the communication from Dennis D. Riley and Jack L. Walker, this REVIEW (September, 1969), pp. 880–899.

TABLE 2
Correlations Between Innovation Scores and Five Social
and Economic Variables, by Time Periods

	Innovation Scores*			
Social-Economic Variables	1870–1899	1900–1929	1930–1966	Composite Score
Per Cent Population Urban:	.62**	.69	.62	.63
Total Population:	.52	.40	.50	.59
Average Income, Per Capita:	—***	.62	.50	.55
Value Added Per Capita by Manufacturing:	.46	.55	.57	.66
Average Value, Per Acre, of Farms:	.70	.52	.52	.54
Per Cent Population Illiterate:	−.58	−.44	−.12	−.23
Median School Years Completed:	—***	—***	.24	.26

*In order to insure that the innovation score and the social and economic variables came from comparable periods, separate innovation scores were calculated for three time periods: 1870–1899, 1900–1929, and 1930–1966. In constructing this table each innovation was placed in the time period during which the first ten states adopted it. Thus, if a program was adopted by only four states during the 1890s, and completed its diffusion during the 1900s, the program is placed in the second time period: 1900–1929, even though its first adoptions took place during the nineteenth century. Social and economic data are taken from the years 1900, 1930, and 1960. The composite score is correlated with social and economic data from 1960.

**The table entries are Pearson product-moment correlations.

***Measures of these phenomena corresponding with these time periods do not exist.

government.[18] If this tendency exists it would also seem likely that state political systems which allow frequent turnover and offer the most opportunities to capture high office would more often develop the circumstances in which new programs might be adopted.[19]

Another prerequisite for the rapid adoption of new programs might be a system of legislative apportionment which fully represented the state's urban areas and which did not grant veto power to groups opposed to change. Such a system might be expected to allow consideration and debate of new policies and programs in all areas. Some recent findings, such as Barber's study of legislators in Connecticut,[20] lead us to speculate that representatives from newly developing urban and suburban areas would be more cosmopolitan, better informed, and more tolerant of change. If nothing else, urban legislators would probably be more willing to deal with problems of sanitation, planning, transportation, and housing peculiar to large metropolitan areas.

[18] Theodore Lowi, "Toward Functionalism in Political Science: The Case of Innovation in Party Systems," this REVIEW (1963), 570–583. Evidence which seems to confirm Lowi's theory may be found in: Charles W. Wiggens, "Party Politics in the Iowa Legislature," Midwest Journal of Political Science (1967), 60–69; and Frank M. Bryan, "The Metamorphosis of a Rural Legislature," Polity (1968), 191–212.

[19] Joseph A. Schlesinger has developed an index of the "general opportunity level" in each state. The index measures the relative number of chances which exist in each state to achieve major political office. See: Ambition and Politics: Political Careers in the United States (Chicago, 1966), pp. 37–56.

[20] James D. Barber, The Lawmakers: Recruitment and Adaptation to Legislative Life (New Haven, 1965). For testimony from legislators about the importance of reapportionment see: Frank M. Bryan, "Who Is Legislating," National Civic Review (December, 1967), 627–633; Allan Dines, "A Reapportioned State," National Civic Review (February, 1966), 70–74, 99.

No matter what the composition of the legislator's constituency, however, it would seem that the presence of competent staff, superior clerical facilities, and supporting services would allow him to give serious consideration to a larger number of new proposals. Several studies of the diffusion of technological innovations have demonstrated that the best informed individuals are most likely to pioneer in the use of new techniques or tools,[21] and so the states which provide the most extensive staff and research facilities in their legislatures ought to pioneer in the adoption of new programs.[22]

In Table 3 efforts to test some of these hypotheses in different time periods are displayed. Measures of political variables are usually based on evidence only from contemporary periods because data are seldom available on state and local elections or the operation of legislatures in earlier decades. Measures are available, however, for the degree of party competition and the extent of legislative malapportionment.[23] As we can see in Table 3 party competitiveness does not seem to be consistently related to the innovation score, at least as it is measured here.[24] Legislative apportionment is not correlated with the innovation score in the 1900–1929 period, but is related in the 1930–1966 period. Since legislatures steadily became less representative of urban populations after 1930, it may be that we have here some empirical evidence of the impact of malapportionment on policy making in the states.

Recent studies of state expenditures have shown that the explanatory effects of political variables could be eliminated if statistical controls for social and economic variables were applied. Therefore, in Table 4 I have presented both the zero-order correlations of the composite innovation score with measures of party competition, turnover in office, legislative apportionment, and legislative professionalism,[25] and also partial correlations with four social and economic variables controlled. The control variables are value added by manufacturing, per cent urban population, total population size, and per capita personal income, all of which earlier proved to be independently related to the innovation score. In Table 4 the

[21] Rogers, op. cit. Also see: Mansfield, op. cit.; James S. Coleman, Elihu Katz, and Herbert Menzel, *Medical Innovation: A Diffusion Study* (Indianapolis, 1966); and John W. Loy, Jr., "Social Psychological Characteristics of Innovators," *American Sociological Review* (1969), 73–82.

[22] For a somewhat different view see: Norman Meller, "Legislative Staff Services: Toxin, Specific, or Placebo for the Legislature's Ills," *The Western Political Quarterly* (June, 1967): 381–389.

[23] There is one other index in existence which deals with political phenomenon: Rodney Mott's Index of Judicial Prestige. The Mott index measures the degree to which state supreme courts were used as models by the legal profession. It is based on a study of citations in federal Supreme Court decisions and all state supreme court decisions, the number of cases reprinted in standard textbooks, and the opinion of a panel of prominent legal scholars; it covers the period 1900 to 1930. The Mott index and the innovation score from the same time period are correlated at .62. This finding might be interpreted to mean that emulative behavior in the judicial arena is not much different from that in the legislative arena. For details of the Judicial Prestige Index see: Rodney L. Mott, "Judicial Influence," this REVIEW (1936), 295–315.

[24] Data for this table was derived from Richard Hofferbert's collection, "American State Socio-economic, Electoral, and Policy Data: 1890–1960" which he has graciously allowed me to use.

[25] The sources are: Richard Hofferbert, "Classification of American State Party Systems," *Journal of Politics* (1964), 550–567; Dennis Riley and Jack L. Walker, "Problems of Measurement and Inference in the Study of the American States" (Paper delivered at the Institute of Public Policy Studies, University of Michigan, 1968); David and Eisenberg, op. cit.; Glendon Shubert and Charles Press, "Measuring Malapportionment," this REVIEW (1964), 302–327, and corrections, 968–970; Schlesinger, op. cit.; and John Grumm, "Structure and Policy in the Legislature" (Paper presented at the Southwestern Social Science Association Meetings, 1967).

TABLE 3
Correlations Between Innovation Scores and Measures
of Political Variables, by Time Periods

	Innovation Scores			
Political Variables*	1870–1899	1900–1929	1930–1966	Composite Score
Party Competition for Governorship:	.36	.02	.14	.24
David-Eisenberg Index of Malapportionment:	**	.07	.55	.65

*The Index of party competition used in this table is the per cent of the total vote going to the gubernatorial candidate coming in second, times 2. This yields a scale from 0 to 100. It was created by Richard Hofferbert. The apportionment Index appears in Paul T. David and Ralph Eisenberg, *Devaluation of the Urban and Suburban Vote* (Charlottesville: Bureau of Public Administration, University of Virginia, 1961).

**Measures of this phenomenon corresponding with this time period do not exist.

TABLE 4
Relationships Between the Composite Innovation Score and Measures
of Legislative Apportionment and Party Competition

Partials						
	Zero-order	Value Added Manufacturing	Per Cent Urban	Total Population	Per Capita Income	Four Factors Combined
Apportionment						
David-Eisenberg Index	.65	.47	.64	.67	.60	.58
Schubert-Press Index	.26	.12	.34	.31	.26	.21
Party Competition						
Hofferbert Index	.54	.35	.34	.50	.26	.12
Riley-Walker Index—Gov.	.40	.33	.22	.47	.09	.17
Riley-Walker Index—Legis.	.31	.24	.17	.34	.04	.07
Turnover in Office						
Schlesinger Index of Opportunity	.53	.40	.39	.32	.34	.24
Legislative Services						
Grumm's Index of Legislative Professionalism	.63	.38	.33	.41	.51	.11

effect of each control variable is displayed separately along with the combined impact of all four. The results tend to corroborate earlier analyses which minimize the independent effects of these political variables on policy outcomes. The Schlesinger index of opportunity, which measures the difference among the states in the average number of times major offices have changed hands, and the Hofferbert index of inter-party competition seem to have some independent impact on innovation, although it is greatly weakened when all four control variables are combined. This finding lends some credence to Lowi's argument that turnover in office fosters change.

Certainly, the most important result depicted in this table is the consistent strength of the correlation between innovation and the David and Eisenberg index of urban representation.[26] Earlier studies, using expenditures as a measure of policy outcomes, have consistently found that apportionment has little importance as an explanatory variable.[27] Our findings indicate that apportionment does make a difference where innovation is concerned. Although the other political factors do not have great independent impact on innovation, the clear implication arising from Tables 3 and 4 is that those states which grant their urban areas full representation in the legislature seem to adopt new ideas more rapidly, on the average, than states which discriminate against their cities.

Given the results of this correlational analysis, we might conclude that New York, California and Michigan adopt new programs more rapidly than Mississippi, Wyoming, and South Dakota primarily because they are bigger, richer, more urban, more industrial, have more fluidity and turnover in their political systems, and have legislatures which more adequately represent their cities. Although these findings are important, they leave many important questions unanswered. The political system does not react automatically in response to the growth of manufacturing industries or to the increase in the percentage of the population living in cities. Developments of this kind obviously cause problems which public officials might try to solve, but the mere presence of such a stimulant does not cause public officials to act, nor does it determine the form the solution will take, or which state might act first to meet the problem. Our analysis has provided us with evidence that change and experimentation are more readily accepted in the industrialized, urban, cosmopolitan centers of the country, but we have not improved our understanding of the institutions and decision-making processes which cause strong statistical relationships between industrial output and innovation. Also, we have not explained the way innovations spread from the pioneering states to those with lower innovation scores. In order to develop explanations of these processes we must go beyond the search for demographic correlates of innovation and develop generalizations which refer to the behavior of the men who actually make the choices in which we are interested.

IV. POLITICAL SCIENCE AND INNOVATION

In one form or another, interest group theories, based on self-regulating systems of countervailing power, are at the heart of much of the recent research into American politics.[28] Studies of the legislative process in the United States, for

[26] Although much simpler than the Schubert and Press measure, the David and Eisenberg index seems to have more relevance to political outcomes. Thomas Dye had the same experience. See Dye, *op. cit.*, pp. 19–20, 63–69, 112–114, 146–148, 174–177, 236–237, 270–281.

[27] Herbert Jacob, "The Consequences of Malapportionment: A Note of Caution," *Social Forces* (1964), 260–266; Thomas R. Dye, "Malapportionment and Public Policy in the States," *Journal of Politics* (1965), 586–601; Richard I. Hofferbert, "The Relation Between Public Policy and Some Structural and Environmental Variables in the American States," this REVIEW (1966), 73–82; David Brady and Douglas Edmonds, "One Man, One Vote—So What?" *Trans-action* (March, 1967), 41–46. A recent article calls some of the conclusions of this research into question: Alan G. Pulsipher and James L. Weatherby, Jr., "Malapportionment, Party Competition, and the Functional Distribution of Governmental Expenditures," this REVIEW (1968), 1207–1219.

[28] Examples of this general approach to policy making are: David B. Truman, *The Governmental Process* (New York, 1960); Edward Banfield, *Political Influence* (New York, 1961); and Richard E. Neustadt, *Presidential Power* (New York, 1960). For an excellent critique of theories which employ concepts of power as a major explanatory variable see: James G. March, "The Power of Power," in David Easton (ed.), *Varieties of Political Theory* (Englewood Cliffs, 1966), pp. 39–70.

example, have been strongly influenced by theories which emphasize the importance of the group basis of politics. Beginning with the efforts of A. Lawrence Lowell[29] political scientists have worked to discover the basic factions within the legislature and have striven to develop operational definitions of power or influence.[30] Extensive efforts have been made to isolate and measure the various influences which come to bear on the individual legislator and motivate him to join one or another legislative bloc: what is a legislator's most important source of cues; is it a lobbyist with whom he has close connections, his party leaders, members of his constituency, the governor, or members of his own family? What impact on his attitudes does the legislative institution itself have; do its informal rules and traditions affect the legislator's decisions, and if so, in what way?[31] Great emphasis has been placed on the analysis of roll-call votes and several sophisticated research techniques have been developed to pursue this work, ranging from Beyle's cluster bloc analysis and Guttman scaling to the more complex, computerized routines presently in use.[32] But all this machinery is useful only in studying those roll-calls which cause divisions in the house; all unanimous votes, nearly eighty per cent of the total in most legislatures, are ignored. Riker has devised a technique in which he uses the percentage of the total membership which is present for the vote and the closeness of the division to determine the relative significance of roll-call votes in legislatures. The more legislators present and the closer the vote, the more significant the issue involved.[33] The full attention of the researcher is thus focused on the relatively small number of decisions which cause significant disagreements, because it is assumed that these are the most important votes; at least, they are the only ones which will provide clues to "the conflicting forces and pressures at work in the legislative system,"[34] and the discovery of those forces and pressures, according to the group theory of politics, is the principal object of political science.

One of the main purposes in this study is to develop an approach to governmental policy making which will serve as a guide in the analysis of *all* legislative decisions, the unanimous as well as the contested ones, and which will lead as well to a better understanding of decisions made by bureaucrats, political executives and other governmental officials. Rather than focus upon the patterns of conflict among factions within the legislature or the administrative agencies, I will search for the criteria employed by legislators and administrators in deciding whether a proposal is worthy of consideration in the first place. This search rests on the belief that whoever the decision maker may be, whether administrator, lobbyist, party leader, governor or legislator, and however controversial a particular issue may become, a set of general criteria exists in every state which establishes broad

[29] A. Lawrence Lowell, "The Influence of Party Upon Legislation," *Annual Report of the American Historical Association* (1901), pp. 321–543.

[30] The best example is: Robert Dahl, "The Concept of Power," *Behavioral Science* (1957), pp. 201–215.

[31] For the best general review of the results of research on the legislative process, see: Malcolm E. Jewell and Samuel C. Patterson, *The Legislative Process in the United States* (New York, 1966).

[32] For a discussion of these techniques see: Lee F. Anderson, Meridith W. Watts, Jr. and Allen R. Wilcox, *Legislative Roll-Call Analysis* (Evanston, 1966). Also see Jewell and Patterson, *op. cit.*, pp. 528–550.

[33] William H. Riker, "A Method for Determining the Significance of Roll Calls in Voting Bodies," in John C. Wahlke and Heinz Eulau (eds.), *Legislative Behavior* (Glencoe, 1959), pp. 337–383.

[34] Jewell and Patterson, *op. cit.*, p. 416.

guidelines for policy making. Regardless of the interests supporting an innovation, no matter whether the decision system is primarily monolithic or pluralistic, if a proposal for change does not fall within those guidelines its chances for acceptance are slim. Many of the propositions I will develop cannot be verified until they are tested with evidence from individual decision makers;[35] they are presented here only as a first, tentative step toward a more comprehensive theory of governmental policy making.

V. EMULATION AND DECISION MAKING IN THE STATES

We are searching for answers to three major questions: (1) why do certain states consistently adopt new programs more rapidly than other states, (2) are there more or less stable patterns of diffusion of innovations among the American states, and (3) if so, what are they? Our answers to these questions will be founded, in part, on the theories of organizational decision making developed in recent years by writers like Simon, March, Cyert and Lindblom.[36] At the heart of these theories is the concept of the decision maker struggling to choose among complex alternatives and constantly receiving much more information concerning his environment than he is able to digest and evaluate. An ordinary decision maker, required to make frequent choices and faced with an inconclusive flood of reports, programs, suggestions and memos, must simplify his task in some way. According to Simon, he does not—cannot—search in every case for the best possible solution to the problems he faces; he has neither the time nor the energy. Instead, he makes decisions by searching until he finds an alternative which he believes is good enough to preserve whatever values are important to him. The limits of rationality imposed by human capacities prevent him from maximizing his benefits in every situation; rather, he "satisfices," or chooses a course of action which seems satisfactory under the circumstances.

The individual in a complex organization, therefore, does not deal directly with all the sources of information potentially available to him, nor does he evaluate every conceivable policy option. In place of the debilitating confusion of reality he creates his own abstract, highly simplified world containing only a few major variables. In order to achieve this manageable simplicity he adopts a set of decision rules or standard criteria for judgment which remain fairly stable over time and which guide him in choosing among sources of information and advice. A decision maker decides both where to look for cues and information and how to choose among alternatives according to his decision rules; these rules also embody the current goals and aspirations of his organization, or the values which the organization is designed to advance and protect. Hence, if we wish to predict the decision maker's behavior, we should try to discover these rules of thumb, or "heuristics" as they are sometimes called, which shape his judgment. His choices could then be explained in terms of the alternatives he considers, his knowledge of each alternative, the sources of his knowledge, and the standard decision rules he applies in cases of this kind.[37]

---

[35] Thanks to a grant from the Carnegie Corporation I have been able to launch a pilot study involving interviews in several states.

[36] I refer to: Herbert Simon, *Administrative Behavior*, Second Edition (New York, 1957); Richard M. Cyert and James C. March, *A Behavioral Theory of the Firm* (Englewood Cliffs, N.J. 1963); and Charles E. Lindblom, *The Intelligence of Democracy* (New York, 1965).

[37] For a comprehensive review of the literature on decision making see: Donald W. Taylor, "Decision Making and Problem Solving," and Julia Feldman and Herschel E. Kanter, "Organizational

Taking cues from these theories of human choice and organizational decision making our explanation of the adoption of innovations by the states is based on the assertion that state officials make most of their decisions by analogy. The rule of thumb they employ might be formally stated as follows: *look for an analogy between the situation you are dealing with and some other situation, perhaps in some other state, where the problem has been successfully resolved.*[38]

We are looking to what has been called the "inter-organizational context,"[39] or the *horizontal* relationships among the states within the federal system, for the principal influences which regulate the speed of adoption and the patterns of diffusion of innovations. Most of the existing work on intergovernmental relations and federalism concentrates on the question of centralization within the American system of government. In line with the general interest of most political scientists in the factors which affect the access of organized groups and the lines of authority within a political system, many writers are concerned with the virtues of centralization or decentralization and try to determine how much of either exists in the system. They have studied primarily the *vertical* relationships among national, state and local governments, and have usually identified the party system and its demands as the institutional influence most responsible for maintaining the present, decentralized, federal relationships.[40] I want to focus attention on the mutual perceptions and relationships among state governments and to show how these relationships affect the behavior of state decision makers.[41]

One of the most common arguments used in state legislatures against raising taxes or passing measures designed to regulate business is the fear that such measures might retard industrial development or force marginal plants to leave the state. Lawmakers often are called upon to deal with the problems which arise

---

Decision Making," in James G. March (ed.) *Handbook of Organizations* (Chicago, 1965), pp. 48–86, 614–649. Also see: W. Richard Scott, "Theory of Organizations," in Robert E. L. Faris (ed.), *Handbook of Modern Sociology* (Chicago, 1964), pp. 485–529.

[38] Decision rules of this kind are mentioned in both Taylor, *op. cit.*, pp. 73–74; and Cyert and March, *op. cit.*, especially pp. 34–43.

[39] William M. Evan, "The Organization-Set: Toward a Theory of Inter-Organizational Relations," in James D. Thompson (ed.) *Approaches to Organizational Design* (Pittsburgh, 1966), pp. 173–191.

[40] Some recent examples are: William Anderson, *The Nation and the States, Rivals or Partners?* (Minneapolis, 1955); M.J.C. Vile, *The Structure of American Federalism* (London, 1961); William Riker, *Federalism: Origin, Operation, Significance* (Boston, 1964); Daniel J. Elazar, *American Federalism: A View from the States* (New York, 1966); Morton Grodzins, *The American System* (Chicago, 1966). For a general critique see: A. H. Birch, "Approaches to the Study of Federalism." *Political Studies* (1966), 15–33.

[41] This is not the first study to discover the important role of emulation and competition in the development of public policy. Richard Hofferbert in: "Ecological Development and Policy Change in the American States," *Midwest Journal of Political Science* (1966), p. 485; and Ira Sharkansky in: "Regionalism, Economic Status and the Public Policies of American States," *Southwestern Social Science Quarterly* (1968) both mention the influence of other states in the calculations of state decision makers. Several earlier students of local government complained that sparsely populated, arid Western states had blindly copied from the heavily populated Eastern states forms of local government which were inappropriately suited for the conditions prevailing in the Great Plains. See: A. Bristol Goodman, "Westward Movement of Local Government," *The Journal of Land and Public Utility Economics* (1944), pp. 20–34; Herman Walker, Jr. and Peter L. Hansen, "Local Government and Rainfall," this REVIEW (1946), 1113–1123. Robert L. Crain has recently used emulation as a principal explanatory variable in his study of the spread of water fluoridation programs among American cities: "Fluoridation: The Diffusion of an Innovation Among Cities," *Social Forces* (1966), 467–476; as did Thomas M. Scott in his: "The Diffusion of Urban Governmental Forms as a Case of Social Learning," *The Journal of Politics* (1968), 1091–1108.

when one or two states establish extremely permissive standards for the granting of licenses, such as the corporation laws in New Jersey and Delaware, or the divorce laws in Nevada. However, interstate competition does not always drive standards down; it has a positive side as well. State decision makers are constantly looking to each other for guides to action in many areas of policy, such as the organization and management of higher education, or the provision of hospitals and public health facilities. In fact, I am arguing that this process of competition and emulation, or cuetaking, is an important phenomenon which determines in large part the pace and direction of social and political change in the American states.[42]

Uncertainty and the fear of unanticipated consequences have always been formidable barriers to reform. Proponents of new programs have always had to combat the arguments of those who predict dire consequences if some innovation is adopted. Even though American history is full of cases where the opponents of change have later had to admit that the dangers they feared never materialized, inertia and the unwillingness to take risks have prevented a more rapid rate of change.

Inertia can more easily be overcome, however, if the proponent of change can point to the successful implementation of his program in some other similar setting. If a legislator introduces a bill which would require the licensing of probation officers, for example, and can point to its successful operation in a neighboring state, his chances of gaining acceptance are markedly increased. As Harsanyi has asserted:

> It is not an overstatement to say that a very considerable part of the social values of most societies is based on sheer ignorance. . . . One of the reasons why other persons' example is so important in encouraging changes in people's values and behavior lies in the fact that it tends to dispel some groundless fears about the dismal consequences that such changes might entail. Another reason is of course that people can more easily face the possible hostility of the supporters of the old values if they are not alone in making the change.[43]

In fact, once a program has been adopted by a large number of states it may become recognized as a legitimate state responsibility, something which all states ought to have. When this happens it becomes extremely difficult for state decision makers to resist even the weakest kinds of demands to institute the program for fear of arousing public suspicions about their good intentions; once a program has gained the stamp of legitimacy, it has a momentum of its own. As Lockard found in studying the passage of Fair Employment Practices laws the actions of other states are sometimes key factors in prompting reluctant politicians to accept controversial programs.

Pressure mounted in New Jersey during 1944 and 1945 for some stronger policy, and when New York passed its FEP law certain key politicians in New Jersey decided to act. Governor Walter E. Edge concluded, apparently reluctantly, that he had to commit himself to such a law. "As the session drew to a close," Edge wrote in his autobiography, "minority racial and religious groups pressed

---

[42] This set of hypotheses is consistent with more general theories concerning the manner in which human beings formulate judgments and establish expectations in all areas of life. See: Leon Festinger, "A Theory of Social Comparison Processes," *Human Relations* (1954), 117–140; and Robert Merton, *Social Theory and Social Structure* (Rev. Ed.; Glencoe, 1957), pp. 225–420.

[43] John C. Harsanyi, "Rational Choice Models v. Functionalistic and Conformistic Models of Political Behavior" (Paper delivered at American Political Science Association Meetings, 1967), p. 17.

for adoption of an antidiscrimination program. While it was a subject which I would have preferred to give greater study, politically it could not be postponed because New York had passed a similar measure and delay would be construed as a mere political expedient."[44]

For similar reasons there have been numerous efforts to enact a program of homesteading in Hawaii as a way of disposing of its arable public lands even though the circumstances there are quite different from other states where homesteading was successfully introduced.[45] And in Connecticut one of the most powerful arguments in favor of introducing the direct primary system during the 1950s was simply that all the other states had adopted one.[46]

The Connecticut case neatly illustrates some of the generalizations we are developing. Lockard points out that the leaders of both political parties privately opposed the introduction of a primary system but felt that an endorsement of the idea had to be put into their platforms to avoid having their opponents charge them with "bossism." Demands for the primary came for the most part from small groups in the state's suburban areas which were interested in the issue as "a consequence of the influx of migrants from states with primaries."[47] Speaking as a professional political scientist as well as a legislator, Lockard was well suited to counter the extreme fears expressed by the party leaders who predicted that party organizations would be completely destroyed if primaries were introduced. Lockard reasoned by analogy to the experience in other states both in countering the opponents of change and in shaping his own moderate position:

> I expressed my considerable doubts about the effect of party primaries on party organization. From observations of politics in some of the most thoroughgoing party primary states, [however,] it seemed that the party organizations had been shattered with many undesirable consequences. In my campaign I expressed support only for a limited form of a primary and not one calculated to wreck the party system.[48]

Events like these illustrate the way in which the agenda of controversy in a state is determined, at least in part, by developments in other states, and they also show how experiences and examples from outside the system help to overcome the natural reluctance of any institutional structure to risk the consequences of change. The constituent units of any federal system are under considerable pressure to conform with national and regional standards or accepted administrative procedures. These norms result primarily from the processes of emulation and competition we have described and also from the efforts of nationally organized interest groups. They are affected also by the growth and development of professional organizations and other forms of communication among state administrators, and the natural circulation of active, politically involved citizens among the states, such as the Connecticut suburbanites who began agitating for a primary system in their adopted political home.

[44] Duane Lockard, *Toward Equal Opportunity* (New York, 1968), pp. 20–21.

[45] Allan Spitz, "The Transplantation of American Democratic Institutions," *Political Science Quarterly* (1967), 386–398.

[46] Duane Lockard, *Connecticut's Challenge Primary: A Study in Legislative Politics* (Eagleton Case #7, New York, 1959).

[47] Ibid., p. 2.

[48] Ibid., p. 22.

VI. REGIONAL REFERENCE GROUPS AND
STANDARDS OF EVALUATION

Nationally accepted standards or norms provide a convenient measure which can be used by interested citizens or political leaders to judge the adequacy of services offered in their own states. But these norms have an ambiguous influence on the performance of state governments. On the one hand, the existence of national standards probably encourages *higher* performance among the *poorer* members of the federation than we could expect if functions and service levels were established independently within each unit of government, solely as a result of internal demands. An example of this tendency was discovered by May in his study of Canadian federalism:

> Newfoundland chose for a long time to remain outside the Canadian federation, thus not subjecting itself to the forces of national reorientation, and when, after joining the Dominion, a royal commission reported on its financial position, the commission observed that Newfoundland's public services were very backward in relation to those of the other provinces, including even the maritimes.[49]

In the United States, Mississippi, Vermont, and North Dakota are good examples of relatively poor states which are making unusually large efforts to bring their public services into closer approximation of national standards. But, on the other hand, national standards and norms can have a *conservative* impact, especially in the richer, industrial states which are able to provide services somewhat above the national averages with relatively little effort.[50] Hansen complains of this tendency when he points out that:

> Some northern states fall considerably below their northern neighboring states in public service standards. . . . Their fiscal problems arise not because they are poor but because their tax levels are low by northern standards. This is notably true for example of a tier of large industrial states—Illinois, Indiana, Ohio and Pennsylvania. . . . These states are not excessively hard pressed by tax burdens relative to the country as a whole.[51]

This statement by Hansen is drawn from an essay in which he expresses disapproval of what he considers the inadequate public services of large industrial states which have relatively low tax burdens. But the statement we have cited contains several ambiguities. For example, Hansen charges that "some northern states fall considerably below their northern neighboring states in public service standards," but then he specifically points as examples to Illinois, Indiana, Ohio, and Pennsylvania, states which border on each other. It is not clear whether we are being asked to compare these states to their neighbors, to other northern states with higher tax burdens, or to "the country as a whole." Within Illinois, however, the states' decision makers are probably comparing their own perfor-

---

[49] Ronald J. May, *Financial Inequality Between States in a Federal System* (unpublished doctoral dissertation submitted to Nuffield College, Oxford University, 1966), p. 168.

[50] For a somewhat similar argument concerning government spending see: Anthony Downs, "Why the Government Budget Is Too Small in a Democracy," *World Politics* (July, 1960), 541–563.

[51] Alvin H. Hansen, *The Postwar American Economy: Performance and Problems* (New York, 1964), pp. 30–31.

mance with their counterparts in Indiana, Ohio, Pennsylvania or New Jersey. Officials in Illinois may know of the procedures and performance levels in New York or California, but they are unlikely to think of events in these states as legitimate guides to action.[52]

When examining the public policy of any state, therefore, it is important to discover in which "league" it has chosen to play. For example, Salisbury, in a statement much like Hansen's, reasons by analogy in arguing that Missouri does not provide as much aid for its schools as its potential resources might warrant. He points out that in 1959 the "state ranked 18th in per capita income but 38th in per capita expenditure for local schools."[53] This relatively low level of support seems to result from the correspondingly low aspirations of the officials of the Missouri State Teachers Association who, according to Salisbury, "have chosen to get what they can with a minimum of agitation or conflict rather than attempt broader public campaigns in behalf of larger objectives."[54] The officials of MSTA "are fully conscious of the gap between the Missouri school aid level and that of, say, neighboring Illinois," but they are quick to point out "that by comparison with other neighboring states—Arkansas, Oklahoma, or Nebraska, for example—Missouri's record is much more impressive."[55] It would seem from this example that Missouri's leaders, at least those concerned with public education, are emulating and competing primarily with the states to their south and west, rather than with the Great Lakes states to their north and east, or the Rocky Mountain states, the Deep South or the Far West. The choice of relatively poor states like Arkansas and Oklahoma as the principal, legitimate reference groups establishes an upper limit of aspirations which is considerably below that which might exist if Missouri's accepted basis for comparison were the public services of Illinois, Wisconsin or Michigan.

VI. REGIONAL GROUPINGS AMONG THE STATES

We have come far enough in our analysis to see that our original presentation of the innovation scores in Table 1 as a linear distribution masked some pertinent information. A more useful representation of the data, which would conform more closely to the actual patterns of diffusion, would have to be in the form of a tree. At the top of the tree would be a set of pioneering states which would be linked together in a national system of emulation and competition. The rest of the states would be sorted out along branches of the tree according to the pioneer, or set of pioneers, from which they take their principal cues. States like New York, Massachusetts, California, and Michigan should be seen as regional pace setters, each of which has a group of followers, usually within their own region of the country, that tend to adopt programs only after the pioneers have led the way. For example, Colorado, which ranks ninth in Table 1, might be seen as the

---

[52] For evidence of this perspective, see Thomas J. Anton, *The Politics of State Expenditure in Illinois* (Urbana, 1966), p. 263.

[53] Nicholas A. Masters, Robert Salisbury, and Thomas H. Eliot, *State Politics and the Public Schools* (New York, 1964), p. 12.

[54] Ibid., p. 25.

[55] Ibid., p. 21. For a similar discussion of the importance of aspirations in determining the speed with which innovations are adopted see: Rufus P. Browning, "Innovative and Noninnovative Decision Processes in Government Budgeting," in Robert T. Golembiewski (ed.), *Public Budgeting and Finance* (Itasca, Illinois, 1968), pp. 128–145.

regional leader of the Rocky Mountain states. The rest of the states in that region are found much further down the list: Utah is twenty-second, Idaho is thirty-third, Arizona is thirty-sixth, Montana is thirty-eighth, New Mexico is forty-first, Wyoming is forty-sixth, and Nevada is forty-seventh. All of these states, with the possible exception of Utah which may share in the leadership of the region, might be seen as Colorado's followers who usually pick up new ideas only after the regional pioneer has put them into practice.

If we are right about the general patterns of competition and emulation, we should discover in our data some evidence of the existence of regional clusters among the states. In an effort to find such groupings, a varimax factor analysis was performed, using a matrix of pair-wise comparisons of all state innovation scores on all eighty-eight issues. If states in the same region are adopting programs in a similar order or pattern over time, a factor analysis should uncover several underlying dimensions in the matrix along which all states would be ordered according to their responses to the programs upon which the innovation score is based. The results of the factor analysis are presented in Table 5.

As we can see, the regional groupings we expected to find do exist, although the patterns are not as neat and clear as we might have hoped. To produce each factor I recorded all loadings which were over .400. The five factors which result bring the states into generally recognizable, contiguous groupings. The states with the largest loadings in each region are not necessarily those with the highest innovation scores. Instead, they are states like Connecticut, Florida, or New Mexico whose innovation scores are closer to the average for their regions. The presence of Nebraska, Iowa and South Dakota on Factor 1, which otherwise identifies Southern states, may indicate that more than one regional cluster is being identified on that factor.

There are several ambiguities in the data. For example, New York, Pennsylvania, West Virginia, Arkansas, and Illinois are loading on more than one factor. The easiest explanation of this may be that the states actually have connections with more than one region. This is especially true of New York, the state with the highest innovation score, which displays fairly strong connections in this analysis with the New England, Mid-Atlantic, and Great Lakes states. I believe that this finding reflects the fact that New York actually serves as a model for states in all three areas. Certainly New York is formally involved in interstate compacts with all three regions, and, if nothing else, enjoys a perfect geographical position from which to carry on relations over such a large area. If the findings concerning New York seem explainable, those concerning California do not. I cannot explain why California loads on Factor V, especially since many of its neighbors load on Factor III. These ambiguous findings concerning New York and California might be merely a reflection of ambiguity in the data. Factor analysis will identify regional groupings in the data only if the regions respond to new programs as a unit, adopting some new ideas with haste and lagging behind on others. Since New York and California consistently lead the country in the adoption of new programs, they may not be members of the cohesive regional group or "league" of states, a fact which may prevent their neat categorization through factor analysis.

There is no accounting at all in this analysis for the behavior of three states: Arizona, Colorado, and Kansas. Both Colorado and Arizona load at the .300 level on Factor III, the one which includes most of the rest of the Rocky Mountain states. Colorado and Nevada both load strongly (.577 and .485 respectively) on a separate factor which was not reported since no other state scored higher than

TABLE 5
Varimax Factor Analysis of Innovation Scores for Forty-eight States

Factor Loading	State	Factor Loading	State
		Factor I (South)	
.756	Florida	.543	Texas
.711	Tennessee	.517	Nebraska
.663	Alabama	.464	West Virginia
.661	Virginia	.460	Louisiana
.656	Georgia	.459	Iowa
.630	Mississippi	.454	South Dakota
.621	Delaware	.433	Nevada
.600	North Carolina		
.590	South Carolina	7.8	Total Factor Contribution
.576	Arkansas		
		Factor II (New England)	
.795	Connecticut	.512	Vermont
.766	Massachusetts	.434	Maine
.758	New Hampshire	.404	Pennsylvania
.659	Rhode Island		
.536	New York	4.1	Total Factor Contribution
		Factor III (Mountains and Northwest)	
.791	New Mexico	.516	Louisiana
.719	Idaho	.503	South Dakota
.702	Montana	.432	Oregon
.694	Utah	.419	Maryland
.638	Washington	.410	Arkansas
.620	North Dakota	.407	West Virginia
.610	Wyoming		
.569	Oklahoma	6.7	Total Factor Contribution
		Factor IV (Mid-Atlantic and Great Lakes)	
.795	New Jersey	.516	Pennsylvania
.637	Wisconsin	.451	Indiana
.605	New York		
.577	Minnesota	4.0	Total Factor Contribution
.536	Illinois		
		Factor V (Border, Great Lakes and California)	
.698	California	.515	Nebraska
.610	Missouri	.458	Illinois
.584	Kentucky		
.577	Michigan	4.1	Total Factor Contribution
.548	Ohio		

.300 on the factor and its contribution score was only 1.7. The same is true for Kansas which was the only state loading strongly (at .658) on a factor whose contribution score was only 1.9.

VII. SPECIALIZED COMMUNICATIONS AMONG THE STATES

Our analysis has provided evidence that a continuum exists along which states are distributed from those which are usually quick to accept innovations to those which are typically reluctant to do so; we also know something about the correlates of innovation and have evidence of regional groupings among the states; but it is not always easy to identify a regional pioneer or to know exactly which states make up each "league" or sub-system of cue-taking and information exchange. Some states seem to have connections with more than one region and may regularly receive cues from states in both groupings. As the American political system has developed, an increasing number of specialized communication systems have been created which cut across traditional regional lines and bring officials from many different regions into contact with each other and with federal and local officials, journalists, academic experts, and administrative consultants.

Several organizations now exist, such as the Council of State Governments, the Federal Commission on Intergovernmental Relations, and the recently established Citizens' Conference on State Legislatures, whose primary function is to improve communications among the states. Most important of these specialized communications networks are the professional associations of state officials, such as the National Association of State Budget Officers, or the National Association of State Conservation Officers. Associations of this kind were first created late in the nineteenth century and more seem to be forming each year. There were only five formed prior to 1900, but by 1930 there were approximately thirty-one, and by 1966 there were at least eighty-six in existence.[56]

These groups serve two general purposes: first, they are sources of information and policy cues. By organizing conferences or publishing newsletters they bring together officials from all over the country and facilitate the exchange of ideas and knowledge among them, thus increasing the officials' awareness of the latest developments in their field. Secondly, these associations serve as "occupational contact networks" which expedite the interstate movement or transfer of personnel. Through the efforts of these groups officials become aware of desirable job openings in other states and are able to create professional reputations that extend beyond the borders of their own states.[57]

By rapidly spreading knowledge of new programs among state officials and by facilitating the movement of individuals to jobs in other states, professional associations encourage the development of national standards for the proper administration and control of the services of state government. Just as in other sectors of American life such as the business, the military and the academic world, as individuals increase their mobility, their role perceptions are likely to change;

[56] Unpublished memo from the Council of State Governments, Chicago, Illinois.

[57] For a discussion of the role of professional organizations in determining career lines see: Fred E. Katz, "Occupational Contact Networks," *Social Forces* (1958), 52–58. Also see: Jack Ladinsky, "Occupational Determinants of Geographic Mobility Among Professional Workers," *American Sociological Review* (1967), 253–264.

TABLE 6
Average Elapsed Time of Diffusion in Years for Innovations in Three Time Periods

Time Periods	For All Adoptions	First Twenty Adoptions
1870–1899:	52.3	22.9
1900–1929:	39.6	20.0
1930–1966:	25.6	18.4

they are likely to adopt a more cosmopolitan perspective and to cultivate their reputations within a national professional community rather than merely within their own state or agency.[58]

Since general awareness of new developments is achieved much more quickly now than ever before, we would expect that the time which elapses from the first adoption of an innovation by a pioneering state to its complete diffusion throughout all the states would be greatly reduced. Certainly, several recent innovations, such as educational television or state councils on the performing arts, have diffused rapidly. In Table 6 we have measured the average speed of diffusion in years for three periods of time: 1870–1899, 1900–1929, and 1930–1966. The results shown in the first column of this table make it very plain that the speed of diffusion has been constantly increasing as time has passed. This measurement, however, is somewhat misleading. The second column of the table indicates the average number of years it took the first twenty states to adopt the programs in each time period. The same trend toward increased speed of diffusion is evident here, but the differences among the three time periods are much smaller.[59] This evidence suggests that the pioneering states, those with high innovation scores, adopted new programs about as quickly in the early part of this century, prior to the development of many specialized communication links, as they did in the 1960s. The total elapsed time of diffusion, however, has decreased primarily because the laggard states, those with low innovation scores, are now reacting more quickly to pick up new programs adopted by the pioneers. This development results partly from the efforts of the federal government to stimulate state action through grants-in-aid, and partly from the increasing professional development in state government. Both these tendencies seem to have had a larger impact on the behavior of the more parochial states than the more cosmopolitan, pioneering states.

VIII. THE PERSISTENCE OF REGIONALISM

Improved communications and greatly increased contacts of all kinds among state officials seem to be accelerating the process of diffusion, but this does not necessarily mean that the regional clusters or "leagues" of states to which we have

[58] Merton, *op. cit.* Also see: Alvin W. Gouldner, "Cosmopolitans and Locals: Toward an Analysis of Latent Social Roles," *Administrative Science Quarterly* (1957), 281–306; and Harold L. Wilensky, *Intellectuals in Labor Unions* (Glencoe, 1956).

[59] A small portion of the difference between the two columns in Table 6 is an artifact of measurement. Since not all the programs in this analysis have been adopted by all forty-eight states, laggard states sometimes remain. As time passes and programs receive widespread acceptance these laggard states slowly fall into line and adopt the programs. Since the programs in the first two time periods have been around longer, they have more likely completed their spread among the states and thus, given our scoring procedure, are also more likely to have a longer period of diffusion.

referred have been destroyed.[60] In order to investigate this question the innovation scores in the time periods from 1870 to 1929 were combined, and two matrices of innovation scores of almost equal size were created, one for 1870–1929 and the other for 1930–1966.[61] Within each of these matrices each state's set of innovation scores (issue by issue) was correlated with the set of innovation scores for each other state. A varimax factor analysis was performed on each matrix, just as was done earlier to produce Table 5.

The results of this analysis are presented in Table 7. The factors derived from 1870–1929 are presented in the left column of the table and those from 1930–1966 are presented in the right column. The factors from each time period are arranged with the highest loadings first and the rest following in descending order. As we can see, the factors from the two time periods are not completely comparable. Some states change their relative rankings on the two factors, and some appear on a factor during only one of the time periods. The state of Georgia, for example, is found at the bottom of Factor 1 during 1870–1929 and moves all the way to the top of the same factor during 1930–1966. Some regional groupings, such as New England, seem to be disintegrating, while others, such as the Middle Atlantic states, seem to be more clearly defined in the later period. The factors for the later period include more states, on the average, and have slightly higher contribution scores, but they are not quite as distinct as those in the early period and include more inappropriate loadings. These data do not contain evidence of any large-scale erosion of regionalism in the United States, but a drift away from clearly defined clusters of states is apparent.

During the last thirty years many new professional associations have been formed and more inter-state and federal agencies have begun facilitating communications and encouraging national uniformity. The diffusion process is operating much faster today than ever before, especially among those states which have traditionally lagged behind in adopting new ideas. The older, established modes of communication and evaluation, based on traditional ties of region and common culture, are persisting, but there are indications in these data that the system is slowly changing. Decision makers in the states seem to be adopting a broader, national focus based on new lines of communication which extend beyond regional boundaries.

IX. CONCLUSIONS

This essay began as an effort to explain why some states adopt innovations more rapidly than others, but in order to explain this aspect of American federalism, we have had to make a more extensive investigation of the complex system of social choice by which we are governed. The approach to policy making which has emerged from our investigation is founded on the perceptions and attitudes of individual state decision makers. Of course, as I have already mentioned, the

[60] The best recent analysis of long-term changes in the American political system is: Donald Stokes, "Parties and the Nationalization of Electoral Forces," in William N. Chambers and William D. Burnham (eds.), *The American Party Systems: Stages of Political Development* (New York, 1967), pp. 182–202. Also see: Norval D. Glenn and J. L. Simmons, "Are Regional Cultural Differences Diminishing?" *Public Opinion Quarterly* (1967), 196–205; and Ira Sharkansky, "Economic Development, Regionalism and State Political Systems," *Midwest Journal of Political Science* (1968), 41–61.

[61] When the data are combined in this manner the 1870–1929 matrix contains 42 issues and the 1930–1966 matrix contains 46 issues.

TABLE 7

Varimax Factor Analysis of Innovation Scores for Forty-eight States in Two Time Periods

1870–1929		1930–1966	
Factor Loading	State	Factor Loading	State
Factor I (South)			
.762	Tennessee	.793	Georgia
.748	Mississippi	.759	Virginia
.745	Florida	.649	Delaware
.705	North Carolina	.629	Tennessee
.662	West Virginia	.623	Florida
.646	Kentucky	.593	Texas
.521	Louisiana	.570	North Carolina
*.499	Arizona	*.541	Utah
.465	Delaware	.524	Alabama
.426	Virginia	.494	Maryland
.425	South Carolina	*.493	Nebraska
*.424	Iowa	.493	South Carolina
.404	Georgia	*.451	Arizona
5.7	Total Factor Contribution	*.432	Montana
		*.426	Kansas
		*.415	Iowa
		*.415	Maine
		.413	Louisiana
		*.410	New Hampshire
		7.1	Total Factor Contribution
Factors II and III (New England—Mid-Atlantic—Great Lakes)			
.851	Connecticut	.800	Connecticut
.814	New Hampshire	.702	Massachusetts
.707	Vermont	.629	New Hampshire
.705	Massachusetts	*.564	Colorado
.67	Rhode Island	*.498	Oregon
.576	Maine	.467	Rhode Island
.509	Delaware	1.7	Total Factor Contribution
.487	New York		
.467	Pennsylvania		
.467	Virginia		
.405	Maryland		
*.405	Alabama		
5.3	Total Factor Contribution		
.808	Kansas	.778	New York
.694	Indiana	.686	Pennsylvania
.643	Wisconsin	.684	New Jersey
.622	Illinois	.666	Wisconsin
.601	Minnesota	.537	Illinois
*.448	Texas	.491	Michigan
4.5	Total Factor Contribution	.486	Indiana
		.474	Minnesota
		.448	Maryland
		4.8	Total Factor Contribution

(continued)

Table 7
(Continued)

Factor Loading	State	Factor Loading	State
1870–1929		1930–1966	

Factor IV (Plains and Mountains)

.769	North Dakota	.71	North Dakota
.762	New Mexico	.683	New Mexico
.722	Montana	.682	Kansas
.709	Utah	.641	Wyoming
.665	Idaho	.633	Oklahoma
.639	Washington	.598	Washington
.567	South Dakota	.572	Oregon
*.494	Maine	.557	Utah
4.7	Total Factor Contribution	*.494	Alabama
.751	Arizona	.462	Idaho
.588	Nevada	*.457	Vermont
.578	Wyoming	*.439	West Virginia
*.469	Arkansas	*.416	Wisconsin
2.5	Total Factor Contribution	.41	Montana
.73	Oregon	*.406	Mississippi
.611	California	6.5	Total Factor Contribution
.645	Colorado		
*.433	Maryland		
2.9	Total Factor Contribution		

Factor V (Mid-America)

.885	Missouri	.726	Missouri
.767	Nebraska	.614	Mississippi
*.639	Michigan	*.600	South Carolina
.419	Ohio	*.589	Idaho
*.400	California	.573	Arkansas
3.4	Total Factor Contribution	.53	Tennessee
		.432	Illinois
		.426	West Virginia
		*.409	South Dakota
		*.409	Montana
		4.5	Total Factor Contribution

*States which are loading on inappropriate factors are marked with an asterisk.

theory cannot be fully elaborated or put to a test until data can be gathered directly from legislators, bureaucrats, governors, and other officials in several states, on a comparative basis. Enough evidence has been presented already, however, to make apparent the major theoretical and practical implications of this approach.

The theory presented here directs our attention to the rules for decision employed by policy makers, rather than their formal group affiliations or their relative power or authority, and thus enables us to offer useful explanations of all policy decisions, not merely those which generate controversy. Emphasis is placed

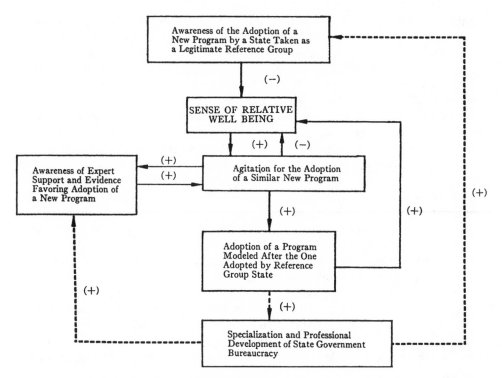

FIGURE 1. Factors Affecting the Adoption of Innovations

on those factors which lead to the establishment of parameters or guidelines for decision, not on the groups or interests supporting one policy over another. In Figure 1 the outlines of the diffusion process are depicted as it operates in a single state. There are undoubtedly many other influences on the level of agitation for change than the ones presented here, and many other secondary effects stemming from the enactment of new programs; this simple diagram is only meant to summarize the fundamental process operating in most cases of diffusion. Relationships are characterized by plus and minus signs but no effort has been made to estimate their relative importance in the system.

The process we have been describing is extremely complex; many influences shape decisions to adopt innovations and no two ideas diffuse in exactly the same way. In all cases, however, the likelihood of a state adopting a new program is higher if other states have already adopted the idea. The likelihood becomes higher still if the innovation has been adopted by a state viewed by key decision makers as a point of legitimate comparison. Decison makers are likely to adopt new programs, therefore, when they become convinced that their state is relatively deprived, or that some need exists to which other states in their "league" have already responded.

Before states may respond to new programs adopted in other states their political leaders must be aware of these developments, so interstate communications are an important factor in the process of diffusion. We have mentioned that many specialized systems of communication among the states have grown up during the last thirty years, mainly through the creation of professional associations among state administrators. These new information networks are spreading into all the states, but even today the isolation of some state capitols from the major cosmopolitan centers of the country is a major obstacle to the adoption of new ideas.[62]

Emerging from this study is the picture of a national system of emulation and competition. The states are grouped into regions based on both geographical contiguity and their place in the specialized set of communication channels through which flow new ideas, information and policy cues. Through this nationwide system of communications a set of norms or national standards for proper administration are established. This system links together the centers of research and generation of new ideas, national associations of professional administrators, interest groups, and voluntary associations of all kinds into an increasingly complex network which connects the pioneering states with the more parochial ones. Because of the limitations of the data presently available to us we can only outline each regional grouping of states, and we cannot yet construct an elaborate theory of the interactions among professional associations, federal officials, private interest groups, and political leaders in setting the agenda of politics within a state. Normative questions arise, which cannot be considered here, concerning the responsiveness of this system and the degree to which it is subject to the control of democratic, representative institutions.[63] Much more investigation will be necessary before we can gain a full understanding of this system and its function as a device for controlling the pace and direction of policy development in the American states. Once we know more, it might be possible to prescribe with confidence some changes in the decision-making system, or the creation of some new governmental institutions, which might accelerate or redirect the process of innovation.

APPENDIX

Note: Following are the eighty-eight programs upon which the innovation score is based.

1. Accountants Licensing
2. Advertising Commissions
3. Agricultural Experiment Stations
4. Aid for Roads and Highways
5. Aid to the Blind (Social Security)
6. Aid to Dependent Children (Social Security)
7. Aid to Permanently and Totally Disabled (Social Security)
8. Air Pollution Control
9. Alcoholic Beverage Control
10. Alcoholic Treatment Agencies

---

[62] See Alan L. Clem's description of the isolation of Pierre, the capitol of South Dakota, in his: *Prairie State Politics: Popular Democracy in South Dakota* (Washington, 1967), p. 137; and Norton E. Long's emphasis on the importance of information sources in his: "After the Voting Is Over," *Mid-west Journal of Political Science* (1962), 183–200. For a general review of communications theory and its application to politics see: Richard R. Fagen, *Politics and Communication* (Boston, 1966), especially pp. 34–69, 88–106. Also see: Karl W. Deutsch, *The Nerves of Government*, Second Edition, (New York, 1966), especially pp. 145–256.

[63] Questions of this kind have been raised already in: Daniel P. Moynihan, "The Professionalization of Reform," *The Public Interest* (1965), 6–16; Theodore J. Lowi, "The Public Philosophy: Interest Group Liberalism," this REVIEW (1967), 5–24; and Philip Green, "Science, Government, and the Case of RAND: A Singular Pluralism," *World Politics* (1968), 301–326.

11. Anti-Age Discrimination
12. Anti-Injunction Laws
13. Architects Licensing
14. Australian Ballot
15. Automobile Registration
16. Automobile Safety Compact
17. Beauticians Licensing
18. Board of Health
19. Budgeting Standards
20. Child Labor Standards
21. Chiropractors Licensing
22. Cigarette Tax
23. Committee on the Aged
24. Compulsory School Attendance
25. Conservation of Oil and Gas
26. Controlled Access Highways
27. Council on the Arts
28. Court Administrators
29. Debt Limitations
30. Dentists Licensing
31. Direct Primary
32. Education Agencies
33. Education Television
34. Engineers Licensing
35. Equal Pay for Females
36. Fair Housing—Private
37. Fair Housing—Public Housing
38. Fair Housing—Urban Renewal Areas
39. Fair Trade Laws
40. Fish Agency
41. Forest Agency
42. Gasoline Tax
43. Geological Survey
44. Highway Agency
45. Home Rule—Cities
46. Human Relations Commissions
47. Initiative and Referendum
48. Integrated Bar
49. Junior College—Enabling Legislation
50. Juveniles Supervision Compact
51. Labor Agencies
52. Legislative Pre-Planning Agencies
53. Legislative Research Agencies
54. Library Extension System
55. Mental Health Standards Committee
56. Merit System
57. Migratory Labor Committee
58. Minimum Wage Law
59. Normal Schools—Enabling Act
60. Nurses Licensing

61. Old Age Assistance (Social Security)
62. Parking Agencies—Enabling Act for Cities
63. Park System
64. Parolees and Probationers Supervision Company
65. Pharmacists Licensing
66. Planning Board—State Level
67. Development Agency
68. Police or Highway Patrol
69. Probation Law
70. Public Housing—Enabling Legislation
71. Real Estate Brokers—Licensing
72. Reciprocal Support Law
73. Retainers Agreement
74. Retirement System for State Employees
75. Right to Work Law
76. School for the Deaf
77. Seasonal Agricultural Labor Standards
78. Slaughter House Inspection
79. Soil Conservation Districts—Enabling Legislation
80. Superintendent of Public Instruction
81. Tax Commission
82. Teacher Certification—Elementary
83. Teacher Certification—Secondary
84. Urban Renewal—Enabling Legislation
85. Utility Regulation Commission
86. Welfare Agency
87. Workmens' Compensation
88. Zoning in Cities—Enabling Legislation

Governance and Public Policy

14

CENTRAL BANKING IN A DEMOCRATIC SOCIETY*
Joseph Stiglitz**

All governments have come to operate a central bank—such as "the Fed" (the Federal Reserve banking system of the United States). This is because central banks allow the orderly processing of transactions in the banking system, which in turn facilitates commerce. But they now do more of course than provide a "back room" for banking.

The Federal Reserve became during 2008 the "bank of last resort" as it struggled to save the American financial system from seizing up and failing. From August 2007 through December 2008 the balance sheet of the Fed grew from $851 billion to $2.245 trillion. It backstopped commercial bank lending and it rescued a giant investment firm. By December of 2008 it sought to drive down interest rates to zero.

What explains the Fed's assumption of such a central role in stabilizing American capitalism? A complete answer has yet to emerge. One factor is the particular economic expertise that Ben Bernanke, the chairman of the Federal Reserve, acquired before his appointment by President Bush, namely, economic history. Bernanke spent much of his academic career studying the performance of the Fed in the late 1920s and early 1930s, during the greatest crisis of American capitalism.

But another part of the explanation is historical and developmental, namely that central banks have acquired a far-reaching responsibility over the course of the twentieth century and most especially since the macroeconomic malaise of the late 1970s—a period during which many advanced industrial democracies experienced slow growth, stubborn unemployment, and price inflation. This new task is discretionary monetary policy, and it is a responsibility of central banks that affects everyone, not just bankers. It is this function that Stiglitz discusses in this article.

Discretionary monetary policy is a tool for regulating macroeconomic performance that works by affecting how much money it costs to borrow. Borrowing money is widespread and entrenched in all parts of American society. Consumers finance cars, houses, college educations, vacations, Christmas spending, and so forth; businesses and farms borrow money to pay for capital investments or to collect profits more efficiently; and nonprofit

Originally published in *De Economist* 146: 2 (1998): 199–226. © Kluwer Academic Publishers. Printed in the Netherlands. With kind permission from Springer Science and Business Media.

* Eleventh Tinbergen Lecture delivered on October 10, 1997, at De Nederlandsche Bank, Amsterdam, for the Royal Netherlands Economic Association.

** The author is on leave from Stanford University. The views expressed here are solely mine, and not necessarily those of any institution with which I am or have been affiliated. I wish to acknowledge the assistance of Jason Furman. Much of the research and ideas reported here are based on joint work with him.

entities, including governments, issue bonds to cover capital investments or to smooth out budgetary outlays. Consequently, the discretionary authority and means to affect how much all of that borrowing will cost are powerful tools to affect consumption, investment, and spending decisions by individuals, firms, and governments.

Affecting consumption, investment, and spending decisions is not, however, the ultimate goal of monetary policy. Instead, these decisions are actually just the immediate targets of monetary policy. There are more important, secondary targets of monetary policy. By affecting literally millions of microeconomic decisions at the margin, those who make monetary policy can help the economy grow—but, ideally, at a pace that, on the one hand, does not trigger accelerating inflation and, on the other hand, also absorbs into the workforce all those who are seeking wage-earning work.

This all sounds like something the president and Congress should be involved in, right? After all, voters hold them accountable for growth, employment, and price inflation.

But, in fact, the president and Congress are only peripherally involved in making monetary policy. People from the White House informally meet with the chairman of the Board of Governors of the Federal Reserve System, and the chairman testifies regularly before Congress. (You can find the congressional testimony, and much else, by navigating to www.federalreserve. gov.) But the president and members of Congress only make requests or offer suggestions: They do not directly affect monetary policy. That is made by our central bank—the Federal Reserve—typically without explicit coordination with elected officials. There is a widespread view, indeed, that to do otherwise—to let the president or members of Congress seriously affect monetary policy—is to court macroeconomic disaster.

Why is political control of the economy thought to be a recipe for economic failure? Presidents and members of Congress will not be able to resist the temptation to grow the economy faster than it should grow. Economists think that there is an optimal growth rate for economies (which in turn is due to the very important idea that there is a rate of employment beyond which accelerating inflation sets in). Politicians might however desire the maximum growth rate in order to get reelected. Yet pushing for the maximum growth rate rather than the optimal growth rate is irresponsible: It is good politics but bad government that will undermine price stability.

Joseph Stiglitz, a Nobel Prize–winning economist, gently unpacks all of this conventional wisdom. Competent macroeconomic policymaking is what can be called a public good: Everyone benefits from it and no one can be excluded from enjoying its benefits. But Stiglitz suggests that discretionary monetary policy via an insulated central bank run by experts is not entirely a public good and that there is a "private good" component to it, that is, there are benefits from it which accrue only to some people and not others. As you read this article, try to figure out who these people are, what the value of the benefits they get is, and whether their receipt of these benefits simultaneously imposes costs on those who do not receive them. Then ask yourself: If Stiglitz is correct, are you willing to give up discretionary monetary policy from an insulated central bank? Try to defend your answer to yourself and *see where that exercise leads you in terms of thinking about the basic issues concerning power that this volume began with.*

• • •

1 INTRODUCTION AND MAIN CONCLUSIONS

IT IS A SPECIAL PLEASURE for me to be here to give this lecture to honor Professor Tinbergen, because his many interests coincide so closely with my own. He spent much of his later life working on the economics of income distribution, a subject with which I began my professional life in my doctoral dissertation, and which has continued to be a focus of my concern. Tinbergen's thesis that the relative wages of skilled and unskilled workers depend on both supply and demand factors resonates throughout my work on optimal taxation.[1] Its importance has been borne out dramatically in wage movements in the United States and elsewhere during the past two decades.

From my present vantage point, I am especially appreciative of his devotion to the economics of development, which became the focus of his concern in the mid-1950s, in order, as Tinbergen (1988) explained in retrospect, "to contribute to what seemed to me the highest priority from a humanitarian standpoint."

But today, I want to focus on other aspects of his work: his contribution to economic policy, particularly the problems of controlling the economy, the relationship between instruments and objectives, and the scope for decentralization, which absorbed him and earned him international recognition in his early days. I have reflected a great deal upon these issues during the past four years, during which I served as economic adviser to the President of the United States, and especially the last two years, when I served as Chairman of the Council of Economic Advisers.

I had the good luck to serve at a time of rising prosperity—and even improved income distribution, lowered poverty, and increased inclusion in our society of previously marginalized groups, such as minorities. The President took much credit for these achievements, and I often quipped that if some of the glory of what was, at least in some dimensions, the strongest economy in three decades should rub off on the President, should not at least some of that rub off on his economic adviser? After all, as my staff jokingly pointed out, while I was Chairman of the Council the misery index—the sum of the inflation rate and the unemployment rate—was half of what it was when Alan Greenspan was Chairman of the Council. Others suggested that it was not the Administration which should get the credit, but the Federal Reserve Board.

To Tinbergen, this debate might have seemed strange indeed. Macroeconomic success depended on coordination of the monetary and fiscal instruments. It was the two working together. Curiously enough, economic policymaking in the United States—and in many other countries—is designed to inhibit this coordination and cooperation. We have created independent central banks, who may, and indeed are instructed to, pursue policies *independently* of the wishes of the elected officials. In the United States, the deliberations of the open market committee which sets interest rates is kept secret—even from the President of the United States. To be sure, in the past, presidents have not been shy about expressing to the Fed what they think it should do, but the Fed has not been shy about ignoring these messages.

[1] See, for instance, Stiglitz (1986, 1998).

Early on in the Clinton Administration, we adopted a policy of not commenting on Fed policy, not because we did not have strong views—at certain critical stages, many in the Administration thought their policies were seriously misguided—but because we thought a public debate would be counterproductive. We thought the Fed would not listen, the newspapers would love the controversy, and the markets, worried by the uncertainty that such controversy generates, would add a risk premium to long-term rates, thereby increasing those rates, which was precisely what we did not want to happen.

There is an irony in all of this. The President is held accountable for how the economy performs—whether or not he has much control. Indeed, econometric models suggest that an infallible predictor of the outcome of presidential elections is the state of the economy;[2] just as the weaknesses of the economy were largely responsible for Clinton's election in 1992, the strength of the economy was largely responsible for his re-election in 1996. The Council's own econometric models in 1995 and 1996 corroborated the findings of others predicting an electoral outcome close to that which emerged—suggesting that President Clinton really did not need to do all that campaigning.

While the President is held accountable, his major tools for affecting the macroeconomy have been removed. Deficit stringency has removed the scope for discretionary fiscal policy (though fiscal impacts played a role in the fine tuning of the 1993 deficit reduction plan),[3] and the independence of the Fed has removed the Executive Branch's influence over monetary policy. Members of the Administration did communicate privately, in weekly, sometimes daily, conversations. We shared our views of what was happening to the economy—but we did not always agree. And according to the rules of the game that we adopted, we did not participate in the public debate on monetary policy.

In a democracy, public discussion and debate about issues of central importance, like the management of the economy, are essential. The Council of Economic Advisers did attempt to contribute to this discussion—but obliquely, especially in the Annual Economic Report of the President.

Today, I want to address two issues which I felt stifled from discussing more openly during my tenure at the Council of Economic Advisers. The first issue concerns the principles of monetary policy in a low-inflation environment such as has prevailed in the United States for the past decade and a half—how should it set its targets? Should it seek to take pre-emptive strikes against inflation? Is it true that it cannot, or at least should not, wait to act until the "white of the eyes of inflation" can be seen? The second issue is more fundamental: What should be the institutional arrangements by which monetary policy is set in a democratic society? How independent should the central bank be? And if it is independent, what should be its governance? Who should choose those who essentially control the economy, and what characteristics should these decision makers have? Though I do not wish to give away my bottom lines, to pique your interest, let me hint at the conclusions I shall draw:

[2] Interestingly, the perception of the state of the economy seems to be a more accurate predictor of electoral outcomes than the actual state of the economy. The incumbent party has won every election in which the University of Michigan's consumer sentiment index in the month before the election was above 92.

[3] Perhaps now that the United States appears on the verge of fiscal surpluses there will be more scope for fiscal policies. But some of the budgetary processes designed to curb public profligacy may inhibit the effective exercise of countercyclical fiscal policy.

1. Monetary policy matters, and the successful conduct of macropolicy in the postwar period has led to far greater stability of the economy. This is not to imply that American economic policy has been perfect—major mistakes, some arising from an imperfect understanding of the economy, have at times contributed to unnecessarily high unemployment or to the economy enjoying a stronger boom than intended.

2. In particular, I will argue that the strategies of opportunistic disinflation or pre-emptive strikes are based on a set of hypotheses about the economy for which there is little empirical support. I will argue, at least in the context of the American economy today, for an alternative, which I call cautious expansionism.

3. There is a rationale for a *degree* of independence of the central bank, even in a democratic society. But the central bank must be accountable, and sensitive, to democratic processes; there must be more democracy in the manner in which the decision makers are chosen and more representativeness in the governance structure. The movement in the opposite direction in some places is particularly disturbing.

2 MONETARY POLICY MATTERS: THE STABILIZATION OF THE POSTWAR BUSINESS CYCLE

Before answering the two questions which are the focus of my concern today, I have to address a prior issue: Does monetary policy matter? For clearly, if monetary policy has no effect, then the design of monetary institutions, the choice of monetary policy strategy, and the coordination of monetary and fiscal policy do not matter. I believe strongly that monetary policy does matter—and it was not just frustration with our inability to use discretionary fiscal policy combined with envy of the economic power of those sitting along Constitution Avenue in the Federal Reserve Board building that led me to this conclusion. This conclusion was based on theoretical work that I had done before entering government[4] and recent empirical work by Francis Diebold and Glenn Rudebusch (1992), which we have confirmed and extended. Their findings have not received the attention they deserve; they shed light on a long-standing controversy about whether there are in fact business cycles or simply random economic fluctuations. Their somewhat surprising conclusion is that there appear to have been cycles prior to the Great Depression, but that in the postwar period, these cycles—in the sense of regular periodic movements in output—have been eliminated. Before turning to the statistical results, let me comment briefly on the circumstances that led up to my work in this area.

Though we did not control monetary policy it was important for us to have views on where the economy was going and what we thought monetary policy should be. My friend Jacob Frenkel (governor of the Central Bank of Israel) once quipped that central bankers have a fascination with fiscal policy—they are always willing to comment on the appropriate size of the deficit (zero), though they thought it inappropriate for the fiscal authorities to comment on monetary policy. By the same token, we had a fascination with monetary policy—and wished we could comment on it.

It is remarkable how little insight into these issues is shed by current macroeconomics. One major school of thought, Real Business Cycles, argues that there

[4] See, for instance, Greenwald and Stiglitz (1990, 1993).

is no involuntary unemployment. It was hard to tell that story to the President, who was elected on a platform of "Jobs, Jobs, Jobs!," or to the voters in California, when unemployment—they did not think it was just a superabundance of leisure—exceeded 10 percent. Another major school, new classical economics, with its emphasis on rational expectations, argues that monetary policy is ineffective, because the private sector would adjust its expectations and actions to undo any *systematic* monetary policies.[5] If correct, concerns about policy coordination are not of much importance! And if correct, the myriad of economists, in government and business, and the multitude of reporters, who were engaged in trying to figure out what the Fed was about to do, are all behaving irrationally. While these schools of thought might have little sway in the real world of government or business, they have had remarkable influence in academia over the past quarter century, especially in America. Both of these schools suggested that our difficulties in the Council of hiring macroeconomists from academia who knew something about the economy was of no consequence: they would be wasting their time in any case. Needless to say, these were perspectives with which I had little sympathy.

As the economy continued the robust recovery from the 1990–1991 recession, I was asked by reporters with increasing frequency, did I expect the recovery to end. Their view was that the economy was perched on a knife-edge, ready to fall off into a recession on one side or rising inflation on the other. Furthermore, they seemed to believe that the longer an expansion lasted, the more likely there was to be a downturn. In contrast, I believed in Keynes' animal spirits, and believed that those animal spirits might be driven, if ever so gently, towards a more favorable view of the economy, and hence stronger investment. The fundamentals of the US economy were clearly sound, but I wanted to make a further argument: that expansions do not end of old age, a popular way of saying that there was no such thing as a business cycle. The results in Figure 1 provide dramatic support for this argument as applied to the post–World War II US economy—the probability of an expansion ending appears to be independent of its length.[6] This result should not come as a surprise, if one makes three assumptions: monetary policy seeks to maintain expansions, monetary policy is forward-looking, and monetary policy is somewhat effective. For if there were any systematic time dependency—or dependency on time and other observable variables—the monetary authorities should seek to take offsetting actions. The result does not require that the monetary authorities be perfectly efficient, only that any errors have no systematic component to them.

From this perspective, downturns come as a surprise, an unexpected event not anticipated, or imperfectly anticipated, or whose consequences were not fully calculated, perhaps because of misunderstandings about the structure of the economy. Monetary authorities seek to offset these effects, to restore the economy

---

[5] In real business-cycle theory, monetary policy is not only not needed, but ineffective. In some variants of rational expectations models, monetary policy can have effects, but only to the extent that the actions of the monetary authorities are imperfectly observed, or observed with a lag.

[6] Diebold and Rudebusch (1992) find no time dependence at all. Our results show a slight time dependence, which disappears once other, easily observed variables are taken into account. The existence of some time dependence, even with an effective monetary policy, is to be expected, if there are variables or events (like large excess inventories) the occurrence of which increases with the length of the expansion, and if monetary policy cannot perfectly offset the effects. Effective monetary policy eliminates any systematic cyclical fluctuation associated with such variables or events.

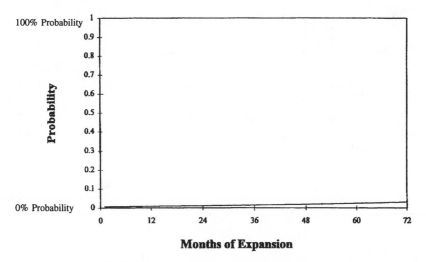

FIGURE 1. Probability of an expansion ending, 1945–1997
Note: Probability estimated using logit regressions on NBER Business Cycle dates.

to its potential. In the short run, there is a tendency of monetary authorities to think of the downturn as a temporary deviation, which will correct itself shortly. Given the lags in the effectiveness of monetary policy, expansionary policies might then complement the natural forces of recovery, leading to inflation. Over time, if the downturn persists, political pressure—even on an independent monetary authority—to do something mounts; the policy of doing nothing, or doing too little becomes hard to maintain. Moreover, information about the true nature of the downturn becomes more apparent.

This pattern is clearly evidenced in the series of pronouncements of the Fed Chairman between 1991 and 1993. Even as the National Bureau of Economic Research was about to declare that the economy was in recession in July 1991, the Fed Chairman's Humphrey-Hawkins testimony (which he is required to give before Congress twice a year) did not indicate that the Fed was worried about recession.[7] To be fair, economic forecasters have almost always missed recessions. (Also, I should add parenthetically that one of the responsibilities of Fed officials is to maintain confidence in the economy. Private views may be more pessimistic than public pronouncements. Still, in this particular case, policy seemed to conform remarkably closely to the public pronouncements. Moreover, the Fed Chairman is a master of Fedspeak—some say a modern version of a Delphic oracle—which is designed to carefully calibrate what information is revealed and what is obscured rather than to provide complete enlightenment. This provides plenty of opportunity for him to make announcements that bolster confidence in the economy while being sufficiently vague so that in retrospect they seem to provide keen insights into the workings of the economy *regardless of what happens*.)

As the downturn persisted the Fed continued to see it as an unexpected shock leading to a "normal" cyclical downturn that would respond to standard policies.

---

[7] The prepared statement reads, "[O]n balance, the economy still appears to be growing, and the likelihood of a near-term recession seems low."

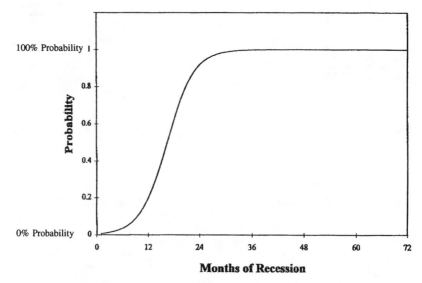

FIGURE 2. Probability of a recession ending, 1945–1997
Note: Probability estimated using logit regressions on NBER Business Cycle dates.

This viewpoint is evident in the Humphrey-Hawkins testimony from February 1991 which reads "[n]onetheless, the balance of forces does appear to suggest that this downturn could well prove shorter and shallower than most prior post-war recessions. An important reason for this assessment is that one of the most negative economic impacts of the Gulf war—the run-up in oil prices—has been reversed. Another is that the substantial decline in interest rates over the past year and a half—especially over the past several months—should ameliorate the contractionary effects of the crisis in the Gulf and of tighter credit availability."

It was not until the economy was on its way to recovery, in February 1993, that the Fed finally recognized the "economy has been held back by a variety of *structural factors*" [emphasis added], most notably fundamental weaknesses in the financial system.[8]

As the nature of the problem became clearer, and as the political pressure to do something mounted, monetary policy was eased 24 times, contributing to the recovery. The pattern evidenced in our most recent recession is typical, as confirmed by the statistical data: Figure 2 shows that there is a strong time dependency in recovery.

These patterns are markedly different from those that prevailed before the Great Depression. Since World War II, expansions are longer and recessions are shorter, as Table 1 shows. Figure 3 shows, using data for the United States for the period 1854 to 1918 that prior to the Great Depression, expansions did end of old age. The probability of an expansion ending increased markedly the longer the expansion continued, with a probability of approximately one-third in the second year, increasing to two-thirds in the fourth. By contrast, recovery from a downturn seems to have been largely a random event, as Figure 4 shows. While

---

[8] In part due to the interaction of the 1986 tax reform which eliminated many of the tax subsidies to real estate that had been enacted in earlier legislation, with the regulatory forbearance that allowed the financial problems to mount, culminating in the savings and loan debacle in 1989.

TABLE 1
Average Duration (in Months) of U.S. Business Cycle Expansions and Recessions

Time period	Recession	Expansion
December 1854–March 1991	18	35
December 1854–August 1929	21	25
October 1945–March 1991	11	50

Source: NBER

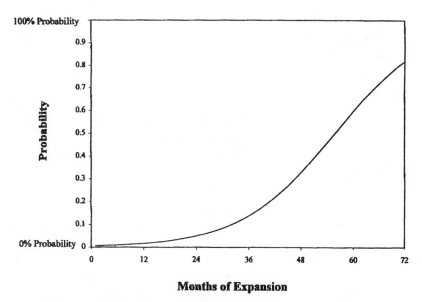

Months of Expansion

FIGURE 3. Probability of an expansion ending, 1854–1929
Note: Probability estimated using logit regressions on NBER Business Cycle dates.

some of these changes could have been accounted for by changes in the structure of the economy, I suspect that it is improved macropolicy (including automatic fiscal stabilizers) that accounts for much of the change.

Incidentally, these results strongly rebut the claim of Christina Romer (1986) that there is no evidence of improved macroeconomic performance in the postwar period. Her argument relies on adjustments in output series which are debatable. Our methodology only requires qualitative assessments about whether the economy is expanding or contracting. Because it does not require measures for every subcomponent of GDP and because it can utilize data from other sources, the timing of expansions and downturns provides a far more robust way of assessing economic performance.

These results, while they show convincingly that monetary policy matters and has been used to improve the overall performance of the economy, do not require us to believe that the monetary authority behaves perfectly or even that it is efficient. I already discussed one example of a mistake: the Fed doing too little and acting too late to avert or minimize the depth and duration of the 1990–1991 recession. A second illustration is the current expansion which can be thought of as also partially attributable to mistakes, at least initially. There is a tendency to

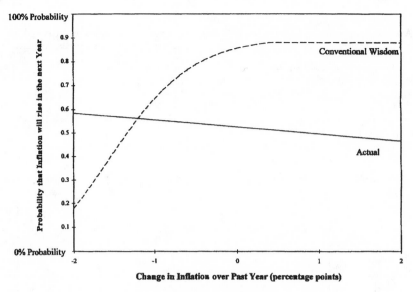

FIGURE 4. Probability of a recession ending, 1854–1929
Note: Probability estimated using logit regressions on NBER Business Cycle dates.

think of mistakes as one-sided—always working to the detriment of the economy. But mistakes, by their nature, should be random, and in at least some cases should work to the benefit of the economy. In this case, there were in fact two errors on the part of the Fed, with one more than offsetting the other.

Throughout the earlier 1990s, the Fed continued to have an overly pessimistic view concerning the NAIRU (non-accelerating inflation rate of unemployment), and the economy's potential for reducing unemployment without inflation increasing. But they also continued to underappreciate the role of financial markets and continued to fail to understand key aspects of banking behavior. Had they better understood these factors, given their beliefs about the NAIRU and given their strong aversion to inflation, they would have prevented the unemployment rate from declining below 6.0 percent to 6.2 percent. It might have been a long time—possibly never—before we learned about the economy's real potential.[9] It was our good fortune that they did not see accurately where the economy was going!

To understand what happened—and why the Fed failed (fortunately) to see the strength of the recovery—we need to return to the early days of the Clinton Administration. When the President took office in February 1993, he moved quickly to introduce a deficit-cutting budget. Eventually the Congress enacted a plan to reduce the deficit by $500 billion over five years (in contrast, the 1997 balanced budget legislation only cut the deficit by $200 billion over five years).

---

[9] Indeed, I have argued that there is a "reverse hysteresis effect"; as the unemployment rate is reduced, previously marginalized workers are drawn into the labor market, develop and maintain worker and job search skills that might otherwise have atrophied, and the economy's NAIRU is thereby actually lowered. If this is the case, then the "mistake" of allowing the unemployment rate to fall below 6 percent was actually crucial in the economy's longer-term improved performance. See Stiglitz (1997).

Old-style Keynesians warned that deficit reduction would undermine the fragile recovery. Those of us who believe that the markets were forward-looking, understood that credible, pre-announced deficit reduction would lower interest rates and thus stimulate the economy. What took us all by surprise was just how much it was stimulated.

Parsing out how credit should be divided up became a preoccupation. To be sure, the strong economy played a role, but this just leads to the further question of how much of the strong economy was attributable to deficit reduction. We were more willing to take credit for higher growth than for the increasing profit share (which led to higher tax revenues), a result partly of the low interest rates, but also partly a reflection of wage performance. But by any reckoning, the tax increases and expenditure reductions in the Omnibus Budget Reconciliation Act of 1993 (OBRA 1993) were directly responsible for more than half of the deficit reduction that followed.

But in spite of all of the rhetoric, the connection between deficit reduction and economic recovery remained somewhat of a puzzle: Should not the Fed be able to manage monetary policy to maintain the economy at full employment, that is, at the NAIRU? Nothing in the modern theory of monetary policy suggested that the Fed's ability to do that should be affected in any way by deficits or deficit reduction, so long as the changes were appropriately anticipated and offsetting actions undertaken. If the government ran a slightly larger deficit, then the Fed would have to run a slightly tighter monetary policy; the short-run macroeconomic performance would be the same, but the composition of output would shift from private investment to government spending, potentially impairing long-run growth.

As I thought about it more, I finally recognized the connection, but it was more subtle and based on the link between financial markets and economic activity. It is an interesting story, and illustrates that while two wrongs do not make a right, in economic policy two mistakes can more than offset each other, and result in an economic boom.

In the 1980s, banks had significant holdings of long-term Treasury bonds. This represented a gamble on falling interest rates. Banks were allowed to take this gamble because accountants valued these bonds at face value and regulators judged risk by the chance of default—which was zero in this case—not by the likely volatility of asset prices (interest rate risk).[10] When interest rates rose in the late 1980s, the value of bank assets fell, which together with substantial losses on loans, forced many banks to curtail their lending. Subsequently, with the 1993 deficit reduction and the lowered inflationary expectations, interest rates declined. The result was a major revaluation of bank assets at the same time that loans were again becoming more profitable. Given their increased net worth and cash flow, banks were both willing and able to increase their lending. And this is precisely what they did. Had this effect been anticipated by the Fed, it is unlikely that they would have allowed the Federal funds rate to stay so low for long.

---

[10] The Fed made a mistake in the way that risk was assessed. This was widely recognized by, among others, members of the Administration who argued with the Fed, but to no avail. But the misguided regulation allowed banks to gamble; and because of the subsequent deficit reduction—and resulting lower interest rates—the gamble paid off. But the gamble could just as well have failed (after all, the market was paying high interest rates on long-term bonds, largely because the market anticipated higher interest rates in the future). And had it failed, the banking system would have been in a disastrous shape.

The effective conduct of monetary policy is extraordinarily difficult. It requires assessing the state of the economy today and in the near future. It requires a detailed knowledge of the economy, so that the consequences of various actions—interest rate increases and decreases—can be carefully assessed. Monetary policy is necessarily conducted in an environment with considerable uncertainty, and therefore requires careful balancing of risks, including the risks of inflation, the changes that it might increase or accelerate, and the costs of disinflation.

One leading monetary policy strategy responds to this uncertainty by recommending that policymakers act to eliminate projected rises in inflation. The argument for aggressive, preemptive strikes against inflation is based on three premises. The most fundamental premise is that inflation is costly. This provides the motivation for trying to avert or lower inflation. The second premise is that once inflation starts to rise it has a tendency to accelerate out of control. This belief provides a strong motivation for erring on the side of caution in fighting inflation. Finally, the third premise is that increases in inflation are very costly to reverse. The implication of this premise is that even if you care much more about unemployment than inflation, you would still keep inflation from increasing today in order to avoid having to induce large recessions to bring the inflation rate down later on. All three of these premises are hypotheses that can be tested empirically.

In many countries throughout the world, monetary policy seems to be based on a belief by policymakers in these three premises, even when these beliefs are not fully incorporated in the formal models that the staffs of the central banks employ. I would like to discuss the evidence underlying each one.

The Costs of Inflation

Many people treat inflation as if it were something that was costly in its own right. This, of course, is not true. Individual utility functions only depend on quantities; prices do not enter because, by themselves, they do not make people better or worse off. The same is true of the social welfare functions that politicians *should* use in guiding their thinking. Putting unemployment or output in the social welfare function might be reasonable, although even here we must worry about a number of finer points, including the valuation of leisure. Putting inflation into the objective function is, however, never justified. Instead, inflation only matters in so far as it effects the two variables we do care about: output and its distribution. When economists or commentators speak about balancing the costs of inflation against the costs of unemployment they are implicitly mixing an objective function (which weights output and distribution) with a model of the economy (which links inflation with these variables) and combining them into a reduced form. This shorthand is acceptable, as long as we remember it is just that—a shorthand. All too often, however, this shorthand turns into a rigid assumption.

What then is the evidence concerning the costs of inflation? There is an old theoretical literature that emphasizes menu costs, shoe-leather costs, tax distortions, and the increasing noise introduced into the price system. Estimates of the deadweight loss imposed by these distortions in countries like the United States have, for the most part, been disappointingly small from the perspective of inflationary hawks.[11] In the last decade, an increasingly sophisticated literature has attempted to measure the costs of both the level and variability of inflation indirectly by examining their consequences for the level of output and growth. Probably the most persuasive studies were done by Bruno and Easterly (1986) who found that when countries cross the threshold of 40 percent per year inflation they fall into a high inflation/low growth trap. But below that level, there is no evidence that inflation is costly.[12]

Others, like Barro (1997) and Fischer (1993), have used cross-country growth regressions in an attempt to quantify the impact of inflation on growth. They have confirmed that high inflation is, on average, deleterious for growth, but again have failed to find any evidence for costs of low levels of inflation. Fischer also found the same results for the variability of inflation.[13] (The strength of the nonlinearity in the relationship between inflation and social welfare is clear from the outcome of research conducted by the United States Federal Reserve Bank. Despite the efforts of their minions of first-rate economists—some of them devoting much of their time to analyzing the costs of inflation—the Fed has still failed to find definitive evidence of costs of inflation in the United States. Should they eventually succeed in finding such results, they will only have proven that data mining does work, not that inflation does not.)

Recent research by Akerlof, Dickens, and Perry (1996) has argued that low inflation is actually beneficial. Some inflation, according to this view, helps maintain full employment by facilitating the downward adjustment of real wages. Their simulation suggests that maintaining zero inflation would be consistent with a 10 percent long-run unemployment rate. This is probably too high—surely people would eventually become less resistant to nominal wage cuts after some experience with zero inflation. Still, their research forcefully reminds us that we need to weigh the costs of low inflation against its benefits.

The Acceleration of Inflation

The second premise of many inflation hawks is that inflation is like a genie, once you let it out of the bottle it will just keep on expanding. Stepping off precipices, sliding down slippery slopes, and falling off the wagon are other metaphors that often dominate popular thinking about inflation. Again, these metaphors can be subject to rigorous testing. Relatively few people have done this, in part because most economic models assume that inflation does not accelerate, a position that is at variance with the conventional journalistic wisdom. My own tests have provided no basis for believing the conventional wisdom.

---

[11] In a recent paper Martin Feldstein (1996) argues that one of the largest costs of inflation is that it exacerbates the distortions in the unindexed tax system, giving rise to costs that are not the usual second-order Harberger triangles but first-order trapezoids. He estimates the present value of the gain from lowering the inflation rate from 2 percent to 0 percent to be 35 percent of the initial level of GDP. One of the main problems with Feldstein's analysis is that it neglects distortions in the tax system that are ameliorated by inflation, like accelerated depreciation.

[12] The null hypothesis in this, as in most other studies of inflation, is that inflation is costless. The failure to reject this null at low levels of inflation does not prove that inflation is costless, only that we have no evidence that it is costly.

[13] Because the level and variability of inflation are so correlated, Fischer reported great difficulty in disentangling their separate effects at any level/variance of inflation. This point holds true more generally: Any study of the consequences of inflation probably also picks up costs associated with the variability of inflation.

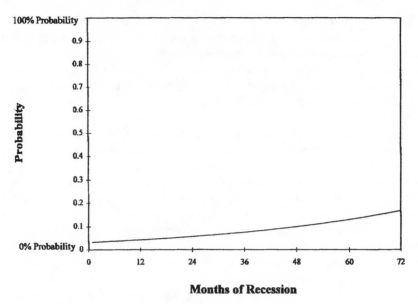

FIGURE 5. Probability of rising inflation
Note: Probability estimated using logit model that controls for the unemployment rate.

One test is to nest non-accelerationism as a special case in an accelerationist model. You can, for instance, estimate empirical Phillips curves in which the change in inflation depends not just on unemployment but also on the past change in inflation. In the United States, this coefficient is insignificant.[14] Alternatively, techniques like logit can be used to infer whether or not the likelihood of inflation increasing depends on, among other variables, the level or the rate of change of inflation. These tests also find no evidence whatsoever that changes in inflation are more persistent than can be accounted for by the persistence of the unemployment rate. In fact, after controlling for the unemployment rate, we find just the opposite: when inflation has been rising it is more likely to reverse course and start falling—the exact opposite of the conventional wisdom (Figure 5). The difficulty of finding evidence—or casual experience—which supports the precipice hypothesis probably explains why it is rarely a feature of standard economic models. However, this hypothesis is still all too present in discussions about the proper stance of monetary policy.

Inflation Is Costly to Reverse

The third premise is that inflation is costly to reverse. The standard mantra is that even if we cared very little about inflation it might be worthwhile to endure a little extra unemployment today in order to avoid increasing inflation leading to a recession down the line. This premise is based on fallacious backward induction. It asks what should the Fed's reaction function be today given a fixed reaction function in the future. Even framed in this way, this argument is based on two somewhat shaky premises.

[14] Results are available on request.

The first premise is that you cannot slow the economy down without creating a recession, and worse, you cannot create a small recession. One rationale for this belief is that slowing growth triggers inventory build-ups that in turn further dampen production. Whatever the merits of this belief, as a matter of logic there is no reason why it should apply any more strongly to a tightening in the future than to a tightening today. If you really believe that fine tuning is impossible and even mild restraints risk triggering a major recession, then there is little argument for pre-emptive tightening.

To be sure, several economic downturns have been due to excessive zeal by the monetary authorities in response to inflation. But one needs to interpret this evidence carefully. The Fed has managed on many occasions "to trim the economy's sails" without inducing a recession. There will be mistakes in monetary policy. Sometimes policymakers will act excessively, and this will cause a downturn. But this does not mean that tightening necessarily must aim to overshoot, and must aim to overshoot by a lot. The fact that occasionally the Fed steps on the brakes too hard does not mean that it always steps on the brakes too hard; it only means that those are the cases which we are most prone to notice.[15]

More generally, the theory of economic adjustment suggests that when firms and households are given time to adjust, they can do so at far lower costs. If they are put on notice that there will be a gradual slowing of economic growth, then the magnitude of the economic fluctuations induced by excess inventory build-ups can be reduced.

The second premise is that low unemployment increases inflation much more than high unemployment lowers it, and that the costs of lowering inflation increase more than proportionately with the magnitude of the inflation reduction—in other words, that the Phillips curve is convex. Prices and wages, according to this view, are downwardly rigid. As a result, decreases in aggregate demand translate more into falling output and employment than into lower inflation. Increases in aggregate demand, however, have just the opposite effect, raising inflation with relatively little gain for output.

The logic behind this belief is not terribly compelling. We often see falling nominal prices and nominal wages. And furthermore, in a world with positive inflation the issue is not whether there is downward price and wage rigidity but whether there is resistance to downward adjustments in the *rate of increase* of prices or wages. Casual observation provides very little reason to believe this is the case.

Other theories suggest the possibility that the Phillips curve might be concave. One intuition comes from strategic price setting in oligopolistic competition. Suppose two competitors, say Coke and Pepsi, are both faced with kinked demand curves. If Pepsi raised its prices, Coke might stand pat in order to gain market share. But if Pepsi lowered its prices, Coke would have to match them in order

---

[15] There is one argument that may have some merit—were it not for the results reported below. Assume that there were large nonlinearities in the *risks of responses*, such that a large increase in the interest rate is far more likely to induce a recession by overshooting. With nonlinearities in the costs of inflation, a higher inflation rate today increases the probability that at some time in the future the inflation rate will be such that the authorities actively seek to reduce it by a large increase in the interest rate, with the concomitant risk of recession. It is worth, in this view, undertaking the risks today of a small increase in interest rates to forestall this risk. Two further assumptions, however, are hidden in this analysis. First, that even high inflation cannot be wrung out slowly (a hypothesis which is not consistent with standard models), and second, that there are increasing costs associated with larger reductions in inflation, a hypothesis which I discuss at greater length below.

to avoid losing market share. The consequence is that prices adjust downward together more easily than they adjust upward. This reverses the logic I just described: expansions in aggregate demand will go more into output than inflation, and vice versa for contractions.

I see no reason for an a priori belief in one shape of the Phillips curve over another when different theories are consistent with such different shapes. Instead, the question is empirical. Unfortunately, it is much easier to assess the sign or even the average magnitude of the relationships between variables than it is to assess the shape of the function relating them. One study conducted by the Council of Economic Advisers found that if you allow a kink in the Phillips curve, the data "choose" a concave shape.[16] When I went to the World Bank I thought it would be interesting to run the exact same regression for other countries. Amazingly, in all but one country we found that the Phillips curve was statistically significantly concave.[17]

These statistical findings corroborate the experiences of case studies. Some of the most dramatic episodes of inflation reduction—most recently, the experiences of Brazil and Israel—show that very large reductions in inflation and inflationary expectations can be achieved at very low costs.

I would caution against drawing overly strong conclusions from the evidence I just discussed. The power of the tests I described is very uncertain. The premises that inflation is not costly or that inflation does not accelerate, for instance, are typically treated as null hypotheses. Failing to reject them may have as much to do with the difficulty of drawing sharp inferences from the data as it does with their substantive merits. And, the concavity result, like all nonlinear regressions, may be sensitive to the choice of functional form. The evidence does, however, decisively refute the extreme versions of all three premises. And in doing so, the arguments underlying the policies of aggressive, pre-emptive strikes against inflation, a stance that is the basis of the rhetoric if not the practice of so many central banks, are undermined. These policies are based on articles of faith, not on scientific evidence.

If monetary policy were conducted under perfect certainty both about the state of the economy and the consequences of policy, the three propositions I just discussed would not matter very much. But because monetary policy is a process of sequential decision-making under uncertainty, all of these questions are very relevant. Consider the problem facing US monetary authorities throughout the 1990s. There is uncertainty about the NAIRU. There is a chance that not engaging in a pre-emptive strike might lead to an unemployment rate below the NAIRU. But if it is true that keeping the unemployment rate below the NAIRU only raises inflation by a small amount, if the costs of this added inflation itself are negligible, and if this mistake is easy to correct by raising the unemployment rate slightly above the NAIRU, then this is a risk worth taking: the economy enjoys a lower unemployment rate and higher output, marginalized groups are brought into the labor force, and through the reverse hysteresis effect, the level of the NAIRU itself may be lowered. We should not follow a policy of pre-emptive strikes, but rather one of cautious expansionism.

[16] Braun and Chen (1996).

[17] The countries were chosen based on the availability of data and comprised Australia, the United States, Canada, France, Germany, Italy, Japan, Mexico, and Brazil. Only in Mexico did the Phillips curve appear to be convex.

4 THE INDEPENDENCE OF THE CENTRAL BANK

So far, I have argued that monetary policy matters, and that it has improved the economy's economic performance, even though it is fallible. I have focused on the United States—showing that the theoretical framework that seems to underlie its rhetoric is not based on empirical evidence, and that its understanding of economic events over the past decade has been, at crucial points, flawed, sometimes to the detriment of the economy. I could have provided similar stories for other central banks or other times. But why should that surprise us. As Shakespeare has said, "To err is human." Why should we expect anything less or more of central bankers than of other mortals.

Our economic institutions should be designed to cope with human fallibility.[18] The United States Constitution created a system of checks and balances, partly because the Founding Fathers were worried about the fallibility of any single individual, especially one who is in a position that wields enormous power.

There is an increasing tendency around the world to devolve responsibility for managing monetary policy on an independent central bank. In many, if not most, countries the deliberations of the central bank are secret, and much, if not most, decision-making power is highly concentrated in the Governor. I find this deeply troubling on several accounts.

The most fundamental is a matter of democratic philosophy. Monetary policy is a key determinant of the economy's macroeconomic performance. The elected government is inevitably held accountable for that performance, as I noted in my introduction; yet, especially as fiscal policy becomes constrained by budget stringency (and it will be even more constrained in Europe with the agreements underlying the monetary unification, and would have become more constrained in the United States had the balanced budget amendment passed), monetary policy is the main instrument for affecting macroeconomic performance. That this key determinant of what happens to society—this key collective action—should be so removed from control of the democratically elected officials should at least raise questions.

Moreover, transparency—openness—is now recognized as a central aspect of democratic processes. There cannot be effective democratic governance without information. Yet central banks continue to operate in secrecy.

The concentration of power in the hands of a single individual raises concerns about fallibility. To be sure, some central bankers may be prescient—though I can think of none today that fall within that category. Some may even have values that are broadly reflective of society as a whole. But the same might be said about dictatorships. A fundamental principle of democratic philosophy is that there should not be a concentration of power in the hands of any single individual; and this is also a fundamental implication of the fact of human fallibility.

The ostensible reason for delegating responsibility to a group of experts is that the decisions are viewed to involve largely technical matters in which politics should not intrude. But the decisions made by the central bank are not just technical decisions; they involve trade-offs, judgments about whether the risks of inflation are worth the benefits of lower unemployment. These trade-offs involve values. I recall a recent meeting with a former central banker in which he expressed his view on

---

[18] This is a line of research which I pursued with Raaj Sah, focusing on the implications of human fallibility for centralization and decentralization. See Sah and Stiglitz (1986, 1988).

the matter: He emphasized the asymmetries of the risk. If inflation increases, there are real costs that have to be borne; if unemployment increases, and it turns out that the economy is operating at an unemployment rate above the NAIRU, then the costs are minimal and the "mistake" can be reversed. Given the evidence on the macroeconomic costs of inflation in the low-inflation environment of the United States, let me translate what he was saying: If inflation increases, real people—bond holders—are hurt, as nominal interest rates increase and prices of bonds fall; unemployment, on the other hand, mainly hurts workers, particularly marginalized workers, since these are the first to lose their jobs as unemployment increases.

Typically, those who make the decisions are not representative of society as a whole, and in some countries, they are chosen in ways which are hard to reconcile with democratic values.[19] In many countries, bankers are disproportionately represented; and even if they do not come from a banking background, they quickly get captured by the banking community in which they are immersed. Few countries ensure that workers and their interests are represented, even though the actions of the central bank have a vital impact on them.

To be sure, we want expertise in running the central bank, and it is natural that we turn to bankers for that expertise. This is the kind of conflict that arises in many aspects of economic regulation: Expertise is concentrated in those who are in the business, and plays an important role in the capture of the regulatory bodies by the industries that they are intended to regulate.[20] But at least in this particular case there are bodies of expertise outside the industry itself, most notably in academia (though this remark may seem self-serving). This is especially true for questions like monetary policy that do not rely on privileged information or detailed hands-on knowledge. Some countries, motivated by these concerns, have taken the bold step of forbidding bankers to serve on the governing board of the central bank. Expertise can be hired. In many other areas, we separate out expertise from governance.

Moreover, the separation between expertise and values is not as clear as it is sometimes depicted. For instance, I was repeatedly struck by how those who, on the basis of their values, worried more about inflation and less about unemployment, also more frequently saw inflation lurking around the corner. As I noted earlier, we shared data with the Fed. We even shared models. We had the same data describing what was happening to wages and prices. But we frequently made different inferences about what was *likely* to happen in the future. We all knew that we had at best a cloudy crystal ball—but policymakers have to do with what they have, and when we each looked into the clouds, we saw different things. But what was interesting was that the inflation hawks focused on the most pessimistic interpretations of the data; while the inflation doves on the most optimistic. As is turned out, in the last several years the latter were far closer to the truth than the former, but the point is not to crow about superior insight, but to remind ourselves both about human fallibility and the *bias* values imparts to what is ostensibly technical analysis.[21]

[19] For instance, in the United States, the open market committee includes presidents of the regional central banks. They are chosen by the boards of the central bank. No elected official—neither Congress nor the President—has a direct say in their appointment.

[20] See Stigler (1971).

[21] To a Bayesian, all of this makes perfect sense: We each formed our best estimate, based on our different loss functions. But Bayesian analysis reinforces the point made earlier about the inability to separate expertise from values.

Value judgments often assert themselves even in what should be purely "positive" discussions of the trade-off between inflation and unemployment. As I noted earlier, the Fed acted as if there was a high cost of inflation—when there was little evidence to support that belief in the low-inflation environment currently in the United States. While we explicitly recognized that there was considerable uncertainty surrounding the value of the NAIRU, I was always struck by how often at least their rhetoric, and sometimes their models, suggested it was at the high end of that range. Again, while there was no evidence of a precipice, and there was evidence that the costs of reversing inflation were not high, their rhetoric suggested otherwise. While in commenting on fiscal policy, on the revision of the cost of living index used for Social Security or taxes, they were willing to provide high estimates of the likely bias in the cost of living index, I never once heard them note the implications for US macropolicy—that the current rate of inflation was not 2.2 percent, but closer to 0.7 percent (using the midpoint of the bias estimate the Chairman of the Fed has frequently mentioned in public)—hardly a threat to the stability of the economy.

The fact that monetary policy involves trade-offs, that values affect not only the choices one makes, but even one's perceptions of magnitude of those trade-offs, has one clear implication in a democratic society. The way those decisions are made should be representative of the values of those that comprise society. At the very least, they should see as their objective the application of their expertise to reflect broader societal values. The central bank should not be seen as a mechanism for the imposition of the values of a subset of the population on the whole.

While values systematically skewed what was supposed to be expert judgment, there was scope for doing so because of the extraordinary difficulties encountered in the wise conduct of monetary policy. Because of the lack of up-to-date data, there is uncertainty about the state of the economy today, let alone about where the economy will be six months from now; and because of the lags in monetary policy—the fact that it takes six months or longer for the full effects of monetary policy to be felt—what one needs to know precisely is just that. The economy is always changing, and so historical data experiences may be of only limited relevance. Fortunately, financial crises like the meltdown of the savings and loan industry in the United States are relatively rare; the last banking crisis was more than a half century earlier. Not only had none of the members of the Board of Governors lived through that experience, but there had been so many changes in the economy in the intervening years that there were questions about its relevance. And economists are a contentious lot: even the experts cannot agree on the appropriate model of the economy, with fads and fashions changing with a frequency comparable to that of the business cycle. Just as monetarism, whose theoretical foundations had always been less than sound, became the flavor of the day, the constancy, and even predictability, of the velocity of money, the empirical regularity upon which it was based, disappeared. Worse still, the advice of two leading American schools of macroeconomics was hardly helpful to the conduct of monetary policy—real business cycle theory and the new classicals said that central banks should essentially just be shut down.

The Federal Reserve does seek advice from a wide set of sources; and even those from whom it does not seek advice offer up their opinions through a variety of media, from scholarly journals to the popular press. There was a group of economists who did recognize the special nature of the 1991 downturn, whose research had focused on the role of financial markets in economic fluctuations,

a group with a long ancestry, going back at least to Fisher's theory of debt defla-
tion.[22] This group saw a need for far stronger, and earlier, actions than those who
continued to subscribe to other traditions. The theoretical foundations had just
recently been bolstered by research on the economics of information, which had
provided insights into the rationale and nature of the resulting capital market
imperfections and their consequences for macroeconomic stability. The empirical
foundations for their positions had been bolstered by evidence showing the role of
credit and equity rationing in investment and consumption behavior. It was ironic
that one of the leading contributors to the empirical literature actually served during this period as vice-chair of the Federal Reserve Board, though his voice was
not reflected in the policies pursued.

Let me be clear: I think the Fed has done a good job managing monetary policy
over the last decade—perhaps not as good as it could have done, and perhaps
worse than it is often given credit for, but still a reasonably good job. In evaluating some of the exaggerated accounts which attempt to endow a single institution
with omnipotence and omniscience, we should remember several qualifications
I have discussed. Once account is taken of the increased ability of the economy
to operate at lower levels of unemployment without igniting rising inflation, the
1990–1991 recession was not the shallow downturn that is often portrayed, but
rather, the lost output was comparable to that of the average of the postwar
recessions. Also, the strong recovery beginning in 1992 could have been said to
have been in spite of the Fed, not because of the Fed. Furthermore, neither the
Administration nor the Fed should be given much of the credit for the changing
structure of the economy that allowed it to operate at such a low level of unemployment without a pickup of inflation. But these are minor qualifications and
pale in comparison to the monetarist policies of the early 1980s which led to high
real interest rates, contributing to the Latin American debt crisis, the lost decade
of development, and the financial debacles that plagued economies throughout
the globe. The cumulative loss of world output relative to its potential—and the
cumulative human suffering—was enormous.

As I said earlier, human fallibility is a fact of life, and even the best designed
institutions will make mistakes. The point of these remarks is not to say, "I told
you so," or to engage in what Americans call Monday-morning quarterbacking.
The point is that all too often the governance structure of central banks makes
these mistakes more likely, and more costly, than they need be. The most important function of the central bank is to make judgments about macroeconomic
policy, questions which deserve a nation's greatest talents; yet the Board typically does not have on its membership anyone who would rank in the top tier
of macroeconomists. There is a vicious cycle: The concentration of power in one
hand, in the chairman, makes appointments to the Fed less attractive to first-
rate economists—those that have come, have come out of real devotion to public
service—and the absence of first-rate economists provides the basis of enhanced
concentration of power in the Chair. (To be fair, the current Chairman deserves
high marks for his political skills in steering the Committee, some of whose members are quite hawkish, to policies which were as reasonable as they were.)

---

[22] In the Great Depression, falling prices combined with fixed interest payments reduced firms' net
cash flows, eroding net worth, and decreasing their investment and further weakening the economy.
As a result, these models are sometimes called debt-deflation models. Modern versions can be found
in Greenwald and Stiglitz (1990, 1993).

The Benefits of Central Bank Independence

Having said all of this, let me say there are good reasons for central bank independence. The conventional argument in favor of central bank independence is that independent central banks will not be tempted to try to enjoy the transitory benefits of lower unemployment at the expense of the permanent cost of higher inflation. There is the worry—and some evidence—that without an independent central bank, politicians may try to stimulate the economy before a recession, knowing that the price—higher inflation—will not be apparent until after the election.[23] Empirically, both the rate and the variance of inflation are lower in countries with independent central banks.[24]

To some degree, institutional changes may not be enough to buy low and stable inflation. Germany does not only have a highly independent central bank, but it also has a culture that is highly averse to inflation. This culture itself, and not the institutional arrangements, may in fact be sufficient to keep inflation down. The Indian Central Bank, for instance, has relatively little legal independence from the government but has consistently delivered low inflation in response to political pressure. In contrast, one transition economy has witnessed the spectacle of a highly independent central banker pushing inflation higher and higher while the government was, initially, unable to remove him.

Interestingly enough, however, the variance of output and employment is no lower in countries with independent central banks.[25] And, as we have seen, among countries with low or moderate rates of inflation, the level and rate of growth of productivity is no higher.

The degree of independence of the central bank also has important impacts on the relationship between key economic variables. An independent central bank, it is claimed, has more credibility; markets are convinced that it will be more committed to fighting inflation. According to new classical theories, this credibility should allow an independent central bank to deflate the economy relatively painlessly. Unfortunately, the evidence suggests just the opposite: economies with independent central banks have substantially higher sacrifice ratios than other countries, even after controlling for a variety of factors.[26] According to Laurence Ball's (1994) estimates of sacrifice ratios, Germany and the United States both need to sacrifice 2 or 3 percentage points of output for each percentage point reduction in inflation. In contrast, France and Japan both have sacrifice ratios on the order of 1 percent. One explanation is that the existence of a highly independent central bank changes the structure of the economy, including the degree of nominal rigidities, as participants come to have more confidence in the stability of prices. Monetary policy in Germany and the United States is more predictable than it is in France or Japan. Consequently, Germans and Americans are less prepared for the abrupt shift in policy that takes place during a disinflation. The higher sacrifice ratios have basically offset the advantages of lower variability in inflation, leading to little change in output variability.

---

[23] See Nordhaus (1975) for one of the original political business cycle studies. Alesina and Rosenthal (1995) is a good recent treatment.

[24] Alesina and Summers (1993).

[25] Ibid.

[26] Furman (1997).

Thus, the gains in economic performance in the dimensions where it really counts—the ability of the economy to live up to, and expand, its productive potential, is little affected by central bank independence. Indeed, the results that the variance of inflation has been reduced, but growth not enhanced, suggest that it is output variability, not price variability, which should be the focus of concern of macroeconomic policy.

Implications for the Design of Central Banks

What implications do these results have for the design of central banks in a democratic society? How independent should they be? What should be their governance structure?

We need to put this question in context. In a democratic society, we often have a desire to depoliticize important decisions, especially in the sphere of economics, and to draw upon expertise. An alcoholic may recognize his weaknesses, and turn over the key to the liquor cabinet to a friend, a form of pre-commitment. So too, we often make collective choices to bind ourselves away from temptation. In the United States, we have created independent regulatory agencies for securities regulation (the Securities and Exchange Commission), for banking regulation (the Controller of the Currency), for energy regulation (the Federal Energy Regulatory Commission), and for telecommunications (the Federal Communications Commission).

This binding cannot, however, fully bind. One of the important, and inherent, limitations on the government's power is that, while it can use its power to enforce private contracts, it cannot enforce its own commitments. It can, however, raise the transactions costs to changes in policies. The PAYGO rules adopted in the 1990 Budget Enforcement Act, for instance, increase the cost of proposing a tax cut by requiring it to be offset by equal or greater spending cuts. Changing the rule itself only requires a majority vote, but there appears to be great political cost associated with changing these rules which reflect a collective commitment to sound budgetary policy; and the rule itself makes it more costly to propose deficit-increasing legislative changes.

No central bank is fully independent. The legislation governing the Fed can be changed or its governors dismissed (a process that itself is very difficult and costly). Although these actions are undertaken rarely if ever, the existence of the threat forces the Fed to anticipate and to some degree act according to the views of elected officials. The Chairman of the Fed must report to the Banking Committees in both the Senate and the House. At various times, the powerful chairmen of these committees have exercised important influence on the Fed. The Fed, as a creation of government, is a political institution. Its most successful governors have recognized this and struck a balance, anticipating the political response to their actions and, to some degree, accommodating it. Paul Volcker, then Chairman of the Fed, testified before a Congressional committee that "the Congress created us and the Congress can uncreate us."[27] Arthur Burns, who served as Chairman of the Fed somewhat earlier, is quoted as saying that the Fed was perpetually "probing the limits of its freedom to undernourish . . . inflation."[28]

[27] Quoted in Orszag (1991) p. 1, citing Greider (1987).
[28] Quoted in Cukierman (1992), p. 162.

The nature of this delicate balance is manifested in numerous examples. The Fed, whose revenues essentially derive from the zero interest rate it pays on reserves, does not depend on Congress for its annual appropriations. It remits to the government the excess of revenues over what it spends. This might appear to give the Fed enormous discretion, yet the Fed realizes that its expenditures are very much in the public eye—a dollar wasted is a dollar less for the public treasury—and its rules are close to those of a purely public agency. Moreover, the salaries of Fed governors are linked to those of cabinet officers, creating the anomaly where some staff are paid more than the governors themselves.

A more important example is the result I discussed earlier—the probability of a recession ending is increasing in the duration of the recession. Under standard assumptions about rational expectations and serially independent stochastic processes, recessions should not die of old age. As the recession goes on, the pressure on the Fed builds and their objective function changes to emphasize unemployment more and inflation less.

Power, however, works both ways. The Fed has an enormous influence over short-term economic activity, and the threat of its exercise can provide an extra incentive for politicians—especially the President—to implement policies that are favored by the Fed. To be sure, the Fed would not use this threat in an extortionist manner. But the Administration could come to believe, for instance, that deficit reduction or capital gains tax cuts would allow the economy to have lower interest rates.

I think the United States has probably struck a good balance in the institutional arrangements governing the Fed. We have got relatively predictable monetary policy, relatively low inflation, and in the recent expansion the Fed has been flexible enough to tolerate the unemployment rate falling below what others might have allowed. More broadly, the success of this balance is manifested in the two results I showed earlier: expansions do not die of old age but recessions do.

But while in practice we seem to have struck a balance regarding the appropriate degree of independence, there are other aspects of governance in which questions may be raised.

Is the concentration of power in the hands of one person compatible with democratic values? Are there compelling arguments for the secret manner in which it operates that offset the presumption in favor of openness and transparency in a democratic society? The Fed itself has moved towards more openness in recent years. Should it go further?

Public accountability is achieved in part not by having decisions made directly by publicly elected officials, but by having them made by those appointed by elected officials. But in the case of monetary policy, many of the decisionmakers are neither appointed nor even confirmed by elected officials. Is this consistent with democratic values? Is this degree of removal from public accountability necessary for achieving the degree of independence that would be warranted by improved economic performance?

Have we marshaled the quality of expertise that the country could, and should, obtain? Recall, the results given earlier on the efficacy of monetary policy only say that there is no systematic component of fluctuations, for instance, no time dependence in economic downturns. It does not say that we have reduced the variability in output to as low a level as we might.

And most importantly, have we achieved the best balance between stabilization and fighting inflation? Again, our earlier results say nothing about where the balance was struck, which depends on the composition and beliefs of the Fed.

Our earlier discussions suggest strongly that, as presently constituted, there are important voices not being heard—voices I dare say that may represent a majority of Americans. These voices ought to have some say on how the intertemporal trade-offs that are central to monetary policy should be made. These voices could be represented, without compromising on the independence of the monetary authority, and indeed, these voices could be represented at the same time that the quality of expertise in the conduct of monetary policy is improved.

There is an old saying that "if it's not broken, don't fix it." Many people believe that our monetary institutions, if not perfect, have been doing a remarkably good job. There is a collective amnesia at work. We forget the criticism our monetary institutions are repeatedly subjected to when the economy goes into a downturn, or when it does not live up to its potential over protracted periods of time. On the contrary, one might argue that the time to improve our institutions is when they are not in crisis, when we can engage in thoughtful deliberations about what kind of society we are striving to create.

But many other societies do not have the leisure of these thoughtful deliberations. As political and economic arrangements change, as monetary unions get formed and dissolved, as economic and political crises necessitate the design of new institutional arrangements, countries will have to face these questions head on. They will have to ask, how much and what form of independence should the central bank have? The answers will depend on the situation and history. Those who have had recent bouts with high inflation are likely to be enticed into having central banks with a greater degree of independence, structured in ways that signal a greater commitment to fight inflation. Those with a more favorable recent history will have harder choices to make. They should not be misled by any myths of magical improvements in economic performance that this latest nostrum of those looking for simple solutions to the complex economic problems have provided. They should be concerned with the role democratic values should play in the making of macroeconomic decisions, which are, after all, among the most important of the collective decisions made by any society.

REFERENCES

Akerlof, G., W. Dickens, and G. Perry (1996), "The Macroeconomics of Low Inflation," *Brookings Papers on Economic Activity*, 1, pp. 1–76.

Alesina, A., and H. Rosenthal (1995), *Partisan Politics, Divided Government, and the Economy*, Cambridge University Press: Cambridge, England.

Alesina, A., and L. Summers (1993), "Central Bank Independence and Macroeconomic Performance: Some Comparative Evidence," *Journal of Money, Credit and Banking* 25(2), May.

Ball, L. (1994), "What Determines the Sacrifice Ratio," in: N. G. Mankiw (ed.), *Monetary Policy*, University of Chicago Press: Chicago.

Barro, R. (1997), *Determinants of Economic Growth*, MIT Press: Cambridge, MA.

Braun, S., and R. Chen (1996), "The NAIRU as a Policy Target: Refinements, Problems and Challenges," A Report by the Council of Economic Advisers to the OECD.

Cukierman, A. (1992), *Central Bank Strategy, Credibility, and Independence*, MIT Press: Cambridge, MA.

Diebold, F. and G. Rudebusch (1992), "Have Postwar Economic Fluctuations Been Stabilized?" *American Economic Review*, 82:4, pp. 993–1005.

Feldstein, M. (1996), "The Costs and Benefits of Going from Low Inflation to Price Stability," NBER Working Paper 5469, Cambridge, MA.

Fischer, S. (1993), "The Role of Macroeconomic Factors in Growth," *Journal of Monetary Economics*, 32, pp. 485–512.

Furman, J. (1997), "Central Bank Independence, Indexing, and the Macroeconomy," unpublished manuscript.

Greenspan, A. (1990), "Testimony of Alan Greenspan, Chairman Federal Reserve Board," July 18, 1990.

Greenspan, A. (1991), "Testimony of Alan Greenspan, Chairman Federal Reserve Board," February 20, 1991.

Greenspan, A. (1993), "Testimony of Alan Greenspan, Chairman Federal Reserve Board," February 19, 1993.

Greenwald, B., and J. E. Stiglitz (1990), "Macroeconomic Models with Equity and Credit Rationing," in: R. G. Hubbard (ed.), *Asymmetric Information, Corporate Finance, and Investments*, University of Chicago Press, pp. 15–42.

Greenwald, B., and J. E. Stiglitz (1993), "Financial Market Imperfections and Business Cycles," *Quarterly Journal of Economics*, 108, pp. 77–114.

Greider, W. (1987), *Secrets of the Temple: How the Federal Reserve Runs the Country*, Simon and Schuster: New York.

Nordhaus, W. (1975), "The Political Business Cycle," *Review of Economic Studies*, 42, pp. 169–190.

Orszag, P. (1991), *Congressional Oversight of the Federal Reserve: Empirical and Theoretical Perspectives*, Princeton University thesis.

Romer, C. (1986), "Is the Stabilization of the Postwar Economy a Figment of the Data?" *American Economic Review*, 76, pp. 314–334.

Sah, R., and J. E. Stiglitz (1986), "The Architecture of Economic Systems: Hierarchies and Polyarchies," *American Economic Review* 76(4), pp. 716–727.

Sah, R., and J. E. Stiglitz (1988), "Committees, Hierarchies and Polyarchies," *Economic Journal*, 98(391), pp. 451–470.

Stigler, G. (1971), "The Theory of Regulation," *Bell Journal of Economics*, pp. 3–21.

Stiglitz, J. E. (1986), "Pareto Efficient and Optimal Taxation and the New Welfare Economics," in: A. Auerbach and M. Feldstein (eds.), *Handbook of Public Economics*, Elsevier Science Publishers/North-Holland: Amsterdam, pp. 991–1042.

Stiglitz, J. E. (1997), "Reflections on the NAIRU Hypothesis," *Journal of Economic Perspectives*, 11(1), pp. 3–10.

Stiglitz, J. E. (1998), "Pareto Efficient Taxation and Expenditure Policies, with Applications to the Taxation of Capital, Public Investment, and Externalities," Paper presented to the *Festschrift* in honor of Agnar Sandmo.

Tinbergen, J. (1988), "Development Cooperation as a Learning Process," in G. Meier and D. Seers (eds.), *Pioneers in Development*, Oxford University Press: New York, pp. 315–331.

15

THE POLITICS OF BLAME AVOIDANCE
R. Kent Weaver[*]

Kent Weaver asks: When do politicians claim credit for a policy and when do they instead pass up any opportunity to claim credit? This question is particularly useful to think through in juxtaposition with the previous article's topic of central bank independence.

Central bank independence, to recall, is regularly justified by the claim that politicians would otherwise exploit monetary policy irresponsibly in order to further their reelection and their careers. They would maximize economic growth just before elections and then take credit for the growth, whatever the delayed costs in accelerating inflation.

Weaver's article suggests, however, that elected politicians may rationally prefer to leave monetary policy to experts in an insulated central bank. In suggesting that point (Weaver does not state it explicitly but the point is easily derived from what he writes), Weaver's insights about politicians' calculations toward policy actions and effects resolve an obvious mystery—one that may have already occurred to you. If monetary policy affects macroeconomic performance—which in turn strongly affects the electoral prospects of incumbent politicians—then how is it that central bank independence is ever sustained or even grows over time? By applying Weaver' analysis, one sees that central bank independence is not something that is jealously protected from irresponsible politicians. Instead, it most likely exists because elected politicians want it to exist.

Politicians' calculus with regard to whether, how, and how much to overtly advertise their causal roles in all types of public policies—and thereby advertise their roles in causing policy effects—is actually rather subtle and complex. Politicians may often prefer to delink themselves from policies and their effects. Weaver offers a simple and persuasive theory of the conditions under which politicians highlight their connections to policies and policy effects—and of the conditions under which politicians blur these connections or erase them altogether.

In reading Weaver, one comes to appreciate a central truth about American governance and public policy, which are both systematically shaped by elected politicians' strategic management of the extent to which voters can cognitively connect policy effects to the policy actions of politicians. Such

Journal of Public Policy 6 (July–September 1986): 371–398. Copyright © 1987 Cambridge University Press. Reprinted with permission.

*The author would like to thank John Chubb, Martha Derthick, Robert A. Katzmann, Samuel Kernell, Paul Peterson, Steven S. Smith, Alice Keek Whitfield and Joseph White for comments on earlier drafts of this manuscript. Research support for this study was provided by the Lynde and Harry Bradley Foundation. Additional support for the larger project of which this study is a part was provided by the German Marshall Fund of the United States and by an anonymous foundation.

anticipation of voters' responses is undoubtedly at work, as well, in state and local governance and public policy.

Note that this perspective on public policy provides further insight into what Rosenberg had to say earlier about the Supreme Court's political independence. Politicians may want the Supreme Court to handle certain highly controversial and difficult issues rather than bring those issues into the national legislative-executive process. A clear example is abortion politics.

• • •

Every time I fill an office, I create a hundred malcontents and one ingrate.
—*Louis XIV*

ONE OF THE MOST IMPORTANT and least studied trends in modern government is the move toward increased "automaticity"—i.e., self-limitation of discretion by policymakers. Examples of this process are manifold. Discretion over benefit levels in many income transfer programs has been replaced by automatic adjustments for inflation (indexation). Civil service mechanisms have replaced patronage appointments as the major means of filling bureaucratic posts in most industrialized countries. Formula grants have replaced discretionary grants in transfers from central to local governments. More recently, automatic mechanisms have even been employed in budget-making, most notably in the Gramm-Rudman-Hollings budget cutting initiative in the United States.

The growth of discretion-limiting devices in government calls into serious question much of the accepted thinking about the way public policy is made. Policymakers are usually seen as seeking through their activities and votes to "claim credit" with constituents and clientele groups for actions taken in their interests (Fiorina, 1977).

While credit-claiming is certainly a major component of policymakers' motivations, it is not the only one.[1] Policymakers may also have *non-electoral* motivations such as vote-trading. In countries with a relatively weak system of legislative party discipline, individual legislators may exchange votes on issues of low salience to themselves and their constituents for other legislators' votes on seemingly unrelated issues. Policymakers may also have "good" policy motivations—i.e., they may act because they think an action is worthwhile even if it has no political payoff. And they may be guided by power considerations within their respective institutions—e.g., their party caucus, legislative chamber or committee, or agency (Fenno, 1973).

A second electoral motivation must also be considered, however. Policymakers are often placed in situations in which the opportunities to claim credit that discretion affords are simply not worth the associated political costs. As Louis XIV

---

[1] David Mayhew (1974: 52–61) argues that credit-claiming is not a strategy that legislators can engage in on all issues: the claim must be credible. This is possible only if (1) legislators can show that they were "prime movers" in the adoption of a measure—e.g., a sponsor or member of the legislative committee with jurisdiction over the issue, or (2) the benefits are particularistic, handed out in an ad hoc fashion, with the legislator playing a role in their distribution. He contrasts this with "position-taking'—issuing a public judgement on an issue, most notably through roll-call votes. The term "credit-claiming" is used here in a broader sense than in Mayhew's book, to include position-taking when it is done in the expectation of political gain rather than to avoid political losses.

discovered in a non-electoral context, even choices that appear to offer substantial opportunities for credit-claiming can also create ill will from constituencies who feel themselves relatively or absolutely worse off as a result of a decision. Politicians must, therefore, be at least as interested in *avoiding blame* for (perceived or real) losses that they either imposed or acquiesced in as they are in "claiming credit" for benefits they have granted.

Credit claiming, "good policy" and blame-avoiding motivations all can influence policy decisions. But do they lead to differences in behavior? And which motivation is likely to dominate when they come into conflict? It will be argued here that blame avoidance leads to patterns of behavior very different from those suggested by the other motivations. Furthermore, when push comes to shove, most officeholders seek above all not to maximize the credit they receive but to minimize blame. In formal terms, they are not credit-claiming maximizers but blame minimizers and credit-claiming and "good policy" satisficers.

This essay sketches out a theory of policy motivations, giving particular attention to blame-avoiding. Specifically, it addresses: (1) how blame avoidance differs from and interacts with the credit-claiming and "good policy" motivations; (2) the situations in which blame-avoiding is most likely to occur; (3) the forces that have led to an increase in the relative importance of blame avoidance in recent years; (4) specific strategies that flow from blame-avoiding; (5) differences in the way that blame avoidance is manifested in the United States and in parliamentary systems; and (6) the consequences of blame avoidance for policy outputs and outcomes.

BLAME-AVOIDING AS A POLICY MOTIVATION

This study will assume that most policymakers are motivated in large part by their desire to maximize their prospects for reelection (or reappointment) and advancement. It will, therefore, give primary attention to electoral motivations. But how can decisionmakers arrange their calculus to enhance their prospects of staying in office? As a starting point, we would expect decisionmakers to attempt to maximize gains realized by their constituents while minimizing losses—i.e., to take actions for which they can maximize credit and minimize blame.

This is not a simple calculation, however. Constituency costs and benefits do not translate directly into political gains and losses for officeholders. Constituents are much less likely to notice widely diffused costs or benefits than those that are relatively concentrated in a smaller group of the constituency; the former will probably be heavily discounted. And groups of constituents that are poorly organized and have few political resources are again likely to have policy effects relating to them heavily discounted.[2]

Taking these caveats into consideration, it might be argued that a policymaker will, given a range of policy alternatives, choose and strongly support the one that maximizes net constituency benefits (i.e., the surplus of concentrated benefits over concentrated costs) to his or her constituency. But even this formulation is still too simplistic. Pursuit of a constituency-benefit maximizing, credit claiming strategy is rational only if constituents respond symmetrically to gains and losses—for

---

[2] Constituency costs and benefits are rarely weighed equally by politicians for a third reason, even if they are equally concentrated. If either costs or benefits fall disproportionately on a group that is unlikely to vote for the officeholder in any case, they will be discounted heavily; the same is true for groups that are unlikely to be shaken from support for the officeholder.

example, if a dollar of income gained by one set of constituents as a result of a policymaker's actions wins as much support as a dollar lost to another group costs. But there is substantial evidence that this is not so (Kahneman and Tversky, 1984). Persons who have suffered losses are more likely to notice the loss, to feel aggrieved and to act on that grievance, than gainers are to act on the basis of their improved state.

In short, voters are more sensitive to what has been done *to* them than to what has been done *for* them.[3] Thus the concentrated losses to constituents need not outweigh benefits for a policymaker to have strong blame-avoiding incentives; it is enough that those costs are substantial. When this situation arises, policymakers will probably attempt not to maximize credit-claiming net benefits but to minimize blame-generating losses.

Much evidence suggests that constituencies are more sensitive to losses than to gains. Using aggregate time-series data for the United States, Bloom and Price (1975, p. 1244) found that members of the incumbent President's party are likely to lose seats in Congress during recession, but an economic upturn does not have an equal reciprocal effect. They conclude that "in bad times the economy becomes a salient issue, whereas in good times it diminishes in importance relative to other determinants of voting behavior."[4] Using individual-level data, Samuel Kernell (1977) found that in midterm Congressional elections, independent voters who disapprove of the President's performance are more likely to vote, and to vote against the President's party, than those who approve of his performance; party identifiers in the President's party who disapprove of the President's performance are more likely to defect to vote against that party than members of the other party who approve of his performance are to defect to support his party.

Disproportionate attention by constituents to questions on which they disagree with policymakers may occur on a variety of other fronts. Gerald Wright (1977) found that Republican supporters of President Nixon on the House Judiciary Committee that considered his impeachment received considerably fewer votes in the 1974 election than would otherwise have been anticipated; Nixon's critics on the Committee did not receive a bonus, however.

The classic case of negativity bias on non-economic issues concerns gun control: opponents of stricter gun control are highly mobilized (primarily by the National Rifle Association), and because many of them view a legislator's opposition to gun control as a vote-determining issue, they are able to exert electoral influence disproportionate to their numbers. Similarly, opponents of abortion or supporters of the proposed Equal Rights amendment to the US constitution might be more likely to see their legislator's position on that issue as a salient, vote-determining issue if it disagrees with their own position than if it is consistent.

Interest groups have also discovered that they can use negativity biases as a tool in fund-raising for specific causes and candidates. By centering their appeal around the danger posed by a specific "devil-figure" (e.g., Jesse Helms or Jane

---

[3] For a discussion of why voters are likely to give a higher weight to negative than to positive information, see Lau (1985) and Fiorina and Shepsle (1986).

[4] Using both aggregate and individual level data, Hibbing and Alford found that the effects of retrospective economic voting in House elections are limited to races in which an incumbent of the President's party is running. Tufte (1978: 126) has disputed the absence of positive electoral effects of an economic upturn, at least for years of very good economic performance. Tufte also notes that party identification affects how individuals perceive changes in their family's financial situation (p. 130).

TABLE 1
Attitudinal Manifestations of Policymakers' Motivations

Dimension:	Good Policy	Credit-Claiming	Blame-Avoiding
Attitude toward costs and benefits:	Maximize net benefits to society	Maximize surplus of concentrated (claimable) constituency benefits over losses	Minimize concentrated losses, even when it means sacrificing greater benefits
Attitude toward discretion:	Indifferent or opposed	Favorable	Suspicious
Attitude toward policy leadership:	Indifferent	Favorable	Suspicious

Fonda) or by raising the spectre of specific losses to the recipient (e.g., of Social Security benefits) they can focus blame while providing an immediate outlet—sending funds—for that blame.

Discounting by politicians of constituency gains (or positive evaluations) relative to losses (or negative evaluations) thus seems quite appropriate. While politicians always have incentives to avoid blame for constituency losses, discounting magnifies and sharpens these effects. Response to blame-avoiding incentives can lead to distinctive patterns of behavior by policymakers on at least three dimensions (Table 1). With respect to choices among policy options that offer differing combinations of social and political benefits, we would expect that policymakers motivated by "good policy" reasoning would seek to maximize net social welfare, although they might disagree as to the exact meaning of that term. Credit-claiming decisionmakers, on the other hand, would focus on political impacts, and hence on the balance between concentrated gains and losses for groups relevant to them. Blame avoiders, finally, would also focus on political consequences, but they would tend to discount potential gains relative to losses in their calculus, and thus to minimize blame before being concerned with building political credit.

The three policy motivations also suggest differing behaviors with respect toward exercising policy leadership and policy discretion. A "good policy" orientation would suggest indifference toward exercising policy leadership, because it is the substantive outcome rather than the political credit or blame that is associated with it that is valued. The same logic is true of maintaining policy discretion—indeed, policymakers may oppose discretion by themselves or others if they believe that it will lead to irresponsible policy choices. Credit-claimers, on the other hand, will seek to exercise policy leadership and maintain discretion because it allows them to make more credible claims for credit from their constituents. Blame-avoiders will be suspicious of exercising both discretion over policy and policy leadership, because these "opportunities" may generate substantial blame as well as credit.

Blame avoidance can be manifested in several ways. Legislators, for example, may try to avoid having to make politically costly decisions or take clear policy positions at all. Failing that, they may vote in favor of legislation about which they have substantial doubts because it would be difficult to explain a contrary vote to their constituents. Or they may cede discretion to the president or an independent agency for making politically costly decisions.

Legislators do not have a monopoly on blame-avoiding, however. This behavior can be found among politicians of all types. Presidential candidates, for example, tend to be more ambiguous on issues where there is a substantial divergence of opinion, presumably because they are more concerned about potential blame from those who might oppose any specific position than they are enticed by potential credit from those who agree with the position (Campbell, 1983; Shepsle, 1972; Page, 1976).

President Reagan's behavior toward Social Security through most of his tenure in office has been a classic example of blame-avoiding. In his first year of office, the administration floated a proposal for drastically cutting Social Security cost-of-living allowances (COLAs) for early retirees and delaying them for all recipients. When the plan was criticized, the President disassociated himself from it—i.e., he sought to avoid blame (Stockman, 1986: 187–192). At the beginning of his second term, Reagan said that he would accept cuts in those COLAs only if they were supported by an overwhelming bipartisan majority in Congress—that is, if others took most of the blame.

Blame avoidance does not always lead to ambiguity and inaction, however. If a president (or any other policymaker) is highly dependent upon a constituency that has come to expect change, he may feel compelled to go along. President Johnson's reasoning for his support of the Civil Rights Act of 1964, for example, had a distinctly blame-avoiding tone:

> I knew that if I didn't get out in front of this issue . . . they [the liberals] would get me. They'd throw my background against me, they'd use it to prove that I was incapable of bringing unity to the land I have loved so much. . . . I couldn't let that happen. I had to produce a civil rights bill that was even stronger than the one they'd have gotten if Kennedy had lived. Without this, I'd be dead before I could even begin. (quoted in Whalen and Whalen, 1985: 239)

Political appointees and bureaucrats in government agencies also seek to avoid blame. The Food and Drug Administration, for example, is often argued to have been overly restrictive in letting new drugs onto the market—prohibiting the use of drugs that would create some costs but greater gains—because of the huge blame-generating potential of another thalidomide case.

Blame avoiding has a different dynamic in the US judiciary because federal judges have lifetime tenure (except in extremely rare cases of impeachment). Thus while they might not like to be blamed for unpopular decisions, they can withstand blame better than legislators and elective and appointed officials in the executive branch. It was the desire to free judges, and judicial decisions, from such fears that led to their being given a constitutional guarantee of lifetime tenure in the first place. Although having decisions overturned by a higher court is an embarrassment most judges would prefer to avoid, it does not threaten a federal judge with unemployment. (Many state and municipal judges do not have this protection, however.) One reason that the federal courts have been able to play an activist policymaking role in the United States over the past thirty years is this greater ability to withstand blame. The judiciary has stood firm in such areas as school prayer and abortion where legislators, subject to extreme blame-avoiding pressures, have attempted to reverse them.

Blame-avoiding motives do not always pose clear conflicts with the other motivations, however. Blame avoidance can also shape the way policymakers attempt to achieve their other objectives. For example, in the early 1970s, Republican lawmakers confronted Democratic initiatives in Congress to raise the real as well as nominal benefit levels for Social Security through ad hoc increases. These fiscal conservatives felt that the benefit changes were not good policy, but they found a vote against them very difficult to explain to their constituents. In an era when reliance on ad hoc changes was perceived as leading to higher real benefits, indexation seemed to offer a way to make a benefit freeze politically palatable—i.e., it reconciled their "good policy" objectives with blame-avoiding ones.

SOURCES OF BLAME-AVOIDING BEHAVIOR

The claim here is not that all politicians and bureaucrats—or even most of them—are pure blame avoiders all of the time. Politicians in equivalent situations may vary in their aversion to risk, and hence in their willingness to be perceived as imposing or acquiescing in losses rather than minimizing or disguising them. Indeed, politicians may, when placed in difficult blame-avoiding situations, simply refuse to pursue strategies consistent with that situation: John Kennedy's *Profiles in Courage* is a chronicle of individuals who pursued their own views of "good policy" when placed in blame-avoiding situations. But for every Edmund G. Ross and Thomas Hart Benton in office who eschews blame-avoiding, there are probably many more J. W. Fulbrights who vote against civil rights legislation and Frank Churches who vote against gun control—if for no other reason than that the latter are likely to stay in office longer.

Socialist parties in many countries face a similar dilemma: should they sacrifice their ideological purity (e.g., by watering down or dropping proposals for nationalization) in order to build political bridges with the middle class? An approach which maximizes political credit with party activists is likely to lead to permanent opposition status or (if the party has won office already) to a loss of power.

The justification given by blame-avoiders is simple: they cannot pursue their other policy objectives if they are not re-elected, and they will not be re-elected if they do not suppress their own views of "good policy" when these views clash with the strongly held opinions of their constituents. Indeed, it might be said that over the long term, *blame avoiding behavior in situations that mandate such behavior is a precondition for pursuing other policy motivations in situations that do not compel that behavior.* Those who fail to avoid blame are likely to find themselves unemployed. Even if voters' judgements are only partially based on a desire to punish behavior or views of which they disapprove, politicians still have strong incentives to minimize potential blame, because (1) they cannot be certain which issues might be picked up by future opponents and used against them, and (2) only some, not all, voters need to pursue retribution as a voting objective for a politician's office to be in danger (Fenno, 1978: 141–143).

The number of parties or candidates competing for votes (which itself reflects the entry barriers posed by electoral laws) may influence whether a party stresses credit-claiming or blame avoiding in its electoral appeals. In a two-party system like the United States, the best strategy is probably to take ambiguous stands and duck divisive issues (i.e., to minimize blame) to avoid offending marginal voters. In a multi-party system, on the other hand, some parties may be better off by tak-

TABLE 2
Cost-Benefit Distributions and Policymakers' Motivations

		Perceived net benefits to constituency of policy choice:	
		High	Low
Perceived net costs to constituency of policy choice:	High	(1) Blame Avoiding	(2) Credit-Claiming
	Low	(3) Credit Claiming	(4) Non-electoral motivations (e.g., good policy or vote-trading)

ing pointed, controversial positions (credit-claiming) in order to build a distinctive political base and avoid becoming lost in a crowded field.

Whether credit-claiming, blame avoiding or non-electoral motivations dominate policymakers' decision-making in a particular policy arena will depend in large part on two factors: (1) how constituent costs and benefits are distributed;[5] and (2) how constituency costs and benefits are translated into political gains and losses.

Blame-Generating Situations: Whereas the absence of concentrated constituency losses may make blame-avoiding motivations irrelevant, at least four situations may lead to blame-avoiding behavior (Table 2). The first is when there is a zero-sum conflict among the policymakers' constituents. Table 2 outlines this situation in its simplest form: a choice between a single alternative policy and the status quo. When concentrated benefits of the alternative policy are high, and costs are low or relatively diffuse, the policymaker can claim credit with constituents for making that choice, as shown in Cell 3.[6] The distribution of "pork barrel projects" such as dams and harbor projects, for example, is virtually pure political "profit," for projects are quite visible and costs are broadly spread. Political analyses that focus on credit claiming have generally examined these "loss-free" activities, and some analysts have even claimed that policymakers skew their own, and government's activities so as to maximize credit-claiming opportunities (Fiorina, 1977: 46).

Politicians can also claim credit when benefits of the alternative are low and costs are high: for example, if a federal facility in a legislator's district is threatened with closure (Cell 2). In this situation, the decisionmaker receives credit for opposing its adoption. (Even here a credit-claiming approach is not without risks, however. If leading the opposition to a measure has little prospect of success, and the policymaker feels that he or she is likely to be blamed for failure in spite of having tried, it might be more fruitful to portray him or herself as powerless to influence the decision—i.e., to "pass the buck" on responsibility to others.)

When both costs and benefits are low, the legislator will be relatively unconstrained, and he or she can act according to non-electoral (e.g., "good policy" or vote-trading) motivations (Cell 4).

[5] Constituents will be used here in a broader sense than simply voters in a legislator's district. It includes potential campaign contributors and elites in interest groups with links to the legislator's electoral constituents as well.

[6] This choice, as well as a vote for the status quo in Cell 2, can also be seen as extreme cases of a blame-avoiding situation: the costs of a contrary vote are so overwhelmingly negative that this option is not even considered. But the more parsimonious explanation is obviously to focus directly on credit-claiming.

Clearly a policymaker's most difficult choice is in Cell 1, where bringing benefits for one part of his or her constituency requires imposing costs on another segment. In this situation the decisionmaker has two options. He or she can attempt to calculate the strength of the impacts and the power of the groups involved, and then back the side that promises the higher political returns, claiming credit for having done so. But this credit-claiming response risks offending the losers, who are more likely to remember that loss and punish him or her for it. So long as the losses (and thus potential blame) are not drastically outweighed by other groups' gains, we would expect policymakers to focus on gaining credit only after attempting to minimize losses—and therefore blame.

A second situation leading to blame avoidance arises when all possible alternatives have strong negative consequences for at least some of the policymakers' constituents. This is a negative-sum game. Here there is no credit to be obtained. Policymakers can only hope to limit their exposure to blame. This form of blame avoidance is particularly likely to arise when government is allocating budgetary cutbacks.

A third blame-generating situation occurs when constituency opinion is overwhelmingly on a single side of an issue. When consensus is so pervasive, there is little credit to be derived from agreement with it—conformity is simply expected. But if a candidate can show that his or her opponent has violated the consensual norm—e.g., is or was a Communist, a drug user or a spouse or child abuser—it can be very damaging indeed. Other forms of personal scandal, such as paternity of an illegitimate child or receipt of bribes, may also lead to an earlier-than-planned exit from the political scene. These can be termed "consensus-violating" situations. A legislator's attendance at roll call votes is a classic example of this type of blame-generating situation: it provides virtually no credit-claiming opportunities (because voters assume that representatives should be present for all votes), but legislators with poor attendance records have had that fact used against them very effectively in the United States.

A fourth situation in which blame-avoiding behavior is likely to occur is when the personal or policy interests of the policymaker and clientele are opposed. Congressional pay raises are perhaps the classic instance of such a conflict. There could hardly be a clearer opportunity for "capture" of a decision-making process by an organized group. But there is little political credit to be gained for legislators who favor pay increases and much blame. Indeed, without the concept of blame avoidance it would be difficult to understand why legislators do not vote themselves huge salaries—it is certainly in their economic interest to do so. Legislators are very concerned about incurring political blame, however. It is for this reason that legislators sought to keep the pay raise issue off their agenda by providing for an automatic process of increases. When this proved impossible to implement, legislators were once again forced to vote down pay raises.

Attributing Blame: The argument for a negativity bias in voting behavior assumes that at least some voters base their voting decisions largely on retrospective considerations (i.e., on officeholders' past records) rather than on prospective considerations (expectations of their future performance) or on other factors such as candidate personality or party identification (Fiorina, 1981; Key, 1966). To the extent that voters make choices on grounds other than retrospective ones, politicians have more autonomy—and less need to blame-avoid—in their own choices.

Policymakers may escape blame and obtain autonomy even where there are real or potential constituency losses. Richard Fenno has shown that legislators in the

US work to develop enough trust on the part of their constituents that they will have "leeway" to vote their conscience on some issues (Fenno, 1978: chapter 5). Legislators from relatively safe districts—whether as a result of their own leeway-building efforts, absence of party competition, or some other factor—presumably do not need to be as concerned with avoiding blame as those with only a marginal hold on office. Any leeway that is achieved is rarely complete, however. There is evidence that US senators seeking re-election moderate their voting decisions as an election approaches, presumably because they believe that their constituents are more likely to remember and punish "deviant" votes than older ones. The pattern is just the opposite among legislators not seeking re-election: in this group, Republicans tend to become more conservative and Democrats more liberal between the fifth and sixth years of their terms (Thomas, 1985).

Voters may also err in attributing blame. On the one hand, they may fail to link policymakers to choices they have in fact made or outcomes to which they have contributed. On the other hand, they may attribute a linkage where the policymaker's influence was really weak or nonexistent. Perhaps the most durable case of over-attribution was the American electorate's blaming the Hoover administration and the Republican party for the onset of the Great Depression—an image which helped the Democrats for decades.

Generating and Avoiding Blame: Policymakers' motivations are not determined entirely by the distribution of costs and benefits among their constituents. They are also determined by the way choices are structured (Riker, 1986). If, for example, alternatives which place policymakers' and constituents' interests in direct conflict can be kept off the agenda, policymakers may be able to reduce blame-avoiding behavior.

On the other hand, the importance of blame-avoiding motivations among policymakers can provide an important boost to those with opposing views. The motives of those opponents may be based on their own notions of good policy or desire to claim credit with their own political constituencies rather than upon blame avoidance. Nor is it necessary that a majority of policymakers (legislators, for example) have strong blame-avoiding motivations for there to be a substantial impact on public policy: it is enough that blame-avoiders hold the balance of power in decision-making. If sponsors of "hard to vote against" legislation such as Congressional pay freezes and Social Security benefit increases can force the issue onto the agenda and shape it in such a way that it activates blame-generating pressures, they can use others' fears of electoral retribution to force blame-avoiders to support their own proposals.

Thus the shaping of alternatives and agendas is an important determinant of which motivations dominate in specific choice situations. And by shaping motivations, political combatants can also affect policy outcomes. In the battle over the 1981 budget reconciliation bill in the House of Representatives, for example, both sides sought to shape the vote in ways that would limit blame for a vote cast on their side, while maximizing the blame-generating potential of a vote for the opposition. The Democrats sought (and the Rules Committee approved) a rule that would have forced separate votes on five sections of the bill. The result was, as David Stockman put it, that "Republicans—and Boll Weevils—were going to be forced to vote against food stamps and Medicaid and Social Security, out loud and one at a time" (Stockman, 1986: 218). The administration and House Republicans, on the other hand, sought a single up-or-down vote on the entire package. This proposal would disguise votes to cut individual programs. It thus maximized the prospects of winning blame-motivated support from wavering Democrats who, in Stockman's words, "weren't even remotely genuine fiscal conservatives . . . [but rather] simply muddle-minded pols who had been scared by the President's popularity in their home districts" (Stockman, 1986: 207). A closed rule was adopted in a House floor vote, ensuring passage of the administration-backed package.

FORCES INCREASING BLAME-AVOIDING BEHAVIOR

Blame-avoiding is by no means a new phenomenon in policymaking. But a number of changes in American society—notably in the economy and fiscal climate, in the way political campaigns are run, and in the way Congress operates—have increased incentives to engage in blame-avoiding behavior.

Fiscal stress has given politics an increasingly zero-sum cast. Programs are forced to compete in the political market-place for funds. Budget deficits have also increased the involvement of budget guardians (notably the Office of Management and Budget and congressional Budget committees) in public policymaking. These developments have undercut the ability of clientele and policy specialists to keep decision-making within a narrow (and favorable) policy subsystem, and have forced politicians to engage in more loss-allocating activities.

Incentives for blame avoidance have also increased in recent years by the decline of party as a determinant of electoral behavior. Incumbent legislators have responded to party decline "[b]y developing a reputation with a minimal amount of partisan or ideological content . . . induc[ing] constituents to evaluate them separately from the state of the nation and the performance of parties and administrations" (Ferejohn and Fiorina, 1985: 94–95). In this situation, voters are likely to continue returning the incumbent *unless they are given a reason not to*. Legislators know it, and their potential opponents know it. Thus legislators must be concerned primarily with avoiding giving their opponents a popular election issue. But challengers have been given new tools as well. In particular, the ability of television advertising to present quick, simple negative images in voters' minds can undermine confidence in the incumbent, reinforcing legislators' reluctance to vote against positions likely to appeal to poorly informed constituencies.

Political and policy changes have also stimulated blame-generating behavior within Congress. Legislators are no longer dependent on their party's apparatus to win the party nomination, or on party funds or party image to win the general election. As a result of the decline of norms of apprenticeship and the growth of formula funding for federal grant programs, junior members are no longer dependent on the largesse of more senior members to win benefits for their districts. In this environment, members are less likely to forgo credit-claiming opportunities that require them to force blame-generating choices on their colleagues. If their colleagues do not like to take an open stand on such classic blame-generating issues as congressional pay raises, federal funding of abortions and a balanced budget amendment to the constitution, that is just too bad.

Interest groups are also getting more sophisticated at generating blame. The Americans for Tax Reform coalition, for example, has attempted to persuade all House and Senate candidates to pledge that they will not raise taxes above levels in the 1986 tax bill. The idea is to raise the salience of the issue and to force legislators to make binding commitments which they otherwise would not make—and will not be able to break without incurring charges of bad faith. Other groups have published "Dirty Dozen" lists (i.e., lists of the dozen legislators with the worst voting records on a particular issue, such as environmental protection) as a means of focusing blame on legislators whom they hope to defeat or whose behavior they hope to modify.

At the same time, a series of Congressional reforms have undercut the ability of legislative specialists to control the legislative agenda. Rules changes enacted in 1970 made it easier for House members to gain floor consideration of amendments. Thus issues like indexation, which might not have reached the floor in prior years because they did not fit the "credit-claiming" interests of the specialists, are reaching the floor. And once non-specialist legislators are forced to take a position on indexation, they find it very difficult to vote no, even if they might prefer to do so. The institution of recorded teller votes in the House of Representatives in 1970 (followed by electronic voting in 1973) dramatically increased the number of issues on which Representatives were forced to take recorded positions, further intensifying the pressures for "blame avoiding" behavior (Oleszek, 1984: 140–142). And because legislators often know little about the precise amendment they are voting on, and cannot predict which issues may be raised and cast in a blame-generating light by a challenger in a future election, they search for politically safe solutions.

Policymakers have not been indifferent to these increasing blame-avoiding forces, however. In the past few Congresses, the House of Representatives has made increasing use of restrictive rules that limit the introduction of "hard to vote against" amendments.

The House has also responded to another consequence of increased roll-call voting—namely, increased pressures to be present for many votes—in a blame-avoiding fashion. The House leadership responded to the universal collective blame-avoiding interest of its peers by scheduling most roll-call votes on Tuesdays through Thursdays, lessening pressures to be in Washington and freeing members' schedules both for committee work and time in their home districts.

BLAME-AVOIDING STRATEGIES

Policymakers can respond to potential blame-generating pressures in several ways. They can, first of all, attempt to prevent a blame-generating situation from arising in the first place. If that fails, they can attempt to deflect blame to others or at least diffuse it broadly. At least eight specific strategies can be identified as flowing from these blame-avoiding motives. (Table 3)[7]

1. Limit the Agenda: The best way for policymakers to keep a blame-generating issue from hurting them politically is to keep it off the agenda in the first place. The successful Republican effort to prevent separate votes on a series of specific program cuts in the 1981 budget reconciliation bill is a good example.

If legislators engage in blame-avoiding behavior only because they have to, why don't they simply band together to make it unnecessary by keeping all blame-generating choices off the agenda? In many cases they do. American political institutions have been shaped to a very substantial degree by policymakers' attempts to limit their need to blame-avoid. The long-time closed rule in the House of Representatives for Ways and Means Committee legislation restrained the enthusiasm

---

[7] This list is not intended to be exhaustive. It is limited, for example, to strategies that are likely to affect future policy choices. It thus excludes strategies that are limited to deflecting blame for past policy choices, but are unlikely to affect future ones.

TABLE 3
Eight Blame-Avoiding Strategies

Strategy:	Approach to Avoiding Blame:	Blame-generating situations where most likely to occur:
1. Agenda limitation	Prevent blame-generating by keeping potentially costly choices from being considered	Policymaker-constituency conflict
2. Redefine the Issue	Prevent blame-generating by developing new policy options which diffuse or obfuscate losses	Any
3. Throw Good Money After Bad	Prevent or delay blame generating by providing resources to prevent constituencies from suffering losses	Zero-sum or negative-sum game
4. Pass the Buck	Deflect blame by forcing others to make politically costly choices	Zero- or negative-sum game
5. Find a Scapegoat	Deflect blame by blaming others	Zero- or negative-sum game
6. Jump on the Bandwagon	Deflect blame by supporting politically popular alternative	Policymaker-constituency conflict
7. Circle the Wagons	Diffuse blame by spreading it among as many policymakers as possible	Negative-sum game
8. "Stop Me Before I Kill Again'	Prevent blame-generation by keeping credit-claiming opportunities that conflict with policy preferences from being considered	Policymaker-constituency conflict

of non-Committee members for proposing budget-busting tax breaks for specific constituencies. Equally important from the Committee's perspective, this agenda limitation allowed Ways and Means members to perform their role of budget guardian for the institution without having to oppose those amendments on the floor—i.e., it prevented a blame-avoiding situation from arising.

Legislators cannot always cooperate to make blame-avoiding behavior unnecessary, however. There are several reasons why. The most important is that some issues pit the blame-avoiding interests of one group of legislators against the credit-claiming and policy interests of others. If some legislators would prefer not to vote on Congressional pay or on granting a Social Security COLA increase, others see this as an opportunity to lead the fight for those issues. The latter group will seek to force these issues onto the agenda, and the institutional changes that have occurred in Congress since 1970 have reinforced their ability to do so. Thus credit-claiming and blame-avoiding behavior may occur together, but in opposing groups: credit-claiming activity forces proposals onto the agenda, and blame-avoiding reactions lead to their adoption.

Even if blame-generating decisions cannot be kept off the agenda completely, policymakers can often at least influence when they must confront them. Thus controversial issues may, for example, be delegated to study commissions with instructions to report just after the election. The issue may thus be removed from the agenda until that time.

Once an issue has made it on to the agenda, blame avoidance suggests several alternative strategies:

2. *Redefine the Issue*: If policymakers cannot keep a blame-generating issue off the agenda, they may be able to reshape it in such a way as to prevent blame. If an issue divides two industries for example, policies may be devised so that each industry obtains satisfactory outcomes, while costs are spread more broadly.

Blame avoidance is oftentimes not an all or nothing matter, moreover. In Congressional roll calls, legislators are of course forced to make simple yes or no decisions. But even in this arena, legislators often provide themselves with a series of votes to soften (or obfuscate) their position on controversial issues.

3. *Throw Good Money After Bad*: Sometimes policymakers know that they will be forced to acquiesce in blame-generating losses eventually. This is most likely to occur in negative-sum games (when all possible outcomes involve losses) or when policies have clearly failed. In these cases, decisionmakers cannot keep the issue off the agenda and they may not be able to diffuse the losses enough that their political impact is small. But they may be able to delay those outcomes by committing extra resources to shore up the status quo. In Indochina, for example, US policymakers were guided in large part by the rule, "Do not lose the rest of Vietnam to Communist control before the next election" (Ellsberg, 1971: 252). Despite pessimism that the war could be won, policymakers did not wish to be branded as having "lost" a country. On a very different political issue, disposal of wastes from nuclear power plants, a similar pattern can be seen. Wastes continue to be stored at power plant sites because of prolonged wrangling over a permanent disposal site. A first site for a repository is unlikely to be named until 1990 or open before 1998–16 years after passage of the act that set up a selection process.

4. *Pass the Buck*: If a blame-generating decision has to be made, policymakers are likely to try to delegate that decision to someone else (Fiorina, 1982). Congress repeatedly passes protectionist trade legislation, relying on the President to veto that legislation and incur the wrath of affected industries. Decisions on siting of nuclear waste repository facilities are another eminently unpleasant activity that Congress has dumped in the President's lap. Independent regulatory commissions are delegated responsibility for many of the most sensitive economic conflicts that pit one firm or industry's interests directly against others (e.g., mergers, rate-making).

Automatic government is a more recent, and increasingly important, manifestation of policymakers' desire to pass the buck to avoid blame. The Gramm-Rudman budget-cutting mechanism is a perfect illustration. Congress sets in motion a process which months or years later causes cuts to be made automatically, with no one directly to blame. Even the officials who would be responsible for sequestering funds are simply following a mandated formula, so they cannot be blamed.

Understanding why politicians would give up discretion over unpopular, cost-generating decisions is relatively easy. But why have they also given up authority over decisions in sectors where there are few or no concentrated losses—for example, over benefit levels in income transfer programs and potential pork barrel decisions in such areas as federal grants?

Understanding that politicians are blame-avoiding and risk averse can help to explain this apparent anomaly. This is clearest for legislators. Congressional incumbents have a number of tools at their disposal—constituency casework, mail to their constituents, etc.—that provide credit claiming opportunities. Thus the primary concern for the bulk of incumbents must be not to give an attractive issue to a challenger. Given this situation, their incentive is to neutralize—i.e., make unlikely to generate blame even if it sacrifices credit-claiming opportunities as well—any issue which has a significant prospect for generating blame. In choosing whether to maintain discretion over any program or give it up, legislators must take into account the prospect that they might in fact lose benefits for their constituents in future rounds, and that a future election opponent could use this as an election issue against him or her. (Indeed, it is not even necessary that actual losses occur—only that the opponent claim that they could do better.) Moreover, resources spent influencing these allocation decisions must be taken from a limited supply, and those resources can be better spent in decisions with less blame-generating potential. Forgoing discretion is, in short, likely to be a politically safer response except where the possibility that one's constituency will suffer real losses is remote.[8]

5. *Find a Scapegoat*: If a politician can't pass the buck for an unpopular decision, he or she may be able to pass the blame for it instead. The usual tactic is to claim that your actions were made necessary by the actions of your predecessors: President Reagan, for example, has claimed that austerity measures were required because of profligate spending by past Democratic administrations and Congresses. Prime Minister Thatcher has made similar claims in Great Britain.

Scapegoating can also be useful when past scandals or policy gaffes are discovered. President Reagan has been able to use his decentralized management style to deflect blame to subordinates on many occasions, giving rise to the term "Teflon presidency" (nothing sticks to the President). The limits to this strategy appear to have been surpassed only in the Iran/Contra arms imbroglio, where there is a broad popular perception that the President either knew more than he was saying or should have exercised more control over his subordinates.

6. *Jump on the Bandwagon*: On issues which pit a policymaker's views versus those of his or her constituents, he or she may be able to switch sides unobtrusively—to jump on the bandwagon—when it becomes evident that other strategies (notably agenda limitation and redefining the issue) have failed to keep a blame-generating situation from arising. If the policymaker's original position has not been made publicly, he or she may even be able to claim credit for holding the popular position all along. This desire to turn blame into credit is the source of the curious Congressional phenomenon of seemingly unimportant procedural votes that are in fact more important than final votes on passage. The unobtrusive procedural vote, which may be closely fought, reveals the balance of forces between the two contending sides. Once it is clear which side is likely to win, legislators may feel that their vote in favor of an unpopular side no longer serves any useful purpose. They can thus switch their vote to support the more popular side on final passage.

A clear example of failed agenda limitation followed by a bandwagon effect can be seen in the 1986 House debate on an omnibus drug bill. With an election less than eight weeks away, members were extremely reluctant to appear "soft on

---

[8] For a similar analysis that stresses universalism in legislative decisionmaking as a form of insurance for a steady stream of benefits, see Shepsle and Weingast (1981). Their analysis, however, focuses only on the provision of benefits and does not directly address the question of their political implications, notably the casting of blame by future political opponents if those benefits are lost.

drugs." Liberal Democrats criticized their own leadership for failing to preclude floor consideration of Republican amendments that would require military participation in anti-drug efforts, limit the application of the "exclusionary rule" on illegally seized evidence, and permit imposition of the death penalty in some drug cases (Rovner, 1986). Forced to take a stand on these issues (in a House atmosphere that two of them described as "a mob mentality" and "panic and hysteria"), many liberal Democrats defected to support them (Feuerbringer, 1986). On final passage they defected overwhelmingly, despite inclusion of all the Republican amendments. The bill passed by a vote of 392–16. The possibility of a Senate filibuster was then dismissed by House Majority Leader Jim Wright, who argued, "Anyone responsible for preventing this legislation from being enacted will have an angry American public to answer to" (Rovner, 1986: 2126).

7. *Circle the Wagons*: This strategy is based on the same principle—safety in numbers—as the "jump on the bandwagon" approach. It is most likely to be found in negative-sum situations, where there are only losses to be allocated and no way of evading the unpleasant choices. If the "pass the buck" and "throw good money after bad" options are no longer viable, decisionmakers may find themselves in a situation where they have a common interest in diffusing the inevitable blame by arriving at a consensus solution. Thus no one has to stick their neck out: everyone provides political cover for everyone else, making it difficult for a future political opponent to raise the issue. When it works best, this approach may even yield political dividends—for taking the hard, gutsy stand (which everyone else is taking as well).

"Circling the wagons" is invariably a risky strategy, however. It will work only if near-unanimity can be maintained. If some participants in the process see an opportunity to deflect the blame to others and claim credit for resisting the loss-producing solution, they will be sorely tempted to defect from the consensus. Thus all participants will be afraid to publicly take the lead in proposing solutions; unless agreements can be negotiated quietly, with commitments of support made in advance, they are unlikely to succeed.

8. *"Stop Me Before I Kill Again"*: Policymakers are not, as has been noted, single-minded seekers of re-election—they are also likely to have preferences for "good policy." Sometimes politicians are faced with a choice between a politically popular position—a credit-claiming opportunity—and what they believe to be a responsible policy position. If they vote against that choice, on the other hand, they may incur a lot of blame. If policymakers are simply credit-claimers, they will sacrifice their policy preferences, "jump on the bandwagon," and support the politically popular position. Thus the analogy to the murderer who asks that he be stopped before he kills again: the policymakers know that what they are doing is wrong, but they can't help themselves. This was the situation that fiscally conservative Republicans in Congress found themselves in as they resisted politically popular Social Security benefit increases in the early 1970s. But as they discovered, jumping on the bandwagon is not the only response: if they limited their discretion over the choice, they could avoid blame and obtain their policy preferences at the same time (Derthick, 1979: 349–350). A similar logic is used by many proponents of constitutional limits on government expenditures: i.e., it is the only way to force legislators to collectively exercise spending restraint, since none of them wishes to vote against individual spending programs (Wildavsky, 1980).

The strategy policymakers choose depends in large part on the nature of the blame-generating situation—e.g., whether it pits constituency versus constituency or policymaker versus constituency (Table 3). A "jump on the bandwagon" strategy may be an effective response to policymaker-constituency conflict. It might not be a viable option in a zero-sum conflict between constituents, however, for no single option may placate all sides. Passing the buck, scapegoating, redefining the issue or throwing good money after bad are all more likely to be more successful in this type of situation. Choice among these options will depend upon the costs and likelihood of success of each option (e.g., if there is a credible scapegoat or entity to which the buck can be passed).

BLAME AVOIDING IN COMPARATIVE PERSPECTIVE

The discussion of blame avoidance has to this point focused on examples drawn from the United States. But the political importance of generating and avoiding blame is by no means a uniquely American phenomenon. It has its roots in a specific set of structural conditions, viz. (1) loss-allocating activity by government, and (2) the ability of citizens and/or politicians to hold government officials accountable, be it through elections, votes of confidence in Parliament, demonstrations, or coups d'etat.

The more governments attempt to do, the more likely they are to be held liable for poor performance, or for policy changes that impose losses, in those sectors. Governments that regulate or subsidize the retail price of basic foodstuffs, for example, are likely to face strong pressures not to raise prices. When they finally do so as a result of rising budget deficits or pressure from the International Monetary Fund, they may face huge protests. Governments that have accepted a responsibility for maintaining full employment, Sweden, for example, make even conservative parties reluctant to allow unemployment to rise when they come to power (Jonung, 1985; Weaver, 1987), whereas in the United States the federal government is partially shielded from attack by public beliefs that it is unemployed individuals rather than government who are to blame for their unemployment (Lau and Sears, 1981; but see also Weatherford 1978; Weatherford, 1983).

The type of resources available to potential "blame generators" and to those who seek to avoid blame will affect both how much blame-avoiding those in power have to do and the strategies with which they choose to do it. If governmental power is highly concentrated, as in Eastern Europe, a pass the buck strategy of avoiding blame may work for individual functionaries and ministries, but it will not work for government (and party) as a whole. Authoritarian governments can suppress blame, but they cannot avoid it. Authoritarian governments occasionally fall, or at least change their leadership, in response to political pressure. Gomulka was deposed in Poland to placate public protest over food price increases; Krushchev fell in the Soviet Union in part due to elite dissatisfaction with his "hare-brained schemes" in agriculture. In short, where centralization of power makes buck-passing less credible as a strategy to avoid blame, scapegoating is likely to be an important blame-avoiding strategy.

Parliamentary institutions also have distinctive impacts on how blame is generated and avoided. Indeed Great Britain, without a written constitution to constrain government, relies ultimately on politicians' fears of attracting blame as a constraint. A full treatment of this topic is not possible here, but a few points can be made. Blame avoiding in the United States is highly decentralized and individualistic, reflecting the great leeway given to individual political entrepreneurs in a system of governmental checks and balances, weak and incoherent parties, and decentralized campaign financing. Both blame-generating and blame-avoiding in parliamentary systems tend to be much more party- and government-centered, reflecting strong party images and party discipline in the legislature. These strong party images make blame-generating much easier. Rose (1984: 49) indicates that party leaders in British election campaigns generally spend more time attacking the other party(ies) than in defending their own party's position and record.

Party discipline seriously constrains the blame-avoiding options for legislators. This is especially true in party list systems, where control over placement on the list gives party leaders a strong mechanism to punish disloyal behavior. Even in a single-member constituency system, the fact that the careers of Members of Parliament are highly dependent on advancing within their party caucus means they cannot do as their American counterparts might: disavow, vote against, and even lead the legislative fight against policies proposed by their party's leaders in the executive.[9] Voters' recognition that their legislator must adhere to party discipline partially shields an MP from *personal* blame for his or her votes, but it cannot absolve completely. MPs can also attempt to insulate themselves from their party's unpopular policies by that quintessential credit-claiming activity, constituency work (Cain, 1983). But this is a substitute for, rather than a form of, individual blame-avoiding.

So long as there is a majority government, opposition parties in parliamentary systems can do little other than generate blame, for they cannot hope to have an effective voice in formulating policy. In countries with Question Time or its equivalent, this blame-generating process has become highly institutionalized. The opposition seeks to embarrass the government, and the government seeks to dodge the questions, obfuscate or counterattack.

Although the opposition can embarrass the government and attempt to force it to consider issues of the opposition's choosing, the government can virtually monopolize the actual legislative agenda. It can refuse to bring up legislation when it does not wish to, and attempt to bury controversial issues by consigning them to commissions or parliamentary committees. Government can also largely control how those issues will be defined in the legislative process. The ability to control agendas also imposes burdens on parties in parliamentary systems. Because governing parties are supposed to govern, evidence of disunity, such as an open backbench rebellion, may have adverse electoral consequences (Jackson, 1968: 300–301). Thus potential rebels may be able to use the blame-avoiding instincts of their Whips to win a favorable behind-the-scenes accommodation of their views.

Parliamentary government also makes it particularly difficult for these governments to dodge blame for losses they have imposed or acquiesced in, because it concentrates authority and accountability in the government-of-the-day and provides regular opportunities to hold government accountable (Weaver, 1985). There is no one to whom the buck can be passed and, in most cases, it is transparently obvious that government could have intervened to prevent the loss, especially for micro-level changes such as a coal mine closure in Wales or a rail line abandonment in Western Canada. Governments in parliamentary systems are thus likely to face very strong pressures to "throw good money after bad" to prop

---

[9] Jackson (1968) found that British MPs were seldom successfully punished for rebelling against the Whip, but that they were less likely to receive rewards such as foreign trips, advancement to ministerial posts, peerages, etc.

up failed policies. Officials in the executive cannot use the legislature as a scapegoat (and vice versa) in the United States. In theory, ministers who are responsible for failed policies can resign as scapegoats, but this usually occurs only in the case of scandal rather than failed policies. The principle of collective cabinet responsibility assures that the government as a whole will share in any blame for failed policies. Governments may, however, have somewhat more freedom in distancing themselves from blame for macro-economic conditions than for micro-level ones: the Thatcher government, for example, was able to win re-election in 1983 in part because "whilst high unemployment has consistently been seen as the most important issue facing the country, expectations as to its solution are low, and the government has been decreasingly singled out as the sole cause of the problem" (Richardson and Moon, 1984: 30).

There are also differences among governments in parliamentary systems, especially between majority governments and minority or coalition governments. There is some evidence that weak coalition governments escape blame for poor economic performance when stronger, single-party, majority governments could not (Paldam and Schneider, 1980; Lybeck, 1985). On the other hand, these governments may be subject to collapse at any time because one or more parties does not wish to be associated with an unpopular policy choice. Hence, policy decisions are especially likely to have a blame-avoiding cast in coalitions. Moreover, because coalition partners are likely to be competing for the same voters in the next election, they may try to generate blame against their partners while trying to build a blame-minimizing record themselves. Indeed, parties' reasons for staying in government may well be based on blame avoidance: a fear that they will be punished by voters for causing the collapse of the government.

BLAME AVOIDANCE AND POLICY OUTPUTS

The analysis outlined above suggests that blame avoidance may lead policy alternatives to be chosen that might otherwise fail. In this sense alone, it has an important impact on policy outputs, if only the passive one of influencing choices made from among a set of alternatives determined by "good policy" advocates and credit-claimers. But blame-avoiding also affects the alternatives considered.

The limitation of policymakers' discretion through indexation, formula grants, merit hiring and promotion and other more or less automatic mechanisms is the foremost example. Blame avoidance can help to produce discretion-reducing decisions in three ways. First, policymakers may themselves seek the reduction of discretion because they believe that it offers few credit-claiming opportunities and high prospects for blame. Louis XIV's rueful comment about malcontents and ingrates reflects this concern. Gramm-Rudman is a more recent manifestation of this phenomenon: discretion to cut popular spending programs is not the kind of discretion that politically astute decisionmakers wish to exercise. Reduction of discretion is, in short, a way of "passing the buck."

Second, policymakers may wish to maintain discretion to take advantage of credit-claiming opportunities, but be forced to reject it when their opponents mobilize opposition to continued discretion. The elimination of patronage when it became an issue of "good government" is an example. Here reduction of discretion follows from a "jump on the bandwagon" mentality.

Finally, policymakers may come to favor a reduction of discretion because they believe that exercising discretion forces them to make unacceptable choices between obtaining substantial credit but very bad policy, on the one hand, or incurring substantial political blame, on the other. The support of conservative Republicans for Social Security indexation as a way to avoid having to vote either for or against real benefit increases was noted earlier as an example of this "stop me before I kill again" motive for reducing discretion.

Several other consequences of blame avoidance are also important. Blame avoidance can, for example, help to explain why policymakers often urge competing interest groups to work out differences among themselves and arrive at a consensus position which is then endorsed by those officials. Doing so limits the ability of decision-makers to claim credit for reaching an agreement. More importantly, it allows them to avoid taking positions and making decisions that will offend one or more of the groups.

Understanding blame avoidance also can help us understand the limits on interest group capture of governmental institutions. Even if a specialist clientele is normally the only "attentive public" for an agency or Congressional committee, those bodies know that they cannot go too far in pursuing that clientele's interest without attracting unwanted outside attention. Regulatory agencies can have their decisions overturned by the courts, Congressional committees by their full bodies. There is also the potential embarrassment of being shown to be too solicitous of a clientele.

This is not to say that catering to specialized interests does not occur. It does. Indeed, it is inevitable—even endemic—in a system such as the US one, which allows agencies and committees substantial autonomy within a system of multiple, intermittently exercised checks. But the "capture" process is one that has natural limits based on blame avoiding—namely, the agency or committee's fear of mobilizing latent constituencies or governmental checks—i.e., of attracting blame.[10]

Blame avoidance also helps to explain why policies are so difficult to change, even if they fail. If policymakers and their constituents perceived costs and benefits symmetrically, they would be willing to change policies quite freely, at least as long as the new policies promised at least as high a surplus of concentrated benefits over costs as the status quo. But substantial vested interests often develop around programs. Because costs and benefits are perceived asymmetrically, policymakers fear that new policies will not win them as much support as dismantling the old ones will lose. They are thus afraid to dismantle policies, and when they do, they may "grandfather" in current beneficiaries so that they do not become losers (Leman, 1980).

Perhaps more important than its potential impact on any specific set of policy outputs, however, are the implications of blame avoidance for the theory and practice of democracy. More specifically, it has implications for at least two constraints that proponents of economic analysis of politics have outlined to an efficient transmission of citizen preferences into government action. The first is that information is costly to obtain (Downs, 1956: chapters 11–13). As a result, most citizens do not in fact have a very good idea of what candidates' and officeholders' positions and records are. Second, because of "free rider" problems, not

[10] The economic analogy is to entry into potentially competitive markets with substantial but not insurmountable entry barriers. A firm operating in those markets can gain some monopoly profits, but attempts to exploit them too far will lead to a challenge to their position. Just how large those profits will be depends on the nature of entry barriers. Similarly, the ability of a clientele and its governmental allies to exploit a policy-making monopoly depends on how easily latent checks and counter-clienteles can be mobilized, which in turn depends on barriers to information and organization by those groups.

all interests are likely to be equally well represented—and thus equally influential in decisions (Olson, 1965). On each of these points, the blame-avoiding perspective suggests both some good news and some bad news.

On the question of information costs, the good news is that political entrepreneurs (both interest groups and candidates) have strong incentives to purvey information about their opponents in a way that imposes as few costs as possible on voters, believing that this information-giving function will provide a substantial return on their investment. On the other hand, this information will be very biased toward the negative, and may contain substantial distortions. In addition, fear of blame causes politicians to be vague in their issue positions, especially where constituencies are divided. Thus voters are denied full information on which to make their choices (Page and Brody, 1972: 995).

On the question of free rider constraints to formation of groups, the good news suggested by the blame-avoiding perspective is that individuals facing major losses probably don't have to be well organized to have attention paid to them. Officeholders are likely to anticipate constituency losses and work to avoid them, since they recognize their dire consequences. On the other hand, the theory of blame avoidance suggests that some groups' views—those that are threatened with losses—will be weighted more than the views of others, because potential losers are more likely to be vocal in expressing their views. It suggests that a Paretian view of the proper role of government (that it should maximize public welfare only when doing so does not make some individuals worse off) may have some empirical grounding, irrespective of its ethical validity. For government will be fearful of trying to maximize net social welfare when doing so forces losses on some interests.

REFERENCES

Bloom, Howard S., and Price, H. Douglas (1975) "Voter Response to Short-Run Economic Conditions: The Asymmetric Effect of Prosperity and Recession," *American Political Science Review*, 69 (December) 1240–1254.

Gain, Bruce E. (1983) "Blessed Be the Tie that Unbinds: Constituency Work and the Vote Swing in Great Britain," *Political Studies*, 31,1 (March) 103–111.

Campbell, James E. (1983) "Ambiguity in the Issue Positions of Presidential Candidates: A Causal Analysis," *American Journal of Political Science*, 27 (May) 284–293.

Derthick, Martha (1979) *Policymaking for Social Security.* Washington, D.C.: The Brookings Institution.

Downs, Anthony (1956) *An Economic Theory of Democracy.* New York: Harper and Brothers.

Ellsberg, Daniel (1971) "The Quagmire Myth and the Stalemate Machine." *Public Policy* 19 (Spring) 217–274.

Fenno, Richard F., Jr. (1973) *Congressmen in Committees.* Boston: Little, Brown.

Fenno, Richard F., Jr. (1978) *Home Style: House Members in their Districts.* Boston: Little Brown.

Ferejohn, John A., and Fiorina, Morris P. (1985) "Incumbency and Realignment in Congressional Elections," in John Chubb and Paul Peterson (eds.) *The New Direction in American Politics.* Washington, D.C.: The Brookings Institution, 91–115.

Feuerbringer, Jonathon (1986) "House Supports Use of Military to Fight Drugs," *New York Times*, September 12.

Fiorina, Morris P. (1977) *Congress: Keystone of the Washington Establishment.* New Haven: Yale University Press.

Fiorina, Morris P. (1981) *Retrospective Voting in American National Elections.* New Haven: Yale University Press.

Fiorina, Morris P. (1982) "Legislative Choice of Regulatory Forms: Legal Process or Administrative Process?" *Public Choice*, 39 33–66.

Fiorina, Morris P., and Shepsle, Kenneth A. (1986) "Negative Voting: An Explanation Based on Principal-Agent Theory," St. Louis, Washington University Political Economy Working Paper 108.

Hibbing, John R., and Alford, John R. (1981) "The Electoral Impact of Economic Conditions: Who Is Held Responsible?" *American Journal of Political Science*, 25 (August) 423–439.

Jackson, Robert J. (1968) *Rebels and Whips: An Analysis of Dissension, Discipline and Cohesion in British Political Parties*. London: Macmillan.

Jonung, Lars (1985) "Business Cycles and Political Changes in Sweden." *Skandinariska Enskilda Banken Quarterly Review*, 2 2–15.

Kahneman, Daniel, and Tversky, Amos (1984) "Choices, Values and Frames," *American Psychologist*, 39 (April) 341–350.

Kernell, Samuel (1977) "Presidential Popularity and Negative Voting: An Alternative Explanation of the Midterm Congressional Decline of the President's Party," *American Political Science Review*, 72 (June) 44–66.

Key, V. O., Jr. (1966) *The Responsible Electorate: Rationality in Presidential Voting, 1936–1960*. Cambridge: Harvard University Press.

Kinder, Donald R., and Kiewiet, D. Roderick (1979) "Economic Judgements and Political Behavior: The Role of Personal Grievances and Collective Economic Judgements in Congressional Voting." *American Journal of Political Science* 23 (August) 495–527.

Lau, Richard R. (1985) "Two Explanations for Negativity Effects in Political Behavior." *American Journal of Political Science*, 29 (February) 119–138.

Lau, Richard R., and Sears, David O. (1981) "Cognitive Links Between Economic Grievances and Political Responses," *Political Behavior*. 3, 4 279–302.

Leman, Christopher K. (1980) "How to Get There from Here: The Grandfather Effect and Public Policy," *Policy Analysis*, 6 (Winter) 99–116.

Lybeck, Johan A. (1985) "A Simultaneous Model of Politico-economic Interaction in Sweden, 1970–1982," *European Journal of Political Research*, 13 135–151.

Mayhew, David (1974) *Congress: The Electoral Connection*. New Haven: Yale University Press.

Oleszek, Walter J. (1984) *Congressional Procedures and the Policy Process* (second ed.). Washington, D.C.: Congressional Quarterly Press.

Olson, Mancur (1965) *The Logic of Collective Action: Public Goods and the Theory of Groups*. Cambridge: Harvard University Press.

Page, Benjamin I. (1976) "The Theory of Political Ambiguity," *American Political Science Review*, 70 (1976) 742–752.

Page, Benjamin I., and Brody, Richard (1972) "Policy Voting and the Electoral Process: the Vietnam War Issue," *American Political Science Review*, 66 (September) 979–995.

Paldam, M., and Schneider, F. (1980) "The Macroeconomic Aspects of Government and Opposition Popularity in Denmark, 1957–1978," *Nationalakonomisk Tidskrift*, 118 149–170.

Price, David E. (1977) "Policymaking in Congressional Committees: The Impact of 'Environmental Factors,'" *American Political Science Review* 71 (March) 548–574.

Richardson, J. J., and Moon, Jeremy (1984) "The Politics of Unemployment in Britain," *Political Quarterly*, 55, 1 (January–March) 29–37.

Riker, William (1986) *The Art of Political Manipulation*. New Haven: Yale University Press.

Rose, Richard (1984) *Do Parties Make a Difference?* (2nd ed.). London: Macmillan.

Rovner, Julie (1986) "House Passes $6 Billion Anti-Drug Package," *Congressional Quarterly Weekly Report*, September 13 2125-2126.

Sears, David O., and Lau, Richard R. (1983) "Inducing Apparently Self-Interested Political Preferences," *American Journal of Political Science*, 27 (May) 223–252.

Shepsle, Kenneth A. (1972) "The Strategy of Ambiguity: Uncertainty and Electoral Competition." *American Political Science Review*, 66 (June) 555–568.

Shepsle, Kenneth A., and Weingast, Barry R. (1981) "Political Preferences for the Pork Barrel: A Generalization," *American Journal of Political Science*, 25 (February) 96–111.

Smith, Stephen S. (1986) "Revolution in the House: Why Don't We Do It on the Floor:" Brookings Discussion Papers in Governmental Studies #5, September.

Stockman, David A. (1986) *The Triumph of Politics: Why the Reagan Revolution Failed.* New York: Harper and Row.

Thomas, Martin (1985) "Election Proximity and Senatorial Roll Call Voting," *American Journal of Political Science*, 29 (February) 96–11.

Tufte, Edward (1978) *Political Control of the Economy*, Princeton: Princeton University Press.

Weatherford, M. Stephen (1978) "Economic Conditions and Electoral Outcomes: Class Differences in the Political Responses to Recession," *American Journal of Political Science*, 22, 4 (November) 917–938.

Weatherford, M. Stephen (1983) "Economic Voting and the "Symbolic Politics' Argument: A Reinterpretation and Synthesis," *American Political Science Review*, 77, 1 (March) 158-174.

Weaver, R. Kent (1985) "Are Parliamentary Systems Better?" *The Brookings Review*. 3–4 (Summer) 16–25.

Weaver, R. Kent (1987) "Political Foundations of Swedish Economic Policy," in Barry Bosworth and Alice Rivlin (eds.) *The Swedish Economy*, Washington, D.C.: The Brookings Institution, 289-317.

Whalen, Charles and Whalen, Barbara (1985) *The Longest Debate: A Legislative History of the 1964 Civil Rights Act.* New York: Mentor.

Wildavsky, Aaron (1980) *How to Limit Government Spending.* Berkeley: University of California Press.

Wright, Gerald C., Jr. (1977) "Constituency Responses to Congressional Behavior: The Impact of the House Judiciary Committee Impeachment Votes," *Western Political Quarterly*, 30, 3 (September) 401–410.

16

PRIVATIZING RISK WITHOUT PRIVATIZING THE WELFARE STATE: THE HIDDEN POLITICS OF SOCIAL POLICY RETRENCHMENT IN THE UNITED STATES

Jacob S. Hacker[*]

Citizens of advanced industrial democracies—like the U.S., Canada, and Germany, among others—have social rights. There is a consensus in such countries, for example, that no member of society should be destitute and lack medical care in his or her old age, and that, furthermore, society, broadly speaking, should assume responsibility for old-age income support and medical care. There is agreement, to take another example, that people who are in the workforce, or who are young but unable to work, ought to be able to consult decent doctors or to stay in hospitals during emergencies without undue financial strain. To realize such social agreements, there exist a range of social policies. They are often referred to as the welfare state. Keep in mind, in passing, that the "welfare state" is a bulky abstraction—in the United States it is actually an intricate array of partnerships among government agencies, the United States Treasury, congressional and presidential budget makers, firms in the private sector, research organizations, policy entrepreneurs such as Senator Edward Kennedy, and advocacy groups of all sorts—for example, labor unions, the American Medical Association, the American Association for Retired People (AARP), and Catholic Charities USA.

But if there are agreements about broad goals there are also disagreements over how far to go with—or even whether to scale back—national commitments to rather expensive public purposes. This fascinating article by Jacob Hacker, one of America's leading experts on social policy, shows that ironically many of the fights over social policy in the United States are below the political radar. They are often fought in the private sector, which is in fact an essential partner in social policy. Such conflicts are not translated into open debates between the political parties.

To be sure, public discussion over health insurance and Social Security are notable exceptions to Hacker's finding. Nonetheless, "retrenchment" is happening, often apparently nonpolitically, through, for instance, changes

From *American Political Science Review* 98 (May 2004): 243–260. Copyright © 2004 by the American Political Science Association. Reprinted with the permission of Cambridge University Press.

* For comments on drafts of this essay, I thank Benjamin Cashore, Alan Jacobs, Oona Hathaway, Stephan Leibfried, Philip Manow, Kimberly Morgan, Kathleen Thelen, Lee Sigelman, Wolfgang Streeck, R. Kent Weaver, three anonymous reviewers, and, especially, Paul Pierson, as well as participants in workshops at Brandeis University, the University of Bremen, and Ohio State University. Nelson Gerew, Rachel Goodman, Joanne Lim, Mary Mason, Julia Sheketoff, Tova Serkin, and Natalie Wigg provided able research and editorial assistance; Nigar Nargis helped develop the index of income volatility; and David Jesuit, Vincent Mahler, and Timothy Smeeding kindly gave me unpublished comparative data on income redistribution. Finally, I thank the Peter Strauss Fund, Yale Institution for Social and Policy Studies, and the William Milton Fund of the Harvard Medical School for financial support.

in private-sector human resource practices. All of the "little retrenchments"
add up to a far-reaching shift—namely that individual experience of social
rights varies enormously across economic sectors, states, companies, and
nonprofit employers. During the economic crisis that deepened in 2008 such
retrenchment accelerated. Many employers cut back on their contributions,
for example, to the old-age pension plans that they provided for their em-
ployees. Others did not. Yet others did not cut as much as some. Meanwhile,
unemployment insurance coverage varied widely among the states.

More generally, everyone is now more vulnerable—in the sense of hav-
ing to personally absorb—the costs of goods whose expense was once more
socialized. There is a quiet shift in social rights in the United States. Hacker's
accomplishment is to characterize that shift and to disentangle its evolution
and origins.

To put it bluntly, the "welfare state" in the United States is not being killed
so much as it is being subtly reconfigured and perhaps hollowed out. Is this
private power at work? Will politicians step in? Or will they stay out because
of what Kent Weaver refers to as "blame avoidance"? Because a compelling
"causal story" is not available? In light of the previous articles in this volume,
these are questions that will occur to you as you read this piece.

• • •

HAS THE WELFARE STATE CONTINUED to provide the inclusive social protection that
defined its goals and operations in the immediate decades after World War II? According to much received scholarly wisdom, the answer is yes. As Paul Pierson
writes in one of the earliest and most influential assessments, "Economic, political,
and social pressures have fostered an image of welfare states under siege. Yet if
one turns from abstract discussions of social transformation to an examination of
actual policy, it becomes difficult to sustain the proposition that these strains have
generated fundamental shifts" (Pierson 1996, 173). A wave of research, relying on
both large-scale statistical modeling and detailed historical analysis, has largely
ratified this evaluation (see, e.g., Bonoli, George, and Taylor-Gooby 2000; Esping-
Andersen 1999; Huber and Stephens 2001; Pierson 1994, 2001; and Weaver 1998).
In this now-conventional view, welfare states are under strain, cuts have occurred,
but social policy frameworks remain secure, anchored by their enduring popularity,
their powerful constituencies, and their centrality within the postwar order.

This article challenges this conventional wisdom and presents an alternative
interpretation based on a comparatively informed historical analysis of the post-
1970s trajectory of the American welfare state—long considered the quintessential example of welfare state stability in the face of fiscal and political challenge
(see, e.g., Huber and Stephens 2001 and Pierson 1996). This alternative account
rests not simply on a reconsideration of the evidence. It rests, too, on a new perspective on social policy reform that broadens the range of policies and forms of
change under consideration. In enlarging and shifting the focus of analysis—from
formal rules to their social consequences, from the welfare state narrowly defined
to the broader public-private economy of welfare, and from the highly visible
politics of large-scale reform to the subterranean political processes that shape
ground-level policy effects—this conceptual framework illuminates and clarifies
the sometimes-covert strategies that political actors adopt when trying to transform embedded policy commitments. In short, this article not only presents a new
interpretation and explanation of the specific trajectory of the American welfare

state, but also offers a new conceptual lens that lays bare the "hidden" means by which policies can be changed by actors employing strategies of stealth, obstruction, and indirection.

Above all, however, the evidence and arguments presented in this article give cause for questioning the conventional story about welfare state resilience in the United States. Although most U.S. public social programs have indeed resisted radical retrenchment, the American social welfare framework has also, in crucial areas, offered increasingly incomplete protection against the key social risks that Americans confront. One reason for this, as suggested by the 1996 overhaul of the Aid to Families with Dependent Children program (commonly known as "welfare"), is that some policies have experienced major formal revision. But this, I contend, is only a relatively small part of the larger story. More crucial are two less visible sources of change, both of which have occurred without significant formal alterations in policy. First, in policy areas that rely substantially on public-private or intergovernmental cooperation, the shifting aims of benefit sponsors and administrators has transformed the ground-level operation of formally stable policies, at times quite radically. Second, and perhaps even more important, recent decades have witnessed an accelerating process that I call "risk privatization," in which stable social policies have come to cover a declining portion of the salient risks faced by citizens. As a result of this process, many of the most potent threats to income are increasingly faced by families and individuals on their own, rather than by collective intermediaries.

For those familiar with comparative research on the welfare state, this last point will resonate with the common observation that advanced industrial societies are marked by a growing mismatch between traditional social policies and the new social risks that citizens face. As Gøsta Esping-Andersen (1999, 5), the dean of welfare state scholars, puts it, "The real 'crisis' of contemporary welfare regimes lies in the disjuncture between the existing institutional configuration and exogenous change. Contemporary welfare states . . . have their origins in, and mirror, a society that no longer obtains." And yet, contrary to the normal framing of this disjuncture as a result of exogenous shocks to stable systems, I argue that many of the most glaring mismatches that have arisen in the United States should be seen instead as a direct outgrowth of political struggle—a manifestation of an important but often hidden "second face" (Bachrach and Baratz 1962) of welfare state debate. No less important, I emphasize that crucial policy changes *have* in fact taken place over the past three decades, despite general stability in formal policies. Their key source, however, is not large-scale legislative reform, but a set of decentralized and semiautonomous processes of alteration *within* existing policy bounds. Thus, in focusing on active changes in policy rules, analysts have missed fundamental ways in which the welfare state's role and effects are changing.

The implications of this argument therefore extend well beyond social policy reform, intersecting with increasingly prominent questions in institutional theory about the causes and character of institutional change (see, e.g., Pierson 2004 and Thelen 2003). The central implication is that there is not one single pattern of institutional change, whether it be the "big bangs" of sudden transformation or the "silent revolutions" of incremental adjustment. Rather, institutional change takes multiple forms, and strategies for institutional change systematically differ according to the character of institutions and the political settings in which they are situated. By exploring these sources of variation, I show that actors who wish to change popular and embedded institutions in political environments that militate against authoritative reform may find it prudent *not* to attack such institutions directly. Instead, they may seek to shift those institutions' ground-level operation, prevent their adaptation to shifting external circumstances, or build new institutions on top of them. These are strategies for change that are little studied and even less well understood. They are also strategies, I shall demonstrate, that critics of the welfare state—rebuffed in their direct assaults on social programs—have increasingly attempted to pursue, sometimes with considerable success.

The choice of the United States as the focus of these claims may appear unconventional. Analysts who disagree on much typically view the American welfare state as lying on a wholly different plane from other regimes, or at least on the outer frontier of the "liberal" world of meager, market-oriented welfare states (Esping-Andersen 1990). Nor can it be denied that the recent American experience is distinctive in a number of crucial respects (Smeeding 2002). At the same time, however, the United States, with its multiple institutional "veto players" (Tsebelis 1995), has long been treated as the quintessential example of welfare state resilience, indeed, as the principal validating case of the leading approach to retrenchment, the "new politics of the welfare state" perspective associated with the work of Pierson (1994, 1996). If, as I argue, the surface stability of U.S. social programs has in fact masked major declines in collective protection, then a strong case can be made that prevailing analytic perspectives have overlooked critical dimensions of policy change—abroad as well as in the United States. Moreover, certain unusual aspects of the U.S. framework are becoming increasingly common elsewhere, making the American experience a guide to the long-term effects of these nascent but powerful trends.[1]

THE ANALYSIS OF RETRENCHMENT

The beginning of the recent wave of interest in retrenchment can be conveniently dated to Pierson's (1994) pathbreaking book on welfare state reform in Britain and the United States, *Dismantling the Welfare State?* A chief reason for the influence of the book is its precision about the dependent variable. "Retrenchment," notes Pierson, "is one of those cases in which identifying what is to be explained is almost as difficult as formulating persuasive explanations for it." Spending cuts alone do not exhaust the definition; analysts need also to consider structural reforms that move the welfare state toward a more "residual" role, in which government does little to shift the distribution of income and services in a progressive direction. Retrenchment thus describes "policy changes that either cut social expenditure, restructure welfare state programs to conform more closely to the residual welfare state model, or alter the political environment in ways that enhance the probability of such outcomes in the future" (Pierson 1994, 17). The last of these—long-term changes in the political environment—Pierson labels "systemic retrenchment," to distinguish it from immediate changes in programs, which he terms "programmatic retrenchment."[2]

---

[1] On the increasing role of private benefits in rich nations, see Adema and Einerhand 1998.

[2] In some respects, then, this article is an attempt to revisit Pierson's arguments about "systemic retrenchment." For the most part, however, the changes I describe fall between systemic and programmatic retrenchment, involving the creation of new policies, internal changes that occur without formal revision, and erosion of programs in the face of external change.

Having defined retrenchment, Pierson goes on to evaluate the success of British and U.S. conservatives in pursuing it. He concludes that "the fundamental structure of social policy remains comparatively stable" (Pierson 1994, 182). Expanding the welfare state involved imposing diffuse costs in return for concentrated benefits. Cutting social programs, by contrast, entails imposing concentrated costs in return for diffuse gains—a far more difficult political prospect. More important, social programs are popular, and they have created powerful constituencies well positioned to fight retrenchment. In short, the chances for retrenchment are—to use a phrase Pierson deploys in more recent writings—highly "path dependent" (Pierson 2000). Past social policy choices create strong vested interests and expectations, which are extremely difficult to undo even in the present era.

Pierson's argument is logical, and it carries a straightforward prescription—namely, that analysts should study efforts to introduce residualizing reforms into existing programs. A large body of writing has followed this prescription and, in doing so, made major advances in our understanding of welfare state reform. Indeed, even predominantly quantitative work now routinely concedes that analysis of retrenchment requires careful probing of political decision-making to verify that spending trends actually reflect collective choices that alter public programs (e.g., Huber and Stephens 2001).

For all its virtues, however, Pierson's approach also has real limits.[3] The first and simplest is its emphasis on authoritative changes in existing social welfare programs. Although this may seem an obvious focus—after all, changing formal policies *is* a central means of changing the distribution of social benefits—it excludes from consideration a host of "subterranean" (Hacker 2002, 43) means of policy adjustment that can occur without large-scale policy change: from "bureaucratic disentitlement" (Lipsky 1984) caused by the decisions of front-line administrators to decentralized cutbacks in social welfare benefits caused by the actions of nongovernmental benefit sponsors and providers. Perhaps more important, in emphasizing affirmative decisions, Pierson also excludes from consideration a wide range of agenda-setting and blocking activities that may well be quite crucial in shaping the welfare state's long-term evolution. Like the pluralists of the 1950s and 1960s, retrenchment scholars have assessed power mainly by tracing observable decisions. The influential critique made against pluralism thus carries weight here too: By looking only at affirmative choices on predefined issues, retrenchment analyses tend to downplay the important ways in which actors may shape and restrict the agenda of debate and prevent some kinds of collective decisions altogether.

Most critical in this regard are deliberate attempts to prevent the updating of policies to reflect changing social circumstance. In the struggle over health care reform in the early 1990s, for example, advocates of expanded government responsibility embarked on an ambitious campaign to extend health coverage to counteract the declining reach of private health benefits (Hacker 1997; Skocpol 1996). Their efforts, in turn, fell victim to a concerted counter-mobilization among affected interests and political conservatives, who denied that government should step in to deal with the increasing hardships caused by skyrocketing costs and dwindling protections. Whether these efforts were necessary or unnecessary,

---

[3] To be fair to Pierson, he has acknowledged some of these limits (Pierson 2001, 2002) and conceded that he underestimated the extent of retrenchment in Britain during the 1980s.

poorly executed or simply doomed to fail, their defeat had enormous implications for the scope and character of U.S. social policy, as well as for judgments about the relative influence of pro- and anti-welfare-state forces in American politics. Yet from the standpoint of the conventional approach to retrenchment, the failure of health care reform is a nonevent.

This example only hints at the broad range of political processes and policy outcomes occluded by a single-minded focus on formal policy change. Historically, welfare states have been directed not just toward ensuring social protection against medical costs, but also toward providing security against a number of major life risks: unemployment, death of a spouse, retirement, disability, childbirth, poverty. Yet the incidence and extent of many of these risks have changed dramatically over the past three decades, leading to potentially significant transformations in the consequences of social policy interventions, even without formal changes in public social programs. To be sure, we should not assume that the welfare state *should* naturally adjust to deal with changing risk profiles, or that gaps between risks and benefits are always deliberate—as they clearly are, for example, in the case of active attempts to prevent policies from being updated to achieve their historical goals in the face of demands to upgrade them. And yet, we cannot ignore these disjunctures either. Welfare states, after all, constitute institutionalized aims as well as an arsenal of policy means for achieving them, and their development over time must be assessed in that dual light.

In fact, even within the relatively narrow conception of the welfare state that Pierson adopts, there are important policies he largely overlooks. Notable here are two overlapping policy realms central to the U.S. social policy framework: tax expenditures with social welfare purposes and regulatory and tax policies governing privately provided social welfare benefits (Hacker 2002; Howard 1997).[4] Recent OECD research shows that the United States has an extremely large employment-based private benefit system that is extensively buttressed and shaped by government policy (Adema 1999; Adema and Einerhand 1998; Adema et al. 1996): Controlling for tax burdens, for example, such "publicly subsidized and regulated private benefits" (Hacker 2002, 11) constituted more than a third of U.S. social spending in 1995. Furthermore, the distribution and character of private benefits have changed dramatically in recent decades, with rates of coverage plummeting among lower-income workers and benefit plans providing increasingly insecure income guarantees. Leaving policies that govern private social benefits out of the analysis entirely, as nearly all retrenchment studies do, thus misses a critically important dimension of social policy change, particularly in the United States.

EVERYDAY FORMS OF RETRENCHMENT: DRIFT, CONVERSION, AND LAYERING

The changes that have taken place within the world of private benefits are an example of what I term "drift"—changes in the operation or effect of policies that occur without significant changes in those policies' structure.[5] The major cause of drift in the social welfare field is a shift in the social context of policies, such as

---

[4] These policy areas correspond nicely with Richard Titmuss's (1976) categories of "fiscal welfare" and "occupational welfare." For an argument along similar lines about the distinctive *regulatory* basis of Australia's welfare state, see Castles and Mitchell 1993.

[5] See the discussion of "utility drift" in Rae 1975.

the rise of new or newly intensified social risks with which existing programs are poorly equipped to grapple. The hallmark of change of this sort is that it occurs largely outside the immediate control of policymakers, thus appearing natural or inadvertent. The question for policymakers becomes whether and how to respond to the growing gap between the original aims of a policy and the new realities that shifting social conditions have fostered.

Esping-Andersen (1999) and others who discuss this type of change imply that it is largely an apolitical process. To the extent that arguments in this vein concern the politics of reform, their ambition is limited to explaining welfare state responses to the disjunction between risks and benefits once that disjunction has become apparent. Yet the emergence of risk-benefit mismatches should itself be seen as a process that is highly mediated by politics. In an environment of new or worsening social risks, opponents of expanded state responsibility do not have to enact major policy reforms to move policy toward their favored ends. Merely by blocking compensatory interventions designed to ameliorate intensified risks, they can gradually transform the orientation of programs. Of course, social policy drift may sometimes be wholly inadvertent. But much of it is quite clearly mediated by politics, a result not of failures of foresight or perception, but of deliberate efforts by political actors to prevent the recalibration of social programs.

An example from the post-1970s American experience will help to clarify the point. In 1974, Congress passed the Employee Retirement Income Security Act (ERISA) to regulate employment-based fringe benefits, especially pensions. Virtually unnoticed at the time was a seemingly minor clause that exempted from state-government regulation all health plans directly financed by employers (commonly called "self-insured" plans). Prior to ERISA, states had sole authority to regulate private health insurance, and most health plans were independently run by insurers and covered multiple workplaces, pooling medical risks across many firms. Yet in the wake of the sweeping law, as the states became by default the primary locus of health coverage expansions, ERISA's "preemption" of state regulation increasingly thwarted efforts to stem the rising tide of medically uninsured Americans (Gottschalk 2000). Seeing an opportunity to escape regulation and limit their sharing of risk with other firms, corporations rushed to set up self-insured plans. And, crucially, once they did so, they needed only to prevent revision of ERISA's preemption clause to hold new government interventions at bay—an aim they relatively easily achieved, given their lobbying strength, the complexity of the issue, and the status-quo bias of American political institutions. The ability of employers and their allies to block a government response to the continued decline of risk-pooling in American health insurance is thus a textbook example of politically mediated policy drift.

Drift is not, however, the only means by which policies may change without formal revision. In addition, what Kathleen Thelen (2003) terms "conversion" may also cause ground-level change. According to Thelen, conversion occurs when "existing institutions are redirected to new purposes, driving changes in the role they perform and/or the functions they serve." Although Thelen does not put the issue this way, adaptation of policies through conversion reflects the reality that most institutions or policies allow actors working within their constraints to pursue multiple ends. This is one reason why institutions are not simply, as William Riker (1980) has put it, "congealed tastes" for favored states of the world—identical, at root, to any other collective choice. Instead of single-use tools, institutions are usually versatile multitaskers (Schickler 2001), and this versatility is itself a crucial variable shaping the strategies of actors who wish to change them. Although mutability of this sort is particularly characteristic of *political* institutions, it is also true of many large-scale public policies—which, as institutional frameworks for the achievement of complex ends, frequently grant substantial flexibility to those carrying out their mandates.[6]

Consider for a moment a highly simplified model of the options open to political actors who wish to change an existing policy. In the starkest calculation, they must decide whether to "work within" this extant policy framework to achieve their ends or "work outside" it by revising or eliminating it. Seen this way, it immediately becomes clear that two questions loom large. First, how easily can these actors achieve their aims through the existing framework? And, second, how costly would it be to replace it with a policy more closely tailored to the ends they desire? If the answer to the first question is "very easily," then the actors may pass up challenging even a policy that would be relatively costless to change. If the answer to the second question is "very costly," then they may try to work within even a policy framework that is heavily biased against the ends they seek.

The place to begin, then, is to distinguish between "internal" policy changes that occur without formal revision, on the one hand, and formal policy changes, on the other. The ability to alter a policy internally is influenced primarily by a policy's specific characteristics: its structure, its goals, its distinctive "feedback" (Pierson 1993) effects. Some policies, for example, have clear and consistent goals; others do not. Some have procedures that are clearly specified and understood; others do not. Some give central leaders strong tools for controlling front-line agents; others do not. At one extreme, then, are policies whose dictates are unambiguous and whose front-line agents have little discretion. On the other are policies whose rules are opaque and contested, and whose implementation by front-line agents is highly variable. In general, the conversion of a policy should be easier when it delegates administration or lacks clear overarching rules or aims, as in decentralized federal-state programs or subsidy arrangements that shape voluntary private benefits.

In the realm of social policy, public retirement programs provide perhaps the best example of the first pole of the continuum, while tax breaks for voluntarily provided workplace benefits exemplify the second (Hacker 2002; Howard 1997). Traditional retirement programs base benefits on minutely specified formulae that account for nearly every aspect of workers' careers and earnings: Once in place, public pensions virtually run themselves. In contrast, tax breaks for voluntary workplace benefits usually allow employers quite wide discretion in the structure and level of benefits, who they are (and are not) offered to, and, ultimately, whether they are offered at all. Indeed, within the typically loose constraints of the tax law, employers are free to use pensions and health benefits—or to not use them—for whatever goals they please: employee goodwill, human capital formation, asset accumulation, union thwarting, and a host of other ends (Hacker 2002).

Nearly all retrenchment studies, however, restrict their scope to policies with explicit and elaborate rules governing eligibility and benefits—such as pensions, unemployment insurance, and sick pay. These are policies for which it makes sense to begin by focusing narrowly on policy rules and attempts to change them. And yet there are many key realms of social policy in which the link between policies and effects is much weaker. To take an example just mentioned, regulatory

---

[6] Large-scale policies are not usually treated as institutions. Yet, as relatively enduring sets of rules that shape and constrain behavior, they are in fact consistent with most definitions.

and tax policies governing private benefits leave virtually unfettered discretion to employers, allowing companies to change what they do within these guidelines fundamentally. This is an extreme but not unique example: Many social policies divide authority between units of government or between government and private actors, such as providers, unions, and employers. And even programs run entirely by public organizations may allow significant "street-level bureaucracy" (Lipsky 1980), making problematic the assumption that what a policy dictates is what is actually done. Moreover, such decentralized arrangements are, it appears, becoming more prevalent (Clayton and Pontusson 1998; Gilbert 2002; Rein and Wandensjö 1997). If this is so, it may become increasingly difficult to judge policy effects simply by reading statute books or examining disputes over policy rules. We will need to look at what really happens on the ground.

The architecture of a policy, however, is not all that matters. A less studied but no less important force shaping the internal mutability of policies is the degree to which a policy gives rise to self-reinforcing "policy feedbacks" that cement in place stable constituencies, operating procedures, and definitions of mission (Mettler and Soss n.d.; Pierson 1993). Although research on the feedback effects of policies is still in its youth, it is clear that social policies do differ markedly in the extent to which they give rise to politically efficacious support coalitions. Social Security, for example, promotes widespread mobilization among the aged, who are well poised to fight cuts (Campbell 2003). Cash assistance for the poor, by contrast, gives rise to an extremely weak, fragmented, and politically demobilized constituency, which was unable to present an effective and united front against the 1996 welfare reform law (Soss 2000; Weaver 2000). In general, policies are more durable if they create or encourage the creation of large-scale organizations with substantial setup costs, directly or indirectly benefit sizable organized groups or constituencies, and embody long-lived commitments upon which beneficiaries and those around them premise crucial life and organizational decisions (Hacker 2002, 55).

In contrast to policy conversion, which hinges principally on policy-specific factors, the ability to formally alter a policy is mainly determined by the basic decision rules and partisan balance that characterize a political system. As institutionalists have long argued, opportunities for policy change are systematically shaped by the distribution of decision-makers' preferences regarding the status quo and alternatives to it, as well as by key institutional features of political systems, particularly the degree to which procedural rules create a status-quo bias (Immergut 1992; Krehbiel 1998; Tsebelis 1995). According to George Tsebelis's (1995) "veto players" framework, for example, policy stability increases when more actors or decision-making bodies must assent to change, when the ideological distance between them is greater, and when they are more internally cohesive. All this suggests that the American political context of the 1980s and 1990s— with bicameral and presidential divisions, frequent periods of split party control, and increasingly polarized parties—was particularly inhospitable to large-scale legislative change.

In sum, although the prospects for internal policy change are shaped by a policy's specific characteristics, formal policy change depends principally on whether the basic political structure and partisan context privileges the status quo. When it does, pragmatic advocates of change may find it more attractive to adapt existing policies to their ends than to wage a frontal assault. For this reason, *political settings that militate against authoritative change encourage reformers to seek the conversion or erosion of existing policies.* In these contexts, not only do reformers

Barriers to Internal Policy Conversion

	High (Low levels of policy discretion, strong policy support coalitions)	Low (High levels of discretion, weak support coalitions)
Barriers to Authoritative Policy Change — High (Many veto players)	**Drift** (Transformation of stable policy due to changing circumstances) Illustrative Example: Erosion of Scope of Protection of Existing Public Social Programs and Private Benefits	**Conversion** (Internal adaptation of existing policy) Illustrative Example: Employers' Restructuring of Publicly Subsidized Voluntary Workplace Benefits
Barriers to Authoritative Policy Change — Low (Few veto players)	**Layering** (Creation of new policy without elimination of old) Illustrative Example: Creation and Expansion of Tax Subsidies for Private Retirement Accounts	**Revision** (Formal reform, replacement, or elimination of existing policy) Illustrative Example: 1996 Welfare Reform

FIGURE 1. Four Modes of Policy Change

find it difficult to establish new policies or replace existing policies, but they are also better able to block efforts to close gaps between a policy's original aims and its actual effects.

Figure 1 sums up the argument. As the bottom-right quadrant indicates, when a policy is both easily convertible and situated in a change-conducive political-institutional setting, it is highly vulnerable to formal *revision*, whether through reform, replacement, or elimination. This is the type of change with which virtually all institutional and choice-theoretic models of policy formation are concerned. It is also, quite obviously, not the normal state of affairs in welfare state politics.

The most illuminating possibilities for the study of retrenchment, therefore, lie in the other three quadrants. When existing policies resist conversion but the political-institutional context permits the creation of new policies, the dominant pattern of change is likely to be what Eric Schickler (2001, 13) terms "layering," in which proponents of change work around institutions that have fostered vested interests and long-term expectations "by adding new institutions rather than dismantling the old." When the political-institutional context poses formidable barriers to authoritative reform but a policy is highly mutable, by contrast, the dominant pattern is instead likely to be "conversion" (Thelen 2003), in which policies are adapted over time rather than replaced or eliminated. Drift, for its part, is most likely when a policy poses high hurdles to internal conversion (meaning it is hard to shift it to new ends) *and* when the status-quo bias of the external political context is also high (meaning it is hard to eliminate or supplant existing policies). Drift, as noted, may be inadvertent. Or it may be the result of active attempts to block adaptation of institutions to changing circumstances. Finally, all these forms of change, if successful in undermining support coalitions or the ability of policies to achieve their goals, should increase the ability to convert, alter, or eliminate existing policies in the future.

As we shall see, each of these forms of retrenchment was on display in the 1980s and 1990s. Drift was the most pervasive dynamic, as critics of the welfare state grew increasingly adept at using the famously fragmented American political system to block legislative reforms that would close the growing gulf between social risks and benefits. It was not, however, the only pattern of the period. When policies posed opportunities for decentralized cutbacks, either because support coalitions were weak or policies relied on public-private or intergovernmental partnerships, opponents of the welfare state were quick to seize them. And when insurgents gained sufficient leverage to enact legislative reforms (yet not to dismantle existing policies outright), the emphasis correspondingly shifted away from conversion and the encouragement of drift and toward the layering of new policies onto old. *Layering* in fact aptly describes conservatives' use of openings in the early 1980s (due to Reagan's election), the late 1990s (due to the GOP capture of Congress), and the early 2000s (due to unified Republican control of Congress and the White House) to create tax breaks encouraging individualized private benefits that compete with public programs.

Because these changes largely occurred without formal revision, examining them calls for an analysis attuned to the internal reworking of otherwise stable policies and the shifting interaction of policies and their environment. This is, of course, a formidable challenge. We are a long way from having good data on what has happened to benefit rules (but see the fledgling efforts by Korpi and Palme 2003; and Scruggs and Allan 2003), much less on how these rules are implemented or actually affect citizens. But the claim that drift, conversion, and layering are crucial does carry with it prescriptions that run counter to the methodological thrust of much previous work on retrenchment. First, and most straightforward, it suggests that we should be interested not only in the structure of policies, but also in their effects—not only in rules governing benefits or eligibility, that is, but also in the outcomes that those rules produce as they are actually carried out by front-line policy actors in the context of other sources of social protection and shifting social conditions. Second, and no less important, it indicates that our *explanations* must take seriously the prospect that policy reformers will seek to change policies without formal revision, employing instead less visible means of change. In all these inquiries, however, one question should be central: Have welfare states continued to provide the inclusive risk protection that once defined their structure and goals?

NEW SOCIAL RISKS, OLD SOCIAL POLICIES

Despite many observations about the "new social risks" and welfare state rigidities in coping with them, the changing ability of social policies to deal with major life contingencies has not been intensively studied. This neglect reflects a larger blind spot in the vast literature on the welfare state. While everyone knows that welfare states serve vital insurance functions, most commentary assumes rather reflexively that income redistribution is, if not the defining goal of social programs, at least the strongest indicator of their performance.[7] Yet the reasons for making risk protection a key independent topic of concern are compelling. Not only are the largest social programs—pensions, health insurance, unemployment compensation, survivors' benefits—centrally about insuring against risks to income, but also many aspects of the welfare state that we do not typically think of as risk protection (such as child care and worker retraining) contain important insurance elements because they cushion families against the income shock of major life events.[8]

Risk protection and income redistribution are related but distinct. Although social insurance does redistribute income, its principal goal is to "moderate the risks of current income loss or inadequacy by providing secure cash or near-cash entitlements on the occurrence of defined risks" (Graetz and Mashaw 1999, 65). The bounds of social insurance thus delimit the scope of shared risk—the degree to which potent threats to income are spread across citizens of varied circumstances (*risk socialization*) or left to individuals or families to cope with on their own (*risk privatization*). To "privatize" risk, in this parlance, is thus to fragment and undermine collective insurance pools that offer reduced-cost protection to higher-risk and lower-income citizens in favor of arrangements that leave individuals and families responsible for coping with social risks largely on their own.

Intuitively, the boundaries of such collective risk pools can be changed in three ways. The first is explicit alterations of rules governing eligibility or benefits—the subject of most retrenchment analyses. The second and more subtle means is a change in those rules' implementation. Do all those eligible receive legally specified benefits? Do policies permit discretion on the part of administrators or providers? The final source of change is a shift in the constellation of risks itself. Risks may become more severe, leading to an effective decline in protection, or new risks can arise that fall outside the universe of shared responsibility. As already noted, neither of the latter two forms of change is likely to be picked up by the conventional focus on active reform. Nor, it should be said, are these forms of change likely to be captured fully by data on redistribution, which can tell us whether more or less is redistributed at any time, but not how well policies protect citizens *over* time.[9]

About one point there can be little question: The constellation of risks that citizens face has changed significantly in the past three decades due to linked changes in work and family (Esping-Andersen 1999; Katz 2001; Skocpol 2000). In the employment sector, the shifts include rising levels of earnings inequality, growing instability of income over time, increased employment in services and in part-time and contingent work, and increased structural (rather than cyclical) unemployment. In the realm of family relations, the changes include rising rates of divorce and separation, declining fertility (a root cause of population aging), and the increasing prevalence of single-parent families. Connecting the two domains is perhaps the most important and fundamental shift in the world of work and family—the

[7] Thus Huber and Stephens 2001 limit their definition of retrenchment to policy changes that decrease the degree of redistribution from rich to poor (and from men to women).

[8] On the central place of social insurance in the welfare state, see, in particular, Baldwin 1990, Barr 1998, Iversen and Soskice 2001, and Moene and Wallerstein 2001. For more general discussions of risk and risk protection, see Baker and Simon 2002, Beck 1992, and Moss 2002.

[9] In response, some scholars have turned to panel studies of income (Burkhauser and Duncan 1991, DiPrete and McManus 2000, and Goodin et al. 1999). But although this research is longitudinal, it does not currently permit assessments of the extent to which family income dynamics have changed over time (the only exception is the preliminary findings reported shortly).

dramatic movement of women into paid employment. Each of these changes has placed new strain on social protections constructed during an era in which the risks that families faced flowed almost entirely out of the employment status of the male breadwinner. In the brave new world of work and family, even stable full-time employment of household heads is not a guarantee of economic security, and citizens are barraged by a host of risks emanating from families themselves.

Foremost among the economic changes is a major transformation in the employment opportunities and earnings of less skilled male workers that began in the 1970s. In a startling break with the past, "the earnings of less skilled American men began dropping after 1973 and fell precipitously during the 1980s" (Blackburn, Bloom, and Freeman 1990, 31). Moreover, average rates of unemployment among these workers escalated dramatically, and the nature of unemployment also changed, shifting from cyclical layoffs during economic downturns toward permanent job losses (Farber 2003). At the same time, employment in the (often low-wage) service sector and in part-time and contingent positions that offered relatively low pay and few or no benefits increased, and the median length of tenure of male workers dropped significantly.

The most easily tracked manifestation of these trends is a marked increase in economic inequality. Between 1979 and 2000, for example, the post-tax and -transfer income of the top 1% of American households on the income scale increased by 201% in real terms, and that of the top fifth by more than 68%. By contrast, the post-tax and -transfer income of the bottom fifth of households increased by just 8.7%, while that of the second fifth and middle fifth rose by 13.3% and 15.1%, respectively (Greenstein and Shapiro 2003). The growth in inequality of wealth during this period was even more dramatic (Wolff 2002).

This is, to many, *the* story of the post-1970s American experience: the reversal of long-standing expectations about rapid across-the-board rises in standards of living. Yet simultaneously, and in many ways in concert, the 1970s ushered in equally profound changes in American families. Most striking by far was the continued entry of women into the paid workforce, a trend that by 2000 had made two-earner families, once an exotic species, the majority of married couples. The increasing prevalence of two-earner families must be seen in part as a private response to the economic pressures families face—a form of intrafamily risk sharing that decreases vulnerability to interruptions of earnings or the high cost of services that housewives once provided yet, at the same time, increases the probability that a breadwinner will be subject to earnings losses (Warren and Tyagi 2003).

But if two-earner families became more common, marriages did not become more durable. Rates of divorce and single parenthood (in most cases, motherhood) increased dramatically. Lone mothers are disproportionately less educated women, who have increasingly delayed marriage but not child-bearing, in part because the men they are most likely to marry have suffered economically. More educated women, by contrast, are delaying child-bearing but not marriage and having fewer children, in part because the opportunity costs of child-bearing have risen (Ellwood and Jencks 2001).

Whatever their causes, these changes in family structure are clearly a significant contributor to inequality and hardship. The rise of two-earner families exacerbated family income inequality because high-earning women tend to marry high-earning men. On the other side of the coin, single-parent families are, unsurprisingly, much more likely to have low incomes than two-parent families. And with dual paychecks now a prerequisite for middle-class life, divorce and separation have come to represent potent risks to family well-being. A partial glimpse of these effects can be gleaned from statistics concerning the characteristics of people in poverty. Although poverty rates dipped in the strong economy of the late 1990s, they rose over the 1970s and 1980s and are rising again. But no less striking than the overall rise is the change in the characteristics of those affected: Poverty among the elderly fell sharply in the 1970s and has remained relatively low since, while a sizable and increasing portion of the poverty population is made up of parents with young children.

A similar, but in many ways more nuanced, portrait is provided by evidence on the number and characteristics of Americans filing for bankruptcy. As is well known, personal bankruptcy has risen dramatically, with filings increasing five-fold between 1980 and 2002, to more than 1.5 million (White 2003, 1). Less well known is that the characteristics of filers have also changed. Elizabeth Warren (2003) reports, for example, that women have emerged as the largest single group of filers, their share of filings rising eightfold between 1981 and 2001. Revealingly, half of filers cite health problems, childbirth, a death in the family, or substantial medical bills as a prime reason for filing. By comparison, a 1970s study found just 11% of filers citing one or more of these reasons in 1964 (cited in Jacoby, Sullivan, and Warren 2001).

The rise in economic inequality and the changing character of the poor and bankrupt are each strongly suggestive of the changing composition of social risks that citizens face. Yet perhaps the most powerful evidence of increased risks to family income is the growing *instability* of income over the past two decades. Robert Moffitt and Peter Gottschalk (2002), for example, have documented a marked increase in the variability of male wages during the 1970s and 1980s—an increase driven more by instability of wages than by instability of employment. Looking specifically at family income, I and Nigar Nargis of the University of Dhaka have recently traced changes in volatility over the past three decades using the Panel Study of Income Dynamics (see Hacker 2003). The analysis confirms that income inequality *across* families increased dramatically over this period. Our results also show, however, that the over-time variance of family income more than doubled between 1974 and 1998, even when controlling for family size and factoring out the secular increase in mean income. Indeed, at its most recent peak in the mid-1990s, family income was roughly five times as unstable as it was in the early 1970s. This is a potent indication of the increased risks to income that American families confront.

These trends have exposed serious gaps in the American framework of social protection—which, although widely criticized, is also widely misunderstood (Marmor, Mashaw, and Harvey 1990). Comparative researchers, for example, commonly describe the American welfare regime as one in which "benefits cater mainly to a clientele of low-income, usually working-class, state dependents" (Esping-Andersen 1990, 26). But although public social spending is lower in the United States than in other affluent democracies, public cash assistance for the poor represents only a tiny fraction of the total, and means-tested benefits as a whole make up less than a third. This picture is considerably reinforced when we consider tax expenditures and private social benefits, both of which primarily benefit upper-income Americans (Hacker 2002; Howard 1997).

The bulk of public and private social spending in the United States, as in other rich democracies, is devoted to major areas of social insurance—particularly health insurance and pensions. In part because the United States is the only nation in which contributory public health insurance is limited to the aged, public spending is highly concentrated on the elderly (Lynch 2000). By contrast, public and private support for working adults and families with children is comparatively anemic. The United States lacks universal government health insurance and family allowances, benefit levels under cash-assistance programs that aid families are low and falling, public and private support for child care is extremely modest, and employers have been reluctant to provide paid family leave even as they have cut back other benefits for spouses and children. Unlike Germany, Japan, and the Nordic countries, the United States also lacks universal long-term health care for the elderly. In some of the key areas affected by the new and newly intensified risks just examined, then, U.S. social policy was already comparatively meager at the outset of the period under study. If anything, as we shall see, that comparative meagerness has only become more glaring over the past three decades.

THE ANEMIC AMERICAN RESPONSE

In principle, U.S. social policy could have adapted to changing realities. As the pathbreaking feminist writings on the welfare state show (e.g., Orloff 1993 and Stetson and Mazur 1995), some nations—most strikingly, the Nordic welfare states—have dramatically increased their provision of services that help families balance work and child-rearing. Many of these same nations have also tackled the new realities of the labor market with active employment and training policies (J. Levy 1999). Putting aside some modest exceptions, however, the United States clearly did not follow this path. Increases in the Earned Income Tax Credit for low-wage workers (Howard 1997), shifts of money from cash assistance to child care and job retraining, and new family leave legislation were all steps toward a response. But low-wage workers continued to receive only meager public supports. Family-leave rules did not apply to small employers and did not provide income support to leave-takers. Government assistance for child care remained scant and frequently unavailable even for eligible families (D. U. Levy and Michel 2002). Despite newly intense job insecurity, unemployment insurance contracted for lower-income and intermittent workers (GAO 2000). And although failing to uphold the direst predictions, the welfare reform legislation of 1996 removed important elements of the safety net for the most disadvantaged (for a comprehensive analysis, see Weaver 2000). Perhaps most striking was a massive decline in employment-based health and pension protections among lower-wage workers—which was only weakly offset by public coverage expansions.

Suzanne Mettler and Andrew Milstein (2003) provide concrete dollar figures for some of these changes. The inflation-adjusted value of the minimum wage, unemployment benefits, and benefits under the Food Stamps and Aid to Families with Dependent Children programs all declined during this period, while unionization rates plummeted in the face of aggressive anti-union policies. Although, as Pierson (1994) argues, declining unionization does not necessarily imperil public programs that enjoy strong support, it is difficult to deny that it has weakened the leverage of those who wish to reorient social policy toward new risks or that it has strengthened the political standing of employers, particularly in negotiations over private benefits.

A further glimpse into these trends is provided by the cross-national measures of redistribution provided by the Luxembourg Income Study (LIS). The LIS statistics show that inequality before taxes and transfers rose sharply during the 1980s in the United States, which has the highest level of inequality among wealthy nations. Yet compared with other countries, the United States appears to have done considerably less to offset the global rise in inequality during this period. Averaging across the 12 other nations for which LIS data exist, for example, the reduction in inequality created by taxes and transfers increased 10% between the first and the last observations. In the United States, by contrast, taxes and transfers reduced inequality slightly less by the end of the series (1997) than at the outset (1986). In short, income inequality increased dramatically in the United States, but income redistribution actually declined. This pattern stands in stark contrast to the experience of nearly every other advanced industrial democracy.

It is important to emphasize that these were not uncontested issues. There were, most obviously, major attempts to scale back public social programs in the early 1980s and then after the ascendance of the GOP in Congress in 1994. Although these efforts had only limited success, they were not without effect. Perhaps more important, these struggles unquestionably helped produce a major shift in policy discourse, immortalized in President Clinton's 1995 declaration that the "era of big government is over." Although in both periods conservatives quickly moved to protect themselves against charges that they were hostile to popular programs, the larger drift was clearly toward the conservative pole of the debate. Proposals for major structural reform of public programs gained ground, liberals found themselves vying with conservatives over the depth of their commitment to make welfare recipients work, tax cuts that threatened future social spending passed into law, and calls for the creation of new social interventions all but vanished from public debate. This new climate has shaped the orientation and structure of the few new policy innovations that have been put in place, leading to an increased emphasis on tax expenditures, market incentives, and private provision. In more decentralized and discretionary programs, it has also shaped the character of front-line administration and even, some evidence suggests, the degree to which citizens take advantage of benefits for which they formally qualify (D. U. Levy and Michel 2002; Zedlewski 2002).

In addition, although few big new policy departures took place, a series of often-unnoticed incremental changes have produced, or seem likely to produce, significant longer-term effects. Most notable here are a deliberate expansion of tax-favored investment accounts for retirement—sold as an alternative to both older company pension plans and Social Security—the creation and expansion of opportunities for private health plans to contract with Medicare and Medicaid, and a significant loosening through both legislative changes and administrative processes (such as waivers) of federal restrictions on state and local social welfare activities. Waivers, in fact, were deliberately used by the Republican-led executive branch in the late 1980s because the "left was strong enough to veto certain policies in the legislative context that it has been unable to stop when pursued through the waiver process" (Teles 1998, 141)—a telling example of strategic adaptation to a political context preventing legislated policy reform. Moreover, all of these more subterranean changes, whether through drift, conversion, or layering, have been aided by the inherent difficulty in a fragmented polity of closing gaps that have opened between original policy aims and ground-level policy effects.

Indeed, overshadowing and dominating these other events were active campaigns to block legislation that might extend social protections to new risks or limit the weakening of existing protections. The Family and Medical Leave Act, for example, passed in 1993 only after it was whittled down for more than a decade—and vetoed twice by President George H. W. Bush. But this was a (marginally) successful example: Most proposals to close the growing gap between social risks and benefits ended up in the political graveyard, stymied by fiscal constraints, actual or threatened filibusters and vetoes, and formidable conservative resistance. The signal case of policy drift of this sort, as discussed earlier, is the failure to pass any proposal for expanded health coverage, despite declining private coverage, President Clinton's strong advocacy, and public enthusiasm for action.

This is an impressionistic tally, to be sure. But, we shall see, its message is confirmed by a closer review of recent developments in the two largest areas of U.S. social policy: health insurance and pensions. These policy areas not only comprise the majority of social spending in the United States (and, indeed, in all affluent democracies); in addition, by virtue of their size and the unambiguous popularity of the policies that constitute them, they are also widely seen as the most resilient components of the postwar welfare order. Yet as the next two sections detail, in both these bedrock areas, relative stability in public programs has masked major declines in the ability of social policies to provide inclusive risk protection. As both employment-based social benefits and government programs have eroded, social risks have shifted from collective intermediaries—government, employers, large insurance pools—onto individuals and families. Efforts to address new and newly intensified risks have failed, and new policies sharply at odds with established ones have been created and expanded. Although the paths of health and pension policy differ in crucial and revealing ways, their overarching trajectories appear the same: toward a significant privatization of risk.

THE UNRAVELING OF AMERICAN HEALTH INSURANCE

By the 1970s, the basic structure of American health insurance was firmly in place. For most Americans—more than 80% by the mid-1970s—private health insurance provided the first line of protection against the risk of medical costs. Historically, employment-based health insurance was provided by large commercial and nonprofit insurers, which pooled risks across many workplaces (and, originally, even charged all subscribers essentially the same rate—a practice favorable to higher-risk groups). Workplace health benefits were (and are) also heavily subsidized through the tax code, which treats virtually all workplace health benefits as exempt from taxation as compensation. (The revenue loss created by this tax break exceeded $188 billion in 2004 [Sheils and Haught 2004].) From 1965 on, the federal Medicare program provided public coverage for elderly—and, later, nonworking disabled—and the joint federal-state Medicaid program covered poor people on public assistance, the working disabled, and the indigent aged.

Since the 1970s, the private foundation of this system has undergone a radical contraction—in what amounts to a textbook case of drift and conversion within the bounds of stable formal policies. From a peak of more than 80% of Americans, private insurance coverage fell during the 1980s and early 1990s to less than 70%. Employment-based protection was the biggest casualty: Between 1979 and 1998, the share of workers who received health insurance from their own employers fell from 66% to 54%—a trend that, in a growing workforce, translates into tens of millions of workers without protection (Medoff and Calabrese 2000). At the same time, employers have grown less willing to cover workers' dependents, and they have required that workers pay a larger share of the cost of coverage, which has discouraged some from taking coverage even when it is offered. The result has been a marked rise in the number of medically uninsured Americans.

For more than a decade, the number of Americans uninsured for the entire year has been rising at the rate of about 1 million a year and now hovers around 43 million, with some 75 million—one of three nonelderly Americans—uninsured at some point during a two-year period (Families USA 2003). Almost nine of 10 uninsured Americans live in families headed by at least one worker.

The gravest effects have been felt by those on the periphery of the labor market: the young, the low-skilled, the low-paid. Among the lowest-paid 20% of workers, for example, the share who receive health benefits from their employers fell from almost 42% to just over 26% between 1979 and 1998 (Medoff and Calabrese 2000). These trends reflect multiple factors, including declining unionization and changing employment patterns. But above all, they mirror the simple reality that medical costs have risen much faster than median wages, outstripping the ability of workers and their employers to finance protection (Kronick and Gilmer 1999). With employers free to drop coverage, and workers under financial pressure to decline it even when it is offered, the risk of medical costs is being shifted from insurers and employers onto workers and their families.

This view is reinforced when we consider one of the most fundamental transformations in American health insurance since the 1970s: the rise of "self-insurance" among employers. As already discussed, corporate self-insurance—the paying of medical claims directly—was encouraged by the 1974 Employee Retirement Income Security Act, which protects self-insured health plans from most state insurance regulations and lawsuits in state courts. But an additional crucial underlying motive for self-insurance has been the desire of larger employers to limit the cross-subsidization of the medical expenses of workers outside their own employment pool. Rather than purchase insurance from external companies that provide coverage to multiple firms (and, as noted, traditionally charged relatively similar rates to all subscribers), employers increasingly financed just their own workers' claims, thereby pooling risks within—and only within—their own labor force. Self-insurance has thus seriously worsened the situation of smaller employers, which have employment groups too small to self-insure safely, while encouraging private insurers to weed out subscribers with high expected costs. The chronically ill, the near-elderly, and those with expensive conditions have all faced increasingly serious barriers to obtaining insurance as a result.

Meanwhile, employers (and in some cases unions, which jointly manage many self-insured plans) have joined with conservative politicians to beat back any attempt to revisit the provisions of ERISA that exempt self-insured health plans from regulation (see Gottschalk 2000). The ERISA Industry Committee, an organization of large employers created in 1976, has been perhaps the most vociferous champion of federal preemption of state regulation, supporting "legislation that preserves and strengthens ERISA preemption and reduces government interference with employers' efforts to provide cutting-edge, comprehensive health care benefits to their employees" (ERIC 2003). As a consequence, government regulation of private health plans has changed relatively little since the mid-1970s, despite a massive swing away from inclusive risk protection in the private sector.

Although Americans' prime source of health protection is eroding, public programs have largely failed to fill the gap. Medicare—a centerpiece of U.S. social insurance—has essentially been caught in a holding pattern (Marmor 2000): Its popularity and the veto-ridden American political structure have prevented radical retrenchment, but it has grown increasingly inadequate as costs have rapidly outstripped the program's constrained spending. In a striking demonstration of drift,

Medicare beneficiaries devote a larger share of income to medical care today than they did at Medicare's passage (Moon 1993, 10–11). At the same time, employment-based coverage for retirees and supplemental private benefits have been in a tailspin, as insurers and employers find that they cannot bear the risks Medicare does not cover. These risks are thus shifting by default to beneficiaries and their families.

Medicare has not been static, of course. But few of the changes made can be described as expansionary. Even the prescription drug benefit enacted in 2003 will cover only a very small share of seniors' expected drug expenses (while outlawing supplemental coverage that fills its huge gaps in protection). And other recent policy changes, including some contained within the 2003 prescription drug law itself, pose the possibility that Medicare's protections could deteriorate even further. The crucial example here is Medicare contracting with private health plans, an effort at policy layering that originated in demonstration projects first pursued by the Reagan administration. Conservatives have aggressively pursued the transformation of contracting into a full-fledged system of competing, risk-bearing private plans, which they hope will undermine the unified constituency that has blocked direct benefit cuts in the past. Although studiously careful not to challenge Medicare directly, the strongest advocates of a competitive system clearly believe that the traditional program should, as Republican House Speaker Newt Gingrich infamously put it in 1995, "wither on the vine." (Gingrich, in fact, was unusually candid about Medicare reformers' covert strategy, noting of Medicare that "we don't get rid of it in Round One because we don't think it's politically smart" [Toner 1995].)

In contrast, coverage of the poor has unquestionably grown: first, with federally mandated extensions of Medicaid in the 1980s and, second, with the creation of the state-federal Childrens' Health Insurance Program (CHIP) in 1997. These were important expansions, all the more remarkable because they occurred in such a hostile climate. Before ending the story, however, three important points should be emphasized. First, the expansion of Medicaid has only partially offset the decline in private coverage. Second, the trend toward expanding coverage appears to have run its course. And third, the 1996 welfare reform bill has created a massive exodus from the welfare rolls, with those who leave moving into the low-wage employment sector, where private coverage is rare. Millions eligible for CHIP and Medicaid are not enrolled, and this is likely to become more true as time limits on welfare kick in. In sum, public coverage expansions appear more like Band-Aids on a festering wound than an inexorable expansion of public protection.

In strategic terms, critics of Medicaid have been greatly aided by the joint federal-state structure of the program, which has facilitated cutbacks by fostering interstate competitive pressures in favor of budgetary stringency, while making cutbacks more difficult to identify and assign responsibility for. Since 2000, federal waivers have been aggressively used to encourage state-based program restructuring by the Bush administration (Park and Ku 2001), which also hopes to shift from the current guaranteed matching formula to so-called block grants, in which the states are provided a fixed amount of funds. Like Medicare reform, Medicaid block grants last became a major issue in the mid-1990s—when, as now, advocates of block grants espoused "an ideological commitment to shrink the welfare state and return power to states from Washington" (Weaver 1996, 52).

No discussion of the recent evolution of U.S. health insurance is complete without mention of the stunning defeat of the Clinton health plan—arguably the most dissected legislative failure in modern history (Hacker 1997; Johnson and Broder 1996; Skocpol 1996). Rather than rehash the saga, I wish simply to emphasize that its defeat represents perhaps the best evidence of politically mediated policy drift. The Clinton health plan and its major competitors reflected a belief that the American policy of relying on voluntary employer provision of health benefits was increasingly unworkable as a secure foundation for risk pooling. The opposition to the plan, centered among hard-core political conservatives, employers, insurers, and private medical interests, in turn reflected not simply the recognition that many of these groups would be immediately hurt by the plan, but also the awareness that its passage would create a new and valued entitlement for anxious middle-class and working-class voters whose long-term political allegiances were very much up for grabs. Thus conservative activist William Kristol warned that the Clinton plan would "relegitimize middle-class dependence for 'security' on government spending and regulation" and "revive the reputation of . . . the Democrats . . . as the generous protector of middle-class interests" (quoted in Skocpol 1996). On the other side, Clinton explicitly cast his crusade as an effort to undo the policy drift of the past two decades—drift that had created, in the words of the White House's *Health Security* report, "growing insecurity." "From the 1940s through the 1970s," the report explained, "the United States made steady progress toward broader health care coverage. . . . Beginning in the 1980s, however, the number of Americans lacking health insurance has increased steadily—while health care costs have increased at ever-rising rates" (Domestic Policy Council 1993).

In the end, the Clinton plan was brought down by much the same dynamic that stymied conservatives' efforts to dismantle public programs: the easily ignited fears of Americans that reform would compromise the social protections on which they relied—in this case, private insurance (Hacker 2002). But what is crucial to emphasize is that U.S. leaders debated whether social policy would adapt to the changing job market and declines in private protection. The privatization of risk in American health insurance occurred without major policy reforms, but it was very much a matter of political struggle.

In sum, when one considers the broader framework of U.S. risk protection in health care, the direction of change is clearly toward a marked narrowing of the bounds of collective protection, driven principally by the conversion and politically mediated drift of policies away from their original scope and purpose. To be sure, major public programs have been preserved. The demise of conservative efforts to scale back Medicare and Medicaid in the mid-1990s is a powerful illustration of the hurdles thrown up by American political institutions and the enduring popularity of established programs. But resilience in the overall framework of American health insurance has not prevented a major shift in the distribution and intensity of the risks faced by citizens. The Medicare program has stagnated in the face of rapidly rising costs. The Medicaid program has expanded, but not nearly enough to offset the implosion of private coverage. There has been a massive decline in private health protection, which has increasingly ceased to be available or affordable for lower-wage workers. Serious efforts to deal with this have been effectively blocked by a formidable constellation of ideologically committed opponents and vested interests. The outcome has been a significant privatization of risk.

INDIVIDUALIZING RETIREMENT SECURITY

The American approach to retirement security is also a public-private hybrid, blending public social insurance and employment-based benefits—and, increasingly, tax-favored savings accounts. But pension policy differs crucially from health policy in the respective roles of public and private benefits. Whereas Medicare and Medicaid emerged after the large-scale development of private health insurance, private retirement pensions largely built on top of the public foundation of Social Security. This supplementary role was embodied most concretely in the practice of "integration," in which employers that qualified for tax breaks for their private retirement plans were allowed to reduce pension benefits sharply for lower- and middle-income workers to reflect expected Social Security benefits. It was also embodied in the 1974 ERISA statute, which regulated private plans to ensure that they would be secure counterparts to the public foundation established by Social Security and even created a quasi-public insurance company to protect defined-benefit plans against insolvency. Put simply, while employers offered health insurance as workers' first line of defense, they offered retirement pensions to "top off" expected Social Security benefits—a role sanctioned, regulated, and insured by the federal government. Thus, in its underlying structure—guaranteed, insured benefits based on earnings and years spent working—the private pension system looked very much like the public, though it was much more favorable to the highly paid than was Social Security.

This vision of the division of labor between public and private still has relevance, but it is much less accurate or widely shared than in the past. First, since the 1970s, Social Security has been under serious financial pressure. Slower wage growth and increases in the ratio of retirees to workers precipitated the passage of two major legislative overhauls, in 1977 and 1983. Although preserving the program, albeit at reduced levels, these reforms have effectively ended its expansion.

Second, employers have rapidly shifted away from the traditional "defined-benefit" plans that were the subject of ERISA. Instead, they have adopted so-called defined-contribution plans (such as the familiar 401[k] plan) that are not tied to Social Security and, unlike defined-benefit plans, place most of the risk of investment onto workers. Although this momentous transformation is mostly a case of conversion, in which employers have restructured their plans within relatively stable federal guidelines, it is important to note that defined-contribution plans were enabled and greatly encouraged by new and expanded federal tax subsidies layered onto the existing retirement system during periods of conservative ascendance. As with health insurance, there has also been a basic decline in employers' support for retirement benefits—and, in tandem, a major privatization of risk.

As employers have moved away from defined benefits and decreased their commitment to pensions since the 1970s, employer pension contributions have significantly decreased as a share of pay. Like the decline in private health insurance, the fall in pension contributions is symptomatic of the broader reversals in the economic outlook of less-educated workers. Between the early 1980s and the mid-1990s, the value of pension benefits to current workers dropped in every income group, but by far most rapidly among the lowest paid workers, who already had the lowest coverage levels (Pierce 1998). In addition, tax breaks for private pensions and other retirement savings options heavily favor better-paid employees: Two-thirds of the nearly $100 billion in federal tax breaks for subsidized retirement savings options accrue to the top 20% of the population (Orzag 2000).

Although the post-1970s economic transformation was the underlying spur for these dramatic forms of conversion and drift, its impact has been deeply mediated by politics. The 1980s signaled the beginning of an ongoing tug-of-war between two increasingly homogenized and polarized parties, with Republicans seeking to create and liberalize individual retirement options and Democrats fighting to place new restrictions on existing pension tax subsidies and limit the top-heavy skew of individual accounts. The overall thrust of policy has nonetheless been in the more conservative direction—toward the expansion of tax-favored plans and toward the loosening of restrictions both on eligibility for them and on the purposes for which they can be used.

The path of IRAs illustrates the overall pattern. Included in ERISA as a retirement savings device available only to workers without private coverage, IRAs were expanded and made available to all workers in the early 1980s. In 1997 and 2001, they were liberalized again, permissible uses of the accounts were broadened to include education and housing expenses, and a new plan—called "Roth IRAs"—was created that would require account holders to pay taxes up front and then avoid all future taxes on their accounts (including estate taxes). Because, at the time, the vast majority of Americans already could establish traditional IRAs, the main effect of these changes has been to make tax-favored accounts more available and attractive to upper-income households.

The story of so-called 401(k) plans is different but similar. In contrast with IRAs, which are individual accounts sponsored by the federal government, 401(k) plans are employer-sponsored retirement accounts that operate under section 401(k)—a provision added with little debate to the tax code in 1978. In 1981, a private benefits expert pressed the IRS to rule that the provision extended to pensions in which workers put aside their own wages, much as in an IRA (Crenshaw 1999). The Reagan IRS agreed, and corporate sponsorship of 401(k) plans exploded. In 2001, as part of that year's tax-reduction plan, Republicans successfully pressed for dramatic liberalization of 401(k)s and IRAs and the creation of "Roth 401(k)s" similar to Roth IRAs.

The explosive growth of 401(k) plans and IRAs over the past decade represents one of the most important developments in the political history of U.S. pension policy. During the 1980s, contributions to IRAs, 401(k)s, and Keogh plans for the self-employed rose dramatically (Venti and Wise 1997, 85), and by 1998, their assets were almost a third as large as the American economy (U.S. Census Bureau 1999, Tables 851 and 852).

Behind this transformation lies a new conception of pensions, for these retirement accounts have few of the characteristics of either Social Security or older defined-benefit plans. These accounts are voluntary for individual workers, participants have a significant degree of control over investment choices, and benefits are often paid as a lump sum upon employment separation or achievement of a specific age and, increasingly, can be accessed for purposes besides retirement. Because they are voluntary, many younger and poorer employees who are offered them choose not to participate or contribute little. And the risk of poor investment decisions or bad financial luck falls entirely on participants—as became painfully clear in the wake of the recent stock-market downturn.

The strength of the stock market in the last decade obviously helps explain the enthusiasm for individualized investment accounts. But the shift must also be seen as rooted in linked economic and political developments of the past two decades. By the 1980s, defined-benefit pensions no longer offered the attractions to employers that they had in the more stable employment climate of the 1950s and 1960s, with its strict managerial hierarchies and large, unionized manufacturing firms. Nor, as Social Security's tax-to-benefit ratio grew less favorable, did employers have a strong incentive to set up integrated plans whose expense would be partially offset by the federal program.

No less important, however, are the underlying political motives that lie behind the expansion of private accounts. For years, conservatives despaired of ever effectively challenging Social Security. Even at the height of Reagan's influence, the conservative push for reform was quickly crushed by the weight of past programmatic choices. These past defeats, however, fostered a new awareness on the part of critics that Social Security could only be fundamentally reformed if there existed a "parallel system" of private individual accounts that could eventually be portrayed as a viable alternative to the public program (Butler and Germanis 1983, 551, 553). Conservatives therefore retooled their strategy to encourage private retirement savings through ever more flexible and individualized means, acclimating Americans to private accounts and layering the institutional infrastructure for a full-fledged private system on top of the core public program of Social Security.

The motives for this approach have been carefully analyzed by Stephen Teles (1998), who argues that "conservatives have slowly built up counter-institutions, counter-experts, and counter-ideas . . . [in] an attempt to solve the political problem of social security privatization." The core of this strategy, Teles concludes, was to "carve out a competing policy path, one that would slowly undermine support for Social Security and preserve the idea of privatization for the day when it was politically ripe" (14–15). This is layering *par excellence*.

Whether the day will ever be ripe remains a very open question. The reluctance of elected politicians to consider plans for even partial privatization of Social Security is overwhelming—all the more so, in light of the stock market and federal budgetary turnaround. The difficulty of reforming mature pay-as-you-go-pensions, which stems from the massive expectations and accumulated fiscal commitments they embody, stands out as the ultimate example of programmatic path dependence and policy feedback. Nonetheless, these barriers should not blind us to the significant change that has already occurred. As corporations and individuals have shifted to more individualized plans, the explicit links between the public and private systems have steadily eroded, undermining some of the self-reinforcing mechanisms that previously secured Social Security's privileged position. And most American employers have lost their direct stake in the program's health, as their own plans have broken off from the public pension core around which they previously revolved. These transformations are perhaps most visible in the growing role of tax-favored retirement accounts linked to the stock market and in the changing balance of public and private pension benefits—a balance that tilted toward the private side of the scale for the first time in the 1980s. Whatever else these momentous shifts foretell, they clearly signal a major privatization of risk.

RETHINKING RETRENCHMENT

In the end, then, the conventional story about retrenchment appears to be only half-right. The path dependence of large-scale social welfare interventions is undeniable. Yet the *character* of path dependence has varied greatly across different programs and policy domains. In some, such as Social Security, path dependence has implied relative stability both in formal policies and in their outcomes. In others, such as employer-provided benefits and some state-based programs, formal policies have been relatively stable but outcomes have not. A critical explanation for this difference is that in the latter areas, departures could occur without active policy change, because formal policies created opportunities for unilateral (or near-unilateral) action by the administrators or providers of benefits. At least as important as internal policy conversion of this sort, however, are politically rooted failures of public action—which retrenchment studies, focused as they are on large-scale policy reform, have largely missed. Even as the scope of American social protection eroded in crucial domains, concerted efforts to close the growing gap caused by this ongoing policy drift were repeatedly stymied.

By no means is this the last word on recent trends in American social protection. The need for comprehensive data on the ground-level effects of risk-protection policies is pressing, and scholars have only started to move toward assembling the types of evidence that might allow more conclusive answers. Nor, I want to stress, is the foregoing intended as a refutation of research on welfare state retrenchment that shows that big programmatic reforms have been quite rare. My point is not that public social policies in the United States have been radically scaled back, but that, for a variety of reasons, their ability to achieve the goals embodied in them has noticeably weakened. This is an argument that, while not infrequently advanced, has not been intensively interrogated, and its refinement could go a long way toward reconciling the conflicting views that continue to characterize the burgeoning body of research on welfare state reform.

The American experience suggests the considerable utility of this shift in focus, demonstrating a general pattern that I have described as "privatization of risk without privatization of the welfare state." Although public social policies have indeed largely resisted the political and economic onslaught of recent decades, efforts to update them to changing social risks have failed (*drift*), their ground-level operation has shifted in directions at odds with their initial goals (*conversion*), and new policies that subvert or threaten them have been put in place (*layering*). The result has been a significant erosion of U.S. social protection, despite the absence of many dramatic instances of policy reform. Because the American experience is widely considered to be the strongest evidence of welfare state resilience in the face of conservative opposition, this is a notable finding in itself. But it also carries lessons for our understanding of welfare state restructuring in other nations, and of the character, cause, and consequence of policy reform more generally.

In extreme form, American developments provide a window into transformations taking place in many affluent democracies, as fiscally constrained welfare states confront new and newly intensified social risks. As Esping-Andersen (1999) argues, these risks have strained the capacity of existing social welfare frameworks. Unlike Esping-Andersen and others, however, I have argued that the growing gap between risks and benefits is not simply a result of exogenous shocks to stable welfare states. Instead, I have highlighted two key respects in which the gap between risks and policies grows directly out of the politics of welfare state reform. First, while the literature on retrenchment has focused on active legislative reform, considerable evidence suggests that changes in policy goals and operation have occurred even in cases where formal policy rules have been relatively stable. Conversion of this sort is especially likely, I have argued, when policies lack powerful support coalitions and when program structures embody principal-agent relationships that leave substantial control over the delivery of benefits to actors other than the authorities charged with establishing policy rules.

Why change of this form has been mostly in the direction of restricted protection is an important question. In the case of subnational policymaking, there are of course the well-known constraints on redistributive spending that states face due to interstate competition for capital and skilled labor (Peterson 1981). But the changing orientation of front-line policy actors, such as caseworkers, also appears crucial, and much more work needs to be done to understand the actions and motives of front-line policy agents. In the case of employment-based benefits, the reasons for the retreat from inclusive risk protection may appear far more obvious. Yet it was employers, after all, who constructed the extensive private systems of risk socialization that they are now so busy dismantling. Their abandonment of the old order appears to reflect not just the declining worth of private benefits for corporate strategies, but also the absence of effective political counterweights in either government or the private sector. The weakening of organized labor may not imperil the welfare state, but in the world of private benefits, the precipitous fall of unions does matter greatly.

The second cause of risk privatization that is endogenous to the politics of reform is precisely the fierce assault on public programs that Pierson (1994, 1996) and others have seen as ultimately so ineffectual. My reason for highlighting conservatives' ability to reframe debates, block new initiatives, and create parallel policy paths is not that I wish to equate these dimensions of accomplishment with the large-scale reforms that retrenchment studies have searched for (and mostly found lacking). Although I believe that U.S. conservatives have been more successful than received scholarly wisdom acknowledges in achieving self-reinforcing incremental reforms, my essential argument is simply that, in a context where social risks are changing and policy drift is ubiquitous and consequential, *critics of existing programs have not had to enact major reforms to move toward many of their favored ends.* Merely by delegitimizing and blocking compensatory interventions designed to correct policy drift, opponents of the welfare state have gradually transformed the orientation of social policy. Fights over the welfare state concern more than whether programs will be cut or scrapped. They also concern the degree to which social policies will uphold long-standing goals and adapt to the world around them. We vastly understate the strength of the welfare state's opponents if we do not see the extent to which they have succeeded in this latter debate.

This "second face" (Bachrach and Baratz 1962) of conservative influence exposes an important soft spot in retrenchment scholarship. Retrenchment studies have argued that fragmented constitutional structures have very different implications in the era of retrenchment than in the era of expansion: The same institutional fragmentation that once hindered the passage of large-scale programs now presents an effective barrier to conservative attempts at retrenchment (Huber and Stephens 2001; Pierson 1994; Swank 2001). Yet this argument does not go far enough in acknowledging the conditional character of institutional effects. In the United States since the late 1970s, conservatives have had two central projects—cutting back existing policies and preventing new initiatives or the updating of existing ones—and whereas institutional fragmentation has indeed hindered the former project, it has facilitated the blocking activities that are the central strategic element of the latter. Furthermore, fragmentation not only creates multiple veto points. It also creates multiple venues in which conservatives can pursue their aims while hindering efforts by defenders of existing programs to undo the policy drift and parallel policy paths that result.

More generally, as we shift our gaze beyond episodes of large-scale retrenchment to take in processes of welfare state adaptation (or failures of adaptation, as the U.S. case seems to be), the political struggles that we find bring together the "old" and "new" politics of the welfare state in interesting ways. In the battle to scale back existing programs, we see the new politics writ large: the perilous obstacle course of veto players, loss aversion, and mobilized constituencies. Yet when we begin to consider the ways in which welfare states have responded to shifting constellations of risk and the weakened ability of established systems of social provision to cope with them, we see more affinities between present struggles and those that lay behind the welfare state's rise. There is good reason to believe, for example, that the power of leftist parties and organized labor—and of emergent forces like feminist coalitions—are quite important in determining whether and how welfare states adapt to new social realities. As just discussed, moreover, there is also good reason to believe that the institutional factors that help explain the size and scope of welfare states have effects similar to those that they had in the past on contemporary efforts to upgrade existing policies. The crucial difference between past and present—and here the effects of past choices indeed loom large—is that current struggles take place in the shadows of massive systems of social provision, which pervasively shape the challenges and opportunities that today's leaders confront.

To capture the interaction of old and new politics, this article has outlined a general framework for studying policy change based on the premise that opponents of existing policies weigh the relative costs of working within an existing policy framework, on the one hand, or of replacing or eliminating the framework through authoritative change, on the other. This calculation suggests that, in political settings that make authoritative change difficult, insurgents may not seek formal revision of policies, but may instead work to alter such policies through active internal reform or the blocking of adaptation to external circumstances. Although I used this framework to illuminate the strategies of opponents of the welfare state—and, in turn, to question the conclusion that there has been limited retrenchment of U.S. social policy—the argument has substantially broader applicability. Indeed, it hints at a solution to the old rational choice conundrum "Why so much stability?" (Tullock 1981) that does not rest on ad hoc distinctions between institutions and outcomes (Riker 1980) or on claims about the inherent uncertainty of reform (Shepsle 1986). Rather, it suggests that policy design choices are not equivalent to preferences regarding states of the world simply because policies can be used to achieve multiple ends. Reformers always face the fundamental question of whether the sacrifices they must make to work within an existing policy outweigh the costs of formal revision.

Within this framework of expectations, I also developed a set of propositions about the strategies that welfare state reformers will follow under different conditions that were well borne out by my analyses of pension and health policy. Faced with status quo–biased political institutions and popular social programs, conservative opponents of the welfare state have turned to strategies designed to abet policy drift, undermining long-standing programs while blocking efforts to adapt policies to shifting social risks. When the support coalitions behind policies have proved weaker or the latitude for internal change greater, they have turned to strategies of internal conversion, altering policies' aims or operation without revamping their formal structure. And when the political barriers have declined in response to favorable electoral or political winds, conservatives have successfully layered new policies that embody new goals on top of existing change-resistant programs.

Moreover, the role that private benefits play in a particular policy area—whether they serve as the core source of benefits, as in health policy, or as a supplementary source, as in pension policy (Hacker 2002)—influences the reform strategies that opponents of the welfare state adopt in the precise fashion that the conceptual framework suggests it should. When private benefits play a core role, as in health care, opponents need only play defense, keeping new state interventions at bay and abetting externally caused policy drift. When private benefits are supplementary, however, much more active use of government power is required to encourage the expansion of private options and undercut public programs, as evidenced by conservatives' layering of new tax breaks onto existing policies in the pension area. This framework thus offers a promising starting point for further analysis of the means by which established public policies are challenged and, at times, transformed.

The pursuit of theoretical advances should not, however, cause us to lose sight of the ultimate concern: the changing role of the welfare state in the lives of citizens. In the new climate of economic and family risks, the welfare state has had to run to stay still—to do more merely to secure past gains. In the United States, it has not done more, and when we examine the broader framework of American social protection, a strong case can be made that it has done less. The scholarship on retrenchment has offered strong reassurance to those who believe that the welfare state is an essential element of a just society. My analysis raises the possibility, however, that formal welfare state policies may turn out to be more resilient than the ideals embodied in them.

REFERENCES

Adema, Willem. 1999. *Net Social Expenditure*. Paris: OECD.

Adema, Willem, and Marcel Einerhand. 1998. *The Growing Role of Private Social Benefits*. Paris: Organization for Economic Cooperation and Development.

Adema, Willem, Marcel Einerhand, Bengt Eklind, Jørgen Lotz, and Mark Pearson. 1996. *Net Public Social Expenditure*. Paris: OECD.

Bachrach, Peter, and Morton S. Baratz. 1962. "The Two Faces of Power." *American Political Science Review* 56 (3): 942.

Baker, Tom, and Jonathan Simon, eds. 2002. *Embracing Risk: The Changing Culture of Insurance and Responsibility*. Chicago: University of Chicago Press.

Baldwin, Peter. 1990. *The Politics of Social Solidarity: Class Bases of the European Welfare State, 1875–1975*. Cambridge: Cambridge University Press.

Barr, Nicholas. 1998. *The Economics of the Welfare State*. 3rd ed. Oxford: Oxford University Press.

Beck, Ullrich. 1992. *Risk Society: Towards a New Modernity*. London: Sage.

Blackburn, McKinley L., David E. Bloom, and Richard B. Freeman. 1990. "The Declining Economic Position of Less Skilled American Men." In *A Future of Lousy Jobs? The Changing Structure of U.S. Wages*, ed. G. Burtless. Washington, DC: Brookings Institution.

Bonoli, Giuliano, Vic George, and Peter Taylor-Gooby. 2000. *European Welfare Futures*. Cambridge: Polity Press in association with Blackwell.

Burkhauser, Richard V., and Greg J. Duncan. 1991. "United States Public Policy and the Elderly: The Disproportionate Risk to the Well-Being of Women." *Journal of Population Economics* 4: 217–31.

Butler, Stuart, and Peter Germanis. 1983. "Achieving Social Security Reform: A 'Leninist' Strategy." *Cato Journal* 3 (2): 547–56.

Campbell, Andrea. 2003. *How Policies Make Citizens: Senior Political Activism and the American Welfare State*. Princeton, NJ: Princeton University Press.

Castles, Francis G., and Deborah Mitchell. 1993. "Worlds of Welfare and Families of Nations." In *Families of Nations: Patterns of Public Policy in Western Democracies*, ed. F. G. Castles. Sydney: Dartmouth.

Clayton, Richard, and Jonus Pontusson. 1998. "Welfare-State Retrenchment Revisited: Entitlement Cuts, Public Sector Restructuring, and Inegalitarian Trends in Advanced Capitalist Societies." *World Politics* 51 (1): 67–98.

Crenshaw, Albert. 1999. "Accidental Beginning for 401(k)s in the Tax Code." *Seattle Times*, 11 April. Available at http://www.seattletimes.com.

DiPrete, Thomas A., and Patricia A. McManus. 2000. "Family Change, Employment Transitions, and the Welfare State: Household Income Dynamics in the United States and Germany." *American Sociological Review* 65 (3): 343–70.

Domestic Policy Council, White House. 1993. *Health Security: The President's Report to the American People*. Washington, DC: Government Printing Office.

Ellwood, David T., and Christopher Jencks. 2001. *The Growing Difference in Family Structure: What Do We Know? Where Do We Look for Answers?* Cambridge, MA: John F. Kennedy School of Government, Harvard University.

ERIC. 2003. *Who We Are*. ERISA Industry Committee (ERIC) [cited September 19 2003]. Available at http://www.eric.org/public/who/overview.htm.

Esping-Andersen, Gøsta. 1990. *The Three Worlds of Welfare Capitalism*. Princeton, NJ: Princeton University Press.

Esping-Andersen, Gøsta. 1999. *Social Foundations of Postindustrial Economies*. New York: Oxford University Press.

Families USA. 2003. *Going Without Health Insurance*. Washington, DC: Families USA.

Farber, Henry. 2003. "Job Loss in the United States, 1981–2001." *NBER Working Paper No. W9707*. Cambridge, Mass.: National Bureau of Economic Research.

GAO. 2000. *Unemployment Insurance: Role as Safety Net for Low-Wage Workers Is Limited*. Washington, DC: United States General Accounting Office.

Gilbert, Neil. 2002. *Transformation of the Welfare State: The Silent Surrender of Public Responsibility*. New York: Oxford University Press.

Goodin, Robert E., Bruce Headey, Ruud Muffels, and Henk-Jan Dirven. 1999. *The Real Worlds of Welfare Capitalism*. Cambridge: Press Syndicate of the Cambridge University Press.

Gottschalk, Marie. 2000. *The Shadow Welfare State: Labor Business and the Politics of Welfare in the United States*. Ithaca, NY: Cornell University Press.

Graetz, Michael J., and Jerry L. Mashaw. 1999. *True Security: Rethinking American Social Insurance*. New Haven, CT: Yale University Press.

Greenstein, Robert, and Isaac Shapiro. 2003. *The New Definitive Data on Income and Tax Trends*. Washington, DC: Center for Budget and Policy Priorities.

Hacker, Jacob S. 1997. *The Road to Nowhere: The Genesis of President Clinton's Plan for Health Security*. Princeton, NJ: Princeton University Press.

Hacker, Jacob S. 2002. *The Divided Welfare State: The Battle over Public and Private Social Benefits in the United States*. Cambridge: Cambridge University Press.

Hacker, Jacob S. 2003, "Call It the Family Risk Factor." *New York Times*. 11 January, A15.

Howard, Christopher. 1997. *The Hidden Welfare State: Tax Expenditures and Social Policy in the United States, Princeton Studies in American Politics*. Princeton, NJ: Princeton University Press.

Huber, Evelyne, and John D. Stephens. 2001. *Development and Crisis of the Welfare State*. Chicago: University of Chicago Press.

Immergut, Ellen. 1992. *Health Politics: Interests and Institution in Western Europe*. New York: Cambridge University, Press.

Iversen, Torben, and David Soskice. 2001. "An Asset Theory of Social Policy Preferences." *American Political Science Review* 95 (4): 875–93.

Jacoby, Melissa B., Teresa A. Sullivan, and Elizabeth Warren. 2001. "Rethinking the Debates over Health Care Financing: Evidence from the Bankruptcy Courts." *New York University Law Review* 76: 375–417.

Johnson, Haynes, and David S. Broder. 1996. *The System: The American Way of Politics at the Breaking Point*. New York: Little, Brown.

Katz, Michael B. 2001. *The Price of Citizenship: Redefining the American Welfare State*. New York: Metropolitan Books.

Korpi, Walter, and Joakim Palme. 2003. "New Politics and Class Politics in the Context of Austerity and Globalization: Welfare State Regress in 18 Countries, 1975–1995." *American Political Science Review* 97 (3): 425–46.

Krehbiel, Keith. 1998. *Pivotal Politics: A Theory of US Lawmaking*. Chicago: University of Chicago Press.

Kronick, Richard, and Todd Gilmer. 1999. "Explaining the Decline in Health Insurance Coverage, 1979–1995." *Health Affairs* 18: 30–47.

Levy, Denise Urias, and Sonya Michel. 2002. "More Can Be Less: Child Care and Welfare Reform in the United States." In *Child Care Policy at the Crossroads: Gender and Welfare State Restructuring*, ed. Sonya Michel and Rianne Mahon. New York: Routledge.

Levy, Jonah. 1999. "Vice into Virtue? Progressive Politics and Welfare Reform in Continental Europe." *Politics and Society*: 27 (2): 239–73.

Lipsky, Michael. 1980. *Street-Level Bureaucracy: Dilemmas of the Individual in Public Services*. New York: Russel Sage Foundation.

Lipsky, Michael. 1984. "Bureaucratic Disentitlement in Social Welfare Programs." *Social Service Review* 58: 3–27.

Lynch, Julia. 2000. "The Age Orientation of Social Policy Regimes in OECD Countries." *Journal of Social Policy* 30 (2): 411–36.

Marmor, Theodore R. 2000. *The Politics of Medicare*. 2nd ed. London: Routledge & Kegan Paul.

Marmor, Theodore R., Jerry L. Mashaw, and Philip L. Harvey. 1990. *America's Misunderstood Welfare State: Persistent Myths, Enduring Realities*. New York: Basic Books.

Medoff, James L., and Michael Calabrese. 2000. *The Impact of Labor Market Trends of Health and Pension Benefit Coverage and Inequality*. Center for National Policy. Washington, DC.

Mettler, Suzanne B., and Andrew Milstein. 2003. "A Sense of the State: Tracking the Role of the American Administrative State in Citizens' Lives Over Time." Presented at the Annual Meeting of the Midwestern Political Science Association, Chicago.

Mettler, Suzanne, and Joe Soss. N.d. "Beyond Representation: Tracing the Consequences of Public Policy for Democratic Citizenship." *Perspectives on Politics*. Forthcoming.

Moene, Karl Ove, and Michael Wallerstein. 2001. "Inequality, Social Insurance, and Redistribution." *American Political Science Review* 95 (4): 859–74.

Moffitt, Robert, and Peter Gottschalk. 2002. "Trends in the Transitory Variance of Earnings in the United States." *Economic Journal* 112 (March): C68–73.

Moon, Marilyn. 1993. *Medicare Now and in the Future*. Washington, DC: Urban Institute Press.

Moss, David A. 2002. *When All Else Fails: Government as the Ultimate Risk Manager*. Cambridge, MA: Harvard University Press.

Orloff, Ann Shola. 1993. *The Politics of Pensions: A Comparative Analysis of Britain, Canada, and the United States, 1880–1940*. Madison: University of Wisconsin Press.

Orzag, Peter R. 2000. *Raising the Amount That Can Be Contributed to Roth IRAs: The Dangers in the Short Run and the Long Run*. Washington, DC: Center on Budget and Policy Priorites.

Park, Edwin, and Leighton Ku. 2001. *Administration Medicaid and SCHIP Waiver Policy Encourages States to Scale Back Benefits Significantly and Increase Cost-Sharing for Low Income Beneficiaries*. Washington, DC: Center on Budget and Policy Priorities.

Peterson, Paul E. 1981. *City Limits*. Chicago: University of Chicago Press.

Pierce, Brooks. 1998. *Compensation Inequality*. Washington, DC: Bureau of Labor Statistics.

Pierson, Paul. 1993. "When Effect Becomes Cause: Policy Feedback and Political Change." *World Politics* 45 (4): 595–628.

Pierson, Paul. 1994. *Dismantling the Welfare State? Reagan, Thatcher, and the Politics of Retrenchment*. New York: Cambridge University Press.

Pierson, Paul. 1996. "The New Politics of the Welfare State." *World Politics* 48 (2): 143–79.

Pierson, Paul. 2000. "Increasing Returns, Path Dependence, and the Study of Politics." *American Political Science Review* 94 (2): 251–67.

Pierson, Paul, ed. 2001. *The New Politics of the Welfare State.* Oxford: Oxford University Press.

Pierson, Paul. 2002. "A Quiet Revolution? Long-Term Processes and Welfare State Restructuring." Presented at Transforming the Democratic Balance among State, Market and Society: Comparative Perspectives on France and the Developed Democracies, Cambridge, Mass.

Pierson, Paul. 2004. *Politics in Time.* Princeton, NJ: Princeton University Press. Forthcoming.

Rae, Douglas W. 1975. "The Limits of Consensual Decision." *American Political Science Review* 63: 1270–98.

Rein, Martin, and Eskil Wandensjö, eds. 1997. *Enterprise and the Welfare State.* Cheltenham, UK: Edward Elgar.

Riker, William. 1980. "Implications from the Disequilibrium of Majority Rule for the Study of Institutions." *American Political Science Review* 774: 432–46.

Schickler, Eric. 2001. *Disjointed Pluralism: Institutional Innovation in the U.S. Congress.* Princeton, NJ: Princeton University Press.

Scruggs, Lyle, and James P. Allan. 2003. "Dynamics of Welfare State Regime Change 1971–2002." Presented at the Annual Meeting of the the American Political Science Association, Philadelphia.

Sheils, John, and Randall Haught. 2004. "The Cost of Tax-Exempt Health Benefits in 2004." *Health Affairs*, Web Exclusive, February.

Shepsle, Kenneth. 1986. "Institutional Equilibria and Equilibrium Institutions." In Herbert F. Weisberg, ed. *Political Science: The Science of Politics.* New York: Algora Publishing.

Skocpol, Theda. 1996. *Boomerang: Clinton's Health Security Effort and the Turn against Government in U.S. Politics.* New York: W. W. Norton.

Skocpol, Theda. 2000. *The Missing Middle: Working Families and the Future of American Social Policy.* New York: W. W. Norton.

Smeeding, Timothy. 2002. *Globalization, Inequality and the Rich Countries of the G-20: Evidence from the Luxembourg Income Study (LIS).* Syracuse, NY: Maxwell School of Citizenship and Public Affairs, Syracuse University.

Soss, Joe. 2000. *Unwanted Claims: The Politics of Participation in the U.S. Welfare System.* Ann Arbor: University of Michigan Press.

Stetson, Dorothy McBride, and Amy G. Mazur, eds. 1995. *Comparative State Feminism.* Thousand Oaks, CA: Sage.

Swank, Duane. 2001. "Political Institutions and Welfare-State Restructuring: The Impact of Institutions on Social Policy Change in Developed Democracies." In *The New Politics of the Welfare State*, ed. P. Pierson. New York: Oxford University Press.

Teles, Steven M. 1998. "The Dialectics of Trust: Ideas, Finance, and Pension Privatization in the U.S. and U.K." Presented at the Annual Meeting of the Association for Public Policy Analysis and Management. New York, NY.

Teles, Steven M. 1996. *Whose Welfare? AFDC and Elite Politics.* Lawrence: University of Kansas Press.

Thelen, Kathleen. 2003. "How Institutions Evolve: Insights from Comparative-Historical Analysis." In *Comparative Historical Analysis in the Social Sciences*, ed. J. Mahoney and Dietrich Rueschemeyer. Cambridge: Cambridge University Press.

Titmuss, Richard M. 1976. *Essays on "The Welfare State."* 3rd ed. London: Allen & Unwin.

Toner, Robin. 1995. "Of Touching Third Rails and Tackling Medicare. *New York Times*, 21.

Tsebelis, George. 1995. Decision Making in Political Systems: Veto Players in Presidentialism, Parliamentarism, Multicameralism and Multipartyism. *British Journal of Political Science* 25: 289–325.

Tullock, Gordon. 1981. "Why So Much Stability?" *Public Choice* 37: 189–202.

U.S Census Bureau. 1999. *Statistical Abstract of the United States*. Washington, DC: U.S. GPO.

Venti, Steven F., and David A. Wise. 1997. "The Wealth of Cohorts: Retirement Savings and the Changing Assets of Older Americans." In *Public Policy toward Pensions*, ed. S. J. Schieber and J. B. Shoven. Cambridge, MA: MIT Press.

Warren, Elizabeth. 2003. "What Is a Women's Issue? Bankruptcy, Commercial Law, and Other Gender-Neutral Topics." *Harvard Women's Law Journal* 25: 19–56.

Warren, Elizabeth, and Amelia Warren Tyagi. 2003. *The Two-Income Trap: Why Middle-Class Mothers and Fathers Are Going Broke (with Surprising Solutions That Will Change Our Children's Futures)*. New York: Basic Books.

Weaver, R. Kent. 1996. "Deficits and Devolution in the 104th Congress." *Publius* 26 (3): 45–86.

Weaver, R. Kent. 1998. "The Politics of Pensions: Lessons from Abroad." In *Framing the Social Security Debate*, ed. R. Douglas Arnold. Washington, DC: Brookings Institution Press.

Weaver, R. Kent. 2000. *Ending Welfare as We Know It*. Washington, DC: Brookings Institution.

White, Michelle J. 2003. "Bankruptcy and Consumer Credit in the U.S." Presented at The Economics of Consumer Credit: European Experience and Lessons from the US, May, at European University Institute, Florence, Italy.

Wolff, Edward. 2002. *Top Heavy: A Study of Increasing Inequality of Wealth in America*. New York: Twentieth Century Fund.

Zedlewski, Sheila R. 2002. *Are Shrinking Caseloads Always a Good Thing?* Washington, DC: Urban Institute.

Public Opinion and Its Roles

17

THE IMPACT OF PUBLIC OPINION ON PUBLIC POLICY:
A REVIEW AND AN AGENDA

Paul Burstein[*]

It is valuable to read Burstein after Hacker, for Hacker's piece raises the unsettling possibility that the public may often not get the policies that it wants. How likely is this in general? Burstein ably surveys the extent to which political scientists have found congruence between the center of public opinion and the introduction or existence of public policy. Burstein reports that quite a bit of the time political scientists believe that they are seeing congruence. If Burstein is right, then Americans should—so his findings imply—eventually get national health insurance.

• • •

MOST SOCIAL SCIENTISTS who study public opinion and public policy in democratic countries agree that (1) public opinion influences public policy; (2) the more salient an issue to the public, the stronger the relationship is likely to be; and (3) the relationship is threatened by the power of interest organizations,[1] political parties, and economic elites (see, e.g., Aldrich 1995; Dahl 1989; Mueller 1999; Stimson, MacKuen, and Erikson 1995; Page and Shapiro 1983; Smith 2000).

There would be much less consensus, however, on the answers to five follow-up questions widely seen as important but seldom addressed directly:

1. How *much* impact does public opinion have on public policy?
2. How *much* does the impact of opinion on policy increase as the importance of an issue to the public increases?
3. To what extent do interest groups, social movement organizations, political parties, and elites influence policy even when opposed by public opinion?
4. Has government responsiveness to public opinion changed over time?
5. How generalizable are our findings about the impact of opinion on policy?

This article distills considerable research directed at these questions. It is not, however, a literature review in the usual sense. Rather than summarizing publications in a conventional narrative, I use each publication as a source of data, tabulating the issues and countries studied, and the authors' predictions, variables, and findings. The analysis will provide the publications' collective answer to each

I would like to thank William Domhoff, Kim Quaile Hill, Lawrence Jacobs, Florence Katz, and Alan Monroe for helpful advice and comments. This study was partially supported by NSF grant SES-0001509.

* From *Political Research Quarterly* 56 (March 2003): 29–40. Publications Inc. Journals. Reproduced with permission of Sage Publications in the format Other book via Copyright Clearance Center.

[1] The term "interest organization" encompasses both interest groups and social movement organizations; for the rationale for treating them together, see Burstein 1998a.

question, and, at times, show how little evidence is available. Highlighting how little we know on some issues will point to an agenda for future research.

It turns out that public opinion influences policy most of the time, often strongly. Responsiveness appears to increase with salience, and public opinion matters even in the face of activities by interest organizations, political parties, and political and economic elites. Claims that responsiveness is changing over time or varies across issues rest on very little evidence.

The next section describes issues that arise in attempts to answer the questions. This is followed by a description of the data, presentation of findings, and conclusion.

ISSUES AND CONTROVERSIES

The Impact of Public Opinion on Public Policy

No one believes that public opinion always determines public policy; few believe it never does. Even dedicated proponents of democratic theory acknowledge that democratic governments sometimes ignore the public (e.g., Page and Shapiro 1983: 189); those whose theories attribute little power to the public concede that governments sometimes follow public opinion (e.g., Block 1987: 66; Domhoff 1998: 301; Korpi 1989: 313). What distinguishes those who believe democracy gives citizens genuine control over their government from those who believe it does not, is thus disagreement over matters of degree: *how much* impact does public opinion have on public policy?

This disagreement is an old one, and one might think it had been resolved, or at least narrowed substantially. But this is not the case. Indeed, it may be argued that the range of predictions about impact based on democratic theory has widened in the past 20 years, not narrowed, and that researchers are no closer to consensus now than they were then.

A good place to begin is Page and Shapiro's (1983) classic article, "Effects of Opinion on Policy." They begin conventionally, delineating theoretical controversies about the impact of opinion on policy: some theories (particularly economists' on electoral competition) predict "a high degree of responsiveness" (175), while others (notably those attributing great power to interest groups) predict much less. Their empirical conclusions are presented in a conventional way as well: on the one hand, the evidence supports one side ("opinion changes are important causes of policy change" [189]), but, on the other hand, problems in the research make them hesitate to accept their own conclusion—it would be "unwise to draw normative conclusions about the extent of democratic responsiveness in policymaking" (ibid).

What has happened in the 20 years since the publication of "Effects of Opinion on Policy"? Theoretically, those expecting responsiveness to be low have generally held fast to their ideas, but the paths of those initially identified with the high responsiveness view have diverged. Some (e.g., Stimson, Mackuen, and Erikson 1995) still argue that democracy works much as it is supposed to, with public officials consistently responding to shifts in public opinion. Others have come to claim, however, that the complexity of modern politics makes responsiveness problematic. Democratic institutions may link opinion and policy on issues that are especially important, relatively simple, and addressed by legislatures straightforwardly, but such issues are few. Jones (1994) argues that inherent limitations in both the cognitive capacities of individuals and the organizational capabilities of Congress mean that responsiveness is likely on only the few issues that the public cares about a great deal at any given time. Zaller (1992) and others (see Glynn et al. 1999: ch. 8) contend that on many issues the public cannot be said to have meaningful political opinions, so policy must be the product of other forces. And Arnold (1990: 271–72) suggests that many issues are so complex, and the legislative process so arcane, that most citizens are unable to ascertain whether their interests are being served.

Thus, predictions about the impact of opinion on policy range from its having a very substantial influence (Stimson MacKuen, and Erikson 1995) to its keeping policy, rather vaguely, "in bounds" in its distance from public opinion (Jones 1994: 238). Increasing theoretical sophistication about opinion and policy has not narrowed the predictions; instead, they have become more diffuse.

One might hope that 20 years of research would enhance the credibility of some theories and reduce that of others. But this does not seem to have happened, partly for a reason rarely discussed: researchers regularly describe their conclusions in terms too vague to be very useful. For example, Wlezien (1996: 81) writes that research "generally corroborates a linkage between public preferences and policy;" Page (1994: 25) that evidence shows "substantial empirical relationships" between opinion and policy; S. Hays, Esler, and C. Hays (1996: 58) that state environmental regulation is "quite responsive" to public opinion, and Erikson, Wright, and McIver (1993: 80) that the relationship between opinion and policy in American states is "awesome." Are they agreeing with each other about the impact of opinion on policy? Or disagreeing?

Faced with this conundrum, a recent review (Glynn et al. 1999: 301) decides to "let the cases and data speak for themselves, so that the reader may judge." This does not seem very satisfactory. Thus, our first task is to develop a way to report findings consistently, so that we can address the first question: what does the evidence show about how much impact public opinion has on policy?

Issue Salience and Government Responsiveness

Issue salience has long been seen as a key element of democratic responsiveness. Citizens who care about an issue are especially likely to take elected officials' actions on that issue into account on election day (Arnold 1990: ch. 6; Jones 1994; see also Lindaman and Haider-Markel 2002). This leads elected officials to be particularly responsive on highly salient issues.

The impact of salience on responsiveness has implications not only for particular issues, but for overall government responsiveness as well. If only a few issues at a time can be salient to the public and the legislature, and if responsiveness is high primarily when salience is high, then responsiveness will be high on only those few issues (Jones 1994: ch. 10). Policy would be kept from drifting too far from public opinion on low-salience issues mainly by elected officials' realization that their salience might increase at some future date.

These arguments about overall responsiveness presume that salience has a powerful impact on responsiveness. But does it? Our second question: How much does the impact of opinion on policy increase as an issue's salience to the public increases?

Interest Organizations, Political Parties,
and Elites vs. the Public

The most common objection to the claim that public opinion influences public policy is that policy is really determined by interest organizations, political parties, and elites, particularly economic elites. The resources available to interest organizations and elites may enable them to get what they want, even in opposition to public opinion (Domhoff 1998; Wilson 1990; Wright 1996), and political parties may, when in office, enact policies favored by their most ardent supporters rather than the general public (Aldrich 1995). Even when opinion and policy are highly correlated, the public's power may be more apparent than real; citizens may have been persuaded that they are getting what they want, while effective power lies elsewhere (Margolis and Mauser 1989; Page and Shapiro 1992: ch. 9).

These points seem obvious to most people, but social scientists have developed important alternative points of view. Many think interest organizations *cannot* get what they want against the wishes of constituents, who can defeat elected officials who ignore them. As Lohmann (1993: 319) writes, "it is puzzling that rational political leaders with majoritarian incentives would ever respond to political action" by interest organizations. Even if interest organizations may be influential, their political activities may be most effective when consistent with public opinion (Denzau and Munger 1986; Kollman 1998).

Indeed, some political scientists argue that interest organizations don't impede responsiveness, they enhance it. Hansen (1991: 227–30), for example, suggests that interest organizations may be influential, in part, because they provide information useful to legislators, including information about what the public wants, serving as useful intermediaries between the public and the government. They represent some groups better than others (see also Baumgartner and Leech 1998: ch. 6), but overall may enhance the impact of public opinion on public policy. Denzau and Munger (1986: 103) argue that it makes sense for interest groups to focus their efforts on legislators whose constituents are divided, ignorant, or indifferent, because it is too costly to influence legislators whose constituents are informed and clearly on one side or the other. The latter group of constituents winds up being effectively represented by their legislators, even if they are unorganized.

Similar arguments have been made about political parties. They may want to serve the interests of their most ardent supporters rather than the public, but electoral competition often mandates responsiveness to the public. They may have some flexibility in how they do this, but inter-party competition may actually increase the impact of opinion on policy (see, e.g., Blais, Blake, and Dion 1993; Burstein 1998b: ch. 5; Kitschelt 1994: ch. 7).

Thus, discovering a relationship between opinion and policy is only a first step toward ascertaining how much power the public has. We also need to know the answer to the third question: To what extent do interest organizations, political parties, and political and economic elites influence policy even when opposed by public opinion?

Trends in Responsiveness

The struggle for democratic responsiveness never ends. There is a long history of institutional reforms intended to increase responsiveness, including extending the suffrage, regulating campaign contributions, nominating candidates through primary elections, and instituting referenda and initiatives. To the extent that such institutional changes have the effects their proponents intend, government responsiveness to the public should increase (see, e.g., Garrow 1978; Rueschemeyer, E. Stephens, and J. Stephens 1992; Haskell 2001; Lijphart and Grofman 1984).

Responsiveness might increase for other reasons as well. Improvements in communications, transportation, and information processing may enhance citizens' connections to their elected officials (Clemens 1997; Hansen 1991; Walker 1991: ch. 1). Public opinion polls may increase politicians' knowledge of citizens' preferences (Geer 1991). And the rise of interest groups may have enhanced responsiveness as well (Clemens 1997).

Increasing responsiveness is hardly inevitable, however. Attempts to reduce the public's influence on policy have occurred often (Markoff 1996)—some blatant (such as denying effective suffrage to blacks after Reconstruction) and others subtle. Jacobs and Shapiro (2000: xvi) recently claimed that in the U.S. "the influence of public opinion on government policy is *less* than it has been in the past" (emphasis in original; also see pp. 326–27), largely because politicians have discovered how to avoid accountability to voters. A "growing body of evidence," they write (4), "suggests that since the 1970s the policy decisions of presidents and members of Congress have become less responsive to the substantive policy preferences of the average American." Both television and new strategies developed by interest organizations have been described as reducing responsiveness (Iyengar 1991: 42–43; Haskell 2001), and it has been suggested that it is reduced responsiveness that has led to the drastic decline in Americans' trust in government over the last 30 years (Bok 1997).

Thus, there is real disagreement about whether changes in politics and society have increased responsiveness or decreased it. Hence, our fourth question: are democratic governments getting more responsive to public opinion, or less?

Generalizing across Issues and Polities

Theories about the impact of opinion on policy are typically stated in general terms, and hypotheses about particular aspects of the opinion-policy relationship are supposed to be derived from general theoretical propositions. For example, the hypothesis that responsiveness will be lower on foreign policy issues than on domestic issues is based on the general propositions that responsiveness increases with salience and with how well informed people are, together with the fact that foreign policy issues are usually of low salience to a poorly informed public (Jones 1994; Kollman 1998; Page and Shapiro 1983).

The way research is usually designed and implemented presents at least a couple of impediments to hypothesis testing and generalization. First, researchers have limited resources and typically devote them to studying one issue they are particularly interested in, making generalization very problematic. Potentially, researchers could accomplish collectively what they could not as individuals, studying enough issues and circumstances to make hypothesis testing and generalization possible. Even collectively, however—here is the second possible impediment—the entire set of issues studied may be so small that it is unrepresentative of the set of all issues and an inadequate basis for generalization (Wittman 1995: ch. 13; cf. Page and Shapiro 1983).

Thus, the fifth and final question: what does the evidence show about our ability to generalize across issues and polities?

DATA

Data Sources

This article presents no new data, instead drawing on the work of others. But it is not a conventional literature review, because it is oriented to hypothesis testing, which most such reviews are not. The approach here is a hybrid; others' research is used as data, with their "output" serving as our "input." Creating the new data set based on others' work required decisions about which studies to include, how to code the variables, and which data to include (cf. Baumgartner and Leech 1998, and Burstein 1998c).

Any review of past work is necessarily selective; for this article relevant studies were drawn from the bibliographies of two recent, fairly extensive literature reviews (Burstein 1998c; Glynn et al. 1999: ch. 9), the three most prestigious journals in sociology (*American Sociological Review, American Journal of Sociology, Social Forces*) and political science (*American Political Science Review, American Journal of Political Science, Journal of Politics*) from 1990 through 2000, and the book in which Jacobs and Shapiro (2000: 4) contend that responsiveness has declined. To be included, a study had to gauge quantitatively (though not necessarily statistically) the relationship between opinion and policy at the aggregate level, utilizing at least one measure of opinion based on a large random (or stratified, random) sample and a clear measure of public policy. Not included were discursive narratives and studies of decisions by individual legislators.

There were 30 such studies, listed in the appendix. Because the focus was on major reviews, top journals, and relatively recent works, their quality should be high.

The unit of analysis is the *effect* of a predictor on a dependent variable, a measure of the relationship between opinion and a policy. Thus, if a particular author analyzes the impact of two distinct measures of public opinion on a policy outcome, that would be two effects.[2]

Studies considering many issues presented a problem. Some (e.g., Erikson, Wright, and McIver 1993; Stimson, MacKuen, and Erikson 1995) combine many issues into a single index (of "policy liberalism," for example). Arguably, such studies should be weighted more heavily, but it is not obvious how much more. Other studies (e.g., Page and Shapiro 1983; Monroe 1998; Brooks 1985) considered hundreds of issues separately before reaching an overall conclusion about responsiveness. If each issue were counted separately, those studies would dominate the results of any review like this one. The decision here was to take each study into account along the lines emphasized by their authors, focusing on coefficients for those relying on indexes and overall estimates of responsiveness (e.g., the percentage of issues on which opinion and policy agree) for the multi-issue studies. On this basis, the 30 studies include estimates of 52 effects. These will be called coefficients, even though not all take that form.

[2] For example, Mooney and Lee (2000) include two measures of attitudes—pertaining to the death penalty and to general ideology—and thus estimate two effects. Ostrom and Marra (1986) consider the impact of opinion on three aspects of defense policy: president's budget request for defense, congressional appropriations, and Department of Defense expenditures. Ostrom and Marra argue convincingly that the three are different in policy terms, and not alternative measures of the same thing, so the effect of opinion on each one is counted separately.

Gauging Impact

Researchers most often describe the impact of independent variables in two ways: in terms of statistical significance, and of substantive significance. The first is by far the more common in studies of policy change. Its virtues are apparent precision and objectivity. It is difficult to argue with, except on highly technical grounds, and provides an answer to what is often the key question in a piece of research: did a variable have an impact?

Statistical significance is not, however, a very satisfactory measure of impact (Gill 1999; Lieberson 1992; McCloskey 1998: ch. 9). It tells us whether there is a relationship (with some uncertainty), but not how strong it is or how important in policy terms. It is thus of little help in answering the first question: how much impact does public opinion have on policy?

Unfortunately, the studies use many measures of impact, and there is no precise way to compare them. That does not mean that nothing meaningful can be said about substantive significance, however. Each relationship between opinion and policy was coded as: 1 not significantly different from zero; 2 statistically significant, substantive significance not discussed; 3 statistically significant, substantive significance discussed and described as of little policy importance; 4 statistically significant, substantive significance discussed and of considerable policy importance; and 5 ambiguous, sometimes statistically significant and sometimes not, in ways unpredicted by the authors.

Many relationships fell into category 2: statistical significance was assessed, but not substantive importance. Authors sometimes used adjectives such as "strong" to describe statistical relationships when their only criterion was the significance level; these descriptions are meaningless in substantive terms, and were ignored.[3]

Discussions of substantive significance used language relevant to the particular policy setting. For example, Fording (1997: 21) found that the "increase in [opinion] liberalism accounted for an increase of about 2,100 recipients (per million population) in state AFDC growth," and concluded (1997: 20) that opinion had the "strongest effect" among political variables. Similarly, Bartels (1991: 466) concluded that public opinion "produce[d] an estimated aggregate impact of almost $16 billion" on fiscal 1982 defense appropriations.

How was it decided whether policy impacts were small (category 3) or considerable (category 4)? Here, the authors were seen as the best judges of their own findings. There is inevitably some subjectivity in such judgments, but a very careful reading of the articles showed them all to be reasonable (even if not absolutely unassailable); accepting their judgments seemed preferable to any obvious alternative.

As already noted, the unit of analysis is a measure of the effect of public opinion on policy. But which relationships should be included? Many statistical analyses present several models; the magnitude of particular relationships depends, to some extent, on which other variables are in the model and sometimes on other factors.

Here, as elsewhere, the choice was to generally reflect the authors' view, coding relationships from what they often call their "final" model. But there is one major exception to this practice. Often authors find during preliminary analyses

---

[3] Jacobs' (1993) study of British and American health policy did not include statistical analysis; his findings were tabulated in ways that seemed most consistent with his own interpretation.

that the impact of some independent variables is not statistically significant; these variables are often dropped from the analysis, not appearing in the final equation (and sometimes referred to only in footnotes). These findings, while negative, are findings nevertheless and are included. If they were not—if only the statistically significant findings in the final equations were included—it would be easy to overestimate how often public opinion and other variables affect policy.

It is necessary to point out that inconsistencies among authors affect the coding. For example, if two authors each have two variables gauging public opinion on an issue, one may include both measures in the final equation, while the other may combine them into an index. The approach taken here is, again, to accept the authors' approach.

RESULTS

The 52 coefficients gauge government responsiveness over a number of issues, and, often, fairly long periods of time (Table 1). Their geographical focus is very narrow, however; 28 pertained to American policies at the federal level, and 19 more at the state level; only 4 pertained to western Europe, 1 to another developed country and 0 to any developing country or to multiple countries as units of analysis. Thus, it is still true, as Brooks remarked in 1985 (250) that "almost all empirical research on the actual nexus between mass opinion and governmental policy has concentrated solely on the United States."

The Impact of Public Opinion on Public Policy

Three-quarters of the relationships between opinion and policy are statistically significant (or a plausible equivalent in qualitative studies; Table 2). Almost half of these were not discussed in substantive terms. When the magnitude of impact was considered, however, it was nearly always substantial.[4] Had the magnitude been assessed in every case, the percentage in which it was substantial surely would have been considerably higher than the 35 percent found in the table.

How should these results be characterized? Is the relationship between opinion and policy "awesome," to use the term Erikson, Wright, and McIver (1993: 80) apply to their own results? Or should we conclude that public opinion "does not have the routine importance" that many attribute to it (Domhoff 1998: 195)?

Social scientists are not very good at addressing this kind of question; that is why, after so many studies, some are willing to say only that there is "a linkage between public preferences and policy" (Wlezien 1996: 81) or that "the reader may judge" (Glynn et al. 1999: 301; on the general issue, see Burstein 1999). At this point, though, I think it would be reasonable to make a claim that, while not very precise, communicates far more than saying merely that a linkage exists: so far as we can tell from published research, policy is affected by opinion most of the time; often—over half the time when public opinion has any effect—the impact really matters substantively.

---

[4] The term "impact" suggests that the relationship between opinion and policy is a causal one. The authors themselves describe the relationship in a variety of ways. Some (e.g., Monroe 1998: 12) state that they are not trying to reach conclusions about causality, while others (e.g., Hill and Hinton-Andersson 1995: 924) state that they are, to the extent feasible. "Impact" is used here for the sake of brevity and because that is what all the authors are ultimately interested in, however cautious they might be in particular publications.

TABLE 1
Issues and Time Periods in Studies of Public Opinion and Policy

Issue	Coefficients	Time Periods	Coefficients
Social welfare	5	Before 1960 only	4
Taxes	1	1960–69	1
Other economic, business	5	1970–79	1
Rights, discrimination	4	1980–89	1
Capital punishment	5	1990-	1
Other domestic*	5	Multiple decades, through 1970s or earlier	13
Defense	10	Multiple decades, through 1980s	16
Policy indexes, multiple issues	17	Multiple decades, through 1990s	15

* Includes one environmental issue, one labor, one abortion, and one "social investment" (Devine 1985) and one "social consumption" (ibid.).

TABLE 2
Impact of Public Opinion on Policy

	%
None	25
Ambiguous	2
Statistically significant, policy importance not discussed	35
Statistically significant, little policy importance	4
Statistically significant, substantial policy importance	35
Total number	52

Note: Total may be greater than 100 percent due to rounding.

There are at least two ways to refine this conclusion and assess its credibility. The first is to see how robust the relationship between opinion and policy is under a variety of circumstances; the second is to examine it in light of theoretical and methodological concerns not necessarily addressed in the studies already taken into account. We consider robustness first. Theories about the relationship consider how it might be affected by salience, interest organizations, political parties, and elites. It is to these influences that we now turn.[5]

Issue Salience and Government Responsiveness

Salience has come to play a central role in theories of responsiveness. It therefore seems vital to know whether it actually has the impact attributed to it theoretically. How much does the impact of public opinion on policy increase as salience increases?

Unfortunately, the theoretical importance of salience has not led to a comparable level of importance in research. Few studies of the impact of opinion on policy include salience (Table 3). But the available data do suggest that the theoretical

[5] Might study results have been affected by study design? Comparisons were made between cross-sectional and time-series analyses, specific and general measures of policy (e.g., capital punishment vs. policy liberalism), and specific and general measures of public opinion (e.g., opinion on defense expenditures vs. ideological liberalism). None affected the results.

TABLE 3
Impact of Public Opinion on Policy When Issue Salience Is Taken into Account

Impact	Salience Ignored %	Salience Taken into Account %
None	32	0
Ambiguous	2	0
Statistically significant, policy importance not discussed	37	27
Statistically significant, little policy importance	2	9
Statistically significant, substantial policy importance	27	64
Total number	*41*	*11*

focus on it is justified. When opinion is related to policy without taking salience into account, opinion has no impact a third of the time. When salience is taken into account, however—when the measure of public opinion incorporates salience as well as substantive preferences—the combination of salience and substantive public opinion always has an effect and is of substantial policy importance over three-fifths of the time. This is consistent with the impact of public opinion increasing as salience increases.

These results should be interpreted extremely cautiously; salience is taken into account in the estimation of only eleven coefficients. Nevertheless, the results do bring together more data on the impact of salience than others have, and increase our confidence that it matters.[6]

Interest Organizations, Political Parties, and Elites vs. the Public

Often the central question in research on public opinion and policy is not whether the two are related, but whether the relationship is spurious. Might interest organizations, political parties, and economic elites be so powerful that when their activities are taken into account, the apparent relationship between opinion and policy decreases, or even disappears? Might interest organizations, political parties, and economic elites, that is, dominate the political process when they choose to?

It would not be surprising to find the apparent impact of opinion on policy going down when the activities of interest organizations, parties, and elites are taken into account. Bivariate relationships usually decrease when other plausible variables are added to the equation. Our question, therefore, is how much the relationship decreases when the new variables are added.

A caveat is in order. Like salience, organizations and elites play a critical role in theories of democratic responsiveness, yet theoretical importance has not been matched by importance in empirical work. Of the 52 coefficients, only 15 are in studies in which the impact of interest organizations is assessed, and of these, 9 are in studies considering only 1. The impact of the party balance is considered much more often—25 coefficients are from studies which estimate the impact of

---

[6] It should be noted that all issues considered in the studies must be of relatively high salience, since all were important to warrant attention from survey organizations or authors. Were all issues, or a random sample of issues, included in the reported analyses, estimates of overall responsiveness might very well decline.

both the party balance and public opinion—but the impact of elites hardly at all (only 7 of the coefficients are from studies considering elite influence).

First, interest organizations: Were interest organizations to get what they wanted, even when opposed by the public, the apparent impact of opinion on policy would decrease as organizations' involvement increased. In fact, though, data show the opposite. The impact of opinion on policy is most likely to be statistically significant when more than one organization is taken into account (83 percent of the time), a bit less likely when one organization is included (78 percent), and least likely when no organizations are included in the analysis (69 percent of the time, 26 of 37 coefficients). What's more, the relationship between opinion and policy is most likely to be of substantial importance when more than one organization is included in the analysis—83 percent of the time with more than one, 11 percent with one, and 32 percent when no organizations are included.

For political parties, the findings are again contrary to expectations. In studies including parties, the impact of opinion is statistically significant 72 percent of the time; in studies not including parties, 74 percent. And, public opinion is more likely to be of substantial importance when the party balance is included than when it is not—48 percent of the time versus 22 percent.

The results for elite influence are the same as for interest organizations and political parties. Taking possible elite influence into account never shows a relationship between opinion and policy to be spurious; all coefficients in studies that consider elite influence are statistically significant.[7]

The data must be interpreted cautiously, of course, but, as they stand, they do not suggest that the relationship between public opinion and policy is often spurious. Indeed—to be as cautious as possible here—the results are consistent with the possibility that interest organizations and parties enhance responsiveness rather than reducing it (for an example, see Burstein 1998b: ch. 5).

Trends in Responsiveness

What is the evidence that government responsiveness to public opinion has declined, at least in the U.S., as Jacobs and Shapiro (2000) claim? They do not provide much. Their conclusion rests on three studies that they cite repeatedly (4 and 297). The first, Monroe's, does support their claim, finding (1998: 13, included in this review) that consistency between preferences and policy change declined from 63 percent in the 1960s and 1970s to 55 percent in the 1980s and early 1990s. A second study (Ansolabehere, Snyder, and Stewart 2001), however, contains no data on public opinion or policy,[8] while the third is Jacobs and Shapiro's (1997: 4) own earlier work, where they refer to their "preliminary results" but

---

[7] We cannot address here how strongly public opinion is influenced by elites, interest organizations, and the political parties. Elites and organizations often influence opinion, but they are constrained by it as well. As it is, almost no one tries to gauge the separate impacts of opinion versus elite and organizational activities when each is affecting the other. Thus, at this point we include the usual note of caution, emphasizing that opinion is not simply the product of elite manipulation. See Hansen 1998; Newman, Just, and Crigler 1992; Jacoby 2000; Zaller 1994.

[8] The authors use congressional district votes for president as an indirect measure of the public's ideology, and their dependent variables are congressional roll call votes, not policies.

present only their conclusions and not their evidence.[9] Thus, their claim rests on one study alone. Do the data analyzed here support them?

Jacobs and Shapiro really make two related claims. The more general one is that responsiveness has simply declined, that it is "less than it has been in the past" (Jacobs and Shapiro 2000:xvi); the more specific claim is that responsiveness declined just since the 1970s.

Several studies, involving twelve coefficients, attempt to gauge changes in responsiveness. Two show it decreasing: Monroe's (1998) on multiple policies and Mooney and Lee's (2000) on specific policy preferences for abolishing the death penalty. Five show no change: Burstein and Freudenburg's (1978) on the Vietnam War, Hartley and Russett's (1992) on defense spending, and Mooney and Lee's (2000) on general policy preferences for abolishing the death penalty and two measures of public opinion on reinstating it. And five show it increasing: Erikson, Wright, and McIver's (1993: ch. 9) on responsiveness in the U.S. South, Fording (1997) on welfare recipients, Ringquist et al.'s (1997) on two measures of state AFDC policy, and Page and Shapiro's (1983) comparison between the 1950s–60s and the 1970s. Nine coefficients compare the periods before and after the 1970s or 1979–80 specifically; the same two show decreasing responsiveness; four, no difference (Hartley and Russett 1992; Mooney and Lee 2000); and three, increasing responsiveness (Erikson, Wright, and McIver 1993; Ringquist et al. 1997).

It is also possible to compare studies of responsiveness before the mid-1970s or so to studies of responsiveness afterward, even though the studies themselves do not compare periods. This procedure is problematic because studies vary in many ways in addition to period studied, but if we nevertheless compare coefficients gauging responsiveness earlier to responsiveness later, across studies (not including those considered above), we find 13 coefficients gauging responsiveness in the earlier period,[10] and 9 in the later.[11] Comparing these coefficients, responsiveness does appear to have declined; before the mid-1970s, only 8 percent of the coefficients showed public opinion having no impact, but after the mid-1970s, a third did.

Thus, data that directly gauge whether responsiveness has declined find more evidence of increase than decline, while a comparison of studies of different periods finds more evidence of decline. From a methodological standpoint, explicit comparisons within studies are the more credible. At this point there is little evidence that responsiveness has declined.[12]

Generalizing across Issues and Polities

Our ability to generalize about the impact of opinion on policy is very much limited by the geographic narrowness of the studies and the range of issues studied.

[9] They also cite Page and Shapiro (1983), whose data end in 1979 and cannot be used to describe change since then; in a footnote (note 3, p. 5) they refer the reader to a study described as documenting nonresponsiveness on a single issue, and to an unpublished paper.

[10] From Brooks 1985; Burstein 1998b; Burstein and Freudenburg 1978; Devine 1985; Erikson 1976; Fording 1997; Jacobs 1993; Page and Shapiro 1983.

[11] Bartels 1991; Grattet, Jenness, and Curry 1998; S. Hays, Esler, and C. Hays 1996; Hill and Hinton-Andersson 1995; Ringquist et al. 1997; Monroe 1998; and Wetstein 1996.

[12] It would be desirable to ascertain whether democratization increases responsiveness. Only two studies looked at this, but both found it did (Erikson, Wright, and McIver 1993: ch. 9; Fording 1997).

As noted, almost all the studies focus on the United States. The studies that compare governments generally find them equally responsive (British and American health care policy, Jacobs 1993) or unresponsive (Britain, Canada, France and the U.S. on a range of issues, Brooks 1987: 470); the sole exception is the finding that southern states in the U.S. were considerably less responsive than northern states (Erikson, Wright, and McIver 1993: ch. 9). But all the comparisons put together totaled only seven coefficients.

Theories about responsiveness have been seen as implying that it is likely to be stronger on some issues than others, and the range of issues covered by the studies permits very modest tests of a couple of hypotheses. Responsiveness is hypothesized to be higher on domestic issues than on foreign policy, because the former will usually be more salient to the public than the latter (Page and Shapiro 1983: 182). It is also hypothesized to be higher on issues of little concern to economic elites than on issues that challenge their interests, because elites are seen as having so much power they can get what they want regardless of public opinion, when it matters to them (Erikson 1976; Smith 2000).

The data on foreign and domestic policy provide no support for the hypothesis. Of the ten coefficients gauging the relationship between opinion and defense policy (nine on expenditures, one on the Vietnam war), all are statistically significant; on defense, government is more responsive to the public than on other policies, not less.

With regard to business interests, the studies are divided. Seven coefficients in studies of specific issues may be seen as referring to economic issues of interest to business: one each to child labor (Erikson 1976) and taxes (Jackson and King 1989), three to federal revenue and expenditures (Hicks 1984), and two to policies affecting business more generally (Smith 1999). All but one of the coefficients is statistically significant; the public has some influence even on such issues.

Brooks' work (1985, 1987) differs from the others by explicitly comparing responsiveness on issues of interest to economic elites with responsiveness on other issues, and his findings differ from the others as well. He made a special effort to identify issues especially likely to provoke strong reactions among economic elites, contrasting redistributive issues (involving reallocation of wealth, property, political rights, or some other related value among broad groups) with others. The British government is just as responsive on redistributive issues as on others (1985: 256), but the Canadian, American, and French governments are quite a bit less so, with an 11 percent difference in the U.S. (38 percent vs. 49 percent), 10 percent in France (34 percent vs. 44 percent; 1987: 473), and the greatest difference, 30 percent, in Canada (27 percent vs. 57 percent). There is thus somewhat more support in the studies analyzed here for the hypothesis that business interests affect responsiveness than for the hypothesis about foreign and domestic policy.

Overall, though, what should be emphasized is how our capacity to generalize is limited by the narrowness of the range of issues studied. The studies of foreign affairs all really focused on defense, and many important issues were touched on little or not at all (Table 1). Only one study each addressed environmental policy, taxes, and health, and none at all considered, for example, education, transportation, agriculture, non-defense aspects of foreign affairs, trade, Social Security, energy, immigration, housing, or technology (some such issues may have been included in the multi-issue studies, but they were not analyzed separately).

CONCLUSIONS AND IMPLICATIONS
FOR FUTURE RESEARCH

This review has shown that: (1) Public opinion affects policy three-quarters of the times its impact is gauged; its effect is of substantial policy importance at least a third of the time, and probably a fair amount more. (2) Salience does affect the impact of public opinion on policy. (3) The impact of opinion on policy remains substantial when the activities of interest organizations, political parties, and elites are taken into account; but the paucity of data on interest organizations and elites mandates great caution when interpreting the results. (4) The hypothesis that government responsiveness to the public has changed over time cannot be definitively rejected, because so little evidence is available; but that evidence does not support the hypothesis. (5) Our ability to generalize about the impact of opinion on policy is severely compromised by the narrow focus of available work, both geographically and in terms of issues.

Overall, the findings about responsiveness seem quite robust, not strongly affected by the activities of political organizations or elites, type of issue, or time. Yet it is also surprising how little has been published in major journals, or referred to in major reviews, about critical topics concerning public opinion and public policy. The publications reviewed suggest two agendas for future research, one substantive and one methodological.

A Substantive Agenda

More work is needed on every topic addressed here, but the findings highlight some avenues of research likely to prove especially fruitful.

It has long been hypothesized that responsiveness varies with salience, and recent theoretical work has emphasized how important salience is to political conflict and overall responsiveness—*if* the connection between salience and responsiveness is in fact strong. Thus, the magnitude of the impact of salience on responsiveness matters greatly.

Simple tests of the hypothesis that salience matters go back decades (e.g., Page and Shapiro 1983), and a great deal of data on salience is available. It therefore seems astonishing that only one study (Jones 1994) assesses statistically whether salience affects responsiveness, and only one more comes close to doing so (Burstein 1998b). More research on the relationship between salience and responsiveness is both feasible and urgently needed.

Another issue of great theoretical importance is how the relationship between opinion and policy is affected by the activities of interest organizations, political parties, and elites. Again it seems surprising how little relevant research has been done. Studies of the impact of opinion neglect organizations and elites, while studies of the impact of interest organizations and parties neglect public opinion (Burstein and Linton 2002).

Why this is the case is difficult to surmise. Contributors to each body of work ought to be able to get together with contributors to the other. Progress, though, would not simply be a matter of each set of researchers incorporating the other's variables into their studies. Some political scientists (Hansen 1991; Lohmann 1993, 1994; Wright 1996) who study interest organizations, for example, have argued that organizations are most likely to influence elected officials when they provide them with information and resources relevant to their re-election prospects. Yet few studies of organizational influence consider the impact of information, and those that consider resources seldom assess their relevance to re-election (Burstein and Linton 2002). Similarly, with regard to public opinion, if salience is theoretically important but seldom investigated, progress will be slight if those studying political organizations simply borrow conventional measures from specialists in public opinion.

A third concern is generalizability. Most studies of opinion and policy focus on issues that the researchers find especially important and of interest to them personally. Almost never considered is how the choice of issues affects our ability to generalize about the impact of opinion on policy. Even important issues are neglected; perhaps even more critically, issues that don't make the headlines are virtually ignored (except in the studies that address hundreds of issues) even though, in the aggregate, the relevant policies affect the public tremendously. The sample of issues studied is very much biased toward those of relatively high salience; if salience influences responsiveness, current estimates of the strength of the relationship between opinion and policy may be too high. But we won't know if this is the case until we study a much wider range of issues—perhaps even something like a random sample of issues.

Another concern about generalizability stems from the exceptionally strong bias in extant work toward studying the United States. Not only does this limit our ability to say much about other long-established democracies, it also may cause us to miss opportunities to study the consequences of democratization. In recent years many countries have democratized their political institutions, including Korea, Taiwan, and some new regimes in eastern and central Europe. Some have moved far along the democratic path; others have not. The time is ripe for studying how transitions to democracy (and failed transitions) affect governmental responsiveness. It is true that before the advent of democratic institutions, public opinion polls on policy questions cannot be conducted or are of doubtful credibility. Nevertheless, polling often begins early in the process of democratization, and the potential for gathering data important for understanding democracy is vast. Doing so in developing democracies (some of which may fail) should be a high priority.

A Methodological Agenda

I would argue that progress in the study of public opinion and public policy depends to a considerable degree on advances in measuring the relevant variables and estimating the relationships among them. Such advances are important not only for the quality of individual studies, but for our ability to synthesize many studies as well.

As a first step, we must ask how decisions about measurement and estimation affect results. Some of this is already being done, but not nearly enough. For example, Brooks (1985; 1987) finds much lower rates of responsiveness than others who study multiple issues, around 40 percent as opposed to 55 (Monroe 1998) or 66 percent (Page and Shapiro 1983). He says nothing about why his results differ from others', and they have responded in kind, referring to his work only in passing (Glynn, et al. 1999: 308) or not at all (Monroe 1998).

One likely reason for the difference is how long-term inconsistency between opinion and policy is counted. Page and Shapiro focus on whether policy moves in the same direction as opinion, counting each issue once. Brooks (1985: 252), in contrast, counts separately each year in which policy and opinion are inconsistent.

This probably means that controversial issues (disproportionately the subject of polls year after year) will be counted many times, while issues more easily resolved with agreement between opinion and policy will drop off the political agenda and out of his data set. Monroe's (1998: 10–11) approach is a hybrid, sometimes including an issue more than once, sometimes not, and his results are intermediate between Page and Shapiro's, and Brooks'. It is not necessarily obvious which approach is best, or even whether the differences among them are responsible for the differences in results, but so far as I can tell, the issue has not even been raised.

A second important step would be to improve the measurement of policy. Some such measures are fairly intuitive, particularly expenditures. Others are the product of long effort, often collaborative (see, e.g., Erikson, Wright, and McIver 1993; S. Hays, Esler, and C Hayes 1996). Often, though, measures of policy are developed on an ad hoc basis in single studies, with little effort being devoted to validating or standardizing them (Burstein 1991). Research on the determinants of policy change is therefore much less cumulative than it might be.

Third, greater effort could usefully be aimed at standardization more generally. One reason it proves so difficult to reach conclusions about the impact of opinion on policy is the great variation among studies in measurement, causal models, estimation of impact, and so on. This makes comparison among studies problematic, and, indeed, makes it difficult to imagine successfully carrying out formal meta-analyses that would provide a more comprehensive and precise summary of what we know (Stanley 2001). It is perhaps no surprise that some writers on opinion and policy figuratively throw up their hands and decline to reach any conclusions, but the field need not remain that way.

Of course, much variation among studies is necessitated by the particularities of issues, available data, political institutions, and historical circumstances. Nevertheless, there has recently been some very real progress toward standardization in measurement. Erikson, Stimson, Wright, and their colleagues (Erikson, Wright, and McIver 1993; Stimson, MacKuen, and Erikson 1995) have developed measures of opinion and policy useful to many researchers (e.g., Barrilleaux 1997; Fording 1997; Grattet, Jenness, and Curry 1998; S. Hays, Esler, and C. Hays 1996; Hill and Hinton-Andersson 1995; Mooney and Lee 2000; Radcliff and Saiz 1998); careful work by all these researchers, in turn, may help to validate the measures. This is most certainly not a claim that progress requires that scholars all use the same measures; rather, our understanding of opinion and policy will advance more rapidly when researchers see themselves as part of a common enterprise, with regard not only to theory, but to research design as well.

Arguably less progress has been made with regard to causal models and estimates of impact, but we can imagine what such progress might look like. Although there are major theoretical controversies about the determinants of policy change, there is considerable consensus as to what factors might be important and should be included in research whenever possible; when they cannot be included, researchers should discuss the implications of their absence. Similar arguments can be made about statistical analysis. Were researchers in different policy areas to incorporate each other's advances in their own work, our understanding of public opinion and public policy would increase more rapidly.

Finally, there is another issue pertaining to generalizability. Studies of the impact of opinion on policy always begin with public opinion—that is, with issues for which public opinion data are available. But such data are available for only a small fraction of all issues, those controversial enough to warrant attention from survey organizations. Thus, even random samples of all issues for which opinion data are available will be biased samples of all issues, weighted toward issues of relatively high salience, and studies based on such samples may exaggerate the impact of opinion on policy. It may be possible to get around this problem to some extent by developing indexes of general public opinion across a very wide range of issues (e.g., Erikson, Wright, and McIver 1993; Stimson, MacKuen, and Erikson 1995), but serious work on this problem has barely begun.

This somewhat unconventional review has led to two types of conclusions. The first pertains to what we know about the impact of public opinion on public policy. The second follows from highlighting what we don't know and how this leads to an agenda for future research. Much progress has been made; what needs to be done is clear.

APPENDIX
Studies of the Impact of Public Opinion on Public Policy

Authors, Date	Policy	Political Units
Barrilleaux 1997	policy liberalism	U.S. states
Bartels 1991	defense	U.S.
Brooks 1985	many	U.S., U.K., Canada
Brooks 1987	many	France
Burstein 1998b	equal employment opportunity	U.S.
Burstein & Freudenburg 1978	Vietnam war	U.S.
Devine 1985	social investment; health, education, others	U.S.
Erikson 1976	capital punishment, child labor, women's rights	U.S. states
Erikson, Wright, McIver 1993	policy liberalism	U.S. states
Fording 1997	AFDC recipient rates	U.S. states
Grattet, Jenness, & Curry 1998	hate crimes	U.S. states
Hartley & Russett 1992	defense	U.S.
Hays, Esler, & Hays 1996	environmental	U.S. states
Hicks 1984	budgets, revenues, expenditures	U.S.
Hill & Hinton-Andersson 1995	policy liberalism	U.S. states
Hill, et al. 1995; Ringquist et al. 1997	welfare benefits	U.S. states
Ignagni & Meernik 1994	many (Supreme Court decisions)	U.S.
Jackson & King 1989	taxes	U.S.
Jacobs 1993	health care	U.S., U.K.
Jencks 1985	defense	U.S.
Jones 1994	defense	U.S.
Monroe 1998	many	U.S.
Mooney 2000	capital punishment	U.S. states
Ostrom and Marra 1986	defense	U.S.
Page and Shapiro 1983	many	U.S.
Radcliffe and Saiz 1998	policy liberalism	U.S. states
Smith 1999	policies favoring business	U.S.
Stimson, et al. 1995	policy liberalism	U.S.
Wetstein 1996	abortion	U.S. states
Wlezien 1996	defense	U.S.

REFERENCES

Aldrich, John H. 1995. *Why Parties? The Origin and Transformation of Political Parties in America*. Chicago: University of Chicago Press.

Ansolabehere, Stephen, James M. Snyder, Jr., and Charles Stewart III. 2001. "Candidate Positioning in U.S. House Elections." *American Journal of Political Science* 45: 136–59.

Arnold, R. Douglas. 1990. *The Logic of Congressional Action*. New Haven, CT: Yale University Press.

Barrilleaux, Charles. 1997. "A Test of the Independent Influences of Electoral Competition and Party Strength in a Model of State Policy-Making." *American Journal of Political Science* 41: 1462–66.

Bartels, Larry M. 1991. "Constituency Opinion and Congressional Policy Making: The Reagan Defense Buildup." *American Political Science Review* 85: 457–74.

Baumgartner, Frank R., and Beth L. Leech. 1998. *Basic Interests: The Importance of Groups in Politics and in Political Science*. Princeton, NJ: Princeton University Press.

Blais, André, Donald Blake, and Stéphane Dion. 1993. "Do Parties Make A Difference?" *American Journal of Political Science* 37: 40–62.

Block, Fred. 1987. "The Ruling Class Does Not Rule." In Fred Block, *Revising State Theory*, pp. 1–68. Philadelphia, PA: Temple University Press.

Bok, Derek. 1997. "Measuring the Performance of Government." In Joseph S. Nye, Jr., Philip D. Zelikow, and David C. King, eds., *Why People Don't Trust Government*. Cambridge, MA: Harvard University Press.

Brooks, Joel E. 1985. "Democratic Frustration in the Anglo-American Polities." *Western Political Quarterly* 38: 250–61.

———. 1987. "The Opinion-Policy Nexus in France." *Journal of Politics* 49: 465–80.

Burstein, Paul. 1991. "Policy Domains." *Annual Review of Sociology* 17: 327–50.

———. 1998a. "Interest Organizations, Political Parties, and the Study of Democratic Politics." In Ann Costain and Andrew McFarland, eds., *Social Movements and American Political Institutions*. Boulder, CO: Rowman and Littlefield.

———. 1998b. *Discrimination, Jobs, and Politics*. Chicago: University of Chicago Press.

———. 1998c. "Bringing the Public Back In." *Social Forces* 77:27–62.

———. 1999. "How Responsive Might Legislatures be to Public Opinion?" Paper presented at the annual meeting of the American Political Science Association, Atlanta.

Burstein, Paul, and William Freudenburg. 1978. "Changing Public Policy: the Impact of Public Opinion, War Costs, and Anti-War Demonstrations on Senate Voting on Vietnam War Motions, 1964–1973." *American Journal of Sociology* 84: 99–122.

Burstein, Paul, and April Linton. 2002. "The Impact of Political Parties, Interest Groups, and Social Movement Organizations on Public Policy." *Social Forces* 81: 380–408.

Clemens, Elisabeth S. 1997. *The People's Lobby: Organizational Innovation and the Rise of Interest Group Politics in the United States, 1890–1925*. Chicago: University of Chicago Press.

Dahl, Robert. 1989. *Democracy and Its Critics*. New Haven, CT: Yale University Press.

Denzau, Arthur T., and Michael C. Munger. 1986. "Legislators and Interest Groups: How Unorganized Interests Get Represented." *American Political Science Review* 80: 89–106.

Devine, Joel E. 1985. "State and State Expenditure: Determinants of Social Investment and Social Consumption in the Postwar United States." *American Sociological Review* 50: 150–65.

Domhoff, G. William. 1998. *Who Rules America: Power and Politics in the Year 2000*. Mountain View, CA: Mayfield.

Downs, Anthony. 1957. *An Economic Theory of Democracy*. New York: Harper and Brothers.

Erikson, Robert S. 1976. "The Relationship between Public Opinion and State Policy: A New Look Based on Some Forgotten Data." *American Journal of Political Science* 20: 25–36.

Erikson, Robert S., Gerald C. Wright, Jr., and John P. McIver. 1993. *Statehouse Democracy*. New York: Cambridge University Press.

Fording, Richard C. 1997. "The Conditional Effect of Violence as a Political Tactic: Mass Insurgency, Welfare Generosity, and Electoral Context in the American States." *American Journal of Political Science* 41: 1–29.

Garrow, David. 1978. *Protest at Selma: Martin Luther King, Jr., and the Voting Rights Act of 1965*. New Haven, CT: Yale University Press.

Geer, John G. 1991. "Critical Realignments and the Public Opinion Poll." *Journal of Politics* 53: 434–53.

Gill, Jeff. 1999. "The Insignificance of Null Hypothesis Significance Testing." *Political Research Quarterly* 52: 647–74.

Glynn, Carroll J., Susan Herbst, Garrett J. O'Keefe, and Robert Y. Shapiro (chapter 9 coauthored with Lawrence Jacobs). 1999. *Public Opinion*. Boulder, CO: Westview Press.

Grattet, Ryken, Valerie Jenness, and Theodore R. Curry. 1998. "The Homogenization and Differentiation of Hate Crime Law in the United States, 1978 to 1995." *American Sociological Review* 63: 286–307.

Hansen, John Mark. 1991. *Gaining Access: Congress and the Farm Lobby, 1919–1981*. Chicago: University of Chicago Press.

———. 1998. "Individuals, Institutions, and Public Preferences over Public Finance." *American Political Science Review* 92: 513–31.

Hartley, Thomas, and Bruce Russett. 1992. "Public Opinion and the Common Defense." *American Political Science Review* 86: 905–15.

Haskell, John. 2001. *Direct Democracy or Representative Government?* Boulder, CO: Westview.

Hays, Scott P., Michael Esler, and Carol E. Hays. 1996. "Environmental Commitment among the States." *Publius: The Journal of Federalism* 26: 41–58.

Hicks, Alexander. 1984. "Elections, Keynes, Bureaucracy, and Class: Explaining U.S. Budget Deficits, 1961–1978." *American Sociological Review* 49: 165–81.

Hill, Kim Quaile, and Angela Hinton-Andersson. 1995. "Pathways of Representation: A Causal Analysis of Public Opinion-Policy Linkages." *American Journal of Political Science* 39: 924–35.

Hill, Kim Quaile, Jan E. Leighley, and Angela Hinton-Anderson. 1995. "Lower-Class Mobilization and Policy Linkage in the U.S. States." *American Journal of Political Science* 39: 75–86.

Ignagni, Joseph, and James Meernik. 1994. "Explaining Congressional Attempts to Reverse Supreme Court Decisions." *Political Research-Quarterly* 47: 353–71.

Iyengar, Shanto. 1991. *Is Anyone Responsible? How Television Frames Political Issues*. Chicago: University of Chicago Press.

Jackson, John E., and David C. King. 1989. "Public Goods, Private Interests, and Representation." *American Political Science Review* 83: 1143–64.

Jacobs, Lawrence R. 1993. *The Health of Nations: Public Opinion and the Making of American and British Health Policy*. Cornell University Press.

———. 2000. *Politicians Don't Pander: Political Manipulation and the Loss of Democratic Responsiveness*. Chicago: University of Chicago Press.

Jacobs, Lawrence R., and Robert Y. Shapiro. 1997. "Debunking the Pandering Politician Myth." *The Public Perspective* 8 (April/May): 3–5.

———. 2000. "Issue Framing and Public Opinion on Government Spending," *American Journal of Political Science* 44: 750–67

Jencks, Christopher. 1985. "Methodological Problems in Studying 'Military Keynesianism.'" *American Journal of Sociology* 91: 373–79.

Jones, Bryan D. 1994. *Reconceiving Decision-Making in Democratic Politics*. Chicago: University of Chicago Press.

Kitschelt, Herbert. 1994. *The Transformation of European Social Democracy*. New York: Cambridge University Press.

Kollman, Ken. 1998. *Outside Lobbying: Public Opinion and Interest Group Strategies.* Princeton, NJ: Princeton University Press.

Korpi, Walter. 1989. "Power, Politics, and State Autonomy in the Development of Social Citizenship." *American Sociological Review* 54: 309–28.

Lieberson, Stanley. 1992. "Einstein, Renoir, and Greeley: Some Thoughts about Evidence in Sociology." *American Sociological Review* 57:1–15.

Lijphart, Arend, and Bernard Grofman, eds. 1984. *Choosing an Electoral System.* New York: Praeger.

Lindaman, Kara, and Donald P. Haider-Markel. 2002. "Issue Evolution, Political Parties, and the Culture Wars." *Political Research Quarterly* 55: 91–110.

Lohmann, Susanne. 1993. "A Signaling Model of Informative and Manipulative Political Action." *American Political Science Review* 87: 319–33.

———. 1994. "Dynamics of Informational Cascades: The Monday Demonstrations in Leipzig, East Germany, 1989–91." *World Politics* 47: 42–101.

Lowi, Theodore. 1972. "Four Systems of Policy, Politics, and Choice." *Public Administration Review* 32: 298–310.

Markoff, John. 1996. *Waves of Democracy: Social Movements and Political Change.* Thousand Oaks, CA: Pine Forge Press.

Margolis, Michael, and Gary A. Mauser. 1989. *Manipulating Public Opinion.* Belmont, CA: Brooks/Cole.

McCloskey, Dierdre N. 1998. *The Rhetoric of Economics,* 2nd ed. Madison: University of Wisconsin Press.

Monroe, Alan D. 1998. "Public Opinion and Public Policy, 1980–1993." *Public Opinion Quarterly* 62: 6–28.

Mooney, Christopher Z., and Mei-Hsien Lee. 2000. "The Influence of Values on Consensus and Contentious Morality Policy: U.S. Death Penalty Reform, 1956–1982." *Journal of Politics* 62: 223–39.

Mueller, John. 1999. *Capitalism, Democracy, and Ralph's Pretty Good Grocery.* Princeton, NJ: Princeton University Press.

Neuman, W. Russell, Marion R. Just, and Ann N. Crigler. 1992. *Common Knowledge: News and the Construction of Political Meaning.* Chicago: University of Chicago Press.

Ostrom, Charles W., Jr., and Robin F. Marra. 1986. "U.S. Defense Spending and the Soviet Estimate." *American Political Science Review* 80: 819–42.

Page, Benjamin I. 1994. "Democratic Responsiveness? Untangling the Links between Public Opinion and Policy." *PS: Political Science and Politics* 27: 25–29.

Page, Benjamin I., and Robert Y. Shapiro. 1983. "Effects of Public Opinion on Policy." *American Political Science Review* 77: 175–90.

———. 1992. *The Rational Public.* Chicago: University of Chicago Press.

Radcliff, Benjamin, and Martin Saiz. 1998. "Labor Organization and Public Policy in the American States." *Journal of Politics* 60: 113–25.

Ringquist, Evan J., Kim Quaile Hill, Jan E. Leighley, and Angela Hinton-Andersson. 1997. "Lower-Class Mobilization and Policy Linkage in the U.S. States: A Correction." *American Journal of Political Science* 41: 339–44.

Rueschemeyer, Dietrich, Evelyne Huber Stephens, and John D. Stephens. 1992. *Capitalist Development and Democracy.* Chicago: University of Chicago Press.

Smith, Mark A. 1999. "Public Opinion, Elections, and Representation within a Market Economy." *American Journal of Political Science* 43: 842–63.

———. 2000. *American Business and Political Power.* Chicago: University of Chicago Press.

Stanley, T. D. 2001. "Wheat from Chaff: Meta-Analysis as Quantitative Literature Review." *Journal of Economic Perspectives* 15: 131–50.

Stimson, James A., Michael B. MacKuen, and Robert S. Erikson. 1995. "Dynamic Representation." *American Political Science Review* 89: 543–65.

Walker, Jack L., Jr. 1991. *Mobilizing Interest Groups in America.* Ann Arbor: University of Michigan Press.

Weissberg, Robert. 1976. *Public Opinion and Popular Government*. Englewood Cliffs, NJ: Prentice-Hall.

Wetstein, Matthew E. 1996. *Abortion Rates in the United States: The Influence of Public Policy*. Albany: State University of New York Press.

Wilson, Graham K. 1990. *Interest Groups*. Cambridge, MA: Basil Blackwell.

Wittman, Donald A. 1995. *The Myth of Democratic Failure*. Chicago: University of Chicago Press.

Wlezien, Christopher. 1996. "Dynamics of Representation: The Case of US Spending on Defence." *British Journal of Political Science* 26: 81–103.

Wright, John R. 1996. *Interest Groups & Congress*. Needham Heights, MA: Allyn & Bacon.

Zaller, John R. 1992. *The Nature and Origins of Mass Opinion*. New York: Cambridge University Press.

———. 1994. "Strategic Politicians, Public Opinion, and the Gulf Crisis." In W. Lance Bennett and David Paletz, eds., *Taken by Storm: The Media, Public Opinion, and U.S. Foreign Policy in the Gulf War*. Chicago: University of Chicago Press.

18

THE CITIZEN AS RESPONDENT:
SAMPLE SURVEYS AND AMERICAN DEMOCRACY,
PRESIDENTIAL ADDRESS, AMERICAN POLITICAL
SCIENCE ASSOCIATION, 1995

Sidney Verba[*]

This address to the American Political Science Association by one of its for-mer presidents takes what is implicit in the previous article by Burstein—that surveys are a new and valuable democratic institution—and makes that point explicitly. It does so by comparing the "participation" of survey re-spondents to the actual participatory patterns of highly motivated citizens who have resources that allow them to participate effectively. Because sur-veys mirror the public's views and policy desires in a way that the voicing of policy preferences by activists do not, the scientific public opinion survey, qua democratic institution, offsets the bias in mobilization that pervades even mass participation, including electoral mobilization. Verba does not presume to know the extent to which the "equality" of a survey offsets the "inequality" of participation. But if Burstein is right, then the offset is per-haps considerable.

• • •

THE STUDY OF POLITICAL PARTICIPATION and the sample survey are closely linked. The latter is the main method by which the former has been studied (Barnes and Kaase 1979; Rosenstone and Hansen 1993; Verba and Nie 1972; Verba, Nie, and Kim 1979; Verba, Schlozman, and Brady 1995). There is a good reason for that connection, since surveys give the researcher access to the "public," an otherwise broad, amorphous, and hard-to-deal-with phenomenon. Surveys tell us what the public does and provide data for analyses of why they do it.

Surveys are especially useful for dealing with issues of democratic representa-tion. Participation is a mechanism for representation, a means by which governing officials are informed of the preferences and needs of the public and are induced to respond to those preferences and needs. It is crucial, therefore, to know how well or how badly the participatory system represents the public to those leaders. But how do we know what the "real" picture is, the interests, preferences, and needs of the public? The sample survey is key to answering this question. In the work on

American Political Science Review 90 (March 1996): 1–7. Copyright © 1996 by the American Po-litical Science Association. Reprinted with the permission of Cambridge University Press. Sidney Verba is the Carl H. Pforzheimer University Professor and Director, Harvard University Library, Harvard University, Cambridge, MA 02138.

*The data for this paper come largely from the Citizen Participation Study, a large-scale survey of activism in U.S. political life supported by the National Science Foundation as well as the Ford, Hewlett, and Spencer foundations. The main analysis of these data can be found in Verba Schlozman, and Brady (1995). I am grateful to Kay L. Schlozman and Henry E. Brady for helpful comments and the collaboration out of which much of this paper grew.

participation by Verba, Schlozman, and Brady (1995), the representative sample survey was used to provide baseline information on the state of the public—its needs and preferences—in order to ascertain the extent to which the messages communicated by the active citizens distort the situation of the public as a whole.

There is a close connection between subject and method in this research, between citizen participation and representative democracy, on the one hand, and survey research, on the other. The sample survey is a major social science tool. In addition, it is technology with an important influence on representative democracy. The nature of the technology, particularly the use of random sampling, has an intimate connection with issues of representation. Social science technology, the political theory of representation, and some real issues in contemporary American politics all come together in relation to political surveys.

Surveys create information that would not otherwise exist. What would our democracy be like if no one had invented them? In particular, I want to consider the social survey as a means of political participation. Citizens participate as voters, protesters, letter writers, campaign contributors, and in many other ways. That participation is one of the major means by which governing officials learn about the needs and preferences of the public. It is not the only means, of course; interest groups and the media also provide input. But citizen activity is perhaps the major way the public's needs and preferences are communicated to governing elites. When citizens participate as respondents, what is added to that flow of information by surveys? In trying to answer this question, I hope to address not only the role of surveys but also some more general questions about the nature of democratic representation.

POLITICAL EQUALITY

The problem in representation with which I wish to deal is as follows: Democracy implies responsiveness by governing elites to the needs and preferences of the citizenry. More than that, it implies equal responsiveness; in the democratic ideal, elected officials should give equal consideration to the needs and preferences of all citizens. This equal consideration is embodied most clearly in the principle of one person, one vote.

Equality, as we all know, is one of the more complex and multidimensioned concepts we have, given the variety of factors on which it can be based and the fundamental heterogeneity of human beings. Let me briefly indicate what I have in mind. I am not concerned with the extent to which the government in fact treats all citizens equally in the policies it produces; what that would mean and whether it is possible is beyond me. I want to deal with a narrower but still basic issue. Rather than looking at the results of the policy process, I want to focus on the extent to which governing officials have the capacity to provide equal consideration, in particular, whether they have equal information about the needs and preferences of all citizens. If some citizens are invisible, one cannot respond to them.

This means, in turn, that citizens have to supply that information. Thus, if the government is to have the capability of giving equal consideration to the needs and preferences of all citizens, the public must be equally capable of providing that information. They must provide information about themselves—who they are, what they want, what they need. If citizen activity is the main way in which that is done, then democratic responsiveness depends on citizen participation, and equal responsiveness depends on equal participation.

Of course, things do not work out that way. Citizen voices are very unequal. Not everyone votes. More important, there are many more ways in which citizens can be active, and here, of course, voices are more unequal. Only small proportions of the citizenry work in campaigns or make contributions. There may be a flood of letters to Washington and, more recently, a flood of faxes and e-mail. But only a small proportion of the public uses these means, and that minority is not a random sample of the population; it comes disproportionately from the more advantaged members of society (Verba and Nie 1972; Verba, Schlozman, and Brady 1995).

Furthermore, not only are some voices raised while others are still, but also those who raise their voices differ in their effectiveness when they do so. In summer 1995, members of the American Political Science Association received a memorandum about threatened abolition of National Science Foundation (NSF) support for the social sciences. Through intense efforts the program was saved. In the office of Congressman Walker, who introduced the amendment to eliminate social science funding in NSF, one staffer is quoted as saying: "Those ladies and gentlemen in the social sciences sure know how to write letters." We ought to. Writing compelling communications is our business.

In our research (Verba, Schlozman, and Brady 1995, chapter 11) we measured the opportunities of our respondents to learn civic skills—how to write a letter, make a public presentation, organize a meeting. As you would expect, there are great differences across social groups in their capacity not only to speak up but also to speak up effectively. The differences in our data are striking. Among people with advanced education and a professional level job, about 90% say they plan meetings and give public presentations. The comparable figure for workers with high school education in lower status jobs is around 5%. The point is obvious but also crucial for understanding political capacity.

That some are active and others are not would be important only if the activists differed in politically relevant ways from the inactive, that is, if they differed in their needs and preferences. Some studies suggest that it does not matter much who is active, since the policy preferences of activists differ relatively little from those of the inactive (Wolfinger and Rosenstone 1980). But that finding concerns the difference between voters and nonvoters in relation to policy preferences (as revealed in standard National Election Studies [NES] questions). The finding does not generalize to political participation more broadly. When one compares activists and inactivists not in terms of responses to issue questions designed by the surveyor but in terms of economic circumstances, need for government assistance, or participatory agendas—the actual issues that animate activity—the discrepancies are much more substantial. In addition, there is variation across activities in the extent to which participants are similar to or different from inactive citizens. Voters are relatively representative of the public. In terms of other forms of participation—acts with both more clout and a greater capacity to communicate information—distortion in participatory input is more substantial (Verba, Schlozman, and Brady 1995, chapter 7). As we noted, the participatory input is tilted in the direction of the more advantaged demographic groups in society. Their voices convey a different message than would be conveyed by the more quiescent.

All this means that governing officials receive more information about needs and preferences from some parts of the public than from others. If we believe that each individual is the best judge of his or her needs and preferences, then the differential expression of these needs and preferences through differential activity levels means that officials receive a biased view of the public.

In a market—in an economic system—such differential engagement is expected and poses no problem. Customer voices, as revealed by their consumer behavior, are not equal. People have different preferences and different budget constraints. No one expects equality in a market-based economy with differential income and wealth.

What about politics? Here, too, preferences vary; some people want things from the government, others do not; and those who want things want different things. Budget constraints also differ. Some people have more resources than others—money, time, skills, connections—and these enable them to act and act effectively. This is what explains differential political activity and the resulting bias in information received by the government.

That some are active and some quiescent is inevitable. But it makes a big difference whether the quiescence is due to preference or resources—to not wanting to act or to being unable to act. If people are not active because they have nothing they want from the government or because they choose to allocate their time to other activities, this poses little challenge to the notion of equal consideration of the needs and preferences of all. But if they are not active because they do not have the resources to be active, that is more of a challenge.

In his recent book, *Inequality Reexamined* (1992), Amartya Sen argues for an approach to equality based on the equal capability to achieve one's goals. It is an attractive notion in relation to political equality. It is something less than equality of outcome—policies that treat everyone equally. But it is something more than the usual notion of equality of opportunity, which ordinarily refers to the absence of barriers to accomplishment. In Sen's approach, equal capability includes the absence of barriers and the presence of the means or the resources needed to accomplish one's objectives. The participatory system in the United States today provides equality of opportunity in that there are few if any legal impediments to political activity. But it is a system based on unequal resources and, therefore, unequal capabilities.

SURVEYS IN AMERICAN POLITICAL LIFE

This is the background to my concern with surveys. Citizens also participate as respondents. The sample survey is a special source of information about the public because the citizen voice expressed does not, as does the participatory voice, depend on having resources or—and this adds an important complexity—on being motivated to participate. This makes the survey a special kind of voice of the people, with some interesting advantages and disadvantages.

The pioneers of political surveys, Gallup, Crossley, and Roper, were optimistic about this new technique. Surveys, they predicted, would be widely used, would bring science and precision into an area where there had previously just been speculation, and would create a new and more responsive democracy (Converse 1987, Gallup and Rae 1940).

They were right about how much surveys would be used. Public opinion polls have become ubiquitous in politics. No political campaign can be conducted without them. Polls provide information that did not previously exist. They allow adjustments of campaign strategies to the winds of opinion, something impossible before polling, when a campaign strategy would be set at the beginning of a campaign and basically adhered to. Anthony Downs predicts that campaign managers will steer their parties and candidates toward the middle of the distribution of opinions. That may be the approach dictated by the logic of vote maximization, but one can only steer in that direction if one knows where the median voter is located. Now, surveys give both parties information on this and may indeed allow campaigners to follow the dictates of theory (Geer 1991).

Polls are closely watched between elections. A presidential administration without a pollster is as unlikely as one without a national security advisor. From the President of the United States on down, elected officials monitor presidential popularity and the response of the public to policy initiatives. The presidential approval questions—one of the longest series of replicated questions—are a running retrospective evaluation of the chief executive's performance. The evidence seems fairly clear that they affect the ability of the president to be effective in Washington (Brody 1991, Edwards 1980, Rivers and Rose 1985). In addition, polls give some content to the level of public support by dealing with the reactions of the public to particular policies. Polls on every issue, large and small, appear in the media. Indeed, virtually every report on a current issue—from Medicare to Bosnia to the O. J. Simpson trial—contains information on what the public thinks. The range is very wide. Surveys hold, as it were, the mirror up to the nation.

Surveys are, I have always believed, a peculiarly U.S. product. The survey industry is now worldwide, but there are good reasons why it developed in and diffused from the United States as an academic research tool, as an instrument in politics, and as a technique for commerce. It fits the consumer-oriented U.S. economy. It fits U.S. culture, where individuals are supposed to have ideas and express them, and where people are accustomed to listening and talking to strangers. And it fits the U.S. polity, where institutions are weak, and therefore the views and attitudes of citizens—as autonomous individuals—make more of a difference in their political behavior than is the case where a person's party, religion, or ethnicity is more predictive.

SURVEYS AS SCIENCE, SURVEYS AS REPRESENTATION

Two main features of the sample survey make it particularly attractive in the U.S. context: its "scientificness" and representativeness (Herbst 1993). Our society vacillates between a belief in science and the expert and a belief in populism and the wisdom of the ordinary citizen. Surveys satisfy both. They give us a scientific measure of the people's will. It is no wonder that surveys play such a major role in the market, in politics, and in academic research.

Surveys produce just what democracy is supposed to produce—equal representation of all citizens. The sample survey is rigorously egalitarian; it is designed so that each citizen has an equal chance to participate and an equal voice when participating. Here is where science and political representation meet. In the social sciences one of the great threats to valid inference, perhaps the most common, is selection bias (King, Keohane, and Verba 1994). Researchers go to great lengths to avoid it. The random sample is a method for eliminating bias. Survey design eliminates bias in two ways: The respondent does not self-select to enter the survey (that is why we reject mail-in polls using forms clipped out of magazines), and the interviewers are given careful instructions as to whom they should select (that is why we reject quota sampling).

Surveys are by no means perfectly random. Poll respondents are not perfectly representative. Some are hard to find; increasingly, many refuse to participate.

Pollsters seek out the respondents, but many cannot be reached, a problem especially severe for telephone surveys. Nor are those who cannot be reached a random group. They tend to be like those uncounted by the census—people with no stable dwelling place, people who are missed by society in general. Once contacted, people may refuse to take part, a growing problem in recent years. In the early days of the NES, refusal rates were below 10%. In recent years, surveys such as NES or the General Social Survey (GSS) of the National Opinion Research Center have been experiencing refusal rates in the 25–30% range.[1]

Surveys are not perfectly representative but offer, nevertheless, a better cross-section of the public than do almost any other means, and certainly they are more representative than any of the modes of citizen activity. Surveys provide us with a relatively unbiased view of the public by combining science and representativeness, indeed, by achieving representativeness through science. They are very like elections in which each individual has an equal voice only better. They get better turnout, since good surveys seek out the participants and do not passively wait for them to come to the polls. They get richer information. The vote says little about the preferences of voters except in the narrow sense of their choice of candidate. Surveys can probe preferences on many issues. Indeed, one of the uses to which surveys are put is the reduction in mandate uncertainty after an election. And surveys are more continuous; they monitor the public between elections.

RANDOM AND BIASED SELECTION: SOCIAL SURVEYS AND THE REAL WORLD OF POLITICS

The essence of the science of surveys and the essence of the representativeness of surveys are both found in the random processes by which participants are selected. But this also makes surveys very unreal. The processes by which participants are selected are fundamentally different in the controlled world of the social survey and the real world of political participation. Politics may be studied with techniques that try to eliminate selection bias—that is what our profession is all about—but real life is dominated by selection bias. We select the circumstances that then affect our social and economic life. We choose schools, jobs, spouses, locations. We choose within constraints to be sure, but the constraints are by no means constant or random across individuals. The constraints are biased as well.

The same happens in political life. The recent analysis by Verba, Schlozman, and Brady (1995) of the processes by which citizens come to be active is, in fact, a study of selection bias in the real world. Citizens differ in motivation and resources; thus, they self-select to take part in politics because of this differential motivation and because they are differentially constrained by resources. This

[1] The nonparticipants in surveys are analyzed by Brehm (1993, chapter 2), who calls them phantom respondents. They differ from the public as a whole but in somewhat surprising ways. Respondents overrepresent the elderly and women, which is not a surprise. According to Brehm's analysis, however, the underrepresentation of the poor and minorities that we might have expected does not appear in the data. The patterns are somewhat varied across survey organizations, but it appears as if the NES and the GSS both overrepresent African Americans and underrepresent the rich. Education is the best single predictor of political activity. NES telephone interviews are consistent with this, as they underestimate the proportion in the population with less than a high school education. Yet, the face-to-face interviews of NES and GSS overrepresent those with lower education levels. Academic surveys, although not perfect, have better response rates than media polls, many of which have rates that call the accuracy of the survey into question (Brady and Orren 1992).

biased selection process produces a biased participatory population. The voices of the well educated and the well heeled sound more loudly.

Each method of selection—unbiased survey sampling and the socially structured real world processes of selection—produces a different result. Random sample surveys are statistically sound, and they treat each individual qua individual the same. Polls provide information about the public as a whole, motivated or unmotivated, resource rich or resource poor, rather than about those who make their presence known through their political participation. Polls are thus an important tool for equal representation. This also means that polls take no account of race or ethnicity, wealth or education, passion or political commitment. In short, they ignore the mainsprings of political life, and this makes them very artificial.

Of what use are such artificial measures of the public? Here is where surveys intersect with one of the basic issues of citizen representation: the meaning of quiescence. Ordinary modes of citizen activity—voting, writing letters, going to a protest, taking part in a campaign or a community project—allow quiescence; they are voluntary, and no one has to take part and express preferences. Surveys do not let people be quiescent; they chase them down and ask them questions. If people are hard to find, the good survey looks for them, calling again and again. And random-digit dialing rather than phone book listings are used in order to catch those would-be shirkers who get unlisted numbers so they can avoid their civic obligation to take phone calls during dinner.

PREFERENCE OR CAPABILITY

How important it is to hear the voice of the otherwise silent depends on why they are silent: because they do not want to voice their preferences or because they do not have the capability to do so. What people do is a result of their choices within constraints, of their preferences and their capacity to achieve them. Much of the debate between liberals and conservatives over government provision of benefits is about the relative importance of choice and constraint. Do people on welfare choose that status by their unwillingness to look for jobs and their earlier willful neglect of education? Or are they constrained by lack of job opportunities and bad schools? The battle is currently being won by those who stress choice. But constraints are also important.

All of this applies to citizen participation. If some are inactive, is it because they lack motivation or lack capability? Distinguishing between motivation and capability is easy conceptually but often hard in practice. The two are related. If people lack the capability, their motivation goes down. If they have little motivation, they do not try to increase their capability. Those who have few resources will be discouraged from taking part in politics; those who are uninterested in public affairs will not care to develop civic skills.

Despite the difficulty, the distinction can be made in particular cases. Let me draw on the data from our civic voluntarism study to present two contrasting situations, one in which differential activity is driven by differential motivation, and one in which it is driven by differential capacity.

Motivation and the Politics of Abortion

Consider motivation or the lack of it. Much activity derives from the greater intensity of preferences among the activists. The examples of the intensely concerned minority are legion; indeed, they are the basis for much of the political action in the United States. I will choose one example from our research, the politics of abortion (Verba, Schlozman, and Brady 1995, chapter 14). The public at large—as revealed by surveys—is divided on abortion rights. Exactly how they divide depends on the questions asked. Most citizens are not pro or anti; they are pro under some circumstances and anti under others. On balance, however, the public tilts in a pro-choice direction. Twice as many respondents in our survey are in the farthest pro-choice position as are in the farthest pro-life position. In addition, those with the strongest pro-choice views have more participatory resources than do those with the strongest pro-life views. They are three times as likely to have a college education and substantially more likely to belong to an organization. They are the kinds of people you would expect to be more active in politics, and they are. That activity, however, is spread across all sorts of issues. Those who take the more extreme pro-life positions are not particularly well endowed with participatory resources, tending on average to be less affluent and less skilled. They are, however, very motivated—intense in their views, concentrated on that particular issue, and likely to act on that issue. Thus, they provide much more of the action, especially the heated action like protesting, on abortion.

The concentration of activity among the pro-life respondents in our study is striking. We asked them about the subject of their activity, whether some issue motivated their letter to a representative, or the protest in which they took part, or their activity in a campaign, and so on. We can then see how much of an individual's activity—across various acts—is focused on the same subject. Eleven percent of the activity of the pro-choice respondents concerns abortion; they are very active but are active about many things. The pro-life respondents, 58% of whose activity concerns abortion, are much more single-minded.

If elected officials heed the voices of the active citizens, they will give greater attention to the pro-life group than its proportion of the population warrants. That does not seem inappropriate, even in the face of the notion that each person's preferences should be given equal weight. There are preferences and preferences, and those strongly held ought to weigh more.

In such a situation, polls do not and should not eliminate the special consideration likely to be given to the intense minority. Rather, they mitigate it somewhat by providing information about preferences in the public at large. Officials can know, at least, that the activists do not represent the population as a whole. And the existence of a gap between the public as a whole and the activists can be used as part of the debate about the proper policy to follow. The quiescence of inactive citizens when they could be active if they cared more justifies paying less attention to them, but knowing their views adds an important ingredient to the political debate.

Resources and the Politics of Benefits Programs

Consider, however, a situation in which the reason for silence is not lack of concern but lack of resources. Being the recipient of a government benefits program creates a motive for political activity, whether in order to protect the program in general or to monitor one's own benefits. Recipients of some programs are less active than recipients of others. It is not that they care less about their program; rather, they lack the money and skills to undertake activity. A properly conducted survey can reveal that fact. It can uncover a part of the population whose silence does not reflect indifference.

An example is found in comparing those who receive Social Security and those who receive AFDC. There is reason to believe that the latter are more needy than the former. For example, our data show that people on AFDC are more than twice as likely to report serious problems in satisfying basic health, housing, and food needs in the previous year. Yet, the AFDC recipients are less well endowed with participatory resources; they have much less education and many fewer civic skills. The result is that three times as many of the Social Security recipients reported activity concerning that program as did AFDC recipients concerning theirs. The former are eight times more likely to belong to an organization concerned with Social Security than are AFDC recipients to belong to an organization concerned with their benefits program. As one would expect, those who receive benefits like Social Security, that is, widespread benefits that are not means tested, not only are more likely to be active in regard to their benefits than those receiving means-tested, welfare-type benefits but also are much more skilled in their activity.

Here, then, is a silent group which can be located through a survey and whose silence does not reflect low motivation but few resources. Note that what is learned through the survey is not the on-the-fly opinion of a group about whether to balance the budget by 2002 or 2007 but information about real needs—needs about which respondents are well informed and, indeed, better informed than anyone.

The ability of polls to get at a sample of individuals who might otherwise not be active is especially useful as a counter to organized expressions of preferences. In one sense, organized interests can benefit more from survey research. Polls are weapons of those who can afford to mount them, and this is more likely to be an organized interest than an unorganized group. Yet, surveys may reduce the monopoly that interest groups might otherwise have over information about the preferences of the public as a whole regarding the interest groups' issues or of their own membership and their purported clientele.

The NRA remains the classic example. Poll results on gun control have not overridden the power of the NRA, but they have been useful as a counterfoil. Legislators may still fear the concentrated resources the NRA can bring to bear, but polls showing that the public at large (and even gun owners) disagrees with the NRA give some ammunition—perhaps the wrong term here—to the other side.[2] Similarly, polls have shown that half the Cuban Americans in the United States disagree with the position of the National Cuban American Foundation, which believes we ought to isolate Cuba,[3] or that many fundamentalist Christians do not support the political agenda of the religious right.

It takes a poll to locate resource poor, unorganized, and otherwise silent citizens. In general, polls can show that the noisy and overt "representatives" of the public or of particular parts of it do not necessarily speak for everyone. If the voices of activists are louder because of their greater intensity of concern, then they deserve the extra clout they have. If their amplified voices result from greater capacity to make themselves heard, however, then the principles of equality of consideration are violated. In the latter case, by searching out the otherwise inactive, asking them questions, and recording their answers, surveys may be thought of as providing the capacity for articulation that some citizens would otherwise lack.

[2] *International Herald Tribune*, May 27, 1995, p. 3.
[3] *New York Times*, June 12, 1995, p. 9.

Survey Democracy?

I am certainly not recommending a government by survey. Gallup referred to the survey as a "sampling referendum," but even he did not think of it as a means of legislating. Rather, I am arguing that one has to view surveys in the context of the participatory process, which exists with or without surveys. Some argue that surveys create a leadership which follows the polls rather than leading. But surveys per se do not make some leaders abandon leadership to follow public whim. In the absence of surveys, such leaders would still sway with the wind of opinion. The wind would just blow from different quarters, more likely from the better parts of town.

Polls are thus a way to give everyone a voice, but they do not reflect the strongest of voices. The information polls communicate may be equal, but it is also limited. And the limitation derives from the strongest feature of polls, the fact that they represent all citizens equally. What message is sent by a method that gives voice to all citizens, with little regard for their level of information or their motivation to participate, and one whose messages are all *in response* to questions selected by and posed by strangers at the door? Certainly, the messages are not the clearest.

One limitation on the role of surveys relates to agendas. First, because the initiative is taken by the surveyor rather than the surveyed, the agenda reflects the interests of the poll taker. It gives the inarticulate a chance to express their views and their concerns, but only on the issues that the surveyor thinks are important. Second, since surveyors have their own agenda—to increase readership, or find information to help a particular candidate, or test a pet academic theory—the set of issues covered may be very different from that which is on the mind of the respondents.

Another limitation has to do with the questions asked: The answers received depend on them. The voice of the citizenry, especially the otherwise quiescent who are of special interest here, can sound very different depending on what is asked.

There is another qualification on the ability of surveys to equalize the voice of the resource poor. Few resources may be needed to respond to a survey, but real resources are required to conduct a survey. Although the selection of respondents may not be biased, the selection of when to have a survey and what to ask (and how to interpret the data) certainly are. This gives a louder voice to the more affluent in several ways. Well-heeled campaigners and wealthy interests can afford to take their own polls. They can then use them as they want, including selective reporting. On top of that, to do a poll one needs to hire professionals, which takes money, and campaigns thus value contributions of money rather than time. Money is, in turn, much more stratified than time; the affluent have money (of course), but time is more equally available to both the advantaged and the disadvantaged (Verba, Schlozman, and Brady 1995, chapter 10). Thus, the survey process reintroduces some of the socioeconomic stratification found in political activity through decisions as to when, what, and whom to survey.

Another qualification is that what people answer—what they think is important, how they evaluate policies and politicians—is in good part a reaction to what they hear from the media or from governing officials. Thus, the questions asked and the answers given do not come from a separate autonomous public but are affected by the processes of politics and policy that they may, in turn, influence. As in so many other areas of politics and political analysis, there is a serious problem of endogeneity.

Finally, polls provide low-grade information. Answers to closed questions do not capture the richness of individuals' views. And the views, themselves, are often ill-formed. Indeed, it is commonplace to note that the opinions are often non-existent until the question is asked and the respondent is faced with the necessity to answer.

This last point, about the quality of information in polls, needs qualification. We have all been trained to be suspicious of survey results on issues far from the consciousness of respondents, when they are asked for opinions on some policy matter. But surveys can give better information than that. It all depends on the subject of the questions. Some information about the public is fairly solid—its positions on issues, its social circumstances, its needs; people know the answers, and the answers are stable. In some of the examples I gave above, questions were asked about whether the respondents participated in Social Security or in AFDC and whether they had faced serious problems paying for necessities in the past year. These are important questions about citizen need, and the individual citizen—of whatever level of sophistication—knows the answers better than anyone. Citizens know their own life circumstances. They also know their own values, and although their values may be in conflict one with another (whose values are not?), they are likely to be fairly stable.[4]

Can the Quiescent Gain a Voice?

This brings me back to my concern with the politically quiescent. How can constraints be broken to achieve the democratic ideal of equal voice? Surveys break the constraints by seeking out those who would otherwise be inactive, but the voice is not very strong or clear. Another means of bringing in the quiescent is political mobilization. Resource poor and apathetic citizens can be brought out to vote or take other actions by social movements or political organizations. There are many historical examples, the civil rights movement being one of the most important. Our research shows, however, that for most activity, the forces of mobilization bring in the same people who would be active spontaneously. There is a vast network of what one might call day-to-day political recruiters, people who call for campaign contributions, get people out to a community meeting, or mobilize citizens to write their representative. These recruiters seek those with motivation and resources. The recruitment process largely reinforces the other biased processes that lead to political activity (Brady, Schlozman, and Verba 1995).

Political inequality is, thus, embedded deeply in American society. Can the ideal of political equality be achieved? More modestly, can we move closer to that ideal? It is hard to see how. The constraint on political participation from unequal resources derives from the basic institutions in society, from differential education and differential economic position. Mobilization breaks the pattern from time to time, but the system of mobilization is also embedded in the same set of institutions, and mobilization generally reinforces the inequality of political voice. Surveys, if done well and used honestly (two significant qualifications), may help, but they can hardly change things. Greater equality in our basic institutions—greater income

[4] Attitudes on complex public policies may be ill-informed and changeable. But as John Zaller (1993) has argued, the "on-the-fly" answers that polls elicit have a certain logic to them. They often reflect a balancing, not a careful balancing but a balancing nevertheless, of alternative values. They are a form of quick-and-dirty reasoning.

equality and, more important perhaps, greater educational equality—would certainly help equalize political resources. That is a tall order, and I certainly have no scheme to achieve it nor any expectation that others do either.

REFERENCES

Barnes, Samuel I., and Max Kaase. 1979. *Political Action: Mass Participation in Five Western Democracies*. Beverly Hills, CA: Sage Publications.

Brady, Henry E., and Gary Orren. 1992. "Polling Pitfalls: Sources of Error in Media Surveys." In *Media Polls and American Democracy*, ed. Thomas E. Mann and Gary R. Orren. Washington, DC: Brookings.

Brady, Henry E., Kay L. Schlozman, and Sidney Verba. 1995. "Prospecting for Participants: A Rational Expectations Approach to Mobilizing Activists." Presented at the Annual Meeting of the American Political Science Association, Chicago.

Brehm, John. 1993. *The Phantom Respondents: Opinion Surveys and Political Representation*. Ann Arbor: University of Michigan Press.

Brody, Richard. 1991. *Assessing the President*. Stanford: Stanford University Press.

Converse, Jean. 1987. *Survey Research in the United States*. Berkeley: University of California Press.

Downs, Anthony. 1957. *The Economic Theory of Democracy*. New York: Harper and Brothers.

Edwards, George C., III. 1980. *Presidential Influence on Congress*. San Francisco: W. H. Freeman.

Gallup, George, Jr., and Saul Rae. 1940. *The Pulse of Democracy*. New York: Simon and Schuster.

Geer, John C. 1991. "Critical Alignment and the Public Opinion Poll." *Journal of Politics* 53:435–53.

Herbst, Susan. 1993. *Numbered Voices: How Opinion Polling Has Shaped American Politics*. Chicago: University of Chicago Press.

King, Gary, Robert O. Keohane, and Sidney Verba. 1994. *Designing Social Inquiry: Scientific Inference in Qualitative Research*. Princeton: Princeton University Press.

Rivers, Douglas, and Nancy Rose. 1985. "Passing the President's Program: Public Opinion and Presidential Power in Congress." *American Journal of Political Science* 29:183–96.

Rosenstone, Steven J., and John Mark Hansen. 1993. *Mobilization, Participation, and Democracy in America*. New York: Macmillan.

Sen, Amartya. 1992. *Inequality Reexamined*. Cambridge: Harvard University Press.

Verba, Sidney, and Norman H. Nie. 1972. *Participation in America: Political Democracy and Social Equality*. New York: Harper and Row. (Reprinted by University of Chicago Press, 1987.)

Verba, Sidney, Norman H. Nie, and Jae-on Kim. 1979. *Participation and Political Equality: A Seven Nation Comparison*. New York: Cambridge University Press, 1978. (Reprinted by University of Chicago Press, 1987.)

Verba, Sidney, Kay Lehman Schlozman, and Henry E. Brady. 1995. *Voice and Equality: Civic Voluntarism in American Democracy*. Cambridge: Harvard University Press.

Wolfinger, Raymond E., and Steven J. Rosenstone. 1980. *Who Votes?* New Haven: Yale University Press.

Zaller, John. 1993. *The Nature and Origins of Mass Opinion*. New York: Cambridge University Press.

19

DEMOCRATIC DISCUSSION
Donald R. Kinder
Don Herzog[*]

In this piece one of the country's most accomplished survey researchers joins forces with a major democratic theorist (they happen to be colleagues at the same institution, the University of Michigan)—and together they try to reconcile what might seem irreconcilable: survey research findings about voter ignorance, on the one hand, with John Stuart Mill's ideal of government by discussion, on the other. Read them carefully to ascertain the basis of reconciliation, for it is subtle: they extrapolate from John Dewey's concept of "contingent social practices." That is undoubtedly a mouthful, but it implies—as you will see—that the relative political sophistication of the citizenry's many members, the extent to which they "get" what is happening with political debates, varies according to how much competitive politics pulls them in. Citizens have the capacity to follow public debate clearly in their own minds, even if they have no immediate plans for writing effective letters to the editor or speaking at local meetings about an issue. But that capacity depends to a considerable extent on how absorbing the larger political environment is. And sometimes that environment can be very absorbing indeed—as the next article, by John Zaller, shows.

• • •

"DEMOCRACY," remarked H. L. Mencken, "is the theory that the common people know what they want, and deserve to get it good and hard." Mencken found American politics a droll spectacle and showered contempt on the dullards he named "the booboisie." Plenty of other intelligent and perceptive observers have concluded that ordinary citizens are flatly incapable of shouldering the burdens of democracy. Uninformed and uninterested, absorbed in the pressing business of private life, unable to trace out the consequences of political action, citizens possess neither the skills nor the resources required for what Walter Bagehot pithily named "government by discussion."

In this light, democratic theorists might appear hopelessly naive or romantic, bent on promoting a politics we haven't seen yet, and likely never will. We want here to take the challenge of antidemocratic thought seriously, particularly on the question of the intelligence of democratic discussion. Our aim is to assess the quality of the political conversations that go on between the American public and American leaders. Our special interest is in what citizens have to say, both

In George E. Marcus and Russell L. Hanson, eds., *Reconsidering the Democratic Public*. (University Park: The Pennsylvania State University Press, 1993), pp. 347–377. Copyright 1993 by The Pennsylvania State University. Reproduced by permission of the publisher.

*We thank Judith Ottmar for impeccable help in preparing the manuscript and Janet Weiss for good advice.

to each other and to their elected representatives. But assessing the quality of such discussions requires an assessment not only of the skills and interests of citizens but of the political environment in which citizens find themselves: the "opportunities for political learning" and the "quality of political information" (Page and Shapiro 1988, 13) that are made available to them. And we want to evaluate both where we are now and where we might be in the future, not in some utopian and unrealizable rendition of American society, but in a foreseeable one. We begin by summarizing Mill's vision of democracy, which accords discussion a central place. Next we review the attack on the possibility of democratic discussion implicitly mounted in recent American survey research, especially as set out in the authoritative and influential writings of Philip Converse. Then, in the heart of the chapter, we examine several different lines of argument and evidence that offer the possibility of modifying Converse's melancholy conclusions. Democratic discussion may be more than just a romantic dream. We needn't be breathless and starry-eyed—determined "to see some blue sky in the midst of clouds of disillusioning facts" (Schumpeter 1942, 256)—to resist the thesis that voters are invincibly ignorant.[1]

MILL'S VISION OF DEMOCRACY

John Stuart Mill would have had no patience for any economistic concept of democracy as a system of preference aggregation; nor for that matter would he have relished any pluralistic conception focusing on the struggles among interest groups.[2] Instead, Mill placed debate over the common good at the heart of democracy. Even majority rule, often thought to be a signally important feature of democracy, faded into the background in his treatment. The majority's vote is important not because it has any right to rule but because it's our best way of seeing what seems the most reasonable view at the moment:

> Unless opinions favourable to democracy and to aristocracy, to property and to equality, to co-operation and to competition, to luxury and to abstinence, to sociality and individuality, to liberty and discipline, and all the other standing antagonisms of practical life, are expressed with equal freedom, and enforced and defended with equal talent and energy, there is no chance of both elements obtaining their due; one scale is sure to go up, and the other down. Truth, in the great practical concerns of life, is so much a question of the reconciling and combining of opposites, that very few have minds sufficiently capacious and impartial to make the adjustment with an approach to correctness, and it has to be made by the rough process of a struggle between combatants fighting under hostile banners. (Mill [1859] 1951b, 28)

The more wide-ranging, the more vibrant, the more well-informed the debate, the better. Only in a richly diverse debate can we have any confidence that emerg-

---

[1] We are deliberately vague about exactly what kind of discussion we have in mind. For an argument that genuine democratic discussion should follow the form of testimony, not deliberation, see Sanders, n.d.

[2] This isn't the place for laborious textual exegesis, so we will present a bald summary account of Mill's conception of democracy, drawn from the *Considerations on Representative Government, On Liberty*, and some of the journalism.

ing views have any rational warrant. That's one reason Mill struggled in and out of Parliament to extend the franchise to workers and women (a campaign giving him a reputation as a crazy radical). Members of Parliament, he urged, could talk all day about the interests of the working class, but they'd never really understand those interests until workers themselves could present them. (Mill had other reasons for extending the franchise, chief among them the pregnant thought that being a citizen, not a subject, is partly constitutive of dignity and equality. However important elsewhere, though, these themes don't cut directly into our topic.)

Critics of liberal democracy have often savaged it as mindless chatter and celebrated instead the cult of action, the heroic leader who firmly grasps what needs to be done. Mill's theory explains why we should want there to be endless talk, in and out of the legislature, and especially between legislators and citizens. We simply can't grasp what might be worth doing and why—we can't learn from our previous mistakes and seek to correct them—without that talk:

> There must be discussion, to show how experience is to be interpreted. Wrong opinions and practices gradually yield to fact and argument: but facts and arguments, to produce any effect on the mind, must be brought before it. Very few facts are able to tell their own story, without comments to bring out their meaning. The whole strength and value, then, of human judgement, depending on the one property, that it can be set right when it is wrong, reliance can be placed on it only when the means of setting it right are kept constantly at hand. (Mill [1859] 1951b, 27)

For other theories of democracy, all that talk poses an explanatory mystery. We needn't talk a lot to register our preferences or to estimate the pressure of competing interest groups. Economists should explain why we don't literally auction off legislation. Pluralists should explain why legislators don't play tug of war in the chamber, why lobbyists don't hire sumo wrestlers to compete on the floor.

The more talk, the more intelligent the talk, the better. Mill here offers an exhilarating contrast to Rousseau, who, weirdly, is still routinely embraced by self-styled ardent democrats. Rousseau's citizens are zealots, enthusiasts for politics who fly to the public assembly. But when they get there, what do they do? Apparently, they participate in a largely silent ritual of communal affirmation. Long debates, Rousseau warns portentously, are a sign of decline in the state, and he adds proudly that his citizens are too stupid to fall for clever and deceptive arguments. Democracy is a capacious enough concept or tradition to include Rousseau, but we see no reason to embrace his vision as any kind of ideal.

No doubt there are important failings in Mill's views. Mill wanted to rig the popular discussion by giving the intelligent plural votes; worse yet, he was willing to entertain taking occupation and wealth as proxies for intelligence. He thought the popularly elected legislature shouldn't be in the business of actually drafting legislation but should tell some career experts what sort of bill they wanted. He tended to underplay the hustle and bustle and crass manipulation of democratic politics, casting it instead as a bloodless debate among intellectually scrupulous citizens bent on getting the right answer. Most important, perhaps, Mill's quasi-utilitarianism sometimes led him to think that political questions are just complicated technical questions, that there's a correct answer to the question what policy would maximize the greatest happiness.

These are genuine defects, and we have no interest in whitewashing Mill. Still, the insight that democracy is government by discussion remains attractive even after we scrap Mill's errors. As Mill knew full well, however, there are lots of prerequisites to fruitful discussion. If democratic debate is to go well, what has to be true?

CONVERSE AND THE IMPROBABILITY OF DISCUSSION

Democratic discussion might seem to require what Walter Lippmann (1922) once called the "omnicompetent citizen," who is attentive to and informed about the persons and problems that animate public life, familiar with the policies and philosophies that divide rival parties and candidates, and in possession of coherent and wide-ranging ideas about government and society. If so, government by discussion is in deep trouble. For it was the omnicompetent citizen that Philip Converse (1964) effectively demolished in his celebrated essay "The Nature of Belief Systems in Mass Publics."

Converse did the job with evidence. Based on a detailed analysis of national surveys carried out in 1956, 1958, and 1960, Converse concluded that qualitative, perhaps unbridgeable differences distinguished the political thinking of elites from the political thinking of ordinary citizens. Imagine a triangle, with elites occupying the apex and the vast majority of citizens crowding into the base. As one descends from the pinnacle of American society to the all too ordinary depths, two striking transformations take place in political comprehension, according to Converse:

> First, the contextual grasp of "standard" political belief systems fades out very rapidly, almost before one has passed beyond the 10% of the American population that in the 1950s had completed standard college training. Increasingly, simpler forms of information about "what goes with what" (or even information about the simple identity of objects) turn up missing. The net result, as one moves downward, is that constraint declines across the universe of idea-elements, and that the range of relevant belief systems becomes narrower and narrower. Instead of a few wide-ranging belief systems that organize large amounts of specific information, one would expect to find a proliferation of clusters of ideas among which little constraint is felt, even, quite often, in instances of sheer logical constraint.
>
> [Second,] the character of the objects that are central in a belief system undergoes systematic change. These objects shift from the remote, generic, and abstract to the increasingly simple, concrete, or "close to home." Where potential political objects are concerned, this progression tends to be from abstract "ideological" principles to the more obviously recognizable social groupings or charismatic leaders and finally to such objects of immediate experience as family, job, and immediate associates. (1964, 213)

Together, these two changes pose a challenge to the very possibility of democratic discussion. They suggest not only that leaders and citizens think about public life in fundamentally different ways, they also question whether citizens are capable of participating in democratic discussion at all. As Converse put it, the fragmentation and concretization of everyday political thinking "are not a pathology limited to a thin and disorganized bottom layer of the *lumpenproletariat*; they are immediately relevant in understanding the bulk of mass political behavior" (213).

Converse came to his gloomy conclusions in part because of Americans' utter unfamiliarity with standard ideological concepts like liberalism and conservatism. Practically nobody relied on such concepts when they commented on what they liked and disliked about the major parties and candidates. Converse also found

that although positions on a variety of pressing domestic and foreign policy issues taken by candidates for the United States House of Representatives revealed
clear ideological inclinations, the views expressed by the general public on the
same issues did not. Candidates were consistently liberal or conservative; citizens
scattered all over the place. Moreover, when citizens were questioned in a series of
interviews, their opinions appeared to wobble back and forth randomly, liberal on
one occasion, conservative on the next. Some citizens seemed to possess genuine
opinions and hold on to them tenaciously, but they appeared to be substantially
outnumbered by those who either confessed their ignorance outright or, when
nudged, invented a "nonattitude" on the spot (Converse 1970). Nor, finally, did
ordinary Americans seem to know very much about politics. Imposing fractions of
the general public do not know whether the Contras were Communist, how William Rehnquist makes a living, who exactly represents them in the United States
Senate: the dreary litany goes on and on. In Converse's analysis, "staggering" and
"astronomical" differences in knowledge set the leadership echelon apart from the
public. "Very little information 'trickles down' very far" (Converse 1964, 212).[3]

All in all, quite an unpretty picture. Most Americans glance at the political
world innocent of ideology and information: indifferent to standard ideological concepts, lacking a consistent perspective on public policy, in possession of
authentic opinions on only a few policy questions, and knowing precious little. Democratic discussion would seem to be out of reach—and not only here
and now. We should keep in mind that Converse's conclusions are directed at an
American public that in historical and comparative perspective is remarkably affluent, extraordinarily well educated, and virtually bombarded with news. What,
if anything, can we say in response?

IT AIN'T SO

Much of Converse's analysis hangs on the contrast between the actual responses
of Americans and the hypothetical responses of a "sophisticated observer." But
we can doubt the sophistication of this observer; that is, we can wonder if Americans have to fit this particular preconceived model in order to think intelligently
about politics. Converse's sophisticated observer, for instance, would have strong
views about whether utilities should be publicly owned or not, but we know of
no evidence that this was pressing business on the public agenda in 1958. Citizens absorbed in the question might well have struck their friends and neighbors
as quaint. More generally citizens who proceeded in the way recommended by
Converse's sophisticated observer could be described not as informed and intelligent but as single-minded and doctrinaire.

Converse emphasizes the advantages of ideology and therefore laments its absence. From his perspective, an ideological framework provides the citizen with a
deeper, richer understanding of politics than is available through other means. In

[3] Estimates of political knowledge, which are unrelievedly depressing, no doubt fail to tell the
grimmer truth. Even the very best sample surveys—like the National Election Study or the General
Social Survey—successfully interview only about 75 percent of the targeted sample. Those who refuse
to be questioned, like those who simply are never contacted in the first place, are unrepresentative of
the public as a whole: they fall disproportionately among those totally disengaged from politics. Were
we to correct for such selection bias, we would discover that the American public is even less well
informed than the reported figures suggest (Brehm 1989).

part this longing for ideology reflects Converse's disdain for these "other means": remember that to Converse, the bulk of the American public thinks about public life in ways that should be regarded as *pathological*. But more than that, Converse believes that ideological frameworks provide an economical and useful way for citizens to make sense of the "swarming confusion of problems" (Lippmann 1925) that constitutes the world of politics. To the ideologically inclined, "new political events have more meaning, retention of political information from the past is far more adequate, and political behavior increasingly approximates that of sophisticated 'rational' models" (Converse 1964, 227).

But as a mode of thinking, ideology also has its disadvantages. Robert Lane (1973), Converse's most persistent critic over the years, worries in particular that ideological thinking is not only economical but also dogmatic and intolerant: "Reference to an ideological posture would not only 'constrain' policy thinking but would confine it. There are meanings of the term *ideology* that suggest defensive postures (Rokeach 1960) such that the main objective of ideological policy thinking is to defend an ideological commitment, not to explore alternative policies" (104). That people don't think the way Converse stipulated they should doesn't necessarily show there's anything wrong with people. It might just show there was something wrong, or at least incomplete, about Converse's specifications (more on this later).

The most devastating element in Converse's original indictment, however, is the nonattitude thesis, the claim that few citizens possess real views on pressing matters of public policy. Because the nonattitude result presupposes nothing about what counts as a valid structure or approach in political deliberation, it would seem to make serious trouble for the wide-ranging discussion that democracy requires.

Fortunately for the prospects of democratic discussion, the nonattitude thesis now seems less persuasive, in light of empirical work of two sorts that has followed in Converse's wake. In the first place, unstable opinions, we now know, are a reflection not only of vague and confused citizens, as Converse would have it, but of vague and confused *questions*, as well; instability is, in part, a product of the very imperfect way survey questions are put to citizens (Achen 1975; Erikson 1979; Brody 1986; and for a review of the evidence, Smith 1984). Second, the political events of the last twenty-five years have made clear that issue publics need not be confined to minuscule fractions of the public as a whole. Most Americans developed real attitudes toward racial busing, capital punishment, abortion, the war in Vietnam, affirmative action, and more (see, e.g., Converse and Markus 1979; Kinder and Rhodebeck 1982; Luker 1984). When policy issues become entangled with moral, racial, religious, and nationalist loyalties, the nonattitude problem appears much less problematic.

These developments leave us somewhat more confident in the public's capacity to develop genuine political commitments than where Converse left things a quarter century ago. Still, what we have said so far does no damage to the contention that Americans know astonishingly little about the political world that whirls around them. Perhaps democratic discussion doesn't require that citizens know more (see below), but nothing we have said to this point gets around the finding of profound and widespread ignorance.

IT AIN'T NECESSARILY SO

Converse clearly understood himself as uncovering not a particular historical contingency but something deeply essential: thus tags like "the nature" of mass publics, and thus his relishing similar findings from France (Converse and Pierce 1986). Now, forty million Frenchmen may be wrong—they may even be empty-headed—but it doesn't follow that all "mass publics" everywhere, even counter-factual mass publics, are or would be wrong and empty-headed.

Like Converse, Lippmann thought his findings depended on nothing but some elementary considerations of psychology. In *The Public and Its Problems* (1927), a veiled response to this part of Lippmann's case, John Dewey suggested that instead of seeing human nature as the cause of political ignorance we should see contingent social practices. Change the practices, and people would become intelligent, acute, incisive.[4] Typically allergic to thinking of psychological predicates as irreducibly "in the head," Dewey emphasized instead the sociological nature of intelligence. The ancient Greeks did a wretched job of economic calculation; we do a surpassingly good job. What explains the difference? Not, surely, that we're brighter than they were. It's that we have a series of social practices and conceptual tools available to us that they didn't have: we have markets, double-entry bookkeeping, the idea of capital depreciation, and the like. Or again: Mark Twain's Connecticut Yankee amazes the gawking yokels of King Arthur's Court, not because he is smarter, but because modern science and technology enable him to do things they can't do.

In a Deweyan view, then, we're not necessarily stuck with the bleak findings of Lippmann and Converse. Change the world, reform our practices, and we can improve the intelligence of citizens. Dewey's argument is the right context for considering the cascade of leftist indictments and reforms offered in recent years. American "democracy," we've been told, is nothing but a spectator sport, a beauty contest, in which voters are systematically distracted from genuinely pressing issues of public policy and fed stupid television advertisements, canned "debates" guaranteeing no real confrontation of competing views, and so on. Or again: a capitalist workplace, a consumerist culture, and the rest explain why the working-class men of Eastport interviewed at length by Robert Lane (1962) were so concerned with buying and selling, so little concerned with social justice and elections. Such critics of liberal democracy as Benjamin Barber (1984) and Joshua Cohen and Joel Rogers (1983) have plenty of antecedents—among them, we note, John Stuart Mill, who himself urged at length that the modern workplace ought to be run democratically and who pressed for unbelievably low spending limits on campaigns.

When Lippmann tells us that politics looms awfully remote on the horizon of the ordinary citizen, he must be talking about social distance, not physical distance. But social distance depends in part on personal identity. Because they identify with Israel, many American Jews know and care a lot about Israeli politics, which (short of intercontinental flights) they can't even participate in. It's flatly implausible to view personal identity as any kind of brute fact: it too depends on contingent social practices, cultural norms, and the like. Americans could think of themselves as citizens concerned with politics; if they did in part have that identity, political issues would no longer be far away.

Remember that we want to keep the conterfactuals reasonably close to the actual world. Some critics of American democracy seem to take perverse pride in insisting that only heroically radical changes could make America truly democratic. One could dispute their programs on the merits, of course, but one could also note

---

[4] This, we suggest, is one thrust of some rather murky Hegelian passages about the public coming to know itself.

that those radical changes just don't seem to be in the cards, not now anyway. We prefer to think about available changes in the name of making America more democratic, even if not fully and ideally democratic according to someone's stern standards.[5] So, for instance, changes in journalism might not have the dramatic implications some attribute to democratic socialism, but those changes are still worth pursuing. If this counts as bourgeois reformism, we are happy to plead guilty.

And if appeals to counterfactual worlds seem unscientifically speculative, consider two real examples pointing in the same direction. In 1964, Senator Goldwater spoke forcefully against the intrusions of national government and for states' rights, making no secret of his staunch opposition to the Civil Rights Act. In this respect, Goldwater was unusual: on matters of policy, American presidential candidates typically seek the safety of ambiguity (Page 1978). When they do not, when they offer clear and distinctive proposals, public confusion and ignorance can diminish, sometimes precipitously. By election day in 1964, more than three quarters of the public claimed some familiarity with the Civil Rights Act, and of those, practically everyone knew that Goldwater opposed the act and that Johnson favored it (RePass 1971). These are extraordinary figures: public perceptions are seldom so clear, and the electoral hazards of clarity—Goldwater *was* slaughtered—have not been lost on the consultants and pollsters who seem increasingly to be in charge of campaigns (and administrations) these days. Still, it is worth keeping in mind that if candidates can be coaxed (or compelled) into presenting their differences, a significant fraction of the public seems capable of appreciating them.

A second example concerns public understanding of congressional candidates, who, compared to their colleagues competing for the presidency, toil for the most part in utter darkness. Immediately following midterm elections, for example, fewer than one in four Americans can recall something about the major party candidates that have just run for the House in their district (Pierce and Converse 1981). That's the way things usually are. But every now and then, things can be quite different. A case in point is the 1958 campaign in the Fifth District of Arkansas. There the incumbent representative had become entangled in the federal government's effort to resolve the Little Rock school desegregation crisis. Hardly an integrationist, the incumbent was nevertheless effectively portrayed as soft on civil rights and was defeated in a write-in campaign by a local hero of Southern resistance. In the Fifth District in 1958, *every* voter claimed to know *both* candidates (Miller and Stokes 1966).

Thus, the melancholy indictment of the American public as "wretchedly informed" need not hold always, everywhere. Whatever hurdles stand in the way of informing the public can be overcome, given the right set of circumstances. Of course, the right set of circumstances may not come along very often. And what voters do with the information once it is in their possession is another matter. In the Fifth District in 1958, they swept a racist into office. This is democracy at work, a discussion (we can presume) really took place, the people got what they wanted (i.e., those who were eligible to vote, in part because of the pale color of their skin). Somehow, though, it is an episode hard to celebrate. Discussion is a necessary but insufficient condition for democratic practice.

What about the claim of ideological innocence, which we regard as a less serious liability for democratic discussion? Many critics argued that Converse's conclusions ignored politics, that his analysis paid too little attention to the nature

---

[5] Keeping in mind that what counts as an available change is in part up for political grabs.

of campaigns and public debate. According to this line of criticism, the quality and sophistication of citizens' understanding of politics mirrors the quality and sophistication of the public debate that they witness. Furnish Americans with a conspicuously ideological politics, and they are perfectly capable of responding in kind.

Certainly the critics have had time on their side. Surely Converse's conclusions reflected in part the comparatively tranquil Eisenhower years, a period of political recovery from the intense ideological debates of the New Deal and from the collective trauma of the Great Depression and world war. Surely the original claim must be modified given the events that have shattered national tranquillity since.

The short answer is no. The long answer is long and complicated, and we have neither the time nor the heart to plow through all the details (for the details, see Kinder 1983; Luskin 1987; Smith 1989). Suffice it to say here that Converse's original claim of ideological innocence stands up reasonably well, both to detailed reanalysis and to political change. Indeed, in some respects, the claim is strengthened. *Despite* the boisterous events, panoramic changes, and ideological debates that have punctuated American politics over the last quarter century, most citizens continue to be mystified by or at least indifferent to standard ideological terminology; most continue, as Lane put it, to "morselize" the items and fragments of political life (Lane 1962, 353). We turn, then, to another question. Does ideological innocence preclude rational democratic discussion? Or is there room for rationality even if we concede the lion's share of Converse's case?

ENOUGH ALREADY ABOUT IDEOLOGY

The great debate over ideology, which took over the study of American public opinion over the last twenty-five years, has taught us more about how Americans *do not* think about politics than about how they *do*. This is a lesson of basic importance for our understanding of public opinion, and one with real practical application. It leads us, for example, to doubt sweeping claims about the American public's embrace of liberalism in the 1960s or the public's supposedly sharp movement to the right during the Reagan years. Detailed and careful investigations reveal, as we would expect, that public opinion actually moved in various ideological directions at once (Gold 1992; Schuman et al. 1985). Although ideological innocence is an important conclusion (especially in light of newly elected leaders' persistence in claiming an ideological mandate), it does not tell us anything in detail about how Americans do in fact participate in democratic discussion.

From this vantage point, a welcome recent development in the study of public opinion has been the investigation of foundations for political belief other than ideology. In the absence of ideological principles, perhaps everyday thinking about politics is determined by the pursuit of self-interest or by the perception of group conflict or by various prejudices and solidarities or by the values Americans embrace, the belief in equality or individualism or limited government. Much of this research follows directly in Converse's footsteps, in the sense that the proper subject of investigation is taken to be the nature of belief systems as a whole. The difference, of course, is that in place of ideology is substituted some other "master idea"—individualism, say. Another and complementary line of empirical analysis attempts to understand public opinion not in general terms but in a particular domain, on a particular topic. By abandoning an analysis of belief *systems*, this approach is necessarily less panoramic and sweeping than the analysis Converse provided. Such work includes research on Americans' willingness to extend political rights to groups they despise (Sullivan et al. 1982), on the American public's view toward relations with the Soviet Union (Hurwitz and Peffley 1987), and on Americans' reactions to affirmative action policies (Kinder and Sanders 1987, 1990). In each of these quite different cases, empirical work has been able to uncover a solid foundation for opinion. The discovery here is not of nonattitudes but of real attitudes, reasonably structured and well embedded in a set of relevant considerations. Public opinion on affirmative action, for example, appears to reflect in systematic ways views on equality and individualism, the expected consequences of affirmative action for family and group, and strongly felt prejudice against affirmative action's intended beneficiaries. Such findings go some distance toward relieving the gloominess that surrounded Converse's original conclusion.

But if public opinion is more intelligible and better structured than Converse's analysis implied, some of the considerations that provide the intelligibility and structure are deplorable. For example, political intolerance has its roots in personal distress and insecurity—in the "psychological burdens of freedom," as Lane (1962) put it. For example, the American public's view toward the Soviet Union was powerfully conditioned by an informationally impoverished response to the symbol of Communism. An important ingredient in whites' opposition to affirmative action programs, probably the most important, is racial prejudice. That public opinion is real does not make it, or the democratic form of government that it shapes, necessarily laudable.

Furthermore, the view of public opinion that we are promoting here—public opinion as a systematic reflection of interests, social attachments and hatreds, and American values—carries with it two potential problems for democratic discussion. First is the problem of *diversity*. Virtually all the empirical results on public opinion assume and address that most hypothetical of creatures, "the average American." Research on political tolerance, like research on U.S.-Soviet relations or on affirmative action, tells just one story, with a single protagonist. This inclination in public opinion research to treat Americans as if they were homogeneous and interchangeable, which is of great statistical convenience, should be resisted. Average results may be quite misleading, disguising "population heterogeneity in much the same way census averages describing the 'average' family as having 2.5 children do: one has trouble finding an average family" (Rivers 1988).

Whether diversity is taken into account in research or, as is more often the case, obliterated, the sheer fact of diversity could spell trouble for democratic discussion. If Americans turned out to be vastly different from one another in ways that were consequential for how they arrived at their views on public issues, then democratic discussion might prove impossible. At the extreme, each of us would possess a private language of politics. We might all be speaking to the same topic—whether government restrictions on abortion should be tightened or relaxed, say—but in ways that our fellow citizens would find quite incomprehensible.

This goes too far. Americans are amazingly diverse, but not all differences count for politics. If this were the case, our "average" results would not be as systematic or powerful as they are. Such results are incompatible with the strong version of diversity: namely, that the American public consists of millions of individual citizens, each operating off an idiosyncratic logic. Moreover, those (regrettably few) studies that have directly investigated the possibility that different kinds of Americans come to their views on politics in fundamentally different ways, often conclude that they do not. Differences marked by education or information or social class or ideas about how the economy works generally do not require a proliferation of qualitatively different models of public opinion. This line of research typically uncovers differences of degree, not kind (see, e.g., Feldman 1982; Stimson 1975; Rivers 1988; Kinder and Mebane 1983; Zaller 1992). Such results, provisional as they are, seem from our angle to be good news: we see no evidence to indicate that diversity precludes democratic discussion.

A companion to the problem of diversity is the problem of *complexity*. If, as we maintain, public opinion is structured by a complex amalgam of interests, attachments, hatreds, and values, is democratic conversation impossible? Does such complexity mean that elites and masses are doomed to talk past each other, the former employing an ideological vocabulary destined to sail past the latter?

Not necessarily. Consider the work of Gamson and his colleagues (Gamson and Lasch 1983; Gamson and Modigliani 1987) on the concept of frame, which holds out both a promise and a threat to democratic conversation. In their account of the public discourse that surrounds political issues, Gamson and Modigliani (1987, 143) portray a frame as "a central organizing idea or story line that provides meaning to an unfolding strip of events, weaving a connection among them. The frame suggests what the controversy is about, the essence of the issue." Frames consist of metaphors, exemplars, catchphrases, depictions, and visual images; they often include a rudimentary causal analysis and appeals to honored principles. We believe that frames lead a double life: that they are structures of the mind that impose order and meaning on the problems of society and that they are interpretive structures embedded in political discourse (Kinder and Sanders 1990). At both levels, frames provide narrations for social problems. Frames tell stories about how problems come to be and what (if anything) needs to be done about them.

The good news here is that frames appear to provide a common vocabulary, one that enables elites and citizens to speak clearly to one another. Take, for example, the controversial issue of affirmative action. Gamson and Modigliani (1987) describe how elites in the United States have framed the debate on affirmative action and how the debate has evolved over the past fifteen years. To identify elite frames, they examined the opinions of Supreme Court justices in pivotal cases, *amicus curiae* briefs, speeches and statements delivered by prominent public officials, and the views expressed in various political journals. Gamson and Modigliani then went on to trace changes in each frame's prominence from 1969 to 1984 by examining national news magazines, network news programs, editorial cartoons, and syndicated opinion columns. According to Gamson and Modigliani's analysis, supporters of affirmative action have typically defended their position throughout this period by referring to the need for "remedial action." Under this frame, race-conscious programs are required to offset the continuing pernicious effects of America's long history of racial discrimination. On the other side of the issue, opponents of affirmative action began by arguing that affirmative action constituted "unfair advantage." This frame questions whether rewards should be allocated on the basis of race and expresses the particular concern that blacks are being handed advantages that they do not deserve. Unfair advantage has gradually given way among elite opponents of affirmative action to "reverse discrimination." Like unfair advantage, reverse discrimination questions whether rewards should be allocated on the basis of race, but this time by raising the particular concern whether the rights of whites must be sacrificed in order to advance the interests of blacks. The important and in certain respects, uplifting point here is that elite frames are widely comprehensible to mass publics: they were created, in part, with this aim explicitly in mind. Through frames, democratic discussion between leaders and citizens seems quite unproblematic.

On the other hand, the creation of artful frames enhances the possibility for manipulation. By sponsoring and promoting rival opinion frames, political elites may alter how issues are understood and, as a consequence, what opinion turns out to be (Kinder and Sanders 1990). We don't mean to suggest that *either* democratic discussion is bloodless, gentlemanly, and overintellectualized *or else* it's passionate, manipulative, and irrational. The introduction of a symbol, even a deliberately created symbol, doesn't itself show that something has gone wrong. Nor does the presence of passion, even stridency. Symbols and emotions aren't the enemies of cognition, or anyway, they aren't necessarily its enemies. Typically democratic discussion is at once rational and emotional, at once a matter of the manipulations of interest and the sorting out of sensible positions on public policy. And that's fine. Our worry about the nefarious possibilities of framing is just that they can become freewheeling exercises in pure manipulation.

ELECTIONS AS GOVERNMENT BY DISCUSSION

Elections do not a democracy make—not even free, fair, and frequent elections. But we need not repeat Schumpeter's (1942) mistake to insist that elections play a special role in democracy and so deserve special attention here. The campaigns that lead up to election day constitute an opportunity for candidates and parties to make their case to the voters. And on election day itself, voters are provided the opportunity to "talk back." What can we say here about how voters make up their minds that bears on the quality of democratic conversation?

It should come as no surprise to learn that voting is seldom driven by ideological concerns. This discovery, like the parallel discovery in the study of public opinion, is no ground for democratic despair. Moreover, recent developments in scholarship on voters and elections suggest several grounds for optimism. We take up three here: the ongoing reassessment of the meaning of party identification, the apparent resurgence of issue-based voting, and the powerful inclination among voters to punish incumbents when things go bad.

Party Identification Revisited

According to *The American Voter*, identification with one of the major parties typically begins in childhood. Such identifications grow stronger but rarely change through the course of adult life. To Campbell et al. (1960), party identification was a standing commitment, a "persistent adherence," one that lent order and stability to a complicated and ever-changing political world:

> To the average person the affairs of government are remote and complex, and yet the average citizen is asked periodically to formulate opinions about these affairs. At the very least he has to decide how he will vote, what choice he will make between candidates offering different programs and very different versions of contemporary political events. In this dilemma, having the party symbol stamped on certain candidates, certain issue positions, certain interpretations of political reality is of great psychological convenience. (Stokes 1966a, 126–27)

This may be convenient for the individual citizen, and it may even mean that democratic discussion is fixed to familiar anchoring points—those provided by the parties. But the preeminence of party identification in the voter's calculus is also troubling for democratic discussion. Mechanical attachment to a party, formed in childhood, seems on the face of it rather discouraging to democratic prospects. It suggests that insofar as campaigns are discussions, no one is really listening: virtually everyone made up their minds long ago.

But this interpretation of party identification has in recent years been vigorously challenged. The central theme here is that party identification should be regarded not as a standing decision, a residue of childhood learning, but, as Fiorina (1977, 618) put it, a "running balance sheet on the two parties." As it happens, party identification is not immovable. The loyalty citizens invest in the parties is at least partly conditioned by what the parties *do*. The Democratic and Republican parties are judged by the candidates they nominate (Markus and Converse 1979; Jennings and Markus 1984); the policy proposals they promote (Jackson 1975; Franklin and Jackson 1983); the peace, prosperity, and domestic tranquillity that they manage to deliver (Fiorina 1981; Kinder and Kiewiet 1981); and the company they keep, as in the political realignment of the American South over the last quarter century (Grofman et al. 1988). Party identification is not merely a blind attachment left over from childhood; it has real political content; it accommodates history.

We should not press this too far, however. Although party identification does respond to the grand events of the day, it does so sluggishly. A deep and sustained "Democratic recession" may weaken the loyalties of the rank and file, but very few will actually abandon their party and cross over to the other side. In this respect, the metaphor of the running balance sheet is misleading. Party identification remains a durable attachment, one not easily relinquished and one that presumably operates both to curtail democratic discussion and to fix it to familiar anchoring points.

The Possibility of Issue-based Voting

Citizens who weigh public policy in their electoral decisions are often commended for their civic responsibility. By supporting candidates whose views on public policy most resemble their own, such citizens supposedly contribute to the formation of policy itself. But according to Converse's diagnosis, the typical voter seemed ill prepared to make such a contribution. Remember that many citizens confessed to having no opinion on policy questions, and some substantial fraction of those who claimed to have an opinion seemed to do so capriciously. Moreover, as revealed in *The American Voter*, few seemed to know current government policy; many thought the parties did not differ appreciably in the policies they advocated. In light of these results, Campbell et al. (1960) concluded that opinions on specific matters of policy ordinarily play a modest role in presidential elections.

This conclusion provoked a strong reaction. Beginning with V. O. Key's posthumously published volume, *The Responsible Electorate* (1966), a major preoccupation of research on voting has been to rehabilitate the ordinary citizen by demonstrating that policy voting is in fact more widespread than originally alleged in *The American Voter*. Succinctly put, Key's argument was that voters were no more foolish than the political choices they confronted; if provided clear alternatives, voters were perfectly capable of being "moved by concern about central and relevant questions of public policy" (1966, 7–8).

And so they are. Clarity about policy differences in the voter's mind does indeed depend on the clarity of the choices available (Pomper 1972). More important, when confronted with real differences, voters take them into account. Policy voting waxes and wanes according to the clarity and aggressiveness with which rival candidates push alternative programs (Nie et al. 1979; Rosenstone 1983).

A clinching demonstration of this point—and its limitations—is provided by Page and Brody's (1972) analysis of the 1968 presidential campaign. They discovered that late in the campaign, opinions on Vietnam policy correlated trivially with voters' comparative assessment of the major party candidates. Page and Brody blamed this result not on voters but on Hubert Humphrey's and Richard Nixon's near total failure to articulate alternative policies for voters to choose between. In contrast, voting in a hypothetical election pitting Eugene McCarthy against George Wallace reflected voters' opinions on Vietnam policy much more faithfully (see also Converse et al. 1969). However—and here is evidence on the limits to policy voting—despite the clarity and extremity of the positions on Vietnam staked out by McCarthy and Wallace, confusion on these matters in the general public was nonetheless widespread. In mid-August, only about two-thirds of the public were able to assign positions to McCarthy and to Wallace, of whom less than one-half placed McCarthy to the left of Wallace. Thus, rival candidates who differ on important matters and say so clearly and conspicuously will certainly encourage policy voting—but many voters will never notice.

Throwing the Rascals Out

This brings us at last to those voters who, when times go bad, seem quite willing to evict incumbents from office. Bad things happen to incumbents who preside over recessions, scandals, international humiliations, domestic turmoil, and the like. Presidents, senators, and governors seeking reelection have much to fear from the voters' inclination to throw the rascals out (see, e.g., Chubb 1988; Fiorina 1981; Kramer 1971; Tufte 1978; Rosenstone 1983).[6]

At first glance, this seems a welcome result: elections become a device, though a crude and retrospective one, for shaping government action. Public officials bent on reelection then "have strong incentives to anticipate their constituents' reactions to the social and economic conditions that result from government actions" (Fiorina 1981, 201). Of course, voters asserting that they don't like what's happened during the preceding administration is not the same thing as giving detailed instructions on what the new administration should do. But such imprecision actually has a certain advantage, as Fiorina points out, "It lays no policy constraint on the governing administration; rather, the government is free to innovate, knowing that it will be judged on the results of its actions rather than their specifics. In a word, the accountability generated by a retrospective voting

[6] Incumbent members of the U.S. House are another matter. It is not that House incumbents are immune to national tides (see, e.g., Kramer 1971; Tufte 1978); it is that incumbent members of the House, when faced with national tides running against them, can compensate through their ability to monopolize resources and deliver benefits to their district. These days, House incumbents are virtually undefeatable (Jacobson 1987).

electorate and reaction anticipating politicians provides latitude for political leadership" (Fiorina 1981, 201).

The pervasiveness of this simple reward-punish calculus leaves wide open the important questions how and how *well* voters decide whether a government's record has been glorious or abysmal or merely ordinary. One possible answer is supplied by the self-interest hypothesis: perhaps voters examine their own circumstances first. Voters motivated by self-interest support candidates and parties that have advanced their own interests and reject candidates and parties that have impeded their own interests. A political calculus based entirely on such private calculations would of course substantially reduce the costs that are normally incurred by becoming informed about the world of politics—costs that Lippmann, Downs, Converse, and many others insist the voter is very reluctant to pay.[7]

The self-interest answer is appealing to many—but not to Mill. Mill would have reviled the "realistic" thought that voters are out to maximize their self-interest. Market rationality isn't what Mill's conception requires. The news that voters are out to maximize their self-interest would have struck him as a fatal blow to democratic politics; voters must pursue instead the common good or sound public policy.

Thus, Mill would have welcomed the news that the self-interest hypothesis has fared poorly in a variety of empirical tests. The electoral effects associated with personal economic well-being appear to be quite modest and seem confined for the most part to that usually small minority of voters who see a connection between their own economic predicament and broader economic trends in the country as a whole (e.g., Feldman 1982; Fiorina 1981; Kinder and Kiewiet 1981; Kinder et al. 1989; Lewis-Beck 1988; Sears et al. 1980; Markus 1988).[8]

A second possibility is that voters pay attention not so much to their own problems and achievements when they reach their political decisions as to the problems and achievements of the country—the "sociotropic hypothesis" (Kinder and Kiewiet 1981). Whereas self-interested voters ask the incumbent, What have you done for *me* lately? sociotropic voters ask, What have you done for the *nation* lately? Voters seem in fact to resemble this sociotropic creature, responding to changes in general economic conditions much more than to changes in the circumstances of personal economic life, in the United States and in Western Europe alike (see, e.g., Feldman 1982; Kinder and Kiewiet 1981; Kinder et al. 1989; Lewis-Beck 1988).

At one level, the sociotropic result can be construed to mean that some significant portion of the electorate is sensible (perhaps even rational). That is, in making political decisions, citizens tend to rely on information about the economy as a whole, instead of information about their own idiosyncratic experiences. But how well do they do this? Perhaps voters can be bamboozled about the real state of the country. They may know very well what has happened to themselves and their families, but as we've seen, such clear-eyed perceptions seem not to matter very much for their political decisions. Assessments of the nation's vitality do not have the same grounding in everyday experience. Edelman (1988), for one, contends

---

[7] Why concede so readily that learning about politics counts as a cost? It's odd for political scientists, who themselves pore over daily newspapers and the like, to talk—and think—this way. Here again, we would insist on the prior place of identity and social practices; given other attachments, other practices, people might see learning about politics as a calling, not a chore.

[8] If voters were motivated by self-interest alone, it would of course never occur to them to vote. That millions do so in the face of this strong prediction is a perpetual embarrassment to economic styles of explanation, as Barry (1970) noted many years ago.

that the public's beliefs about government success and failure are among the most arbitrary of political constructions: "Assessing governmental performance is not at all like evaluating the plumber by checking whether the faucet still drips. Officials construct tests that show success, just as their opponents construct other tests that show failure. The higher the office the more certain that judgments of performance depend upon efforts to influence interpretations by suggesting which observations are pertinent, which irrelevant, and what both mean" (41). Edelman reminds us that the sociotropic calculus is subject to manipulation and distortion, that there is no necessary correspondence between the public's diagnosis and the actual health and vitality of the nation.

That voters are sociotropic is promising: it means they may be capable of shouldering Mill's burden of relegating concern with mere self-interest and thinking about (something like) the common good. But we'd like to know more. Given a more detailed account of sociotropic voting, will Mill's account be adequate? Or (as we suspect) will it need sharpening, recasting, more nuance? Perhaps we should emphasize yet again that it is not appropriate to adjust our normative standards so they fit whatever the facts are. Maybe it will turn out that current sociotropic voters aren't good enough.

THE MIRACLE OF AGGREGATION

If the public is "that miscellaneous collection of a few wise and many foolish individuals," as Mill maintained, the public *as a whole* may behave quite wisely. This can happen in part through the sheer mechanical process of statistical aggregation, the law of large numbers applied to public opinion. Aggregating from individuals to the public as a whole drives out the noisiness that is so visible to analysts of individual opinion. The signal that emerges from the miracle of aggregation, as Converse calls it, may be determined disproportionately by the relative handful of citizens who are paying careful attention. Thus, it is quite possible "to arrive at a highly rational system performance on the backs of voters most of whom are remarkably ill-informed much of the time" (Converse 1990; see also Converse 1975, 135; McKelvey and Ordeshook 1990).

The citizenry may behave wisely, even if made up largely of foolish citizens, also because of what Page and Shapiro call *social aggregation*, a phrase that is meant to point to the division of political labor in society:

> Experts and researchers and government officials learn new things about the political world. They make discoveries and analyze and interpret new events. These analysts pass along their ideas and interpretations to commentators and other opinion leaders, who in turn communicate with the general public directly through newspapers, magazines, and television and indirectly through social networks of families, friends, and coworkers. Members of the public think and talk among themselves and often talk back to elites, questioning, criticizing, and selecting ideas that are useful. Most citizens never acquire much detailed information about politics, but they do pay attention to and think about media reports and friends' accounts of what commentators, officials, and trusted experts are saying the government should do. And they tend to form and change their policy preferences accordingly.

As a result, new information and ideas can affect collective public opinion even when most members of the public have no detailed knowledge of them.

Even when most individuals are ill informed, collective public opinion can react fully and sensibly to events, ideas, or discoveries. (this volume, 42)

If this seems Panglossian, it is. Are experts and officials really so determined to turn up the "truth"? Is it reasonable to assume that most members of the public who know so little nevertheless hang on the words of friends for advice about what the government should do? Even in a society featuring an efficient division of political labor, can the public really be expected to react *fully* to new information? Well, no.

Still, statistical and social aggregation together can work wonders. A particularly illuminating illustration of this can be found in research devoted to explaining fluctuations in public support for the president. This is an important topic, not least because popular support is a vital political resource, perhaps the president's single most important base of power (Neustadt 1960; Rivers and Rose 1985; Ostrom and Simon 1985). We now know that a president's support depends upon the prevailing economic, social, and political conditions of the times. Unemployment, inflation, economic growth, flagrant violations of public trust, the human toll of war, international crises, dramatic displays of presidential authority—all these affect the president's standing in the public at large (Hibbs et al. 1982a, 1982b; Kernell 1978; MacKuen 1983; Ostrom and Simon 1985). These results suggest a certain reasonableness of public opinion *in the aggregate* to conspicuous events on the national and international stage.

Much the same conclusion emerges from the study of elections. Although the typical voter seems ill informed, the typical *electorate* seems to behave as if it were well informed. For example, Feld and Grofman (1988) have shown that the electorate can express preferences among candidates exactly congruent with an ideological ordering, despite the fact that a large fraction of the voters who constitute the electorate express preferences that are ideologically incoherent. This result—ideological consistency as a collective phenomenon, a kind of Arrow's paradox running in the opposite direction—may hold not only for the electorate as a whole but for most major social groups as well. Feld and Grofman argue that "it is a 'fallacy of composition' to believe that collective decision making will be ideological *only* when all or most members of the collectivity, as individuals, are ideological" (774).

Change in electoral outcomes from one contest to the next—again, an aggregate phenomenon—displays the same kind of coherence. Such change seems provoked primarily by the emergence of new candidates and by alterations in national circumstances (see, e.g., Stokes 1966b; Popkin et al. 1976; Rosenstone 1983; Markus 1988; Kramer 1971). The overriding point for our purposes is that electoral change appears to be both intelligible—see especially Rosenstone's (1983) model's ability to *predict* presidential election outcomes months before they happen—and sensible. Voters in the aggregate behave as though a real discussion had taken place.[9]

The results on presidential popularity and on election outcome are quite representative of the empirical returns from a wide range of inquiry into the dynamics of public opinion taken as a collectivity. During the last fifteen years, there has

[9] This kind of intelligibility, we grant, can also be taken as a threat to democratic debate. For it can be (mis-?)read as suggesting that campaigns make no difference, that all that talk is surface blather, obscuring our view of the deep causal mechanisms, like economic growth, that really drive election outcomes.

been an explosion of research of this sort: on the American public's attachment to political parties (Converse 1976), support for racial integration (Schuman et al. 1985), opposition to war (Mueller 1973), support for government policy (Page and Shapiro 1988), assessments of the national economy (Markus and Kinder 1988), and more. A very general conclusion across such investigations is how finely responsive public opinion is to social, economic, and political change. Viewed from this vantage point, public opinion looks extremely sensible, reasonable, perhaps even rational (Page and Shapiro 1989).

The construction of a rational public in this fashion is certainly possible, but not foolproof. The claim for aggregation has an illustrious history: roughly parallel arguments litter the history of political thought. The miracle of aggregation is reminiscent of Condorcet's jury theorem. It may well be what Rousseau had in mind in a notoriously obscure passage in *The Social Contract* about the pluses and minuses canceling out in voting. And it must be what Madison was hoping for in thinking that after public opinion was refined and filtered by large districts, indirect elections, and the like, republican devotion to the common good would outweigh the din of faction.

Like their modern counterparts, these arguments are tempting, but they're all a bit too convenient. Put in terms of signal and noise, the essential problem is that the noise we want to drown out may not be random; it may instead be systematic, structured by cynical television advertisements, appeals to racism, and the like. There's no reason a priori to expect that these various forces will neatly cancel themselves out. In fact, the noise may add up to a tightly unified signal that will drown the signal we're interested in. It is—no surprise here—an empirical question how often aggregation produces miracles. Perhaps the answer is frequently. But it is wise to remember that aggregation is no magical mechanism that somehow guarantees systematic rationality on the backs of ignorant and confused voters.

BLUE SKY AND CLOUDS OF DISILLUSIONING FACTS

"Democracy," wrote Mencken, "is the art and science of running the circus from the monkey-cage." Or, for those who like their theory formal, "If x is the population of the United States and y is the degree of imbecility of the average American, then democracy is the theory that $x \times y$ is less than y." Such sentiments tempt not just cynics but those anguished by the undeniable shortcomings of the American citizen—and of American politics. But are they justified?

Not completely. Granted, there is much that Americans just flatly don't know about politics, and their ignorance does indeed threaten the very possibility of government by discussion. The bleak results of Converse and others can't be lightly dismissed. But as we've discovered here, citizens are capable of expressing real opinions on government policy, opinions that are systematically rooted in their interests, social attachments, and political values. Citizens sometimes think sensibly about politics, and in the right context, they can learn quite a bit, quite rapidly, about the candidates who compete for their support. Broadly speaking, many voters seem to behave in reasonable ways, given the discourse and choices they are presented: they reassess their attachments to party in light of political, economic, and social change; they select the candidate that more closely resembles their own views on policy, the more so on those comparatively rare occasions when opposing candidates actually stake out alternative positions; and they are quite prepared to evict incumbents from office when, as they see it, things have run downhill on their watch. And however ill informed and eccentric individual voters may seem, through the miracle of aggregation, the public as a whole may often behave quite sensibly.

Those content with bleak conclusions seem to us sadly mistaken about the problems and possibilities of democratic politics. Theories of democracy that focus on preference aggregation or the pluralistic clash of interests are portraits of a polity in trouble, not any kind of ideal worth affirming. The real hope lies in reforming our politics and practices, not in lowering our aspirations. Given what passes for democratic debate these days, we shouldn't be too surprised by the bleak empirical findings—by the clouds of disillusioning facts. Still, it is not difficult to discern patches of blue sky, and not utopian to press for more.

REFERENCES

Achen, Christopher H. 1975. "Mass Political Attitudes and the Survey Response." *American Political Science Review* 69:1218–31.

Barber, Benjamin. 1984. *Strong Democracy*. Berkeley and Los Angeles: University of California Press.

Barry, Brian. 1970. *Sociologists, Economists, and Democracy*. Chicago: University of Chicago Press.

Brehm, John. 1989. "How Survey Nonresponse Damages Political Analysis." Paper presented at the annual meeting of the American Political Science Association, Atlanta, Georgia.

Brody, Charles J. 1986. "Things Are Rarely Black and White: Admitting Gray into the Converse Model of Attitude Stability." *American Journal of Sociology* 92:657–77.

Campbell, Angus, Philip E. Converse, Warren E. Miller, and Donald E. Stokes. 1960. *The American Voter*. New York: Wiley.

Chubb, John E. 1988. "Institutions, the Economy, and the Dynamics of State Elections." *American Political Science Review* 82:133–54.

Cohen, Joshua, and Joel Rogers. 1983. *On Democracy*. New York: Penguin.

Converse, Philip E. 1964. "The Nature of Belief Systems in Mass Publics." In *Ideology and Discontent*, ed. David E. Apter, 206–61. New York: Free Press.

———. 1970. "Attitudes and Non-attitudes: Continuation of a Dialogue." In *The Quantitative Analysis of Social Problems*, ed. Edward R. Tufte, 168–89. Reading, Mass.: Addison-Wesley.

———. 1975. "Public Opinion and Voting Behavior." In *Handbook of Political Science*, ed. Fred I. Greenstein and Nelson Polsby, 4:75–168. Reading, Mass.: Addison-Wesley.

———. 1976. *The Dynamics of Party Support: Cohort-Analyzing Party Identification*. Beverly Hills, Calif.: Sage Publications.

———. 1990. "Popular Representation and the Distribution of Information." In *Information and Democratic Process*, ed. James Kuklinski and John Ferejohn, 369–88. Urbana: University of Illinois Press.

Converse, Philip E., and Gregory B. Markus. 1979. "Plus ça change . . . : The New CPS Election Study Panel." *American Political Science Review* 73:32–49.

Converse, Philip E., Warren E. Miller, Jerrold G. Rusk, and Arthur C. Wolfe. 1969. "Continuity and Change in American Politics: Parties and Issues in the 1968 Election." *American Political Science Review* 63:1083–1105.

Converse, Philip E., and Roy Pierce. 1986. *Political Representation in France*. Cambridge, Mass.: Harvard University Press.

Dewey, John. [1927] 1952. *The Public and Its Problems*. Columbus: Ohio State University Press.

Edelman, Murray. 1988. *Constructing the Political Spectacle*. Chicago: University of Chicago Press.

Erikson, Robert S. 1979. "The SRC Panel Data and Mass Political Attitudes." *British Journal of Political Science* 9:89–114.

Feld, Scott L., and Bernard Grofman. 1988. "Ideological Consistency as a Collective Phenomenon." *American Political Science Review* 82:773–88.

Feldman, Stanley. 1982. "Economic Self-Interest and Political Behavior." *American Journal of Political Science* 26:446–66.

Fiorina, Morris P. 1977. "An Outline for a Model of Party Choice." *American Journal of Political Science* 21:601–26.

———. 1981. *Retrospective Voting in American National Elections*. New Haven: Yale University Press.

Franklin, Charles H., and John E. Jackson. 1983. "The Dynamics of Party Identification." *American Political Science Review* 77:957–73.

Gamson, William A., and K. E. Lasch. 1983. "The Political Culture of Social Welfare Policy." In *Evaluating the Welfare State*, ed. S. E. Spiro and E. Yuchtman-Yaar, 397–415. New York: Academic Press.

Gamson, William A., and Andre Modigliani. 1987. "The Changing Culture of Affirmative Action." In *Research in Political Sociology*, ed. Richard D. Braungart, 3:137–77. Greenwich, Conn.: JAI Press.

Gold, Howard J. 1992. *Hollow Mandates: American Public Opinion and the Conservative Shift*. New Haven: Yale University Press.

Grofman, Bernard, Amihai Glazer, and Lisa Handley. 1988. "Three Variations on a Theme by V. O. Key." Paper delivered at the annual meeting of the American Political Science Association, Washington, D.C.

Hibbs, Donald A., Jr., R. Douglas Rivers, and Nicholas Vasilatos. 1982a. "The Dynamics of Political Support for American Presidents Among Occupational and Partisan Groups." *American Journal of Political Science* 26:312–32.

———. 1982b. "On the Demand for Economic Outcomes: Macroeconomic Performance and Mass Political Support in the United States, Great Britain, and Europe." *Journal of Political Science* 44:426–62.

Hurwitz, John, and Mark Peffley. 1987. "How Are Foreign Policy Attitudes Structured?" *American Political Science Review* 81:1099–1120.

Jackson, John E. 1975. "Issues, Party Choices, and Presidential Votes." *American Journal of Political Science* 19:161–85.

Jacobson, Gary C. 1987. *The Politics of Congressional Elections*. 2d ed. Boston: Little, Brown.

Jennings, M. Kent, and Gregory B. Markus. 1984. "Partisan Orientation over the Long Haul." *American Political Science Review* 78:1000–1018.

Kernell, Samuel. 1978. "Explaining Presidential Popularity." *American Political Science Review* 72:506–22.

Key, V. O., Jr. 1966. *The Responsible Electorate*. Cambridge, Mass.: Harvard University Press.

Kinder, Donald R. 1983. "Diversity and Complexity in American Public Opinion." In *The State of the Discipline*, ed. Ada Finifter, 389–425. Washington, D.C.: American Political Science Association.

Kinder, Donald R., Gordon S. Adams, and Paul W. Gronke. 1989. "Economics and Politics in the 1984 American Presidential Election." *American Journal of Political Science* 33:491–515.

Kinder, Donald R., and D. Roderick Kiewiet. 1981. "Sociotropic Politics." *British Journal of Political Science* 11:129–61.

Kinder, Donald R., and Walter R. Mebane, Jr. 1983. "Politics and Economics in Everyday Life." In *The Political Process and Economic Change*, ed. Kristi R. Monroe, 141–80. New York: Agathon.

Kinder, Donald R., and Laurie A. Rhodebeck. 1982. "Continuities in Support for Racial Equality, 1972 to 1976." *Public Opinion Quarterly* 46:195–215.

Kinder, Donald R., and Lynn M. Sanders. 1987. "Pluralistic Foundations of American Opinion on Race." Paper delivered at the annual meeting of the American Political Science Association, Chicago.

———. 1990. "Mimicking Political Debate with Survey Questions: The Case of White Opinion on Affirmative Action for Blacks." *Social Cognition* 8:73–103.

Kramer, Gerald H. 1971. "Short-term Fluctuations in U.S. Voting Behavior, 1896–1964." *American Political Science Review* 65:131–43.

Lane, Robert E. 1962. *Political Ideology*. New York: Free Press.

———. 1973. "Patterns of Political Belief." In *Handbook of Political Psychology*, ed. Jeanne Knutson, 83–116. San Francisco: Jossey-Bass.

Lewis-Beck, Michael S. 1988. *Economics and Elections*. Ann Arbor: University of Michigan Press.

Lippmann, Walter. 1922. *Public Opinion*. New York: Macmillan.

———. 1925. *The Phantom Public*. New York: Harcourt, Brace.

Luker, Kristin. 1984. *Abortion and the Politics of Motherhood*. Berkeley and Los Angeles: University of California Press.

Luskin, Robert C. 1987. "Measuring Political Sophistication." *American Journal of Political Science* 25:617–45.

McKelvey, Richard, and Peter Ordeshook. 1990. "Information and Elections: Retrospective Voting and Rational Expectations." In *Information and Democratic Process*, ed. James Kuklinski and John Ferejohn, 281–312. Urbana: University of Illinois Press.

MacKuen, Michael. 1983. "Political Drama, Economic Conditions, and the Dynamics of Presidential Popularity." *American Journal of Political Science* 27:165–92.

Markus, Gregory B. 1988. "The Impact of Personal and National Economic Conditions on the Presidential Vote." *American Journal of Political Science* 32:137–54.

Markus, Gregory B., and Philip E. Converse. 1979. "A Dynamic Simultaneous Equation Model of Electoral Choice." *American Political Science Review* 73:1055–70.

Markus, Gregory B., and Donald R. Kinder. 1988. "Reality and Perception in Economic Assessments." Paper delivered at the annual meeting of the American Political Science Association, Washington, D.C.

Mill, John Stuart. [1861] 1951a. *Considerations on Representative Government*. In *Three Essays*. Oxford: Oxford University Press.

———. [1859] 1951b. *On Liberty*. In *Three Essays*. Oxford: Oxford University Press.

Miller, Warren E., and Donald E. Stokes. 1966. "Party Government and the Saliency of Government." In *Elections and the Political Order*, ed. Angus Campbell, Philip E. Converse, Warren E. Miller, and Donald E. Stokes, 194–211. New York: Wiley.

Mueller, John E. 1973. *War, Presidents, and Public Opinion*. New York: Wiley.

Neustadt, Richard E. 1960. *Presidential Power: The Politics of Leadership*. New York: Wiley.

Nie, Norman H., Sidney Verba, and John R. Petrocik. 1979. *The Changing American Voter*. Enlarged ed. Cambridge, Mass.: Harvard University Press.

Ostrom, Charles W., and Dennis M. Simon. 1985. "Promise and Performance: A Dynamic Model of Presidential Popularity." *American Political Science Review* 79:334–58.

Page, Benjamin I. 1978. *Choices and Echoes in Presidential Elections*. Chicago: University of Chicago Press.

Page, Benjamin I., and Richard A. Brody. 1972. "Policy Voting and the Electoral Process: The Vietnam War Issues." *American Political Science Review* 66:979–95.

Page, Benjamin I., and Robert Y. Shapiro. 1988. "Democracy, Information, and the Rational Public." Paper delivered at the annual meeting of the American Political Science Association, Washington, D.C.

———. 1989. "The Rational Public and Democracy." Paper delivered at the conference "Reconsidering American Democracy," Williams College, August.

Pierce, Roy, and Philip E. Converse. 1981. "Candidate Visibility in France and the United States." *Legislative Studies Quarterly* 3:339–71.

Pomper, Gerald M. 1972. "From Confusion to Clarity: Issues and American Voters, 1956–1968." *American Political Science Review* 66:415–28.

Popkin, Samuel, J. W. Gorman, Charles Phillips, and Jeffrey A. Smith. 1976. "What Have You Done for Me Lately? Toward an Investment Theory of Voting." *American Political Science Review* 70:779–805.

RePass, David E. 1971. "Issue Salience and Party Choice." *American Political Science Review* 65:389–400.

Rivers, Douglas R. 1988. "Heterogeneity in Models of Electoral Choice." *American Journal of Political Science* 32:737–57.

Rivers, Douglas R., and Nancy L. Rose. 1985. "Passing the President's Program: Public Opinion and Presidential Influence in Congress." *American Journal of Political Science* 29:183–96.

Rokeach, Milton. 1960. *The Open and Closed Mind: Investigations into the Nature of Belief Systems and Personality Systems*. New York: Basic Books.

Rosenstone, Stephen J. 1983. *Forecasting Presidential Elections*. New Haven: Yale University Press.

Sanders, Lynn M. N.d. "Against Deliberation." *Political Theory*. Forthcoming.

Schuman, Howard, Charlotte Steeh, and Larry Bobo. 1985. *Racial Attitudes in America*. Cambridge, Mass.: Harvard University Press.

Schumpeter, Joseph A. 1942. *Capitalism, Socialism, and Democracy*. New York: Harper and Brothers.

Sears, David O., Richard R. Lau, Tom Tyler, and Harris M. Allen, Jr. 1980. "Self-Interest Versus Symbolic Politics in Policy Attitudes and Presidential Voting." *American Political Science Review* 74:670–84.

Smith, Eric R.A.N. 1989. *The Unchanging American Voter*. Berkeley and Los Angeles: University of California Press.

Smith, Tom W. 1984. "Nonattitudes: A Review and Evaluation." In *Surveying Subjective Phenomena*, ed. Charles F. Turner and Elizabeth Martin, 2:215–56. New York: Russell Sage Foundation.

Stimson, James A. 1975. "Belief Systems: Constraint, Complexity, and the 1972 Election." *American Journal of Political Science* 19:393–418.

Stokes, Donald E. 1966a. "Party Loyalty and the Likelihood of Deviating Elections." In *Elections and the Political Order*, ed. Angus Campbell, Philip E. Converse, Warren E. Miller, and Donald E. Stokes, 125–35. New York: Wiley.

———. 1966b. "Some Dynamic Elements of Contests for the Presidency." *American Political Science Review* 60:19–28.

Sullivan, John L., James Piereson, and George E. Marcus. 1982. *Political Tolerance and American Democracy*. Chicago: University of Chicago Press.

Tufte, Edward R. 1978. *Political Control of the Economy*. Princeton: Princeton University Press.

Zaller, John. 1992. *The Nature and Origins of Mass Opinion*. Cambridge: Cambridge University Press.

20

MONICA LEWINSKY'S CONTRIBUTION TO POLITICAL SCIENCE

John R. Zaller

However hopeful the Kinder-Herzog piece is, a discerning reader might nonetheless have finished it with the unsettling thought that Kinder and Herzog forgot something very important, namely, the role of the media, in particular, of "media frenzies." Can't the public be distracted by media frenzies? How can we talk about the things that really matter if, in a cable television and blog-saturated 24/7 media environment, we lurch from one media frenzy about some fascinating but sensationalized topic to the next?

To get at the role and impact of media politics, Zaller closely investigates the astonishing improvement in President Bill Clinton's approval ratings after the scandal over his relationship with Monica Lewinsky became the focus of a media frenzy. Zaller ends up showing something very important: the public stuck to the basics it cared about during the Lewinsky scandal, namely, peace and prosperity. This finding may or may not be entirely attractive. As Zaller says, the public would seem rather amoral. It is, however, consistent with the conclusion of the Kinder-Herzog discussion: "There is much that Americans just flatly don't know about politics, and their ignorance does indeed threaten the very possibility of government by discussion. . . . But . . . citizens are capable of expressing real opinions on government policy, opinions that are systematically rooted in their interests, social attachments, and political values."

• • •

THE BOUNCE in President Clinton's job ratings that occurred in the initial 10 days of the Lewinsky imbroglio may offer as much insight into the dynamics of public opinion as any single event in recent memory. What it shows is not just the power of a booming economy to buttress presidential popularity. It shows, more generally, the importance of political substance, as against media hype, in American politics. Even when, as occurred in this case, public opinion is initially responsive to media reports of scandal, the public's concern with actual political achievement reasserts itself. This lesson, which was not nearly so clear before the Lewinsky matter as it is now, not only deepens our understanding of American politics. It also tends, as I argue in the second half of this article, to undermine the importance of one large branch of public opinion research, buttress the importance of another, and point toward some new research questions.

PS: Political Science and Politics 31 (June 1998): 182–189. Copyright © 1998 by the American Political Science Association. Reprinted with the permission of Cambridge University Press. Thanks to Larry Bartels, Dick Brody, Mo Fiorina, Fred Greenstein, John Petrocik, and Daron Shaw for advice on early drafts of this paper.

Whatever else may have transpired by the time this article gets into print, the Lewinsky poll bounce is something worth pondering. In a half-dozen commercial polls taken in the period just before the story broke, Clinton's job approval rating averaged about 60%. Ten days later, following intensive coverage of the story and Clinton's State of the Union address, presidential support was about 10 percentage points higher.[1] The fact that no analyst of public opinion could have credibly predicted this outcome makes the poll bounce especially important to examine. It is, in statistical parlance, a high leverage case.

I begin my analysis with an attempt to establish the parameters of the initial public response to the Lewinsky matter. Toward this end, the results of some three dozen commercial polls, gleaned from published sources, are summarized in Table 1. Although question wordings differ somewhat, all poll results refer to approval of Clinton's job performance as president. Also reported in Table 1 are the results of a content analysis of network TV news coverage during this period.

The content analysis, as shown in the top three rows of the table, gives average minutes of each network news program that were favorable or unfavorable to Clinton. Favorable references include Clinton's denials, attacks on Independent Prosecutor Ken Starr, statements of support for Clinton, and any other information (including non-scandal information) that might tend to enhance public support for the president. Unfavorable references include all statements indicating that the president had an affair with Lewinsky or tried to cover it up, attacks on Clinton or defense of Starr, and any other information that might tend to undermine public support for Clinton. I emphasize that, although journalists played a major role in creating the Lewinsky imbroglio, other actors, notably politicians, initiated some of the information that was reported.

What the content analysis shows is that the frenzy began with two days of heavily negative coverage, but that coverage was relatively balanced after that (given that the matter continued to attract media attention at all). In fact, if the first two days are removed, the remaining period has about as many positive minutes as negative ones, including two days on which Clinton's coverage was decidedly positive.

I have divided the poll data into four partially overlapping periods. As the table indicates, the first two days of heavily negative scandal reportage had a considerable impact on public opinion. On the basis of a half-dozen polls, Clinton's public support seems to have dropped about six or seven points.[2]

The scandal broke on a Wednesday, with the most heavily negative coverage on that day and Thursday. From Friday on, coverage was more balanced and public

---

[1] Documentation of the sources of polls cited in this paper may be found in a PC Excel 5.0 file labeled "Lewpols" on my web page (www.sscnet.ucla.edu/polisci/faculty/zaller). The polls used in determining the overall effect of the Lewinsky matter are: ABC News–*Washington Post*, January 19 and 31, job approval rates of 59% and 67%; ABC News, January 13 and 30, job approval of 62% and 69%; CBS News, January 18 and February 1, 58% and 72%; *Newsweek*, January 18 and 30, 61% and 70%; *Time*-CNN, January 15 and 31, 59% and 72%; *U.S. News and World Report*, January 11 and February 1, 58% and 66%. In cases in which polling occurred over several days, the date given is for the final day. Although wordings of the questions differ, all refer more or less directly to Clinton's job performance rather than to the Lewinsky matter *per se*.

[2] Gallup conducted a poll on the afternoon of the first day of the episode, prior to the evening news. This poll showed Clinton's support rising to 62% from 60% two days earlier. However, I do not count this poll on the grounds that, although the story had broken at the time of the poll, few Americans could yet have learned about it.

TABLE 1

Trends in Presidential Job Approval in the Initial Phase of the Lewinsky Matter

	Pre-event Baseline	Jan. 21 Story Breaks	22	23	24	25	26	27 Before Speech	27 After Speech	28	29	30	31	Feb. 1	Change
TV News Content															
Positive news minutes		0.7	2.0	4.2	2.5	2.4	2.9	4.9	—	4.6	1.9	4.0			
Negative news minutes		7.9	8.3	5.3	5.2	1.6	5.3	3.4	—	1.5	2.4	2.4			
Net news (positive minus negative)		−7.2	−6.3	−1.1	−2.8	+0.8	−2.5	+1.5	—	+3.1	−0.4	+1.6			
Phase I: Initial Frenzy (first two days)															
NBC News	62 (1/18/98)		61												−1
CBS News-NYT	58 (1/18)		55												−3
ABC News	62 (1/13)				57										−6
Time/CNN	59 (1/15)			52											−7
Newsweek	61 (1/18)			54											−7
Gallup 60 (1/18)					58										−2
ABC News-Wash. Post	59 (1/19)				51										−8
Phase II: Charge & Counter-charge (up to State of Union)															
NBC			61			61	63								+2
CBS News/NYT			55		56	56	57								+2
ABC News					57	59	60								+3
Gallup					58	60	59	67							+9

Source	Readings	Change
ABC News	60 60	0
NBC	63 68	+5
CBS News (respondents telephoned ahead to watch speech)	73	16?

Phase IV: Coverage of State of Union address

Source	Readings	Change
Gallup	67 69	+2
CBS News	57 73 72	+15
ABC News	60 68 69	+9
Los Angeles Times	59 68	+9
Time/CNN	52 68 68	+16
Averages:	58 53 56 59 60 67 70 68 69 68 72	

Note: For sources of polls, see a PC Excel 5.0 file labeled "Lewpols" on my webpage, http://www.sscnet.ucla.edu/polisci/faculty/zaller/. Sizes and designs of polls vary.

support for the president rose. By Monday, Clinton had regained everything lost in the first two days, and in Tuesday's Gallup poll, support for the President rose above pre-Lewinsky levels. There were two notable events in this period, both of which were amply reported on TV news. The first was Clinton's appearance on camera on Monday to make an emotional denial of a sexual relationship with Lewinsky; the other was Hillary Clinton's appearance on NBC's *Today Show* on Tuesday morning, where she charged the existence of a right-wing conspiracy against her husband.

If there is any particular spike in the data, it is the Tuesday Gallup poll, which was taken between six and nine in the evening and was therefore able to reflect news of Hillary Clinton's appearance on the *Today Show* that morning. Indeed, the poll was taken just as or just after many Americans were getting news of Mrs. Clinton's appearance; it may therefore, as other polls hint, have overstated its lasting importance on opinion. This poll showed a gain of eight percentage points from the day before, a difference that is statistically significant on a two-tailed test.[3]

Clinton's State of the Union address occurred on Tuesday evening, the end of the seventh day since the Lewinsky story broke. The speech attracted an unusually large audience, presumably because people wanted to see how the crisis-stricken President would perform. According to virtually all the pundits, he performed extremely well. "Good speech, too bad," as one commentator put it.[4]

Two national surveys were taken immediately after the speech. From baselines on the day before the speech—and therefore before Hillary Clinton's charge of right-wing conspiracy—one survey showed no change and the other showed a gain of five points, for an average gain of 2.5%.[5] There was also a CBS poll involving reinterviews with a panel of respondents who had been asked by telephone to watch the speech so that they could be polled afterward. This survey found that Clinton's post-speech job approval rating was 73%. No immediate pre-speech baseline for this poll is available, but if we take the best baseline we have—Clinton's 57% job approval in the CBS–*New York Times* poll from the day before the speech—then the combination of the speech and Mrs. Clinton's defense netted the president some 16 percentage points in support.

A little back-of-the-envelope arithmetic shows that these two sets of post-speech results—an average 2.5% gain in two polls and a 16-point gain among those asked to watch the speech—are not as far apart as they might seem. According to the Nielsen research firm, 53.1 million Americans saw the speech ("TV Ratings for Speech," 1998). This is a lot of people, but only about 25% of the adult population. If 16% of the 25% who watched the speech became more supportive of the president, the overall increase in public support would be only 4.0 percentage points ($.16 \times .25 = .04$). If we assume that viewership of the speech was higher than 25% among those asked to watch it in preparation for a survey but still well under 100%, there is no real disagreement among the three polls on the size of the "speech plus Hillary" effect.

From the bottom panel of Table 1, it appears that public support for Clinton rose another three or so points after the State of the Union, perhaps in response

[3] The sizes of the two surveys were 864 and 672.

[4] Peter Jennings, quoting an anonymous politician.

[5] The baseline for the ABC poll was actually January 25–26, with a sample of 1023. The size of the ABC postspeech survey was 528. The NBC pre- and post-speech surveys both have reported sizes of 405.

to favorable news coverage of that event. But this gain, if real, is apparently small in relation to gains that had already occurred.

It is tempting to pursue more detailed analyses of particular events, but I have already pressed dangerously close to the limits of the data. Instead, I will step back and offer a somewhat less detailed and, I therefore hope, safer summary: In response to sharply negative media coverage of the Lewinsky matter, public support for the president fell. But support rebounded and then surpassed its initial level as the president, his wife, and their allies fought back.

One point seems especially clear and important: In the period in which Clinton's support fell about 7 percentage points, media coverage was sharply negative, but in the period in which he gained back those 7 points and added an additional 8 to 10 points of support, coverage was essentially balanced. Thus, while media coverage of the Lewinsky matter explains part of the opinion change that occurred, it cannot explain all of it. In particular, the notion that the public responded mechanically to media coverage cannot explain how Clinton ended up with higher job approval ratings than he began with. Additional explanation is needed.

An obvious possibility is to argue that the public makes a distinction between approving the way the president does his job and approving of the president as a person. There is, as it happens, some evidence for this view, but not a great deal. The president's personal favorability ratings fell more sharply than his job approval ratings and also recovered less well. In three NBC News polls, Clinton's favorability ratings were 57% before the Lewinsky matter broke, 40% after three days of scandal coverage, and 50% after the State of the Union. In what is apparently the only other set of surveys that made three such soundings of opinion, *Time*-CNN found that Clinton's favorability ratings went from 60% to 50% and then back to 60%.[6]

These data on favorability seem to me to do little to alleviate the mystery of Clinton's bounce in job approval ratings, since they show essentially the same trend. Even if we were examining the favorability data alone, we would still be hard-pressed to explain why Clinton, who looked nothing like a Teflon president when he was pressing for gays in the military and health reform, stood up to the scandal coverage as well as he did. Nor could we explain why, amidst continued media attention to scandal, he actually recouped most of his initial loss.

Another argument might be that Clinton's specific defense against the allegations of sex and cover-up was simply very persuasive. But I find this hard to swallow—not because I disbelieve Clinton, but because he presented so little evidence to support his side and got so little support from witnesses that were in a position to give it. In particular, Clinton got no help from Lewinsky herself, who was semi-publicly negotiating a plea bargain with the independent prosecutor throughout this period. As I parse Clinton's defense, it has consisted of two flat assertions: "I didn't do it" and "my enemies are out to get me."

If the public believed this defense, it was because it wanted to. I suggest, therefore, that we consider the political context that presumably made the public want to believe Clinton's defense, namely, his record of achievement in office. Clinton made an excellent statement of this record in his State of the Union address. Although the address reached too few people and came too late to explain the bulk

---

[6] For sources of these and other favorability polls, see the PC Excel file labeled "Lewpols" on my webpage (www.sscnet.ucla.edu/polisci/faculty/zaller).

of Clinton's recovery in the polls, it is reasonable to suppose that the presidential record that the speech touted was well-known to the majority of the public.

Clinton's speech was, first of all, a celebration of a list of "accomplishments" that would be any president's dream: The economy was the strongest in 25 years, the federal budget was on the verge of balance for the first time in 20 years, crime was falling for the first time in living memory, and the country was at peace. In the main section of the speech, the president proposed a series of programs designed to appeal to the ideological center, as exemplified by a plan to use surplus funds to put Social Security on a sound footing, improve public education, and build more highways. Thus, what the president trumpeted in his speech—and what he would presumably continue by remaining in office—was a record of peace, prosperity, and moderation. Or, more succinctly, it was a record of "political substance." This record was so unassailable that, to much of what the president said in the State of the Union, the Republican leadership could only offer polite applause.

Can political substance, thus defined, move public opinion? Certainly it can. Thanks to a distinguished series of studies—including Key (1966), Kramer (1971), Mueller (1971), Fiorina (1981), and Rosenstone (1983)—political scientists have been aware of the importance of "bottom line" politics for some time. Brody's (1991) work on presidential popularity, which stresses the effects of "outcomes" news coverage on approval, points in the same direction. In light of this, it seems entirely plausible to suggest that the poll bounce that Clinton got at the time of the Lewinsky matter was driven by the same thing that drives presidential election outcomes and presidential popularity in general—political substance. It was not admiration for Bill Clinton's character that first buttressed and then boosted his approval ratings. It was the public's reaction to the delivery of outcomes and policies that the public wants.

This argument is much more than a claim that "It's the economy, stupid." In fact, Clinton's economic performance has been only middling through most of his presidency. Taking the average four-year growth in Real Disposable Income (RDI) for every president elected from 1948 on, Clinton's first term economy ranks tenth of 13. If presidential terms are rank-ordered by growth in the 12-month period prior to Election Day, Clinton's first term is still a mediocre tenth of 13 since World War II. Only recently has Clinton's economic performance become as strong as he described it in his State of the Union.

If Clinton's economy cannot by itself explain why he won by nine percentage points over Bob Dole in 1996, neither can it explain trends in his approval ratings. One big but easy-to-overlook factor is peace, which is a virtual prerequisite for popular support. Popular support for Presidents Truman and Johnson was so damaged by bloody wars that, despite reasonably good economies, they chose not to run for reelection.[7] Clinton's administration has not only avoided war, it has enjoyed a very notable success in Bosnia, for which the President was nominated for a Nobel Peace Prize.

The other big and also easy-to-overlook plus for Clinton is his ideological moderation. This is a factor that scholars, with the exceptions of Rosenstone (1983) and Alesina et al. (1993), have too often ignored. Let me first show anecdotally how moderation affected Clinton's support and then, insofar as possible, make a systematic case.

---

[7] President Bush showed that short, successful wars that cost few American lives do not harm popularity; but neither are they much help over the longer run.

Since gays in the military and the debacle of health care reform, Clinton has hewed to centrist policies, including ones, like welfare reform (and NAFTA earlier on), that are hard for Democratic presidents to endorse. In his confrontation with the Republican Congress over balancing the budget, it was the president, rather than the Republicans, who held middle ground. And finally, after two decades of massive budget deficits, the president has, by means of an initially unpopular budget package in his first term, helped bring the centrist goal of a balanced budget within apparent grasp.

Consistent with the notion that moderation matters is this fragment of hard evidence: President Clinton's approval ratings were weaker at the midpoint of his first term, when the economy was stronger but he identified himself with noncentrist policies, than at the end of his first term, when the economy was weaker but he had remade himself as a policy moderate. Clinton's average job approval rating in Gallup polls taken in the sixth, seventh, and eighth quarters averaged 44.3% and the average percent change in RDI in these same quarters was 4.7%. In quarters fourteen through sixteen, these figures were 55.5% and 1.5%.

Systematic evidence that policy moderation affects presidential popularity is, as far as I know, non-existent. But as regards presidential elections, the evidence, though limited, is clear. The only published evidence comes from Rosenstone's *Forecasting Presidential Elections* (1983), which finds centrism to be a major determinant of cross-state and cross-time voting. In another cut at this problem, my research assistant rated each of the candidates in elections from 1948 to 1996 on a seven-point scale, running from liberal (+3) to conservative (–3). The ratings of each pair of candidates were then summed to produce a measure of relative distance from the center—i.e., a measure of relative extremism—such that higher scores indicated greater relative distance from the midpoint by the candidate of the incumbent party. For example, Lyndon Johnson was rated +2 in 1964 and Barry Goldwater as –3, so that Goldwater was one point further from the center than Johnson. Obviously, such ratings are subject to error and bias. But I note that they were developed in connection with another project (press bias in presidential primaries), and that they correlate highly with the ratings of Rosenstone with which they overlap. These ratings also correlate well with a new set of ideological location scores produced by Poole (forthcoming) for presidential candidates who earlier served in Congress.[8]

The results for a standard voting model are shown in Table 2. War is coded as "1" in 1952 and 1968 and "0" otherwise. Economic performance is measured as average percent change in RDI in the four quarters prior to the election; that is, in the 12th through 15th quarters of each term. As examination of the regression coefficients in Table 2 shows, ideological extremism rivals economic performance as a determinant of vote for the incumbent party. Being one point closer to the center on a seven-point ideology scale (as Johnson was in 1964) is worth about 3 percentage points of the vote; by way of comparison, each additional percent of growth in RDI is worth about 2.1 percentage points. Finally, war costs the incumbent party about 4.5 percentage points of the vote.[9]

From all this I conclude that peace, prosperity, and moderation very heavily influence the dynamics of presidential support, probably in matters of presidential

---

[8] Full details of the ideological coding are available upon request.

[9] Though going beyond the direct evidence, this analysis suggests that Clinton's confrontation with Congress over the budget in early 1996, in which he reestablished his reputation as a defender of centrist policies, may have been as important to his November win as the economy.

TABLE 2
The Effect of Peace, Prosperity, and Moderation on Presidential Vote, 1948–1996

	B	S.E.	Two-sided p-value
War (52, 68 = 1, else = 0)	−4.5	2.3	.04
Real Disposable Income[a] (range: 0% to 7.7%)	2.1	0.40	.001
Relative Extremism (see text)	−3.3	1.0	.005
Constant	43.6		
Adjusted r-square	.77		
N = 13			

Note: Dependent variable is percentage of the two-party vote for the incumbent party candidate.
[a]From *Survey of Current Business,* August, 1997, Table 4, p. 164–67.

popularity and certainly in general elections, for Clinton as well as for other presidents. What the Lewinsky bounce adds to this conclusion is confidence. Although evidence of the importance of political substance has been accumulating for some three decades, no one could have predicted that Clinton would survive the opening round of the Lewinsky affair nearly so well as he did. This is because it has never been quite so starkly clear just how relentlessly the majority of voters can stay focused on the bottom line. Nor, to my knowledge, has it ever been quite so clear that it is possible for public opinion and media opinion to go marching off in opposing directions.

To argue, as I am, that the public stays focused on a bottom line consisting of peace, prosperity, and moderation is not to say that the public is either wise or virtuous. For one thing, its sense of substance seems, in the aggregate, rather amoral—usually more like "what have you done for me lately" than "social justice." Nor is it clear that its decision criteria are very sophisticated. Suppose, for example, that the Watergate investigation of Richard Nixon had taken place in the context of Bill Clinton's booming economy rather than, as was the case, in the context of gasoline shortages and "stagflation" (the combination of high inflation and high unemployment). Would Nixon have been forced from office under these circumstances? Or, if Clinton were saddled with Nixon's economy, would Clinton be, at this point, on the verge of impeachment? These are, I believe, real questions, and the fact that they are does not speak well for the public's wisdom or virtue.

Perhaps future events will shed clearer light on these questions. From the vantage point of early April, when this essay is being finalized, I am keenly aware that issues relating to Lewinsky, Whitewater, and Paula Jones have by no means reached a conclusion. If clear evidence of sexual harassment, perjury, or obstruction of justice emerges, the public might still turn on Clinton. If so, one's judgment of public opinion would need to be more favorable: It waits for clear evidence before reaching a verdict, and it is, after all, concerned with higher values. My personal hunch, however, is that public support for Clinton will be more affected by future performance of the economy than by the clarity of the evidence concerning the charges against him.

I said in opening this article, the Lewinsky affair buttresses some work in political science and undermines the importance of other work. The tradition of studies on economic and retrospective voting, which maintains that the public responds to the substance of party performance, seems strengthened by the Lewinsky matter. On the other hand, the tradition of studies that focuses on the mass media, political psychology, and elite influence, including such diverse studies as Edelman's *Symbolic Uses of Politics* (1964) and my own *Nature and Origins of Mass Opinion* (1992), seems somewhat weaker. It is reasonable to contend that the ground has shifted beneath these two traditions in a way that scholars will need to accommodate. However poorly informed, psychologically driven, and "mass mediated" public opinion may be, it is capable of recognizing and focusing on its own conception of what matters. This is not a conclusion that comes naturally to the second tradition.

Let me amplify the nature of the aspersion I have just cast. A major development in American politics in the last 50 to 100 years has been the rise of what has been variously called *The Rhetorical Presidency* (Tulis 1987), the "political spectacle" (Edelman 1988) and, more simply, Media Politics. This form of politics stands in contrast to an older model of politics, Party Politics. The defining feature of what I prefer to call Media Politics is *the attempt to govern on the basis of words and images that diffuse through the mass media*. This communication—whether in the form of presidential speeches, press conferences, TV ads, media frenzies, spin, or ordinary news—creates a sort of virtual reality whose effects are arguably quite real and important. Typical of the attitude that prevails in this style of politics is Republican strategist Frank Luntz's assessment of the events I have just analyzed: "The problem with [the Lewinsky matter] is we are not going to learn the real impact for years. . . . It's going to leave an indelible mark on our psyche but I don't know what the mark will be" (quoted in Connolly and Edsall 1998). Freely translated, what Luntz is saying is: "It may take us in the spin business a little time to figure out how to play this, but you can be sure we'll keep it alive until we come up with something that works for our side."

As a Republican strategist, Luntz has an obvious partisan interest in taking this view. But his occupational interest is equally great. He and his colleagues in both parties have an interest in "constructing" a public discourse in which events like the Lewinsky affair are important and in which political substance—in the sense of peace, prosperity, and moderation—is unimportant, except insofar as it is useful to emphasize it.

A sizeable part of political science has organized itself to study this new political style. My analysis of the Lewinsky affair, however, suggests that political science not go too far down this road, since old-fashioned political substance of the kind that party competition brings to the fore is not only thriving in the media age, but quite likely still dominant.

This is not to say that the new style of Media Politics is without importance. If only for the resources it consumes and the public attention it commands, Media Politics matters. More, perhaps, than we would like, Media Politics defines our political culture. But beyond that, the effects of Media Politics on political outcomes must be demonstrated on a case-by-case basis, because sometimes the effects are real and lasting and other times they are not.

One illuminating example of Media Politics that produced lasting effects is Gerald Ford's pardon of Richard Nixon in 1974. Coverage of the event was, of course, overwhelmingly negative. On the basis of the same coding categories as in Table 1, Ford got 11 minutes of negative coverage on the network news on the night following the pardon, as against two minutes of positive coverage. The next night, these figures were 10 and 2 minutes. Reporters were by no means the only source of the bad news. In the first two news days after the pardon, 12 Democratic members of Congress, including the House Speaker and Senate Majority Leader, were quoted on the network news attacking Ford, and within the first week the Democratic Congress passed a resolution condemning the pardon. Three Republican leaders also criticized Ford. In these circumstances, Ford's approval rating fell 17 percentage points in the first two days and about 30 points over the longer run.

The contrast with the Lewinsky case is striking. In the first two days of this case, only three Republican members of Congress, none from the leadership, were willing to be quoted on network TV news attacking Clinton—and not for want of opportunity. Reporters were scouring Capitol Hill for volunteers, but politicians (including Democratic politicians) were playing it safe. Thus, the media were forced to shoulder a much larger part of the Lewinsky story on their own. In these quite different circumstances, Clinton suffered limited short-term damage and made gains over the longer run.

It is a tempting conclusion that when the partisan opposition joins a media frenzy, the two together can move public opinion, but that the media alone cannot do it. But even if systematic research were to establish that this pattern is general, there would still be an obvious concern: namely, that opposition politicians attack when they see an opportunity to score points and hold fire otherwise. By this account, Democratic politicians attacked Ford because they knew the attacks would play well, but Republican politicians refrained from attacking Clinton because they feared the attacks would backfire. If this argument is considered plausible, as I think it must be, it further underscores the central claim of this essay: that American politics tends to be driven more by political substance—in this case, public disapproval of the pardon of Nixon—than by the antics of Media Politics. It also points to a difficult future research problem: sorting out whether partisan attacks and other media messages are the causes of public attitudes or their hidden (i.e., endogenous) effects. Surely, the answer is some of both.

Another media frenzy from the Ford administration is worth a brief look. When Ford stated in the second presidential debate that "there is no Soviet domination of Eastern Europe," the mass audience hardly noticed but reporters instantly saw the remark as a gaffe. Polls showed that, citizens polled immediately after the debate judged 44% to 33% that Ford had won. Once the media frenzy of this famous gaffe had run its course, however, the public's judgment was reversed: Several days after the debate, the public thought by a margin of 62–17% that Carter had won. More significantly, Ford also lost ground in straw poll surveys on how people intended to vote. But by about 10 days later, Ford's poll standing had recovered and the gaffe was left for political scientists to ponder (Chaffee and Sears 1979; Sabato 1993, 127–29).

According to a study by Daron Shaw (1995), this pattern is typical. Media frenzies over gaffes and alleged gaffes in presidential campaigns do affect public support for the candidates, but only briefly. The time it takes public opinion to bounce back may, as in the Ford example, disrupt a candidate's momentum and perhaps thereby affect the election, but the lasting direct effect of most media frenzies tends to be nil.

One way to think about this pattern is to assume that there is some "natural" level of support for candidates that is determined by political fundamentals such as the strength of the economy, the candidates' positions on issues, and other such matters. Media frenzies can briefly undermine a candidate's natural level of support, but cannot permanently lower it. Thus, what happened to Clinton in the Lewinsky matter is similar to what happens to candidates who misstep in elections; he recovered from the initial attack. The fact that Clinton gained back more support than he lost is harder to explain in these terms, but I offer the following conjecture: In non-electoral periods, the public tunes out from politics, failing, *inter alia*, to keep its evaluation of presidential performance fully up-to-date. But when, as in the early days of the Lewinsky matter, Clinton's capacity to remain in office came into question, the public took stock and reached a conclusion that led to higher levels of overall support for the threatened leader.

These observations suggest a rough generalization about when media frenzies have lasting effects on opinion and when they don't: The closer media frenzies get to what I am calling political substance, the more likely the effects are to be lasting. The example of Ford's pardon of Nixon would seem to fit this pattern. To take one other example, it seems likely that sympathetic press coverage of attacks by racist southerners on peaceful civil rights protesters in the 1960s had an important effect on northern opinion and thereby congressional action. This was exactly what the Rev. Martin Luther King Jr. expected to happen, and it had lasting importance.

One lesson for political science from the Lewinsky poll bounce, then, is that more attention needs to be given to the general question of when Media Politics (in the sense of trying to mobilize public support through mass communication) matters and when it doesn't, and to do so in a manner that doesn't presuppose the answer. A current research project of Larry Bartels shows how this can be done: With a measure of the "real economy" from the Commerce Department and a measure of the "media economy" from content analysis of media coverage, he hopes to find out which has more influence on presidential approval. Among the auxiliary variables whose impact on presidential approval he will assess is the white-collar unemployment rate in Manhattan. The results will be interesting however they come out.

Another lesson for political science from the Lewinsky poll bounce is that the public is, within broad limits, functionally indifferent to presidential character. "Don't Ask, Don't Tell," as my colleague Art Stein summarizes the mass attitude. Given this, it seems appropriate to consider carefully whether research on the public's assessment of presidential character really helps us to understand the dynamics of American politics.

Contrary to this suggestion, it might be argued that private sexual misbehavior is different from public character, especially in light of changing sexual mores in this area, and that voters' assessments of public character will remain important. Perhaps. But if we view the character issue more broadly, it seems unlikely that voter concern about character has ever been very great. For example, Richard Nixon's peculiar shortcomings were deeply felt by a large number of voters from the moment he stepped onto the national stage in the 1940s. Further, the concerns about Nixon's public character were more serious than any that have been raised about Clinton's. Yet Nixon was elected to the presidency twice, once over Hubert Humphrey, a man whose sterling character has been almost universally acknowledged. Nixon's campaign against Humphrey was, of course, framed by urban riots and a stalemated war in Asia, and in these circumstances, Nixon chose to emphasize substance rather than character. "When you're in trouble," he told voters, "you don't turn to the men who got you in trouble to get you out of it. I say we can't be led in the '70s by the men who stumbled in the 60's."[10] Voters agreed with this emphasis, as they almost always do.

REFERENCES

Alesina, Alberto, John Londregan, and Howard Rosenthal. 1993. "A Model of the Political Economy of the United States." *American Political Science Review* 87(1): 12–33.

Brody, Richard. 1991. *Assessing the President: The Media, Elite Opinion, and Public Support.* Stanford: Stanford University Press.

Chaffee, Steven, and David Sears. 1979. "Uses and Effects of the 1976 Presidential Debates: An Overview of Empirical Studies." In *The Great Debates: Carter vs. Ford*, ed. Sidney Kraus. Bloomington: University of Indiana Press.

Connolly, Cecil, and Thomas B. Edsall. 1998. "Political Pros Looking for Explanations: Public Reaction Seems to Rewrite the Rules." *Washington Post*, February 9, A6.

Edelman, Murray. 1964. *Symbolic Uses of Politics.* Urbana: University of Illinois Press.

———. 1988. *Constructing the Political Spectacle.* Chicago: University of Chicago Press.

Fiorina, Morris. 1981. *Retrospective Voting in American National Elections.* New Haven: Yale University Press.

Key, V. O. Jr. 1966. *The Responsible Electorate: Rationality in Presidential Voting, 1936–60.* New York: Vintage.

Kramer, Gerald H. 1971. "Short-Term Fluctuations in U.S. Voting Behavior, 1896–1964." *American Political Science Review* 65(l):131–43.

Mueller, John. 1973. *War, Presidents, and Public Opinion.* New York: Wiley.

Poole, Keith. Forthcoming. "Recovering a Basic Space from a Set of Issue Scales." *American Journal of Political Science* 42 (August).

Rosenstone, Steven. 1983. *Forecasting Presidential Elections.* New Haven: Yale University Press.

Sabato, Larry. 1993. *Feeding Frenzy: How Attack Journalism Has Transformed American Politics.* New York: Free Press.

Shaw, Daron. 1995. "Strong Persuasion? The Effect of Campaigns in U.S. Presidential Elections." Ph.D diss. UCLA.

Tulis, Jeffrey. 1987. *The Rhetorical Presidency.* Princeton: Princeton University Press.

"TV Ratings from Speech." 1998. *Los Angeles Times*, January 29, A11.

Zaller, John. 1992. *Nature and Origins of Mass Opinion.* Cambridge: Cambridge University Press.

---

[10] Quoted in *Newsweek*, November 4, 1968, p. 28.

Forming Groups

21

THE POLITICAL ECONOMY OF GROUP MEMBERSHIP
John Mark Hansen[*]

This challenging piece by a very senior scholar now at the University of Chicago amply repays the time that you will spend on it. It first presents an elegant calculus of the individual-level decision to participate in an organized group. Do not be put off by the notation of the "model" for this decision; it is actually quite simple and commonsensical.

Notice, incidentally, the emphasis in the model on loss aversion as a motivation for "defensive" expenditure of the dues required to join a dues-collecting organization that can provide policy benefits. This is the second time in this reader that loss aversion (a concept that results from the fusion of economics and psychology) has been brought into political analytic use—the previous instance was in the piece by Kent Weaver.

After presenting his probabilistic model, Hansen then reports the results of statistical tests using membership from three different organized groups and discusses the extent to which the results of these tests illuminate—and are illuminated by—his individual-level model. Interestingly, the most difficult part of the article is the exceptionally subtle "discussion" section at the end. Pay close attention there to how Hansen suggests something quite important: organizations can form—and survive—to transmit strong policy demands for very large constituencies (such as farmers) far more easily than the famous "free rider" paradox suggests, but their future is far from assured. This is both good news and bad news, as Hansen points out. Control of even a small part of the federal government by "special interests" is quite unlikely. On the other hand, the self-organization of citizens is enormously difficult and often results, if it happens, only from government intervention. All of this means, in turn, that there are many gaps in the group representation of demands, concerns, values, and interests to elected and non-elected officials.

If—after reading this article—you want to spend more time on group politics and group formation, you should reread the articles by Paul Pierson, Kent Weaver, and Sidney Verba. They also contain analysis and observation of organized groups in American politics.

• • •

American Political Science Review 79 (March 1985): 79–96. Copyright © 1985 by the American Political Science Association. Reprinted with the permission of Cambridge University Press.

[*]I would like to thank a number of people who have kindly read this article, contributed information or comments, or criticized earlier formulations of the arguments herein. They are Henry E. Brady, Jason D. Cheever, Allan J. Cigler, James DeLizia, Victoria Fillgrove, Shanto Iyengar, Joseph LaPalombara, Burdett A. Loomis, David Priebe, Gerald N. Rosenberg, and Laura J. Scalia. The contributions of Steven J. Rosenstone and Peter VanDoren are especially appreciated. I remain responsible for errors.

OBSERVERS OF AMERICAN DEMOCRACY have greeted political interest groups with praise and with condemnation, but seldom with both. According to some commentators, associations are the upholders of the interests of intense minorities; according to others, they are the selfish saboteurs of majority rule.

These normative conclusions, however, depend vitally on an empirical premise about why people join interest groups. If, as Truman (1971, pp. 26–43) hypothesized, people create and join organizations in response to "disturbances" in the social environment, then interest groups represent legitimate grievances that should be heeded in a democratic political system. But suppose, as Olson (1965) argued, that people who share interests with a large group join less readily than people who share interests with a small one, and suppose that joiners of large groups act in the collective interest only as an unintended consequence of their seeking benefits unrelated to the association's political purpose. Then interest groups, if they have any influence at all, bias public policy away from majority preferences.

Here I argue that political mobilization of large groups does indeed reflect political concerns, but only under certain conditions. I develop a model of interest group membership in which group incentives interact with individual circumstances and test the model's propositions against membership data from three prominent lobbies. My conclusions are at once encouraging and sobering. Political benefits do matter, especially when groups are threatened, but they do not always matter.

A CONTEXT-SENSITIVE MODEL OF
INTEREST GROUP MEMBERSHIP

Olson's by-product theory focuses on two classes of benefits derived from group membership: collective and selective (Olson, 1965, Chap. 6). Collective or political benefits (I use the terms interchangeably) are received jointly by both members and nonmember constituents of the group, and for that very reason are insufficient inducements toward activity. Selective benefits, in contrast, are essential for cooperation because they can be provided to dues payers alone. In concept, the class of selective inducements is varied, although Olson by that term understands goods and services that can be expressed monetarily. Others cast the term more broadly, adding intangible inducements of two kinds: solidary benefits—"rewards created by the act of associating" like fun and friendship—and expressive benefits—"rewards that derive from a sense of satisfaction at having contributed to the attainment of a worthwhile cause" (Wilson, 1973, p. 34).

The context of the incentive model remains unspecified, however, and explicitly or implicitly, interest group theorists assume three things about it: the existence of associations offering political benefits, the extent and nature of the information available to individuals, and the configuration of individual preferences and resources. The first, of course, is simply an assumption that interest groups exist, that they supply the incentives outlined above at some cost, and that some of the benefits supplied are political. I, too, follow convention and assume that interest groups exist, although I return to the question of supply in the conclusion.

The content of the last two assumptions, my primary concern here, is usually stated as fixed and immutable, if indeed it is stated at all. But no single set of assumptions about information, preferences, and resources is universally applicable; rather, the set of appropriate assumptions changes as circumstances change. People in different contexts have different information about alternatives. Depending upon the circumstances, people will be differentially uninformed and misinformed about the actual benefits, costs, and risks of collective action.

More important, people in different contexts have different preferences and resources and hence different subjective weightings of the benefits and costs of group participation. When resources like income and time are ample, people can more easily bear costs; when people have particular needs and preferences, they are more attracted by certain benefits; and when people take different attitudes toward risk, they are more or less willing to engage in actions whose success is uncertain and contingent on the actions of others. In short, information, preferences, and resources that arise in particular situations interact with the actual incentives that organizations offer, forming the subjective assessments of benefits and costs that enter into personal calculations. In equation form, this conceptual model of the individual calculus is:

$$M = E(B_g^s) + \Sigma B_s^s - \Sigma C^s$$
$$= (B_g{}^a I_g T_g)\,(P I_p A_p) + \Sigma\,(B_s{}^a I_s T_s)$$
$$- \Sigma\,(C^a I_c R_c)$$

where

> M = membership (if $M > 0$, the individual joins; if $M \le 0$, the individual does not)
>
> B = benefits
>
> P = probability that the collective good will not be provided if the individual does not join
>
> C = costs
>
> I_g, I_p, I_s, I_c = information about collective benefits, probabilities, selective benefits, and costs
>
> T = preferences and needs
>
> R = resources
>
> A = risk attitudes
>
> subscript g = collective or political benefits
>
> subscript s = selective benefits (services, and solidary and expressive benefits)
>
> superscript s = subjective levels
>
> superscript a = actual levels

An individual joins an interest group if the subjective benefits (B^s) he derives from membership exceed the subjective costs (C^s) he incurs. His subjective assessments depend, however, upon the information (I) that he has about actual benefits (B^a), costs (C^a), and probabilities (P) (cf. Moe, 1980). In addition, the assessments depend upon environmental and dispositional factors that impinge upon specific elements of the calculus: resources (R) on costs, preferences (T) on benefits, and risk attitudes (A) on probabilities. As information, resources, preferences, and risk attitudes change, so too does the attractiveness of group affiliation.

To see how they change, consider in turn each of the three major terms in equation (1).

Expected Political Benefits: $E(B_g^s) = (B_g^a I_g T_g)(PI_p A_p)$

At base, collective action is a strategic problem (Hardin, 1982). The benefits of cooperation indisputably are large. Even a small construction firm with a $100,000 payroll (approximately 10 employees), for example, will save $1000 a year if the unemployment tax is reduced by a single percentage point. But if the political good is won, group constituents receive the windfall regardless of whether or not they cooperated. Given the choice, then, a prospective member would rather remain prospective, reaping any benefits while avoiding all costs.

The strategic aspect, then, is in avoiding costs while being sure that the benefits keep coming. The individual has some idea of what the present and potential benefits are worth to him (B_g^s). He also has some notion of the likelihood that those benefits will *not* be provided, now or in the future, if he does not cooperate (P).[1] In large groups and in normal times, the product of the two, the expected political benefits [$E(B_g^s)$], will for many people be smaller than costs, although not perhaps as small as some have imagined.

Threatening times, be they political, economic, or social, alter three of the premises that underlie the conclusion that political benefits lack motivational force in large groups. First, different kinds of information are available and different kinds of information are salient in times of threat. Groups are always fending off threats; that is, the benefits are always there, but people do not notice them until they are brought to their attention. Threats bring defensive benefits to people's attention. As the adage goes, "You don't know what it's worth until you need it."

Second, potential losses weigh more heavily in people's minds than potential gains (Kahneman & Tversky, 1979). In other words, the utility of a given amount lost exceeds the utility of the same amount gained.

Finally, threats change people's risk attitudes. Faced at most times with potential political gains or at worst small losses, people are risk averse. Given a choice between a certain outcome and a probabilistic outcome of slightly greater expected value, they will choose the sure thing. Faced with large losses, however, people are risk seeking. They will gamble on a probabilistic loss of greater expected value rather than take a sure loss (Kahneman & Tversky, 1979). Realistically, a single individual's contribution to an interest group will make no more difference to its ability to ward off a loss than its ability to secure a gain, but people are more willing to take a chance that it might avert a loss.

In sum, people are more easily mobilized in response to threats than in response to prospects. Threats increase awareness (I_g) of the collective benefits of group membership. Political benefits that avoid losses are weighed more heavily than political benefits that promise gains (i.e., T_g is higher). And instead of discounting collective benefits for risk, threatened people place a premium upon them (i.e., A_p changes from less than one to greater than one). This is the insight that prompted Truman's (1971, pp. 26–43) emphasis on the motivational force of socioeconomic disturbances, and this is the insight that inclines interest group

---

[1] This conditional probability corresponds to Hardin's (1982, chaps. 9–11) notion of collective action as an iterated game in which anticipated reprisals of noncooperation for noncooperation provide an incentive for cooperation that would not exist in single play games.

leaders to emphasize threats over prospects in their appeals. The environmental lobbies, for example, stress the environmental deterioration that will occur if the person solicited does not act, rather than the environmental improvement that will come about if he does (Mitchell, 1979). After James Watt's resignation, these same groups scrambled to find a new *bête noire* as convincing as Reagan's Secretary of the Interior.

The motivational force of political benefits also varies, of course, with other elements of context. First, actual political benefits (B_g^a) change as the political agenda changes. Promoting or staving off regulation of business, for instance, is a political benefit only if policymakers can conceive of business regulation. Second, the probability that collective goods will not be provided if an individual does not cooperate (P) decreases, roughly, with group size. If the political context (for instance, a decentralized political system) makes possible provision of collective goods by local chapters, then a national federation can provide still other benefits on a more inclusive scale (cf. Hardin, 1982, pp. 195–197).

Political benefits, in short, will have different motivational value in different milieux. Like any other good, they are more or less in demand according to people's needs at the moment.

Selective Benefits: $\Sigma (B_s^s) = \Sigma (B_s^a I^s T^s)$

As with collective benefits, demand is more stable for some selective incentives than for others. Some services, such as insurance, are necessities. As a Farm Bureau officer pointed out, "You don't cancel your insurance when things get bad." On the other hand, solidary and expressive benefits by and large are luxury goods. This distinction is implicit in the frequently made assertion that associations offering only intangible incentives are less stable than those offering tangible benefits (Salisbury, 1969; Wilson, 1973), but it need not be unalterably true. For many people, for instance, religious rewards are more important than discount travel tours, and organizations offering the former intangible benefit are apt to be more enduring than those offering only the latter tangible good.

Still, the generalization that services are often necessities whereas expressive and solidary incentives are luxuries allows three predictions. First, demand for intangible incentives will be highly income elastic—that is, small fluctuations in income will produce large shifts in quantity demanded—whereas demand for tangible incentives will be income inelastic. Consequently, income changes that scarcely disturb interest groups offering tangible benefits may be catastrophic for groups relying on intangible inducements. Second, demand for intangibles will be quite price elastic, that is, sensitive to the level of dues. Price elasticity will be higher still if close substitutes exist.[2] Because substitutable expressive and solidary benefits are so widely available—and not only in organizations—interest groups relying upon intangibles are all the more vulnerable to income and price fluctuations (cf. Knoke & Wright-Isak, 1982, p. 243).

Finally, demand for intangible selective goods will be extremely sensitive to changes in fashion. The Sierra Club, for example, has existed since 1892, yet only

---

[2] This holds true if consumers' demand functions are such that relative quantities purchased do not change if income and all prices are multiplied by the same scalar. Given this assumption, the sum of the own-price elasticity (almost always negative), the income elasticity (almost always positive), and cross-price elasticities (positive for substitutes, negative for complements) equals zero. This is known in microeconomics as the homogeneity condition.

recently has it attracted a large following. Clearly, part of the reason is the height-ened salience of conservation in the wake of Earth Day in 1970. In some circles Sierra Club membership is a status good, a symbol of the member's environmental consciousness. Sierra, like the other public interest lobbies, traffics in status. In exchange for dues no more costly than a subscription to the *New Yorker*, Sierra Club members receive a handsome magazine for their coffee tables and a distinc-tive decal for their car windows.

To sum up, demand for selective material incentives depends less upon context than demand for intangible selective goods. Stability of demand for incentives translates into membership stability, if members are equally able to bear costs.

Costs: $\Sigma\ C^s = \Sigma\ (C^a_c I_c R_c)$

Material costs, such as dues and demands on time, often are not the only price of membership. Costs might also be solidary or expressive. Many people, for ex-ample, are put off by Ralph Nader. For them, associating with Nader would be a solidary cost of joining Public Citizen. Likewise, imagine the expressive costs faced by a liberal outdoor enthusiast who joins the National Rifle Association to obtain discounts at hunting lodges (cf. Moe, 1980, pp. 608–609). In the two examples, the tastes that interact with actual costs are clear: expressive costs of NRA membership are higher for ideological liberals than for conservatives.

In general, however, for the same reasons outlined in the preceding section, the most important costs are material. People join interest groups by and large because they can afford to; studies of interest groups virtually always find income effects (e.g., Salisbury, 1969; Tontz, 1964). Yet high income hardly implies infinite resources. When consumers choose to join interest groups, they forgo other prod-ucts they might have purchased, other avenues of political participation (e.g., con-tributing to parties or candidates), or other consumption goods. Hence, subjective costs will be altered by the existence of substitutes (cf. Hirschman, 1971, chap. 2). Full-time employment and membership in the League of Women Voters, for ex-ample, require an identical resource (time) and offer similar benefits (social inter-action and intellectual engagement). Thus, when career opportunities for women increase, as they did during the seventies, the opportunity costs of membership in a participatory group like the League also increase.

ADDITIVITY

In some cases, the same contextual factor interacts with both benefits and costs, but because benefits and costs are additive, the ultimate effect on participation de-pends upon whether the factor affects benefits or costs more strongly. Income, for example, clearly is a resource that enables one to bear material costs. Some peo-ple, however, use income as a psychological indicator of personal economic well-being, affecting how they weight political benefits. The total effect of a change in income, then, depends upon which interaction is stronger.

The model's additivity also underscores the importance of quantity and qual-ity of information. People obviously lack the time and capacity to perform all of the calculations seemingly required by equation (1). In everyday life, though, the decisional elements that people consider are the ones that are available, those that most easily come to mind (Taylor, 1982). The media hoopla that surrounded the financial irregularities of the 1972 Nixon reelection campaign, for example, heightened people's awareness of the political and expressive benefits of Common Cause membership. Moreover, the format of the information people receive greatly influences its evaluation, a psychological phenomenon known as framing (Tversky & Kahneman, 1981). If people buy lottery tickets more readily when the purchase is described as insurance against loss rather than as a gamble on gain—as they do—people will more readily join an association when the information they receive about group membership is framed in the same way. As I noted earlier, interest groups go to great pains to cast their appeals in just that manner.

In conclusion, a theory that looks only at benefits or only at costs misses a great deal of what is important. Benefits and costs do not simply exist; rather they exist in particular milieux. The effects that costs and benefits have on group membership depend upon what people know about them, upon whether people need or want the benefits, and upon whether or not they can afford the costs. In the next section, which analyzes changes in membership in three lobbies, I explore empirically the context-dependence of interest group incentives.

AN OVERVIEW OF THE ANALYSIS

Devising tests of interest group theories has proven far more difficult than devising the theories themselves. Two modes of inquiry predominate: appeals to anecdotal evidence and case studies of particular interest groups, based sometimes upon surveys of their members.

I take a different approach, examining the annual changes in the memberships of three groups: the American Farm Bureau Federation, the League of Women Voters, and the National Association of Home Builders.[3] The Farm Bureau and the Home Builders are "economic" lobbies representing large constituencies, groups for which Olson's by-product theory is most suited. They were chosen for that very reason. The League is ordinarily thought to be a social and expressive organization; it is included to demonstrate the range of the theory.[4]

Because the theory is dynamic, the data are time series. Benefits, costs, risks, context, and membership are all constants at a single slice in time. Joining and quitting interest groups are behaviors that vary only over time, and the things that cause those behaviors vary only over time.

Because the analysis is multivariate, moreover, I can properly test a model that posits multiple causes. In each equation, my explanatory variables are environmental factors, such as actual benefits and costs, resources, and events, with which subjective benefits and costs (and hence membership levels) should be associated, given my earlier argument. The theory predicts that membership can be expected to increase with the development of additional selective incentives. It predicts membership increases when people have higher incomes or more free time. It holds that political and economic disturbances heighten the attractiveness of political benefits, and that people consequently are more likely to join when they are threatened. When school budgets are inadequate, for example, people

---

[3] Few aggregate time series analyses of group membership exist. See Tontz (1964) and Russell (1937) for casual analyses of farm group membership, and Ashenfelter and Pencavel (1969) (plus a comment by Mancke, 1971) for an econometric analysis of union membership.

[4] I contacted a number of organizations within the categories of farm, business, public interest, and labor groups. Most organizations (notably unions) claimed not to have past membership tallies at all, and several more declined to divulge the information. Only the Farm Bureau had already compiled figures. These three groups, then, were selected both for variety and because they were willing to release the membership data they did have.

who value public education will rally to its support. When farmers and builders are in financial binds, they will flock to organizations that claim to have obtained vital subsidies for them. Finally, the theory asserts that group benefits are more available psychologically when the group has a high profile, so that greater visibility alone will stimulate joining. In short, the theory predicts that political and economic context affects membership because context influences subjective evaluations of benefits and costs. In turn, subjective evaluations of incentives determine membership.[5]

THE AMERICAN FARM BUREAU FEDERATION (AFBF)

> The county agent has been the John the Baptist of the farm bureau movement.
>
> —*Extension official W. A. Lloyd*[6]

By any standard, the American Farm Bureau's success in recruiting members has been phenomenal. When it burst onto the scene in 1919 as a federation of state farm bureaus it was already, with 317,000 members, the second largest farm organization in the country, after the Grange (Figure 1). Like the other farm groups, its membership waned in the 1920s and early 1930s, then shot up quickly during and immediately after the Second World War. Now it is by far the largest farm group; its membership of 3.5 million dwarfs the memberships of the four other general farm organizations combined.

Two features of the Farm Bureau have figured prominently in conventional explanations of its organizational success. First, to an unusual degree it was created and nurtured by a government agency, the Cooperative Extension Service (Olson, 1965/1971, pp. 148–157). The Extension organized many local farm bureaus, assisted in forming the state and national federations, recruited for Farm Bureau, and sometimes favored Farm Bureau members in allocating the county agent's services. Over time, however, the Federation's reliance upon the Extension has declined markedly. Efforts to separate the public agency from the private association began as early as 1920 and proceeded slowly (Block, 1960), but even the most hostile contemporary accounts make it clear that the present relationship is but a shadow of what it was (Berger, 1971).

Second, the state farm bureaus offer their members an impressive array of services, including everything from life insurance to farm supplies. Although nominally independent, Farm Bureau businesses are legally controlled by the state lobbying organizations (Berger, 1971, chap. 4; Olson, 1965/1971, pp. 153–156). Illinois pioneered both with insurance services and with the legal arrangement when it launched the County Mutual Insurance Company in 1925. By 1940, about a quarter of the nation's farmers, mostly in the Midwest, could purchase insurance from Farm Bureau companies. By 1950, however, nearly 85% were in

---

[5] Two problems should be mentioned. First, material resources and preferences for material benefits are more easily quantified than nonmaterial resources and preferences for intangible benefits. As a consequence, my estimates are biased if the omitted intangibles are causes of group membership and are associated with the included independent variables. Second, any aggregate analysis risks committing the ecological fallacy, i.e., equating the effects of the independent variables on individuals with their effects on the population. Where possible, then, I supplement the econometric evidence with historical evidence.

[6] Quoted by Baker (1939, p. 21).

FIGURE 1. American Farm Bureau Federation Membership, 1920–1980
Source: American Farm Bureau Federation.

the Farm Bureau insurance trade area, owing to the incorporation of companies in the South and West.

The estimates reported in Table 1 confirm the contribution of insurance services to the Farm Bureau's growth. A four-point increase in the percentage of U.S. farms for which Farm Bureau insurance was available boosted AFBF membership more than 1% in the year before introduction, anticipating the offering, and by 1% in the year of introduction.[7] Insurance was an even better selling point in the

[7] In none of the equations I estimated are the dependent variables normalized, that is, standardized by dividing by the relevant population. Undeniably, they should be. Changes in the size of the potential membership pool are causes of changes in the size of membership, and if population changes are associated with other independent variables, the coefficients are biased. The simple methodological problem, however, masks a thorny theoretical one: what is the proper normalizing population? In each of my cases the answer would seem to be clear, but a moment's reflection makes the quandary apparent. Farm Bureau membership since 1977 has exceeded the number of U.S. farms; the League, which has never considered itself a "women's" organization, has admitted men since 1972; and two-thirds of NAHB membership is drawn from "derived demand" occupations, such as architects, realtors, and bankers. Conceptually, the market is clearly bounded (all who benefit from the policies espoused by the group), but operationally the market is ill-defined and ever-shifting. One of the strategies of leaders, after all, is broadening the group's appeal. Hence, normalizing by the wrong population does not insure that the bias is avoided or obviated.

The solution offered here is, I believe, more palatable. Expressing the dependent variables as percentage changes in raw membership levels introduces a sort of normalization; it narrows the relevant comparison from all observations to adjacent observations. Thus, the estimates in the equation are unbiased if the percentage change in the size of the true normalizing population is uncorrelated with

Table 1

Determinants of Percentage Changes in American Farm
Bureau Federation Membership, 1922–1980
(Weighted maximum likelihood estimates)

	Coefficient	Standard Error
Change in percentage of farmers in a Farm Bureau insurance trade area		
$(t + 1)$	.30	.17
(t)	.26	.17
$(t - 1)$	.32	.17
Log (real agricultural income per farm in thousands of dollars)	5.59	4.10
Percentage change in real subsidy payments/(Real agricultural income per capita in thousands of dollars)		
(t)	.14	.03
$(t - 1)$	.08	.03
$(t - 2)$	.12	.03
$(t - 3)$	.07	.03
Active farm protest group	−5.61	2.29
Constant	−18.82	28.65

$R^2 = .57$
rho = .35
D.W. = 2.07
$N = 59$

See Appendix for data sources and definitions.

year after its offering—percentage point increases in membership followed from 3% increases in coverage.

It would overstate the importance of insurance services, however, to give them the full credit for the huge increases in Farm Bureau membership after World War II. As Table 1 shows, there were other factors involved, such as political benefits, rival groups, and income. Farm Bureau insurance was available to three times as many farmers after the war, but real agricultural income per farm was also about 65% higher. Farm Bureau benefits attracted new members or retained old ones only when farmers had income sufficient to pay dues (Russell, 1937; Salisbury, 1969; Tontz, 1964). Even a casual inspection of Figure 1 shows that membership trends most parallel economic trends. The twenties and thirties were bad both for farmers and the AFBF; the postwar period was good for both. The estimates in Table 1 verify powerful income effects. Roughly a threefold increase

the other independent variables (few of which are themselves percentage changes). Such an assumption is not unreasonable.

The Farm Bureau equation is estimated on data that were weighted to correct for nonconstant error variance and differenced to correct for autocorrelation, with rho estimated by maximum likelihood methods. The League equation likewise corrects for autocorrelation, and the Home Builders equation likewise corrects for heteroskedasticity. Both the Farm Bureau and Home Builders data are weighted by the square root of time.

in real agricultural income per farm produced a 6 percentage point increase in Farm Bureau membership. Membership was subjectively less costly when resources were ample.

Part of the reason for the Farm Bureau's revival in the late 1930s, then, was the revival of the farm economy brought about by the subsidy programs of the New Deal. But another factor in its resurgence was the AFBF's success in obtaining those subsidies. The Farm Bureau was an important—and well publicized—proponent of the 1933 Agricultural Adjustment Act (AAA), and its political success paid big dividends. As shown in Table 1, increases in agricultural subsidy payments boosted Farm Bureau membership then and for several years after, but the magnitude of the increase was contingent upon the level of farm income. When income was at its lowest point, each additional 5 percentage point current-year increase in farm subsidy payments boosted AFBF membership by 1 percentage point (Figure 2). When income was at its highest point, however, it took nearly a 100 percentage point increase in government payments to produce a percentage point increase in AFBF membership. The response to the Federation's political benefits, in short, depended upon the seriousness of the economic threat.

Of course it is impossible to tell from aggregate estimates whether joiners really were responding to political benefits. They might, for instance, have been attracted by expressive incentives. The history of the Farm Bureau, however, argues against that possibility. Although farmers have been prone to expressiveness, the AFBF has not. Even while lobbying aggressively for fundamental changes in agricultural policy, the AFBF was cool, if not hostile, toward all radical agrarian groups from the Nonpartisan League to the American Agriculture Movement. Expressive benefits have not been absent, of course. During the New Deal, Farm Bureau rhetoric emphasized that parity prices meant "equality for agriculture," and one critic has characterized its recent ideology as "right-wing in overalls" (Berger, 1971, p. 5). By and large, however, farmers seeking expressive benefits have had to look elsewhere.

In fact, the expressively motivated farmers have looked elsewhere. Farm Bureau membership dropped by over 5 percentage points in years when the Farmers Holiday, the National Farmers Organization, and the American Agriculture Movement were active and visible (Table 1). The Farm Bureau simply did not provide the expressive benefits that farmers often sought, and when other groups did provide them, many substituted protest group activity for AFBF membership.

A more formidable alternative interpretation of the finding has it that payments under the AAA were seen by farmers not as a collective good but as a selective benefit contingent upon Farm Bureau membership. The Extension Service initially administered the AAA, and Olson (1965/1971, pp. 151–152) argues that the Farm Bureau's influence over the Extension enabled it to coerce subsidy recipients into joining. County agents "encouraged" farmers to enlist with local farm bureaus, implying that those who failed to do so would notice the difference in their checks.

The historical record indicates, however, that an explanation emphasizing collective goods cannot be dismissed so easily. Two elements of Olson's empirical argument need revision. First, the administrative authority of the Extension Service *and* the influence of the AFBF over the Extension varied by farm program and by region. County-agent control over administration was greatest in areas where Farm Bureau strength was least and vice versa. The Extension possessed the most authority in the tobacco, cotton, and peanut programs of the South

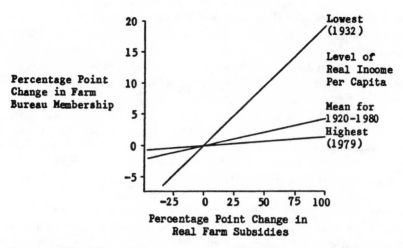

FIGURE 2. The Effect of Changes in Farm Subsidies on Farm Bureau Membership for Different Income Levels
Source: Table 1.

(Baker, 1939, pp. 75, 94), but during the thirties the Southern farm bureaus were relatively small and weak and often subservient to, rather than dominant over, the Extension services (Baker, 1939, p. 141). The influence of the farm bureaus over the Extension was greatest in the Midwest, but there the wheat and corn programs were administered mainly by committees elected by local farmers. This did not, of course, preclude Farm Bureau influence. In fact, an estimated 85% of AAA committeemen in New York, Illinois, and Iowa (all AFBF strongholds) were Farm Bureau members (Baker, 1939, p. 73; Kile, 1948, p. 205). My point here is not that coercion was insubstantial. Rather, it is that the potential ability to coerce was greatest in regions where Farm Bureau had the least to gain from it.

Second, and more important, the Extension did not administer the farm programs for very long. After the passage of the 1936 Soil Conservation and Domestic Allotment Act,

> responsibilities for local administration were withdrawn from the county agents of the Extension Service. . . . The [Agricultural Adjustment Administration] had its own county offices and its own farmer committeemen. While the Farm Bureau was in some cases able to dominate the farmer committeemen of the A.A.A., the influence of the Farm Bureau with a centralized agency was not likely to be as strong as with a decentralized agency like the Extension Service, since the organization and development of the Farm Bureau virtually paralleled that of the Extension Service (Campbell, 1962, p. 157; Block, 1960, pp. 16–17).

The replacement of one bureaucracy with another makes no appreciable difference to the quality of the model; the equation predicts membership changes for 1937 to 1940, the prewar years during which the AAA administered the subsidy programs, just as well as for 1933 to 1936, when the Extension possessed the authority.[8]

---

[8] The mean residual for 1933 to 1936 is 5.0. The mean for 1937 to 1940 is 3.0.

The AAA subsidy programs were important for two other reasons. First, the AFBF feared that the local committees set up by the farm programs might be organized into a rival interest group, especially in the South. Hence, starting in 1935, it waged an aggressive campaign to enlist Southern committeemen as farm bureau members and leaders (Campbell, 1962, chap. 6). The informational (and, perhaps, coercive) campaign paid off—membership growth in the South in the 1930s outpaced growth in all other regions. Second, the New Deal farm legislation was popularly associated with the Farm Bureau, the AFBF encouraged that association, and farmers joined out of responsibility or gratitude or simply to insure the flow of benefits in the future. "In states where the Farm Bureau had an active program," Baker (1939, p. 7) reports, "it claimed considerable credit for the enactment of the AAA. In these states, nonfarm bureau members often felt a moral obligation to become members and promoters of the county farm bureau organization." (See also Campbell, 1962, p. 63.) The benefits that produced the aggregate relationship were not wholly selective, as Olson asserts, but also were collective. Political success and high visibility combined to boost Farm Bureau membership growth past the level determined only by income and selective benefits.

Similar circumstances may have occasioned the Federation's best recruiting year ever, 1921. By all accounts, membership should have dropped. Real income was off about 20% from 1920. More important (from Olson's standpoint), Dr. A.C. True of the States Relations Bureau (precursor of the Extension Service) and AFBF President J. R. Howard had concluded a "memorandum of understanding" that forbade county agents from recruiting for Farm Bureau.

Instead of falling, though, membership jumped by 50%, AFBF's largest percentage gain ever.[9] May 1921 saw the creation of the infamous Farm Bloc in the Washington office of AFBF lobbyist Gray Silver. By the end of the year, the Farm Bloc had passed six priority pieces of legislation, including bills regulating meat packers and the grain exchanges (Kile, 1948, chap. 7). The Federation's legislative clout was no doubt an important selling point in the recruitment campaign the new organization undertook (Kile, 1948, chap. 5).

And what of the True-Howard Agreement? Clearly, if the memorandum had any effect at all, it was not immediate. Farm Bureau membership began to drop a full year after its signing. Of course, in August 1922 the agreement was reissued as USDA policy, and this separation of the Farm Bureau and the Extension Service may have provoked the 1922 membership decline, but it is doubtful. Neither edict, it is clear, changed long-standing practice. The separation of the Extension and the Farm Bureau proceeded slowly and by starts (Block, 1960), and as late as 1954 the USDA saw fit to reprimand the county agents for performing Farm Bureau tasks (Berger, 1971, chap. 8). The importance of the True-Howard Agreement has been overstated.[10] Farm Bureau membership declined in 1922 and throughout the twenties because of a long and severe farm depression.

---

[9] Because of the differencing used in autocorrelation correction procedures, the coefficients for 1921 and 1922 dummies cannot be reported. Weighted least squares estimates indicate a 52 percentage point increase in membership in 1921 over what would be expected on the basis of other variables in the equation. The 1922 decline not accounted for by lower income, on the other hand, is only 17 percentage points.

[10] Part of the confusion stems from unfamiliarity with the time frame. The agreement was signed in April, 1921, but AFBF membership figures are current as of November 30.

Even under the most cautious interpretation, then, this analysis of Farm Bureau membership is solid in its support of the theory. Political success begot membership success, especially when farmers were threatened. But the Farm Bureau's influence over the Extension is a compelling alternative explanation that cannot, and should not, be dispelled totally. This ambiguity is not present in the two remaining cases.

THE LEAGUE OF WOMEN VOTERS (LWV)

What does the average member want when she joins the League? . . . She wants to feel that the *League as a group* is effective in doing something to improve the governmental situation. . . . She wants sociability(?)[*sic*].
—*From materials prepared for the 1938 LWV Board of Directors meeting.*

The League of Women Voters is a social and political organization nonpareil. Organized in 1920 at the victory convention of the National American Woman Suffrage Association, the League offers only one tangible selective incentive—policy study groups to inform its members on a broad range of political issues. As the memorandum quoted above and their own surveys indicate, its primary benefits are political and social (Cantril & Cantril, 1974, pp. 7, 15).

As a consequence of its reliance on intangible incentives, League membership has been particularly sensitive to changes in income and in fashion (Figure 3). Its membership remained high during the early 1920s but began to drop in the latter part of that decade as the enthusiasm of the suffragette days wore thin. Then came the Depression—at its nadir in 1935 League membership stood at only 40% of its total in the early twenties. But membership revived with prosperity, and only recently has it again begun to lag. Since the late 1960s, the League has had to compete with careers and with new women's groups.

Women's entry into the workforce had contradictory effects on the League. On the one hand, jobs boosted the discretionary incomes of upper-middle-class women, making membership more affordable. On the other hand, jobs provided many of the same benefits as League membership—sociability and intellectual engagement—and consumed time, a resource especially precious to the highly participatory League. The estimates in Table 2 reflect the contradiction. A percentage point increase in the workforce participation rate for females decreased LWV membership by 1.5 percentage points a year later. Two years later, however, the effect of a percentage point increase was the opposite, but not offsetting—a percentage point increase in LWV membership.[11] For the League, then, the coinci-

[11]The equation is estimated on only part of the data available because yearly workforce participation rates for females do not exist before 1940. Omitting this variable for the period from 1925 to 1940 would introduce a serious specification error. Moreover, unlike the membership change series for the Farm Bureau and Home Builders, the membership change series for the League is not stationary. Hence, the equation was estimated on differenced data to insure that the patterns of association found here are not the result of both the dependent variable and the independent variables exhibiting parallel trends (this is in addition to the correction for autocorrelation).

Differencing also reduces drastically the collinearity between school expenditures and disposable income (aux. R^2 = .39), allowing their effects to be distinguished. But even here, disposable income has no effect on changes in LWV membership—while the coefficient is positive, it is dwarfed by its standard error (p = .55). The problem would seem to be the inability to measure adequately the competition from new women's groups in the 1970s. This omitted variable, which is associated with high levels of disposable income, probably biases downward the estimate of the income effect.

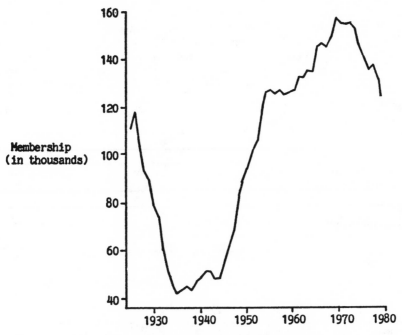

FIGURE 3. League of Women Voters Membership, 1925–1980
Source: Compiled from League of Women Voters records and archives.

dence of the influx of women into the workforce and the creation of the National Organization for Women (NOW), the National Abortion Rights Action League (NARAL), and other women's groups was doubly debilitating. The existence of both career and group substitutes increased the price (in this case, time) elasticity of demand for LWV membership. Because jobs produced greater discretionary income, the new women's groups, which made greater monetary demands but lesser time demands, were aided at the League's expense. A change in the relative availability of different resources affected the relative attractiveness of groups with different cost structures.[12]

The League's decentralized, participatory character, though, made it better able to provide an important collective benefit. In many communities, the League of Women Voters was most prominent as a lobbyist of school boards.[13] Quality of

[12] Entry into the workforce and the founding and growth of NOW were, of course, both a consequence and cause of rising women's consciousness, and the connection between workforce participation and League membership may be as much the result of the relatively greater attractiveness of NOW benefits as of price advantages. It is clear, however, that as of 1970 few women had dropped out of the League to join other women's groups but that dropouts were more likely to be holders of full-time jobs (Cantril & Cantril, 1974, pp. 12–13). Although the League appears to have lost members as a result of its equivocal stance on the Equal Rights Amendment, the competition between LWV and NOW seems to be for women who were not members of any women's groups. The argument here is that many of these women would have joined the League had NOW and NARAL not been available. League membership held its own in the 1940s, when women entered the war economy in large numbers but no alternative women's political groups existed. The most recent LWV membership decline, however, dates from 1969, which coincidentally or not is only three years after NOW's founding.

[13] The importance of local educational issues to the League, which did not initially occur to me, was emphasized by a staffer in the LWV's membership division.

TABLE 2
Determinants of Percentage Changes in League of
Women Voters Membership, 1946–1980
(Maximum likelihood estimates on differenced data)

	Coefficient	Standard Error
Change in female workforce participation rate		
$(t-1)$	−1.63	.32
$(t-2)$	.97	.31
Real per capita state and local expenditures on public schools (in dollars)	−.11	.05
Presidential election years	4.90	.82
Constant	.69	.59
$R^2 = .67$ rho = −.35 D.W. = 2.22 N = 35		

See Appendix for data sources and definitions.

public education was just the sort of highly salient issue that could mobilize educated, upper-status women, many with school-aged children of their own. The League's 1974 self-study found, for example, that one and a half times as many women with children at home were very active in local leagues as women without children at home (Cantril & Cantril, 1974, p. 5). League involvement in school politics, moreover, was invariably directed toward *defense* of existing educational services, and relative to the more specialized teachers' unions and parent-teachers' associations, it was rather episodic. Zeigler and Jennings (1974, p. 117) conclude, for example, that "non-issue-specific groups, such as the . . . Leagues of Women Voters, . . . provide support for the ongoing system, but inject little conflict. . . . They constitute a resource from which decision makers may draw in times of crisis." Accordingly, my estimates indicate that LWV membership grew by a percentage point when per capita state and local support for public education fell by $10, in other words, when support for public education was inadequate. In some measure, then, membership in this national federation reflects neither attention to national affairs nor responsiveness to selective inducements, but rather the great salience of the political benefits offered by its locals.

The LWV's voter education and get-out-the-vote crusades naturally were no less important, but primarily because of the publicity and excitement they generated. The League has been most active, and most visible, in presidential election years. In the 1928 Hoover-Smith contest, for example, it sponsored a weekly series of pre-election radio programs, and in 1976 and 1980 it staged the presidential debates. The favorable light these events cast on the LWV boosted membership by about 5 percentage points.

Two lessons emerge, then, from this analysis of the League of Women Voters. First, League membership responds to the same stimuli to which Farm Bureau membership responds—changes in resource availability and visibility—even though the League relies more on intangible incentives. Second, threats to valued collective goods mobilized League members to the same extent as threats mobilized farmers. These conclusions apply equally strongly to the final case I consider, the National Association of Home Builders.

THE NATIONAL ASSOCIATION OF HOME BUILDERS (NAHB)

[NAHB members] have a tendency to swing erratically and sharply with
the trends in homebuilding: When building drops, then they get radical; but
when times get good and they get fat, then they go conservative.
—*A National League of Cities–U.S. Conference of Mayors official*[14]

The years after World War II brought unprecedented prosperity to the residential construction industry. As a result of forced savings during the war, federal loan and tax subsidies, population growth, and affluence, the stock of owner-occupied housing increased 246% between 1940 and 1980, compared to a population increase of only 72%. The National Association of Home Builders rode the crest of the postwar housing boom (Figure 4). Founded in 1942, NAHB grew spectacularly from its original 500 members to its current 124,000, most organized into local chapters. Only one-third are builders, "anyone who at any point in his lifetime has constructed one home for sale" (Lilley, 1971, p. 444); the majority are associates—subcontractors, architects, realtors, banks, and other suppliers.

The estimates in Table 3 confirm that money in builders' pockets meant builders and suppliers on NAHB rolls and cash in NAHB coffers. A 2-billion-dollar increase in aggregate industry income upped membership by over a percentage point.[15]

But if prosperity was the road to organizational success for the Home Builders, it was a bumpy, uncertain ride. Federal monetary manipulations designed to stabilize the economy fell especially hard on the interest-rate-sensitive residential construction industry. Because building activity fluctuated widely, future prospects were always uncertain. Accordingly, when housing starts were below about 2 million annually, NAHB growth was greatest when starts were low, but for new construction activity above that level, growth was greatest when starts were high. At the lowest level of building activity, a decrease of 10,000 starts produced an NAHB membership increase of a percentage point (Figure 5). At the highest level, a decrease of 10,000 produced a small membership drop of approximately .2 of a percentage point.

The nonlinearity results, I suspect, from a difference between the type of firms that populated the industry in good times and the type that remained in bad times. When building activity and potential profits were high, new firms, which tended to be smaller and undercapitalized, entered the industry. In bad times, however, these marginal firms exited, leaving the large-volume, well-capitalized operations. Thus, decreases in building activity when it already was high mainly affected the small, low-volume builders, who, even though threatened, lacked the accumulated resources to pay dues. Decreases in starts when activity already was low affected

---

[14] Quoted by Lilley (1971, p. 445).

[15] Unlike the independent variables in the Farm Bureau and League equations, the explanatory variables in the NAHB equation are not normalized. The Census Bureau stopped tabulating the number of firms in contract construction in 1963. Estimation of the equation with normalized independent variables for those 20 years, however, demonstrates only one specification change—the coefficient for construction income fails to attain significance.

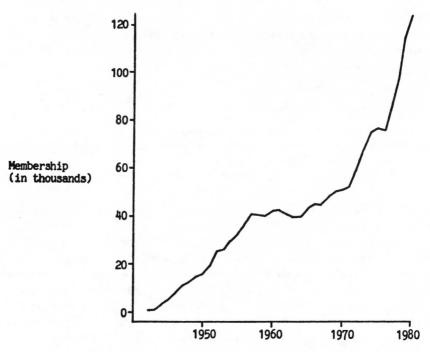

FIGURE 4. National Association of Home Builders Membership, 1942–1980
Source: Compiled from National Association of Home Builders records.

TABLE 3
Determinants of Percentage Changes in National
Association of Home Builders Membership, 1943–1980
(Weighted least squares estimates)

	Coefficient	Standard Error
Real residential construction income in billions of dollars	.60	.17
Housing starts in thousands	.12	.02
Housing starts (in thousands) squared (× 1000)	.30	.07
Housing starts under FHA insurance or VA loan in thousands/(Real residential construction income in billions of dollars)	4.41	.73
Constant	49.7	20.3
R^2 = .87 D. W. = 2.06 N = 38		

See Appendix for data sources and definitions.

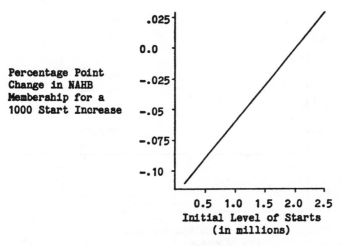

FIGURE 5. The Effect of Changes in Housing Starts on National Association of Home Builders Membership
Source: First derivative, with respect to starts, of equation reported in Table 3.

large builders, who had resources even in hard times. Housing starts for builders, like educational expenditures for upper-status women, were a psychological indicator of well-being, an indicator to which large builders were better poised to respond.

Of course if homebuilders' woes stemmed from policy decisions made by the Federal Reserve Board, there clearly was little that a lobbying organization could do to help. The alternative was to seek help elsewhere, in the bureaucracies that administered the most important and extensive housing subsidy programs, federally backed Federal Housing Administration (FHA) and Veterans Administration (VA) loans. "FHA," as NAHB's chief executive lobbyist put it, "is our major point of contact with the federal bureaucracy" (Lilley, 1971, p. 441). Even in good times the loan subsidies were of considerable importance: "NAHB membership is responsible for a [significant] percentage—90 percent or higher—of houses built under some government insurance or subsidy program" (Lilley, 1971, p. 433).

The effect of realized building subsidies on NAHB membership paralleled the effect of realized farm subsidies on AFBF membership. As shown in Table 3, the value of the collective benefits depended upon builders' incomes. The effect was greatest when income was low. When income was least adequate, a rise of only 1000 government-backed starts swelled NAHB rolls by 1 percentage point (Figure 6). When income was at its highest, the same percentage point membership increase required an additional 25,000 federally subsidized starts. The home builders did indeed get radical in hard times; they did indeed go conservative when they got fat.

As before, of course, the finding may reflect an associated selective benefit provided to members. Although FHA and VA guidelines are legislated, the agencies decide who meets the loan criteria and who does not. If the Home Builders were able to intercede on behalf of particular builders' customers, preferential treatment might constitute sufficient explanation.

Not only does such a contention lack supporting evidence, it is also implausible. NAHB does lobby FHA on behalf of individual members, but the thrust of

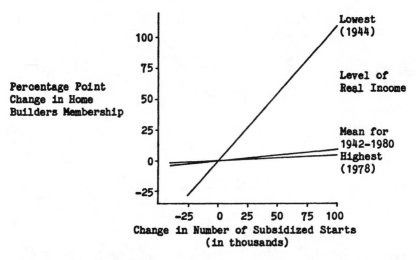

FIGURE 6. The Effects of Changes in Housing Subsidies on Home Builders Membership for Different Income Levels
Source: Table 3.

such efforts is settlement of disputes over building code requirements for FHA-insured houses (Lilley, 1971, p. 441). The FHA and VA bureaucracies are simply not as open to NAHB influence as the decentralized Extension Service was to the Farm Bureau.

A more plausible explanation is that the Home Builders could at least put on a show of pressuring FHA and VA. As an NAHB membership division staffer commented to me, when the industry is emerging from a recession, "NAHB benefits if it has fought hard to end the crunch." FHA, like its parent bureau of Housing and Urban Development (HUD), "is renowned for slowness bordering on catatonia" (Headey, 1978, p. 193; Weicher, 1980, pp. 113–114). The Association of Home Builders could press FHA and VA to speed processing of loan applications so that builders could build.

Until recently, moreover, the loan insurance and subsidy programs were "off budget." Hence, faster processing and more lenient evaluations of loan applicants were perhaps a handy means by which the federal government could compensate the construction industry for the hardships it suffered as a result of anti-inflation policy. Whether NAHB pressure was responsible for the subsidies or not is immaterial. All NAHB had to do was claim the credit for it. Like farmers joining the Farm Bureau, builders joined the Home Builders out of gratitude, responsibility, or to insure that the flow of benefits was not interrupted.

The National Association of Home Builders, in sum, presents a strong case: mobilization in response to threats and mobilization in response to political benefits offered in times of stress.

DISCUSSION

Interest group incentives do not exist in a vacuum. As my three case studies have shown, incentives have different effects in different contexts. Two consistencies are especially important. First, political benefits matter. Although the case of the Farm Bureau is murky because of its influence over the Extension and over local committeemen, the case of the Home Builders is not. Membership responded to realized subsidies, a collective benefit. Second, political benefits matter most when groups are threatened. Subsidy benefits interacted with lower income to swell AFBF and NAHB rolls. Inadequate expenditures on public schools stimulated League growth. Contrary to Olson's claim, then, individuals do indeed join interest groups in response to collective benefits.

My conclusion, however, sets aside a complementary question, that of supply. It makes little difference whether or not members of large groups respond to collective incentives if associations representing large groups never come into being; that is, for individuals to respond to political incentives (or to *any* incentives) they first must exist. Developing membership benefits is extremely costly, and the larger the group, the more costly the organizing endeavor. For a group even to be organized, therefore, it must be subsidized by entrepreneurs, by other groups, or by governments.

The key to understanding which organizations form, then, is understanding which groups get subsidized and when. Producer groups predominated early in the twentieth century, for example, because of smaller size and easier access to organizing resources. The concentration of U.S. industry insured numerous small groups and monopoly rents, that is, lower initial costs and greater resources. Producer groups, moreover, held a privileged position with government (Lindblom, 1977, chap. 13). Political leaders needed the support of business and hence were often eager to create groups as a conduit for communication. The greatest impetus to business (and labor) organization, for example, was war, when government most needed to secure the concurrence of producers. During World War I the federal government encouraged cooperation among firms in vital war industries (McConnell, 1966, pp. 60–64) and hastened the creation of local farm bureaus by the States Relations Bureau in an effort to boost food production (Baker, 1939, p. 44; Kile, 1948, p. 42). Finally, producer groups were more likely than consumers to call forth entrepreneurs willing to bear initial costs. Miller et al. (1981) have documented the importance of group identification in predicting other forms of participation. Part of the advantage of producer groups over diffuse groups, then, was more natural identification with the former and hence greater responsiveness to intrinsic, group-centered rewards such as solidary and expressive benefits.

The proliferation of consumer and environmental groups in the 1970s reflected an expansion of subsidization. Foremost among the developments was the growth of charitable foundations, the bread-and-butter of the public interest sector (Berry, 1977, pp. 72–74; Walker, 1983). Second, government programs in the 1960s often mandated or encouraged the creation of countervailing groups. And finally, entrepreneurs' consciousness of membership in more diffuse groups preceded that consciousness among the masses. Nader's experience with the Corvair certainly alerted him to the marketability of consumer crusading, but it probably also made him more willing to subsidize the consumer movement for its own sake.[16]

There is, in sum, a Say's law of interest groups: supply creates its own demand. Individuals can only respond to whatever incentives are there. Subsidization does

[16] Clearly, many large groups organized by entrepreneurs will fail, but one cannot conclude from that fact alone that rational individuals will not undertake organizing endeavors (Hardin, 1982, pp. 36–37). We commonly presume, after all, that economic entrepreneurs are rational, yet each year many thousands optimistically launch small businesses even though 62% will fail within four years (Small Business Administration, 1983).

not end with creation, however; it extends even to maintenance. In a sense, politics subsidizes services. Interest groups' service organizations quite ironically are by-products of their lobbying organizations, not the other way around. In all but a few cases, services were added to political benefits, not political benefits to services (Hardin, 1982, p. 34). Interest groups entered into competition with commercial firms. If service markets are competitive and if interest groups and commercial companies face similar cost structures, no service provider can undercut the market price, and the only competitive avenue left is product differentiation. In addition, out of the many firms that offer a particular service, *only interest groups offer political benefits in addition*. Part, therefore, of the politically induced changes in interest-group membership levels stems from competitive advantage.

One can, then, identify three classes of joiners motivated by political benefits. For some people, political benefits are sufficient of themselves. Others join both for services and for policy, but either alone is insufficient (Moe, 1980, p. 607). For still others, political benefits are the crucial quality difference; they make the difference between buying from the interest group and buying from a commercial firm. In each case, political benefits are the pivotal component because they subsidize services. Far from being a marginal phenomenon, therefore, responsiveness to political incentives is more widespread and noteworthy than heretofore believed.

Two implications follow. First, the organizational prospects for interests common to large groups are not nearly so bleak as critics of group theory have asserted. On the other hand, because start-up costs are related directly to group size, subsidization is essential for organization. In a sense, this conclusion is more pessimistic even than Olson's, pointing as it does to the explicitly political calculations that give rise to group formation. If certain associations do not exist, it is because it was not in the political interests of resource holders to put them there. That is not to say, of course, that subsidization is the *sine qua non* of organizational success. Demand for interest group benefits must also exist. Perhaps this seems equivocal; that is, to argue that the high risk of failure among expressive groups, to take one instance, results from the absence of effective demand. But groups offering material services fail or lose members as well. The Farmers Alliance, for example, offered a variety of farm services but collapsed when the 1893 depression undercut its members' buying power and the People's Party stole its political program. In short, there are no sufficient conditions for interest group formation and maintenance, only a host of necessary—and highly contingent—conditions.

APPENDIX: DATA SOURCES

Unless otherwise noted, the data were drawn from *Historical Statistics of the U.S. from Colonial Times to 1970* and updated from the *Statistical Abstract of the United States*, both published by the U.S. Commerce Department. Real money series are in 1980 dollars, and all were deflated by the personal consumption price deflator. The deflator for 1920 to 1970 is drawn from *Long Term Economic Growth, 1860–1970*, a U.S. Commerce Department publication (1973), pp. 222–223, and updated from the *Statistical Abstract*.

American Farm Bureau Federation membership as of November 30, 1920–1982: Courtesy of the American Farm Bureau Federation.

League of Women Voters membership as of approximately January 1, 1925–1982: Compiled from League records and archives by the author.

National Association of Home Builders membership as of January 1, 1942–1982: Compiled from NAHB records by the author.

Agricultural income: 1929–70: National income from agriculture, forestry, and fisheries, Series F-227. 1921–28: Robert F. Martin, *National Income in the United States, 1799–1938*. New York: National Industrial Conference Board, p. 65.

Direct subsidy payments to farmers: Series K-326. When expressed as a percentage change, 1933, the year payments commenced, is coded zero.

Farm population: Series K-1.

Number of farms: Annual: Series K-4. Quinquennial, by state: Series K-17 to K-81.

States with Farm Bureau insurance companies: *Farm Bureau Insurance*, pamphlet, American Farm Bureau Federation, 1981; *Best's Insurance Reports: Property/Casualty, Life/Health*. Oldwick, N.J.: A.M. Best Co., 1983; Kile, 1948, pp. 346–352; Berger, 1971, chap. 4. States were considered to have Farm Bureau insurance from the date at which the company *currently* offering *either* property and casualty or life insurance (whichever was earliest) was founded. Because one company often serves several states, this estimate probably errs toward crediting states with an insurance program before they actually had one. For other states, however, it errs toward lateness, because many contracted for insurance through the Nationwide Insurance Company (an Ohio Farm Bureau affiliate) before forming their own companies.

Active farm protest groups: A dummy variable for the Farmers Holiday Association strikes and penny auctions (1932 and 1933), the National Farmers Organization protests and holding actions (1956–1962, 1964, 1967 and 1968), and the American Agriculture Movement tractorcades (1978 and 1979).

State and local expenditures for public schools: Series Y-686. Data are annual for 1952–1980 and are interpolated from biannual data for 1924–1952.

Labor force participation rate for females: Series D-36.

Housing starts: Series N-156.

New privately owned housing units started under FHA insurance or VA guarantee: Series N-180 and N-181.

Residential construction income: Value of new residential construction put in place, Series N-3.

REFERENCES

Ashenfelter, O. & Pencavel, J. American trade union growth: 1900–1960, *Quarterly Journal of Economics*, 1969, *83*, 434–448.

Baker, G. *The county agent*. Chicago: University of Chicago Press, 1939.

Berger, S. *Dollar Harvest*. Lexington, Mass: D.C. Heath, 1971.

Berry, J. *Lobbying for the people*. Princeton, N.J.: Princeton University Press, 1977.

Block, W. *The separation of the Farm Bureau and the Extension Service*. Urbana: University of Illinois Press, 1960.

Campbell, C. *The Farm Bureau and the New Deal*. Urbana: University of Illinois Press, 1962.

Cantril, A., & Cantril, S. D. *The report of the findings of the League self-study*. Washington, D.C.: League of Women Voters, 1974.

Hardin, R. *Collective action*. Baltimore: Resources for the Future, 1982.

Headey, B. *Housing policy in the developed economy*. London: Croom Helm, 1978.

Hirschman, A. *Exit, voice, and loyalty*. Cambridge, Mass.: Harvard University Press, 1971.

Kahneman, D., & Tversky, A. Prospect theory: An analysis of decisions under risk, *Econometrica*, 1979, *47*, 263–291.

Kile, O. *The Farm Bureau through three decades*. Baltimore: Waverly, 1948.

Knoke, D. & Wright-Isak, C. Indivdual motives and organizational incentive systems. *Research in the sociology of organizations*, 1982, *1*, 209–254.

Lilley, W. Washington pressures/home builders' lobbying skills result in success, "good guy" image. *National Journal*, February 27, 1971, 431–445.

Lindblom, C. *Politics and markets*. New York: Basic Books, 1977.

Mancke, R. B. American trade union growth, 1900–1960: A comment. *Quarterly Journal of Economics*, 1971, *85*, 187–193.

McConnell, G. *Private power and American democracy*. New York: Knopf, 1966.

Miller, A., Gurin, P., Gurin, G., & Malanchuk, O. Group consciousness and political participation. *American Journal of Political Science*, 1981, *25*, 495–511.

Mitchell, R. National environmental lobbies and the apparent illogic of collective action. In C. Russell (Ed.) *Collective decision making*. Baltimore: Resources for the Future, 1979, 87–136.

Moe, T. A calculus of group membership. *American Journal of Political Science*, 1980, *24*, 593–632.

Olson, M. *The logic of collective action*. Cambridge, Mass.: Harvard University Press, 1965/1971.

Russell, R. Membership in the American Farm Bureau Federation, 1926–1935, *Rural Sociology*, 1937, *2*, 29–35.

Salisbury, R. An exchange theory of interest groups. *Midwest Journal of Political Science*, 1969, *13*, 1–32.

Small Business Administration. *The state of small business*. Washington: Government Printing Office, 1983.

Taylor, S. The availability bias in social perception and interaction. In D. Kahneman, P. Slovic, & A. Tversky (Eds.), *Judgments under uncertainty*. Cambridge: Cambridge University Press, 1982, 190–200.

Tontz, R. Membership in the general farmers' organizations, United States, 1874–1960, *Agricultural History*, 1964, *38*, 143–157.

Truman, D. *The governmental process* (2d ed.). New York: Knopf, 1971.

Tversky, A., & Kahneman, D. The framing of decisions and the psychology of choice. *Science*, 1981, *211*, 453–458.

Walker, J. The origins and maintenance of interest groups in America. *American Political Science Review*, 1983, *77*, 390–406.

Weicher, J. *Housing: Federal policies and programs*. Washington: American Enterprise Institute, 1980.

Wilson, J. Q. *Political organizations*. New York: Basic Books, 1973.

Zeigler, L. H., & Jennings, M. K. *Governing American schools*. North Scituate, Mass.: Duxbury, 1974.

SECTION 6

Elections

22

ELECTORAL CONTINUITY AND CHANGE, 1868–1996
Larry M. Bartels

In addition to (1) public opinion and (2) group influences on government, citizens communicate with (and they control) public officials via regularly (indeed constitutionally) scheduled elections—which are largely conducted by political parties. (Please note that political parties form the focus for the next section, Section 7, after this section on elections, Section 6.) Here Larry Bartels shows (in a very careful and accessible statistical treatment of presidential elections since 1868) that general elections are very competitive—so competitive that one can safely say that there has never been anything like a one-party system in this country at the national level. Neither major political party can be said to predominate over the other.

Some elections are more long-lasting in their effects than others, to be sure—but it is not possible to discern regular "realignments" in the record, that is, "big elections" in which one party comes to the fore in such a way that its issues and ideas dominate government by discussion (recall Kinder and Herzog's term here) at the expense of the other party's issues and ideas. In fact, competitive parties and entrenched partisanship among voters would seem, on Bartels' account here, to be extremely strong influences on elections—much stronger in their impact on elections than particular candidates or personalities or voter fickleness and manipulability.

• • •

ELECTORAL CONTINUITY AND CHANGE, 1868–1996[1]

Confronted with the limited configurations of the present, the survey analyst will more and more be tempted to search for similar phenomena in the nearer and farther past. Far from being necessarily antihistorical, as they are sometimes supposed to be, survey studies can provide a fresh stimulus to historical analysis.

—*Campbell et al., 1966, 159*

THE STUDY OF ELECTORAL POLITICS has been revolutionized in the last fifty years by the availability of massive amounts of high-quality survey data providing unprecedented access to the attitudes and perceptions of prospective voters. Much

Electoral Studies vol. 17, no. 3, pp. 301–326, 1998. © 1998 Elsevier Science Ltd. Reproduced with permission of Elsevier Science and Technology Journals via Copyright Clearance Center.

[1] This is a revised version of a paper originally presented at the Donald Stokes memorial panel, Annual Meeting of the American Political Science Association, Washington, DC, August 1997. I am grateful to Princeton University and the John Simon Guggenheim Memorial Foundation for generous financial support for the research reported here, and to Daniel Carpenter, John Zaller, and anonymous referees for helpful reactions to the original version.

of that information has been gathered by the authors of *The American Voter* (Campbell *et al.*, 1960) and by their successors in what have come to be called the American National Election Studies. Not surprisingly, easy scholarly access to this treasure-trove of data has done a great deal to shape the contours of the field. The modern scholarly literature on electoral politics is primarily about presidential elections rather than state and local races (or primary elections, or elections in other political systems), primarily about individual political psychology rather than elite behavior or mass-elite linkages, primarily about voting behavior rather than aggregate election outcomes, and primarily about the present rather than the past—all, at least in significant part, because that is where the best data are.

While this scholarly development has produced an unusually rich and technically sophisticated body of political research, it has also encouraged a sort of provincialism, in which the totality of electoral politics is sometimes too readily equated with the psychology of voting behavior in the dozen U.S. presidential elections since 1952. Apparent changes within this fairly narrow compass are taken as reflections of momentous social or political transformations, while apparent continuities are taken as evidence of the way things have always been and will always be. What is one to make of a scholarly literature in which successive decades have witnessed the unveiling of *The American Voter* (Campbell *et al.*, 1960), *The Changing American Voter* (Nie *et al.*, 1976), *The Unchanging American Voter* (Smith, 1989), and *The New American Voter* (Miller and Shanks, 1996)?

In view of these developments, it is well worth recalling that the authors of *The American Voter*—and Donald Stokes perhaps foremost among them—clearly recognized the limitations of the contemporary survey data on which their classic work was based, and strove in a variety of ingenious ways to produce a more complete and nuanced understanding of electoral politics than could be afforded by those data alone. Their efforts to extend the scope of electoral research beyond the reach of national opinion surveys are reflected in the cross-national collaborations of Campbell and Valen and of Converse and Dupeux (both reprinted in Campbell *et al.*, 1966), in the classic works on representation by Miller and Stokes (also reprinted in Campbell *et al.*, 1966), and in Stokes's work with David Butler on the British political system (Butler and Stokes, 1969); they are also reflected in a somewhat different way in the series of historical essays by Stokes considered here, which represent the core of his scholarship in the decade separating *The American Voter* in 1960 and *Political Change in Britain* in 1969.[2]

Within two years after the publication of *The American Voter*, Stokes was consciously attempting to project the framework and findings of that work onto a broader canvas. "The contemporary voting studies," he wrote (Stokes, 1962, 689),

> have disposed of many questions whose answers could only be guessed a few years ago. Yet any such cumulation of findings brings to the fore a number of "second-generation" problems that could hardly be stated except in terms of the theoretical ideas evolving out of current work. This has especially been true in the voting studies as interest has extended from the population of voters to a population of elections; concepts that could explain a good deal about individual choice inevitably spawned additional questions about elections as total social or political events.

[2] I have attempted elsewhere (Bartels, 1997) to provide a more detailed assessment of the aims and significance of the whole corpus of Stokes's work on electoral politics.

Given the limitations of contemporary survey data, an interest in "elections as total social or political events" impelled Stokes to examine the historical record of aggregated electoral data, primarily but not only in the United States. In the process, he organized previously fugitive election returns,[3] developed innovative statistical models and methods for analyzing historical electoral data,[4] and played a major role in defining as well as resolving the "second-generation" problems" posed for the broader field of electoral studies by the findings of contemporary survey research.

My aim here is to revisit the issues of electoral continuity and change raised by Stokes in three important works from this period (Stokes, 1962; Stokes and Iversen, 1962; Stokes, 1967), applying models and methods he would (I like to think) have applied himself had he written these works thirty years later, and using the intervening thirty years' data both to shed additional light on the broad sweep of American electoral history and to shed some light on our current political circumstances. That the specific questions Stokes formulated seem as theoretically and historically relevant in the 1990s as they did in the 1960s is, I submit, a testament to his remarkable intellectual vision.

COMPONENTS OF THE VOTE

The data for my analysis consist of state-level presidential election returns for the 33 elections from 1868 through 1996.[5] I focus here on the Republican popular vote margin in each state, defined as the difference between the Republican and Democratic percentages of the total vote cast for president. I prefer this measure to the Republican share of the two-party vote because the latter measure tends to overstate the winning party's dominance in elections with strong third-party showings.[6]

I make no concerted effort to analyze support for third-party and independent candidates, largely because that support has been so sporadic and ephemeral in the period covered by my analysis. The total vote cast for candidates other than the Republican and Democratic nominees has averaged only five percent in these

[3] Stokes and Iversen (1962) presented the first time series of national congressional vote percentages going back to the Civil War, a forerunner of the ambitious historical data collection carried out under the auspices of the Inter-University Consortium for Political and Social Research.

[4] Stokes's (1962) use of a normal error model and Stokes and Iversen's (1962) use of a random walk model were both, to the best of my knowledge, unprecedented in political science. Later, Stokes devoted considerable scholarly energy to addressing methodological problems arising in analyses of aggregated data (Stokes, 1969) and developing and applying a "variance components" model for what are now commonly referred to as hierarchical data (Stokes, 1965, 1967).

[5] The data are taken from Congressional Quarterly (1995), updated with 1996 returns from *Congressional Quarterly Weekly Report*. These data are derived from Scammon and McGillivray (1994), but differ in minor respects from those compiled by Robinson (1934) and Petersen (1963).

[6] Including third-party voters in the denominator, as I do, implicitly assumes that they would divide their support evenly between the two major candidates if forced to choose between them; excluding third-party voters implicitly assumes that they would divide their support in the same proportions as those who actually voted for the two major candidates. Both these assumptions are surely false, but the first is probably closer to the truth than the second, since the major party that loses more of its usual supporters to a strong third-party challenge is likely to lose the election, as the Republicans did in 1912 and 1992. Most of Theodore Roosevelt's supporters in 1912 were surely Republicans, while polling data from 1992 suggest that Ross Perot drew as much or more from George Bush as from Bill Clinton.

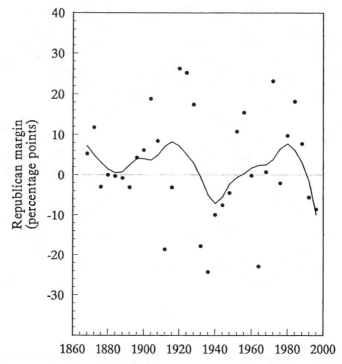

FIGURE 1. Election outcomes, 1868–1996

33 elections, and the half-dozen cases in which it reached ten percent or more (1912, 1992, 1924, 1968, 1892, and 1996) have displayed rather little continuity in voting patterns.[7]

The Republican vote margins in the 33 presidential elections from 1868 through 1996 are shown as dots in Fig. 1. The figure also shows a moving average through time of the individual election outcomes, which provides a clearer visual representation of historical shifts in party dominance.[8] By this moving average measure, the Republican party was dominant (at the presidential level) from the Civil War until the accession of Franklin Roosevelt, and again from Eisenhower through Bush—albeit at times only narrowly, and with reversals in specific elections, most spectacularly in 1912 and 1964. It is also interesting to note, however, that despite these long periods of Republican dominance, the median vote margin is exactly zero, and 20 of the 33 margins are smaller than ten percentage points.

[7] For example, even with Ross Perot in both the 1992 and 1996 races, the correlation between the total vote shares for third-party and independent candidates in those two elections was only 0.71, while the corresponding correlation between Republican vote margins in 1992 and 1996 was 0.88. Defections from the two-party system in 1996 were also correlated with previous defections in 1980 (0.63), 1968 (–0.63), 1924 (0.59), and 1912 (0.50). However, these correlations mostly reflect the relative appeal of third-party candidates in the South; the corresponding correlations for non-southern states only are 0.23., –0.25, 0.35, and 0.04.

[8] The moving averages shown in this and subsequent figures were generated by locally weighted regressions of election outcomes on time using the *ksm lowess* procedure in the Stata software package. Beck and Jackman (1998) provide an introduction to locally weighted regression and related techniques. All of my locally weighted regressions employ bandwidths of 0.3, meaning that 40 years' worth of data are used to calculate the summary value at each point, with temporally proximate observations receiving more weight than those more distant in time.

The election outcome in each state in each election year may usefully be thought of as a sum of three distinct components: a partisan component reflecting standing loyalties carrying over from previous elections, an election-specific component reflecting the shifting tides of national electoral forces, and an idiosyncratic component reflecting new sub-national electoral forces at work in the specific state. I propose to measure these three distinct components of the vote by regressing state election outcomes in each election year on previous election outcomes in the same state plus a constant. The regression model is

$$R_{st} = \alpha_t + \beta_{1t} R_{st-1} + \beta_{2t} R_{st-2} + \beta_{3t} R_{st-3} + \varepsilon_{st},\qquad(1)$$

where R_{st} represents the Republican vote margin in state s in election year t, and R_{st-1}, R_{st-2}, and R_{st-3} represent the Republican vote margins in the same state in the three immediately preceding elections. α_t, β_{1t}, β_{2t}, and β_{3t} are election-specific parameters to be estimated, and ε_{st} is a stochastic term reflecting state-specific idiosyncratic forces in election year t; I will assume for purposes of estimation that ε_{st} is drawn from a probability distribution with mean zero and election-specific variance σ_t^2.

The parameters of this regression model correspond directly to the three components of the vote distinguished here: the parameters β_{1t}, β_{2t}, and β_{3t} on lagged state votes reflect standing partisan loyalties carrying over from previous elections, the intercept parameter α_t measures the overall vote shift attributable to national electoral forces in a given election, and the stochastic variance parameter σ_t^2 measures the magnitude of new sub-national forces in a given election.

Estimates of these parameters for each of the 33 presidential elections examined here are presented in Table 1. Each row of the table represents one regression, with the number of observations corresponding to the number of states voting in that election year.[9] In order to reflect national voting behavior, all of the data are weighted by the number of votes cast in each state in each election year, so that more populous states receive more weight in the regressions.

The first column of Table 1 shows the square root of the estimated stochastic variance of sub-national forces in each election year (σ_t) in percentage points; the second column shows the estimated national partisan swing (α_t) in percentage points (with positive values indicating Republican swings, negative values indicating Democratic swings, and standard errors of the estimates in parentheses); the third, fourth, and fifth columns show the estimated persistence of previous state-level outcomes in each election year (β_{1t}, β_{2t}, and β_{3t}); and the sixth column shows the sum of these three lagged partisan effects (again, with its standard error in parentheses).[10]

For example, the parameter estimates for the 1996 election presented in the first row of Table 1 show that the state-level voting pattern in 1996 basically replicated the pattern in 1992, but with an across-the-board shift of five percentage points toward Clinton. (The national shift is reflected in the intercept of −5.198,

---

[9] Actually, because lagged election outcomes appear as explanatory variables in Table 1, each state appears in the regressions twelve years after it entered (or, in the case of the former Confederate states following the Civil War, reentered) the electorate. Thus, the number of observations ranges from 20 in 1868 to 51 (including the District of Columbia) since 1976.

[10] The sum of the three lagged partisan effects in a given election year is often estimated more precisely than the separate effects themselves. This fact reflects the positive correlations among the three separate measures of past election outcomes, which make it harder to disentangle their separate effects but easier to measure their joint effect.

TABLE 1
Components of the Presidential Vote, 1868–1996

Election Year	σ_t (Sub-National Forces)	α_t (National Forces)	β_{1t} (4-year Lag)	β_{2t} (8-year Lag)	β_{3t} (12-year Lag)	$\Sigma\beta_t$ (Partisan Loyalties)
1996	5.755	-5.198 (3.610)	1.087 (0.187)	-0.060 (0.184)	0.164 (0.178)	1.191 (0.092)
1992	4.518	-15.664 (1.963)	0.404 (0.153)	0.379 (0.191)	-0.016 (0.097)	0.767 (0.073)
1988	4.298	-9.975 (1.491)	1.085 (0.088)	-0.240 (0.135)	-0.085 (0.119)	0.760 (0.074)
1984	3.884	1.026 (1.345)	0.582 (0.101)	-0.029 (0.109)	0.467 (0.044)	1.020 (0.071)
1980	5.233	9.991 (1.797)	0.742 (0.098)	0.036 (0.074)	0.322 (0.114)	1.100 (0.095)
1976	7.658	2.871 (4.636)	-0.274 (0.132)	0.712 (0.134)	-0.043 (0.087)	0.395 (0.107)
1972	8.141	30.323 (2.366)	0.686 (0.229)	0.356 (0.086)	-0.324 (0.225)	0.717 (0.144)
1968	5.293	6.250 (1.295)	0.234 (0.058)	0.782 (0.102)	0.009 (0.091)	1.024 (0.122)
1964	12.613	-7.988 (3.111)	0.927 (0.299)	-0.708 (0.283)	-0.385 (0.355)	-0.165 (0.234)
1960	6.444	-3.435 (2.058)	-0.350 (0.142)	0.798 (0.138)	-0.019 (0.094)	0.429 (0.097)
1956	6.683	10.572 (2.123)	0.595 (0.122)	0.123 (0.109)	0.098 (0.087)	0.816 (0.104)
1952	8.311	14.679 (1.532)	0.101 (0.136)	0.488 (0.367)	-0.101 (0.329)	0.488 (0.111)
1948	8.555	2.078 (3.432)	0.104 (0.394)	0.207 (0.361)	0.136 (0.179)	0.446 (0.089)
1944	3.269	2.368 (1.406)	0.820 (0.061)	0.055 (0.095)	0.004 (0.056)	0.879 (0.031)
1940	7.703	10.841 (3.124)	1.113 (0.159)	-0.189 (0.136)	0.193 (0.083)	1.117 (0.089)
1936	7.388	-12.256 (3.663)	0.703 (0.099)	-0.030 (0.088)	0.021 (0.080)	0.694 (0.077)
1932	10.683	-28.393 (3.100)	-0.150 (0.147)	1.070 (0.215)	-0.496 (0.210)	0.424 (0.129)
1928	10.751	13.994 (4.381)	0.976 (0.164)	0.767 (0.202)	0.047 (0.178)	0.257 (0.090)
1924	9.851	3.675 (5.181)	0.879 (0.127)	0.144 (0.174)	0.134 (0.150)	1.157 (0.098)
1920	9.480	19.478 (4.250)	0.249 (0.184)	0.046 (0.160)	0.904 (0.187)	1.200 (0.093)
1916	8.105	-3.216 (3.644)	0.247 (0.124)	0.946 (0.176)	-0.192 (0.121)	1.001 (0.080)
1912	9.832	-25.556 (2.014)	0.557 (0.270)	0.049 (0.144)	0.083 (0.252)	0.689 (0.095)
1908	5.678	-1.383 (1.212)	0.311 (0.095)	0.620 (0.206)	0.028 (0.083)	0.958 (0.062)
1904	8.192	9.864 (1.499)	1.617 (0.204)	-0.446 (0.123)	0.291 (0.107)	1.462 (0.080)
1900	5.726	3.171 (0.994)	0.471 (0.058)	0.079 (0.130)	0.504 (0.202)	1.053 (0.074)
1896	16.688	4.130 (2.866)	-0.825 (0.335)	2.573 (0.719)	-0.648 (0.630)	1.100 (0.206)
1892	8.273	-2.798 (1.376)	1.167 (0.271)	-0.289 (0.370)	0.243 (0.200)	1.121 (0.101)
1888	4.923	-2.124 (0.900)	1.019 (0.146)	0.392 (0.181)	-0.395 (0.148)	1.016 (0.063)
1884	6.032	1.022 (2.019)	0.764 (0.171)	0.069 (0.217)	-0.117 (0.116)	0.715 (0.070)
1880	6.294	6.863 (2.075)	1.112 (0.142)	-0.357 (0.126)	0.096 (0.075)	0.851 (0.084)
1876	4.765	-7.501 (1.706)	0.541 (0.103)	0.230 (0.131)	0.009 (0.106)	0.780 (0.082)
1872	7.295	6.712 (2.318)	0.428 (0.192)	-0.151 (0.188)	0.365 (0.091)	0.642 (0.117)
1868	6.410	-2.286 (2.077)	0.740 (0.104)	0.136 (0.075)	0.235 (0.072)	1.111 (0.110)

while the stability of relative support from 1992 to 1996 is reflected in a coefficient close to one for four-year lagged votes and coefficients close to zero for eight-year lagged votes and twelve-year lagged votes.) Sub-national forces are captured by the standard error of this regression, which gauges the extent to which the 1996 outcome in specific states deviated from the overall pattern. (For example, Clinton did notably worse in Kansas—Robert Dole's home state—in 1996 than in 1992, and considerably better in several northeastern states than the overall regression relationship would suggest.) The estimated magnitude of these sub-national forces was slightly larger in 1996 than in the previous four election cycles, but smaller than in most of the elections before 1980.

The results presented in Table 1 provide the basis for the analyses in the next three sections of this paper, each focusing on a single aspect of American electoral history. The first of these sections deals with the persistence of partisan loyalties, the second with the magnitudes of national and sub-national electoral forces, and the third with the identification of "critical elections." Subsequent sections on the dynamics of party competition and on the volatility of election outcomes are based upon national-level rather than state-level analysis of the same election returns.

THE PERSISTENCE OF PARTISAN LOYALTIES

One of the most widely accepted generalizations in the whole scholarly literature on voting behavior and elections is that party loyalties count for less in contemporary American politics than they did a generation or more ago. For example, Wattenberg (1990, 1991) has used data from the National Election Studies and other sources to document *The Decline of American Political Parties* and *The Rise of Candidate-Centered Politics*, while Burnham (1989, 24) has referred more colorfully to "a massive decay of partisan electoral linkages" and to "the ruins of the traditional partisan regime." These developments have sometimes been taken to imply that the whole theoretical framework presented in *The American Voter*, with its emphasis on the causal priority of long-standing partisan loyalties, has become increasingly irrelevant in the contemporary American context.

Characteristically, Stokes expressed curiosity about the extent and causes of temporal and spatial variation in the strength of party identification even before contemporary survey data began to register noticeable departures from the levels of partisanship documented in *The American Voter*. "The reality which parties have as objects of mass perception," he wrote (Stokes, 1967, 183),

> is the more remarkable in view of the actual fragmentation of party structure and the diffusion of authority produced on all levels of government by the doctrine of separated powers. Indeed, the ambiguity of parties as stimulus objects suggests that the focus of partisan attitudes may vary a good deal and that the modern American experience may differ from that of other liberal democracies or earlier periods of our own politics.

Lacking direct measures of party identification from contemporary surveys in most "other liberal democracies or earlier periods of our own politics," it seemed reasonable to Stokes—and still seems reasonable today—to look for evidence of party loyalties in the continuity of partisan voting patterns over time. To the extent that successive elections with different candidates, issues, and political conditions produce essentially similar voting patterns, it seems safe to infer that these patterns somehow reflect the organizing force of partisanship. Of course, whether that organizing force is manifested through party machines, party symbols, parental socialization, or other specific mechanisms may vary from time to time and place to place, and the mere fact of continuity does nothing to illuminate the actual workings of the relevant electoral processes. Nevertheless, the mere fact of continuity in partisan voting patterns over significant periods of time *does* seem to provide *prima facie* evidence of the importance of partisanship in one form or another.

The logic of this inference is nicely captured by Stokes's (1962, 691) own example:

> [W]e may suppose that any one judging the candidates according to the dominant values of American culture, rather than in purely partisan terms, would have found Grover Cleveland a more estimable man than James G. Blaine in the campaign of 1884. Yet we can be sure that the public's actual response to these new presidential personalities was colored almost completely by its prior partisan loyalties, as the smallness of the vote swing from 1880 to 1884 suggests.

Of course, the national vote swing from one election to the next might be small for a variety of reasons having little to do with the public's partisan loyalties. For example, positive responses to Cleveland's personality in some parts of the country might (despite Stokes's assessment of the candidates) have been counterbalanced by positive responses to Blaine's personality in other regions, or by defections from the Democratic platform planks on silver, regulation, or other policy issues of the day. However, the same pattern of countervailing election-specific deviations would be much less likely to occur simultaneously in each state than in the nation as a whole. Thus, the fact that more than three-quarters of each state's partisan popular vote margin in the election of 1880 persisted in the election of 1884—despite the intervening assassination of President Garfield, the recession of 1884, and the emergence of Cleveland and Blaine as their parties' nominees—seems to provide considerable support for Stokes's inference that voters' responses to the immediate candidates and issues were strongly colored by their partisan loyalties. Nor is Stokes's example historically atypical; the estimates of lagged partisan effects for 11 of the 32 other elections in Table 1 are even larger, and the *average* combined effect of the three most recent past elections (in the last column of Table 1) for the entire 130-year time span is 0.825. Clearly, party loyalties have produced a good deal of continuity in presidential voting patterns at many points in American electoral history.

While the magnitude of partisan effects evident in Table 1 is impressive, the variability of these effects is also impressive. There is far more election-specific variation in the estimated strengths of party loyalties than could be attributed to random fluctuation in the parameter estimates themselves. The historical evolution underlying this election-specific variation is indicated by the locally weighted regression trend line drawn through the plotted party loyalty estimates (the sums of 4-year, 8-year, and 12-year lagged effects from the last column of Table 1) in Fig. 2.

Two aspects of the historical evolution shown in Fig. 2 may be surprising. First, the persistence of partisan loyalties appears to have declined throughout the first half of the 20th century from the very high level of the Gilded Age. The first half of this decline is largely attributable to the election of 1912, in which a long-standing Republican majority was fractured by the split between William Howard Taft and

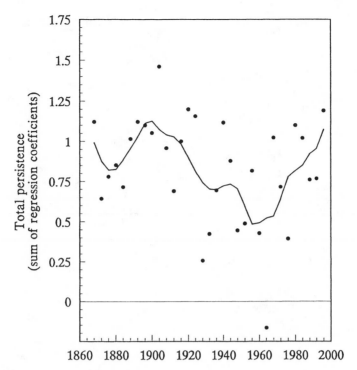

FIGURE 2. Partisan forces, 1868–1996

Theodore Roosevelt. However, the second half of the decline reflects a series of elections in the New Deal era in which pre-existing partisan loyalties were significantly eroded. The first two of these, in 1928 and 1932, mark the end of the Progressive era party system and the beginning of the New Deal era itself. Whereas the election of 1896 superimposed new sub-national forces on a basically stable party system (as evidenced by estimated partisan persistence levels in Table 1 of 1.12 in 1892, 1.10 in 1896, 1.05 in 1900, and 1.46 in 1904), the New Deal realignment erased much of the existing party system (as evidenced by estimated partisan persistence levels of 0.26 in 1928, 0.42 in 1932, and 0.69 in 1936). Moreover, what Sundquist (1983) has referred to as the aftershocks of the New Deal, especially in the South, produced a great deal of further reshuffling in 1948, 1952, 1960, 1964, and 1976 (with estimated partisan persistence levels of 0.45, 0.49, 0.43, – 0.16, and 0.40, respectively). It seems fruitless to argue about which one of these elections marked the end of the New Deal party system, when the evidence suggests that the system was in considerable partisan flux almost throughout its existence.

The other potentially surprising feature of the historical evolution graphed in Fig. 2 is the notable resurgence of partisan forces in the last 20 years. The five most recent presidential elections have been characterized by a persistence of party loyalties unsurpassed over any comparable time span since the turn of the last century. The strong correlation between state-level election returns in 1984 and 1988 adduced by Bartels (1992) to illustrate the continuing relevance of party identification in presidential elections appears from the parameter estimates presented in Table 1 to be fairly typical of the whole period. Whatever prospective voters may say in response to survey questions, and whatever academics may write and believe, actual presidential election outcomes suggest that we have been

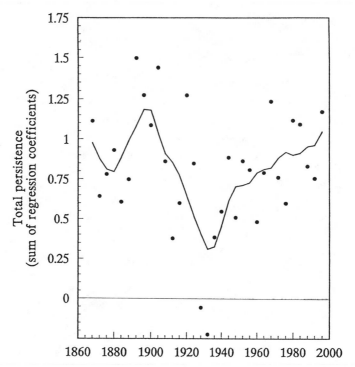

FIGURE 3. Partisan forces, Non-south

living through an era marked by unusually strong partisan continuity in state-level voting patterns.

The revival of partisanship evident in Fig. 2 is even more striking in Fig. 3, which tracks the persistence of partisan voting patterns outside the South.[11] Whereas Fig. 2 shows a fairly steady decline in the persistence of partisan voting patterns through the first six decades of the twentieth century, Fig. 3 shows a shorter and sharper decline, followed by a longer and even more impressive increase in the strength of partisan forces over the last sixty years. The difference between these patterns reflects the fact that Democratic loyalties in the "Solid South" survived the New Deal realignment intact, but began to erode significantly in the 1950s and 1960s, when the rest of the country was already in a period of historically typical partisan persistence. It seems clear, however, that the unusually high—and still increasing—levels of partisan persistence in recent presidential elections are no mere artifact of the breakup of the Solid South, since they appear clearly even in an analysis limited to non-southern states.

NATIONAL AND LOCAL FORCES

Stokes's interest in "Parties and the Nationalization of Electoral Forces" stemmed primarily from his interests in legislative behavior and political representation. "Many influences affect the solidarity of a legislative party," he wrote (Stokes, 1967, 184),

[11] The calculations presented in Fig. 3—and in Fig. 7 below—are based on regression analyses paralleling those reported in Table 1, but omitting data from the eleven former Confederate states.

but the members' perception of forces on their constituents' voting behavior is surely among them. . . . If the member of the legislature believes, on the one hand, that it is the national party and its leaders which are salient and that his own electoral prospects depend on the legislative record of the party as a whole, his bonds to the legislative party will be relatively strong. This is the situation posited by the model of responsible party government. But if the legislator believes, on the other hand, that the public is dominated by constituency influences and that his prospects depend on his own or his opponent's appeal or on other factors distinctive to the constituency, his bonds to the legislative party will be relatively weak.

Stokes set out to measure the influence of national and local forces on turnout and voting behavior in legislative elections, not only in the contemporary United States, but over a 90-year span of American history (from the 1870s through the 1950s) and in Britain as well. He found a substantial and fairly regular decline in constituency-specific variation in turnout in congressional elections, and a somewhat later decline (first evident in the 1930s) in local influences on the partisan vote division in congressional races. "If the nationalization of political forces has carried less far in America than in Britain," he concluded (Stokes, 1967, 202), "it seems nevertheless an outstanding aspect of our elections for Congress over the life of the modern party system."

My own historical analysis of presidential election returns allows for a roughly parallel analysis of changes over time in the extent to which voting behavior has been dominated by national or local forces. Indeed, the absence of cross-sectional variation in the identity of the competing candidates makes presidential elections especially useful for gauging changes in the extent to which the electorate itself has become more or less homogeneous in its voting behavior.

A natural measure of the magnitude of national forces in presidential elections is the absolute value of the α_t coefficient reflecting overall shifts in the presidential vote in each election year. These absolute values are charted in Fig. 4. The three highest values shown in the figure, each corresponding to a national vote shift of 25 to 30 percentage points, represent the Republican debacle of 1912, the repudiation of Herbert Hoover in 1932, and the Nixon landslide of 1972. The national vote shift in a typical election year is, of course, much smaller in magnitude—about nine percentage points. Even this modest historical average was not reached in any of the nine elections between 1868 and 1900. However, the magnitude of national forces increased markedly over the first three decades of the 20th century, reaching a peak at the beginning of the New Deal era before subsiding to a fairly consistent average of ten percentage points for the remainder of the century.

An equally natural measure of the magnitude of sub-national forces in each election year is the standard deviation σ_t of state-specific political shocks. These sub-national forces, graphed in Fig. 5, display much less temporal variation than the national forces graphed in Fig. 4. There are notable outliers of 17 percentage points in 1896 and 13 percentage points in 1964, but relatively constant averages of eight percentage points over the whole period from 1868 through 1928 and seven percentage points over the whole period from 1932 through 1996. It is interesting to note that the pattern of local forces in presidential elections shown in Fig. 5 is roughly similar to the pattern Stokes (1967) found in congressional elections, with a gradual increase from the 1870s into the 1920s followed by a decline from the 1920s through the 1940s. It is also interesting to note that the

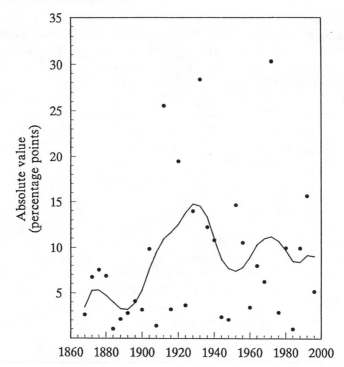

FIGURE 4. National forces, 1868–1996

eight most recent elections have clustered near the lower end of the historical distribution, suggesting that the decline in the magnitude of sub-national effects may have resumed in the last twenty years.

The national and sub-national forces charted in Figs 4 and 5, respectively, are directly comparable in the sense that both are measured on the same scale of percentage point changes in the popular vote. Thus, it is possible not only to assess fluctuations in the magnitude of each force over the 13 decades covered by the figures, but also to assess the relative magnitude of national and sub-national forces at any given point, in much the way Stokes (1967) did for congressional and British parliamentary elections. Fig. 6 displays the relative magnitude of national forces—represented by the ratio of national variance (the square of the national tide coefficient α_t in Table 1) to national variance plus sub-national variance (the square of the state-specific shock coefficient σ_t in Table 1)—in each election year.

The pattern of relative nationalization in Fig. 6 suggests that national and sub-national forces have been relatively evenly balanced throughout most of this century, but with the balance tipping toward national forces at the beginning of the New Deal and in the most recent elections and toward sub-national forces during the racial sorting-out of the 1950s and '60s. By contrast, sub-national forces were predominant through most of the late 19th century, with national variance exceeding sub-national variance in only two of the first nine elections shown in Fig. 6. On a broad historical scale, Fig. 6 might be read as a reflection of long-term nationalization of the mass media and of American political culture more generally. However, the notable reversals of this long-term trend evident in the 1880s and '90s and again during the New Deal era suggest that technological and social

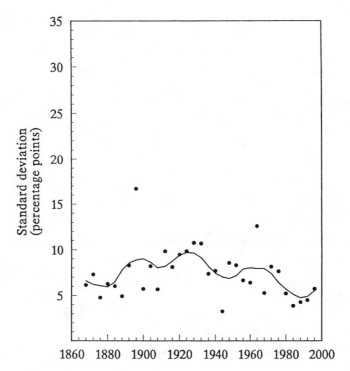

FIGURE 5. Sub-National forces, 1869–1996

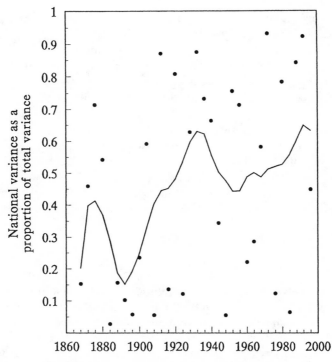

FIGURE 6. Relative nationalization of electoral forces, 1868–1996

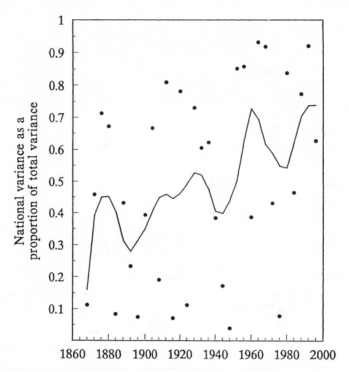

FIGURE 7. Relative nationalization of electoral forces, Non-south

forces producing greater nationalization have, at least at times, been stymied by deep sectional political cleavages.

The political significance of the most important such sectional cleavage is evident from comparing the pattern of nationalization in Fig. 6 with the corresponding pattern in Fig. 7, which is based upon parallel calculations of national and sub-national forces derived from regression analyses omitting the southern states. The general pattern in Fig. 7 suggests a more consistent nationalizing trend than in Fig. 6, with the trough following Reconstruction and the peak marking the advent of the New Deal party system both considerably smoothed. While there are still substantial ebbs and flows in the nationalization of electoral forces evident in Fig. 7 (marking, for example, disparate reactions in the various non-southern states to the political changes of the 1960s and '70s), the contemporary period stands out even more clearly than in Fig. 6 as a period of unprecedented electoral nationalization.

CRITICAL ELECTIONS

In addition to shedding light on the magnitude of partisan and short-term electoral factors or national and sub-national forces in any given election or historical period, the decomposition of election outcomes presented in Table 1 provides a framework for assessing the long-term impact of each election on the subsequent movement of the party system. Each election outcome may have direct effects 4, 8, and 12 years later, and indirect effects over an even longer time horizon.[12] These direct and indirect effects constitute the historical legacy of a specific election. When they are unusually large and persistent, it seems reasonable to refer to the election as a "critical election" in the sense developed by Key (1955, 1959), Burnham (1970), Sundquist (1983), and others.

My calculation of the long-term impact of each election takes into account the magnitude of new national and sub-national forces in that election (reflected by the estimates of α_t and σ_t, respectively, in Table 1) as well as the persistence of those forces in subsequent elections (reflected by the estimates of β_{1t}, β_{2t}, and β_{3t} for subsequent elections in Table 1). More specifically, I average the immediate impact of new national and sub-national forces in each election (represented by the square root of the sum of α_{t2} and σ_t^2), the direct impact four years later (consisting of the immediate impact multiplied by β_{1t+1}), the total impact eight years later (consisting of the immediate impact multiplied by β_{2t+2} plus the fourth-year impact multiplied by β_{1t+2}) and so on, over a total of seven elections spanning a quarter-century.[13] The long-term effects calculated in this manner for each election from 1868 to 1972 are shown in Fig. 8, which displays the average impact of each election over a 24-year horizon.[14]

The estimates of the long-term impact of each election represented in Fig. 8 conform in some respects to expectations derived from the scholarly literature on critical elections. Most obviously, the election of 1932 stands out as the most influential single election of the entire 100-year period, with an average impact over a quarter-century of more than 15 percentage points. This was a critical election by any reasonable standard, and the calculation on which Fig. 8 is based nicely captures that fact.

In some other respects, however, the results presented in Fig. 8 must be regarded as strongly counterintuitive. For one thing, the distribution of long-term effects seems a good deal more diverse than one would expect from a scholarly literature so strongly fixated on the electoral significance of a handful of critical elections. Rather than consisting of a few great peaks separated by broad plateaus reflecting long periods of political stasis, the distribution of long-term effects in Fig. 8 reflects a complex intermixture of large, medium and small effects.[15]

---

[12] In principle, the indirect effects of any given election can persist indefinitely or even increase over time. In practice, given the magnitudes of the estimated continuity coefficients in Table 1, the effects tend to decline fairly monotonically, so that the impact of each election outcome gradually fades with the passage of time.

[13] Thus, the seven terms in each average are; $\omega_t = (\alpha_t^2 + \sigma_t^2)^{1/2}$, $\omega_{t+1} = \beta_{1t+1}\,\omega_t$, $\omega_{t+2} = \beta_{1t+2}\omega_{t+1} + \beta_{2t+2}\,\omega_t$, $\omega_{t+3} = \beta_{1t+3}\omega_{t+2} + \beta_{2t+3}\omega_{t+1} + \beta_{3t+3}\omega_t$, $\omega_{t+3} = \beta_{1t+3}\omega_{t+2} + \beta_{2t+3}\omega_{t+1} + \beta_{3t+3}\omega_t$, $\omega_{t+4} = \beta_{1t+4}\omega_{t+3} + \beta_{2t+4}\omega_{t+2} + \beta_{3t+4}\omega_{t+1}$, $\omega_{t+5} = \beta_{1t+5}\omega_{t+4} + \beta_{2t+5}\omega_{t+3} + \beta_{3t+5}\omega_{t+2}$, $\omega_{t+6} = \beta_{1t+6}\omega_{t+5} + \beta_{2t+6}\omega_{t+4} + \beta_{3t+6}\omega_{t+3}$.

[14] These calculations of long-term effects may be usefully contrasted with the "real time" approach to the study of political realignments developed by Cavanagh (1997). Cavanagh's calculations using county-level election returns grouped by regions are consistent with mine in suggesting that "the stability of the presidential alignment during the contemporary era from 1980–96 has attained *the highest level in the history of the American party system*" (Cavanagh, 1997, 7; emphasis in original), but his classification of realigning elections based solely on breaks from the recent past—without reference to their subsequent durability—produces results that look more like Sundquist's (1983) than like those presented here.

[15] In addition to flying in the face of much of the classic literature on "critical elections," these results stand in marked contrast to the statistical results reported by Nardulli (1995, Fig. 1) which display clear peaks in 1896 and 1932 and lesser peaks in 1928 and 1960. However, these discrepancies may reflect the fact that Nardulli's (1994, 1995) analysis is based on an interrupted time-series analysis that

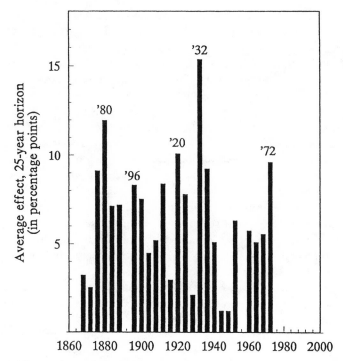

FIGURE 8. Critical elections, 1868–1972

What is more, the long-term importance attached to specific presidential elections in Fig. 8 is in several cases quite out of keeping with the estimates of previous political observers. A sense of the nature and bases of these discrepancies may be provided by considering in some detail two specific elections. One of these, the election of 1896, has been considered "one of the decisive elections in American history" by Schattschneider (1960, 76) and many subsequent analysts. The other, the election of 1880, has not figured at all in the literature on critical elections, but appears in Fig. 8 as the second most important election of the century following the Civil War.

The voting pattern of 1896 was unusual in being marked by a set of sub-national shocks more than twice as large in magnitude as those observed on average in the other 32 elections examined here. These shocks reflect the regional reorientation of the party system precipitated by the Democrats' nomination of William Jennings Bryan on a Populist platform, which drove much of the industrial Northeast and Midwest strongly into the Republican camp. Thus, in an immediate sense, the election of 1896 marked an important shift in the existing party system.[16] However,

---

"requires the analyst to specify the point at which major, enduring interruptions in long-term electoral trends (critical elections) are hypothesized to begin, as well as the form of those interruptions" (Nardulli, 1995, 11), whereas the approach adopted here incorporates no theoretical preconceptions regarding the timing or nature of critical elections.

[16] This discontinuity is perhaps best captured by the simple correlation across states between the Republican vote margins in 1892 and 1896: 0.43. The corresponding correlations between current and immediately preceding vote margins from 1880 through 1892 ranged from 0.91 to 0.94, while those from 1900 through 1924 ranged from 0.80 to 0.93. In the whole data series analyzed here, the discontinuity apparent in 1896 was only exceeded in 1960 (0.33), 1964 (0.12), and 1976 (0.02).

when we consider the combined effect of national and sub-national forces, the election of 1896 appears to have had a good deal less immediate impact than the elections of 1912, 1932, or 1972, which produced less sub-national reshuffling but much larger national shifts;[17] it ranks in immediate impact with the elections of 1920, 1928, 1936, 1952, and 1964.

This short-term calculation alone seems to shed some doubt upon the conventional classification of 1896 as a critical election. However, the longer-term calculation reflected in Fig. 8 sheds even more doubt upon that classification by indicating that the electoral pattern established in 1896 was much less durable than previous scholarship has suggested, despite the persistence of the Republican majority—with one eight-year interruption—for another generation. According to the calculations presented in Table 1, the electoral impetus of 1896 was diminished by half within four years; the state-by-state voting pattern in 1900 reflected the divisions of 1888 (with a coefficient of 0.504) as much or more than those of 1896 (with a coefficient of 0.471). Moreover, the direct carryover of the 1896 voting pattern was actually negative in 1904 (with a coefficient of –0.446), and negligible in 1908 (with a coefficient of 0.028). Thus, if we focus not only on the extent to which the electoral pattern of 1896 was discontinuous with those of the immediate past, but also on the extent to which the distinctive electoral forces that emerged in 1896 persisted into the future, it seems difficult to sustain Schattschneider's (1960, 76) characterization of this as "one of the decisive elections in American history."

By contrast, the election of 1880 appears in Fig. 8 as the second most significant election of the entire 100-year period, despite its virtual invisibility in the scholarly literature. The immediate impact of the election of 1880 amounted to 9.3 percentage points—about half the immediate impact of the election of 1896, and a third that of 1932. This immediate impact was roughly evenly divided between a national shift toward the Republicans (counteracting the Democratic tide of 1876) and a reshuffling of sub-national voting patterns reflecting the end of Reconstruction. For example, Louisiana and South Carolina reported Republican majorities in 1872 and 1876, but reverted to Democratic control as soon as federal troops were withdrawn in 1877, and supplied Democratic popular vote margins of 25 and 31 percentage points, respectively, in 1880. In an important sense, this was not a *new* partisan alignment, but a reconstitution of the *status quo ante bellum*.[18]

What made the election of 1880 so significant, at least by the calculations summarized in Fig. 8, was not its short-run impact but the persistence of the renewed partisan cleavages it reflected. Having returned to the Democratic fold in 1880, both Louisiana and South Carolina—and most of the rest of the South—remained there for 80 years. Moreover, even outside the South, the period of stable partisan competition following the settlement of 1876 perpetuated the electoral pattern

---

However, even this discontinuity is somewhat more complicated than it appears at first sight; the more detailed regression analysis reported in Table 1 shows that the pattern of vote margins in 1896 combined a strong *negative* carryover from 1892 (– 0.825) with an even stronger *positive* carryover directly from 1888 (2.573).

[17] Despite the reality of widespread Republican gains in the nation's urban industrial areas in 1896, the Republican share of the total popular vote only increased by eight percentage points (from 43 percent in 1892 to 51 percent in 1896), while the Democratic share remained almost unchanged.

[18] For example, the correlation between the Republican vote margins in 1880 and 1856—for the thirty states that participated in both elections—was 0.84. This correlation over a quarter-century exceeds most of the correlations between adjacent elections in the whole period covered by my analysis!

established in 1880 for the next three decades, despite the interventions of populism, depression, and a colonial war. Thus, for example, while the impact of the election of 1896 had declined by my calculations from eight percentage points in 1900 to six by 1908, the impact of the election of 1880 had nearly doubled from seven percentage points in 1884 to almost 14 percentage points in 1908.

It is worth noting that the electoral pattern of 1880 persisted despite the apparent absence of any significant "realigning issue." According to one historian (Hicks, 1949, 162),

> both parties were completely bankrupt. The issues that divided them were historical merely. . . . The platforms of the two parties in 1880 revealed few real differences of opinion as to policies and no real awareness of the problems that confronted the nation. Neither Democrats nor Republicans seemed to sense the significance of the vast transformation that was coming over business, nor the critical nature of the relationship between labor and capital, nor even the necessity of doing something definite about civil service reform, the money problem, and the tariff. The Republican Party existed to oppose the Democratic Party; the Democratic Party existed to oppose the Republican Party. . . . With issues lacking, the campaign turned on personalities.

Here, clearly, was an election bearing few of the hallmarks of the ideal-typical critical election envisioned by political scientists and historians. Nevertheless, the distinct electoral pattern established in 1880 persisted longer and more powerfully than that of all but one of the 32 other presidential elections examined here. That fact is a testament to the intensely organized partisan struggle of the Gilded Age, but also to the limitations of a theoretical perspective that strains to find in the complex historical record of partisan struggles a stately procession of more or less static issue-based party alignments.

THE DYNAMICS OF PARTY COMPETITION

One of the most striking features of the time series of presidential election outcomes displayed in Fig. 1 is that the Republican popular vote margin never strays very far or very long from the competitive equilibrium represented by an even partisan division of the vote. There are few instances of 20-point vote margins, and no instances of 30-point vote margins, in this 130-year period.[19] Only once has either party maintained even a 10-point vote margin for three successive elections, and this impressive 8-year run (by the Republicans from 1920 to 1928) was immediately followed by the Democrats' most impressive 8-year run (from 1932 to 1940).

In their piece "On the Existence of Forces Restoring Party Competition" Stokes and Iversen (1962, 159–160) suggested a variety of possible explanations for this regularity:

> Restoring forces have been seen in such diverse factors as the tendency of interest groups to remember the favors an administration has dispensed less than the favors it has not; the ability of the party out of power to make

---

[19] Of course, an even longer time horizon would have included the suspension of partisan competition at the presidential level during the Era of Good Feeling following the War of 1812.

more flexible and extravagant promises of future benefit whereas the party in power is limited by what it can actually deliver; the greater motivational strength of the public's negative response to an administration's mistakes than of its positive response to an administration's successes; the liability of the party in power to disastrous splits as its majority grows and its sense of electoral pressure lessens; movements of the business cycle, generating new support for the opposition party in periods of economic decline; the alternating moods of liberalism and conservatism that have marked our national temper; and a vigorous popular belief in rotation in office, which turns the peccadilloes of a party long in power into convincing evidence that the time for a change has arrived.

Stokes and Iversen (1962) demonstrated the reality of "restoring forces" by positing as an alternative a non-parametric "random walk" model in which the partisan division of the presidential vote could move in either direction with equal probability in each election, and showing that the persistent competitiveness of observed election outcomes was extremely unlikely given such a model. They also noted in passing (1962, footnote 7) that "if the division of the vote at one presidential election is correlated with the *change* of the vote from that election to the next, a negative correlation of –.55 is obtained. In other words, the greater a party's share of the vote at one election, the greater is its share likely to be reduced at the next."

My own analysis of the dynamics of party competition in presidential elections builds upon this latter result, using the observed change in the Republican vote margin in each election year as the dependent variable in a regression with vote margins in the previous two elections as explanatory variables. If equilibrating forces are at work, we should expect previous vote margins to have a negative impact on current changes in the vote margin, producing Democratic shifts following Republican victories and Republican shifts following Democratic victories. The parameter estimates reported in Table 2 clearly conform to this expectation, with each percentage point of the winning party's vote margin producing direct negative effects of about half a percentage point in each of the two subsequent elections.[20]

The second and third columns of Table 2 present comparable parameter estimates separately for the periods from 1868 through 1928 and from 1932 through 1996. The separate parameter estimates for the two periods are virtually identical, suggesting that the equilibrating forces explored by Stokes and Iversen have persisted essentially unchanged through several generations of American partisan struggles.[21] Neither the replacement of traditional patronage-based party machines with modern media campaigns nor the vast expansion of the scope and

[20] Allowing for serial correlation in the residuals from this regression would leave the results virtually unchanged; the estimated serial correlation is 0.03 with a standard error of 0.18. The results are equally impervious to adding the vote margin 12 years earlier as an additional explanatory variable (the resulting coefficient is 0.015 with a standard error of 0.181) or adding the number of consecutive years the incumbent party has been in office (the resulting coefficient is –0.111 with a standard error of 0.243).

[21] The estimated serial correlations of the stochastic disturbances are –0.22 (with a standard error of 0.26) in the pre–New Deal period and 0.10 (with a standard error of 0.22) in the post–New Deal period. Adjusting the analysis to allow for these serial correlations would change the estimated lagged effects to –0.309 (0.219) and –0.719 (0.257) in the pre–New Deal period and –0.635 (0.224) and –0.491 (0.211) in the post–New Deal period. The dynamics for each period implied by these estimates are quite similar to those shown in Fig. 9.

TABLE 2
Competitive Equilibration. Parameter estimates (with standard errors in
parentheses) from ordinary regression analyses of changes in presidential
vote margins (in percentage points) on previous margins

	1868–1996	1868–1928	1932–1996
Margin$_{t-4}$	−0.474 (0.156)	−0.438 (0.234)	−0.561 (0.222)
Margin$_{t-8}$	−0.525 (0.157)	−0.602 (0.261)	−0.496 (0.206)
Intercept	2.59 (1.98)	5.59 (2.86)	−0.10 (2.94)
adjusted R^2 –	0.47	0.42	0.51
std error of reg	10.90	9.88	12.00
Durbin-Watson	1.97	1.97	1.60
N	33	16	17

activities of the federal government in the period covered by this analysis seems to
have produced any significant alteration in the appetite or ability of losing politicians to reclaim the reigns of government through electoral competition.

The impact of the equilibrating forces measured in Table 2 is illustrated in
Fig. 9, which traces the implied dynamic response of the political system to a
typical electoral shock in each of the 60-year periods covered by my analysis.
Here, too, the similarity of the two distinct sets of estimates is evident. In each
period, half of a typical gain (or loss) of ten to twelve percentage points in the
Republican vote margin is likely to persist four years later. But in the next two
elections after that, the net effect is reversed, with Democrats actually doing noticeably *better* than they would have in the absence of the original Republican
gain (or vice versa). This reverberation produces its own correspondingly smaller
reverberation another decade later, and so on, as the original electoral shock is
gradually dissipated.

Of course, these long-term equilibrating movements would not be directly observable in any actual sequence of election outcomes, since each election overlays
new shocks on the dissipating electoral forces inherited from the past. Nevertheless, the pattern of equilibration identified by Stokes and Iversen accounts for
the marked tendency of the electoral system to produce fairly regular alterations
between Republican and Democratic possession of the White House—and thus,
arguably, for the remarkable persistence of the two-party system itself through the
last thirteen decades of American political history.

ELECTORAL VOLATILITY

Stokes's studies of electoral politics (Stokes *et al.*, 1958; Campbell *et al.*, 1960;
Stokes, 1962; Stokes and Iversen, 1962; Stokes, 1966; Butler and Stokes, 1969)
are marked by an intense recurring interest in the balance and interplay of long-
term and short-term political forces. As he put it in one of those pieces (Stokes,
1962, 689–690),

> By measuring a limited set of political orientations (among which party loy-
> alty is preeminently important) we are able to say with increasing confidence
> what the behavior of the American electorate would be in any given election
> if the vote were to express only the influence of these basic dispositions.
> But the election returns reflect, too, the public's reaction to more recent and

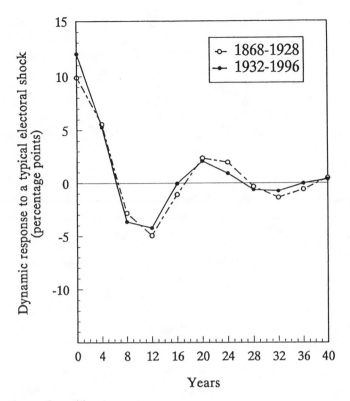

FIGURE 9. Electoral equilibration

transitory influences (think for the moment of candidate personality) that deflect the vote from what it would have been had these short-term factors not intruded on the nation's decision. Therefore, any national election can be thought of as an interplay of basic dispositions and short-run influences. Yet the freedom of these "disturbing" influences to modify the effects of long-term dispositions is not well understood. Their capacity to do so is not of trivial importance; there have been few presidential elections in a hundred years that we could not imagine having gone to the loser, had the right combination of short-term factors appeared in time. And yet each election is not a fresh toss of the coin; like all good prejudices, the electorate's basic dispositions have a tremendous capacity to keep people behaving in accustomed ways. The freedom of short-run influences to deflect the vote has an obvious bearing on how well long-standing party loyalties are able to explain a total election outcome. Plainly, a closer estimate of the ease with which short-term electoral tides may run to one party or the other would tell a good deal about the importance of party identification in a predictive theory of elections.

Stokes treated the distinction between long-term and short-term forces both as an organizing framework for survey-based research on the components of individual vote choices (Stokes et al., 1958; Stokes, 1966) and as an aggregate-level property of electoral systems. In "Party Loyalty and the Likelihood of Deviating Elections" (Stokes, 1962), he used the observed distribution of presidential election outcomes around their long-term average (calculated alternatively from 1892 through 1928 and from 1892 through 1960) to estimate the probability of what Campbell *et al.* (1960, 531–538) had referred to as a "deviating" election.

Subsequent analysts who have argued that the long-term stabilizing force of party identification has declined substantially since the 1950s have seemed to assume as a matter of course that the magnitude of short-term forces has increased concomitantly, driven by the reactions of large numbers of unanchored "independent" voters to candidate images and performance. For example, Wattenberg (1991, 21) argued that "the focus of the campaign" has turned "from long-term to short-term issues. Being less tied to the patterns of the past, the American electorate is far more volatile compared to three decades ago, and has grown accustomed to looking directly at the candidates through the mass media."

This perception of increased volatility was presumably fueled by the evident variability of presidential election outcomes since the 1950s, with substantial popular vote landslides won by both parties (in 1964, 1972, and 1984) and only one twelve-year stretch of uninterrupted control of the White House by either party (from 1981 through 1993). But how does that level of volatility compare with the level observed at other periods in American electoral history? Fig. 10 displays the time trend of volatility in presidential elections over the entire period of my analysis, as measured simply by the magnitude of the national popular vote swing in each election—the absolute values of the changes in vote margin analyzed in Table 2.

Fig. 10 shows two clear peaks in the volatility of presidential election outcomes. One of these, of about twenty years' duration, encompasses the break-up of the prevailing Republican majority in 1912, its reinstitution in 1920, and its replacement by the New Deal majority in 1932; the second, somewhat shorter and sharper, reflects the electoral turbulence of the 1960s and '70s, including the Goldwater and McGovern debacles in 1964 and 1972. This second peak of electoral volatility seems to confirm the widespread perception that presidential elections in the television age have become significantly more volatile than they used to be.

Unfortunately, any such simple generalization must collapse in the face of the subsequent time trend of electoral volatility in Fig. 10. Whereas the presidential elections of the 1960s and '70s were highly volatile by historical standards, the five most recent presidential elections have evidenced levels of volatility *below* the long-run historical average. It is certainly not true now, as it would have been in the 1970s, that "the American electorate is far more volatile compared to three decades ago" (Wattenberg, 1991, 21). It would seem to follow that any plausible explanation for the volatility of the 1960s and '70s must be based upon specific features of that historical period rather than secular technological or other trends.

Fig. 11 displays an alternative historical record of volatility based upon residual popular vote swings from the analysis in Table 2. This more sophisticated measure reflects the magnitude of the vote swing in each election net of the reequilibrating forces carrying over from previous elections. Thus, it probably provides a better estimate of the extent to which the actual election outcome deviated from the "expected" outcome in Stokes's sense.

Not surprisingly, the residual vote swings shown in Fig. 11 tend to be considerably smaller in magnitude than the total vote swings shown in Fig. 10. The contrasts in volatility between historical peaks and troughs are also less pronounced. However, the basic pattern in Fig. 10 is essentially replicated in Fig. 11.[22] The

[22] The most notable difference between the patterns in Fig. 10 and Fig. 11 is that the periods of high electoral volatility appear somewhat later and last somewhat longer in Fig. 11. Thus, the first major

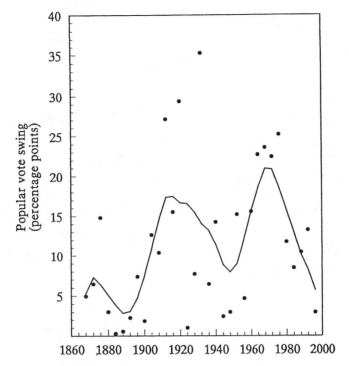

FIGURE 10. Electoral volatility, 1868–1996

historically low volatility of the last two decades of the 19th century and the periods of high volatility from 1912 through 1932 and in the 1960s and '70s appear clearly in Fig. 11, just as they do in Fig. 10. The return to historically low levels of volatility in recent presidential elections also appears clearly in Fig. 11, reinforcing the conclusion that the high volatility of the 1960s and '70s was a temporary phenomenon rather than a sea change in the nature of American electoral politics.

ELECTORAL CHANGE IN HISTORICAL PERSPECTIVE

Three decades ago, Stokes (1967, 183) worried that "[t]he very richness of contemporary American survey data poses the danger that conclusions of unwarranted generality will be drawn from the evidence at hand." That worry seems amply justified by the results reported here, but in a way that Stokes might have found surprising. Rather than mistaking contemporary American political conditions for eternal regularities—as some critics of *The American Voter* and Stokes himself seem to have feared—observers have, in my view, overstated the particularity of contemporary political conditions while overlooking important elements of continuity with previous eras of American electoral history.

period of high volatility in Fig. 11 encompasses much of the early New Deal period, as the Democratic majority established in 1932 withstood for some time the usual pattern of competitive erosion; and the second major period of high volatility in the 1960s and '70s is also slightly later and longer, since the Republican gains in 1968 and 1972 are counted in the calculations underlying Fig. 11 as partly predictable reequilibrations following the Democratic landslide of 1964.

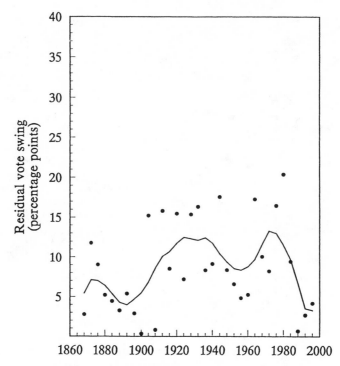

FIGURE 11. Residual volatility, 1868–1996

Despite the widespread belief among political scientists that the American electoral system is more volatile and unconstrained by partisan loyalties than ever before, systematic analysis of election returns suggests just the opposite: the unusual political turmoil of the 1960s and '70s has given way to a period of partisan stability and predictability unmatched since the end of the 19th century.

No doubt, every generation is tempted to imagine itself unique, and one of the most important uses of history is to dispel the illusion that we live in an era of unprecedented this or that. The historical questions addressed by Stokes in the works I have revisited here continue to serve that purpose very well, providing a bracing perspective on the nature of continuity and change in the American electoral system.

REFERENCES

Bartels, L. M. (1992) The Impact of Electioneering in the United States. In *Electioneering: A Comparative Study of Continuity and Change*, ed. D. Butler and A. Ranney. Clarendon Press, Oxford.

Bartels, L. M. (1997) Donald Stokes and the Study of Electoral Politics. *PS: Political Science and Politics* 30, 230–232.

Beck, N., and Jackman, S. (1998) Beyond Linearity by Default: Generalized Additive Models. *American Journal of Political Science* 42, 596–627.

Burnham, W. D. (1970) *Critical Elections and the Mainsprings of American Politics.* W. W. Norton, New York.

Burnham, W. D. (1989) The Reagan Heritage. In *The Election of 1988: Reports and Interpretations*, ed. G. M. Pomper et al. Chatham House, Chatham, NJ.

Butler, D., and Stokes, D. (1969) *Political Change in Britain: Forces Shaping Electoral Choice*. St. Martin's Press, New York.

Campbell, A., Converse, P. E., Miller, W. E. and Stokes, D. E. (1960) *The American Voter*. John Wiley and Sons, New York.

Campbell, A., Converse, P. E., Miller, W. E. and Stokes, D. E. (1966) *Elections and the Political Order*. John Wiley and Sons, New York.

Cavanagh, T. E. (1997) *Assessing Realignment in Real Time: The Contemporary American Party System in Historical Context*. Paper prepared for delivery at the annual meeting of the American Political Science Association, Washington, DC.

Congressional Quarterly, 1995. *Presidential Elections: 1789–1992*. Congressional Quarterly Inc., Washington, DC.

Hicks, J. D. (1949) *The American Nation: A History of the United States from 1865 to the Present*, 2nd ed. Houghton Mifflin Company, Boston.

Key, V. O. (1955) A Theory of Critical Elections. *Journal of Politics* 17, 3–18.

Key, V. O. (1959) Secular Realignment and the Party System. *Journal of Politics* 21, 198–210.

Miller, W. E., and Shanks, J. M. (1996) *The New American Voter*. Harvard University Press, Cambridge, MA.

Nardulli, P. F. (1994) A Normal Vote Approach to the Study of Electoral Change: Presidential Elections, 1828–1984. *Political Behavior* 16, 467–503.

Nardulli, P. F. (1995) The Concept of a Critical Realignment, Electoral Behavior, and Political Change. *American Political Science Review* 89, 10–22.

Nie, N. H., Verba, S. and Petrocik, J. R. (1976) *The Changing American Voter*. Harvard University Press, Cambridge, MA.

Petersen, S. (1963) *A Statistical History of the American Presidential Elections*. Frederick Ungar Publishing Company, New York.

Robinson, E. E. (1934) *The Presidential Vote: 1896–1932*. Stanford University Press, Stanford, CA.

Scammon, R. M., and McGillivray, A. V. (1994) *America at the Polls*. Congressional Quarterly, Washington, DC.

Schattschneider, E. E. (1960) *The Semisovereign People: A Realist's View of Democracy in America*. Harcourt Brace Jovanovich, 1975, Fort Worth.

Smith, E.R.A.N. (1989) *The Unchanging American Voter*. University of California Press, Berkeley, CA.

Stokes, D. E. (1962) Party Loyalty and the Likelihood of Deviating Elections. *Journal of Politics* 24, 689–702. Reprinted in *Elections and the Political Order*, A. Campbell, P. E. Converse, W. E. Miller, and D. E. Stokes. John Wiley and Sons, 1966, New York.

Stokes, D. E. (1965) A Variance Components Model of Political Effects. In *Mathematical Applications in Political Science*, ed. J. M. Claunch. Arnold Foundation, Dallas.

Stokes, D. E. (1966) Some Dynamic Elements of Contests for the Presidency. *American Political Science Review* 60, 19–28.

Stokes, D. E. (1967) Parties and the Nationalization of Electoral Forces. In *The American Party Systems: Stages of Political Development*, ed. W. N. Chambers and W. D. Burnham. Oxford University Press, New York.

Stokes, D. E. (1969) Cross-Level Inference as a Game against Nature. In *Mathematical Applications in Political Science IV*, ed. J. L. Bernd. University Press of Virginia, Charlottesville, VA.

Stokes, D. E., Campbell, A. and Miller, W. E. (1958) Components of Electoral Decision. *American Political Science Review* 52, 367–387.

Stokes, D. E., and Iversen, G. R. (1962) On the Existence of Forces Restoring Party Competition. *Public Opinion Quarterly* 26, 159–171. Reprinted in *Elections and the Political*

Order, A. Campbell, P. E. Converse, W. E. Miller, and D. E. Stokes. John Wiley and Sons, 1966, New York.

Sundquist, J. L. (1983) *Dynamics of the Party System: Alignment and Realignment of Political Parties in the United States*, revised ed. Brookings Institution, Washington, DC.

Wattenberg, M. P. (1990) *The Decline of American Political Parties: 1952–1988*. Harvard University Press, Cambridge, MA.

Wattenberg, M. P. (1991) *The Rise of Candidate-Centered Politics: Presidential Elections of the 1980s*. Harvard University Press, Cambridge, MA.

23

THE TURNOUT RATE AMONG ELIGIBLE
VOTERS IN THE STATES, 1980–2000
Michael P. McDonald

Recall from the previous article by Bartels that the national electoral process has historically been highly competitive. The political environment of American citizens is therefore salient and mobilizing on a regular basis over the lifetime of a citizen. But do Americans respond by voting? It is a commonplace that citizens today are turned off by electoral politics and that they do not in fact vote at very high levels.

In this article Michael McDonald forces one to reconsider the supposed "stylized fact" of dropping turnout. The "vanishing voter idea" is based on putting voting age population into the denominator of the turnout ratio rather than voting eligible population. But that second population, McDonald shows, has shrunk, due both to immigration and to felony disenfranchisement. Accordingly the relevant turnout rate has been higher than suspected. In fact, it may be the case that McDonald underestimates the number of citizen ineligibles, which would kick the turnout rate up even higher. His estimates for the impact of felony disfranchisement are smaller than estimates at the website of The Sentencing Project, an advocacy group that collects and disseminates statistics on felony disenfranchisement (navigate to http://www.sentencingproject.org/).

Thus McDonald's article suggests both good news and bad news. If one focuses on the relevant turnout rate, then one sees that Americans vote far more than many commentators have long thought. But, by the same token, felony disenfranchisement has also grown. You will want to decide for yourself whether you consider felony disenfranchisement a serious problem for American democracy. Bear in mind, though, that the United States is exceptional among advanced democracies with respect to widespread felony disenfranchisement. The consensus among other such democracies is that if you have served your time you deserve to be fully politically reincorporated into your nation's politics. Indeed, analysts who have looked into American public opinion on the matter find that Americans largely hold this view as well (which, incidentally, poses another challenge to Burstein's suggestion— see his article earlier in the book—that there is considerable congruence between policy and public opinion). Finally, you might consider that the disproportionately racial impact of felony disenfranchisement has generated concern among election law specialists. On this view, felony disenfranchisement undercuts the democratic gains of the 1965 Voting Rights Act.

• • •

From *State Politics and Policy Quarterly* 2 (Summer 2002): 199–212. Copyright 2002 by the Board of Trustees of the University of Illinois. Used with permission of the University of Illinois Press.

DEMOCRATIC GOVERNMENTS and the people they govern are linked by the act of voting. Voting is a voluntary act in the United States. How many of those people eligible to vote in a polity who actually cast a ballot—that is, the voter turnout rate—figures large in many explanations of political processes. The United States' decentralized federal government, and the heterogeneity of population and electoral laws among its 50 states, provides a natural experiment to assess the causes and effects of voter turnout. Using these advantages, researchers have investigated, for example, how electoral laws affect state turnout rates (Fenster 1994; Knack 1995; Rhine 1995; Franklin and Grier 1997; Martinez and Hill 1999; Alvarez et al. 2001), how racial diversity affects turnout (Hill and Leighley 1999), how the number of initiatives on a ballot affects turnout (Tolbert, Grummel, and Smith 2001), and how turnout affects voting for presidential candidates (Radcliff 1994; Erikson 1995).

Despite the importance of this variable in these and many other studies of questions central to understanding political behavior and policy-making, the empirical measure of voter turnout that has typically been used is problematic. Voter turnout rates have typically been measured in these studies as the ratio of the ballots cast to the voting-age population (VAP), persons 18 years of age and older. This is not a true measure of the turnout rate for those eligible to vote, because the VAP includes some persons who are not legally eligible to vote, such as non-citizens and felons (Andrews 1966; Wolfinger and Rosenstone 1980; Bruce 1997; Day 1998). Despite this limitation of the VAP, political scientists have used it because, unlike the voting-eligible population (VEP), the VAP is readily available from the Bureau of the Census (Gans 1997).[1] The implications of using the VAP rather than the VEP as the denominator for calculating turnout rates should not be underestimated. For example, McDonald and Popkin (2001) find that the much vaunted decline in the United States turnout rate since 1972 is actually just an artifact of the growing ineligible population. And perhaps more important for students of state politics, if distribution of the ineligible population is not random across states, as I demonstrate to be the case, this measurement error may bias studies of voter turnout that use aggregate state data.

In this article, I outline a methodology to calculate a VEP-based turnout rate for the 50 states using Current Population Survey (CPS) and Department of Justice (DOJ) reports. The advantages of this approach are that it gives a truer indicator of the concept of voter turnout and that, unlike attempts to adjust VAP for citizenship (Barnham 1987; Hill and Leighley 1999), it does not rely on interpolation between censuses. The drawback of my approach is that it relies upon a survey, the CPS, for its estimate of non-citizens, and is thus subject to the errors of survey methodology.

CONSTRUCTING STATE TURNOUT RATES

Conceptually, the voter turnout rate is easily defined. It is a ratio in which the numerator is the number of persons who cast a ballot and the denominator is the number of persons eligible to vote. Clearly, if someone is not eligible to vote, there should be no expectation that he or she will vote, and thus he or she should not be

---

[1] Notable exceptions to the standard approach are Burnham (1987) and Hill and Leighley (1999) who derive the citizen VAP by interpolating the population of United States' citizens in each state between decennial censuses. Of course, this measure cannot be used for years following the most recent census.

included in the turnout rate's denominator. However, operationalizing this simple concept has been difficult because reliable estimates of those ineligible to vote are not readily available. In this section, I describe a method of approximating these numbers. In doing so, I draw attention to the presence of measurement error in government statistics of which casual consumers of data are often unaware.

The scope of this research is limited by data availability. State-level voting-age population estimates are available from the first U.S. census in 1790. However, reliable estimates of the non-citizen population in each state are only available since 1978 from the Current Population Survey, and reliable state-level tallies of the number of felons in the correctional system are only available since 1980. For this reason, this research covers 1980 to 2000.

The Numerator: Votes

United States elections are highly decentralized. Typically, county election boards (or their local equivalents) organize elections for the voting precincts in their jurisdictions and report the results for statewide, congressional, and national elections to their state counterparts, who in turn publish the aggregate results. To avoid the potentially onerous task of collecting election data from each of the 50 states, I rely on a voting report to the U.S. Congress produced by the Congressional Research Service (Crocker 1996, 1997, 1999).[2]

Even with such a central data source, the decentralized United States' election system thwarts a uniform turnout standard of measurement. The question arises as to how you count a person who votes for one office on a ballot, but not another. Although many states report the most desirable measure of turnout, the total number of persons who cast any ballot, reporting varies over time and across states. For example, some states only report tallies of the number of votes cast in specific races. Thus, using total turnout in the calculation of state turnout rates is impractical since it is not reported for all years and states.[3] Instead, I use a measure that is reported comparably over time and space, the vote for the highest office on the ballot. In presidential election years, this is defined as the total votes cast for the presidential candidates, and in non-presidential election years, it is the largest number of persons casting a vote in a statewide race. If no statewide race was on a state's ballot in a non-presidential election year, I use the aggregate vote for its congressional races (Crocker 1996, 6). Of course, the vote for the highest office may underestimate total turnout, as persons may cast ballots that do not include a vote for the highest office. For those states that report it, total turnout in presidential elections—not the turnout rate—is, on average, a nearly consistent 2.1 percent greater than the vote for highest office (McDonald and Popkin 2001, 964).

The Denominator: The Voting-Eligible Population

The voting-age population (VAP) is commonly used as the denominator of the turnout rate in reports of voting participation in the United States. But a central

[2] 2000 turnout data was provided by the ABC News Polling Unit, compiled by the Associated Press, obtained by personal correspondence with Gary Langer, April 26, 2001.

[3] In the dataset accompanying this article, I report total turnout for those states that report it so that researchers can make their own calculations of turnout rates using total turnout, for those states and years where it was reported.

point of this article is that the VAP is not the eligible population, as is explicitly stated in the U.S. Census Bureau definition:

> The voting-age population includes all U.S. residents 18 years and over. This consists of both people who are eligible to vote and those not eligible to vote, such as non-citizens, convicted felons, and prison inmates. These projections do not cover Americans living overseas who may vote. (Day 1998, 1)

I estimate a state's voting-eligible population from its VAP by removing non-citizens and ineligible felons from the latter to reflect more accurately the eligible electorate. This adjustment is not perfect, since reliable estimates of permanently disfranchised felons and persons declared mentally incompetent by a court of law are not available. Furthermore, overseas citizens are incorrectly excluded from the VAP, but cannot be added to my estimate of VEP because no method exists to allocate these people among the states.

Voting-age population

The Census Bureau calculates monthly estimates of the United States population by adjusting the last census for the number of deaths, births, immigrants, emigrants, and persons moving in and out of the military. This estimate is then adjusted to age the population each month. The estimate of the number of persons 18 years and older in the November of an election year is my estimate of the VAP for counties, states, and the nation.

This VAP estimate is not error-free. Inaccuracies enter with errors in the decennial census and the method of estimating the monthly population. The errors in the decennial census are a combination of not counting some people and counting others more than once. According to the U.S. General Accounting Office (1997), the estimated net under-coverage of the U. S. Census was 5.8 percent of the total population in 1940, 4.1 percent in 1950, 3.1 percent in 1960, 2.7 percent in 1970, 1.2 percent in 1980, and 1.8 percent in 1990. For 2000, the undercount is estimated to be between 0.96 and 1.40 percent (Bureau of the Census 2001). The increasing reliability of the census lowers the estimated turnout rate, *ceteris paribus*. By counting more people, the turnout rate's denominator is increased, decreasing the estimated turnout rate.

The monthly estimate of the United States population uses the last decennial census as the baseline, adjusting for deaths, births, and so forth. This estimate is subject to subsequent revisions as the Bureau of the Census acquires additional data. A final estimate for a given month is not released for years following the first estimate, and even this estimate is subject to further revision to bring a decennial estimate in line with the subsequent census' numbers. Therefore, the population estimates for the most recent years reported here must be considered preliminary.

Non-citizens

While non-citizens are included in the VAP, they do not enjoy voting rights in the United States, and therefore should not be included in the VEP.

The Current Population Survey (CPS) provides an election year estimate of the number of non-citizens among the VAP. The CPS is a survey with a sample size of more than 100,000 persons nationwide. Its primary purpose is to determine monthly labor statistics, but in the November of election years, a battery of additional questions on voting behavior is asked, including on citizenship.

The CPS includes a representative sample drawn for each state and weighted accordingly. No state has fewer than 1,300 respondents and most have thousands more. Thus, even for the smallest states, the CPS sample size rivals the best national polls. Still, there remain unavoidable errors inherent in these data as a consequence of survey methodology. The Bureau of the Census estimates the standard error of their CPS percentages based on their sampling methodology. In the worst case (for small, homogenous states such as North Dakota, which has a non-citizen population estimated at 0.79 percent and a standard error of 0.64), the 95 percent confidence interval covers 0.0 percent. Furthermore, the degree of error associated with the survey methodology of the CPS is unknown, although the Census Bureau expends considerable effort to assure its reliability because of the important government uses of the CPS.[4]

Despite this inherent statistical uncertainty, the CPS's large samples in each of the states limit the degree of error of my estimates. Undoubtedly, the CPS provides a more accurate measure of the citizen VAP for panel and cross-sectional analysis than the unadjusted VAP that fails to account for non-citizens. My approach is also more flexible than the alternative of interpolating citizen VAP between censuses (Burnham 1987; Hill and Leighley 1999). The latter is possible only if there are two censuses to interpolate between, and it may miss important intra-decade trends. The validity of my citizen VAP measure is supported by the fact that Immigration and Naturalization Service statistics of legal immigration track the CPS estimate of total non-citizens quite well. Both exhibit a peak in 1991 and a subsequent modest decline.

Ineligible Felons

The voting rights of convicted felons depend on state law. Only Maine, Utah, and Vermont currently allow their incarcerated felons to vote (a 2000 referendum disfranchised incarcerated felons in Massachusetts). All other states deny the franchise to felons in prison, and some states go even further. Table 1 lists the states' voting restrictions on felons. Thirty-two states deny felons on parole the right to vote, and 29 deny that right to those on probation. Thirteen states restrict in some form the voting of those convicted of a felony even after they have served their full time in the correctional system (Love and Kuzma 1996).[5]

Correctional Populations of the United States is an annual publication of the Department of Justice that lists the number of felons in prison, on probation, and on parole in each state. I calculate the number of persons in the correctional system ineligible to vote in each state by matching the state law to the number of persons in each stage of the correctional system. However, not all of these persons are felons. A Department of Justice report states that nearly all prisoners and half of probationers have been convicted of a felony (U.S. Department of Justice 2000). Therefore, for this study, I assume all prisoners and parolees are felons and half of probationers. I use data reported for December 31 of each year since monthly

---

[4] Besides the sampling error described here, the CPS is also prone to other errors. For example, the weighting scheme is based on the decennial census, and this changes as new final counts are tallied. The other usual suspects of survey methodology may also affect the CPS estimates, such as interviewer, respondent, and question-wording biases.

[5] Felons in these states can regain their voting rights only through a pardon. Because of the Full Faith and Credit clause of the federal constitution, felons are subject to the voting restrictions of the state in which they were convicted, not their state of residence.

TABLE 1
Felons Disfranchised Under State Law

State	Prison	Probation	Parole	Ex-felons
AL	Y	Y	Y	Y
AK	Y	Y	Y	
AZ	Y	Y	Y	2nd felony
AR	Y	Y	Y	
CA	Y		Y	
CO	Y		Y	
CT	Y	Y	Y	
DE	Y	Y	Y	Y
DC	Y			
FL	Y	Y	Y	Y
GA	Y	Y	Y	
HI	Y			
ID	Y			
IL	Y			
IN	Y			
IA	Y	Y	Y	Y
KS	Y			
KY	Y	Y	Y	Y
LA	Y			
ME				
MD	Y	Y	Y	2nd felony
MA	Post-2000			
MI	Y			
MN	Y	Y	Y	
MS	Y	Y	Y	Y
MO	Y	Y	Y	
MT	Y			
NE	Y	Y	Y	
NV	Y	Y	Y	Y
NH	Y			
NJ	Y	Y	Y	
NM	Y	Y	Y	Y
NY	Y		Y	
NC	Y	Y	Y	
ND	Y			
OH	Y			
OK	Y	Y	Y	
OR	Y			
PA	Y			
RI	Y	Y	Y	
SC	Y	Y	Y	
SD	Y			
TN	Y	Y	Y	Pre-1986
TX	Y	Y	Y	2 Years
UT				
VT				
VA	Y	Y	Y	Y
WA	Y	Y	Y	Pre-1984
WV	Y	Y	Y	
WI	Y	Y	Y	
WY	Y	Y	Y	Y
Total	48	29	32	13

Note: "Y" indicated felons in this category are disfranchised.
Sources: Love and Kuzma (1996) and author's notes.

figures are not available. The state of origin of felons in the federal corrections system is unknown, so these people are excluded from my analyses.

Remaining Outstanding VEP Adjustments

There are several other corrections to the VAP that should be made to arrive at the true VEP population for each state, but for which the appropriate data are currently unavailable. Thus, my VEP measure remains subject to these errors.

I do not correct for felons who have been permanently disfranchised. These data needed to do this (e.g., recidivism, death rates, and migration of felons) are not available. A study by Human Rights Watch and The Sentencing Project estimated that 1.4 million ex-felons had permanently lost their voting rights in the 1996 presidential election (Fellner and Mauer 1998). These people are concentrated in those states that permanently restrict felons from voting (see Table 1), and thus the VEP in these states is overestimated by an unknown amount.

The number of non-citizens in state correctional systems should be subtracted from the number of ineligible felons to avoid double counting them in the calculated VEP. A Department of Justice (1996) report found in 1991 that there were 30,718 non-citizens in state prisons. Non-citizens comprised 18.9 percent of California's prison population, 12.1 percent in Texas, 9.3 percent in Arizona, 5.0 percent in Florida, 5.0 percent in Illinois, 4.1 percent in New York, and 2.6 percent in New Jersey; the distribution of the small remainder is unknown. A similar study (Clark and Anderson 2000) found that the non-citizen population in these same state prisons declined by over 50 percent to 14,262 by 1995.[6] Unfortunately, these are the only data available on this subject. Lacking a data for the entire series, I do not adjust for these non-citizen prisoners in my VEP calculations. However, the resulting error should be very small. Even for California in 1991, with 18.9 percent of its prisoners being non-citizen, this adjustment would result in only a .05 percent decrease in the VEP turnout rate.

Persons found mentally incompetent by a court of law are disfranchised in many states. Since these people cannot care for themselves, a rough estimate of their numbers might be obtained from the number of people in high-level-care nursing homes. However, the only source for this information, the National Nursing Home Survey, was conducted only twice during my study period and, more important, it does not report these data disaggregated by state. Therefore, no adjustment will be made for the mentally incompetent. But again, the error should be small since there were only a quarter of a million people in high-level-care nursing homes in 1995. Furthermore, since there is little reason to believe that the mentally incompetent are not distributed evenly among the states, any resulting bias would be evenly reflected among the states.

Finally, citizens of voting-age living overseas are not included in the VAP but they should be included in the VEP. The number of United States citizens living overseas can be obtained through military, census, and State Department publications (McDonald and Popkin 2001). Unfortunately, the home state of these citizens residing overseas is unknown, so no adjustment to the state-level VAP can be made to account for them.

---

[6] Immigration and Naturalization Services publications suggest that efforts to deport non-citizens in the correctional system were increased, perhaps to reduce the burden of federal laws that require the federal government to reimburse states for the costs of incarcerating their non-citizen felons.

ANALYSIS

Limited space prevents the entire 1980–2000 50-state series from being presented here, so I will discuss only some of the highlights. An electronic dataset that can be used to calculate the VAP and VEP turnout rates, using the corrections outlined above, is publicly accessible at the Inter-Consortium for Political Science Research publication-related archives as study #1248 (www.icpsr.umich.edu).

From World War II through the early 1970s, the non-citizen and ineligible felon population was small relative to the voting age population, and thus the adjustment to the VAP to obtain the VEP was small. Beginning in the mid-1970s, a dramatic increase in the non-citizen population occurred, peaking in 1991 (McDonald and Popkin 2001). Furthermore, since 1984, a substantial increase in the ineligible felon population has also occurred. These trends have resulted in a significant divergence between the VAP and the VEP. This divergence will lead to serious underestimation of the turnout rate among eligible voters in some states when using the VAP. Although these trends are not fully captured in my dataset, due to the data limitations discussed above, the general increase in non-citizens and ineligible felons is evident in my data for most states.

In Table 2, I present the 2000 data as an example of what is available in my dataset, including all of the raw numbers needed to calculate each state's 1980–2000 VAP and VEP turnout rates. Table 2 differs from the dataset in some minor ways. Not reported here, but included in the dataset, is the number of persons casting any ballot, for those states that report this number. In the dataset, I provide the CPS estimate of the non-citizen population only as a percentage of the VAP, while in Table 2, I also present this as a raw number (i.e., the percentage multiplied by the VAP). I also provide, in the dataset, the individual components used to calculate the totals of the ineligible felons (those in prison, on probation, or on parole), while in Table 2, I only present the total of these numbers to save space. In the dataset, but not in Table 2, I also provide the total number of persons casting a ballot for those states that report this figure.

As Table 2 shows, the larger of the two adjustments, the non-citizen population, is very unevenly distributed among the states. In 2000, 14 of the 50 states had non-citizen populations of less than 2.0 percent of their VAP. These states were primarily located in the deep South, the border states, and the upper tier of the country. On the other hand, states that border Mexico, plus Florida, Hawaii, New Jersey, and New York, had non-citizen populations greater than 9.0 percent of their VAP. The extreme case is California, with a non-citizen population of 19.9 percent of its VAP, more than six percentage points above the next highest state, New York.

The percentage of VAP that a state's ineligible felon population accounts for depends both on state law on felons' civil rights and state incarceration rates. The 20 states with ineligible felon populations of less than 1.0 percent of their 2000 VAP are all located above a line horizontally bisecting the lower 48 states. Southern states generally have restrictive felony disfranchisement laws, as do some non-Southern states. Georgia leads the nation in ineligible felons with 6.3 percent of its 2000 VAP ineligible due to felony status. The next highest state, Delaware, has 4.9 percent of its 2000 VAP ineligible, followed by Texas at 4.8 percent.

The final column in Table 2 shows the most telling data in this analysis—the difference between 2000 VAP turnout rate and the turnout rate adjusted to be based more closely on the VEP. Note that this bias of the VAP turnout rate is both

TABLE 2
2000 VAP and VEP Turnout Rates

State	VAP	Vote for Highest Office	VAP Turnout Rate	Non-citizens	Percent Non-citizen	Ineligible Felons	Percent Ineligible Felon	VEP	VEP Turnout Rate	Turnout Rate Difference
AL	3,333,000	1,665,473	49.97	45,293	1.36	52,108	2.19	3,235,599	51.47	1.84
AK	430,000	284,492	66.16	13,681	3.18	6,924	2.14	409,395	69.49	3.72
AZ	3,625,000	1,531,846	42.26	406,194	11.21	58,763	2.41	3,160,043	48.48	6.66
AR	1,929,000	921,781	47.79	43,145	2.24	34,800	2.59	1,851,055	49.80	2.43
CA	24,873,000	10,965,822	44.09	4,936,534	19.85	277,047	1.11	19,659,419	55.78	11.69
CO	3,067,000	1,741,368	56.78	195,613	6.38	22,096	0.72	2,849,291	61.12	4.34
CT	2,499,000	1,458,257	58.35	182,004	7.28	47,416	3.00	2,269,580	64.25	6.69
DE	582,000	327,529	56.28	24,103	4.14	18,043	4.90	539,854	60.67	5.60
DC	411,000	201,355	48.99	34,825	8.47	7,456	1.81	368,719	54.61	5.62
FL	11,774,000	5,963,070	50.65	1,570,535	13.34	223,936	3.14	9,979,528	59.75	10.00
GA	5,893,000	2,583,206	43.84	227,093	3.85	220,061	6.34	5,445,845	47.43	4.98
HI	909,000	367,951	40.48	89,863	9.89	5,053	0.56	814,084	45.20	4.72
ID	921,000	489,323	53.13	35,459	3.85	5,526	0.60	880,015	55.60	2.47
IL	8,983,000	4,742,062	52.79	751,521	8.37	45,281	0.50	8,186,198	57.93	5.14
IN	4,448,000	2,180,305	49.02	77,565	1.74	20,125	0.45	4,350,310	50.12	1.10
IA	2,165,000	1,313,866	60.69	104,336	4.82	20,306	1.39	2,040,357	64.39	4.02
KS	1,983,000	1,072,216	54.07	48,734	2.46	8,344	0.42	1,925,922	55.67	1.60
KY	2,993,000	1,544,026	51.59	78,027	2.61	29,281	1.30	2,885,692	53.51	2.09
LA	3,255,000	1,765,656	54.24	53,378	1.64	52,606	2.16	3,149,016	56.07	2.14
ME	968,000	651,790	67.33	12,612	1.30	0	0.00	955,388	68.22	0.89
MD	3,925,000	2,022,079	51.52	254,688	6.49	79,188	3.05	3,591,124	56.31	5.43
MA	4,749,000	2,698,952	56.83	378,922	7.98	0	0.00	4,370,078	61.76	4.93
MI	7,358,000	4,231,314	57.51	272,065	3.70	47,718	0.65	7,038,217	60.12	2.61
MN	3,547,000	2,438,657	68.75	100,869	2.84	61,696	3.21	3,384,434	72.06	4.43
MS	2,047,000	994,204	48.57	28,208	1.38	27,821	1.66	1,990,971	49.94	1.52
MO	4,105,000	2,359,892	57.49	80,039	1.95	65,017	2.22	3,959,943	59.59	2.50
MT	668,000	411,038	61.53	7,596	1.14	3,105	0.46	657,299	62.53	1.00

(continued)

TABLE 2
(Continued)

State	VAP	Vote for Highest Office	VAP Turnout Rate	Non-citizens	Percent Non-citizen	Ineligible Felons	Percent Ineligible Felon	VEP	VEP Turnout Rate	Turnout Rate Difference
NE	1,234,000	697,019	56.48	29,330	2.38	14,738	2.02	1,189,932	58.58	2.60
NV	1,390,000	608,970	43.81	148,838	10.71	19,798	1.85	1,221,363	49.86	6.29
NH	911,000	567,795	62.33	45,474	4.99	2,257	0.25	863,269	65.77	3.45
NJ	6,245,000	3,187,226	51.04	665,644	10.66	107,069	2.74	5,472,287	58.24	7.90
NM	1,263,000	598,605	47.40	72,611	5.75	12,909	1.47	1,177,479	50.84	3.69
NY	13,805,000	6,821,997	49.42	1,858,164	13.46	128,154	0.93	11,818,682	57.72	8.31
NC	5,797,000	2,910,620	50.21	303,281	5.23	88,202	2.43	5,405,517	53.85	4.16
ND	477,000	288,256	60.43	4,549	0.95	1,233	0.26	471,218	61.17	0.74
OH	8,433,000	4,701,988	55.76	160,911	1.91	45,833	0.54	8,226,256	57.16	1.40
OK	2,531,000	1,234,229	48.76	58,842	2.32	38,706	2.08	2,433,451	50.72	2.25
OR	2,530,000	1,530,549	60.50	221,283	8.75	10,630	0.42	2,298,087	66.60	6.11
PA	9,153,000	4,912,185	53.67	268,641	2.94	36,847	0.40	8,847,512	55.52	1.85
RI	753,000	408,783	54.29	40,349	5.36	14,223	3.29	698,427	58.53	5.14
SC	2,977,000	1,383,742	46.48	32,744	1.10	48,186	2.37	2,896,070	47.78	1.67
SD	543,000	316,269	58.24	5,122	0.94	2,616	0.48	535,262	59.09	0.84
TN	4,221,000	2,075,753	49.18	107,717	2.55	49,534	1.65	4,063,749	51.08	2.16
TX	14,850,000	6,406,933	43.14	1,630,495	10.98	490,857	4.81	12,728,648	50.33	8.09
UT	1,465,000	770,932	52.62	93,266	6.37	0	0.00	1,371,734	56.20	3.58
VT	460,000	293,794	63.87	7,077	1.54	0	0.00	452,923	64.87	1.00
VA	5,263,000	2,736,640	52.00	268,896	5.11	52,077	1.29	4,942,027	55.37	3.56
WA	4,368,000	2,487,433	56.95	238,138	5.45	36,659	1.33	4,093,203	60.77	4.14
WV	1,416,000	648,100	45.77	7,931	0.56	8,011	0.78	1,400,058	46.29	0.62
WI	3,930,000	2,597,251	66.09	130,880	3.33	56,207	2.12	3,742,913	69.39	3.81
WY	347,000	213,726	61.59	2,304	0.66	3,062	1.15	341,634	62.56	1.14

Definitions: VAP: Voting-age population, residents aged 18 and older. VEP: Voting-eligible population, those persons eligible to vote. *Vote for Highest Office:* Vote for president in presidential election years (presented here), vote for highest statewide office or sum of congressional vote in midterm elections.

Sources: VAP and *Vote for Highest Office:* Crocker 1995, 1997, 1999, 2000 vote for highest office provided by ABC News Polling Unit, compiled by the Associated Press. *Non-Citizen:* Bureau of the U. S. Census, various years. *Ineligible Felon:* U. S. Department of Justice, various years.

substantial in many states and that it varies dramatically among the states. For example, California shows the largest difference between its 2000 VAP and VEP turnout rates. The California 2000 VAP turnout rate was 44.1 percent. When adjusted for only those eligible to vote, California's voter turnout rate climbs to 55.8 percent, a difference of 11.7 percentage points. Of those states with a greater than five percentage point upwards adjustment in the 2000 turnout rate, all are either located in the Southwest, have large cities, or, like Georgia and Florida, have restrictive felony disfranchisement laws. Those states with small ineligible populations, and therefore small differences between the VAP and VEP, tend to be small or predominantly rural. All of the states with only one congressional district (except Delaware, which has strict felony disfranchisement) fall below the median VAP turnout rate bias, with most having very small ineligible populations. The other states with small ineligible populations and small VAP turnout rate bias tend to be border states, such as Indiana, Kentucky, Ohio, Tennessee, and West Virginia.

Overall, there is less variation in the turnout rate among the states using the VEP measure. The standard deviation of the 2000 VAP turnout rate is 6.9 percentage points, while the standard deviation for the 2000 VEP turnout rate is 6.5 percentage points. This narrowing of the distribution of the turnout rate among the states is due primarily to the VEP turnout rates of those states with the largest ineligible populations being brought more in line with the norm by this adjustment. These states tend to fall at the low end of the VAP turnout rate distribution (because of their large VAP turnout rate bias), and move closer to the mean when their ineligible populations are removed from the turnout rate calculation.

CONCLUSION

As of 2000, nearly 10 percent of the persons of voting age living in the United States were ineligible to vote (McDonald and Popkin 2001), and these ineligible persons are unevenly distributed among the states. For studies of political processes using state-level turnout rate as a dependent or independent variable, the VEP turnout rate provides a better measure than the traditional VAP turnout rate measure. The VEP turnout rate is less susceptible to the confounding influences of these ineligible persons and the bias of the VAP turnout rate measure. For example, liberalizing voter registration laws (Fenster 1994; Knack 1995; Rhine 1995; Franklin and Grier 1997; Martinez and Hill 1999; Alvarez et al. 2001) could have no effect on encouraging ineligible persons to vote, unless they are first granted the franchise. The effect of direct democracy on the propensity to vote (Tolbert, Grummel, and Smith 2001) might be confounded by the outlier case of California, which has both a high level of direct democracy and many ineligible persons in its population.

The diversity of a state's population is related closely to the number of ineligible persons among its VAP, largely because ineligible non-citizens often come from various countries. Currently, people of Hispanic origin are driving this trend, and they will comprise an increasing share of the VAP in states beyond the Mexican-- U.S. border as they diffuse through the country. This is already occurring in urban areas across the country, in states like New York, New Jersey, and Illinois. Population diversity is also related to the severity of felony disfranchisement laws. Perhaps it is no coincidence that in an ethnically diverse state (Massachusetts), voters approved an amendment to the constitution in 2000 to deny incarcerated felons the right to vote. With a disproportionate number of minorities incarcerated as felons in the United States, a remaining challenge for the civil rights movement is to rectify not only patterns of minority incarceration, but also restrictive disfranchisement laws.

While I have not made all the corrections necessary to arrive at a true measure of the turnout rate among eligible voters in the states, I will continue to update my dataset to provide scholars with an improving alternative to the standard measure.

REFERENCES

Alvarez, Michael R., Steven Ansolabehere, Erik Antonsson, Jehoshua Bruck, Steven Graves, Thomas Palfrey, Ron Rivest, Ted Selker, Alex Slocum, and Charles Stewart III. 2001. "Voting: What Is, What Could Be." Pasadena, CA: Caltech/MIT Voting Technology Project.

Andrews, William. 1966. "American Voting Participation." *Western Political Quarterly* 19: 636–52.

Bruce, Peter. 1997. "Measuring Things: How the Experts Got Voter Turnout Wrong Last Year." *The Public Perspective* October: 39–43.

Burnham, Walter Dean. 1987. "The Turnout Problem." In *Elections American Style*, ed. A. James Reichley. Washington, DC: The Brookings Institution.

Clark, Rebecca L., and Scott A. Anderson. 2000. "Illegal Aliens in Federal, State, and Local Criminal Systems." Washington, DC: The Urban Institute.

Crocker, Royce. 1996. "Voter Registration and Turnout: 1948–1994." CRS Report for Congress: CRS-122. Washington, DC: Congressional Research Service.

Crocker, Royce. 1997. "Voter Registration and Turnout: 1996." Memorandum. Washington, DC: Congressional Research Service.

Crocker, Royce. 1999. "Voter Registration and Turnout: 1998." Memorandum. Washington, DC: Congressional Research Service.

Day, Jennifer C. 1998. "Projections of the Voting-Age Population for States: November 1998." Current Population Reports, P25–1132. Washington, DC: U.S. Dept. of Commerce, Bureau of the Census.

Erikson, Robert S. 1995. "State Turnout and Presidential Voting: A Closer Look." *American Politics Quarterly* 23(4): 387–96.

Fellner, Jamie, and Marc Mauer. 1998. "Losing the Vote: The Impact of Felony Disenfranchisement (sic) Laws in the United States." Washington, DC: Human Rights Watch and The Sentencing Project.

Fenster, Mark J. 1994. "The Impact of Allowing Day of Registration Voting on Turnout in U.S. Elections from 1960 to 1992: A Research Note." *American Politics Quarterly* 22(1): 74–87.

Franklin, Daniel P., and Eric E. Grier. 1997. "Effects of Motor Voter Legislation: Voter Turnout, Registration, and Partisan Advantage in the 1992 Presidential Election." *American Politics Quarterly* 25(1): 104–17.

Gans, Curtis. 1997. "Measuring Things: How the Experts Got Voter Turnout Wrong Last Year." *The Public Perspective* October: 44–8.

Hill, Kim Quaile, and Jan E. Leighley. 1999. "Racial Diversity, Voter Turnout, and Mobilizing Institutions in the United States." *American Politics Quarterly* 27(3): 275–95.

Knack, Steven. 1995. "Does 'Motor Voter' Work? Evidence from State-Level Data." *Journal of Politics* 57(3): 796–811.

Love, Margaret C., and Susan M. Kuzma. 1996. "Civil Disabilities of Felons: A State-by-State Survey." Washington, DC: U.S. Department of Justice, Office of the Pardon Attorney.

Martinez, Michael D., and David Hill. 1999. "Did Motor Voter Work?" *American Politics Quarterly* 27(3): 296–315.

McDonald, Michael P., and Samuel Popkin. 2001. "The Myth of the Vanishing Voter." *American Political Science Review* 95(4): 963–74.

Radcliff, Benjamin. 1994. "Turnout and the Democratic Vote." *American Politics Quarterly* 22 (3): 259–76.

Rhine, Staci L. 1995. "Registration Reform and Turnout Change in the American States." *American Politics Quarterly* 23(4): 409–26.

Tolbert, Caroline J., John A. Grummel, and Daniel A. Smith. 2001. "The Effects of Ballot Initiatives on Voter Turnout in the American States." *American Politics Research* 29(6): 625–48.

U.S. Department of Commerce, Bureau of the Census, various years. *Current Population Survey: Voter Supplement File,* various years [Computer File]. ICPSR version, Washington, DC: U.S. Dept. of Commerce, Bureau of the Census [producer], various years. Ann Arbor, MI: Inter-university Consortium for Political and Social Research [distributor], various years.

U.S. Department of Commerce, Bureau of the Census. 2001. "Preliminary Estimates Show Improvement in Census 2000 Coverage." Washington, DC: Department of Commerce.

U.S. Department of Justice, Bureau of Justice Statistics. various years. *Correctional Populations in the United States,* various years. Washington, DC: U.S. Department of Justice.

U.S. Department of Justice, Bureau of Justice Statistics. 1996. "Non-Citizens in the Federal Criminal Justice System, 1984–1994." NCJ-160934. Washington, DC: Department of Justice.

U.S. Department of Justice, Bureau of Justice Statistics. 2000. "U.S. Correctional Population Reaches 6.3 Million Men and Women, Represents 3.1 Percent of the Adult U.S. Population." Washington, DC: U.S. Department of Justice, Bureau of Justice Statistics.

U.S. General Accounting Office. 1997. "2000 Census: Progress Made on Design But Risks Remain." Washington, DC: U.S. General Accounting Office.

Wolfinger, Raymond E., and Stephen J. Rosenstone. 1980. *Who Votes?* New Haven, CT: Yale University Press.

24

THE EVOLUTION OF THE GENDER GAP
Barbara Norrander

A central fact about voter attachments to one political party or another is that they are not random. The process of voters' attachment to either the Republicans or the Democrats is mediated and actually reinforced in considerable degree by voters' social characteristics (and by other attributes as well, such as associational affiliation). Norrander subtly explores here the role of gender in influencing voter attachment to one party or another and she nicely captures how that process in the aggregate is itself a composite of sorting by men and women into the two political parties over time and across political jurisdictions. If your appetite for more information is whetted by Norrander's article, and you would like a succinct bird's-eye view of how voters' attributes and party attachment have interacted, navigate to the following page at the American National Election Studies: http://www .electionstudies.org/nesguide/gd-index.htm#1.

• • •

MOST STUDIES OF THE GENDER GAP focus on the greater attraction of the Democratic party for women than for men. Scholars and journalists first noticed the gender gap in connection with the 1980 presidential election (Mueller 1988). Thus, initial explanations of the gender gap centered on how Ronald Reagan's opposition to abortion and the Equal Rights Amendment led women to be less likely than men to vote for Reagan. These women's issues, however, were subsequently found not to explain the gender gap, since men's and women's positions on these issues tended to be the same (Cook, Jelen, and Wilcox 1992; Mansbridge 1985). Subsequent explanations for the gender gap turned to issue areas where men's and women's positions diverged, such as use of force abroad or at home and compassion issues (Conover and Sapiro 1993; Fite, Genest, and Wilcox 1990; Shapiro and Mahajan 1986; Smith 1984). Feminist attitudes also were debated as the source of the gender gap (Conover 1988; Cook and Wilcox 1991). Finally, varying economic positions and differences in weighting economic factors in voting decisions also have been argued to underlie the gender gap (Chaney, Alvarez, and Nagler 1998; Erie and Rein 1988; May and Stephenson 1994; Miller 1988; Seltzer, Newman, and Leighton 1997; Welch and Hibbing 1992). Despite the focus on different sets of issues, most research still attempts to explain why women have a greater attraction to the Democratic party than do men.

Scholars are increasingly using a longitudinal perspective to understand the origins of the gender gap, and these researchers are finding that the greatest movement in partisan preferences in recent decades has occurred among men who left the Democratic party more quickly than did women (Kaufmann and Petrocik

Norrander, Barbara. "The Evolution of the Gender Gap," *Public Opinion Quarterly* 63: 566–576. By permission of Oxford University Press.

1997; Kenski 1988; Miller 1991; Wirls 1986). In addition, men's and women's voting patterns diverged before the 1980 election. Men were more likely than women to vote for George Wallace in 1968 and Richard Nixon in 1972 (Norrander 1999). To better understand the long-term evolution of the gender gap two factors need to be considered. First, changes in partisan preferences have been greater in the South than in the rest of the nation. Thus, the development of the gender gap in the South may be different from that in the North or West. Second, men have a greater tendency than women to profess an independent identification (Norrander 1997). If this independence gap is not taken into account, the growth in men's preference for the Republican party can be understated to the extent that researchers continue to focus on women's attraction to the Democratic party rather than men's movement into the Republican party.

ADJUSTING THE GENDER GAP FOR
INDEPENDENT PREFERENCES

An independence gap, in which men are more likely to consider themselves political independents, and women are more likely to claim a partisan identity, is evident in 70 percent of the American National Election Surveys (ANES) from 1952 to 1996 and in 65 percent of the General Social Surveys (GSS) from 1972 to 1994 (Norrander 1997). The gap averages 6 percentage points in the ANES and 5.6 percent points in the GSS. The independence gap exists among almost every demographic group, including divisions by age, education, race, region, marital status, and religion. The exact location of the independence gap is between the leaning independent category, where more men are located, and the weak partisan classification, which more women choose.

Because of the independence gap, a gender gap measured solely on differences between Democratic and Republican adherents underestimates the partisan preferences of men versus women. Thus, women can be more prevalent in both parties, as was true nationwide in 1952, 1958–60, 1964–66, 1970–80, and 1986. This pattern even reaches statistical significance in 1976 and 1978. For these two years, the traditional measure of party identification, which excludes leaners, would indicate a gender gap of more women than men adherents in both the Democratic and Republican parties. To compensate for men's greater propensity to declare an independent preference, leaning independents need to be incorporated with the appropriate partisan category before calculating the partisan gender gap. With this measurement adjustment, trends in male and female partisan preferences become more distinct. The new measure will clearly identify when a gender gap arose in the Democratic party, composed of more women than men, and when a gap appeared for the Republican party, constituted by more men than women identifiers.

Since the largest amount of partisan change in recent years has occurred among white southern males, it is necessary to divide the population by race and region when tracing the evolution of the gender gap. African Americans have remained much more Democratic than the rest of the nation. The sample of blacks in the ANES is, unfortunately, too small to consistently examine gender differences, though a gender gap is apparent among African Americans in some of the larger exit polls.[1] To demonstrate how the gender gap arose from the exodus of men

---

[1] The average number of African American men with responses to the ANES party identification question is 74; the number for African American women is 116.

from the Democratic party, this analysis will be confined to white Americans. "South" is defined as the eleven ex-Confederate states.

LONGITUDINAL ANALYSIS OF THE GENDER GAP

Figure 1 illustrates the growth of the gender gap between white southern men and women using the redefined measure of Democratic support (including leaners). In this figure, men are represented by solid lines and women by dotted lines. Southerners are distinguished from northerners by black circles on each data point. As the left side of the graph shows, southern men were more Democratic than southern women through 1960, with this pattern reaching statistical significance at the .05 level in 1956.[2] In 1964, the gender pattern reversed itself with women being more Democratic than men. A statistically significant gender gap in white southerners' preferences for the Democratic party existed in 1974, 1988, and 1992–96. Table 1 lists the gender gap for each year, using both the redefined measure, which includes leaning independents, and the traditional measure, which excludes independents. The traditional and the redefined measures of the gender gap produce similar patterns for the gap in Democratic identification in the South, with the exception that the traditional measure does not find a gender gap in 1992. More differences between the two measures of the gender gap occur for Republican preferences. The traditional measure does not find a Republican gender gap in 1992 and 1994, and the size of the gender gap is generally smaller than that found when independent leaners are included. The traditional measure, by excluding the larger proportion of men under the leaning independent label, underestimates the movement of southern white men into the Republican party.

The southern gender gap arose mainly from the more dramatic movement of men away from the Democratic party and into the Republican party. Table 2 quantifies the changes in each sex's partisanship by using percent Democratic (or Republican) as the dependent variable and year as the independent variable. Support for the Democratic party among southern white men declined four-fifths of a percentage point per year ($b = -.86$), while southern women's support was reduced by one-half a percentage point per year ($b = -.53$). Over the 44-year period of 1952–96, these coefficients describe a drop in white southern men's support for the Democratic party of 38 percentage points, while southern women's support declined 23 percentage points. Movement of white southerners into the Republican party was slightly less dramatic, with men's support for the Republican party increasing by three-fourths of a percentage point per year ($b = .75$) and women's preferences increasing by only one-third of a percentage point per year ($b = .36$). Thus, the southern gender gap surfaced in a two-step process. First came the greater movement of men than women away from the Democratic party beginning in the 1960s, and second came a slower conversion to Republican ranks.

Miller (1991) found that the gender gap arose foremost from the movement of southern males. However, with the inclusion of male independent leaners and a few additional years for analysis, a gender gap appears among nonsouthern whites as well. Figure 1 also shows a decline in Democratic preferences fluctuate somewhat but do not exhibit a consistent upward or downward trend. As a result, northern white women significantly outnumbered men in the Democratic party in 1980–82, 1986, and 1992–96 (see table 1). The traditional measure of the gender

[2] Statistical significance is measured by a difference in proportions test.

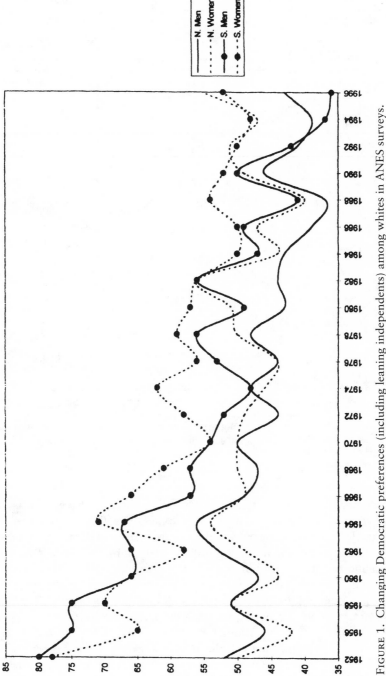

FIGURE 1. Changing Democratic preferences (including leaning independents) among whites in ANES surveys.

TABLE 1
Partisan Gender Gap among White Americans Measured
With and Without Leaning Independents Included

	South				North			
	Democratic Gap		Republican Gap		Democratic Gap		Republican Gap	
Year	With Leaners	Without Leaners	With Leaners	Without Leaners	With Leaners	Without Leaners	With Leaners	Without Leaners
1952	−2	−1	4	3	−2	2	5	5
1956	−10*	−10*	11**	7	−5	1	6	9**
1958	−5	−1	6	4	−1	3	0	1
1960	0	−1	−1	−1	−3	6*	4	7*
1962	−7	−6	5	7	−4	−2	7*	6
1964	3	2	−4	−1	−2	3	4	4
1966	8	10	−4	0	0	−1	−1	2
1968	4	7	−5	−1	3	3	−4	−1
1970	0	4	0	0	0	2	0	3
1972	5	6	−1	3	4	5*	−3	2
1974	13**	15**	−6	−1	−2	4	1	3
1976	4	1	2	5	0	4	3	7**
1978	3	4	2	5	2	4	2	7**
1980	8	7	−2	2	8*	9**	−3	1
1982	0	0	−3	0	12**	13**	−7	−3
1984	3	6	−5	3	2	5	−1	0
1986	1	2	0	4	8**	8**	−8**	0
1988	12**	11**	−14**	−8*	3	5	−1	4
1990	3	7	−6	−5	3	3	−5	−2
1992	8*	4	−13**	−7	10**	8**	−6*	−4
1994	11*	11**	−12**	−3	9**	8**	−7**	−4
1996	16**	12**	−14**	−11*	13**	11**	−14**	−8**

Source: American National Election Surveys.

Note: Numbers are percent of men subtracted from percent of women. Thus, positive numbers indicate more women adherents and negative numbers, more men identifiers.

* $p \leq .05$.

** $p \leq .01$.

gap, excluding leaners, tends to produce a similar pattern for a gap measured on Democratic preferences. Once again, the two measures differ more when considering a gender gap measured on Republican preferences. The traditional measure does not find a gender gap in the Republican party until 1996, while the measure including independent leaners finds greater male support for the Republican party in 1986 and from 1992 to 1996. In an unexpected pattern, the traditional measure of the gender gap has more women than men identifying with the Republican party in 1976 and 1978. By excluding the greater proportion of independent leaners who are men, the traditional measure of the gender gap underestimates the growing attraction of the Republican party for men versus women.

The gender gap in the North arose from the greater movement in partisan preferences among males than females. As table 2 shows, men's preferences for the Democratic party declined by one-fourth of a percentage point per year ($b = -.28$), while no trend exists in the partisan preferences of nonsouthern women ($b = .02$). Unlike the South, the decline in northern male support for the Democratic party is

TABLE 2

Summarizing Yearly Changes in Party Identification for
White Americans from 1952 to 1996

	South		North		Both Regions, Both Sexes
	Men	*Women*	*Men*	*Women*	
Changes in Democratic identification:					
Year	−.86**	−.53**	−.28**	.02	.03
	(.07)	(.06)	(.05)	(.07)	(.06)
Male					639.40**
					(127.05)
Year × male					−.33**
					(.06)
South					1,107.50**
					(127.05)
Year × South					−.56**
					(.06)
Constant	1,755.24**	1,096.58**	598.79**	4.43	−6.97
	(147.45)	(128.12)	(104.52)	(135.48)	(110.03)
Adjusted R^2	.86**	.75**	.56**	−.04	.82**
Number	22	22	22	22	88
Changes in Republican identification:					
Year	.75**	.36**	.23**	−.07	−.09
	(.07)	(.06)	(.06)	(.07)	(.05)
Male					(125.05)
Year × male					.35**
					(.06)
South					−952.61**
					(125.05)
Year × South					.48**
					(.06)
Constant	−1,450.74**	−681.19**	−418.31**	177.58	221.05*
	(136.22)	(109.88)	(125.67)	(136.19)	(108.30)
Adjusted R^2	.85**	.66**	.37**	.00	.79**
Number	22	22	22	22	88

Source: American National Election Studies Surveys.

Note: Entries are unstandardized coefficients from ordinary least squares regression. Values inside parentheses are standard errors.

* $p \leq .05$.

** $p \leq .01$.

reflected in an equal movement into the Republican party. Northern male support for the Republican party increased by one-fourth of a percentage point each year ($b = .23$), while female support for the Republican party has not changed over the years ($b = .07$).

The source of the gender gap is the same in the North as in the South. The movement of men away from the Democratic party left the party's composition to become more dominated by women. Greater movement by men than women into the

Republican party produced a gender gap in the GOP as well. The difference between the two regions is in the amount of partisan change and whether the decline in Democratic identification is coupled with an equal growth in Republican supporters. The final regression analyses presented in table 2 examine changing partisan preferences for both sexes in both regions. The statistical significance of the interaction terms between year and sex confirms that the rate of partisan change has been greater for men than women. On average, men's partisan preferences have changed by one-third of a percentage point more than that of women in each subsequent year since 1952 ($b = -.33$ for declining Democratic identification and $b = .35$ for increasing Republican preferences). The significance of the interaction terms between year and region similarly verifies that the rate of partisan change has been greater in the South than in the rest of the nation. For each year, the partisan preferences of southerners have changed by one-half a percentage point more than those of nonsoutherners ($b = -.56$ for Democratic identification and $b = .48$ for affiliation with the Republican party).[3]

CONCLUSION

In both the North and the South, the partisan gender gap arose as white men left the Democratic party and moved into the Republican party at a swifter pace than did women. Partisan preferences of the two sexes began changing in the 1960s, and the first indications of both a partisan and electoral gender gap occurred in the 1970s. The partisan gender gap became more frequent in the 1980s and by 1992 became a permanent pattern for both Democratic and Republican identification in all regions of the country. Why men have been more willing than women to leave the Democratic party and enter the Republican party is beyond the scope of this article. Nevertheless, the increasing conservatism of men and women's greater support for government programs that fall under the rubric of compassion issues (Norrander 1999) may explain why men have become more attracted to the Republican party while women feel comfortable remaining within the Democratic fold.

The nature of changing partisanship in the last few decades becomes clearer when examined by region and with the inclusion of independent leaners. The greater attraction of the Republican party for men becomes clearer when leaning independents are included along with partisans. This modification compensates for the greater tendency of men to adopt a leaning independent identification. Differences between the North versus the South are found in the greater amount of change in the South, where both men and women have become less Democratic and more Republican. The rate of change for southern white men, however, exceeds the shift among southern white women by one-third. Northern men also changed their preferences, but at a slower rate than southern men, and northern women have not changed partisanship in any consistent pattern over the past 40 years. The gender gap evolved from these varying rates of partisan change.

[3] Using the traditional measure of the partisanship, which excludes independent leaners, to measure partisan change across the two regions and the two sexes produces similar regression results. The major difference is that the traditional measure produces statistically significant coefficients for the year variable, as the increasing number of independents over these years reduced both the number of Democrats and Republicans. Excluding independent leaners, the values for changes in Democratic identification are as follows: year = $-.12$*, male = 456.03**, year $\times$ male = $-.23$**, South = 1253.25**, year $\times$ South = $-.63$**, constant = 277.13*, adjusted $R^2 = .87$**. The values for the Republican regression included the following: year = -18** male = -434.33**, year $\times$ male = $.22$**, South = -764.81**, year $\times$ South = $.38$**, constant = 387.28**, adjusted $R^2 = .71$**.

REFERENCES

Chaney, Carole Kennedy, R. Michael Alvarez, and Jonathon Nagler. 1998. "Explaining the Gender Gap in U.S. Presidential Elections, 1980–1992." *Political Research Quarterly* 51 (June): 311–40.

Conover, Pamela J. 1988. "Feminists and the Gender Gap." *Journal of Politics* 50 (November): 985–1010.

Conover, Pamela J., and Virginia Sapiro. 1993. "Gender, Gender Consciousness, and War." *American Journal of Political Science* 37 (November): 1079–99.

Cook, Elizabeth Adell, Ted G. Jelen, and Clyde Wilcox. 1992. *Between Two Absolutes: Public Opinion and the Politics of Abortion.* Boulder, CO: Westview.

Cook, Elizabeth Adell, and Clyde Wilcox. 1991. "Feminism and the Gender Gap—a Second Look." *Journal of Politics* 53 (November): 1111–22.

Erie, Steven P., and Martin Rein. 1988. "Women and the Welfare State." In *The Politics of the Gender Gap: The Social Construction of Political Influence*, ed. Carol M. Mueller, pp. 173–91. Newbury Park, CA: Sage.

Fite, David, Marc Genest, and Clyde Wilcox. 1990. "Gender Differences in Foreign Policy Attitudes: A Longitudinal Analysis." *American Politics Quarterly* 18 (October): 492–512.

Kaufmann, Karen M., and John R. Petrocik. 1997. "The Revenge of the Soccer Moms? Gender as a Party Cleavage in American Politics." Paper presented at the American Political Science Association Washington, DC, August 28–31, 1997.

Kenski, Henry C. 1988. "The Gender Factor in a Changing Electorate." In *The Politics of the Gender Gap: The Social Construction of Political Influence*, ed. Carol M. Mueller, pp. 38–60. Newbury Park, CA: Sage.

Mansbridge, Jane E. 1985. "Myth and Reality: the ERA and the Gender Gap in the 1980 Election." *Public Opinion Quarterly* 49 (Summer): 164–78.

May, Ann Mari, and Kurt Stephenson. 1994. "Women and the Great Retrenchment: The Political Economy of Gender in the 1980s." *Journal of Economic Issues* 28 (June): 533–42.

Miller, Arthur. 1988. "Gender and the Vote: 1984." In *The Politics of the Gender Gap: The Social Construction of Political Influence*, ed. Carol M. Mueller, pp. 258–82. Newbury Park, CA: Sage.

Miller, Warren E. 1991. "Party Identification, Realignment, and Party Voting: Back to the Basics." *American Political Science Review* 85 (June): 557–68.

Mueller, Carol M. 1988. "The Empowerment of Women: Polling and the Women's Voting Bloc." In *The Politics of the Gender Gap: The Social Construction of Political Influence*, ed. Carol M. Mueller, pp. 16–36. Newbury Park, CA: Sage.

Norrander, Barbara. 1997. "The Independence Gap and the Gender Gap." *Public Opinion Quarterly* 61 (Fall): 464–76.

———. 1999. "Is the Gender Gap Growing?" In *Reelection 1996: How Americans Voted*, ed. Herbert F. Weisberg and Janet M. Box-Steffenmeier, pp. 145–61. New York: Chatham House.

Seltzer, Richard A., Jody Newman, and Melissa Voorhees Leighton. 1997. *Sex as a Political Variable: Women as Candidates and Voters in U.S. Elections.* Boulder, CO: Lynne Rienner.

Shapiro, Robert Y., and Harpreet Mahajan. 1986. "Gender Differences in Policy Preferences: A Summary of Trends from the 1960s to the 1980s." *Public Opinion Quarterly* 50 (Spring): 42–61.

Smith, Tom W. 1984. "The Polls: Gender and Attitudes toward Violence." *Public Opinion Quarterly* 48 (Spring): 384–96.

Welch, Susan, and John Hibbing. 1992. "Financial Conditions, Gender, and Voting in American National Elections." *Journal of Politics* 54 (February): 194–213.

Wirls, Daniel. 1986. "Reinterpreting the Gender Gap." *Public Opinion Quarterly* 50 (Autumn): 316–30.

25

THE AMERICAN PROCESS OF SELECTING A PRESIDENT: A COMPARATIVE PERSPECTIVE

Matthew Soberg Shugart[*]

How Americans pick their president is remarkably strange in comparative perspective, as Shugart shows in this lively and informative piece. But maybe "strange" is also "not so bad." Consider that the electorates of the two parties nominate their candidates in sequential contests. (There is a modest amount of strategic, cross-over voting, to be sure, in some of the states where presidential primaries are so-called open primaries.) Such a sequential nomination process leads to candidates trying both to prove their appeal to their party electorate in many different places and to develop unstoppable momentum. Meeting those twin challenges requires constant fund-raising and enormous physical and psychic stamina. In the process successful candidates become better candidates than they were when they started. They also develop or deepen their connections with organized groups, activists, and party officials and co-partisans across the country.

As for the general election, the Electoral College forces presidential candidates to assemble two kinds of majorities—a popular majority and a territorial majority. Generating a second, territorial majority via the Electoral College has the effect—usually, but not always—of weighting and augmenting the first majority. Thus the Electoral College seals the winning candidate's accomplishment in the popular contest. This is no small accomplishment, since fair elections should generate crystal-clear winners if voters are to have confidence, after the election, in governance by that winner.

Nonetheless, there are potential problems—which is a central fact of electoral institutions. They all have problems one way or another, it happens. The Arrow Theorem—which won its author, Kenneth Arrow, the Nobel Prize in Economics—demonstrated this blunt truth about election institutions when it was published in 1952. (For technical details, go to Wikipedia, as good a place to start as any.)

Consider the Electoral College. As everyone knows, thanks to the 2000 election, there have been enormously consequential instances in which the second majority, which is to say, the Electoral College majority, has been larger than the first, the popular majority. Under the rules, the Electoral College majority trumps—apparently frustrating popular will. Besides the case of the 2000 presidential election, there is also the presidential election

Shugart, Matthew Soberg. "The American Process of Selecting A President: A Comparative Perspective," *Presidential Studies Quarterly*, vol. 34:3, 2004, pp. 632–655. Reprinted with permission of Blackwell Publishing LTD.

*Author's Note: I am grateful to Marty Wattenberg for comments, Mark Jones for assistance locating information on Latin American primary elections, and Mónica Pachón-Buitrago for research assistance. I maintain responsibility for any errors.

of 1888. (Most readers will know that the 1876 election is always cited as a third example, but in actuality it is not obvious that the 1876 election counts as an Electoral College "misfire"—little-known scholarly reanalysis of the contested outcomes in Florida, Louisiana, and South Carolina has shown that Rutherford B. Hayes probably won the popular vote in these contested states.) Perhaps, though, the Electoral College should not be assessed by its failure rate (roughly 4 percent since the 12th Amendment to the Constitution) but rather by its success rate (roughly 96 percent) over two hundred years of presidential elections.

Nonetheless, there seems to be another signal weakness in the Electoral College, namely (as Shugart points out) vulnerability to "spoilers." That weakness raises a troublesome possibility, namely, that a major political party can finance a spoiler who will siphon off just enough of the opposition's strength to cost that opposition candidate the election. A full analysis of such vulnerability requires a consideration, however, of the high cost of ballot access. Only billionaire candidates, such as Ross Perot, can pay that cost.

Then there is the issue of whether there is any evidence in such a case of coordination between the supposed "spoiler" and one of the major party candidates. Perot may have undercut George H. W. Bush's reelection in 1992—but there is no evidence at all that the Clinton presidential campaign coordinated its strategy with Perot's campaign. All of the evidence shows that Perot was motivated by sincere public spirit and a large ego. Neither is there any evidence that the Bush presidential campaign coordinated with Ralph Nader in 2000 to block Al Gore from succeeding President Clinton. There too the explanation for Nader's role is to be found in his sincere purpose and strong personality. In short, while the possibility of a grand strategy of voter manipulation would seem to be facilitated by the Electoral College, it has so far remained just that, a possibility—which is an interesting puzzle for you to ponder for what it says about American politicians.

• • •

THE UNITED STATES was the first country to have a chief executive selected through an electoral process distinct from the election of legislators. Despite the absence to this date of a constitutional mandate for states to hold popular elections for presidential electors, by early in the nineteenth century nearly all states did so. In the two centuries since, many more countries have implemented popular elections for a president. France in 1848 was probably the next example, although French presidential elections soon thereafter became indirect again until 1965. In the second half of the nineteenth century and in the early twentieth century, nearly all countries of Latin America established popular presidential elections, and in more recent decades the number of countries with such elections has grown immensely.

The United States may have started the trend toward popular presidential election, but in more recent times it has fallen behind worldwide trends in the methods by which those elections are conducted. The United States has continued to use its electoral college, while elsewhere the trend has been unmistakably toward methods that are not only popular (voters allowed to vote for presidential candidates) but direct (popular voting is decisive and final). Indirect methods raise the possibility that one candidate could win the popular vote yet not be selected president, as happened in 2000 in the United States. In the world today, the only other country in which such an outcome could occur is Bolivia.

In addition to the trend toward direct election, there is also a trend in the decision rules away from the plurality method, because of that method's vulnerability to so-called spoilers. A spoiler is a candidate with no realistic chance of winning the election outright, but whose presence in the race may affect which of the other candidates does win, by siphoning votes disproportionately from one of those other candidates. To guard against spoilers, while simultaneously permitting a wide range of partisan options to participate in the campaign for president, more and more countries are adopting runoff procedures. The U.S. use of an electoral college, in which the electors are chosen by plurality (usually statewide) stands against these two trends.

In a third trend, on the other hand, the United States has been the pacesetter. More and more countries are joining the United States by using primary elections to select parties' presidential nominees. Interestingly, however, even in this one area where the United States is ahead of the curve in presidential selection methods, it still retains features not found elsewhere that mirror the general-election process. First, primaries are indirect, whereby voters select party convention delegates rather than decisively determine the nominee. Second, like the electoral college, primaries take place on a state-by-state basis—in this case, spread out over time rather than on a single date. No country in the world uses a similar set of rules in its primary elections.

Before turning to the variety of election methods used elsewhere in the world, and how U.S. methods compare, let us first turn to some theoretical considerations regarding executive elections. To do so, we need to consider variations in the nature of the office being elected, as not all popularly elected presidencies are clear analogues to the U.S. presidency within their respective political systems. We also need to ask ourselves, what is the purpose of having an elected national executive, particularly in a federal system, with all the emphasis such systems put on preserving the (constitutionally delimited) sovereignty of sub-national governments?

TYPES OF PRESIDENCIES

In parliamentary systems, the head of government depends on the majority in parliament to obtain and maintain power, and the head of state may be a hereditary monarch or a largely ceremonial president, often selected by parliament and rarely by popular election. In what I shall term "pure" presidential systems, on the other hand, the roles of head of state and head of government are combined into one office selected separately from the legislature. Thus, executive power does not depend on the composition of the legislature, and may even be held by a party opposed to the legislative majority—a possibility, conventionally known as "divided government" in the United States, that is ruled out in parliamentary systems.

However, not all countries that hold presidential elections can be considered pure presidential systems (Shugart and Carey 1992). In the Fifth Republic of France, for example, there is an elected presidency in the role of head of state, but there is also a prime minister who heads the government and is accountable to the majority in the National Assembly, just as in parliamentary systems. In France, then, the possibility of a head of government opposed by the legislative majority is ruled out, but the possibility of a president and prime minister of different parties—known as "cohabitation"—is a very real possibility, and has been common since first occurring in 1986. The French president is, of course, no mere ceremonial figure, but rather is a major partisan player in French politics, and has the right to dissolve parliament and call new elections (once per year at most), among other powers.

Thus, whether in the form of pure presidentialism as in the United States or the hybrid form seen in France, the presence of popular election for a non-ceremonial presidency raises the possibility that the president and the legislative majority may be of different political tendencies. In fact, that is one of the principal theoretical justifications for having a presidency in the first place. Legislatures may be fragmented by multiple political parties, as in France, for example, or by regional divisions, as in many federal systems, including the United States. The presidency in such a context may serve to counter the fragmentation of legislative elections by creating a single national office whose occupant is chosen by the people. Some political scientists see the separation of the elected executive from other sources of authority in the polity as a potential advantage (for a review, see Shugart and Carey 1992), while others see it as fraught with perils that endanger effective governance or even democracy itself (Linz 1994). I shall not enter into this debate here. Rather, my purpose is to note that this idea of the chief executive being distinct from the legislative parties and the states of a federation implies that the president is the people's agent in the government formation and policy-making processes.

If the purpose of executive election is to counter the potentially disaggregating effects of legislative and sub-national competition, then it follows that presidential selection processes should be *bipolarizing* and *nationalizing*. By bipolarizing, I mean an electoral process that encourages high "identifiability" of executive choice (Strom 1990; Huber and Powell 1994; Shugart 2001). Unlike a legislature, particularly one elected by proportional representation, a presidency is almost always held by a single person,[1] and thus is an indivisible prize, and is elected to a fixed term. There is only one president at a time, and his or her term of office is constitutionally established, rather than subject to changes in the balance of power in the legislature. Thus, it is probably desirable that the election process promote broad popular support for the president's election, ideally a majority. It is probably also desirable that the election process produce two major alternatives, to clarify choices for voters and thus enhance identifiability. The bipolarization of presidential elections may even reshape a fragmented legislative party system into two blocs, as in France after the initiation of direct presidential elections in 1965 (Duverger 1986, 80–82). Several more recently established democracies have emulated the French model of direct elections of the presidency as a counterweight to legislative fragmentation, including Portugal after 1976 and Poland after 1990.

The second criterion that promotes the presidency as a counterweight to the disaggregating tendencies that sometimes result from legislative elections and especially from federalism is nationalization. For instance, legislative elections under some electoral systems tend to focus competition around local issues or legislators' personal attention to constituents, which may inhibit the articulation of broader national issues in legislative elections. This effect is often magnified in federal systems including the United States. The national election of a chief executive is a potential counter to such localizing effects because it generates competition around large national issues such as the economy and national security. If the nationalization of competition for the presidency is a desirable feature, then it is

---

[1] Rare exceptions include the multiperson-elected executive council of Bosnia-Herzegovina, and similar models being debated for Iraq.

probably also desirable for presidential elections to be conducted in such a way as to promote articulation of national issues rather than local concerns.

It is worth noting that it is a *normative* statement to claim that bipolarization and nationalization are desirable features of presidential elections. It is just as plausible to construct an alternative argument that limiting bipolarizing and nationalizing tendencies is desirable. In a multiparty system with a diverse ideological spectrum, it may be argued that it is advantageous to encourage the president to have support in the legislative party system to attain or retain office. Thus, ratification by the legislature may be a requirement for gaining the office, or a legislative majority may be empowered to remove the elected executive and call new elections. Few countries have followed such procedures, although Bolivia currently requires and Chile formerly required legislative assent for a president to take office (except in the rare case of a popular vote majority), while Finland formerly used an electoral college in which representatives of its many political parties assembled to elect the president. Israel briefly provided for a directly elected prime minister who needed to maintain parliamentary confidence, thus bypassing the fragmented parliament in the selection of the head of government, but requiring that the prime minister have partisan support to remain in office.

Similarly, in a regionally diverse federation, it may be desirable to ensure that presidents do not overlook those very regional differences, and hence the election process may be designed to ensure that local preferences are injected into the selection of the executive. Few countries have gone this route, although it does provide a normative justification for the electoral college in the United States (Best 1975),[2] and formerly in Argentina. Without settling these normative debates—which really have no right or wrong answer—I would simply observe two points. First, the logic of injecting legislators or sub-national interests into executive selection or retention of office is a distinctly "counter-presidentialist" argument, in that it seeks to restrain the inherent tendency of electoral competition for a single indivisible national leadership to promote bipolar and nationalized competition. Second, whatever the logic of the argument for restraining those tendencies, the empirical trend worldwide is clearly against imposing such restraints on the election of presidents, as we shall see next.

PRESIDENTIAL ELECTION METHODS AROUND THE WORLD

In order to consider trends in executive-election methods, we need to establish what sorts of methods promote bipolarizing and nationalizing effects: (1) an election method that encourages a face-off between two major contenders, and (2) direct election.

The most reliable way to ensure a two-candidate face-off is, of course, to mandate it. No democratic system would legally restrict the field of competitors to two. Thus, the most common way to promote bipolarization is to restrict a *second round* to the two competitors with the most votes in a preliminary round. Thus, the majority/runoff method is widespread in the election of presidents. This method is not without its problems. For instance, the two-round procedure may

---

[2] Although, interestingly, not the normative justification that the Founders themselves gave in the Federalist Papers. They were more concerned about the lack of nationally known politicians at the time, and thus fearful of having multiple regional candidates.

encourage candidates to enter the first round even if they have no realistic chance of winning, but rather to show their support and bargain with one of the leaders in advance of the second round (Shugart and Taagepera 1994).

Occasionally, the incentives of candidates to enter the first round of a two-round election may produce highly aberrant results, such as in France in 2002, when the far-right candidate, Jean Marie Le Pen, qualified for the runoff against the mainstream conservative, Jacques Chirac. This left French voters with a clear choice, but for most it was no choice at all, because the entire left of the spectrum was excluded from the runoff, because none of its several candidates finished in the top two. In an effort to encourage more bipolarization in the *first* round, some countries have turned to *qualified plurality* methods, similar to that first proposed by Shugart and Taagepera (1994).[3] Under such rules, a candidate can win in the first round with less than a majority, provided he or she has some stipulated lead over the closest challenger. The intent is to discourage fragmentation in the first round, by making the probability of a runoff depend not on whether any candidate obtains over 50 percent of the votes, but rather on the closeness of the race. At the same time, the intent of qualified plurality rules is to prevent the very high risk of spoilers in single-round plurality elections. Qualified plurality rules have been adopted since 1995 in Argentine, Ecuadorian, and Nicaraguan general presidential elections, and in Uruguayan primaries.

Some presidential elections, including those in the United States, are indirect. Two alternatives exist: election by the legislature or election by an electoral college. Pure legislative selection, with no popular voting, is clearly in a different category, and is, in any event, very rare for politically important presidencies. Combined methods have been used, however, whereby there is an initial popular election, followed by a "runoff" in the legislature (possibly involving more than the top two candidates) in the event there is no candidate with a popular-vote majority. Selection by an electoral college implies a process of popular voting, but instead of these votes being decisive, they are aggregated by districts or states, and electors make the final decision. An election settled in the legislature or an electoral college retains influence, possibly decisive, for political parties and/or representatives of sub-national interests in the selection of a president.

In Table 1, we see 23 countries that elect a politically powerful presidency. The cases are disaggregated by those in which the president is the head of government (without a prime minister or with one who is clearly subordinate), as in the United States, and those hybrid systems in which there is a prime minister who is accountable to parliament.[4] The countries shown all have populations over three million and have held competitive elections since some time around 1990, if not longer. The table indicates the current rules used to elect the president, as well as rules used previously. Several of these countries have recently re-inaugurated a democratic period after an authoritarian interlude, or have adopted new constitutions or executive-election procedures within an ongoing democracy. Thirteen countries—all of those with an entry in the column for previous rules—either have adopted a new constitution or have changed their executive-selection procedure since around 1990. When we compare the previous to the new rules, the

---

[3] I owe the term "qualified plurality" to Colomer (forthcoming).

[4] One could quibble about whether the prime ministers in Russia and Taiwan can be effectively held accountable by parliamentary majorities, or whether these systems really belong with the (pure) presidential systems.

TABLE 1
Presidential Election Methods

Country	Current Rules (and Date Adopted)	Previous Rules, if Applicable
Presidential systems (president as head of government, no prime minister, or prime minister agent of president)		
Argentina	1995: Qualified plurality[a]/runoff[b]	1983–89: Electoral college (federalist)
Bolivia	1993: Majority/congress (from top 2)	1985: Majority/congress (from top 3)
Brazil	1989: Majority/runoff	1945–61: Plurality
Chile	1989: Majority/runoff	1925–70: Majority/congress (from top 2)
Colombia	1994: Majority/runoff	1958–90: Plurality
Costa Rica	1948: 40%/runoff	—
Dominican	1996: Majority/runoff	1966–94: Plurality
Rep. Ecuador	1998: Qualified plurality[c]/runoff	1948–60: Plurality
		1979: Majority/runoff
Honduras	1980: Plurality[d]	—
Korea, South	1987: Plurality	—
Mexico	1994: Plurality	—
Nicaragua	1995: Qualified plurality[e]/runoff	1990: Plurality
Philippines	1992: Plurality	1946: Plurality
United States	1790: Electoral college (federalist)	—
Uruguay	1999: Majority/runoff	1984–94: Double simultaneous plurality[f]
Venezuela	2000: Plurality	1958–98: Plurality
Hybrid systems (president politically important, but prime minister accountable to parliament)		
Finland	1994: Majority/runoff	1925–82: Electoral college (partisan)
		1988: Majority/electoral college (partisan)
France	1965: Majority/runoff	—
Poland	1990: Majority/runoff	—
Portugal	1976: Majority/runoff	—
Romania	1990: Majority/runoff	—
Russia	1993: Majority/runoff	—
Taiwan	1996: Majority/runoff	1990: Electoral college (partisan)

[a] Forty-five percent is sufficient for election, or 40 percent with at least a ten percentage-point lead over the runner-up.

[b] When a slash is used, the criterion to the left is that required in a preliminary round of direct popular voting. The criterion to the right is how a final result is obtained if the initial criterion is not met in the first round. "Runoff" means a second round of popular voting involving the top two candidates from the first round. "Congress" means the legislature decides, by majority vote (from the indicated number of leading candidates in the first round); "electoral college" means electors are elected on the same ballot on which voters vote for presidential candidates, and the electors assemble to elect a president only if the popular-vote criterion is not met.

[c] Forty percent is sufficient provided that the runner-up is at least ten percentage points behind.

[d] One election (1985) was held under double simultaneous plurality (see note on Uruguay).

[e] Forty percent is sufficient for election, or 35 percent with at least a five percentage-point lead over the runner-up.

[f] Winner is candidate with the plurality within the party whose candidates collectively held the plurality.

trend is unmistakable: Six countries have shifted to a runoff method, after a prior period of using plurality: Brazil, Colombia, the Dominican Republic, Ecuador, Nicaragua, and Uruguay.[5] Only two countries, the Philippines and Venezuela, that adopted a new constitution after a previous democratic period stayed with plurality rule.[6] Most new presidential democracies in the last three decades have opted for majority runoff. Clearly, single-shot winner-take-all methods, which are vulnerable to spoilers, are falling out of favor.

Table 1 also includes six countries that have used partly or fully indirect methods. Chile formerly required congress to select from the top two candidates in the event that there was no popular majority. The (in)famous election of socialist Salvador Allende in Chile in 1970 was carried out under this procedure. Allende won a narrow plurality of the popular vote, but this vote was not decisive. Congress was legally empowered to choose the conservative runner-up, but selected Allende after first requiring him to sign a Statute of Constitutional Guarantees that, in retrospect, was a portent of the deep lack of trust among political forces in Chile that would eventually precipitate the coup in 1973 and usher in the dictatorship of General Augusto Pinochet (Valenzuela 1978). After Pinochet's defeat in a plebiscite on granting him a new eight-year term in 1988, Chile returned to democracy, this time with direct election via majority/runoff.

Argentina, Finland, and Taiwan have all recently abolished electoral colleges, leaving the United States with the world's last electoral college to select a president who is either head of government or otherwise possesses significant political powers.[7] These electoral colleges varied in the way in which they were constructed. Argentina's, like that of the United States, was "federalist," in that it weighted the representation of states (provinces in Argentina) in the electoral college such that smaller states were over-represented relative to their share of the national population. Those of Finland and Taiwan were "partisan," in that they were elected much like their countries' respective legislatures. Candidates for elector campaigned as individuals as well as representatives of a party promoting a specific presidential candidate, and the electoral college assembled and was empowered to take multiple ballots, if necessary, to produce a winner.

Contrast these partisan electoral colleges with the federalist procedure used in the United States, whereby the electors assemble only in their respective state capitals and transmit their result to the federal capital, thereby giving states a role in presidential selection, but avoiding deliberation among electors at the national level. If there is no majority, a contingent-election procedure devolves upon the House of Representatives. When this happens, the House selects from the top

---

[5] Uruguay—and Honduras in 1985—formerly used an unusual variant of plurality in which a party could present more than one candidate, and pool its votes. The winner would be the candidate with the most votes within the party whose various candidates combined had the most votes, whether or not that candidate had the most votes of all candidates individually.

[6] Mexico has so far stayed with the plurality rule that it has used since 1917, under single-party hegemony prior to 1988.

[7] Some parliamentary systems continue to use an electoral college to select their head of state—for instance, Germany, India, and Italy. However, these electoral colleges are distinct in two senses. First, electors are selected *ex officio*, rather than popularly elected, in that they are national or state legislators or delegates of local council members. Second, the president they are selecting is clearly a less important figure than the prime minister. An electoral college comprised of delegates primarily selected by local councils was employed in France in the Fourth Republic, and initially under the Fifth Republic, until Charles DeGaulle held and won a referendum converting his post into a directly elected one (see Pierce 1995, 8).

three electoral-vote winners, with each state delegation casting a single vote—a further federalist aspect to U.S. presidential selection rules. Broadly, these procedures (except for the one state, one vote requirement if the Congress must settle an election) were followed in Argentina, as well.

Indirect methods are clearly on their way out. Whereas there previously were six such examples out of the 23 countries shown in Table 1, now there are only two: Bolivia and the United States. Except for these two countries, recent reforms have replaced indirect procedures with direct popular voting, always with a provision for a runoff to protect against spoilers. Argentina uses a "qualified plurality," meant to strike a balance between plurality and majority/runoff methods. The others use two-round majority.

In Bolivia, the selection method remains indirect, but no longer may congress select the second runner-up in the popular vote. In 1989, the third-place finisher in the popular vote had been selected, and this event helped generate momentum to restricting congress's choice to the top two, as has been the case since 1994 (Mayorga 2001). Given Bolivia's extreme fragmentation—Gonzalo Sánchez de Losada was selected by congress in 2002 after having won a plurality of just 22.5% of the popular vote—the idea of direct election remains on the agenda as a way to promote bipolarization of political competition. Sánchez de Losada's perceived illegitimacy, due to his low popular vote and the political deals that got him into power, contributed to a popular rebellion that forced his resignation in 2003.

This discussion has highlighted two trends in presidential elections worldwide. The first is the movement away from methods that are vulnerable to minor-party spoiler effects.[8] The second trend is the movement away from indirect methods. Notably, this trend is observed even in federal systems. Argentina is a federal system in which an electoral college was abolished. Russia is a vast federation—much larger territorially than the United States and with many of its sub-national units serving as homelands for distinct ethnic groups—but apparently an electoral college was not seriously considered after the fall of the Soviet Union. Other large federal systems such as Brazil and Mexico have long practiced direct election.[9] Thus, the United States stands against both trends—using plurality rule to select electors to an indirect-election procedure even as third-party and independent candidates (i.e., potential spoilers) have arisen in importance in recent years. I shall now elaborate on these points more fully.

REGIONALISM AND MULTIPARTISM:
THE ROLE OF THE ELECTORAL COLLEGE
AND PLURALITY RULE

When viewed through a comparative lens, perhaps the most striking effect of the U.S. process of electing a president is the extent to which it regionalizes the contest. For instance, media commentary in advance of the 2004 presidential election routinely refers to the "red states" and the "blue states," meaning those that are

---

[8] Avoiding such outcomes is clearly the motivation behind the adoption of runoff provisions. In several of the countries that have left behind the single-round plurality method—notably Colombia, the Dominican Republic, and Uruguay—the change was preceded by decreasing dominance of the two largest parties.

[9] An electoral college established in Brazil under military rule (1964–1985) was abolished after a series of *Diretas ja!* (direct [elections] now!) mass protests in the late 1980s.

likely to give their entire slate of electoral votes to the Democrat or Republican, regardless of the margin of victory. A small number of states is likely to be decisive in any given election year, as relatively small swings of the popular vote in a few states can shift the outcome in the electoral college and hence determine the presidency. Under a direct-election procedure, attention would be unlikely to focus on swing states (and, within them, crucial voting blocs), because the goal would be to win a national plurality (or majority or qualified plurality, depending on the rules), rather than to amass a majority of electoral votes. However, it is not the electoral college alone that is responsible for this regionalization, but the fact that nearly all states give their entire electoral-vote contingent to one candidate, with the winner determined by plurality. For instance, if electors were awarded proportionally,[10] small vote shifts in specific states would be much less decisive in the final outcome.

OVER- AND UNDERREPRESENTATION OF STATES IN THE ELECTORAL COLLEGE

In the United States, the electoral-vote winner may not be the popular-vote winner because the percentage of electoral votes in each state is only roughly proportional to the population of the state. No state has less than three electoral votes, or about 0.56 percent of the total, because each state has a number of electoral votes equal to its representation in the House and Senate combined. Some of the states that have just three electoral votes have far less than 0.56 percent of the national population, with the greatest discrepancy being that for Wyoming (0.18 percent of the population).

We can calculate an *advantage ratio* for each state by simply dividing its share of the total electoral vote by its share of the national population. These ratios range from about 0.85 for California and Texas to 3.18 for Wyoming. In other words, California's weight in electing a president is only 85% of its contribution to the national population, while Wyoming's is more than three times as great as its population. Figure 1 plots each state's advantage ratio against its population (based on population estimates from 2002 and the electoral college apportionment that will be effective in 2004 and 2008). It shows very clearly how the smallest states are significantly overrepresented. Only states with around five million population have an electoral college weight about equal to their share of the population. There are 13 states with an advantage ratio greater than 1.5. Together, these states hold 4.7 percent of the population, but cast 9.1 percent of the electoral votes.

This lack of proportionality of state representation is magnified by the winner-take-all electoral rule. A close state may turn out to give the decisive margin of electoral votes to a candidate without that candidate's having obtained the nationwide plurality. Of course, this is what happened in 2000, when the razor-thin and judicially contested margin in Florida resulted in that state's 25 electoral

---

[10] It is sometimes said that two states award their electors proportionally, but this is incorrect. In Maine and Nebraska, two electoral votes are awarded to the candidate who wins the statewide plurality, and the others are awarded to the winner of the plurality in each congressional district. This is not proportional representation (PR). For instance, in Maine in 1992, Bill Clinton won all four electoral votes, despite winning well under 50% of the votes. With PR, Clinton would have won two electors, and George H. W. Bush and H. Ross Perot would have won one each.

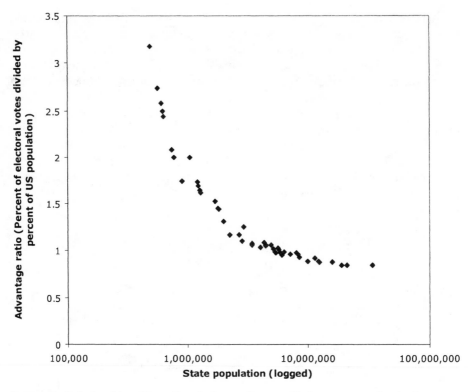

FIGURE 1. Relationship of State Population to Over- or Underrepresentation in the Electoral College

votes all being awarded to George W. Bush, while Al Gore had the uncontested plurality of the nationwide popular vote. Given the outcome in the remainder of the 50 contests (49 states, plus the District of Columbia), it just happened that Gore needed only three additional electoral votes to obtain the presidency, while Bush needed 24 to win. Florida would award all of its 25 electoral votes to the candidate who was determined to have won the plurality of votes in the state.

Thus, given the winner-take-all rule, the stakes in Florida were vastly higher than they would have been in a direct vote—Florida's disputed popular vote would not have altered the outcome in such an election. It is worth noting that close state-level outcomes would have far less impact if the electoral votes of a state were allocated by almost any other method aside from winner-take-all plurality. As noted earlier, three other countries have used an electoral college to select a politically powerful president in recent decades—Argentina, Finland, and Taiwan. However, the United States is unique among these in its use of winner take all (plurality). Argentina, although emulating the federalist allocation of electoral votes to its provinces in its former electoral college, used proportional representation to allocate each province's electors among the candidates. This proportionality somewhat mitigated the very high malapportionment of the electoral college itself. While the smallest provinces were more overrepresented in Argentina than are the smallest states in the United States, no province could deliver its entire voting weight to one candidate. Finland and Taiwan elected presidential electors in districts whose proportion of electors more closely matched their proportion of the national population, and, like Argentina, did not use plurality to allocate those electors. Thus, the U.S. electoral college, uniquely, is doubly disproportional—states are given a weight that typically does not correspond to their share of the population, and the winning candidate obtains 100% of a state's electoral vote regardless of his margin of victory.

This dual disproportionality is especially magnified in the case of a close election or an election with a prominent independent or third-party challenger. While no candidate other than the Democrat or Republican has won a single electoral vote since George Wallace won 46 (of 538) in 1968,[11] the votes won by minor candidates may have been important in other cases as potential spoilers. Because the elections were not close between the Democrat and Republican, the 1992 and 1996 outcomes were probably not affected by H. Ross Perot's voting support in any state, though the presence of Perot and the absence of a popular-vote runoff surely undermined the legitimacy of Clinton's two victories in the eyes of his opponents. The extremely close 2000 election, which reversed the popular-vote plurality, undermined his legitimacy in the eyes of a different segment of the electorate. It is worth reiterating that these sorts of election outcomes are *inherent in the use of plurality voting and indirect election*. Plurality voting—the rule used at the state level in U.S. presidential elections—implies that some winners will obtain less than half the votes. Indirect election—the electoral college—implies that sometimes the president will not have won the most popular votes.

By now the story of the election contest in Florida in 2000 is well known, but most of the popular commentary on the election almost ignored other states in which razor-thin pluralities were critical to the electoral-vote margin. Although more than 96 percent of the national popular vote was cast for either Gore or Bush, the electoral college magnified the impact of minor candidates in some states. As discussed earlier, countries that use direct popular voting to determine the winner often employ second rounds to eliminate the so-called spoiler effect. In the 2000 U.S. election, the minor candidates did not change the popular-vote outcome. Gore won a nationwide plurality in spite of the presence in the race of Green Party candidate Ralph Nader to Gore's left. Yet Nader's presence in the race may have affected the outcome, both by tipping Florida and maybe New Hampshire to Bush as well as by shifting Gore's optimal ideological position further left to avoid losing votes to Nader (Magee 2003). The votes of a minor conservative candidate, Patrick Buchanan of the Reform Party, would not have been sufficient to give Bush the national plurality (nor, according to Magee, did Buchanan affect Bush's optimal ideological position). Nonetheless, it is possible that even Buchanan—who won less than half a percent of the national vote—could have tipped Iowa, New Mexico, or Oregon to Gore (given the presence also of Nader in these states).[12]

Gore was three electoral votes short of victory while Florida hung in the balance. New Hampshire awarded its four electoral votes to Bush, who won the state by less than two percentage points, while Nader won almost 4 percent of the state's votes. There is some possibility that Nader was a spoiler in New Hampshire (Magee 2003), a state that could have given the presidency to Gore regardless of the outcome in Florida.

---

[11] Perot narrowly missed winning one elector in Maine in 1992.

[12] If Bush had won any one of these closely fought states where Buchanan was stronger than he was nationally, Bush would not have needed Florida, just as Gore would not have needed Florida had he won New Hampshire, which was one of Nader's strongest states.

It is a fallacy to assume that all of the votes won by any candidate beyond the leading two would have gone to just one of the major candidates had the additional candidate been out of the race. Any additional candidate is likely to bring in some voters who would otherwise sit the race out, and such a candidate exploits dimensions of policy that are distinct from those articulated by the major candidates. This latter factor means that each of the major candidates would pick up some of a third-party candidate's voters were that candidate to drop out. For instance, Magee (2003) conducts simulations based on survey data and concludes that Gore would have received 32 percent to 40 percent of Nader's vote and Bush 14 percent to 17 percent, with the remainder to abstention or other minor candidates.

The point is not that we can know who would win in the absence of entrants other than the two main parties' candidates. In fact, the point is precisely that *we cannot know*, and this is the reason that more and more countries have incorporated runoff provisions into the process of electing presidents via a direct vote: to enhance the legitimacy of the eventual winner by preventing the election of candidates who might have been opposed by a majority.

Thus, the electoral college in the United States, with its overrepresentation of smaller states and its winner-take-all allocation of electoral votes, magnifies the impact of closeness and of third parties. During the tense standoff over the Florida outcome in 2000, many commentators suggested that a nationwide vote would be even more conflict-ridden in the case of a very close election and potential recount of the result. However, in assessing that argument it is worth recalling that this was the closest presidential election in U.S. history, yet the popular vote margin was still over 540,000 votes. While this was only about half a percent of the vote, even the decisive vote swing reflected by that result is far greater than the votes that did in fact determine the margin. Bush's final margin in Florida, 537 votes, was 0.009 percent of that state's votes, and 0.0005 percent of the national votes. (The New Hampshire margin, at 1.27 percent of that state's votes, was 0.007 percent of the national votes.)

In the next section, I explore whether the impact of third parties and regionalized plurality voting in the 2000 presidential election is likely to have been unique, or whether an incipient multipartism in American elections might suggest that it could become the norm in elections that are closely fought between the major parties.

WAS THE IMPACT OF MINOR PARTIES IN 2000 A HARBINGER OR AN ABERRATION?

The impact of state-level competition and winner-take-all rules is magnified when the number of competitors is greater than two. In plurality contests, the impact of potential spoilers is magnified, especially if a third-party or independent candidate has greater strength in some closely fought states than he or she has nationally. This is particularly significant if recent trends in U.S. elections—both presidential and congressional—can be interpreted as heralding a long-term presence of minor parties in U.S. elections. If 2000 was an aberration—not only in the sense of a razor-thin margin and judicial intervention, but also in the impact of minor-party candidates—then discussion of alternative election methods is unlikely to advance. On the other hand, if 2000 was a harbinger of a rising prominence of minor parties in shaping national election outcomes, the prospects might increase that the United States would join the worldwide trend in adopting methods to guard against spoilers.

To the extent that the literature has addressed the potential for a third-party breakthrough in U.S. politics, it has done so almost exclusively through analysis of voter attitudes in presidential elections in which third-party or independent candidates have done better than the norm (Abramson et al. 2000; Gold 1995). The standard of third-party "success" has tended to be whether or not the larger-than-normal surge in votes for a third-party or independent candidate heralds a potential for a new party to displace one of the major parties (e.g., Sundquist 1983). However, another way to approach the question is from the standpoint of congressional elections, and with an eye not to whether one of the two major parties will be displaced, but whether they will both be joined by new parties. A close examination suggests that they already have been, and that this could impact presidential elections again in the future, given the rules used in the United States.

This question is relevant to placing the U.S. method of presidential selection in comparative perspective precisely because the congressional party system has been so much less responsive to third-party and independent presidential candidates in the past, but appears to have become more so recently, since 1992. In other presidential systems, multiple presidential candidates are the norm. That is one of the reasons for the trend noted above toward runoff methods. Additionally, in other presidential systems, it is the norm for a slate of congressional candidates associated with non-major presidential candidates to perform better in legislative than in presidential voting. In other words, while voters may be somewhat less likely to vote for a presidential candidate with no realistic chance of winning, they are more likely to support an allied legislative slate. Not so in the United States, where third parties typically poll far better in the presidential contest. In fact, as Abramson et al. (2000) note, John Anderson in 1980 and Ross Perot in 1992 did not even run with affiliated congressional candidates. George Wallace in 1968 did so only in his home state of Alabama.

Apparently the barriers against minor parties are greater in the United States in congressional than in presidential elections. However, there is some evidence that this may have changed recently, as third-party voting in House elections rose substantially in the 1990s. Figure 2 shows the percentage of votes won by third parties and independents in House, Senate, and presidential elections over time. House elections are probably the best indicator of trends in third-party voting because the greater number of contests means they are less subject to the effects of specific popular candidates than either presidential or Senate elections. As the figure shows, the third-party vote in presidential elections has bounced around a lot from election to election. In the House, on the other hand, no election from 1950 to 1988 saw more than 2.5 percent of the votes won by third parties, and then every election since 1990 has been above 4 percent. Senate elections have shown some past volatility from election to election, but appear to have tracked the rise in third-party voting in the House rather closely since 1992.[13]

It is unlikely that this rise in minor-party voting signals a demise of either of the major parties—Sundquist's standard for third-party success. On the other hand, it could signal a greater volatility in presidential election outcomes, given the use of plurality voting and indirect election. If third parties gain (or have gained already) a toehold, even with no prospects of winning the presidency, their impact could

---

[13] Data were not available for some Senate elections before 1956.

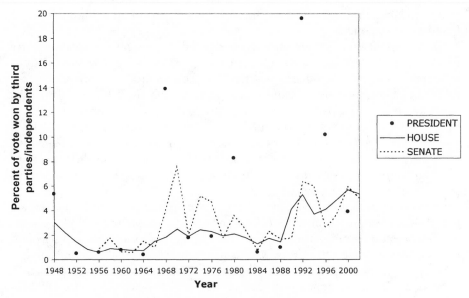

FIGURE 2. Third-Party Voting in U.S. Elections, 1948-2002
Source: Reports by the Clerk of the U.S. House of representatives. Available from
http://clerk.house.gov/members/electionInfo/elections.html.

increase, given U.S. presidential-election rules. Let us look at the data displayed in Figure 2 more closely, and consider their implications for future presidential elections.

Whether there is an upward trend in presidential elections is hard to ascertain, given that third-party voting has been subject to short-term spikes in past decades, notably in the single elections of 1968 and 1980. The high percentage in 1992 and 1996 is, of course, partly explicable by two campaigns of one very rich man, Ross Perot. However, even in 2000, without Perot, third-party voting in both chambers of Congress increased over the 1998 midterm election. Moreover, the rise in third-party voting for the House predates Perot's first candidacy, as can be seen by the spike in 1990.

Third-party congressional, and particularly House, voting has been less volatile. For instance, the Wallace and Anderson campaigns were associated with no noticeable upward tick in the House. As I alluded to above, in most presidential systems, third parties tend to perform better in legislative than in presidential elections. Largely, that can be explained by the use of proportional representation in most countries' congressional elections, which encourages even nonviable presidential candidates to run with slates of candidates for congressional elections. However, a notable change takes place in the 1992 U.S. elections. Third-party voting ticks upward in both houses of Congress to over 5 percent of the vote in each house, despite the absence of any congressional candidates explicitly running with Perot. In no election from 1948 through 1990 had the third-party share in the House been even half as high, and in only two Senate elections (1970 and 1974) had the third-party share exceeded 5 percent. McWilliams (1993) offers a partial explanation. Perot's voters were more likely to be critical of their member of Congress than supporters of either Bush or Clinton; yet, as Figure 2 shows, the spike in House voting actually began in 1990. The recent growth in third-party voting is large, by U.S. standards, and it is surprising that the political science literature has had little or nothing to say about it.

Of course, the flipside of third-party voting increasing is the likely absence of any party having over 50 percent of the vote. Indeed, in three consecutive elections (1996, 1998, and 2000), no party won a majority of the House vote.[14] Prior to 1996, the last time even two consecutive elections had failed to produce a majority of the votes for one party in the House was 1950–1952. Three or more consecutive occurrences of this phenomenon had not happened since 1908–1916.

These trends in third-party House voting are most important, at least for our purposes, in what they might indicate for future presidential elections. That third-party voting has not fully subsided to pre-1990 levels in the six subsequent congressional elections suggests it might not be a mere short-term effect. In the 1994 election, in which Republicans took control of Congress, third-party voting dropped substantially in the House—probably because the *Contract with America* appealed to some voters who had been voting for third parties out of protest. It did not drop much in the Senate, however, and even in the House remained well above its pre-1990 levels.

Third-party voting rose again from 1996—coincident with Perot's second presidential campaign—to 2000. In the latter year, it may have been fueled by minor-party presidential candidates actually (and unusually) running with parties that nominated candidates for some down-ballot offices: Pat Buchanan with the (Perot-launched) Reform Party and Ralph Nader with the Green Party. In fact, in 2000, third-party voting was actually higher in both houses of Congress than it was in the presidential election, unlike in the other presidential elections since 1948 in which the third-party share of the presidential vote exceeded 2 percent. Thus, 2000 was more similar to other presidential systems with multiparty competition, where third parties almost always perform better in congressional than in presidential contests.

These numbers hardly suggest a crash of the American two-party system, and 2004 or 2006 could see a return to "normal," just as have previous elections after periods of increased third-party voting. However, combined with the close division of the nation between Republican and Democrat, even a small rise in the presence of minor parties can inject unpredictability into the relationship between the popular vote for the presidency and the electoral college outcome. Given the use of plurality rule to allocate electors, and the overrepresentation of smaller states, even a very small party nationally can be a spoiler in a presidential election.

We have seen that the U.S. method of electing a president is unique. While some of its features have been employed elsewhere, the U.S. process is distinctive in several respects. The United States is now the only country that elects a politically powerful presidency via an electoral college, and one of only two in which a candidate can become president without having obtained the highest number of votes in the sole or final round of popular voting (the other such country being Bolivia). The U.S. electoral college regionalizes the contest of presidential elections, all the more so because of the use of winner-take-all allocation of almost

[14] Moreover, the Federal Election Commission's data show that the plurality was reversed in the 2000 House elections just as it was in the presidential election: Democrats won more votes than Republicans, yet Republicans won the majority of seats. Other sources disagree, and given that there is no central electoral-data agency in the United States (yet another way in which U.S. elections differ from probably all other countries!), we cannot say for sure. All sources seem to agree that Republicans did not win a majority of votes.

every state's electors. At a time when most other countries have shifted toward rules meant to reduce the "spoiler" problem, U.S. presidential elections continue to be vulnerable to spoilers. Now, let us turn our attention to the process that comes before the final election of a president, the selection of parties' nominees.

PRESIDENTIAL NOMINATION PROCESSES

Up to now, my focus has been entirely on general elections. Now I turn the spotlight on the selection of the major parties' candidates. Here is where the United States has been no laggard behind worldwide trends, but rather has been the pacesetter. Long before any other country adopted popular voting to select party nominees for the presidency (or any other office), the United States established its system of primary voting.[15] Several other countries in recent years have likewise adopted primaries, to the extent that we can say that there is a trend toward increasing participation of voters in selecting nominees. However, even in this area in which the United States is the trendsetter, elements of the contrary nature of U.S. election methods are to be found. For, while the United States permits voters to take part in nominations, the process mirrors general-election rules in its indirect and regionalized nature.

The U.S. presidential nomination process is indirect because primaries select convention delegates—a partial analogue to the electors in the general-election phase.[16] Additionally, there remains no national vote in the primary process, but rather a sequence of state-level contests (often and increasingly with groups of states voting on a common day) that inevitably gives greater weight to voters in some states than in others.

By contrast, other countries that have held presidential primaries have generally done so in a direct national vote. An exception to the directness of the process can be found in some primaries in Costa Rica, where voters have elected delegates to party conventions much as in the United States. However, the most recent primaries, in 2001, were direct. A partial exception to the nationalization of the primary process was found in Mexico's then-ruling Institutional Revolutionary Party (PRI) in 1999. In that case, the election was held on the same day throughout the country, but the decision rule was that the candidate who won pluralities in the most congressional districts would be the party's nominee, even if that candidate did not have the plurality of the national popular vote. Because congressional districts are drawn to equalize population but not necessarily PRI voters across districts, this process effectively gave greater weight to localities where the party was weaker relative to other parties. Given that the party was going to face a tough general-election battle, a process that encouraged candidates to reach out to voters outside the party's strongest congressional districts may have assisted the nomination of a more appealing candidate over the candidate of the traditional party machinery. As it turned out, the winner of the most congressional districts also had the most votes nationwide—and then lost the general election.

[15] I will ignore the caucus system employed in some states, notably Iowa. To my knowledge, there is nothing comparable outside the United States.

[16] One difference is that the party conventions allocate states' voting power more proportionally than does the electoral college (proportionate to votes for the respective party's presidential candidate in the state in past elections). The convention delegates further differ from presidential electors in that they are deliberative, at least in principle.

TABLE 2
Countries and Parties That Have Held Primaries in Latin America

Country	Parties and Dates	Status
Argentina	FREPASO (1994) FREPASO-UCR (1999)	Party-administered
Bolivia	MNR (1999), MIR (1999)	State-administered, party option
Chile	Concertación alliance (1993, 1999, 2001)	Party-administered, direct
Colombia	Liberal Party (1990, 1994, 2002)	State-administered
Costa Rica	National Liberation and Social Christian Parties (2001)	State-administered
Mexico	PRI (1999)	Party-administered; winner was candidate with a plurality of votes in a plurality of congressional districts
Uruguay	All parties (1999)	State-administered, constitutionally mandated; if no candidate obtains a qualified plurality in a party primary (40% with at least a 10% lead), a concurrently elected party convention decides the nominee

Note: Decision rule is direct vote decided by national plurality of votes cast in the respective party's primary, unless otherwise noted.

Source: Adapted from Freidenberg and Sánchez López (2002); additional detail on Uruguay provided by Mark P. Jones (personal communication).

Presidential primaries are being adopted in increasing numbers of countries in Latin America (Alcántara Sáez n.d.; De Luca, Jones, and Tula n.d.). There have been no presidential primaries outside of the Americas, to my knowledge. Before 1993, no country in Latin America other than Costa Rica (Sánchez n.d.) had opened up the selection of presidential candidates (or delegates who select the nominee) to voters. Since 1993, as Table 2 shows, at least one primary has been held in six additional countries of the region. Unlike the earlier Costa Rican and 1999 Mexican examples cited above, and unlike the United States, these are national and direct elections, with one partial exception. In Uruguay, if a candidate obtains a majority of the votes cast in the respective party primary, that candidate is elected outright. Additionally, if there is no majority but a qualified plurality is met—at least 40 percent of the vote with at least a ten percentage-point lead over the closest rival—the leading candidate is elected outright. If neither the majority nor qualified plurality is met, then a convention decides, with the delegates having been elected pledged to the various candidates in proportion to their votes.[17]

In some cases, presidential primaries are required by the constitution or national electoral law, and are administered by the national electoral authorities. In other cases, they are administered by the party. A similar variation in administration is found among U.S. states, with most states that hold primaries having them administered by a state agency, but a few are party administered (e.g., South

[17] With the exception of the qualified-plurality clause, this is essentially the hybrid direct/indirect method Finland used in 1988, only applied within parties, rather than in the general election.

Carolina). There is some variation in Latin America similar to that found in U.S. states in whether a primary is "open" to any registered voter, or "closed" to those who have not registered in advance their preference for the specific party. For instance, in Colombia and Chile, there is no registration of voters by party, so primaries are necessarily open. In Argentina, voters may indicate a party preference when they register to vote, and some parties have held closed primaries, some open, and still others "semi-open," where unaffiliated voters may participate, but not voters registered with other parties (see De Luca, Jones, and Tula 2002).[18]

In all of the direct primaries, with the exception of Uruguay, the election is decided by a plurality of votes. Of course, the risk of that decision rule is that in a multicandidate field, the nominee may not be the majority choice of the party's voters. So far, no country or party has adopted a popular runoff, such as exists for non-presidential primaries in some U.S. states (mainly in the South). Perhaps a trend toward runoffs will develop in primaries if they become more competitive, just as runoffs have been increasingly adopted in general elections as they have come to feature more candidates. However, a look at some data will suggest a simple reason for why there are no runoff provisions in Latin American presidential primaries: There has been no need for them.

To explore the degree of fragmentation in primary elections, it is best to use a widely accepted indicator of party-system fragmentation: the "effective" number of parties (N). This index is actually just a weighted average of party sizes, where the weighting is by their own size: Each party's vote share is squared, and then these squares are summed. The index is the reciprocal of this sum. For instance, if there are two parties that equally split the vote, N = 2.00. If one of the parties grows at the expense of the other, such that their vote shares are 65–35, N should decrease to reflect the reduced competitiveness. Indeed it does, as N = 1.83. Now suppose instead that one of two equal-sized parties splits into two equal-sized fragments, such that we have 50–25–25. Now, N must rise, because we have a more fragmented system.[19] Indeed, we get 2.67. More generally, N will thus indicate the extent to which we have two-party (or two-candidate) competition (N = 2.0), or the extent of fragmentation (if N is much greater than 2.0).

Table 3 shows the results of calculating effective N on candidates' vote shares in 17 presidential primaries held in six countries in Latin America since 1989. The average over these elections has been 2.06, signifying that competition has tended to be quite bipolar. The effective number has not been greater than 2.8 in any of them. With such a strong tendency toward bipolar competition in primaries, the spoiler problem has tended not to be present. While the number of cases is too small and the extant literature too thin to draw firm conclusions, it could be that contests for nominations determined via a national primary tend to be less fragmented than general elections because of intraparty bandwagoning effects. In other words, as the primary draws near, groups within the party may tend to bet on one or the other of the two leading candidates, while other potential challengers for the nomination drop out. A similar phenomenon is some-

[18] In some other countries, some parties have held selection processes open to their enrolled memberships, but if the party organization itself controls the roll, the implication is that the party can choose to limit the breadth of popular participation. Thus, these processes are potentially much more closed than the closed (state-administered) primaries of some U.S. states.

[19] The largest party is, of course, more dominant, but this constellation of parties is clearly farther from two-partisan.

TABLE 3
Effective Number of Candidates in Presidential Primary Elections, Latin America

Country	Party	Year	N
Argentina	PJ	1989	1.99
Argentina	UCR	1989	1.24
Argentina	Frepaso	1995	2.00
Argentina	UCR	1995	1.83
Argentina	Alianza	1999	1.85
Chile	Concertación	1999	1.69
Colombia	PL	1990	2.83
Costa Rica	PUSC	2001	1.63
Costa Rica	PLN	2001	2.52
Costa Rica	PLN	1985	1.93
Costa Rica	PLN	1989	2.12
Costa Rica	PLN	1993	2.63
Costa Rica	PLN	1997	2.30
Mexico	PRI	1999	2.27
Uruguay	EP-FA	1999	1.40
Uruguay	PC	1999	2.01
Uruguay	PN	1999	2.81
Mean			2.06

Note: Data were not available for all primaries listed in Table 2.

what less likely to happen in general elections, even when plurality rule is used, because separate parties seek to maintain their identity—including a presence in the legislature—and to differentiate themselves from one another. Separate campaigns within a party, on the other hand, tend to agree on the desirability of unifying around their shared party label, whatever their specific differences about the party's priorities.

In the United States, on the other hand, the primary season often starts out with far more fragmented fields of candidates than does the typical Latin American presidential primary. Over time, the field tends to consolidate and two leading contenders emerge. This trend can be captured by a look at two states that have voted at opposite ends of the primary-election sequence. New Hampshire has traditionally held the first primary, usually in February.[20] California has held its primary much later. Prior to 1996, it was in June, on one of the last days of primary voting. Since 1996, it has been in March, but even so, it has been effectively the last day of the race, often with the final serious challenger dropping out a day or two afterward. Thus, comparing these two primaries, as in Table 4, shows the considerable degree of fragmentation at the beginning, and the winnowing that takes place later on. In nine contested primaries since 1984, the average effective number of candidates in the New Hampshire presidential primary has been 3.73, while in California it has been 2.13. In New Hampshire it has been as high as 4.98 (Democratic, 1992) and never lower than 2.20 (Democratic, 2000). In California, on the other hand, the most fragmented primary in this period had an effective

[20] In 2004, it was in late January, as New Hampshire responded to other states' "front-loading" and moved its primary to an earlier date to preserve its privileged position.

TABLE 4
Effective Number of Presidential Candidates in New Hampshire
and California Presidential Primaries, 1984–2004

Year	Party	NH	CA
1984	Democrat	4.15	3.20
1988	Democrat	4.57	2.02
	Republican	3.83	2.02
1992	Democrat	4.98	2.54
	Republican	2.40	1.67
1996	Republican	4.73	2.08
2000	Democrat	2.20	1.44
	Republican	2.87	2.04
2004	Democrat	3.88	2.18
Average		3.73	2.13

number of candidates of 3.20 (Democratic, 1984), still (an effective) half a candidate below New Hampshire's average.

The likely cause for this early fragmentation, followed by consolidation, lies in the sequential nature of the U.S. presidential primary process. Far from being a single-shot contest, U.S. primaries are spread over a period ranging from several weeks to several months. In recent primary election seasons, there has been a marked tendency for shortening the period in which the majority of states conduct their primaries,[21] but the United States continues to stand out for the regionalized nature of its presidential primaries, with some (mostly smaller) states voting early in the process when there are more candidates in the running. Other (including the largest) states vote later, when the field has already been winnowed.

Ironically, given the lack of spoiler-protection rules in U.S. general elections for the presidency, the U.S. presidential primary process contains at least two forms of protection. First of all, the nondecisive nature of any given day of primary voting, up until some candidate has clinched the nomination, means that there are always opportunities for voters in later states to assess the field and make strategic shifts of support from trailing candidates to more viable candidates. That is, bandwagoning may occur after voting has started. Of course, this has the drawback of meaning that voters in earlier states lack the opportunity to transfer their votes from a trailing candidate to one who is revealed, only after subsequent contests, to have a better chance. Additionally, voters in later-voting states, which have always included many of the largest states, lack the opportunity to help shape the field. A candidate who may have proven viable in a larger, later-voting state, may have already been eliminated early in the process.

Another way in which the U.S. process contains protection against spoilers is in the use of proportional representation to elect delegates to the party nominating conventions that formally choose the nominee. For the Democratic Party previously and at present for the Republican Party, many states have awarded all their delegates to the candidate with the plurality in the state, much like the electoral

[21] For an overview of the change in the primary schedule over the years through 2000, see Cook (2000).

college. However, the Democratic Party now uses proportional representation (PR) in all states, and Republicans use PR in some states.[22] Thus, while Americans often tend to view PR as foreign and complex, in fact, a large percentage of the voters who have voted in presidential primary elections in recent cycles have voted in PR elections, perhaps without even realizing it.[23] PR means that even candidates who trail the frontrunners can win delegates, and thus potentially remain viable for future contests where they may have greater strength.

The U.S. presidential candidate nomination process thus stands out from those used elsewhere, not so much by its use of primaries—which are no longer unique to the United States—but due to its indirect and regionalized nature. Of course, these are the same features that stand out about the general-election process in the United States, so we could say that the primary process mirrors that of the general election in critical respects. Indeed, the primaries are even more indirect and regionalized than is the general election. It is more indirect in that party convention delegates, unlike electors, can deliberate on the choice of candidate if no candidate has obtained a majority. However, the concept of the "brokered" convention now seems a quaint historical phenomenon, remembered and even longed for by many a pundit, but unlikely to recur. Nonetheless, presidential primaries in the United States remain indirect, because they elect delegates, who formally select the nominee. In fact, they could not be direct, as long as the process continues to be regionalized as it is now, with the sequence of elections in different states. Because there is no single day on which all voters who wish to take part in their party's nomination are summoned to the polls, the mediation of delegates is necessary, to have some counting mechanism that bridges the separate contests and ultimately ties them together to determine a winner.

The sequential process inevitably means some states weigh more heavily than others. Moreover, the sequential state primaries encourage candidates to visit states one by one and speak to specific concerns of voter blocs that are important in those states. Like the consideration of direct versus indirect general elections, discussed above, whether this is seen as an advantage or drawback to the process is largely a matter of taste. However, what we can say as a matter of fact is that the way primaries are conducted in the United States largely prevents bipolarization of the contest (by keeping multiple candidates within a party viable at least for a time, especially if they have regionally concentrated support) and restrains nationalization (because there is no single national contest). In this respect, the U.S. presidential nomination process contains counter-presidentialist features, inhibiting both identifiability (especially for voters in early contests) and perhaps also reducing the relative attention to national issues, as opposed to issues of importance to blocs of party voters in key states.

[22] For a general discussion of the allocation methods used in the Republican Party, see Republican National Committee (2000).

[23] Often there is a high threshold, typically 15 percent, much higher than is found in any country that uses PR to elect its legislature. Still, above the threshold, a candidate's share of the delegates will closely reflect its share of the "effective" votes (those cast for all candidates who clear the threshold). Some states apply PR at the level of their congressional districts, from which multiple delegates are elected. Only rarely, for example in New York, do voters vote for delegates by name. That is, the method used in most states is what the electoral systems literature refers to as "closed list," whereby the voter simply selects the candidate (or, in other countries' legislative elections, party). The slate of delegates and the order in which they will be elected is predetermined by the candidate's (party's) campaign organization.

CONCLUSIONS

We have seen that the United States uses a series of procedures for selecting its president that is distinctive from those used elsewhere. If we conceive of the role of a presidency to be transcending political divisions that are articulated in congressional and state electoral processes and facilitating the articulation of nationally oriented campaigns, then the U.S. presidency actually performs this function less than those of other countries probably do, and less than if the rules were changed. Whereas most countries that elect presidents have moved toward direct voting with the possibility of a popular runoff, the United States retains an indirect electoral college, even as three consecutive presidents have won less than a majority of the votes and one did not win the national plurality. It is possible that recent trends in both presidential and congressional voting could signal a more permanent presence of third parties in the system. If so, it is likely that future presidents could face doubts about their legitimacy in the eyes of a large portion of the electorate, and it is likely that third-party spoilers may affect outcomes.

Despite falling behind worldwide trends toward nationalization and spoiler protection in general elections, the United States has been the worldwide leader in promoting voter participation in the process of selecting its parties' presidential nominees. Only recently have many other countries begun to implement primaries. Even here, though, the United States uses methods that are distinctly different from elsewhere. The process of presidential nomination is highly regionalized due to the state-by-state primary calendar, and the initial field of candidates is often far more fragmented than in primaries elsewhere.

In the various ways in which the United States differs from other countries, it is not necessarily the case that U.S. methods are inferior. That is a normative matter. However, if we accept the basic "presidentialist" premise that a politically powerful president should be supported by a majority (or close to it, and not less than a plurality) and should represent the nation at large, then the U.S. procedures would seem to fall short. It is possible that the United States could ultimately follow worldwide trends—for example, by abolishing the electoral college—and the prospects of such a development would probably rise if third parties and close elections raise doubts about other election outcomes over the next decade or so. It is also possible that the United States could one day adopt a national primary. However, at the moment, it is hard to imagine the United States remaining anything other than idiosyncratic in the way it chooses the most powerful political leader in the world.

REFERENCES

Abramson, Paul R., John H. Aldrich, Philip Paolino, and David W. Rohde. 2000. Challenges to the American two-party system: Evidence from the 1968, 1980, 1992, and 1996 presidential elections. *Political Research Quarterly* 53 (3): 495–522.

Alcántara Sáez, Manuel, n.d. Experimentos de democracia interna: Las primarias de partidos en America Latina. Unpublished.

Best, Judith. 1975. *The case against direct election of the president: A defense of the electoral college.* Ithaca, NY: Cornell University Press.

Colomer, Josep M. Forthcoming. The Americas: General overview. In *Handbook of electoral system choice,* edited by Josep M. Colomer. London: Palgrave.

Cook, Rhodes. 2000. *Race for the presidency: Winning the 2000 nomination.* Washington, DC: Congressional Quarterly Press.

De Luca, Miguel, Mark P. Jones, and María Inés Tula. 2002. Back rooms or ballot boxes? Candidate nomination in Argentina. *Comparative Political Studies* 35 (4): 413–36.

De Luca, Miguel, Mark P. Jones, and María Inés Tula. n.d. Partidos políticos, sistema de partidos y selección de candidatos en la Argentina (1983–2001). Unpublished.

Duverger, Maurice. 1986. Duverger's law: Forty years later. In *Electoral laws and their political consequences*, edited by Bernard Grofman and Arend Lijphart. New York: Agathon Press.

Freidenberg, Flavia, and Francisco Sánchez López. 2002. ¿Cómo se elige un candidato a presidente? Reglas prácticas en los partidos políticos de América Latina. *Revista de Estudios Políticos* 118: 321–61.

Gold, Howard J. 1995. Third party voting in presidential elections: A study of Perot, Anderson, and Wallace. *Political Research Quarterly* 48 (4): 751–73.

Huber, J. D., and G. B. Powell, Jr. 1994. Congruence between citizens and policymakers in two visions of liberal democracy. *World Politics* 46 (3): 291–326.

Linz, Juan J. 1994. Democracy, presidential or parliamentary: Does it make a difference? In *The failure of presidential democracy*, edited by Juan J. Linz and Arturo Valenzuela. Baltimore: Johns Hopkins University Press.

Magee, Christopher S. P. 2003. Third-party candidates and the 2000 presidential election. *Social Science Quarterly* 84 (3): 574–95.

Mayorga, Rene. 2001. Electoral reform in Bolivia: Origins of the mixed-member proportional system. In *Mixed-member electoral systems: The best of both worlds?* Edited by Matthew Soberg Shugart and Martin P. Wattenberg. Oxford: Oxford University Press.

McWilliams, Wilson Carey. 1993. The meaning of the election. In *The election of 1992*, edited by Gerald Pomper. Chatham, NJ: Chatham House.

Pierce, Roy. 1995. *Choosing the chief: Presidential elections in France and the United States*. Ann Arbor: University of Michigan Press.

Republican National Committee. 2000. Nominating future presidents. Report commissioned on behalf of the Republican National Committee: Advisory Commission on the Presidential Nomination Process.

Sánchez, Fernando F. n.d. The twilight of a predominant party: Institutional crisis of the Partido Liberación Nacional in Costa Rica. Unpublished.

Shugart, Matthew Soberg. 2001. "Extreme" electoral systems and the appeal of the mixed-member alternative." In *Mixed-member electoral systems: The best of both worlds?* Edited by Matthew Soberg Shugart and Martin P. Wattenberg. Oxford: Oxford University Press.

Shugart, Matthew Soberg, and John M. Carey. 1992. *Presidents and assemblies: Constitutional design and electoral dynamics*. New York: Cambridge University Press.

Shugart, Matthew Soberg, and Rein Taagepera. 1994. Majority versus plurality election of presidents: A proposal for a "double complement rule." *Comparative Political Studies* 27 (3): 323–48.

Strom, K. 1990. *Minority government and majority rule*. Cambridge: Cambridge University Press.

Sundquist, James L. 1983. *Dynamics of the party system: Alignment and realignment of political parties in the United States*. Washington, DC: Brookings Institution.

Valenzuela, Arturo. 1978. *The breakdown of democratic regimes: Chile*. Baltimore: Johns Hopkins University Press.

26

SENDING THEM A MESSAGE—GETTING A REPLY: PRESIDENTIAL ELECTIONS AND DEMOCRATIC ACCOUNTABILITY

Kay Lehman Schlozman
Sidney Verba*

What do election results mean? The simple and enormously interesting answer provided by this article is that an election outcome means what important people say it means. The actual election results by themselves communicate nothing about what was at stake, why the winner won and the loser lost, and what voters had on their minds when they voted. Certain kinds of candidates exist, Schlozman and Verba note, and certain kinds of voters also exist. Plug the two together and all you get are two columns of numbers that have to be interpreted and given meaning.

The imperative of determining electoral meaning is built into "government by discussion" (to recall the conceptualization of Kinder and Herzog). Discussion, talking, debating, and communication pervade the electoral process, and they also permeate the post-election assessment among all those who participated. However, the democratic requirement of imputing content and significance to election results does not mean that "anything goes"— that is, that any possible (and therefore some unreasonable) construction of a presidential election's results will emerge and become accepted wisdom among members of Congress, editorial boards, officials of party organizations, columnists and talking heads, and ultimately voters. Winners and losers, indeed all sides, look to the same sources of information for interpreting results: the exit polls, unusual and unexpected results (for example, whether states that had long voted for one party surprisingly switched to the other), the size of the margin, the state of the economy, whether or not America is at war or peace, and whether it was "time for a change," (i.e. whether the party holding the presidency was seeking a third term or not).

A modified version of Deborah Stone's concept of "causal stories" applies, in other words—in the sense that there will be competing causal stories (or "narratives" if you like that term better) about what happened and why. Such discursive competition is disciplined by the common availability of the same facts about the election context. Moreover, post-election debate is a familiar kind of democratic discussion with which the country has had long, indeed unbroken experience. Americans have been at the business of

Originally published in *Elections in America*, ed. Kay Lehman Schlozman (Winchester, MA: Allen and Unwin, 1987). Reprinted courtesy of the Trustees of Boston College.

*We wrote this essay in the summer of 1985. Were we to start from scratch today, we would surely produce a somewhat different essay—one that updated the examples and acknowledged such significant changes in American opinions on policy matters and their partisan commitments. Still, we stand by the underlying concepts.

explaining what elections mean for over two hundred years—an instance, to borrow again from Kinder and Herzog, of a Deweyan "contingent social practice."

• • •

THERE HAVE BEEN MANY INTERPRETATIONS of the part played by elections in popular government. Elections have been viewed as a legitimating institution, functioning to give elected leaders the wherewithal to govern. Alternatively, they have been construed as a republican institution, functioning as a mechanism for choosing meritorious individuals in whom to entrust governmental power. Our concern is with the election as a democratic institution, particularly with the way in which American presidential elections serve as an agency by which an incumbent president is held accountable to the public. That is, our concern is to understand whether and how presidential elections give voters a meaningful opportunity to render the president responsive to their wishes and to make judgments about his conduct in office.

To consider the election as an instrument of accountability requires making a link between the analysis of the behavior of citizens and the analysis of the behavior of presidents. Political scientists have attempted to make this connection in various ways. Students of elections study the consequences for the presidency of the nature of the electoral process. For example, there has been much concern with the impact on the nature and quality of presidential candidates of the recent changes in presidential nominating procedures and campaigning.[1] Conversely, students of the presidency deal with the reaction of the president to the public: his attempts to monitor and manipulate public opinion, as well as the relationship between his behavior in office and public preferences, public expectations, and the promises he has made in the past.[2]

In the vast literature on presidential elections and presidential behavior, however, concern with citizens usually is kept separate from concern with incumbents. Works on voting and elections focus on the behavior of individual voters and the aggregate electorate, presenting alternative perspectives on voting behavior— whether it is rational or not, policy oriented or not, party dominated or not, prospective or retrospective—and on the factors that influence shifts in the voting preferences of the electorate as a whole. The literature on the presidency deals with the way in which decisions are made in office, the role of presidential style and personality, the structure of the presidential office, the relations between the president and the rest of the Washington community. The link between the behavior of the electorate and the behavior of the president is less often considered.

[1] See, for instance, Byron F. Shafer, *Quiet Revolution* (New York: Russell Sage Foundation, 1983; and Nelson W. Polsby, *Consequences of Party Reform* (New York: Oxford University Press, 1983). Many of the issues are summarized and extensive bibliographic citations are contained in Robert E. DiClerico and Eric M. Uslaner, *Few Are Chosen* (New York: McGraw-Hill, 1984), chaps. 1–3, 6.

[2] Benjamin I. Page and Robert Y. Shapiro have analyzed the relationship between public opinion and presidential policy in "The Effects of Public Opinion on Policy." *American Political Science Review* 77 (1983): 1071–1089, and in "Presidents as Opinion Leaders—Some New Evidence," *Policy Studies Journal* 12 (1984): 649–661. For a comprehensive account of the way presidents have been "going public" more frequently recently in order to increase their influence in Washington—an approach that requires careful monitoring and manipulation of public opinion—see Samuel Kernell, Going Public (Washington D.C.: CQ Press, 1986). For an analysis of the relationship between presidential performance and the promises made in a campaign, see Jeff Fishel, *Presidents and Promises* (Washington, D.C.: CQ Press, 1985), esp. chaps. 2 and 7.

Our purpose is to attempt such a link: to see how well the various models of electoral behavior articulate with what we know of presidential behavior. In so doing, we add neither new research nor new data. Instead, we use existing research on the American electorate and on presidential behavior to see how well the two bodies of research hold together. And, as we see, the fit is imperfect. There is a disjunction across three levels of analysis—the individual voter, the electorate in the aggregate, and the president—in terms of which of several models commands the greatest explanatory power. The electoral model that best fits the behavior of the individual voter does not fit the behavior of the electorate as a whole. And incumbents behave in ways that do not fit either model neatly. In trying to solve the puzzle of this disjunction, we hope to shed light not only on political science literature on elections but on the substance of political representation in the United States.

MODELS OF VOTERS AND MODELS OF INCUMBENTS

Let us begin by suggesting three models of voter behavior and three corresponding models of presidential behavior that might help to illuminate various ways in which elections can function to facilitate presidential accountability. We can delineate three kinds of voters: policy voters, retrospective voters, and "Michigan" voters;[3] and three parallel kinds of incumbents: instructed delegates, nervous performers, and trustees. We propose these categories as ideal types in order to clarify the electoral links between voters and presidents, and do not wish to reify them. In short, we would not expect all presidents or all voters—or even any particular voter or particular president—to conform perfectly to a single type.

Our three types of voters are derived from the literature on voting. Because of our particular concern with the relationship between voters and incumbents, however, these categories do not correspond to any well-known typology. *Policy instruction voters* evaluate the policy alternatives presented to them in an election and choose that which best fits their policy preferences. Such prospective choices on policy matters are possible only when candidates or parties offer the electorate clearly identifiable options on the issues of greatest salience. Voters select from among these alternatives and choose a government committed to carrying out the promises made during the campaign. Voters retain control by refusing to reelect an incumbent party or candidate that has reneged on these promises or by changing allegiance to a challenging party or candidate that seems to offer a more attractive program.

This model is really a more generalized version of the party government model. The party government model involves clearly identifiable policy alternatives being presented by strong parties. Although the existence of such recognizable party programs may be necessary for elections to act as policy instruction mechanisms, we specify only that there be such clearly articulated choices, not that strong parties act as the vehicle. Policy instruction can take place under weak parties as long as parties or candidates offer voters comprehensible alternatives.

[3] We have searched unsuccessfully for an alternative, and more appropriate, designation for such voters. We use the quotation marks deliberately, to indicate our awareness that our use of the term reflects the caricature of the voter that often emerges in discussions of *The American Voter* (Angus Campbell, Philip E. Converse, Warren E. Miller, and Donald Stokes, *The American Voter* [New York: Wiley, 1960]). The portrait of the average voter contained in that work is painted with a much less broad brush than is often presumed to be the case.

Retrospective voters cast ballots on the basis of their evaluation of the performance of the incumbent candidate or party rather than on the basis of their preference for alternative programs. Dissatisfied retrospective voters exercise control by punishing the incumbent who fails to deliver—whose administration is characterized by foreign policy humiliation, political scandal, or economic sluggishness.[4] This is a form of constraint that is blunter, but no less potent, than that exercised by the policy voter. Unless the incumbent is running again or unless the incumbent's party has placed a successor candidate in the field, however, retrospective voters cannot hold the incumbent accountable in this way. Thus, retrospective voting depends on some continuity in the electoral system.

"Michigan" voters are the residual category. Concerned neither to choose among policy alternatives nor to render retrospective judgments, "Michigan" voters respond to any of a wide array of forces in making ballot choices: unstinting party loyalty that is not tied to issues, preference for the personal style or ethnicity of one of the candidates, persuasion by a friend, media coverage, and so on. While the ballot cast by each such voter is equal in weight to that cast by a retrospective or policy voter in the collective decision to retain the incumbent or his party, this type of voting is the loosest form of electoral constraint.

Analogous to these three kinds of voters are three categories of incumbents. These ideal types are derived from the normative theory of representation. Once again, however, we have juggled what are familiar categories by adding one for the incumbent whose actions reflect a concern with the constraint imposed by the retrospective voter. The *instructed delegate* is well known from the theory of representation. He construes his responsibilities as to reflect, insofar as possible, the wishes of the electorate. Such a conception of the representative role places distinct limits around the president's autonomy in governing, for he feels the need to be responsive to the specific policy preferences of the public. There is an additional requirement, however. In order to assume such a role a president needs detailed information about those preferences.

Like the instructed delegate, the nervous performer feels constrained by the public. Nevertheless, he strives to satisfy voters by governing effectively rather than by following their specific policy preferences. Although his actions are informed by a concern for his own, or his party's, success in the next election, he exercises much more discretion in governing than does the president who adopts the role of instructed delegate. The nervous performer will probably find it useful to monitor public satisfaction, but he will require much less precise information about citizen preferences than the instructed delegate. That is, it will be critical for him to know *that* the public wants something done, but much less important for him to know exactly *what*.

The trustee is also familiar from representation theory. Political observers from Burke to Schumpeter have argued that political leaders who seek to govern in the best interests of the public cannot be slavish in their devotion to the preferences of the public. Like the nervous performer, the trustee is guided by his own judgment in attempting to govern effectively. Unlike the nervous performer, he does not

[4] In applying their famous measure of the "levels of conceptualization," Campbell et al., (ibid., chap. 10) discussed those individuals who cited only the "nature of the times" in explaining their votes and cast ballots for or against a candidate because times were good or bad. Such voters, considered to be relatively apolitical in the original formulation, have been raised in status over the years so that we now recognize them as retrospective voters.

have his eye fixed on his own or his party's success in the next election. Because he does not feel constrained by the public, the trustee does not need information about either their policy preferences or their level of satisfaction.[5]

Implicit within our discussion of ideal-typical voters and presidents has been a concern with two dimensions central to electoral accountability—information and control. We have shown that all three kinds of voters retain ultimate control over the selection of political leaders, although they vary in the degree to which they seek to constrain the actions of the incumbent and to pressure him to respond to their preferences. Similarly, we have contrasted three kinds of incumbents in terms of the degree to which their behavior is guided by a desire to respond to such pressure and the level of information required for each representative role. We have not yet confronted the issue of how these various kinds of voters communicate what has animated their electoral choices and how the instructed delegate and nervous performer get the information they need.

THE VOTE AS A SOURCE OF INFORMATION

The policy instruction model—and to a lesser extent the retrospective model—of electoral control depend on the transmission of information to incumbents about the views of the public. To what extent can an election act as the vehicle of such information? We can differentiate the information communicated to political leaders by various participatory acts along two dimensions. The information about citizen preferences communicated by different modes of participation can be differentiated in terms of its bias: the degree to which it emanates from a representative group of citizens. It can also be distinguished with respect to its precision: the degree to which it provides a detailed guide to public preferences.

With respect to bias, voting, like all political acts, is not universal; in recent American presidential elections, nearly half the eligible electorate has failed to turn out. Furthermore, nonvoters are, at least in demographic terms, somewhat different from voters. Nonvoters are more likely to be of lower social status—to have less education, lower income, and less prestigious occupations, to be from minority and non-English-speaking groups—than voters.[6] What is more, compared with other democracies, voting in the United States is both less widespread and more stratified. That is, a smaller proportion of the eligible electorate actually goes to the polls, and there is a closer relationship between turnout and measures of social status in the United States than in other democracies.[7]

---

[5] The portrait is somewhat overdrawn. Trustees would still want information about public preferences if they needed to satisfy some of those preferences in order to remain in office to continue their trustee activities.

[6] The main causal variable appears to be education rather than other status characteristics. But that does not change the descriptive statement that poorer people and minorities are likely to be underrepresented among voters. See Raymond E. Wolfinger and Steven J. Rosenstone, *Who Votes?* (New Haven: Yale University Press, 1980).

[7] See Sidney Verba, Norman Nie, and Jae-on Kim, *Participation and Political Equality: A Seven-Nation Comparison* (New York: Cambridge University Press, 1979); and G. Bingham Powell, Jr., "American Voter Turnout in Comparative Perspective," *American Political Science Review* 80 (1986): 17–44. The reason why it is less stratified in other nations is not unrelated to the ease of voting. While voting is the easiest participatory act in the United States, it requires greater effort and resources than in democracies where registration requires less initiative (often being the responsibility of the government) and where strong political parties take a more important role in getting voters to the polls. Under such circumstances it may take more activation not to vote than to do so.

Even so, voting—the political act which requires the least initiative and investment of the fewest resources of money, information, and skill—is the most nearly universal.[8] In addition, since those who command few political resources are likely to vote if they participate at all, the relationship between participation and measures of socioeconomic status—income, education, and occupation—is lower for the vote than for any other participatory act. The electorate is much more representative of the population as a whole than is any other group of activists— letter writers, organization members, campaign donors, and so on. In short, in comparative terms voting is the most egalitarian form of political participation.

Ironically, although voting is the political activity that involves the most nearly representative group of citizens, in comparison with other forms of participation— particularly the direct expressions of opinion by individuals and groups—voting permits the conveyance of rather imprecise messages. Totally apart from the capacities of individual citizens and their propensity to use the incumbent's position on disarmament, his performance in office, his haircut, or his party affiliation as criteria in making electoral decisions, voting as an act clearly carries little information; in casting a ballot a single individual communicates only his or her secret preference for a particular candidate.[9]

Even if citizens are inclined to act as policy voters and to use issue positions as the only criterion in making vote choices, presidential elections, for several reasons, provide uncertain mandates and cannot be expected to supply to the instructed delegate the information he needs to govern.[10] First, the nature of governing undermines the election as an instrument for the communication of information about public preferences. The process of electing and the process of governing are very different. Elections involve intermittent choices; governing goes on continuously. New issues that did not even exist at the time of the campaign—the overthrow of a dictator in Haiti or the Philippines, the explosion of the space shuttle—arise all the time and demand presidential attention and judgment. Under such circumstances, even a certain electoral mandate provides the president who would be an instructed delegate with no guidance to popular opinion. In addition, even when issues are given a full airing during the campaign and even when the electoral returns give an indication of the public temper on various matters of policy concern, issues inevitably assume a very different form in the halls of government from what they were during the campaign. Even at their most elevated, the terms of election debate are necessarily general. In comparison, the terms of policy action are complex and nuanced. When policy is made, discussion of broad outlines gives way to discussion of the details that dictate the nature and extent of its impact. Proposals are refined and adjusted; there is bargaining

---

[8] Sidney Verba and Norman Nie, *Participation in America* (New York: Harper & Row, 1972), p. 31, show that, of the large number of political acts they study, voting is the only one in which more than half of the population engages.

[9] Students of elections know that there is more information in the ballot than this discussion implies. Sophisticated scholars can tease out information about public attitudes and preferences from patterns of voting: split-ticket voting, drop off, roll off, and ballot spoiling. Such information can tell a lot about the importance of partisanship in elections (split-ticket voting, drop off, roll off), the relative salience of various offices (roll off), and the degree of alienation (spoiled ballots.) See Walter Dean Burnham, "The Changing Shape of the American Political Universe," *American Political Science Review* 59 (1965): 7–28.

[10] A strong and well-reasoned statement of this position is contained in Nelson Polsby and Aaron Wildavsky, *Presidential Elections*, 6th ed. (New York: Scribner's, 1984), chap. 7.

and negotiation among many actors and lots of tinkering at the margin. Even an interpretable electoral mandate cannot be a source of cues when the discussion is at this level of specificity.

In addition, the American party system with its two relatively weak and undisciplined parties exacerbates the inability of electoral outcomes to transmit precise messages about public sentiment. Where parties are stronger, they tend both to reinforce a single fundamental cleavage, thus moderating competing conflicts, and to create an environment in which it is more difficult for candidates to obfuscate issues and for the media to treat national elections as sporting events. Where there are more parties, they can permute issues in multiple ways and thus offer citizens a wider variety of issue bundles.

In the United States, an agenda of citizen concerns that includes many issues of differential salience to various individuals is not easily accommodated by the dichotomous presidential vote choice. Not all the issues about which potential policy voters are concerned are necessarily discussed in a particular campaign. Voters who care deeply about an issue, say, abortion, may find that the major-party candidates offer no choice—because they take the same position or because they say nothing about it at all. Furthermore, if there are other issues of substantial concern—say, aid to the poor or competition from foreign imports—policy voters might find that the candidate who takes the preferred position on the first issue may adopt less congenial postures on the others. Under such circumstances, in choosing one candidate or the other, voters—individually and collectively—express very little about their policy concerns. Correspondingly, the victorious candidate cannot know whether he won because of (or in spite of) his stand on abortion, welfare reductions, or import restrictions—or because of his predecessor's performance in office or his photogenic smile. In short, on its own the electoral outcome does not permit the victor to discriminate among the policy, retrospective, and "Michigan" voters.[11]

OTHER SOURCES OF INFORMATION
ABOUT CITIZEN PREFERENCES

Of course, our argument about the inevitability of mandate uncertainty ignores the other ways in which an incumbent who is so inclined can gather information about popular attitudes. Political leaders, from the Turkish caliph who visited the bazaar in disguise to Ed Koch, who inquires incessantly how he is doing, have sought information about the public's frame of mind. Contemporary politicians have a tool that can give them information with a new level of precision and validity, the public opinion poll. Exit polls, which have large samples, an immediacy to the voting act, and the ability to include voters only, provide a particularly important mechanism for understanding the motivations of voters and their policy preferences.

---

[11] We should note that the existence of minor-party candidates does not obviate the problem. Minor-party candidates—for example, Strom Thurmond in 1948 and George Wallace in 1968—sometimes offer voters meaningful choices on policy issues and, thus, the opportunity to register their views. Nevertheless, the logic still applies: There may be no like-minded minor-party candidate; the minor-party candidate may adopt a congenial position on one issue, but an uncongenial stand on others; and so on. Hence, even when there is a minor-party option—and there is not always—mandate uncertainty remains.

As a source of information, polls are distinctive in that they are unbiased. Modern sampling techniques can guarantee within a specifiable margin of error that the opinions expressed in the poll are representative of the electorate as a whole. Polls are much more limited, however, when it comes to the precision of the information they contain. As our comments with respect to the contrast between the level of generality of public discourse about political issues and the level of specificity of the terms of policymaking should make clear, polls cannot provide the kind of detailed information needed when policy is being made. Their questions necessarily oversimplify policy choices and cannot deal with the complex contextual nature of policymaking. Futhermore, rival polls using different sampling techniques and different versions of questions often elicit different results. In consequence, although the meaning of a poll is probably less ambiguous than that of an electoral mandate, it still may be subject to alternative interpretations.

In view of these characteristics, poll results place a lower level of constraint on the president than do electoral results. Although an incumbent cannot ignore the electoral defeat that sweeps him from office, there is nothing to force the president to pay attention to the polls. Indeed, he has wide latitude in how he treats the results of public opinion polls: He can ignore them; he can read them in ways that suit his political or ideological purposes; he can consult them as a guide to public approval of his performance; or, if he wishes, he can use them to gain a much clearer picture of what is on the minds of voters than he can from the returns alone.

Direct contacts between citizens—especially such political elites as campaign activists, campaign contributors, and pressure group representatives—and the president or his aides constitute a second source of information about citizen preferences that can supplement an uncertain mandate, information that is in several ways well suited to the process of governing. First, while elections must occur at fixed intervals, there are no restrictions on the timing of direct communications. Hence they are more likely to coincide with the rhythms of policymaking and to provide guidance with respect to citizen views on subjects not contained on the campaign agenda at the time those issues are being considered. In addition, these communications permit the transmission of much more precise messages than are possible through voting, more precise even than the information contained in polls. One implication of this level of detail is that it is more difficult for the president to misread or read self-servingly such direct communications. At least individually, if not collectively, such messages are much less likely to be ambiguous—and, thus, amenable to alternative readings—than are either public opinion polls or electoral mandates.

Although the information derived from direct contacts—particularly direct contacts with political elites—is more precise than that contained in electoral mandates or even in polls, it is considerably more biased than the information derived from either of these two sources.[12] Those who engage in the forms of political activity demanding the highest levels of information, skill, contacts, and financial resources—writing letters, working in campaigns, making contributions, being active in organizations—are in critical ways less representative of the public at large than both those who turn out to vote and, especially, those who respond to polls. In part, the skew is socioeconomic: It is well known that political

[12] See E. E. Schattschneider, *The Semisovereign People* (New York: Holt, Rinehart and Winston, 1960), chap. 5.

activists are drawn from the ranks of those of high economic, educational, and occupational status.[13] However, the bias is ideological as well. Such activists are more likely than less involved voters to care intensely about particular, often quite narrow, policy matters and to have less moderate views.[14] Thus, the set of the messages conveyed by such political activists overrepresents not only the opinions of the socioeconomically advantaged but also points of view that are farther from the political center.

How much freedom the president and his advisers have in deciding whether to ignore or to pay attention to such direct communications is a complicated issue. Clearly, while such contacts yield much less ambiguous information than do electoral mandates, they do not carry the kind of ultimate consequences that give to elections their potential as mechanisms of democratic control. Only elections can deprive incumbents of office. Thus the president may often discount or disregard what he is told. Under certain circumstances, however, direct communications do constrain the president and his aides to listen to the messages being conveyed. Campaign activists, contributors, and representatives of large and powerful organizations command resources—among them, political and electoral support, contributions, and information—that the president needs if he is to make sound policy, govern effectively, and win reelection.[15] Not surprisingly, the president who values such assistance has an incentive to pay attention to those who provide it.

Our discussion leads to an ironic conclusion about the information conveyed to policymakers. Participatory acts vary in their difficulty and in the amount of information, skill, contacts, and money they demand. In general, the less exacting the form of participation, the more demographically and ideologically representative the group of participants. Voting is a relatively easy form of participation. It is also both the most nearly universal and representative. Nevertheless, the information conveyed by electoral outcomes, even elaborated by public opinion polls, is very imprecise. The more difficult forms of participation, on the contrary, afford activists with wider latitude for presenting detailed and complex arguments on policy matters. They are also characterized by more pronounced levels of ideological and socioeconomic skew. Thus, there is a built-in dynamic such that increasing amounts of information about public preferences are accompanied by increasing bias in its sources.

---

[13] See Verba and Nie, *Participation in America*, chaps. 8 and 12; and Lester W. Milbrath and M. L. Goel, *Political Participation*, 2d ed. (Chicago: Rand McNally, 1977), pp. 90–106. On the socioeconomic bias of pressure politics in particular, see Kay Lehman Schlozman and John T. Tierney, *Organized Interests and American Democracy* (New York: Harper & Row, 1986), esp. chaps. 4, 5, and 15.

[14] This generalization has found support in studies of various kinds of political activists. See, among others, Herbert McClosky, Paul J. Hoffman, and Rosemary O'Hara, "Issue Conflict and Consensus among Party Leaders and Followers," *American Political Science Review* 56 (1960): 406–429; Jeane Kirkpatrick, *The New Presidential Elite: Men and Women in National Politics* (New York: Russell Sage and Twentieth Century Fund, 1976); and Norman H. Nie, Sidney Verba and John R. Petrocik, *The Changing American Voter*, Enlarged Edition (Cambridge, Mass.: Harvard University Press, 1979), chap. 12.

[15] These political elites, particularly the organized interest representatives, mobilize certain resources— for example, honoraria, invitations on fact-finding trips, and future jobs—that are less important to the president than to legislative and state-level policymakers. On the degree to which organized interest activity constrains policymakers, see Schlozman and Tierney, *Organized Interests and American Democracy*, pp. 310–317, 323–330, 391–398.

EVALUATING THE MODELS

We have delineated several models of how voters might behave and how presidents might respond to them, and have indicated both the different levels of constraint imposed by various kinds of voters and the different levels of information required by presidents who construe their policy responsibilities in various ways. We have also discussed the limitations of the election as a medium of information to the incumbent who seeks information about public preferences. It is now appropriate to evaluate these models in terms of the actual behavior of voters and incumbents. In so doing, we distinguish the behavior of individual voters from that of the electorate taken in the aggregate, and distinguish both, in turn, from the response of the incumbents.

What Voters Do

We have delineated three types of voter: policy instruction voters, retrospective voters, and "Michigan" voters. Although few controversies have figured so importantly in American political science as that over the best explanation of the individual vote choice, support can be found for each mode of voting. The earliest studies of the vote painted a portrait of the model American voter as essentially impervious to policy concerns, not well informed about politics, and animated by habitual partisanship or the personal qualities of the candidate in making vote choices.[16]

Recent literature has placed more emphasis on the ability of the average voter to make politically relevant choices. But there has been considerable controversy among academic analysts of politics with respect to the degree to which such choices are based on specific forward-looking policy preferences and the degree to which they are retrospective evaluations of performance.[17] There is evidence that voters respond in ways that are consistent with the policy instruction model. Particularly when given a clear choice on an issue of salience, voters are likely to be able to state a policy preference, to understand reasonably accurately the difference between the candidates on the issue, and to vote for the proximate candidate.[18]

In addition, there is evidence that voters make retrospective judgments. They consider the performance of the incumbent administration and reward or punish

[16] The original statement of this point of view is contained in Campbell, Converse, Miller, and Stokes, *The American Voter.* For a later statement, see Philip E. Converse, "Public Opinion and Voting Behavior" in *The Handbook of Political Science,* ed. Fred Greenstein and Nelson Polsby (Reading, Mass.: Addison-Wesley, 1975), vol. 4, chap. 2.

[17] On the issue voting controversy, see the discussions and bibliographic references contained in Herbert B. Asher, "Voting Behavior Research in the 1980s: An Examination of Some Old and New Problem Areas," in *Political Science: The State of the Discipline,* ed. Ada Finifter (Washington, D.C.: American Political Science Association, 1983), pp. 339–368; Herbert Asher, *Presidential Elections and American Politics,* 3d ed. (Homewood, Ill.: Dorsey Press, 1984), chap. 4; and Richard G. Niemi and Herbert F. Weisberg, eds., *Controversies in Voting Behavior,* 2d ed. (Washington, D.C.: CQ Press, 1984), pt. A.II.

[18] See Nie, Verba, and Petrocik, *The Changing American Voter,* chaps. 17, 18, and 20. For a recent paper that provides clear evidence for issue voting, see Merrill Shanks and Warren Miller, "Policy Direction and Performance Evaluation: Complementary Explanations of the Reagan Elections," paper presented at the annual meeting of the American Political Science Association, New Orleans, September 1985.

that performance depending on whether they deem it successful.[19] It seems that they are especially likely to base their votes on such judgments when the performance of the previous administration has been perceived as outstanding—especially when it has been perceived as being outstandingly bad.[20] We should note that such judgments about governmental performance might rest on several bases—perceptions of foreign policy successes or failures, governmental efficiency or corruption, economic prosperity or downturn.[21] Perhaps because it is deemed more salient by voters and perhaps because it is least tied to particular episodes and thus easiest to measure on a sustained basis, analyses of retrospective voting tend to emphasize economic performance as the basis for judgments about the capability of those in office.[22] At the same, however, it is clear that the older view of the voter has not lost its relevance. Some voters are impervious to both policy and performance concerns and cast ballots on the basis of a variety of other concerns, particularly party loyalties and candidate appeal.

To summarize, evidence suggests that individual vote choices have multiple sources, among them policy preferences, retrospective evaluations, and a panoply of additional factors consistent with a "Michigan" model of the voter. For some voters, a single model of voting is appropriate. For others, a single model has explanatory power in one election, another model in the succeeding one. For some voters, however, a multidimensional explanation is needed because, for example, partisan loyalties or candidate preferences can interact with views on policy issues or contaminate judgments about the success of the incumbent. Of course, there is dispute about the relative weight that should be assigned to various determinants

[19] The classic statement is in V. O. Key, *The Responsible Electorate* (New York: Vintage, 1966). In *Retrospective Voting in American National Elections* (New Haven: Yale University Press, 1981), Morris Fiorina explores this concept in depth. For analyses of recent elections from this perspective, see D. Roderick Kiewiet and Douglas Rivers, "The Economic Basis of Reagan's Appeal," in *The New Direction in American Politics*, eds. John E. Chubb and Paul E. Peterson (Washington, D.C.: Brookings, 1985), chap. 3; and Douglas A. Hibbs, Jr., *The American Political Economy: Macroeconomics and Electoral Politics in the United States* (manuscript, 1985), chap. 7. For an evaluation of the elections literature that stresses the centrality of Key's insights, see Peter Natchez, *Images of Voting, Visions of Democracy* (New York: Basic Books, 1985).

[20] See Fiorina, *Retrospective Voting*. Shanks and Miller, "Policy Direction and Performance Evaluation," provide the most extensive analysis of the relative role of policy and performance voting in the 1980 and 1984 elections—and find both.

[21] Although most of the literature on retrospective voting deals with voter response to economic conditions, the model can be applied to performance evaluation in other areas. There is evidence that at various times during the Vietnam war, the public was divided on what policy the government ought to pursue, and that those policy preferences were rather loosely held. But the public was more strongly convinced that whatever was being done was inadequate and that some solution needed to be found. See the discussion of the role of Vietnam in the 1968 election in Verba and Nie, *Participation in America*, pp. 107–108.

[22] In making judgments about economic performance, retrospective voters who cast ballots on the basis of economic conditions seem to give more weight to their perceptions of national economic health than to their own personal economic circumstances. See Donald E. Kinder and D. Roderick Kiewiet, "Economic Discontent and Political Behavior: The Role of Personal Grievances and Collective Economic Judgments in Congressional Voting," *American Political Science Review* 23 (1979): 495–527; Kinder and Kiewiet, "Sociotropic Politics: The American Case," *British Journal of Political Science* 11 (1981): 129–161; Richard A. Brody and Paul M. Sniderman, "From Life Space to Polling Place," *British Journal of Political Science* 7 (1977): 337–360; Kay Lehman Schlozman and Sidney Verba, *Injury to Insult* (Cambridge, Mass: Harvard University Press, 1979), chap. 6; and Gerald Kramer, "The Ecological Fallacy Revisited: Aggregate versus Individual Level Findings on Economics and Elections, and Sociotropic Voting," *American Political Science Review* 77 (1983), 92–111.

of the vote. The relative effects of such factors seem to vary with the characteristics of the voters themselves, the nature of the choices they are offered, and the particular statistical model used. Still, no single model suffices to explain fully the motivations of individual voters.

What Electorates Do

When we ask what affects the outcome of an election, rather than what animates individual voters, the recent evidence tends to support the performance evaluation model. Those who have considered the relationship between the outcome of presidential elections and the performance of the economy before the election find that a substantial portion of the vote shift from election to election can be explained by economic performance. Many of the recent presidential elections have hinged on retrospective evaluations of the incumbents.[23]

How can individual voting behavior appear so multidimensional, while relatively simple assumptions about performance evaluations seem to fit the data on election outcomes? The answer has to do with the fact that we are now attempting to explain aggregate vote shifts rather than individual votes. Of the various determinants of individual vote choices, performance evaluations are probably the most volatile; that is, performance evaluations are relatively likely to vary from election to election. Furthermore, changes in performance evaluations are more likely to be unidirectional across the electorate; that is, changing performance evaluations are likely to confer a clear advantage on one candidate or the other. Although a poor economic performance for the economy as a whole does not affect all voters in the same way, it will on average reduce the favorable rating of the incumbent, a tendency enhanced by the fact that, as we have seen, voters tend to be influenced by their perceptions of the state of the economy as a whole more than they are by their own economic circumstance.

Policy preferences, in contrast, are more viscous. Not only are policy preferences less likely to undergo change but, if they do, such changes are less likely to be unidirectional in their impact on the election outcome. If a candidate with a strong issue position comes along—even more so, if a pair of candidates with strong and opposed issue positions comes along—voters will be likely to consider this issue in casting ballots.[24] As voters sort themselves out in terms of their preferences on this issue, there will be movement in both directions. Some of these movements will cancel each other out, and the resultant impact on a particular candidate's support may be relatively small.[25] Thus the net effect of changes in performance evaluations is likely to be substantially stronger than the net effect of changes in policy preferences. It is for this reason that economic performance is

[23] See Hibbs, *American Political Economy*, chap. 7; and D. Roderick Kiewiet and Douglas Rivers, "The Economic Basis of Reagan's Appeal."

[24] See Nie, Verba, and Petrocik, *The Changing American Voter*. They find strong issue voting in 1964 and 1972 when there was a candidate offering a true issue choice, and even stronger issue voting in a mock election between Barry Goldwater and George McGovern. Recent work finds issue voting also in the Reagan elections although it may be muted by the role of other factors such as personality and the effects of the negative retrospective evaluation of Carter.

[25] Miller and Shanks, "Policy Direction and Performance Evaluation," distinguish carefully between the effects of various factors on individual votes and the effects on the net vote outcome. They show that in 1984 individual votes were affected by policy preferences, but the policy effects cancelled each other out on the aggregate level.

so powerful in explaining aggregate electoral outcomes, while many factors play a role in individual vote decisions.

What Presidents Do

If the retrospective voting model stands up to empirical test better than the policy instruction model as an explanation of the outcome of elections, it cannot be said to have as decisive an advantage when it comes to explaining how policymakers behave. Presidents appear, at one time or another, to fit each of the three models we have discussed. They often act as trustees, their behavior unaffected by the outcome of the last election or by the anticipation of the next. They also often appear as nervous performers, calculating the electoral effects of their acts with an eye to the coming election. But what may be surprising is that they often act as if they had received policy instruction at the previous election. In light of what we have said about the limited capacity of elections to convey information and the tendency of aggregate election outcomes to reflect retrospective performance evaluations rather than prospective policy directives, this is somewhat puzzling.

It is hardly astonishing that presidents often act as trustees. Public policy analysts know that many factors have consequences for policy outcomes, only one of which is the preferences of citizens. Especially if the issue is highly technical and relatively invisible, there is likely to be little electoral guidance that the president can take even if he were so inclined. Under such circumstances, in making policy the president must rely on cues from a wide variety of sources ranging from his advisers to congressional leaders to interest groups to his own conscience. Thus the president is inevitably a trustee, no matter how concerned he may be about his own electoral future or that of his party.

Presidents also behave as nervous performers. According to this model, the incumbent who wishes to be reelected, or who wishes to be succeeded by a fellow partisan, must concentrate simply on being effective. Certainly the politician whose principal goal is to become a celebrity, to line his pockets, or to retire from office might not be motivated to concentrate on governing successfully. Nevertheless, most elected officials seem to care about how they perform and to have the public good, however they might define it, at heart. Hence, almost by definition, we might conclude that presidents are responding to the fact that winning electoral margins are created out of retrospective judgments of performance.[26]

There is a more rigorous empirical test that is relevant to the question of whether presidents behave as nervous performers. It has been argued that there is a political business cycle; that is, that incumbent presidents, knowing they will be judged on the health of the economy, pull whatever economic levers they control in order to guarantee that the economy is purring at the time of the election. The evidence that presidents actually engage in such preelection manipulation of the economy is mixed. There is evidence of successful and possibly self-conscious economic expansion under Nixon in 1972 and Reagan in 1984, but no evidence that this

[26] Clearly, the incumbent who wants to run again and is eligible to do so will be more concerned about the potential punishment meted out by retrospective voters. Even the president who anticipates retirement will not be impervious to such considerations. He will probably be concerned to maintain public approval for several reasons: He knows that erosion of public support can jeopardize the realization of his policy objectives; he will not want his party—and with it his performance—to be repudiated at the next election; and he will wish to receive kind treatment from historians, who may judge harshly a president who is unable to lead the public.

has been a persistent pattern for preelection years.[27] Since long before electoral analysts arrived on the scene with their sophisticated statistical models, presidents have been aware of the fact that Americans will vote their pocketbooks. But it is not clear that presidents control the economic levers necessary for the short-term manipulation of the economy for political ends or that they are willing to engage in such manipulation at the expense of other policy goals.[28]

The interesting fact is that, despite what we have said about the inevitability of mandate uncertainty, evidence suggests that presidents behave as if they have been instructed by a policy mandate. If presidents simply responded to the pressures generated by the possibility of electoral punishment by voters making retrospective evaluations, then they would be interchangeable—except insofar as they differed in their managerial capabilities. We know, however, that it matters who wins a presidential election. In spite of the pressures on a president to move to the center and to avoid policies that will alienate voter support, presidents do not all behave alike. According to a recent study, contrary both to popular wisdom about how candidates behave and to great pressures on them to obfuscate issues, presidential candidates make a large number of promises—promises sufficiently specific that it is possible to test whether they have been kept.[29] What is more, victorious candidates take their promises seriously—initiating proposals on a substantial number of them—and are likely to face punishment if they renege. Moreover, it seems to matter not only which particular individual is elected but which party's candidate is successful. Especially with respect to macroeconomic policy, there are aggregate differences between presidents of the two parties in terms of the policies they pursue; for example, compared with their Democratic counterparts, Republican presidents are more likely to tolerate high levels of unemployment and less likely to support redistributive measures.[30]

In addition, presidential victories, especially decisive ones, are often accompanied by substantial departures in the direction of public policy. This is most obviously the case during periods of electoral realignment when the response to national crisis is not simply a reformulation of electoral coalitions but major changes in policies affecting broad categories of people.[31] But even non-realigning elections can have such an impact on policy.[32] This is especially likely when the

[27] See Hibbs, *American Political Economy*, chap. 9.

[28] Kiewiet and Rivers, "The Economic Basis of Reagan's Appeal." Hibbs argues that such overt manipulation of the economy would soon be noticed and discounted by the public (*The American Political Economy*, chap. 9).

[29] Fishel, *Presidents and Promises*, esp. chaps. 2 and 7.

[30] See Hibbs, *The American Political Economy*, chap. 8; Edward R. Tufte, *Political Control of the Economy* (Princeton: Princeton University Press, 1978), chap. 4; and Schlozman and Verba, *Injury to Insult*, chap. 11.

[31] For an elaboration of the policy consequences of electoral realignments, see Walter Dean Burnham, Jerome M. Clubb, and William H. Flanigan, "Partisan Realignment: A Systemic Perspective," in Joel H. Silbey, Allan G. Bogue, and William H. Flanigan, *The History of American Electoral Behavior* (Princeton: Princeton University Press, 1978), pp. 45–77. See also David Brady, "A Reevaluation of Realignment in American Politics," *American Political Science Review* 79 (1985): 28–49, for the way in which realigning elections affect long-term changes in Congressional policy.

[32] See Hibbs, *The American Political Economy*, chap. 8; Tufte, *Political Control*, chap. 4; Susan Hansen, *The Politics of Taxation: Revenue without Representation* (New York: Praeger, 1983): Gerald Pomper, *Elections in America: Control and Influence in Democratic Politics* (New York: Dodd, Mead, 1970); Benjamin Page, *Who Gets What from Government* (Berkeley: University of California Press, 1983), p. 92; and Schlozman and Verba, *Injury to Insult*, chap. 11.

electoral result is a landslide. It seems that, although newly elected presidents take concrete steps to fulfill a substantial number of their policy promises, they cannot guarantee the passage of proposals they initiate.[33] That is why landslides are particularly likely to produce policy departures. A landslide gives a president the wherewithal to govern. The wider the electoral margin, the more likely that political observers will interpret it as a mandate for policy change and the more likely that the president will face a supportive Congress; hence, the greater his capacity to deliver on his campaign promises.

This logic raises a conundrum. If voters are animated by concern with governmental performance rather than by commitment to a policy program, and if presidential candidates have every incentive to take ambiguous issue positions and face political opposition if they go back on their campaign pledges, why do presidential candidates even make specific promises? And if electoral mandate contains so little policy content, why does policy alternate with a fair amount of regularity and predictability, as if there were a policy mandate? For even a partial answer to the puzzle, we must look beyond the loose constraints imposed on the president by the electoral outcome to those placed on him by his ideology and the elite political community in the country, especially in Washington to which he is especially sensitive.

WHY AREN'T PRESIDENTS INTERCHANGEABLE?

The very uncertainty of an electoral mandate—even an electoral mandate supplemented by polls—permits the president wide latitude in interpreting the election result, which he may do in ways that serve his ideological and political purposes. The message conveyed by the electoral outcome may be insubstantial as a cloud, but the clever victor will see in it the shape of the political ends he wishes to pursue and will manage (as Hamlet did with Polonius) to convince others that they see the same thing. Yet we need not assume that the victorious president who reads a mandate into his electoral triumph is merely being manipulative. It is only natural for a president who believes sincerely in what he has been saying to interpret the electoral outcome, especially if it is decisive, as a mandate to pursue the policies he advocated during his campaign.

The president's freedom in interpreting his uncertain mandate is exemplified by Ronald Reagan's comportment in office. The main theme of various scholarly and journalistic analyses of the 1980 election is that the outcome reflected dissatisfaction with an incumbent who was widely perceived to be incompetent.[34] As

---

[33] Fishel, *Presidents and Promises*, esp. chaps. 2 and 7.

[34] This appears to be the view of most political science analyses of the 1980 election. See, for instance, William Schneider. "The November 4 Vote for President: What Did It Mean?" in *The American Elections of 1980*, ed. Austin Ranney (Washington, D.C.: American Enterprise Institute, 1981), pp. 177–211; and Douglas A. Hibbs, Jr., "President Reagan's Mandate from the 1980 Election: Shift to the Right?" *American Politics Quarterly* 10 (1982): 387–420. As we have pointed out, Miller and Shanks ("Policy Direction and Performance Evaluation") differ somewhat from this interpretation. They find substantial policy voting in 1984 as well as in 1980. The effects of policy voting are, however, felt more on the individual than on the aggregate level, that is, policy voting explains individual vote choices better than it explains who won the election. For 1980 they conclude that conservative policy preferences were marginally more important in explaining the election outcome than were negative evaluations of President Carter's performance. But for 1984, the situation is the opposite and they find, as do others, that performance evaluations were more important in explaining the overall outcome. See also, Warren E.

such, it did not provide a clear message as to how to improve on President Carter's performance. Nevertheless, Reagan seems to have been impressively successful in interpreting it as an indication of a public preference for a more conservative departure in policy. Although there was a vast amount of polling data available in the Reagan presidential elections, the data allowed of selection and interpretation. And although almost all observers read these data as indicating little ideological shift to the right, the Reagan administration could find evidence for such a shift in the poll results.[35] To repeat, then, a president who finds it politically expedient or ideologically congenial has considerable latitude in reading the meaning of the election.

The uncertainty of the mandate, even when accompanied by extensive polling, creates a situation in which it is difficult to know whether a president is acting as a trustee or as a delegate. Given the alternative interpretations that can be read into either the results of an election or the welter of survey data and analyses that accompany it, and given the natural tendency for all of us—especially elected officials—to read into data that which we would most like to see, it is no wonder that a president will consider his victory as a mandate for the positions that he would like, in any case, to pursue. When he does so, it is difficult to evaluate whether he is behaving as a sincere delegate, honestly convinced of public support for his program, or whether he is behaving cynically, acting self-consciously as a trustee while dressing in delegate's clothes.

There is another dynamic at work—implicit in none of the three models of electoral democracy—that helps to explain why elections produce changes in policy. What it takes to get nominated and to run a campaign is quite different from what it takes to get elected. In order to gain a nomination and to conduct a campaign it is necessary to cultivate the support of party activists and campaign supporters and donors, as well as various other political influentials in Congress, the media, and interest groups. These political elites have policy concerns, and they communicate their views much more effectively than either the average citizen or the electorate as a whole. This explains why candidates actually make commitments when the logic of majority building gives them every reason to obfuscate. These elites are likely to demand that presidential candidates take positions, to monitor how presidential incumbents treat their pledges, and to hold them accountable if they fail to live up to their promises.

These elite groups differ in significant ways from the electorate as a whole. As we have seen, they tend to be drawn disproportionately from higher socioeconomic groups. In addition, their political views are likely to be stronger, more precise, and less centrist than those of the public at large. The need to curry favor with those whose support he needs thus constrains the president to respond to a set of activists who differ from ordinary citizens in important ways and exposes

---

Miller and Merrill Shanks. "Policy Directions and Presidential Leadership: Alternative Interpretations of the 1980 Presidential Election," *British Journal of Political Science* 12 (1982): 299–356.

The best overall summary of the literature on the two Reagan elections is that they were retrospective evaluations of performance—inadequate performance by Carter in the 1980 election, much better performance by Reagan in the 1984 election. See also, Kiewiet and Rivers, "The Economic Basis of Reagan's Appeal."

[35] As an illustration of the fact that presidents can see within public opinion polls a number of things—including a clear mandate—if they want to, we might mention that the one interpreter of the 1984 election that we have heard call it a mandate for conservative change is Richard Wirthlin, President Reagan's chief pollster. (Comment by Richard Wirthlin at the Thomas P. O'Neill Symposium on Presidential Elections, Boston College, 4–5 October 1985.)

him to expressions of preference about policy matters that are relatively precise in their content, but not necessarily representative of the opinions of either the public at large or the electorate. In addition, this introduces a countervailing tendency to the centrism implicit in American two-party electoral politics: The logic of building an electoral majority is centripetal, pushing candidates to converge at the center; the logic of dealing with political activists is centrifugal, pushing candidates to diverge ideologically.

It is, however, too simplistic to pose responsiveness to elites as an alternative to, or a replacement for, responsiveness to citizen preferences. Attention to elite preferences does not necessarily mean that citizen preferences are unrepresented, only that representation is more complex than it would be if the intermediate elite level of information and constraint were missing. Although the campaign activists, party leaders, interest group advocates, and other political elites that provide the incumbent with information and support have their own sets of preferences and concerns, which differ from those of the citizenry as a whole, they do not inhabit a realm totally cut off from the public. Their commitments to particular organizations (especially to the political parties) and to particular constituencies sometimes place them in a position to act as conduits for expressions of public preference. Furthermore, some of these elite groups, particularly media elites, may have as one of their highest priorities ensuring that the incumbent pays attention to broadly defined public preferences.[36] Nevertheless, although attention to elite-generated information is not necessarily antithetical to responsiveness to public preferences, it is hardly the same thing. Elites may speak for the public—or they may speak for themselves. And the public they speak for is likely to be a highly skewed one, far from representative of the public at large.

CONCLUSION:
PRESIDENTIAL RESPONSIVENESS AND
ELITE ACCOUNTABILITY

Thus we are forced to alter our understanding of the nature of presidential accountability. To whom is the president accountable? Two-party competition in America brings pressure on presidential incumbents to be responsive to broad majorities and to be accountable to citizens on a relatively equal basis. The need to be responsive to political influentials introduces a serious bias into the relatively egalitarian tendency of electoral politics, however. Although the political activists who must be cultivated are drawn disproportionately from the ranks of those of high economic, educational, and occupational status, this bias is more ideological than socioeconomic. If the overall thrust of electoral politics is broadly majoritarian and centrist, the process just described puts candidates under pressure to be responsive to those with narrower concerns and to those farther from the political center.

The result may be a dual form of accountability. The dynamics of aggregate electoral outcomes force a president who seeks reelection for himself or his party to be responsive to a public that will reward or punish him for his performance in office. It may not be easy to measure the effects of this mechanism of accountability, since it does not always manifest itself in crude presidential attempts to manipulate the economy for electoral purposes, and it otherwise consists of a

---

[36] Furthermore, the media may increase the likelihood that an incumbent will fulfill campaign pledges, since they will criticize him for not so doing.

general injunction to "try hard." Nonetheless, the prospect of the next election undoubtedly looms large in the minds of incumbents. The general pressure from the public evaluating the state of the nation is supplemented by pressures from more elite groups: from campaign activists, from those in the president's entourage, from leaders of supportive interest groups, from the congressional delegation of the president's party. To these people, the president will have made more specific pledges during the campaign, and they expect at least some follow-through. Furthermore, the media will carefully monitor the president's pledges and their fate in the new administration. Thus these special publics are a source of detailed policy instruction to the president. Moreover, their attentiveness to the administration is a source of constraint that the president cannot afford to ignore. In short, we must add still another to our models of presidential accountability. The dictates of the electoral process force the president to be accountable to political elites—and to elites who are much more capable of giving specific content to that accountability than is the public at large.

Political Parties and the Party System

27

WHO NEEDS POLITICAL PARTIES?
Rick Valelly

Many people think that parties and partisanship warp democratic politics. Given a chance—or so the results of the Gallup Poll would clearly suggest—millions of Americans would report that they are not partisans but are independents. (To check on this fact, navigate to http://www.gallup.com/ poll/15370/Party-Affiliation.aspx.)

Is it true that so many millions of Americans are not partisan? It cannot be true, as shown in the previous article by Larry Bartels, "Electoral Continuity and Change, 1868–1996." Consider too Norrander's discussion of how partisan attachments and social characteristics are tightly linked. Partisanship—on this view—is a part of how each of us constructs our personal identity.

Nonetheless, the Gallup Poll is telling us that many people have trouble revealing their partisanship or, alternatively, like to present themselves to a stranger on the phone as dispassionate and thoughtful. In that sense they agree with the only professional political scientist who ever became president, Woodrow Wilson. Wilson thought that parties and partisanship inhibited the open-mindedness required for public deliberation about important issues—for government by discussion, in other words.

On the other hand political scientists truly admire political parties. They think that a voter's attachment to a political party prepares her or him for government by discussion. They would agree with the notion that one has to start thinking about politics from some distinctive standpoint. Given the rich political histories of major American political parties and their enormous policy impact, partisanship is a perfectly good starting point.

With the exception of David Mayhew (recall that he is the author of one of the selections on Congress in Section 2), contemporary political scientists suspect that democratic politics is fundamentally unworkable without parties and partisanship. Parties connect the ordinary citizen to government and politics and offer them broad policy choices, thereby giving voters a chance to direct and control government through party politics. Think about whether you agree with them as you read this short piece.

• • •

As the major political parties convene this summer, with all the usual noise, pomp, and expense, Americans can be counted on to let out a collective yawn, or maybe a grimace. But not so for political scientists. Academic experts see a lot to like—or at least a lot to study—in the American two-party system. In their considered view, a competitive party system ensures the legitimacy of opposition to government, promotes public debate about policy options, and gets citizens involved in the public sphere. The two-party system never does these things perfectly, but it does them well enough. Without it our system would collapse overnight, leaving gridlock and hyperpluralism—or so most political scientists think.

But if one looks closely at the views of those who are researching, thinking about, and writing about political parties, one finds an interesting division of opinion. One school of thought is that parties are in decline and consequently, that we have a major problem. The public is right to be irritated. A second view holds that parties have changed dramatically but that they are just as strong as they used to be. The public ought to get used to the transformation and stop griping. A third school best articulated by David Mayhew of Yale University, is that political scientists have attributed too much importance to party dynamics. They matter, but less so than the professional literature has suggested. In this light, the public's gripes are beside the point.

To make sense of the disagreement, we must first sift through the ruins of realignment theory. For about 20 years, American government students were instructed in this line of thinking. Its concepts still echo in political punditry. But the theory died a decade ago when it became clear it wasn't explaining with any precision the events of the actual political world.

Still, it was an elegant idea. Realignment theory held that not all elections were the same. In certain highly charged elections or in a string of two or three such elections, big and lasting shifts occurred in how voters behaved. A new voter coalition would assert control over our system, determining policy outcomes for a generation. Walter Dean Burnham, the theory's best-known proponent, suggested such elections might be a uniquely American surrogate for political revolution. Before realignment, there might be a third-party challenge, protests, and even civil disorder. Eventually, ambitious politicians would pick up the pressing issues and make them their own.

With the image of periodic political renewal, there was a soothing message in all this. Realignments allowed the political system to adjust to social and political stress, and to bring those citizens who might otherwise be absorbed in personal concerns into political action. The party system periodically restored its own vitality and that of the system as a whole. Burnham explicitly warned, however, that the party system's capacity for "peaceful revolution" was not automatic. If and when the party system lost its ability to adapt, the branches of government would lock up. Governmental remedy as both an ideal and a practice would wither. Gradually, a propensity toward broad-based oligarchy would set in. After all, the wealthy are best protected by government that is deadlocked. Simultaneously, a huge class of unmobilized people would emerge as a "party of nonvoters." Their influence on the system would necessarily be weaker.

Scholars in the "party decline" school have inherited Burnham's worry. They agree that as a party system weakens it tends to pull the rest of the order down with it. Sidney Milkis of the University of Virginia, who is close in spirit to Burnham, makes such a case in *Political Parties and Constitutional Government*, a study of the rise and development of political parties since the founding. While Milkis does not share Burnham's open distaste for markets, capitalism, and social inequalities, he does adopt Burnham's democratic nationalism. For Milkis the weakening of parties has promoted broad discontent with American government and has generated an anemic civic culture.

In Milkis's account—and this is what makes his work so provocative—the cause of party decline, and thus of public cynicism, is not the depoliticizing force of market values, as Burnham has long argued. Instead, it is the particular development of the presidency. To put Milkis's claim bluntly, FDR killed the parties when he built a government competent enough to run a welfare state. In doing that, he changed the constitutional balance that had been supported by the parties since the time of Madison, Jackson, and Van Buren. Subsequent presidents failed to reverse Roosevelt's legacy.

Party competition first emerged, Milkis argues, when James Madison and Thomas Jefferson sought to develop a political opposition to Alexander Hamilton, John Adams, and the Federalist legatees of George Washington's two-term presidency. Madison, in particular, feared for the future of federalism and the separation of powers if Hamilton's economic nationalism were left politically unchecked. Milkis takes pains to point out that there was a second Madison, one less well-known but just as important as the more familiar Madison who framed the Constitution. The first disliked parties and factions; the second had no trouble embracing them in order to save his overall institutional design. Happily for Madison, the party system that he helped to launch evolved (thanks to the genius of Martin Van Buren) into a stable contest between two large confederations of state and local parties. And happily for the system as a whole, Milkis says, the parties won the political loyalties of voters scattered across a vast geographic expanse.

Americans came to appreciate the full range of national, state, and local institutions contemplated by the founders. Voters liked their town and county governments; they valued their state institutions; and they came to treasure not only the presidency but the Senate, the House, and the Supreme Court. America's elaborate mix of national, state, and local jurisdictions and offices might never have taken hold without the early development of decentralized but nationally competitive parties. This accomplishment helps to explain the persistence of the Constitution of 1787 despite the extraordinary events of the Civil War and the Reconstruction, and the huge expansion of the republic's size.

But our party system and institutions were never particularly well-suited for strong, positive government, Milkis argues. They were good for participation and office-seeking, but not for supple macroeconomic management or the competent bureaucratic delivery of social benefits, such as old-age income security or work relief. Here Milkis carries forward a long line of thinking about party politics and public administration that dates to the work of Herbert Croly and other progressives in the early decades of the 1900s.

FDR was the first president, in Milkis's view, who was forced to cope with the lack of fit between the institutional forms given to him and new executive tasks. He keenly understood the limits of the party system he inherited, and sought briefly to do something about them, through the ill-fated 1938 "Roosevelt purge" in which New Deal liberals were encouraged to run against reactionary and conservative Democratic incumbents in Congress. He hoped to transform his party into a programmatic, responsible organization. He failed miserably.

FDR did not try again, opting instead for the independent regulatory commissions, new bureaucracies, court-packing, and executive reorganization that he or congressional liberals had already launched or planned before the purge effort. Roosevelt grasped that he could, and probably should, soft-pedal his party as an instrument of executive governance. It was too loaded with southern conservatives and stand-pat careerists. Time was short, and there was much work to be done to save liberal capitalism from its enemies within and without.

But there was a hidden price for this understandable decision. The cost to the polity, one that was not immediately obvious, was reduced voter involvement. As Kennedy, Johnson, and Nixon perfected the New Deal state, they did so on the backs of social movements, professors, experts, and government executives and lawyers. Their mission was not to revitalize the remnants of the urban machines or to reform the conservative state parties and party factions that they scorned. They made the same choice Roosevelt did. So the decentralized system of confederated parties—imagined by Madison and perfected by Van Buren—collapsed, as one ward club or county committee after another (with the notable exception of Chicago) died on the liberal vine. These local institutions were the vital foundation of voter involvement; without them voter turnout began its long decline.

Not all political scientists are alarmed by such developments. In his important 1995 work, *Why Parties?*, John H. Aldrich responds to the passing of the ward heelers by saying, in effect, "so what?" He wants us to face up to a stark proposition: The forms of parties are going to change. As he notes, trenchantly, "The major political party is the creature of the politicians. . . . These politicians do not have partisan goals per se, and the party is only the instrument for achieving them." Politicians run the parties, and they will inevitably change the ways in which parties help them to be politicians.

Aldrich is no iconoclast, to be sure. His book is deeply thoughtful, gently argued, and quite rigorous. At the heart of Aldrich's case lies an extended comparison between two party systems: the system that emerged in the North during the 1820s and 1830s and that lasted until the Civil War, and the more familiar two-party system that has structured our politics since the 1960s. The first was intensely mobilizing and generated sharp increases in voter turnout until it reached extraordinary, indeed uniquely high levels. This was also a period of "team parties," in which politicians subordinated their individual identities to the corporate identity of their party since the path to power lay through making that trade-off.

Today's parties, in contrast, are service-providing organizations. They resemble a franchise for entrepreneurs. The individual candidates of the two parties meet certain programmatic requirements related to party ideology, but in terms of campaigning they act as freelancers. They have no trouble behaving as highly competitive teams within government, particularly within the House of Representatives, but they do not cooperate with each other to rally voters. Stimulating turnout is up to an individual candidate if he or she chooses.

The point of Aldrich's contrast is not that there has been decline relative to some golden age. Instead, these are fundamentally different systems. Juxtaposed to this claim is a lucid demonstration of the central tendency of any competitive party system, regardless of differences in the campaign styles of politicians. Using simple modeling, Aldrich posits that a party system will solve pathologies that would otherwise plague politicians. Without a competitive party system, politicians could not cooperate around mutual policy gains, which can only come through repeated interaction and binding commitments that hold up across time. They would instead treat all their interactions with each other as one-shot games and thus fall prey to the noncooperative trap epitomized by the "prisoner's dilemma."

Second, without parties' resources and their capacity to stimulate, motivate, and inform voters, politicians could never solve a major dilemma facing voters, i.e., the propensity to avoid voting and to instead "free ride" on those who take the trouble to vote out of an irrationally strong sense of civic duty. If most of us were freeriders, there could be no genuinely popular electoral system.

Third, without the partisan organization of legislatures and government, politicians could never efficiently restrict the agenda of conflict and debate to a basic set of important issues. They would instead stumble in and out of fragile log-rolls that would incorporate many unrelated items. The result would be policy immobility, rendering deliberation and participation beside the point.

Professional politicians in a democracy obviously need parties to satisfy their policy and office-seeking ambitions. But the rest of us also need parties. No parties, no "positive externalities" (in the language of welfare economics)—no streams of consistent and related policies, no agenda for public debate, and little prospect of even a modicum of voter attachment to the polity and its concerns. Thus, our current party system provides essentially the same "positive externalities," Aldrich is saying, as the earlier party system.

But a somewhat different take on the same facts is offered by Steven Schier in *By Invitation Only*. During the golden age of party politics, roughly the period from 1830 to 1890, we had something approaching a genuinely participatory democracy in this country. Today we have, in its place, a vast congeries of professionally managed "activation," that is, the stimulation and enlistment of thousands of small subsets of the citizenry in service of the ambition of an interest group or a candidate. Several kinds of professional consultancies are available to the well-heeled or the well-organized to accomplish their preferred strategy of activation: pollsters, media consultants, fund-raisers, gatherers of demographic data, opposition and issue researchers, speechwriters, schedulers, and so forth. Schier catalogues them all succinctly.

The basic idea here is that parties now compete in a broad marketplace of service providers for the politically ambitious. Their historic monopoly on access to office and influence disappeared with the rise of primaries, referenda, campaign finance regulation, and a privately operated system of broadcast communications.

The loser in the shift toward a competitive market in political techniques is the mass of ordinary citizens. Following politics and getting involved in it is up to them. If they do not have the education, confidence, partisanship, or time to do so, no one will ask them. Expending resources to activate the already motivated voters is cost-effective. It is less cost-effective to pursue those who are not listed in the databases of the consultants.

In this way, the political system is a bit like the medical system: technologically advanced, expensive, and replete with a variety of coverages and exclusions. As a nation, we spend a huge amount of money on electoral politics and employ all the latest campaign techniques, but we do not get much average-voter turnout in return.

Schier's final chapter offers an exceptionally thoughtful treatment of possible cures for this state of affairs. The bottom line for reform, he suggests, is making party affiliation more salient to political candidates than it currently is. In response, politicians might have stronger incentives to cooperate with one another in mobilizing voters, rather than worrying only about their own constituency.

We should reorganize campaign finance so that parties control more resources than they do now. And the states could provide ballots that are organized as party slates. More states could do what Maine and Nebraska do, which is to allocate votes in the electoral college to whomever carries a congressional district and give the "Senate votes" to the statewide winner. These are among the most plausible reforms of the many that Schier discusses.

Could it be that such reforms overemphasize the importance of political parties to democracy? David Mayhew is the one leader of the political science profession who has consistently resisted such enthusiasms. In the course of his career, he has helped to show that political parties have little to do with whether Congress works well, that states with weak parties are not necessarily less generous with social policies (and are sometimes more generous), and that from 1947 to 1990 divided government at the national level simply had no effect on the production of important public policy, budgetary balance, or the frequency or disruptiveness of congressional investigations of the White House or the executive bureaucracies.

It could also be the case that the party system, as Aldrich says, is not in decline but simply has acquired new forms. One might retort that the earlier system made for more active citizens. But cross-national survey research does not show that countries with party systems more like our earlier system have citizens more satisfied with how their democracy works than ours.

Nonetheless, Walter Dean Burnham was right to think as long and as hard as he did about cycles of decline and renewal in American party politics. Perhaps critical realignments never really existed, but political decline and renewal are hardly fanciful inventions of Burnham's towering intellect. They are the oldest and most important issues of political thought, going back to Aristotle.

For all their faults, political parties have been the essential foundation of both citizen involvement and citizen awareness of the issues facing a democratic polity. Perhaps nothing will come of letting our two-party system continue to become just one among many channels for citizen involvement, rather than the premier channel. It is more likely, though, that good things would come from trying, as Schier suggests, to make our party system more salient for voters and politicians than it currently is.

28

TOWARD A ONE-PARTY SOUTH?

Danny Hayes
Seth C. McKee[*]

*The stability and age of the American party system are often remarked
upon—sometimes with dissatisfaction over obstacles to third parties, sometimes with satisfaction about the extent to which the party system's stability
and age ease the cognitive burdens of voters in following government and
policy. Either perspective tends to obscure the fact that in one large part of
the country—the South—party politics has always been unusual. There, one
major party or the other has rebuilt itself or entrenched itself in power. This
succinct and precise piece by Hayes and McKee looks at the most recent
case of party (re)building: the Republican party's remarkable comeback in
the ex-Confederacy. That process of party (re)building, they further suggest,
confirms the predictive and analytic utility of what is known as the "median
voter" theorem, namely, the idea that parties must converge on the policy
preferences of the "median voter" in the electorate.*

• • •

THE POLITICAL HISTORY of the American South is well known. For the 80 years
following Reconstruction, the Democratic Party dominated regional politics, producing famous accounts of the one-party South (Key, 1996). In the past half century, however, the Democratic hammerlock has loosened. The Republican Party,
helped along by the civil rights movement (Carmines & Stimson, 1989), economic
growth in the South's burgeoning metropolitan areas (Bartley & Graham, 1975;
Shafer & Johnston, 2006), and the Reagan realignment of White conservatives
(E. Black & M. Black, 2002), has grown increasingly strong, turning the once
solid Democratic South into the country's most reliably Republican region.

Even after the Republican Party's "thumping" in the 2006 elections,[1] the GOP
in the South holds 7 of 13 governorships, 21 of 26 U.S. Senate seats, and 85 of
142 U.S. House seats.[2] In the 2000 and 2004 presidential elections, Republican
George W. Bush won every southern state. Democratic presidential candidates
since 1964 have won a plurality of the southern vote only twice, in 1976 and
1996 (Lamis, 1999). Still, political observers have not been prepared to suggest

American Politics Research 36 (January 2008): 3–32. Copyright 2008 by Sage Publications Inc.
Journals. Reproduced with permission of Sage Publications Inc.

*Authors' Note: The authors' names are in alphabetical order. A previous version of this article
was presented at the 2006 Citadel Symposium on Southern Politics. Brian Arbour, Neal Allen, Charles
Prysby, Rick Valelly, Jeremy Teigen, Mathieu Turgeon, and three anonymous reviewers offered valuable comments. All errors remain ours.

[1] This was the language George W. Bush used to describe the result in a postelection press conference.

[2] Unless stated otherwise, the South in this article is defined as the 11 former Confederate states—
Alabama, Arkansas, Florida, Georgia, Louisiana, Mississippi, North Carolina, South Carolina, Tennessee, Texas, and Virginia—plus Kentucky and Oklahoma.

that the pendulum of southern party competition has swung to the opposite end of its arc—toward one-party dominance again, this time under the thumb of the GOP. "[I]f the old solid Democratic South has vanished, a comparably solid Republican South has not developed" write E. Black and M. Black (2002, p. 3). "Nor is one likely to emerge."

Although we are not prepared to predict a return to the days of one-party dominance reminiscent of the post-Reconstruction South, recent developments spell major trouble for the Democratic Party. The political landscape, we argue, is shifting in ways that make it worthwhile to ask whether Democrats will, in the foreseeable future, be able to compete effectively in southern statewide elections.[3]

Three factors tip the scales heavily in favor of the GOP. First, and most important, the party's ideological orientation lines up much more closely with the region's electorate than does the Democratic Party's. This is especially critical in an era in which ideology appears to play a major role in the formation of individual party identification (Abramowitz & Saunders, 1998; Schreckhise & Shields, 2003). Second, the Democratic Party's most loyal age cohort is the pre–civil rights generation: those over the age of 65. At the same time, young voters are the most reliably Republican group, a discrepancy that will produce a GOP skew in the distribution of party identification in the southern electorate as time wears on. Third, because the majority White electorate continues to shift Republican, the incumbency advantage accrued and cultivated by Republican candidates may cement and reinforce Republican electoral gains. It also appears that other factors will break in the GOP's favor. For instance, many of the offices held by White Democrats who are reaching the end of their political careers will likely be won by Republican candidates.

In this article, we present evidence that speaks to the mounting strength of the GOP in the South and the daunting challenges facing the Democratic Party. To be sure, the overwhelming Democratic support from African Americans places an upper limit on Republican hegemony, which prevents the sort of one-party dominance exhibited by southern Democrats from 1880 through the 1950s (Lublin, 2004). But what makes the current state of southern politics all the more remarkable is the ascendancy of the GOP despite the presence of an electorate that is only limited by citizenship—an impediment to the number of Hispanic voters, but certainly not a barrier to African American participation. Because the current electorate is more racially diverse than its pre–civil rights predecessor, there is an obvious limitation to Republican advancement in district-based contests. The jury, however, is still out with respect to statewide elections, and this is admittedly

[3] Let us be clear—the solid Democratic South, which still flourished when V. O. Key published *Southern Politics in State and Nation* in 1949, is gone with the wind. Never again do we anticipate a scenario in which one party can essentially sweep the region's elections aside from a handful of contests confined to isolated pockets of minority-party strongholds (i.e., the mountain Republican sections of eastern Tennessee and western North Carolina preceding and following the Civil War). The expansion of the franchise and the diversity of interests in the contemporary South (racial and ethnic, economic, religious, in-migration patterns, etc.) are such that one-party control will never be as solid and unifying as it once was when Democratic unity rested on blocking federal intrusion of the South's artificially White electorate. But though we acknowledge the unlikelihood of a solid Republican South that mirrors the erstwhile one-party Democratic South, we raise the possibility of a growth in Republican strength to the point that the GOP is the dominant partner in most elections, and especially in statewide contests.

what makes our question provocative. Because of increasing partisan polarization in the political preferences of Whites as compared to minorities, a one-party Republican South in statewide elections is a possibility that merits consideration.

We begin by providing a brief overview of the recent partisan change that has taken place in the South, present new data on statewide elections from 1990 through 2006, and lay out a sketch of our argument. We then use a variety of individual- and aggregate-level data to document the increasing ideological distance between the Democratic Party and southern voters, the dramatic generational divide in partisan support that presages a growth in GOP strength, and the mounting Republican incumbency advantage. We also use the results of the 2006 midterm elections to underscore the solidity of the Republican Party's support in the South. In the discussion, we consider several possibilities for the revival of the Democratic Party's success. Our research points to the conclusion that the South remains exceptional—historically, because of Democratic dominance, and currently, because southern Republican growth persists even while it declines in the rest of the nation.

PARTISAN CHANGE IN THE SOUTH

Since the 1950s, the South has seen massive changes, both societal and political (E. Black & M. Black, 1987). As the architecture of racial segregation has been dismantled by the civil rights movement, the region has undergone a political transformation that has had a profound effect not only on the South itself but also on national politics (E. Black & M. Black, 2002). At the heart of the transformation are changes at both the mass and elite levels.

At the mass level, the most obvious is the shift in partisan allegiance. As African Americans have become a solidly Democratic constituency, White southerners have in increasing numbers moved into the GOP. This has dramatically reshaped the distribution of party identification in the South.

In 1952, just 20% of southerners identified as Republicans, underscoring the regional dominance of the Democratic Party, which claimed the support of more than three out of every four voters. But over the next half century, as shown in Figure 1, support for the GOP continued to grow, so that by 2002, nearly half of the southern electorate identified as Republican.[4] At the same time, the Democratic Party watched its ranks dwindle as the region's White electorate moved in large numbers to the GOP. In 1952, 78% of southerners identified as Democrats. By 2004, that number had dropped by 30 percentage points. More than any other change, it is the growth in White support that has given the Republican Party a firm toehold in the region (E. Black & M. Black, 2002).

The shift in partisan loyalty has had consequences at the elite level. As the numbers cited in the introduction attest, Democratic presidential candidates have for the most part found the South to be fallow ground, with the region typically going for Republican candidates (E. Black & M. Black, 1992). In Congress, Republicans now hold 81% of the southern Senate seats and 60% of House seats. Whereas in 1960, Republicans held less than 5% of the seats in the region's state

[4] The lines for Republican and Democratic identifiers include those who say they lean toward one party. We consider these individuals partisans because of the evidence that such citizens tend to behave more like partisans than independents (e.g., Keith et al., 1992).

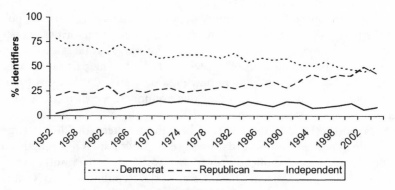

FIGURE 1. Party Identification Among Southerners, 1952–2004
Source: National Election Studies Cumulative Data File

legislatures, they now have nearly reached a majority, with 49%.[5] The GOP's state parties have grown in strength (Ceaser & Saldin, 2005), which has produced benefits for its candidates throughout the region.

The growth in Republican strength at the elite level is striking, as shown in Figure 2, which documents the GOP's rise in the South from 1952 to 2006. The line displays David's Index of party strength (David, 1972), a composite of U.S. House, U.S. Senate, and gubernatorial election data.[6] In the earliest years of the time series, prior to the civil rights movement, the GOP's strength was decidedly anemic, but its movement has been healthily upward since the 1980s, though with a small dip in 2006.

The growth in Republican statewide office-holding is also notable, and as far as we know, previously undocumented. Figure 3 displays the percentage of statewide offices in the South held by the GOP over the past decade and a half.[7] As recently as 1990, Republicans held just 17% of statewide offices, illustrating the persistence of the Democrats' grip on the region. But the jump-shift in the early 1990s is remarkable, suggesting the existence of a new competitive equilibrium. As of 2006, Republicans held a majority (53%) of southern statewide offices.

It is on these statewide contests that we train our focus, suggesting that the growing ideological alienation of voters from the Democratic Party, the Republican trend in the youngest voting cohorts, and the benefits of incumbency predict a continued upward slope of the line in Figure 3.

[5] The 1960 figure was computed by Alexander Lamis and Andrew Lucker, who graciously shared their data with us. We compiled the contemporary data from Congressional Quarterly's *Politics in America* biennial volume. In raw numbers, the GOP now holds 1,013 of the 13 states' 2,069 state legislative seats.

[6] Figure 2 displays David's Index for Republican strength in Composite B form (combined returns for the U.S. House, U.S. Senate, and gubernatorial elections). We thank Alexander Lamis and Andrew Lucker for providing these data for 1952–1998. We have updated the data for 2000–2006. For a detailed explanation of how the index is constructed, see David (1972) and Lamis (1999, p. 407).

[7] Statewide offices include governor, lieutenant governor, secretary of state, attorney general, adjutant general, treasurer, auditor, comptroller, agriculture commissioner, election commissioner, state land commissioner, chief financial officer, education superintendent, education commissioner, labor commissioner, insurance commissioner, corporation commissioner, general land office commissioner, and railroad commissioner. A complete list of offices in each state used in these calculations is available from the authors.

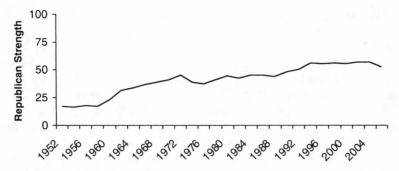

FIGURE 2. Republican Strength in the South, 1952–2006
Source: David's Index for Republican Strength, provided by Alexander Lamis and Andrew Lucker (1952–1998). Data for 2000–2006 were compiled by the authors. The South is defined as the 11 former Confederate states plus Kentucky and Oklahoma.

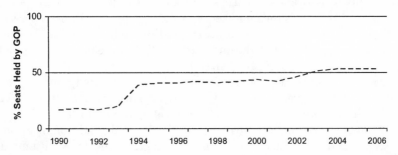

FIGURE 3. Percentage of Republicans in Southern Statewide Elective Offices, 1990–2006
Source: Data compiled by the authors.

TOWARD A ONE-PARTY SOUTH?

We take a Downsian (Downs, 1957) approach in considering the current—and future—status of the Republican and Democratic parties in the South. Over the long-term, it is the positioning of the parties and their candidates that determines the size of each party's base of voters (see McDonald, Mendes, & Budge, 2004; Stimson, 2004; Sundquist, 1983). We argue that the Republican Party is better positioned spatially because, with regard to ideology, it is closer to the median southern voter—and particularly White voters, who constitute a decided voting majority.[8]

We acknowledge that many voters—probably most—do not engage in thoughtful consideration of why they happen to identify with a political party (Campbell, Converse, Miller, & Stokes, 1960; Converse, 1964; Green, Palmquist, & Schickler, 2002). It is well known that partisanship is mainly acquired through socialization, specifically the transfer of party identification from parent to child (Campbell, Converse, Miller, & Stokes, 1960). Nonetheless, on those rare occasions when the parties are represented by candidates who take opposing positions on a highly

[8] Among southern voters, based on the 2004 National Election Pool exit poll data, the racial and ethnic breakdown was the following: 70.7% White, 18.3% Black, 8.7% Hispanic, 0.7% Asian, and 1.5% Other.

salient issue, voting behavior is immediately affected (Carmines & Stimson, 1989). And if the parties and their candidates persist in taking opposing positions, partisanship will eventually be altered.

Partisanship lags considerably behind vote choice, but vote choice becomes a leading indicator of partisan change. If voters become habitual in their defection toward the opposite party, eventually we expect these voters to at least dealign, if not realign. In the long term, as Fiorina (1981) would argue, if voters' running tally of party evaluations disproportionately favors the party they do not identify with, then they may finally switch in favor of that party.

The gradual increase in the number of Republican identifiers and the gradual decline in the number of Democratic identifiers are a consequence of the political parties running candidates who are generally differentiable and consistent in their position-taking—with Republican candidates spatially closer to the median southerner. There is a strong element of path dependency: As Democratic and Republican candidates consistently stake out opposing positions on salient issues, voters eventually associate the parties with anchoring different ideological positions. And over time, it is the consistency of the ideological distinctiveness of the candidates who run under the Democratic and Republican banners that makes short-term partisan tides—like the one in 2006—little more than a deviation from the long-term pattern of partisan change.

We trace the Republican spatial advantage back to the civil rights movement, and in particular, the passage of the 1964 Civil Rights Act and the 1965 Voting Rights Act. As discussed at length by Carmines and Stimson (1989), the opposing positions taken by the national parties and their presidential nominees on civil rights set in motion an issue evolution that triggered an almost instantaneous switch in the voting behavior of southern Whites. In presidential contests since 1964, southern Whites have always cast a majority Republican (two-party) vote (E. Black & M. Black, 2002).[9] With the franchise for African Americans secured by the 1965 Voting Rights Act, the Democratic Party has reaped the benefits of a bloc vote. But African Americans' overwhelming support of the Democratic Party has also had the effect of placing the party at a spatial disadvantage. Because of the substantial ideological distance between southern Whites and southern Blacks, coupled with the fact that the White population constitutes a much greater share of the electorate, the Democratic Party is noticeably further away from the median southern voter than is the Republican Party, as we show below.

The spatial advantage of southern Republicans was certainly not inevitable. It materialized steadily over decades as a result of the increasing polarization of Democratic and Republican candidates. The partisan sorting of elites (see Fiorina, Abrams, & Pope, 2006) exhibits a strong generational component. As older Democratic candidates and officeholders are replaced by the next generation of Democrats, the latter are more liberal and thus moving away from the median southern voter. In addition, as conservative Democrats retire, they are usually replaced by Republicans, which further polarizes the parties (E. Black & M. Black, 2002).

[9] Often overlooked, southern Republicanism received its initial (although much smaller) boost following World War II, as economic conservatism proved a compelling motive for voters located in the rapidly urbanizing "New South" to cast Republican presidential ballots (see Bartley & Graham, 1975; Lublin, 2004; Phillips, 1969; Shafer & Johnston, 2006). We contend, however, like other scholars (e.g., E. Black & M. Black, 2002; Carmines & Stimson, 1989; Valentino & Sears, 2005), that race was paramount in setting in motion southern partisan change. Furthermore, economics and race are complementary, because the GOP has staked out the conservative ground on both issues.

Similarly, at the mass level, generational change has led to an increase in the number of southern White Republicans (Green et al., 2002). The process is slow, with older generations of southern Democrats dealigning and then younger generations finally realigning in favor of the Republican Party. If, however, we focus on ideology as the grounds for partisan change, then partisan realignment has been fairly rapid among certain subgroups. For example, during the Reagan presidency, conservative southern Whites realigned in favor of the GOP (E. Black & M. Black, 2002). It is now the case that an historic event has occurred: For the first time in southern politics, a generation of Republican parents is now transferring their Republican identification to the next generation of southern voters.

Biracial coalitions are the winning formula for Democrats who are able to secure an overwhelming Black vote with enough of the White vote to comprise a voting majority (E. Black & M. Black, 1987, 1992, 2002). By the 1990s, however, biracial coalitions have increasingly failed to garner voting majorities for Democrats, because the increase in Republican identifiers has made it more difficult for Democrats to meet their White vote share targets (Hayes & McKee, 2004). By comparison, the Republican strategy of securing White supermajorities has met with increasing success because of the rise in the number of Republican identifiers.

We posit that for the foreseeable future, the electoral predicament of the southern Democratic Party will only worsen, because the racial composition of rank-and-file Democrats can no longer deliver voting majorities. In short, throughout the South, Democrats have lost, or are on the brink of losing the necessary White share of the vote to win elections. Candidate-positioning reinforces the Democratic Party's dilemma: Democratic candidates take positions that win a majority of Democratic votes, but what the party needs are candidates who can win the votes of independents and even some Republicans—yet this most likely is not possible without alienating Black voters.[10]

In short, the Democratic Party is in a spatial bind. Moving closer to the median southern voter is likely to come at the cost of losing Black electoral support. Put plainly, Democrats are damned if they move to the right because they risk upsetting their African American base, and damned if they stay put because their White constituency is shrinking. In the next section, we present empirical support for our argument that the Republican Party is better positioned than the Democratic Party.

PARTY POSITIONING IN IDEOLOGICAL SPACE

To estimate the longitudinal trend in ideology among southerners and their perceptions of the political parties, we take advantage of the National Election Studies Cumulative Data File. Every 2 years since 1972,[11] the National Election Studies has asked survey respondents to place themselves on a 7-point ideology scale, ranging from (1) *extremely liberal* to (7) *extremely conservative*, and to identify the ideological positions of the Republican and Democratic parties. The survey is

---

[10] E. Black and M. Black (1992, 2002) emphasize that successful southern Democratic candidates are adept at mixing liberal/progressive and conservative themes to secure a biracial voting majority. This is indeed the appropriate strategy for Democrats. But with the increasing polarization of partisan elites, it is harder for Democrats to win White votes, because the Republican Party has more credibility when its candidates take conservative positions.

[11] The lone exception is that the Cumulative Data File does not include responses to the questions about the political parties' ideological positions in 2002, which necessitated its omission from Figure 4.

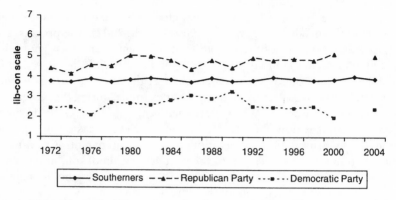

FIGURE 4. Mean Ideological Placements: Southerners, the Republican Party, and the Democratic Party
Source: National Election Studies Cumulative Data File

national in scope but typically includes 300 to 500 southern respondents, enough to generate fairly reliable estimates.[12]

Figure 4 presents the median self-placement scores for southerners and the median ideological perceptions of the political parties for each year since 1972. Consider first the middle (solid) line, which represents the median southern voter. Of note is the considerable stability in ideological self-placement. Since 1972, the typical southerner has been moderate, hovering slightly to the left of the midpoint of the ideology scale.[13]

But the perceptions of the parties tell a story of change, not stability. There has been a notable growth in the distance of the Democratic Party from the region's electorate. Although the GOP has typically been perceived as closer to the median voter, the gap between southerners and the Democratic Party has widened remarkably since 1990. That year, the distance between the median southerner and the Democratic Party was 0.49 on the 7-point scale. By 2004, however, that gap had tripled to 1.48. At the same time, the distance between southerners and the Republican Party stands at 1.09. In other words, the typical southern voter now perceives the Democratic Party to be about 40% further from him or her than the GOP.[14]

The polarization in the figure deserves attention. Perceptions of the parties have become more extreme since the start of the time series. The Republican Party was seen as more conservative in 2000 (with a rating of 5.09) than at any other

[12] The number of southerners who respond to the ideology measures ranges from a low of 217 (2000) to a high of 512 (1978).

[13] The precise medians represented in Figure 4 are available from the authors on request.

[14] Although our focus here is on the political parties and statewide elections, further evidence of the ideological alienation of the Democratic Party appears in southern perceptions of its presidential candidates. It is not surprising that the widest gulf between the typical southerner and a Democratic presidential candidate came in 1972, when George McGovern's antiwar campaign alienated many of the region's more conservative voters. But more troubling for the Democrats, and speaking loudly to the growing ideological divide, is that the distance between the typical southerner and John Kerry was nearly as large as that between McGovern and the region's electorate. Whereas in 2000, George W. Bush was perceived as about one point more conservative than the typical southerner, Kerry in 2004 was perceived as more than two times as liberal. Although perceptions of both parties have polarized, views of the Democrats have become much more extreme.

time in the series. The story for the Democrats is similar but more pronounced. The perception of the party in 2004 (2.39) is only slightly less liberal than it was in 2000, and those years represent the most extreme perceptions of the party since the 1970s. Not only are southern voters becoming more likely to identify with the GOP but they are also seeing the Democratic Party as increasingly moving away from the electorate's generally moderate policy positions.[15]

Voters' perceptions of where the parties stand ideologically are powerful indicators of future electoral competition. As we show in the next section, younger cohorts of southern Whites are more likely to identify with the GOP, supporting our contention that voters will reward candidates affiliated with the party that is ideologically closer.

GENERATIONAL CHANGE AND REPUBLICAN GROWTH

In this section, we narrow our focus to White southerners, the segment of the electorate that is driving partisan change in favor of the Republican Party. Since the 1960s, there has been relatively little movement in the partisan allegiance of African Americans in the South.[16] Beginning with the 1964 presidential election, African Americans have overwhelmingly identified with, and supported, Democratic candidates. It has even become a rule of thumb that the Democratic Party in general elections typically receives 90% or more of the Black vote (E. Black, 1998; E. Black & M. Black, 1987, 1992, 2002; Petrocik & Desposato, 1998). Given the stability of African American loyalty to the Democratic Party, we focus here on the dynamic growth of Republican identification among White southerners.

Generational changes in the southern White electorate do not augur well for the Democratic Party's electoral prospects. One of the brakes on Republican growth is the well-known fact that older voters comprise a disproportionately large share of the active electorate, and in the South, older voters are the most Democratic. But as time marches on, generational replacement favors the Republican Party, because younger cohorts are more likely to identify with the GOP. Also, we show that although younger cohorts of southern Whites are more Republican, the Republican trend has affected every cohort of White southerners.

In the South, the ideological positioning of the parties and their candidates has been remarkably consistent. As we have shown, southerners rate the Republican Party as more conservative than the Democratic Party—and furthermore, southerners now consistently place themselves ideologically closer to the GOP. The relative stability of the ideological placement of the parties ensures that as younger cohorts of southerners enter the electorate, the decision of which party to identify with and vote for is made long before entering the voting booth.

Over the past 30 years, there has been a dramatic increase in the number of southern White voters who identify with the Republican Party. And this growth in Republican identification is disproportionately fueled by younger citizens. Figure 5 plots the percentage of southern White voters affiliated with the GOP,

[15] A comparison with the non-South is instructive. According to National Election Studies data, the median voter outside the South is more liberal and sees the Democratic Party as ideologically closer. For example, in 2004, the distance between the median non-southerner and the Republican Party was 1.66 on the 7-point scale, but just 1.34 for the Democratic Party. In stark contrast to the state of affairs in the South, the Democratic Party holds an ideological advantage in the non-South.

[16] According to E. Black and M. Black (2002), "[s]ince the mid-1960s the partisan division of the Black vote has been the principal constant in southern politics" (p. 29).

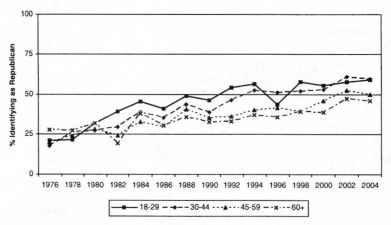

FIGURE 5. Southern White Voters: Republicans, by Age Cohort, 1976–2004
Source: Data are from national exit polls. The South consists of the 11 ex-Confederate states plus Kentucky and Oklahoma. Individual states are not identified until the 1984 exit poll. From 1976 to 1982, the South is coded according to its region label in these polls and the region label consists of exactly those states we define as the South. Also, with respect to race, "White" is combined with "Other" in the 1976 and 1980 exit polls. 1976–1978 = CBS; 1980–1988 = CBS/New York Times; 1990 = Voter Research and Surveys/CBS/ New York Times; 1992 = Voter Research and Surveys; 1994–2002 = Voter News Service; 2004 = National Election Pool. All data are weighted.

broken down into four age groups: (1) 18 to 29, (2) 30 to 44, (3) 45 to 59, and (4) 60 and older. Because these are not panel data, the lines do not represent the same voters over time. Instead, we illustrate that each age category is becoming more Republican, especially the two youngest cohorts. In other words, it is apparent that as older, more Democratic Whites exit the southern electorate, they are replaced by younger, more Republican Whites.

It is worth pointing out that before 1982, there is no clear generational distinction with respect to Republican identification. In fact, in 1976, the highest percentage of Republican identifiers (27.6%) comes from the oldest voter cohort. But from 1982 forward, the two youngest age groups are always the most Republican. By 2004, the percentage of Republican identifiers for each age group is as follows: 59% for 18- to 29-year-olds, 60% for 30- to 44-year-olds, 50% for 45- to 59-year-olds, and 46% for southern White voters age 60 and older.

Another useful way to document the trend in Republican identification among age groups is to display the difference in the percentage of Republicans compared to the percentage of Democrats. Figure 6 shows the percentage difference in Republican versus Democratic voters by age group for southern White voters from 1976 to 2004. A positive (negative) value means there is a higher percentage of Republicans (Democrats) than Democrats (Republicans) in a given age group. From 1976 to 1980, Democrats outnumber Republicans in every age group. In 1982, the only Republican plurality is registered among 18- to 29-year-olds. Since 1984, the two youngest voter cohorts are always more Republican.

In 2002, it is finally the case that within all four age groups, more voters identify with the Republican Party. The large Republican surplus of southern White voters in 2002 and 2004 speaks to the growing and overwhelming electoral advantage redounding to Republican candidates. As time passes, because younger southern

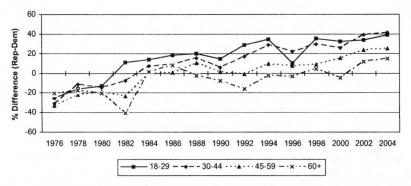

FIGURE 6. Percentage Difference in Southern White Republican and Democratic Identifiers, by Age Cohort, 1976–2004
Source: Data are from the same sources identified in Figure 5.

Whites are more Republican than their predecessors, generational replacement equals an increasingly Republican electorate.

THE INCUMBENCY ADVANTAGE

The ideological and generational advantage of the GOP is likely to manifest itself in a growing incumbency advantage. Much of the incumbency advantage that accrues to representatives of either party is earned, not guaranteed (Desposato & Petrocik, 2003; Erikson & Wright, 2005; Petrocik & Desposato, 2004). Stated another way, the incumbency advantage is variable, dependent on constituent service and the possible effect of short-term political conditions to the prospects of the incumbent's party (Desposato & Petrocik, 2003; Petrocik & Desposato, 2004). To the dismay of southern Democrats (see Fenno, 2000) since at least the 1980s—and especially the 1990s—cultivating the personal vote has become more difficult because of the revival of partisan voting (Bartels, 2000) and a greater emphasis on national politics (Fiorina, 2005).

Although the incumbency literature is almost completely based on U.S. House elections, many of the findings are portable to any electoral contest. Most incumbents, irrespective of the political office, garner a share of the vote that they otherwise would not capture except for the fact that they are the incumbent. To be sure, apart from greater name recognition, simply being an incumbent should not translate into a higher vote. But it is the activities incumbents pursue that serve to increase their electoral support. Incumbents, in their capacity as representatives, engage in constituency service, and this behavior attracts the votes of many constituents who reward their incumbent for being responsive (Cain, Ferejohn, & Fiorina, 1987; Fenno, 1978; Fiorina, 1977; Mayhew, 1974).

Conceptually, the incumbency advantage is the share of the vote that an officeholder receives that is separable from partisan support. Thought of in this way, incumbents receive a higher share of the vote than open-seat candidates, because only the former secure some votes on the basis of performance in office.[17] Candidates who win elective office thus have the opportunity to use their office to secure

---

[17] This, of course, also means that incumbency can be a disadvantage when representatives are punished by voters for performing poorly.

additional votes that could mean the difference between winning and losing during a tough reelection. As Petrocik and Desposato (2004) put it, "[i]ncumbency anchors voters by limiting their reaction to the party bias of the election environment" (p. 371). The incumbency advantage is an electoral insurance policy paid for by cultivating the personal vote.

For decades after it was evident that southern Democrats were politically vulnerable to the challenges of Republican candidates—because the latter are spatially closer to southern voters—the incumbency advantage served to maintain Democratic majorities (E. Black & M. Black, 2002). The incumbency advantage does not simply protect officeholders from strong challengers. Perhaps more important, it also deters the emergence of strong challengers (Cox & Katz, 1996), because the most viable candidates know that the likelihood of winning is much greater in an open-seat contest (Jacobson & Kernell, 1983). Thus, the long-standing incumbency advantage enjoyed by southern Democrats retarded the growth of southern Republicanism.

Unfortunately for the Democratic Party, incumbents eventually retire. In open-seat contests, southern Republicans clearly have an advantage, because they are ideologically closer to the views of the electorate. Not only is it the case that southern Republicans are better positioned to win statewide elections but also because the incumbency advantage is by definition nonpartisan, Republican officeholders can reap the rewards of a personal vote—a portion of the vote that is not as important for the GOP, because the party is already better positioned to win voting majorities. The electoral bonus earned through the incumbency advantage makes it that much harder for southern Democrats to win back Republican seats, because Republican voters now outnumber Democrats.[18] So just as southern Democrats used the incumbency advantage to insulate themselves from Republican competition, as Republicans make further electoral gains, these gains will be protected by the GOP incumbency advantage.[19]

Consider Figures 7 and 8, which display the percentage of elections in three time periods won by Republicans in gubernatorial and U.S. Senate races, respectively. The upward slope of the six lines in both figures demonstrates yet again the rising tide of Republican strength. It is not surprising that as the South has trended Republican, the GOP has been increasingly successful in running candidates for open seats and against Democratic incumbents. For example, before the 1980s, Republicans won just 14% of open-seat contests for governor, and not once did they defeat a sitting Democrat. The story is the same for the Senate, as GOP candidates from 1946 to 1979 won just 21% of open seats and succeeded in knocking off Democratic incumbents a mere 4% of the time. Since 1990, however, Republicans

[18] According to data from the 2004 National Election Pool General Election exit poll, the partisan breakdown for southern voters was the following: 37% Democrats, 44% Republicans, and 19% Independents.

[19] Consider another gain made by the GOP as the next decennial redistricting approaches. Heading into the 1992 elections, Republicans did not control redistricting ("control" means having a majority Republican State House and State Senate and a Republican governor) in any southern state, whereas the Democratic Party was in control in Arkansas (an independent commission has the task of congressional redistricting), Florida, Georgia, Kentucky, North Carolina, Oklahoma, Tennessee, Texas, and Virginia. There was divided control in Alabama, Louisiana, Mississippi, and South Carolina (Niemi & Abramowitz, 1994). Currently, the GOP is in control in Florida, Georgia, South Carolina, and Texas, whereas the Democratic Party has control in Arkansas, Louisiana, and North Carolina. Divided control prevails in Alabama, Kentucky, Mississippi, Oklahoma, Tennessee, and Virginia (data are from the National Conference of State Legislatures: http://www.ncsl.org/).

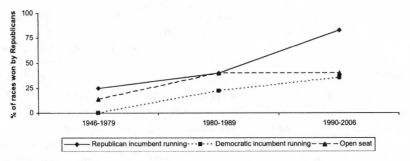

FIGURE 7. GOP Success Rates in Southern Gubernatorial Elections, 1946–2006
Source: Data compiled by the authors.

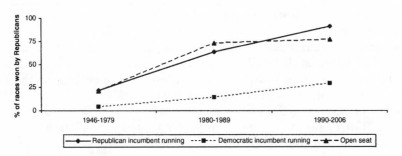

FIGURE 8. GOP Success Rates in Southern U.S. Senate Elections, 1946–2006
Source: Data compiled by the authors.

have won roughly 40% of the gubernatorial elections as both open-seat candidates and challengers to Democratic incumbents. In the Senate contests, the GOP has won three-quarters of open-seat races since 1990 and defeated Democratic senators 30% of the time.

But it is the lines that represent the reelection rates of Republican incumbents that are of greatest interest. Before 1980, Republican governors won reelection in one of four tries, a figure that increased to 40% during the 1980s. With the onset of the 1990s, however, and continuing into the first years of the 21st century, the success rates of GOP governors more than doubled, climbing to 83%. In Senate elections, the change is even more dramatic. GOP senators won 22% of their reelection bids between 1946 and 1979, 63% in the 1980s, and a remarkable 91% from 1990 on. In both gubernatorial and Senate contests, the slope is steepest for the races involving Republican officeholders, indicating that the growth in the incumbency advantage was outpacing GOP success in the other two types of elections. In other words, although the GOP was winning more southern elections than it had in decades, its success rates were highest when a Republican officeholder was running for reelection. Once in office, Republican incumbents since 1990 have been exceedingly difficult for Democrats to dislodge, a trend that is likely to continue.

We can also conceptualize electoral success not only in terms of victories but also as the share of the vote received. For example, in the earliest era (1946–1979), Republican Senate candidates won an average of 32.5% of the two-party vote in open-seat races. By the 1990s and 2000s, however, that figure had risen more than

20 points, to 52.8%. Meanwhile, GOP incumbents increased their average vote share from 54.5% to a robust 62.9%. The same pattern appears in gubernatorial contests, though the absolute numbers are smaller. The average Republican vote share in open-seat races increased from 29% to 47.6% from the 1940s to the early 2000s, and the incumbent vote share grew from 44% to 54.1%. Conceptualized as either electoral victories or vote share, the performance of GOP candidates—especially incumbents—has continued to improve.

Republican growth in gubernatorial contests is particularly striking, given that such contests are fairly insulated from national party images and issues. Historically, Republican top-down advancement in the South has been more promising in federal elections (Aistrup, 1996), where the images of the parties are more distinct than their state counterparts. Nonetheless, the identities of the national and state parties have tightened with the passage of time, because the polarization of political elites has permeated the ranks of national, state, and local party leaders (Clark & Prysby, 2004).

Among statewide contests, we would expect gubernatorial elections to constitute the GOP's greatest challenge, because candidates for both parties are afforded more ideological leeway. Outside the South, no one better displays the political independence of California Republican Governor Arnold Schwarzenegger. In the South, Florida Republican Governor Charlie Crist and Virginia's Democratic Governor Tim Kaine are prime examples of post-partisan politicians. But these examples are likely exceptions to the general trend in favor of increased partisan polarization, which will make it more difficult for gubernatorial candidates to obfuscate their ties to parties that have become more distinct, salient, and relevant to an increasingly partisan (Bartels, 2000) and ideological (Abramowitz & Saunders, 1998) southern electorate.

THE 2006 MIDTERM ELECTIONS

Although the evidence presented thus far documents the growing Republican strength in the South, the results of the 2006 elections may seem to suggest a reversal of fortune. Even in the South, the GOP lost a U.S. Senate seat (Virginia), a governorship (Arkansas), and several U.S. House seats. But although the Republican Party indeed took its lumps, a closer look suggests that the Democratic tide that swept the country did not swell to full crest in the South.

Table 1 presents data on Republican seat losses in 2006 in the non-South and South for federal contests (U.S. Senate and U.S. House) and state-level elections (Governor, State Senate, and State House). For every type of election, Republican losses were substantially greater outside the South. Contests for the U.S. House warrant specific mention, because half of the six southern seats Republicans lost resulted from "very unusual circumstances" (Klinkner & Schaller, 2006, p. 4). The resignation of scandal-plagued Republicans Tom DeLay (TX 22nd) and Mark Foley (FL 16th) led to Democratic pickups in what are two otherwise reliably Republican districts.[20] In addition, Republican Henry Bonilla (TX 23rd) lost his

[20] Despite the fact that the Republican option was for a write-in candidate in Texas's 22nd and Mark Foley's name remained on the ballot in Florida's 16th, both these contests remained competitive. In District 22 in Texas, former Democratic Congressman Nick Lampson beat his nearest write-in opponent (there were two other write-in candidates) with 55% of the vote, and in District 16 in Florida, Democrat Tim Mahoney beat Republican Joe Negron (who was the choice a voter selected

TABLE 1
Percentage of Republican Seats Before and After the
2006 Elections, Non-South and South

	Non-South			South		
	Before 2006	After 2006	Difference	Before 2006	After 2006	Difference
U.S. Senate	44.6 (33)	37.8 (28)	–6.8	84.6 (22)	80.8 (21)	–3.8
U.S. House	48.1 (141)	39.9 (117)	–8.2	64.1 (91)	59.9 (85)	–4.2
Governors	54.1 (20)	40.5 (15)	–13.6	61.5 (8)	53.8 (7)	–7.7
State Senate[a]	48.7 (696)	44.7 (638)	–4.0	49.4 (268)	49.4 (268)	0.0
State House[a]	49.6 (1,928)	43.0 (1,669)	–6.6	49.7 (759)	48.8 (745)	–0.9
Total	49.3 (2,818)	43.2 (2,467)	–6.1	51.0 (1,148)	50.0 (1,126)	–1.0

Note: The N of Republican seats appears in parentheses.

Source: Data were compiled by the authors from news sources and the National Conference of State Legislatures.

[a] Excludes Nebraska, which has a unicameral legislature with nonpartisan elections.

bid for reelection as a direct consequence of a redistricting that increased the Hispanic population in his district, thus tipping the runoff in favor of his seasoned challenger, former Democratic Congressman Ciro Rodriguez.

It is also worth noting that the GOP in the South claimed the same number of state Senate seats before and after the elections, and lost only a tiny fraction of state House seats. Overall in 2006, the decline in Republican seats outside the South was six times greater than in the South, and only in the South did a majority of voters cast Republican ballots in U.S. House contests (Klinkner & Schaller, 2006).[21]

Ultimately, our interpretation is that the 2006 midterm elections delivered a wake-up call to the Bush administration and the Republican Party but does not represent a reversal in the growth of the GOP in the South. As we read the political tea leaves, it appears that a jump in support for Democratic candidates was more evidence of frustration with the political status quo than a clear endorsement of the Democratic Party's ideas or ideology. In the South, in particular, the small Democratic gains speak loudly to a deviating election and certainly not a lasting departure from the erstwhile Republican trend. Indeed, the underlying electoral structure in the South, as we have documented in this article, bolsters our contention that the region will continue to shift toward the GOP despite a short-term setback in 2006.

DISCUSSION

One potential objection to our approach is that the analyses to this point have considered the South as a region and not as a collection of heterogeneous states.

by choosing Mark Foley on the ballot) with 51% of the vote. Data are from the Texas and Florida Secretary of State Web sites, respectively.

[21] In election cycles that clearly favor one party, we should expect that the disadvantaged party has a much smaller number of "free rides" or uncontested seats. In the 2006 U.S. House elections, Democrats had 46 (46 out of 435 = 10.57%) uncontested seats, whereas Republicans had free rides in just 10 districts (10 out of 435 = 2.3%). Seven out of the 10 uncontested Republican districts were in the South.

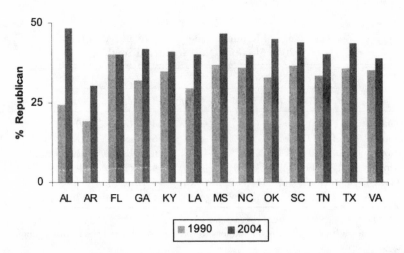

FIGURE 9. Republican Party Identification of Southern Voters, by State, 1990 and 2004
Note: Data points for Louisiana, Mississippi, and Virginia are from 1992 rather than 1990.
Source: See Appendix table.

Indeed, the 13 southern states do differ in terms of partisanship, demographics, and other salient characteristics. But despite this diversity, the growing Republican trend is evident across the region. Figure 9 presents exit polling data on the percentage of voters in each southern state identifying as Republican in 1990 and 2004. Over that 14-year period, the percentage of Republican identifiers in every state has grown.

Whether it is Arkansas, where the GOP has admittedly struggled in no small measure because of Bill Clinton's large political shadow,[22] or Mississippi, where the specter of race has resulted in the most extreme partisan polarization, the GOP has increased its share of the southern electorate. Overall, the Republican portion of the southern electorate has grown from one third in 1990 to 44% in 2004. The base of Republican strength in the South is quite variable depending on the state, but the upward trend is universal.[23] The appendix shows the growth in Republican identification for each of the eight elections between 1990 and 2004.

Although Republican growth is occurring across the South, it is important to note two possible paths to a revival of Democratic success. The first is rooted in demographic change. The Hispanic population is expanding at a striking rate, particularly in Texas, Florida, Georgia, North Carolina, and Virginia. To the extent that Democrats can tap into and mobilize votes among Latinos in the South, the party may enable itself to put together coalitions that challenge the growing Republican dominance in statewide elections.

[22] The political acumen of Bill Clinton is legendary, and his skill at staking out the majority position as a southern governor illustrates the difficulties the GOP has encountered in winning these statewide contests. In the words of E. Black and M. Black (2002), "Like most southern Democrats holding statewide office, Clinton had spent his entire political career learning how to bob and weave liberal and conservative themes in order to create and maintain a successful biracial coalition" (p. 27).

[23] Although it is difficult to tell in the figure, Florida's Republican share of the electorate increased from 40.1% to 40.2%. In 2002, the number was 43%.

This endeavor, however, is not without formidable challenges. For one, a large segment of the Hispanic population is composed of noncitizens who cannot vote, and this situation is likely to persist for several decades (see Bullock & Hood, 2006).[24] Second, unlike African Americans, Hispanics are not unified in their partisanship or voting behavior (Leal, Barreto, Lee, & de la Garza, 2005). Cuban Americans in Florida, for example, continue to lean Republican, and estimates from the 2004 presidential election show Bush polling between 32% and 44% among Latinos (Leal et al., 2005).[25] In addition, upwardly mobile Hispanics in the South are attracted to the Republican Party (E. Black & M. Black, 2002). Finally, the increasing diversity of the southern electorate is counteracted by the increasing partisan polarization of White and minority voters (Bullock, Hoffman, & Gaddie, 2005; Valentino & Sears, 2005). In several Deep South states where recent Republican growth is most pronounced—in particular, Alabama, Georgia, and Mississippi—the Black populations are among the largest in the region, but Democratic strength is more than offset by the highest degrees of racial polarization in party identification and vote choice.

The second and perhaps more likely route to Democratic revival passes through the GOP itself. Although data on southern political activists[26] in 1991 and 2001 show a marked increase in ideological cohesion and a concomitant reduction in intraparty factionalism (see McGlennon, 2004), the Republican Party is susceptible to division along a religious and secular cleavage. To the extent that Republican primaries become divisive along this fault line, in those instances where religious right candidates have prevailed, the party has often succumbed to defeat in subsequent general elections (Glaser, 2005, 2006; Lamis, 1999). This fits with our Downsian explanation of party positioning: Candidates of the religious right are further from the median southerner than is the typical White Democratic candidate.

The bad news for the Democrats is that, more often than not, Republican fringe candidates do not win primaries.[27] And to the extent that the Democratic Party takes positions that are ideologically incongruent with the preferences of most southern Whites to satisfy the party's proportionally smaller and more racially diverse core of supporters (M. Black, 2004), we expect that the GOP will

[24] The most striking growth among Hispanics in the South is occurring in states such as Georgia and North Carolina, where the vast majority of Hispanic residents are noncitizens.

[25] Not surprisingly Hispanics did increase their Democratic support considerably in 2006. Exit poll data show the small population of Hispanic voters (8% of the electorate) casting 69% of their U.S. House votes in favor of Democratic candidates (http://www.cnn.com/ELECTION/2006/pages/results/states/US/H/00/epolls.0.html).

[26] These data consist of surveys of county party chairs and county executive committee members in the 11 ex-Confederate states (see Clark & Prysby, 2004).

[27] As Glaser (2005, 2006) points out, the runoff primary in most southern states has come to serve the purpose of blocking the nomination of fringe candidates who are often capable of winning the most votes in the initial round of primary voting but then end up losing the runoff to the more centrist candidate who rallies greater support from voters backing the candidate(s) failing to make the runoff. The runoff primary is indeed an opportunity for voters to reevaluate candidates. And at this stage, it is likely that one of the factors accounting for vote choice is general election viability. Regarding the religious versus secular factions in the southern GOP, Glaser (2006) writes, "[t]his cleavage runs through the Republican electorate in many southern districts now and it is a cleavage that the party will have to bridge, though the primary runoff offers a means by which a majority can at least counter a 'mischievous' faction—as it long has done. This has been overlooked in discussions of how the Christian Right might threaten the growth and dominance of the party as a whole by turning off more centrist general election voters" (p. 784).

continue to gain in strength by positioning itself to meet the demands of its over-whelmingly White constituents.

CONCLUSION

With the passage of time, it appears increasingly evident that the two-party South will soon be eclipsed by a majority- and minority-party South. E. Black and M. Black (2002), at the time of their writing, convincingly demonstrate that the South consists of two minority parties reliant on swing voters to secure majorities in statewide elections. But the current structure of competition is moving in favor of the GOP, irrespective of the level of elections one chooses to investigate.

Although the thrust of our argument focuses on statewide elections, the pattern of contemporary congressional politics provides a window to the future of southern politics in general (see Shafer & Johnston, 2001). As discussed by E. Black (1998), there are generally three kinds of districts in southern U.S. House contests: (a) majority–minority districts where minority representatives can win election based solely on the votes of racial and ethnic minorities, (b) districts represented by Republicans who rely on the votes of Whites, and (c) districts represented by White Democrats who depend on a coalition of White and minority voters. Racial redistricting has disproportionately harmed the electoral prospects of White Democrats (Lublin & Voss, 2000, 2003) who must appeal to a segment of White and Black voters who often have different concerns and disagree on many issues (Lamis, 1988). Furthermore, in many cases, these White Democrats find themselves barely surviving reelection and others losing to strong GOP challengers who recognize that the partisan balance of these districts (based on presidential returns) favors the Republican Party (see Abramowitz, 1995; E. Black & M. Black, 2002; Jacobson, 1996, 2000).

In the case of district-level contests, such as U.S. House, State House, and State Senate races, there is clearly a floor of Democratic viability that places a limit on GOP advancement so long as a substantial portion of districts are configured to secure minority representation (Shotts, 2001). For Democrats, this reality is certainly not cause for celebration, because the GOP already controls a majority of U.S. House seats and is on the cusp of attaining majority status in the number of state legislative seats, without even coming close to exhausting the possible number of winnable districts. The uniform trend of Republican advancement in office-holding in the South, regardless of the level of contest and whether it is statewide or district-based, speaks loudly to our contention that the near future of southern politics entails a majority Republican Party and a minority Democratic Party.

If we conceptualize each southern state as a single district for the sake of considering Republican prospects in statewide elections, then, to the extent that these contests reflect the dynamics in district-level contests, the GOP is greatly advantaged. Given the fact that Whites comprise a clear majority in every southern state but Texas, further movement of Whites in favor of the GOP necessarily dims the prospects for Democrats in statewide elections.

In Downsian (Downs, 1957) spatial parlance, the GOP occupies the ideological real estate where most southerners reside. The ideological constraint that African American voters place on Democratic candidates forecloses the likelihood of the Democratic Party positioning itself to not only win back, let alone maintain, the political allegiance of enough White southerners to sustain a political system characterized by two competitive minority parties. And as we have stated previously, the factors that we claim are most influential in shaping future partisan competition all tend to advantage the GOP. In addition to ideological proximity, younger White voters are decidedly more Republican, and satisfactory performance in governance and constituency service reinforces support for Republican candidates. In addition, success in office undoubtedly affects the political calculations of the next generation of strategic politicians who see a greater probability of making a career in elective politics by running under the Republican label (Aldrich, 1995).

One major difficulty for Democrats is that the party appears positioned to lose more and more White votes. The evidence presented by M. Black (2004) suggests the southern Democratic Party is in a state of disequilibrium and its current transformation may render it an uncompetitive minority party. The problem rests with the incongruence between the Democratic Party in office vis-à-vis the Democratic Party in the electorate. As M. Black (2004) points out, 70% of "Democratic statewide officeholders in 2003 were White men, even though they comprised only 21 percent of the party in the electorate."[28] Given the fact that the contemporary southern Democratic Party is majority female, approximately 52% White, 38% African American, and 10% Hispanic (M. Black, 2004), there will be increasing pressure for the recruitment and support of candidates who not only advocate Democratic positions but also share the gender, race, and ethnicity of most Democratic voters. We expect the Democratic Party will be further disadvantaged by running candidates for statewide office who are not White, because White swing voters are less likely to vote for minority candidates.

In the 1960s, George Wallace made the famous remark that "there wasn't 'a dime's worth of difference' between the Democratic and Republican parties" (Watson, 1996, p. 152). At the time, Wallace was at least partially correct, because so many un-Reconstructed Democrats held power in the Deep South by "out-segging" Republican challengers. In the newest southern politics, however, the Republican and Democratic parties differ sharply on most political issues, and the electorate continues to realign according to the positions the parties stake out. For example, although it still may be possible for a conservative Democrat to win the election in a Republican-leaning district, time is not on the Democratic Party's side; eventually, voters are likely to support a candidate who shares their partisan affiliation (Cottrill, 2004; Erikson & Wright, 2005).

The current positioning of southern Democrats prevents them from recapturing the long-term political support of the median southern voter. According to David Rohde (1996), "the likelihood and stability of future Republican gains rests in large measure on the choices of candidates and office-holders of both parties. Which party prospers, and how much, depends on the platforms candidates adopt and the policy agendas presidents and Members of Congress pursue" (p. 30). We think Rohde is correct and thus agree that there is nothing inevitable about GOP ascendancy. But as the world of southern politics stands now, the Democrats find themselves in a difficult fight against a rising Republican tide.

It is nothing short of fascinating to reflect on the copious southern politics literature that for several decades has pointed to the end of southern exceptionalism (see Shafer & Johnston, 2006). Most political observers considered the advent of a two-party South to hasten the death knell of southern distinctiveness. The rise of the southern Republican Party meant that the region's politics would now reflect the rest of the nation's more competitive partisan balance. The evidence presented

---

[28] M. Black's (2004) data are limited to the 11 former Confederate states.

here offers an alternative interpretation: The South remains exceptional, because Republican growth persists, even as it has declined in the rest of the country. We doubt that the GOP will ever attain the one-party dominance once exhibited by the Democratic Party, but the current structure of southern politics remains promising for further Republican growth.

APPENDIX

Republican Party Identification of Southern Voters, by State, 1990–2004

State	1990	1992	1994	1996	1998	2000	2002	2004	Change (1990–2004)
Alabama	24.4	33.5	29.1	35.8	29.6	36.6	42.7	48.3	+23.9
Arkansas	19.3	28.4	22.5	24.8	22.4	25.2	—	30.3	+11.0
Florida	40.1	36.6	40.2	38.4	39.5	37.9	43.0	40.2	+0.1
Georgia	31.8	34.0	35.4	34.1	36.9	37.7	44.0	41.8	+10.0
Kentucky	34.7	35.5	—	35.4	34.8	39.4	42.3	40.9	+6.2
Louisiana	—	29.3	—	28.8	27.2	34.0	36.2	40.2	+10.9
Mississippi	—	36.8	—	37.1	—	41.6	51.5	46.5	+9.7
North Carolina	35.9	37.0	—	39.1	38.8	37.6	53.1	39.7	+3.8
Oklahoma	32.9	37.2	41.3	39.7	42.0	45.3	—	44.8	+11.9
South Carolina	36.5	39.5	42.3	39.3	36.0	39.0	—	43.8	+7.3
Tennessee	33.4	30.7	37.8	36.8	41.0	37.4	65.2	40.0	+6.6
Texas	35.5	35.8	38.9	37.5	38.1	41.2	43.6	43.4	+7.9
Virginia	—	35.1	37.8	36.3	—	36.5	51.6	38.7	+3.6
South	33.4	36.8	37.6	37.0	37.9	39.7	45.9	44.0	+10.6

Source: Data are from exit polls. The South consists of the 11 ex-Confederate states plus Kentucky and Oklahoma. With the exception of 2002 and the South (both calculated with national exit poll data), these data are compiled from polls conducted in each state for the given election year. Blank entries indicate the absence of a state poll for that election. In 2002, the data for each state were drawn from the national exit poll, because there were no individual state polls; the number of observations range from $N = 182$ in Mississippi to $N = 1,402$ in Texas. There were no observations for Arkansas in 2002, and the number of cases were too small in Oklahoma ($N = 85$) and South Carolina ($N = 12$). The percentage of Republican voters is calculated by dividing the total number of Republicans by the sum of the total number of Republicans, Democrats, and Independents. In the last column, "difference" equals the percentage of Republican voters in 2004 subtracted by the percentage of Republican voters in the earliest election (either 1990 or 1992). The exit polls are as follows: 1990 = Voter Research and Surveys/CBS/*New York Times*; 1992 = Voter Research and Surveys; 1994–2002 = Voter News Service; 2004 = National Election Pool. All data are weighted.

REFERENCES

Abramowitz, A. I. (1995). The end of the Democratic era? 1994 and the future of congressional election research. *Political Research Quarterly, 48*(4), 873–889.

Abramowitz, A. I., & Saunders, K. L. (1998). Ideological realignment in the U.S. electorate. *Journal of Politics, 60*(3), 634–652.

Aistrup, J. A. (1996). *The southern strategy revisited: Republican top-down advancement in the South.* Lexington: University of Kentucky Press.

Aldrich, J. H. (1995). *Why parties? The origin and transformation of political parties in America.* Chicago: University of Chicago Press.

Bartels, L. M. (2000). Partisanship and voting behavior. *American Journal of Political Science, 44*(1), 35–50.

Bartley, N. V., & Graham, H. D. (1975). *Southern politics and the Second Reconstruction.* Baltimore: Johns Hopkins University Press.

Black, E. (1998). The newest southern politics. *Journal of Politics, 60*(3), 591–612.

Black, E., & Black, M. (1987). *Politics and society in the South.* Cambridge, MA: Harvard University Press.

Black, E., & Black, M. (1992). *The vital South: How presidents are elected.* Cambridge, MA: Harvard University Press

Black, E., & Black, M. (2002). *The rise of southern Republicans.* Cambridge, MA: Harvard University Press.

Black, M. (2004). The transformation of the southern Democratic Party. *Journal of Politics, 66*(4), 1001–1017.

Bullock, C. S. III, Hoffman, D. R., & Gaddie, R. K. (2005). The consolidation of the white Southern congressional vote. *Political Research Quarterly, 58*(2), 231–243.

Bullock, C. S., III, & Hood, M. V., III. (2006). A mile-wide gap: The evolution of Hispanic political emergence in the Deep South. *Social Science Quarterly, 87*(5), 1117–1135.

Cain, B., Ferejohn, J., & Fiorina, M. P. (1987). *The personal vote: Constituency service and electoral independence.* Cambridge, MA: Harvard University Press.

Campbell, A., Converse, P. E., Miller, W. E., & Stokes, D. E. (1960). *The American voter.* Chicago: University of Chicago Press.

Carmines, E. G., & Stimson, J. A. (1989). *Issue evolution: Race and the transformation of American politics.* Princeton, NJ: Princeton University Press.

Ceaser, J. W., & Saldin, R. P. (2005). A new measure of party strength. *Political Research Quarterly, 58*(2), 245–256.

Clark, J. A., & Prysby, C. L. (Eds.). (2004). *Southern political party activists: Patterns of conflict and change, 1991–2001.* Lexington: University of Kentucky Press.

Converse, P. E. (1964). The nature of belief systems in mass publics. In D. Apter (Ed.), *Ideology and discontent* (pp. 206–261). New York: Free Press.

Cottrill, J. B. (2004, January). *Surviving in the electoral jungle: The role of environmental factors in congressional elections.* Paper presented at the annual meeting of the Southern Political Science Association, New Orleans, LA.

Cox, G. W., & Katz, J. N. (1996). Why did the incumbency advantage in U.S. House elections grow? *American Journal of Political Science, 40*(2), 478–497.

David, P. T. (1972). *Party strength in the United States: 1872–1970.* Charlottesville: University Press of Virginia.

Desposato, S. W., & Petrocik, J. R. (2003). The variable incumbency advantage: New voters, redistricting, and the personal vote. *American Journal of Political Science, 47*(1), 18–32.

Downs, A. (1957). *An economic theory of democracy.* New York: Harper & Row.

Erikson, R. S., & Wright, G. C. (2005). Voters, candidates, and issues in congressional elections. In B. I. Oppenheimer & L. C. Dodd (Eds.), *Congress reconsidered* (8th ed., pp. 135–158). Washington, DC: CQ Press.

Fenno, R. F., Jr. (1978). *Homestyle: House members in their districts.* Boston: Little, Brown.

Fenno, R. F., Jr. (2000). *Congress at the grassroots: Representational change in the South, 1970–1998.* Chapel Hill: University of North Carolina Press.

Fiorina, M. P. (1977). *Congress: Keystone of the Washington establishment.* New Haven, CT: Yale University Press.

Fiorina, M. P. (1981). *Retrospective voting in American national elections.* New Haven, CT: Yale University Press.

Fiorina, M. P. (2005). Keystone reconsidered. In B. I. Oppenheimer & L. C. Dodd (Eds.), *Congress reconsidered* (8th ed., pp. 159–177). Washington, DC: CQ Press.

Fiorina, M. P., Abrams, S. J., & Pope, J. C. (2006). *Culture war? The myth of a polarized America.* New York: Pearson Education.

Glaser, J. M. (2005). *The hand of the past in contemporary southern politics.* New Haven, CT: Yale University Press.

Glaser, J. M. (2006). The primary runoff as a remnant of the old South. *Electoral Studies 25*(4), 776–790.

Green, D., Palmquist, B., & Schickler, E. (2002). *Partisan hearts & minds: Political parties and the social identities of voters*. New Haven, CT: Yale University Press.

Hayes, D., & McKee, S. C. (2004). Booting Barnes: Explaining the historic upset in the 2002 Georgia gubernatorial election. *Politics & Policy, 32*(4), 708–739.

Jacobson, G. C. (1996). The 1994 House elections in perspective. *Political Science Quarterly, 111*(2), 203–223.

Jacobson, G. C. (2000). Reversal of fortune: The transformation of U.S. House elections in the 1990s. In D. W. Brady, J. F. Cogan, & M. P. Fiorina (Eds.), *Continuity and Change in House Elections* (pp. 10–38). Stanford, CA: Stanford University Press.

Jacobson, G. C., & Kernell, S. (1983). *Strategy and choice in congressional elections*. New Haven, CT: Yale University Press.

Keith, B. E., Magelby, D. B., Nelson, C. J., Orr, E., Westlye, M. C., & Wolfinger, R. E. (1992). *The myth of the independent voter*. Berkeley: University of California Press.

Key, V. O., Jr. (1996). *Southern politics in state and nation*. Knoxville: University of Tennessee Press.

Klinkner, P. A., & Schaller, T. F. (2006). A regional analysis of the 2006 midterms. *The Forum, 4*, Article 9.

Lamis, A. P. (1988). *The two-party South*. Oxford, UK: Oxford University Press.

Lamis, A. P. (Ed.). (1999). *Southern politics in the 1990s*. Baton Rouge: Louisiana State University Press.

Leal, D. L., Barreto, M. A., Lee, J., & de la Garza, R. O. (2005). The Latino vote in the 2004 election. *PS: Political Science & Politics, 38*(1), 41–49.

Lublin, D. (2004). *The Republican South: Democratization and partisan change*. Princeton, NJ: Princeton University Press.

Lublin, D., & Voss, S. D. (2000). Boll-weevil blues: Polarized congressional delegations into the 21st century. *American Review of Politics, 21*, 427–450.

Lublin, D., & Voss, S. D. (2003). The missing middle: Why median-voter theory can't save Democrats from singing the boll-weevil blues. *Journal of Politics, 65*(1), 227–237.

Mayhew, D. (1974). *Congress: The electoral connection*. New Haven, CT: Yale University Press.

McDonald, M. D., Mendes, S. M., & Budge, I. (2004). What are elections for? Conferring the median mandate. *British Journal of Political Science, 34*(1), 1–26.

McGlennon, J. J. (2004). Factionalism transformation in the two-party South: It's getting harder to pick a fight. In J. A. Clark & C. L. Prysby (Eds.), *Southern political party activists: Patterns of conflict and change, 1991–2001* (pp. 91–106). Lexington: University of Kentucky Press.

Niemi, R. G., & Abramowitz, A. I. (1994). Partisan redistricting and the 1992 elections. *Journal of Politics, 56*(3), 811–817.

Petrocik, J. R., & Desposato, S. W. (1998). The partisan consequences of majority-minority redistricting in the South, 1992 and 1994. *Journal of Politics, 60*(3), 613–633.

Petrocik, J. R., & Desposato, S. W. (2004). Incumbency and short-term influences on voters. *Political Research Quarterly, 57*(3), 363–373.

Phillips, K. P. (1969). *The emerging Republican majority*. New Rochelle, NY: Arlington House.

Rohde, D. W. (1996). The inevitability and solidity of the 'Republican solid South.' *American Review of Politics, 17*, 23–46.

Schreckhise, W. D., & Shields, T. G. (2003). Ideological realignment in the contemporary U.S. electorate revisited. *Social Science Quarterly, 84*(3), 596–612.

Shafer, B. E., & Johnston, R. (2001). The transformation of southern politics revisited: The House of Representatives as a window. *British Journal of Political Science, 31*(4), 601–625.

Shafer, B. E., & Johnston, R. (2006). *The end of southern exceptionalism: Race, class, and partisan change in the postwar South*. Cambridge, MA: Harvard University Press.

Shotts, K. W. (2001). The effect of majority-minority mandates on partisan gerrymandering. *American Journal of Political Science, 45*(1), 120–135.

Stimson, J. A. (2004). *Tides of consent: How public opinion shapes American politics.* Cambridge, UK: Cambridge University Press.

Sundquist, J. L. (1983). *The dynamics of the party system.* Washington, DC: Brookings Institution.

Valentino, N. A., & Sears, D. O. (2005). Old times there are not forgotten: Race and partisan realignment in the contemporary South. *American Journal of Political Science, 49*(3), 672–688.

Watson, S. J. (1996). Race and realignment reconsidered: Issue evolution in the South since 1972. *American Review of Politics, 17*, 145–170.

29

THE LEGAL STATUS OF POLITICAL PARTIES: A REASSESSMENT OF COMPETING PARADIGMS

Nathaniel Persily[*]

Bruce E. Cain[**]

Political scientists and citizens are not the only people who have distinctive and complex views of political parties: so do judges and election lawyers. All told, in fact, there are several "competing paradigms" of political parties, as Persily and Cain show. Surveying them, they provide a concise catalogue of the different ways to understand what political parties do well—and the values that they can facilitate or sometimes undermine. Persily and Cain also underscore a central fact about party politics, namely, that it is influenced by judicial correction and intervention.

Finishing Gillman and Rosenberg, earlier in this volume, one might have wondered just what the Supreme Court does reasonably well. One thing it has done with some care is attend to our associational rights by inserting itself into the regulation of political parties. Indeed this article is a useful counterpoint to Gillman and Rosenberg.

• • •

INTRODUCTION

IN THE PAST FORTY YEARS, the caselaw and legal scholarship on the regulation of politics have erected a subdiscipline in American law.[1] Courts, with some assistance from Congress, have become forums for political disputes previously dismissed as mere political questions or as something generally beyond the province

Columbia Law Review, Vol. 100, No. 3, Symposium: Law and Political Parties. (Apr. 2000), pp. 775–812. Copyright 2000 by Columbia Law Review Association, Inc. Reproduced with permission of Columbia Law Review Association, Inc. via Copyright Clearance Center.

* Staff Attorney, Brennan Center for Justice at NYU School of Law. The author was part of the legal team representing Senator John McCain in Molinari v. Powers, 82 F. Supp. 2d 57 (E.D.N.Y. 2000), and assisted in the Brennan Center amicus brief in California Democratic Party v. Jones, 984 F. Supp. 1288 (E.D. Cal. 1997), aff'd, 169 F.3d 646 (9th Cir. 1999), cert. granted, 120 S. Ct. 977 (U.S. Jan. 21, 2000). Both cases are discussed herein. The authors would like to thank the Brennan Center for Justice, the Institute of Governmental Studies, and the Institute for Humane Studies for their support, the participants in the Columbia Law Review symposium for their helpful comments, and Gaurav Shah, Wendy Cassity, Bryan Diederich, and the Columbia Law Review staff for their editorial assistance.

** Robson Professor of Political Science and Director of the Institute of Governmental Studies, U.C. Berkeley. The author was the expert witness for the plaintiffs in California Democratic Party v. Jones.

[1] Two casebooks, for example, now deal exclusively with issues of the legal regulation of politics: Daniel Hays Lowenstein, Election Law: Cases and Materials (1995); Samuel Issacharoff et al., The Law of Democracy: Legal Structure of the Political Process (1998). See generally Symposium, Election Law as Its Own Field of Study, 32 Loy. L.A. L. Rev. 1095–1272 (1999).

of the judiciary.[2] Despite the innovation in caselaw on patronage, ballot access, voting rights, racial and political gerrymandering, and campaign finance, however, the subject of the legal status of political parties has only recently joined these other topics as a focus for legal scholarship.

Unique challenges face lawyers and scholars who seek to make sense of the caselaw in this area. The chief difficulty may be the ill-fitted and limited array of tools in the legal scholar or judge's analytical toolbox. These cases, after all, come in two contexts—either in a dispute over statutory interpretation[3] or in an individual or group's constitutional challenge to a law or other governmental action. The constitutional cases are also quite limited to (1) disputes centered on First Amendment rights of association and speech[4] (or as incorporated through the Due Process Clause of the Fourteenth Amendment) or (2) governmental action that treats individuals differently or burdens fundamental interests such as the right to vote and thus violates Equal Protection.[5]

The judicial framework for constitutional cases involving political parties generally involves four familiar steps. First, characterize the parties: Who is the state actor and whose rights were violated? In some cases the party is the state actor violating the rights of a citizen; in others, the state violates the rights of an individual or of a party as a free association of individuals. Second, define the rights claim: How severe was the deprivation of the private actor's rights? Third, characterize the state interest: Is it sufficiently weighty to justify the restraint on the non-state actor's rights? And then, depending on the outcome of steps two and three, decide whether the means the state chose were appropriately tailored (i.e., narrowly or rationally related) to the ends it was trying to achieve.[6]

Simple mechanics but, as we read the caselaw, unforeseeable results. Something else is at work here. We think it has to do with the worldview that judges and

---

[2] There are, of course, a few earlier cases, such as the White Primary cases, where courts dabbled in this area, but finding more than a few Supreme Court cases in this area of the law before 1955 presents a challenge. See the White Primary cases: Terry v. Adams, 345 U.S. 461 (1953); Smith v. Allwright, 321 U.S. 649 (1944); Nixon v. Condon, 286 U.S. 73 (1932); Nixon v. Herndon, 273 U.S. 536 (1927). See also United States v. Classic, 313 U.S. 299, 314–20 (1941) (holding that Louisiana electoral officials infringed the right to vote by stuffing primary ballot boxes).

[3] See, e.g., Morse v. Republican Party, 517 U.S. 186 (1996) (interpreting Section 5 of the Voting Rights Act to apply to party primaries).

[4] See, e.g., Timmons v. Twin Cities Area New Party, 520 U.S. 351 (1997) (upholding Minnesota law banning fusion candidacies); Eu v. San Francisco County Democratic Comm., 489 U.S. 214 (1989) (striking down California law preventing parties from endorsing candidates in primaries); Elrod v. Burns, 427 U.S. 347 (1976) (establishing First Amendment bar to patronage-based dismissals for low level employees). See generally Anderson v. Celebrezze, 460 U.S. 780, 787 n.7 (1983) (comparing First Amendment, Due Process, and Equal Protection cases).

[5] See, e.g., Williams v. Rhodes, 393 U.S. 23 (1968) (striking down restrictive ballot access law as denying minor parties equal protection of the laws); Herndon, 273 U.S. at 536 (striking down Texas law that prevented African-Americans from participating in the Democratic Party primary).

[6] See, e.g., Timmons, 520 U.S. at 358 ("Regulations imposing severe burdens on plaintiffs' rights must be narrowly tailored and advance a compelling state interest. Lesser burdens, however, trigger less exacting review, and a State's important regulatory interests will usually be enough to justify reasonable, nondiscriminatory restrictions.") (internal quotation marks and citations omitted); Tashjian v. Republican Party of Conn., 479 U.S. 208, 213–14 (1986) (The court must "consider the character and magnitude of the asserted injury to the rights protected by the First and Fourteenth Amendments that the plaintiff seeks to vindicate" against "the precise interests put forward by the State as justifications for the burden imposed by its rule" considering "the extent to which those interests make it necessary to burden the plaintiff's rights").

lawyers bring to these cases and particularly their differing philosophies as to the function political parties play in American democracy.[7] With this Article, we hope to explain the varying schools of thought in the caselaw and scholarship on the legal status of political parties. Our principal argument is that each school of thought comprises a set of assumptions and normative positions with respect to the proper role of political parties in American politics. After describing in Part I the nature of the problem of characterizing the legal status of political parties, Part II isolates and critiques five schools of thought: the Managerial, Progressive, Political Markets, Libertarian, and Pluralist. Having rejected any one of these paradigms as achieving desirable or even determinate results in all cases, in Part III we propose some middle range principles that might guide courts in deciding two specific types of political regulation cases: ballot access cases and regulation of party nomination procedures.

I. THE NATURE OF THE PROBLEM

The crux of the problem political parties pose for lawyers and judges derives from parties' uncertain constitutional and legal status. Are they state actors and therefore subject to constitutional restraints imposed by the Bill of Rights and the Fourteenth Amendment or are they private associations, similar to churches and bowling clubs, that can use the Constitution as a shield against state power?[8] A substantial amount of the caselaw in this area rests on whether judges switch on the state actor toggle. For if parties are state actors, then they have no right to condition membership on the basis of race or other protected characteristics,[9] they cannot raise associational rights claims when the state regulates how they select their members or leaders, and perhaps they would not even have standing to sue the government (or the same level of government, depending on whether we are talking about state or federal parties)[10] for any imposition whatsoever. As most recognize, this sticky state actor question is probably best answered by some categorization of parties as state actor hybrids or, as we suggest later, by the familiar law review refrain, "it depends."[11]

An interrelated, but uniformly overlooked, question concerns whether there might be several, perhaps conflicting, dimensions to political parties that have different legal properties about them. In a foundational work of political sci-

---

[7] For example, the Constitution is thoroughly unhelpful in determining which right a restrictive ballot access requirement infringes. Does it violate First Amendment rights of speech and association? Equal Protection? Any answer would require us to depart from the constitutional text to arrive at a more intuitive principle: that "excessive" restrictions violate some innate quality of democracy the Constitution ought to protect. Similarly, for state laws that regulate party nomination methods or restrict fusion candidacies, do they really impinge on rights of association, as the opinions suggest? Regardless of such laws, party members can gather together and perform the normal functions of associations. Nevertheless, judges try to hang on this First Amendment hook an intuitive proposition we all feel: Such regulations of the primary or general election ballot affect a party's message to the voters, and if excessive should be struck down.

[8] But see Samuel Issacharoff & Richard H. Pildes, Politics As Markets: Partisan Lockups of the Democratic Process, 50 Stan. L. Rev. 643 (1998) (expressing dismay over the Supreme Court's preoccupation with the state actor question).

[9] See the White Primary cases, cited in supra note 2.

[10] See Democratic Party of the United States v. Wisconsin, 450 U.S. 107 (1981) (upholding Democratic National Committee's decision not to seat delegates elected under Wisconsin's open primary rules).

[11] See infra note 103 (describing theory of contractarian moments).

ence rarely cited by lawyers before this symposium, V. O. Key disaggregated the simple description of "party" into three components:[12] the party-in-the-government,[13] professional political workers,[14] and the party-in-the-electorate.[15] Scholars writing in this area throw around the word "party" as if it had a consistent meaning across the range of legal terrain.[16] This carelessness actually reveals while it obscures. We spend a large part of this Article arguing that certain legal decisions follow from one's conception of "party" and preferred hierarchy of power within the party. In other words, one who prefers party organizations as the prime locus of power in the party system will come out differently, for example, on the topic of state regulation of party primaries than one who believes the power should be concentrated in the party-in-the-government or party-in-the-electorate.[17]

In addition to preferring a certain power hierarchy within the party, each paradigm we describe in Part II has a distinct view of the role parties should play in American politics, how the state should regulate the party system, and the ideal number of political parties. (We set out the main components of the paradigms in the table below.) Of course, although we have set out each of these paradigms as distinct, individual judges or scholars may gravitate toward different paradigms in different legal contexts. Often, the Justices will even shift paradigms within a given case or will coalesce with adherents of other paradigms on an identical result in a given case. Our task here is merely to characterize the worldviews that compete for judicial and scholarly attention in disputes involving political parties. By laying bare their empirical assumptions and implicit normative positions, we hope to find some coherence in what is one of the most complicated and ad hoc areas in the legal regulation of politics.

II. LEGAL PARADIGMS OF POLITICAL PARTIES

A. The Managerial Paradigm

What we call the managerial paradigm, for lack of a better term, has its roots in the approach that dominated the Supreme Court's jurisprudence at least until the White Primary cases and probably through the 1950s. Within this approach, which treated controversies involving parties as something akin to political

---

[12] See V. O. Key, Jr., Politics, Parties & Pressure Groups 163–65 (5th ed. 1964).

[13] For Key, this slice of the party includes the President and representatives from his party in the legislative branch and executive departments. Here we use it to apply to all elected officials with a given party label. See id. at 164.

[14] This refers to the party's national and state committees and all the people who worked for the party organization at any level. See id.

[15] Quite simply, this refers to individuals who identify with a party, namely voters whose main form of party work is voting in primaries and general elections. See id.

[16] While not citing Key, the Court has on a few occasions made passing reference to this multidimensionality of political parties. See Eu v. San Francisco County Democratic Comm., 489 U.S. 214, 230 (1989) ("A party might decide, for example, that it will be more effective if a greater number of its official leaders are local activists rather than Washington-based elected officials."); Elrod v. Burns, 427 U.S. 347, 361 (1976) ("[C]are must be taken not to confuse the interest of partisan organizations with governmental interests.").

[17] See generally Daniel Hays Lowenstein, Associational Rights of Major Political Parties: A Skeptical Inquiry, 71 Tex. L. Rev. 1741, 1757 (1993) (describing much of the Supreme Court's jurisprudence in this area as dealing with intraparty disputes).

Legal Paradigms for Political Parties

Paradigm	Primary Purpose of Political Parties	Preferred Number of Parties	Preferred Power Hierarchy Within Political Party	State Interest in the Party System	Role of Judiciary
Managerial	Foster regime stability	Two	Government/Organization/Electorate	Preserve stability of the two party system	Noninterventionist
Libertarian	To express political opinions of their members	Indifferent	Organization/Electorate/Government	Stay out	Interventionist—preserve ballot box as public forum
Progressive	Interfere with democracy	None	Electorate/Government/Organization	Enhance democracy	Intervene to avoid partisan capture or corruption
Political Markets	Foster electoral choice	More than one—as many as necessary?	Electorate/Organization/Government	Manage political competition	Intervene to prevent "partisan lockups"
Pluralist	To aggregate interest groups into policy-making coalitions	Two broad parties	Organization/Government/Electorate	To ensure party system is responsive to organized interests	Intervene to protect party autonomy; otherwise non-interventionist
Critical	To represent social and ethnic cleavages in society	As many as necessary to accurately represent populations	Electorate/Organization/Government	Achieve proportional representation	Intervene to compensate for biases of social and political system

questions,[18] states had near plenary authority to regulate political parties, and judges were loathe to use the Constitution to interfere with political parties' internal structures or autonomous decisions. In its current incarnation, the paradigm's influence appears in cases where judges recoil once the state asserts interests in preserving electoral stability or maintaining the two-party system—interests that always seem to dwarf the associational or other rights advanced by the plaintiffs.[19]

Drawing on the fears of faction so central to the Constitution's creation, the Manager enforces a worldview on the party and electoral system that has as its primary goal the preservation of political order. That order finds its purest expression in the maintenance of the traditional two-party system, in general, and perhaps in the preservation of the Republican and Democratic parties, in particular.[20] Managers place their faith in the democratic process "to work things out" and assume that all important interests can find expression through one of the two major parties. Viewing the party system as the state's tool for channeling political participation, Managers also consider the judiciary as ill-suited and institutionally incapable of intervening to disrupt the self-regulation of the political branches. Since the party system is largely a state instrumentality, Managers accord little importance to a political party's "freedom to associate." Given their lack of fear of political manipulation of the government for partisan ends, the Managers, according to Key's tripartite design,[21] see the party-in-the-government as the preferred location of power in the party system. The party *is* the government for the Manager. And the professional party organization represents, at most, a private arm of a public institution, while the party-in-the-electorate is irrelevant.

To their credit, the Managers appreciate a fundamental problem posed by majoritarian electoral systems, such as the first-past-the-post districting structures employed in nearly all legislative elections in the United States. With more than two parties or candidates appearing on the ballot, there always exists the risk that a candidate or party will govern with a mandate of less than fifty percent of the electorate.[22] When the familiar liberal arguments are waged against the managerial

[18] See Samuel Issacharoff & Richard H. Pildes, Not by "Election Law" Alone, 32 Loy. L.A. L. Rev. 1173, 1180 (1999) ("The Warren Court opinions . . . [broke] the restraints of the political question doctrine that had long kept the issues of democratic design outside of the constitutional law arena.").

[19] See, e.g., Timmons v. Twin Cities Area New Party, 520 U.S. 351, 367 (1997) ("The Constitution permits the Minnesota Legislature to decide that political stability is served through a healthy two-party system."); Rutan v. Republican Party of Ill., 497 U.S. 62, 107 (1990) (Scalia, J., dissenting) ("The stabilizing effects of such a [two-party] system are obvious."); Davis v. Bandemer, 478 U.S. 109, 144–45 (1986) (O'Connor, J., concurring) ("There can be little doubt that the emergence of a strong and stable two-party system in this country has contributed enormously to sound and effective government."); Anderson v. Celebrezze, 460 U.S. 780, 803 (1983) (citing Storer v. Brown, 415 U.S. 724, 735–36 [1974]).

[20] See supra note 19.

[21] See supra notes 12–15 and accompanying text.

[22] It should be noted that such is often the case in Presidential elections. Of the last five elections, the winner garnered a majority of the electorate in only two elections, 1984 and 1988. "Why not hold a run-off between the two highest vote-getters?" a critic of the Managerial approach might ask. The answer is that there is no guarantee that either of the two highest vote-getters would actually defeat the third candidate in a head-to-head contest. A majority of the electorate might prefer party A over B, while a differently constituted majority from the same electorate will prefer B over C and another, C over A. In fact, as Kenneth Arrow ably demonstrated in his Nobel Prize–winning work, there is no value-neutral means of determining an electorate's most preferred outcome between more than two alternatives. See Kenneth Arrow, Social Choice and Individual Values 92–96 (2nd ed. 1963). This so-called "cycling" problem is well explored in the public choice literature and need not occupy

paradigm—namely, that it stifles competition, entrenches an ideologically homogeneous duopoly, stultifies political discourse by silencing voices that should be heard, and leads to underrepresentation of the range of political interests held by a diverse electorate[23]—the advocate for the two-party system cites tradition, stability, and the guarantee of a governing coalition.[24] However, even the most ardent defenders of single-member, simple plurality rules must concede that they do not *guarantee* a majority winner, and that plurality winners, because of their uncertain mandate, enjoy a shallower legitimacy, undercutting the government's authority to speak for the majority. Managers, therefore, might conclude that the state and the courts have a duty to prevent the siphoning of votes to third parties. By keeping entry costs relatively high, the Managers might want to discourage frivolous third party efforts, to channel voters into more realistic choices, and avoid mere plurality winners. To the degree that the two-party duopoly can be maintained as purely as possible, it increases the likelihood that the plurality winner will also enjoy the formal consent of the majority.

While there is something to be said for the Managerial paradigm, especially for its insight that parties serve important functions for and derive valuable resources from the state, its major weaknesses lie in its reification of the state and deceptively simple treatment of party. The state is not simply a unitary actor devoid of party influence, and the party itself, as we stated earlier, is actually composed of three parts.[25] In essence, the state is often controlled by one of the parties for at least some discrete period of time. More accurately, we should say that the state is at that point controlled by the elected official component of one dominant party. Giving the state total authority to set the rules of party organization translates in many circumstances to giving the elected officials of one party the right to set the rules for other parties as well as for their own.

This leads to several problematic consequences. First, the Managerial approach potentially favors the elected official party component over the non-elected parts of the parties, turning the parties into service instruments for incumbent office holders and candidates and depriving activists of playing any meaningful role in brokering interests and formulating policies. Second, the approach creates the possibility that governing party office holders might try to prevent competitor parties from organizing themselves in the most effective manner possible. For instance, a plausible interpretation of *Tashjian v. Republican Party of Connecticut*[26] was that Democratic office holders in Connecticut were threatened by the possibility that Republicans would develop better ties with independent voters if they were allowed to open up their primary elections to them. The Democrats then tried to use their control of the legislature to prevent the Republicans from pursuing that electoral strategy. *Tashjian* showed the dangers of granting the state the unchecked power to alter party rules of membership and nomination and thereby determine a party's message and prospects. If parties have no right to self-determination, then we cannot be sure that the rules they operate under are the ones they would have chosen themselves. Nor for that matter can we be sure that the party is able

---

us now. Suffice it to say that there is something magical about the number two when it comes to electoral choice—as between two alternatives, at least you can tell which choice is the most preferred.

[23] See generally Richard Hasen, Entrenching the Duopoly, 1997 Sup. Ct. Rev. 331.

[24] See supra note 19.

[25] See supra notes 12–16 and accompanying text.

[26] 479 U.S. 208 (1986).

to compete as effectively as it might otherwise with the message that it wanted to adopt. Had the Connecticut Republicans opened their primaries to independents, they probably would have broadened and moderated their appeals. Not being allowed to do so likely had the opposite effects on their appeals to voters.

In short, the problem with the Managerial perspective is that it cannot effectively check the possible "tyranny" of the party as elected officials. It overlooks the fact that the party as elected officials controls the state, and hence, that actions the state takes can be manipulated to serve the interests of either elected officials generally or elected officials of the governing party specifically.

B. The Libertarian Paradigm

Libertarians take the direct opposite view of the Managers regarding the electoral and party system. Far from instruments to serve the state, parties are merely a species of private, organized interest groups, which should thus be accorded maximal rights of association, privacy, expression, and freedom from state discrimination. Parties' public role and power are, like those of corporations or religious institutions, merely incidental effects of their private operations and in any event, not the proper subject of state regulation.[27]

For the Libertarian, the electoral and party systems should be as separate as possible. More specifically, parties should not receive any state benefits (e.g., public financing of party primaries) or be subject to state regulation (e.g., state law requiring parties to conduct primaries as the means of selecting general election candidates). Therefore, any regulation of primaries or a party's internal processes could only be justified, if at all, by a truly compelling state interest—a test that almost all such regulations would fail.

While Libertarians view parties as merely one type of interest group, they perceive elections as serving several different ends. Elections are, of course, the means of choosing leadership for the government, but for the Libertarian, they also serve additional functions: They provide an outlet for protest against or influence of the governing party or parties, they embody a citizen's right to have his viewpoint counted equally to that of other citizens, and, perhaps, they also provide the means toward a periodic reaffirmation of the social contract between citizens and their government.[28] For the Libertarian, the polling booth is a public forum where dissent must be tolerated and regulation of "speech" (in this case, the expression entailed in deciding whether to vote or not, coupled with the expression of a preference through the casting of ballots) violates the First Amendment.[29]

---

[27] See Colorado Republican Fed. Campaign Comm. v. FEC, 518 U.S. 604, 616 (1996) ("The independent expression of a political party's views is 'core' First Amendment activity no less than is the independent expression of individuals, candidates, or other political committees."); *Tashjian*, 479 U.S. at 224 (The Constitution protects a party's "determination . . . of the structure which best allows it to pursue its political goals. . . ."); Rosario v. Rockefeller, 410 U.S. 752, 764 (1973) (Powell, J., dissenting) ("Self-expression through the public ballot equally with one's peers is the essence of a democratic society.").

[28] See generally Adam Winkler, Note, Expressive Voting, 68 N.Y.U. L. Rev. 330 (1993) (arguing that irrespective of its instrumental function, voting is a meaningful participatory act through which individuals create and affirm their membership in the community and thereby transform their identities both as individuals and as part of a greater collectivity).

[29] See id. at 378–88; David Perney, Note, The Dimensions of the Right to Vote: The Write-in Vote, Donald Duck, and Voting Booth Speech Written-Off, 58 Mo. L. Rev. 945, 965–66 (1993).

The judiciary performs an important and active role in enforcing those rights, as the political branches cannot be trusted to rein in their own power. Thus, ballot regulations that limit the choices available to voters (through difficult signature requirements[30] or the absence of a write-in voting option,[31] for example) are viewed as limiting core political speech. And surely, any measure that presents differential obstacles for the two established parties and for minor parties (i.e., makes it more difficult for a third party to form or poses different requirements for ballot access by new parties) is seen as content-based state action that favors certain speech over others.[32]

Naturally, then, Libertarians tend to view more parties as preferable to two or a few, although by considering elections as forums for expression, they concentrate less on the multi-party result of an election than on the opportunity the system provides for that result.[33] Libertarians would also appear to place power primarily in the professional party organizations, since their conception of party is so fundamentally intertwined with a strong conception of First Amendment freedom of association.[34] Fearing co-optation of governmental power for partisan ends, Libertarians would also seek to hobble the party-in-the-government as much as possible. To that end, they would encourage judges to use every tool in their arsenal (the First Amendment, substantive due process, equal protection) to protect parties' rights to associate and preserve individuals' rights to express their electoral preferences for any party they choose.

The advantage of the Libertarian paradigm is that it provides a counterweight to the claim that parties are a mere state instrumentality. It reminds us that parties can originate among the voters and groups in the polity. Maurice Duverger, for instance, distinguishes between parties that originated as legislative factions (e.g., the Liberal and Conservative Parties in the U.K.) and parties that emerged as the political arms of external organizations (e.g., the Labor Party in the U.K. or the Christian Democratic Party in Italy).[35] Not only might the origins of parties differ, but parties might also differ in the degree to which they operate as state instruments. The Democratic and Republican parties enjoy far more state

---

[30] See Williams v. Rhodes, 393 U.S. 23 (1968).

[31] See Dixon v. Maryland State Admin. Bd. of Election Laws, 878 F.2d 776 (4th Cir. 1989); Paul v. Indiana Election Bd., 743 F. Supp. 616 (S.D. Ind. 1990). But see Burdick v. Takushi, 504 U.S. 428 (1992) (holding a prohibition against a write-in vote does not infringe voters' First Amendment rights).

[32] See *Rhodes*, 393 U.S. 23. Cf. Buckley v. Valeo, 424 U.S. I, 68–74 (1976) (suggesting that even a facially neutral disclosure law for campaign contributions could be unconstitutional as applied to minor parties, given the different character of minor parties); Brown v. Socialist Workers '74 Campaign Comm., 459 U.S. 87, 95–102 (1982) (applying *Buckley* rationale to campaign disbursement law).

[33] To the degree that Libertarians distrust government in general (i.e., the classical liberal fear of governmental domination of the private sphere) and generally prefer systems that cripple the government's ability to pass legislation, they might see in multipartyism the promise that no one party might be able to take its winning for granted in any given election and the prospect that a more frequent cleansing of the system (i.e., throwing the bums out) would be possible.

[34] Although what we have said thus far about Libertarians is not intended to refer to the minor political party of the same name, we note that the Libertarian Party of California is the only party in that state which asks its members to pay dues and sign a pledge called the "certification against the initiation of force." See The Membership Webpage of the Libertarian Party of California (visited April 4, 2000) <http://www.ca.lp.org/lpcmembership.html>. To the degree that the Libertarian Party embraces the philosophy we have elucidated here, this datum offers some support for the notion that professional party organizations are the Libertarian's preferred repository for power in the party system.

[35] See Maurice Duverger, Political Parties: Their Organization and Activity in the Modern State 62–71 (Barbara & Robert North trans., John Wiley & Sons, Inc. 1963) (1951).

resources than most minor parties by virtue of the fact that they hold office. The major parties plausibly serve a central function in a two-party duopoly by giving choices to voters and forcing exaggerated majorities, but one can hardly say the same of the American Independence, Reform, or Green Parties. They receive little from the state and do not perform central functions for the state (although we will argue later that they have a role in making major parties more responsive). What justifies minor party regulation by the state?[36]

However, like the Managerial paradigm, the Libertarian paradigm overlooks the heterogeneity of political parties: heterogeneity, that is, both in terms of type of party (i.e., major or minor) as well as the particular features of each state's laws that define and structure parties. Since some parties do act as instruments of the state and since the two party duopoly forces voters into a limited number of choices, a democracy cannot ignore the anti-democratic actions of major parties. If, as in the White Primary cases, whole blocs of voters are excluded from participation on the basis of race, ethnicity, or some other attribute, then they can be effectively cut out of meaningful participation, particularly in noncompetitive, one party dominant situations.[37] On the other hand, we might care less if a minor party that takes no resources from the state and has no role in government organizes itself in anti-democratic ways. The state interest in regulating such minor parties is much less than their interest in the major parties. In a balancing framework that weighs interests against rights, this would argue for cutting the minor parties much more slack in their internal affairs. The point here is only that just as the Managers go too far in the state interest direction, the Libertarian paradigm goes too far in the party rights direction, neglecting the heterogeneity of parties and the legitimate state interests that arise in matters where basic voting rights are effectively denied. If the danger of the first paradigm can be called the "tyranny of the party as elected officials," then the corresponding problem raised by the Libertarian approach is the "tyranny of the party as organization."

C. The Progressive Paradigm

Emerging at the beginning of this century in response to what was seen as the corrupting influences of party machines on American politics, the Progressive Movement viewed parties, at least in their Americanized form,[38] as an impediment to democracy.[39] This generalized hostility to parties was part of a larger program of institutional reform that included direct democracy, direct election of senators, direct primaries, women's suffrage and an enhanced non-partisan civil service.[40] The target of Progressive ire was the party machine, accused of excessive patronage,

---

[36] See Brief for the Brennan Center for Justice at New York University School of Law as Amicus Curiae in Support of Neither Party at 24–26, California Democratic Party v. Jones, 169 F.3d 646 (9th Cir. 1999), cert. granted, 120 S. Ct. 977 (U.S. Jan. 21, 2000) (No. 99-401) [hereinafter Brennan Center Brief].

[37] See Issacharoff & Pildes, supra note 8, at 652–60.

[38] Many Progressives, such as Woodrow Wilson, favored centralized parliamentary-style parties as they existed in Europe. See generally Woodrow Wilson, Congressional Government: A Study in American Politics (1885) (contrasting congressional and parliamentary governments).

[39] See generally Nathaniel A. Persily, The Peculiar Geography of Direct Democracy: Why the Initiative, Referendum and Recall Developed in the American West, 2 Mich. L. & Pol'y Rev. 11, 21–32 (1997).

[40] See id.; Key, supra note 12, at 393–94.

graft, wasteful spending, extortion and intimidation, rigging elections, and a host of other unseemly acts.[41] Parties impeded democracy, it was thought, by turning elections into sham competitions while the true kingmakers decided the winner behind closed doors in the prototypical smoke-filled room.[42]

Today, reformers in the Progressive tradition have found new avenues for expression of their hostility to parties. Most recently, in California, for example, a set of politicians and political scientists proposed to the voters that party primaries should be "opened up" so that any voter, regardless of affiliation, could vote in any primary for any office.[43] Proponents of this "blanket primary" initiative, which more than 60% of all voters and comfortable majorities in each party supported, justified the measure as a remedy for particular problems posed by so-called "closed primaries," where only party members choose candidates for the general election. The initiative's proponents argued that the blanket primary would produce more centrist (i.e., less partisan) candidates because primary winners would be closer to the median voter in the electorate, rather than the median voter in the party.[44]

For these modern-day Progressives, parties remain obstructive forces for the realization of the general will of the electorate.[45] Progressives therefore tend to favor state regulations that vitiate party autonomy or freedom of association and make parties less relevant for electoral purposes. Thus, the party-in-the-electorate remains the preferred power center for the Progressive with party organizations at the bottom of the pecking order of Key's taxonomy. Seeking to make parties an irrelevancy, Progressives tend not to concentrate on the issue of new or minor parties.[46] If anything, Progressives' preferred number of parties is zero. For similar reasons, they see the state's interest in the party system as ensuring that party factions or machines do not capture official governmental institutions. Consequently, judges should stay out when confronted with legal regulations that trespass on parties' autonomy or limit their power. But Progressive judges should step in when parties seek to entrench themselves through manipulation of the rules of the game or the use of state machinery to bias elections in their favor.

From our perspective, the real problem with the Progressive paradigm is that it does not recognize the essential role that parties play in brokering group interests and solving voters' collective action problems. A polity without parties places a

---

[41] See Leon D. Epstein, Political Parties in the American Mold 170–71 (1986); Richard L. McCormick, From Realignment to Reform: Political Change in New York State 1893–1910, 256–57, 267–68 (1981); Austin Ranney, Curing the Mischiefs of Faction: Party Reform in America 17–19, 80–81, 119–21 (1975).

[42] See Persily, supra note 39, at 22–25.

[43] See generally California Democratic Party v. Jones, 984 F. Supp. 1288, 1289–93 (E.D. Cal. 1997) (discussing Proposition 198, the Open Primary Act), aff'd, 169 F.3d 646 (9th Cir. 1999), cert. granted, 120 S. Ct. 977 (U.S. Jan. 21, 2000) (No. 99-401).

[44] See id. at 1302.

[45] See Davis v. Bandemer, 478 U.S. 109, 177 (1986) (Powell, J., concurring and dissenting) ("There is no evidence that the public interest in a fair electoral process was given any consideration [by architects of a political gerrymander]."); Elrod v. Burns, 427 U.S. 347, 369 (1976) ("The [democratic] process functions as well without the practice [of patronage], perhaps even better, for patronage dismissals clearly also retard that process. Patronage can result in the entrenchment of one or a few parties to the exclusion of others."); O'Hare Truck Serv., Inc. v. City of Northlake, 518 U.S. 712, 717 (1996) ("Absent some reasonably appropriate requirement, government may not make public employment subject to the express condition of political beliefs or prescribed expression.").

[46] Indeed, we think the blanket primary portends the worst effects for smaller parties whose low-turnout primary elections may now be swamped with Democratic and Republican voters. See infra note 96.

greater cognitive burden on individual voters and weakens the collective responsibility of political agents.

On the first point, parties provide voters with an important heuristic that organizes and lessens the expense of information about candidates and policies.[47] Even in the era of weakened parties, party identification remains the most valuable predictor of what a voter will do in the polling booth.[48] Knowing that a candidate is running under a certain party label allows the voter to make reasonable predictions about what that candidate stands for and what he or she will do in office. Moreover, by tying candidates to teams that collectively pursue election goals and policy making, political parties create a collective responsibility for actions in office that allows voters to reward or punish based on the policies and conditions that they observe. In the absence of parties, individual candidates would more easily distance themselves from actions the government takes or claim credit for things that they did not help to produce.

Parties also serve the legislative function of lowering the costs of cooperation among legislators. In a system as decentralized as the United States, parties are one of the few coordinating forces that make positive action possible. They provide a common agenda for legislators at many levels of government as well as provide common ground between partisans in the executive and legislative branches. Courts that translate the Progressives' animosity towards parties into judicial decisions exacerbate the more atomistic and fractionalizing forces in the American political system.

D. Political Markets

Attempting to bring the virtues of law and economics and public choice analysis to the field of election law, adherents to the Political Markets paradigm fault the Managers and Libertarians for the limited usefulness of their conceptual tools for deciding political regulation cases. By forcing such controversies into the rigid model of individual rights versus state interests, they argue, judges and scholars inevitably fail to address the chief danger lurking in the background of these cases: the risk posed by partisan manipulation of the rules of the game to secure permanent political advantage.[49] Therefore, to resolve cases of ballot access, campaign finance restrictions, and regulation of primaries, for example, judges should "discern which regulation of politics are anticompetitive and lock up democratic competition in impermissible ways."[50] Whether one analogizes the judicial role to

---

[47] At times, the Court has recognized this function. See Tashjian v. Republican Party of Conn., 479 U.S. 208, 220 (1986) ("To the extent that party labels provide a shorthand designation of the views of party candidates on matters of public concern, the identification of candidates with particular parties plays a role in the process by which voters inform themselves for the exercise of the franchise.").

[48] See Bruce E. Keith et al., The Myth of the Independent Voter 200–03 (1992) (finding that despite the rise in number of voters identifying themselves as independents, partisanship remains a reliable predictor of vote choice); Warren E. Miller & J. Merrill Shanks, The New American Voter 283–88 (1996).

[49] See Issacharoff & Pildes, supra note 8, at 644–52. See also Elizabeth Garrett, The Law and Economics of "Informed Voter" Ballot Notations, 85 Va. L. Rev. 1533, 1557–63 (1999) (applying the Political Markets paradigm to ballot notations); Bruce E. Cain, Garrett's Temptation, 85 Va. L. Rev. 1589, 1600–03 [1999] (responding to Garrett and attacking the Political Markets paradigm); Richard H. Pildes, The Theory of Political Competition, 85 Va. L. Rev. 1605 (1999) (responding to Cain and defending the Political Markets paradigm).

[50] Issacharoff & Pildes, supra note 8, at 680.

that of a trustbuster or watchdog for political lockups,[51] the end result is the same: Judges ought to use the Constitution to break down barriers to competition.[52]

For the Political Marketeer, the primary purpose of political parties is to offer voter-consumers electoral choices. For it is through unfettered partisan competition that an invisible political hand will operate to supply voter-consumers with goods (in this case, candidates and/or policy positions) that are purchased with votes at the polls. The political market breaks down when incumbent officeholders use their dominant position to place legal or other barriers in the way of those who seek to displace them. In such cases, the political market becomes inefficient—defined and measured, we suspect, by the gap between voters' demand for candidates and parties of a particular ideological brand, and the "unnaturally low" supply of such candidates and parties due to the incumbents rigging the rules of the game.

It thus follows from such an approach: the more parties, the better. After all, one would not limit restaurant choices to McDonald's and Burger King when consumer demand is better sated with the addition of Arby's and Pizza Hut, let alone Le Cirque and Tavern on the Green. If we take the Political Markets model to its logical conclusion, the optimal number of parties (or for that matter, candidates on the ballot) is the number that will attract votes when costs of entry into the market are zero. Of course, recognizing the logistical difficulties of having ballots quite literally the length of grocery lists, Political Marketeers would not go so far, and we should not force them. But the values to be maximized, we must keep in mind, are choice and competition, and given the diversity of political beliefs in America, a small number of political parties would not satisfy the existing demand.

It also follows from the Political Markets paradigm that the party-in-the-electorate is the preferred location of power in the party system. After all, the entire paradigm is geared toward satisfying voter-consumer demand. As Professors Issacharoff and Pildes maintain:

> [A]ppropriate democratic politics [is] akin in important respects to a robustly competitive market—a market whose vitality depends on both clear

[51] Although Professors Issacharoff and Pildes devote most of their article to the economic analogy of corporate lockups, see, e.g., id. at 647–49, we find the antitrust metaphor apropos. See also id. at 710 (discussing the antitrust metaphor as used in John Hart Ely, Democracy and Distrust 102–03 [1980]). None of the explanatory power of the Political Markets approach is lost, however, if we trade corporate law analogies: Both focus our attention on maximizing competition and avoiding political monopoly and market breakdowns. In fact, we think this shift makes the paradigm's strengths and shortcomings easier to understand. See also Leon D. Epstein, Political Parties in the American Mold 155–99 (1986) (comparing political parties to public utilities); Richard L. Hasen, The "Political Market" Metaphor and Election Law: A Comment on Issacharoff and Pildes, 50 Stan. L. Rev. 719, 720, 725–26 (1998) (describing the limits of the corporate lockup analogy).

[52] See Timmons v. Twin Cities Area New Party, 520 U.S. 351, 382 (1997) ("[T]he entire electorate, which necessarily includes the members of the major parties, will benefit from robust *competition* in ideas and governmental policies. . . .") (emphasis added); Anderson v. Celebrezze, 460 U.S. 780, 794 (1983) ("By limiting the opportunities of independent-minded voters to associate in the electoral arena to enhance their political effectiveness as a group, such restrictions threaten to reduce diversity and *competition* in the marketplace of ideas. . . . In short, the primary values protected by the First Amendment . . . are served when election campaigns are not *monopolized* by the existing political parties.") (emphasis added); Williams v. Rhodes, 393 U.S. 23, 32 (1968) ("There is, of course, no reason why two parties should retain a permanent *monopoly* on the right to have people vote for or against them. *Competition* in ideas and governmental policies is at the core of our electoral process and of the First Amendment freedoms.") (emphasis added).

rules of engagement and on the ritual cleansing born of competition. Only through an *appropriately competitive partisan environment* can one of the central goals of democratic politics be realized: that the policy outcomes of the political process be responsive to the interests and views of citizens.[53]

The success of a political system is thus determined by its ability to satisfy as many voter-consumers as possible—that is, by its ability to present electoral choices best matched to each voter's political consumption function. The party-in-the-government is viewed with plutocratic suspicion, since with it lies the power to manipulate the rules of the game for partisan gain. Professional party organizations, in their capacity as manufacturers of political consumer goods, are servile and responsive to shifting voter-consumer demand. Their purpose is to provide customers with brands that inspire loyalty from the greatest number of consumers possible.

For Political Marketeers, the state interest in the party system and the role of the judiciary is the same: to construct rules that maximize (or at least provide "adequate") competition among parties. A state, like an economy, is best served, under this view, when the relevant actors compete with each other so as to make their product (i.e., platforms and policy promises) more efficient[54] and popular. As with antitrust law, the judge should intervene to prevent market breakdowns posed by monopolistic partisan practices[55]—that is, some brand of "heightened scrutiny" should be triggered by laws passed by "ins" that make it more difficult for the "outs" to gain control.[56] Thus, judges should be deeply suspicious of laws passed by incumbent parties that, for example, make it difficult for other parties to develop and gain strength,[57] impose differential burdens on the party controlling the government and on the party currently out of power,[58] or otherwise give preference to the two established parties.

---

[53] Issacharoff & Pildes, supra note 8, at 646 (emphasis added).

[54] Political efficiency might be determined by the party's ability to construct a platform that includes the minimum amount of political commitment necessary to garner the maximum number of votes. In other words, the party "managers" (whoever they are) should make the fewest commitments possible to secure the number of votes needed to attain a majority. This notion of efficiency, like the market metaphor itself, runs into a problem, however, because unlike a corporation and its shareholders whose appetites for profits are unlimited, the value of a marginal voter drops off sharply after a party gains one voter above the fifty percent mark. Such a voter (while still valued) becomes only insurance against the possible loss of another voter.

[55] Also like antitrust law, the devil is in the details of when a market breakdown occurs. The central question—what level of political competition is *appropriate*—is impossible to answer.

[56] We might as well note here that there is nothing special about political parties that makes them the unit of analysis for this approach. Indeed, that might serve as a fundamental criticism of this paradigm. The Political Markets paradigm could be used just as well to regulate moves by incumbent politicians (individually or collectively) to entrench themselves in office. By expanding the concept of political lockups, the paradigm would then call into question a range of political phenomena, including: incumbents' use of the franking privilege to send constituent mail; incumbents' privileged position to raise disproportionate sums of campaign contributions that have the predictable effect of preventing opposition by possible challengers; and bipartisan gerrymanders that create safe seats insulating incumbents from challengers from another party.

[57] See Issacharoff & Pildes, supra note 8, at 668–87 (discussing Timmons v. Twin Cities Area New Party, 520 U.S. 351 [1997], and Burdick v. Takushi, 504 U.S. 428 [1992]).

[58] If taken to its logical extreme, this paradigm would therefore increase scrutiny on partisan gerrymanders, for example. Cf. Davis v. Bandemer, 478 U.S. 109, 118–27 (1986) (holding partisan gerrymandering claims justiciable).

While there is much to be said for a paradigm that promotes electoral competition, this approach suffers from some important weaknesses. To begin with, it overlooks the role of "voice" in politics and relies far too heavily on "exit."[59] Parties may respond to voters because of the threat that they will "exit" the party and vote for another, but they may also respond because important factions within the party want change, and party leaders feel that they cannot ignore these valued members. Parties listen to and rely on their activists to a significant degree since activists provide money and resources that are valuable to winning elections. The issue is not competition for its own sake, but how to produce responsiveness. Maximizing the threat of exit by lowering the barriers to entry into the system is one way to achieve responsiveness, but not the only way. In a two-party system, the incorporation of new groups within existing coalitions is as important as the threat of new parties forming in terms of making the existing parties more adaptable. Encouraging groups to form new parties when they do not get their way only lessens compromise and coalition-building in the electoral stage and postpones it to the legislative stage.

Second, the Political Markets paradigm places its entire faith in the electorate. As consumers, they are sovereign. As such, it is a strongly populist approach that leaves little room for leadership, guidance, and assistance from the politically active. Only the choices at the ballot box matter. There is no allowance for differences between those who are more active and knowledgeable than others. "Civic slackers" rely on parties to provide cues about where candidates stand and which policies will benefit them, but if elected officials and party activists have no important role in setting the platform and choosing the nominees of the parties, then "information" is lost, and the "civic slacker" must look elsewhere (e.g., the press or interest groups) for the information and cues that they need to operate effectively.[60]

The Political Markets paradigm merely allows for the articulation of and response to consumer preferences. It does not allow for deliberation and the transmission of information within party networks, particularly in a two-party system. Denied the easy ability to exit, groups are forced to work together to forge a common platform and to agree upon acceptable candidates.[61] The absence of exit can enhance deliberative actions and encourage voice. To be sure, a two-party system must have competition between the two parties, but it does not necessarily require the entry of a third party. In fact, the high costs of exit may actually increase internal compromise and coalition building. Sometimes, negotiations work best when the doors are locked.

E. The Pluralist Paradigm

Pluralism takes as its point of departure the importance of organized groups in the political process.[62] The Pluralists view the political world as filled with

---

[59] See Albert O. Hirschman, Exit, Voice, and Loyalty: Responses to Decline in Firms, Organizations, and States 4–5 (1970); infra text accompanying notes 85–85.

[60] See Daniel R. Ortiz, The Democratic Paradox of Campaign Finance Reform, 50 Stan. L. Rev. 893, 903 (1998) (describing politically disengaged voters as civic slackers).

[61] For a discussion of the Principle of Electoral Influence, see infra text accompanying notes 122–126.

[62] The literature of the Pluralist school is quite extensive. Some great works include: Arthur F. Bentley, The Process of Government (Peter H. Odegard ed., 1967); Robert A. Dahl, Who Governs? Democracy and Power in an American City (1961); Nelson W. Polsby, Community Power and Political Theory (1963); David B. Truman, The Governmental Process: Political Interests and Public Opinion (1951); Jack L. Walker, Jr., Mobilizing Interest Groups in America: Patrons, Professions, and Social Movements (1991); The Federalist No. 10 (Madison) (Clinton Rossiter ed., 1961).

group-based competition, bargaining, coalition formation, vote-trading and the like.[63] Democracy in America, the Pluralist recognizes, is less "government by the people" or even "majority rule" and better described as "minorities rule"[64]—that is, operating under widely understood rules of democratic engagement, teams of factions gather together to advance each other's particular causes or advocate collectively for broader public policy programs. These minority factions—or as we call them today, interest groups—can take the form of racial or regional groupings or groups defined, for example, by occupation, ideology, or economic interest.[65] They are sometimes organized by social entrepreneurs from the top down, at other times they result from the banding together of individuals with shared interests (usually from the dedication of a few who are most resourceful), and infrequently they spring forth as by-products of mass social movements.[66]

With interest groups as their preferred unit of political analysis, Pluralists advance a particular view of American political parties. Unlike the ideologically rigid and well-defined parties of other democracies,[67] American parties, according to the Pluralist, should be broader, decentralized coalitions of interest groups.[68] This is not just the Pluralists' objective description of the uniquely American party system. (Indeed, this is increasingly inaccurate as a description of the current party system.)[69] Rather, it represents a normative preference for a party system that can aggregate and account for the intensity of group preferences in the most politically, economically, and ethnically diverse country in the world.[70] A highly ideological party system, such as that prevalent in Europe, would inevitably fail to satisfy the preferences of large population segments of American society.[71] If

[63] Cf. *Bandemer*, 478 U.S. at 132–33 ("[T]he question is whether a particular group has been unconstitutionally denied its chance to effectively influence the political process . . . [i.e.,] the opportunity of members of the group to participate in party deliberations in the slating and nomination of candidates, their opportunity to register and vote, and hence their chance to directly influence the election returns and to secure the attention of the winning candidate.").

[64] See Robert A. Dahl, Democracy and Its Critics 150 (1989).

[65] See generally Truman, supra note 62, at 33–39 (defining "interest groups" and supplying various examples); Walker, supra note 62, at 1–17 (discussing various categories of interest groups and their development in the American political system).

[66] See Walker, supra note 62, at 12–13.

[67] See generally Arend Lijphart, Patterns of Democracy: Government Forms and Performance in Thirty-Six Countries 243–57 (1999) (describing party systems in parliamentary democracies).

[68] See Dahl, supra note 62, at 5 (analogizing parties to "molecules" and interest groups to "atoms"); Key, supra note 12, at 330 ("All the factors that contribute to the grouping of sectors of the electorate into each of the party followings assure a degree of cohesiveness within the national party machinery. When it is said that national party is a coalition, the reference may be to the coalition or combination of social interests for which the party speaks. That combination induces unity within the political machinery, narrowly defined, and the combination may, of course, be to a degree a product of the workings of the party machinery.").

[69] See William J. Keefe, Parties, Politics, and Public Policy in America 287–317 (7th ed. 1994); Martin P. Wattenberg, The Decline of American Political Parties 1–29 (1994); Morris P. Fiorina, Whatever Happened to the Median Voter? (Oct. 2, 1999) (paper Presented at the MIT Conference on Parties and Congress) (unpublished manuscript, on file with the *Columbia Law Review*).

[70] See Leon D. Epstein, Political Parties in the American Mold 23–30 (1986) (describing the Pluralists as "defenders of indigenous institutions").

[71] See, e.g., Herbert Agar, The Price of Union xv–xvi (1950) (American parties "are unique. They cannot be compared to the parties of other nations. They serve a new purpose in a new way. . . . It is through the parties that the clashing interests of a continent find grounds for compromise."); id. at 689 ("Instead of seeking 'principles,' or 'distinctive tenets,' which can only divide a federal union, the party is intended to seek bargains between the regions, the classes, and the other interest groups. It is intended to bring men and women of all beliefs, occupations, sections, racial backgrounds, into a

representatives are less able to adapt their voting behavior to the needs of their constituencies (geographic or programmatic) and must instead follow a party line, the party in the government will fail to capture the diversity and perhaps even ideological inconsistencies of the party-in-the-electorate.

To enhance the function of interest group aggregation performed by the American party system, Pluralists would concentrate internal decision making power in the professional party organizations, particularly at the local level. The party organizations have the flexibility to adapt their policy agenda and promote candidates (to the degree such power resides in organizations) attentive to the unique political culture and legal terrain of each state. The Democratic Party of New York City or Chicago, the Pluralist would argue, faces different challenges and must cater to different constituencies than the party organization in Little Rock or Salt Lake City. Although there is a seemingly elitist side to this preference for party organizational power (i.e., transferring power from the party-in-the-electorate—"the people"—to unelected aparatchiks), the Pluralists respond that the organizations are the glue that holds the party-in-the-electorate and the party in all branches of government together.[72]

Because they favor broad parties with weak ideological ties and downplay the expressive theory of voting,[73] Pluralists do not place much importance on third or minor parties—except as those parties influence the policy positions and direction of the two major parties.[74] As we explain more fully in our discussion of Albert Hirschman's concepts of exit and voice,[75] an interest group's power derives, in part, from the threat of its potential exit from one party either to join another or to start a party of its own. By threatening to bolt the party, interest group leaders can influence a party's choice of candidate, running mate, or policy position.[76]

In sum, the Pluralist school treats questions of regulation of the electoral and party system from the perspective of what changes would further interest group aggregation and coalition formation. This preoccupation with coalition formation does not stem merely from a romantic notion of team building. The Pluralist sees the party system as the main mechanism in American democracy for representing both the size of the group and the intensity of its interest. An unmediated electoral system treats each voter as an equal individual and weights his or her preferences (as expressed at the ballot box or in the legislature) equally: One person = one vote = one electoral preference equally weighted by candidates competing for votes.

In the process of party coalition formation, however, groups that are unified and organized by their collective interest can have bargaining power disproportionate to their actual numbers. When preferences are more intense and well-defined, interest groups can focus on those few group-defining issues and exact

---

combination for the pursuit of power. The combination is too various to possess firm convictions. The members may have nothing in common except a desire for office."); Nelson W. Polsby, The Presidential Campaign, British Style, *in* Alan Brinkley et al., New Federalist Papers, 45–49 (1997) (comparing American and British party systems and nomination methods).

[72] See generally Giovanni Sartori, Parties and Party Systems 25 (1976) (arguing that the collective benefits resulting from party-driven activity are preferable to the self-serving nature of factions).

[73] See Timmons v. Twin Cities Area New Party, 520 U.S. 351, 363 (1997) ("Ballots serve primarily to elect candidates, not as forums for political expression.") (citing Burdick v. Takushi, 504 U.S. 428, 438 (1992); id. at 445 (Kennedy, J., dissenting).

[74] See Steven J. Rosenstone et al., Third Parties in America: Citizen Response to Major Party Failure 8–9 (1984).

[75] See infra text accompanying notes 87–91.

[76] See Anthony Downs, An Economic Theory of Democracy 114–41 (1957).

selective promises from party leaders even if the "majority" of party adherents are indifferent or slightly opposed.[77] Of course, Pluralists must admit that even a weak and porous two-party system can shortchange minorities, particularly those with an array of intense policy preferences all solidly situated at an extreme of the liberal-conservative continuum or those without the resources needed to participate in any coalition.[78] The process of coalition formation favors those minorities with intense preferences on specific issues, especially distributive ones, such that their inclusion in the coalition will not cause the defection of an even larger faction from the party.

Indeed, this vision of the party system also forces interest group leaders to moderate each individual demand by the long-term value of being part of a policy-making coalition. Interest group leaders must pick their fights and cede ground on those non-crucial issues upon which they disagree with other groups in the coalition. Unlike a multiparty system in which parties have strong incentives to distinguish themselves from each other and interest groups bargain for coalition position only in the process of forming a government,[79] the American two-party system frontloads the coalition formation process, forcing groups to form electoral unions (especially for presidential elections).[80]

The American party system also has the fortunate benefit of being well-tailored to the American separation-of-powers system (that is, a system that splits law-making power between a legislature and a chief executive).[81] Ideologically unified parties heighten the hurdles to policymaking that are already quite daunting in the American system. Under conditions of divided government, for example, an executive must have the ability to peel off votes from the governing party of the legislature to have any hope of passing legislation or executing his agenda. Conversely, under unified government, the executive faces no obstacles and the minority party in the legislature has no power either to obstruct the passage or to affect the substance of legislation. Unified parties in a separation-of-powers system create a choice between stalemate and tyranny of the majority.[82]

The Pluralist values a *porous* party system: one in which legislators are not afraid of defecting from the party-line (to the degree that there is one), one where

---

[77] See, e.g., Epstein, supra note 41, at 27 ("[A] major American party is a bundle of compromises, a cross section not a segment of the community, and even with majority voting support it has policies that are the product of pluralistic bargaining.") (citing Austin Ranney & Wilmoore Kendall, Democracy and the American Party System 523 [1956]); E. E. Schattschneider, Party Government 85 (1942) ("A large party must be supported by a great variety of interests sufficiently tolerant of each other to collaborate, held together by compromise and concession, and the discovery of certain common interest, and so on, and bearing in mind the fact that a major party has only one competitor and that party managers *need not meet every demand made by every interest.*") (emphasis in original).

[78] See E. E. Schattschneider, The Semisovereign People: A Realist's View of Democracy in America 35 (1960) ("The vice of the groupist theory is that it conceals the most significant aspects of the system. The flaw in the pluralist heaven is that the heavenly chorus sings with a strong upper-class accent. Probably about 90 per cent of the people cannot get into the pressure system.").

[79] See Downs, supra note 76, at 114–63.

[80] See generally Nelson W. Polsby, Consequences of Party Reform (1983).

[81] See Epstein, supra note 41, at 43 ("The American separation-of-powers doctrine, firmly embedded in constitutional letter and practice, makes the Congress capable of operating apart from or against executive leadership . . . The constitutional prohibition against holding both executive and legislative offices precludes a parliamentary system. . . .").

[82] See Bruce E. Cain & Nathaniel Persily, Creating an Accountable Legislature: The Parliamentary Option for California Government, *in* Constitutional Reform in California: Making State Government More Effective and Responsive 163 (Bruce E. Cain & Roger G. Noll eds., 1995).

interest groups can penetrate and bargain for position in the electoral coalition, and one where professional party organizations, particularly at the local level, are free to broaden a party's tent to cover the diversity of interests that exist in this country. However, Pluralists may exaggerate the representativeness of the interest group system. They tend to downplay the potential for autonomous party organizations to ignore large interest groups with dispersed interests and small groups outside the mainstream or without the resources to make their voice heard. Finally, given their weak ideological cohesion, Pluralist parties at the legislative level often prove ineffective as policy making bodies and can blur accountability such that no party ever appears "responsible" for anything.

III. SOME MIDDLE RANGE PRINCIPLES[83]
AND NORMAL SCIENCE[84]

As the fight between paradigms rages in the background of the party decisions, the courts have not come close to adopting even middle range principles that could bring some coherence to the caselaw. Recognizing that each paradigm has its own strengths and weaknesses, we attempt to draw from their best features to propose a set of such principles applicable to two areas of the law: (1) ballot access restrictions and (2) regulation of candidate nomination methods. A different set of principles, drawing on different aspects of the various paradigms, would apply in a different legal context—for example, campaign finance or gerrymandering. By exploring these context-specific principles, however, we mean to show that certain paradigms (or a combination of paradigms) have particular utility for certain areas of the law, while those same ways of thinking about political parties might not work in a different context. In any event, we think that an emphasis on principles, rather than paradigms, might bring some sense and could help foster some predictability in this area of the law.

A. Exit and Voice in Legal Regulation of the Party System

We begin with the Pluralists' unit of analysis: the interest group. While others have argued that most political regulation cases involve group rights,[85] we think the group-based analysis particularly apropos when considering questions of ballot access or party nomination regulations. As aggregations of interest groups,

---

[83] See Robert K. Merton, Social Theory and Social Structure 39–72 (1968) (distinguishing middle range theories from comprehensive political philosophies such as Marxism).

[84] See Thomas S. Kuhn, The Structure of Scientific Revolutions 10–34 (1970) (distinguishing normal science from paradigm shifts).

[85] See generally Vikram David Amar & Alan Brownstein, The Hybrid Nature of Political Rights, 50 Stan. L. Rev. 915, 924–28 (1998); Samuel Issacharoff, Groups and the Right to Vote, 44 Emory L.J. 869, 883–84 (1995) (analyzing voting rights claims through the group-based legal regime of racial and ethnic classifications); compare Davis v. Bandemer, 478 U.S. 109, 167 (1986) (Powell, J., concurring in part and dissenting in part) ("The concept of 'representation' necessarily applies to groups: groups of voters elect representatives, individual voters do not. Gross population disparities violate the mandate of equal representation by denying voters residing in heavily populated districts, *as a group*, the opportunity to elect the number of representatives to which their voting strength otherwise would entitle them."), with id. at 148–52 (O'Connor, J., concurring) (rejecting the group conception of the right to vote in defense of a more individualist notion).

parties' claim to autonomy or for space on the ballot necessarily entails a claim made by the groups that compose the party.[86] We then ask the question: What constitutional rules will ensure that the party system serves to aggregate and to represent interest groups? Obviously, if the party system somehow operates to shut out large interest groups, leaving them "voiceless" and unrepresented as were African-Americans in the White Primary cases, we would say the system is broken and somehow judges should intervene to tweak the party system so all can participate. At the other extreme, interest group leaders should not be able to seek judicial intervention to rewrite rules of party membership or nomination procedures merely because they do not find the candidates on the general election ballot appealing or they find that the requirement of affiliation prevents them from exerting maximum influence in the selection of candidates for the general election ballot.

Like other contexts of political or economic organization, the party system must provide two alternative avenues for interest group influence. The first option, which Albert Hirschman termed "voice,"[87] includes those means through which a group can work within the organization (in this case, a political party) to influence its positions, decisions and leadership. The state often regulates the process of interest group influence within the party through laws that, for example, require parties to use primaries as their mode of nomination, specify who can vote in such primaries (i.e., whether limited to party members or "open" to non-party members as well), or require certain organizational forms for the party (such as a nominating committee or local party committees). Through such regulations, the state can bias the party system in favor of certain interests and in favor of certain strategies of influence (e.g., open campaigning versus smoke-filled-room elite politics).

When the voice option is unavailable, however, the group must have the ability to exit from the party in order to run its own slate of candidates. The exit option legitimizes the party system by leaving theoretically possible the practically impossible scenario of a defecting interest group or minor party replacing one of the established parties. Minor parties' chief mode of service to the two-party system, as we noted above, is their effect on the composition and policy positions of the major parties. As the premier text on the subject explains:

> [T]he power of third parties lies in their capacity to affect the content and range of political discourse, and ultimately public policy, by raising issues and options that the two major parties have ignored. In so doing, they not only promote their cause but affect the very character of the two-party system. When a third party compels a major party to adopt policies it otherwise may not have, it stimulates a redrawing of the political battle lines and a reshuffling of the major party coalitions.[88]

[86] As for the right of an individual to appear as a candidate on the ballot, the significant aspect of such a "right" is the opportunity and choice that the candidacy gives the group of voters who wish to support it. The right to appear on the ballot is really just a right to have the opportunity to garner group support for your candidacy.

[87] See generally Hirschman, supra note 59, at 4–5 (describing "voice" as the mechanism by which one influences an organization from within and "exit" as the process of exercising influence from outside).

[88] Rosenstone et al., supra note 74, at 8–9; see also Sweezy v. New Hampshire, 354 U.S. 234, 250–51 (1957) (Warren, C. J.).

Or as an earlier writer put it, "let a third party once demonstrate that votes are to be made by adopting a certain demand, then one or the other of the older parties can be trusted to absorb the new doctrine."[89]

Thus, the exit option provides a forum where an otherwise "voiceless" group can be heard.[90] The decision to exit is a serious one; the potential third party must decide that they have more to gain from bolting and losing than from staying and influencing. The existence of the exit option itself, however, gives credibility to interest group leaders' threat that they will take their votes with them unless the major party shifts its policy positions to accommodate them. The mere availability of the threat may help prevent the party from becoming overly unified ideologically—i.e., the more ideologically homogeneous they become, the greater the risk that they will alienate groups that do not share in the ideological vision. For example, the prospect of the Christian Coalition or Right-to-Life Party running its own candidates in a general election ensures that the Republican candidates, such as George W. Bush, will think twice before alienating them from the Republican Party by compromising their position on abortion. Were the exit option taken away, interest group leaders threatening to defect would be forced to choose between allying with the opposing party (which is usually worse than the one from which the group would defect) or convincing their adherents to stay home from the polls. An election boycott, sometimes employed in other countries, is a poorly tailored and highly ineffective means for brokering influence. Better to demonstrate one's strength at the polls than to brag ex post that your group members influenced the election by sitting this one out.[91]

By reiterating Hirschman's conceptualization here, we mean to stress the interrelatedness of the voice and exit options for legal regulation of the party system and the need for judicial protection of both avenues of interest group influence.

B. Principles from Paradigms

In this next section, we offer our own set of decision rules that we think flow from the strengths of each paradigm we discussed. These rules will not decide every case, but may reformulate the judicial inquiry in these cases toward what we see as more productive ends.

1. *Principle of Electoral System Symbiosis. —The constitutionality of any given regulation of the party system will usually depend on what other laws accompany it. Judges should be careful not to consider the impact of a single law in isolation.*

States vary considerably in how they define political parties, regulate party internal organization and nomination methods, and restrict access to the ballot.[92] In one context, a law might have the effect of decreasing electoral competitive-

---

[89] Rosenstone et al., supra note 74, at 8 (quoting John D. Hicks, The Third Party Tradition in American Politics, 20 Miss. Valley Hist. Rev. 26–27 [1933]); see also Anderson v. Celebrezze, 460 U.S. 780, 794 (1983) ("Historically political figures outside the two major parties have been fertile sources of new ideas and new programs; many of their challenges to the status quo have in time made their way into the political mainstream.").

[90] See Alexander M. Bickel, Reform and Continuity 87–88 (1971) ("The characteristic American third party, then, consists of a group of people who have tried to exert influence within one of the major parties, have failed, and later decide to work on the outside.") (quoted in *Anderson*, 460 U.S. at 805).

[91] See Downs, supra note 76, at 118.

[92] See, e.g., E. Joshua Rosenkranz, Voter Choice '96: A 50-State Report Card on the Presidential Elections (1996).

ness or weakening a party's ability to aggregate interest groups into coalitions. In another, it might have no effect at all. Yet courts' morselized approach to party system regulations hampers the current caselaw. Judges adjudicate challenges to individual electoral regulations at the time legislatures or voters enact them. If upheld, their constitutionality is forever presumed regardless of subsequent action by policy makers. If struck down, the legislature is forced to achieve the goals of the nullified law through other means.

Perhaps this is the natural consequence of Article III's "case and controversy" requirement. Judges do not make broad policy recommendations or evaluate the sum total effect of a regime of political regulation. They adjudicate cases, usually in the form of a specific challenge to a specific law. But the case method need not always prevent judges from taking a more holistic view of their task in regulating the party system.[93]

The harm of the piecemeal approach was evident in the California blanket primary case, *California Democratic Party v. Jones*.[94] Judge Levi (and the Ninth Circuit panel that upheld his decision without an opinion) glossed over the fact that California not only requires a party's primary ballot to be open to all voters, but a party has no option other than primary elections for it to nominate its candidates for state office.[95] In other words, the blanket primary, existing alongside California's other party regulations, eviscerates both the voice and exit options from the party system. Parties, on the one hand, cannot require party membership as a precondition to primary voting, thus inhibiting their ability to build coalitions to which the party and its candidates will be responsible over time. Nor can parties, on the other hand, use nominating conventions or some other method for selecting state candidates—i.e., to opt out of the primary system altogether.

The court also failed to recognize the different character of minor and major parties and the differential effects the blanket primary would have on them. While fears of raiding and massive cross-over voting to major party primaries have uncertain empirical foundations, such fears are certainly valid for minor parties' primary elections, which are often squeakers where winning candidates may win by fewer than a hundred votes. The blanket primary operates to ensure that non-party members will determine who will be minor party candidates. As strong as we think the argument against the blanket primary is for the major parties, the minor parties have the additional argument that their very purpose is threatened by the initiative.[96] For those groups that wish to exit from the two-party system,

[93] See Williams v. Rhodes, 393 U.S. 23, 39 (1968) ("Cumbersome election machinery can effectively suffocate the right of association, the promotion of political ideas and programs of political action, and the right to vote. The totality of Ohio's requirements has those effects."); Molinari v. Powers, 82 F. Supp. 2d 57 (E.D.N.Y. 2000) (finding that the totality of the 2000 New York Republican presidential primary regulations posed an undue burden on the right to vote of John McCain's supporters and also, holding two sections of the electoral law unconstitutional as applied to the 2000 presidential primary).

[94] 984 F. Supp. 1288 (E.D. Cal. 1997), aff'd, 169 F.3d 646 (9th Cir. 1999), cert. granted, 120 S. Ct. 977 (U.S. Jan. 21, 2000).

[95] See id. at 1299; Cal. Const. art. II, § 5 ("The Legislature *shall* provide for primary elections for partisan offices. . . .") (emphasis added); Cal. Elec. Code § 337 (West 1999) (defining a partisan office as "an office for which a party may nominate a candidate"); Cal. Elec. Code § 15451 (West 1999) ("The person who receives the highest number of votes at a primary election as the candidate of a political party for the nomination to an office is the nominee of that party at the ensuing general election.").

[96] See Brennan Center Brief, supra note 36, at 22–28; Christian Collet, Openness Begets Opportunity: Minor Parties and the First Blanket Primary in California, *in* California's Open/Blanket Primary:

they are now faced with an electoral system that removes from them the power to choose their own candidates. For those that wish to stay and exercise their voice, theirs is lost in the din of independents and non-party members who may determine primary nominees.

2. *Principle of Party Autonomy.* —*State laws that dictate party membership, organization, or nominating procedures infringe on the party's protected freedom of association unless they are necessary for expanding interest group participation in the party system.*

It should come as no surprise then that we think the Supreme Court got it right (at least in the result) in *Tashjian v. Republican Party of Connecticut*[97] and *Democratic Party of the United States v. Wisconsin ex rel. LaFollette*,[98] and the Ninth Circuit got it wrong in *California Democratic Party v. Jones*.[99]

The party system, as we noted above, serves as a filter for interest group activity and under certain conditions can counteract the majoritarian bias of the American plurality-based electoral system. Throughout the ongoing process of coalition formation, party leaders and candidates make promises to interest groups and attempt to translate those promises into public policy by whipping the votes of elected officials. This process of aggregation accounts for both the intensity of interest group preferences and the size of the interest group.

Freedom from state interference in the organization of political parties is a crucial element in preserving party leaders' ability to broker their influence and nominate candidates that respond to the party's electoral coalition. For example, in *Tashjian*, the Connecticut legislature (dominated by Democrats) passed a law that prohibited political parties from allowing non-party members to vote in their party primaries. The state proffered interests in "administrability of the primary system, prevention of raiding, avoiding voter confusion, and protecting the responsibility of party government."[100] The Republican Party wanted to allow independents to vote in its primary, challenged the constitutionality of the law, and won.

We agree with *Tashjian*'s result because the Connecticut law inhibited the party's ability to field candidates that catered to the needs of the interest groups whose support the party sought. The party organization decided that an open primary would help broaden its coalition to include interest groups that were not affiliated with either party. Despite the state's admonitions to the contrary, the closed primary law served one purpose only: to prevent parties from catering to individuals and groups that chose not to identify with a party.[101] To allow such a law would permit the state to define the meaning of party membership, and, more importantly, to substitute its judgment for that of party leaders as to what interests should form the basis of its electoral coalition. The law does not fall into the exception to our rule—that such restrictions pass constitutional scrutiny if they are necessary for expanding interest group participation in the party system—so the law fails.

A Natural Experiment in Electoral Dynamics (Bruce E. Cain & Elisabeth R. Gerber eds., forthcoming 2000).

[97] 479 U.S. 208 (1986).

[98] 450 U.S. 107 (1981).

[99] 169 F.3d 646 (9th Cir. 1999), cert. granted, 120 S. Ct. 977 (U.S. Jan. 21, 2000) (No. 99–401).

[100] *Tashjian*, 479 U.S. at 217.

[101] We deal with the state interest in prevention of raiding and the party responsibility issue under a later principle—that the state cannot regulate parties for their own good. The state's articulated interest of avoiding voter confusion would seem to fail even a rational basis test; we cannot fathom how voters would be confused by the Republicans allowing independents to vote in their primary.

But what about California's blanket primary?[102] Perhaps we should support that law because it forces parties to allow all interest groups to participate in the process—i.e., any group can vote for any candidate in any primary. We disagree. The core of our disagreement with the Court arises from the law's removal from party organizations altogether the power to broker interest group influence in the candidate selection process or even, as the Libertarians might view it, the power to define what the party is. Without the blanket primary law, a party organization can recruit a candidate, for example, whom it believes remains true to the party's ideological bias and interest group alignment, and test its choice in the primary election against other possible competitors to see if the party-in-the-electorate supports the party professionals' choice. The blanket primary, however, nullifies any notion of and prevents any opportunity for a "party's choice." The primary becomes a preview for the highly median dominated general election, with party organizations functionally removed from the process, no organizational filter for interest group aggregation, and the promise of eroding interest group influence within the parties, as opposed to outside the parties, over time. Even if this seems a bit extreme, a less apoplectic diagnosis for the blanket primary predicts that the party organizations will be less able to craft a distinct party message, less able to recruit candidates that respond to that message and win, and less able to organize interest group coalitions that support a party nominee. Let us also not forget the obvious: Prior to the blanket primary, all California voters were able to vote in the primary of their choice; they merely needed to take the relatively costless step of affiliating with a party.

The Libertarians would also support such a principle even without its exception. Party autonomy for the Libertarian is a core component of the First Amendment freedom of association. Just as one would not want the state determining qualifications for membership in the Rotary Club, so should it not invade the associational sanctum of political parties. Our exception to this principle represents an attempt to temper the Libertarian approach with the Progressive one. The Progressive suspicion of parties arose, in part, from parties' tendency toward parochialism and oligarchy (hence the advocacy of primaries over nominating conventions). Under certain conditions, such as existed in the South during the times of the White Primaries, parties' associational autonomy must give way to the larger interest of open participation of interest groups in the party system.[103]

3. *Anti-Paternalism Principle.*—*Any state interest that can be achieved through parties' regulation of themselves is impermissible as a justification for formal state regulation of political parties.*

With this principle we hope to rein in the state when it tries to regulate parties for their own good. So, for example, state interests in preventing party raiding[104]

---

[102] See *California Democratic Party*, 984 F. Supp. 1288.

[103] We must admit that there is a serious analytical drawback to this principle: It treats all parties as if they were created equal. In future work, we hope to explain more fully a two-tier system of legal analysis for political parties: one that applies to major parties and another that will apply to minor parties. We have glossed over the state action problem for now (i.e., whether a minor party should be treated differently than a major party with regard to decisions that impact its members and the capacity of the state to regulate them). We expect that one could develop an approach based on "contractarian moments" that looks at a series of decisions by party leaders, for example, to accept public funding for the party or to use the organs of the state to run purely intraparty affairs. At a certain stage of commingling of state and party rules and functions, a party may cede its associational rights to such a degree that even its nomination process must be subject to constitutional rules similar to a general election.

[104] See *Tashjian*, 479 U.S. at 217.

or reducing intraparty factionalism[105] represent illegitimate excuses for state laws when those values can be achieved through internal party regulation. When a party uses the official governmental machinery to regulate itself and its opposition for their own good, judges should be particularly suspicious. Most often, the state's articulated interest in party-building masks incumbents' strategic decisions to regulate their opposition.

In *Timmons v. Twin Cities Area New Party*, the state justified its prohibition of fusion candidacies (i.e., where multiple parties endorse the same candidate) by "its interests in avoiding voter confusion, promoting candidate competition[,] . . . preventing electoral distortions and ballot manipulations, and discouraging party splintering and 'unrestrained factionalism.'"[106] Finding the fusion ban rationally related to the achievement of those state interests, as well as interests in preserving stability and the two-party system, and finding it an insignificant burden on parties' First Amendment rights, the Court upheld the law in a five to four decision.[107] Both the majority and principal dissent in *Timmons* viewed the fusion ban in isolation (violating principle number one).[108] In the Libertarian tradition, Justice Stevens's dissent saw the law as infringing upon the party's right to self-expression, i.e., its right to choose a "standard bearer" regardless of the fact that another party also chose him.[109] The state could achieve its articulated interests through less intrusive means, he thought, and thus the ban on fusion could not pass heightened scrutiny. Like the majority, the dissent emphasized that "[t]he members of a political party have a constitutional right to select their nominees for public office and to communicate the identity of their nominees to the voting public."[110]

We think both opinions miss the point of Minnesota's fusion ban. The Court should have asked the question whether state laws, rather than party regulation, were necessary to achieve the party-system effects the state sought with its fusion ban. Indeed, we think parties without the aid of official regulation could have accomplished the state's paternalistic interests.[111] Both the party in the legisla-

---

[105] See Timmons v. Twin Cities Area New Party, 520 U.S. 351, 367 (1997); Eu v. San Francisco Democratic Comm., 489 U.S. 214, 233 n.23 (1989).

[106] *Timmons*, 520 U.S. at 364.

[107] See id. at 369–70.

[108] Both the majority and the dissent failed to appreciate that Minnesota's primary laws prevent party organizations from limiting the qualifications of its members or candidates. Minnesota's election laws specify the qualifications for candidates' participation in a party primary. Prospective candidates must be eligible voters, who have lived in their electoral district for 30 days before the general election and will be over the age of 21 should they be elected. They cannot file for more than one office and if they seek a major party's nomination, they must sign an affidavit that says they "either participated in that party's most recent precinct caucus or intend[ ] to vote for a majority of that party's candidates at the next ensuing general election." See Minn. Stat. § 204B.06 (1992). If a candidate with those qualifications wins the party's primary, then he is that party's nominee at the general election. The official party organization cannot require additional qualifications (e.g., rejection of third party endorsement if nominated) and cannot stand in the way of the primary electorate's choice being the general election candidate. Telephone interview with the Office of Minnesota's Secretary of State (Oct. 19, 1999).

[109] *Timmons*, 520 U.S. at 373 (Stevens, J., dissenting) (quoting *Eu*, 489 U.S. at 224).

[110] Id. at 371 (Stevens, J., dissenting); see also id. at 359 (majority opinion) ("The New Party's claim that it has a right to select its own candidate is uncontroversial, so far as it goes.") (citing Cousins v. Wigoda, 419 U.S. 477 [1975]).

[111] The majority in *Timmons*, 520 U.S. at 365, recognized other non-paternalistic state interests such as preventing the ballot from becoming a billboard for small candidate-created parties with slogans such as "Stop Crime Now" or "No New Taxes." Those interests reflect a legitimate, non-paternalistic desire to combat a sort of prisoners' dilemma where parties compete with each other to destroy the ballot as a system of electoral choice and convert it into a system of electioneering. See

ture and the professional party organizations, if they fear cross-endorsement by a minor party, can use all the sanctions at their disposal to prevent or retaliate against candidates who accept multiple endorsements. By directing soft money, allocating choice committee or leadership assignments, or mobilizing electoral support, a party organization can enact its own fusion ban without the aid of a state apparatus by using various carrots to solidify party loyalty or sticks to sanction candidates who divide their loyalties. Instead of relying on parties to organize themselves, Minnesota thought it better to use the hammer of state law to force a fusion ban on both parties.

4. *Principle of Equal Treatment. —State laws that impose unique and disproportionate burdens of ballot access on minor parties violate the Equal Protection Clause.*[112]

We are firm believers in the utility and value of the two-party system for American politics. We buy the Pluralist/Managerial argument that has swayed Supreme Court majorities for much of the past half century: Factionalism in the form of multipartyism at the legislative level is incongruous with the American separation-of-powers system and system of legislative representation.[113] In addition, a choice between two parties provides additional legitimacy by increasing the probability that the winning candidate will have won a majority of the vote and decreasing some of the "cycling" problems we described earlier.[114]

While endorsing the two-party system, we do not mean to endorse the two incumbent parties in particular,[115] nor do we think those parties ought to be able to add to their incumbency advantages by preventing defecting interest groups from securing places on the ballot. But any attempt at a universal rule governing access to the ballot ultimately devolves into a balancing test, where access restrictions should be struck down when they are "too severe." Some balancing is inevitable to protect the right of exit[116] while alleviating the Managers' real concerns about factionalism and ballot integrity. Hence, Laurence Tribe describes the Court's current law of ballot access restrictions as allowing "states [to] condition access to the ballot upon the demonstration of a '*significant,* measurable quantum of community support,' but cannot require *so large* or *so early* a demonstration

---

Note, Associational Rights of Political Parties, 111 Harv. L. Rev. 309, 318–19 (1997) (characterizing the fusion issue as one of "time inconsistency of preference"). The dissent rightly dismissed that interest and the billboard scenario as farfetched. See *Timmons*, 520 U.S. at 375–76 (Stevens, J., dissenting). At the very least, some empirical showing of such a danger should be required.

[112] We note that the Court has paid lip service to this principle in some cases. See Anderson v. Celebrezze, 460 U.S. 780, 793–94 (1983) ("A burden that falls unequally on new or small political parties or on independent candidates impinges, by its very nature, on associational choices protected by the First Amendment. It discriminates against those candidates and—of particular importance—against those voters whose political preferences lie outside the existing political parties.") (citing Clements v. Fashion, 457 U.S. 957, 963–64 [1982]).

[113] See supra text accompanying notes 79–82.

[114] See supra note 22; Polsby, supra note 71, at 38–43.

[115] See *Anderson*, 460 U.S. at 803 n.30; Williams v. Rhodes, 393 U.S. 23, 32 (1968).

[116] The Libertarians might also conceive of ballot access as an individual right—i.e., the right of any American to run for office. We do not attach much value to that putative right. The value of the right of running for office, as we see it, derives not from mere access to the ballot, but from the opportunity it gives groups to gain political power. As we noted in our discussion of exit and voice, ballot access provides groups with two routes to political power: (1) the right to place their candidates in elective office or (2) the ability to affect the outcome of an election. See supra text accompanying notes 84–91.

of support that minority parties or independent candidates have *no real chance* of attaining ballot positions."[117]

While we see no way around using some balancing test along the lines currently in use, the principle of equal treatment stated above can operate to rectify some of the more egregious abuses incumbent parties inflict on possible new entrants. In particular, we see this rule as targeting states that pass laws that privilege incumbent parties by regulating *only* access by minor parties, giving incumbent parties automatic ballot access. Most state laws specify, for example, that a party gets on a ballot automatically if it polled 20% of the vote in the previous election, but new parties must collect a number of signatures equal to 5% of the voters in the last statewide election. Compliance with signature requirements such as these tends to gobble up most of a minor party's expenditure on an election,[118] thus adding to the head start incumbent party candidates already have in the campaign.

On questions of ballot access, no less than voting,[119] courts should strike down laws that impose burdens only on minor parties. Thus, a ballot access law that allows the two established parties automatic access, but forces new parties to gain a substantial number of signatures, should be unconstitutional under the Fourteenth Amendment. For the same reasons that we would not allow the government, for example, to impose heightened voter registration requirements or other impediments to voting on an unprotected class such as farmers, the government should not be able to employ ballot access laws that specifically and intentionally prevent a new Farmer's Party from developing. Such a rule would force established parties to internalize the start-up costs they are imposing on new parties—costs many of them never even had to pay.

Such a rule, if implemented, could have a widespread short-term effect since most states employ a two-tiered system of ballot access.[120] But the effect would be quite minor since states would probably respond by passing universally applicable signature requirements set at a level that both accounts for the rule's inconvenience on all parties and serves the two parties' interest in preventing factionalism and voter confusion. Although abstract notions of fairness familiar to Equal Protection law by themselves might justify this rule, the rule has particular attraction for Pluralists, we think, because it ensures that the incumbent parties do not use their incumbent status to impose costs on defecting interest groups that the parties themselves would be unwilling to bear.[121] We are well aware that this decision rule does not remove the impediments to minor party ballot access,

---

[117] Laurence H. Tribe, American Constitutional Law 1110–11 (2d ed. 1988) (emphasis added).

[118] See Bradley A. Smith, Note, Judicial Protection of Ballot-Access Rights: Third Parties Need Not Apply, 28 Harv. J. on Legis. 167, 200 (1991) (estimating costs at one dollar per signature).

[119] See *Williams*, 393 U.S. at 31 ("[T]he right to vote is heavily burdened if that vote may be cast only for one of two parties at a time when other parties are clamoring for a place on the ballot. In determining whether the State has power to place such unequal burdens on minority groups where rights of this kind are at stake, the decisions of this Court have consistently held that 'only a compelling state interest . . . can justify limiting First Amendment freedoms.'") (quoting NAACP v. Button, 371 U.S. 415, 438 [1963]); Harper v. Virginia Board of Elections, 383 U.S. 663, 670 (1966) ("[T]he right to vote is too precious, too fundamental to be so burdened or conditioned.").

[120] See Rosenkranz, supra note 92, at 90–91 (state-by-state charts reflecting ballot access information).

[121] The rule might be applicable to other areas of the law as well, such as public financing of presidential elections. Then-Justice Rehnquist seemed to apply a variant of this rule in his partial dissent in *Buckley v. Valeo*, which stressed Congress's discriminatory treatment in the public financing of the two major party candidates in presidential elections. Justice Rehnquist thought that the Federal Election Campaign Act

and, for that matter, does not prevent state parties from solidifying the two-party system. Indeed, as true believers in the value of the two-party system, we would not want the rule to do so. But we think it might add some predictability and coherence to this area of electoral regulation, while preventing incumbent parties from imposing unique costs on new political actors.

5. *Principle of Electoral Influence.*—*A party that can demonstrate the requisite ability to affect the outcome of an election has the right to appear on the ballot.*[122]

As we noted above, any universal rule of access will ultimately require one to reject restrictions that in some respect are "too severe." This principle attempts to parse "severity" down to its purposes. As our discussion of exit and voice indicated, we believe that access to the ballot should be limited to groups that can influence elections because (1) they have support equal to or exceeding that of incumbent parties, or (2) they have the capacity to cause one of the incumbent parties to lose an election. Following from the second, and more permissive, option, courts should guarantee ballot access only to those groups with support equal to or greater than the expected margin of victory between party candidates in an upcoming election.

Operationalizing this principle presents some difficulties, although no more than the current standardless approach. Of course, courts can only make assumptions about the expected margin of victory by observing previous elections and deriving some average margin from competitive races in a given electoral district. Although in theory we would want judges to analyze where the new party would garner its support,[123] in practice we should only expect judges to look at raw numbers.

This approach rejects the extreme Libertarian view of expressive voting[124] and any natural rights approach to ballot access. To the degree the ballot under this approach serves any "expressive" purpose, it is only to allow minor factions to demonstrate their potential influence to the major parties. However, we regard

---

enshrined the Republican and Democratic Parties in a permanently preferred position, and has established requirements for funding minor-party and independent candidates to which the two major parties are not subject. Congress would undoubtedly be justified in treating the Presidential candidates of the two major parties differently from minor-party or independent Presidential candidates, in view of the long demonstrated public support of the former. But because of the First Amendment overtones of the appellants' Fifth Amendment equal protection claim something more than a merely rational basis for the difference in treatment must be shown, as the Court apparently recognizes. I find it impossible to subscribe to the Court's reasoning that because no third party has posed a credible threat to the two major parties in Presidential elections since 1860, Congress may by law attempt to assure that this pattern will endure forever. I would hold that, as to general election financing, Congress has not merely treated the two major parties differently from minor parties and independents, but has discriminated in favor of the former in such a way as to run afoul of the Fifth and First Amendments to the United States Constitution.

Buckley v. Valeo, 424 U.S. 1, 293 (1975) (Rehnquist, J., concurring and dissenting).

[122] As we noted prior to our discussion of the paradigms, ballot access restrictions do not clearly impinge on identifiable constitutional rights. See supra note 7. Nevertheless, we would expect a court to hang this principle, as it does its current approach, see, e.g., Munro v. Socialist Workers Party, 479 U.S. 189 (1986), on the First Amendment, substantive due process under the 14th Amendment, or the fundamental interest strand of Equal Protection jurisprudence.

[123] In other words, a party whose support comes only from the perpetual losing party cannot affect the outcome of an election. For example, if the Republicans in an electoral district always beat the Democrats by 5%, a new Liberal Party formed exclusively from a faction of Democrats will not affect the expected outcome of an election.

[124] See supra note 28 and accompanying text.

this goal as instrumental, rather than expressive: Parties' ballot access rights depend only on their ability to *influence* an election, not their ability to make a statement. As this principle follows a more Managerial approach, we expect it may be somewhat less permissive than the Court's current approach.[125] However, nothing would prevent the Court from merely adopting this principle alongside its current approach, i.e., treating the electoral influence principle as a ceiling for access restrictions but not a floor. Thus, the Court might say that one, but not the only metric to measure the constitutionality of a ballot access restriction is whether the relevant law requires a demonstration of support beyond that needed to change the outcome of a typical election.

The Marketeers might respond that this approach does nothing to curtail the growth of dominant parties operating under uncompetitive situations. After all, the larger the gap between the two parties, the higher a demonstration of support that judges would permit the state to require for access to the ballot.[126] Recognizing, as we did above, that this principle could operate alongside other ad hoc "severity" or "competitiveness" tests, we would also respond that this approach actually enhances competition in a way best suited to plurality-based systems. This principle could enhance coalition building among "out groups" by forcing interest groups defecting from highly dominant parties to join with opposition parties to increase the probability of uprooting incumbents. Seeking two-party competition when it is most needed, the principle directs judges to strike down only those laws that prevent interest group exit when such exit has any electoral significance. By enhancing two-party competition when one party is dominant, and by decreasing costs of entry under conditions of duopoly or active two-party competition, the principle should allay the Marketeers' fears of non-competitiveness while maintaining the Managerial/Pluralist emphasis on broad-based political parties.

CONCLUSION

Our principal argument in this Article has been that one must look to alternative philosophies of the party system rather than constitutional provisions to explain the Court's decisions and individual judges' opinions in party regulation cases. Managers, Libertarians, Progressives, Marketeers, and Pluralists have different philosophies when it comes to the relationship between the party and the state, where power should be located in the party system, and what the preferred number of parties is. Judges then filter these philosophical predispositions through constitutional provisions in order to arrive at decisions in concrete cases.

In a subsequent work, perhaps we, or others, could deconstruct these paradigms even further and concentrate on specific aspects of judges' political philosophies. There appear to be several dimensions along which decisions on regulation of the party system are made: a "representativeness" dimension with poles at descriptive and substantive representation, a "liberal" dimension along which one locates one's fear of state authority, an "activism" dimension that measures one's preference for legislative, as opposed to judicial, action, and an "efficiency" dimension that cali-

[125] See Burt Neuborne & Arthur Eisenberg, The Rights of Candidates and Voters 57 (1980) (suggesting that the Court abides by an implicit 5% signature requirement).

[126] For example, under conditions where the Republicans routinely beat the Democrats by 20%, a ballot access law requiring a demonstration of 20% electoral support to get on the ballot would be constitutional. Remember, though, that pursuant to the Equal Treatment Principle this 20% demonstration would need to be required of all parties.

brates one's preference for governmental institutions well-fitted for the achievement of public policy goals. We hope others can operationalize this multi-dimensional approach and that this Article will spur some new thinking in this area.

After recognizing the strengths and weaknesses of these paradigms, we proposed five middle-range principles relevant to cases involving ballot access restrictions and regulation of a party's method of candidate selection. A similar set could be constructed for other cases of party regulation, such as those involving patronage, gerrymandering, and campaign finance. Neither the paradigms we discussed nor the principles we float here represent an exhaustive or sufficient list.[127] However, acknowledgement that the relevant constitutional provisions are of limited utility and that each paradigm provides a valuable perspective to be considered in the development of principles to govern individual cases, we hope, will lead to a more honest and coherent jurisprudence of political parties.

EPILOGUE[128]

The law of political parties has developed further since we wrote this Article. At the same time that the U.S. Supreme Court considered arguments in the California blanket primary case,[129] Senator John McCain's candidacy in the 2000 Republican presidential primary raised new issues about legal regulation of the party system.

The experience of John McCain should fascinate scholars for a number of reasons. For the first time in American history, a presidential candidate maintained his viability through much of the primary season by winning the votes of non-party members. Between the New Hampshire primary and Super Tuesday, McCain consistently won the votes of Democrats and Independents while George Bush garnered a majority of Republicans.[130] Reminding voters of the

---

[127] For example, we have excluded from our discussion here—but have included in the table—a skeletal description of what might constitute a Critical paradigm. Adherents to such an approach would seek to use the party system to maximize proportional representation, maybe even calling into question the constitutionality of single member districts themselves. Distrusting elites, whether elected or elevated through the party ranks, the Critics would probably prefer to locate power in the party-in-the-electorate. They would advocate aggressive judicial intervention to counteract the median voter tendencies of the American system of representation and separation of powers, and might even urge the judiciary to view substantive policy results as one form of representation. In other words, public policies that work to disadvantage one group would be considered evidence of discrimination to be counterbalanced by judicial intervention in the system of representation. Advocates would probably prefer a high number of parties, each with the right to have a proportional share of governmental power, with such proportions regulated by judicial overseers. We do not discuss this paradigm at length because we do not find much in the court decisions or legal literature to support it.

[128] We are grateful to the *Columbia Law Review* for allowing us to offer a few additional thoughts at this late date.

[129] California Democratic Party v. Jones, 984 F. Supp. 1288 (E.D. Cal. 1997), aff'd, 169 F.3d 646 (9th Cir. 1999), cert. granted, 120 S. Ct. 977 (U.S. Jan 21, 2000) (No. 99–401).

[130] Rhodes Cook, Race for the Presidency: Winning the 2000 Nomination viii–ix (2000) (detailing the type of presidential primary systems used in each state). Primary election results for each state are available on the ABC News website. See ABC News, Returns by State (visited May 1, 2000) <http://abcnews.go.com/sections/politics/2000vote/returns_by_state.html>. Connecticut is the only primary McCain won where the primary electorate was limited to Republican registrants. However, in New Hampshire, which allows Independents to vote in the Republican primary, exit polls show that McCain also beat Bush among registered Republicans. See Derek Rose, Pollster Predictions Poleaxed by McCain's Broad Victory, Manchester Union Leader, Feb. 2, 2000 (available at <http://www.theunion leader.com/Articles_show.html?article=6245&archive=1> [the online edition of New Hampshire's

importance of "Reagan Democrats" to earlier Republican presidential victories, McCain viewed his candidacy as one that would broaden the Republican Party tent. Frequently invoking the Progressive spirit of his hero, President Theodore Roosevelt, McCain took on the party establishment and delivered a message of political reform that provided engaging political drama even if it did not result in his nomination.

McCain's Progressivist mission found its way into the courts as well. Unable to maneuver the burdensome ballot access laws that governed the New York Republican presidential primary, McCain and his supporters filed suit to force the party and the state to place his delegates' names on the ballot statewide.[131] Applying general election ballot access rules to the 2000 Republican primary, the Court found, as the same judge and the Second Circuit had in a successful challenge to the 1996 Republican primary ballot access laws,[132] that "the New York ballot access scheme as applied to the Primary poses an undue burden in its totality on the right to vote under the First Amendment."[133] Placing McCain, as well as all other Republican candidates, on the ballot statewide, the Court embraced the Progressive argument that party members, not leaders or machines, should determine the party's presidential nominee:

> The legislative scheme, which was chosen by the Republican State Committee and enacted into law as part of the accommodation that the Republican and Democratic Parties in the Legislature make to each other, "consistently and decisively advantages the candidate [the Republican State Committee] supports and discourages and disadvantages the candidates it has rejected." *Rockefeller* [v. *Powers*], 917 F. Supp. at 164. While this may further the interest of the Republican State Committee, as distinguished from the 3.1 million New York voters affiliated with the Republican Party, it undermines the very purpose of a primary, which is "to protect the general party membership against this sort of minority control [by the party leadership]," *Tashjian v. Republican Party of Connecticut*, 479 U.S. 208, 236 (1986) (dissenting opinion of Scalia, J.).[134]

Molinari and the *Rockefeller* decision upon which it was based are two in a small set of cases since the White Primary cases where the courts have applied constitutional rules developed for general elections to primary elections. They also appear to be the first cases where a party organization's interest in skewing primary rules to favor its candidate of choice was deemed an illegitimate state interest.

McCain's Progressive mission spilled over into the Supreme Court's consideration of the appeal in *California Democratic Party v. Jones*, a case in which Mc-

---

daily newspaper]). Of course, in many states that allow non-party members to vote, such as South Carolina, Democratic or Independent crossovers were insufficient to give McCain a victory.

[131] See Molinari v. Powers, 82 F. Supp. 2d 57 (E.D.N.Y. 2000). As specified by New York law, not internal party rules, the ballot access rules for the 2000 New York Republican presidential primary required candidates to collect 5000 signatures statewide from registered Republicans to earn the opportunity to have their delegates appear on the ballot. Then, in each of New York's 31 congressional districts, the slate of delegates needed to collect signatures from 0.5% of the registered Republicans in that district who had not yet signed another candidate's petition. See id. at 59–61.

[132] See Rockefeller v. Powers, 917 F. Supp. 155, 164 (E.D.N.Y. 1996), aff'd, 78 F.3d 44 (2d Cir. 1996).

[133] *Molinari*, 82 F. Supp. 2d at 71.

[134] Id. at 77.

Cain filed an amicus brief supporting the blanket primary law.[135] Judging from the oral argument,[136] McCain's passion and the lower courts' reasoning were not well received by the Justices. Opting for the Libertarian over the Progressive paradigm, the Justices did not appear to consider the state's interests in expanding participation in the primary election, and certainly not the alleged interest in producing moderate candidates, as justifying the blanket primary's intrusion on party autonomy.[137] Justice O'Connor asked Thomas Gede, who represented the state of California, "What's left [of party autonomy], if this can stand? . . . [T]ell me what would remain after your so-called balancing test of a party's right at all."[138] Justice Scalia, whose dissent in *Tashjian* rejected the party's right to open its primary to independent voters, clearly felt this case, where the party sought to close itself from independents and crossovers, presented a different issue. Defending this one-way ratchet of party autonomy, Justice Scalia argued passionately for the right of party organizations to exclude. He hypothesized: "[H]ere we have a party that's committed to an ideal, and if we stay committed to it, we will, in fact, eventually persuade people. But we cannot stay committed to that ideal when, because of random considerations, basically, we find ourselves saddled with a gubernatorial candidate who may not even share that ideal."[139]

From the tone of the questioning, the most difficult challenge confronting the Justices comes in drawing a line between California's blanket primary, which allows voters to switch party primaries as they migrate down the ballot, and the various types of open primaries, which allow all voters to choose either party's entire ballot on the day of the primary.[140] As we noted earlier, we view with suspicion any state-imposed rules that dictate party nominating procedures, but we expect that the Court will be less eager to cast a shadow over the open primary laws that govern almost half the states.[141] The Court seemed poised to create a rule that rested on the point of affiliation: that a state could require a party to allow any voter to affiliate with it even up until the day of the primary, but it could not force a party to allow unaffiliated voters to vote for any office on its primary ballot. Given that in several open primary systems the process of "affiliation" appears out of view in the voting booth when the voter chooses one primary ballot over another, the Court must identify the moment of "party affiliation" somewhat tautologically by the point at which a voter commits to voting on a primary ballot.

Seeking to limit this case to its facts, the Court might instead emphasize that, unlike the open primary systems currently in effect, California's blanket primary was imposed upon the party organizations without their consent. As the opinion in *Molinari* suggested, in most cases the "laws" governing primary ballot access and membership are the result of collusive bargains between the parties to formalize in law what the parties have agreed serves both of their interests. Perhaps a

---

[135] See Brief for Amici William E. Brock and John McCain et al., California Democratic Party v. Jones, 984 F. Supp. 1288 (E.D. Cal. 1997), aff'd, 169 F.3d 646 (9th Cir. 1999), cert. granted, 120 S. Ct. 977 (U.S. Jan. 21, 2000) (No. 99–401).

[136] See California Democratic Party v. Jones, No. 99–401, 2000 WL 486738 (oral argument transcripts).

[137] See id.

[138] Id. at *26.

[139] Id. at *31.

[140] See Elisabeth R. Gerber & Rebecca B. Morton, Primary Election Systems and Representation, 14 J. L. Econ. & Org. 304 (1998) (describing the variety of primary systems).

[141] See id. at 306 (listing states with open primary laws).

challenge to the open primary has not surfaced because all parties operating under them see them as to their advantage or at least not worth overturning. Given the embarrassment the McCain candidacy inflicted on various Republican party machines from New Hampshire to Michigan and the correlative glee it provided Democrats, however, a challenge to a state open primary law may be just around the corner.

Challenges to American Democracy

30

THE PARTISAN POLITICAL ECONOMY
Larry M. Bartels

Earlier in this reader Valelly emphasized that political scientists like political parties a great deal because they frame broad policy and philosophical choices, enable government by discussion (to use the phrase introduced by Kinder and Herzog), and attach voters to their polity. In this chapter from his very important book on the political economy of increasing income inequality in the United States, Larry Bartels pours a bucket of ice-cold water on such enthusiasm. Bartels shows that the two parties differ profoundly in how they arrange the social rewards of the macroeconomy's performance. Republicans increase income inequality, Democrats do not. The American party system, as a result, generates income inequality simply because—as Bartels showed in his piece earlier in this volume—alteration in party fortunes is inevitable. National elections are after all very competitive.

Had Democrats been in control more often in the postwar era there would be less income inequality today. But who would want such one-party government? Ultimately there seems to be a surprising and stark trade-off between economic fairness and democratic political competition. This is an exceptionally challenging claim to make about American politics and government.

Bartels's bracing portrait of the partisan origins of increasing income inequality raises several questions for you. First, can you argue the evidence away? If you cannot, then what would mitigate the trade-off that is framed by Bartels's analysis? Social policy? Recall, however, that Hacker's portrait of the welfare state highlights how little the American welfare state now does to cushion economic risks for those who are not wealthy or do not have high incomes. Should we then have stronger social policies? If so, under what conditions would we get them? Think about which articles earlier in the volume address such questions—and whether the answers are gloomy or hopeful.

• • •

... as our economy grows, market forces work to provide the greatest rewards to those with the needed skills in the growth areas. . . . This trend . . . is simply an economic reality, and it is neither fair nor useful to blame any political party.

—*Treasury Secretary Henry Paulson, 2006*[1]

Bartels, Larry M. In *Unequal Democracy: The Political Economy of the New Gilded Age.* © 2008 by Russell Sage Foundation. Published by Princeton University Press. Reprinted by permission of the Princeton University Press.

[1] Remarks Prepared for Delivery by Treasury Secretary Henry H. Paulson at Columbia University, August 1, 2006, http://www.treas.gov/press/releases/hp41.htm.

SECRETARY PAULSON'S ATTRIBUTION of increasing economic inequality to impersonal "market forces" is politically convenient, given his prominent position in an administration that has presided over booming corporate profits but stagnant wages for most working people. Nonetheless, his perspective is symptomatic of a much more general tendency to think of the economy as a natural system existing prior to, and largely separate from, the political sphere.

In the run-up to the 2004 presidential election, for example, the Associated Press (AP) reported that, "Over two decades, the income gap has steadily increased between the richest Americans, who own homes and stocks and got big tax breaks, and those at the middle and bottom of the pay scale, whose paychecks buy less." While the AP story noted that Democratic presidential candidate John Kerry was attempting to make the economy a campaign issue, the last word went to the chief economist for Wells Fargo: "This really has nothing to do with Bush or Kerry, but more to do with the longer-term shift in the structure of the economy." Similarly, in the run-up to the 2006 midterm election business columnist Ben Stein noted that "there is extreme income inequality in this country. It is hard to say whether it's the fault of President Bush, since there was also extreme income inequality under former President Bill Clinton, and in fact there has always been extreme income inequality."[2]

The tendency to think of economic outcomes as natural and inevitable is politically significant because it discourages systematic critical scrutiny of their causes and consequences. If escalating inequality is "simply an economic reality," it seems pointless to spend too much energy worrying about how and why it arises. Moreover, if "there has always been extreme income inequality" under Republicans and Democrats alike, it seems pointless to hope that public policies might mitigate that inequality. As prominent policy analyst Lawrence Mead rather breezily put it, in a response to the report of the American Political Science Association's Task Force on Inequality and American Democracy cited in chapter 1, "The causes [of growing economic inequality] are not well understood and have little tie to government."[3]

My aim in this chapter is to refute the notion that the causes of economic inequality in contemporary America "have little tie to government." Indeed, I suggest that the narrowly economic focus of most previous studies of inequality has caused them to miss what may be the most important single influence on the changing U.S. income distribution over the past halfcentury—the contrasting policy choices of Democratic and Republican presidents. Under Republican administrations, real income growth for the lower- and middle-income classes has consistently lagged well behind the income growth rate for the rich—and well behind the income growth rate for the lower and middle classes themselves under Democratic administrations.

In addition to documenting these substantial partisan disparities in income growth, the analyses presented in this chapter address a variety of potential explanations for them. I show that the dramatic differences in patterns of income growth under Democratic and Republican presidents are quite unlikely to have occurred by chance; nor can they be attributed to oil price shocks or changes in the structure of the labor force or other purely economic factors, or to cyclical

---

[2] Associated Press, "Gap Between the Rich, Others Grows," *Trenton Times,* August 17, 2004, A6; Ben Stein, "You Can Complain, or You Can Make Money," *New York Times,* October 15, 2006, BU 3.

[3] Mead (2004), 671.

corrections by each party of the other party's policy excesses. Rather, they reflect consistent differences in policies and priorities between Democratic and Republican administrations. In the first half of the post-war era, these differences were expressed primarily in macroeconomic policies and performance, with Democrats presiding over significantly less unemployment and significantly more overall economic growth than Republicans. Since the 1970s some of these macroeconomic differences have been muted, but significant partisan differences in tax and transfer policies have continued to produce significant partisan disparities in patterns of post-tax income growth, with the middle class and, especially, the working poor experiencing significantly more income growth under Democratic presidents than under Republican presidents.

The cumulative effect of these partisan differences has been enormous. My projections based on the historical performance of Democratic and Republican presidents suggest that income inequality would actually have *declined* slightly over the past 50 years—completely erasing the substantial increase in inequality documented in chapter 1—had the patterns of income growth characteristic of Democratic administrations been in effect throughout that period. Conversely, continuous application of the patterns of income growth observed during periods of Republican control would have produced a much greater divergence in the economic fortunes of rich and poor people than we have actually experienced—a Platinum-Gilded Age.

PARTISAN PATTERNS OF INCOME GROWTH

As suggested in chapter 1, economists have generally paid only perfunctory attention to potential *political* explanations for increasing economic inequality in contemporary America. They have paid even less attention to *partisan* political explanations—perhaps because marked partisan differences in economic outcomes are difficult to account for within the framework of standard economic models.[4] While political economists have documented consistent partisan differences in economic policy, they have seldom focused on the implications of those differences for income inequality or for the specific economic fortunes of people in different parts of the income distribution.[5]

The most notable exception to this pattern of neglect is the work of Douglas Hibbs, who produced pioneering studies of the impact of partisan politics on a variety of macroeconomic outcomes, including the money supply, unemployment, real output, and income inequality. Using data from 1948 through 1978 (that is, before most of the substantial increase in income inequality documented in chapter 1), Hibbs found that the ratio of the share of post-tax income received by the top 20% of the income distribution to the share received by the bottom

[4] A rudimentary search of *JSTOR,* an online archive including articles from more than 50 economics journals, turned up 228 articles published since 1987 with the phrase "economic inequality" in the text; but only 19 of these made any mention of "political parties," "political party," "partisan," "Democrat," or "Republican," and only one brief piece (Bartels and Brady 2003) focused significantly on the role of partisan politics in exacerbating or mitigating economic inequality. In addition, Atkinson (1997) and Putterman, Roemer, and Silvestre (1998) argued for the general significance of political factors (and more specifically for the potential utility of models in which political parties may generate nonmedian policy outcomes) in the course of surveying economic research on income distribution and egalitarianism, respectively.

[5] Hibbs (1977, 1987); Keech (1980); Beck (1982); Alesina and Sachs (1988).

40% declined during periods of Democratic control but increased during periods of Republican control. Applying these estimates to his entire period, Hibbs concluded that inequality declined markedly (by a total of about 25%) during the 14 years of Democratic control covered by his analysis, while remaining essentially unchanged during the 17 years of Republican control. Hibbs and Christopher Dennis extended this analysis through the early 1980s and embedded it in a somewhat broader analysis of partisan differences in macroeconomic policy.[6]

The analysis presented in this chapter extends Hibbs and Dennis's analyses in a variety of ways—most notably by incorporating 20 years of additional historical experience, including most of the period of escalating inequality described in chapter 1. My focus is on partisan patterns of real income growth for affluent, middle-class, and working poor families. I employ the tabulations from the U.S. Census Bureau's Historical Income Tables introduced in chapter 1 to examine year-to-year changes in real pre-tax income for families at the 20th, 40th, 60th, 80th, and 95th percentiles of the income distribution from 1948 through 2005.

It will not be surprising, in light of the discussion in chapter 1, that the average rate of real income growth during this period was higher for affluent families than for those lower in the income distribution. These average growth rates, which appear in the first column of table 1, range from 2% for families at the 95th percentile down to 1.4% for families at the 20th percentile.

What may be surprising is that this pattern of differential growth is entirely limited to periods in which Republicans controlled the White House. The second and third columns of table 1 present separate tabulations of real income growth during Democratic and Republican administrations, respectively. Since it seems unreasonable to expect a new president to have an immediate impact on income growth in his first year in office, my measure of partisan control is lagged by one year; thus, income changes in 2001 are attributed to Democrat Bill Clinton, despite the fact that Republican George W. Bush took office in January of that year. The assumption of a one-year lag in partisan policy effects is consistent with macroeconomic evidence regarding the timing of economic responses to monetary and fiscal policy changes; it also fits the observed data better than a zero-, two-, three-, four-, or five-year lag.[7]

Figure 1 provides a graphical representation of the patterns documented in the second and third columns of table 1. The starkly different patterns of income growth under Democratic and Republican administrations are very clear in the figure. Under Democratic presidents, poor families did slightly better than richer families (at least in proportional terms), producing a modest net decrease in income inequality; under Republican presidents, rich families did vastly better than poorer families, producing a considerable net increase in income inequality. In both cases, the patterns are essentially linear over the entire range of family incomes represented in the figure (that is, for incomes ranging from about $25,000 to $200,000 in 2005).

[6] Hibbs (1987), 232–243. The t-statistic for this partisan difference is 1.8, suggesting that it is very unlikely to be due to chance (Hibbs and Dennis 1988).

[7] Christiano et al. (1999); Blanchard and Perotti (2002). I have investigated the statistical fit of alternative lags by replicating the analysis presented in table 3 using current (unlagged) presidential partisanship, as well as presidential partisanship lagged by two, three, four, or five years. In every case the resulting regression model fit the data 4 to 5% less well than the model with presidential partisanship lagged by one year.

TABLE 1

Real Income Growth Rates by Income Level and Presidential Partisanship, 1948–2005

Average annual real pre-tax income growth (%) for families at various points in the income distribution (with standard errors in parentheses). Partisan control measured from one year following inauguration to one year following subsequent inauguration.

	All Presidents	Democratic Presidents	Republican Presidents	Partisan Difference
20th percentile	1.42 (.50)	2.64 (.77)	.43 (.61)	2.21 (.97)
40th percentile	1.54 (.39)	2.46 (.58)	.80 (.49)	1.67 (.75)
60th percentile	1.73 (.34)	2.47 (.52)	1.13 (.43)	1.33 (.67)
80th percentile	1.84 (.33)	2.38 (.50)	1.39 (.42)	.99 (.65)
95th percentile	2.00 (.38)	2.12 (.65)	1.90 (.46)	.22 (.77)
N	58	26	32	58

Source: Calculations based on data from Census Bureau Historical Income Tables.

If patterns of income growth differ so dramatically under Democratic and Republican presidents, it seems natural to wonder whether similar differences are attributable to Democratic and Republican members of Congress. Unfortunately, the historical pattern of change in the partisan composition of Congress in the post-war era makes it very hard to tell. With Democrats holding an uninterrupted majority in the House of Representatives from 1955 through 1994 and Republicans in control from 1995 through 2006, any effect of variation in the partisan composition of Congress is likely to be confounded with the effects of broader economic trends. Thus, although simple tabulations of income growth levels suggest that they have generally been higher when Congress has been more Democratic, those differences cannot be considered dispositive.[8]

A PARTISAN COINCIDENCE?

The partisan differences in characteristic rates of income growth documented in figure 1 would seem to be of immense economic and political significance—if they are real. They suggest that middle-class and poor families in the post-war era have routinely fared much worse under Republican presidents than they have under Democratic presidents. By this accounting, economic inequality in contemporary America is profoundly shaped by partisan politics.

But to what extent are these patterns really attributable to partisan politics rather than to accidental historical factors? One way to address this question is to examine their consistency across a range of presidents and circumstances. To that end, figure 2 shows the level of income inequality in each year of the post-war period as reflected in one standard measure of inequality, the ratio of incomes at the 80th percentile of the income distribution to those at the 20th percentile.

[8] Adding a measure of the average proportion of Democrats in the House and Senate to the regression equations reported in table 3 suggests that Democrats in Congress probably had positive effects on income growth, at least for low-income families; but the relevant parameter estimates are small (implying that even the largest observed shift in the partisan composition of Congress had much less effect on income growth than a shift in partisan control of the White House) and very imprecise (with an average *t*-statistic of .35).

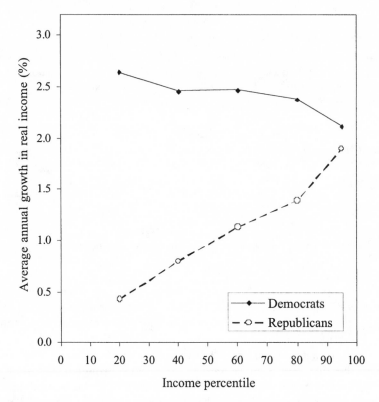

FIGURE 1. Income Growth by Income Level under Democratic and Republican Presidents, 1948–2005

By this measure, income inequality was essentially constant from the late 1940s through the late 1960s, with families at the 80th percentile of the income distribution earning about three times as much as families at the 20th percentile. Inequality increased fairly steadily through the 1970s and 1980s before leveling off once again in the 1990s. These broad temporal trends reinforce the impression that growing inequality is significantly related to long-term technological and social changes.

Despite these long-term forces, distinguishing between Democratic and Republican administrations (the white circles and black diamonds in the figure, respectively) reveals the regularity with which Democratic presidents reduced and Republican presidents increased the prevailing level of economic inequality, regardless of the long-term trend. Indeed, the effect of presidential partisanship on income inequality turns out to have been remarkably consistent since the end of World War II. The 80/20 income ratio increased under each of the six Republican presidents in this period—Eisenhower, Nixon, Ford, Reagan, George H. W. Bush, and George W. Bush. In contrast, four of five Democratic presidents—all except Jimmy Carter—presided over declines in income inequality. If this is a coincidence, it is a very powerful one.[9] Even in the highly inegalitarian economic climate of the 1990s, Bill Clinton managed to produce slightly stronger income growth for

[9] The probability of observing no more than one exception to the partisan pattern of increasing inequality under Republicans and decreasing inequality under Democrats in a random sequence of 11 increases and decreases would be $12 \div 2{,}048 = .006$.

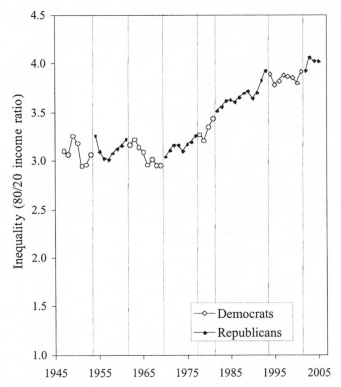

FIGURE 2. Income Inequality under Democratic and Republican Presidents, 1947–2005

families at the 20th percentile than at the 80th percentile, though families at the very top of the income distribution did even better.

The strikingly consistent partisan pattern of changes in income inequality in figure 2 seems hard to attribute to a mere coincidence in the timing of Democratic and Republican administrations. That conclusion is reinforced by additional analyses focusing on various subsets of the 58-year period represented in figure 2. For example, families at the 20th percentile of the income distribution experienced much more robust income growth under Democratic presidents than under Republican presidents in both the first and second halves of the post-war era.[10] Substantial partisan differences appear even if any one or two administrations are omitted from the comparison,[11] if years with unusually high or low growth are ignored,[12] or if presidential election years or partisan transition years are

[10] From 1947 to 1974, average income growth for families at the 20th percentile of the income distribution was 1.5% under Republican presidents and 3.8% under Democratic presidents; the partisan difference is 2.32 (with a t-statistic of 1.3). From 1974 to 2005, average income growth for families at the 20th percentile was –0.3% under Republicans and 1.3% under Democrats; the partisan difference is 1.59 (with a t-statistic of 1.7).

[11] Omitting each of the 11 post-war presidents in turn from the comparison reported in table 1 produces estimates of the partisan difference in income growth at the 20th percentile ranging from 1.49 (with a t-statistic of 1.5), omitting Lyndon Johnson, to 2.77 (with a t-statistic of 3.0), omitting Dwight Eisenhower.

[12] Excluding years in which real income growth at the 20th percentile was greater than 5% or less than –2% produces a partisan difference of 2.02 (with a t-statistic of 4.0).

TABLE 2
The Impact of Partisan Turnover on Partisan Differences
in Real Income Growth Rates, 1948–2005

Average annual real pre-tax income growth (%) for families at various points in the income distribution (with standard errors in parentheses). Partisan control measured from one year following inauguration to one year following subsequent inauguration. "Partisan turnover" refers to first-term Democrats who succeeded Republicans or first-term Republicans who succeeded Democrats.

	All Presidents	Democratic Presidents	Republican Presidents	Partisan Difference
20th percentile	1.38 (.75)	2.28 (1.00)	.71 (1.08)	1.57 (1.52)
40th percentile	1.52 (.54)	2.07 (.75)	1.11 (.76)	.96 (1.09)
60th percentile	1.60 (.47)	2.00 (.63)	1.30 (.67)	.71 (.95)
80th percentile	1.80 (.45)	2.19 (.62)	1.51 (.63)	.68 (.91)
95th percentile	1.89 (.45)	1.93 (.69)	1.86 (.61)	.07 (.92)
N	28	12	16	28
No partisan turnover				
20th percentile	1.46 (.68)	2.95 (1.19)	.16 (.61)	2.80 (1.29)
40th percentile	1.56 (.56)	2.80 (.88)	.48 (.63)	2.31 (1.06)
60th percentile	1.86 (.51)	2.86 (.82)	.97 (.57)	1.89 (.98)
80th percentile	1.87 (.48)	2.55 (.78)	1.27 (.57)	1.28 (.95)
95th percentile	2.10 (.62)	2.28 (1.07)	1.95 (.70)	.34 (1.25)
N	30	14	16	30

Source: Calculations based on data from Census Bureau Historical Income Tables.

excluded.[13] In each of these analyses, the overall pattern of partisan differences in income growth is qualitatively similar to the wedge-shaped pattern in figure 1.

It may be tempting to suppose that the very different patterns of income growth under Democratic and Republican presidents in figure 1 reflect a cycle of partisan equilibration in which Democrats pursue expansionary policies in reaction to Republican contractions and Republicans produce contractions as an antidote to Democratic expansions. However, a detailed analysis of the timing of partisan differences in income growth provides no support for that notion. Table 2 provides tabulations of average income growth paralleling those in table 1, but separately for administrations in which the president was of the opposite party as his predecessor (in the top panel of the table) and those in which the president succeeded himself or a member of his own party (in the bottom panel).

If slow growth for middle-class and poor families under Republican presidents represented an antidote to unsustainable expansion under Democratic presidents, and vice versa, we would expect to see the greatest partisan differences in administrations where Republicans succeeded Democrats or Democrats succeeded Republicans. However, the actual pattern is exactly the opposite: the partisan differences in average growth rates at every income level were about twice as large in terms with no partisan turnover as they were in the first terms of new partisan

[13] The partisan difference in income growth at the 20th percentile excluding presidential election years is 3.27. The corresponding estimate in a model excluding partisan transition years (1953, 1961, 1969, 1977, 1981, 1993, and 2001) is 2.47. The t-statistics for these estimates are 3.0 and 2.3, respectively.

regimes. Democratic presidents generally presided over similar income growth rates for families in every part of the income distribution, regardless of whether they were in their first or second terms; but average income growth was consistently higher (by a little more than half a percentage point) when Democrats succeeded Democrats than when Democrats succeeded Republicans. Conversely, most families (except the most affluent) did better under first-term Republican presidents than in subsequent Republican administrations; these differences, too, were on the order of half a percentage point.

Income growth was also considerably more unequal in Republican administrations with no partisan turnover than it was under first-term Republican presidents. In both cases there was a steady increase in average growth rates with each step up the income ladder; but the gap in economic fortunes between the rich and the poor was almost twice as large when Republican presidents were well-entrenched in the White House than when they succeeded Democrats. Clearly, these differences cannot be attributable to short-term corrections of misguided Democratic policies.

Another way to gauge the robustness of the partisan pattern of income growth in figure 1 is to consider a variety of potential nonpolitical explanations for the pattern. Perhaps Republican presidents have just been unlucky in occupying the White House at times when powerful external forces depressed income growth for middle-class and poor families. In order to explore this possibility, table 3 presents the results of a series of parallel statistical analyses relating each year's real income growth at each of the income levels tabulated by the Census Bureau to a variety of potentially relevant economic and social conditions. The estimated effects of partisan control in these analyses represent the difference in average income growth under Democratic and Republican presidents for families at each income level, net of any differences attributable to historical trends or current economic circumstances.[14]

One economic circumstance of particular significance for income growth rates is the real price of oil—perhaps the most volatile and economically important commodity in modern industrial economies. Since major oil price shocks are largely outside the control of presidents, it would be misleading to attribute income changes associated with those shocks to partisan politics. As it turns out, however, fluctuations in oil prices have had little impact on income *inequality*; the statistical results presented in table 3 suggest that a 50% increase in the real price of oil would reduce the real incomes of families at every income level by a similar amount, about 1.5 percentage points.[15]

Income growth rates are also sensitive to changes in labor force participation, since adding another family member to the workforce is likely to produce a significant increase in family income. The proportion of adults in the labor force

[14] The Seemingly Unrelated Regression (SUR) estimator (Zellner 1962) exploits cross-equation correlations of the regression disturbances to produce more efficient parameter estimates than with ordinary least squares regression. Not surprisingly, the residuals from the parallel regression models considered here are strongly correlated, reflecting the extent to which economic shocks affect families at all income levels in similar ways. The 10 cross-equation correlations range from .27 to .90, with an average value of .68. As a result, some of the SUR parameter estimates reported in table 3 are a good deal more precise than the corresponding ordinary least squares parameter estimates.

[15] Annual percentage changes in the real price of oil are derived from monthly spot prices (for West Texas Intermediate) compiled by Dow Jones & Company and published by the Federal Reserve Bank of St. Louis, http://research.stlouisfed.org/fred2/series/OILPRICE/. By this measure, the real price of oil increased by 142% in 1974, by 52% in 2000, and by 48% in 1980. The largest decline was 47% in 1986.

TABLE 3

Statistical Analysis of Income Growth, 1949–2005

Annual real pre-tax income growth (%) for families at various points in the income distribution. Parameter estimates from Seemingly Unrelated Regression models (with standard errors in parentheses). Partisan control measured from one year following inauguration to one year following subsequent inauguration. "Linear trend" and "Quadratic trend" reflect cumulative change from 1949 through 2005.

	20th percentile	40th percentile	60th percentile	80th percentile	95th percentile
Democratic president	2.32 (.80)	1.60 (.56)	1.53 (.52)	1.23 (.51)	.50 (.64)
Oil prices (lagged %Δ)	-.032 (.016)	-.031 (.011)	-.035 (.011)	-.030 (.010)	-.032 (.013)
Labor force participation (Δ%)	4.66 (1.44)	4.46 (1.02)	2.95 (.95)	2.69 (.93)	3.58 (1.16)
Lagged growth	-.191 (0.84)	-.249 (.074)	-.286 (.077)	-.296 (.090)	-.040 (.114)
Lagged 95th percentile	.395 (.151)	.244 (.111)	.201 (.104)	.187 (.109)	—
Linear trend	-12.84 (5.88)	-13.71 (4.17)	-8.76 (3.88)	-5.30 (3.75)	-4.18 (4.71)
Quadratic trend	9.68 (5.75)	10.18 (4.06)	5.33 (3.78)	2.54 (3.67)	2.83 (4.61)
Intercept	2.68 (1.26)	3.80 (.89)	3.60 (.83)	3.17 (.81)	2.80 (1.01)
Standard error of regression	2.89	2.02	1.89	1.84	2.31
R^2	.41	.52	.45	.37	.29
N	57	57	57	57	57

Source: Calculations based on data from Census Bureau Historical Income Tables.

has increased from 59% in the late 1940s and 1950s to 67% at the turn of the twenty-first century, largely due to an increase in the number of working women. The statistical results presented in table 3 indicate that this increase significantly bolstered the incomes of American families, especially those in the bottom half of the income distribution.[16]

The price of oil and the increasing participation of women in the labor force are just two of a great many economic and social forces beyond the control of presidents that might be expected to affect the American economy and, perhaps, patterns of income inequality. For example, college education is much more common today than it was at the end of World War II, immigrants and the elderly make up larger shares of the population, the average size of families has become smaller, and imports constitute a larger share of the economy than they once did. Any or all of these changes may have contributed to changing patterns of income growth over the past half-century. However, because these long-term trends have been so glacial, and so intertwined, it is very difficult to discern their distinct effects on the shape of the income distribution.[17]

Fortunately, from the standpoint of *political* analysis, the very fact that these social and economic trends have been gradual and fairly steady implies that their effects are unlikely to be confounded with the effects of alterations in control of the White House, which occur episodically and have produced only a very slight increase over time in the frequency of Republican governance.[18] Thus, rather than attempting to pinpoint specifically how these and other long-term trends have affected patterns of income growth, I simply allow for the possibility that expected income growth rates have changed over time by including linear and quadratic trend terms in my analysis. Given the crudeness of this strategy for capturing long-term trends in income growth, it is important to note that the apparent effects of presidential partisanship are insensitive to a variety of alternative strategies for taking account of secular changes in the structure of the American economy and society. The statistical evidence for a partisan political effect turns out to be surprisingly robust in this respect.[19]

The estimated effects associated with the linear and quadratic trend terms in table 3 imply that average real income growth for families below the 95th percentile has declined by a little more than half a percentage point per decade over

[16] My measure is the annual change in the percentage of noninstitutionalized civilians over the age of 15 who are employed or seeking work, as tabulated by the Bureau of Labor Statistics, http://www.bls.gov/cps/cpsaat1.pdf.

[17] Correlations between annual levels of labor force participation, college education, immigration, elderly population, family size, and imports as a share of GDP range from .76 to .99 and average .89. Correlations between these measures and a simple linear trend range from .83 to .99 and average .93.

[18] The correlation between time and partisan control of the White House over the period covered by my analysis is .10. Correlations between partisan control and the social and economic indicators mentioned in the text range from .04 to .14 and average .10.

[19] For example, adding a cubic trend term to the regression models in table 3 increases the apparent impact of presidential partisanship by 11%, on average; the parameter estimates for Democratic presidents decline in roughly linear fashion from 2.54 (with a standard error of .77) at the 20th percentile to .66 (with a standard error of .61) at the 95th percentile. Replacing the linear and quadratic trend terms with an indicator variable for the period after 1973 decreases the apparent impact of presidential partisanship on income growth rates by an average of 8%; the parameter estimates for Democratic presidents decline in roughly linear fashion from 2.25 (with a standard error of .80) at the 20th percentile to .34 (with a standard error of .61) at the 95th percentile. Including social and economic trend variables, singly or in combination, also produces generally similar patterns of estimated partisan effects. For example, in the best-fitting model I have examined, which includes the value of imports as a share of GDP, the estimated partisan effects are all within 2% of the values reported in table 3.

the post-war era. However, the negative trend in income growth was much milder for families near the top of the income distribution—only one quarter of a percentage point per decade.[20] In this respect, among others, there is a fairly striking disconnection between the pattern of income growth for families at the 95th percentile and the pattern for less affluent families. Income growth at the 95th percentile was also virtually unrelated to growth in the previous year and was relatively unaffected by presidential partisanship. Thus, the most affluent families represented in the Census Bureau's tabulations have been surprisingly insulated from the structural shifts in the U.S. economy that have eroded income growth among less affluent families over the past half-century; and they have fared very well regardless of which party controls the White House.

Income growth among these affluent families does seem to have spurred significant subsequent income growth among middle-class and, especially, working poor families. This "trickle-down" phenomenon is reflected in the positive effects of the previous year's growth rate for families at the 95th percentile on current growth for families at lower income levels in table 3. Conversely, current growth for families at each income level was negatively related to the previous year's growth rate at the same income level, suggesting some tendency toward equilibration (with growth spurts in one year leading to slumps the following year, and vice versa), or perhaps some measurement error in the year-by-year growth rates derived from the Census Bureau's Current Population Surveys.

Despite the complicating effects of the constellation of explanatory factors represented in table 3, the impact of presidential partisanship emerges clearly in these analyses. Indeed, the partisan differences between Democratic and Republican presidents estimated in table 3 are remarkably similar in magnitude to those reported in table 1, declining in a roughly linear fashion from 2.3 percentage points at the 20th percentile to 0.5 percentage points at the 95th percentile of the family income distribution. These statistical results provide strong evidence that the striking differences in the economic fortunes of rich and poor families under Democratic and Republican administrations are not an artifact of the different conditions under which Democrats and Republicans have happened to hold the reins of government, but a reflection of the fundamental significance of partisan politics in the political economy of the post-war United States.[21]

PARTISAN DIFFERENCES IN MACROECONOMIC POLICY

Probing the remarkable partisan differences in patterns of income growth over the past half-century suggests that these differences are real, not a historical coincidence or a statistical illusion. But how do Democratic and Republican presidents actually *produce* such strikingly different patterns of income growth? That would constitute a fruitful research agenda for a small army of economists. Here, I merely attempt to sketch some consistent partisan differences in key policy areas in the

---

[20] My time trend variable runs from 0 in 1949 to 1 in 2005. Thus, the total decline in annual income growth rates at each income level over the entire period covered by my analysis is captured by the sum of the "Linear trend" and "Quadratic trend" coefficients in the corresponding column of table 3. The implied declines per decade in average income growth rates are .55, .62, .60, .48, and .24, respectively, for families at the 20th, 40th, 60th, 80th, and 95th percentiles of the income distribution.

[21] The partisan differences for all but the 95th percentile are too large to be plausibly attributable to chance, with *t*-statistics ranging from 2.4 to 2.9.

post-war era, provide some examples of contrasting Democratic and Republican policy initiatives, and trace the connection between partisan differences in macroeconomic performance and partisan patterns of inequality. The case studies presented in chapters 6, 7, and 8, though still far from comprehensive, are intended to supplement this brief overview with more detailed examinations of partisan politics in two especially important areas, tax policy and minimum wage policy.

One important source of partisan differences in income growth is that Democratic and Republican presidents have consistently pursued rather different macroeconomic policies, and those policies have had significant consequences for the changing shape of the U.S. income distribution. As Edward Tufte wrote, summarizing cross-national research through the mid-1970s, "Party platforms and political ideology set priorities and help decide policy. The consequence is that the governing political party is very much responsible for major macroeconomic outcomes—unemployment rates, inflation rates, income equalization, and the size and rate of expansion of the government budget."[22]

In the United States, as in many other industrial democracies, differences in the class composition of the parties' respective supporting coalitions have encouraged them to adopt distinctive macroeconomic priorities. Douglas Hibbs, writing in the mid-1980s, summarized these distinctive priorities simply and forcefully: "Democratic administrations are more likely than Republican ones to run the risk of higher inflation rates in order to pursue expansive policies designed to yield lower unemployment and extra growth." Hibbs added that "six of the seven recessions experienced since the Treasury–Federal Reserve Accord of 1951, which made possible activist monetary policies coordinated with fiscal policies, occurred during Republican administrations. Every one of these contractions was either intentionally created or passively accepted, at least for a while, in order to fight inflation."[23]

The testimony of policy makers, both contemporary and retrospective, provides ample evidence of important differences in economic philosophies and priorities between Republican and Democratic administrations. For example, Tufte noted that "the Eisenhower administration memoirs, fiscal histories, and diaries . . . bristle with determined statements on the need to avoid inflation and reduce the federal budget. Stimulative interventionist policies by the government were to be avoided because they ultimately stifled creative business initiative and because they served little purpose, since economic downturns and unemployment were seen as self-curing."

In stark contrast, within weeks of John Kennedy's inauguration, the new Democratic administration was being bombarded with pleas from a future Nobel laureate, Paul Samuelson, for stimulative interventionist policies: "WHAT THIS COUNTRY NEEDS IS AN ACROSS THE BOARD RISE IN DISPOSABLE INCOME TO LOWER THE LEVEL OF UNEMPLOYMENT, SPEED UP THE RECOVERY AND THE RETURN TO HEALTHY GROWTH, PROMOTE CAPITAL FORMATION AND THE GENERAL WELFARE, INSURE DOMESTIC TRANQUILITY AND THE TRIUMPH OF THE DEMOCRATIC PARTY AT THE POLLS."[24]

Two more future Nobel laureates, James Tobin and Robert Solow, were among the key members of Kennedy's economic policy-making team who drafted the

---

[22] Tufte (1978), 104.
[23] Hibbs (1987), 218.
[24] Tufte (1978), 17, 7.

administration's blueprint for economic recovery, a report by the Council of Economic Advisers entitled "The American Economy in 1961: Problems and Policies." In their diagnosis, "the real challenge of economic policy in the months ahead" was to absorb some $50 billion in slack economic capacity. To that end, Kennedy had already "proposed programs in education, health, natural resources and highways, which, while fully justified on their own merits, promise additional benefit in the form of speedier recovery." If more stimulation proved necessary, "A further program for economic recovery might consider a speed-up in Government construction and related projects, an expansion of housing programs, and tax reduction."[25]

Income growth under Kennedy was substantially stronger than it had been under Eisenhower for middle-class and working poor families, although affluent families fared less well.[26] Kennedy's successor, Lyndon Johnson, presided over five years of extraordinarily rapid, broad-based income growth. From 1964 through 1969, the real incomes of families at the 95th percentile of the income distribution grew by 4.2% per year. The corresponding growth rates for families at the 80th, 60th, and 40th percentiles were 4.3%, 4.3%, and 4.5%, respectively. The only group that deviated from this remarkable pattern of proportional income growth was the working poor; their incomes grew even more rapidly than those of more affluent families, by 5.6% per year. That fact was at least partly attributable to a variety of new antipoverty policies and programs implemented as part of Johnson's "Great Society," including Medicare and Medicaid, Job Corps, Food Stamps, and the Community Action Program.

Johnson's successor, Richard Nixon, is sometimes viewed as a rather unconventional, nonideological Republican president, at least in the realm of domestic policy. However, the first few years of Nixon's presidency "fit the stylized pattern of Republican economic priorities well: An orthodox policy of fiscal and monetary restraint was pursued to raise the rate of unemployment and contain the inflationary pressures inherited from the Johnson administration." The result of these policies was also consistent with the typical Republican pattern: the robust egalitarian income growth that had persisted for five years under Johnson screeched to a halt in 1970, replaced by slow growth for the affluent and sharp declines in income for the working poor. Only in August 1971, with a reelection campaign on the horizon, did Nixon launch a New Economic Policy including "fiscal stimulation, monetary expansion, a wage-price freeze, and a devaluation of the dollar."[27]

Nixon's New Economic Policy produced a booming economy in 1972, with real income growth ranging from 4.5% for working poor families to 6.6% for families at the 95th percentile of the income distribution. This robust growth contributed significantly to Nixon's landslide reelection. However, income growth slowed considerably in 1973 and disappeared in 1974. By the time Nixon resigned in disgrace in the wake of the Watergate scandal, in August 1974, the country was sliding into a severe recession.

[25] Tobin and Weidenbaum (1988), 54, 46, 48–49.

[26] The average real income growth rate for families at the 20th percentile of the income distribution increased from 2.1% under Eisenhower to 3.8% under Kennedy. Middle-class incomes grew by 2.3% under Eisenhower and 3.3% under Kennedy, while the growth rate for families at the 95th percentile declined from 3.2% to 1.4%.

[27] Hibbs (1987), 271. Real income growth rates in 1969 had ranged from 3.9% to 5.7%; in 1970 they declined monotonically from 1.9% for families at the 95th percentile of the income distribution to –2.7% for families at the 20th percentile.

The recession of 1974–1975 was triggered by a massive oil price shock engineered by the Organization of Petroleum Exporting Countries (OPEC). The real price of oil increased by 140% in 1974, throwing the industrial sector of the United States and other advanced economies into a tailspin. Accidental president Gerald Ford entered the White House in the midst of a major economic crisis not of his own making.

Although every president's economic performance is shaped by unpredictable and uncontrollable events, presidents' *responses* to those events are often strongly colored by their partisan priorities and predispositions. Given President Ford's conventional Main Street Republican background, it is perhaps unsurprising that he "initially refused to respond" to the OPEC price shock "with policies to restore aggregate demand," as most Democrats would have done. Instead, he "launched the 'Whip Inflation Now' program of fiscal and monetary restraint, which helped prolong the deep post-OPEC slump in employment and output through 1974 and into 1975. . . . Only after a long and sharp decline in real output did President Ford finally propose a one-year tax rebate in January 1975. The Democratic-dominated Congress passed the bill two and a half months later, after increasing the amount of the rebate substantially and redistributing it in favor of low-income and middle-income individuals."[28] Real incomes, which had declined significantly in 1975, rebounded in 1976—almost, but not quite, enough to get Ford reelected.

The economic recovery that had begun in President Ford's final year in office accelerated under his Democratic successor, Jimmy Carter. Real income growth in 1978 exceeded 5%, and the unemployment rate fell from 7% to 6%. From a distributional standpoint, the nature of the recovery shifted markedly. Under Ford, both the recession and the recovery were marked by the class bias characteristic of Republican administrations: low-income families lost more real income than affluent families in 1975 and gained less in 1976 and 1977. In marked contrast, real income growth in 1978 was robust across the board, with families at the 20th and 40th percentiles gaining 5.6% and 5.9%, respectively.

President Carter's economic policies were surprisingly consistent with traditional Democratic tendencies and priorities, given his own ideological moderation, his often-rocky relations with the Democratic leadership in Congress, and the difficult economic times in which he governed—"An Age of Limits," as one scholarly account put it. Carter and Congress negotiated a stimulus package including tax cuts and increased government spending, as well as an increase in the minimum wage and an expansion of federal employment programs. The administration refused to tolerate higher unemployment in order to check inflation, reckoning that "the human and social costs of this approach are prohibitive," according to one White House policy memorandum.[29]

Within months of taking office, Carter obtained congressional support for almost $10 billion in new funding for employment programs, much of it through the Comprehensive Employment and Training Act (CETA). The new money, channeled through local governments, paid for training grants, full-time public service jobs for up to two years, and summer jobs for low-income high school students. Four years later, Carter's secretary of labor announced proudly that he had presided over "more than a two and a half fold increase" in funds for employment and training, and that "about 4 million economically disadvantaged persons

[28] Hibbs (1987), 272.
[29] Bivin (2002), 198, 71, 128.

received training and job opportunities" under CETA in each year of the Carter administration.[30]

The unemployment rate declined through most of Carter's term but spiked back up in the wake of a second major oil price shock in 1979–1980. Slow growth was coupled with double-digit price inflation—an unprecedented combination of economic ills dubbed "stagflation." Running for reelection in the midst of recession, as well as foreign crises in Iran and Afghanistan, Carter was defeated by a popular vote margin of almost 10 percentage points.

When Carter's Republican successor, Ronald Reagan, assumed office in 1981, the unemployment rate stood at 7.5%—exactly the same level as four years earlier. However, Reagan's response to the unemployment problem stemming from an oil price shock was dramatically different from Carter's. Reagan's first budget gutted the controversial public service employment component of CETA and significantly reduced funding for job training programs. When CETA expired in 1982, the Reagan administration reluctantly agreed to support a much smaller successor program, the Job Training and Partnership Act (JTPA), with no public service employment and primary reliance on the private sector rather than local governments. "At its peak," one summary of domestic policy in the Reagan years noted, "CETA had funded more than three-quarters of a million full-time public service jobs. JTPA funds training, but not wages, for a smaller number of participants, who are enrolled, on average, for less than half the year. Spending on employment and training programs fell from about $22 billion to about $8 billion (in 1992 dollars) between 1979 and 1982. . . . Spending was also reduced for Food Stamps, school lunches, legal services, and social services."[31]

President Reagan's broader macroeconomic policies reflected a decisive choice between the horns of the "stagflation" dilemma. As Hibbs put it, "Monetary policy during the Reagan years leaned harder and longer against inflation than at any time since the Eisenhower administrations. The monetary restraint succeeded in breaking the inflationary legacy of the 1970s, but at the cost of the highest unemployment rates since the last years of the Great Depression."[32]

MACROECONOMIC PERFORMANCE AND INCOME GROWTH

The contrasting responses of Jimmy Carter and Ronald Reagan to the economic ills of "stagflation" are emblematic of surprisingly consistent partisan differences in the macroeconomic policies and priorities of Democratic and Republican presidents in the post-war era. Rather than multiplying examples, I turn in this section to the question of how those contrasting policies have affected the economic fortunes of American families. As it turns out, they have resulted in striking differences in macroeconomic performance between Democratic and Republican presidents, and those differences account for much of the partisan difference in income growth patterns evident in figure 1.

Here, too, my analysis builds on pioneering work by Douglas Hibbs. His empirical analyses, based on data from 1953 through 1983, documented significant

---

[30] Ray Marshall, "The Labor Department in the Carter Administration: A Summary Report—January 14, 1981," U.S. Department of Labor, http://www.dol.gov/oasam/programs/ history/carter-eta.htm.
[31] Danziger and Gottschalk (1995), 25.
[32] Hibbs (1987), 281.

TABLE 4

Macroeconomic Performance under Democratic and Republican Presidents, 1948–2005

Average values of macroeconomic indicators (with standard errors in parentheses). Partisan control measured from one year following inauguration to one year following subsequent inauguration.

	All Presidents	Democratic Presidents	Republican Presidents	Partisan Difference
Unemployment (%)	5.63 (.19)	4.84 (.24)	6.26 (.24)	–1.42 (.34)
Inflation (%)	3.85 (.39)	3.97 (.71)	3.76 (.43)	.20 (.80)
Real per capita GNP growth (%)	2.15 (.31)	2.78 (.41)	1.64 (.43)	1.14 (.60)
N	58	26	32	58

Source: Calculations based on data from Bureau of Labor Statistics and Bureau of Economic Analysis.

partisan differences in macroeconomic performance between Democratic and Republican administrations. In particular, Hibbs found that "after adjustment lags the unemployment rate tends to be about 2 percentage points lower under the Democrats than under the Republicans" and that "real output tends to be about 6 percent higher."[33]

Table 4 and figure 3 present comparisons of overall macroeconomic performance between Democratic and Republican administrations over the longer (58-year) period covered by my analysis. Unlike Hibbs's nonlinear regression estimates, these are simple average values of unemployment, GNP growth, and inflation under each party's presidents, again assuming a one-year lag in presidential influence.[34] Despite these differences, the comparisons of unemployment and GNP growth rates are quite consistent with Hibbs's: the average level of unemployment over the entire post-war era has been almost 30% higher under Republican presidents than under Democrats, while the average rate of real per capita GNP growth has been more than 40% lower. However, despite Republicans' traditional emphasis on curbing inflation, the average inflation rate has been virtually identical under Republican and Democratic presidents over this period.[35] While differential sensitivity to inflation may have contributed to partisan differences in unemployment and GNP growth, as Hibbs suggested, it is less obvious that Republican presidents have actually been more successful than Democrats in containing inflation.[36]

[33] Ibid., 226. For an earlier version of these analyses, see Hibbs (1977).

[34] The annual unemployment rate for the civilian labor force is reported by the Bureau of Labor Statistics, http://www.bls.gov/cps/home.htm#empstat. The GNP growth rate is calculated from annual data on real GNP per capita (chained dollars) reported by the Bureau of Economic Analysis, http://www.bea.doc.gov, table 7.1. The inflation rate is calculated from the Census Bureau's consumer price index CPI-U-RS, http://www.census.gov/hhes/income/income03/cpiurs.html.

[35] The average annual *change* in the inflation rate, not shown in table 4, is also virtually identical under Republican and Democratic presidents (–0.18 versus+0.03; the *t*-statistic for the difference is 0.3).

[36] The simple averages reported in table 4 may obscure an important partisan difference in inflation performance by ignoring the possibility of secular trends in the "natural" rate of inflation. Adding linear, quadratic, and cubic trend variables to a regression of inflation on (lagged) presidential partisanship produces some statistical evidence of higher inflation rates under Democratic presidents: the relevant regression parameter estimate is .75. Unfortunately, the estimate is quite imprecise (with a standard error of .72), making it very hard to tell how much, if any, of the apparent Republican

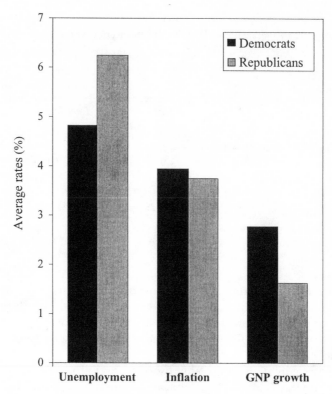

F_{IGURE} 3. Macroeconomic Performance under Democratic and Republican Presidents, 1948–2005

As with the partisan differences in income growth documented in figure 1, the partisan differences in macroeconomic outcomes documented in figure 3 cannot plausibly be attributed to differences in the circumstances in which Republican and Democratic presidents have occupied the White House. Embedding the partisan comparisons in a statistical analysis paralleling the analysis of income growth presented in table 3 provides strong evidence of significant partisan differences in unemployment and GNP growth between Republican and Democratic administrations, even after allowing for differences in specific economic circumstances and general historical trends.[37]

The partisan differences in macroeconomic performance documented in table 4 account for the lion's share of the partisan differences in income growth

---

advantage in constraining inflation is real. Adding lagged inflation to the analysis implies a smaller but longer-lasting partisan effect, with a coefficient of .53 (.56) and a coefficient for lagged inflation of .54 (.11). Adding trend variables to a regression of unemployment on presidential partisanship reduces the estimated difference between Democratic and Republican presidents by 16%, from –1.42 to –1.19 (with a standard error of .30). The apparent effect of Democratic presidents on GNP growth actually increases slightly, from 1.14 without trend variables to 1.21 (with a standard error of .64).

[37] In regression analyses paralleling those presented in table 3, the average unemployment rate is .76 percentage points lower under Democratic presidents (with a *t*-statistic of –4.0), and the average rate of GNP growth is 2.10 percentage points higher under Democratic presidents (with a *t*-statistic of 4.6). Allowing for delayed effects produced by lagged unemployment, inflation, and GNP growth in these models, the partisan differences implied by these statistical results are quite similar in magnitude to the raw partisan differences reported in the right-most column of table 4.

evident in table 3. Once differences in unemployment, inflation, and GNP growth are taken into account, the additional income growth attributable to Democratic presidents (in the first row of table 5) is only about half a percentage point—and that modest additional income growth is virtually constant across the income spectrum.

The rest of the statistical results presented in table 5 provide a clearer sense of how partisan differences in macroeconomic performance get translated into partisan patterns of income growth for middle-class and poor families. Unemployment and GNP growth have substantial effects on income growth rates for poor and middle-class families, but very little impact on the incomes of families near the top of the income distribution. Thus, the lower unemployment rates and higher GNP growth rates that have generally prevailed during Democratic administrations are much more beneficial to families near the bottom of the income distribution than to those near the top. Conversely, the impact of inflation is negligible near the bottom of the income distribution but much more significant at higher income levels.[38]

The statistical evidence presented in tables 4 and 5 provides a clear explanation for the partisan differences in pre-tax income growth for lower- and middle-class families documented in table 1. The policies of Democratic presidents have produced more employment and output growth, disproportionately benefiting poor and middle-class families. Republican presidents have tended to focus more on containing inflation, which has negligible effects on real income growth near the bottom of the income distribution but substantial effects at the top.

The notion that these partisan differences in income growth reflect conscious policy choices on the part of Republican and Democratic presidents is reinforced by a more detailed analysis of their political timing. Alberto Alesina has noted that Democratic and Republican administrations are characterized by distinct cycles of economic growth, with expansion in the second year of a Democratic president's term followed by slower growth in the third and fourth years, and contraction in the second year of a Republican president's term followed by more robust growth in the third and fourth years.[39] These cycles are unsurprising in light of the fact that presidents have their greatest influence over policy in the first year of each new administration—the "honeymoon" period immediately following election or reelection; the effects of that influence are felt one year later, in the second year of each four-year term.

The political economic cycle identified by Alesina appears conspicuously in data on growth rates in real GNP per capita over the entire post-war era. In the second year of each four-year cycle Democrats presided over average GNP growth of 4.4%, while Republicans presided over average growth of −0.8%.[40] By contrast, in the first, third, and fourth years of each president's term average GNP growth rates were virtually identical: 2.3% for Democrats versus 2.5% for Republicans.

---

[38] Substituting the annual *change* in the inflation rate produces a similar but somewhat stronger pattern of differential effects on income growth. Indeed, the results suggest that efforts to rein in inflation may actually *reduce* real income growth among the working poor, other things being equal.

[39] Alesina (1988); Alesina and Rosenthal (1989); Alesina, Londregan, and Rosenthal (1993).

[40] The *t*-statistic for this difference is 5.5. The average partisan difference is virtually identical in "honeymoon" years with and without partisan turnover; thus, as with the partisan differences in income growth in table 2, there is no indication in the data that this effect reflects corrections of the opposition party's macroeconomic failings.

TABLE 5
Statistical Analysis of Income Growth Including Macroeconomic Conditions, 1949–2005

Annual real pre-tax income growth (%) for families at various points in the income distribution. Parameter estimates from Seemingly Unrelated Regression models (with standard errors in parentheses). Partisan control measured from one year following inauguration to one year following subsequent inauguration. "Linear trend" and "Quadratic trend" reflect cumulative change from 1949 through 2005.

	20th percentile	40th percentile	60th percentile	80th percentile	95th percentile
Democratic president	.51 (.64)	.45 (.41)	.52 (.37)	.61 (.42)	.51 (.62)
Unemployment (%)	-.849 (.307)	-.672 (.187)	-.577 (.167)	-.484 (.187)	-.115 (.267)
Inflation (%)	-.134 (.127)	-.269 (.082)	-.307 (.073)	-.376 (.084)	-.513 (.123)
GNP growth (%)	.798 (.144)	.523 (.091)	.481 (.079)	.293 (.089)	.126 (.129)
Oil prices (lagged %Δ)	-.005 (.013)	-.00 (.008)	-.008 (.007)	-.005 (.009)	-.007 (.013)
Labor force participation (Δ%)	2.72 (1.09)	3.34 (.71)	2.02 (.63)	2.35 (.72)	4.03 (1.05)
Lagged growth	-.110 (.089)	-.195 (.073)	-.213 (.074)	-.290 (.092)	-.044 (.108)
Lagged 95th percentile	.137 (.117)	.060 (.082)	.033 (.073)	.093 (.092)	—
Linear trend	.63 (5.69)	.29 (3.63)	4.85 (3.22)	8.01 (3.72)	7.73 (5.47)
Quadratic trend	-2.54 (5.43)	-2.59 (3.45)	-7.07 (3.06)	-9.69 (3.54)	-8.13 (5.20)
Intercept	4.99 (1.74)	5.61 (1.11)	5.01 (.98)	4.54 (1.08)	2.70 (1.51)
Standard error of regression	2.05	1.31	1.17	1.36	1.97
R^2	.70	.80	.79	.66	.48
N	57	57	57	57	57

Source: Calculations based on data from Census Bureau Historical Income Tables.

TABLE 6
Political Timing of Partisan Differences in Real Income Growth Rates, 1948–2005

Average annual real pre-tax income growth (%) for families at various points in the income distribution (with standard errors in parentheses). Partisan control measured from one year following inauguration to one year following subsequent inauguration. "Post-election ('honeymoon') years" are the second years of each four-year term (beginning one year following inauguration).

	All Presidents	Democratic Presidents	Republican Presidents	Partisan Difference
Post-election ("honeymoon") years				
20th percentile	1.72 (1.18)	5.74 (.89)	−1.29 (1.04)	7.03 (1.44)
40th percentile	1.48 (.90)	4.55 (.84)	−.82 (.68)	5.37 (1.07)
60th percentile	1.32 (.79)	3.96 (.61)	−.66 (.72)	4.62 (.99)
80th percentile	1.70 (.68)	4.08 (.47)	−.08 (.56)	4.16 (.76)
95th percentile	2.35 (.67)	4.28 (.71)	.90 (.69)	3.38 (1.01)
N	14	6	8	14
Other years				
20th percentile	1.33 (.55)	1.71 (.87)	1.01 (.71)	.71 (1.12)
40th percentile	1.56 (.43)	1.83 (.66)	1.33 (.57)	.50 (.87)
60th percentile	1.86 (.38)	2.02 (.63)	1.73 (.47)	.29 (.77)
80th percentile	1.88 (.38)	1.88 (.59)	1.88 (.49)	−.01 (.76)
95th percentile	1.89 (.46)	1.47 (.76)	2.23 (.56)	−.76 (.93)
N	44	20	24	44

Source: Calculations based on data from Census Bureau Historical Income Tables.

Alesina's political economic cycle also appears clearly in income growth rates for families in every part of the income distribution. Table 6 provides a comparison of average income growth rates under Democratic and Republican presidents in the second years of their terms (in the top panel of the table) and in the rest of each four-year term (in the bottom panel). The largest partisan differences by far appear in the second year of each administration—the first year in which the president's policies could be expected to have a significant economic effect. Democratic presidents in those years presided over average real income growth for the working poor of 5.7%, while the corresponding average growth rate under Republican presidents was −1.3%—a remarkable partisan difference of 7 percentage points. The corresponding partisan differences in income growth for middle-class and affluent families were also substantial, ranging from 5.4 percentage points at the 40th percentile down to 3.4 percentage points at the 95th percentile.

By comparison, partisan differences in income growth in other years were much more muted. Democratic presidents produced somewhat more income growth for middle-class and poor families in those years, while Republican presidents produced somewhat more income growth for affluent families; but neither of these partisan differences is large enough to be statistically reliable. Nor was the inequality in income growth between rich and poor families under Republican presidents nearly as stark in other years as in "honeymoon" years—the average growth rate was 1.2 percentage points higher for families at the 95th percentile than for families at the 20th percentile in other years, but 2.2 percentage points higher in the second year of each four-year term.

The dramatic differences in output and income growth associated with Democratic and Republican "honeymoon" periods are a testament to the ability of presidents in the post-Keynesian era to shape the economy to their partisan ends. Democratic presidents have routinely used these periods to produce vibrant economic growth for families in every part of the income distribution; in contrast, Republicans have routinely presided over economic contractions and declining incomes for middle-class and poor families. Partisan differences in macroeconomic priorities and performance have clearly had a very significant impact on the economic fortunes of American families over the past half-century, and that impact has been especially marked at the point in the electoral cycle when presidents are most politically influential.

PARTISAN POLICIES AND POST-TAX INCOME GROWTH

The partisan differences in income growth documented in table 1 are especially striking in light of the fact that the tabulations reported there focus entirely on pre-tax income figures. Those figures include cash benefits from the government such as Social Security and unemployment benefits; but they do not reflect any partisan differences in the distribution of noncash government benefits or in effective tax rates. Since taxes and transfers are the most obvious policy levers available to presidents with partisan distributional goals, the pre-tax income tabulations seem likely to miss much of what is distinctive about Democratic and Republican policies.

Partisan differences in economic philosophy and distributional priorities are especially striking in the realm of tax policy. The history of major postwar tax cuts is especially illuminating. Presidents of both parties have implemented significant tax cuts; but they have done so in very different ways and for very different reasons. For example, when President Kennedy's economic team argued for a tax cut in the early 1960s, they reasoned that "the beneficiaries of a personal income tax cut, especially in the lower brackets, would promptly spend a large part of the proceeds on goods and services, thereby stimulating production, employment, and income." In contrast, the supply-side theory adopted in the Reagan administration suggested that tax cuts "could not be given to the middle class or even the poor. In order to be successful, tax cuts had to be directed primarily toward the wealthy because of their larger role in saving and investing. . . . Tax cuts for everyone else might stimulate additional consumption, but that was not what supply-side economics was all about."[41]

President Reagan's tax policies reinforced preexisting trends contributing to increasing economic inequality. As Sheldon Danziger and Peter Gottschalk have pointed out, because of "technological changes, the globalization of markets, and other structural changes in the labor market . . . government tax and transfer policies would have had to become more redistributive than they had been in the 1970s just to keep poverty and inequality constant. Instead, because of the Reagan philosophy and legislative changes, income tax and antipoverty policies became less progressive." Similarly, Hibbs noted that Reagan "succeeded in reversing the trend of increasing federal commitments to the poor and near-poor," adding that, "most important of all, Reagan achieved a dramatic redistribution of the federal tax burden from corporations and high-income classes to moderate- and low-income groups.[42]

[41] Tobin and Weidenbaum (1988), 49; Karier (1997), 76.
[42] Danziger and Gottschalk (1995), 29; Hibbs (1987), 281.

When Bill Clinton entered the White House in 1993, he apparently felt a good deal more constrained by the Federal Reserve Board and the bond markets than previous Democratic presidents had been. Rather than relying on macroeconomic stimulation or across-the-board tax cuts to complete the economy's recovery from the recession of 1991, Clinton focused on reducing the ballooning federal budget deficit. Nevertheless, in his first year in office he proposed, and Congress passed, a major expansion of the Earned Income Tax Credit for working poor people. Higher up the income ladder, tax brackets were revised to make them somewhat more progressive while increasing total revenue.[43]

Clinton succeeded so well at reining in the budget deficit that his successor, George W. Bush, inherited a substantial budget surplus. Bush took advantage of the opportunity to engineer a series of major tax cuts. However, in marked contrast to Clinton's strategy of targeting tax cuts to mitigate the effects on the income distribution of technological changes, globalization, and shifting labor markets, Bush exacerbated those effects by reverting to President Reagan's emphasis on reducing the tax burden of wealthy individuals and corporations.

I examine the politics and economic impact of the Bush tax cuts in much more detail in chapter 6. My aim here, however, is to provide a more general accounting of the impact of tax and transfer policies on the shape of the income distribution under Republican and Democratic presidents. Unfortunately, consistent Census Bureau tabulations of the distribution of post-tax income are only available from 1979 through 2003. Thus, the scope for systematic historical analysis of partisan effects on post-tax income growth is quite limited; rather than five Democratic and six Republican presidents over 58 years, the data encompass only 10 years of Democratic control (two under Carter and eight under Clinton) and 14 years of Republican control (eight under Reagan, four under George H. W. Bush, and two under George W. Bush). With that caveat, figure 4 shows the average rates of real after-tax income growth since 1980 under Democratic and Republican presidents for households at the 20th, 40th, 60th, and 80th percentiles of the income distribution.[44]

In qualitative terms, the partisan pattern of post-tax income growth in figure 4 is strikingly similar to the partisan pattern of pre-tax family income growth in figure 1. Households at every income level did about equally well under Carter and Clinton, with average growth rates ranging from 1.4% to 1.6%. On the other hand, Republican presidents presided over weaker income growth for households in the top half of the income distribution and little or no income growth for households in the bottom half of the income distribution. As with the partisan differences in pre-tax growth presented in figure 1, these partisan differences in

[43] As one sympathetic account had it, "Taxes were raised a bit and made more progressive (helping to balance the budget). What followed, contrary to alarmist predictions, was not an economic crash, but rather a sustained economic boom." Page and Simmons (2000), 158.

[44] "Table RDI-6: Income Limits for Each Fifth of Households, by Selected Definition of Income: 1979 to 2003," http://www.census.gov/hhes/income/histinc/rdi6.html. The table reports 15 different "Experimental Measures" of income. The one employed here is the most expansive, Definition 15, which subtracts federal and state taxes from the standard measure of pre-tax income and adds capital gains, health insurance supplements to wage or salary income, noncash government transfers, and net imputed returns on home equity. Unlike the pre-tax income tabulations included in the Census Bureau's Historical Income Tables, these tabulations of "experimental measures" of income have not been updated to include more recent years, nor do they include information on households at the 95th percentile of the income distribution.

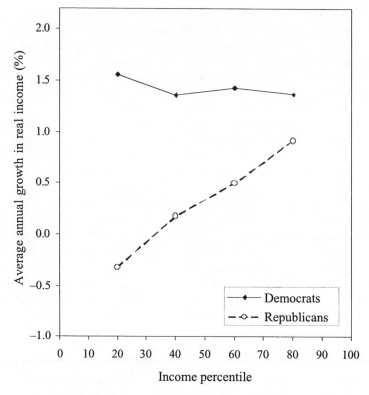

FIGURE 4. Post-Tax Income Growth under Democratic and Republican Presidents, 1980–2003

post-tax growth are concentrated in the second year of each administration, when the policy initiatives adopted in the "honeymoon" period immediately following Inauguration Day are most likely to take effect.[45]

Despite the qualitative similarity, a comparison of the magnitude of partisan differences in figures 1 and 4 suggests that post-tax income growth was somewhat less subject to partisan effects than pre-tax income growth. That impression is confirmed by comparing the magnitudes of partisan differences in post-tax income growth, which are reported in the top panel of table 7, with the corresponding partisan differences in pre-tax income growth in table 1. For example, average pre-tax income growth for middle-income families was about 1.5 percentage points higher under Democratic presidents than under Republican presidents in table 1, but the corresponding difference in average post-tax income growth in table 7 is only about 1 percentage point.

It seems odd to suppose that presidents have had less influence on the distribution of post-tax income than on the distribution of pre-tax income—especially in light of the dramatic differences in tax policies between Republican and Democratic presidents over the past quarter-century. This peculiarity is more apparent than real,

[45] In "honeymoon" years, the differences in average post-tax income growth between Democratic and Republican presidents range from 5.0% for households at the 20th percentile of the income distribution to 3.0% for households at the 80th percentile. The corresponding differences in nonhoneymoon years range from 0.9% to –0.3%.

however. A direct comparison of the magnitudes of partisan differences in figure 1 and figure 4 is quite misleading because the two figures refer to very different time periods—1947 through 2005 in figure 1 and 1980–2003 in figure 4.[46]

The tabulations presented in the lower panel of table 7 summarize pretax household income growth over the same 24-year period covered by the post-tax calculations in the upper panel of the table.[47] Here the partisan differences in average income growth rates are much smaller than in table 1, ranging from a bit less than one percentage point for households at the 20th percentile to only one-tenth of a percentage point at the 80th percentile.[48] These differences suggest that it has become much more difficult in the past quarter-century for presidents to influence the distribution of pre-tax income. The most plausible explanation for this difference is that the increasing impact on the American economy of global trade and credit flows, and the increasing domestic prestige and political independence of the Federal Reserve Board, have reduced the ability of presidents to pursue distinctive partisan macroeconomic policies.[49]

However, even as contemporary presidents have been increasingly constrained in their pursuit of partisan macroeconomic policies, they seem to have been quite successful in using taxes and transfers to shape the post-tax income distribution along familiar partisan lines. That impression is reinforced by the statistical analysis reported in table 8, which parallels the analysis of pre-tax income growth in table 3 using the available post-tax data. As in table 3, the statistical analysis shows that the partisan differences in income growth evident in simple tabulations persist even after taking systematic account of the differing economic circumstances in which Democrats and Republicans have held the White House. Indeed, in this case the estimated partisan effects are even larger than the corresponding raw differences in post-tax income growth in figure 4, ranging in roughly linear fashion from 3.1 percentage points for households at the 20th percentile of the income distribution to 1.5 percentage points for households at the 80th percentile.[50] These results provide surprisingly strong statistical evidence of characteristic partisan differences in post-tax income growth paralleling—and

[46] An additional difference is that the data summarized in figure 1 are for families of two or more people, while those summarized in figure 4 are for households. However, that distinction is inconsequential here; parallel calculations employing the pre-tax family and household data from 1980 through 2003 produce very similar results.

[47] The data employed in the lower panel of table 7 are based on the same definition of pretax income as in table 1 but for households rather than families to maximize comparability with the data in the upper panel.

[48] These partisan differences in pre-tax growth are nowhere close to being "statistically significant," even for households at the 20th percentile. However, the *declines* in partisan differences apparent in the post-1979 data by comparison with the earlier post-war period are not "statistically significant" either. Indeed, a variety of elaborations of the regression model in table 3 to allow for changes in the magnitude of partisan effects produced no statistically reliable evidence of either structural breaks or secular trends.

[49] The partisan difference in unemployment evident in table 4 persists even when the comparison is limited to the period from 1980 through 2003: the average unemployment rate was 6.9% under Republican presidents and 5.4% under Democratic presidents, for a difference of 1.49 (with a standard error of .54). However, the earlier partisan difference in average GNP growth entirely disappeared: real per capita growth averaged 1.8% under both Republicans and Democrats.

[50] As with the parallel analysis of pre-tax income growth presented in table 3, the estimated partisan effects in table 8 are insensitive to plausible variations in model specification. For example, excluding the quadratic trend term does not change any of the estimated partisan effects by as much as 5%, while excluding both trend terms reduces the estimated partisan effects by only 8% to 11%.

TABLE 7
Partisan Differences in Real Pre- and Post-Tax Income Growth, 1980–2003

Average annual real income growth (%) for households at various points in the income distribution (with standard errors in parentheses). Partisan control measured from one year following inauguration to one year following subsequent inauguration.

	All Presidents	Democratic Presidents	Republican Presidents	Partisan Difference
Post-tax income growth				
20th percentile	.46 (.42)	1.56 (.59)	−.32 (.49)	1.89 (.76)
40th percentile	.67 (.32)	1.36 (.46)	.18 (.39)	1.17 (.60)
60th percentile	.89 (.30)	1.43 (.44)	.50 (.38)	.93 (.58)
80th percentile	1.11 (.31)	1.37 (.44)	.92 (.44)	.45 (.64)
N	24	10	14	24
Pre-tax income growth				
20th percentile	.39 (.47)	.93 (.89)	.00 (.50)	.93 (.95)
40th percentile	.47 (.40)	.67 (.75)	.33 (.46)	.33 (.83)
60th percentile	.63 (.39)	.74 (.72)	.55 (.45)	.19 (.81)
80th percentile	1.03 (.34)	1.10 (.60)	.98 (.42)	.12 (.71)
N	24	10	14	24

Source: Calculations based on data from Census Bureau Historical Income Tables.

surpassing in magnitude—the differences in pre-tax income growth evident over the entire post-war period.

Unfortunately, the limitations of the post-tax income data make it impossible to distinguish between two possible interpretations of the changing partisan political economy of the United States over the past quarter-century. One possibility is that contemporary presidents, faced with the increasing difficulty of influencing the macroeconomy, have resorted to tax and transfer policies as alternative means to achieve their partisan ends. In this interpretation, redistribution through taxes and transfers (for example, Clinton's significant expansion of the Earned Income Tax Credit) is the modern Democrat's *substitute* for pre-tax redistribution through expansionary macroeconomic policies. The other, perhaps more likely, possibility is that earlier presidents relied on both macroeconomic policies and tax and transfer policies to pursue their partisan ends, producing larger partisan effects than appear in the pre-tax data—and larger partisan effects than contemporary presidents are able to achieve.

In any case, the partisan differences in post-tax income growth since 1980 are sufficiently large, and sufficiently familiar in their pattern, to reinforce the conclusion that partisan politics has a profound impact on the economic fortunes of poor and middle-class households in contemporary America. While Republican and Democratic presidents may have lost a considerable portion of their influence over the distribution of pre-tax income, they have managed to continue to produce marked partisan differences in the distribution of post-tax income, with Democrats presiding over higher average income growth across the board and substantially higher average growth for people of modest means. Here, too, the partisan political economy seems to be of fundamental importance for the economic fortunes of ordinary Americans.

TABLE 8

Statistical Analysis of Post-Tax Income Growth, 1981–2003

Annual real post-tax income growth (%) for households at various points in the income distribution. Parameter estimates from Seemingly Unrelated Regression models (with standard errors in parentheses). Partisan control measured from one year following inauguration to one year following subsequent inauguration. "Linear trend" and "Quadratic trend" reflect cumulative change from 1949 through 2005.

	20th percentile	40th percentile	60th percentile	80th percentile
Democratic president	3.07 (.76)	2.34 (.52)	2.23 (.45)	1.51 (.64)
Oil prices (lagged %Δ)	-.039 (.014)	-.034 (.010)	-.037 (.009)	-.032 (.012)
Labor force participation (Δ%)	1.40 (1.56)	2.03 (1.10)	2.29 (.96)	2.49 (1.33)
Lagged growth	.004 (.131)	-.112 (.099)	-.196 (.089)	-.205 (.141)
Linear trend	19.01 (37.41)	-27.61 (26.23)	-62.70 (22.84)	-87.79 (31.55)
Quadratic trend	-14.31 (24.80)	17.28 (17.39)	39.90 (15.14)	56.78 (20.89)
Intercept	-6.87 (13.83)	10.42 (9.69)	24.04 (8.44)	33.62 (11.68)
Standard error of regression	1.34	.94	.18	1.12
R^2	.56	.62	.68	.46
N	23	23	23	23

Source: Calculations based on data from Census Bureau Historical Income Tables.

DEMOCRATS, REPUBLICANS, AND
THE RISE OF INEQUALITY

Economists associate the escalation of inequality over the past 30 years with important structural changes in the American economy, including demographic shifts, globalization, and technological change. I see no reason to doubt that these factors have played an important role in increasing the income gap between rich and poor people in the contemporary United States; but if this is "simply an economic reality," as Treasury Secretary Paulson asserted, it does not follow that nothing can be done to mitigate the economic and social consequences of that reality. Nor does the fact that "there has always been extreme income inequality," as Ben Stein observed, imply that presidents and their policy choices can have no significant effect on the extent of inequality at any given time.

The cumulative impact of these partisan policy choices is illustrated in figure 5. The dotted line in the center of the figure represents the actual course of inequality over the past half-century, as measured by the ratio of family incomes at the 80th and 20th percentiles of the income distribution. (This portion of the figure is simply repeated from figure 2.) The solid upper line represents the projected course of the 80/20 income ratio over the same period given the pattern of income growth that prevailed under Republican presidents during this period, while the lower line represents the projected course of the 80/20 income ratio under Democratic presidents. (These projections are constructed on the basis of the statistical analysis reported in table 3, the upper line assuming continuous Republican control and the lower line assuming continuous Democratic control throughout the period.)

The projections in figure 5 imply that continuous Democratic control would have produced an essentially constant level of economic inequality over the past three decades, despite all the technological, demographic, and global competitive forces emphasized in economists' accounts of escalating inequality. In contrast, continuous Republican control would have produced a much sharper polarization between rich and poor than has actually occurred over the past 30 years, with the 80/20 income ratio reaching a level about one-third higher than it actually did.[51]

The projections presented in figure 5 are based on an arguably unrealistic assumption: that if either party had uninterrupted control of the White House, it would do all the time what it in fact does only half the time. It is impossible to know whether either party would actually have the political will or the political power to produce economic redistribution of the cumulative magnitude suggested by these projections. Nevertheless, the cumulative differences portrayed in figure 5 convey the fundamental significance of partisan politics in ameliorating or exacerbating economic inequality over the past half-century.

In the first 25 years of the post-war era, the partisan differences in income growth patterns documented in this chapter implied robust growth for middle-class and poor families under Democratic presidents and more modest growth under Republicans. In the less propitious economic circumstances prevailing in the early twenty-first century, not even a steady succession of Democratic presidents and policies would be likely to reproduce the robust broad-based income growth

---

[51] The 80/20 income ratio increased by 27% between 1975 and 2005. The projections in figure 5 suggest that it would have increased by 45% under continuous Republican control but by only 3% under continuous Democratic control.

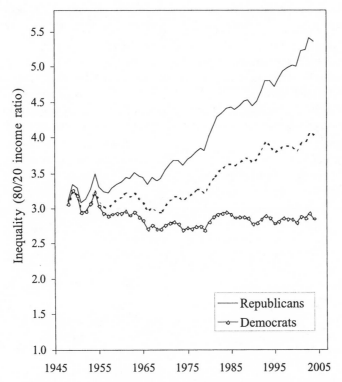

FIGURE 5. Projected Income Inequality under Republican and Democratic Presidents, 1947–2005

of the 1960s. However, that does not make the choice between Democrats and Republicans any less consequential.

The magnitude of what is at stake in partisan control of economic policy may be demonstrated by considering the ramifications of a few hundred votes in a single presidential election. In his first four years in office, President George W. Bush presided over a 2% cumulative increase in the real incomes of families at the 95th percentile of the income distribution, but a 1% *decline* in the real incomes of middle-class families and a 3% decline in the real incomes of working poor families. (Meanwhile, Piketty and Saez's tabulations of IRS data indicate that the real incomes of taxpayers at the 99th percentile increased by more than 7% over this period, while the real incomes of taxpayers at the 99.99th percentile increased by almost 18%.) However, the statistical analyses presented in table 3 imply that, had President Al Gore governed under the same economic circumstances, the real incomes of working poor families would probably have grown by about 6% (1.5% per year) over those four years, and the real incomes of middle-class families would probably have grown by about 4.5% (1.1% per year), while the real incomes of families at the 95th percentile would have remained unchanged.

As Edward Tufte insisted 30 years ago, "economic life vibrates with the rhythms of politics."[52] Thus, while it may be "neither fair nor useful to blame any political party" for the structural changes in the economy that make income growth and income inequality much more pressing issues now than they were in the post-war

[52] Tufte (1978), 137.

boom years of the 1950s and 1960s, it certainly seems fair—and perhaps even useful—to hold political parties accountable for the profound impact of their policies on the way those structural changes shape the economic fortunes of wealthy, middle-class, and poor American families.

Of course, whether voters *do* hold political parties accountable for the profound impact of their policies is another question. I address that question in chapters 3 and 4, which turn Tufte's maxim on its head by exploring the ways in which American political life vibrates with the rhythm of economics.

31

DEMOGRAPHY AND THE SOCIAL CONTRACT

2002 Presidential Address
Population Association of America

Marta Tienda[*]

The previous contribution by Bartels asks, in effect, What kind of democracy do we have if its ordinary processes of political competition subtly generate distributive injustice? Bartels's analysis implies that Americans face a major political philosophical issue.

This piece by renowned sociologist Marta Tienda suggests something similar, as it deftly weaves demography, political philosophy, and analysis of representation. Due to decades of immigration, a far-reaching question is now on the agenda of our government by discussion: What kind of citizenship and political membership do we want to develop in the years to come?

• • •

DEMOGRAPHY AND THE SOCIAL CONTRACT

The bosom of America is open to receive not only the opulent and respectable stranger, but the oppressed and persecuted of all nations and religions; whom we shall welcome to a participation of all our rights and privileges . . .[1]

—*George Washington, 1783*

SINCE THE FOUNDING OF THE UNITED STATES as a sovereign nation, population diversity has challenged the values of *inclusiveness* and *equality*. Historically, these tensions manifested themselves in debates over taxation and representation; apportionment; and suffrage. In modern times these values are disputed in controversies about the differential undercount and census adjustment; immigrants' rights to representation; access to higher education; and the entitlements of citizenship, among many other social issues. Essentially the question is about the rights of membership in a liberal democracy and whether citizenship is a special membership status.

Copyright © 2002 by Marta Tienda from *Demography* 39 (November 2002): 587–616. Reprinted with the permission of the Population Association of America.

*Acknowledgments: I gratefully acknowledge the able research assistance and technical support of Michael F. Maltese, programming assistance of Chang Chung, and the bibliographic support of Elana Broch and Jackie Druery. I am also indebted to several colleagues who offered helpful comments on drafts of this manuscript: Sigal Alon, Noreen Goldman, Germán Rodríguez, James Trussell, and Charles Westoff. Institutional support was provided by a grant from NICHD (P30HD32030) to Princeton University's Office of Population Research and Woodrow Wilson School of Public and International Affairs.

[1] Washington, George. "Letter to the Members of the Volunteer Association and Other Inhabitants of the Kingdom of Ireland Who Have Lately Arrived in the City of New York," 2 December 1783. As quoted in Fitzpatrick (1938).

The antecedents of the debate over membership date back to classical political theorists, particularly Thomas Hobbes, John Locke, and Jean-Jacque Rousseau. Their notion of membership derives from consent to be governed: individuals willingly concede some of their personal freedoms in exchange for security and other social benefits (Walzer 1995). Members maintain autonomy and avoid being subjected to the will of others by obeying laws they give themselves (Arneson 2001: 4724–29). Ideally, the "general will" creates unity by subordinating individualism in the interest of the collective well-being. However, recognizing the challenge of forging unity from diversity, Rousseau warned of special interests—"partial societies"—within the state, which could undermine the ability of the general will to serve the common good. To prevent the emergence of social cleavages, Rousseau argued for democratic equality.[2] Should factions arise, maintaining *equality* among them was essential to prevent the general will from dissolving into particular interests and undermining shared interests (Rosseau 1762).[3]

Of course, the real world is far more complicated than 18th century political theorists envisioned, yet these simple premises bear profound lessons for understanding the civic implications of recent demographic trends. The ideals of American democracy, which have influenced liberal democracies around the world, rely crucially on the notion of consent as the basis of citizenship even though few have specified what precisely constitutes consent (Bosniak 2000). Modern political theorists and legal scholars have elaborated the primitive Rousseauean vision of social contract theory, making distinctions between nominal citizenship, which is based on participation in social life, to formal citizenship, which guarantees the right to vote and to exercise political power (Raskin 1993; Smith 1997; Marshall 1964; Schuck 1997). And while the U.S. political system has been heralded as the gold standard of liberal democracy, according to Rogers M. Smith (1997:15), "... for over 80% of U.S. history, American laws declared most people in the world legally ineligible to become full U.S. citizens solely because of their race, ... nationality or gender." In short, American democracy has violated the sacred values of inclusiveness and equity.

Against a backdrop of rising income inequality since 1973 (Levy 1987), the historically unparalleled diversification of the U.S. population compels a reexamination of the social contract to ask whether the terms of membership are qualified as heterogeneity increases, and if so, for whom and why. I argue that, as the principle motor of contemporary and past population diversity, immigration strains commitment to the democratic principles of inclusion and equity by redrawing the boundaries of membership based on ascription and an ever more narrow definition of citizenship. As long as membership confers different rights to different groups, future progress toward reducing social and economic inequality will be stymied. I conclude that population diversification warrants a realignment of democratic ideals with demographic realities.

---

[2] "As the citizens, by the social contract, are all equal, all can prescribe what all should do, but no one has a right to demand that another shall do what he does not do himself" (Rousseau 1762: book III, 16).

[3] "From whatever side we approach our principle, we reach the same conclusion, that the social compact sets up among the citizens an equality of such a kind, that they all bind themselves to observe the same conditions and should therefore all enjoy the same rights. Thus, from the very nature of the compact, every act of Sovereignty, i.e., every authentic act of the general will, binds or favours all the citizens *equally* (emphasis added); so that the Sovereign recognizes only the body of the nation, and draws no distinctions between those of whom it is made up" (Rousseau, 1762: book II, 4).

In order to illustrate the powerful role of demography for understanding the evolution of social justice in the United States, I first sketch 20th-century immigration trends and highlight nativity differentials in poverty and educational inequality. Historical debates about membership, as played out in controversies about representation and immigrant suffrage, illustrate some potentially deleterious civic consequences of recent demographic trends. I also identify several contemporary issues that show how immigration has sharpened group boundaries and strengthened civic hierarchies. This need not be so if the rules of membership are made more inclusive and the commitment to equity renewed.

My conception of citizenship as a social contract conceding the right to be governed in exchange for privileges, rights and social obligations emphasizes the liberal ideas of T. H. Marshall (1964), who considers equity and social welfare as core features of mature citizenship; Jamin Raskin (1993), who differentiates among citizenship as presence, as integration, and as standing; and Rogers Smith (1997), who views citizenship as an institution for distributing life opportunities. In what follows I argue that the relative openness of U.S. borders makes immigration central to the project of democracy for the 21st century (Smith 1997).

DEMOGRAPHY OF DIVERSIFICATION

The ebb and flow of immigration during the 20th century is evident in the changing race, ethnic, and nativity composition of the U.S. population (see Table 1). In 2001, over 10% of U.S. residents were foreign born; this share has more than doubled since 1970 (U.S. Census Bureau 2001:2). The absolute number of immigrants is much larger now than at the turn of the century because the population base was much smaller (U.S. Census Bureau 2001:9). Both at the turn of the 20th and 21st centuries, immigration was and is a highly politicized social issue.

Four decades of high-volume immigration from virtually every country, rising intermarriage, and persisting fertility differentials have transformed the United States into the most demographically complex country in the world (Prewitt 2001). Since 1960, the changed source countries of immigrants have visibly altered the U.S. ethno-racial landscape, just as the shift in source countries from Western to Eastern European countries did during the latter half of the 19th and early 20th century. At the turn of the 19th century, 12% of the U.S. population was black and an additional 1% combined either Hispanic, Asian, or American Indian. Half a century later, these same groups combined accounted for 13% of the U.S. population, except that the black share had fallen from 12% to 10%. Yet, over the next 50 years the combined share of blacks, Hispanics, Asians, and Native Americans swelled to just under 30% of the total population (Gibson and Lennon 1999; U.S. Census Bureau 2000a).

The force of immigration is evident in the changing nativity composition of these pan-ethnic groups. Whereas only one-third of Asians were foreign born in 1960, this share rose to 63% during the 1990s. In like fashion, the foreign-born share of the Hispanic population nearly doubled from 1970 to 2000 (Gibson and Lennon 1999; U.S. Census Bureau 2001). By contrast, the foreign-born share of the non-Hispanic white population has declined slightly, from six to three percentage points, while the black share has risen from 1%–6%. Although differential fertility also has altered the ethno-racial composition of the U.S. population, I focus on immigration because it is the single most powerful force driving the demography of diversification, and because nativity differentials at best maintain

TABLE 1

Changing Population Composition, 1900–2000

| Year | Race and Hispanic Origin | | | | | |
	Whites	Blacks	Hispanics	Asians	AIND	Total FB %
1900	87.9	11.6	—	0.2	0.3	13.6
1950	89.5	10.0	—	0.2	0.2	6.9
1960	88.6	10.5	—	0.5	0.3	5.4
(%FB)	5.9	0.7	—	31.9	0.0	
1970	83.5	11.1	4.5	0.8	0.4	4.7
(%FB)	4.2	1.1	19.9	35.7	1.9	
1980	79.7	11.7	6.4	1.6	0.7	6.2
(%FB)	3.9	3.1	28.6	58.6	2.5	
1990	75.6	12.0	8.8	2.9	0.8	7.9
(%FB)	5.0	4.9	35.8	63.1	2.3	
2000	70.6	12.3	12.5	4.0	0.7	10.4
(%FB)	3.6	6.2	39.0	61.4	—	

Note: (%FB) = Percent Foreign-Born. All percentages may not sum to 100 due to rounding and estimation. For 1970–2000, White, Non-Hispanic data were used in the Whites column.

Source: Gibson and Lennon, 1999: Table 8; U.S. Census Bureau 2000: Table 1, 2001: Table 9–1.

or at worst increase aggregate socioeconomic inequality. A brief overview of poverty and educational differentials suffices to make this point.

The decline in poverty, from 22% to 17% between 1960 and 1965, and to 12.3% a decade later, is one of the stellar achievements of the War on Poverty (Dalaker 2001:18). However, sizeable nativity differentials persist. In 1999, when 11.8% of the U.S. population was poor, immigrant poverty exceeded that of natives by 5.6 percentage points—16.8% versus 11.2%, respectively. Moreover, recent immigrants are more likely to be poor than earlier arrivals, and noncitizen poverty is over twice that of naturalized citizens. Specifically, just over one in five noncitizens were poor in 1999 compared to less than one in ten naturalized citizens (U.S. Census Bureau 2001:47).

Immigrants from Latin America are much more likely to be poor than those hailing from Europe, Asia, or Africa (U.S. Census Bureau 2001:46). In 1999, less than 10% of European immigrants lived in poverty compared to 13% of those from Asia and Africa, and over one-in-five immigrants from Latin America. Mexicans and Central Americans are the poorest among the foreign born, with one in four below the poverty threshold in 1999. Because Mexicans now account for over one-quarter of the foreign-born population, up from 8.2% in 1970, their high poverty rate weighs heavily on the aggregate immigrant poverty rate and especially the poverty rate for Latin Americans (U.S. Census Bureau 2001:12).

To a considerable extent, differentials in economic well-being are rooted in large and persisting educational disparities among demographic groups, which are exacerbated by the influx of immigrants with very low and very high educational levels. Among college graduates, there are small differences between native and foreign-born adults because the majority of immigrants who gain admission under the occupational preferences are highly selected toward advanced degrees. However, the nativity differential in high school graduation is appreciable: 87% of native born persons ages 25 and over are high school graduates, compared to 67% of the foreign-born (U.S. Census Bureau 2001:36). Aggregate differentials in high school completion reflect the comparatively low educational levels of recent immigrants from Central and South America, but especially Mexico.

The diversification narrative would be of little socioeconomic or civic consequence if the promises of the Great Society had been delivered. Some were; others were rescinded; and still others have been threatened by restrictive legislation that deprives immigrants of their full rights of civic membership. By comparison with studies of socioeconomic inequality, demographers have paid considerably less attention to what Milton Gordon (1964) characterized as *civic assimilation*—that is, membership, statutory citizenship, and political participation. These primary rights are pillars of a liberal democracy committed to the values of inclusion and equality, and essential for preventing the re-emergence of what Rogers M. Smith (1997) dubbed "ascriptive democracy"—that is civic hierarchies defined by race, birthplace, sex, and age, with their attendant social and economic consequences.

U.S. immigration history dramatically illustrates ascriptive democracy in play.[4] This story has been thoroughly scripted and warrants no elaboration except to underscore three points. First, the 1924 Immigration Act, frequently called the National Origins Act, set the first numerical limits on immigration, set country quotas based on 2% of resident nationalities according to the 1890 census, and established a commission to determine the country quotas (Briggs 1993).[5] However, heated debate ensued about whether to apportion the quotas using the 1890 census as the law stipulated, or the 1920 census. This controversy centered fundamentally on protecting a Tocquevillian image of American national identity as white and Anglo Saxon (Smith 1997; King 2000). The 1890 census did this, but the 1920 census did not because almost 90% of all immigrants enumerated in 1890 were from Northern and Western Europe or Canada, but by 1920 only 45% were (Gibson and Lennon 1999). Originally scheduled to go into effect in 1927, the political struggle over the apportionment of quotas delayed implementation of the 1924 Immigration Act until 1929. In the end, quotas were based on the 1920 census.

Second, the 1952 Immigration Act, which was passed over President Truman's veto, repealed the Asiatic exclusion clause that had damaged American prestige overseas, but retained the 1920 census as the basis for apportioning quotas. This legislation reinforced the pro-European bias of U.S. visas by explicitly restricting Eastern European immigration through numerical ceilings. As a concession to the social value of inclusiveness, this legislation ended the ban of nonwhite immigration imposed in 1790 (King 2000). If the architects of the 1924 Immigration Act were in denial about *demography* in America, they were even more naïve about how the politics of exclusion extol their price as unintended consequences. References to the restrictions imposed by the 1924 legislation emphasize the quotas imposed to *exclude* groups by limiting new admissions to tiny shares of the resident national origins, yet its long term impact derives more from the groups *exempt* from the quotas. Explicitly excluded from the numerical quotas were immigrants from: Canada, Newfoundland, Mexico, Cuba, Haiti, the Dominican Republic, the Canal Zone, and the independent countries of Central and South America, along

---

[4] One of the most striking illustrations of ascriptive democracy, the Immigration Act of 1924, is noteworthy both for its racist criteria governing admissions and the pseudo-scientific eugenic arguments used to justify the decisions. King (2000) provides a richly textured discussion of the congressional debates.

[5] Immigration Act of May 26, 1924 (43 Statutes-at-Large 153).

with their immediate dependent family members (68th U.S. Congress 1924). Since 1980, Mexico has been the leading source country of U.S. immigrants, and along with Haiti and the Dominican Republic, is a major contemporary source of undocumented immigration.

Third, the heightened volume and changed composition of U.S.-bound migration since 1970 was seeded in the 1924 Act, and bolstered by the 1965 Amendments to the 1952 Immigration Act. Designed to atone for the discriminatory foundations of the 1924 national origins quota system, the 1965 Amendments accomplished several things. One, by abolishing the quota system, the Amendments opened doors to immigration from countries previously excluded, notably Asian and African nations, albeit with strict country limits. Two, an annual ceiling of 120,000 was extended to Western Hemisphere immigrants and individual countries were subjected to the 20,000 annual country maximum to which Eastern hemisphere countries had been subjected. Finally, the 1965 Amendments shifted the emphasis of the visa allocation preference system from labor market priorities to family reunification. Initially, 74% of total visas available each year were reserved for relatives of U.S. citizens and permanent resident aliens, but this share of the numerically regulated visas was raised to 80% in 1980 (Briggs 1993:15).

Co-sponsor of the 1965 immigration legislation, Emanual Celler (D-N.Y.) argued during the floor debate that few Asians or Africans would enter the country because they had no family ties to the United States (Briggs 1993:18). In signing the bill into law, President Lyndon Johnson reassured his critics of benign consequences: "This bill that we will sign today is not a revolutionary bill. It does not affect the lives of millions. It will not reshape the structure of our daily lives" (Public Papers of the Presidents of the U.S. 1966: 1037–1040). Then Attorney General Robert Kennedy predicted approximately 5,000 immigrants from the Asia-Pacific triangle and very few thereafter (U.S. House 1964:418); Secretary of State Dean Rusk anticipated 8,000 immigrants from India over 5 years (U.S. Senate 1965a:65); Senator Edward Kennedy argued that the ethnic mix of the country would not be upset (U.S. Senate 1965b:2). History scripted otherwise, as European immigration plummeted following post–World War II reconstruction, while rising inequality and political strife in Latin America and Asia swelled the ranks of workers aspiring better opportunities for earning a living.

Not only did the 1965 Amendments usher in a new period of mass migration, but the law *did* affect the lives of millions of residents already here and those yet to come. Immigrants from the Americas comprised about one-third of those admitted during the 1930s and 1940s and nearly 40% of new arrivals during the 1950s (INS 2002:9). Since 1960, roughly half of all immigrants admitted hail from the Americas, and about one-third from Asia. Owing to the legalization program authorized by the 1986 Immigration Reform and Control Act (IRCA), during the 1990s, the number of legal immigrants exceeded nine million, of which 42% originated in Latin America (INS 2002:9).

If the diversification narrative broadened the cultural space to forge a core American identity from many race and ethnic strands, participation in the reformulated "WE" required rewriting the social contract to realign democracy with demography (Prewitt 2001). This is the project of U.S. democracy for the 21st century—forging and governing a "world nation" within a framework of social justice. As such, historical and contemporary debates over apportionment and suffrage provide key lessons about how changing population composition evolved into civic hierarchies that undermine the commitment to values of inclusiveness and egalitarianism, and they highlight future challenges to civic integration of the foreign-born. I discuss each in turn.

APPORTIONMENT, SUFFRAGE, AND THE POLITICS OF EXCLUSION

> . . . as nearly as is practicable, one man's vote in a congressional election is to be worth as much as another's.[6]
> —*Justice Hugo L. Black, 1964*

Constitutional guarantees of representation and suffrage were integral to forging the social contract, yet both rights have been contested terrain since the nation's founding. The 14th Amendment of the U.S. Constitution clearly states that, "*Representatives shall be apportioned among the several states according to their respective numbers, counting the whole number of persons in each state, excluding Indians not taxed.*"[7] That all *persons* residing in the United States are counted for the purposes of apportionment, but only *citizens* are permitted to vote in national elections, presumes that the right to representation is more fundamental than the right to exercise the franchise. However, the value of representation is eroded to the extent that growing numbers of "new Americans" have no voice in selecting who represents them. This need not be so, and for a large part of our history, including most of the last period of mass migration, non-citizens were allowed to vote (Keyssar 2000; Harper-Ho 2000; Neuman 1993; Raskin 1993; Rosberg 1977). Although the landmark "one-person, one-vote" decision[8] responded directly to inequities in representation and exercise of the franchise, the presence of immigrants continues to defy the value of inclusiveness.

Apportionment

The *method* used to apportion the seats in the U.S. House of Representatives conveys commitment to equality as a social value; the question of *who* should be included in the apportionment population conveys the value of inclusiveness (Davis 1981). Since 1790, five different methods have been used to allocate the seats among states (Davis 1981; Balinski and Young 2001).[9] All methods emphasize *equity relative to population size*; the current method of equal proportions in use since 1940 has the advantage of minimizing the proportional difference in the average district size between two states, with a bias favoring small states (Davis 1981). Because the Constitution neither requires apportionment after every census nor specifies *how* to apportion, these decisions are entirely within the purview of Congress.

---

[6] *Wesberry v. Sanders*, 376 U.S. 1.

[7] U.S. Constitution. Amendment. XIV § 2.

[8] *Reynolds v. Sims*, 377 U.S. 533 (1964) held that "an individual's right to vote for state legislators is unconstitutionally impaired when its weight is in a substantial fashion diluted when compared with votes of citizens living in other parts of the State."

[9] The five methods are: "Jefferson" method of greatest divisors (used from 1790–1830), "Webster" method of major fractions (used in 1840), "Vinton" or "Hamilton" method, which established a predetermined number of Representatives for each apportionment (used from 1850–1900), "Wilcox" revised method of major fractions (used in 1910 and 1930), and "Huntington" or "Hill" method of equal proportions (used from 1940 to present) (Schmeckebier 1941; Balinksi and Young 2001; U.S. Census Bureau 2000b).

The matter of *who* should be included in the apportionment base has been controversial since the Constitution was ratified, so it is remarkable that its provisions for representation have withstood the test of time and numerous legal challenges.[10] The Civil War raised the value of slaves from 3/5ths to full persons for purposes of representation; the 14th Amendment defined statutory citizenship, provided equal protection for all *persons*, and reaffirmed the principles of representation on the basis of *persons*, including non-citizens. Since that time, the collision of political interests with the moral principles of justice and fairness has precipitated several legal challenges to the practice of including immigrants—both legal and undocumented—in the apportionment base (Wood 1999; Woodrow-Lafield 2001; Poston et al. 1998; Congressional Record 1940:4366; *Federation for American Immigration Reform (FAIR) v. Klutznick* 1980[11]). For example, to support claims that the framers of the Constitution were unable to envision the emergence of undocumented immigration, advocates of a citizen-only apportionment base argue that the absence of immigration policy prior to 1875 made this category inconceivable in 1787, and that the words inhabitants, persons, and citizens are deliberately used interchangeably in the Constitution. However, Gerald Neuman (1993) dismisses these claims because prior to 1875, legislation regulating foreign admissions was largely a state concern, and once slavery ceased to be a divisive issue, systematic federal regulation was possible.

The first major 20th-century apportionment controversy involved the 1920 census, which singled out immigrants as a source of "distortion" in the rural-urban population distribution. Representatives from rural states slated to lose Congressional seats to urbanized states with large immigrant populations proposed a panoply of reapportionment bills designed to correct the alleged immigration distortion. Even though they paid taxes and had been legally admitted to the United States, the anti-immigrant Representatives considered immigrants unworthy of representation in Congress. The ensuing vitriol found ample pseudo-scientific support in the 42-volume *Dillingham Commission Report* (1911), which claimed that immigrants from eastern and southern Europe were intellectually inferior and unworthy of naturalization (King 2000:76). Kansas Representative Homer Hoch argued that exclusion of non-citizens from apportionment not only would alter the allocation of seats in 16 states, but would allow farming states to retain their seats (Bacon et al. 1995). The bitter and protracted political struggle culminated in several unsuccessful constitutional amendments to exclude all aliens for purposes of apportionment. In the end, the rural states won the debate because there was no reapportionment based on the 1920 census. Although the balance of power was preserved, the passage of restrictive immigration legislation in 1924 testified that the admission of foreigners had assumed center stage in Congress. In anticipation of the 1930 census and to avoid a similar spectacle, in 1929 Congress passed legislation requiring reapportionment after each census.[12]

Apparently the lessons from the 1920 apportionment dispute faded quickly because the 76th Congress again debated the immigration-apportionment question. New York Representative Hamilton Fish (R), conceded that "it is one of the

---

[10] See *United States Department of Commerce v. Montana*, 503 U.S. 442 (1992) and *Franklin v. Massachusetts*, 505 U.S. 788 (1992).

[11] 486 F.Supp. 564 (D.D.C.), appeal dismissed, 447 U.S. 916.

[12] The Apportionment Act of 1929 (46 Stat. 26), which was amended by the Apportionment Act of 1941 (54 Stat. 162), calls for an "automatic reapportionment" every decade using census data.

most difficult problems for the House to solve on a fair and nonpartisan basis" (Congressional Record 1940:4368). Not surprisingly, Representatives from New York and Illinois, two states where immigration had figured prominently in population growth, strongly supported including aliens in the apportionment base. By contrast, Representative John Elliot Rankin, a Mississippi Democrat, claimed that "... the reapportionment must be based upon persons, and that means *American* persons; it does not mean alien persons who owe no allegiance to the United States" (Congressional Record 1940:4369, emphasis added).

On matters of immigration, political interests did not follow partisan lines. The fight was *not* about the disappearance of a Jeffersonian agrarian society; at stake was the balance of power between those states growing rapidly through immigration, and the sparsely populated rural states. As shown in Figure 1, combined, the six immigrant-receiving states gained 16 seats in the House between 1900 and 1910, signaling a shift in political power that threatened the interests of rural states should immigration continue.[13] And continue it did, until Congress passed legislation to restrict who and how many were admitted. Between 1960 and 2000, these same six states, which currently house 75% of the foreign-born population (Frey and Devol 2000), increased their share of House seats from 153 to 171, so that currently they hold nearly two of every five seats. There are 435 seats in the House of Representatives—a number that has been fixed since 1911, but was variable before that time.[14]

Given how much ink and energy have been expended on the politics of immigrant exclusion in matters of representation, and in light of the growing political dominance in the U.S. House of Representatives of the six immigrant receiving states, it is instructive to imagine how representation and apportionment *would have* changed if a Constitutional Amendment to exclude all immigrants from apportionment had succeeded; if the restrictionists in Congress had succeeded in averting the two great waves of 20th-century immigration; or if rural states had succeeded in eliminating non-citizens from apportionment.

To develop these counterfactuals, I simulated three scenarios each for the period 1900 through 1930, which covered the first wave of 20th-century mass migration, and from 1960 to the present, which represents the second wave of 20th-century mass migration. These three scenarios simulate the world that the politics of exclusion sought to create under the banner of ascriptive democracy, namely: apportionment restricted to the native-born—designated *"natives only"*; apportionment assuming no immigration between 1900 and 1930, and none again after 1960—denoted *"halt immigration"*; and apportionment that excludes non-citizens—dubbed *"citizens only."* Stopping immigration in 1900 or 1960 is not only less stringent than excluding all of the foreign-born from apportionment, but also is more in keeping with liberal ideology to embrace those already here, while lifting the gangplank to future arrivals. *"Citizens only"* is the least restrictive of all, implicitly stipulating a "qualified membership" for those who do not pledge allegiance.

Table 2 summarizes the results from this simulation exercise, and Appendix Tables A-1 and A-2, respectively, report the state-specific detail for the first and

[13] Partly this reflects an increased number of seats in the House, which rose from 391 in 1900 to 435 in 1911; still, over one-third of these were allocated to the 6 immigrant states (Congressional Quarterly, 1991).

[14] The House of Representatives' size was fixed at 435 by the Apportionment Act of 1911 (37 Stat. 13).

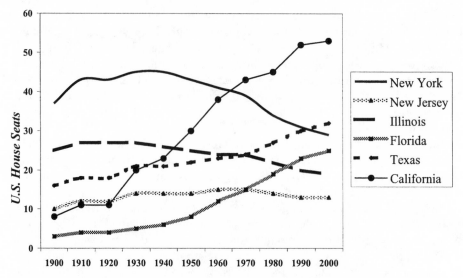

FIGURE 1. Seats in U.S. House of Representatives Held by Six Leading Immigrant Receiving States, 1900–2000
Source: U.S. Census Bureau 2002.

second periods of 20th-century mass migration.[15] That the total number of re-shuffled seats for a given scenario is usually less than the number of states affected reflects the high residential concentration of immigrants, the highly unequal populations of the 50 states, and the small state bias of the formula used to apportion seats in Congress (Davis 1981; Balinski and Young 2001). To simplify the exposition, I summarize the results for each period by counterfactual, beginning with the most restrictive scenario (*"natives only"*) and concluding with the least restrictive (*"citizens only"*). This strategy helps illustrate how layers of qualified membership undermine the spirit of equal representation.

First Period of 20th-Century Mass Migration

Had apportionment excluded all immigrants in 1910, when 15% of the population was foreign born, 24 seats would have been reshuffled among 29 states, with 17 states gaining and 12 losing seats. As the primary hub of European immigrants during the 19th century, New York would have sustained the greatest losses, with eight fewer seats than were actually assigned, and Mississippi would have claimed two of the reshuffled seats. For 1920, the *"natives only"* scenario would have reallocated 22 seats—two fewer than in 1910—among 28 states, with 15 gaining and 13 losing seats. Following a decade of numerical restrictions

[15] For the census data of 1900 through 1930, the number of Indians not taxed constitutes the difference between the total residential population and the apportionment population (Schmeckebier, 1941:11). From 1940 to the present, Indians have been included in the apportionment population. In 1970, 1990, and 2000, the apportionment population includes U.S. Armed Forces personnel and federal civilian employees stationed outside the United States (and their dependents living with them) that can be allocated back to a home state in addition to the residential population (U.S. Census Bureau, 2000c). I included declarant aliens, who had filed their first papers among the noncitizens because very few states allowed noncitizens to vote during the 20th century (Harper-Ho, 2000; Keyssar, 2000).

TABLE 2
Reapportionment Summary for Three Scenarios about Representation of the Foreign-Born

	Natives Only			Stop Immigration*			Citizens Only		
	Seats Reshuffled	States Affected		Seats Reshuffled	States Affected		Seats Reshuffled	States Affected	
		Gainers	Losers		Gainers	Losers		Gainers	Losers
Period 1									
1910	24	17	12	8	8	6	7	7	6
1920	22	15	13	12	8	9	12	9	8
1930	15	12	8	12	12	8	7	7	5
Period 2									
1970	6	6	3	3	3	3	3	3	3
1980	8	8	3	6	6	3	6	6	3
1990	12	12	4	11	11	4	8	8	4
2000	16	16	5	14	14	5	9	9	4

* In Period 1, Recent Immigrants are defined by those who arrived after 1900, while in Period 2 Recent Immigrants refer to those who arrived after 1960.

on immigration, by 1930 only 15 seats would have been reshuffled among 20 states had apportionment been restricted to native-born persons. Seat losses affected eight states, with New York sustaining over one-third of the losses, while 12 different states would have increased their congressional power.

A less stringent scenario, "*halting immigration in 1900*," excludes recent immigrants from the apportionment. Because two-thirds of the resident foreign born in 1910 arrived prior to 1900, stopping immigration in 1900 would have reshuffled only eight seats among 14 states in 1910, with eight gaining and six losing seats in the U.S. House of Representatives. Under this scenario, New York would have lost three instead of eight seats, and Mississippi would have reclaimed one seat. Had there been no immigration after 1900 and had Congress actually been reapportioned in 1920, 12 seats would have been reallocated among 17 states, with eight gaining and nine losing votes in Congress. Because immigration restrictions were actually implemented during the 1920s, a 1930 reapportionment that assumed no immigration after 1900 would have reshuffled the same number of seats as in 1920, except that 20 rather than 17 states would have been affected, with 12 gaining and eight losing seats. New York alone would have lost five seats if 2.3 million immigrants who arrived after 1900 had been excluded from the 1930 reapportionment, while California, Connecticut, Illinois, Massachusetts, Michigan, New Jersey, and Washington would have each lost one seat.

The third scenario, which responds to Representative Rankin's views about representation and citizenship, restricts the apportionment to "*citizens only*." This counterfactual produces the smallest effects on reapportionment because naturalization rates were relatively high at the beginning of the 20th century, particularly following the Americanization movement to naturalize the foreign born (King 2000). Only seven seats would have been reshuffled in 1910 by restricting congressional apportionment to citizens, with seven states gaining and six losing seats. Under this scenario New York would have only lost two seats. By 1920, however, the "*citizens only*" counterfactual would have reallocated 12 congressional seats among 17 states, with nine gaining and eight losing votes in Congress. Iowa,

Maine, Missouri, Pennsylvania, Rhode Island, and Vermont would each have lost one seat, while Massachusetts and New York would have lost two and four seats, respectively, had congressional representation been restricted to statutory citizens. Because the Americanization movement to increase naturalization rates was relatively effective in reducing the number of resident aliens (King 2000), excluding non-citizens from the 1930 reapportionment would have reshuffled only seven seats, costing New York three and assigning one of these to Mississippi.[16]

Second Period of 20th-Century Mass Migration

The hiatus in immigration following the Great Depression reduced the foreign-born share of the national population to around 5% by 1960, where it stabilized until after 1970 (U.S. Census Bureau 2001:9). Therefore, the reapportionment simulations are less dramatic—at least until the second wave of mass migration unfolded. Thus, rather than decrease over time, the impact of immigration on the distribution of congressional power rose during the second period of mass migration. A second difference between the first and second periods of 20th-century mass migration is that the states gaining and losing political power due to immigration changed, signaling a shift in congressional influence from the East and Midwest to the South and West.

Using the most restrictive "*natives only*" scenario for assigning congressional seats in 1970 would have reshuffled six seats among nine states, with six gaining and three losing seats. New York alone would have shouldered half of the lost seats, with California and Florida rounding out the losses at two and one, respectively. Beneficiaries of a 1970 reapportionment that excluded immigrants include Alabama, Maryland, Oregon, Pennsylvania, Tennessee, and Wisconsin—each with one additional seat. However, the increased volume of immigration over the next decade had more sizeable consequences for the 1980 distribution of power in Congress, as eight seats would have been reshuffled if apportionment had been restricted to natives. California, New York, and Florida would have lost four, three, and one seats, respectively. Of the eight states gaining seats under this scenario, five are in the South and three in the Midwest.

The rising momentum of immigration during the 1980s and 1990s, which included the legalization of 2.7 million undocumented immigrants, had a more sizeable impact on the distribution of congressional power compared to the prior two decades. In 1990, the "*natives only*" counterfactual implies a reshuffling of 12 seats, of which 11 were due to post-1960 immigrants. In the most recent apportionment, 16 congressional seats would have been reshuffled among 21 states if the apportionment were based on the "*natives only*" scenario. Five states would sustain seat losses (nine in California, two in Florida, one in New Jersey and Texas each, and three in New York) while 16 states would gain one seat each.

Because the 1965 Amendments to the Immigration and Nationality Act did not go into effect until 1968, the volume of immigration during the decade was relatively low. Therefore, "*halting immigration in 1960*" would have had a very modest effect on the 1970 distribution of congressional power—reshuffling only three seats among six states. Moreover, reapportionment based on "*citizens only*"

---

[16] Mississippi would have actually lost seats in 1920 had a reapportionment been implemented using the constitutionally mandated criteria to represent all inhabitants, hence the lack of any gain from this counterfactual in 1920 reflects this fact.

would have identical effects because in 1970 nearly 66% of foreign-born residents were naturalized citizens (U.S. Census Bureau 2001:20). But as the volume of immigration increased, so too did its consequences for the distribution of congressional votes among states. Owing to low naturalization rates among recent immigrants, for 1980 both the "*halt immigration*" and the "*citizens only*" scenarios would have reshuffled six seats among nine states, with six gaining and three losing seats. Under both counterfactuals, California would have borne the lion's share of the losses by forfeiting three seats, and New York would have lost two seats and Florida one seat.

In the 1990 reapportionment, the "*halt immigration*" scenario would have reshuffled 11 seats among 15 states, with California losing seven seats, New York two seats, and Texas and Florida one apiece. By 2000, the impact of recent immigration on the distribution of congressional power approached the magnitude witnessed in 1930. Apportioning seats assuming no immigration after 1960 would have reshuffled 14 congressional seats among 19 states in 2000, with California alone forfeiting eight seats, Florida and New York two each, and Texas and New Jersey one apiece. The 14 beneficiaries of the reshuffled seats, each receiving one additional vote in Congress, were dispersed throughout the country, and included Montana, Utah, and Oklahoma, among other states (Appendix Table A-2).

Because the naturalized share of the foreign-born population had fallen to 40% by 1990 (U.S. Census Bureau 2001:20), reapportioning using the "*citizens only*" scenario would have reshuffled eight seats among 12 states, with California alone forfeiting five, and Florida, New York and Texas each giving up one seat for the benefit of three southern states (Georgia, Kentucky, and Louisiana), along with four states in the north central region (Kansas, Montana, Michigan, and Ohio) and Pennsylvania in the East. Confining the 2000 apportionment to birthright and naturalized citizens would have reshuffled one more seat than in 1990—with California forfeiting the additional seat. However, the profile of beneficiary states in each year differed. Owing to shifts in population distribution and the small state bias of the apportionment formula, Oklahoma, Indiana, Utah, Mississippi, and Wisconsin would have gained a seat in 2000 had apportionment been restricted to statutory citizens, but Georgia, Kansas, Louisiana, and Ohio would not have.

Of course, these counterfactuals produce very conservative estimates of the impact of immigration on the distribution of Congressional power because they ignore the compounding demographic effects from immigrant fertility and internal migration in response to immigration. Moreover, because the Supreme Court (447 U.S. 916) unequivocally ruled that *all persons* are to be included in the population base for purposes of apportionment, these scenarios will not materialize. Nevertheless, they provide several important lessons. First, the effects of immigration on Congressional apportionment of immigration declined from 1900 to 1930 as political anxiety about the impact of the foreign born on representation rose, but the impact has risen appreciably since 1960 and particularly after 1980. This is also evident by comparing the difference between the "*natives only*" and "*halt immigration*" scenarios in Table 2. Furthermore, the states losing seats are more concentrated during the latter period, reflecting the higher concentration of immigrants in six states.

Second, based on the number of seats and states involved, the impact of immigration on the distribution of congressional power is most similar in 2000

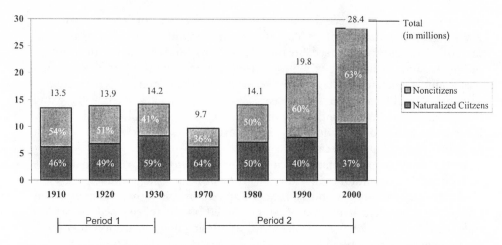

FIGURE 2. Citizenship Status of Foreign-Born Population for Two Periods of Mass Migration
Source: Gibson and Lennon 1999; U.S. Census Bureau 2001.

and 1930 across all scenarios, except that there has been a shift in the balance of power among the six immigrant receiving states to California, Texas, and Florida from New York, New Jersey, and Illinois, at the expense of other states (See Figure 1). In 1930, New York, New Jersey, and Illinois collectively held one in five House seats; currently, California, Texas, and Florida combined hold one in four House seats. These conditions are ripe for another round of restrictions on immigration to stem the flow, as well as new variants of ascriptive democracy, as I discuss below.

Third, the consequences of the *"citizens only"* scenario rise before declining during the early period, but rise continually during the latter period. As Figure 2 shows, this is because the proportion of naturalized immigrants was relatively high at the turn of the century, ranging from a low of 46% to a high of 60% during the first period of mass migration (Thernstrom 1980:747). Although the Americanization movement during this period was partly responsible for the high naturalization rates (King 2000), naturalization rates declined during the most recent period, falling about 50% from almost two out of every three immigrants in 1970 to just over one in three by 2000 (U.S. Census Bureau 2001:14).

Fourth and more important, the *"citizens only"* scenario raises a real (rather than simulated) moral dilemma because non-citizens, who are a growing share of the immigrant population, do not have a voice in selecting their Representatives and because residential concentration of immigrants creates serious problems of malapportionment (Edmonston and Schultze 1995; Davis 1981; Goldfarb 1995). For example, Illinois did not redraw congressional districts between 1900 and 1940, and although its number of Congressional seats held relatively stable, the disparity between the smallest and largest Illinois Congressional district rose from 105 thousand to 752 thousand persons (Congressional Record 1940:4371).

Nationally, the problem of malapportionment increased such that by 1960, the 20 most populous districts represented a combined population of 14 million compared to 4.6 million residents for the smallest 20 districts (Edmonston and Schultze 1995:244). Although disparities in the sizes of congressional or legislative districts are not due entirely to immigration, problems of *malapportionment* are particularly harsh for districts containing large numbers of immigrants who can't vote because they are not citizens.

The problem of unequal voice has two solutions: one is to *equalize the voting* power across districts (*Baker v. Carr*, 369 US 186, 1962); the other solution is to strive for truly equal representation by *allowing non-citizens to vote*. However, both solutions are problematic from an operational or a legal standpoint. Equalizing voting power would appear to be straightforward, but immigration complicates the solution because the residential concentration of the foreign-born poses moral and practical dilemmas for achieving equal representation. Essentially, the solution involves a choice between an exclusive apportionment that protects *citizens'* right to voting equality, and an *inclusive* apportionment that ensures equal representation for *all persons*, including non-citizens. The dilemma is moral because decisions about inclusion or exclusion of non-citizens from congressional and state legislative districts invoke issues of fairness, the spirit of equal representation, and the fundamental rights of membership implicit in the social contract; it is practical because population-based allocation of state and local monies could perpetuate inequities between the included and excluded residents, thereby effectively blocking the emergence of a Marshallian conception of social citizenship.

Figure 3 for Los Angeles County illustrates the dilemma of balancing the democratic values of *electoral equality* and *representational equity* in districts with a high concentration of noncitizens. Electoral equality emphasizes proportionality of registered voters across districts, while equal representation dictates redistricting using population proportions as the base (Goldfarb 1995). Applying electoral equality on the basis of citizenship produced districts in Los Angeles County with highly unequal populations: in 1971, district 4 had a population 70% larger than district 9, despite similar proportions of registered voters. But an alternative plan proposed for 1990, which balances total residents without taking direct account of differences in citizenship, violates the spirit of "one-person, one-vote" by weighting more heavily the votes of citizens residing in districts with larger shares of unnaturalized immigrants compared to those with few immigrants. In effect, representational equality is traded for electoral inequality; that is, demographic equity implies unequal membership in a democratic society.

An alternative solution to the problem of malapportionment in places with large immigrant populations is to equalize voting privileges. The difficulty here is that the Constitution explicitly restricts voting in *national* elections to citizens, but not necessarily in state and local elections (Rosberg 1977; Neuman 1993, 1996). Legislation passed in 1996 made alien voting in federal elections a felony, and voting in violation of any federal, state or local law grounds for removal (Schuck 1997). However, states retain great latitude in their local apportionment and voting criteria, provided that they do not engineer discriminatory impacts in violation of the Voting Rights Act (Pub. L. No. 89–110, 79 Stat. 445). Voting equality is possible at the state and local level if non-citizens are allowed to vote legally. This requires going beyond citizenship as *presence*, which recognizes that the resident foreign-born shape the lives of their communities (Keyssar 2000; Bosniak 2000), and embracing Raskin's concept of citizenship as *integration*, which involves socializing newcomers in the activities that lead to formal citizenship, including participating in the governance of their communities. A review of alien suffrage makes this point more forcefully.

A. Plan Based on Electoral Equality

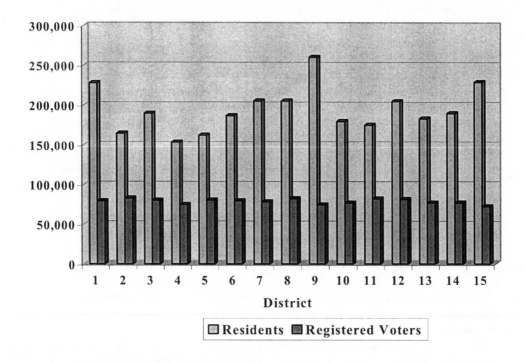

District

Residents ■ Registered Voters

B. Plan Based on Representational Equality

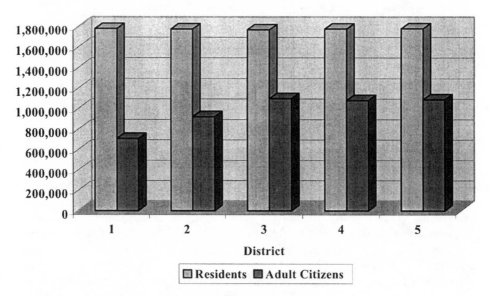

District

Residents ■ Adult Citizens

Figure 3. L.A. Redistricting Plans. Source: Goldfarb (1995).

CITIZENSHIP AS PRESENCE AND STANDING

> Citizenship is man's basic right for it is nothing less than the right to have
> rights.[17]
>
> *—Chief Justice Earl Warren, 1958*

As a master status, citizenship defines membership, confers rights and privileges, and distributes life opportunities (Marshall 1964; Smith 1997). The right to hold public office and the franchise are two of the most sacred privileges of citizenship, which distinguish this status from aliens, including those admitted as legal residents. The 14th Amendment, ratified in 1868, defines *citizens* as "All persons born or naturalized in the United States . . . ,"[18] while the 15th Amendment guarantees all *citizens* the right to vote.[19] Congress legislated itself power to enforce voting rights, but enforcement was irresponsibly lax until the Voting Rights Act of 1965 and its various reauthorizations put teeth into monitoring activities.

The chapter of African American's quasi-citizenship has been well documented in legal and academic scholarship (Smith 1997; Mills 1997). Less well known is the story of immigrant suffrage and its role in nation-building, particularly how states used the state franchise instrumentally to increase population and gain seats in Congress (Williams 1912; Rosberg 1977; Raskin 1993; Neuman 1996; Harper-Ho 2000). In fact, non-citizen voting was common through the early 20th century because federalism permits considerable discretion in civil matters, including specifying the privileges of state citizenship and deciding matters of legislative apportionment (Neuman 1996; Goldfarb 1995).

Although the federal Constitution restricts the national franchise to citizens, "categorical denial of noncitizens' voting is neither constitutionally required nor historically normal" (Raskin 1993:1391; Rosberg 1977). But, the story of alien suffrage was neither linear nor smooth, involving periods of expansion and retrenchment along the way (Keyssar 2000). During the Colonial Era, non-citizens not only voted, but also held public office (Harper-Ho 2000). Neuman (1996) claims that the early instances of alien suffrage occurred because of the confused relationship between state and federal citizenship, which was only partly clarified by the Fourteenth Amendment. According to Rousseau, such ambiguity in the boundaries of political communities are natural to emerging states, whose values and principals are being forged in their social contract.[20]

Historically, access to the franchise not only excluded blacks, women, and the young but also selected non-Protestant groups. Rhode Island precluded Jews from voting until 1842; Catholics and Jews were denied the franchise in most colonies, while Quakers and Baptists could not vote in others (Congressional Quarterly 1991). On the eve of the Civil War in 1860, aliens were allowed to vote in as many

---

[17] *Perez v. Brownell*, 356 U.S. 44.

[18] U.S. Constitution. Amendment XIV § 1.

[19] Rosberg (1977) contends that inclusion of the word "citizens" in the 15th Amendment does not prevent noncitizen suffrage, but the courts have ruled otherwise. However, this restriction refers to federal elections, not voting in state and local matters, which is entirely up to discretion of states, as stipulated by Article Ten (Raskin, 1993; Neuman, 1996:63).

[20] "There is for nations as for men a period of maturity, which they must wait before they are subjected to laws; but it is not always easy to discern when a people is mature, and if time is rushed, the labor is abortive. One nation is governable from its origin, another is not so at the end of ten centuries" (Rousseau, 1762: book II, Chapter IX).

states as blacks—six (Porter 1918: 148).[21] As barriers of property, race, sex, literacy, age, and other impediments to universal suffrage were eliminated through Constitutional Amendments and legislative acts, the suffrage rights of noncitizens were eroded and ultimately terminated, except in a few localities (Raskin 1993; Neuman 1996; Keyssar 2000).

Secondary sources on the subject of alien suffrage disagree about how many, which, and when states allowed non-citizens to vote. A tally based on certain end-dates indicates that at least 22 states and territories allowed non-citizens to vote in the nineteenth century and that several permitted aliens to vote and hold public office during the early post-Colonial period (Aylsworth 1931; Harper-Ho 2000). Thus, a count of all states recognized for ever permitting noncitizens to vote produces an upper limit of 35, as shown in Figure 4 (Porter 1918; Rosberg 1977; Raskin 1993; Neuman 1996; Harper-Ho 2000; Keyssar 2000).[22]

When the right to vote was linked mainly to property, age, sex, and race rather than to citizenship, and before the 14th Amendment was ratified, a legal interpretation of "inhabitants" easily included immigrants. As the United States consolidated its state and national identities during the late 18th and through most of the 19th centuries, state citizenship was a salient identity from which immigrants benefited and to which they contributed. The militant nationalism and xenophobia following the War of 1812 precipitated the first retrenchment of alien suffrage, largely involving the relatively well-populated eastern states, including New York, Vermont, Tennessee, Pennsylvania, and Massachusetts (Raskin 1993; Harper-Ho 2000; Keyssar 2000).

According to Porter (1918:22), between 1820 and 1845 state suffrage debates lost sight of the foreigner, especially those occupied with the "free Negro" and reaming property tests. Even as the franchise was being rescinded in some states, other states capitalized on the paradigm of strong electoral federalism for instrumental purposes by declaring unnaturalized aliens as *state* citizens—assuming, of course, that they were white men 21 years and older (Porter 1918; Smith 1997). At that time, women and persons under 21 were ineligible to vote. Neither, of course, were slaves, and naturalization was closed to most Asian nationals until 1952 (Smith 1993; Keyssar 2000). Despite the ratification of the 14th and 15th Amendments, in many southern states, African Americans were voiceless until the enactment and enforcement of the Voting Rights Act.

Even after the federal government's exclusive power to naturalize aliens was clarified,[23] distinctions between state and national citizenship permitted states to grant aliens the franchise, by declaring them state citizens. Beginning with Wisconsin in 1848, states that allowed immigrants to vote required declarations of an

---

[21] Six states allowing blacks to vote were: Maine, Massachusetts, New Hampshire, New York, Rhode Island, and Vermont. Aliens were allowed to vote in: Indiana, Kansas, Louisiana, Minnesota, Oregon, and Wisconsin (Porter, 1918:148).

[22] Both Raskin (1993) and Harper-Ho (2000) include Oklahoma and Washington among the states that permitted noncitizen voting, but we were unable to verify this claim using corroborating sources.

[23] The process of naturalization became the exclusive domain of the federal government in the late 1870s as a result of the companion 1876 Supreme Court cases *Henderson v. Mayor of New York* (92 U.S. 259) and *Chy Lung v. Freeman* (92 U.S. 275), after the divisive issue of slavery was settled and the uniform regulation of admissions was politically feasible (Kurian 1998; Neuman 1993). However, a standard citizenship application form was only made available in 1906, wresting discretion from States and municipalities, which were adhering to a wide range of naturalization policies that suited their political objectives.

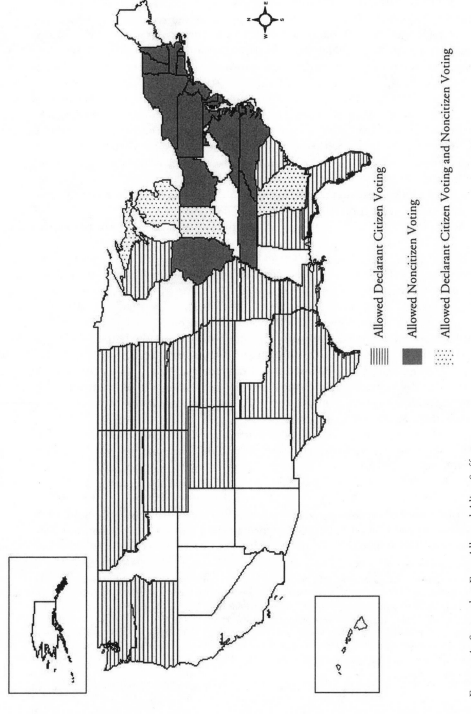

FIGURE 4. States that Ever Allowed Alien Suffrage
Source: Rosberg 1977; Raskin 1993; Neuman 1996; Harper-Ho 2000; Keyssar 2000.

Allowed Declarant Citizen Voting

Allowed Noncitizen Voting

Allowed Declarant Citizen Voting and Noncitizen Voting

intention to become U.S. citizens as a condition for voting, and several imposed a minimum residency requirement (Raskin 1993; Keyssar 2000: Table A-12).[24] Thus, at least during the mid- to late 19th century, non-citizen voting was pre-citizen voting. Williams (1912) suggests that "naturalization was practically a state affair" until 1882 because of lax federal supervision over the records and procedures. Moreover, vigilance over the process by which first papers were filed was also weak to nonexistent.[25] In Nebraska, for example, immigrants who took out their first papers for national citizenship were allowed to vote in national elections even before the 6-month waiting period (Williams 1912).[26]

The issue of non-citizen voting was embroiled in the national division over slavery: the North wanted to expand the privilege, while Southerners wanted to restrict suffrage to limit the political influence of the North. Alien suffrage actually *expanded* during the tense pre-war period, but during the Civil War alien suffrage carried an enormous price—namely, conscription, which was *apportioned* among states based on the apportionment population (Keyssar 2000). Immigrants who attempted to rescind their declarations to become citizens in order to avoid conscription faced deportation (Raskin 1993).

After the Civil War 13 new states, including former Confederate states, adopted declarant alien suffrage as a way of repopulating their states, settling public debt, and regaining political power in Congress (Rosberg 1977; Raskin 1993; Keyssar 2000). The contraction of alien suffrage gained momentum in the wake of the 1890s recession, when several states repealed provisions that granted noncitizens voting rights, yet as late as 1900, 11 states still permitted noncitizen voting (Harper-Ho 2000; Keyssar 2000). The resurgence of nativism coupled with legal changes in voting rights of other citizen groups during and after World War I led to further contraction of alien suffrage, which terminated completely in the late 1920s (Keyssar 2000; Harper-Ho 2000; Neuman 1996).[27] Thus, the suffrage chapter of immigration history illustrates how the boundaries of membership were expanded and then contracted as matters of economic and political expediency within the guise of democratic values.

If in the past the *instrumental goals* of attracting immigrant settlers to populate newly admitted states and settle debt motivated political leaders to offer the franchise to non-citizens (Keyssar 2000; Neuman 1996), *democratic principle* might compel a similar state and local policy in the 21st century (Bosniak 2000). For blacks, the 13th and 14th Amendments formalized a social contract of rights and responsibilities by declaring them full-fledged citizens; the process of naturalization does the same for immigrants by formalizing their statutory status. For non-citizens, voluntary immigration provides more explicit consent to be governed than

[24] Censuses from these periods differentiate the foreign born as "aliens" or "declarant aliens," (who filed their first paper or declaration of intent to become a citizen) and naturalized citizens (who had obtained the certificate of naturalization). However, filing a declaration of intention imposed no obligation to naturalize after the five-year waiting period (Porter 1918).

[25] Hattie Plum Williams (1912) provides a detailed case study of the process of naturalization in Lancaster county, Nebraska, which illustrates the casualness of the process and the opportunities for widespread political corruption led to the Corrupt Practices Act of 1899. Nebraska allowed declarant immigrant suffrage from 1867 to 1918.

[26] On the books, there was a 5-year residence requirement for naturalization from 1795, which was increased to 14 years in 1798, and then restored to 5 years with the Act of 1802 (Jasso and Rosenzweig 1990).

[27] Keyssar (2000:Table A12) dates the end of alien suffrage in 1926, when Arkansas abolished noncitizen voting, but Harper-Ho and others use 1928 as the end of alien suffrage.

birthright citizenship. Therefore, and in contrast to ancient democracies where the distinctions between citizens and foreigners were sharply defined and rigid, in a liberal democracy non-citizens *should be* virtually indistinguishable from citizens because legal admission ostensibly guarantees equal access to the privileges, rights, and civil guarantees accorded to citizens, save the franchise (Bosniak 2000).[28] However, in practice the citizen-alien distinction appears to be deepening (Gosewinkel 2001; Schuck 1997).

This need not be so. The citizen-alien distinction *can* be blurred because both are entitled to representation in Congress; because both are required to pay taxes; because both serve in the armed forces; and because both are bound by the same laws and obligations. Hence both are putatively eligible for the rights and privileges enjoyed by citizens through birthright or naturalization, except voting in federal elections, and where stipulated by law, also state elections. That states retain authority to grant non-citizen voting in state and local affairs is a socially meaningful way to fade the distinction between aliens and citizens (Neuman 1996; Raskin 1993; Rosberg 1977).[29] Some have argued that the citizen-alien distinction *should* be blurred because it is morally consistent with the values of *equity* and *inclusiveness* professed by a liberal democracy, and because political participation in local affairs ostensibly can prepare aliens for statutory U.S. citizenship (Raskin 1993; Bosniak 2000).[30] But as the history of black suffrage testifies, morality is never sufficient to compel compliance with the letter, let alone the spirit, of the law.

Not only are concerns about conflicts of allegiance less relevant in local compared to national politics, but the expansion of dual citizenship among immigrant sending countries (including Mexico) renders moot the question of loyalty to either source or host country. More generally, as the era of mass migration unfolds throughout the world (Massey et al. 1998), the meaning of national citizenship comes into sharp relief and questions the relationship between rights and membership. According to Linda Bosniak (2000:963), non-citizen residents as a social class render problematic "citizenship-as-rights" and "citizenship-as-status." Her perspective parallels Raskin's notion of citizenship as integration and as standing, which the 1992 Maastricht Treaty on the European Union brings into sharp relief (Neuman 1996).

As economic imperatives and adoption of a common currency compel making national boundaries porous in order to harness the benefits of scale in matters of trade and labor market specialization, questions of nationality and strict allegiance to a nation-state assume back stage, even in the face of persisting cultural and language diversity.[31] The underplaying of national boundaries against the

[28] Hume (1748:153) notes that even in Athens, the most extensive democracy in history, only one-tenth of the residents were signatories to the laws that governed the republic.

[29] The 10th Amendment specifically stipulates that, "The powers not delegated to the United States by the Constitution, nor prohibited by it to the States, are reserved to the States respectively, or to the people." The paradigm of strong federalism allows states great discretion in the conduct of state governance, which was liberally exercised during the period of nation-building (Raskin 1993). The Dred Scott (*Scott v. Sandford*, 60 U.S. 393, 1856) decision recognized the rights of citizenship that states may confer within their own limits, except for naturalization.

[30] Anti-immigrant groups such as FAIR disagree, arguing that no one should receive the franchise without a Pledge of Allegiance because divorcing voting from citizenship strips its meaning. Rosberg (1977) and others (Raskin 1993; Bosniak 2000) rebuke the idea that citizenship and voting are synonymous.

[31] Switzerland, Sweden, Denmark, and Great Britain have not adopted the Euro as their sole currency, and the question about whether the British Isles are part of Europe is still a matter of debate in some quarters.

backdrop of pan-European citizenship is evident in the movement to increase the portability of political rights that EU citizens can use in any member country. The Maastricht Treaty commits member states to grant nationals of other member states the right to vote and run for office in municipal elections (Neuman 1993). Currently, 5.5 million EU citizens hold limited political rights throughout Europe, but the extension of suffrage and other privileges of citizenship do not extend to resident aliens and third-country nationals (Day 2000).

This unique social experiment, and its historical antecedents, bears important lessons for the political incorporation of U.S. immigrants. In the 1980s, Sweden seriously considered an initiative that would grant foreigners the right to vote, but these efforts were stymied by ardent nationalists. Eventually Sweden, along with Norway, Finland, Denmark, the Netherlands, and Ireland, granted active and passive local and regional voting rights to foreigners (1994a, 1994b; Johnson 1993). In France and Germany the debate over extending the local franchise to noncitizens did not favor immigrants. Moreover, in the fall of 1990, Germany's Federal Constitutional Court reversed the statutes of two states that allowed resident aliens to vote in municipal matters, and reconfirmed the exclusivity of political voice for citizens only. Despite the efforts of the German government to revise its inefficient naturalization process, the privileged position of German-ancestry immigrants remains intact, reifying a membership hierarchy within the subset of foreigners (Neuman 1992).

The EU is not alone in limiting the national franchise to statutory citizens. A recent study by Blais and colleagues (2001) found that 76%, or 48 of 63, of the democratic countries in their sample restricted the right to vote to citizens. Moreover, among the countries that did permit non-citizen voting, many imposed extended residency requirements. For example, while New Zealand grants permanent residents the franchise, in Uruguay non-citizens must reside in the country for 15 years before they can vote. At least 11 countries relax the citizenship requirement for suffrage for nationals from specific countries. This practice is particularly common among many former British colonies and Portugal (Blais et al. 2001). Notwithstanding its symbolic value of full membership, only when exercised is the franchise socially and politically meaningful. When granted the right to vote, non-citizens are less likely than citizens to exercise the franchise (Harper-Ho 2000) and naturalized citizens are less likely to vote than native-born citizens (Bass and Casper 1999).

In raising the issue of qualified membership, I am not advocating non-citizen voting. Rather, my purpose is to illustrate how, in the shadows of a history of ascriptive democracy, national but especially local interests are not well served by muffling the voices of a growing share of the U.S. population. "Because aliens are a significant part of many contemporary political communities, their presence inevitably shapes the nature and practice of citizenship within" (Bosniak 2000: 975). Hence, if recent laws that explicitly prohibit immigrant voting disadvantage legal immigrants as a class, the political salience of citizenship through naturalization is bound to increase—and it has (Singer 2000). More significant, however, is that concerns about fairness in governance will become more discordant with the principles of *equity* and *inclusion* as long as entire communities remain voiceless in decisions that govern their life options and those of their children. But, for immigrant rights to become the civil rights of the 21st century, as Raskin (1993) claims, requires a realignment of democracy with demography.

Admittedly, the United States would be a very different country had immigration been stopped at the turn of the 20th century; or had the second era of mass migration not materialized after 1970. History scripted otherwise, and the future promises to do so even more. The U.S. Census Bureau predicts that 36% of the U.S. population will consist of minority groups by 2020, and 47% by mid-century (U.S. Census Bureau 2000d). Immigration will play a major role in this future diversification. Even if immigration levels are cut, the offspring of immigrants will maintain the force of diversification for at least 30 to 40 years—the time required for significant changes in the childbearing behavior of the foreign-born (Smith and Edmonston 1997:111). Although the children of immigrants are citizens by birth, their place in the status hierarchy will be shaped by the reception and rights accorded their parents.

According to Linda Bosniak (2000:983), ". . . the category of alienage poses a special challenge to the liberal vision of citizenship, because the concerns with status and rights which lie at the heart of this vision necessarily engage the questions of how far—and, especially, to whom—the liberal-democratic project of universality should be understood to extend." Fortunately, history provides lessons about how to prepare for that future within a framework of social justice. The main lessons are about how immigration challenges commitment to values of inclusion and equality given voice in the Declaration of Independence and the U.S. Constitution by requiring a broadened conception of membership that embraces both T. H. Marshall's (1964) notion of *social citizenship* and Raskin's (1993) notion of *citizenship as integration*. Maximal civic incorporation of immigrants is crucial for reinvigorating the shared commitment to values of liberty, democracy and equal opportunity (Prewitt 2001; Bosniak 2000). At a minimum, social justice dictates that non-citizens be treated as functional citizens.

However, several legislative measures targeting the foreign-born threaten the social contract and expose the vulnerability of immigrants' rights to political manipulation. For example, in 1980 the Supreme Court denied a lawsuit initiated by FAIR against the Commerce Department that aimed to exclude undocumented immigrants from the apportionment base.[32] Former counsel to the Senate Judiciary Committee on immigration, Charles Wood, alleges that both the Constitutional provisions to include undocumented immigrants in the apportionment population and the provisions that grant birthright citizenship to children of undocumented immigrants are cracks in the social contract that will "undermine the civic foundation of national unity" (Wood 1999). He proposes to seal these cracks by *excluding* undocumented immigrants from the apportionment population and denying birthright citizenship to their offspring. Both objectives require constitutional amendments, which to date have not succeeded. Once again, history teaches that inclusive approaches to sealing cracks in the contract are not only more enduring, but also consistent with the values of a liberal democracy.

Legislative measures targeting the foreign-born expose the vulnerability of immigrants' membership to political manipulation. Some have been revised or rescinded after public scrutiny and legal review, while others have been allowed to stand. If anti-immigrant initiatives in California, Florida, and Texas are the

[32] Ibid., note 11.

bellwether of the future, prospects for equality between natives and immigrants, and between citizens and non-citizens are worrisome. For example, passed in November 1994, by a 59% majority of California voters, Proposition 187 targeted both legal and undocumented immigrants by advocating that children of non-U.S. citizens be denied access to public schools as well as health and social welfare benefits except in cases of emergency.[33] That it was declared unconstitutional does not erase the strong symbolic message about membership and inclusion—rather, alienage and exclusion—and the strong popular support adds an aura of legitimacy to the intent.

Temptations to muffle immigrants' voice and limit social participation show no signs of abating. Even the extra protections afforded by statutory citizenship were threatened when INS interpreted a provision in the 1990 Immigration Act as granting the agency the ability to revoke citizenship as an administrative rather than a judicial matter (Kim 2001). Although the practice of "administrative denaturalization" as proposed by the Attorney General's Office was declared unconstitutional (*Gorbach v Reno*, 219 F.3d 1087, 9th Cir), accusations of election fraud or partisan politics could lead to similar initiatives in a climate where nativism has re-sharpened boundaries between citizens and unnaturalized immigrants (Harvard Law Review 1997). According to Gopal (2001), the current system of administrative denaturalization renders the revocation of citizenship easier than ever and with fewer safeguards for naturalized citizens.

In 1996 President Clinton signed the Personal Responsibility and Work Opportunity Reconciliation Act (Pub.L. 104–193) into law, which restricted the eligibility of some groups of legal immigrants from federal, state, and local benefits and services. This flagrant anti-immigrant legislation was further buttressed by the Illegal Immigration Reform and Immigrant Responsibility Act of 1996 (Pub.L. 104–208), which restricted access to social benefits for undocumented immigrants, including in-state tuition for postsecondary education (Harvard Law Review 2002).[34] As Peter Schuck (1997:12) aptly notes, "Until the statutory changes adopted by Congress in 1996, the differences between the legal rights enjoyed by citizens and those enjoyed by LPRs (legal permanent residents) were more political than legal or economic, and those differences had narrowed considerably over time." Both Acts deepen the divide between statutory and functional citizenship and underwrite inequality between immigrants and natives. In view of the volume of immigration in the recent past, sealing cracks in the social contract are essential to prevent the demography of difference and foreignness to shape the contours of inequality.

On a more positive note, there are several signs that democratic values are being realigned with the demographic realities of immigration. Local initiatives to promote inclusion by permitting noncitizens to vote in school board and municipal elections are an important stride toward building a sense of community by giving voice to immigrants and reducing the salience of foreignness. Several localities currently permit non-citizen voting. In Chicago and New York City, non-citizens have voted in school board elections for a long time. More recently Takoma Park,

<hr/>

[33] See full text of Proposition 187 at University of California Hastings College of the Law. *Proposition 187*. California Ballot Propositions Database. Online: <http://holmes.uchastings.edu/cgi-bin/starfinder/27148/calprop.txt>. (Date reviewed 12 April 2002).

[34] See: Davila (2002), Federation for American Immigration Reform (2001), Arenson (2001), and Purnick (2002).

Maryland, granted non-citizens, including undocumented immigrants, the right to vote in local elections (Harper-Ho 2000; Keyssar 2000).[35] Yet these cases currently are the exception, not the norm. Similar initiatives have been proposed in several other localities with mixed success, and some opposition comes from members of the African American community, whose opportunities to gain seats on school boards and hold municipal office may be diminished if the local franchise is granted to Latino, Asia, and Arab parents (Tamayo 1995). How diversity will play out in local politics will shape the contours of the national agenda about inclusion and equity.

Another powerful gesture toward the twin goals of equity and inclusiveness is recent legislation that grants in-state tuition privileges to undocumented immigrants who graduate from U.S. high schools.[36] That Texas and California along with Utah have assumed leadership in authorizing this benefit is all the more impressive because these states contain over half of the undocumented population; because these states achieved notoriety during the mid-1990s for their anti-immigrant and antiaffirmative action legislation; and because their decisions defy the federal ban on in-state tuition benefits for undocumented aliens included in the 1996 Illegal Immigration Reform and Immigrant Responsibility Act. Other states have proposed similar initiatives, which have been defeated. In a world where the value of college education signals large differences in lifetime earnings and general well-being, denying youth the opportunity to maximize their educational investment will surely compromise a future where immigrants' and their offspring will be major contributors to economic productivity. Philosophically, denying children of undocumented immigrants equal access to public education not only falls short of a liberal conception of social citizenship that includes social welfare rights along with full civic membership, but by raising the threshold of the tolerable limits of inequality, also breaches the social contract.

CONCLUSION

As we look toward the future with the benefit of hindsight, the looming question is whether immigration, broadly construed, will strain fractures in the social contract to the breaking point. The answer, I think, depends on whether the symbolic commitment to inclusiveness and equity can adhere in practice to the Marshallian conception of mature citizenship, giving full and equal access to education, employment, and all forms of services provided by the welfare state. The answer depends on whether the distinction between functional and statutory citizenship is minimized to the extent the Constitution permits, and particularly how states with high immigrant populations, resolve the dilemma of electoral and representational equity at all levels of government. The answer depends on whether adequate safeguards are put in place to prevent the re-emergence of ascriptive democracy, and to reinvigorate the cherished values of equity and inclusiveness. Ultimately, the answer depends on whether legislators shift their policy focus from *immigration* to *immigrants*.

With so many unknowns it is hard to visualize the final answer beyond its vaguest contours, but history shows that our nation has been particularly adept

---

[35] In November 1991, citizens residing in Takoma Park, Maryland, voted 1,199 to 1,107 (51–49%) to allow alien residents to vote (Kaiman and Varner 1991). See also: Howard (1991) and Sontag (1992).

[36] Ibid., note 33.

in adapting to changing social conditions. If we can find strength rather than weakness in our increased diversity, then the social contract will emerge not just unbroken, but stalwart in its renewed promise to fulfill the dream of rights and privileges that George Washington offered to Irish immigrants in 1783.

REFERENCES

Arenson, K.W. 2001. "CUNY Raises Tuition Rates for Foreigners Here Illegally." *The New York Times* 3 November: D3.

Arneson, R.J. 2001. "Equality (Philosophical Aspects)." Pp. 4724–29 in *International Encyclopedia of the Social and Behavioral Sciences*, edited by Baltes. N.J. Smelser, P.B. and Amsterdam: Elsevier Science.

Aylsworth L.E. 1931. "The Passing of Alien Suffrage." *American Political Science Review* 25: 114–116.

Bacon, D.C., R.H. Davidson, and M. Keller, eds. 1995. *The Encyclopedia of the United States Congress*. New York: Simon and Schuster.

Balinski, M.L., and H.P. Young. 2001. *Fair Representation: Meeting the Ideal of One Man, One Vote* (2nd ed.). Washington, D.C.: Brookings Institution Press.

Bass, L.E. and L.M. Casper. 1999. "Are There Differences in Voting Behavior Between Naturalized and Native-born Americans?" *Population Division Working Paper* 28. Washington, D.C.: U.S. Census Bureau.

Bauböck, R. 1994a. "Changing the Boundaries of Citizenship: The Inclusion of Immigrants in Democratic Polities." Paper presented at the *90th Annual Meeting of the American Political Science Association*, 1–4 September, New York, NY.

———. 1994b. *Transnational Citizenship. Membership and Rights in International Migration*. Brookfield, VT: Edward Elgar.

Blais, A., L. Massicotte, and A. Yoshinaka. 2001. "Deciding who has the right to vote: a comparative analysis of election laws." *Electoral Studies* 20: 41–62.

Bosniak, L. 2000. "Universal Citizenship and the Problem of Alienage." *Northwestern University Law Review* 94: 963–982.

Briggs, V. 1993. "Immigration and the U.S. Labor Market: Public Policy Gone Awry." *The Jerome Levy Economics Institute of Bard College Public Policy Brief* 7: 9–38.

Congressional Quarterly. 1991. *Guide to Congress* (4th ed.) Washington, D.C.: Congressional Quarterly.

Congressional Record. 1940. Proceedings and Debates of the Congress. House of Representatives. 11 April.

Dalaker, J. 2001. "Poverty in the United States: 2000." *U.S. Census Bureau Current Population Report* P60–214.

Davila, F. 2002. "Bills Would Ease Tuition Rules for Undocumented Immigrants—Legislature 2002." *Seattle Times*. 24 January: B1.

Davis, S.T. 1981. "Reapportionment: Numerical Politics." *American Demographics*. November: 24–29.

Day, S. 2000. "Dealing with Alien Suffrage: Examples from the EU and Germany." Paper presented at the *Ionian Conference*, Corfu, Greece. 19–22 May.

Edmonston, B., and C. Schultze, eds. 1995. *Modernizing the U.S. Census*. Washington, D.C.: National Academy Press.

Federation for American Immigration Reform. 2001. "Taxpayers Should Not Have to Subsidize College for Illegal Aliens." Online: <http://www.fairus.org/html/04182108.htm>. (Published August, 2001.)

Fitzpatrick, J.C., ed. 1938. *The Writings of George Washington [1931–44]*. Washington, D.C.: U.S. Government Printing Office. Vol. 27: 257.

Frey, W.H., and R.C. Devol. 2000. "America's Demography in the New Century: Aging Baby Boomers and New Immigrants as Major Players." *Milken Institute Policy Brief* 9.

Gibson, C.J., and E. Lennon. 1999. "Historical Census Statistics on the Foreign-Born Population of the United States: 1850–1990." *Population Division Working Paper* 29. Washington, D.C.: U.S. Census Bureau.

Goldfarb, C.E. 1995. "Allocating the Local Apportionment Pie: What Portion for Resident Aliens?" *Yale Law Journal* 104: 1441–1472.

Gopal, V. 2001. "Comment: From Judicial to Administrative Denaturalization: For Better or for Worse?" *University of Colorado Law Review* 72: 779–815.

Gordon, M. 1964. *Assimilation in American Life: The Role of Race, Religion, and National Origins*. New York: Oxford University Press.

Gosewinkel, D. 2001. "Historical Development of Citizenship." Pp. 1852–1857 in *International Encyclopedia of the Social and Behavioral Sciences*, edited by N.J. Smelser, P.B. Baltes. Amsterdam: Elsevier Science.

Harper-Ho, V. 2000. "Non-citizen Voting Rights: The History, the Law and Current Prospects for Change." 18 *Law and Inequality Journal* 18: 271–322.

Harvard Law Review, eds. 1997. "Note: The Constitutional Requirement of Judicial Review for Administrative Deportation Decisions." *Harvard Law Review* 110: 1850–1867.

———. 2002. "Recent Legislation: Immigration Law—Education—California Extends In-state Tuition Benefits to Undocumented Aliens—Act Relating to Public Postsecondary Education." *Harvard Law Review* 115: 1548–1554.

Howard, M. 1991. "Vote to extend voting rights seen as likely to start a trend." *Washington Times*. 7 November: B3.

Hume, D. [1748] 1948. *Of the Original Contract*. Pp. 147–166 in *Social Contract: Essays by Locke, Hume and Rousseau*, edited by E. Barker. London: Oxford University Press.

Immigration and Naturalization Service (INS). 2002. *Statistical Yearbook of the Immigration and Naturalization Service, 2000*. Washington, D.C.: U.S. Government Printing Office.

Jasso, G. and M.R. Rosenzweig. 1990. *The New Chosen People: Immigrants in the United States*. New York: Russell Sage Foundation.

Johnson, K.R. 1993. "Los Olvidados: Images of the Immigrant, Political Power of Non-citizens, and Immigration Law and Enforcement." *Brigham Young University Law Review* 3: 1139–1241.

Kaiman, B., and L.K. Varner. 1991. "Maryland: Takoma Park Residents Favor Vote for Non-Citizens in City Elections." *Washington Post*. 6 November: A30.

Keyssar, A. 2000. *The Right to Vote: The Contested History of Democracy in the United States*. New York: Basic Books.

Kim, C.Y. 2001. "Revoking your citizenship: Minimizing the Likelihood of Administrative Error." *Columbia Law Review* 101: 1448–1478.

King, D. 2000. *Making Americans: Immigration, Race, and the Origins of the Diverse Democracy*. Cambridge, MA: Harvard University Press.

Kurian, G.T., ed. 1998. *A Historical Guide to the U.S. Government*. New York: Oxford University Press.

Levy, F. 1987. *Dollars and Dreams: The Changing American Income Distribution*. New York: Russell Sage Foundation.

Marshall, T. H. 1964. *Class, Citizenship, and Social Development*. Garden City, NY: Doubleday.

Massey, D.S., G. Hugo, J.E. Taylor, J. Arango, A. Kouaouci, and A. Pellegrino. 1998. *Worlds in Motion: International Migration at the End of the Millennium*. Oxford: Clarendon Press at Oxford University Press.

Mills, C. 1997. *The Racial Contract*. Ithaca: Cornell University Press.

Neuman, G.L. 1992. " 'We Are the People' Alien Suffrage in German and American Perspective," *Michigan Journal of International Law* 13: 259–335.

———. 1993. "The Lost Century of American Immigration Law: 1776–1875." *Columbia Law Review* 93: 1833–1901.

———. 1996. *Strangers to the Constitution: Immigrants, Borders, and Fundamental Law*. Princeton: Princeton University Press.

"Note: The Constitutional Requirement of Judicial Review for Administrative Deportation Decisions." 1997. *Harvard Law Review* 110: 1850–67.

Perez v Brownell, 356 U.S. 44 (1958).

Porter, K. 1918. *A History of Suffrage in the United States*. Chicago: University of Chicago Press.

Poston, D.L., S.A. Camarota, L.F. Bouvier, G. Li, and H. Dan. 1998. "Remaking the Political Landscape: How Immigration Redistributes Seats in the House." Center for Immigration Studies. Online: <http://www.cis.org/articles/1998/Reapportionment/remaking.html> (Published October 1998).

Prewitt, K. 2001. "Beyond Census 2000: As a Nation, We Are the World." *Carnegie Reporter* 1(3): 3–11.

Public Papers of the Presidents of the U.S. 1966. "Lyndon B. Johnson, 3 October 1965." Vol. II, Entry 546. Washington, D.C.: Government Printing Office.

Purnick, J. 2002. "Tuition, Out of State and Beyond." *The New York Times*. 18 February: B1.

Raskin, J.B. 1993. "Legal Aliens, Local Citizens: The Historical, Constitutional and Theoretical Meanings of Alien Suffrage." *University of Pennsylvania Law Review* 141: 1391–1470.

Rosberg, G.M. 1977. "Aliens and Equal Protection: Why Not the Right to Vote?" *Michigan Law Review* 75: 1092–1136.

Rousseau, J.J. [1762] 1948. "The Social Contract." Pp. 169–307 in *Social Contract: Essays by Locke, Hume, and Rousseau*, edited by E. Barker. London: Oxford University Press.

Schmeckebier, L.F. 1941. *Congressional Apportionment*. Washington, D.C.: Brookings Institution Press.

Schuck, P. 1997. "The Reevaluation of American Citizenship," *Georgetown Immigration Law Journal* 12: 1–34.

Singer, A. 2000. "Naturalization under Changing Conditions of Membership: Dominican Immigrants in New York City." Pp. 157–186 in *Immigration Research for a New Century: Multidisciplinary Perspectives*, edited by N. Foner, R. Rumbaut, and S.J. Gold. New York: Russell Sage Press.

Sixty-eighth U.S. Congress, 1924. Session I, Chs. 185–190.

Smith, R.M. 1993. "Beyond Tocqueville, Myrdal, and Hartz: The Multiple Traditions in America." *American Political Science Review* 87(3): 549–566.

———. 1997. *Civic Ideals: Conflicting Visions of Citizenship in U.S. History*. New Haven: Yale University Press.

Smith, J.P. and B. Edmonston, eds. 1997. *The New Americans: Economic, Demographic, and Fiscal Effects of Immigration*. Washington, D.C.: National Academy Press.

Sontag, D. 1992. "Non-citizens and Right to Vote: Advocates for Immigrants Explore Opening Up Balloting." *The New York Times*. 31 July: B1.

Tamayo, W.R. 1995. "When the 'Coloreds' Are Neither Black Nor Citizens: The United States Civil Rights Movement and Global Migration." *Asian Law Journal* 2: 1–32.

Thernstrom, S., ed. 1980. Entry for "Naturalization and Citizenship." *Harvard Encyclopedia of American Ethnic Groups*. Cambridge, MA.: Belknap Press of Harvard University Press.

U.S. Census Bureau. 2000a. "Census 2000 Redistricting (Public Law 94–171) Summary File." Washington, D.C.: Government Printing Office. Tables PL1 and PL2.

U.S. Census Bureau. 2000b. "Apportionment of the U.S. House of Representatives." Online: <http://www.census.gov/population/www/censusdata/apportionment/history.html>. (Published December 01, 2000.)

U.S. Census Bureau. 2000c. "Apportionment—Who's Counted." Online: <http://www.census.gov/population/www/censusdata/apportionment/who.html>. (Published December 01, 2000).

U.S. Census Bureau. 2000d. "Projections of the Resident Population by Age, Sex, Race, and Hispanic Origin: 1999 to 2100." Population Division Paper NP-D1-A.

U.S. Census Bureau. 2001. "Profile of the Foreign-Born Population in the United States: 2000." Current Population Report P23–206.

U.S. Census Bureau. 2002. "Congressional Apportionment." Historical Charts. Online: <http://www.census.gov/population/www/censusdata/apportionment.html>. (Data Reviewed 12 April 2002.)

U.S. House. 1964. Hearings of Subcommittee Number 1 of the Committee on the Judiciary, 2 July. Washington, D.C.: Government Printing Office.

U.S. Senate. 1965a. Hearings of Subcommittee on the Immigration and Naturalization of The Committee on the Judiciary Hearings, 24 February. Washington, D.C.: U.S. Government Printing Office.

U.S. Senate. 1965b. Hearings of Subcommittee on the Immigration and Naturalization of the Committee on the Judiciary Hearings, 10 February. Washington, D.C.: U.S. Government Printing Office.

Walzer, M. 1995. Entry for "Contract, Social." In *The Oxford Companion to Philosophy*, edited by Ted Honderich. Oxford: Oxford University Press.

Williams, H.P. 1912. "The Road to Citizenship." *Political Science Quarterly* 27(3): 399–427.

Wood, C. 1999. "Losing Control of America's Future: The Census, Birth Right Citizenship, and Illegal Aliens." *Harvard Journal of Law and Public Policy* 22(2): 465–522.

Woodrow-Lafield, D.A. 2001. "Implications of Immigration for Apportionment." *Population Research and Policy Review* 20: 267–289.

APPENDIX TABLE A-1

Differences in Theoretical and Actual Apportionment of
U.S. House Seats under Three Counterfactuals

States	Natives Only			Immigration Stopped in 1900			Citizens Only		
	1910	1920	1930	1910	1920	1930	1910	1920	1930
Alabama	2	1	2	1	0	1	0	0	1
Alaska*	—	—	—	—	—	—	—	—	—
Arizona	0	0	0	0	0	0	0	0	0
Arkansas	2	1	0	1	1	0	1	1	0
California	−1	2	−1	0	2	−1	0	2	−1
Colorado	0	0	0	0	0	0	0	0	0
Connecticut	−1	0	−1	0	0	−1	0	0	−1
Delaware	0	0	0	0	0	0	0	0	0
Florida	0	0	1	0	0	1	0	0	0
Georgia	2	2	2	1	1	1	1	1	1
Hawaii**	—	—	—	—	—	—	—	—	—
Idaho	0	0	0	0	0	0	0	0	0
Illinois	−2	−2	−1	−1	−1	−1	−1	0	0
Indiana	1	0	0	0	0	0	0	0	0
Iowa	0	−1	0	0	−1	0	0	−1	0
Kansas	1	0	0	0	0	0	0	0	0
Kentucky	1	0	1	0	0	1	0	0	1
Louisiana	1	0	0	0	0	0	0	0	0
Maine	0	−1	0	0	−1	0	−1	−1	0
Maryland	1	0	0	0	0	0	0	0	0
Massachusetts	−3	−3	−2	−1	−1	−1	−1	−2	−1
Michigan	−1	1	−1	0	2	−1	0	2	0
Minnesota	−2	−1	0	0	0	0	0	0	0
Mississippi	2	1	1	1	0	1	1	0	1

(continued)

States	Natives Only			Immigration Stopped in 1900			Citizens Only		
	1910	1920	1930	1910	1920	1930	1910	1920	1930
Missouri	1	−1	1	0	−1	1	0	−1	0
Montana	0	0	0	0	0	0	0	0	0
Nebraska	0	−1	0	0	0	0	0	0	0
Nevada	0	0	0	0	0	0	0	0	0
New Hampshire	0	0	0	0	0	0	0	0	0
New Jersey	−2	0	−1	−1	0	−1	0	0	0
New Mexico	0	1	0	0	0	0	0	0	0
New York	−8	−7	−7	−3	−4	−5	−2	−4	−3
North Carolina	2	2	2	1	1	1	1	1	1
North Dakota	−1	−1	0	0	0	0	0	0	0
Ohio	1	2	0	1	2	0	1	2	0
Oklahoma	1	2	0	0	1	0	0	1	0
Oregon	0	0	0	0	0	0	0	0	0
Pennsylvania	−1	−1	0	−1	−1	0	−1	−1	0
Rhode Island	−1	−1	0	−1	−1	0	−1	−1	0
South Carolina	1	1	1	0	0	1	0	0	0
South Dakota	0	0	0	0	0	1	0	0	0
Tennessee	2	1	1	1	0	1	1	0	1
Texas	2	3	1	1	2	0	1	1	0
Utah	0	0	0	0	0	0	0	0	0
Vermont	0	−1	0	0	−1	0	0	−1	0
Virginia	1	1	1	0	0	0	0	0	0
Washington	0	0	−1	0	0	−1	0	1	−1
West Virginia	0	1	1	0	0	1	0	0	0
Wisconsin	−1	−1	0	0	0	1	0	0	1
Wyoming	0	0	0	0	0	0	0	0	0

* Alaska became the 49th state in 1959, thus data are not available for this analysis.

** Hawaii became the 50th state in 1959, thus data are not available for this analysis.

APPENDIX TABLE A-2

Differences in Theoretical and Actual Apportionment of U.S. House Seats Under Three Counterfactuals

States	Natives Only				Immigration Stopped in 1900				Citizens Only			
	1970	1980	1990	2000	1970	1980	1990	2000	1970	1980	1990	2000
Alabama	1	1	1	1	0	1	1	0	0	1	0	0
Alaska	0	0	0	0	0	0	0	0	0	0	0	0
Arizona	0	0	0	0	0	0	0	0	0	0	0	0
Arkansas	0	1	0	1	0	1	0	1	0	1	0	0
California	−2	−4	−8	−9	−1	−3	−7	−8	−1	−3	−5	−6
Colorado	0	0	0	0	0	0	0	0	0	0	0	0
Connecticut	0	0	0	0	0	0	0	0	0	0	0	0
Delaware	0	0	0	0	0	0	0	0	0	0	0	0
Florida	−1	−1	−1	−2	−1	−1	−1	−2	−1	−1	−1	−1
Georgia	0	1	1	0	0	1	1	0	0	1	1	0
Hawaii	0	0	0	0	0	0	0	0	0	0	0	0

States	Natives Only				Immigration Stopped in 1900				Citizens Only			
	1970	1980	1990	2000	1970	1980	1990	2000	1970	1980	1990	2000
Idaho	0	0	0	0	0	0	0	0	0	0	0	0
Illinois	0	0	0	0	0	0	0	0	0	0	0	0
Indiana	0	1	0	1	0	1	0	1	0	1	0	1
Iowa	0	0	0	0	0	0	0	0	0	0	0	0
Kansas	0	0	1	1	0	0	1	1	0	0	1	0
Kentucky	0	0	1	1	0	0	1	1	0	0	1	1
Louisiana	0	0	1	1	0	0	1	1	0	0	1	0
Maine	0	0	0	0	0	0	0	0	0	0	0	0
Maryland	1	0	1	0	0	0	0	0	0	0	0	0
Massachusetts	0	0	0	0	0	0	0	0	0	0	0	0
Michigan	0	0	1	1	0	0	1	1	0	0	1	1
Minnesota	0	0	0	0	0	0	0	0	0	0	0	0
Mississippi	0	0	0	1	0	0	0	1	0	0	0	1
Missouri	0	1	1	0	0	1	1	0	0	1	0	0
Montana	0	0	1	1	0	0	1	1	0	0	1	1
Nebraska	0	0	0	0	0	0	0	0	0	0	0	0
Nevada	0	0	0	0	0	0	0	0	0	0	0	0
New Hampshire	0	0	0	0	0	0	0	0	0	0	0	0
New Jersey	0	0	0	−1	0	0	0	−1	0	0	0	0
New Mexico	0	0	0	0	0	0	0	0	0	0	0	0
New York	−3	−3	−2	−3	−1	−2	−2	−2	−1	−2	−1	−1
North Carolina	0	1	0	0	0	1	0	0	0	1	0	0
North Dakota	0	0	0	0	0	0	0	0	0	0	0	0
Ohio	0	1	1	1	0	0	1	1	0	0	1	0
Oklahoma	0	0	0	1	0	0	0	1	0	0	0	1
Oregon	1	0	0	1	1	0	0	0	1	0	0	0
Pennsylvania	1	0	1	1	0	0	1	1	0	0	1	1
Rhode Island	0	0	0	0	0	0	0	0	0	0	0	0
South Carolina	0	0	1	1	0	0	1	1	0	0	0	0
South Dakota	0	0	0	0	0	0	0	0	0	0	0	0
Tennessee	1	0	0	0	1	0	0	0	1	0	0	0
Texas	0	0	−1	−1	0	0	−1	−1	0	0	−1	−1
Utah	0	0	0	1	0	0	0	1	0	0	0	1
Vermont	0	0	0	0	0	0	0	0	0	0	0	0
Virginia	0	1	0	0	0	0	0	0	0	0	0	0
Washington	0	0	0	0	0	0	0	0	0	0	0	0
West Virginia	0	0	0	0	0	0	0	0	0	0	0	0
Wisconsin	1	0	0	1	1	0	0	1	1	0	0	1
Wyoming	0	0	0	0	0	0	0	0	0	0	0	0